The 1988 Election: The Senate in the 101st Congress

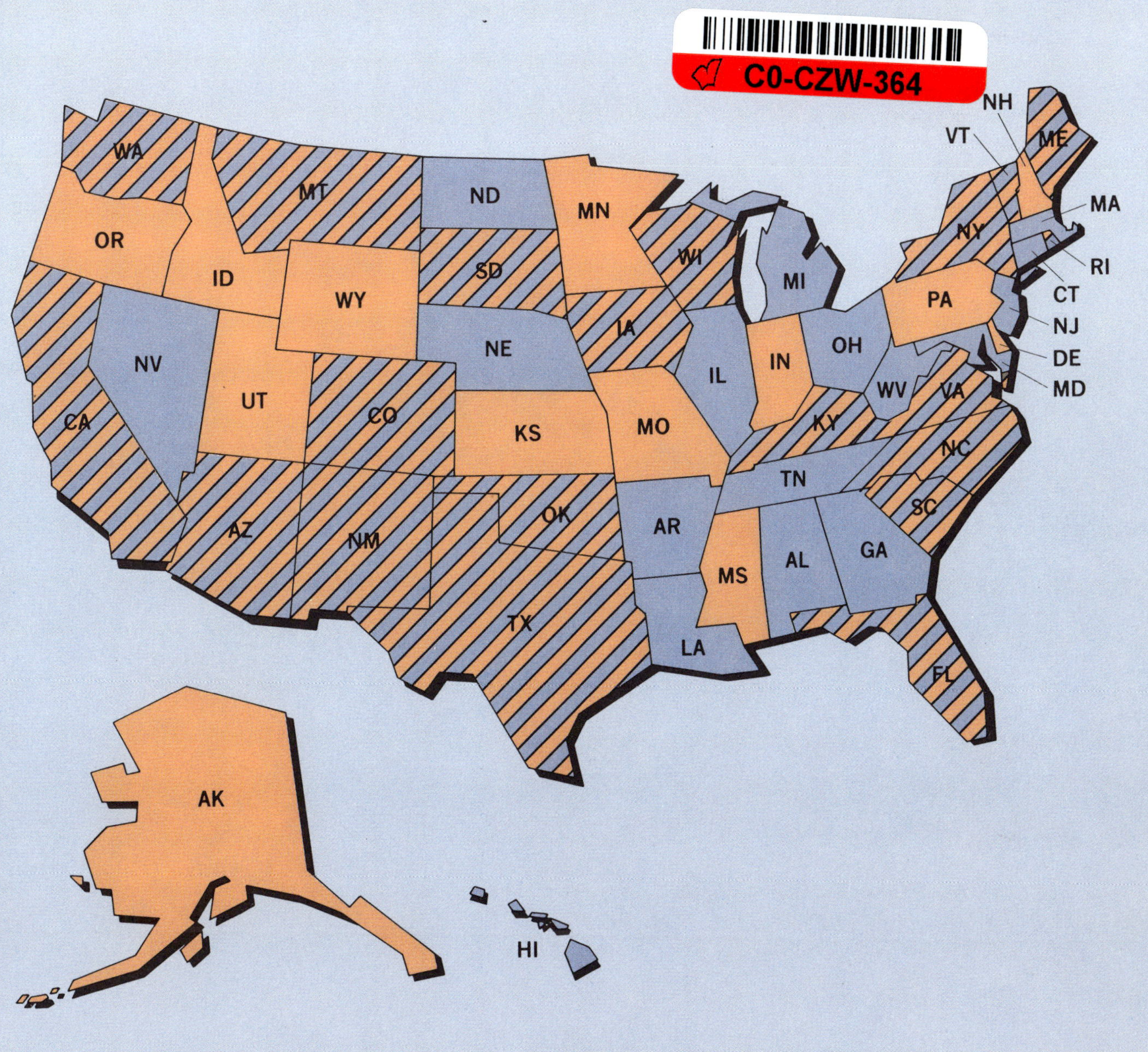

Both Senators Democratic

Both Senators Republican

Split Party Control

Party	1972	1974	1976	1978	1980	1982	1984	1986	1988
Democratic	56	61	61	58	46	46	47	55	55
Republican	42	37	38	41	53	54	53	45	45
Others	2	2	1	1	1	0	0	0	0

American Democracy

Student:

To help you make the most of your study time and improve your grades, we have developed the following supplement designed to accompany Keefe et al.: *American Democracy: Institutions, Politics, and Policies, 3/e:*

- Study Guide, by Michael Margolis and Christopher Bosso 0–06–043583–6

You can order a copy at your local bookstore or call Harper & Row directly at 1-800-638-3030.

American Democracy

Institutions, Politics, and Policies

THIRD EDITION

William J. Keefe
University of Pittsburgh

Henry J. Abraham
University of Virginia

William H. Flanigan
University of Minnesota

Charles O. Jones
University of Wisconsin

Morris S. Ogul
University of Pittsburgh

John W. Spanier
University of Florida

1817

HARPER & ROW, PUBLISHERS, New York
Grand Rapids, Philadelphia, St. Louis, San Francisco, London, Singapore, Sydney, Tokyo

Sponsoring Editor: Lauren Silverman
Development Editor: Jonathan Haber
Project Editor: Steven Pisano
Art Direction: Kathie Vaccaro
Text Design: Richard Stalzer Associates, Ltd.
Cover Coordinator: Teresa J. Delgado
Cover Design: Delgado Design, Inc.
Cover Photo: Frederic Petters Photography
Photo Research: Cheryl Mannes
Production: Willie Lane

American Democracy: Institutions, Politics, and Policies, Third Edition

The Picture Credits for this book can be found on p. 747, and constitute an extension of this copyright page.

Library of Congress Cataloging-in-Publication Data

American democracy / William J. Keefe . . . [et al.].—3rd ed.
p. cm.
1. United States—Politics and government. I. Keefe, William J.
JK274.A54725 1989
320.973—dc20 89-38477
ISBN 0-06-043582-8 (Student Edition) CIP
ISBN 0-06-043584-4 (Teacher's Edition)

89 90 91 92 9 8 7 6 5 4 3 2 1

"If men were angels, no government would be necessary."

— The Federalist

Brief Contents

Brief Contents

Contents

Chapter Ten
Interest Groups

Chapter Eleven
Mass Media Politics

Chapter Fourteen
Executive–Legislative Relations

Chapter Eighteen
Domestic Policy Growth 586

Chapter Nineteen
Domestic Policy Issues: The 1990s 616

Preface

The authors of *American Democracy* have been teaching courses in American government and politics for more than a century and a half. (Fortunately for everyone, that is a group claim.) Our experience leads us to believe that we know what students find interesting and are likely to remember. We think we know what they need to understand if they are to interpret the American political system, to think critically about it, and to discover for themselves their role in it.

Objectives

A text in American government should be just as aware of how students learn and instructors teach. Our aim was to write a book that, without sacrificing analytical rigor, met that key test.

Clear, Comprehensive Discussions

What students and instructors expect, we believe, are analyses and interpretations laid out clearly and coherently, with a minimum of jargon. For us, that meant examining fewer topics comprehensively rather than numerous ones sparingly.

A Balanced but Challenging Presentation

We offer a balanced, mainstream interpretation of American government. In addition, we have sought to give students a firm basis for evaluating the political system while laying the groundwork for further study. To these ends, we focus on features of American political processes and institutions that are important and interesting in their own right—and that challenge students and invite their questions.

A Focus on Politics

Of key importance, we provide instructive ways to think about, plus a variety of answers to, the classic practical question in democracies: How can citizens get hold of their government? The centrality of that question to this book is expressed in an unusually heavy emphasis on *politics* and, in particular, *political institutions* and *political processes.* The truth is that no introductory text rivals this one in attention to all aspects of politics. *American Democracy* begins and ends with politics.

Up-to-Date Information

While we have taken pains to provide the legal and historical background needed to understand the present, we believe that students are best engaged by the events of today. Moreover, a text in the 1990s has the obligation to explore *in depth* the 1988 presidential election, issues and events that have faced the Bush administration, and the challenges of the new decade. No other text has yet met that obligation; indeed, none has had the chance to try.

Specialization

American Democracy also benefits from specialization, for each author wrote his chapter(s) in his special field(s) of research and interest. Keefe authored the chapters on American politics, the Constitution, federalism, the political parties, interest groups, the media, and Congress. Abraham analyzed civil rights, civil liberties, and the judiciary. Flanigan contributed his expertise on political participation, public opinion and ideology, and voting behavior. Jones described domestic policy growth, policy processes, and policy issues. Ogul appraised the presidency, executive–legislative relations, and the bureaucracy. Finally, Spanier addressed today's foreign policy issues.

Thorough Integration

"Too many cooks," an old aphorism contends, "spoil the broth." What about that? Is it true? Our response is just this side of conceit: "Only if they are poor cooks!" The fact is that each of the authors made a more than determined effort to integrate his work with that of the others. Additionally, Keefe played the role of general editor, actively helping to blend together organizational features and individual writing styles.

In particular, each author took pains to link institutions, processes, and policies. Foreign and domestic policy chapters, for example, are closely tied to the institutional and process chapters that precede them. Many of the chapters are grounded in analyses of relevant constitutional arrangements and provisions discussed at the outset of the book. *Politics* was a key theme for everyone.

Our specialization had its advantages here, in creating connections like these, as well. Above all, it allowed us to wring the most from different approaches to American politics. We relied throughout the text on a comprehensive assortment of current legal, behavioral, normative, and historical studies. The only criteria invoked was their appropriateness to clarifying American government.

The broad point is that each author was sensitive to the unity of the text and the requirements of classes and students. "Turf problems" were virtually nonexistent. We hope the effort to preserve common aims was as successful as reviewers—who gave us excellent ideas about how to achieve a fully integrated text—say it was.

Features: Providing Perspectives

Concretely, our approach meant that we place important issues in perspective. To this end, we set goals and structural features for each chapter.

Up-to-Date Illustrations

We developed apt, lively illustrations of propositions that matter. These examples fully reflect the time this book was written, concluding well beyond the first days of the Bush administration. Some of these examples are also the subject of the *Impact* boxes found in many chapters.

Studies of Interrelationships

We show—and also account for—interrelationships among political institutions, both throughout the text and in *Political Linkage* boxes in almost every chapter. Examples include linkages of many issues to ideology (discussed primarily in Chapter 7), political action committees (introduced in Chapter 10), and the meaning and character of American democracy (first explored in Chapters 1 and 2).

A Range of Voices

To expose students to pertinent scholars and politicians, we quote them liberally. A range of voices appears not only in *Perspectives* boxes in each chapter, but throughout the text.

Comparative Approaches

We provide helpful comparisons: between American political systems and those of other countries, between the federal and local perspectives that are equally essential to the American constitutional system, and between past and present issues and policies. Many of the latter comparisons form the basis of the *Continuity & Change* boxes. Coverage of state politics within the federal system appears most notably in Chapters 3, 9, and 16–18.

The Data of Political Science

In the age of specialization, it is important that students be taught to draw conclusions from charts, maps, and tables. We have printed several that offer useful comparative perspectives on American democracy on the book's inside covers and included a wealth of all of these tools in our analyses. In Chapters 2, 7–9, and 11 especially, the student will be exposed to hard data, including surveys of public opinion and studies of the print and electronic media.

Annotated Readings and Documents

This edition includes the text of the Declaration of Independence and *Federalist* papers 10, 51, and 78. In addition, we have taken the unusual step of annotating the Constitution, so that students can read this document with greater interest and understanding.

Other Pedagogical Aids

Along with the abundant maps, graphs, and tables, a variety of cartoons offer substantive insights—and, we trust, a little humor—into the issues. Unusually detailed captions to photographs add context and help link them to the issues in the text. These features, along with outlines, summaries, and annotated readings in each chapter and the concluding glossary, are designed to help the student better approach American government and politics.

New to This Edition

Political scientists familiar with the second edition of *American Democracy* will find the third edition familiar as well—but just barely. With some allowance for hyperbole, this edition is only a brick or two shy of being a new book, from the maps and charts that now appear on the inside covers to the selections from the *Federalist* added at the end. Some of the key features new to this edition include five timely new chapters, a new array of informative boxes to challenge your students, and, of course, a renewed commitment to make this text up to date. Every chapter has been rethought to bring out the themes enunciated above and to bring in the critical issues and events of the most recent years, and the following substantial additions have been made.

Five New Chapters

With the addition of five new chapters, the text is more comprehensive, up to date, and focused on politics than its previous edition. Each of these new chapters expands on emphases that will, we trust, already be evident.

Chapter 1—Politics, Continuity, and Change. A new opening chapter now introduces students to American politics and political institutions, shows their relation to conflict and political change, and sketches the organization of the rest of the book. It describes relationships between politics, continuity, and change in the nation's "Madisonian" system.

Chapter 5—Civil Rights and Liberties: Freedom and Equality. This added chapter substantially expands the analysis of civil rights and civil liberties. It makes the point that these issues remain a center of political controversy.

Chapter 11—Mass Media Politics. Coverage of the role of the media is increasingly essential. Chapter 11 is unique, we believe, in stressing not the media for their own sake, but rather their impact on political institutions and public policy.

Chapter 14—Executive–Legislative Relations. A new chapter on executive–legislative relations maintains the text's emphasis on politics. Chapter 14 focuses on conflict, conflict resolution, and cooperation between branches.

Chapter 19—Domestic Policy Issues: The 1990s. With the addition of a separate chapter analyzing the policy questions that will dominate the government's agenda in the 1990s, policy issues, policy processes, and the budgetary agenda now receive unusually thorough coverage. Chapters 17–19 on domestic policy also help reinforce the importance of political economy in American government.

New Informative Boxes

Together, the four kinds of boxes in this edition offer serious analysis of such important topics as racial polarization in voting, campaign spending, voting in Congress on gun control legislation, hazardous waste sites, and the facts behind such recent election issues as pollution in Boston Harbor and the record of the American Civil Liberties Union.

Perspectives. Boxes in each chapter feature a collage of quotes from politicians and political scientists. These "mini-reader" collections pose contemporary and classic questions for students.

Continuity & Change. These boxed discussions contrast past and present, helping students to understand how features of the American political system both change and resist change.

Political Linkage. These boxes illustrate a variety of relations among institutions, processes, and behavior. They address the student's need to tie together subjects covered in separate chapters.

Impact. Finally, these boxes make it clear that political institutions, processes, and decisions make a difference in American society.

Ancillary Instructional Materials

Our aim of a teachable but challenging text could not be achieved without the support of a full selection of teaching and learning resources.

Study Guide

Michael Margolis, at the University of Pittsburgh, and Christopher Bosso, at Northeastern University, have written a superb study guide that, like *American Democracy* itself, aims to help students not only remember the essentials, but also examine and discover further perspectives on American government. The study guide contains learning objectives, reviews, and summaries for each chapter, along with discussions of the key terms and concepts, alternative perspectives, "Test Yourself" questions for review, and essay and discussion questions that demand a critical approach to the material.

Instructor's Manual

Michael Margolis and Christopher Bosso have also written the instructor's manual, which closely parallels both the text and the study guide. In addition to providing teaching objectives, chapter outlines, and a recapitulation of key terms and concepts, they suggest alternative perspectives and discussion questions for the classroom. Also included are answers to the "Test Yourself" questions in the study guide.

Test Bank

The test item file provided by Michael Margolis consists of 1,500 multiple-choice, true/false, and completion test items. Each item was extensively reviewed, and each is referenced by page number to *American Democracy.*

HarperTest

The test questions are also available on *HarperTest.* This flexible test-generating system can be obtained for use with either the IBM-PC and most compatibles, or the Apple IIe and IIc.

Media Program

A comprehensive media program includes a wide selection of highly praised films and videos for use both as "lecture-launchers" and in conjunction with classroom teaching. The *American Government Media Handbook,* designed to help instructors integrate the media program with the text and their teaching plans, describes audiovisual options in detail, and suggests follow-up discussion questions.

Instructors have several excellent choices. *The Power Game,* Hedrick Smith's popular four-part PBS documentary on the elected—and unelected—government in Washington, and *Eyes on the Prize,* the award-winning six-part series on the civil rights movement, are each available through the Harper & Row media policy. So is "The Thirty-Second President," Bill Moyers's look at the office in an age of soundbites, from his PBS series *A Walk Through the Twentieth Century. The Challenge of the Presidency,* a one-hour videotape, combines the thoughtful interviews by David Frost with each of the last four former presidents. For adopters of this text, Harper & Row has compiled a unique Newsreel Video—a selection of authentic newsreel footage that captures the key American political events of the past six decades. Finally, instructors may choose a number of complimentary film and video rentals from Indiana University's invaluable archives in U.S. history and government, which at last count had upward of 600 titles.

Transparencies

Transparency acetates of 35 figures taken from the text, also free to instructors, reinforce our emphasis on helping students to interpret the visual presentation of important data. They should make it easier to integrate student assignments with the lectures.

Student Software

A computerized Student Tutorial Guide is available to help students retain key concepts and ideas. This flexible drill-and-practice software contains multiple-choice, true/false, and short-answer questions for each chapter in the text. Lively graphics provide immediate student reinforcement. Students can also print chapter outlines or consult an easy-to-use tutorial guide. In addition, a FlashCard program is available to drill students on all terms in the text's glossary.

Grades

Grade-keeping and class-management software, free to instructors, maintains data for up to

200 students. It is suitable for the IBM-PC and most compatibles.

Acknowledgments

Our debts for counsel and assistance are substantial. We want to begin by thanking friends and colleagues for their good work on our behalf. Jonathan Hurwitz, at the University of Pittsburgh, prepared a number of excellent boxes for this edition and gave us good advice on several chapters. Holbert N. Carroll, also at the University of Pittsburgh, carefully reviewed several chapters and made valuable suggestions for their improvement. We are grateful too for contributions from Janet Adamski, Christopher Bosso, Jack Burkman, Robert E. Burtt, Mark Hall, Rebecca Dick-Hurwitz, Robert L. Donaldson, David Fitz, Jane Flanders, Zheya Gai, E. Brooke Harlowe, Vera M. Jones, John Keefe, Martha Keefe, Ellis Krauss, Michael Margolis, Linda McClain, Kathryn Keefe McCurdy, Kolawole Olugbade, Barbara Perry, Guy Peters, Chris Rogers, Drew Slaven, Kathy Uradnik, and Robert S. Walters. Our book is much better for their efforts.

We also want to thank the scholars across the country who reviewed our second edition and one or more drafts of chapters for this edition. The analyses throughout the book reflect their insights:

Thomas J. Baldino, *Juniata College*
John F. Bibby, *University of Wisconsin–Milwaukee*
David Billeaux, *Oklahoma State University*
Fredric N. Bolotin, *Case Western Reserve University*
Christopher J. Bosso, *Northeastern University*
Carl P. Burney, *San Jacinto College*
Allan J. Cigler, *University of Kansas*
David Louis Cingranelli, *State University of New York at Binghamton*
James W. Davis, *Western Washington University*
Charles R. Embry, *East Texas State University*
Osbin Ervin, *Southern Illinois University*
Dave Flint, *Moorhead State University*
Kevin Gleason, *Marquette University*
Marshall R. Goodman, *Georgetown University*
Leroy C. Hardy, *Claremont McKenna College, California State University, Long Beach*
Richard J. Herzog, *Stephen F. Austin State University*
Paul Holder, *McLennan Community College*
Thomas Keating, *Arizona State University*
William E. Kelley, *Auburn University*
Henry C. Kenski, *University of Arizona*
Steve J. Mazurana, *University of Northern Colorado*
William C. Meulemans, *Southern Oregon State College*
Bradley J. Miller, *Northeastern University*
Curtis G. Reithel, *University of Wisconsin, La Crosse*
John Roos, *University of Notre Dame*
Carmine Scavo, *East Carolina University*
E. Patrick Smith, *Broward Community College*
J. Owen Smith, *California State University, Fullerton*
June Sager Speakman, *Rutgers University*
Robert P. Steed, *The Citadel*
Denis Thornton, *Illinois State University*
William L. Wallis, *California State University, Northridge*

We are also indebted to reviewers who helped shape the first two editions. *American Democracy* continues to reflect their valuable suggestions. In addition to those mentioned above, we again thank Thad L. Beyle, University of North Carolina, Chapel Hill; William H. Harader, Indiana State University; Paul Light, The National Academy of Public Administration; Sandy Maisel, Colby College; Donald J. McCrone, University of Washington; Alan D. Monroe, Illinois State University; Albert Papa, University of Pittsburgh; Samuel C. Patterson, Ohio State University; Michael D. Reagan, University of California, Riverside; David W. Rohde, Michigan State University; A. Jay Stevens, California State University, Long Beach; Walter J. Stone, University of Colorado; and Eugene A. Taylor, Jr., Citrus College.

We want to thank Marianne Russell, the editorial director at Harper & Row, and Lauren Silverman, sponsoring editor, for their lively interest in this book and for greatly facilitating its completion. From the outset, John Haber, our development editor, proved to be one of the most dedicated and creative editors to be found anywhere; his assistance was simply indispensable. Lastly, Steve Pisano, project editor, capably directed the book through the various stages of the production process. Harper & Row, all of us learned, is an outstanding publishing house, and we are delighted to be associated with it.

William J. Keefe
Henry J. Abraham
William H. Flanigan
Charles O. Jones
Morris S. Ogul
John W. Spanier

To the Student: Thinking About Democracy

Governments everywhere are troubled by popular discontent. When students march in China, or workers in Poland, or average citizens in East Germany or Czechoslovakia, that discontent is page 1 news. But the demands of people on governments are not just faraway affairs. In a democracy, how the people regard their government matters even more. Our own government attracts discontent, because what it does—or fails to do—really matters.

Virtually all of society's problems eventually land on the government's doorstep. Inflation, unemployment, race relations, equal rights, abortion rights, nuclear power, crime, drugs, the relations between labor and business, environmental protection—there is an endless list of issues, new and old, about which government is asked to do something. Issues like these make up the changing agenda of our government, and they are nothing quite so much as an array of conflicts that individuals and groups have not been able to solve among themselves.

Discontent, then, can mean only that government really does matter. But an absence of pervasive trust in government today, documented by one poll after another over the years, is still a troublesome feature of American democracy. Popular unease, and even disillusionment, make governing more difficult and public decisions less acceptable. Government's legitimacy itself soon suffers.

Yet America's democratic ideals and the institutions of our government are in no danger of withering away. In this text, you will learn that democracy is firmly rooted in our Constitution, our system of government, and our political processes. You will also see how democratic values are a central element of American culture. The democratic way of life is taught in schools and in the family; it is celebrated by political leaders; it is closely monitored by the media and the public. Not surprisingly, then, we find it comfortable to accept the general values of popular government, liberty, and equality. We can never forget that democracy in America has endured for more than 200 years. It has survived—and should continue to outlast—the dislocations of wars, depressions, and long periods of international tension.

Democracy in America is as vital as ever. And by better understanding it, you can help make it even stronger. A crucial part of its vitality is the willingness of its citizens to take politics seriously. The more you learn about America and its politics, the better you will be able to protect our freedoms and to influence how we are governed.

We hope that your study of our nation's government will not only expand your understanding, but also encourage you to take politics seriously. If the authors of this book have done their job well, you will soon come to share some of their fascination with American government and politics.

W. J. K.
H. J. A.
W. H. F.
C. O. J.
M. S. O.
J. W. S.

Chapter 1

Politics, Continuity, and Change

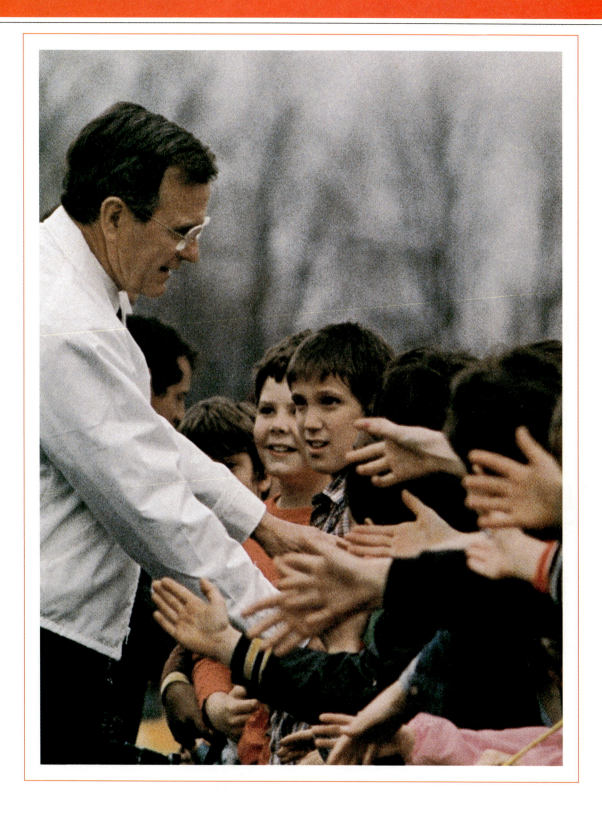

Politics. American politics. What is it? By one definition, politics is the science and art of government. To some it means simply participation in public affairs. In the ancient Greek city-state of Plato and Aristotle, politics was viewed as a public duty of citizens.

To many Americans, politics carries an unsavory connotation. "That's just politics," one hears again and again. It is said, for example, that politics is unprincipled and that public business is rife with "political" deals, with favors, graft, and maneuvering. Just as commonly, politics is seen as dominated by self-interest and "sleaze." Clearly, much of the American public takes a cynical view of political activity and of politicians. Its impression, of course, is not necessarily accurate. At the least, it is incomplete—a partial view of a complex reality.

Contemporary political science generally treats politics in neutral, or value-free, terms. It seeks to understand and explain this activity. And for a very good reason, politics needs to be properly understood: It is the centerpiece of American political life. Politics emerges from the complexity and diversity of society, from relationships of political power between governors and governed,[1] and from the need to make binding decisions. All institutions of government and all policy-making processes are threaded by it; hence it is an illusion to think that "politics" can somehow be eliminated from "governing." Politics is, in fact, the essence of governing, especially in democratic systems.

Politics as Who Gets What, When, and How

The dynamics of politics are captured in Harold Lasswell's classic definition. Politics, he wrote, is "who gets what, when, and how." Using this framework, Figure 1–1 presents a broad and contemporary sketch of the political process, showing a variety of linkages between the key factors of participants (who), goals (what), and methods (how).[2]

"But let us try to forget politics for the moment."

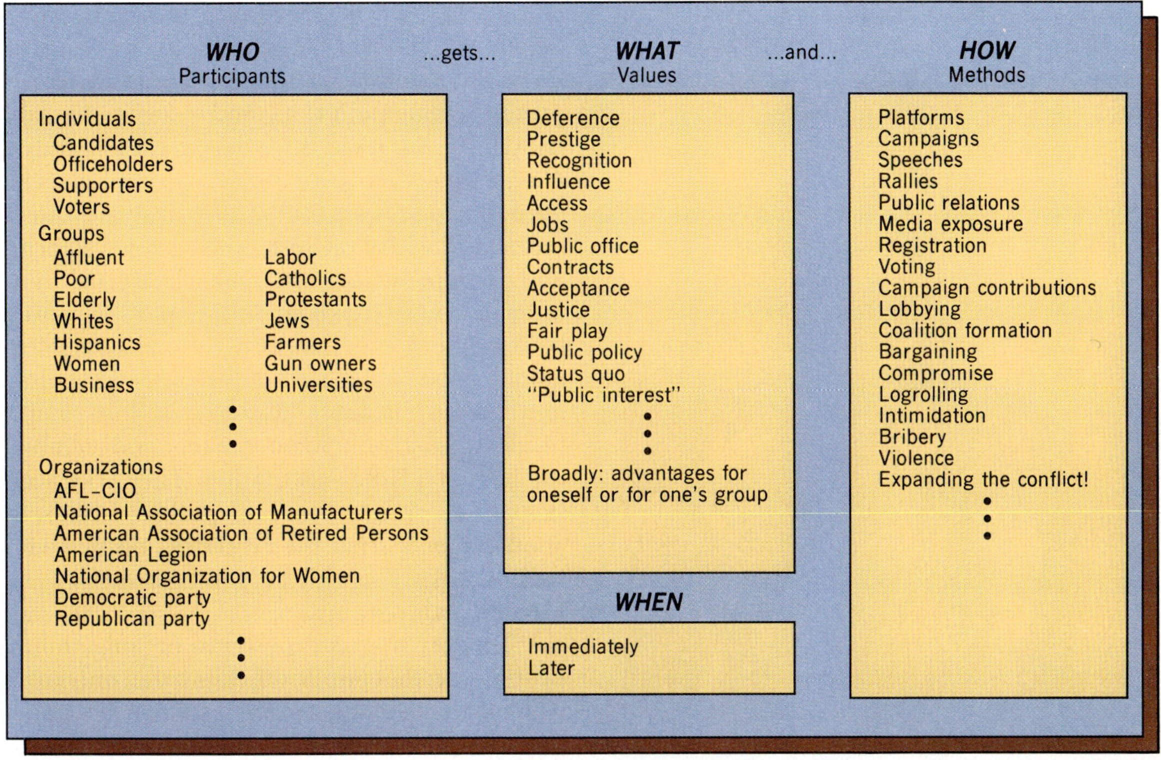

Figure 1–1 Politics—who gets what, when, and how. This simplified picture of the Lasswell model discussed in the text focuses on only some of the possible participants, their values, and their methods. But the questions are the same: Who participates? What do they want? How and when do they get it?

Participation in Politics: Individuals

People participate in politics as individuals, acting independently, and as members of groups. In political campaigns, for example, individuals write letters, discuss issues, make telephone calls, ring doorbells, address envelopes, make campaign contributions, display bumper stickers, contact officeholders, and vote, among other things. Some people are involved in nearly all of these activities, some in just a few, and a surprising number in none. Democratic political systems permit individuals to be participants in the political process, active critics, or simply spectators.

Life experiences help to shape political behavior. The most important factor in participation is education. College graduates are more likely to engage in a range of political activities, from voting to running for office. Persons with higher incomes are more likely to participate than those with lower incomes. Professionals, such as physicians and lawyers, are much more active politically than laborers. Social class is clearly a key factor in explaining differences in involvement in politics.

Older persons (except the very old) participate more than young persons, men participate more than women (particularly in campaign activities), and whites participate more than blacks.[3] Nevertheless, differences in participation linked to race, ethnicity, and gender are much less pronounced today, largely as a result of the adoption of voting rights legislation and a narrowing of differences in educational attainment and occupation.

No feature of American democracy is of greater significance for the conduct of politics than freedom of speech. Here Dennis Banks, American Indian activist, carries a child in one arm while speaking at a rally on the rights of American Indians.

Participation in Politics: Groups

Individuals also participate in politics as members of groups and organizations. Although Americans place great emphasis on individualism, they eagerly form and join groups to promote political objectives. They band together to save the whales, defend the interests of labor or of business, curb the use of nuclear power, advance Indian interests, protest ocean pollution, and restrict the sale of handguns. As David B. Truman's classic study *The Governmental Process* argues, in complex societies "group experiences and affiliations" are the chief means "by which the individual *knows, interprets,* and *reacts* to the society in which he exists."[4] Voters often evaluate candidates and parties against a backdrop of group interests. Union leaders, for example, know which side of their bread is buttered, and so do business leaders, welfare mothers, blacks, Christian fundamentalists, and members of the National Rifle Association. They vote accordingly. The group theory of politics insists, with good evidence, that the attitudes and behavior of individuals are significantly influenced by their affiliations with groups.

The key to group power is organization. The proposition that public officials listen only to those who make the loudest noise is not wholly true. But there is little doubt that political decision makers are seldom as attentive to sounds coming from the unorganized public. It could hardly be otherwise amid the noisy clamor of organized voices. Is it easier for government to hear the appeals of migrant workers or those of organized agriculture?

The demands of individual workers, businesspersons, farmers, or physicians for responses from government may not be heeded. But the preferences of their organizations—such as the AFL-CIO, the Chamber of Commerce of the United States, the American Farm Bureau Federation, or the American Medical Association—are certain at least to catch the attention of public officials. The women's vote in elections may be critical—when it differs significantly from the men's vote—but the continuing influence of women on public policy is more likely to depend on the resourcefulness of their organizations that press claims on government. The picture is clear: "All power is organization and all organization is power. . . . A man who has no share in any form of organized power is not independent of organized power. He is at the mercy of it."[5]

Objectives in Politics

What do participants want from politics? The main answer is that participants want the institutions of government to make decisions that protect their existing advantages or confer new advantages on them. It follows that the decisions of government typically are conflictual because they benefit individuals and groups differently. Collisions occur because a policy that benefits one group often costs another.

Participation in politics carries a variety of inducements. Figure 1–1 included some of the values Americans seek in political activity. Some citizens become local precinct committeemen and committeewomen because party office gives them access to local government, a measure of community recognition, occasions for camaraderie and socializing, opportunities to influence the distribution of public goods (perhaps additional street lights and stop signs in their neighborhoods), and a job in city or county government. Scope is the key element in political positions. The more prominent the position—representative, senator, governor, president—the greater the opportunities for its occupant to gain personal indulgences (deference, recognition, prestige, influence), to be in the network and "in the know," to shape public policy on matters of importance, and often, as a matter of fact, to advance a conception of the public interest. Politics is thus not aimless participation, indifferent relationships, or ambiguous expression. Ultimately it concerns matters that count.

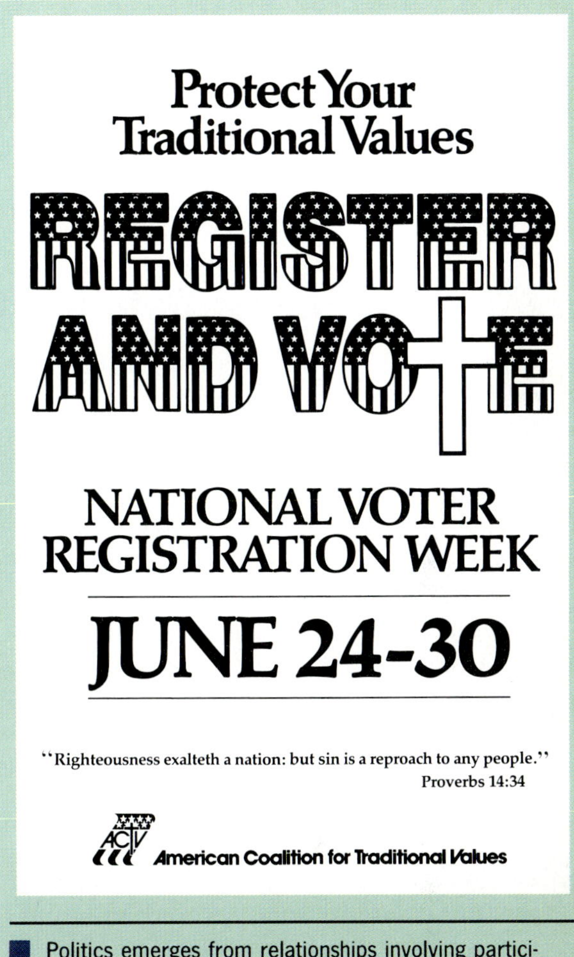

Protect Your Traditional Values
REGISTER AND VOTE
NATIONAL VOTER REGISTRATION WEEK
JUNE 24-30
"Righteousness exalteth a nation: but sin is a reproach to any people."
Proverbs 14:34
ACTV
American Coalition for Traditional Values

Politics emerges from relationships involving participants, values, and methods—or "who gets what, when, and how." This poster links religious values and symbols with voting. People are urged to register and vote in order to uphold traditional values, such as expressed by a well-known maxim from the Bible.

Most individuals and groups are interested in public policy rather than in public or party office. What do *they* want? Consider a few examples, large and small. College students and administrators lobby Congress for the continuation and expansion of such programs as Pell grants, guaranteed student loans, and the College Work Study Program. Groups such as the National Education Association regularly descend on Congress to lobby for additional funds for elementary, secondary, and vocational education. Major research universities urge, first, that research funding be increased and, second, that funds be allotted through a process of peer review rather than through the pork barrel (or earmarking) method that rewards universities in the home states of influential lawmakers. Institutions know what they want: Higher education wants more money.

Environmental groups, working for clean air and clean water, press for legislation to restrict

Politics and Ideas: Defining the Key Concepts

Power: The ability in politics to control or change the behavior of human beings in a way favored by the power-wielder. Some political analysts link influence and force with power, whereas others regard them as distinct techniques employed in the pursuit of objectives. ["Power" often connotes the use of force, while "influence" does not.] Power can be divided into political, economic, social, and military categories. Power can also be viewed as a means, an end, or both, and as actual or potential. As a practical matter, A can be said to exercise power over B if A can get B to do something that B would otherwise not do, or had refused to do.

Influence: The power of a person or group to produce effects without the exertion of physical force or authority, based on wealth, social position, ability, etc.

Authority: Power and influence based on legitimacy. Authority involves the acceptance by others of the right to rule, to issue commands, to make rules, and to expect compliance with them. If an individual or a group recognizes and accepts another's control and direction, the latter functions in a legitimate or rightful capacity and exercises authority over the former.

Legitimacy: Recognition and acceptance of the exercise of political power. Legitimacy is based on the conversion of the exercise of political power or the assumption of a political position into a situation of "rightful" authority. Within a nation, legitimacy means that the people accept the government and the role of the rulers in exercising power. Election victories thus assign power and create legitimacy.

Source: Jack C. Plano and Milton Greenberg, *The American Political Dictionary* (New York: Holt, Rinehart & Winston, 1985).

emissions of pollutants such as chlorofluorocarbons, which deplete the ozone layer, and to impose strict standards for the use of pesticides. Businesses (worried about their factories, products, and the bottom line), farmers (worried about their crops), and even some cities (worried about losing federal grants by failure to meet clean-air standards) line up in opposition.

Year in and year out, organized labor's policy "wish list" is one of the most comprehensive of all. In the 100th Congress (1987–1988), for example, labor lobbied Congress to increase the federal minimum wage, to require employers to give advance notice of plant closings and mass layoffs, to increase funding for child care (both parties' "hot ticket" item in the 1988 presidential campaign), to institute mandated minimum health benefits for all workers, to require employers to notify workers who may be at risk of developing occupational diseases, and to require public and private employers to grant unpaid family and medical leaves to employees. On all of these issues, major elements of organized business, such as the Chamber of Commerce of the United States, were arrayed in opposition. Struggles between labor and business are never far below the surface during any administration.

Not all participants in the policy-making process are American nationals. Foreign governments and businesses care intensely about American public policy. Many hire American law firms and well-known lobbyists to represent them in Congress and before administrative agencies. And many law firms solicit contracts to represent foreign interests. Some members of Congress become ardent advocates for certain countries.

When trade legislation is under consideration in Congress, foreign countries seek tariff reductions for their products and oppose various protectionist provisions that would restrict their access to U.S. markets. They also oppose legislation that would limit foreign ownership of U.S. assets or that would require them to disclose information about their investments. Third World countries lobby for debt relief. Some countries urge Congress and especially the administration (which has considerable discretion in these matters) to sell them particular weapons systems, such as fighter bombers and air-to-ground missiles, and other countries lobby against these sales; conflict between foreign countries occurs in the halls of Congress and elsewhere in Washington as well as "back home." Economic and military aid is of critical importance to many countries, and they press hard for increased funding and maximum discretion in spending these funds. Foreign countries also oppose congressional sanctions for countries that fail to cooperate with U.S. efforts to reduce drug trafficking, and they oppose bans against the sale of their products in the United States, such as the sales ban against Toshiba Corporation of Japan for having sold certain equipment to the Soviet Union that could be used to improve the performance of Soviet submarines.

The salient point is that the American political process is less insular than might be supposed. American politics is vitally important to foreign nations, and the system's overall openness encourages those nations to participate in it. Even Deng Xiaoping, China's senior leader, got into the act in 1988, remarking to visiting Secretary of Defense Frank Carlucci that he hoped George Bush would be elected president.

To complete this analysis of political goals, we need to point out that groups are often as concerned with protecting the status quo—securing exemptions from general policies and preventing the adoption of new legislation—as they are with changing policies. Physicians typically oppose extensions of governmental health care programs; many industries fight tighter clean-air requirements; the tobacco industry opposes more comprehensive health warning labels (for example, adding that smoking is addictive as well as an agent in heart disease and cancer); the coal industry resists acid rain controls; and businesses advantaged by free trade combat protectionist measures, such as textile quotas, because they fear that other nations will retaliate against their products. Efforts to preserve the status quo frequently appear to dominate Washington policy making.

Methods in Politics ■

Understanding American government, however, means more than simply knowing "who gets what." Politics is also about the strategies or methods that participants use to achieve their objectives.

In democratic institutions, the "how" of politics means collaboration. Consider Congress, where persuasion, bargaining, and compromise are accepted ways of doing business—as they are in democratic legislatures everywhere. Lawmaking consists of working out major and marginal compromises among ideas advanced for legislation. The sifting and sorting of proposals accompanies the search for agreement—in the party caucus, in

IMPACT

People in Politics: Officeholding

People participate in politics for social, economic, and psychological rewards and advantages. Some politically active persons concentrate on winning *elective* public office. What are their chances? Not bad—particularly at the grass roots level. Here is what a recent inventory of elected officials by the Census Bureau shows:

Municipal	137,688
Township	120,790
School	86,772
Housing, water and sewer, and other special districts	80,509
County	59,932
State	18,171
Federal	542
Total	504,404

The federal officials include the 435 members of the House of Representatives, 100 senators, five delegates to Congress from U.S. territories and the District of Columbia, the vice president, and the president.

Who holds these positions? Eighty percent are men; only 2 percent are black and 1 percent Hispanic. Women are most likely to be elected to school boards, where they make up 26.5 percent of the total, or to township office (23.1 percent). Blacks are most often elected to positions in municipal government—but only as 3.3 percent of elected public officials. In terms of their proportions in the population, women, blacks, and Hispanics are all substantially underrepresented.

Source: *New York Times,* January 25, 1987.

committee, on the floor, in negotiations with the executive, in dealing with interest groups. Politics in democratic institutions, such as legislatures, is distinguished by discussion, tolerance, a disposition to bargain, a willingness to examine issues from others' perspectives (which contributes to logrolling, or vote trading), and compromise.

Like other activities, politics also has a seamy side. Sometimes its methods are unconventional, objectionable, even illegal. Intimidation, coercion, bribery, and violence have all been used to shape political decisions and induce compliance. Elections have sometimes been debased by corrupt practices. Legislators, executives, judges, and bureaucrats occasionally have been bribed and blackmailed to deliver votes and decisions (perhaps more often in novels than in the real world). Abuses of power and utter disregard for the rule of law, as in the Iran-contra scandal, have tainted government and shaken popular confidence in the system. A president and a vice president—Richard M. Nixon in 1974 and Spiro Agnew in 1973—have been driven from office amid criminal charges. Violence and public law have been used to repress citizens and obstruct the suffrage and other forms of political participation—the central story of white-black relations in the South from the collapse of the Reconstruction governments to the passage of the Voting Rights Act of 1965.

But politics in America is not just stories like these, and one does not have to repudiate politics to deplore the excesses and abuses of power and trust. And if Washington journalists wake up every morning and go to bed every night savoring thoughts of winning a Pulitzer Prize for a thundering exposé of some official wrongdoing—well, that, too, is politics.

"Who gets what, when, and how": These questions are as relevant to analyzing politics today as when Lasswell asked them in the 1930s. Systems change, administrations come and go, politicians fade away, but politics remains largely the same. In this interpretation, politics is relational. Thinking about it requires analysts to focus on three key benchmarks: participants, methods, and outcomes ("values") in political life.

Politics as Conflict

Politics in free societies emerges from the collision of competing interests. Sometimes conflicts can be settled privately and directly through economic competition, negotiations, bargaining, boycotts,

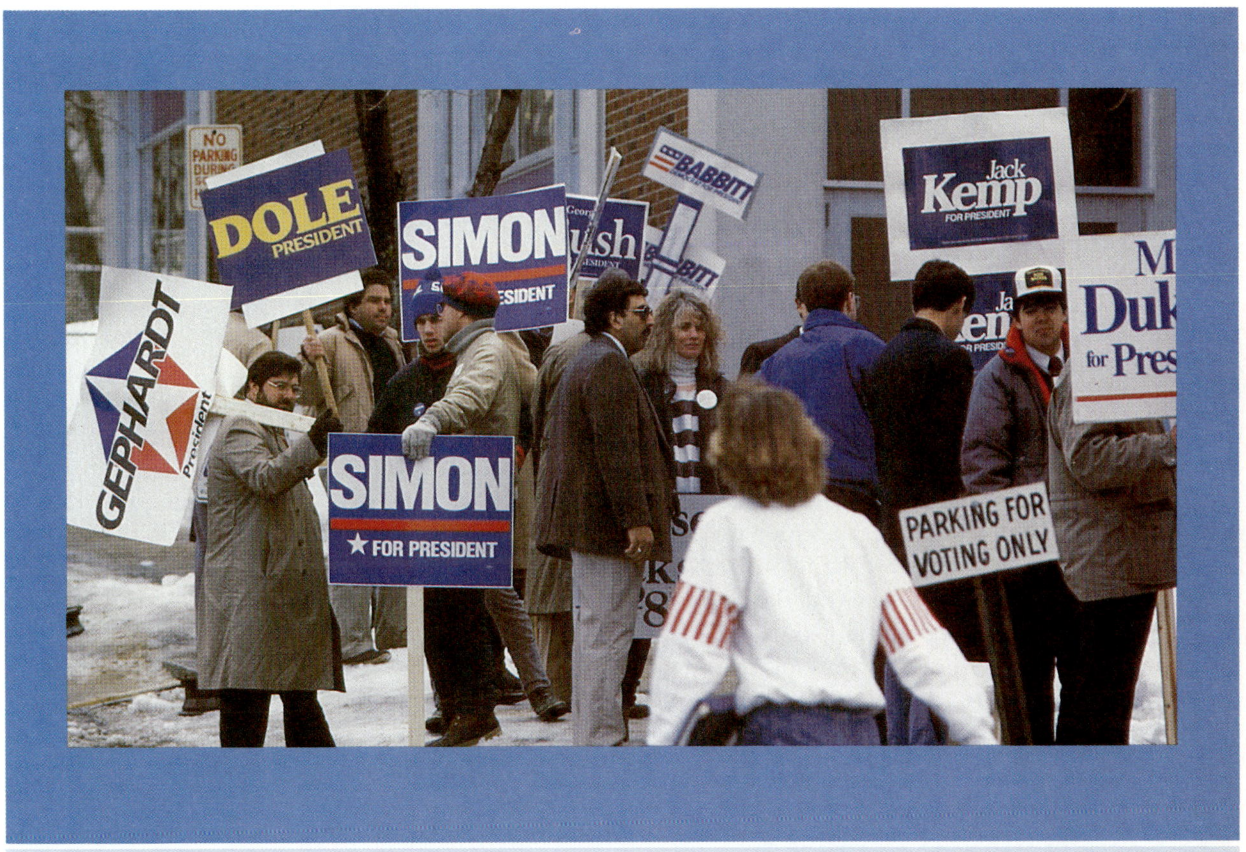

Electioneering is a major method of democratic politics. Here candidate organizations in both parties compete for support among New Hampshire primary voters in 1988. Whatever else primaries may do, they screen out "losers" in the political struggle.

"Do we have enough might to make it right?"

picketing, sanctions, protests, accommodation, and the reciprocal denial of goods and services. As long as disputes are confined to relationships between those immediately involved, as E. E. Schattschneider observes, no political process is initiated. "Conflicts become political only when an attempt is made to involve the wider public." The essence of politics is the "struggle between the conflicting tendencies toward the *privatization* [restriction or localization] and *socialization* [expansion or nationalization] of conflict." Schattschneider's approach both complements and extends our earlier framework. Politics, he concludes, "has its origin in strife."[6]

The Socialization of Conflict

Looking at politics as the socialization of conflict means focusing on the *method* of politics. Individuals and groups who are losing—ignored, limited, repressed—in private disputes or are disadvantaged by existing law and practice seek outside help in order to improve their position.

This model of politics is sketched in Figure 1–2. Losers in private or localized conflicts may, of course, decide that the odds are so stacked against them that expanded conflict is likely to be fruitless. Lacking confidence, anticipating more losses, and fearful of retaliation, they pack it in, at least for the time being.

More commonly, however, the losing side in the political battle searches for reinforcements. It knows that conflict is elastic and that opportunities to win in other arenas may be available. Leaders, resources, and, above all, compelling ideas and symbols are needed to draw the attention of the press and television. Stories on network television, or in the *New York Times* or *Washington Post,* can transform local conflicts into national issues in a matter of days and, at the same time, catch the eye of political leaders. The basic strategy is thus to get more people, and eventually government, involved. New participants change the nature of the fight. "The outcome of every conflict," Schattschneider writes, "is determined by the *extent* to which the audience becomes involved in it." "If a fight starts," he continues, "watch the crowd, because the crowd plays the decisive role."[7]

Private, localized conflicts are inherently unstable—one side is winning most of what can be won while the other chafes under the pressure of accumulating losses. Sooner or later, grievances growing, the weaker side seeks outside intervention to redress the balance. "The flight to government is perpetual."[8]

Ideas to Expand and Contract Conflict ■

The struggle to capture the government's attention and to gain a place on its agenda takes place largely in the realm of ideas and symbols, as shown

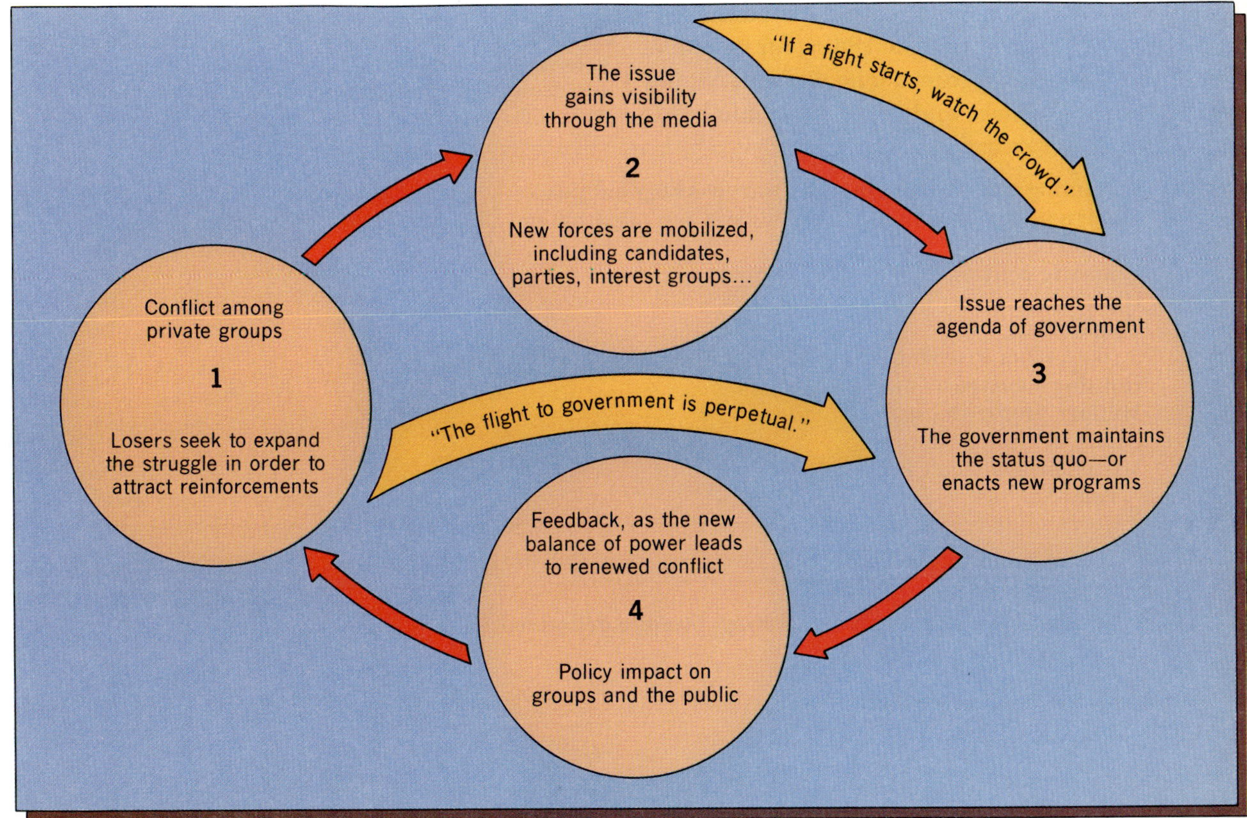

■ **Figure 1–2** Politics as conflict expansion. In the Schattschneider model pictured here, "democratic government is the greatest single instrument for the socialization of conflict." Democratic governments provide an arena in which to resolve private disputes. What ultimately happens to conflicts on the "agenda" depends on four factors: (1) the scope of the conflict, (2) the importance of other conflicts competing for attention in government, (3) the intensity and influence of the competing groups, and (4) the range of governmental powers and resources.

Continuity & CHANGE

Policy Agendas over Four Decades

Several times each year, the Gallup Poll attempts to chart the concerns of the nation in a random sample of American adults. A useful question has proved to be this: "What do you think is the most important problem facing this country today?" In the table below are shown the answers that have emerged over 40 years.

Whereas some issues, mainly economic ones, are chronically on the public's mind, others emerge and disappear. During the late 1940s, for instance, the nation was turning from a long war and coping with shortages, strikes, and other economic hardships of a postwar economy. These concerns were replaced in the late 1960s by Vietnam, race relations, and crime. Today, it is the budget deficit and illegal drugs. The political agenda in Washington reflects those changes.

Source: George H. Gallup, *The Gallup Poll: Public Opinion 1935–1971* (New York, Random House, 1972), vol. I, pp. 726–727, vol. III, p. 2128; Gallup Poll press release, September 18, 1988. The polls were conducted on March 19–24, 1948; May 2–7, 1968; and September 9–11, 1988. The responses in the first two polls total more than 100 percent because some respondents cited more than one problem; after 1987 Gallup changed the procedures to record only the first response.

1948	
Preventing war, peace, danger of war, working out peace	38%
Foreign policy, getting along with Russia and other nations, helping Europe recover from war	27%
Domestic politics, presidential election	9%
Higher prices, cost of living, inflation	8%
Communism	7%
Strikes, labor problems	2%
Housing shortage	2%
Military preparedness	1%
Future of United Nations	1%
Miscellaneous, don't know	6%
Total	101%
1968	
Vietnam situation	42%
Race relations	25%
Crime and lawlessness (rioting, looting, juvenile delinquency)	15%
High cost of living, taxes	8%
Poverty	4%
General unrest in nation	3%
Other, don't know	12%
Total	109%
1988	
Budget deficit	12%
Economy (general)	12%
Other economic problems	12%
Drugs	11%
Unemployment	9%
War, international problems	9%
Poverty	7%
Other, don't know	28%
Total	100%

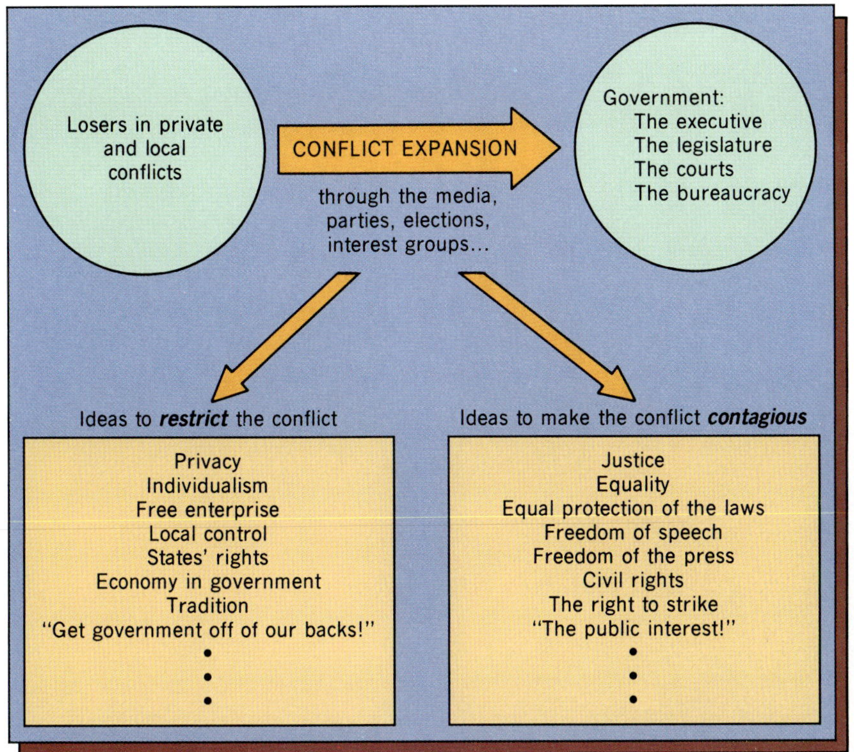

Figure 1–3 Expanding the conflict. In this model, discussed further in the text, groups use more than just competing parties and politicians to control a conflict or invite public support. They depend as well on ideas and symbols—many of which we think of as American democracy itself. The figure depicts only a few of the possibilities.

in Figure 1–3. Efforts to expand the scope of conflict are not necessarily successful. Those on the winning side attempt to exclude the audience and keep the government from intervening, invoking such powerful ideas (values, doctrines) as individualism, free enterprise, privacy, local control, states' rights (to keep Washington out of their fight), tradition, and the need for economy in government. Even the size of the federal budget deficit can be used to discourage new governmental undertakings. Winners in local and private struggles also have friends in government who will be less inclined to use government to break open private conflicts. "Government is not the solution to our problem," Ronald Reagan said in his inaugural address. "Government is the problem!" Acceptance of that position contracts the government's agenda and limits the socialization of conflict.

By contrast, losers rest their appeals on such contagious ideas as justice, equality, liberty, equal protection of the laws, the First Amendment freedoms, fair play, and standards of the public interest. In addition to stirring up public opinion, these ideas encourage the government to intervene—to see that "justice is done," constitutional protections upheld, minorities defended, or the interests of the broader public safeguarded. Ideas are the critical element in determining the scale of conflict in American politics. One set compresses conflict, the other inflates it.

The Contagion of Conflict ■

Conflict is inherently contagious. And for many reasons conflicts spread easier today than in the past. One reason is that the *suffrage has been extended*—more "players" are involved. The first major expansion of the electorate in the twentieth century came with the adoption of the Nineteenth Amendment (1920), giving women the right to vote.

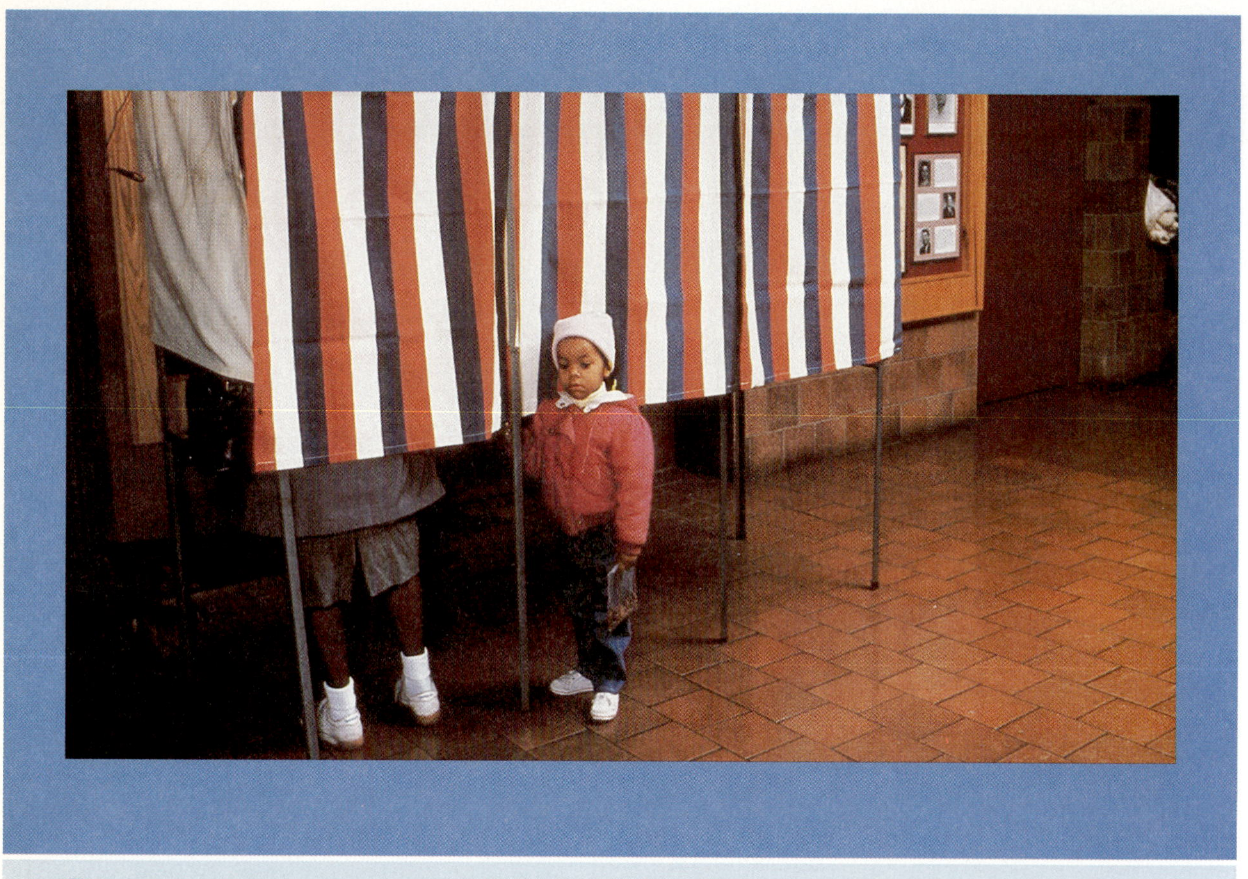

Voting, a political resource for one, an interlude for the other. This photo also illustrates the phenomenon of "political socialization," the process by which persons (particularly during childhood) acquire their political beliefs and orientations—including their attitude toward voting.

With adoption of the Twenty-third Amendment in 1961, residents of the District of Columbia were given the right to vote for president. Passage of the Voting Rights Act of 1965 brought blacks into the political process in unprecedented numbers after generations of exclusion. And young voters between 18 and 21 entered the electorate following the ratification of the Twenty-sixth Amendment in 1971.

Every extension of the suffrage carries major repercussions for society: Old grievances are illuminated, new interests are consolidated, and new participants enter the political process. The result of changing the electorate is that it becomes more difficult to keep the lid on old, often discriminatory, practices and settlements. Changing electorates ultimately culminate in policy shifts.

A second reason why opportunities to expand conflict are greater today turns on the *emergence and development of new political skills, patterns, and institutions.* Organized protests—marches, parades, cavalcades, demonstrations, rallies, flotillas, sit-ins, boycotts, fasts, and the like—have become a major form of political activity since the civil rights movement of the 1950s. Groups lacking in economic resources are particularly prone to de-

“ Perspectives ”

On the Public Interest

People may participate in public life to promote their conception of "the public interest" (or "the common good"). But what is meant by the term? Neither scholars nor politicians agree on its meaning. It is viewed broadly and narrowly, as goal and as symbol, and as policy result and as process. Consider this sampling of definitions:

"*If a majority are capable of preferring their own private interest, or that of their families, counties, and party, to that of the nation collectively, some provision must be made in the constitution, in favor of justice, to compel all to respect the common right, the public good, the universal law, in preference to all private and partial considerations.*"

—John Adams

"*The public interest may be presumed to be what men would choose if they saw clearly, thought rationally, acted disinterestedly and benevolently.*"

—Walter Lippmann

"*The public interest may be described as the aggregate of common interests, including the common interest in seeing that there is fair play among private interests. The public interest is not the mere sum of the special interests, and it is certainly not the sum of the organized* special interests. Nor is it an automatic consequence of the struggle of the special interests (a struggle in which everyone demands too much and feels entitled to it)."

—E. E. Schattschneider

"*[The will of the people] serves as a symbol to legitimize the acts of any group that can successfully identify itself with it in the public mind.*"

—Norton Long

"*The public interest rests not in some policy emerging from the settlement of conflict, but with the method of that settlement itself, with compromising in a peaceful, orderly, predictable way the demands put upon policy.*"

—Frank J. Sorauf

"*By theorizing that governing is something above and beyond the mere compilation of pressure group demands, the public interest model threatens to take the politics out of governing. . . . By comparison with Europeans, Americans put little stock in the public interest as a doctrine. This is not because Americans have a weaker sense of national pride or desire to do good than do Europeans, but rather because Americans have tended to reject government as the chief means of providing for the public good.*"

—Richard Rose

Sources: John Adams, *A Defense of the Constitutions of Government of the United States of America* (London: 1788), vol. 3, pp. 215–216; Walter Lippmann, *The Public Philosophy* (New York: Mentor, 1955), p. 40; E. E. Schattschneider, "Political Parties and the Public Interest," *The Annals* (March 1952), p. 22; Norton Long, "Bureaucracy and Constitutionalism," *American Political Science Review* (September 1952), p. 809; Frank J. Sorauf, "The Public Interest Reconsidered," *Journal of Politics* (November 1957), p. 638; Richard Rose, *What Is Governing? Purpose and Policy in Washington* (Englewood Cliffs, N.J.: Prentice-Hall, 1978), pp. 80–81. For a wide-ranging critique of the concept, see Glendon Schubert, *The Public Interest* (Glencoe, Ill.: Free Press, 1960).

monstrative activity. In general terms, protests are triggered by crises, heightened discontent, discrimination, and inability to adjust to change. Today, organized protests are common on such issues as civil rights, abortion, pollution, ocean dumping, welfare policy, nuclear power, gay rights, pesticides, public health, law enforcement, gun control, school prayer, equal rights, social security, pornography, and conditions of employment. A new openness in society and the public's greater toleration for dissent assure groups of an opportunity to press their case intensely. Almost anything goes in contemporary "piece-of-the-action" politics. And groups worry less about retaliation. Washington itself has become a "demonstration city."

At no time in American history has it been easier to challenge the status quo, start fights, embroil others, and press for the redress of grievances. Everywhere, things are up for grabs. Hierarchy has been replaced by bargaining and accommodation. Discipline in institutions is easily set aside in favor of personal expression and the defense of narrow interests. No one waits for party leaders, for example, to give them the nod before running for office. Almost everyone holding major public office can entertain fantasies about running for president. And with the weakening of the norms of apprenticeship and specialization in Congress, even the greenest member can make his or her presence felt immediately:

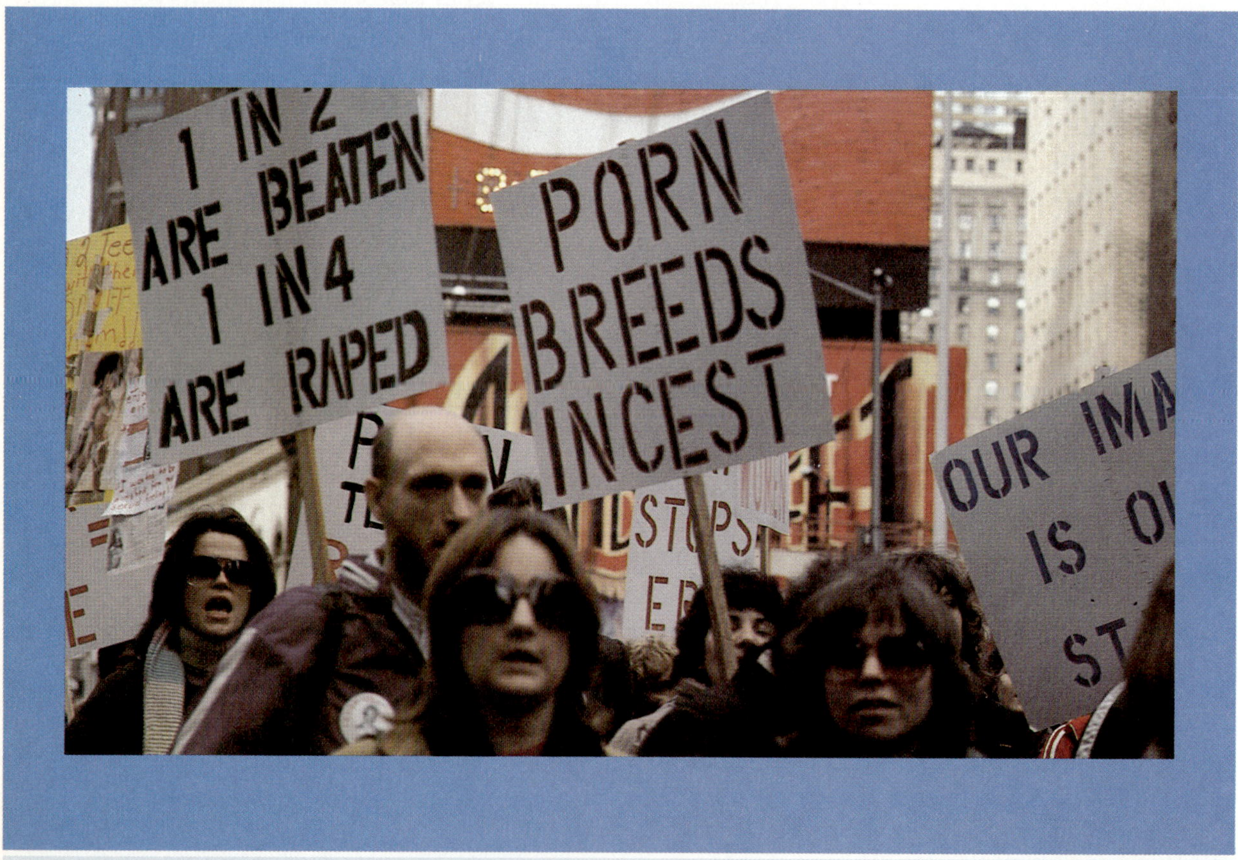

Rallies and marches have become increasingly important methods for groups to reflect their values, express discontent, and mobilize support for a course of action (such as banning pornographic literature and movies).

> It's terribly frustrating. You come out of a committee with some kind of a proposal that seems to be rather reasonable and then all of a sudden it's like a dog in heat trotting down the street. You attract every conceivable idea, wild, weird and otherwise, that ever penetrated the mind of a human being. . . . When I came to the Senate, you almost waited for the senior members to speak first. You weren't really so audacious as to speak first, let alone challenge on the floor or elsewhere.[9] *Senator Mark Hatfield (R-Ore.)*

> Party discipline doesn't matter because parties don't matter. There's no discipline, just 30,000 special interests that we're all serving in one way or another.[10] *Senator David F. Durenberger (R-Minn.)*

> If Lyndon [Johnson] were here today and tried to crack the whip, [a member] would simply go out on the Capitol steps before the TV cameras and raise hell. . . . that man would be a hero.[11] *Former Senate leader Howard H. Baker, Jr. (R-Tenn.)*

A third explanation for the relative ease with which conflicts are expanded lies in the *widespread acceptance of the idea of the positive state*—a theory that it is both appropriate and necessary for government (in particular, the national government) to initiate social and economic programs designed to enhance individual security and promote social goods. Government does more than provide for the common defense. It is now expected to address problems that confound and threaten the lives of its citizens. At issue are such matters as justice, income, jobs, education, health, safety, and equal opportunity.

The two major parties are not equally committed to the positive state. Nor, however, do they hold altogether different perspectives. Many of the differences appear in the *extent* to which they would use government to solve problems and in the *level of government* to bear responsibility for programs. The Democratic tendency is liberal, expansive (government role), and national (level of government); the Republican tendency is conservative, circumscribed (government role), and state (level of government).

Taken as a group, Democrats are more likely than Republicans to favor social welfare programs, job programs through public works, labor rather than management, tax policies that aid lower-income families, government regulation of business, and new and expanded federal programs to address private inequities or dislocations. The conservative alternatives posed by Republicans often prescribe smaller expenditures for various programs, general fiscal prudence, state government and private initiative rather than federal responsibility, and policy formations that favor business over labor, middle- and upper-income groups over lower-income groups, and, to an extent, defense expenditures over domestic programs. Republicans would lower capital gains taxes while Democrats would raise the minimum wage. When viewing the overall economy, most Republicans worry more about inflation, most Democrats more about unemployment. American parties are parties of contrasting central tendencies, shown clearly in terms of their relative willingness to use government to break open private conflicts.

Acceptance of the idea of the positive state has a major corollary: the development of activist governmental institutions. People look to the president, Congress, and the courts for solutions to their problems. Presidents develop legislative programs in response to various demands. Congress is accessible to everyone (president, constituents, interest groups, political parties, and bureaucrats) in making laws, and the courts play a significant role in public policy formation by protecting individual rights, balancing personal liberty and social equality, and defining the power and authority of public and private institutions. In the last analysis, the energy that governments require to make decisions is generated by conflicts and the claims that flow from them.

Important as the foregoing factors are in the socialization of conflict, they are still not as important as the *media*. Conflicts expand because the audience hears about them and becomes involved—

visibility of the issue is the sine qua non in conflict expansion. Hence all strategies for seeking reinforcements begin with efforts to attract the attention of the press and television. Since conflicts compete with one another for coverage, there is no assurance that any issue will receive more than cursory attention from the media. But when the media do focus sharply on an issue (candidate, theme), even people who spend their lives in caves learn about it. In the 1988 presidential campaign, scarcely any voter could have failed to learn that presidential candidate Michael Dukakis had vetoed a bill requiring teachers in Massachusetts public schools to lead their students in reciting the Pledge of Allegiance or that vice presidential candidate Dan Quayle had joined the Indiana National Guard at the height of the Vietnam War, thereby reducing his risk of being sent into combat.

In quest of news, the media expose and examine disputes, inform and activate the public, and ultimately help to shape political decisions and outcomes. Although their impact is unintended, the media's coverage of an issue invariably leads to wider controversies and, as a result, changes in the odds favoring one side or the other. Concretely, what the media do is to break up power monopolies—everywhere. And in this activity, television leads the way.[12] The broad point is that the scope of conflict is as useful in understanding issues and candidacies in campaigns as it is in understanding policy formation in governmental institutions.

The Socialization of Conflict Theory in Practice ■

In the typical pattern of conflict expansion, conflicts become more intense and visible and move from the private to the public arena and from local and state levels to the national level.

The history of race relations can be written in terms of the theory of socialization of conflict. The embarrassing truth is that it took nearly a century following the Civil War to move critical questions of race relations onto the national agenda. For decade after decade, race was hidden, treated as a local or private matter, shielded by the doctrine of states' rights. Throughout the South, blacks were excluded from the political system. Shortly after the Civil War, the Ku Klux Klan emerged to harass and intimidate the black community. Then came state legislation providing for discriminatory registration and voting systems, poll taxes (taxes on the right to vote), literacy tests, more abstruse tests based on the voter's understanding of the Constitution, grandfather clauses (to permit whites to vote if their grandfathers had been registered to vote prior to the adoption of the Fifteenth Amendment), and the privatization of the party system by limiting participation in primaries to whites. Despite the promise of the Civil War Amendments (Thirteen, Fourteen, and Fifteen), by 1900 blacks were generally disfranchised in the South.

The first major cracks in the structure of white supremacy were created by the court system. In 1915, the Supreme Court held the grandfather clause unconstitutional (*Guinn* v. *U.S.*). Challenges to the white primary began in 1927, and in 1944 the legal doctrine on which this discriminatory device rested was eliminated by the Supreme Court (*Smith* v. *Allwright*). Understanding-the-Constitution tests fell in 1949 (*Davis* v. *Schnell*). In a historic decision in 1954, the Court held that racial discrimination in public schools was unconstitutional (*Brown* v. *Board of Education*). The use of the poll tax in federal elections was outlawed by adoption of the Twenty-fourth Amendment in 1964, and the poll tax in state elections was eliminated by the Supreme Court in 1966 (*Harper* v. *Virginia Board of Elections*). One system after another was thus toppled by the courts.

Congress next became involved, passing four civil rights acts between 1957 and 1965. The Civil Rights Act of 1964 barred discrimination in public accommodations, in employment, and in any activity receiving federal funds. It remained for the Voting Rights Act of 1965 to shatter the legal basis of black disfranchisement throughout the South. Under its provisions, literacy tests or other voter qualification devices used for discriminatory purposes were suspended in any state or county in which less than 50 percent of the voting-age residents were registered to vote in November 1964 or less than 50 percent voted in the 1964 presidential election. Black registration and voting have risen dramatically since then. The point is that race relations (and the distribution of political power) in the United States were fundamentally changed by the socialization of conflict—that is, by the intervention of the national government on the side of those who had been losing in state and local arenas. Intensive media coverage of civil rights demonstrations, led by Martin Luther King, Jr., and others, undoubtedly played a major role in putting civil rights issues at the top of the federal government's agenda in the 1950s and 1960s.

Changes in politics and policies depend on the spread of information inducing others to enter the fray. At work are the dynamics of "widening the circle," as Hedrick Smith writes in *The Power Game.* Using Schattschneider's theory, he explains shifts in U.S. policy toward Nicaragua:

> Initially [in the agency's covert war against the Sandinistas] the CIA began secretly to arm the Nicaraguan *contras.* Only a few people in the government and in Congress knew what the CIA was doing. . . . By early 1984, internal critics felt the CIA had overstepped its

Leaders of the March on Washington in August, 1963: Dr. Martin Luther King, A. Philip Randolph (far right), and Roy Wilkins (second from right). Civil rights demonstrations played a major role in moving certain issues, such as voting rights, onto the federal government's agenda.

bounds—blowing up oil depots, attacking coastal installations, and finally mining Nicaraguan harbors. Then, à la Schattschneider, these dissenters appealed to a wider audience: Critics inside the government fed information to allies on Capitol Hill. Congressional intelligence committees, the first of the wider circles, joined the fight. When policy did not change, the weaker side kept leaking embarrassing disclosures until the full Congress became involved. House Democrats, fearing a wider war, blocked further military aid to the Nicaraguan *contras* after July 1984.

As the administration was thrown on the defensive, President Reagan adopted the Schattschneider tactic: He took his case to a still wider audience, trying to revive aid to the *contras.* All pretense of a covert war was abandoned: The power game went public. Reagan threatened congressional opponents with future blame if Central America "went communist." The fear of a political backlash among voters threatened enough fence-sitting congressmen to revive military aid in 1986. Politically, the battle followed a Schattschneider scenario: What began as covert policy and an inside policy dispute escalated into an open confrontation . . . each side trying to gain the upper hand by summoning reinforcements.

This is how Washington works, again and again. . . . Those who are in control of policy, whether the president and his top advisers or bureaucrats buried in the bowels of government, will try desperately to keep the information loop small, no matter what the issue; those who are on the losing side internally will try to widen the circle. As the audience grows and the circle is widened, control over policy shifts, the conflict spreads, and the very nature of the game changes.[13]

Our examination of the "who gets" and "socialization" theories should confirm these broad, underlying notions: (1) The first principle of political analysis is that politics is everywhere. (2) The first principle of political systems is that politics can never be removed from governing. (3) The first principle of political reality is that politics is as American as apple pie.

Politics, Continuity, and Change

Politics has a profound impact on society at large: It is either an instrument for change or an instrument for stability. In Lasswell's frame of reference, people participate in politics both to alter and to protect existing conditions. In Schattschneider's framework, some people (losers) seek to expand conflict to change policy while others (winners) seek to constrict it in order to preserve advantages. Most politics is not grounded in altruism. In one way or another, participants attempt to manage the political system to secure favorable outcomes. They know much better than nonparticipants that *the most important thing that government does is to take sides.*

When faced with conflict, government has a range of options. It can look the other way, ignore demands, reinforce the status quo, take symbolic action, introduce marginal alterations, or turn things inside out by making substantial changes. The important question in all of this is whether the American system facilitates or impedes change. One approach to this question is to examine key institutions and system features in terms of their broad effects on political change. The analysis that follows focuses on elections, parties, and a basic system characteristic, decentralization of power.

Elections, the "Madisonian System," and Change ■

American campaigns and elections are occasions for promises of change. When politicians seek votes, change is always in the air. And changes do occur as a result of elections: New politicians with different philosophies and agendas, representing different constituencies, assume power, prepared to change things. It makes a difference whether the voters choose Ronald Reagan or Walter Mondale, elect George Bush or Michael Dukakis, or give control of Congress to the Democrats or the Republicans.

Occasionally the changes fostered by elections are dramatic—as in the case of the New Deal of Franklin D. Roosevelt (1933–1945), the Great Society of Lyndon B. Johnson (particularly during the 89th Congress, 1965–1966), and the presidency of Ronald Reagan (particularly during the 97th Congress, 1981–1982). With the New Deal came a national government more active than at any time in the past, distinguished by its interventions in the economy (typically taking the side of labor) and its eagerness to develop social welfare programs. The Johnson administration ushered in Medicare and Medicaid, the Voting Rights Act of 1965, massive increases in federal aid to education, a panoply of grant-in-aid programs for the states, a heightened concern for protecting the environment, and new agencies (including the Department of Housing and Urban Development).

By focusing sharply on the economy, with a largely "contractive" agenda, the Reagan administration moved the nation in new directions through reduced domestic spending, sizable reductions in individual and business taxes, the largest peacetime defense appropriations in the nation's history, significant cutbacks in federal regulations, and a moderate reordering of federal-state relations that gave the states greater discretion in the use of (reduced) federal aid funds.[14] In addition, and of large significance, President Reagan added a distinctively conservative cast to the federal judiciary through his court appointments (much as Roosevelt gave a markedly liberal tilt to the judiciary during his terms). In sum, the elections won by Roosevelt, Johnson, and Reagan were "critical" in the sense of reshaping both the role of the federal government (expansion, expansion, contraction) and the thrust of public policy (liberal, liberal, conservative).

Election-based policy outcomes on this scale, however, are the exception, not the rule. The American constitutional system, on the whole, impedes efforts to make major change. The framers of the Constitution established an intricate system of divided powers, checks and balances, and auxiliary precautions to reduce the government's vulnerability to factions. The "Madisonian system"—separation of powers, staggered terms of office, bicameralism, federalism, life appointments for federal judges, an independent judiciary, fixed terms of office for the president and members of Congress—makes it difficult for any group to gain firm control of the political system. The party that captures the presidency may not capture both

The "great communicator" of his time, Franklin D. Roosevelt (1933–1945) addresses a nationwide radio audience in 1940 shortly before his election to a precedent-breaking third term.

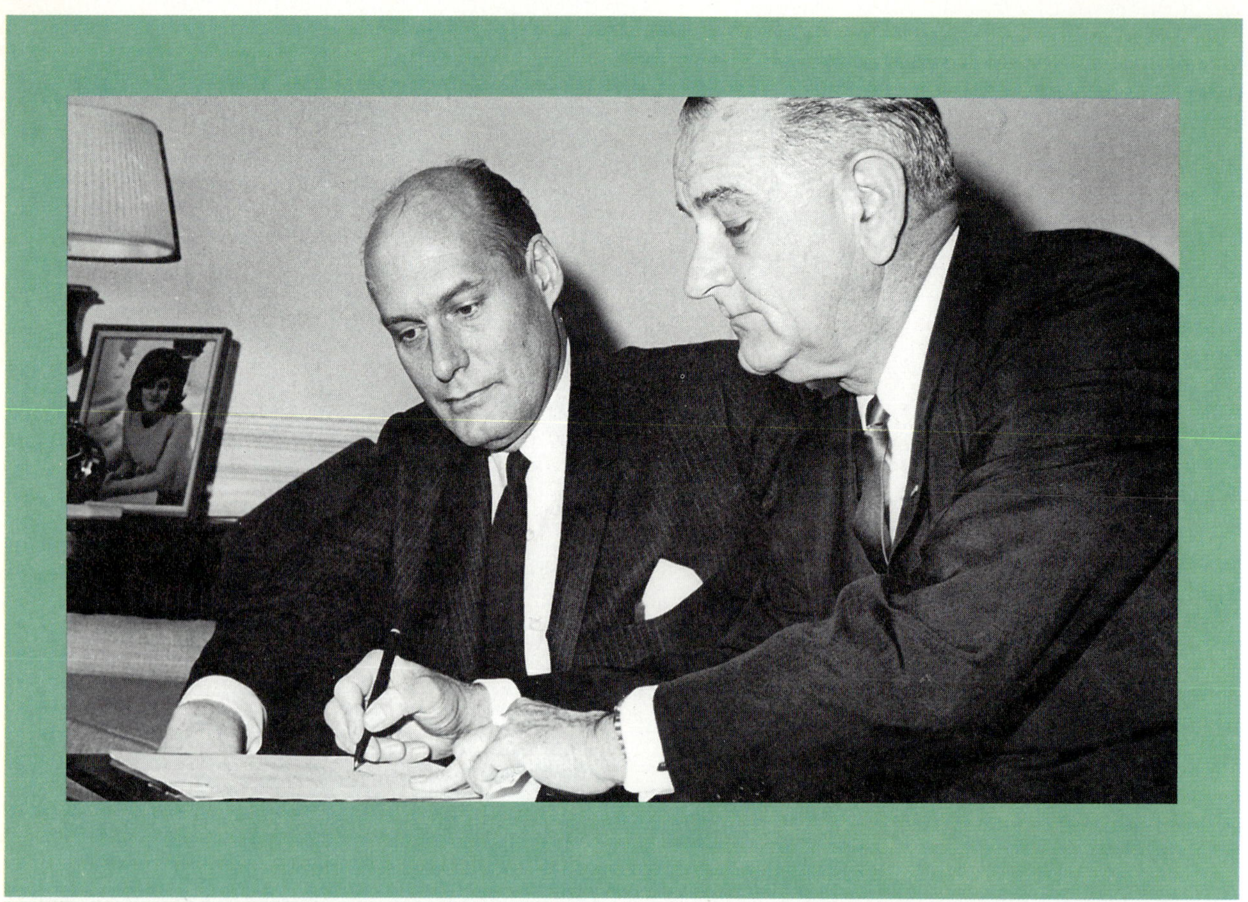

■ In the presence of Attorney General Nicholas Katzenbach, President Lyndon B. Johnson signs a letter to Congress, urging support for a bill on voting rights. Passed in 1965, the Voting Rights Act is often described as the most important civil rights legislation in the nation's history. This act banned all "voter qualification devices," such as literacy tests, that could be used to restrict black suffrage.

houses of Congress; and even if it does, it may lose one or both two years later. Justices and judges, with lifetime tenure, may be the product of previous, philosophically different administrations. The branches of the 50 state governments may be held by all manner of party and ideological combinations.

The framers knew what they wanted: a governmental system stacked against change but, at the same time, one that would not preclude it. There is more than a trace of "muddling through" in their design.

Political Parties and Change ■

The character of the American major parties also bears on opportunities for change. The parties' two dominant features are *moderation* and *inclusivity.* Because the major parties contain divergent interests, they are limited in their capacity to move sharply in any one direction. They are pushed and hauled by the groups in their coalitions. The Democratic party must deal with more conservative southerners in its ranks, the Republican party with more liberal easterners in its ranks. Neither party is monolithic. Neither one moves impetuously. Neither one is altogether predictable. Interested party elements can contest any new proposal. Every affected interest expects to be heard, bargaining occurs as a matter of course, and conciliation usually takes place. Accommodation invariably leads to tempered rather than drastic change.

The broad consequences of these patterns, ordinarily, are first, that policy making is a slow process; second, that policy changes are made incrementally; and third, that general policies are often patched together with particularistic provisions inserted simply to attract the support necessary to win. American politicians tend to be pragmatists, habituated to dealing in increments and margins. They may know next to nothing about certain issues but they know virtually everything about splitting differences. Their moderation and the moderation of the parties ordinarily mean that no one wins completely, no one loses completely. In this environment, abrupt changes are difficult to bring about.

Decentralization of Power and Change ■

No characteristic of the American political system is more pronounced than that of decentralization of power. Both the party system and the governmental system are heavily decentralized. Power slops around—here, there, and everywhere. The result is that it is difficult to fashion comprehensive or distinctly new ways of addressing public problems. As James L. Sundquist has argued: "With power dispersed, Congress remains organized to deal with narrow problems but not with broad ones. Its structure impels it to think parochially. It can skirmish for limited objectives but it cannot think strategically."[15]

Decentralization of power also affects the success of groups—in differential fashion. All the evidence suggests that groups opposed to changes in public policy have an enormous built-in advantage over groups seeking changes. This is especially evident in the congressional process. Any group, including party, that hopes to advance legislation must create successive majorities in the legislative process: first in the standing committee, then on the floor, and last in the conference committee. In the House a majority will also be needed in the Rules Committee, which schedules bills for floor consideration. Failure to achieve a majority at any stage usually dooms a proposal. And the president, waiting in the wings, may also play a role in resisting change through the veto power.

The opponents of legislation have only one requirement: to splice together a majority at any one stage in the decision-making process. Defeating legislation requires neither exceptional resources nor unusual imagination. It is simply the case that the adoption of a new public policy is immeasurably more difficult than the preservation of an old one.

Normal Politics ■

Major change in policy directions in the American setting is thus ordinarily a slow, drawn-out process. Adopted in 1965, Medicare was 25 years in the making. And after tinkering with the welfare system for half a century (since its adoption during the Great Depression), Congress in 1988 agreed to a sweeping reform bill (the Family Support Act of 1988) that, among other things, was designed to reduce welfare dependency by requiring welfare recipients to participate in job training and education programs ("workfare") or risk losing their benefits.

Legislation to protect the environment has come in fits and starts and much more slowly than environmentalists believe conditions warrant. Attempts to overhaul the Clean Air Act to add acid rain controls, for example, have failed in one Congress after another since the act's adoption in 1977. Failure stems from the inability to fashion a compromise acceptable to the coal industry, coal miners' union interests, coal-using industries such as utilities, and environmentalists.

Normal politics and normal policy making are characterized by incrementalism—a step at a time, a change here and there.

Significant change is usually predicated on the determination of a vigorous president and the existence of a cohesive, persistent, imaginative legislative majority. Disarray within the opposition party sometimes makes it easier to launch new ventures; the "Reagan revolution" of the early 1980s, for example, owed much to the support of conservative southern Democrats in both houses of Congress. But the general rule is that even under the best of circumstances, it is hard to "get hold" of the American government—and even harder to maintain control. This book illustrates this fundamental point in dozens of ways.

"The making of governmental decisions [in the American system]," Robert A. Dahl wrote some years ago, "is not a majestic march of great majorities united on certain matters of basic policy. It is the steady appeasement of relatively small groups." At the same time, the advantages of such a system are not inconsiderable: it is "a relatively efficient system for reinforcing agreement, encouraging moderation, and maintaining social peace in a restless and immoderate people operating a gigantic, powerful, diversified, and incredibly complex society."[16] That nicely sums up the thrust of our argument.

Politics and *American Democracy*

This introductory chapter of *American Democracy* has focused on two main questions:

1. What is politics?
2. How does politics influence such critical features of political systems as continuity and change?

Politics, as the argument developed, means different things to different people. It is a vocation, an activity, a disposition, a strategy, and a way of doing business in institutions. It is important to understand the term by itself and to understand the bearing of politics on the work and functions of government. The interpretation presented has borrowed mainly from realist perspectives that see politics as who gets what, when, and how and as the struggle between the socialization and privatization of conflict. Under either definition, politics can and often does include the pursuit of some version of the public interest. Popular views to the contrary, cynicism in politics is no greater, and often less, than cynicism anywhere else in American society.

Politics is the engine of democratic political systems. Constitutions and governments are shaped and driven by politics. Competing politicians and political organizations engage in it; presidents, members of Congress, judges, and bureaucrats "do" politics every day. The opportunities of the people to participate in governing themselves are part of politics. Finally, the public policy choices that governments make are informed by politics. Government without politics is a contradiction in terms, as improbable as fire without oxygen.

An emphasis on politics and political institutions is thus a major feature of this book. Here a word or two about the book's organization is appropriate. *American Democracy* opens with an analysis of the Constitution. It next considers federalism—a key principle of the constitutional system and the most innovative feature of the framers' design. Two chapters on civil rights and liberties, fundamental to American democracy, follow. Part One (Chapters 2 through 5) thus focuses on the constitutional foundations of the nation's political system and provides a basis for analyzing the political behavior of its citizens, the workings of its institutions, and the thrust of its public policies.

Part Two (Chapters 6 through 11) examines the linkages between the public and government. Public opinion, political participation, elections, political parties, and political interest groups are the major means through which citizens become involved in politics, express consent, influence government, and hold political leaders accountable. This section concludes with an analysis of the increasingly important role of the media and, in par-

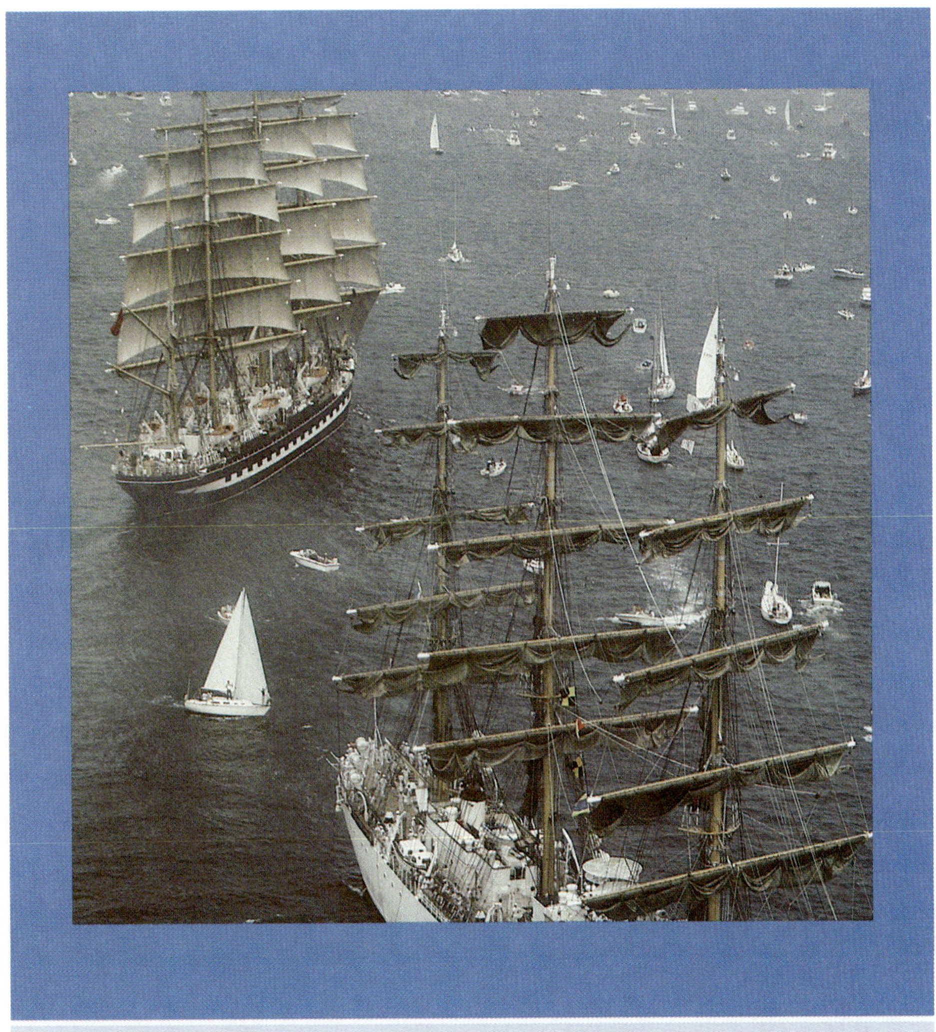

One of the newest concerns of the environmental movement is ocean pollution. Shown here is a flotilla of tall ships and pleasure boats, massed in New York harbor to protest ocean dumping. Contamination of the world's oceans has become a central problem for modern government.

ticular, their impact on political campaigns, government, and public policy.

Part Three (Chapters 12 through 16) describes and analyzes the principal institutions of the federal government: Congress, the presidency, the bureaucracy, and the judiciary. Chapter 14 explores changing relations between the executive and legislative branches. The chapters in this section are thus concerned with the policy-making and policy-implementing institutions of American government. Their decisions have repercussions throughout society, and their performance can be used to gauge the system's vitality.

Part Four (Chapters 17 through 20) examines

"Perspectives"

On Politics and Politicians

"*How praiseworthy it is for a prince to keep his word and live with integrity rather than craftiness. . . . Yet we see from recent experience that those princes have accomplished most who paid little heed to keeping their promises, but who knew how craftily to manipulate the minds of men. In the end, they won out over those who tried to act honestly.*"

—Niccolò Machiavelli

"*Politics is as much a regular business as the grocery or the dry-goods or the drug business. You've got to be trained up to it or you're sure to fail. . . . The politicians who make a lastin' success in politics are the men who are always loyal to their friends, even up to the gate of the state prison, if necessary.*"

—George Washington Plunkitt, of Tammany Hall

"*Politics [is] the adjudication through public compromise of whatever is in serious dispute. If you are not willing to become party to compromise, then do not get into serious dispute.*"

—T. V. Smith

"*In government offices which are sensitive to the vehemence and passion of mass sentiment public men have no sure tenure. They are in effect perpetual office seekers, always on trial for their political lives, always required to court their restless constituents. They are deprived of their independence. Democratic politicians rarely feel they can afford the luxury of telling the whole truth to the people. . . . With exceptions so rare that they are regarded as miracles and freaks of nature, successful democratic politicians are insecure and intimidated men. They advance politically only as they placate, appease, bribe, seduce, bamboozle, or otherwise manage to manipulate the demanding and threatening elements in their constituencies. The decisive consideration is not whether the proposition is good but whether it is popular—not whether it will work well and prove itself but whether the active talking constituents like it immediately. Politicians rationalize this servitude by saying that in a democracy public men are the servants of the people.*"

—Walter Lippmann

"*A superior politician combines two contrasting qualities: In the details of his work he is flexible, yet the outlines of his personality are definite. The flexibility is necessary to do justice under the democratic process, and also to permit him to survive in politics. His nature must be clearly enough defined for him to know who he is, so that his policies may be guided by some rational framework of principles as well as for his satisfaction with himself. Few great public men have differed from this pattern, and in none of them was it reversed—none was without direction or identity yet stiff in execution of detail.*"

—Stimson Bullitt

"*Mothers all want their sons to grow up to be president, but they don't want them to become politicians in the process.*"

—John F. Kennedy

Sources: Niccolò Machiavelli, *The Prince* (New York: Norton, 1977), p. 49; William L. Riordin, *Plunkitt of Tammany Hall* (New York: Dutton, 1963), pp. 19, 35; T. V. Smith and Eduard C. Lindeman, *The Democratic Way of Life* (New York: New American Library of World Literature, 1951), p. 107; Walter Lippmann, *The Public Philosophy* (New York: Mentor, 1955), p. 28; Stimson Bullitt, *To Be a Politician* (New York: Doubleday, 1961), p. 5; Jay M. Shafritz, *Dictionary of American Government and Politics* (Chicago: Dorsey Press, 1988), p. 420.

policy making in domestic and foreign policy issue domains. The policy process is government at work: forming goals, sifting issues, developing agendas, reconciling differences and conflicts, balancing interests, mobilizing support, creating majorities, writing and implementing legislation, and evaluating results.

Government is not an end in itself, but a means to an end. In the American design, that end is the security of each citizen's right to "life, liberty, and the pursuit of happiness." What American democracy promises and delivers is the opportunity for people to do something about public issues that concern them—the opportunity, in other words, to participate in politics.

The study begins with an account of American political participation more than 200 years ago, leading to the Declaration of Independence, the writing of the Constitution, and the formation of a new nation.

Part One

The Constitutional System

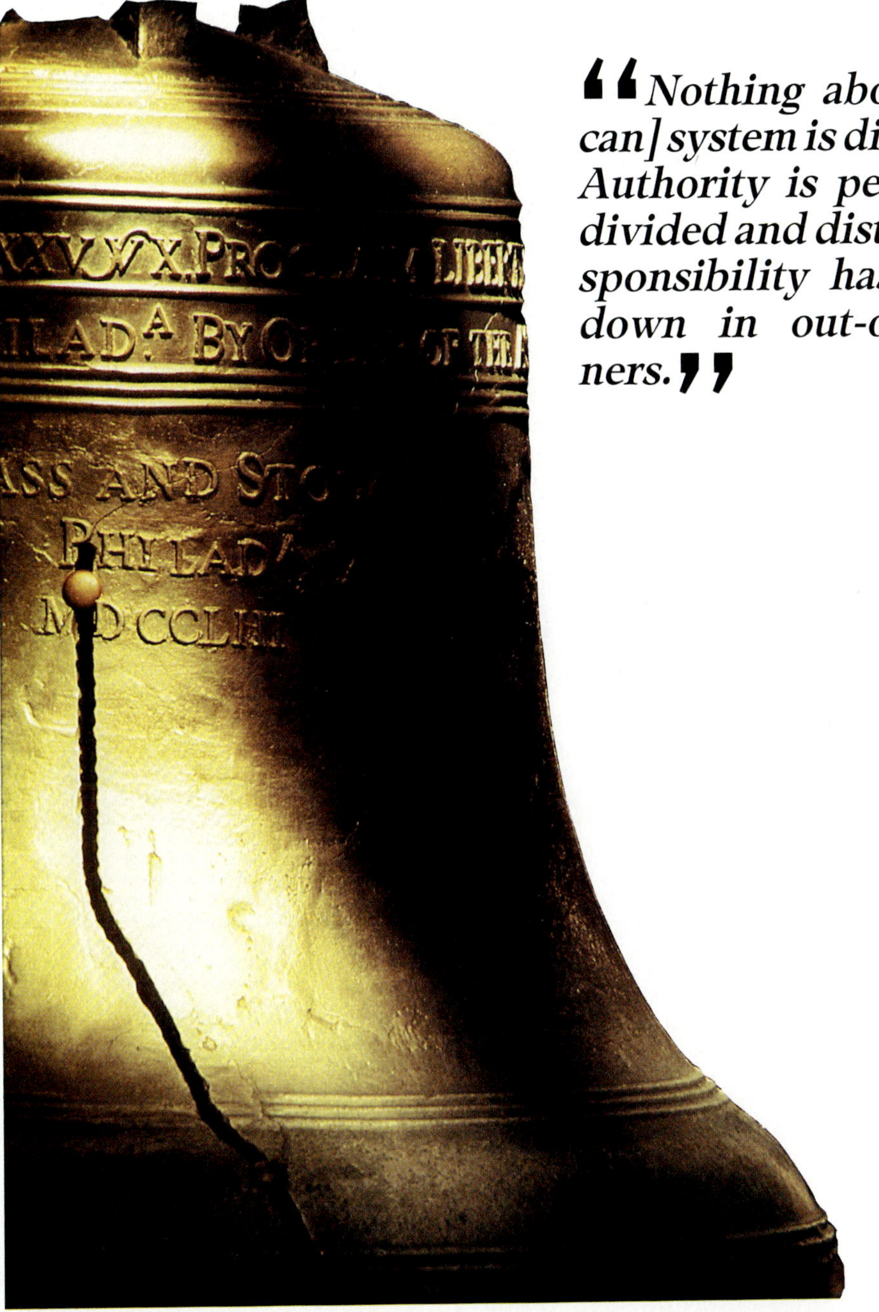

"Nothing about the [American] system is direct and simple. Authority is perplexingly subdivided and distributed, and responsibility has to be hunted down in out-of-the-way corners."

— Woodrow Wilson

Chapter 2

The Constitution and American Politics

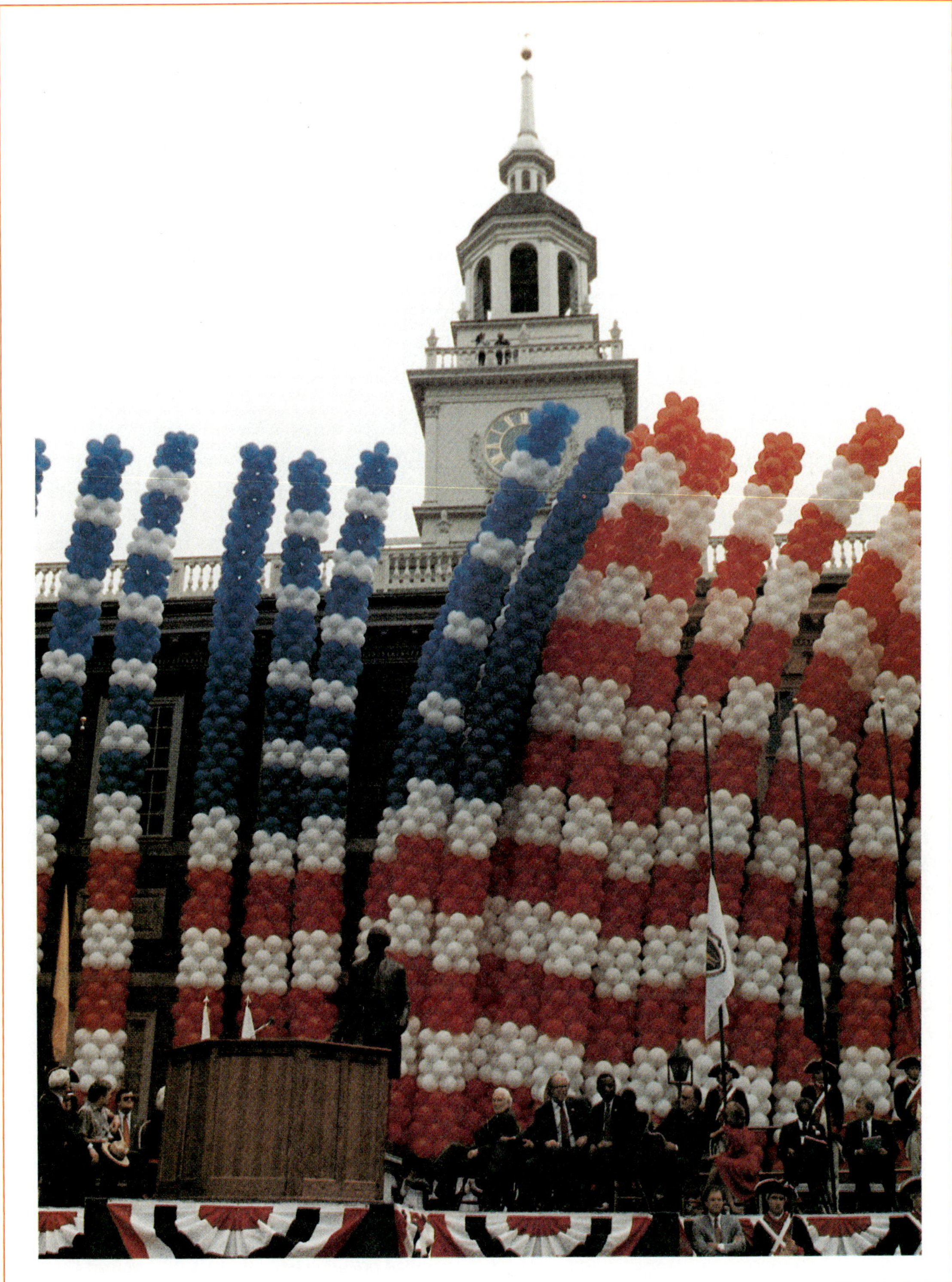

The Constitution of the United States, the supreme law of the land, is now over 200 years old. Drafted in Philadelphia during the summer of 1787, signed by its authors on September 17, 1787, and approved by most of the new states in 1788, it is the oldest written constitution in the world. The Constitution is the nation's special document: Schoolchildren study (and memorize) its lines; jurists and scholars ponder its provisions; politicians celebrate its virtues; other nations adopt its designs; and the general public gains reassurance from it. Its language on limited government and individual liberties resonates for people everywhere.

The Constitution is much more than a special document housed in the National Archives. Purely and simply, it is the foundation of the American system of representative government. Its democratic values profoundly shape the conduct of politics—in elections, in institutions, and in the policy process.

The Constitution is straightforward in some respects and ambiguous in others. So central is it to the nation's politics that hardly any important public action can be taken without the question arising: "Is that constitutional?" If the question is raised persistently, the matter may be settled by the courts.

Every constitution has a profile of its own. This chapter examines the distinctive features and provisions of the American Constitution, focusing on why they were put in place and how they have shaped the nation's politics, political institutions, and policy making. For two centuries the Constitution has marked the main paths leading to the development and consolidation of American democracy. A look at its origins will help us understand its structure and its contributions to the development of a free society.

The Making of the Constitution

The Constitution is a product of the American Revolution—the war that was fought by the colonies to gain independence from Great Britain.

Independence and Self-Government ■

The government created by the Constitution was not Americans' first effort at self-government. Even under British control, the colonies enjoyed a fairly large measure of self-rule. With the drive for independence, colonial politicians gained experience in ordering their own affairs by forming political groups and small governments, such as committees of correspondence and provincial (local) congresses. Most of these, of course, were on a small scale.

A major step in the development of a central government came in 1774. The First Continental Congress was called to air complaints against England and to assert colonial rights. With an armed rebellion already under way in 1775, a Second Continental Congress was called; it raised an army and named George Washington to head it. The rebellion meanwhile grew in intensity. On July 4, 1776, the Congress unanimously approved the Declaration of Independence, formally separating the colonies from Great Britain.

The Declaration's broad purpose was to set forth the right of nations to form their own governments. It provided a political philosophy for a revolutionary time, inspired a love for free government, and expressed the fundamental principle of democracy—that government must rest on the *consent of the governed.* The Declaration of Independence is filled with eloquent lines, and none more so than these:

> We hold these truths to be self-evident, that all men are created equal, that they are endowed by their Creator with certain unalienable Rights, that among these are Life, Liberty and the pursuit of Happiness. That to secure these rights, Governments are instituted among Men, deriving their just powers from the consent of the governed.

The Declaration of Independence marked the end of an era; it signaled the need for free and independent governments to replace those of the colonial period. The logical place to begin this

"If you hold those truths to be so self-evident, how come you keep harping on them?"

process of creating government was in the states—the center of political activity. Between 1776 and 1780, all but two states adopted written constitutions.[1] At the same time, efforts were made in the Continental Congress to establish a national government—one that was able to coordinate and conduct the struggle for independence and other affairs of state. The outcome was the nation's first constitution, the Articles of Confederation. Submitted to the states in 1777, the document was not formally ratified until 1781.

The Articles of Confederation were not an ambitious attempt to solve the problems of governing a new nation. They can be thought of as a "halfway house" on the road to a strong central government. On the crucial question of state power, the Articles were clear: The states retained their "sovereignty, freedom, and independence" in a pact described simply as a "league of friendship." There were few authentic national powers. Congress was authorized to conduct foreign policy, declare war, and coin money—its main powers—but it could not levy taxes or regulate commerce. The Articles made no provision for either an executive or a judiciary. Laws were hard to enact. They required a two-thirds majority, with each state (regardless of size) having one vote. Finally, the document itself was rigid; amendments required a unanimous vote of all 13 states.

The nation's first constitution failed because it did not create a government capable of governing. The national government had little success in securing money from the states or settling disputes between them. It could not enforce its decisions. Its efforts to develop commercial treaties with foreign countries turned out badly. Its financial system was a disaster, and it could do little to meet the economic problems of the time. Growing discord and disorder, highlighted by Shays's Rebellion in 1786 (an armed rebellion by debt-ridden Massachusetts farmers), brought fear that the confederation itself might not survive. Demands for a

George Washington (1732–1799), presiding at the Constitutional Convention. The nation's first president, Washington held office from 1789 to 1797.

stronger central government no longer could be denied. In 1787, Congress passed a resolution for a meeting of state delegates to consider changes in the Articles.

The Constitutional Convention

The 55 delegates who met in Philadelphia during the spring and summer of 1787 decided that revising the Articles would not suffice. They set out to write a new constitution, to form a national government that would directly involve the people (unlike the Confederation, whose authority was drawn from the states).

The Participants. The Constitutional Convention was made up of an extraordinary group of political leaders—"an assembly of demi-gods," said Jefferson. They were the most prominent citizens of their states. Most important, they were *practicing politicians.* A large majority had served in the Congress under the Articles of Confederation; many had served in state legislatures; and several were former governors. By the standards of the time, they were unusually well educated; about half were college graduates. Many were lawyers. Nearly all the delegates had played an active role in the Revolution, many in the continental army. And they were comparatively young, mainly in their thirties and forties. James Madison was 36; Alexander Hamilton was 32; and Benjamin Franklin, the oldest member, was 81.

George Washington, the nation's leading citizen, presided at the convention. Other key leaders in the Virginia delegation were James Madison, Edmund Randolph, and George Mason. The most prominent members of the Pennsylvania delegation were Benjamin Franklin, Gouverneur Morris, and James Wilson. Other delegates who played leading roles were Roger Sherman of Connecticut, Elbridge Gerry and Rufus King of Massachusetts, Charles Pinckney and John Rutledge of South Carolina, William Paterson of New Jersey, Luther Martin of Maryland, and Alexander Hamilton of New York. It is generally agreed that the major figure in this august group was Madison, a brilliant scholar and astute politician whose contributions to the constitutional design earned him the title "Father of the Constitution."

The Main Issues. Constitutions deal with basic questions of *place*—the place of government in society and the place of people in the political system. For the framers, the basic question involved the place of states in the nation: What should be the relationship between these two levels of government? The answer was crucial to the new political system. The framers agreed to a resolution "that a national government ought to be established consisting of a supreme legislative, executive, and judiciary." This decision fixed the place of the new government. It was to be a *national* government, not a league of states, and *supreme* in its domain. Few decisions were more important than this one.

A constitution requires concrete ideas for the organization of government. The first proposal put before the convention came from the Virginia delegation. Mainly the work of Madison, the Virginia Plan provided for a strong central government with a bicameral (two-house) legislature, an executive, and a judiciary. The members of the lower house would be popularly elected; they in turn would choose the members of the upper house from nominees sent by the state legislatures. The legislature was given power to "legislate in all cases to which the separate states are incompetent" and to veto laws passed by state legislatures that would violate the constitution. In addition, the legislature would choose both the executive and the judiciary. The key features of this plan were a superior national government and a powerful Congress.

The Virginia Plan was controversial. Delegates concerned to protect states' rights viewed it with skepticism. Also, its provisions for legislative representation clearly favored the large states; seats in each house would be allocated to states on the basis of population or wealth. Under this scheme, the populous states of Virginia, Pennsylvania, and Massachusetts would control the Congress.

In all forms of politics, proposals produce counterproposals. The answer of the small states was the New Jersey Plan—in essence, a revision of the Articles. It called for a unicameral (one-house) Congress, with each state given one vote; members would be chosen by the state legislatures. These were familiar features of government under the Articles. But it also added two branches: a plural executive chosen by Congress and a judiciary whose members would be appointed by the executive. In harmony with the drive for a stronger central government, it gave Congress the right to tax and regulate commerce and made its laws supreme over those of the states.

In the view of many delegates, the New Jersey Plan had two key drawbacks. First, the national government would continue to rest on the states rather than on the people—the Articles all over again! Second, the interests of the large states would be threatened in a plan for equal representation of all states.

The main difference between these proposals involved *representation:* Should the government be founded on the people or on the states? Based on the principle of equal representation for all states or on proportionality?

Politics is often marked by deadlock. After weeks of wrangling, the impasse was broken by the

"Remember, gentlemen, we aren't here just to draft a constitution. We're here to draft the best damned constitution in the world."

adoption of the Connecticut Compromise. Each side won something. The lower house was to be based on population. It was given the right to initiate revenue (tax) bills. The upper house was tailored to the measure of the small states. Each state was given two members who would be elected by the state legislatures. This was the price of union—in effect, ***a compromise between nationalism and state sovereignty.*** With this matter settled, the success of the convention was largely assured.

Other conflicts were less intense. The issue of slavery was largely avoided, although it was agreed to count a slave as three-fifths of a person for purposes of representation and taxation. To protect southern trade, levying export taxes was forbidden and a two-thirds vote in the Senate was required to ratify treaties. Some issues were skirted by leaving them to the judgment of the states (qualifications for voting) or to Congress (design of the lower court system). Others were handled with ambiguous language, such as the powers of the executive.

The work of the delegates was aptly summed up by John P. Roche.

> Drawing on their vast collective experience, utilizing every weapon in the politician's arsenal, looking constantly over their shoulders at their constituents, the delegates put together a Constitution. . . . [It] was a patchwork sewn together under the pressure of both time and events by a group of extremely talented democratic politicians. . . . For two years, they worked to get a convention established. For over three months, in what must have seemed to the faithful participants an endless process of give-and-take, they reasoned, cajoled, threatened, and bargained amongst themselves. The result was a Constitution which the people, in fact, by democratic processes, did accept, and a new and far better national government was established.[2]

Ratification. The government formed by the Constitution was not anyone's exact idea of a "proper" government. But for most delegates—politicians used to compromise—it was a reasonable structure for managing a diverse nation. Most important, it established a republican (or representative) form of government with ample powers to govern. Of those present when the document was finished, all but three signed it.

The campaign for ratification by state conventions, which were popularly elected, began right away. Approval by 9 of the 13 states was needed for the Constitution to go into effect. No one thought the campaign in the states would be easy; and it was not.

Three aspects of the ratification struggle stand out:

A scientist, inventor, and writer, Benjamin Franklin (1706–1790) was the elder statesman of the Constitutional Convention.

1. **The campaign of the Constitution's backers (who described themselves as Federalists) was better organized than that of the opponents (dubbed Antifederalists by the Federalists).** The Federalists had a concrete program. They could also point to the failures of government under the Articles and to the need for a strong union. Most newspapers rallied to their cause. The Federalists had the biggest names in politics: George Washington and Benjamin Franklin headed the list. Finally, they had a reasoned defense of their plan in the essays by Madison, Hamilton, and John Jay. (In assembled form, these essays became known as *The Federalist.*)

2. **The campaign rhetoric of the Antifederalists contained a variety of themes.** The delegates had exceeded their powers by writing a new Constitution; the independence of the states would be destroyed; the new government was designed to serve the wealthy (or, some Antifederalists said, the poor and propertyless); the government's tax powers would be abused; the Senate would become an aristocracy; the Constitution would lead to tyranny. Most important, the document lacked a bill of rights. (To meet this charge, the Federalists pledged that the first Congress would add one.)

3. **The outcome of the campaign was as close as had been expected, especially in the large states.** Massachusetts ratified the Constitution by a vote of 187 to 168, Virginia by 89 to 79, and New York by 30 to 27. Delaware was the first state to accept the Constitution, Rhode Island the last (in 1790).

The Constitution was adopted because the politicians who drafted it had a sure sense of political strategy; they knew where the best opportunities lay for reaching agreement on basic issues and knew how to present their work to the people. From beginning to end, they were adept in the art of democratic politics: conciliation. Their document, political in the best sense, deserves careful study.[3]

Continuity & CHANGE

The Constitution's Prospects: Washington's Pessimism

Popular and scholarly interest in the Constitution has been intense during the bicentennial era. More than 150 previously unknown documents on the Constitutional Convention were published in 1988 by Yale University Press. One of the highlights in this collection is the account of a Georgia delegate of his informal conversations with George Washington. Abraham Baldwin's notes disclose that Washington was quite pessimistic about the Constitution's prospects. Debates were contentious and agreements were elusive. More than once, Washington said, the convention was "upon the point of dissolving without agreeing on any system." Of special interest is this observation attributed to the Constitutional Convention's presiding officer: "I do not expect the Constitution to last for more than 20 years."

Source: See an interesting account in the *New York Times,* July 4, 1987.

Constitutional Concepts and Institutions

Whether described in detail or in general, *power* is the central concept, the organizing principle, of all constitutions. The major challenge of constitution writers is to provide for the distribution and exercise of power. Few tasks are more complicated:

1. The *principal powers* of government must be expressed.
2. *Distributions of power* among branches and levels of government must be settled.
3. *Limitations* must be fixed within which officials may use their powers.
4. Provisions must be made for *constituent power*—in other words, how citizens are to participate in government.

A remarkable feature of the Constitution is its durability. One reason it has survived for two centuries is that its plan for the disposition of power has seemed reasonable to ever-changing publics and politicians. The Constitution's treatment of power can be seen from a review of its basic concepts and institutions.

A Government Based on Popular Consent Through Representation

The architects of the Constitution did not intend to create a "direct" or "pure" democracy where citizens debate and decide the chief questions of government. Such a system would be impractical in a large country. And history had taught them that direct democracy meant turbulence, excesses, and disorder. This was reinforced by their observations of the new state governments—whose legislatures, self-consciously "democratic," passed law after law granting relief to debtors, overriding the claims of creditors, ignoring property rights, and otherwise threatening traditional arrangements.

Many delegates no doubt agreed with Elbridge Gerry that "the evils we experience flow from the excess of democracy"; but they were not tempted to design a government beyond the control of the people. They sought a middle ground. A partial solution lay in the creation of a *republican* system, one in which the majority rules by electing representatives. Over the years, this system has had various labels, including *representative democracy, democratic republic, constitutional democracy,* and *deliberative democracy.* Each is an apt description.

"When the framers rejected direct popular participation in the governing process, they put their faith instead in political institutions."[4] In a word, they put their faith in representation. It is in the nature of a republic, Madison wrote in *Federalist* no. 10,

> to refine and enlarge the public views, by passing them through the medium of a chosen body of citizens, whose wisdom may best discern the true interest in their country, and whose patriotism and love of justice, will be least likely to sacrifice it to temporary or partial considerations. Under such a regulation, it may well happen, that the public voice, pronounced by the representatives of the people, will be more consonant to the public good, than if pronounced by the people themselves, convened for the purpose.[5] [But it should be noted Madison also recognized that leaders of "sinister designs" might "betray the interests of the people."]

The American government was designed to rest on popular consent. The public consents to government through free elections, which permit citizens to choose those who will make decisions on their behalf. The framers laid the basis for popular rule by providing for the election of House members "by the people of the several states" (Article I, Section 2). The Senate and the president would also be elected, but in a manner that involved the public only indirectly: Senators would be chosen by state legislatures, and the president by a select group of electors.[6] Figure 2–1 sketches this design for a balanced government, one branch under the direct control of the voters, the other branches under their indirect yet ultimate control.

Representative government and responsible government go hand in hand. Those entrusted with political power must account to those who elect them. Representation also endows the officeholder's decisions with legitimacy. Elections, representation, legitimacy, and responsibility—these are the central concepts in a government based on majority rule. They reflect a major theme of the Declaration of Independence: Governments derive all "their just powers from the consent of the governed."

A Government Limited in Power ■

Liberty is a congenial idea to democrats. Naturally, so is its protection. Influenced by the writings of the English philosopher John Locke and by their experiences, the framers knew that individual liberty cannot be taken for granted; it is always vulnerable to government invasion. So they gave much thought to restraints on political power.

With no tested formula for limiting the scope and power of government, the framers introduced a mixture of limitations. First, the powers awarded to the federal government were stated in specific terms, such as the power to coin money or to declare war (Article I, Section 8). No general power was granted to the government. Additionally, in Article

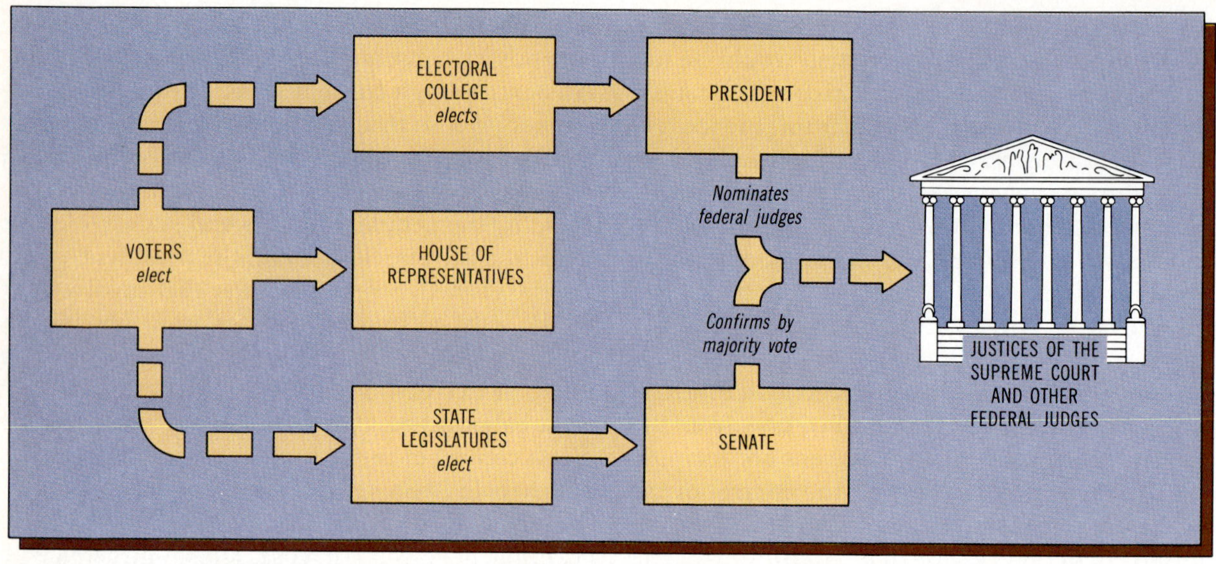

Figure 2–1 The electoral system under the original Constitution: direct and indirect popular control. Under the Constitution's original provisions, only the members of the House of Representatives were directly elected by the people. The president was chosen by electors, expressing their independent judgment, and senators were chosen by the state legislatures. The justices of the Supreme Court and other federal judges were appointed by the president "by and with the advice and consent of the Senate." This method of judicial selection continues to the present, but the president and members of the Senate are now chosen by the voting public. Presidential electors run as party candidates and are expected to vote for their party's presidential candidate if the candidate wins a plurality of the popular vote in the state. (Cases of "faithless electors"—those who fail to cast their vote for their party's presidential candidate—are extremely rare.) Since the passage of the Seventeenth Amendment in 1913, senators have been directly elected by the people. These changes reflect the democratization of American politics.

I, Section 9, the government was enjoined from certain practices: It cannot suspend the writ of *habeas corpus* (the right of an imprisoned person to be brought before a judge to decide the legality of his or her detention) except during invasion or rebellion; it cannot pass a *bill of attainder* (a law that finds a person guilty of a crime without a trial); it cannot pass an *ex post facto* law (a law that declares an act to be criminal retroactively—that is, after it has been done). Elsewhere, provisions grant persons the right to a trial by jury in criminal cases (Article III, Section 2) and prevent the imposition of a religious test for holding public office (Article VI). Extending its reach, the Constitution also restricts the powers of the states (Article I, Section 10).

The Bill of Rights places major limitations on the federal government. Most important is the First Amendment: "Congress shall make no law respecting an establishment of religion, or prohibiting the free exercise thereof; or abridging the freedom of speech, or of the press; or the right of the people peaceably to assemble, and to petition the government for a redress of grievances." Covering "the great rights of mankind" (Madison), the Bill of Rights is a safeguard against the abuse of power by government. (See Chapter 4 for a detailed analysis of these rights.)

Constitutional development never ends. After the Civil War came the Fourteenth Amendment, which forbids the states to deprive any person of life, liberty, or property without due process of law or to deny any person the equal protection of the laws. Interpretation of this amendment by the Supreme Court later made many guarantees of the Bill of Rights applicable to state governments (see Chapter 4).

Drafting a constitution consists of finding major and marginal compromises to the issues that divide a society and its people. The task of the framers was to strike a balance between liberty and order, or between a government limited in scope and authority (hence, less threat to people's rights) and one powerful enough to ensure stability. They succeeded in remarkable degree. The Constitution proved to be adaptable. Its flexibility allowed the national government to expand its role to meet the changing needs of society and the changing values of the people.

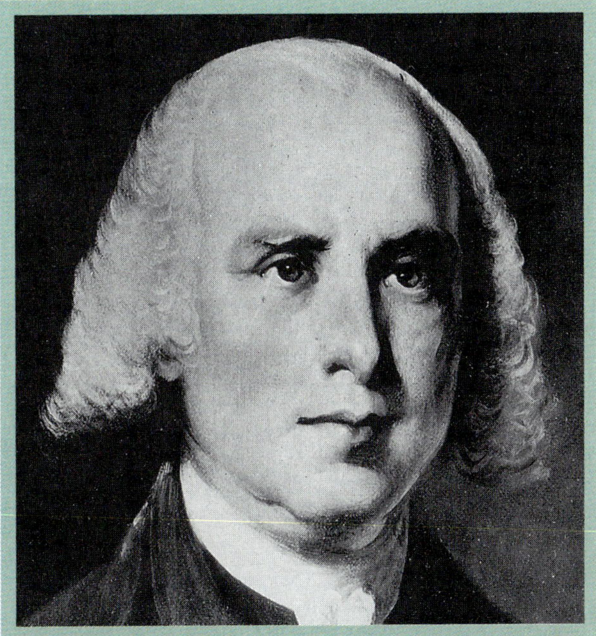

James Madison (1751–1836), "Father of the Constitution," was only 36 years old at the time of the Constitutional Convention. A leader in the movement to establish a strong national government, Madison later served as the fourth president of the United States (1809–1817).

A Government of Divided and Shared Powers

The belief that citizens can govern themselves, the essence of democracy, is basic to the Constitution. But the framers also believed that every form of government had defects. For democracy, the chief danger was thought to be majority tyranny, the oppression of the minority by a majority of the citizens. How could they guard against this? A government with limited purposes and authority was one safeguard against the abuse of power. The other was in the internal structure of the government—in a plan for divided and shared powers.

The logic of a system of internal checks is best explained by Madison, especially in *Federalist* no. 51:

> Ambition must be made to counteract ambition. The interest of the man must be connected with the constitutional rights of the place. It may be a reflection on human nature, that such devices should be necessary to control the abuses of government. But what is government itself, but the greatest of all reflections on human nature. If men were angels, no government would be necessary. If angels were to govern men, neither external nor internal controls on government would be necessary. In framing a government, which is to be administered by men over men, the great difficulty lies in this: You must first enable the government to control the governed; and in the next place, oblige it to control itself. A dependence on the people is, no doubt, the primary control on the government; but *experience has taught mankind the necessity of auxiliary precautions.*[7]

“ Perspectives ”

On Governing in *The Federalist*

The political philosophy underlying the Constitution is best explained in *The Federalist,* a series of 85 essays written by Alexander Hamilton, James Madison, and John Jay in 1787 and 1788. Published originally in the New York press as part of the ratification campaign, these papers became both a classical interpretation of the Constitution and a major contribution to the history of political philosophy. (The number of the essay from which each excerpt is drawn is shown in parentheses. Perhaps the most famous of all the essays is the tenth, written by Madison, on the danger of factions. It appears in its entirety at the end of this book.)

A Vigorous Executive

“*Energy in the Executive is a leading character in the definition of good government. It is essential to the protection of the community against foreign attacks; it is not less essential to the steady administration of the laws; to the protection of property against those irregular and high-handed combinations which sometimes interrupt the ordinary course of justice; to the security of liberty against the enterprises and assaults of ambition, of faction, and of anarchy.*”

—(No. 70)

The Danger of Factions

“*The latent causes of faction are . . . sown in the nature of man; and we see them everywhere brought into different degrees of activity, according to the different circumstances of civil society. A zeal for different opinions concerning religion, concerning government, and many other points . . . have, in turn, divided mankind into parties, inflamed them with mutual animosity, and rendered them much more disposed to vex and oppress each other, than to cooperate for their common good. . . . But the most common and durable source of factions has been the various and unequal distribution of property. Those who hold and those who are without property have ever formed distinct interests in society. Those who are creditors, and those who are debtors, fall under a like discrimination. A landed interest, a manufacturing interest, a mercantile interest, a moneyed interest, with many lesser interests, grow up of necessity in civilized nations, and divide them into different classes, actuated by different sentiments and views. The regulation of these various and interfering interests forms the principal task of modern legislation. . . .*”

—(No. 10, the work of Madison, and perhaps the most famous of all the essays)

The Purpose of a Constitution

"*The aim of every political constitution is, or ought to be, first to obtain for rulers men who possess most wisdom to discern, and most virtue to pursue, the common good of the society; and in the next place, to take the most effectual precautions for keeping them virtuous whilst they continue to hold their public trust.*"

—(No. 57)

The Place of the Senate

"*Such an institution may be sometimes necessary as a defense to the people against their own temporary errors and delusions.*"

—(No. 62)

The Place of the Courts

"*The complete independence of the courts of justice is peculiarly essential in a limited Constitution. Limitations [on legislative authority] can be preserved in practice no other way than through the medium of courts of justice, whose duty it must be to declare all acts contrary to the manifest tenor of the Constitution void.*"

—[This was the view of Hamilton. The Constitution did not directly empower the courts to invalidate legislative acts.] (No. 78)

The Place of the House of Representatives

"*As it is essential to liberty that government in general should have a common interest with the people, so it is particularly essential that the [House of Representatives] should have an immediate dependence on, and an intimate sympathy with, the people. Frequent elections are unquestionably the only policy by which this dependence and sympathy can be effectually secured.*"

—(No. 52)

The Need for Government

"*Why has government been instituted at all? Because the passions of men will not conform to the dictates of reason and justice, without constraint.*"

—(No. 15)

Democracy Versus Republic

"*The two great points of difference between a democracy and a republic are: first, the delegation of the government, in the latter, to a small number of citizens elected by the rest; secondly, the greater number of citizens, and greater sphere of country, over which the latter may be extended.*"

—(No. 10)

Alexander Hamilton (1757–1804), a key member of the Constitutional Convention, one of the authors of *The Federalist* (along with James Madison and John Jay), became the first Secretary of the U.S. Treasury (1789–1795).

One does not have to look hard to find the "auxiliary precautions" in the Constitution. They are in the key devices of separation of powers, checks and balances, and federalism.

Separation of Powers. "The accumulation of all powers, legislative, executive, and judicial, in the same hands . . . may justly be pronounced the very definition of tyranny." This conviction of the framers—stated here by Madison in *Federalist* no. 47—was expressed in the Constitution through the creation of equal and independent legislative, executive, and judicial branches. The concept of the separation of powers did not spring from the genius of the framers; the system was already used in the new state governments. Some delegates were probably attracted to the idea by their understanding of *The Spirit of the Laws,* the eighteenth-century work of the French philosopher Montesquieu.

The writers of the Constitution sought to ensure the independence of the separate branches by the way officials were selected. Their arrangements have survived largely intact. Chosen by the president with the consent of the Senate, judges are appointed for life ("shall hold their Offices during good Behaviour," the Constitution reads), thus contributing to an independent judiciary. Fixed terms of office support the independence of the president and members of Congress. Terms are staggered—two years for the House, six years for the Senate, and four years for the president. These arrangements do more than protect branch boundaries, helping each "to resist encroachments by the others" (*Federalist* no. 51). In harmony with the broad aims of creating a balanced government and dividing power to limit its misuse, these provisions make it difficult for any group (faction or party) to control all three branches at the same time.

Congress is the first branch of government. Its structure and powers are established in Article I of the Constitution; more lines are devoted to the legislative branch, in fact, than to the other two combined. The attention lavished on Congress was not accidental. It came from a belief in a republican form of government and a concern that, of the three branches, the legislature was most likely to try to expand its powers.

The legislature that emerged from the convention's drawing board had four key features. First, it was a *bicameral* (two-house) legislature, consistent with the framers' desire to divide power. Second, the two chambers were to reflect the interests of different segments of society. The House of Representatives was to be the popular chamber, in keeping with democratic tenets; the Senate was to represent the "aristocracy." Their modes of election were thus different: Members of the House were elected by the people; members of the Senate were chosen by state legislatures. (Since the passage of the Seventeenth Amendment in 1913, senators have been popularly elected.) Third, to keep the legislature (and thus the national government) in its proper place, its powers were specifically listed. Powers not given to Congress were reserved for the states. Finally, as will be shown later, the Constitution had numerous provisions to link Congress with the other branches of government. The purpose was to blend legislative, executive, and judicial powers and duties.

The organization of the executive branch proved especially troublesome. Members sifted and debated a variety of plans for the presidency: Should the office be strong or weak? Single or plural? Should its occupant be chosen by the national legislature, the state legislatures, the people, or some other means? Should the president's term be short or long (a life term was preferred by Alexander Hamilton)? Should the president be eligible for reelection? With such questions, the final compromises that made up Article II came late in the convention.

The settlements are now familiar. The Constitution provided for a single president, elected independently, "strong enough to protect himself under ordinary circumstances against the abuse of power by the legislative branch of the government and to that extent prevent it from destroying the equilibrium among the three branches."[8] The president's term was set at four years, with no limitation on reelection. (Ratified in 1951, the Twenty-second Amendment limits the president to two elected terms, or a total of 10 years in office.)

An ingenious idea for shaping the new government was the *electoral college,* designed for the election of the president. Each state was given as many electors as it had representatives and senators. The electors were chosen by the voters or by the legislature (as each legislature determined); and they were expected to be well-known, respected citizens—like the framers themselves. Using their best judgment, the electors, not the voters, would pick the president (and vice president).

Neither the ideas incorporated into a constitution nor the language used to convey them ensure a predictable line of political development. The emergence and institutionalization of political parties, for example, fundamentally changed the role of the electors, eliminating their discretion in choosing the president. Since the early nineteenth century, electors have appeared on the ballot as party candidates, morally obligated to cast their votes for the presidential candidate of their party if that candidate wins a *plurality* of the popular vote in their state. ("Faithless" electors—those who fail to vote for their party's candidate—are few and far between.) Political change has made the electoral college a fully democratic institution (see Chapters 8 and 9).

The Constitution gives the president many powers. One is an undefined grant of "executive power." In addition, the president is commander in chief of the armed forces, is empowered to make treaties, has authority to appoint judges and high officials of the executive branch, is authorized to send messages to Congress (including recommendations for legislation), and is given veto power by a provision in the legislative article. And from the vague enjoinder to "take care that the laws be faithfully executed" comes the president's responsibility to serve as "chief administrator." Resting on Article II and defined further by the actions of individual presidents, the presidency has become one of the most powerful executive offices in the world. But only the most far-seeing framers could have anticipated this in 1787. (See Chapter 13 for a detailed analysis of the president's powers.)

Article III provides for the organization of the judicial branch. Only about 400 words long, it is the briefest of the three articles that describe the system of separated powers. The main thrusts of Article III are to establish a Supreme Court and to sketch the jurisdiction of the federal judiciary. It leaves to Congress the authority to create such "inferior courts" as it finds necessary. Thus invited by the Constitution, Congress has filled out the judicial structure with an elaborate array of *district courts* and *circuit courts of appeal,* along with various specialized courts such as the Court of Customs and Patent Appeals, the Court of Claims, and the Court of Military Appeals. The structure

Democracy: Ideas and Constitutional Structures

Democratic governments rest on an idea: that governments derive their powers from "the consent of the governed." But political ideas require implementation, and implementation requires structure. In broad terms, the three key structural features of American democracy found in the Constitution and its amendments are:

- a democratic political process centering in majority rule through representation;
- general and specific limitations on the power of government in order to protect individual rights and liberties; and
- divided and shared powers—reflected in the separation of powers, checks and balances, and federalism—as a design for controlling the exercise of authority and preventing abuses of political power.

of the federal judiciary owes more to the decisions of Congress than to those of the Constitutional Convention.

The Founding Fathers intended to establish a rule of law. The listing of legislative powers and the restrictions placed on both national and state governments, for example, reflect the idea that the new union was to be a government of laws, not of people. The courts were responsible for interpreting the law. But what if a law was challenged as being in conflict with the Constitution? Could the Supreme Court find it unconstitutional and set it aside? Some members of the convention favored such authority—a "judicial veto"—but it is not mentioned in the Constitution.

Constitutional silences create opportunities for constitutional development. In this instance, the Supreme Court itself settled the issue. In the case of *Marbury* v. *Madison,* decided in 1803, the Court held that an act of Congress is invalid if it is in conflict with the Constitution. Known today as *judicial review,* this doctrine permits the Court to declare acts of Congress, the president, and states to be unconstitutional and thus null and void. The acceptance of judicial review signaled an important shift of power to the judicial branch, more than enough to compensate for the "thinness" of Article III. (See the analysis of judicial review in Chapter 16.)

Checks and Balances. The separation of powers is both a principle of organization and a device for containing power. The same can be said for the Constitution's scheme of checks and balances, the means for maintaining the separation of powers. Together they make up the basic framework of the national government.

The design of American government reflects a search for equilibrium—balance or equality among legislative, executive, and judicial forces. The fram-

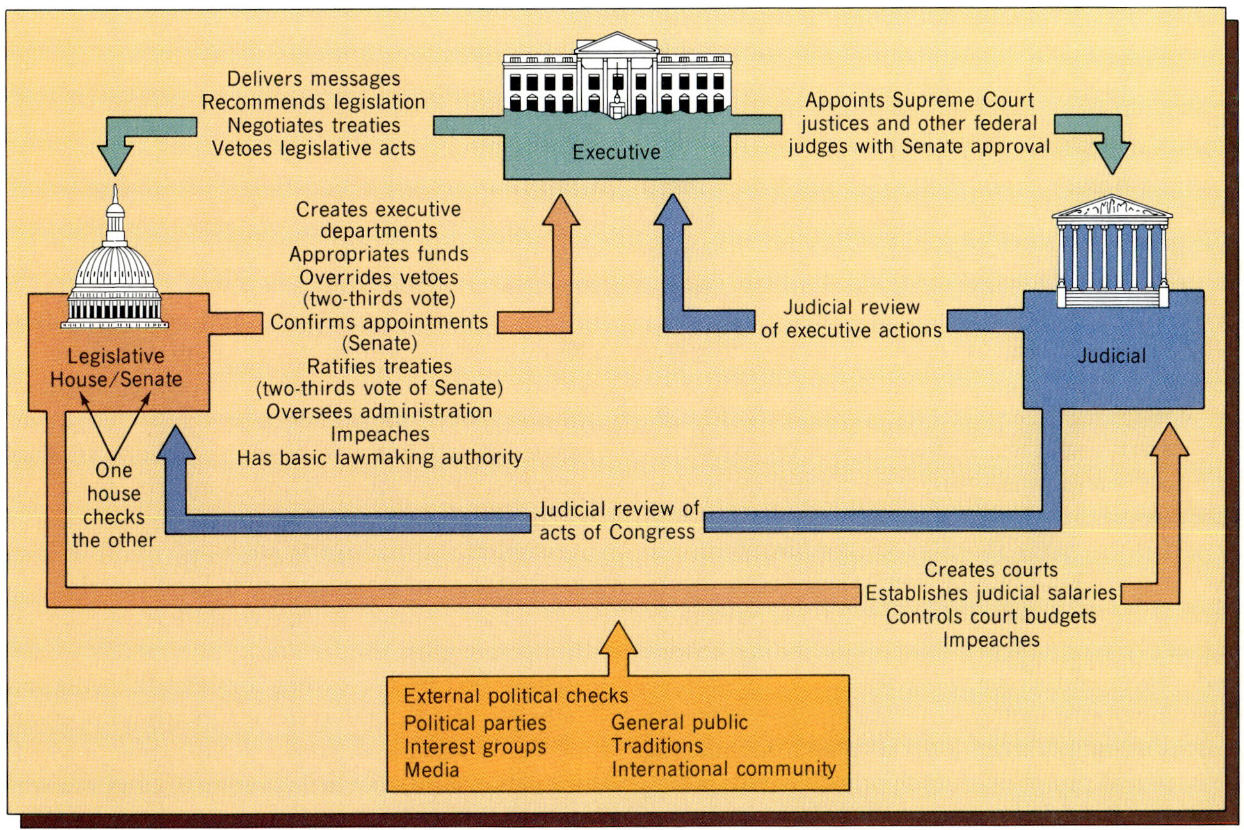

Figure 2–2 "Ambition must be made ready to counteract ambition": The separation of powers and checks and balances.

ers found it in linkages that permit and encourage each branch to check and balance the other two. The details of this complex system are shown in Figure 2–2.

The most interaction occurs between the executive and legislative branches. A law is passed with the concurrence of both houses—a check in itself—but the president may veto it. Yet by a two-thirds vote of each house, the president's veto can be overridden. "All legislative powers" are conferred on Congress; but the president is authorized to recommend measures "as he shall judge necessary and expedient." Modern presidents do this with a vengeance. The executive establishment is headed by the president; but both its organization and funding are determined by Congress. In addition, custom and legal recognition (including court decisions) permit Congress to "oversee" the executive branch, checking on the implementation of its laws and the expenditure of money, investigating administrative behavior, and controlling the conduct of bureaucrats. In a special constitutional form of legislative oversight, the Senate may approve or reject both presidential appointments and treaties the president has negotiated. The policy-making process, in this prudent scheme, demands great cooperation between the legislative and executive branches.

Still other linkages are shown in Figure 2–2. Chief among them is the power of the judiciary to interpret laws by defining their meaning and examining their constitutionality. On occasion, the Court settles disputes involving the branches. An example occurred in 1974 when the Court ruled that President Nixon must release White House tapes that revealed his complicity in the cover-up of the Watergate burglary. (The burglary was a break-in of the Democratic National Committee headquarters in the Watergate complex to plant wiretap devices.)

Designing a constitution is a formidable task. It is a stern test of the drafters' ingenuity to fashion political compromises and create institutions (and relationships) that will endure. The formula of *separated institutions sharing powers* has stood the test of time. One branch sometimes gains ascendancy over the others, to be sure, but the advantage is usually temporary. Because conditions change and power shifts, rough parity is soon regained. Forty-one presidents and 101 congresses after the Constitutional Convention, this plan for managing government power, with each branch participating in the work of the others, remains intact.

Federalism. To the separation of powers and checks and balances the framers added a third "auxiliary precaution": a division of power between the national government and the states. In theory, each is supreme in its own jurisdiction. This is the principle of federalism. The main reason for its adoption was that there was no other choice. A highly centralized, or *unitary,* form of government would not have been acceptable to the states, which by then were accustomed to their independence. But that is only a partial explanation. The federal idea was also a key element in the Madisonian system, marked by intricate restraints on the powers of both national majorities and government itself. "In the compound republic of America," Madison argued, "the power surrendered by the people is first divided between two independent governments [federalism], and then the portion allotted to each subdivided among distinct and separate departments [separation of powers]. Hence a *double security* arises to the rights of the people. The different governments will control each other, at the same time that each will be controlled by itself."[9]

The Constitution is a place for ideas and principles, but not for blueprints. This is surely true for federalism. The Constitution has no clear-cut boundaries that divide the central (federal or national) government from the states. Rather, it sets up a framework for dual governing systems, nation and state, leaving them to define jurisdictions.

Divisions of responsibility between national and state governments never have reflected a consensus. The proper role of each has been steadily disputed. Ordinarily, when conflicts have occurred, the "winning" side has been the national government. No pattern is more apparent, in fact, than the massive expansion of federal functions in the last half-century. If they could have a glimpse of American government today, the framers would be astounded by the extent to which Washington dominates the federal system. Equally important, they would also be surprised by the extent to which the levels of government cooperate to carry out various functions. (Chapter 3 examines the changing nature of federalism.)

A Government Capable of Governing

New governments are created from disillusionments and experiences with old ones. There were good reasons for unhappiness with the government formed by the Articles of Confederation (1781–1789). The central government consisted of a single organ—a Congress with minimal authority. With no direct links to the people and heavy dependence on the governments of the 13 states, this Congress scarcely qualified as a national government.

Although the Constitutional Convention was called for the sole purpose of *revising* the Articles, the delegates soon set aside that mission. Their task was to form a government capable of governing but confined to prevent it from threatening individual liberties. The fabric of a strong central government

President George Bush, the nation's 41st chief executive, addresses a joint session of Congress in 1989. He faced a Congress dominated by the Democratic party for more than half a century, including his earlier years as a Republican House member from Texas.

was woven from several strands. First, three independent branches were formed to replace the single legislature of the Articles. Second, Congress was given broad power, including the authority to lay and collect taxes and to regulate commerce among the states and with foreign nations. Third, the foundation was laid for a vigorous executive. Fourth, bypassing the states, the Constitution established an electoral link between the people and the national government. Fifth, limits were placed on the states; they were forbidden, for example, from entering into treaties, coining money, or passing laws impairing the obligation of contracts. Finally, for good measure, the framers added a "supremacy" clause:

> This Constitution, and the laws of the United States which shall be made in pursuance thereof; and all treaties made, or which shall be made, under the authority of the United States, shall be the supreme law of the land; and the judges in every state shall be bound thereby, any thing in the Constitution or laws of any state to the contrary notwithstanding. (Article VI)

A government capable of governing, over the long haul, is a flexible government, one able to address ever-changing problems and public needs. In today's perspective, the ultimate wisdom of the framers was their willingness to define the powers of government in language sufficiently general and evocative that future generations would be able to use government in ways appropriate to their times.

"The Constitution," Thomas Jefferson observed, "belongs to the living and not to the dead." Or as others have said, it is a "living" constitution. How it earned this title should become clear in the next section.

Changing the Constitution

One secret to the lasting nature of the Constitution is its adaptability. Although the Constitution is a product of the framers' "systematic reflection and purposeful choice,"[10] it has also been shaped by society's changing needs. Some changes have come through formal amendment. Others have emerged through informal means. Clearly, the Constitution is not a museum piece: It has been remarkably receptive to new ways of thinking about government and its role in society.

Formal Change: The Amending Process

The methods for amending the Constitution are set forth in Article V. An amendment may be proposed by a two-thirds vote of both houses of Congress or by a national constitutional convention called by Congress in response to the petition of two-thirds of the state legislatures. Ratification takes place in the states, either by the legislatures in three-fourths of the states or by special conventions held in three-fourths of the states. Under the usual method, proposals are passed by Congress and approved by the state legislatures. (See Figure 2–3.)

Amending the Constitution is far from easy. Consider the evidence of about 200 years. The first ten amendments, the Bill of Rights, were adopted by Congress in 1789 and ratified by the states in

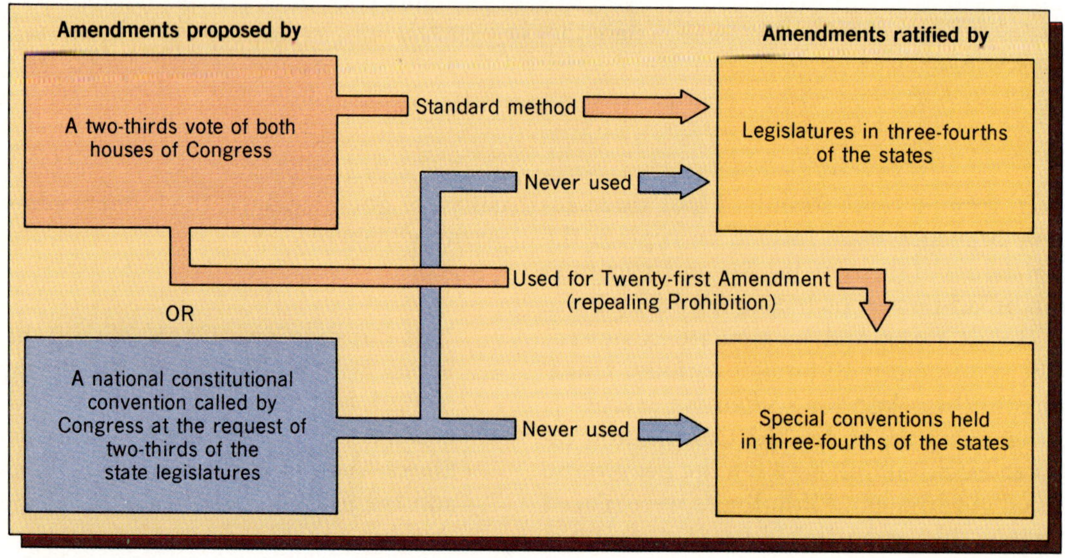

Figure 2–3 Amending the Constitution: a two-stage process.

The First Ten Amendments: The Bill of Rights

American democracy owes much to the adoption of the first ten amendments known as the Bill of Rights. These basic guarantees were adopted by the first Congress in 1789 and approved by the states in 1791. Their broad thrust is to secure the liberties of the people against infringement by the government. Initially, the first ten amendments were thought to apply only to the national government. As a result of various Supreme Court decisions in the twentieth century, these rights now *restrain* state governments about as fully as they do the national government. (See Chapter 4.)

Amendment 1: Congress shall make no law respecting an establishment of religion, or prohibiting the free exercise thereof; or abridging the freedom of speech, or of the press; or the right of the people peaceably to assemble, and to petition the Government for a redress of grievances.

Amendment 2: A well regulated Militia, being necessary to the security of a free State, the right of the people to keep and bear Arms, shall not be infringed.

Amendment 3: No Soldier shall, in time of peace be quartered in any house, without the consent of the Owner, nor in time of war, but in a manner to be prescribed by law.

Amendment 4: The right of the people to be secure in their persons, houses, papers, and effects, against unreasonable searches and seizures, shall not be violated, and no Warrants shall issue, but upon probable cause, supported by Oath or affirmation, and particularly describing the place to be searched and the persons or things to be seized.

Amendment 5: No person shall be held to answer for a capital, or otherwise infamous crime, unless on a presentment or indictment of a Grand Jury, except in cases arising in the land or naval forces, or in the Militia, when in actual service in time of War or public danger; nor shall any person be subject for the same offence to be twice put in jeopardy of life or limb; nor shall be compelled in any criminal case to be a witness against himself, nor be deprived of life, liberty, or property, without due process of law; nor shall private property be taken for public use, without just compensation.

Amendment 6: In all criminal prosecutions, the accused shall enjoy the right to a speedy and public trial, by an impartial jury of the State and district wherein the crime shall have been committed, which district shall have been previously ascertained by law, and to be informed of the nature and cause of the accusation; to be confronted with the witnesses against him; to have compulsory process for obtaining witnesses in his favor, and to have the Assistance of Counsel for his defense.

Amendment 7: In Suits at common law, where the value in controversy shall exceed 20 dollars, the right of trial by jury shall be preserved, and no fact tried by a jury, shall be otherwise reexamined in any Court of the United States, than according to the rules of the common law.

Amendment 8: Excessive bail shall not be required, nor excessive fines imposed, nor cruel and unusual punishments inflicted.

Amendment 9: The enumeration in the Constitution, of certain rights, shall not be construed to deny or disparage others retained by the people.

Amendment 10: The powers not delegated to the United States by the Constitution, nor prohibited by it to the States, are reserved to the States respectively, or to the people.

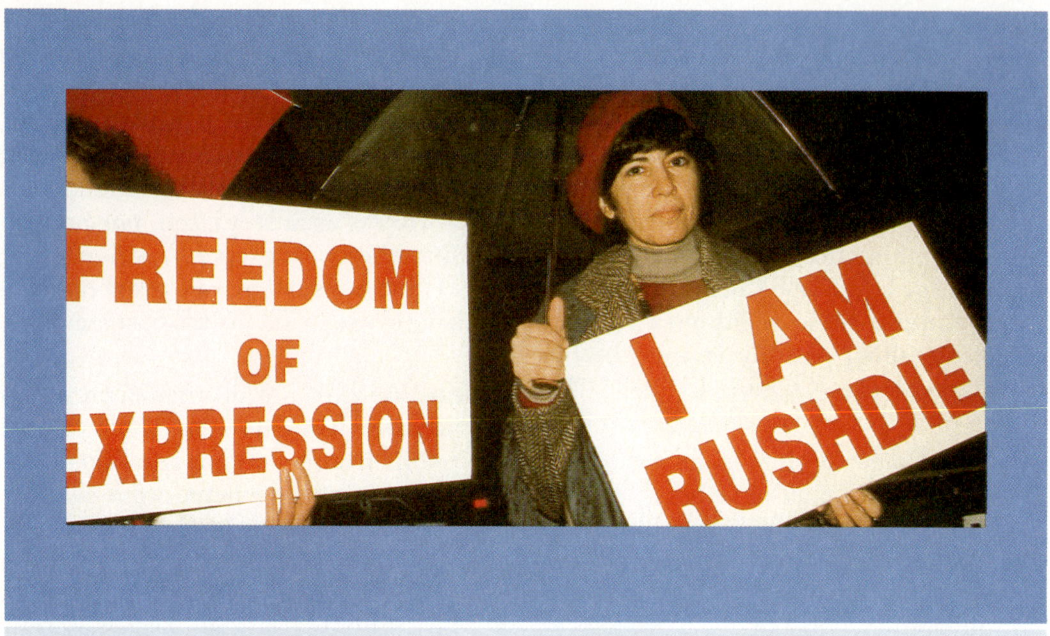

Our basic freedoms are protected by a written bill of rights. In other nations, citizens depend on legal and cultural traditions. Salman Rushdie knows how different these can be. His novel *The Satanic Verses* brought him a death sentence in 1989 from the Islamic government of Iran. But in Great Britain, where the Indian-born writer lives, protestors insisted on their right to obtain the book, which several bookstores had withdrawn.

1791. Since then, of nearly 6000 amendments introduced in Congress, only 23 have passed both houses and been sent to the states. Sixteen have been adopted, making a total of 26 amendments. No amendment has been adopted since 1971, when voting for 18-year-olds was approved. In recent years, two amendments have come before the states, one guaranteeing equal rights for women and the other giving congressional representation to the District of Columbia. Neither was successful, although the Equal Rights Amendment barely fell short, winning adoption in 35 of the necessary 38 states. Other current efforts to change the Constitution would ban abortions, provide for a school prayer, end busing to achieve racial equality in schools, and require a balanced budget.

Amendments have had a major impact on the political system, especially civil rights and suffrage. From the Bill of Rights come basic freedoms (religion, speech, press, assembly, and petition) and protections for citizens against the power of the federal government (prescribing, for example, the rights of persons accused of crimes). The Thirteenth Amendment (1865) outlawed slavery. In addition to granting citizenship to former slaves, the Fourteenth Amendment (1868) placed sharp limits on the states; they are prevented from making or enforcing "any law which shall abridge the privileges or immunities of citizens of the United States," from depriving "any person of life, liberty, or property, without due process of law," and from denying "to any person within [their] jurisdiction the equal protection of the laws."

The Fifteenth, Nineteenth, and Twenty-sixth Amendments extended suffrage to blacks (1870), women (1920), and youth (1971). The Seventeenth Amendment (1913) provided for the popular election of senators, the Twenty-third Amendment

(1961) gave citizens of the District of Columbia the right to vote for president and vice president, and the Twenty-fourth Amendment (1964) outlawed poll taxes (taxes on the right to vote). American politics would be markedly less democratic if these provisions had not been adopted.

Informal Change

If basic political change could be brought about only through amendments, the Constitution would have been a barrier to viable government. That, of course, has not been the case. Rather, the Constitution has lent itself to informal change. Politics, in a broad sense, is the means for "modernizing" the Constitution. The meaning of the Constitution is altered by acts of Congress, court decisions, presidential interpretations, and the institutionalization (or development) of political arrangements and customs.

Acts of Congress. The role of Congress in adapting the Constitution to the times derives from the last provision of Article I, Section 8. This clause permits Congress to make all laws that are "necessary and proper" for carrying out those powers specifically given to it. This key grant was first tested when an early Congress passed a law setting up a national bank, even though it lacked explicit power to do so. In *McCulloch* v. *Maryland,* decided in 1819, the Supreme Court upheld the constitutionality of the act, finding it an appropriate way for Congress to discharge its specified financial powers.

Major acts often add to the meaning of the Constitution. Consider two examples. The Voting Rights Act of 1965 was perhaps the most important civil rights act in American history. It brought blacks into the electorate in record numbers by suspending state and county voter qualification devices (such as literacy tests) that had been used to keep them from voting. (See Table 2–1.) This act ranks in importance with most of the suffrage amendments; it delivered, in fact, what the Fifteenth Amendment promised. At the same time, it extended federal policy making into a domain (election law) previously controlled by the states.

TABLE 2–1

Expanding the Constitution Through Legislation: The Impact of the Voting Rights Act of 1965 on Black Registration in Southern States

	Percentage of Eligible Blacks Registered to Vote	
State	**1964**	**1986**
Alabama	23.0	68.9
Georgia	44.0	52.8
Louisiana	32.0	60.6
Mississippi	6.7	70.8
South Carolina	38.8	52.5
Virginia	45.7	56.2

Sources: *Congressional Quarterly Weekly Report,* April 11, 1981, p. 635; and U. S. Bureau of the Census, *Statistical Abstract of the United States, 1988* (Washington, D.C.: U.S. Government Printing Office, 1988), p. 250.

The other example is also instructive. When Congress passed the War Powers Resolution in 1973, limiting the president's authority to commit troops abroad, it strengthened its own constitutional power over the declaration of war. (See an analysis of the War Powers Resolution in Chapter 14.)

Statutes and the Constitution cover similar ground. The passage of a major law, in fact, may relieve the pressure for a constitutional amendment.

Court Decisions. The meaning of the Constitution depends in large part on the way it is interpreted by the judiciary, particularly by the Supreme Court. The Court explains the language of the document, setting forth the meaning of such spare (if elegant) phrases as "due process of law" and "equal protection of the laws."

The meanings of constitutional provisions change over the years—new times, justices, theories, and politics make a difference. In 1896, for instance, the Supreme Court held that segregation by race in public facilities was not unconstitutional if the facilities for blacks and whites were substantially equal (*Plessy* v. *Ferguson*). This doctrine lasted for more than half a century. But in 1954, the Court reversed its position: "Separate but equal" facilities, it then found, failed to meet the equal protection requirements of the Fourteenth Amendment (*Brown* v. *Board of Education*). School desegregation soon began in earnest. The language of the amendment, of course, had not changed at all between 1896 and 1954.

Cases that involve the political process itself come before the courts. Consider an aspect of representation. Must all legislative districts have about the same number of people? On that key question (as on so many others) the Constitution is silent. When a case involving congressional districts came before the Supreme Court in 1946—one Illinois district had nine times as many people as another—the Court took the position that apportionment was a "political question" that should be handled outside the judicial process (*Colegrove* v. *Green*).

In 1962, the Court reversed its view. Apportionment became a *justiciable* issue—meaning that a court could consider a case on this subject (*Baker* v. *Carr*). Soon a string of court decisions brought equal apportionment to the states and the U.S. House of Representatives (see Chapter 5). The doctrine of "one man, one vote" was consolidated, accepted by the state legislatures that make the districts. Today there are no malapportioned legislatures—that is, legislatures where some areas have more representation than their population entitles them to have. For this achievement, fashioned in the spirit of the Constitution, the courts get credit.

Presidential Interpretation. The Constitution is also changed through the president's view of the presidency and its powers. Unmentioned in the Constitution, the *cabinet* is the president's creation. President Washington found the institution useful, and it became a fixture in later administrations.

The emergence of the president as the nation's "chief legislator" was similar. The Constitution (Article II, Section 3) awards only three "legislative" powers to the president: power to propose measures to Congress, to veto its acts, and to convene either or both houses in special sessions (and under certain circumstances, to adjourn them as well). Using the message and veto powers, modern presidents have established a firm legal base for active involvement in the legislative process. Politicians, the press, and the public wait to hear what the president wants from Congress (and all guess what the president will get). But program development, reflected in administration bills, is only the first step. Using the leverage of office, the president seeks to mobilize support for administration bills by lobbying members of Congress, attracting media attention, and courting the public. Aggressive presidents pull out all the stops; they are aware that their administrations will be judged by their successes in Congress. It comes down to this: Pliable and open to change, the Constitution permits the president, Woodrow Wilson observed, "to be as big a man as he can."

TABLE 2–2

The American Public's Knowledge of the Constitution

	Percentage of the Public Identifying Statement as Accurate
Accurate statements	
Citizens are entitled to a lawyer in a criminal trial if they cannot afford to pay for one	92
Citizens are entitled to a trial by jury	83
The Constitution can be amended by a two-thirds vote of both houses of Congress, provided that three-quarters of the states approve	76
Under the Constitution, only a person born in the United States can be elected the country's president	71
The original Constitution left voting requirements up to the individual states	68
The Constitution was written to create a federal government and define its powers	54
The Bill of Rights is the first ten amendments to the original Constitution	41
	Percentage of Public Failing to Identify Statement as Inaccurate
Inaccurate statements	
The (Gettysburg Address) phrase "of the people, by the people, and for the people" is found in the Constitution	82
The (Declaration of Independence) phrase "all men are created equal" is found in the Constitution	80
The Constitution guarantees every citizen's right to a free public education through high school	75
The Constitution establishes English as the national language, requiring that it be used in schools and government	64
The president acting alone can appoint a justice to the Supreme Court	60
Local schools may require children to pledge allegiance to the U.S. flag	57
The President can suspend the Constitution in time of war or national emergency	49
A state can give money to religious schools provided it gives it to all religious schools equally	46
A state has a right to declare an official state prayer	45
The president can adjourn Congress when he sees fit	35
The presidential candidate who gets the most votes in a popular election automatically becomes president	31

Source: *The American Public's Knowledge of the U.S. Constitution: A National Survey of Public Awareness and Personal Opinion* (New York: Hearst Corporation, 1987), passim.

TABLE 2–3

The Original Constitution and Popular Control of Government

Limitations on Popular Control	Extensions of Popular Control
Indirect election: President chosen by the electoral college Senators chosen by state legislatures and given a long term of office The design of government: Separation of powers Checks and balances Bicameralism Staggered terms of office Suffrage left to the states Federal judges appointed for life (barring impeachment)	A government that emanates from the people: "We the people of the United States, in order to form a more perfect union . . ." (from the Preamble to the Constitution) The states guaranteed a republican form of government Direct election of members of the House of Representatives for a short term of office No restrictions on political participation (such as a religious test for holding public office)

Political Development. Few things about the constitutional system are as enduring as its tendency to change—gradually. It grows through accretion, through analysis and interpretation, and from chance and events as well as from intent.

Unknown at the time the Constitution was written, political parties are today a central feature of American politics. Their status is protected by the First Amendment (see Chapter 9). No framer of the Constitution foresaw their formation as agencies for implementing democratic ideas. Yet since the earliest days, the parties have helped recruit and select leaders, educate and channel public opinion, serve as brokers among organized interests, and control and direct government. Their functions are so important that it is hard to imagine how the government could operate without them. And cooperating and competing with the parties are political interest groups—they are similarly important for advancing popular (if segmental) views and without mention in the Constitution.

And consider Congress. The committee system, seniority rule, congressional parties, and other informal networks all affect legislative performance. They shape the way Congress goes about its business and the policies it adopts. Could Congress function without policy groups, customs, and understandings? Almost surely not. Their lack of constitutional status in no way lessens their importance for the institution or the larger political system.

The Public's Knowledge of the Constitution

The data of Table 2–2 provide evidence concerning the public's understanding of the Constitution. This portrait is less than flattering. Clearly, the public lacks a good grasp of the history and purposes of the Constitution. It perceives the original Constitution as a much more democratic document than it actually was and, not surprisingly, confuses it with other documents. Only four of ten persons know that the first ten amendments make up the Bill of Rights. The public tends to overestimate the powers of the president and, to some extent, the powers of the states. Americans are best informed about the criminal justice system; they know, for example, that citizens are entitled to a jury trial and to a lawyer in a criminal trial.

But there is also more than a little popular confusion concerning personal rights and government authority. Three of four people incorrectly believe that citizens have the constitutional right to a free public education through high school, and two of three believe that English is the official national language. More than half of the public believe erroneously that government (local school boards) may require students to pledge allegiance to the flag. Indeed, the Pledge of Allegiance became a compelling issue in the 1988 presidential campaign when George Bush successfully portrayed Michael Dukakis as "weak on patriotism" for having vetoed a bill to require teachers to lead children in saying the pledge. "What is it about the Pledge of Allegiance that upsets him so much?" the vice president asked. Dukakis stood by a 1943 Supreme Court decision that schoolchildren could not be forced to recite the pledge if to do so violated their religion.

On the whole, the American public takes a complaisant view of the constitutional system. It is firmly attached to inherited institutions and arrangements, even when it knows little about how they work or what purposes they serve. It knows intuitively, it would seem, that the Constitution is not an anachronism, that it is rather the centerpiece of American democracy. The reality is that the constitutional system is stable and predictable, which makes it easy to take for granted. Thus, despite numerous popular misconceptions concerning it, the Constitution appears to be in excellent health as it enters its third century.

The Constitution, the People, and Political Power

The Constitution is a series of compromises between delegates who had confidence in the ability of people to govern themselves and those who thought institutional devices were needed to refine popular views. For the most part, the compromises fell on the "conservative" or "aristocratic" side. They were reflected in key arrangements for "filtering" popular views and moderating majority rule. Put another way, the framers accepted the democratic form, but as Martin Diamond observed, theirs was a "cautious acceptance."[11]

Table 2–3 shows the main features of the system spliced together by "accommodating conservatives" moving "in a democratic direction."[12]

Today the nation's political system differs in major ways from that shown in the table. National political parties have changed the electoral college, bringing it under the control of the voters. Parties have also helped to bridge the gaps created by the separation of powers and bicameralism. The parties, through their officeholders, have become the "managers" of the political system; they are accountable to those on whom they depend for votes.

Democracy, history shows us, is contagious. Since the early twentieth century, senators have been chosen through elections rather than by state legislatures. Presumably this link increases their responsiveness to the public. In the national nominating process, party leaders no longer have much voice in the choice of the presidential nominee. The recent democratization of the process permits voters, participating in primaries and caucuses, to choose the delegates to the national convention. And a raft of constitutional amendments, laws, and court decisions has broadened the electorate—bringing in women, youth, and blacks—and recast representation so that one person's vote is equal to that of any other person. Opportunities for people to take part in politics and to influence public actions, typically through the strategy of expanding conflict, are much greater now than in the past. And on another front, blacks, women, and Hispanics are being elected to office in record numbers today, though still well under their shares of the population. (For example, in the 101st Congress, 1989–1990, there were only 25 women, 24 blacks, and 12 Hispanics.)

The main structural feature of the government is the division of power. This system has both costs (disadvantages) and benefits (advantages), as shown in Figure 2–4. A glance at the figure shows the nature of the argument between critics and sup-

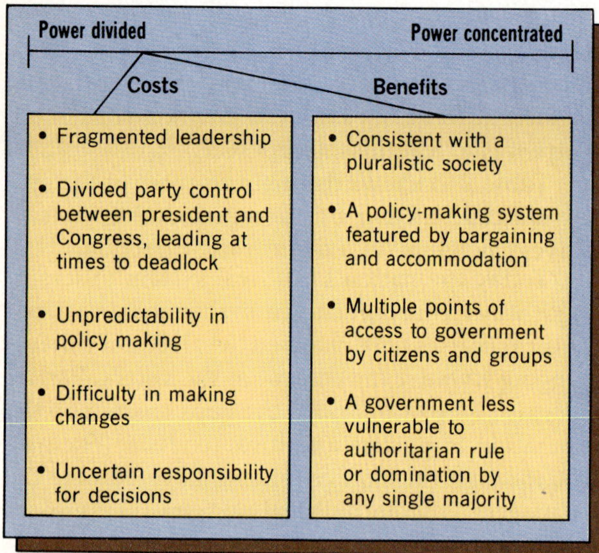

Power divided
Power concentrated
Costs
Benefits
• Fragmented leadership
• Divided party control between president and Congress, leading at times to deadlock
• Unpredictability in policy making
• Difficulty in making changes
• Uncertain responsibility for decisions
• Consistent with a pluralistic society
• A policy-making system featured by bargaining and accommodation
• Multiple points of access to government by citizens and groups
• A government less vulnerable to authoritarian rule or domination by any single majority

Figure 2–4 The Constitution and political power.

porters of this design. To divide power, say the critics, is to invite internal conflict, making it difficult for leaders to form goals, to lead, to create majorities, and to develop coherent policies. Stalemates between president and Congress are common. Policy making tends to be awkward, often unpredictable, and usually drawn out. (See Chapter 20 for an analysis of the impact of the separation of powers on foreign policy.) A system of divided powers produces mysteries as to "who gets what, when, and how." The public finds it hard to fix responsibility for actions taken or claims ignored.

The benefits of this system, on the other hand, cannot be dismissed. Policy making in a *deliberative* mode increases the prospects for evenhandedness, permitting many voices to be heard and a range of options to be posed. For citizens and groups, there are numerous "access points" where they can press their claims for favorable action. Such a system ensures that there are no unrivaled winners. Negotiations proceed slowly. In the end, public policy is the result of bargaining and accommodation at all points in the political process.

Finally, the diffusion of power also meshes well with a diverse society in which no single majority can speak authoritatively for all the people. In this system, Herbert Agar points out:

> Most politics will be parochial, most politicians will have small horizons, seeking the good of the state or the district rather than of the Union; yet by diplomacy and compromise, never by force, the government must water down the selfish demands of regions, races, classes, business associations, into a national policy which will alienate no major group and which will contain at least a small plum for everybody. *This is the price of unity in a continent-wide federation.*[13]

Two summary points may be useful. The first is that neither the critics nor the defenders of the framers' design have an airtight case: Appraisal turns finally on one's preferences in policy making. The second is that the framers' plan is unlikely to be undone in any event. This nation's political institutions have a matchless capacity for survival.

The Constitution and American Politics

The Constitution's contributions to the nation's life are well known. It created a durable union; it laid a firm basis for the orderly development of a new nation composed of diverse elements; and it formed a superior tier of government for solving conflicts and making public decisions. It also fostered the growth of a democratic form of politics.

The framers did not create a democracy in the ancient Greek sense of "rule by the people." That was not their aim. Rather, they established a system that would permit democracy to evolve. And that happened.

Although there is room for argument over its meaning, democracy is usually said to include these ideas:

Representatives Charles B. Rangel (D-N.Y.), right, and William H. Gray (D-Pa.), left, meet with Jesse Jackson at a National Black Leadership Roundtable conference held to assess the impact of black voters on elections. After four years as chairman of the House Budget Committee, Representative Gray was elected chairman of the House Democratic Caucus in 1989, making him the highest-ranking black public official in the Democratic party.

1. Citizens must have the right to vote in free and competitive elections.
2. They must have the right to form political groups to express their views and interests.
3. There must be means for discussion between leaders and citizens.
4. Those in power are responsible for those who elect them.

These requirements are a tall order—never, of course, wholly met.

The Constitution's design for a self-governing republic, limited in its powers over the people, was the essential first step in launching the nation's experiment in large-scale democracy. Free elections promptly became the centerpiece in the scheme for enforcing the responsibility of public officials to the voters. And with its guarantees of

“ Perspectives ”

On Democracy

“*A pure democracy, by which I mean a society consisting of a small number of citizens, who assemble and administer the government in person, can admit of no cure for the mischiefs of faction. . . . A republic, by which I mean a government in which the scheme of representation takes place . . . promises the cure.*”

—James Madison, *Federalist* No. 10

“*. . . government by the consent of the governed.*”

—Thomas Jefferson

“*. . . government of the people, by the people, and for the people.*”

—Abraham Lincoln

“*The democratic way implies the conviction on the part of both the majority and the minority that the majority has the right to rule, but also the acceptance by the majority of the duty to exercise this right, and to exercise it circumspectly.*”

—T. V. Smith

“*Democracy does not mean and cannot mean that the people actually rule in any obvious sense of the terms 'people' and 'rule.' Democracy means only that the people have the opportunity of accepting or refusing [those] who are to rule them.*”

—Joseph Schumpeter

“*Democracy is a competitive political system in which competing leaders and organizations define the alternatives of public policy in such a way that the public can participate in the decision-making process.*”

—E. E. Schattschneider

Sources: T. V. Smith and Eduard C. Lindeman, *The Democratic Way of Life* (New York: New American Library of World Literature, 1951), p. 12; Joseph Schumpeter, *Capitalism, Socialism, Democracy* (New York: Harper & Row, 1950), pp. 284–285; E. E. Schattschneider, *The Semisovereign People: A Realist's View of Democracy in America* (Hinsdale, Ill.: Dryden Press, 1960), p. 138.

free speech, petition, and association, the First Amendment brought the basic liberties that support political organization (such as competitive parties), political speech, and political activity. The growth of democratic politics was assured. If the Constitution was not a solidly democratic document at the outset, it is now—or at least, not a bad imitation of one.

Summary

- The Constitution reflects a quest for a fresh formula with which to govern a new nation. In the end, the framers produced a mixed government designed to balance the competing interests of people and property, of democrats and aristocrats, of the many and the few.

- The Constitution was the work of skilled politicians who treated politics as the "art of the possible." Without compromise, the Constitution could not have been adopted. The crucial compromise provided for Senate representation on the basis of state equality, House representation on the basis of population.
- A government based on popular consent through representation, limited in authority, with divided and shared powers, and capable of governing is the design created in Philadelphia in 1787. The "bottom line" is that the government was formed to protect the fundamental freedoms of individuals.
- Division of power, designed to prevent a faction from taking control of government, is the chief structural feature of the American system. Independent branches, staggered terms of office, bicameralism, an intricate system of checks and linkages, and federalism make up this Madisonian model. The fragmentation of power makes bargaining and compromise essential in policy making. At the same time, it makes it hard to fix responsibility for the actions or inactions of government.
- The American system is based on a living Constitution. Formal change in the constitutional system occurs through amendments. The difficulty of the amending process is shown by the fact that only 26 amendments have been adopted in 200 years. Yet change also occurs informally, through acts of Congress, presidential interpretation, court decisions, and the development of political institutions. Adaptability is a key feature of the Constitution.
- The Constitution created a republican, or representative, form of government. Events, time, political leaders, the courts, and the public itself have contributed to its further democratization. The system is known by a variety of names, such as representative democracy, democratic republic, and constitutional democracy. But whatever the name, the key fact is that the government is subject to control by the people.

Readings on the Constitution

Agar, Herbert. 1950. *The Price of Union.* Boston: Houghton-Mifflin. American constitutional history from 1763 to 1909.

Beard, Charles A. 1960. *An Economic Interpretation of the Constitution of the United States.* New York: Macmillan. Argues that the Constitution was designed to protect the property of the elites rather than to protect life, liberty, and the pursuit of happiness.

Brown, Robert E. 1956. *Charles Beard and the Constitution: A Critical Analysis of "An Economic Interpretation of the Constitution."* Princeton, N.J.: Princeton University Press. An analysis and critique of Beard's work (see above).

Farrand, Max. 1913. *The Framing of the Constitution of the United States.* An interpretation of the Constitutional Convention.

Goldwin, Robert A., and William A. Schambra, eds. 1980. *How Democratic Is the Constitution?* Washington, D.C.: American Enterprise Institute. A variety of perspectives focusing on the ability of the Constitution to protect rights democratically.

Kelly, Alfred H., and Winfred A. Harbison. 1976. *The American Constitution: Its Origins and Development,* 5th ed. New York: Norton. Examines major constitutional decisions in the context of American history.

Peltason, J. W. 1988. *Corwin and Peltason's Understanding the Constitution,* 11th ed. New York: Holt, Rinehart & Winston, Inc. An explanation of the meaning and significance of the main features of the Constitution.

Rossiter, Clinton L. 1966. *1787: The Grand Convention.* New York: Macmillan. The story of 1787, the "most fateful year in the history of the United States."

Smith, David G. 1965. *The Convention and the Constitution: The Political Ideas of the Founding Fathers.* New York: St. Martin's Press. Examines the political philosophy of the framers in relation to the development of the Constitution.

Chapter 3

The American Federal System

ELECT
ON BIRD
FOR
NTY COUNCIL
Re-Elect
SCOTT
FOSLER
COUNTY
COUNCIL
FOSLER
HOGAN
FOR
U.S. SENATE
The Washington Post
ENDORSES
GILCHRIST
FOR COUNTY EXECUTIVE
GAZETTE
GILCHRIST
COURIER
GILCHRIST
SCHOOL BOARD
EDITORIALS
KLEIN & O'SHEA
CAROL F.
ALLACE
OOL BOARD

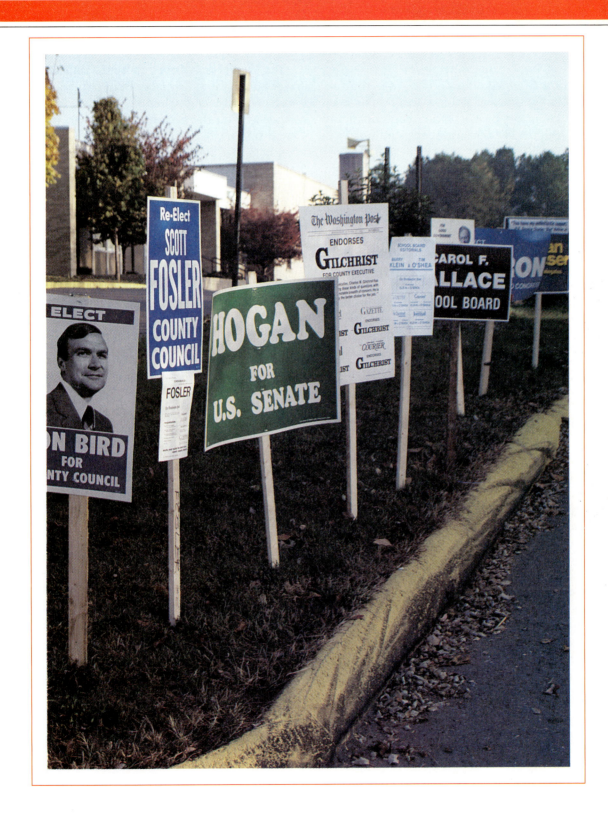

The most important contribution of the Constitutional Convention of 1787 was the formation of a government subject to popular control—a government based on the consent of the governed. But the most original contribution of the framers of the Constitution was the design of a federal system under which two levels of government, national and state, each with substantial authority, would govern the same territory, respond to the same people. Like government itself, federalism evolves. It is complex, creative, and dynamic: complex because it requires separate and competing governments to sort out powers and responsibilities, creative because it encourages them to interact in solving public problems, and dynamic because intergovernmental relations shift in response to politics, elections, and the requirements of public policy. The one constant in federalism is change.

The Constitution and Federalism

Acceptance of the federal principle was a response to practical necessity. It was unlikely that the proposed Constitution would be ratified if it provided for a centralized government. The states, after all, were the hub of political activity and policy making under the Articles of Confederation. They were not about to give this up, at least not knowingly.

The basic problem for the framers was the need to form a strong national government while permitting the states to retain major responsibilities. The solution lay in the creation of a healthy federal system, marked by a strong national government and strong states. Over the years, the relationship has become one of sharing, thus making the federal union basically a *partnership*.

Constitutional Bases of Federalism ■

American federalism is firmly rooted in the Constitution. It is based on the following provisions:

1. **The Connecticut Compromise Settlement.** This specified a national legislature of two houses, one based on the federal principle (the Senate) and the other based on the people (the House). When the Constitution was changed to provide for the popular election of senators (Seventeenth Amendment, 1913), this feature of federalism became less important; state legislatures were removed from the selection process.

2. **Article I, Section 8.** Here the Constitution delegates *enumerated* powers to the central government. Included are the powers to tax, to borrow and coin money, to declare war, to regulate interstate and foreign commerce, to raise and support an army, to maintain a navy, and to establish post offices and post roads.

3. **Article I, Section 10.** This part of the Constitution prohibits the states from such activities as entering into treaties with foreign nations, coining money, taxing imports or exports (without the consent of Congress), and passing laws that would impair the obligation of contracts. Other major restrictions on the states are found in the Bill of Rights and in later amendments (Fourteenth, Fifteenth, Nineteenth, Twenty-fourth, and Twenty-sixth).

4. **Article VI, Clause 2, the National Supremacy Clause.** This key provision reads: "This Constitution, and the laws of the United States which shall be made in pursuance thereof; and all treaties made . . . under the authority of the United States, shall be the supreme law of the land; and the judges in every state shall be bound thereby, any thing in the constitution or laws of any state to the contrary notwithstanding." Quite simply, this clause provides that if state laws or constitutions conflict with the national Constitution, laws, or treaties, the national position prevails. The supremacy clause has often been invoked to support the exercise of national powers. In a nutshell, "it makes federalism work."[1]

5. **The Tenth Amendment.** Inserted in the Constitution to placate the opponents of a strong central government, this amendment declares: "The pow-

ers not delegated to the United States by the Constitution, nor prohibited by it to the states, are reserved to the states respectively, or to the people." In earlier years, this amendment was sometimes used by the Supreme Court to limit the powers of the national government. In *Hammer* v. *Dagenhart* (1918), for example, the Court ruled unconstitutional an act of Congress that restricted the movement in interstate commerce of goods produced by child labor; this statute, the Court held, was an intrusion on state power and violated the Tenth Amendment.[2]

By the 1940s, however, the Court's outlook had changed, and laws of this type were regularly upheld. Today the Tenth Amendment is less important, although states' rights advocates still consider it a barrier to the expansion of national power. A more realistic view is found in Chief Justice Harlan Stone's observation: The amendment, he said, is "but a truism that all is retained which has not been surrendered.[3]

The Range of Powers ■

Another way to bring American federalism into focus is to examine the kinds of powers held by each level of government. There are five: delegated, implied, inherent, reserved, and concurrent.

Delegated powers are awarded to the national government by the Constitution. They are sprinkled throughout the document, set forth in both specific and general terms. Of the general variety, Article I grants "all legislative powers" to Congress, Article II vests "the executive power" in the president, and Article III assigns "the judicial power" to "one supreme Court, and in such inferior courts as the Congress may from time to time ordain and establish." Of special importance in defining federal-state relations are the specific (express or enumerated) national powers in Article I, Section 8 (see above). Listed as powers of Congress, they are the constitutional "hooks" on which national policies are fastened.

In the development of the federal system, the national government has had many advantages over the states. The enumeration of powers in Article I, Section 8 limited national authority less than expected. Hidden in this section was the *elastic clause*—the authorization to Congress to make such laws as are "necessary and proper" to carry out its listed powers. As interpreted by the Supreme Court, this clause became the basis of the doctrine of *implied powers:* The national government would thus enjoy powers not specifically granted if they could be reasonably inferred from the list of specific powers. This ensured the growth of national power.

The national government also has *inherent* powers in foreign affairs. These result, the Supreme Court has held, from its status as a sovereign nation, necessarily engaged in external relations with other nation-states. Its powers in foreign relations do not depend on the Constitution and hence are not limited to the express powers found in it, such as the power to declare war or make treaties.[4]

Powers not delegated to the national government, the Tenth Amendment declares, are *reserved* to the states or to the people. These are undefined. Traditionally, the powers of the states to regulate the health, safety, and morals of their citizens (called "police powers") have been in this category. Control over public education rests mainly with the states—less today, however, than a generation ago.

Concurrent powers are exercised by both levels of government. Powers to tax and spend, which are necessary to policy making, fall into this group.

Federal Guarantees to the States ■

Because the Constitution is filled with restrictions on government, it is easy to miss the fact that it also specifies government obligations. Those placed on the federal government are found mainly in Article IV. The federal government must guarantee to all states a republican (which has come to mean "representative") form of government, protect them against foreign invasion and domestic violence, and preserve the integrity of their territory. (For example, no new state can be formed by taking territory from an existing state, unless the latter gives its consent.) Article IV also provides for the admission of new states to the union. (The last states to be admitted were Alaska in 1958 and Hawaii in 1959.) Finally, Article V guarantees that no state "shall be deprived of its equal suffrage in the Senate."

Although the obligations of the federal government to the states are usually not matters of concern, they can be important. In 1957, for example, President Dwight Eisenhower sent federal troops to Little Rock, Arkansas, to enforce a judicial decree on desegregation. The source of the president's authority was the obligation, delegated to him by Congress, to prevent "domestic violence."

Interstate Obligations

The obligations of the national government to the states are matched by certain obligations the states have in their relations with each other. Article IV outlines three of these.

1. "Full faith and credit shall be given in each state to the public acts, records, and judicial proceedings of every other state." Designed to promote interstate cooperation, this clause requires states to recognize the civil judgments of other states. Private contracts made under the laws of one state must be upheld by other states. In the realm of "full faith and credit," divorce is an especially tangled matter; under limited circumstances, the Supreme Court has ruled, a state may refuse to recognize a divorce granted by another state.

2. "The citizens of each state shall be entitled to all privileges and immunities of citizens in the several states." In general, this clause prevents states from favoring their own citizens by discriminating against citizens of other states. Thus, the citizens of one state may acquire property in another state, engage in normal business there, and have access to that state's courts. But the "privileges and immunities" clause does not prevent a state from making reasonable distinctions between its own residents and those from out of state. For example, tuition fees at state universities, as well as fees for hunting and fishing licenses, are usually higher for nonresidents than for residents.[5]

3. "A person charged in any state with treason, felony, or other crime, who shall flee from justice and be found in another state, shall, on demand of the executive authority from the state from which he fled, be delivered up, to be removed to the state having jurisdiction of the crime." This process is known as interstate rendition or extradition. Under ordinary conditions, extradition is routine: A fugitive from justice who flees across a state line, and is apprehended, is promptly surrendered to the state from which he or she fled. The courts have held, nevertheless, that a governor cannot be forced to return a fugitive. One reason a governor might deny a state's request for rendition is the belief that the accused person would not receive a fair trial.

Interstate Compacts

Through the federal principle the Constitution permits the states to carve out their own spheres. It also permits them to cooperate in meeting problems that cross state lines. The instrument for this is the interstate compact provided for by Article I, Section 10. Today there are numerous compacts between the states; these cover such diverse subjects as water and air pollution, conservation, bridges, harbors, parks, education, transportation, civil defense, and highways. Probably the best known compact is the one between New York and New Jersey that formed the Port of New York Authority. Founded in 1921, the authority manages a variety of transportation functions, including port facilities, interstate bridges, airports, and bus terminals. Interstate compacts also have a national presence, since (with some exceptions) Congress must consent to them.

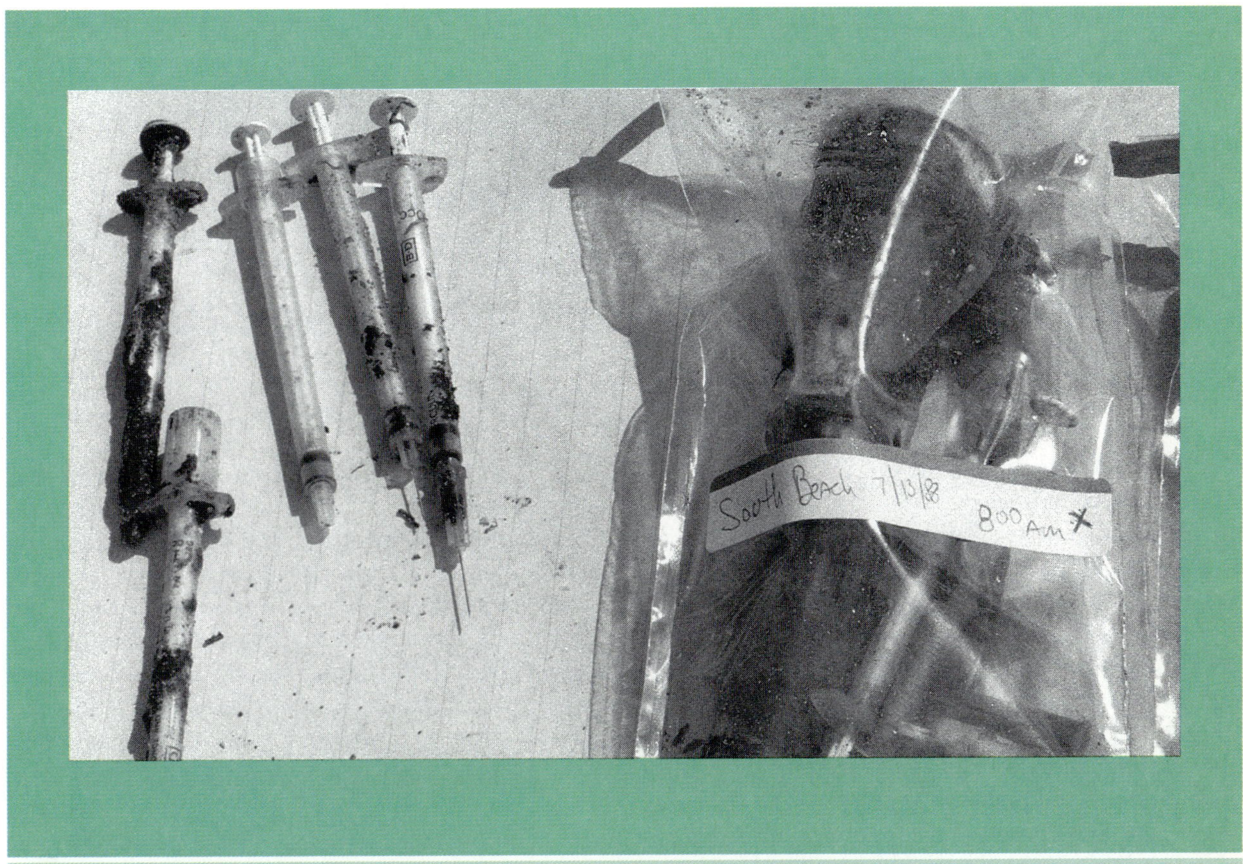

■ Pollution knows no state boundaries. Wastes dumped off the shore of one state may wind up on the beaches of another. Shown here is some of the medical waste, including syringes, recently found on the South Beach of Staten Island, N.Y. Combatting ocean dumping requires a high degree of interstate cooperation.

Disputes Between States ■

One of the by-products of a federal system is controversy between states. Their interests are not identical. Whereas it is an advantage for midwestern states to have weak emission controls, thus permitting industries to burn the high-sulfur coal produced in that region, it is not in the interest of northeastern states, where these emissions fall as acid rain on soil, streams, and lakes. Severance taxes (duties levied by a state on its exports to other states of coal, natural gas, oil, or other nonrenewable resources) raise revenues for energy-rich states (in the West, Southwest, and South) to run their governments, but they add to the financial woes of energy-consuming states. When one state diverts water from interstate streams, there may be major repercussions for other states in need of water. States also come into conflict over the attraction (and relocation) of businesses. New York officials, for example, complain that New Jersey is engaged in pirating New York businesses and sports teams (the "New York" Giants and Jets now play football in the New Jersey Meadowlands sports complex).

“ Perspectives ”

On Federal–State Relations: Nullification Versus National Supremacy

Only one vice president of the United States has ever resigned because of policy differences with the president—John C. Calhoun, who served under President Andrew Jackson from 1825 to 1832. What was the source of disagreement?

President Jackson believed that decisions of the federal government must apply to each of the states in the nation. But Vice President Calhoun argued for the principle of *nullification,* or the belief that a state can nullify an act of Congress within its own borders. Termed "interposition" (because states may interpose themselves between their citizens and the national government in order to prevent the enforcement of national law within the state), the doctrine has now long been rejected by federal courts as contrary to the national supremacy clause of Article VI of the Constitution. In 1832, however, it was a controversial expression of the rights of states—controversial enough to force Calhoun to resign.

". . . in order to maintain the Union unimpaired, it is absolutely necessary that the laws passed by the constituted authorities should be faithfully executed in every part of the country, and that every good citizen should, at all times, stand ready to put down, with the combined force of the nation, every attempt at unlawful resistance, under whatever pretext it may be made or whatever shape it may assume."

—Andrew Jackson, Farewell Address (1837)

"This right of interposition, . . . be it called what it may,—state-right, veto, nullification, or by any other name,—I conceive to be the fundamental principle of our system, resting on facts historically as certain as our revolution itself. . . ."

—John C. Calhoun, Fort Hill Address (1831)

A $40 million grant from the federal Department of Housing and Urban Development to Jersey City was assailed by New York politicians, who contended that the money was being used illegally to lure New York's businesses across the Hudson River.[6] At stake in these rivalries are jobs, unemployment costs, and tax revenues, not to mention states' images.

State and regional controversies often crop up in national politics. In the 101st Congress (1989–1990), for example, northern and midwestern members sought unsuccessfully to require those states in which there had been numerous failures of savings and loan institutions (as in Texas, California, and Florida) to foot a larger share of the bill for bailing out the industry. A report of the Northeast–Midwest Coalition, a caucus of members from those regions, disclosed that Texas savings and loans were responsible for an extraordinary 65 percent of the funds needed in the first year of the bailout. Overall, the federal government's rescue of insolvent thrifts in the 1990s promised to cost the nation's taxpayers more than $100 billion. Other federal programs were certain to be adversely affected by this monumental crisis brought about by relaxed state regulation of thrifts, profligacy, mismanagement, and fraud.

When disputes between states cannot be settled by negotiation, interstate compacts, or national law (and a real "case or controversy" is present), the matter goes to the Supreme Court, which has *original jurisdiction* in all "controversies between two or more states" (Article III, Section 2).

The Supreme Court and Federalism

There have been divisions of opinion over the proper role of the national government in the federal system since the framers of the Constitution set out to form "a more perfect Union." In general, the clash has been between advocates of states' rights and nationalists. The latter group has favored a "loose construction" of the Constitution—one that permits the national government to engage in activities that go well beyond its express powers. Bent on protecting state domains, states' rights advocates believe in a national government with limited powers; they argue from the vantage point of a "strict construction" of the Constitution.

Disputes between these levels of government naturally occur. When they do, the Supreme Court serves as umpire. The landmark case of federal-state relations is *McCulloch* v. *Maryland,* decided by the Supreme Court in 1819.[7] The controversy arose when the state of Maryland levied a tax on the Baltimore branch of the Bank of the United States, which had been established by Congress. The cashier (McCulloch) refused to pay the tax, contending that a state had no power to tax an instrument of the national government.

The suit posed two key questions. The first was whether Congress had the power to charter a bank, since there was no mention of it in the Constitution. The opinion of the Supreme Court, written by Chief Justice John Marshall, a nationalist, left no doubt. Congress's power to establish a bank could be *im-*

John Marshall (1755–1835), Chief Justice of the United States from 1801 to 1835. Under the leadership of Marshall, the power of the Supreme Court increased dramatically; its decisions, moreover, played a major role in the expansion of national power.

plied from the other great powers given to it, such as the powers to levy taxes and borrow money. In other words, Congress could do what was "necessary and proper" to execute its express powers. "Let the end be legitimate," Marshall declared, "let it be within the scope of the Constitution, and all means which are appropriate, which are plainly adapted to that end, which are not prohibited, but consist with the letter and spirit of the Constitution, are constitutional."

That matter settled, the Court turned to the second question: Could the state of Maryland tax a branch of the national bank? The answer was no, for "the power to tax involves the power to destroy." If the states were allowed to tax instruments of the national government, "the declaration that the Constitution, and the laws made in pursuance thereof, shall be the supreme law of the land, is empty and unmeaning declamation."

The *McCulloch* decision reflected the nationalist concept about the development of the United States; essential, in this view, was a strong central government. Yet this case did not settle the issue of national supremacy for all time. A civil war was fought that was as much a struggle between national and state power as it was a struggle over slavery. And from the late nineteenth century to the middle 1930s, the Supreme Court found reasons to invoke the Tenth Amendment to deny power to the federal government.

The permanent legacy of *McCulloch* v. *Maryland* is that it established the principle of implied powers. Ultimately, this became the vehicle for the growth and consolidation of a federal government with wide-ranging powers over the states and the nation. Few decisions in our constitutional history have had greater significance.

The Growth of National Power

The development of the American federal system has been marked by many twists and turns. Yet one trend is clear: The power of the national government has grown enormously, especially during this century. The following reasons help to account for the growing domination of Washington (see Table 3–1).

1. The Electoral Successes of Political Leaders Committed to the Positive State. This school of thought holds, among other things, that the national government has an obligation to develop economic and social programs that promote individual security and social goods. Among presidents, Franklin D. Roosevelt (1933–1945), Harry S Truman (1945–1953), John F. Kennedy (1961–1963), and Lyndon B. Johnson (1963–1969) fit this mold. By contrast, President Ronald Reagan fits just as clearly in the "Tenth Amendment" school.

Congress, too, has often been influenced by members hoping to expand the activities of the federal government. A study of certain major programs (public assistance, unemployment, higher education, elementary and secondary education, and the like) concludes:

> If there is one "primary causal factor" in the growth of government, it has been the hyperresponsiveness to almost every conceivable stimulus—large and small; important and trivial; of national significance and of local interest—of the modern congressional entrepreneur. . . . [The] trend on Capitol Hill increasingly has been toward Congress as an individual rather than toward Congress as an institution. In other words, *government has grown because the individual member of Congress responds*—in part, exactly what he or she is supposed to be doing.[8]

2. Widespread Disillusion with the States. The turn toward the national government reflects, in part, a lack of confidence in state government. Politicians and citizens alike have found fault with the states. Terry Sanford, former governor of North Carolina and currently a U.S. senator from that state, summarizes the case made against them: ". . . indecisive, . . . antiquated, . . . timid and ineffective, . . . not willing to face their problems, . . . not responsive, . . . not interested in cities. These half

TABLE 3–1

Who Makes the Federal Government Grow? The Relative Importance of Various Actors and Environmental Influences in the Development and Growth of the Federal Government (by Policy Fields)

	Public Assistance	Elementary and Secondary Education	Higher Education	Environment	Unemployment	Libraries	Fire Protection
Internal policy actors							
Congress	■	■	■	■	■	■	■
President		■			■		
Interest groups		■		■		■	■†
Bureaucracy				■	■		■
Courts		■		■			
External policy actors							
Public opinion	■*			■			
Elections							
Political parties					■		
Press	■*			■			
Environmental influences							
Demographic and social trends	■	■	■				
Dislocations (war, depression)	■		■		■		

* Food stamps only.
† Interest groups were crucial in the creation of the U.S. Fire Administration only.
Source: Advisory Commission on Intergovernmental Relations, *The Federal Role in the Federal System: The Dynamics of Growth, an Agenda for American Federalism—Restoring Confidence and Competence* (Washington, D.C.: U.S. Government Printing Office, 1981), p. 105 (as modified). These seven policy fields make up about 40 percent of the federal government's grant-in-aid outlays.

dozen charges," he continued, "are true about all of the states some of the time and some of the states all of the time."[9]

3. Crises. The federal system has been affected by three crises in this century: World War I, the Great Depression, and World War II. Meeting these emergencies required a sharp expansion of national government activities. Military spending increased dramatically during World War II and the Vietnam War. And in the 1980s, increased military spending became a major priority of the Reagan administration. Defense spending reaches to every corner of the country, affecting all major aspects of American life. Industries are formed around it, business and labor depend on it, and states (especially in the Sunbelt) benefit from it.

The economic collapse of the 1930s also contributed to changing federal-state relations. With state and local governments helpless to meet the crushing problems of the depression, the people turned to the national government for help. And Washington responded. Emergency programs of public works and direct relief were launched. The Social Security Act was passed in 1935, providing for old-age insurance, unemployment insurance,

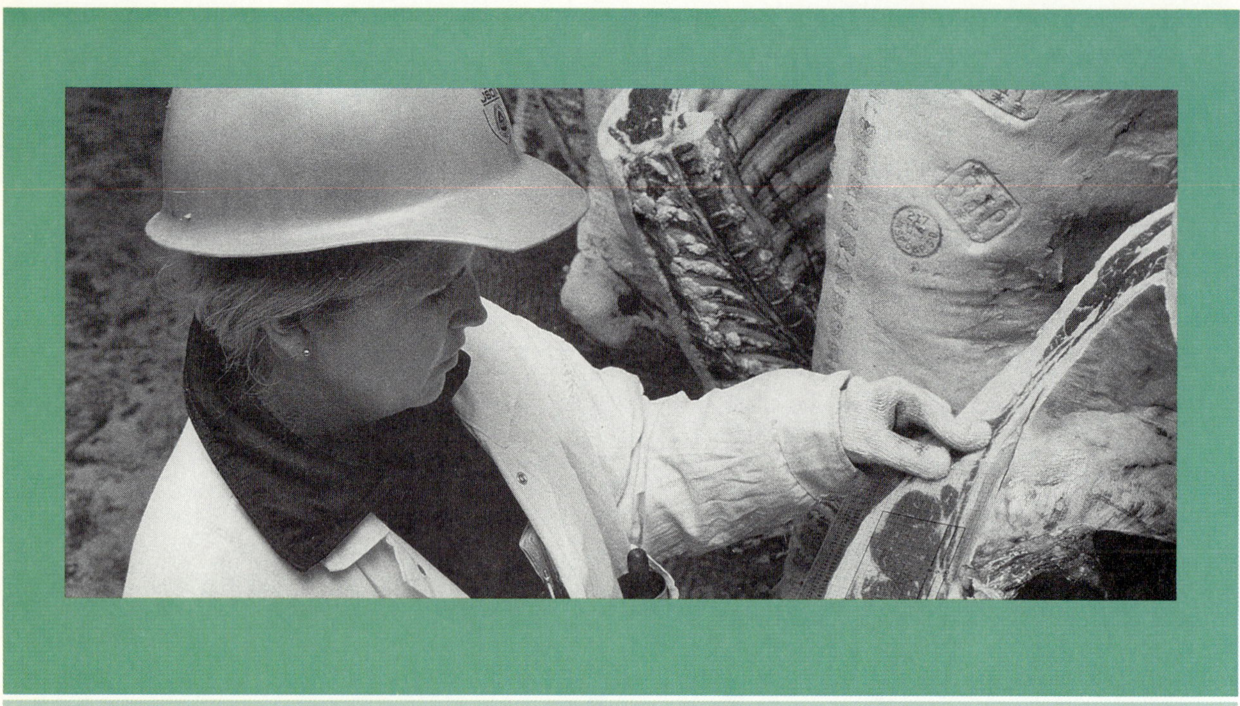

Protecting the consumer from dangerous and adulterated food and drugs has been a major responsibility of the federal government since passage of the Food and Drug Act of 1906. This photo shows a federal meat inspector examining a beef carcass in a Chicago packing plant.

and public assistance grants. Federal aid to state and local governments increased from $232 million in 1932 to $945 million in 1940;[10] climbing more or less steadily, it reached $7 billion in 1960.[11] By 1987, spurred by both inflation and program expansion, federal aid had soared to about $108 billion—a 15-fold increase from 1960. Even so, the *rate* of growth in federal spending for domestic programs declined in the 1980s, the result of budget cuts and a shift of certain responsibilities from Washington to the states under the Reagan administration.

These crises did more than shift power to the national government; they also strengthened the presidency. The president's capacity for leadership, more than Congress's, seemed to promise relief from these national troubles. To help the president do the job, Congress enlarged the "presidential establishment," creating new agencies and increasing staff support. By increasing the president's pool of experts, Congress gave the president greater resources with which to press for legislative goals. The president's role as "chief legislator" became firmly fixed. The broad point is that these crises of war and depression not only altered the balance of power between nation and state but also altered that between president and Congress.

4. Growth in Population and Social Complexity. Although the federal government was not heavily involved in domestic affairs until well into this century, the basis for an expanded role was laid by earlier social changes. Industrialization, urbanization, increased interstate and foreign commerce, national transportation and communications systems, the flow of people across state lines, the centralization of business, and the growth of organized labor—each posed problems too complex for individual states to solve. It has been a long time since the state of Michigan, for example, was a match for the automobile industry, or the state of Texas a match for the oil industry. Each industry is multinational. Similarly, it has long been clear that no single state can handle such large problems as unemployment, welfare, health, and urban decay. The national government has thus become a "dumping ground" for the problems of an interdependent society in an age of high technology and concentrated economic power.

5. **A New Set of Expectations.** No government, least of all a democratic one, operates in a vacuum. What it does depends, in large part, on what is asked of it. The growth in power of the national government came in response to claims made on it by the public at large and particularly by organized interests (including state and local governments). Now almost everyone looks to Washington for aid, and few, if any, government units or citizens are untouched by federal programs.

The demands made on Washington are endless. They include the following:

Aid to elementary, secondary, and higher education
Health care
Price supports for agricultural products
Facilities for runaway youth
Clean air
Enriched educational experiences for disadvantaged children
Safe drinking water
Meals on wheels
Child nutrition programs
Fair packaging and labeling regulations
Community and regional development
Crippled children's services
Wholesome meat
Bikeways
Housing
Promotion of the arts
Occupational safety
Pothole repair
Alcoholism prevention
Employment training
Mine safety
Indian education
Safe streets
Urban rat control
Equal employment opportunities
Reduced-price school lunches
Poultry inspection
Interstate highways
Pesticide control
Bridge replacement
Noise control
Flood prevention
Police disability payments
Protection of voting rights
Law enforcement training
Curtailment of violence on television

The demands generate laws, agencies (federal and state) to administer them, funds, benefits, and agency rules and regulations to be complied with by citizens, the private sector, and state and local governments. What is more, the creation (or expansion) of a federal program helps existing interest groups and launches new interest groups—all concerned with protecting their special forms of aid (see Chapter 10). The "glue" of new, bigger, and better federal programs is politics: For elected officials, programs are translated into endorsements, campaign funds, and, most important, votes.

Programs and political gain, one writer argues, make up the "Washington system":

> [There] is an identifiable Washington system, composed of Congress and the federal bureaucracies operating in a seemingly antagonistic but fundamental symbiotic relationship. . . . [By] working to establish various federal programs (or in some cases fighting their establishment) congressmen earn electoral credit from concerned elements of their districts. Some federal agency then takes Congress's vague policy mandate and makes the detailed decisions necessary to translate the legislation into operating programs. The implementation and operation of the programs by the agencies irritate some constituents and suggest oppor-

"Bottoms up" for children at a day care center. Child care is now a prominent issue on the national agenda. The main question before Congress is *how* the federal government should help working parents to pay for the costs of child care. Should federal *grants* be made to the states to subsidize child care, which most liberals prefer, or should the child-care needs of families be met through giving them *tax credits and deductions,* which most conservatives prefer? Or should some combination of the two be used?

tunities for profit to others. These aggrieved and/or hopeful constituents then appeal to their congressman to intervene in their behalf with the bureaucratic powers that be. The system is connected when congressmen decry bureaucratic excesses while riding a grateful electorate to even more impressive electoral showings.

Thus congressmen appropriate all the public credit generated in the system, while the bureaucracy absorbs all the costs. The bureaucrats may not enjoy their status as objects of public opprobrium, but so long as they accommodate congressmen larger budgets and grants of authority will be forthcoming. All of Washington prospers as ever larger cadres of bureaucrats promulgate ever more numerous regulations and spend ever more money. Meanwhile, ever fewer congressmen meet electoral defeat. This is the Washington system.[12]

6. The Expansion of National Power Through Court Decisions. Federal-state relations have been sharply changed by court decisions of the last several decades. Their main thrusts have been to *expand* the legal basis of national power and to *re-*

strict state and local discretion. Consider several examples.

One express power of the national government is to "regulate commerce . . . among the several states." Under Chief Justice Marshall, the interstate commerce clause was interpreted broadly, which gave Congress wide latitude in passing laws to regulate commercial transactions. In the late 1800s, however, the Court began to narrow the meaning of the clause. Congress could regulate the movement of goods and persons and also carriers (such as railroads) across state lines, the Court said, but it had no authority to regulate manufacturing, marketing, and mining; these were *intrastate* activities, beyond the reach of Congress. It made no difference, for example, that manufactured goods were shipped across state lines. Manufacturing itself was local in nature.

This narrow interpretation lasted until the late 1930s. Since then, with new justices and changed conditions, the commerce clause has been given a broad meaning. Nearly all commerce, including that within a single state, has become subject to national regulation. Interestingly, the commerce clause became the basis for various federal civil rights acts. Citing this clause, the Court has upheld the right of Congress to ban racial discrimination in public accommodations (hotels, restaurants, and the like) and in housing sales and rentals. A landmark decision by the Supreme Court in 1985 even requires that city transit workers (and by extension all other state and local government employees) be paid in accordance with federal minimum wage and hour standards.[13] Today, few activities, commercial or otherwise, fall outside the scope of the commerce power.

The Supreme Court not only has enlarged the legal basis of national action, as in its "broad construction" of the commerce power, but also has intervened in policy domains traditionally governed by state law, such as education, election systems, police, and morals. It has become "a major domestic policymaker" through its decisions on such matters as school desegregation, reapportionment, criminal justice, abortion, and obscenity laws.[14] (See Chapters 4 and 5.) Numerous state laws, constitutional provisions, and practices have given way in the face of the Court's decisions on individual rights and democratic political structures and processes. The reapportionment cases of the 1960s were especially dramatic; they revealed that the states could not even control their own political institutions.

All in all, the Supreme Court is a force for the nationalization of American life and politics as much today as it was in the days of Chief Justice Marshall. Perhaps even more so now. It is not surprising that advocates of states' rights see the Court not as the "umpire" of the federal system, but as a participant on the national side.

7. The National Government's Superior Financial Resources. The growth of federal activities in this century owes much to the Sixteenth Amendment (1913), which gave Congress the power to levy an income tax. An income tax produces much greater revenues than the taxes primarily relied on by the states (sales)[15] or local governments (property). The result, in terms of federal-state relations, is a fiscal mismatch. Limited in their fiscal capacity, state and local governments have become more reliant on federal revenues (through grants-in-aid or, for a time, revenue sharing) to support state and local services.[16] One reason for this is that it is easier to ask Congress for help than to risk the wrath of voters by raising taxes. Whatever the complete explanation, the independence of the states suffers.

8. The Political Strategy of "Losers." All politics, E. E. Schattschneider argued, is the struggle between those who want to restrict conflict and those who want to expand it.[17] The rule is simple: Political interests on the winning side of any issue seek to keep conflict localized or private; "losers" want to "socialize" or expand it, bringing more people into the fight to change the balance of forces. Ultimately, the scope of the conflict—the number of people involved—decides the outcome. In the typical pattern of conflict expansion, conflicts become more intense and visible and move from local and state levels to the national system.

Governments shape their agendas by choosing

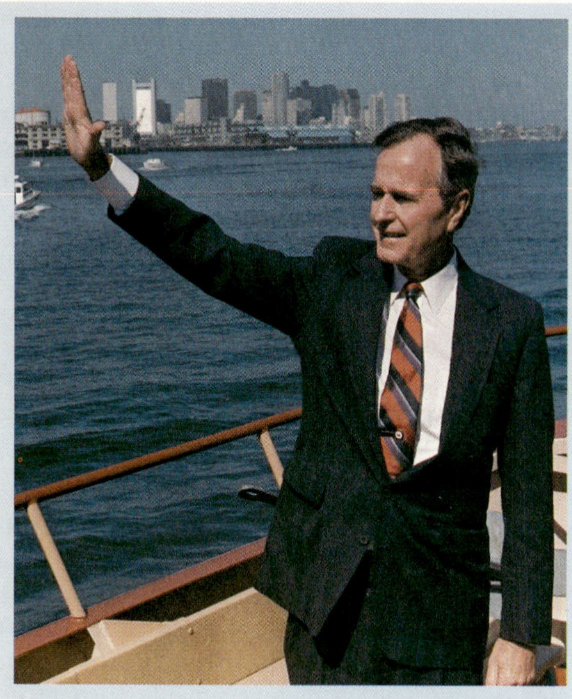

Campaign 1988: With the Deer Island sewerage treatment plant as a backdrop, Vice President George Bush attacks Massachusetts Governor Michael Dukakis's handling of the Boston Harbor cleanup during a news conference aboard a passenger ferry in the harbor. Bush was greeted by a flotilla of Dukakis supporters on other ferries, rubber rafts and sailboats with critical allegations of their own.

which conflicts they want to exploit. They thrive on conflict. They take sides. Their willingness to pick up fights begun elsewhere assures a steady flow of power to them. The nationalization of American politics is one result of Washington's sustained involvement in political conflicts formerly settled in private domains or by lower governments.

Federal–State Relations

In broad terms, there have been two major eras in American federalism. The dominant pattern during most of the nineteenth century was *dual federalism.* On the whole, the federal and state governments occupied separate spheres. Although there was limited sharing of functions, such as federal land grants to the states to support education and certain internal improvements (canals, railroads, and the like), the main thrust of public policy reflected the separateness and independence of the two levels. The federal government itself grew slowly. Most matters of domestic policy were within the legal authority of state and local governments.

The relationship between the federal government and the states in the modern era has been very different. The idea of dual federalism all but vanished (at least until the Reagan administration), replaced by a scheme of *cooperative federalism* under which national and state governments share responsibilities and powers in carrying out public functions. The turn toward cooperative federalism was not because government functions were taken away from the states; it rather represented a new sharing of functions that once were the province of states.[18]

Even with the slowdown of federal funding for state programs during the Reagan years, the federal commitment in grant-in-aid money continues to be enormous. Almost every government function now involves intergovernment collaboration.

> From public welfare to public recreation, from national defense to local police protection, the system of sharing has become so pervasive that it is often difficult for the uninitiated bystander to tell just who is doing what under which hat. The highly institutionalized system of federal-state cooperation which has developed has become part of the nation's constitutional tradition. Under this cooperative system, the federal government, the states, and the localities share the burden for the great domestic programs *by making the larger governments primarily responsible for raising revenues and setting standards, and the smaller ones primarily responsible for administering the programs.* For each program, all governments involved contribute toward making policy in

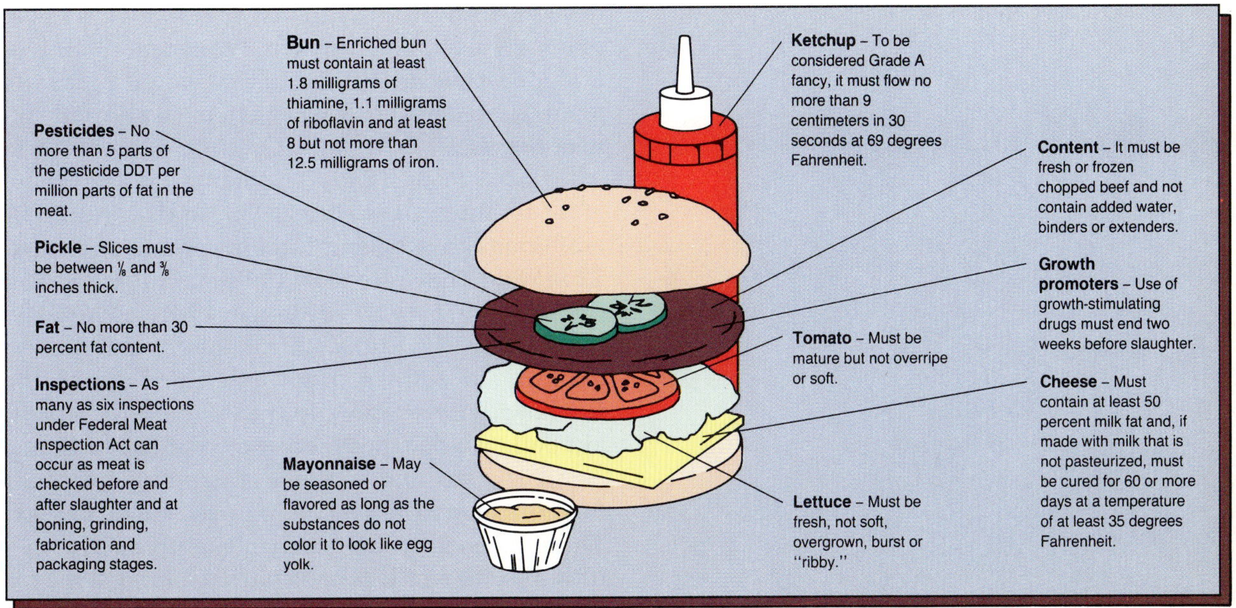

■ **Figure 3–1** Your hamburger: 41,000 regulations. The illustration here is only a sampling of the rules and regulations governing the burger you buy at the corner sandwich stand. The 41,000 federal and state regulations, many stemming from 200 laws and 111,000 precedent-setting court cases, touch on everything involved in meat production—grazing practices of cattle, conditions in slaughterhouses, and methods used to process meat for sale to supermarkets, restaurants, and fast-food outlets. According to a three-volume study by Colorado State University, these regulations, add an estimated 8 to 11 cents per pound to the cost of a hamburger. So where's the beef? There are two answers: (1) under the scrutiny of government inspectors, enforcing countless federal and state regulations, and (2) adjacent to the ketchup (which must flow no more than 9 centimeters in 30 seconds at 69 degrees Fahrenheit) and between the buns (which must contain at least 1.8 milligrams of thiamine, 1.1 milligrams of riboflavin, and at least 8 but nor more than 12.5 milligrams of iron). Source: Adapted from *U.S. News & World Report,* February 11, 1980, p. 64.

ways which often depend upon the forms of sharing involved.[19]

Cooperative federalism is part of a larger theme: the expanded range of activities of *all* governments. To deal with an infinite variety of economic and social problems, government at all levels has become the "great regulator." A maze of federal, state, and local rules and regulations governs individuals, associational life, and businesses, making it all but impossible to mark where the authority of one government stops and that of another begins. It boggles the mind (while perhaps calming the stomach) to learn that there are 41,000 state and federal regulations governing the production and processing of meat! (See Figure 3–1.)

Federal Grants-in-Aid ■

The most important feature of intergovernment relations in the United States is the *grant-in-aid system*—a mix of programs under which federal money is provided to state and local governments.[20] There are, for example, grant programs to aid the blind and families with dependent children, to construct highways and airports, to provide for public assistance and public housing, to provide employment training and child welfare services, to help low-income persons pay fuel bills, and to help local governments build sewage treatment plants. Altogether, by 1981, more than 500 different federal grant programs were in place. During the Reagan administration the number was cut to about 370.

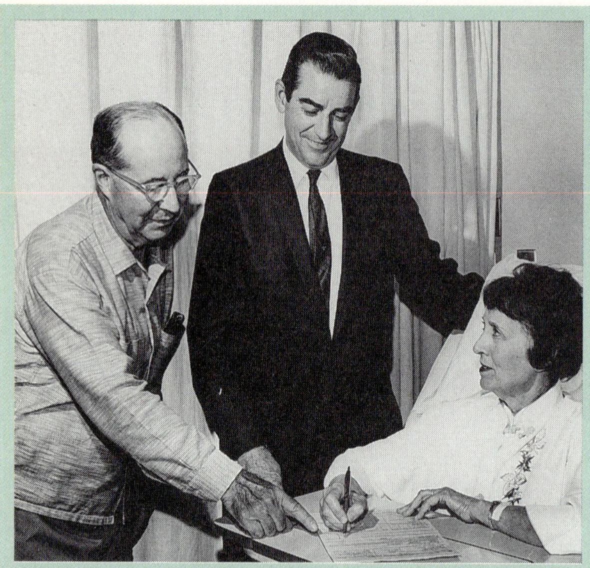

In 1965, Congress passed a health insurance program, popularly known as Medicare, to provide medical assistance for the elderly. Administered by the Department of Health and Human Services, the main thrust of Medicare is to provide hospital insurance for persons 65 and over who are covered by Social Security. Another program, Medicaid, helps the poor to pay their medical bills. About 50 million people now receive benefits from these two programs. This photo shows the nation's first Medicare beneficiary in 1966: Mrs. Lillian Grace Avery of Naperville, Illinois.

Programs were eliminated outright or consolidated as the Reagan administration won congressional approval for reduced federal spending and for grant programs that gave the states wider discretion in the uses to be made of federal money.

Currently, the leading grant programs are Medicaid, interstate highway construction, Aid to Families with Dependent Children, and subsidized housing. Medicaid is the largest grant-in-aid program; it assists state and local governments in providing health services to some 25 million low-income persons. Major changes have occurred in the distribution of grant outlays over the years. Only 3 percent of federal aid in 1960, for example, was devoted to health programs; in 1989, these programs received an estimated 29 percent of all federal aid. Almost half of all grant-in-aid funds are administered by the Department of Health and Human Services.[21]

The data of Table 3–2 depict the growth of grant-in-aid outlays since 1950. In that year, federal grants to state and local governments totaled $2 billion. They rose to $11 billion in 1965, to $50 billion in 1975, to $95 billion in 1981, and to $108 billion in 1987. Adjusted for inflation, however, grant-in-aid outlays actually declined during the Reagan administration. In the early 1990s, federal aid outlays are expected to exceed $125 billion.

It is a striking fact that grants-in-aid account for more than $1 of every $10 in the federal budget. These payments, moreover, make up nearly one-fifth of state and local revenues. Federal money is crucial in state and local spending. Nonetheless, as the data of Table 3–2 make clear, grants-in-aid have declined as a proportion of the federal budget and as a proportion of state and local expenditures. These shifts stem in large part from the Reagan administration's success in reducing the growth rate of federal domestic spending. And, of course, rapidly rising federal deficits (interest on the national debt now exceeds $150 billion annually!) and increased military spending, each a major trend in the 1980s, make it more difficult to put together majorities in Congress for grants-in-aid. Programs, in other words, compete for dollars, for a share of the federal pie.

In addition to the purely financial objective of helping state and local governments provide services, federal grants also serve less obvious purposes. They may be designed to (1) establish minimum national standards in certain programs (to provide, for example, an income floor in aid to dependent children), (2) equalize resources among the states (by providing more aid to poorer states), (3) improve state services through technical assistance, (4) promote interstate cooperation in meeting problems that cross state lines (such as air pollution), (5) encourage experimentation in meeting problems (such as Project Head Start), (6) improve the administration of state programs, (7) attain cer-

TABLE 3–2

Historical Trend of Federal Grant-in-Aid Outlays

	Total Grants-in-Aid ($ billion)	Federal Grants as a Percentage of: Federal Outlays — Total	Federal Outlays — Domestic Programs*	State and Local Expenditures
Five-year intervals				
1950	2.3	5.3	11.6	10.4
1955	3.2	4.7	17.2	10.1
1960	7.0	7.6	20.6	14.6
1965	10.9	9.2	20.3	15.2
1970	24.1	12.3	25.3	19.2
1975	49.8	15.0	23.1	22.7
Annually				
1980	91.5	15.5	23.3	25.8
1981	94.8	14.0	21.6	24.6
1982	88.2	11.8	19.0	21.6
1983	92.5	11.4	18.6	21.3
1984	97.6	11.5	19.6	20.9
1985	105.9	11.2	19.3	20.9
1986	112.4	11.3	19.8	20.5
1987	108.4	10.8	18.9	18.2
1988 estimate	116.7	11.0	19.0	NA†
1989 estimate	119.0	10.9	18.7	NA
1990 estimate	121.9	10.6	18.1	NA
1991 estimate	124.3	10.3	17.6	NA
1992 estimate	127.7	10.3	17.3	NA
1993 estimate	131.5	10.3	17.0	NA

* Excludes outlays for national defense, international affairs, and net interest.
† NA, Not available.
Source: "Special Analysis H," in *Special Analyses, Budget of the United States Government, Fiscal Year 1989* (Washington, D.C.: U.S. Government Printing Office, 1988), p. H-20.

tain social objectives (such as the elimination of discrimination in public services), and (8) of large political significance, meet problems without apparently increasing the size of the federal bureaucracy.[22]

Federal grants often bring about major changes in the public policies of the states. In response to a public outcry over drunken driving, lobbied heavily by Mothers Against Drunk Drivers (MADD) and less conspicuously by the insurance industry, Congress in 1984 entered a domain previously left to the states to decide: the drinking age. Supported by President Reagan, who was initially an opponent, Congress passed a federal highway aid bill to induce states to raise their drinking age to 21. (About half of the states then had a lower drinking age.) Under its terms, any state that failed to enact a minimum drinking age of 21 by 1988 would have

M.A.D.D., Mothers Against Drunk Driving, was launched by a mother whose child was killed by a teenage drunken driver. This organization can claim primary credit for the adoption of legislation raising the national drinking age to twenty-one.

up to 15 percent of its federal highway funds withheld (5 percent in 1987 and 10 percent in 1988 and thereafter). In a 1987 case, *South Dakota* v. *Dole,* the Supreme Court upheld the constitutionality of the act, stating that the "encouragement" given states to raise their minimum drinking age was "a valid use of the spending power." Lawyers for South Dakota had contended that the Twenty-first Amendment, which repealed Prohibition, empowered the states to control the sale of liquor.[23]

Money is an ever-present inducement in federal-state relations. In 1988, faced with the loss of highway funds, Wyoming became the last state to raise its drinking age to 21. In effect, using the grant-in-aid device, Congress imposed a uniform drinking age on the nation.

Channels for Federal Money

Three principal methods have been used to channel federal money to state and local governments: categorical grants, block grants, and general revenue sharing.

Categorical Grants. The oldest form of federal aid, categorical grants, is awarded for specific purposes, such as highway construction, urban mass transit systems, pollution control, employment training, food stamps, Medicaid, or the control of hazardous wastes. Carrying detailed requirements ("strings"), these grants give state and local governments little discretion in how the funds are spent. About 85 percent of all federal aid is in the form of categorical grants. Once enacted, the grants are hard to terminate. Interest groups develop around them to lobby Congress for "their" program's renewal.

Members of Congress are equally fond of categorical grants. One reason for their appeal is that

> they constitute answers to the perennial question: What have you done for me lately? A narrowly defined category is ideal from this standpoint. It is custom-made to suit the requirements of some key group of constituents and the Congress can plainly label it "from me to you." Revenue sharing, whether "general" or "special," altogether lacks this advantage. It gives benefits not to constituents directly but in wholesale lots to state and local politicians who will package them for retail distribution under their own labels, taking all of the credit.[24]

Grant programs share a common feature—the tendency to expand. The food stamp program, begun in 1964, is an especially good example. In 1970, federal outlays for food stamps were well under $1 billion; fueled mainly by inflation and unemployment, appropriations for this program in the late 1980s reached nearly $14 billion. The food stamp program now helps about 19 million people to pay their grocery bills. Its supporters contend that it is critical in meeting the nation's problems of hunger and malnutrition. Critics say it is laced with "fat" and infested by "parasites."[25] Lobbying to protect

"It's too bad you can't get federal matching funds, whatever they are."

Federalism, Environmental Issues, and the 1988 Election

One of the drawbacks of a federal system is that it is often difficult to fix blame for policy failures and to hold the appropriate leaders accountable. Consider an issue that became prominent during the 1988 presidential election: the polluted waters of Boston Harbor. Democratic candidate Michael Dukakis, a self-proclaimed environmentalist, was accused by his Republican rival, Vice President George Bush, of being unable to attend to environmental concerns in his own state and of "dumping sludge from Massachusetts off of the beaches . . . of New Jersey." The Bush campaign steadily hammered away at this issue with television ads that showed the sewage in the harbor. The ads were widely seen as unfair, but they left little doubt in the minds of many voters that Dukakis was responsible for the mess. In fact, they won an award for their producer after the election.

Was Dukakis really to blame for this environmental diaster? Yes, in part. On two occasions (1976 and 1984), Dukakis applied to the Environmental Protection Agency (EPA) for waivers from the Clean Water Act so that he could postpone cleanup of the harbor. Had Dukakis made an effort to clean up the harbor in those earlier years, when more federal funds were available, the estimated cost for the job would have been about $1 billion. By 1988, however, the same project carried a price tag between $3 and $6 billion—a cost that would be borne mainly by Boston households.

On the other hand, the Reagan administration, with the support of Vice President Bush, made major cuts in funding for environmental cleanup, including a $250 million reduction in the EPA's 1988 fiscal budget. Of that sum, $96 million was sliced from the municipal wastewater construction grants program and $50 million from the Superfund hazardous waste cleanup program. The vice president also supported two vetoes of the Clean Water Act in 1986 and 1987. Thus, Dukakis could appropriately claim that his hands were tied by a lack of funding and blame the Reagan administration for "doing everything [it] could to kill the Clean Water Act and [the] grants to make it possible for states and local communities to clean up rivers and harbors and streams."

In federal systems, there is often no simple answer to the question: "Who is to blame?"

Sources: *Environment,* January/February 1988, pp. 7–9; *Time,* August 15, 1988, pp. 16–17.

the program has been led by the National Anti-Hunger Coalition, supported by various poor people's, welfare, and food industry groups (food stamps, of course, increase food sales).

Most categorical grants require state or local matching funds; in other words, recipient governments must put up some of their own funds to qualify for federal money. Prior to 1960, most grants provided for 50:50 sharing of costs. Since then, the federal share of most programs has increased; ratios of 1:2 and 1:3 are now common. For the interstate highway system, the federal government pays 90 percent of the costs and the states only 10 percent.

A special form of categorical grant is the *project grant.* Designed to handle specific problems, project grants are made selectively rather than across the board. Potential recipients compete for grants—for example, to fund community health centers or slum clearance—by writing proposals to fit federal guidelines. Ingenuity counts in writing proposals and lobbying for their approval. Some states and communities are much more successful than others in capturing project money, in playing the "federal grantsmanship game." Many states and cities operate a Washington office to facilitate efforts to obtain grants. A common type of aid, project grants have become especially important for local governments. Evidence shows that the strength of a city's representation in the House of Representatives (coupled with representation on the relevant committee) has a major impact on its ability to capture project grants and on the level of the funding made available. In the distribution of project grants, political linkage turns out to be more important than a city's needs.[26]

Under the Reagan administration, many project grants were switched to *formula grants;* using this method, funds are allocated automatically on the basis of a certain formula, thus removing the discretion of federal authorities. In the view of the Reagan administration, formula grants reduce federal intrusion in local decision making; in particular, they weaken the spending ties between grant recipients and their federal benefactors (members of Congress and agency bureaucrats).[27]

Block Grants. A newer form of federal aid is the block grant—one in which funds are committed to a broad functional area, such as health or community development. State and local officials have substantial discretion in how they spend federal funds. A well-known example of a block grant is the Partnership in Health Act of 1966, which combined several categorical grants (such as those dealing with cancer, tuberculosis, heart, venereal, and mental diseases) into a single program.

Block grants are an effort to return power to the states, to permit state and local officials to tailor programs to fit their needs. They have fewer details, carry fewer strings, and require less paperwork; the "federal octopus" is thus less evident. Grants are made for general rather than specific purposes. On the whole, Republicans are more likely to support this broad-based approach than Democrats, in part because it meshes with the party's states' rights ideology. Many congressional Democrats oppose block grants because they fear that social programs supported by categorical grants (enacted by earlier Democratic majorities) might be shortchanged in a consolidated program.

Many state and local politicians prefer that federal aid be given with fewer strings or mandates. They complain that the mandates are unfair and poorly designed to meet the needs of their constituents. But politics is also involved: the fewer the strings, the greater the opportunity for state and local politicians to use federal money in ways calculated to build and maintain coalitions for future elections.[28]

Block grants thus have a strong appeal in certain quarters. During the Reagan administration, block grants came to be seen as a means of overhauling the federal system, since these grants give states greater freedom from federal controls. Many proposals for merging grant programs were made, and some were adopted. Congressional resistance prevented larger changes. Overall, the states gained added flexibility in the use of federal money, but at the administration's price: a reduction in funding. Despite President Reagan's preference for block grants, categorical grants continued to dominate direct aid to state and local governments. In-

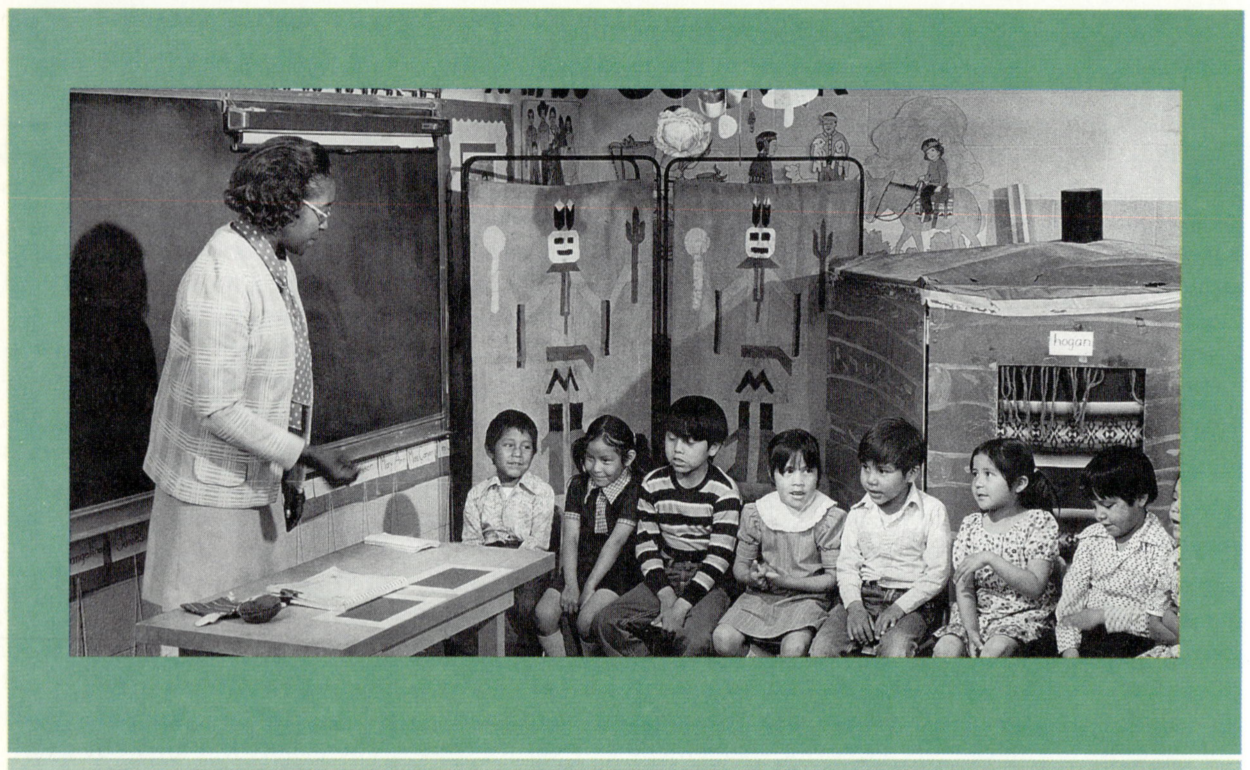

Funding for education is a good example of cooperative federalism. Today, virtually every school district in the country benefits from some form of federal aid. Shown here is a kindergarten class at a Tuba City, New Mexico boarding school for Indian children.

deed, in 1988, only about 13 percent of all federal aid was allocated in broadly discretionary grants.[29]

Revenue Sharing. A third major form of federal aid, general revenue sharing, was used from 1972 to 1986. A key feature of the Nixon administration's New Federalism, revenue sharing provided states and localities with about $6 billion annually during the 1970s, with one-third awarded to the states and two-thirds to some 39,000 local governments (cities, counties, and townships). Despite intensive lobbying by governors and other state officials, the states were dropped from the program in 1980. Local governments continued to receive about $4.6 billion a year in revenue-sharing money until 1986, when, pressured by the Reagan administration, Congress terminated the program. Growing national budget deficits also influenced Congress's decision to abandon revenue sharing.

Introduced with much fanfare, revenue sharing was designed to reverse "the flow of power in America" by strengthening state and local governments. The charm of revenue sharing for beneficiaries was that the money was given with few strings attached. Matching funds were not required. Governments were free to use the money in almost any way they chose; they spent it on police protection, education, highways, health, libraries, housing, parks, and dozens of other things. Understandably, no federal aid program has been more popular among state and local officials. Attempts by the U.S. Conference of Mayors and other organizations to revive it thus far have been unsuccessful.

The Scope of State and Local Expenditures

So much has been said about the expansion of the federal government's role in domestic affairs that it is easy to overlook the place of state and local governments in providing services. Not so long ago, state and local government expenditures were much larger than those of the federal government. In 1929, states and cities outspent the "feds" by a 3:1 ratio. Of course, the situation today is much different. Federal money now makes up nearly two-thirds of all public spending. Even so, state and local units spend more than $650 billion annually of their own funds on public services—not exactly a drop in the bucket. The burden of providing for education, public welfare, health and hospitals, and highway construction (among other things) weighs heavily on all states and cities, even with the benefit of federal aid. (See Table 3–3 for data on the most expensive state programs.)

TABLE 3–3

State Spending and State Services: Where the Money Goes

Programs: The Big Four	Percentage of State Expenditures*
Education	29.4
Higher education	8.0
Local schools	20.1
Miscellaneous	1.3
Public welfare	10.6
Health and hospitals	7.6
Highways	6.9

* Other expenditures support such functions as police and fire protection, sanitation and sewage, housing and urban renewal, parks and recreation, employee retirement, and unemployment compensation.
Source: Developed from data in *Statistical Abstract of the United States, 1988* (Washington, D.C.: U.S. Government Printing Office, 1988), p. 262.

Federalism in Transition

In the nation's formative years, the federal government rarely touched the lives of average people. Almost all federal employees were either members of the armed services or engaged in revenue collection.[30] Citizens seldom pressed for federal benefits or services, and few were available. In this highly decentralized political order, domestic policy making was largely a function of state and local governments. The role of the federal government was more that of observer than of participant.

Time, events, and political leaders combined to change the notion of a federal government with limited reach. In one way or another, everyone is now directly affected by the policies of the federal government. Consider these statistics: Over 80 percent of the population is covered by the individual federal income tax, about 90 percent of employed persons fall under the social security system and unemployment insurance, about 8 percent of all persons receive some kind of public assistance, and more than 90 percent of the elderly (over 65) receive social security payments. And that is only a small part of the story. Businesses, other private-sector organizations, and state and local governments have been affected to a similar degree by an expanding federal presence.[31]

In recent decades, nearly all shifts in functions have been toward greater federal influence. For example, the most important public policies affecting civil rights (civil liberties and voting rights) are now federal rather than state. Other major shifts have taken place in aid to the poor, health services and regulations, and control over the production and distribution of goods; in these domains the federal government now dominates. Local control over education has also declined. For example, at the urging of President Reagan, Congress passed an equal-access law that denies local school boards the right to bar student religious groups from using public school facilities during nonclass hours. Even in

“Perspectives”

On Federalism

“The federal system is not accurately symbolized by a neat layer cake of three distinct and separate planes. A far more realistic symbol is that of the marble cake. Wherever you slice through it you reveal an inseparable mixture of differently colored ingredients. There is no neat horizontal stratification. Vertical and diagonal lines almost obliterate the horizontal ones, and in some places there are unexpected whirls and an imperceptible merging of colors, so that it is difficult to tell where one ends and the other begins. So it is with federal, state, and local responsibilities in the chaotic marble cake of American government.”

—Morton Grodzins,
political scientist

“The spending power and the commerce power as construed by the Supreme Court have afforded national government hegemony over all affairs of the citizens and residents of this nation. The national government is free to regulate everything, except that it must conform to the Supreme Court's interpretation of the limitations imposed by the Bill of Rights and other specific limitations spelled out in the Constitution itself. From a government of delegated powers it has become a sovereignty with jurisdiction no different from that of the nation from which it seceded in 1776.”

—Philip B. Kurland,
constitutional lawyer

“The states test whether the opinions by which we live our lives and run our governments are myths or facts. This is federalism at its best—always probing, always testing, always seeking a better way. The states allow experimentation, change, and local leadership, especially in controversial subjects involving deep societal values in which feelings run high and attitudes vary all across the nation.”

—Senator Terry Sanford,
former governor of North Carolina

“This government is acknowledged by all to be one of enumerated powers. The principle that it can exercise only the powers granted to it . . . is now universally admitted. But the question respecting the extent of the powers actually granted is perpetually arising, and will probably continue to arise, as long as our system shall exist.”

—Chief Justice John Marshall

“[We] have now arrived at a point in our constitutional history when no sphere of life is beyond the reach of the national government. Since we no longer question the constitutionality of federal acts, the deciding factor becomes one of policy rather than legality.”

—Michael D. Reagan,
political scientist

Sources: Morton Grodzins “Centralization and Decentralization in the American Federal System,” in *A Nation of States,* ed. Robert A. Goldwin (Chicago: Rand McNally, 1963), pp. 3–4; Philip B. Kurland, *Watergate and the Constitution* (Chicago: University of Chicago Press, 1978), p. 174; Terry Sanford, *Storm Over the States* (New York: McGraw-Hill, 1967), p. 4; *McCulloch* v. *Maryland* (1819); Michael D. Reagan, *The New Federalism* (New York: Oxford University Press, 1972), p. 13.

matters of morality, long the sole province of state and local governments, the federal government's presence can now be detected. It appears, for example, in laws and court decisions involving abortion, fair campaign practices, truth in lending, and truth in labeling.

A second major conclusion is easier to miss: Despite the growth of federal involvement in all government functions in this century, the federal-state relationship is basically a *partnership.* For the most part, responsibilities are shared—sometimes equally, sometimes tipped on the side of the federal government, sometimes tipped on the side of the states. More often than not, of course, the senior partner is the federal government.[32] Put another way, modern American federalism is a "*nationally dominated system of shared power and shared functions.*"[33]

A New Federalism?

The present division of responsibilities between nation and states is subject to change. The federal system will certainly be different in the years to come—more or less interdependent, more or less in equilibrium, more or less under the sway of one or the other level.

Truism or not, the Tenth Amendment is not dead. A change in national administrations often ignites a fresh debate over federalism. A shift of power and functions from Washington to the states becomes a possibility. Indeed, this became a central goal of the Reagan administration: "It is my intention," the president stated in his inaugural address, "to demand recognition of the distinction between the powers granted to the federal government and those reserved to the states and to the people. All of us need to be reminded that the federal government did not create the states; the states created the federal government."

In 1982, in his first State of the Union address, President Reagan unveiled his New Federalism program. Breaking with the past, his proposal called for the transfer of some 40 federal programs (involving more than 100 categorical grants) back to the states, along with two core welfare programs—Aid to Families with Dependent Children (federal-state) and the food stamp program (federal). In return, the federal government would take over Medicaid (federal-state), a health program for the poor. Thus, a major feature of the proposal was a swap of costly programs: "We'll take care of your sick," as one writer put it, "if you'll take care of your poor." In addition, the president proposed the creation of a short-term federal trust fund with revenues (derived from federal excise and oil windfall profits taxes) that would be available to the states to help meet the costs of programs shifted to them. By 1991, with the transfer concluded, total funding of these programs would be assumed by the states.

Reactions to the Reagan program were mixed. Among the advantages seen for the New Federalism were relief from the growing centralization of power in the federal government, growth of state initiative and responsibility, greater efficiency, dollar savings, less cumbersome administration, and development of programs that would be more responsive to the people. A leaner federal government would emerge. Critics were just as certain that the New Federalism would lead to a "crazy quilt" of regional and state differences in programs (see Table 3–4), "winners" and "losers" among the states, reduction or elimination of certain social programs, migration of poor people to states with more generous welfare programs ("voting with their feet"), loss of influence for groups that speak for the poor since they would be forced to lobby in 50 state capitals, and putting local governments at the mercy of state governments for funds.

The key feature of President Reagan's New Federalism—the program swap—was extensively debated in Washington, the state capitals, and the press. Strong resistance from members of Congress and state and local officials, along with division within the Reagan administration itself, kept the proposal from getting off the ground. Interestingly, legislation to provide for the "swap and turnback" was never introduced in Congress. Other features of the Reagan federalism initiative, joined with budget cutting, nevertheless brought a number of changes to intergovernmental relations.

TABLE 3–4

Federalism in Action: Wide Differences Among the States in Expenditures for Public Elementary and Secondary Education, Shown as Average per Pupil, 1987

Expenditures									
Top Fifth		**Second Fifth**		**Third Fifth**		**Fourth Fifth**		**Lowest Fifth**	
Alaska	$8842	R.I.	$4574	Mich.	$3954	N.C.	$3473	S.C.	$3005
N.Y.	$6299	Vt.	$4459	Va.	$3809	Neb.	$3437	W.Va.	$2959
Wyo.	$6229	Hawaii	$4372	Wash.	$3808	N.H.	$3386	Tenn.	$2842
N.J.	$6120	Minn.	$4241	Ohio	$3769	Ind.	$3379	Ark.	$2795
Conn.	$5552	Ore.	$4236	Nev.	$3768	Mo.	$3345	Ariz.	$2784
Mass.	$4856	Kan.	$4137	Calif.	$3751	La.	$3237	Okla.	$2701
Del.	$4776	Colo.	$4129	Iowa	$3740	N.D.	$3209	Ala.	$2610
Pa.	$4752	Mont.	$4070	Maine	$3650	S.D.	$3190	Idaho	$2555
Wis.	$4701	Fla.	$4056	Tex.	$3584	Ga.	$3167	Miss.	$2534
Md.	$4659	Ill.	$3980	N.M.	$3537	Ky.	$3107	Utah	$2455

Source: Developed from data in *Statistical Abstract of the United States, 1988* (Washington: U.S. Department of Commerce, Bureau of the Census, 1988), p. 133. The national average was $3970.

The Reagan federalism box score looks like this: Several dozen minor federal aid programs were eliminated outright. Matching rates were lowered or eliminated for certain categorical grants, saving federal dollars and reducing the spending incentives of state and local governments. Other categorical grants were consolidated into broader and more flexible grants, giving the states more latitude in the use of their resources; the larger block grants covered such programs as elementary and secondary education, community development, preventive health and health services, and alcohol, drug abuse, and mental health. The new block grants, with reduced funding, made the states (rather than local governments) the aid recipients; each state could thus shape its own aid policies for local governments. (During the 1960s and 1970s, the states frequently were bypassed by grants given directly to local governments.) Various federal regulations governing grant programs were relaxed. General revenue sharing was permitted to lapse, thus severing the major link between federal and local governments. Numerous project grants were replaced by formula grants in an effort to curb "pork barrel" politics in the grant structure.

Of major significance, along with grant consolidation, federal funding itself was cut. In constant dollars (adjusted for inflation), federal aid was pared by 15 percent during the Reagan years.[34] These reductions prompted some states and local governments to increase their taxes in order to preserve existing programs and others to dip into reserves, reduce services, and experience deficits. Overall, as a percentage of state-local expenditures, federal aid dropped markedly—from 26 to 18 percent between 1981 and 1988. (Refer back to Table 3–2.)

With respect to intergovernmental relations, the Reagan administration's basic objective was to realign the federal system by reducing the financial

Continuity & CHANGE

The Changing Thrust of Federal Grant-in-Aid Outlays

Function	Percent of Total	
	1960	1989
Health	3	29
Income security, including food and housing assistance	38	27
Education, training, employment, and social services	7	18
Transportation	43	15
Miscellaneous (in such areas as natural resources, agriculture, and community development)	9	11

The functions served by federal grants have changed dramatically in the last three decades. Almost half (43 percent) of all grant funds in 1960 were earmarked for state transportation programs; by 1989, only 15 percent of grant funds were used for this purpose. Funds for education, training, employment, and social services were, proportionately, two and one-half times larger in 1989 than in 1960. But the real "winner" has been the health function. Government today is deeply involved in providing health services. Health grants increased from 3 percent in 1960 to 29 percent in 1989. Concretely, more than 25 percent of all grant-in-aid funds in 1989 were allocated simply for Medicaid—a range of health services for low-income families.

Source: Developed from data in "Special Analysis H," in *Special Analyses, Budget of the United States Government, Fiscal Year 1989* (Washington, D.C.: U.S. Government Printing Office, 1988), pp. H-10–H-18.

interdependence of the levels of government. This change would require a sorting out of responsibilities by level of government—in essence, setting aside cooperative federalism and reviving dual federalism. More responsibility, authority, money, and discretion were to be transferred to state and local governments. In the Reagan theory of federalism, the states would bear primary responsibility for domestic policy, as they had half a century earlier. Federal aid would be cut sharply and pressure on the federal budget eased. This theory of federalism meshed comfortably with the administration's central goal of cutting the size of the federal government by reducing federal domestic expenditures and taxes.

The Reagan administration's thrust in federalism focused debate in Washington and elsewhere on the issue of devolving power to the states. States

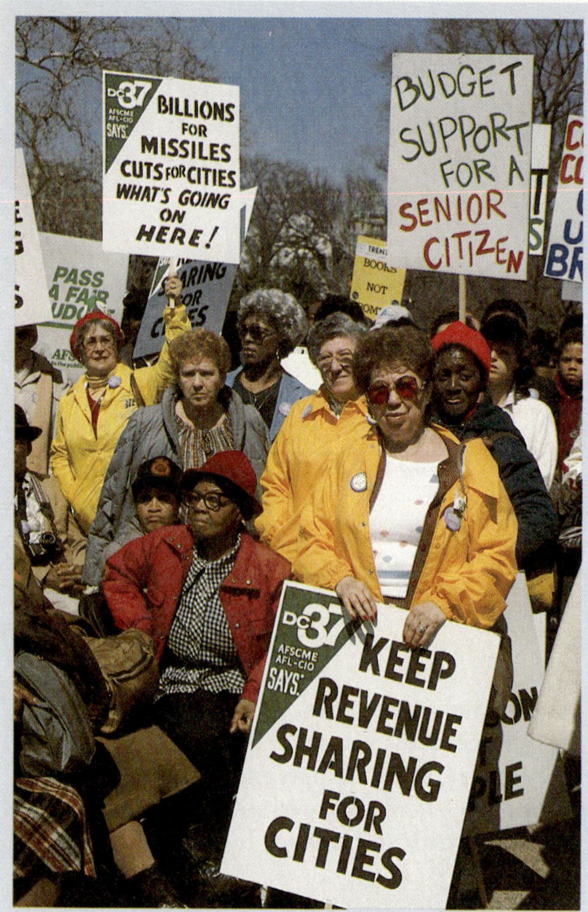

Members of the American Federation of State, County, and Municipal Employees and other organizations protest President Reagan's budget cuts, including the elimination of general revenue sharing for cities.

were alerted quite early that Washington expected them to bear more responsibility in domestic policy. In program terms, the Reagan budget cuts were focused on certain redistributive grants-in-aid—such as housing, job training, food stamps, child nutrition, and a variety of social services—and accordingly hit hardest the "working poor."[35] The impact of these early cuts was softened as Congress subsequently restored some federal aid funds and as state and local governments used more of their own funds to provide services.

Several summary observations on the Reagan federalism record appear to be warranted. First, the federalism policies of this administration did not culminate in a sharp reversal of past policies. No large-scale devolution of federal responsibilities and functions took place.[36] The Reagan federalism record rather reflects incremental change. Second, Reagan policies succeeded in slowing the growth of federal aid—a development of genuine consequence. Plainly, by the end of the Reagan administration, states were operating in more of a "fend for yourself" fiscal environment. Moreover, the administration's tax and budget policies, reflected in a massive federal deficit, seemed likely to restrain succeeding administrations and congresses in providing financial assistance to state and local governments. Third, the Reagan initiative encouraged states and localities to become more self-reliant and to assume larger roles in the provision of services for their residents. On the whole, losing funds and gaining discretion, the states were more resilient and adaptive in "coping" than most observers expected. "The most important federalism change brought about by Reagan's policies," Richard Nathan's and Fred Doolittle's comprehensive study concludes, "was the way in which the combination of Reagan's social program retrenchment goals and his block grant and related devolutionary policy initiatives *activated state governments and enhanced their role in the nation's governmental system.*"[38]

The chief question in American federalism now and in the past concerns the proper division of responsibilities between the federal government and the states. Are the nation and states to be more or less of a partnership? Losing on its centerpiece proposal, the Reagan administration nevertheless made a moderate adjustment in the intergovernmental system, moving away from collaboration, paring federal involvement (especially financial) in state affairs, and simultaneously increasing state responsibilities (especially financial).

IMPACT

The Federal System: Where Do Poor People Have the Best Chance to Obtain Quality Care Under Medicaid?

Medicaid is a program to provide medical care for the needy. Adopted in 1965, the program is financed jointly by federal and state revenues. Operating within federal guidelines, each state determines the criteria for eligibility and the scope of benefits to be made available. The more each state spends of its own money in offering health services, the more federal money it receives. Because states differ in their commitment to Medicaid and in their financial resources, there are wide differences across the nation in health services for low-income persons. The map here ranks the states in terms of such factors as scope of services offered, money spent on health care for the needy, ease of qualifying for the program, and availability of nursing homes and physician care. In 1988, for example, Medicaid spending averaged about $1,600 per poor person in New York and about $100 per poor person in Mississippi. The five best Medicaid programs were found in Minnesota, Wisconsin, New York, Massachusetts, and Connecticut and the five worst in Mississippi, Wyoming, Arizona, Alabama, and Missouri. The sharp differences found among the states prompt central questions: Should the federal government set uniform eligibility standards and reimbursement provisions for all states? Are needy persons everywhere entitled to equal health services?

Source: The data are derived from a study by the Health Research Group of Public Citizen, Inc. (a Ralph Nader organization), as reported in the *New York Times,* December 22, 1987.

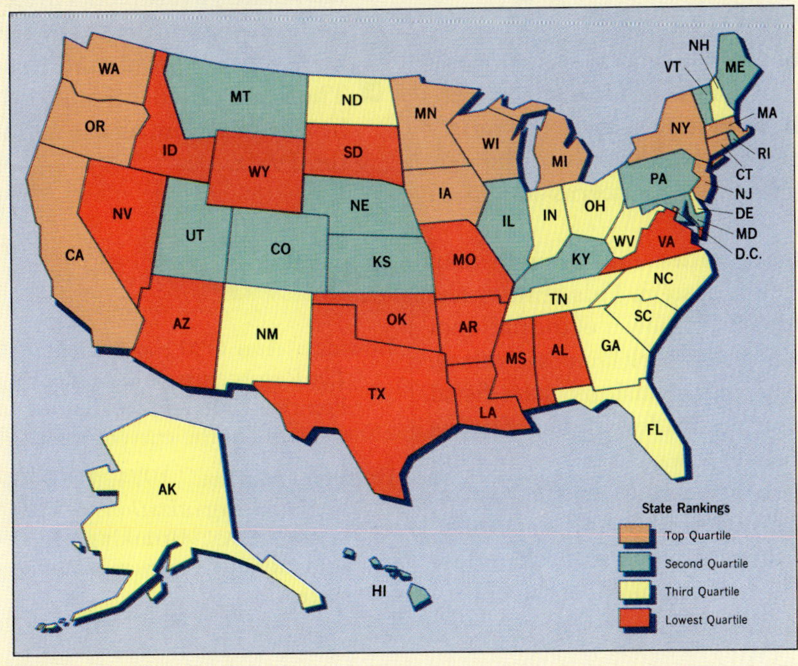

With rare exceptions, changes in American politics come slowly, and the rhetoric that describes them is more dramatic than the changes themselves. Changes in the federal system cannot be set in cement. Federalism has no final answers. The safest prediction of all is that the durability of the Reagan policies and arrangements will be tested repeatedly by new political leaders, in Washington and the states, under new circumstances. What they will face, however, will be old realities centering in multiple demands from the constituencies (and organized groups) and limited resources with which to meet them. And they will also confront nagging old questions: What *services* should be provided? What *existing programs* should be kept, strengthened, or cut back? What *new programs,* if any, should be initiated? How should programs be *administered?* And most important of all—the overarching question in contemporary federalism—how should programs be *financed?* Answers to these questions cannot be found in the Constitution, in past practice, or in political theory. Tentative and piecemeal in the American system, the answers emerge from politics: candidates, parties, and elections make a difference!

Summary

- The formation of a viable federal system was a key achievement of the Constitutional Convention in 1787. The need for a structure to satisfy the states and to meet the diversity of the new nation—practical political concerns—dictated its acceptance.
- The Constitution provides only a rough map of the modern federal system. This century has seen a sharp growth in the power of the national government—induced by such factors as crises, social complexity, court decisions, state fiscal needs, and changing attitudes (among citizens and politicians alike) toward the role of government. Congress appears to be the central force in the expansion of national programs.
- Federal-state relations are constantly changing. The dual federalism of the nineteenth century evolved into cooperative federalism during the twentieth century. Independence gave way to interdependence. National and state governments now share countless powers and functions.
- The growth of the national government's role in domestic affairs has come about primarily through financial assistance to state and local governments. The major forms of aid are categorical grants and block grants. Under block grants, state and local governments enjoy greater discretion in the use of federal funds. Federal aid grew rapidly during the past quarter-century but tapered off during the Reagan adminstration. Even so, nearly one-fifth of all state and local revenue is currently supplied by the federal government.
- The relationship between the federal government and the states is best described as a partnership. Commonly, domestic programs are financed primarily by the federal government and administered by state and local authorities according to federal guidelines. The basic policy choices, on the whole, are made at the national level. During the Reagan administration, however, a number of changes designed to strengthen the states' role were adopted. Today, state governments are clearly more active and self-reliant than they were at the outset of the Reagan administration.
- The issue of federal-state relations is likely to be a central item on the nation's agenda during the 1990s.

Readings on Federalism

Bowman, Ann O'M., and Richard C. Kearney. 1986. *The Resurgence of the States.* Englewood Cliffs, N.J.: Prentice-Hall. Argues that revitalized states are key elements in the current political system.

Derthick, Martha. 1974. *Between State and Nation: Regional Organizations of the United States.* Washington, D.C.: Brookings Institution. The role of subfederal governments and agencies in the federal system.

Dilger, Robert J., ed., 1986. *American Intergovernmental Relations Today: Perspectives and Controversies.* Englewood Cliffs, N.J.: Prentice-Hall. Diverse perspectives on the relationships among different levels of government: local, state, and federal.

Elazar, Daniel J. 1972. *American Federalism: A View from the States,* 2d ed. New York: Crowell. A discussion of the states as participants in a system of cooperative federalism.

Goldwin, Robert A., ed. 1974. *A Nation of States: Essays on the American Federal System.* 2d ed. Chicago: Rand McNally. Differing views on American federalism.

Grodzins, Morton. 1966. *The American System: A New View of Government in the United States.* A discussion of a "marble cake" of shared powers between local, state, and federal governments.

Nathan, Richard P., Fred C. Doolittle, and associates. 1987. *Reagan and the States.* Princeton, N.J.: Princeton University Press. A critical analysis of the impact of Reagan's federalism initiatives on state governments.

Reagan, Michael D., and John G. Sanzone. 1981. *The New Federalism.* 2d ed. New York: Oxford University Press. The role of the federal government in the fiscal dilemmas facing state and local governments.

Riker, William H. 1964. *Federalism: Origin, Operation, Significance.* Boston: Little, Brown. An analysis of federalism in comparative perspective.

Salamon, Lester M., and Michael S. Lund, eds. 1985. *The Reagan Presidency and the Governing of America.* Washington, D.C.: Urban Institute Press. Explanations of the Reagan adminstration's attempts to shift relationships between federal and subfederal authorities.

Chapter 4

Civil Rights and Liberties: Constitutional Fundamentals

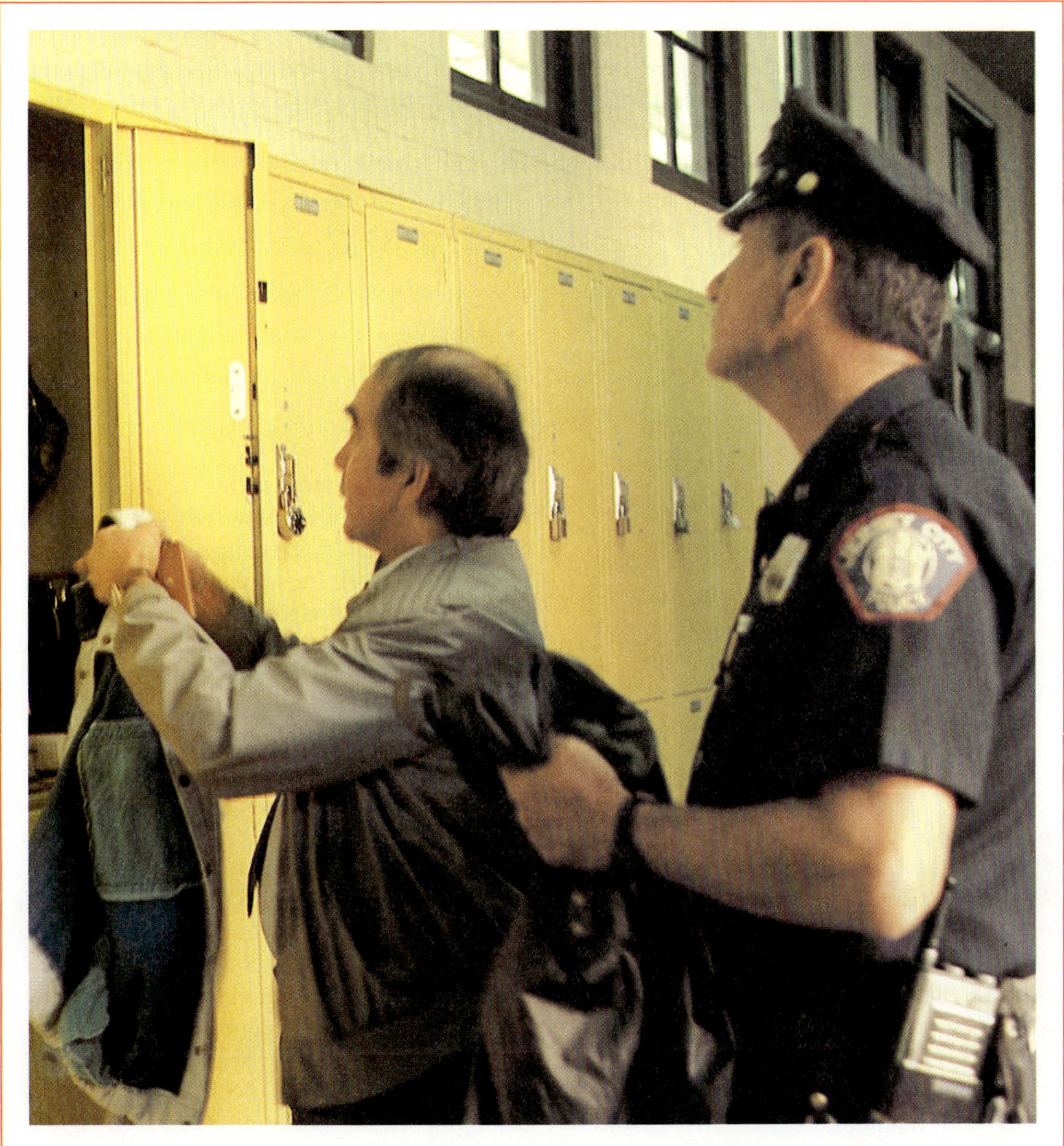

The central meaning of our Constitution lies in the fundamental rights and liberties it was designed to protect. The terms *civil rights* and *civil liberties* can be used interchangeably. Usually, however, we reserve the former for matters of racial, ethnic, and sex discrimination. Civil liberties include freedom of speech, freedom of the press, and freedom of worship. Both are distinguished from other individual rights and freedoms: They are rights protected by government—against invasion by the public or private sector.

A former Supreme Court justice, Robert H. Jackson, stated it eloquently:

> Those who begin coercive elimination of dissent soon find themselves exterminating dissenters. Compulsory unification of opinion achieves only the unanimity of the graveyard. . . . If there is any fixed star in our constitutional constellation it is that no official, high or petty, can prescribe what shall be orthodox in politics, nationalism, or religion, or matters of opinion, or force citizens to confess by word or act their faith therein.[1]

The words carved above the entrance to the Supreme Court of the United States echo these freedoms: "Equal Justice Under Law."

But equal justice under law is not equal justice at any cost. The Founding Fathers resolved to create a Constitution that would allow for majority rule with careful regard for minority rights. Drawing the line between social and individual rights has been essential ever since. Almost every political issue raises that dilemma. Candidates debate a woman's right to an abortion versus a state's right to regulate it. One group's claim to "affirmative action" is another's cry of "reverse discrimination." Freedom of the press collides with a reporter's obligation as a citizen to aid in the pursuit of criminal justice. Words like "obscenity" and "illegally obtained evidence" come up for interpretation again and again.

Each of these issues points to the need to draw a line of acute complexity. Debate on public versus private rights should never cease; it is the essence of constitutional law. The federal court system, with the Supreme Court at its apex, must interpret the meaning and legality of the laws as they relate to our civil rights and liberties. This and the next chapter look at the search for an accommodation between our rights and obligations under our governmental system.[2]

Civil Rights and Liberties: The Explosion of Litigation

"When I first came on the bench I never had a discrimination case. Now that is all you have." Speaking in 1977, District Court Judge Oren R. Lewis was describing an explosion of suits alleging violations of civil rights.

Although a civil rights act was first passed in 1871, only 21 related cases were tried by 1920; in 1976 alone, 17,543 suits were filed. That year 5320 such suits were brought in federal courts against employers—a 1500 percent increase in just six years. And these trends have since continued at an even faster pace. Civil rights suits against state prison inmates alone soared from 5000 in 1973 to 22,000 in 1986. The title of a book by A. E. Dick Howard, an expert in constitutional law, tells the story: *I'll See You in Court.*[3] Today more than half the docket, or case load, of the U.S. Supreme Court concerns our basic freedoms.

Each new decade brings tremendous social change. The growth and decline of cities, migration, changing sexual mores, and the civil rights movement all help bring an expanding number of civil rights cases before the courts. The institutional causes of the growth in litigation are less clear. We will look at three important ones. First, the Bill of Rights has been applied to state as well as federal law. Second, the constitutional amendments passed just after the Civil War have been interpreted more liberally by the courts. Finally, under what is often called the judicial double standard, civil rights and civil liberties are the province of the judiciary, while economic issues fall to the legislatures.

Obscenity may not be the most important issue raised by the First Amendment, but it has certainly made the constitutional guarantee of freedom of expression a center of controversy. Some contend that obscenity ought to be entirely protected. Others, like Tipper Gore (shown here)—whose husband, Albert Gore, failed in his 1988 bid for the Democratic presidential nomination—disagree. Alas, one person's smut may well be another's song lyrics.

Incorporation: Nationalization of the Bill of Rights

In 1833, the Bill of Rights was interpreted as applying to the federal government only—not to the states, by virtue of Chief Justice John Marshall's opinion, backed by a unanimous Court vote, in *Barron* v. *Baltimore.* The rights, Marshall wrote, "contain no expression indicating an intention to apply them to the state governments. This court cannot so apply them." Marshall based his interpretation on the language of the Bill of Rights.

There is one possible exception—the concept of *eminent domain.* This is the right of government to take over private property for public use, provided just compensation is granted, and it is embedded in the due process clause of the Fifth Amendment. The Court deemed this concept applicable to the states as well as the federal government in a railroad case in 1897.[4] Otherwise, Marshall's view prevailed until the second decade of the twentieth century.

In a 1925 dictum by Justice Edward T. Sanford,[5] the Court ruled that First Amendment guarantees applied to the states through provisions of

Abortion and the 1988 Presidential Election

When Americans voted for president on November 8, 1988, they were also, in a sense, "electing" members of the federal bench. One judicial issue that received considerable attention during the 1988 campaign was abortion. The candidates took opposing positions, with Republican George Bush opposing legalized abortion and Democrat Michael Dukakis supporting it. Presumably, their differences over this issue would affect their judicial appointments, especially to the U.S. Supreme Court. And these appointments, in turn, will affect millions of women and men into the future.

But why was the issue particularly important during the 1988 campaign? Of the seven original justices constituting the majority in *Roe* v. *Wade,* the landmark 1973 decision establishing the right to an abortion during the first two trimesters of pregnancy, only three—Justices Brennan, Marshall, and Blackmun—were still on the Court at the time of the election. And all of these men are at least 80 years old. Further, of the four remaining justices who constituted the 5:4 majority (Justice Powell retired in 1986) in *Thornburgh* v. *American College of Obstetricians and Gynecologists* (90 L Ed. 2d 779; 1986)—a decision holding unconstitutional a Pennsylvania law designed to deter women from having abortions—only one (Justice Stevens) is under 70 years of age. In short, the "pro-choice" bloc on the Court is both numerically smaller and substantially older than it once was.

Indeed, that proved to be the case when Justice Powell's replacement, Anthony M. Kennedy, joined the other two Reagan appointees, Sandra Day O'Connor and Antonin Scalia, plus the two dissenters in *Roe* sixteen years earlier, William H. Rehnquist (now Chief Justice) and Bryon R. White, in a dramatic weakening of *Roe* in July 1989. Without overruling that crucial decision, the Court nonetheless made clear that it would henceforth be much more hospitable than heretofore to efforts by the several states to enact provisions restrictive of abortions. By a 5:4 vote it thus upheld a series of the latter by Missouri in *Webster* v. *Reproductive Services,* and the several opinions on the victorious side gave promise of possible further chipping away at the original *Roe* holding. The Court docketed three new abortion issue cases for 1989–1990, but the immediate battle ground would now lie at the state level in the political arena.

the first section of the Fourteenth Amendment. (A dictum is an "aside" in the opinion in a case, in which the author propounds an issue that is not central to the decision.) In 1927, a Court majority began to "incorporate" or "absorb" the provisions of the First Amendment, aspects of the Sixth (providing for counsel in capital criminal cases), and the concept of a "fair trial" under the Seventh and Eighth.

Extending the Bill of Rights to areas previously

covered only by state law caused controversy. Between World Wars I and II, hitherto disenfranchised Americans began to seek their full civil rights and liberties guaranteed by the Constitution; they turned increasingly to the federal government for solutions.

The "incorporation" process attracted attention in a crucial decision concerning the application of the Bill of Rights. This was Justice Benjamin N. Cardozo's celebrated opinion in *Palko* v. *Connecticut* (1937), with only one justice dissenting.[6] Cardozo's ruling created what has been called an "honor roll" of superior rights. He separated constitutional rights into two kinds: One was "of the very essence of a scheme of ordered liberty"; these were "fundamental principles of liberty and justice which lie at the base of all our civil and political institutions"; they were principles of justice "rooted in the traditions and conscience of our people." These rights guaranteed freedom of speech, press, religion, assembly, and petition, plus due process of law, the right to a fair trial, and a limited right to counsel—rights that, as a result of Cardozo's momentous ruling, now applied to the states as well as to the federal government.

The other kind of rights were those that were properly safeguarded by the states but were not "incorporated" or "absorbed" through the Fourteenth Amendment. These rights were not deemed to be "of the very essence of a scheme of ordered liberty." Cardozo argued that "justice would not perish" without them; unlike freedom of speech, they did not constitute a "matrix, [an] indispensable condition of nearly every other form of freedom." In this list of "nonmatrix" rights were the Fifth Amendment's grand jury and self-incrimination provisions; the Sixth's provisions pertaining to trial by jury, the compulsory process of witnesses, accuser confrontation, and broad rights to assigned counsel; and the Eighth's guarantees against excessive bail and fines and against cruel and unusual punishment.

As the Court—and the country—became more sympathetic to a generous view of civil rights and liberties, incorporation became almost total. Table 4–1 shows the result of a succession of opinions of the Court under Chief Justice Earl Warren between 1961 and 1969. Now the words that once limited the federal government extend rights to all 50 states. Only the following provisions are still "out": grand jury indictment (Fifth Amendment), trial by jury in civil cases (Seventh), excessive bail and fines (Eighth), the right to keep and bear arms (Second), and the Third Amendment's safeguards against quartering troops in private homes. But controversy persists, for incorporation has dramatically altered the federal system. Even justices disagree.

Judges of the Supreme Court have held essentially four major positions. The first grows out of Cardozo's opinion—the concept of the "honor roll," or *selective incorporation.* This position has commanded a majority of the Court since 1937. It has the virtue of emphasizing generally agreed-upon essentials while retaining some flexibility. Its vices are selectivity and uncertainty.

The second major doctrine was first advocated at the turn of the century by Justice John Marshall Harlan (whose grandson and namesake later served on the Court as well)—simply incorporate the Bill of Rights lock, stock, and barrel. Harlan stressed the fundamental nature of *all* the provisions of the Bill of Rights, and he called for their absorption by the Fourteenth Amendment. More recently, Justice Hugo Black and others have argued that, even if history does not provide an entirely sure guide on this, democratic society in the last quarter of the twentieth century demands it. *Total incorporation* possesses the virtues of certainty and simplicity, the vice of dogmatism.

The third position is really an extension of the second—*total incorporation plus.* This view was expressed in a 1947 dissent by Justice Frank Murphy. In his words, the guarantees of the Bill of Rights should be "carried over intact" into the first section of the Fourteenth Amendment. But he went further:

> Occasions may arise where a proceeding falls so short of conforming to fundamental standards of procedure as to warrant constitutional condemnation in terms of a lack of due process despite the absence of a specific provision in the Bill of Rights.

TABLE 4–1

Chronological Record of the Incorporation or Absorption of the Bill of Rights

Year	Issue and Amendment	Case	Vote
1897	Eminent domain (V)	*Chicago, Burlington and Quincy RR.* v. *Chicago,* 166 U.S. 226	9:0
1927	Speech (I)	*Fiske* v. *Kansas,* 274 U.S. 380	9:0
1931	Press (I)	*Near* v. *Minnesota,* 283 U.S. 687	5:4
1932	Counsel in *capital criminal cases* (VI)	*Powell* v. *Alabama,* 287 U.S. 45	7:2
1934	Free exercise of religion (I)	*Hamilton* v. *Regents of the Univ. of CA,* 293 U.S. 245	9:0
1937	Assembly and petition (I)	*De Jonge* v. *Oregon,* 299 U.S. 253	9:0
1947	Separation of church and state (I)	*Everson* v. *Board of Education of Ewing Township, N.J.,* 330 U.S. 1	5:4
1948	*Public* trial (VI)	*In re Oliver,* 333 U.S. 257	7:2
1961	Unreasonable searches and seizures (IV) (exclusionary rule)*	*Mapp* v. *Ohio,* 367 U.S. 643	6:3
1962	Cruel and unusual punishment (VIII)	*Robinson* v. *California,* 370 U.S. 660	7:2
1963	Counsel in *all criminal* cases (VI)†	*Gideon* v. *Wainwright,* 372 U.S. 335	9:0
1964	Compulsory self-incrimination (V)	*Malloy* v. *Hogan,* 378 U.S. 1, and *Murphy* v. *Waterfront Comm. of New York Harbor,* 378 U.S. 52	5:4 9:0
1965	Confrontation of *hostile* witnesses (VI)	*Pointer* v. *Texas,* 380 U.S. 400	9:0
1966	*Impartial* jury (VI)	*Parker* v. *Gladden,* 385 U.S. 363	8:1
1967	Confrontation of *favorable witnesses*	*Washington* v. *Texas,* 388 U.S. 14	9:0
1967	Speedy trial (VI)	*Klopfer* v. *North Carolina,* 386 U.S. 213	9:0
1968	Jury trial in nonpetty criminal cases (VI)	*Duncan* v. *Louisiana,* 391 U.S. 145	7:2
1969	Double jeopardy (V)	*Colgrove* v. *Battin,* 413 U.S. 149	7:2

* *In theory,* the Fourth had been "incorporated" 6:3 in *Wolf* v. *Colorado,* 338 U.S. 25 (1949), but not in reality. It took *Mapp* to do it.

† Extended even to incarcerable offenses in "petty" criminal cases in a 9:0 holding in *Argersinger* v. *Hamlin,* 407 U.S. 25 (1972).

The most powerful judicial body in the free world—the 1988–1989 Supreme Court of the United States. Alexander Hamilton styled the Court "the least dangerous branch of government." Yet while the people, in theory, have the last word, the Court is the arbiter of what is and is not constitutional. What differences will the three Reagan appointees—Sandra Day O'Connor, Anthony Kennedy, and Antonin Scalia—make in the years ahead?

Justice William O. Douglas was the most forceful advocate of this approach to full justice for all until his retirement in 1975, after more than 36 years of service on the Court. It is fair to say that, on today's court, William Brennan and Thurgood Marshall embrace Douglas's position.

The fourth position is becoming increasingly important for the 1990s. It was Justice Felix Frankfurter who best expressed the doctrine of *judicial restraint.* He and such recent supporters as Byron R. White reject total incorporation; that, they argue, is contrary to the commands of the Constitution, and it clearly violates the structure and principles of federalism. Such "judicial legislating" creates unwarranted, artificial distinctions among basic rights. Instead, they advocate a "fair trial" or "case-by-case approach." In this approach, the Court would test each case on its merits against the requirements of due process of law. Frankfurter's position has generally appealed to the five Nixon and Ford appointees to the Burger Court: Chief Justice Warren Burger and Justices Harry Blackmun, Lewis F. Powell, William Rehnquist (now Chief Justice), and John Paul Stevens. Although it is a bit too soon for a conclusive judgment, President Reagan often attacked the power of the Court over the states, and his appointees—Sandra O'Connor, Antonin Scalia, and Anthony Kennedy—seem likely to increase the fourth doctrine's influence. It has the virtue of leaving the Court considerable latitude to examine individual cases closely. Its vices are unpredictability and subjectivity.

New Interpretations of the Civil War Amendments ■

Another clear development is the dramatic change in the judiciary's interpretation of the three Civil War amendments, especially the Fourteenth. These amendments reflected a spirit of postwar triumph. But hope that they would rapidly and dramatically improve the status of blacks proved to be false. After Reconstruction, new barriers were erected to withhold full citizenship from blacks, and in three historic decisions, the Supreme Court made this antilibertarian spirit law.

The first came in the so-called *Slaughterhouse Cases* of 1873, which separated state from federal citizenship. The Court's 5:4 decision held that the privileges or immunities clause of the Fourteenth Amendment did not apply to states. In Justice Samuel F. Miller's words, "There is a citizenship of the United States, and a citizenship of a state, which are distinct from each other, and which depend upon different characteristics or circumstances in the individual." [7] With that sharp distinction, Miller could rule that only federal citizenship was protected by the amendment. In short, the privileges or immunities clause now meant nothing to the states.

The second blow came when the Civil Rights Act of 1875 was declared unconstitutional in 1883. This was an 8:1 decision; only Justice Harlan dissented. The 1875 law had made discrimination against blacks in public accommodations a federal crime. No owner or operator of a hotel, public conveyance, or theater, among other enterprises, could "deny the full enjoyments of the accommodations thereof" because of a customer's race or color. But Justice Joseph F. Bradley ruled that Congress had exceeded its powers under the Fourteenth Amendment. He argued that the amendment applied only to *state* action; it did not forbid discrimination by *private* individuals. Owners of public accommodations were neither "agents" nor "instrumentalities" of the state, but private individuals. If the state did not help citizens to discriminate, exclusionary activities were purely private. Such private racial discrimination was not covered by the "no State shall" clauses of the Civil War amendments, in general, or the first section of the Fourteenth, in particular.[8]

The third decision came in 1896. Homer Adolph Plessy unsuccessfully challenged Louisiana's "separate but equal" accommodations as unconstitutional. Racially separated accommodations were widespread throughout the South and in some other parts of the land. Plessy's case asked whether the Fourteenth Amendment, which promised U.S. citizens "equal protection of the laws," therefore forbade state-mandated or state-authorized separate accommodations according to race. In a 7:1 decision, the Court, with a majority of northern members, ruled that separate facilities for whites and blacks did *not* run afoul of the equal protection clause. The reasoning was that whites were separated just as much from blacks as blacks were from whites; such a racial classification did not "stamp the colored race with a badge of inferiority"; if such inferiority was perceived, it was "not by reason of anything found in the act, but solely because the colored race chooses to put that construction upon it." [9] Justice Harlan cried out in vain, "Our Constitution is colorblind, and neither knows nor tolerates classes among citizens." [10] How times would change during his grandson's tenure on the Court (1956–1971)!

While the duality of citizenship from the Slaughterhouse Cases has never been overruled, its teeth have been judicially pulled. A civil liberties revolution began to stir shortly after World War I with the incorporation movement described earlier. The campaign for civil rights for blacks grew noticeably before World War II, climaxing after the war. The Warren Court (1953–1969) was decisive in advancing the cause of civil rights. It battled but also propelled Congress and the president into action. Its work resulted in a host of antidiscrimi-

Rosa Parks is greeted by Coretta Scott King 25 years after she made history. By refusing to yield her seat on an Alabama public bus to a white, Parks inspired the civil disobedience that was to become one of the most effective tactics of Dr. Martin Luther King and others in the civil rights movement. Their peaceful protests were crucial to eliminating the doctrine of "separate but equal."

natory executive orders, although some of them had originated in the Roosevelt and Truman administrations. By the late 1950s, major federal laws were passed prohibiting segregation, crowned by the tough, far-reaching Civil Rights Act of 1964. Backed by the courts, the legal profession, and the people as a whole, these laws have made it much easier to take a discrimination case to court.

The philosophy of the 1883 decision on civil rights is no longer the law of the land. That decision limited the power of the Fourteenth Amendment to protect civil liberties. Today, "equal protection" and "due process of law" apply to most public activities and even certain private ones. The battle for equal rights for minority groups has extended to equal access to employment, schooling, housing, transportation, public accommodations, athletics, entertainment, and even private clubs. Success has not been complete in every field, of course. But recent rulings continue to support federal laws that allow suits against states and cities. Although the Supreme Court majority has often been narrow, these rulings have opened the door for additional libertarian claims against government agencies and instruments. Thus, they have expanded the broad area already covered by federal court jurisdiction.

The last discriminatory decision was overturned when the Supreme Court overruled the separate but equal holding of *Plessy* v. *Ferguson* (1896). The famed school desegregation case of

Brown v. *Board of Education of Topeka, et al.* of May 17, 1954 has been called justly the "greatest social revolution of this generation." [11] Racial equality led the way, but claims for equality for all persons regardless of sex, ethnic and national origin, and age soon followed. The once toothless "equal protection of the laws" clause of the Fourteenth Amendment was given new meaning; more cases arise under it today than under any other constitutionally articulated right. (See Chapter 5.)

The groundwork for abandoning the separate but equal concept had been laid in a series of cases: The first concerned admission to the University of Missouri law school (*Missouri ex rel Gaines* v. *Canada,* 1938). Other important cases were *Sweatt* v. *Painter* (1950) and one concerning the University of Oklahoma graduate school of education, *McLaurin* v. *Oklahoma State Regents* (1950).[12] Less than two years later, Thurgood Marshall, then a young lawyer, aided by lawyers, historians, and social scientists, brought five cases to the Supreme Court. Of these, *Brown* v. *Board of Education,* headed the list. The Court's unanimous ruling under Chief Justice Earl Warren came in 1954. Although it was confined to public schools, it led to the downfall of the separate but equal doctrine in general. The *Plessy* v. *Ferguson* ruling of 1896 was dead.

The struggle was not over, but the government's part in allowing racial segregation was no longer constitutional. Persons of all races were now legally entitled to equal access to bus, streetcar, taxicab, and rail transportation, waiting rooms, comfort stations, drinking fountains, state and local schools, state colleges and universities, hospitals, jails, cemeteries, sports facilities, beaches, bath houses, swimming pools, parks, golf courses, courthouse cafeterias, libraries, private dwellings, theaters, hotels, restaurants, barber and beauty shops, and employment agencies. Interracial marriages were no longer illegal. And it was only a matter of time until private organizations, once covered by the concept of state action, were also affected by desegregation laws. (See Chapter 5.)

It was perhaps inevitable that the drive to end discrimination because of race (and later, because of sex) would go beyond calling for equality of *opportunity* to calling for equality in fact or *result.* It was not enough to claim that everyone had an equal chance at education, employment, and social dignity if the end result was no improvement in their status. This accounts for the controversy surrounding practices termed *affirmative action* and/or *reverse discrimination.* (See Chapter 5.) That emotion-charged issue has also contributed to the increase in court cases concerning civil rights.

The Judicial Double Standard ■

The third major reason for the explosion in civil rights cases is that since 1937 the courts have followed a double standard in examining the law. Cultural, political, and human freedoms are given greater weight in the courts than traditional property rights. Thus, the rights of property are placed on a different plane of values from "human" rights. Human rights are (1) due process of law in criminal justice; (2) political equality in suffrage and apportionment or districting; (3) equality regardless of sex, race, age, national origin, and alien status; (4) free exercise of religion and separation of church and state; and (5) freedom of expression, encompassing freedom of speech, press, assembly, and petition.

This double standard, now 50 years old, contrasts markedly with earlier Court attitudes. Before the New Deal, the Court focused on economic and property rights more than human rights. This was especially true under Chief Justices Melville W. Fuller (1888–1910), Edward D. White (1910–1921), William Howard Taft (1921–1930), and Charles Evans Hughes (1930–1941). Fuller's Court "rediscovered" the tool of substantive due process—the Court's purported right to evaluate the content, the substance, of laws—and declared 15 federal laws unconstitutional. Marshall had created that tool with his freedom of contract decisions in the *Fletcher* and *Dartmouth College* cases of 1810 and 1819.[13] With rare exceptions, Fuller and his three successors used it to strike down laws enacted by Congress and state legislatures to regulate ec-

“Perspectives”

On Basic Constitutional Guarantees

“Under our constitutional system courts stand against any winds that blow as havens of refuge for those who might otherwise suffer because they are helpless, weak, outnumbered, or because they are nonconformist victims of prejudice and public excitement.”

—Justice Hugo L. Black, opinion for the Court, *Chambers* v. *Florida,* 309 U.S. 227 (1940), at 241

“Dissent and dissenters have no monopoly on freedom. They must tolerate opposition. They must accept dissent from their dissent.”

—Justice Abe Fortas, *Concerning Dissent and Civil Disobedience* (New York: New American Library, 1968), p. 126

“To declare that in the administration of the criminal law the end justifies the means—to declare that the government may commit crimes in order to secure the conviction of a private criminal—would bring terrible retribution. Against that pernicious doctrine this court should resolutely set its face.”

—Justice Benjamin N. Cardozo, dissenting opinion, *Olmstead* v. *United States,* 277 U.S. 438 (1928), at 485

“There is danger that if the Court does not temper its doctrinaire logic with a little practical wisdom, it will convert the constitutional Bill of Rights into a suicide pact.”

—Justice Robert H. Jackson, dissenting opinion, *Terminiello* v. *Chicago,* 337 U.S. 1 (1949), at 37

“Like St. Paul's freedom, religious liberty with a great price must be bought. And for those who exercise it most fully, by insisting upon religious education for their children mixed with secular, by the terms of our Constitution the price is greater than for others.”

—Justice Wiley B. Rutledge, dissenting opinion, *Everson* v. *Board of Education of Ewing Township,* 330 U.S. 1 (1947), at 59

“The spirit of liberty is the spirit which is not too sure that it is right; the spirit of liberty is the spirit which seeks to understand the minds of other men and women; the spirit of liberty is the spirit which weighs their interests alongside its own without bias. . . .”

—Judge Learned Hand, “I Am an American Day” speech, New York City, 1944.

onomic affairs; they ruled that these laws violated the virtually absolute *liberty of contract,* a freedom they viewed as guaranteed by the due process clauses of the Fifth and Fourteenth Amendments.

Similarly, Hughes's Court declared 14 federal laws unconstitutional between 1934 and 1937. It upheld the legal philosophy of the Fuller Court, using a somewhat different rationale: Hughes argued that the federal government exceeded its authority in entering the economic sphere, which he viewed as an invasion of areas of authority reserved for the states under the Tenth Amendment. With but a few exceptions, the Court struck down states' attempts to legislate in economic and property matters. It was a policy consistent with the old substantive due process concept.

But the emphasis on the sacredness of the economic sphere ended with the 1937 "switch in time that saved nine" (so called because Hughes and Roberts began to cast their votes in favor of the New Deal on most major issues). The New Deal Court, dating from the retirement of Justice Willis Van Devanter and Franklin Roosevelt's appointment of Justice Hugo Black, was preoccupied with basic human freedoms.[14]

Is the double standard justified? It gives state legislatures and Congress legal control over economic issues; however, the courts give close scrutiny to cases charging that laws violate basic human freedoms. In other words, today's Court would be unlikely to uphold charges of violation of due process in a case involving a state or federal law about hours and wages or child labor. Such a complaint would have been received enthusiastically by the Fuller Court, but today's Court might even refuse to hear it. The Supreme Court justifies this policy on the grounds of judicial self-restraint. The argument is that legislators must be given more authority on economic proprietarian issues, because they are best equipped to understand them. However, the Court will hear a complaint that state or federal law or executive-administrative practice in criminal law enforcement has violated an individual's right to due process. And any court today will readily judge whether a state statute or official practice has infringed on the constitutional rights of racial minorities or women.

Is the double standard defensible? Any justification poses a moral dilemma. It attributes political maturity to the people's representatives in one area but not in another. Yet even Justices Holmes and Brandeis supported this double standard. The two great jurists had considerable faith in the legislative process, but they preferred to trust the judiciary on human rights. In particular, they trusted the courts to interpret the First Amendment's protections of freedom of religion, speech, press, assembly, and petition. However, they could argue for denying the courts' role in economic questions. The basic idea is that the Court must guard against denying itself adequate power to speak out, lest our basic freedoms "be eroded to the point where their restoration becomes impossible."[15]

Four reasons are often given for this double standard. First, the Bill of Rights has explicit language regarding civil rights. Its First Article opens with the ringing injunction that "Congress shall make no law respecting an establishment of religion, or prohibiting the free exercise thereof; or abridging the freedom of speech, or of the press." To quote Justice Black:

> It is my belief that there are "absolutes" in our Bill of Rights, and that they were put there on purpose by men who knew what words meant, and meant their prohibitions to be "absolutes.". . . The phrase "Congress shall make no law" is composed of plain words, easily understood; . . . the language of this Amendment [is not] anything less than absolute.[16]

Black's "absolutist" concept might be questioned, however generous and attractive its sentiment. Yet no one can deny the explicitness of the First Amendment's language. On the other hand, rulings on economic matters are not so clear: The language of "due process of law" in the Fifth and Fourteenth Amendments and "equal protection of the laws" in the Fourteenth is more general and vague.

Closely allied to the first reason is a second contention: *The Bill of Rights deals with the most basic of all our freedoms, those on which all the others rest.* The right to vote itself would be worth a good deal less if the rights of petition for the redress of grievances and assembly were gone. The effect would be just as dramatic if prior censorship denuded of meaning the rights of freedom of speech and of the press. In short, when these most basic rights are gone, the rest become irretrievable as well.

It was this reasoning that in 1938 persuaded Justice Harlan Fiske Stone, with assistance from Chief Justice Charles Evans Hughes, to write an influential footnote to an otherwise unimportant case. Stone argued that the Constitution commanded active, even painful scrutiny of the effect of our laws on civil liberties. On economic issues, where the Constitution is less specific, he expected greater judicial restraint:

> Legislation which restricts those political processes which can ordinarily be expected to bring about repeal of undesirable legislation is to be subjected to more exacting judicial scrutiny . . . than are most other types of legislation.[17]

Stone followed this two years later with a stirring dissenting opinion in the case of Pennsylvania Jehovah's Witnesses and their children who had been convicted of refusing to salute the American flag.[18] It would become majority opinion with Justice Jackson's often-quoted words two years later:

> The Constitution expresses more than the conviction of the people that democratic processes must be preserved at all costs. It is also an expression of faith and a command that freedom of mind and spirit must be preserved, which government must obey, if it is to adhere to that justice and moderation without which no free government can exist.[19]

A third reason the Court has given special weight to civil liberties is simply that *no other agency of our government is as willing and able to do it.* In Britain, the legislative branch has the ultimate power to preserve and defend these vital freedoms. In America, however, our political traditions see jurists as the most qualified to afford that necessary protection. This role is enhanced by their prerogative to determine the kind of cases that reach the Supreme Court.

On the other hand, the judiciary has neither the expertise nor the time to make complex economic judgments. The legislative branch of government alone has day-to-day responsibility for economic planning. As Justice Hugo Black wrote, "Whether the legislature takes for its textbook Adam Smith, Herbert Spencer, Lord Keynes or some other is no concern of ours." [20] Probably no one has stated the case as colorfully as Oliver Wendell Holmes to Harlan Fiske Stone. The 90-year-old justice had lost none of his sharpness as he addressed his 61-year-old colleague:

> Young man, about 75 years ago I learned that I was not God. And so, when the people want to do something I can't find anything in the Constitution expressly forbidding them to do, I say, whether I like it or not, "Goddamit, let 'em do it." [21]

Or, as he put it to John W. Davis, the 1924 Democratic nominee for President:

> Of course I know, and you know, and every other sensible man knows, that the Sherman [Antitrust] Law is damned nonsense, but if my country wants to go to hell, I am here to help it.[22]

On the Bill of Rights, however, particularly the First Amendment, Holmes took a different view. Like many other thoughtful jurists, he simply did not regard the average legislator as very "enlightened"—to use Justice Robert H. Jackson's phrase[23]—on basic civil rights and liberties.

Fourth, *by and large, private interests and pressure groups have special access to the legislative process.* Unpopular minorities can often obtain redress of grievances only by litigation. Whatever average Americans think about the activities of economic interests, they are more likely than not to regard political minorities as troublemakers of one sort or another. As Felix Frankfurter once observed, the average civil liberties litigants "are not very nice people." [24]

Repeatedly, cases involving accused criminals have extended our constitutional rights to due process of law. There was nothing particularly endearing about Arthur Culombe, who was convicted for two grisly murders at a Connecticut gas station. Yet in 1961 the Supreme Court ruled that his confession was obtained by force and so could not be voluntary.[25] Nor, surely, Ernesto Miranda, the convicted rapist and kidnapper whose name has become a household word for our safeguards against self-incrimination.[26]

It is not easy for people like these to obtain their day in court, let alone in Congress. The success of civil rights groups in having their grievances heard—and litigated—represents a revolutionary change in our governmental process. Today they are often aided by public interest lawyers with government support, as well as by civil rights and civil libertarian interest groups like the National Association for the Advancement of Colored People (NAACP) and the American Civil Liberties Union (ACLU).

More often than not, "respectable" private interests have no such difficulty gaining the attention of elected representatives. There is nothing evil about this fact of public life. Yet it does mean that economic interests can often take steps to redress court-imposed grievances. Perhaps the influence of your corner grocer is hardly on a par with that of such powerful firms as du Pont de Nemours. But this does not negate the basic argument: Even the lone economic individual has an influence on politics that those accused of crime or those in the political minority never will.

The traditional double standard has begun to change. In the 1960s, the Supreme Court began to extend "strict judicial scrutiny" to many more types of equal protection and due process cases, especially the former. Yet the Court still looks at different kinds of laws differently. For matters of private property, it still uses the traditional "equal protection" and "due process" test to determine whether the legislature had a "reasonable" or "rational" basis for making classifications.[27] Basic civil rights and liberties still raise a different standard. When the Court is satisfied that it is dealing with a law or an executive action that affects fundamental interests, like voting rights[28] or the right to interstate travel[29]—or that touches a "suspect" category, like race[30] or national origin or alien status[31]—its scrutiny will be particularly exacting.

Even when the subject matter is not "suspect," it may still be accorded close attention. Sex discrimination, for example, is second only to race in equal protection litigation.[32] But once an issue has been placed in the suspect category, the Court in effect shifts the burden of proof. It requires that government demonstrate a "compelling state interest." [33] The result is greater judicial protection of our basic rights.

In essence, then, the Court uses a complicated double standard *within* a double standard. For this reason, it has faced widespread accusations of taking on legislative power. It has certainly triggered constitutional confusion. Still, most people concede that "within often ill-defined limits, the case of special judicial protection of civil liberties is strong": Taken together, as well as separately, the four reasons outlined above represent the case for a justification of a double standard. The latter may not be entirely convincing, either morally or logically. It raises very serious, indeed fundamental, questions about the nature of judicial power and judicial process under our system. Yet it is a practical recognition of one of the crucial and realistic facets of government and politics.

The Range and State of Civil Rights and Liberties

Americans enjoy many civil rights and liberties not always found in other countries. There has been great progress, although some feel we have not gone far enough. The revolution in civil rights and liberties has raised major questions of limits and balancing apparently contradictory constitutional rights. For example, the rights of equality and liberty sometimes conflict. Illustrations are the freedom of association in private clubs, for example, and, as Justice Brandeis put it, "the right to be let alone—the most comprehensive of rights and the right most valued by civilized men." [34] William O. Douglas, who was the leading libertarian activist on the Court during this century, dedicated his life to protecting the right to be left alone. He wanted to "get the government off the backs of the people." Perhaps ironically, this was also the theme of Ronald Reagan's successful campaign in 1980. Let us look at a key component of the protection of civil rights and liberties—due process of law.

Due Process of Law

There are two kinds of due process of law—*substantive* and *procedural.* Substantive due process refers to the contents or subject matter of a law or executive ordinance; procedural due process means how the legislative and/or administrative process is carried out. This may cover the law enforcement activities of civil executives, civil servants, or judges. In both categories, the court decides on the constitutionality of an issue according to whether an action has been "capricious," "invidious," "irrational," "irrelevant," "arbitrary," or "unreasonable," [35] as applied to the constitu-

Do "compelling state interests" include the threat to society from illegal drugs? The answer to that question will decide whether citizens may be forced to undergo drug tests, like that to which Ben Johnson submitted. Johnson, a Canadian sprinter who won the 100-meter dash in the 1988 Seoul Olympics, was stripped of his gold medal for unauthorized drug use.

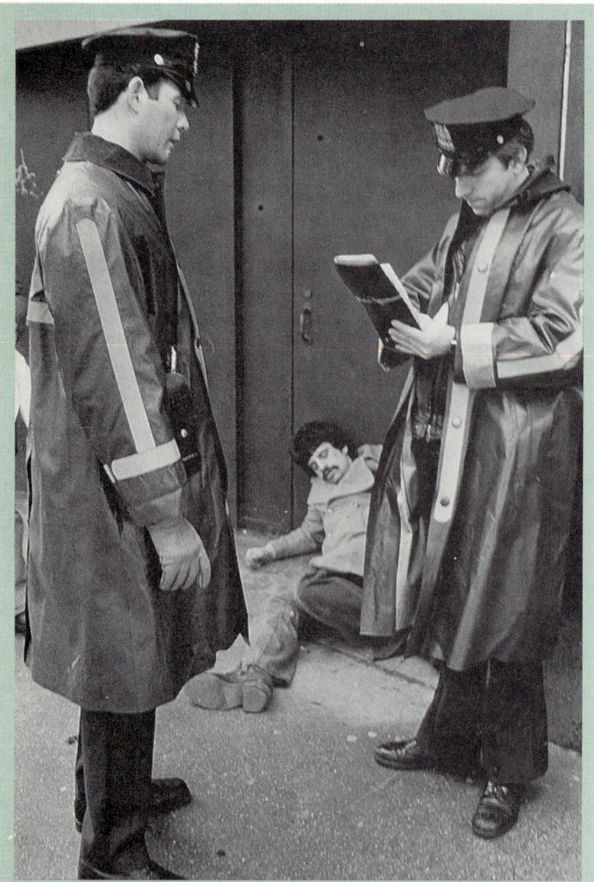

Police powers include the regulation of business, labor, and agriculture—as well as the work of this officer. Under our Constitution, both federal and state governments have a role in such areas as health, welfare, safety, and morals. As Justice Oliver Wendell Holmes used to say, with our taxes "we buy civilization." But police must follow "due process of law." Is the man being ticketed here a danger or a victim of homelessness? Should it matter to our vagrancy laws?

tional guarantees. If the answer is yes, the law or order falls on either substantive or procedural grounds, sometimes both.

Until the nineteenth century, the concept of due process of law was viewed as wholly procedural. But after the famous New York court decision in *Wynehamer* v. *People* (1856),[36] courts began to examine the substance of legislation. Deciding between substantive and procedural due process has proved to be one of the most controversial aspects of the judicial role; it involves the basic question of whether the courts may "legislate" as well as "judge" (see Chapter 16).

Substantive Due Process. An illustration of violation of substantive due process was a Jacksonville, Florida, ordinance against vagrancy. Echoing the poor laws of Elizabethan England, it outlawed as vagrants and "rogues and vagabonds" persons who "use juggling or unlawful games," are "common nightwalkers" or "habitual loafers," and are "able to work but habitually live upon the earnings of their wives or minor children." Plaintiff Papachristou had been convicted under that quaint statute for "prowling by auto." Justice Douglas spoke for a unanimous Court in declaring the law unconstitutionally vague; it did not tell citizens clearly what conduct was forbidden, and it encouraged arbitrary and erratic arrests and convictions.[37]

Procedural Due Process. Procedural violations occur more frequently and have a more immediate effect on the average person. Procedural due process requires a general standard of fairness in law enforcement; it prevents government agents from taking away private rights by improper methods. Examples are coerced confessions, denial of counsel, "stacked juries," and *unreasonable* searches and seizures.

The famous case of *Rochin* v. *California* was a clear violation of procedural due process. Three Los Angeles County deputy sheriffs entered Antonio Richard Rochin's home, charging him with selling illegal narcotics. They had neither arrest nor search warrant. Before the law enforcement agents could stop him, Rochin swallowed two morphine capsules he had allegedly obtained illegally. In an attempt to make him cough up the evidence, the agents pummeled and kicked him. When this failed, they tied, gagged, and transported Rochin to a hospital, where they ordered a physician to give him an emetic through a stomach tube. This caused him to vomit the morphine, which the police then presented as evidence at his trial.

Rochin was convicted. He appealed, contending that he had been deprived of procedural due process. His claim was rejected by the California courts because, although the evidence was obtained through an unconstitutional search and seizure in *federal* terms, California *state* law did not then proscribe such evidence. It made no difference that the district court of appeals acknowledged that Rochin had been treated outrageously. However, the Supreme Court of the United States reversed Rochin's conviction; it ruled that it violated procedural due process of law guaranteed by the Fourteenth Amendment. Justice Frankfurter, speaking for the Court, held that the proceedings constituted "conduct that shocks the conscience . . . bound to offend even hardened sensibilities. . . . States in their prosecutions [must] respect certain decencies of civilized conduct. . . . Due process of law [means that these] convictions cannot be brought about by methods that offend 'a sense of justice.' "[38]

In separate concurring opinons, Justices Black and Douglas opposed Frankfurter's reasoning, saying that the case was rightly decided but for the wrong reasons. This illustrates the basic clash about the application of the Fourteenth Amendment. Black and Douglas argued that the constitutional issue was *not* violation of procedural due process of law under the Fourteenth Amendment: *Rather,* California's agents had clearly violated individual liberties specifically safeguarded under the Bill of Rights, such as the Fifth Amendment's protections against self-incrimination. Their viewpoint ultimately prevailed. Twelve years after *Rochin,* the Supreme Court ruled 5:4 that "the Fourteenth Amendment secures against invasion by the states the same privilege that the Fifth Amendment guarantees against federal infringement."[39]

Due Process and Criminal Justice ■

Each alleged violation of a procedural due process right must be resolved case by case. Based on Anglo-Saxon common law, the basic procedural due process requirements, enunciated in the Constitution, are as follows (the appropriate amendment is indicated in parentheses):

1. The right of people to be secure in their persons, houses, papers, and effects against unreasonable searches and seizures (IV).
2. The issue of a search and/or arrest warrant only upon probable cause, supported by oath or affirmation, and particularly describing the place to be searched and the person or things to be seized (IV).
3. Indictment by grand jury for capital or otherwise infamous crime (V).
4. No double jeopardy (V).
5. Immunity against compulsory self-incrimination (V).
6. The right to a speedy and public trial, by an impartial jury, in the state and district wherein the crime was committed (VI).
7. The right to be informed of the nature and cause of the accusation (VI).
8. The right of the accused to be confronted with adverse and favorable witnesses (VI).
9. The right for compulsory process to obtain witnesses in the accused's favor (VI).
10. Counsel in criminal cases (VI).
11. Safeguards against excessive bail, excessive fines, and cruel and unusual punishment (VIII).

These constitutional safeguards *originally* applied only to the federal government; however, as we have seen, by virtue of their "incorporation," all of the above except the third and the bail and fine aspects of the eleventh now also apply to the states as a result of court decisions. And even if many states do not provide *all* the remaining safeguards, they are expected to provide procedures that amount to due process of law. So the concept of a fair trial demands minimum safeguards of due process: among others, freedom from arbitrary arrest, questioning, and imprisonment; unreasonable

A Pauper Makes Constitutional History

How much of a difference can one person—especially one without financial resources—make in our political system? Consider Clarence Earl Gideon, who spent many of his 51 years in prison. Gideon ran away from his home in Hannibal, Missouri, at the age of fourteen, after completing only eight years of formal education. A gambler and a drifter, he was to serve time for four felonies.

In 1961 Gideon was sentenced to five years imprisonment in Florida for "having broken and entered a poolroom with intent to commit a misdeameanor." Gideon was unable to afford an attorney, and his request for counsel was refused. The trial judge cited a Florida law, based on a 1942 decision of the U.S. Supreme Court, that demanded the appointment of a lawyer only in capital cases. Gideon had to defend himself. The crucial testimony came from a man who later turned out to be the culprit himself.

Unwilling to accept jail without a fight, Gideon filed suit against the Florida director of corrections, Louie Wainright. He appealed his case to the U.S. Supreme Court *in forma pauperis*—in the manner of a pauper. This procedure waives many of the costs and legal technicalities in order to give the poor access to justice. While typical petitions to the high Court are formally drafted by attorneys, that of Florida prisoner No. 003826 was scratched in pencil on lined sheets provided by the prison. It was replete with spelling and grammatical mistakes. Yet the case of *Gideon* v. *Wainwright* changed the constitutional history of the United States.

With Abe Fortas, himself a future associate justice, as his appointed attorney, and with the support of 23 states filing as "friends of the court," Gideon argued that the 1942 decision (in *Betts* v. *Brady*) was anachronistic. Speaking for the majority, Justice Hugo Black agreed with this opinion: It is "an obvious truth" that "in our adversary system of criminal justice any person hailed into court who is too poor to hire a lawyer cannot be assured a fair trial unless counsel is provided for him." The Court held that failure to appoint counsel in a criminal case deprived the indigent man of due process of law under the Fourteenth Amendment and of the right to counsel under the Sixth Amendment.

searches and seizures; third-degree interrogation; compulsory self-incrimination; "stacked juries"; "quickie" trials; and the absence of proper representation by counsel. The right to counsel—to be represented by a lawyer at all stages of the criminal justice process—was secured in three dramatic Supreme Court decisions in 1963, 1964, and 1966. The first was *Gideon* v. *Wainwright,* the second *Escobedo* v. *Illinois,* the third *Miranda* v. *Arizona.* Although they were bitterly attacked, they are the law of the land.[40]

Not only the Bill of Rights but also the original Constitution contain additional due process safeguards. Some are procedural, some substantive.

Among them is the historic *habeas corpus* safeguard, often considered the most crucial right of all. According to Article I, Section 9, this right may not be suspended except "when in cases of rebellion or invasion the public safety may require it." Even then, *congressional* sanction is required. *Habeas corpus* (Latin for "you should have the body") is designed to protect a person from capricious arrest and unlawful imprisonment. Authorities may not imprison someone and then throw away the key. Any legally imprisoned person may petition a court for a *writ of habeas corpus;* this requires the magistrate who authorized the jailing to show cause for continuing the imprisonment. A hearing on such a petition does not prove guilt or innocence; it only determines whether there is sufficient reason to believe that the detained person may have committed a crime. After learning the reason for the arrest, the accused may hire a lawyer, or, if too poor, may be assigned one. At the same hearing, the judge decides whether or not the arrest was reasonable. If the evidence presented is deemed too flimsy to justify further restraint, the writ of habeas corpus is issued to free the prisoner instantly. This does not preclude rearrest if further evidence indicates that the suspect is guilty.

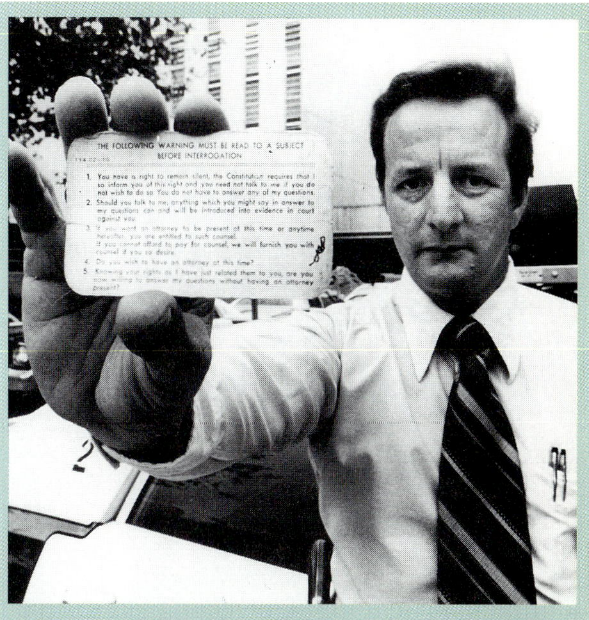

"Being read our rights" is now familiar police procedure. But the conduct of police was bitterly contested in 1966, when a divided Court ruled in *Miranda* v. *Arizona.* Chief Justice Earl Warren laid out a six-part requirement for police making arrests. Hailed by civil libertarians, the Miranda warnings were seen by many police authorities as making their job—and the conviction of criminals—unnecessarily difficult.

Because our federal system provides for a tiered system of justice, particularly in criminal procedures, the Supreme Court increasingly must adjudicate conflicts between individuals and society. Many state officials have felt that the Court has thus made it more difficult to bring accused lawbreakers to trial. Law enforcement officers, from the late J. Edgar Hoover on down, have protested against what they have viewed as "undue sentimentality toward lawbreakers." They have charged the courts with making the job of the police more difficult, and sometimes impossible.

Judges themselves view with alarm the tough due process standards imposed by the Warren Court, particularly in criminal cases. In 1958, 36 state chief justices, headed by Justice Brune of Maryland, protested what they considered "a dangerous development in Supreme Court adjudication." The Brune report expressed alarm over the "erosion of the federal system"; it exhorted the Court to return to the "greatest of all judicial powers—the power of judicial self-restraint"; and it censured the Court for most of the controversies that have engulfed it in recent years. It particularly criticized the application of the due process and equal protection clauses of the Fourteenth Amendment to state-level law enforcement, and it concluded that the Court had assumed legislative authority and had acted without judicial restraint. It charged that the Court had thus expanded national power at the expense of the states.

Not everyone agrees with these charges. Paul A. Freund contends, for example, that all the Court has demanded of the states is that lower courts obey existing constitutional safeguards; they should

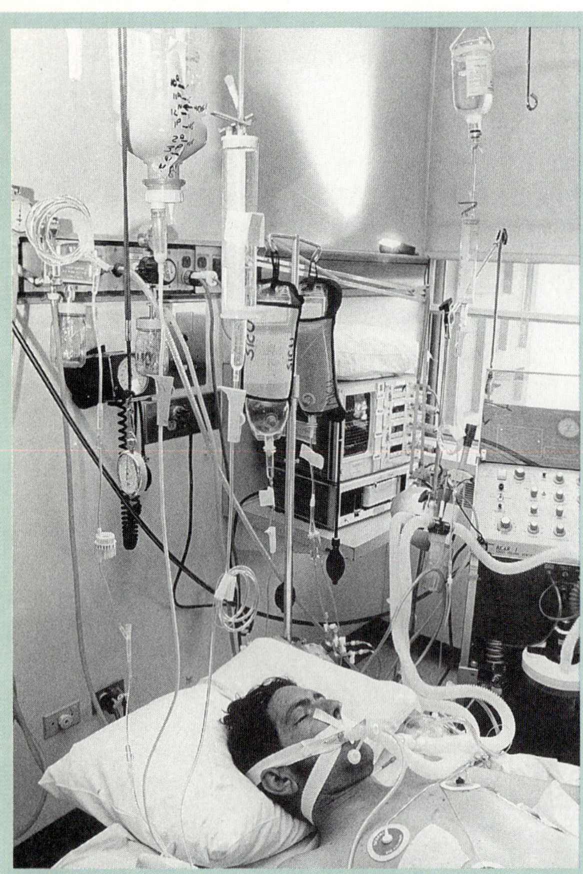

Our right to privacy under the Ninth Amendment includes the right to make decisions about our own welfare. Yet government has responsibility for the welfare of society as a whole. Where do we draw the line? Consider the rights of families faced with the life or death of loved ones in a world of complex technology. In the case of Karen Ann Quinlan, the Supreme Court approved turning off a woman's life-sustaining equipment, but she survived, comatose, for nearly ten more years.

"turn square corners" in dealing with sensitive areas of human liberty.[41] Eugene V. Rostow concluded that the Brune report's findings represent "not so much a protest against the Court as against the tide of social change reflected in the Court's opinions." [42]

Still, widespread concern remains about the limits the judicial branch has been establishing on its authority. Our rising crime rate heightens these fears. Many Americans seconded Chief Justice Burger's warning in his 1981 "state of the judiciary" address, when he said that Americans were no longer secure in their homes, on their streets, or in their schools.

Privacy

The range of civil rights and civil liberties is vast. We will look at some of them in the next chapter. But how is a new realm of constitutional freedoms defined? Let us end this chapter with a case in point—the right to privacy.

The right of each of us to be protected from intrusive government may seem basic to American democracy, but the word *privacy* never appears in the Constitution. Instead, we—and the courts—must generally rely on the Fourth Amendment and its implications:

> The right of people to be secure in their persons, houses, papers, and effects, against unreasonable searches and seizures, shall not be violated. . . .

Privacy is a vexing notion, and it is likely to become more controversial in the years ahead. In fact, the Supreme Court has recognized at least *three* distinct rights to privacy.[43]

One rests on "privacy that inheres in the place or property." The case of Dollree Mapp fell squarely in that category. So did that of "T.L.O," a 14-year-old New Jersey student whose claim was less successful. An administrator at her high school, alerted to her smoking in school, suspected the freshmen was also selling marijuana. He insisted on seeing and searching the young woman's purse. There he found a pack of cigarettes, a packet of rolling papers, a pipe, a small amount of marijuana, some empty plastic bags, $40 in cash, a card that appeared to be a list of students who owed the girl money, and two letters showing clearly that she dealt in "pot." Tried as a juvenile and found de-

Government and the Citizen

How much power does government have to invade our private lives? In a landmark 1961 decision, the U.S. Supreme Court ruled that definite restrictions prohibit any government—federal or state—from illegally searching the premises of a citizen.

In 1957 Cleveland police, acting on information that Dollree Mapp was hiding a fugitive and "policy paraphernalia" (that is, pornography) in her dwelling, forced their way into her home. On the strength of the seized evidence, Mapp was convicted of the possession of "obscene materials." Although the Ohio Supreme Court upheld her conviction, the case of *Mapp* v. *Ohio* reached the U.S. Supreme Court because of the way the evidence was obtained: The police had forced their way in without a warrant. (They actually brandished a blank sheet of stationery!)

Speaking for the majority, Justice Tom Clark overruled long-standing precedent. He argued that

> All evidence obtained by searches and seizures in violation of the Constitution is, by that same authority, inadmissible in a state court. . . . Since the Fourth Amendment's right of privacy has been declared enforceable against the States through the due process clause of the Fourteenth, it is enforceable against them. . . .

The case illustrates how the federal judiciary has been able, by the Fourteenth Amendment, to apply certain restrictions against *federal* actions to the states. Although subsequent rulings have weakened the *Mapp* decision, it remains a landmark: It restricts government intrusion into citizens' lives.

linquent, "T.L.O." was sentenced to one year on probation. On appeal, the New Jersey Supreme Court overturned her conviction on Fourth Amendment grounds—the prohibition of unreasonable searches and seizures. The U.S. Supreme Court agreed that the amendment applies to students, but it reversed the lower court's decision 6:3. Drug use and violence in public schools, it said, are "major social problems" that give school officials broad power. They could search students suspected of carrying weapons, dealing drugs, or even violating school rules.[44]

A host of other cases have involved private places and private property. One concerned the right of Robert Stanley to watch films of "successive orgies of seduction, sodomy, and sexual intercourse." Mr. Stanley found himself convicted of violating a Georgia law forbidding possession of obscene matter. Speaking for a 9:0 court, Justice Thurgood Marshall held that "a state has no business telling a man, sitting alone in his own house, what books he may read or what films he may watch."[45]

A second category of claims to privacy centers on the person. An example was the right of the comatose Karen Ann Quinlan to have life-sustaining apparatus disconnected. The New Jersey Supreme Court was unanimous in upholding her family's privacy claims, and the U.S. Supreme Court denied review.[46] The Court promised to take another look at the right of terminally ill patients to request cessation of life-sustaining methods in its 1989–90 term.

Another person-centered claim to privacy clashed with the First Amendment. A Connecticut family sued when *Life* magazine reviewed *The Desperate Hours,* a play based on their horrifying struggle with a intruder. Despite a New York law that limited photographic and textual invasions of privacy, the family's claims narrowly lost in the Supreme Court to the stronger claims of freedom of the press. So did the agonized plea of a Florida father, whose daughter had been brutally raped and murdered, to keep the Cox Broadcasting Corporation from publishing her name. His claim, too, was supported by state law, but it lost 9:0 to counterclaims based on the First and Fourteenth Amendments.[47] Press freedom, which we will discuss in detail in Chapter 5, is usually a good bet to win out over competing rights.[48]

No constitutional issue has been fought more passionately in the last decades than abortion rights. In 1973, the Court in *Roe* v. *Wade* declared a fundamental legal right to abortion on demand, based on the right to privacy, buttressed by the safeguards of "due process." Sex counseling, shown here, is designed to avoid the abortion problem by reducing the high rate of teenage pregnancies. But the government's role in teenage counseling is nearly as controversial as abortion itself.

"This is OUR parade!"

A third category includes claims based on personal, and especially sexual, relationships. The case of *Griswold* v. *Connecticut,* for instance, struck down an arcane statute prohibiting not just the sale of contraceptives, but even advice about them or their use by married couples. Justice Douglas's majority opinion strongly affirmed "the zone of privacy created by several fundamental constitutional guarantees." [49] Down, too, went New York's ban on the sale of contraceptives to minors and five years later, in 1977, a law forbidding birth control advertisements.

This last category contains what must be the most famous and controversial privacy claim of all. In the 1973 decision *Roe* v. *Wade,* the Supreme Court defined a woman's fundamental constitutional right (within certain calendar restrictions) to an abortion, which it called a matter of "free choice." Fighting that decision was a sensitive issue for George Bush in his successful campaign for the presidency. The Court's 7:2 ruling cited a claim now rooted in the Ninth and Fourteenth Amendments—the privacy of a woman's body.[50]

Claims of a right to practice one's "sexual preference" have not fared as well. In 1976, for example, the Supreme Court upheld without formal opinion a Virginia antisodomy law, a decision reconfirmed in 1978.[51] And in 1986 a bitterly divided court ruled 5:4 for Georgia's statute making anal or oral sex a crime.[52]

The issues raised by these decisions are more complex than ever since the AIDS epidemic, and they should remain emotionally charged in the 1990s. Other privacy issues now before the Court relate to mandatory drug testing. As the following chapter demonstrates, it is but one of the many controversial matters on which we look to the judiciary for ultimate judgments.

IMPACT

Defining the Right of Privacy

The concepts debated in the courts are not static. The judiciary began to treat privacy as constitutionally protected only well into the 1960s. A broad right of privacy first began to emerge respecting personal decisions about birth control (*Griswold* v. *Connecticut,* 1965) and abortion (*Roe* v. *Wade,* 1973). Since then, the courts have been asked to define and protect new types of privacy. Does that right extend, for instance, to those who refuse to take certain medical tests? Two issues have made this an important question—illegal drugs and AIDS (acquired immune deficiency syndrome).

Employers are increasingly demanding that workers submit to random urinalysis designed to detect illegal drugs. Drug tests, they argue, are important when the safety of the public may be at stake (e.g., for airline pilots) or the employee is a role model for children (e.g., professional athletes). Several cases came before the Supreme Court in the 1980s. In *Burnley* v. *Railway Labor Executives' Association,* the Court was asked to look at federal regulations requiring alcohol and drug testing of rail employees involved in accidents. Do the tests violate the Fourth Amendment ban on unreasonable searches? And in *National Treasury Employees Union* v. *Von Rabb,* the justices were asked to rule on a Custom's Service policy of testing employees before promotion. The Court's answer came in 1989, upholding both searches (7:2 and 5:4, respectively).

The Court is also likely to hear cases dealing with another type of privacy, that of AIDS patients. The first case may well address any of several issues. But it could ask the judiciary to do what Congress has so far refused to do—to guarantee that the results of AIDS-related blood tests remain confidential. In late 1988, Congress passed a health bill that included numerous AIDS-related amendments, but a confidentiality clause was deleted at the last minute. The extent of the guarantee of privacy remains open.

Source: *Congressional Quarterly Weekly Report,* October 22, 1988, pp. 3067–3071; November 5, 1988, p. 3196.

Summary

- Since the heyday of the New Deal, there has been a massive increase in the number of civil rights and liberties cases handled by the courts.
- A major reason for this explosion in civil liberties litigation is the "nationalization" of the Bill of Rights—that is, the application of the Bill of Rights to the states via the Fourteenth Amendment. This amendment had been seriously weakened by Supreme Court decisions in the later nineteenth century, but it was restored to prominence after the 1940s.
- Another reason for the increase in civil rights cases is the liberal application and interpretation of the three Civil War amendments. These were passed to protect the freedom of the newly emancipated slaves. The Fourteenth

Amendment, with its "equal protection" and "due process" clauses, was the principal judicial-legislative instrument in the struggle to end social injustice.

- A third reason is the adoption of a judicial "double standard" that gives closer scrutiny to allegations of government violations of fundamental or cultural freedoms than to alleged violations of economic liberties.
- Major strides have been made in the past half century in expanding civil rights and liberties in the United States. Not only have the First Amendment and other basic substantive civil rights and liberties been extended, but their application to those accused of crimes has been strengthened markedly—often accompanied by criticism that "criminal forces" were being advantaged over "peace forces."
- Claims to privacy have found increasing support by the judiciary, which has expanded many aspects of privacy by a generous interpretation of the Ninth and, to a lesser degree, the Fourth Amendments in the Bill of Rights.
- One of the major areas of contention under privacy has become the issue of sexual freedom or orientation.

Readings on Civil Rights and Liberties

Abraham, Henry J. 1988. *Freedom and the Court: Civil Rights and Liberties in the United States,* 5th ed. New York: Oxford University Press. Analyzes and evaluates the history, development, and status of civil rights and liberties, with particular attention to the posture of the judicial branch.

Berger, Raoul. 1977. *Government by Judiciary: The Transformation of the Fourteenth Amendment.* Cambridge, Mass.: Harvard University Press. A controversial attack on the contemporary judiciary's expansive interpretation of the original meaning of the Fourteenth Amendment, in particular its application of the Bill of Rights to the states.

Black, Hugo L. 1967. *A Constitutional Faith.* New York: Knopf. A valedictory work written by one of our country's great jurists and devoted constitutionalists.

Cortner, Richard C. 1981. *The Supreme Court and the Second Bill of Rights.* Madison: University of Wisconsin Press. An excellent, full-length study of the development and application of the incorporation doctrine.

Curtis, Michael K. 1986. *No State Shall Abridge: The Fourteenth Amendment and the Bill of Rights.* Durham, N.C.: Duke University Press. A potent defense of the justification of the incorporation doctrine and its broad application to the states.

Lewis, Anthony. 1964. *Gideon's Trumpet.* New York: Random House. An eloquent account of Clarence Earl Gideon's struggle to attain the application of the right of counsel to the states.

O'Brien, David M. 1979. *Privacy, Law, and Public Policy.* New York: Praeger. An able study of the claims for and conflicts surrounding the range and extent of the privacy entitlement.

Rutland, Robert. 1983. *The Birth of the Bill of Rights, 1766–1791.* rev. ed. Boston: Northeastern University Press. The definitive history of the Bill of Rights' genesis.

Siegan, Bernard H. 1980. *Economic Liberties and the Constitution.* Chicago: University of Chicago Press. A call for the rejection of the "double standard" by arguing for equal treatment of economic-proprietarian rights.

Wilson, James Q. 1985. *Thinking About Crime,* rev. ed. New York: Random House. A realistic analysis of crime in the United States and its causes, emphasizing that it is "suicidal" to blame "society" for all criminals.

Chapter 5

Civil Rights and Liberties: Freedom and Equality

A commitment to civil rights and liberties characterizes a free people. Like Thomas Jefferson, in words inscribed on his memorial in the nation's capital, Americans "have sworn upon the altar of God eternal hostility against every form of tyranny over the mind of man." Yet, as the last chapter showed, the Bill of Rights needs constant interpretation and affirmation.

The sweep of the U.S. Supreme Court, the nation's highest judicial body, is as broad as it is often controversial. "We, the people" are the final authority—but people differ profoundly on the range of our basic freedoms. This chapter looks at these major components: freedom of religion, freedom of speech, and political, racial, and sexual equality.

Freedom of Religion

Article 1 of the Bill of Rights begins in an emotion-charged realm—religious liberty:

> Congress shall make no laws respecting an establishment of religion, or prohibiting the free exercise thereof. . . .

Note the two separate but related protections. The first, "the establishment clause," guarantees the separation of church and state. The second, the right to free exercise of religion, is less controversial but just as fundamental.

Free Exercise of Religion

The First Amendment was designed to mean what it says: Neither Congress nor, by incorporation, the states (see Chapter 4) may interfere with religious belief or exercise—the freedom to *believe* or the freedom to *act.* Obviously, however, as Justice Owen Roberts wrote for a unanimous Court in 1940, "the first is absolute, but . . . the second cannot be. *Conduct* remains subject to regulation for the protection of society." [1] In every case, he continued, "the power to regulate must be so exercised as not, in attaining a permissible end, unduly to infringe the protected freedom." Since then, the Court has shown a growing commitment to that freedom.

A regard for free exercise protects sometimes unpopular sects, such as Jehovah's Witnesses or Seventh-Day Adventists. It also safeguards practices that may not always sit well with the majority. In a campaign debate in 1988, for example, President Bush made one of those protections a key issue—the right not to recite the Pledge of Allegiance. Other Court rulings have supported refusals to salute the flag—even to burn it (*Texas* v. *Johnson,* 1989)—to mount license plates with patriotic phrases, to attend school beyond the eighth grade, to refuse to work on the Sabbath, and even to have a photograph taken for a driver's license.

Limits on free exercise have been considerably less controversial than questions involving the separation of church and state. For example, citizens cannot hold parades on major highways without a permit, refuse outright to pay taxes, become tax exempt for $25 in a mail-order ministry, handle poisonous snakes in church, or grow marijuana or wheat in excess of federal rules. (It has been argued that regulating the fruits of the soil interferes with God's will.) The Court reaffirmed a ban on polygamy as recently as 1984.

One controversial issue, conscientious objection to military service, has been neutralized for the time being by the end of the draft. Before that, the Court had generally banned only "selective C.O.'s" from claiming a right to distinguish just from unjust wars. However, students may be required to register for the draft to receive financial aid.

Justice William O. Douglas's lone dissent in the just-war case points to the high value Americans place on religious freedom: "I had assumed that the welfare of a single human soul was the ultimate test of the vitality of the First Amendment." [2] If there are limits, it means only that lines must be drawn under the Constitution. The rule of law cements our society.

Americans have always prided themselves on a full measure of free exercise of religion. Here members of an Amish family in Pennsylvania are seen listening intently to a Red Cross volunteer before receiving their polio vaccine. The Amish consented to take the vaccine to help protect their neighbors after several confirmed cases of polio in the area. Elsewhere, however, the rights of religious communities could well clash with the power of government to protect the public health.

Separation of Church and State

The complex issue of the "establishment" of religion cannot be understood apart from religious liberty itself. The founders' views would *seem* to be clear. Jefferson objected to a "preferred position of the favored church," and in 1786 he acted to remove the status of Anglicanism as the established church of Virginia. For children of the Enlightenment, the Virginians represented the secular, humanistic position that supported religious liberty. Justice Hugo Black stated the doctrine forcefully:

> Neither a state nor the Federal government can, openly or secretly, participate in the affairs of any religious organizations or groups and vice versa. In the words of Jefferson, the clause against establishment of religion by law was intended to erect a "wall of separation" between church and state.[3]

IMPACT

The Courts and Religious Freedom

Not every claim based on the First Amendment succeeds. But each shows the importance of our religious freedoms—simply because the courts took the claims seriously. Here are just some of the arguments *unsuccessfully* advanced in only the last few years. How might you have decided?

- A teacher claimed that a public school celebration of Halloween violated his conscience as a "pagan observance of every evil and wicked thing in the world." An American Indian objected to being assigned a social security number because "numbers are an instrument of the devil."
- The National Bible Association, along with the National Foundation for Fairness in Education, objected to an exhibit held at the Smithsonian Institution in Washington, D.C. By omitting the biblical account of the creation of the universe, they argued, it established a "religion of secular humanism."
- Madalyn Murray O'Hair has become well known for suits like one to remove the phrase "In God We Trust" from U.S. currency. Another unsuccessful claim garnered more support, as she sought to restrain a mass by Pope John Paul II on the mall in Washington, D.C.
- Air Force Captain S. S. Goldman contended that he was entitled to wear a yarmulke, or skullcap, while in uniform; and Hindu Sikh James Cooper claimed a right to don white clothes and a turban while teaching elementary school. Both claims were rejected, but they helped get Congress to act. Religious garb now is permitted if the wearer's duties are not affected.
- A Christian evangelical group, the Tony and Susan Alamo Foundation, protested the federal minimum wage requirement. Its 300 "associate members" worked in foundation-owned construction firms, retail stores, a motel, hog farms, and service stations.
- A Philadelphian tried to bring federal suit against public policies because he was "God's prophet." The judge accepted the U.S. attorney's contention that the court had no jurisdiction over God!

Since Jefferson's time, the Court has acted to support that wall of separation. For example, in a 1972 case it struck down a Louisiana law that required the teaching of "creationism" alongside the teaching of evolution.

Yet the Court has never found it easy to draw the line. If some argue that the Constitution prohibits government from any recognition or aid for religion, others believe that sometimes government action is a duty. Even history is an unreliable guide. All that can be said with certainty about James Madison—a leading author of the Bill of Rights' religion clauses—is that he wanted no law ever to respect a state religion or a state church.

The Child Benefit Theory. Black's own words, however memorable, are a case in point. They came in 1947, in *support* of a New Jersey law providing free bus transportation to parochial school children. Black argued for a 5:4 court that the law benefited the child rather than the church.

The Court has applied a similar principle to defend many "indirect services" to religion. These include grants for school lunches and nonsectarian textbooks, the use of chaplains in the armed forces, and tax exemptions for nonprofit activities of religious institutions. On the other hand, the Court has upheld state bans on free bus transportation to other than public school children. Evidently judicial restraint matters, too.

Prayers and Bible Reading. In the early 1960s, the Warren Court began to interpret the separation clause more strictly. Few decisions have caused as much outcry as a 1962 case concerning a 22-word prayer. The New York State Board of Regents had recommended (but not required) that classes read the nondenominational prayer at the start of each school day. A group of Long Island parents objected, and a majority of the Court agreed. Justice Black's opinion put it bluntly:

> It is neither sacrilegious nor antireligious to say that each separate government in this country should stay out of the business of writing or sanctioning official prayers. . . .[4]

A year later the Court struck down similar policies, such as the long-standing Baltimore practice of daily Bible readings in the schools. Justice Tom Clark wrote, with an eye toward soothing the public:

> The place of religion in our society is an exalted one, achieved through a long tradition of reliance on the home, the church and the inviolable citadel of the individual heart and mind. We have come to recognize through bitter experience that it is not within the power of government to invade that citadel. . . . In the relationship between man and religion, the State is firmly committed to a position of neutrality.[5]

That ruling received significant church support and lengthy concurring opinions by William Brennan, a Roman Catholic, and Arthur Goldberg, a Jew. Yet it seemed only to increase the uproar. State and local officials frequently encouraged the many violations of the Court's decision, and by 1986 some 385 proposed constitutional amendments supported school prayer—a handful narrowly failing passage in Congress. (Two attempts to curb the Court's jurisdiction in school prayer cases actually passed the Senate.) Constitutional amendments to accomplish what simple laws cannot seem unlikely to pass, but the controversy is still very much alive.

Several states have tried instead to allow teachers to lead silent prayer. It is conceivable that simple moments of silence might surmount constitutional challenge, but those labeled as "prayers" or even "meditations," Justice John Paul Stevens wrote in 1984, impermissibly "endorse religion as a favorite practice." [6]

Financial Aid to Parochial Schools. Another prohibition covers direct public funds for sectarian schools, even if that aid promotes the teaching of secular subjects. "Under our system," concluded Chief Justice Warren Burger in 1971, "the choice has been made that government is to be entirely excluded from the area of religious instruction. . . ." [7]

Partisans of state aid have continued to press, generally without success, for tax relief and tuition reimbursement (see Table 5–1). In each case, the Court has set a three-part standard: First, a law must have a secular purpose. Second, its principal effect must neither advance nor inhibit religion. And, finally, it must not foster "excessive entanglement in religion by government." So far, textbook loans have passed that standard. Services such as counseling, remedial classes in speech and hearing therapy, and funds for audiovisual equipment often have not. Private schools can be reimbursed for testing, *if* the tests are state mandated, and parents for tuition, *if* the tax deduction provides relief for *both* public and parochial schools.

TABLE 5–1

Recent Supreme Court Decisions on Aid to Nonpublic Schools

Case	Year	Upheld	Struck Down
Walz	1970	Tax exemption of property used exclusively for religious purposes (7:1)	
Lemon [I]	1971		Partial payment of salaries of parochial school teachers (1:8)
Early	1971		Purchases of secular services for sectarian schools (1:8)
Tilton	1971	Construction funds for religiously affiliated colleges and universities (5:4)	
Essex	1972		Direct tuition rebates per child of $90.00 (1:8)
Nyquist	1973	Lending of textbooks (6:3)	Maintenance, repair, tuition, equipment, and record keeping and tuition reimbursement (3:6 and 1:8)
Meek	1975	Lending of textbooks (6:3)	Counseling, testing, remedial classes, instructional materials and equipment, speech and hearing therapy, psychological services (3:6)
Roemer	1976	Noncategorical financial (Maryland) aid to church-related colleges, if not used for sectarian purposes (first time in history Court approved general-purpose subsidies) (5:4)	
Blanton	1976	Tuition grants to college students, no matter where enrolled (9:0)	
Wolman	1977	Therapeutic, remedial, and guidance counseling on "neutral" sites off grounds (7:2); lending of textbooks (6:3); diagnostic services on grounds (8:1); standardized texts and test scoring (provided by public schools) (6:3)	Field trip financing (4:5); providing to parents or pupils (loan) classroom paraphernalia—e.g., wall charts, maps, projectors, tape recorders (3:6)

TABLE 5–1 (*Continued*)

Case	Year	Upheld	Struck Down
Cathedral	1977		Direct financial aid for testing and record keeping (3:6)
Byrne	1979		Income tax deductions for parents of parochial school students (3:6)
Regan	1980	Reimbursement for expenses incurred by nonpublic schools in connection with keeping official attendance and other records, for administering three state-prepared tests, and for grading two of these (5:4)	
Mueller	1983	Tax deduction of up to $700 yearly for parents of children in *all* elementary and secondary schools, whether public, private, or parochial (5:4)	
Grand Rapids	1985		"Shared Time" (4:5) and "Community Education" (2:7) programs
Aguilar	1985		Instructional services, funded under Title I of the FAESS, on parochial school premises (4:5)
Kendrick	1988	Governmental funding of community teaching programs that deal with the problem of teenage pregnancy by encouraging sexual abstinence, adoption, and other alternatives to abortion.	

The Court has agreed to aid for church-related *colleges.* By 5:4, the Court upheld a Maryland law over fervent, often biting dissent. Colleges, the majority reasoned, can better separate secular and religious functions, and college students are simply less impressionable than younger pupils.

Accommodation and the 1990s. If the 1980s suggest a new majority for a more "accommodationist" approach to church and state, they also reflect deep divisions and bitter dissents. Often the Court has split many ways, with no single opinion speaking for the majority.

In 1984 the Court permitted public support of an annual Christmas display in a private park, including a life-sized Nativity scene, calling it "a historical symbol rather than a religious endorsement."[8] Over outraged dissent from four members of the Court, Chief Justice Warren Burger observed that total separation is neither possible nor required. But the "creche" issue was again before the Court in 1989: In a combined case, involving the City of Pittsburgh and Allegheny County, a seriously divided Court handed down two rulings that may well have settled little and gave promise of almost certain future litigation on the issue. Dividing 5:4 and 6:3 the Justices held, in two opinions authored by Justice Harry A. Blackmun, that (a) displaying a nativity scene inside the Allegheny County courthouse in Pittsburgh violates constitutionally required separation of church and state because it appears to endorse Christian principles; but that (b) a Hanukkah menorah, placed on the steps of the city-county building, joined by a Christmas tree and a homily to the Statute of Liberty, was allowable because it was placed in a physical setting that, in Blackmun's words, "conveyed the city's secular recognition of different traditions for celebrating the winter holiday season." (*Allegheny County* v. *Greater Pittsburgh ACLU*). Also recently, the Court divided 5:4 in upholding the Adolescent Family Life Act. This federal act grants funds to a variety of groups, including religious organizations; its goal is to foster counseling for prevention of adolescent sexual relations and for pregnant teenagers and teenage parents. The narrow majority in 1988 included President Reagan's final appointee, Anthony M. Kennedy. In the 1990s we can expect continuing disagreement on the delicate issue of church and state.[9]

Freedom of Expression

Freedom of expression includes far more than what we tend to think of as freedom of speech. In the words of the First Amendment:

> Congress shall make no law . . . abridging the freedom of speech, or of the press; or the right of the people peaceably to assemble, and to petition the Government for a redress of grievances.

The First Amendment, which also applies to the states as well as Congress (see Chapter 4), means freedom to communicate—without prior restraint. It allows each of us to express opinions orally or in writing, through books, movies, and plays—even, at least since 1976, in purely "commercial speech"—i.e., speech that is related to business transactions. Expression includes a host of other basic liberties; picketing, for example, is just as much a mode of communication as speaking.

Freedom of expression protects campaign spending (but not unlimited spending) by and for a candidate for elective office. It has been related to the right of banks and corporations to spend money to influence referenda not "materially affecting" their business. It allows views on controversial issues to be slipped in with our electric bills. As of 1976, it defends most government workers from dismissal for mere patronage reasons.

"Symbolic speech" includes acts like wearing black armbands in school as an antiwar protest, wearing uniforms in a play unfavorable to the military, or sporting a jacket with a four-letter insult to the draft on it. It protects unpopular groups and unpopular acts—from religious pamphleteering in airports, to advertising civil disobedience, to viewing stag movies in private. The special protection accorded even to these freedoms is part of the "judicial double standard" discussed in Chapter 4.

Free Expression and Its Limits ■

These guarantees are sweeping and unequivocal, but they are not absolute. Yelling "fire" in a crowded theater is an exercise of freedom of speech, but only if there really is a fire. The laws protect advocating the overthrow of our government *in theory,* but not language inciting violence. Newspapers cannot be *required* to print replies from political candidates, but they are subject to libel suits by ordinary citizens.

Under our system of government, the majority is obliged to respect the rights of others, but not to give in to a "tyranny of the minority." Illegal picketing, trespassing, and breach of the peace are

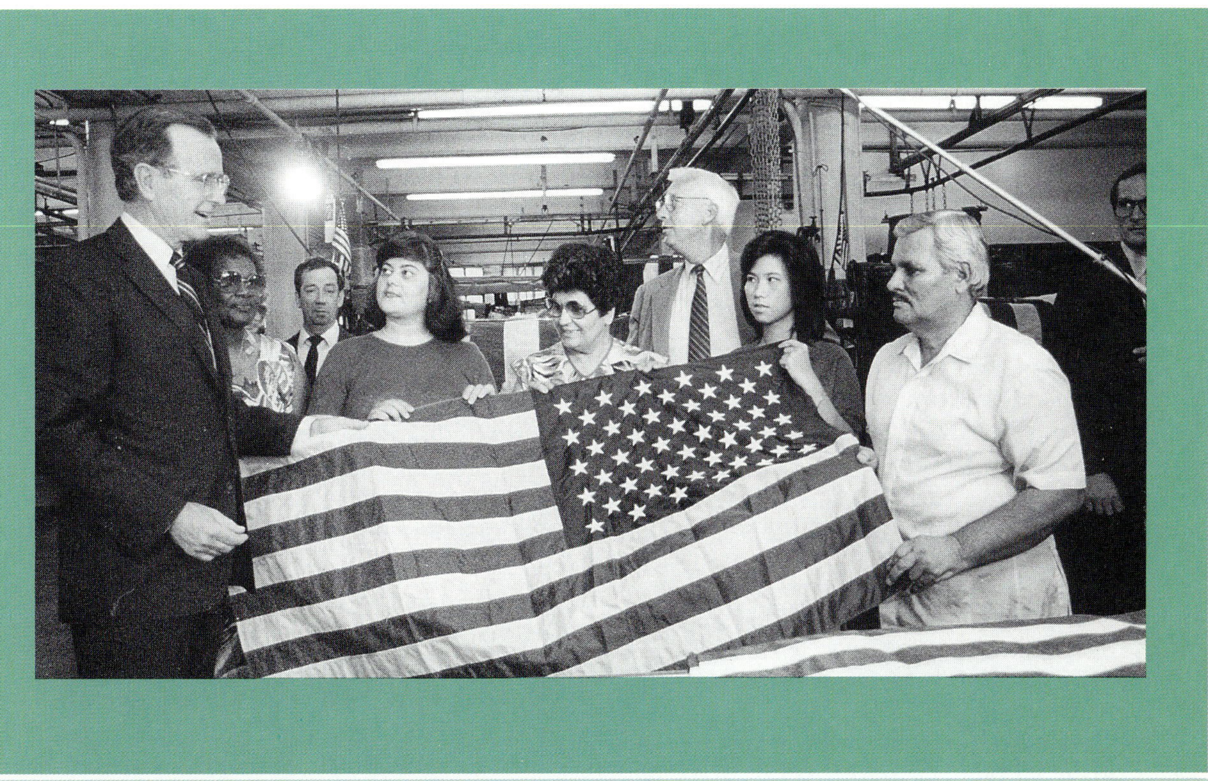

People everywhere express themselves by symbols, and the First Amendment protects that freedom of expression. While governor of Massachusetts, Michael Dukakis vetoed a bill that required school children to say the pledge of allegiance. He cited a 1943 Court decision that compulsory flag salutes cannot be imposed on those who see venerating a flag as offensive to their religion. George Bush steadily used this veto in 1988 to question his opponent's patriotism. To drive home the point, he visited a New Jersey flag factory during the campaign. Echoing the patriotism theme of the 1988 campaign, the Supreme Court ruled in 1989 that burning the American flag in political protest is protected by the Constitution's free-speech guarantees in the First Amendment.

not protected expression. Nor are burning draft cards, walking about in the nude, selling pornography to children, using mailboxes for unstamped material, or sleeping in parks—even when 60 tents for the homeless were set up in protest near the White House. Laws against sodomy have generally been upheld. School boards and police departments can require haircuts, and journalists can be sent to jail if they do not reveal confidential sources in civil and criminal cases.

The courts must draw the line between the individual's right to free expression and society's needs. Not just where to draw the line but *how* it shall be drawn remains a problem. The courts have set no single, definitive standard.

The "Clear and Present Danger" Test. The best-known standard remains the earliest one. Charles T. Schenck had been jailed during World War I for urging young men to resist the draft. The language he had used was intemperate, but was it protected by the First Amendment? In 1919 the Court unanimously upheld his conviction under the Espionage Act of 1917, a law designed to safeguard national security. Oliver Wendell Holmes outlined the new test:

> We admit that in many places and in ordinary times the defendants in saying all that was said . . . would have been within their constitutional rights. But the character of every act de-

The American Civil Liberties Union as a Political Issue

One of the most emotional issues of the 1988 presidential campaign concerned candidate Michael Dukakis's membership in the American Civil Liberties Union (ACLU). George Bush repeatedly ridiculed his opponent's affiliation. He observered in one presidential debate, for example, that:

> "*I don't want my ten-year-old grandchild to go into an X-rated movie. . . . I don't think they're [the ACLU] right to try to take the tax exemption away from the Catholic church. I don't want to see their kiddie pornographic laws repealed. I don't want to see "under God" come out from our currency. Now these are all positions of the ACLU. And I don't agree with them.*"

(The ACLU subsequently pointed out that Bush was wrong in attributing to it all but the last of these four positions.) What is this organization which Bush portrayed as so controversial and so radical in its politics?

In 1917, Norman Thomas and Roger Baldwin established the American Civil Liberties Bureau (ACLB) to defend conscientious objectors during World War I. In 1920, the ACLB became the ACLU and served, during the 1920s, to protect the rights of individuals during the rein of U.S. Attorney General A. Mitchell Palmer—who, among other things, sought to deport aliens with "radical" political beliefs, interfere with the establishment of trade unions, and imprison American citizens for speaking out against this country's involvement in World War I.

From the beginning, the ACLU's mission has been to ensure "that the Bill of Rights—amendments to the Constitution that guard against unwarranted governmental control—are preserved for each new generation." The ACLU often becomes involved in disputes involving First Amendment rights, equal protection, due process of law, and the right to privacy. Some of its more renowned efforts include:

1925 Clarence Darrow, on behalf of the ACLU, defended John T. Scopes, a science teacher, against a Tennessee law forbidding the teaching of evolution.

pends upon the circumstances in which it was done. . . . The question in every case is whether the words used . . . create a clear and present danger that they will bring about the substantive evils that Congress has a right to prevent. It is a question of proximity and degree.[10]

Justice Louis Brandeis wrote that this "rule of reason" would preserve free speech both "from suppression by tyrannous, well-meaning majorities and from abuse by irresponsible, fanatical minorities." One week later, two more convictions under the act were upheld—again based on a "clear and present danger" test.

1933 The ACLU successfully fought censorship laws which prevented James Joyce's novel *Ulysses* from being sold in the United States.

1942 The ACLU expressed strong and repeated objection to the federal government's policy of relocating 110,000 Japanese Americans (mostly U.S. citizens) from their West Coast homes to inland "internment camps" during World War II.

1954 The ACLU joined forces with civil rights groups in the *Brown* v. *Board of Education of Topeka, Kansas* case, which held that segregated schools are unconstitutional.

1964 The ACLU argued successfully before the Supreme Court in *Reynolds* v. *Sims* that legislative districts should be of equal size rather than be drawn so as to discriminate against minorities.

1977 The ACLU defended the rights of American Nazis to demonstrate in the predominantly Jewish Chicago suburb of Skokie, Illinois.

1981 The ACLU challenged an Arkansas law requiring science teachers to present the biblical story of creation as a "scientific alternative" to the theory of evolution.

Plainly, the union does not shy away from defending the rights of despised individuals or groups—a major reason for the ACLU's controversial image.

Although the ACLU's main arena has been the judiciary (it has taken more cases to the Supreme Court than any other private organization), this 250,000-member group has become more active in legislative politics in recent years. Since 1970 the union, with its 11 full-time lobbyists in its Washington office, has encouraged Congress to bring impeachment charges against President Richard Nixon, lobbied for the extension of the 1965 Voting Rights Act, and actively opposed the nomination of Robert Bork to the Supreme Court.

As if to show how little the standard had settled, barely six months later Holmes and Brandeis found themselves in the minority. The case began after World War I, when 29-year-old Jacob Abrams and four young "anarchist-Socialist associates" who had fled Tsarist Russia threw leaflets from rooftops on New York's Lower East Side. They urged the "workers of the world" to resist American military intervention against the Bolsheviks in Russia, bitterly denounced President Wilson, and called for a general strike to prevent the shipment of munitions to the anti-Soviet forces. In a world torn by war, did Americans resent foreign influence, or at least *German* influence? "It is absurd to call us pro-German," the leaflets concluded. "We hate and despise German militarism more than do your hypocritical tyrants. We have more reasons for denouncing German militarism than has the coward in the White House." [11] Abrams and two others were sentenced under the Sedition Act of 1918, which forbade certain kinds of expression and conduct inimical to national security, to the maximum of 20 years in federal penitentiary and a $4000 fine; the lone woman among the defendants, Mollie Stein, drew 15 years and a $500 fine. The Supreme Court upheld their conviction, applying the "clear and present danger" test, but Holmes wrote a memorable dissent:

> I think that we should be eternally vigilant against attempts to check the expression of opinions that we loathe . . . unless . . . an immediate check is required to save the country. . . .[12]

In 1921 President Harding released the four, on condition that they embark for Russia at their own expense. They did.

The "Bad Tendency" Test. The Court first officially modified the "clear and present danger" doctrine in 1925. The *Gitlow* test was whether verbal or written expression constituted a "bad tendency" to bring about a danger.[13] This effectively shifted the balance between the state and the individual in favor of the state.

The "Imminence" Test. Throughout much of the 1930s and 1940s, the Court returned to a liberalized version of the "clear and present danger" standard. It was Justice Brandeis who argued, in the 1927 *Whitney* case, that the danger must be not only clear and present but also *imminent* to justify suppressive state action:

> Fear of serious injury cannot alone justify suppression of free speech and assembly. . . . There must be reasonable ground to fear that serious evil will result if the free speech is practiced. . . . There must be reasonable ground to believe that the danger apprehended is imminent. . . .[14]

Free Expression and National Security

Still, it is understandable that the courts will be more careful where public opinion sees a threat to national security. Since the Cold War began, the Court has more than ever been mindful of its complex role as a political institution as well as a branch of government and, above all, a court of law.

In 1946 Frederick M. Vinson became chief justice. The Vinson Court preserved the "imminence" test for press freedom and street corner oratory. On national security issues, however, it tended to be far less liberal in its application of the First Amendment. To some observers, the test of "clear and present danger" had been transformed into a "grave and probable"—or perhaps even "possible and remote"—threat to security.

More recently, however, beginning during the term of the Warren Court around 1960, the Court has consistently applied the "imminence" test to all First Amendment cases. That generous interpretation of our freedoms seems likely to hold in the coming years under the Rehnquist Court. Where national security issues are raised, the Court has at times gone out of its way to support statutes, but it has insisted that laws be executed fairly. Most often it has chosen to curb Congress by *statutory interpretation.* As we shall learn in Chapter 16, that means interpreting the laws rather than declaring them unconstitutional.

Congressional Investigating Committees. Congress's power of investigation enables it to legislate intelligently, inform the public, and oversee the administrative branch. But that power readily lends itself to abuses, especially in investigations of "subversive activities." Matters came to a head during the anti-Communist crusades of the 1950s, led by men like Senator Joseph R. McCarthy (R–Wis.). Under the Fifth Amendment, a witness may refuse to answer questions that might lead to self-incrimination. But what if a witness invokes First Amendment freedoms?

In 1957 the Supreme Court supported John T. Watkins's refusal to discuss activities of some of his associates before the House Committee on Un-American Activities. Chief Justice Earl Warren wrote that Congress has no authority to expose private lives merely "for the sake of exposure." An inquiry must further a "legitimate task" of Congress.

Reaction to the decision was vehement. If legislation that sought to limit judicial power failed to be enacted, it may be because, two years later, the Court—and, arguably, Congress—seemed in part to back down. Still, the Court has repeatedly shown that it will not allow patently unconstitutional investigations.

The Smith Act. The Smith Act of 1940 was the first of a series of controversial anti-Communist statutes. In 1951 eleven leaders of the American Communist party fell victim to that act. They were convicted of a conspiracy to teach and advocate the violent overthrow of the United States. *Dennis v. United States* let that conviction stand. Chief Justice Vinson found a "clear and present danger" in the "conspiratorial nature" of the defendant's activities. He cited Learned Hand: The courts "must ask whether the gravity of the evil, discounted by its improbability, justifies such invasion of free speech as is necessary to avoid the danger." [15]

Two passionate dissents argued for what William O. Douglas called "full and free discussion of ideas we hate." Justice Douglas belittled the alleged strength of the American Communist party, and Hugo Black ended his dissent with an expression of hope:

> Public opinion being what it now is, few will protest the conviction of these Communist petitioners. There is hope, however, that in calmer times, when present pressures, passions and fears subside, this or some later Court will restore the First Amendment liberties to the high preferred place where they belong in free society.[16]

By the time that hope was vindicated, the government had obtained 145 indictments and 89 convictions under the act.

In 1957 the Court first limited the Smith Act, and in 1961 it ruled that no one can be punished for mere membership in any group. Only active members with "a specific intent to bring about violence" were subject to prosecution. One year later, it drew a crucial line—between statements of belief and advocacy of illegal action. The Smith Act stood, but the federal government could never again legitimately punish people for their beliefs.

The McCarran Act. The McCarran Act, or Internal Security Act of 1950, forced members of the Communist party to register with the government, and it denied them passports. The Court ruled that the forced disclosure of party membership did not violate the First Amendment. With characteristic deference to the Congress, the long 1961 opinion by Justice Felix Frankfurter deliberately avoided other constitutional issues.

The McCarran Act was eventually defeated, but not on First Amendment grounds. Since the Smith Act had made membership in the Communist party a criminal conspiracy, the Court of Appeals said in 1963, "mere association with the party incriminates," and registration violated the Fifth Amendment. The Supreme Court let that decision stand; and, two weeks later, on the final day of its 1963–1964 term, it struck down the section on passports for restricting "too broadly and indiscriminately" the liberty to travel. Another law, the Communist Control Act of 1954, has been rarely enforced and never tested conclusively in court.

National Security and the Court Today. The judiciary has been increasingly willing to enter the troublesome national security sector—within limits. Those issues were raised, for example, when Colonel Oliver North's involvement in the "Iran-contra" scandal put the power of Congress and an independent special prosecutor to the test. Even where freedom of expression is at stake, the Court can never get entirely away from balancing liberty and authority. If Justice Black denounced that con-

“Perspectives”

On the First Amendment

Freedom of Religion

“The ‘establishment of religion’ clause of the First Amendment means at least this: Neither a state nor the Federal Government can set up a church. Neither can pass laws which aid one religion, aid all religions or prefer one religion over another. Neither can force nor influence a person to go or remain away from church against his will or force him to profess a belief or disbelief in any religion. No person can be punished for entertaining or professing religious beliefs or disbeliefs, for church attendance or nonattendance. No tax in any amount, large or small, can be levied to support any religious activities or institutions, whatever they may be called, or whatever form they may adopt to teach or practice religion.”

—Justice Hugo L. Black
Everson v. *Board of Education of Ewing Township*
(330 U.S. 1, at 15–16)

Freedom of Speech

“The vitality of civil and political institutions in our society depends on free discussion. . . . [I]t is only through free debate and free exchange of ideas that government remains responsive to the will of the people and peaceful change is effected. The right to speak freely and to promote diversity of ideas and programs is therefore one of the chief distinctions that sets us apart from totalitarian regimes. . . . That is why freedom of speech, though not absolute . . . is nevertheless protected against censorship or punishment, unless shown likely to produce a clear and present danger of a serious substantive evil that rises far above public inconvenience, annoyance, or unrest. . . . There is no room under our Constitution for a more restrictive view. For the alternative would lead to standardization of ideas either by legislatures, courts, or dominant political or community groups.”

—Justice William O. Douglas
Terminiello v. *Chicago*
(337 U.S. 1, 69 S.Ct. 894, 1949)

cept throughout a long and noble career, he could at least be a little reassured. Where balancing is called for, in the absence of a clear, present, and imminent danger we must presume the scale to be weighted on the side of the individual.

Equality

No issue has so dominated public policy as America's striving for full equality for all. In the last decades, "equal protection of the laws" has meant more than the right to be fairly represented in government. It has also demanded freedom from discrimination on the basis of race or gender. The struggle for equal protection affects every level of government and society. The words just quoted appear in the Fourteenth Amendment, which applies to the states, but they pertain just as much to the

Freedom of the Press

"*The First Amendment was designed to enlarge, not to limit, freedom in literature and in the arts as well as in politics, economics, law, and other fields. . . . Its aim was to unlock all ideas for argument, debate, and dissemination. No more potent force in defeat of that freedom could be designed than censorship. It is a weapon that no minority or majority group, acting through government, should be allowed to wield over any of us.*"

—Justice Earl Warren, Dissent
in *Times Film Corp.* v. *Chicago*
(365 U.S. 43, 81 S.Ct. 391, 1961)

Freedom of Assembly

"*The greater the importance of safeguarding the community from incitement to the overthrow of our institutions by force and violence, the more imperative is the need to preserve inviolate the constitutional rights of free speech, free press and free assembly in order to maintain the opportunity for free political discussion, to the end that government may be responsive to the will of the people and that changes, if desired, may be obtained by peaceful means. Therein lies the security of the Republic, the very foundation of constitutional government. . . . The holding of meetings for peaceable political action cannot be proscribed. . . . The question, if the rights of free speech and peaceable assembly are to be preserved, is not as to the auspices under which the meeting is held but as to its purpose; not as the to the relations of the speakers, but whether their utterances transcend the bounds of the freedom of speech which the Constitution protects.*"

—Justice Charles Evans Hughes
DeJonge v. *Oregon* (299 U.S. 366,
365, 57 S.Ct. 255, 1937)

Source: *DeJonge* v. *Oregon* quotation taken from: Fred W. Friendly and Martha J. H. Elliott, *The Constitution: That Delicate Balance* (New York: Random House, 1984), p. 80.

federal government through the Fifth Amendment pledge of due process of law. Their promise has been increasingly fulfilled, but it stands in need of further progress.

The Right to Vote ■

Universal suffrage refers to the right of everyone to vote. It required decades to overcome discrimination at the polls against Quakers, Catholics, and Jews. Amendments granting the vote to women and 18-year-olds passed only in 1920 and 1972. The chief struggle, however, has been the quest of black Americans for the political equality due all citizens under the Constitution. Despite a long civil war and the command of the Fifteenth Amendment, it took many blacks until 1965 to secure that right.

Passage of the 1965 Voting Rights Act helped open the way for full participation for all in American politics, regardless of color, religion, or gender. Jesse Jackson in 1988 called on a "rainbow coalition" as he campaigned for the presidency. Jackson ran a strong race for his party's nomination, winning six state caucauses and seven primaries. His organization also played a major role in drafting the Democratic platform.

The first court victories came in the 1920s, but it was only in 1944, in *Smith* v. *Allwright,* that an 8:1 majority declared the all-white primary to be unconstitutional. Federal Civil Rights Acts of 1957, 1960, and 1964 and the ban on poll taxes in the Twenty-fourth Amendment (ratified in 1964) were other important steps toward making black suffrage a reality. The emerging civil rights movement and the beatings and other outrages committed against marchers led by Dr. Martin Luther King, Jr., in Selma, Alabama, also served as a great catalyst for change. So did the commitment of Lyndon Johnson to the ideals of racial justice declared by President Kennedy.

In 1965 President Johnson could finally hail a new, tough Voting Rights Act as "a proud moment for this nation." The act, broadened and extended in later years (most recently in 1982), outlawed such widespread tools of discrimination as literacy tests. Black suffrage is now a potent fact of political life, and so is the possibility of a black seeking and holding any public office. Millions of black voters have been registered—at 73 percent, roughly on a parity with whites. The difference in black and white voter turnout had shrunk to 6 percent by 1988.

Some 6600 blacks held elective office following the 1988 elections—over 3000 in the 11 states of the former Confederacy. By mid-1988 there were 300 black mayors, including six in America's ten largest cities; over 700 judges (14 of them on the highest state courts); and thousands of law enforcement officials nationwide, including 379 black FBI agents. The largest number of black elected officials was found in the heart of the formerly segregated southern Alabama and Mississippi. Reverend Jesse Jackson's "rainbow coalition" dramatized the potential appeal of black candidates to black and white voters alike.

Fair Representation ■

The right to vote depends closely on the right to a fair share of representation in government. Discrimination long kept urban and suburban voters, including most black Americans, from that right. Rurally dominated state legislatures often apportioned electoral districts to *under*represent urban voters—by as much as 99 to 1 in Georgia and by up to 1000 to 1 in Vermont. The Supreme Court, meanwhile, dismissed the issue as a "political question." As Felix Frankfurter was to write in his last signed opinion, rather than entering a "mathematical quagmire," the Court must "sear the conscience of the peoples' representatives."

The year 1962 brought a revolutionary change. For 60 years the Tennessee state legislature had refused to redistrict in the face of state constitutional demands to do so regularly. In the case of *Baker* v. *Carr* (with the dissent of Frankfurter quoted above), the Supreme Court held that the distribution of seats in the legislature was subject to the equal protection clause of the Fourteenth Amendment.[17] A year later, in striking down the Georgia "county unit" system, which blatantly discriminated against urban areas such as Atlanta, Justice Douglas held that *"one person, one vote . . . is the only conception of political equality under historical standards."* [18]

In a series of cases throughout the 1960s, the "one person, one vote" standard became the law for Congress, the states, and local governments:

> Legislators represent people [wrote Chief Justice Warren], not trees or acres. Legislators are elected by votes, not farms or cities or economic interests. . . . To the extent that a citizen's right to vote is debased, he is that much less a citizen. The weight of a citizen's vote cannot be made to depend on where he lives.[19]

In the 1970s the Burger Court began to back down slightly from strict numerical tests for gerrymandering. And Congress threatened to counterattack several times; a bill proposed by Senator Everett Dirkson (R–Ill.) to permit one house of legislative bodies to be apportioned other than on the basis of population passed both houses in 1967, only to die in the Senate's conference committee. Yet by 1972 every state had undertaken redistricting, and the Court has continued to be tough indeed with Congress. Thus, in 1984 it disallowed a New Jersey district variation of less than one-seventh of 1 percent! [20] And in 1989 it unanimously ordered New York City to devise a new form of government, holding the old one to be in violation of the "one person, one vote" principle.

Equality and Racial Justice

The abolition of slavery, the Civil War, and the Fourteenth Amendment actually intensified the problem of black and white in the United States. Particularly in areas of the South [21] where blacks still outnumber whites, racial inequality continues to be a critical issue. As the ghetto riots of the 1960s demonstrated only too clearly, however, a "racial problem" is hardly regional. If in 1900 almost 90 percent of America's blacks lived in the 15 states below the Mason-Dixon line, by 1978, following years of migration to northern cities, that figure had declined to about 53 percent—with more blacks now moving *to* than *from* the South.

Discrimination against blacks, who today make up about 11.8 percent of Americans, has long taken place. For many years state and local laws permitted, and sometimes required, it. Buses and railroads, waiting rooms and drinking fountains, schools, parks, and hospitals—all were segregated. So were libraries, beaches, jails, and even cemeteries. Interracial marriages could be illegal. Private groups meanwhile denied blacks access to social clubs, churches, sporting events, barber shops, and, crucially, housing and employment. Little, if anything, was covert about either public or private discrimination. It was simply a fact of life.

Soon after the "Hayes Compromise" ended Reconstruction, blacks began to battle public discrimination. Today, as we shall see, the law has increasingly relegated bias to the private sphere (see Table 5–2). As we shall also see, however, the distinction between public and private intolerance is not easy to define.

"Separate but Equal"

At first the black community seemed doomed to failure, for in 1896 the Supreme Court declared "separate but equal" to be the law. A Louisiana statute had commanded "equal but separate accommodations for the white and colored races" in intrastate railways. In *Plessy* v. *Ferguson*, Justice Henry B. Brown's majority opinion called that law a reasonable exercise of the state's police power:

> If the civil and political rights of both races be equal, one cannot be inferior to the other civilly or politically. . . . Enforced separation of the two races stamps the colored race with the badge of inferiority . . . . simply because the colored race chooses to put that construction upon [it].[22]

Homer Plessy, whose plea for equal protection was denied, was seven-eighths white. The lone dissent came from a former Kentucky slaveholder, John Marshall Harlan: "Our Constitution is colorblind and neither knows nor tolerates classes among citizens."[23]

The "separate but equal" doctrine stood, de-

TABLE 5–2

America's Changing Views on Race

	1963	1977
Do you think white students and black students should go to the same schools, or to separate schools? Percent responding "same":	63%	85%
How strongly would you object if a member of your family wanted to bring a black friend home to dinner? Percent responding "not at all":	49%	71%
White people have a right to keep blacks out of their neighborhood if they want to, and blacks should respect that right. Percent disagreeing:	44%	56%
Do you think there should be laws against marriage between blacks and whites? Percent responding "no":	36%	71%

Source: Data drawn from Michael Corbett, *Political Tolerance in America* (New York: Longman, 1982), p. 68.

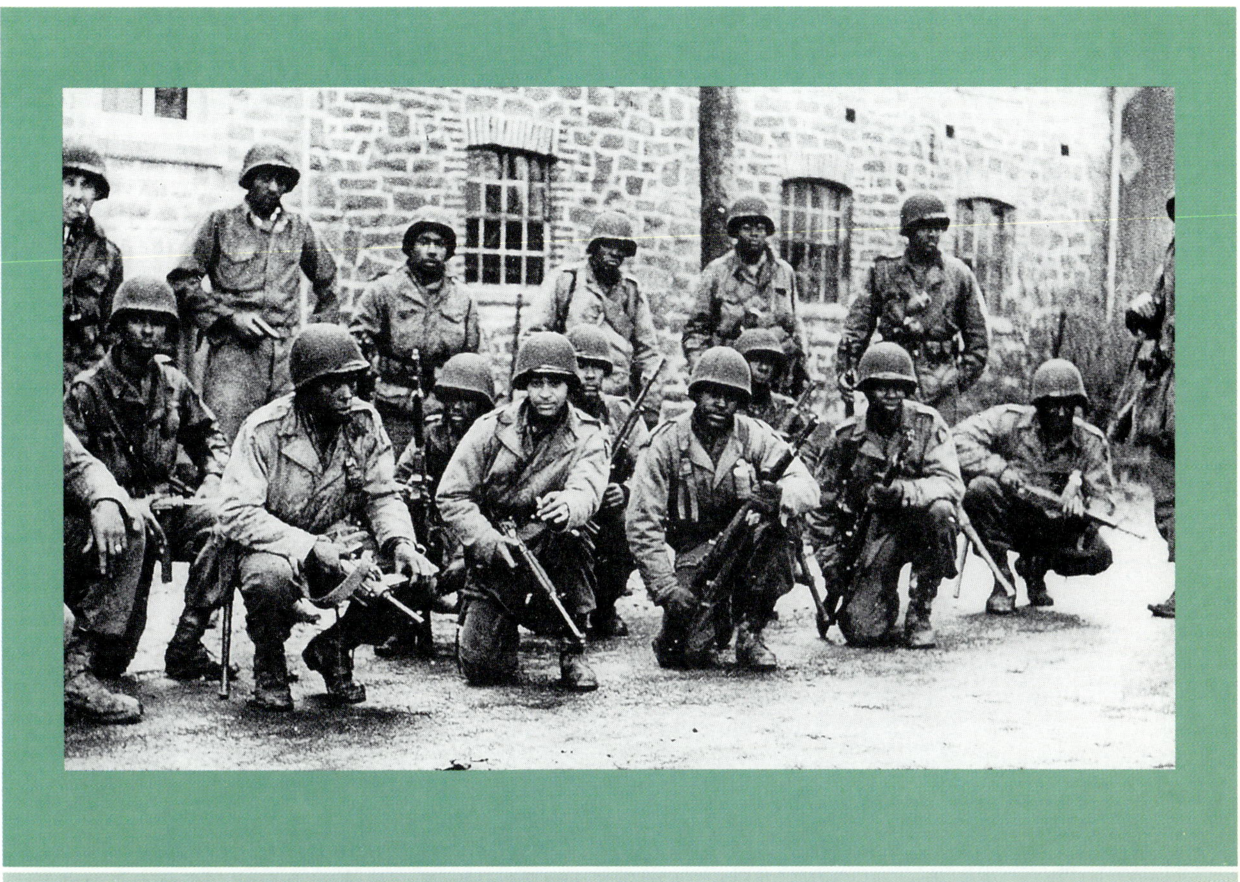

The doctrine of "separate but equal" died in 1954, with *Brown* v. *Board of Education,* but only after a long and bitter struggle. As this photograph shows, there were still segregated fighting units in World War II. This platoon of black soldiers had just captured a large contingent of German SS troops.

spite increasing legal attacks, until 1954; and more than one-third of the states plus the District of Columbia put it into practice. Time and again the Court struck down certain laws as *unequal,* but the standard remained.

Yet its days were numbered. Beginning in the 1930s, the Court ordered law schools and universities to admit qualified blacks or else provide truly equal facilities, which was probably literally impossible. In 1950 it found the Texas law school for blacks to be "clearly inferior" and a denial of the equal protection of Texas law to black citizens.[24] Two years earlier, it held that restrictive covenants, or agreements, to keep blacks out of housing could not be enforceable. As early as 1946 statutes segregating interstate busing started to fall.

In other areas the president and Congress led the way. In 1941 President Roosevelt created a Fair Employment Practices Committee, which became the Fair Employment Board under President Truman; Truman outlawed segregation in the armed forces in 1948. President Eisenhower formed a committee to monitor bias in the administration of federal contracts. By the 1940s laws in half the states promoted equal opportunity even in the private sector, and the courts increasingly rejected attempts to segregate public facilities by leasing them to private entrepreneurs.

Brown v. *Board of Education* and the Civil Rights Acts

On May 17, 1954, the Supreme Court, after deliberating for two years, initiated what has been called the greatest social revolution of its generation. *Brown* v. *Board of Education of Topeka* struck down "separate but equal" forever.[25] Compulsory segregation in public schools was simply unconstitutional:

> In the field of public education the doctrine of "separate but equal" has no place. Separate educational facilities are inherently unequal. . . .[26]

Chief Justice Warren's opinion called public education "the very foundation of good citizenship." Drawing on the findings of psychologists and sociologists, he wrote that in segregated schools "a sense of inferiority affects the motivation of a child to learn." Therefore black children were "deprived of the equal protection of the laws guaranteed by the Fourteenth Amendment."

Warren was well aware of the crushing affect his decision would have on the South and its traditions. He understood how difficult compliance would be. The Court deliberated for two years because Warren saw the need for unanimity; two decades later, he credited the three southerners who joined in the single, brief opinion. And the Court delayed issuing an enforcement order for one more year while it invited the views of interested authorities; few offered any. Finally, on May 31, 1955, the Court called for "a prompt reasonable start" under the eye of district courts, which were to consider local problems. Nevertheless, it left no doubt that it expected compliance "with all deliberate speed." [27] As Justice Goldberg put it nine years later, the Court

> never contemplated that the concept of "deliberate speed" would countenance indefinite delay in elimination of racial barriers in schools, let alone other public facilities. . . . The basic guarantees of our Constitution are warrants for the here and now.[28]

Yet compliance was slow. Customs that have stood for years, whatever their moral implications, are not readily altered. All but the border states used every conceivable strategy to delay. In 1957 federal troops had to be sent to Little Rock, Arkansas, to overcome Governor Orval Faubus's interference with enforcement orders. By 1964 almost 200 state segregation laws had been tried to frustrate the hated judgment. Many legal and physical battles were ahead—but no state remained completely untouched by public school desegregation.

While *Brown* never directly mentioned integration, it led to important progress. Congress passed its first Civil Rights Act since Reconstruction in 1957; others were to follow in 1960, 1964, 1968, and 1988. Presidents Kennedy and Johnson banned discrimination in federally constructed or financed housing, and the Supreme Court, in a host of decisions, repeatedly struck down state laws permitting segregation in public facilities. Public transportation was opened to blacks in 1955, when the Interstate Commerce Commission issued a blanket order forbidding segregation in interstate buses and trains, as well as public waiting rooms; the Court made that ban stronger still in 1960. Laws forbidding interracial cohabitation and marriage went down in 1964 and 1967.

Building on the growing civil rights movement, the legacy of President Kennedy, and the persuasive power of President Johnson, the Civil Rights Act of 1964 aimed a death blow at segregated public accommodations and unequal employment opportunities. Its strict Title VI provisions withheld funds for school districts not in compliance with *Brown* and provided tools accelerating its enforcement. Meanwhile the Court made it clear that "delays are no longer tolerable." In October 1969, after 14 years, it used the case of Holmes County, Mississippi, schools to overrule the guideline of "all deliberate speed." All school districts now must end segregation "at once" and operate integrated schools "now and forever." [29]

A Nationwide Problem

In the 1960s, what had long been anticipated became fact: racial inequality was clearly a nationwide issue. The North, which all too often had gloated over the southern predicament, found itself deeply involved in the controversy. It was not a matter of legal or publicly mandated inequality—that no longer existed in the North. But discrimination in employment and housing did exist; and the vast gap in income and housing between blacks and whites, so prevalent in the cities of the North and West, led in practice to segregation in public schools. If the new civil rights acts blunted those facts, much remained to be done—against a backdrop of increasingly militant action in urban ghettos and other black communities throughout the land.

In August 1965, in the Watts section of Los Angeles, the era of boycotts, sit-ins, and other acts of nonviolent protest ended in sporadic bloodshed. By the close of 1969 some 260 cities had experienced riots, resulting in over 180 deaths—34 in Watts, 43 in the 1967 riots in Detroit. Thousands

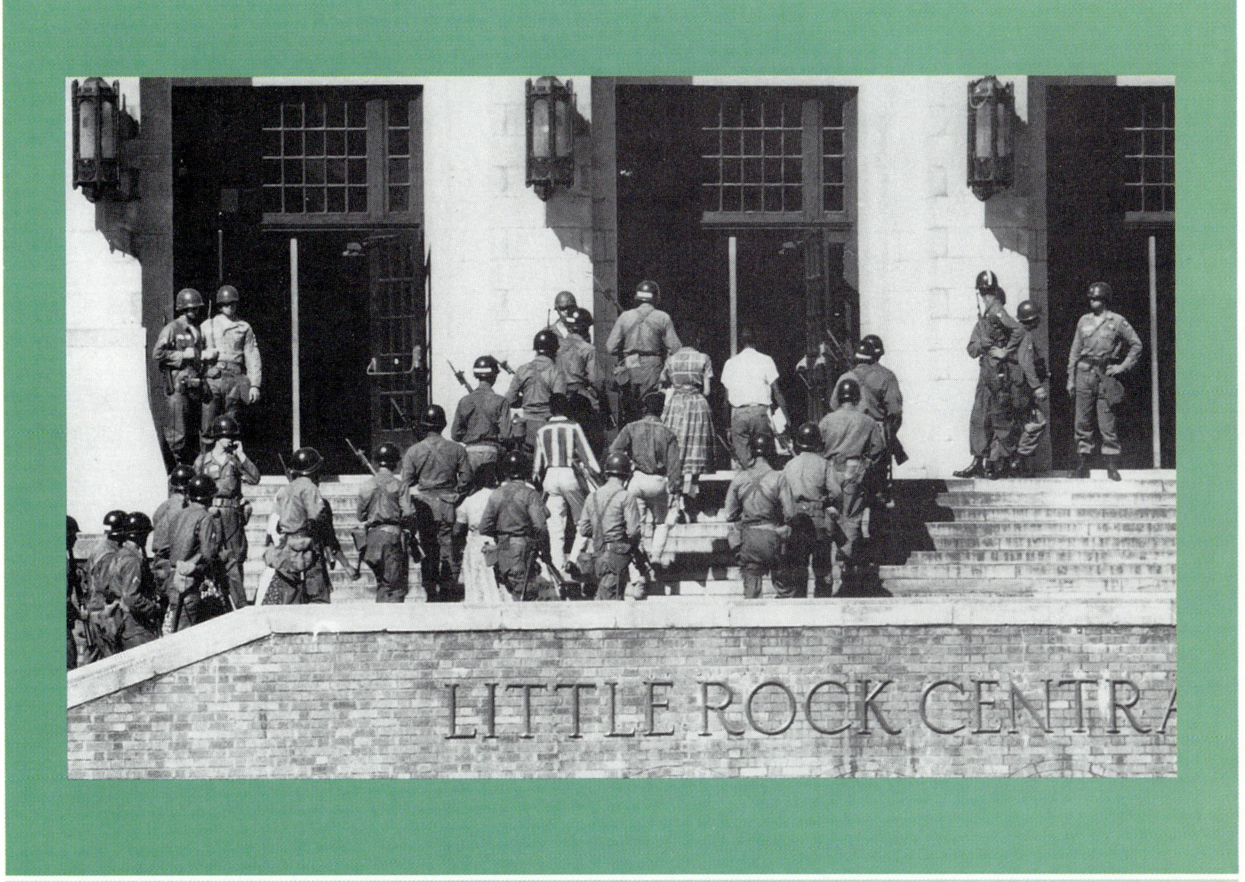

Resistance to the Supreme Court's desegregation decisions was both widespread and determined in the eleven old Southern states. In Little Rock, Arkansas, Governor Orval Faubus used the National Guard to keep Central High School, a public school, all white. President Eisenhower nationalized the Guard and sent units of the 101st Airborne to implement the Court's desegregation order. The admission of nine black students was a milestone toward racial integration.

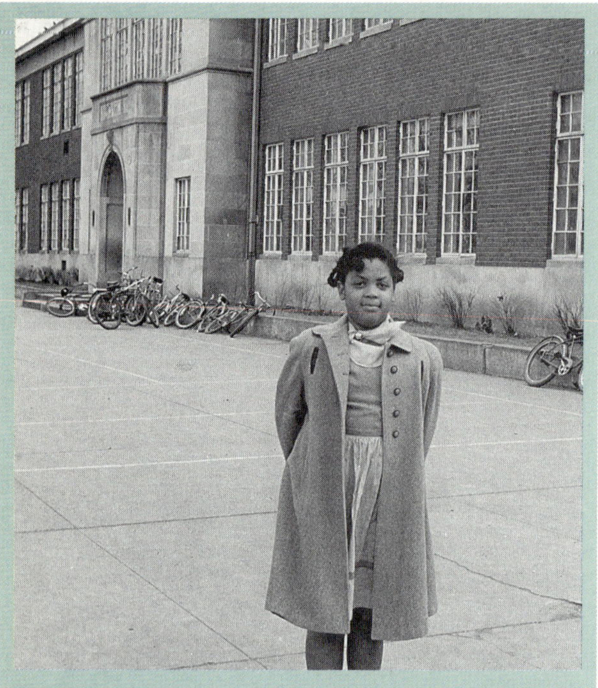

Linda Brown will always be associated with the 1954 and 1955 desegregation rulings that bear her name. Her case arose not in the South, but in Topeka, Kansas, in a pocket of Northern public schools that practiced segregation under state and local laws. Like other black children, she was bused beyond the all-white public school nearest her home to attend one that was entirely black. When she finally won her case for future generations, she was long past school age—and a mother.

were injured, tens of thousands arrested, and billions of dollars in property damaged.[30]

When the period of "all deliberate speed" came to an end in 1969, only 35 percent of black students in northern states went to integrated schools, compared to 38 percent in the South. That same year brought the first desegregation suit in the North. (District Court Judge Julius J. Hoffman, who ruled in that case against a suburban Chicago school district, is now better known for the "Chicago Seven" case. The trial of antiwar demonstrators at the 1968 Democratic National Convention turned into a colorful confrontation between the judge and the defendants; to many it seemed to typify the new period of turbulence.)

In 1977 the Supreme Court was to approve far-reaching court-ordered programs in city schools; these costly programs include remedial reading classes, teacher training, and counseling. But how could *desegregation* come about in the cities and suburbs of the nation? Where blacks and whites live apart, how could they be educated together? Chapter 19 takes up the growth of federal welfare and housing programs for the needy. The courts and the nation were divided by another answer.

Busing and Racial Quotas ■

According to Earl Warren, in 1954 the Supreme Court never even considered enforced busing of students to achieve desegregation. By 1971 it was an explosive issue. In one case, parents from Charlotte and Mecklenburg, North Carolina, pointed to the words of the *Brown* decision itself: if schools were to be "color blind," why not the assignment of students, too? The answer must have surprised not only much of the country but especially the most highly placed opponent of school busing, President Nixon. In April, speaking for a unanimous court, Chief Justice Warren Burger upheld not only busing but also all other devices to "remove all vestiges of state imposed segregation. . . . *Desegregation plans cannot be limited to the walk-in school.*" [31] The Court's decision did not in fact apply to northern-style segregation, based on neighborhood patterns, and it stopped short of requiring racial balance in schools. But it said that all-black schools created a presumption of discrimination, and it gave district judges broad discretion to use racial quotas as a guide in their desegregation decrees:

> All things being equal, with no history of discrimination, it might be desirable to assign pupils to schools nearest their homes. But all things are not equal in a system that has been deliberately constructed and maintained to enforce racial segregation.[32]

Two decades of unanimity on segregation ended the next year, when the four Nixon appointees to the Supreme Court dissented from what they called an effort to require racial balance rather than desegregation. The Court has rarely been unanimous on the issue since.

Defiance echoed in cities across the country, including Cleveland, Detroit, and Los Angeles, where the courts sometimes ordered busing across district lines, from the heavily black core cities to the surrounding suburbs. In 1972 Judge Robert R. Merhige, Jr., ordered public schools in Richmond, Virginia, which were 70 percent black, to merge with the overwhelmingly white schools of suburban Chesterfield and Henrico, but the Supreme Court ultimately disallowed it.[33]

Antibusing sentiment quickly grew. State legislatures tried to block busing by law and even by constitutional amendment. In a televised address, President Nixon asked for legislation to bring about a "moratorium" on busing, and Congress complied at least in part. Governor George C. Wallace of Alabama received a huge boost in his race for the presidency—and not only in the South. The uproar over Richmond led directly to a decisive Wallace victory in the 1972 Florida Democratic primary; and again in 1976 he ran almost exclusively on the busing issue, with striking success in urban Michigan and Massachusetts.

The reaction in urban centers of the North reached its peak in 1975. That year the heavily white, ethnic neighborhood of South Boston confronted District Court Judge W. Arthur Garrity, Jr. When the Boston School Committee, a popularly elected body, consistently refused to follow court orders, Garrity deprived it of much of its power. He continued to administer the strife-torn school system until 1985.

Already the courts had begun to take a softer line. Busing was overruled in Richmond and Detroit. After 1974, the Supreme Court generally insisted on proof of intent to discriminate before busing could begin. Also, once a school system has complied with a court-ordered plan, the Court has increasingly refused to order new busing zones to keep up with a changing population. While it let stand desegregation plans in Delaware and Kentucky, a minority of the Court (typically White, Marshall, Douglas, and Brennan) saw, in the words of Justice Marshall, "a giant step backward."

Riders to welfare and labor legislation have tried to strike at enforced racial busing as recently as 1982. Yet where there is proof of past or continuing discrimination, it would take a constitutional amendment to alter decisively the judiciary's power under the "equal protection" clause. No such amendment has passed either house of Congress, and none is likely to do so.

Affirmative Action ■

On other fronts, the pace of government pressure to remedy race and sex discrimination quickened. The Department of Labor and the Department of Health, Education and Welfare, relying on the Civil Rights Acts of 1964 and 1968, gave stiff mandates to labor, business, and educators. So did executive orders from Presidents Johnson, Nixon, and Ford. The Carter administration applied both forms of pressure even more strictly. By threatening to withhold federal contracts and grants, it insisted on specific goals for minority employment, school admissions, and personnel practices.

The Civil Rights Act of 1964 expressly forbids quotas, as well as "preferential treatment."[34] However, many states and federal agencies have required some form of *goals* or *guidelines,* in such sectors as business, industry, telephone service, and federally aided colleges and universities. At first the Supreme Court avoided addressing the issue. In 1974, when Marco De Funis sued the University of Washington, an unsigned (5:4) opinion declared the case moot (or closed). The law school had admitted 36 minority applicants with lower predicted first-year averages than De Funis's, but at the time of the ruling he had been admitted by order of a lower court. Justice Douglas alone attacked what is sometimes called "reverse discrimination":

> The Equal Protection Clause commands the elimination of racial barriers, not their creation, in order to satisfy our theory as to how

Continuity & CHANGE

Milestones in the Battle to Protect Civil Rights

Perhaps the most volatile and recurrent issue on the political agenda in America is civil rights; for our entire history one group or another has complained of unequal treatment and made demands for redress. Although the involvement of the federal government in the civil rights domain has been uneven, certain eras (especially during the Civil War Reconstruction period and the civil rights movement of the 1950s and 1960s) have seen flurries of legislation designed to rectify inequalities. Among the most important civil rights acts are these:

Civil Rights Act of 1866: granted citizenship rights to former slaves (who had been emancipated by the Thirteenth Amendment) born in the United States.

Civil Rights Act of 1871: provided means for enforcement of the equal protection clause of the Fourteenth Amendment, with the specific intention of prosecuting groups (e.g., the Ku Klux Klan) attempting to deny such rights as voting and office holding by blacks.

Civil Rights Act of 1875: the first law mandating equality in public accommodations (held to be unconstitutional by the U.S. Supreme Court in 1883).

Civil Rights Act of 1957: established a Civil Rights Division of the Justice Department, provided for means of enforcing the right-to-vote guarantee of the Fifteenth Amendment, and created the U.S. Commission on Civil Rights for the purpose of investigating civil rights violations.

Civil Rights Act of 1960: established a procedure to referee instances in which individuals are denied the right to vote; enables children of military personnel to attend

> society ought to be organized. The purpose of the University of Washington cannot be to produce black lawyers for blacks, Polish lawyers for Poles, Jewish lawyers for Jews, Irish lawyers for the Irish.[35]

It would be four years before the Court again looked at the volatile issue.

In 1976 it did reject a challenge to the Washington, D.C., police force: While blacks failed the application test in higher proportion than whites, an official act is not unconstitutional just because it places a "substantially disproportionate" burden on one race.[36] (An example came two years later. The Court upheld the National Teachers Examination, which failed four times as many blacks as whites, because it had a valid relationship to professional skills.) Already a 1971 ruling that put the burden of proof on the employer seemed to be qualified. Two other decisions—written by the Court's only black member, Thurgood Marshall—noted that the Civil Rights Acts of 1866 and 1964 also desegregated schools; enlarged the powers of the Civil Rights Commission; legislates criminal penalties for obstruction of federal court orders and other racially motivated belligerent acts.

Civil Rights Act of 1964: among its 11 titles, Title II prohibits discrimination in public accommodations, Title VI withholds federal monies from any institution practicing racial discrimination, and Title VII established the Equal Employment Opportunity Commission to protect individuals from unfair and discriminatory employment practices. The 1964 act is considered the most far-reaching civil rights measure ever legislated by the federal government.

Voting Rights Act of 1965: enables the federal government to monitor elections in order to protect minorities from discrimination in voting; requires bilingual ballots in certain precincts; bans literacy tests. This act has had an enormous impact on black voting.

Civil Rights Act of 1968: defines the rights of American Indians, forbids discrimination in housing sales and rentals, and establishes penalties for obstructing any individual's rights through violence or intimidation.

Civil Rights Restoration Act of 1988: has the effect of overturning a 1984 Supreme Court ruling (*Grove City College* v. *Bell*) which held that when an institution receives federal monies, only the program or activity actually receiving the money—not the entire institution—is bound by previous antidiscrimination laws. As a consequence of the Restoration Act, all programs and activities must comply with federal law if the institution receives any federal funds.

Source: Various issues of *Congressional Quarterly Weekly Report.*

prohibit discrimination against *whites.*[37]

The Bakke Case. The long-awaited decision on affirmative action came in June 1978.[38] The *Bakke* case had no clear winners or losers—and that may be precisely what the justices intended. Compared to the brief, unanimous opinion in *Brown* v. *Board of Education* a quarter of a century earlier, the six separate judgments, adding up to 154 pages, could not pretend to settle matters. If each side felt disappointment then, the controversy lingers today.

The University of California at Davis had twice rejected Allan Bakke, a white applicant to its medical school. Davis had set aside 16 of its 100 openings for minority students, and it frankly admitted that Bakke was more highly qualified than those minority students admitted under the quota system. No racial discrimination had ever been charged against the university. The Court's decision narrowly upheld affirmative action—and just as narrowly rejected rigid quotas. It ordered Bakke admitted.

Essentially, the justices formed three groups, with Lewis F. Powell, Jr., the key, swing vote in each part of the 5:4 ruling. Chief Justice Burger and William Rehnquist, John Paul Stevens, and Potter Stewart joined Powell in declaring Davis's admission system a violation of the "equal protection" clause. But the four went further: they rejected any system of "rigid" racial quotas in government-supported programs like higher education because it violated Title VI of the Civil Rights Act of 1964. In dissent, Harry Blackmun, William Brennan, Thurgood Marshall, and Byron White called for more permissive use of race as a factor in "compensatory" action to redress past wrongs generally. Powell agreed that race could be a factor, a "plus," but not the way Davis used it. Pointing to Harvard's policies, he wrote that a state university has a "substantial interest" in a diverse student body. That interest "legitimately may be served by a properly devised admissions program involving the competitive consideration of race and ethnic origin."

The *Bakke* case left intact most affirmative action programs aimed at minority groups and women, while it served a warning on obvious, rigid quotas—and perhaps other quotas as well. The *Wall Street Journal* termed it "The Decision Everyone Won." [39] It was also a decision needing further explication.

Weber. The *Weber* case started that process. At issue was a voluntary affirmative action program in the steel industry, at the Kaiser Aluminum and Chemical Corporation's plant then in Grammercy, Louisiana. With the agreement of the United Steel Workers Union, Kaiser reserved half the positions in an on-the-job training program for blacks. Excluded solely because he was white, Brian Weber filed suit in federal courts.

Weber based his claim on Title VII of the Civil Rights Act of 1964, which bans any racial discrimination in employment—against blacks or whites. Title VII states that the provisions of the act do not "require any employer . . . to grant preferential treatment to any individual or to any group because of the race . . . of such individual or group." If any doubt remained, the record of 83 exciting days of floor debate in 1964 could have dispelled it; the bill's backers had taken pains to reassure doubters. The U.S. District Court and Court of Appeals therefore both found the affirmative action plan illegal.

In a startling 5:2 decision, with Justices Powell and Stevens abstaining, the Supreme Court reversed the lower courts, however. Writing for the majority in 1969, Justice Brennan conceded that the lower courts had followed the letter of the law, but they had failed to follow its spirit. Since Congress had been concerned for "the plight of the Negro in our economy," it would be "ironic indeed" if Title VII could be used to prohibit "all voluntary, private, race-conscious efforts to abolish traditional patterns" of discrimination.[40]

In their dissents, Chief Justice Burger and Justice Rehnquist accused the majority of judicial activism—of having "totally rewritten a crucial part" of the law. As a member of Congress, wrote Burger, he would have sided with the majority, but here "Congress expressly *prohibited* the discrimination against Brian Weber" that the Court approved. Rehnquist, in what may be the angriest dissenting opinion in modern times, compared the Court to Harry Houdini, the escape artist. Congress, he concluded, sought to require racial equality; yet

> there is perhaps no device more destructive to the notion of equality than . . . the quota. . . . With today's holding, the Court introduces . . . a tolerance for the very evil that the law was intended to eradicate, without offering even a clue as to what the limits on that tolerance may be. . . . The Court has sown the wind. Later courts will face the impossible task of reaping the whirlwind.[41]

The *Weber* decision confirmed that some racial quotas could be legal—if adopted on a "voluntary" and "temporary" basis. But the growing split on the Court showed that it had not settled the affirmative action issue. When the Court next applied its ruling in the public sector, Justice White, who was beginning to regret his vote in *Weber,* joined in the dissent.

A Shifting Consensus. Surprisingly, the chief justice himself, who had so strongly dissented in *Weber,* in 1980 wrote a majority opinion in support of racial quotas. *Fullilove* v. *Klutznick* let stand a law setting aside 10 percent of a $4 billion public works program for "minority business enterprises." Rejecting the claim that Congress must be "color blind," Burger noted that it has the power "to enforce by appropriate legislation" the Constitution's equal protection guarantees. He repeatedly cited the temporary nature of the "narrowly tailored program" designed by Congress to correct long-standing wrongs.[42]

The passage of the law had demonstrated how controversial it was: the provision came in a floor amendment adopted without hearings. So now did the 6:3 split on the Court. Again several justices supported the decision but on far more permissive grounds, while the dissent bristled with anger. Justice Stewart accused the Court of a "racist" decision, virtually spitting out the word as he read his dissent in full from the bench.[43] Justice Stevens, who had abstained in *Bakke,* warned that the quota could breed more resentment than it corrects and compared it to Nazi attempts to define who is a Jew: How much "oriental blood or what degree of Spanish-speaking skill," he asked, "is required for membership in the preferred class?"[44] Nine years later, the Court would rule quite differently in a Richmond, Virginia, seemingly similar set-aside ordinance (discussed below). Justices Black mun, Brennan, and Marshall meanwhile now clearly formed a core supporting quotas to promote racial equality.

The Court first *overruled* an affirmative action plan in 1984. A lower federal court had forced layoffs or demotions of white fire fighters in Memphis, Tennessee, to protect gains in black hiring and promotion under an earlier court-ordered plan. That plan, a result of long-growing pressure for civil rights, had rapidly increased the proportion of black fire fighters—from 4 percent in 1974 to 11½ percent in 1980. But in a 1981 budget crunch, the city began to lay off fire fighters, beginning with those most recently hired, a group that included many blacks. A federal district court intervened, and three whites lost their jobs to blacks with less seniority. Both the fire fighters union and Memphis appealed to the Supreme Court. Justice White wrote that Title VII of the Civil Rights Act of 1964 clearly "protects bona fide seniority systems." The *Stotts* vote was 6:3; Justices Blackmun, Brennan, and Marshall were now the only dissenters.[45]

Two years later, *Wygant* v. *Jackson Board of Education* seemed to say both yes and no to racial preferences.[46] Again whites had been laid off before blacks with less seniority—this time schoolteachers in Michigan—and again the Court held that the mere fact of racial discrimination in the United States need not justify reverse discrimination. But the six separate opinions offered something for everyone, and the concurring opinion from Justice Sandra O'Connor, the newest Reagan appointee, recognized that "a carefully constructed affirmative-action program . . . need not be limited to the remedying of specific instances of identified discrimination." She saw "a degree of unanimity" in *rejecting* the Reagan administration's argument that affirmative action can be used only to remedy discrimination against *individuals.* With O'Connor, Powell, and Stevens in the center (the latter most often siding with those in favor of affirmative action), the Court seemed resigned to a case-by-case approach in the future.

Affirmative Action Today. Since 1986 the Supreme Court has twice ruled in favor of "hiring goals," "timetables," and "targets" for minorities—first in the case of Cleveland fire fighters, and again for sheet metal workers in New York.[47] It is clearly willing to support hiring and promotion programs that apply to minority groups generally, not just individual victims of discrimination. And it has left little doubt that states and cities have broad discretion to adopt plans that go well beyond court orders.

Just as clearly, the Court remains divided.

Rarely does any single written opinion command a majority. Two excerpts in the New York case, one from Justice O'Connor in dissent, the second from Justice Brennan in the majority, respectively, show that disunity:

> The legislative history, fairly read, indicates that such racial quotas are impermissible . . . and that even racial preferences short of quotas should be used only where clearly necessary if these preferences would benefit nonvictims at the expense of innocent nonminority workers.

> The availability of race-conscious affirmative relief . . . as a remedy for violation of Title VII also furthers the broad purposes underlying the statute. . . . We do not mean to suggest that such relief is always proper. . . . [The] court should exercise its discretion with an eye towards Congress's concern that race-conscious affirmative measures not be invoked simply to create a racially balanced work force.

Two holdings in early 1987 gave promise of providing the latest word on the issue, but they would do so only for two years. In *United States v. Paradise* the Court ruled that judges can order strict quotas for minority promotion to overcome "long-term, open and pervasive discrimination." [48] The decision supported an Alabama district court judge, who had commanded the state to promote one black state trooper for each white until it could develop acceptable promotion practices. Justice Powell made the controlling argument: the rigid quota was likely to be brief, "relatively diffuse" in its effect on innocent white workers, and appropriate where Alabama "had engaged in persistent violation of constitutional rights and repeatedly failed to carry out court orders." The minority asked only for a more "narrowly tailored" solution.

Four weeks later brought an even more far-reaching judgment. Justice Brennan's landmark opinion made it permissible to take both sex and race into account in employment.[49] Paul Johnson, who for 13 years had worked for the Transportation Agency of Santa Clara County, had scored higher on a qualifying interview for road dispatcher than Diane Joyce, the successful applicant. The 6:3 decision, in March 1987, was the Court's first decision giving job preferences to women:

> Given the obvious imbalance in the skilled craft division and given the agency's commitment to eliminating such imbalances . . . it was appropriate to consider as one fact the sex of Ms. Joyce in making its decision.

It meant that employers could use racial and sexual preference in hiring and promotions, without any proof of past discrimination, to bring their work force into line with the local labor market.

As so often on this issue, the dissent was blistering. A new Reagan appointee, Antonin Scalia, charged that the decision

> effectively requires employers, public as well as private, to engage in intentional discrimination on the basis of race or sex. . . . This is an enormous expansion, undertaken without the slightest justification or analysis. . . . A statute designed to establish a color-blind and gender-blind work place has thus been converted into a powerful engine of racism and sexism.

And again the center faction of the Court was decisive. In casting her vote with the majority, Justice O'Connor scolded it for going too far but resolved to go along "with the reality of the course that the majority of the Court has determined to follow . . . in light of our precedents."

No one could be so foolhardy as to conclude that these cases would indeed be the last word. Justices Rehnquist, Scalia, and White stood firmly opposed to most minority and sex preferences—and Justices Blackmun, Brennan, and Marshall, and usually, but by no means always, Stevens now, rested just as firmly in support. Justice O'Connor is a swing vote on the troubling problem as she would prove by her authorship of the Court's 6:3 holding in early 1989 that struck down as a violation of the equal protection of the laws provision of the Fourteenth Amendment the City of Rich-

The passion that ignited the civil rights movement sometimes went beyond the peaceful civil disobedience urged by Dr. Martin Luther King. The late 1960s saw bloody riots in such cities as Detroit and Los Angeles, leaving hundreds dead and thousands injured. The disorder was accompanied by heavy looting. As shown here, Miami has continued to experience sporadic violence through the much calmer 1980s.

mond (Va.) rigid thirty-percent "set aside" for minorities ordinance. With only Justices Marshall, Brennan, and Blackmun in dissent, she ruled for the majority of six that such wide-sweeping rigid racial quota programs in effect constitute unconstitutional reverse discrimination,[50] as being "suspect" and not "narrowly tailored." The impact of the final Reagan appointment, Anthony Kennedy, became clear in a series of 1989 decisions handed down by the Court in the waning days of its 1988–1989 term. Following the tenor of the Richmond "set aside" ruling, the Justices, closely divided, gave notice that change was in the wind in the heretofore generous judicial stances on affirmative action issues. Thus, it ruled:

- 5:4 that in attempts by employees to sue to try to show by use of statistical evidence that an employer's policies have resulted in discrimination against broad groups of workers, the burden of proof under Title VII of the Civil Rights Act of 1964 falls upon the employees. It is they who must prove that the policies they are challenging cannot be justified as necessary to the employer's business. [In effect, the decision overturned the 1971 *Griss* v. *Duke Power Co.* opinion (401 U.S. 424), in which the then Court had placed the legal burden on employers to justify policies that had the statistical effect of screening out women or minorities.] (*Wards Cove Packing* v. *Atonia*)

- 5:4 that Court-approved settlements (consent decrees) are open to subsequent legal challenges by white workers. The ruling, which also applies to sex discrimination cases, was based on the mandates of the equal protection of the laws provisions of the Fourteenth Amendment. (*Martin* v. *Wilks*)
- 5:3 that filing of lawsuits challenging seniority systems alleged to be discriminatory must be brought within 300 days of their adoption, in accordance with requirements regarding filing of such suits in the Civil Rights Act of 1964. (*Lorance* v. *A.T.&T. Technologies*)
- 5:4 that the Civil Rights Act of 1966 cannot be used to bring damage suits against state or local governments for acts of racial discrimination; that the Civil Rights Act of 1871 provides the

For many, abortion rights have become central to the battle against gender discrimination. As the controversy again came before the Supreme Court in 1989, a mass rally in Washington, D.C., called these rights essential to a full measure of equality for women. It seems likely that no Court ruling will soon settle the personal and moral passions on both sides of the issue.

only means to bring damage suits against state and local governments for the type of discrimination banned by the 1866 law. (*Jett* v. *Dallas Independent School District*)

Notwithstanding these decisions, it still seems clear that public and private agencies may adopt voluntary programs to hire and promote qualified minorities and women. Where there is a "manifest imbalance" in representation in various job categories, there need be no evidence of past discrimination. Job layoffs and firings face a tougher standard. Executive orders may—and generally do—require that federal contractors employ minorities. Finally, the courts may, and do, sometimes impose numerical quotas. But, as the quintet of 1989 decisions indicated, there are limits to affirmative action, and the current Court will not permit it to turn into reverse discrimination.

Sexual Equality

The *Johnson* case may have introduced gender into the debate over quotas, but discrimination on the basis of sex is part and parcel of the American dilemma. A women's movement existed for decades before it transformed the public conscience. Today the National Organization for Women, formed as recently as 1966, has 160,000 members, including both men and women. In many recent elections, men and women have tended to cast their votes differently; the importance of this "gender gap" in 1988 (see Chapter 8), like the run for the vice presidency by Geraldine Ferraro four years before, shows the changing status of women. Each also suggests how much women's special status in America remains an issue.

The obstacles facing women, of course, stem from their historically subordinate role in society. Sexually stereotyped, they could expect limited economic, political, and educational opportunities. While black Americans strove against a double standard devised to keep them subservient, women had to struggle against a deeply ingrained tradition designed to accord them a *protective* status as well. For example, a 1903 statute in Oregon limited women working in factories and laundries to a ten-hour day. In defending that law, Louis Brandeis, a future justice of the Supreme Court, devoted more than 100 pages to data on health, morals, and legislation abroad—all to protect women. David Brewer then spoke for a unanimous Court:

> The two sexes differ in structure of body, in the functions to be performed by each, in the amount of physical strength, in the capacity for long-continued labor, particularly when done standing, . . . self-reliance which enables one to assert full rights, and in the capacity to maintain the struggle for subsistence. This difference justifies a difference in legislation and upholds that which is designed to compensate for some of the burdens which rest upon her.[51]

Few jurists would agree now. Discrimination based on gender is today against the law. As with racial discrimination, the courts have had the task of defining equal opportunity and equal protection of the laws. However, they approach the problems of race and gender somewhat differently. The Supreme Court has been unwilling to treat distinctions based on gender as "suspect" or automatically invalid without a compelling state interest. While four justices do tend to put sex on the same footing as race, a majority, so far at least, has not. Where the law treats men and women differently, the court has demanded only "close" or "very close" scrutiny. As Table 5–3 shows, that can mean asking for a compelling state interest—or just "rationality."

One distinction that survived was in the draft registration law of 1980, which excluded women. A group of male registrants filed a class action suit: either men were being singled out, or else women were being denied *their* constitutional rights of due process of law. The Court disagreed. It ruled in 1981 that Congress had acted within its power to raise and regulate armies and navies, an area where its judgment is "particularly appropriate." When students refusing to obey were later denied federal funds, the Court called it "a plainly rational means to improve compliance." [52]

TABLE 5–3

Representative Decisions by the United States Supreme Court in Recent Gender-Based Discrimination Cases

Case	Year Decided	Issue and Disposition	Vote	Dissents
Reed v. *Reed,* 404 U.S. 71	1971	State of Idaho gave preference to males in intestate administration. Declared a violation of the equal protection clause of the Fourteenth Amendment, based on the Court's "rationality" test.	9:0	None
Frontiero v. *Richardson,* 411 U.S. 677	1973	Federal law that automatically qualified male service personnel for spousal benefits but that required female personnel to show proof of dependency. Declared unconstitutional infringement of due process clause of the Fifth Amendment, since Court found no "compelling" state interest.	8:1	Rehnquist
Kahn v. *Shevin,* 416 U.S. 351	1974	Florida law granting widows but not widowers $500 property tax exemption. Declared constitutional because a woman's loss of spouse imposed greater financial disability usually than a man's loss of spouse.	6:3	Douglas Brennan Marshall
Geduldig v. *Aiello,* 417 U.S. 484	1974	State of California disability insurance payments to private employees not covered by workmen's compensation, *excluding* normal pregnancies, among other disabilities. Upheld as a rational choice by state.	6:3	Douglas Brennan Marshall

TABLE 5–3 (*Continued*)

Case	Year Decided	Issue and Disposition	Vote	Dissents
Schlesinger v. *Ballard,* 419 U.S. 498	1975	Federal law on mandatory Navy discharges: women guaranteed 13 years of service; men automatically discharged after failing twice to be promoted. Upheld as rational because women have less opportunity for promotion.	5:4	Douglas Brennan Marshall White
Taylor v. *Louisiana,* 419 U.S. 522	1975	Louisiana statutory and constitutional provisions excluded women from juries unless they manifest a desire to serve via a written request. Declared unconstitutional as violation of equal protection clause of the Fourteenth Amendment.	8:1	Rehnquist
Stanton v. *Stanton,* 421 U.S. 7	1975	Utah law that provides for lower age of majority for girls than for boys in connection with parental obligation to pay child support. Struck down as "irrational" legislative action.	8:1	Rehnquist
Weinberger v. *Wiesenfeld,* 420 U.S. 636	1975	U.S. Social Security Act provision for payment of death benefits to surviving spouse and minor children in case of husband's death, but only to the latter in case of wife's demise. Struck down as violative of Fifth Amendment's due process of law guarantees.	8:0	None

TABLE 5–3 (*Continued*)

Case	Year Decided	Issue and Disposition	Vote	Dissents
General Electric Co. v. *Gilbert,* 429 U.S. 125	1976	Private employer's disability plan excluded pregnancies from coverage. Upheld as not invidiously discriminatory under due process of law clause of the Fifth Amendment. (Later overturned in corrective legislation by Congress.)	6:3	Brennan Marshall Stevens
Craig v. *Boren,* 429 U.S. 190	1976	Oklahoma statute prohibiting sale of 3.2 percent beer to males under 21 years of age but to females only under 18. Held to be invidiously discriminatory under equal protection clause of the Fourteenth Amendment, the Court here introducing the "heightened scrutiny" test.	7:2	Burger Rehnquist
Califano v. *Webster,* 430 U.S. 313	1977	Section of federal Social Security Act providing that wives may exclude three more of their lower earning years in computing average wage for retirement benefits than husbands may. Upheld as "benign," not illogical, and thus not constitutionally defective. Cf. *Califano* v. *Goldfarb,* 430 U.S. 199 (1977).	9:0	None
Vorchheimer v. *School District of Philadelphia,* 430 U.S. 703	1977	Philadelphia's existence of some "all-boy" and some "all-girl" public schools is permissible, provided enrollment is voluntary and quality is equal.	4:4	Brennan Marshall Blackmun Stevens

TABLE 5–3 (*Continued*)

Case	Year Decided	Issue and Disposition	Vote	Dissents
Nashville Gas Co. v. *Satty*, 434 U.S. 136	1977	Distinguishing *Gilbert, supra,* Court holds that losing all accumulated seniority when returning to work after pregnancy violates Title VII of Civil Rights Act of 1964.	9:0	None
City of Los Angeles Department of Water v. *Manhart*, 435 U.S. 702	1978	Municipal regulation that required female employees to pay 15 percent more into pension fund than male employees because women expect statistically to live longer than men. Declared unconstitutional as violation of equal protection of the laws clause of Amendment Fourteen.	6:2	Burger Rehnquist
Orr v. *Orr*, 440 U.S. 268	1979	Alabama law providing that husbands but not wives are liable to pay postdivorce alimony. Struck down as violation of equal protection clause of Fourteenth Amendment.	6:3	Burger Powell Rehnquist
Califano v. *Westcott*, 443 U.S. 76	1979	Section of federal Social Security Act providing benefits to needy dependent children only because of father's unemployment, not because of mother's. Struck down as violation of the due process clause of the Fifth Amendment.	9:0	None

TABLE 5–3 (*Continued*)

Case	Year Decided	Issue and Disposition	Vote	Dissents
Wengler v. *Druggists Mutual Insurance Co.,* 446 U.S. 142	1980	Section of Missouri's workmen's compensation law that requires a husband to prove actual dependence on his spouse's earnings but does not require wife to prove such dependence. Declared unconstitutional as violation of the equal protection clause of the Fourteenth Amendment.	8:1	Rehnquist
Michael M. v. *Superior Court,* 450 U.S. 464	1981	California statutory rape law punishing males, but not females, for sexual intercourse with an underage partner of the opposite sex upheld as not irrational becausc "only women may become pregnant." Law defines unlawful sexual intercourse as "an act of sexual intercourse accomplished with a female not the wife of the perpetrator where the female is under the age of 18."	5:4	Brennan White Marshall Stevens
Rostker v. *Goldberg,* 453 U.S. 57	1981	Draft Registration Act of 1980, confined to males. See text, *supra,* for discussion.	6:3	Brennan White Marshall
McCarty v. *McCarty,* 453 U.S. 210	1981	Federal law to preserve regular and reserve commissioned officers' military pensions as the service member's "personal entitlement" *not* subject to being considered for anyone else's benefit in a property or divorce settlement. (Later overturned by corrective legislation by Congress.)	6:3	Brennan Stewart Rehnquist

TABLE 5–3 ***(Continued)***

Case	Year Decided	Issue and Disposition	Vote	Dissents
Kirchberg v. *Feenstra,* 450 U.S. 455	1981	Louisiana law giving husband the unilateral right to dispose of property jointly owned by husband and wife declared unconstitutional as invidious discrimination by gender.	9:0	None
Mississippi University for Women v. *Hogan,* 458 U.S. 718	1982	Single-sex public institution of higher learning discriminates against males. See text, *supra,* for discussion.	5:4	Blackmun Powell Rehnquist Burger
Arizona v. *Norris,* 464 U.S. 808	1983	Title VII of Civil Rights Act of 1964, which outlaws employment discrimination on the basis of both race and sex, requires employees to be treated as individuals rather than as members of a group (here women's level of pensions).	5:4	Burger Blackmun Powell Rehnquist
Roberts v. *U.S. Jaycees,* 465 U.S. 555	1984	Rejecting freedom of association argument by the Jaycees, Court rules through Brennan that the "large and basically unselective" nature of the organization could not vitiate Minnesota's law forbidding discrimination in "public accommodations." See text, *supra,* for discussion.	7:0	None

TABLE 5–3 (*Continued*)

Case	Year Decided	Issue and Disposition	Vote	Dissents
Hishon v. *King & Spaulding,* 467 U.S. 69	1984	The no-gender-discrimination mandate of Title VII of the Civil Rights Act of 1964 reaches the issue of promotion of lawyers to the status of *partners* in a law firm. Burger's opinion overturns two lower federal court holdings to the contrary, rejects the argument that "partners" are not "employees" under Title VII and should therefore not be covered by its terms. Also turned aside freedom-of-association claims.	9:0	None
Grove City College v. *Bell,* 465 U.S. 555	1984	Title IX of the Federal Education Act of 1972 subjects noncompliant institutions to federal fund cutoffs, since any aid to students constitutes aid to their colleges. However, the law's verbiage "any educational program or activity receiving federal financial assistance" means *only* the *specific* program of a college and *not* the *entire* institution. The holding was reaffirmed 6:3 in 1986 in *Department of Transportation* v. *Paralyzed Vets of America,* 55 LW1004. (But Congress took corrective action in 1988 over President Reagan's veto.)	6:3	Brennan Marshall Stevens

TABLE 5–3 ***(Continued)***

Case	Year Decided	Issue and Disposition	Vote	Dissents
Board of Directors of Rotary International v. *Rotary Club of Duarte,* 55 LW 4606	1987	Decision similar to *Roberts, supra:* states may outlaw gender discrimination by certain types of private clubs. See text, *supra,* for discussion.	7:0	None
California Savings & Loan Association v. *Guerra,* 55 LW 4077	1987	Upheld a California law requiring employers to grant up to four months of unpaid leave to women "disabled" by pregnancy and childbirth, even if similar leaves are not granted for other disabilities. Dissenters saw a violation of the 1978 federal law prohibiting employers from treating pregnant employees differently from other employees who are "similar in their ability or inability to work."	6:3	White Rehnquist Powell
Johnson v. *Transportation Agency of Santa Clara County,* 55 LW 4379	1987	Civil Rights Act of 1964 permits employers to promote a woman over a more qualified man. See text, *infra,* for discussion.	6:3	Rehnquist White Scalia
New York State Club Assn. v. *New York,* 108 S.Ct. 2225	1988	Unanimously upheld city ordinance, against racial challenge, that prohibits discrimination based on race, creed or sex by institutions (except benevolent orders or religious corporations) with more than 400 members that provide regular meal service and receive payment from nonmembers for the furtherance of trade or business.	9:0	None

TABLE 5–3 (*Continued*)

Case	Year Decided	Issue and Disposition	Vote	Dissents
Watson v. *Forth Worth Bank and Trust,* 56 LW 5922	1988	In a further expansion of federal antidiscrimination law, the Court rendered it easier for women (and minorities) to prove discrimination in hiring or promotions, by ruling that employees—in cases challenging employers' "subjective" decisions—need not prove *intentional* discrimination. Instead, they may use statistical evidence showing "under-representation" of women (or minorities) in the work place.	8:0	None
Price Waterhouse v. *Hopkins,* LW	1989	Significantly altering the burden of proof plaintiffs must carry to prevail in many lawsuits based on alleged sex (and race and age) discrimination, the Court ruled that once a woman presents evidence that she was denied promotion because of illegal "sex stereotyping," it is up to the employer to prove that there were other, legitimate, reasons for denying the promotion.	6:3	Kennedy Rehnquist Scalia

Still, the standards have been strict enough to demand far greater fairness in employment. The Court has agreed with most claims of "invidious discrimination," and in 1981 it concluded that the Civil Rights Act of 1964 not only entails equal pay for equal work but also may extend to a standard of equal pay for *comparable* work.[53] It has concluded that Title IX of the Education Amendments of 1972 bars most sex-based discrimination in any education program receiving federal aid. And it has supported the resulting regulations issued by the Department of Health and Human Services.

The movement toward equality for women had its first success in the pioneering West. Wyoming granted women the right to vote in 1869. It was an isolated victory, but when Congress objected to "this petticoat provision" in the territory's application for statehood in 1890, the legislature replied that it would stay out of the Union for 100 years rather than enter without suffrage for women. Led by the West, over half the states had granted that right by the end of World War I, and the Nineteenth Amendment in 1920 extended it to all federal and state elections. Still, as Judge Ruth Bader Ginsburg of the U.S. Circuit Court has said, "the Constitution remained an empty cupboard for sex equality claims." It would take another 50 years to achieve the changes that many now take for granted.

One catalyst was *The Feminine Mystique,* by Betty Friedan. The eagerly read book by the feminist and activist challenged the notion of a woman's proper role as wife, homemaker, and mother. The upheavals of the 1960s certainly also helped to change the consciousness of men and women. Yet surprisingly, the Warren Court, which decisively attacked racial discrimination, stayed passive. It generally upheld legal differences between men and women by invoking the standard of a "reasonable man," while women continued to be denied equal rights and equal pay. The Burger Court finally began to remove the disabilities imposed by federal and state laws in the early 1970s.

The feminist movement has not fully achieved its goals. The defeat of the Equal Rights Amendment, however, only underscores the actual economic, social, legal, and political gains. Women can point to such visible triumphs as a Supreme Court justice; nine members of the cabinets of Presidents Carter, Reagan, and Bush; several governors in the last decade; mayors of many of America's largest cities, including San Francisco, Chicago, Dallas, and Houston; and some 18,000 elective posts, among them about 15 percent of all state legislators. Women serve as presidents at the University of Chicago and the University of Wisconsin, to mention only two, and as deans of such prestigious law schools as Columbia University's.

Genuine change in the status of American women will surely continue. And the nation's commitment to affirmative action has clearly played a major role in the quest for equality.

Private Discrimination and State Action

In 1960 four black students sat down at a "whites only" lunch counter in North Carolina and refused to leave. It was the birth of the sit-in movement, giving new force to the battle against discrimination. As this event illustrates, the cause of equal rights for minorities and women involves the call for an end to private discrimination. Under the Constitution, however, private individuals are free to do what they choose—as long as they get no assistance from the state and violate no laws.

As long ago as 1883 the Court held that the Fourteenth Amendment forbids only the states and the federal government to discriminate, not the individual. The Constitution protects the freedom of all Americans—a freedom for intolerance *if* no laws are violated, but also the freedom from illegal discrimination. It requires drawing the line between *public* discrimination and *private* action. As Hugo Black noted:

> This Court has never said . . . that the prejudice of individuals could be laid to the state. . . . The worst citizens, no less than the best is entitled to equal protection of the laws of his state and his nation.[54]

Housing. In 1948 and 1953, the Court first began to define "state action." It held that, in the absence of legislation, restrictive housing covenants (private agreements to keep minorities out) are not unconstitutional; however, government could not help enforce those covenants. An example came in 1967, when the Court barely (5:4) overturned a California initiative that enabled owners to "decline to sell, lease, or rent" property "in their absolute discretion." [55] But if California could not enforce discrimination in housing, it could let local communities veto proposed public housing by special referendum.

The 1968 Civil Rights Act brought fresh safeguards. So did new court decisions based on an almost forgotten civil rights law of 1866. Discrimination in the sale or lease of property was now held illegal, and since 1988 the Secretary of Housing and Urban Development has had power to seek heavy fines against property owners who discriminate. That power also shields the handicapped and families with children. Still, private discrimination continues to exist.

Public Services. The sit-in movement raised new questions. Can a private entrepreneur refuse service or ask the police to eject intruders? When does peaceable assembly become simple breach of the peace or trespassing? In 1963 the Supreme Court reversed the conviction of demonstrators in many southern states, because in each case the local authorities had required segregation by law, public policy, or declared custom. It acted thus again barely ten days before passage of the Civil Rights Act of 1964.

This act advanced a new defense against bigotry in "public accommodations":

> All persons shall be entitled to full and equal enjoyment of goods, services, facilities, privileges, advantages and accommodations of any place of public accommodations . . . without discrimination or segregation on the ground of race, color, religion or national origin.[56]

The Court unanimously upheld the law that same year, relying on Congress's power over interstate commerce. The 1964 act covers even a recreation club in an out-of-the-way corner of Arkansas: Lake Nixon, some 12 miles west of Little Rock, had advertised widely for "membership," which cost only 25 cents and grew to 100,000 in a single year. Since food and equipment, such as a jukebox and canoes, came from outside the state, the club fell under the reach of federal law.[57]

One of the Court's first rulings on public accommodations, however, again went back to the long-neglected Reconstruction laws. It used the 1866 Civil Rights Act when a suburb excluded a black family from its park and swimming pool.

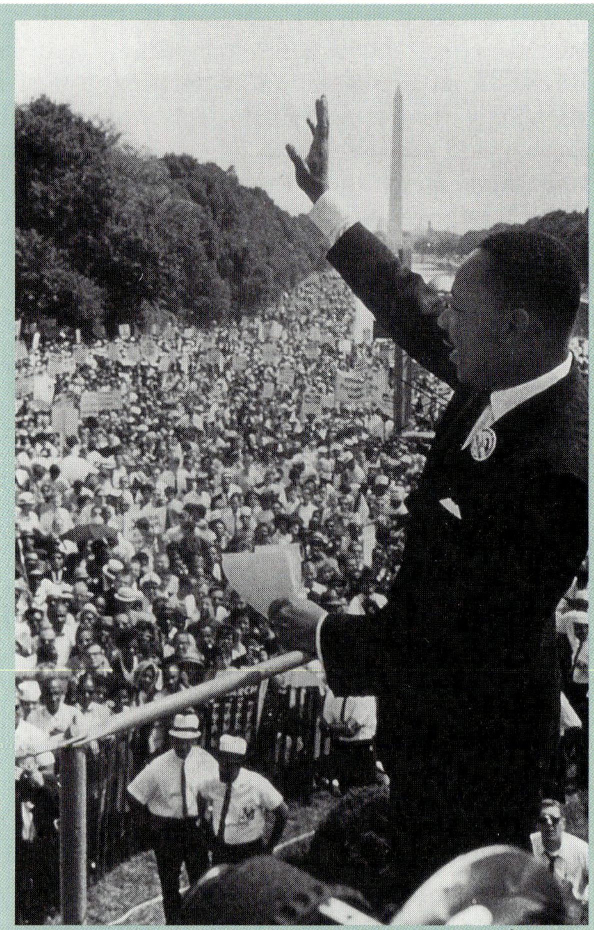

The movement toward full legal and constitutional rights for all races has turned on court decisions, the passage of federal law—and active political participation. A leading figure in the fight for civil rights was Dr. Martin Luther King, shown here as he delivered his historic "I Have a Dream" speech during the 1963 march on Washington. His assassination in 1968 was a major American tragedy.

Similarly, the Court denied that a "recreation association" could fairly draw its members from whites—and whites only—living within three-fourths of a mile of its swimming pool. It has also struck down wills barring blacks from a public park or private school. One city *did* manage to avoid desegregation: it closed all its public swimming

School Desegregation and a Historic Ruling

What was really meant by the Supreme Court's order to desegregate "with all deliberate speed"? Consider what actually happened in Prince Edward County, Virginia.

In 1951, black students there went on strike over conditions at the all-black high school, demanding facilities equal to those of whites. Black parents later filed suit for their children to be admitted to white schools. Their suit became one of the four cases that formed *Brown* v. *Board of Education.* That historic ruling held that the county schools were unconstitutional. Here is what happened next:

1959: Under federal court order to desegregate the public schools in the fall semester, the county board of supervisors instead closes them.

Fall 1959: The private Prince Edward Academy opens for 1200 white children.

September 1963: An emergency "free school" for black students opens in Prince Edward County under a Kennedy administration initiative.

September 1964: Under federal court order, public schools reopen to about 1400 blacks and whites.

July 1976: Civil rights groups and black parents file a class action suit against the Internal Revenue Service. That suit challenges the tax-exempt status of Prince Edward Academy and other private white schools.

August 1978: The IRS revokes the academy's tax-exempt status after the school refuses to adopt a nondiscriminatory admissions policy.

January 1982: The Reagan administration tries to revoke the policy that had ended the tax-exempt status of Prince Edward Academy and 100 other allegedly discriminatory schools.

May 1983: The Supreme Court rules that the federal government can and should withhold tax-exempt status from schools that practice racial discrimination.

August 1985: The IRS restores the academy's tax-exempt status, retroactive to October 1984.

Spring 1986: The academy appoints its first black director. It also advertises that it is seeking black students and creates a fund to help black families pay for tuition.

Fall 1986: The academy admits its first black students.

Source: *The Washington Post,* December 15, 1986.

pools rather than admit blacks [58] (but the city voluntarily reopened its pools on a desegregated basis a few years later).

Private Clubs. In one of these cases, the Court noted that it refused to acknowledge the facilities as a "private club at any level." For a truly private club, liberty to associate freely appears to outweigh egalitarianism. Can the Loyal Order of Moose limit membership in its 2000 lodges to adult white males who are of "good moral character" and "express a belief in a supreme being"? If it pays its taxes and receives no government aid? The answer depends on the terms and status of state law.

K. Leroy Irvis, black majority leader of the Pennsylvania House of Representatives, tested that notion in 1972. As a guest of Lodge 107, he had been refused food—and a drink. The Supreme Court ruled that the state liquor license alone does not involve the state in discriminatory action.[59] But the Court was later to open the Minnesota Jaycees and 19,000 Rotary Clubs to women, given their "large and basically unselective nature." [60] It also unanimously upheld in 1988 a New York law that bans discrimination in private clubs with more than 400 members that provide meal service and receive payment from nonmembers "for the furtherance of trade or business." [61]

Private Schools. In 1976 the Court ruled 7:2 that nonsectarian private schools may not deny "admission to prospective students because they are Negroes." [62] In the case, involving two Virginia schools, Justice Stewart again went back to the Civil Rights Act of 1866, which accords "all persons the same rights to" make and enforce contracts. Privacy and parental rights, he wrote, "do not provide easy or ready escapes" to "contravene laws enacted by Congress to enforce the Constitutional right to equality."

Justice White's dissent in the *Runyon* case accused the Court angrily of undertaking "the political task" of revising laws, "a task appropriate for the legislature, not the judiciary." [63] A few years later, however, "the Christian School cases" extended that decision: a *religious* school may exclude blacks—but then it may also lose its tax-exempt status. A public interest in outlawing discrimination in education "substantially" outweighs the burden that taxes may place on the exercise of religious beliefs.[64]

In a bombshell development, on April 25, 1988, the Court voted 5:4 to reconsider its *Runyon* ruling, and it heard intensive oral arguments that fall.[65] In June 1989 it rendered a divided verdict: On the one hand it upheld unanimously the reconsidered *Runyon* v. *McCreary* precedent and with it the here-at-issue application of the Civil Rights Act of 1866 as a tool in combatting discrimination in the private sector *at the initial hiring stage.* However, the Court held 5:4, with the newest Justice, Anthony M. Kennedy, writing the opinion, that the law could *not* be used to combat discriminatory treatment *on* the job, because Congress had not intended that 1866 statute to go that far. Other laws, of course, may be invoked against discrimination. (*Patterson* v. *McLean Credit Union*)

The explosive issue of private rights and public discrimination is far from settled. The Court must continue to defend and interpret our basic freedoms. It is at once a legal, political, and human institution. As such, it can never escape controversy—nor should it.

Equal Protection and the Constitutional System. This chapter and the last have shown the central place of freedom, liberty, and equality in our constitutional system. They have also shown the growth of government action to interpret and defend those civil rights and liberties. These actions have included all branches of government—acts of Congress, executive order and presidential leadership, regulations, and, crucially, judicial interpretation to articulate and defend our basic freedoms. Under a federal system, these sometimes parallel the actions of the states and sometimes preserve freedoms against claims of "states' rights." Under that system, it is "we, the people" who shoulder the final responsibility. The following chapters build on these ideas as they examine the institutions and processes of government and the public policy decisions of the 1990s.

Summary

- The religion clauses of the First Amendment are as important to our concepts of freedom and liberty as they are controversial. This is particularly true of the first of the two, which mandates against the establishment of a state religion.
- Protected by the First Amendment, freedom of expression signifies the freedom to communicate without prior restraint. Freedom of expression is nevertheless not absolute.
- The major public policy issue in constitutional law since the end of World War II has been that of achieving equal political, racial, and gender rights for all. The Fourteenth Amendment's "equal protection of the laws" clause and the Fifth's "due process of law" clause have been at the center of decisions involving claims of political, racial, and gender discrimination.
- *Brown* v. *Board of Education* (1954), plus its implementation decision in 1955, was a critical decision in ending racial discrimination and, ultimately, discrimination based on sex and ethnic or national origin. Although much remains to be done, the gains for equal justice have been dramatic.
- Controversy continues over affirmative action and its by-product, reverse discrimination. The Supreme Court is sharply divided over the issue.
- One of the most difficult questions facing the Court is that of balancing the alleged private right to discriminate—as long as no law is violated—and the public right to be constitutionally protected against illegal discrimination.

Readings on Freedom and Equality

Abraham, Henry J. 1988. *Freedom and the Court: Civil Rights and Liberties in the United States,* 5th ed. New York: Oxford University Press. Analyzes and evaluates the status of civil rights and liberties, with particular attention to the role of the judiciary.

Berns, Walter. 1976. *The First Amendment and the Future of American Democracy.* New York: Basic Books. A book that raises fundamental questions about the nature and value of First Amendment rights.

Chafee, Zechariah, Jr. 1954. *Free Speech in the United States.* Cambridge, Mass.: Harvard University Press. Still the classic study of free speech.

Glazer, Nathan. 1987. *Affirmative Action,* rev. ed. Cambridge, Mass.: Harvard University Press. An analysis and evaluation of the difficult line between affirmative action and reverse discrimination and its impact on both equality and liberty.

Kluger, Richard. 1975. *Simple Justice: The History of Brown v. Board of Education and Black America's Struggle for Equality.* New York: Knopf. The seminal work on the desegregation movement.

Oaks, Dallin H., ed. 1963. *The Wall Between Church and State.* Chicago: University of Chicago Press. A carefully compiled anthology of views by a host of experts on the issue of church and state separation.

O'Neil, Robert M. 1975. *Discriminating Against Discrimination.* Indianapolis: Indiana University Press. A sympathetic treatment of the affirmative action movement.

Miller, Robert T., and Ronald B. Flowers. 1987. *Toward Benevolent Neutrality: Church, State and the Supreme Court,* 3d ed. Waco, Texas: Baylor University Press. An up-to-date overview of the basic issues informing the separation problem and the perceived role of the government.

Schwartz, Bernard. 1986. *Swann's Way: The School Busing Case and the Supreme Court.* New York: Oxford University Press. An in-depth analysis of the compulsory school-busing-by-race controversy.

Thernstrom, Abigail M. 1987. *Whose Votes Count? Affirmative Action and Minority Voting Rights.* Cambridge, Mass.: Harvard University Press. A significant treatment of the voting process in relation to egalitarian claims of electoral practices and results.

Wilkinson, J. Harvie, III. 1979. *From Brown to Bakke.* New York: Oxford University Press. An excellent historical account of the desegregation movement by an ex-Supreme Court clerk, professor, journalist, and now federal judge.

Part Two

Political Institutions and Processes

> *"Who shall speak for the people?*
> *Who has the answers?*
> *Where is the sure interpreter?*
> *Who knows what to say?"*
>
> — Carl Sandburg

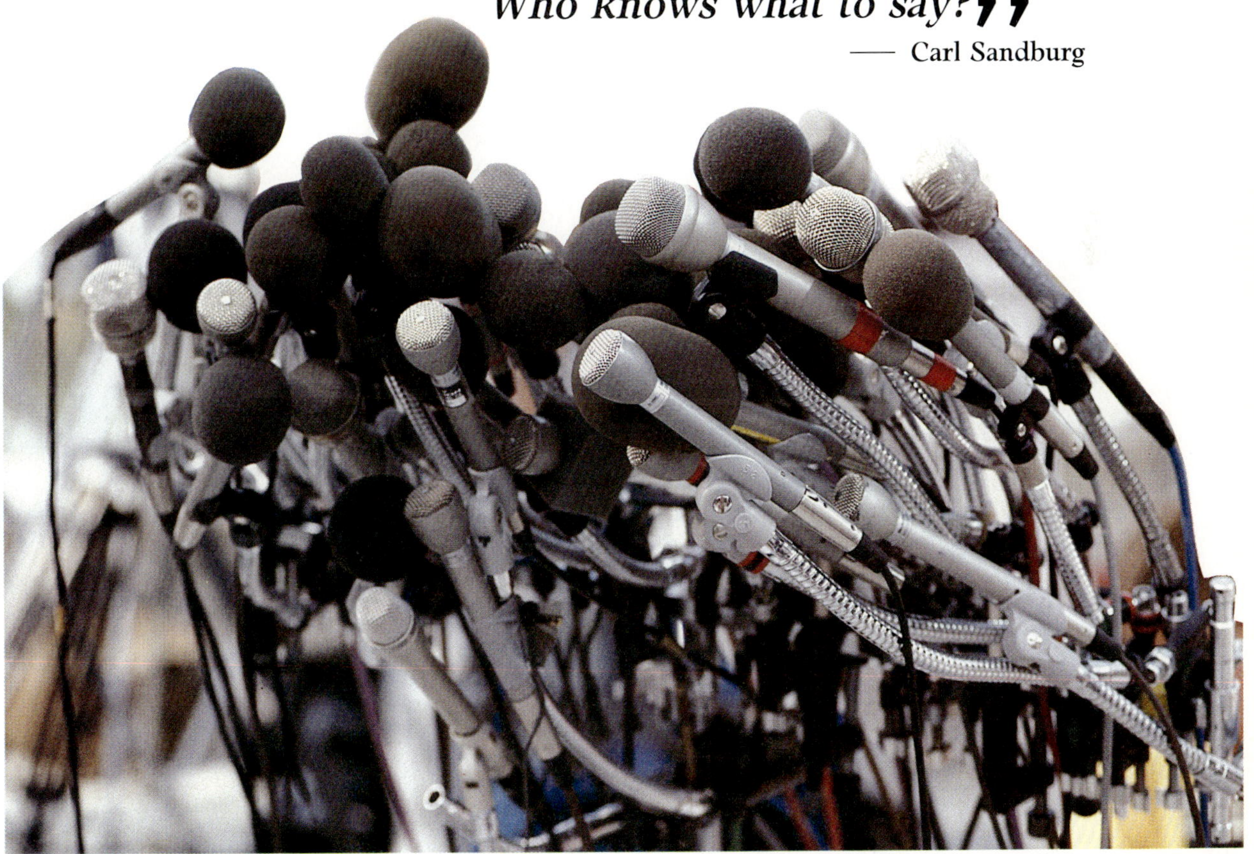

Chapter 6

Citizens, Participation, and Democracy

Active Political Participation

- Voting
- Turnout in Elections
- Election Campaigns
- Direct-Influence Attempts
- Protests and Demonstrations

Passive Participation

- American Political Culture
- Popular Support for Democracy
- Political Tolerance
- Trust and Cynicism

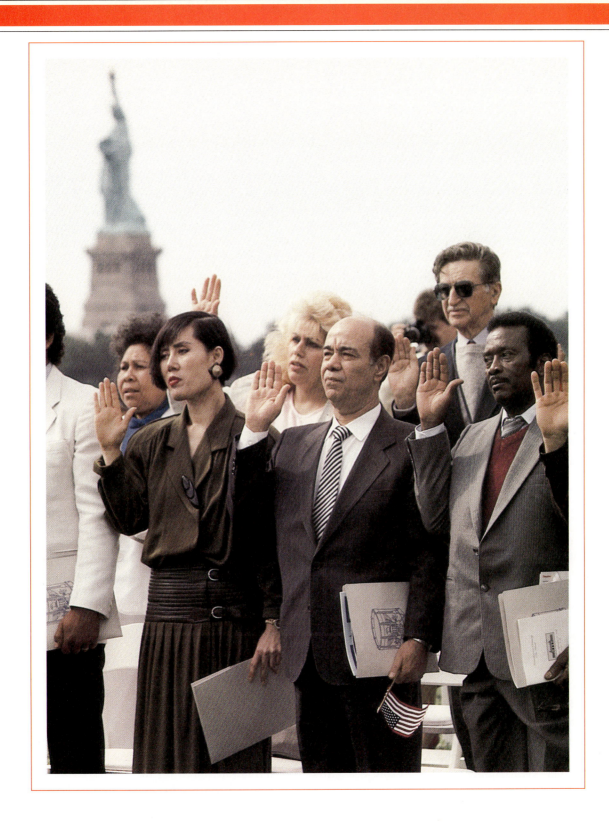

Central to any discussion of democracy are "the people." The rhetoric of democracy expresses faith in the ability of ordinary people to govern themselves. At the same time, the support of the people is crucial to the survival of a democratic government. Indeed, the people's support is important to the survival of any government.

Democracy provides for rule by the people. In a complex political system such as that of the United States, however, the people are rarely involved directly in governance. Government is run by leaders, representatives of the people. In a democratic republic, the people are a source of political demands; the public reminds political leaders that some things are more important than others, that some things are not going well, that changes need to be made. One measure of performance in a democracy is the extent to which a government responds to the demands of the people.

The people not only make demands on a political system, they also provide support for it. There is, in fact, a close link between political demands and popular support of government in a democracy. To maintain the loyalty and support of citizens, a political system must respond to their demands. Successful democracies encourage widespread participation because political activity by citizens is one way leaders find out what people want. Participation permits a person to register demands with political leaders.

The participation of ordinary citizens also allows them to express the basic values of society. When political leaders respect individual liberty, promote equality, tolerate diversity, or manage the political system, they are to a considerable degree responding to what the people want. The people help shape the *political culture*—those widely shared values and beliefs about the nature of political life and the activities of government.

To understand American democracy, then, we must focus attention on the people. But during the past 200 years in the United States, the idea of "the people" has itself changed greatly. From a small number of white male property holders in the early days of the republic, the *people* have grown today to include all adults. The number of adult citizens has increased from less than 1 million in 1790 to over 180 million in 1990. During these years, the country has grown from 13 states along the Atlantic coast to 50 states across a continent and beyond. The country has changed from a farm economy with a simple transportation and communication system into a complex industrial-service economy. The public has become a highly diverse collection of people.

This chapter examines the main forms of active participation by citizens in this complex society and the range of popular attitudes toward the nation's political institutions and leaders.

Active Political Participation

There is a basic distinction between active and passive political roles. A politically active person makes demands, expresses values, and uses time and energy to pursue goals. Political activity may be as simple as voting in an election or as unusual as a special meeting with the president to ask a favor. Political activity may consist of putting a bumper sticker on a car, going to a neighborhood meeting, or giving money to a political organization. Active political participation is the way ordinary citizens express demands and achieve goals. Although a president or governor has much more influence than the average person, millions of ordinary people can be a powerful political force.

Voting

The act of voting is crucial to democratic government for several reasons. First, most important leaders in the political system are selected by election. Second, voting permits the public to "throw the rascals out." And third, elections provide a major opportunity for people to tell political leaders what they want.

Active participation in politics is not limited to people who are eligible to vote. Women were active in politics long before they had the vote. Today some people who are too young to vote be-

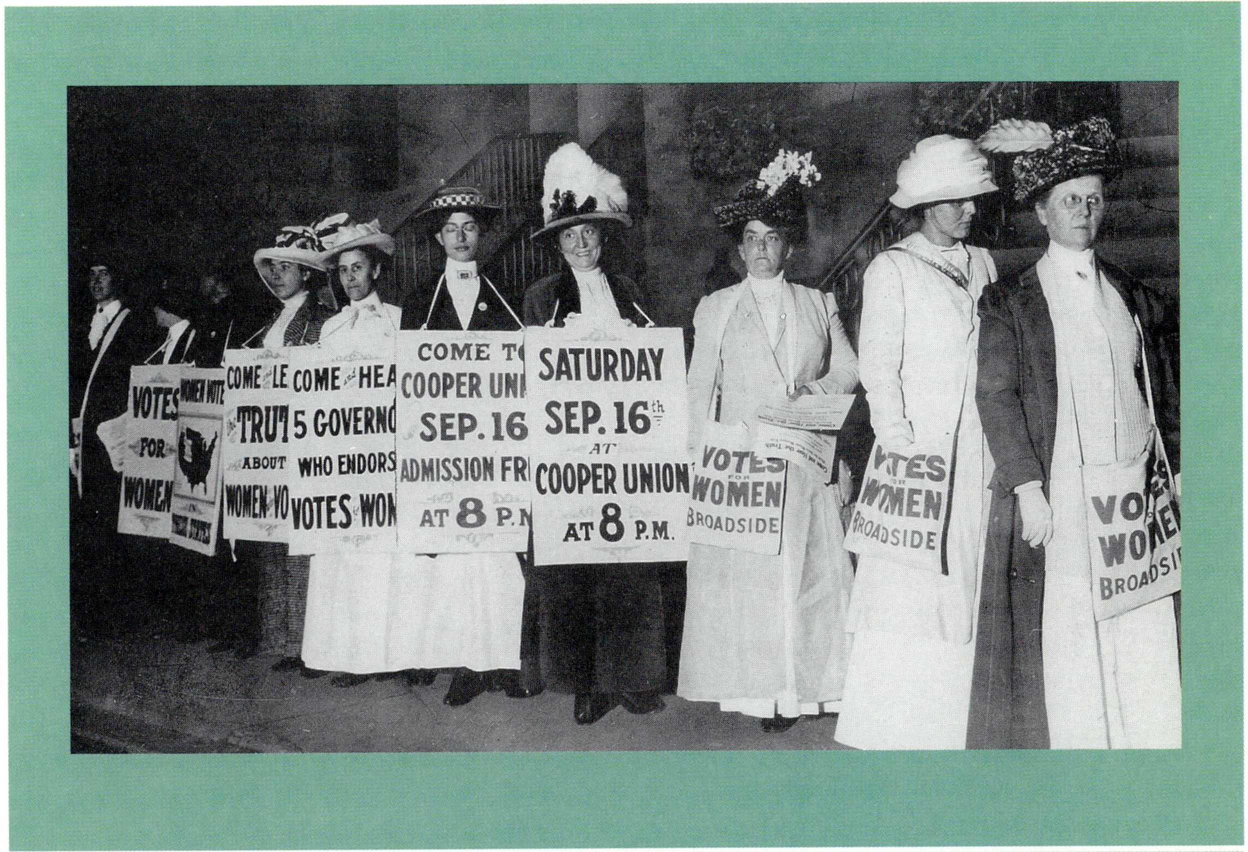

Early in the twentieth century women actively demonstrated to win the right to vote. The advocates of suffrage for women believed that the addition of women to the electorate would improve the quality of politics in the United States.

come active in politics. But voting has a special quality; it enhances other political activities. Leaders pay attention to the everyday claims of citizens because they recognize that sooner or later there will be another election.

Suffrage. A basic aspect of political development in America has been the expansion of *suffrage.* Although the American colonial experience was remarkably democratic compared with other countries, active participation in politics was not widespread. Political power was broadly shared by community leaders, but America was not a mass democracy. Voting was limited to property-owning males, and in some places the barriers to voting were high. Political parties and interest groups were yet to develop. Gradually, in the early decades of the nineteenth century, suffrage was extended to all white males in most elections in most states.[1] The story since then is told in Table 6–1.

In the early 1800s, two issues were raised over major extensions of voting rights. One clash was over women's suffrage. That would take a long time to resolve; women did not win the right to vote until the Nineteenth Amendment was passed prior to the election of 1920. The other conflict began with the issue of slavery but eventually included voting rights for blacks. That would take a war to resolve. Following the Civil War, suffrage was extended to black males; but by the latter part of the nineteenth century, most southern states had devised ways to disenfranchise blacks. The most recent extension of voting rights in 1971 changed the legal age from 21 to 18. This was less controversial than the extension of suffrage to blacks and women.

The battles over the extensions of suffrage resemble other political conflicts, with interests lined up on opposite sides. Perhaps clashes over the franchise are particularly important because they decide who will participate in other political disputes. Arguments over extending voting rights are usually stated in lofty democratic terms, but often simple policy goals lie behind that language. The long fight over women's suffrage, for example, was waged by people who believed that most women would vote for Prohibition. People who wanted to close the bars and prohibit the sale of alcohol fought hard to win voting rights for women. Those against Prohibition opposed women's suffrage. As it turned out, both sides were mistaken. Women as a group did not vote in a distinctively different way from men on policy or partisan choices.

Clashes over the right to vote are likely to be intense when the new additions to the electorate may change the balance of political power. The extensions of suffrage to blacks and women were expected to change the political system; by contrast, the enfranchisement of 18- to 20-year-olds was not viewed as politically significant.

Extensions of suffrage are changes in the legal conditions of electoral participation. But legal conditions do not determine who will take advantage of the opportunity to participate.

Voter Registration. Having the right to vote does not mean that a person will be eligible to vote in a particular election. A person must first be registered. To register in most places, one must have established a residence; 30 days is a typical requirement. States and localities differ greatly in how easy they make it for people to register. Five states now permit registration on the day of the election.

A basic purpose of registration requirements has been to prevent people from voting more than once by going from one polling place to another.

TABLE 6–1

The Expanding Electorate Since the Civil War

1870	Fifteenth Amendment—guaranteed suffrage to blacks (after it appeared the Fourteenth Amendment had failed to do so).
1920	Nineteenth Amendment—guaranteed women the right to vote.
1961	Twenty-third Amendment—extended the right to vote in presidential elections to the District of Columbia.
1964	Twenty-fourth Amendment—provided that failure to pay a poll tax or any other tax cannot be used to deny the right to vote.
1965	Voting Rights Act—banned the use of tests or other similar devices to deny the right to vote in certain parts of the country, mainly the South; voting examiners were to handle registration of voters in these areas.
1970	Voting Rights Act—suspended literacy tests throughout the nation.
1971	Twenty-sixth Amendment—extended the vote to 18-year-olds.
1972	*Dunn* v. *Blumstein*—Supreme Court ruled that long residency requirements were unconstitutional.
1975	Voting Rights Act—required bilingual voting information in parts of 24 states.
1982	Voting Rights Act—extended for 25 years.

The Constitutional Framework and Political Culture: Becoming a Citizen

There are two ways of becoming a citizen of the United States: by birth and by naturalization.

U.S. citizenship is conferred by birth:

- On anyone born in the United States.
- On the children of U.S. citizens born anywhere in the world.

U.S. citizenship is conferred by naturalization:

- On anyone of good moral character with five years residency who passes an examination. (These requirements may be relaxed for the spouse of a citizen, for members of the armed forces, and for elderly aliens of long residence.)
- On children under 16 living in the United States when both parents are naturalized.
- Through a special act of Congress.

Throughout American history, registration requirements have made it difficult for some people to vote and easy for others. Some states imposed strict registration procedures for cities and lenient rules for rural areas. Literacy tests were used in some states to bar voting by immigrants not fluent in English.

The most extensive use of registration to limit participation in politics occurred in the South. From the late 1800s until the Voting Rights Act of 1965, a variety of techniques were used to prevent blacks from voting. Some of these worked so well that they also prevented many white southerners from voting. The two most restrictive devices were *literacy tests* and *poll taxes.*[2] In the South, the requirement to pay a poll tax was often cumulative, so that taxes for past years would have to be paid as well. Wherever it was used, the poll tax discouraged the poor from voting. The use of poll taxes for federal elections was eliminated by the Twenty-fourth Amendment, adopted in 1964. The Supreme Court ruled in *Harper* v. *Virginia Board of Electors* in 1966 that a poll tax could not be used in any election.

In 1976, 63 percent of all southern blacks were registered to vote, compared with only 29 percent in 1960. By 1980, the impact of earlier practices on black voting had disappeared; blacks were registered in the South at levels comparable to whites. In 1984 and 1988, large-scale efforts were launched to register black voters. Attention focused on the drive to register blacks by Jesse Jackson's campaign. Other black leaders also urged their followers to register.

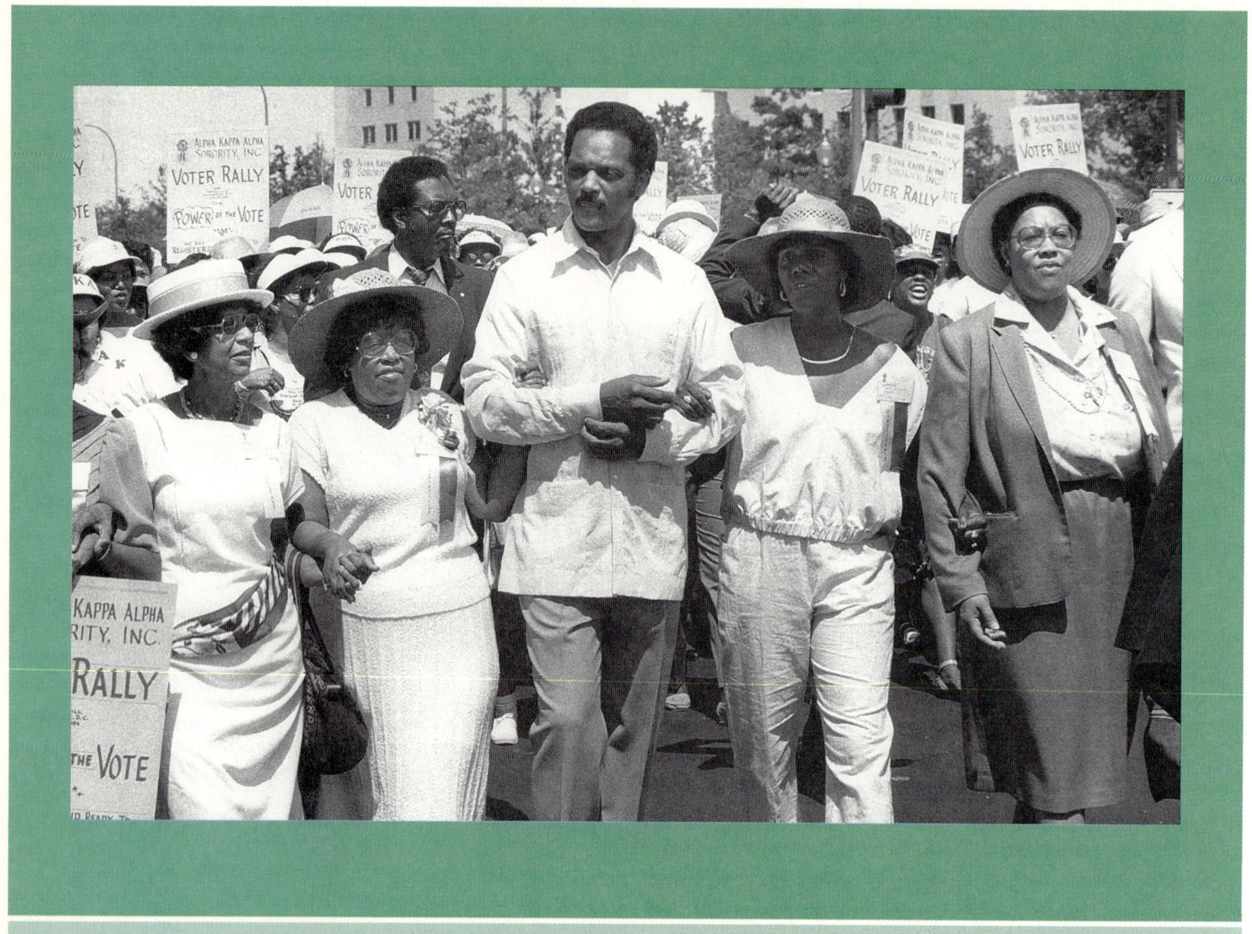

Jesse Jackson participates in a voter rally with members of the nation's first black sorority. Jackson, more than most candidates for the presidency in recent years, has used mass rallies and parades in his campaigns.

Registration requirements sharply affect participation. Three out of four nonvoters in 1988 were not registered. A major study of turnout by Wolfinger and Rosenstone estimated that relaxing registration laws would increase voting by 9 percent[3] and that most of that increase would be among the less educated and the poor. To state the importance of registration another way, 85 to 90 percent of registered voters go to the polls in presidential elections. Registering more people would almost certainly increase turnout.

In Australia and Belgium over 95 percent of the voting-age population participates in national elections, and the figure is barely lower for a dozen other nations, including Italy, Austria, Venezuela, Turkey, Sweden, Portugal, and Germany. Indeed, one can easily list over two dozen countries with higher turnout than the United States, which ranks barely above 50 percent. One reason is that some nations, such as Australia and Belgium, have compulsory voting—laws requiring electoral participation. Another is that other nations commonly hold elections on nonworkdays. But a third major reason is that other countries automatically register all persons eligible to vote, rather than requiring the individual to take the initiative. Registration

TABLE 6–2

Voter Registration in the United States

	Yes	No		Yes	No
National	72%	27%	*Occupation*		
Sex			Professional and business	77	22
Men	71	28			
Women	72	27	Clerical and sales	68	30
Age			Manual worker	64	35
18–24 years	48	51	*Income*		
25–29 years	59	40	$40,000 and over	82	18
30–49 years	74	25	$30,000–$39,000	78	22
50–64 years	84	15	$20,000–$29,000	73	26
65 and older	84	15	$10,000–$19,000	69	30
			Under $10,000	65	34
Region			*Religion*		
East	73	26	Protestant	73	26
Midwest	78	21	Catholic	72	27
South	68	31			
West	69	30	*Labor union*		
			Labor union family	78	21
Race			Non-labor union family	70	29
White	72	27	*Urbanization*		
Black	73	26	Center city	72	27
Hispanic	58	41	Fringe	73	26
			All others	71	28
Education					
College graduate	82	17			
College incomplete	77	22			
High school graduate	69	30			
Less than high school graduate	64	35			

Source: *Gallup Report*, no. 224 (May 1984), p. 10. Surveys from November 1983 to April 1984 were combined. Roughly 1 percent in each category in these surveys gave the response "Don't know."

laws in the United States on the whole do little to *facilitate* voting.

In many ways, Americans who are registered to vote resemble citizens who are not registered. As shown in Table 6–2, men and women register with about the same frequency as do blacks and whites. Throughout the nation, poor, less educated citizens are less likely to register than those who are well-off. Young people have a particularly dismal rate of registration. More than half the population between 18 and 24 was not registered in 1984.

Hispanics show unusually low levels of registration because so many are not citizens. But beyond that legal barrier, Hispanic citizens are less likely to be registered than either blacks or other whites. Registered Hispanics, however, are about as likely to vote as registered blacks and other whites. The lingering barriers for Hispanics are probably associated with language.

Overall, the failure to register is partially the result of individual social and economic conditions, but there is also a strong connection between political interest and registration. Most people who are not registered indicate that they do not care about politics and have no interest in the election

TABLE 6–3

Reasons for Not Registering and Not Voting

	Percent
Reason for not registering	
Recently moved	8
Permanent illness or disability	4
Time or place of registration inconvenient	3
Did not like any of the candidates	12
Not interested, did not care	42
Other reasons	13
No reason, did not know why	11
Reason for not voting when registered	
Out of town, away from home	15
Could not leave work, too busy	20
Illness or family emergency	16
Did not like any of the candidates	8
Not interested, did not care	7
Other reasons	10
No reason, did not know why	22

Source: Recalculated from data in CBS news release, November 18, 1984, CBS News/*New York Times* Poll, November 8–14, 1984; "The People, the Press, and Politics," *Los Angeles Times Mirror,* November 1988. Poll conducted by the Gallup Organization.

(see Table 6–3). The legal and administrative barriers to registration are a nuisance, to be sure, but the main obstacles are motivational.

Turnout in Elections

In recent years there has been a growing concern about the low turnout in American elections. Only about *half* the electorate votes for president. Even fewer turn out for less prominent elections. Since 1920, almost all adult citizens have had the constitutional right to vote. Yet, as Figure 6–1 shows, turnout of eligible voters in presidential elections has rarely reached 60 percent. Turnout in congressional elections is even lower; it declines steeply when there is no presidential election. Turnout in recent elections has been lower than during World War II (see the dip in the middle of Figure 6–1) and almost as low as in the 1920s.

Evidence suggests that groups given the right to vote do not immediately exercise that right. In recent elections, young people have not voted at a high rate—always well below 50 percent. Since the passage of the Twenty-sixth Amendment in 1971, the addition of 18- to 20-year-olds to the electorate has contributed to a lower turnout. After the passage of the Nineteenth Amendment in 1920, many women were slow to use their new right. The difference in turnout between men and women has not been significant in recent decades, though. By the 1988 presidential election, it was fairly easy for most Americans to register and vote; yet only about 50 percent turned out to vote. What causes low turnout? How serious is it?

A major cause is *indifference.* Many people are not interested in elections and do not care who wins

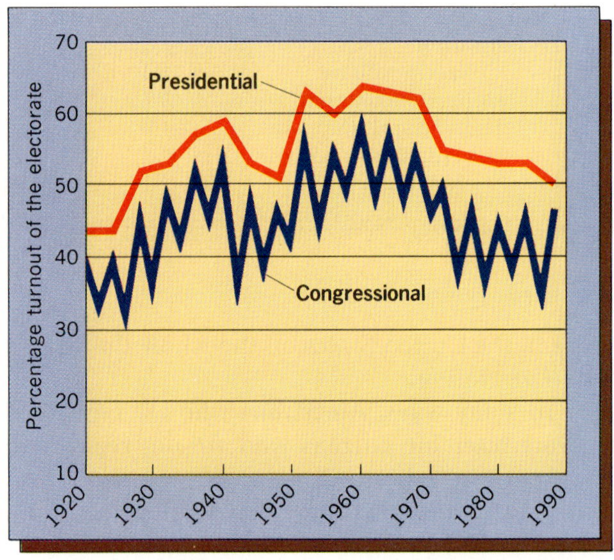

Figure 6–1 Turnout in presidential and congressional elections, 1920–1988. Source: U.S. Bureau of the Census, *Statistical Abstracts of the United States, 1971, 1987* (Washington, D.C.: U.S. Government Printing Office, 1982, 1988); *New York Times,* November 10, 1988.

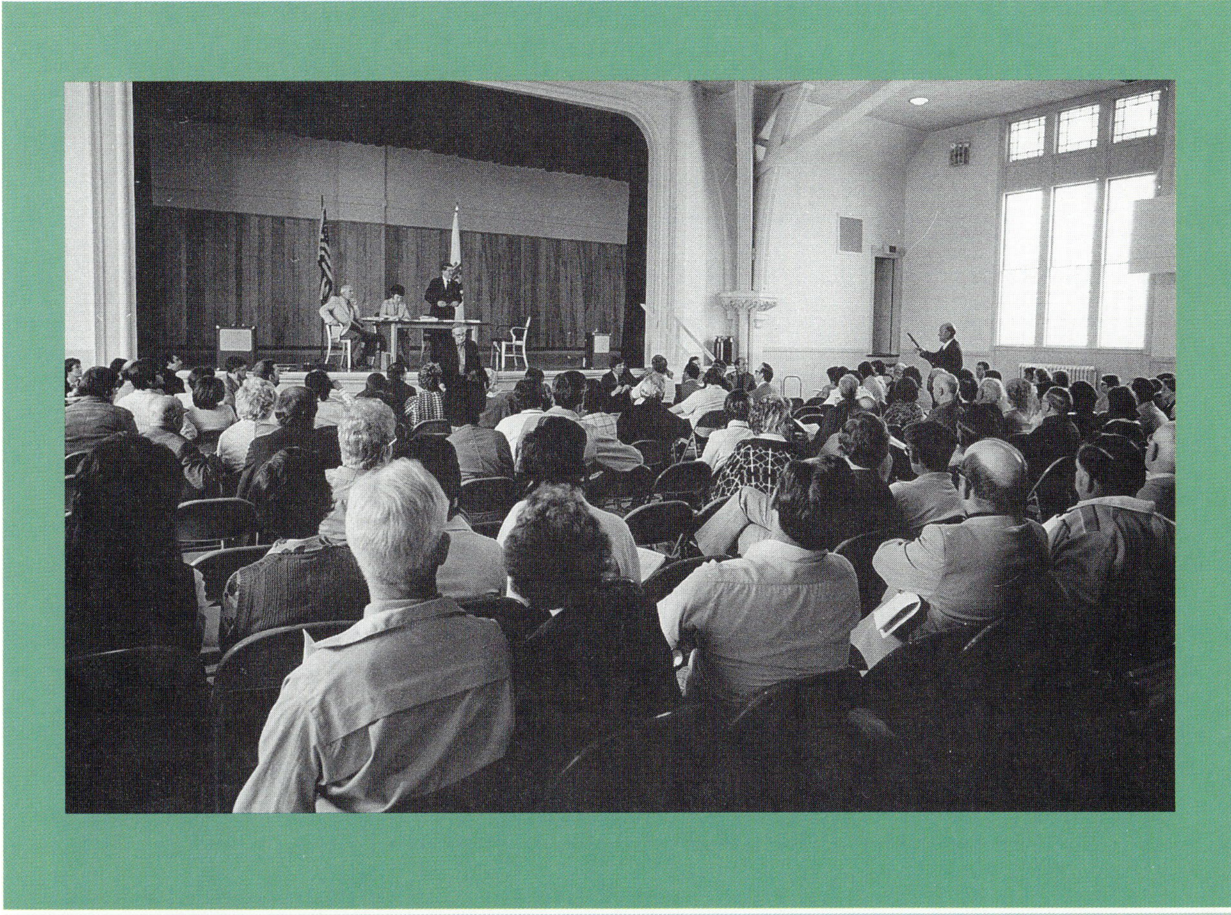

■ This town meeting in Massachusetts illustrates an unusually active form of political participation at the local level. In comparison with voting in an election, attending town meetings requires much more time and commitment from citizens. Not many Americans engage in political activities as actively as do these New Englanders.

(see Table 6–3 above). For a long time—at least since the 1920s—this has been the major cause of nonvoting. There are two ways to view this condition. We might be relieved that the uninterested (and perhaps uninformed) are not voting. Or we might argue that it is a failure of our political system. Of course, many people who do vote may not be interested in politics or be especially well informed.

Some citizens are discouraged from voting because they think it makes no difference or they find the election choices unattractive. This positive alienation is not too common in the United States. People who are well enough informed to be unhappy with all the candidates usually have other reasons for voting. Some voters may abstain because they are dissatisfied with their party's nominee and want to register their dismay. In an expected landslide election a few voters may not bother to vote.

Some groups in America regularly vote at high rates and others do not. Habitual nonvoters risk

Would Michael Dukakis Have Been Elected President If All Nonvoters Had Voted?

	Percent of Voters Who	Percent of Nonvoters Who
Preferred George Bush for president	53	50
Preferred Michael Dukakis for president	45	34

Source: Developed from survey data appearing in the *New York Times,* November 21, 1988.

The answer to the question, of course, is that there is no way to know for certain. But a *New York Times*/CBS News survey taken shortly after the election found that George Bush would have won by an even larger margin (11 percent rather than the actual 8 percent) if all nonvoters had voted. Forty percent of those who did not vote were young (under 30 years of age); this large group was actually more pro-Bush than the younger persons who voted. As contrasted with voters, nonvoters were younger, poorer, less educated, more likely to regard themselves as independents than as partisans, and less likely to perceive differences between the parties.

having their interests ignored by the candidates. Nonvoters give up their chance to influence the outcome of the election. Contrary to popular belief, there are no great differences in turnout among social groups. Members of the large religious groups participate in elections at roughly the same rate. The same is true for the major ethnic groups, men and women, and blacks and whites. The main differences in voting participation turn on age and social status. We know that young people are not as likely to vote as older people. We also know that better-educated people are more likely to vote than the less well educated. Age and education are related. Young people are better educated. This leads to contradictory expectations—that as young people they will fail to vote and that as well-educated citizens they will vote.

Figure 6–2 shows how these characteristics—age, education, and turnout—are interrelated.[4] We describe the pattern in this way. At each age, the better educated have higher turnout. This does not permit us to say definitely whether *age* or *education* is a more important influence on voting, but the pattern describes a long-standing characteristic of American voting behavior.

As Figure 6–3 shows, geography is another factor. Historically, turnout has been lowest in the South, where the substantial legal barriers to voting have only recently been removed. Turnout estimates can be unreliable, however, in the Southwest,

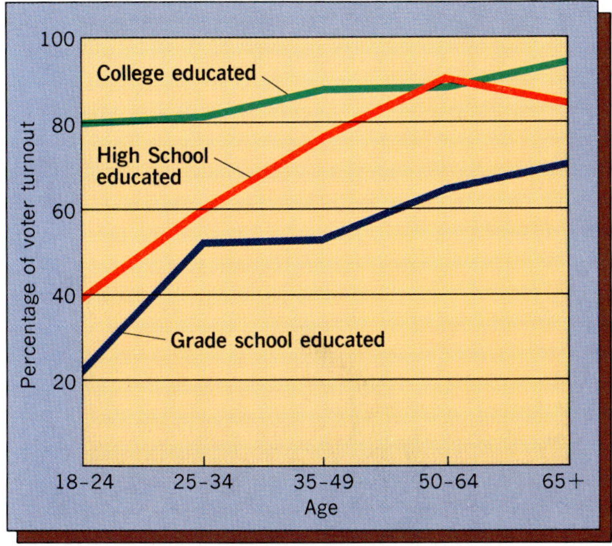

Figure 6–2 Turnout in the 1984 presidential election by age and education. Source: *1984 National Election Study,* Center for Political Studies.

Figure 6–3 Turnout across the nation for the 1988 presidential election.

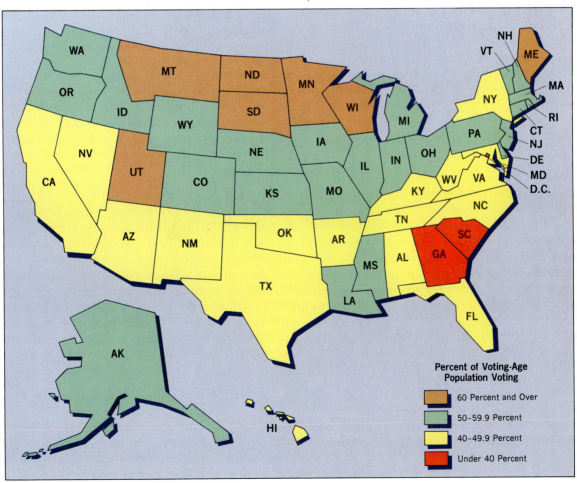

"And now I appeal to you non-voters. According to the latest polls, I have a substantial lead. Please do not spoil this by surprising us and coming out to vote."

where many adults are noncitizens. While noncitizens are not eligible to vote, they can easily be included in estimates of the total electorate, since the U.S. census does not distinguish them from citizens.

Almost all Americans believe that citizens have a duty to vote. In the 1980s over 88 percent of all adults *disagreed* with the statement that "so many other people vote in national elections that it doesn't matter much to me whether I vote or not." [5] Nevertheless, substantial numbers of people who believe it is everyone's obligation to vote do not always exercise their right. The evidence is that two attitudes are strongly related to turnout; one is the strength of partisan loyalty, the other the belief that people can have an effect on what government does.[6] Those most supportive of a political party, the so-called strong partisans, are most likely to register and vote; those who feel that they can make a difference are, too. Put another way, citizens who have no great attachment to either political party and no sense of political effectiveness feel less reason to register and vote.

Surge and Decline. A familiar pattern in American politics is that turnout in congressional elections is far less than turnout in presidential elections. Turnout is higher in elections that create interest and attract attention. This combination of high and low turnout was described by a prominent analyst, Angus Campbell, as "surge and decline." [7]

The idea of surge and decline is that in high-turnout elections, many less interested voters are attracted to the polls by the excitement of the campaign. These less interested people do not vote in low-turnout elections. Low-turnout elections are dominated by voters who are more interested, more partisan, and better informed about politics. This means that voters in low-turnout elections (such as primaries or congressional elections in nonpresidential years) are different from voters in high-turnout elections.

Continuity & CHANGE

Concern over Turnout in the United States

A total of 91,602,291 persons—50.16 percent of the *voting-age* population—cast ballots in the 1988 presidential election. This was the lowest level of participation in any presidential election since 1924. Yet concern over low turnout is not unique in American history. In the 1920s turnout was *lower* than it is today. There was probably greater worry over turnout in that era than today, and more organized efforts were made to increase turnout.

Writing about nonvoting in the 1920s, Harold Gosnell introduced his book with these words:

> In the fall of 1924 there were more Get-Out-the-Vote clubs organized than in any recent presidential election campaign. Shocked by figures which show the declining interest in politics manifested by the American electorate since 1896, party managers, editors, businessmen, leaders of women's clubs, and secretaries of civic organizations all over the United States united in a drive to increase the proportion of the eligible voters that took part in the presidential election. From the national headquarters of the two major parties, minute instructions went to all the local managers urging them to exert their best efforts in getting out the vote. An energetic lawyer established a National Get-Out-the-Vote Club, with headquarters in Washington and branches in the various states. The National League of Women Voters arranged for house-to-house canvasses and enlisted the services of a volunteer motor corps. The American Bankers' Association, the United States Chamber of Commerce, and the National Association of Manufacturers organized their membership for the purpose of registering a full businessmen's vote. Over two million Boy Scouts took part in the campaign of reminding citizens of their privileges and duties as voters. The pulpit, the daily press, the trade journal, the radio, the theater, and the lecture platform were all used as advertising media for the election.*

The reasons given for nonvoting in the 1920s were quite similar to those given today. The main reason for not voting was indifference; voters did not care or know about the election. The second most common reason was inability to get to the polling place. Another reason for nonvoting was the belief among women that women should not vote. Few people in the 1920s—or today—were positively hostile to the political parties or candidates.

* From Harold F. Gosnell, *Getting Out the Vote* (Chicago: University of Chicago Press, 1927), pp. 1–2.

This difference has political consequences. Less interested voters in high-turnout elections are more easily swayed by the campaign. One result is that congressional candidates from the party of the winning presidential candidate gain extra votes. Two years later in a low-turnout election, the same candidates win fewer votes because the uninterested voters stay at home (see Chapter 12).

This pattern of surge and decline explains in part why the president's party almost always loses congressional seats two years after the president is elected. Often the loss of seats is interpreted as an unfavorable judgment of the president. A more complete explanation would find the loss to be the result, in part, of the changing pattern of turnout. This is another way of emphasizing the importance of voting or not voting in the political system.

Americans are strongly committed to the values of elections. Even nonvoters believe everyone should vote. Most Americans see elections as a key factor in keeping political leaders in line. Both the leaders and the public recognize that the threat of electoral defeat is a crucial power in the hands of the people. Voting is the ultimate weapon in a democracy.

Election Campaigns

Since elections are so important in American democracy, it is surprising that so few people participate actively in election campaigns. Many citizens run for public office in the United States. A good guess is that about 1 million people run for some office every year or so. About a half million people serve in an elective office at any time. As a percentage of the adult population—perhaps one-third of 1 percent—that seems small. In actual numbers, however, that is a great many people.

Voting is the most common political activity in American society—next to just talking about politics. Compared with voting, relatively few people are actively engaged in political campaigns. And most people involved in a campaign do not do anything exciting; they prepare mailings, telephone, and distribute literature.

Less than 5 percent of all citizens work for a candidate or party during a campaign. Another 2 or 3 percent attend a campaign meeting or rally or some similar function. This does not constitute large-scale involvement by the public. Viewed in this way, active participation is not great. If we say, however, that around *10 million* Americans are actively involved in election campaigns in some way, it seems more impressive. In fact, millions of people sounds like a lot, and one might wonder how many more could become usefully involved.

In 1988 Americans were reminded that the disruption of a candidate's speeches is a form of campaign activity. Opponents of abortion were active once again in demonstrating against the Democratic ticket. Demonstrators disrupted several appearances by Michael Dukakis, although not as many—or as aggressively—as those of the Mondale-Ferraro campaign in 1984. George Bush also endured loud demonstrations at times during his campaign speeches. Perhaps only a few thousand people at most were active in these demonstrations, but they gained media attention and bothered the candidates. Hecklers raise some difficult problems for the political system. Must they be tolerated because they are exercising their freedom of speech? Or must they be stopped because they are interfering with the candidates' freedom of speech? American political and legal traditions provide no simple answers. There is some indication that hecklers become discouraged because their tactics discredit their cause.

Large numbers of people—over 10 percent—make financial contributions to candidates, parties, or other political causes. For most people, this is more of a token gesture than real political effort. Yet it is significant that Americans make a real contribution to political activities. The involvement of Americans in political campaigns is a driving force of the political system. Political interests and goals are converted into time, energy, and resources on which political campaigns help make elections an effective means for selecting and rejecting leaders. Indeed, it is difficult to imagine how American democracy would function if most people lost interest in voting and few were willing to work in campaigns.

Direct-Influence Attempts

Campaign activities connected with elections by no means exhaust the political activities people find useful. There are more straightforward ways for ordinary citizens to attempt to influence political leaders and shape government policy. People

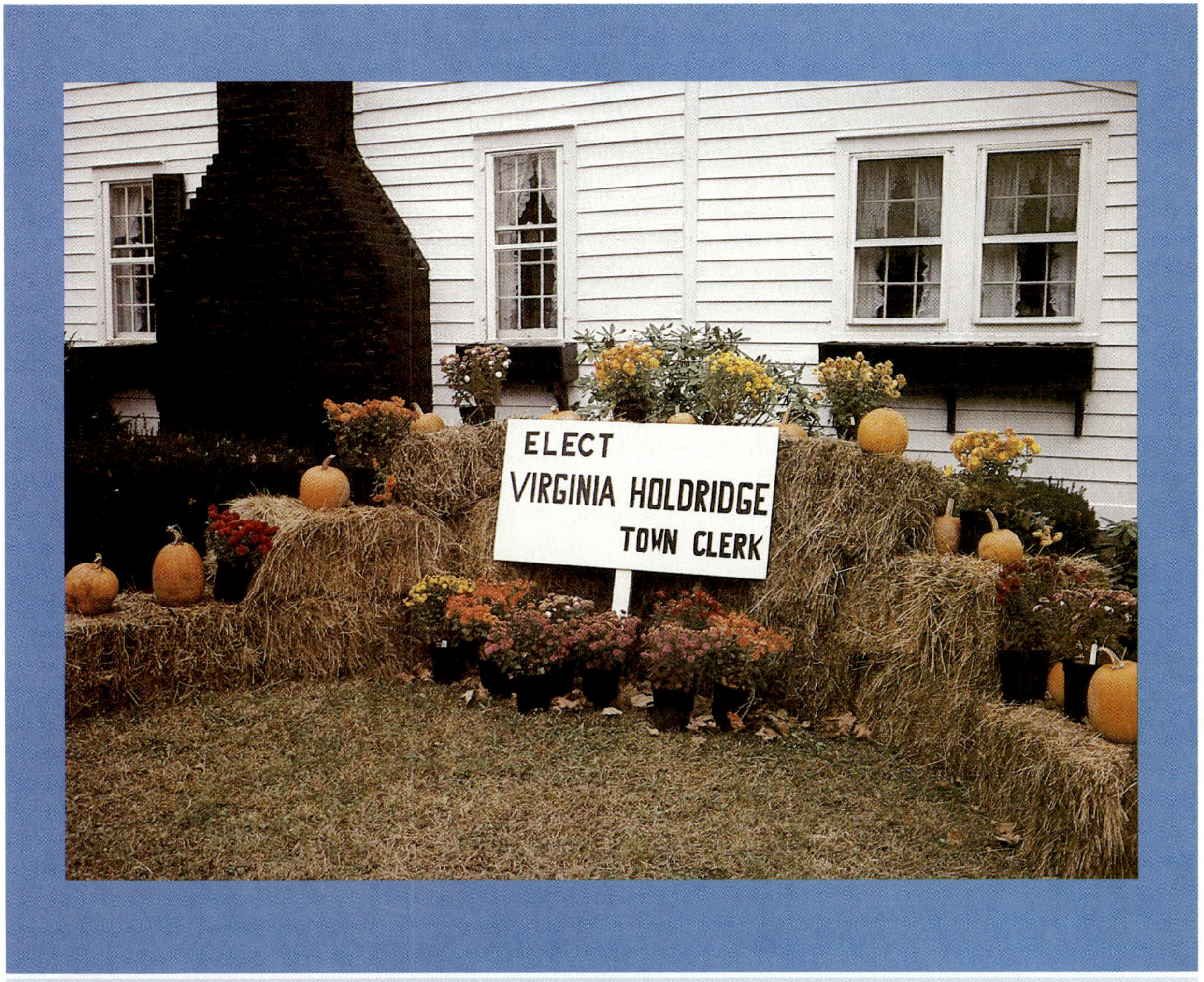

Most election campaigns are modest affairs based on hard work but not much money. Only candidates for the most important offices spend millions of dollars and advertise on television. In local elections more informal techniques are quite effective.

who want to gain specific political goals usually focus their efforts on the appropriate policymakers. Because campaign activity and modest financial contributions do not buy political influence, people may approach politicians directly or work through organizations with specific goals. More Americans are engaged in nonpartisan political activities than work actively in election campaigns.[8]

Large numbers of people engage in simple political activities such as writing letters, making phone calls, or perhaps signing a petition. Almost *half* of all adults report that they have engaged in some local political activity in the past few years. Over a *quarter* of all citizens report some activity related to a national problem. Almost all these activities are simple, direct, and uncomplicated. What is more, most people feel that their efforts are worthwhile.

Does Election Night Media Coverage Reduce Turnout?

On election day in 1972, at 5:30 P.M. Pacific Standard Time, NBC television news declared that Richard Nixon had been reelected president. This announcement came several hours *before* the polls were closed in the western part of the United States. In 1988, polls in a dozen western states were still open when CBS and ABC announced that George Bush had been elected president. These developments point to the continuing controversy over the impact of election night coverage on voter turnout.

First, it has been alleged that exit polls, based on interviews with voters as they leave the polling place, discourage others from voting, because they believe that a candidate has already won in their state. And second, many believe that voters in the western states will refrain from voting if they hear the networks declare a winner based on the results back east. In California, for example, about 3 percent of the population reports *not* voting because of early projections.*

The three networks have now agreed not to report exit poll results until after the polls have closed in a given state. But will that answer the concerns? Consider these points:

Question: Is turnout lower in the West?
Answer: Actually, turnout is slightly higher in the West and has increased in recent elections.

Question: Are certain types of potential voters discouraged from voting?
Answer: Political folk wisdom has held that Democrats vote late in the day, but there is no convincing evidence on this point. Wolfinger and Linquiti concluded that the highly educated might be more attentive to news and therefore more likely to be influenced.

Question: Why not delay television coverage of the election in a state until the polls are closed?
Answer: This is done in Canada, and Tannenbaum and Kostrich suggest it could be done in the United States.† Actually, most television stations across the country do not start national coverage until prime time anyway.

Question: Could the government prevent the television networks from declaring winners early?
Answer: Probably not, for such action would restrict the freedom of the press. Moreover, the problem is not always with network coverage. In 1980, for example, President Carter conceded the election at 6:45 P.M Pacific Standard Time (prior to poll closing in most of the West).

Question: Are there other possible solutions?
Answer: A uniform poll closing has been suggested, wherein polls in all states would close simultaneously (e.g., 9:00 Eastern, 8:00 Central, 7:00 Mountain, and 6:00 Pacific Standard Times). If the networks continued to withhold exit poll information until poll closing within a state, then elections in western states would not be "contaminated" by the election returns from eastern states. (These proposals usually ignore Hawaii and Alaska.)

* Raymond Wolfinger and Peter Linquiti, "Tuning In and Turning Out," *Public Opinion* (February–March, 1981), p. 56.

† Percy H. Tannenbaum and Leslie J. Kostrich, *Turned-On TV/ Turned-Off Voters* (Beverly Hills: Sage Publications, 1983), p. 208.

The simple forms of political activity are engaged in by typical citizens. The more complex forms of activity, however, are engaged in by fewer people. And these highly active participants are different from the rest of the public.[9] The most active citizens are better educated and better off financially than the average person. They are likely to be middle aged. They have experience and skills that give them confidence in dealing with political leaders or governmental officials. And they expect to be successful in their attempts to influence policy.

Unlike most voting, these forms of political activity may focus on particular problems or issues. Only referenda give voters a chance to indicate directly how they feel about an issue, and these chances do not occur often. But a letter or phone call to an official gives an individual an opportunity to express a view at any time. Elections are a cumbersome way to change public policy. Direct attempts at political influence are likely to be much more effective in achieving policy goals.

Groups organized for political purposes are so important in our society that it is surprising we know so little about their bases of support. Only about 10 percent of the public think of themselves as involved in political organizations, but actually most Americans are involved in groups that are active in politics. Labor unions, veterans, farm organizations, and churches are among the largest groups that engage in political activity (see Chapter 10). Smaller special-interest groups also have the support of millions of Americans.

The National Rifle Association (see Chapter 10) has a small but intensely committed following along with strong financial support, which has made the organization a powerful participant in American politics. Recently, political groups concerned with the environment and consumers' interests have also grown. Groups working for and against the Equal Rights Amendment have been well publicized. Older organizations such as the NAACP and the Urban League deal with many issues for a single clientele. Even though only a small percentage of the public actively supports these organizations, for most purposes that is all that is needed. Loyal, insistent supporters have influence out of proportion to their numbers. During election campaigns, as many Americans make contributions to political interest groups, usually to political action committees or PACs, as to political parties. It is possible that these various political groups will take more and more influence away from the political parties.

Protests and Demonstrations ■

There have been many episodes of great violence in American history. The Civil War is an obvious case. In the decades of frontier warfare with the Indian tribes, many people lived with violence around them. Labor disputes often led to violence. Business competitors such as railroad tycoons and newspaper publishers have at times fought each other with small, private armies. In some periods, lynchings were common.

In many dramatic ways, violence has disrupted society in recent years. Urban riots, antiwar demonstrations, and prison riots create the impression that violence is all around us. The assassination of one president, John F. Kennedy, the attempted assassination of two others, Gerald Ford and Ronald Reagan, as well as the killing of Martin Luther King, Jr., and Senator Robert Kennedy show violence to the political system in a terrible and unmistakable way.

Of course, very few people engage in violent political acts. Even peaceful demonstrations are not common political activities for most Americans. Ten percent of the public report they have picketed during a labor strike, 4 percent have been in a civil rights demonstration, and 5 percent have participated in an antiwar demonstration. Five percent of the public say they have taken part in a school-related demonstration.[10] Most of these demonstrations were peaceful and legal.

The public thoroughly disapproves of riots and violent demonstrations. On this matter, as on most others, opinions depend on the interest at stake. Although most people disapprove of political violence regardless of race, changing the question makes a difference among blacks and whites. When

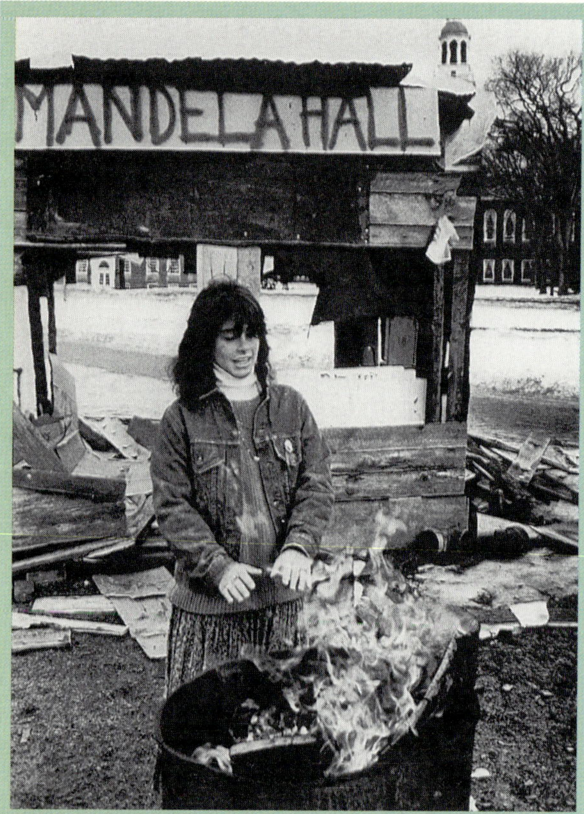

Protests and demonstrations take many forms. Students at Dartmouth College built shanties on the campus protesting apartheid in South Africa. Specifically, they opposed the school's investment in companies doing business in South Africa. Other Dartmouth students subsequently destroyed the shanties, escalating the conflict over the school's policies.

they read this statement, "The only time the federal government really pays attention to black problems is when blacks resort to violent demonstrations or riots," blacks and whites give different responses. Blacks agree with the idea overwhelmingly—by a margin of 70 to 30 percent. Whites answer just the reverse; only 30 percent agree and 70 percent disagree.[11] Quite possibly, many whites would change their answer if the question focused on them.

So very few people participate in demonstrations and protest marches. On the other hand, just one-tenth of 1 percent of the population would be a huge parade. A small demonstration may appear large on a television screen and attract a great deal of news coverage and publicity. A demonstration may draw more attention to a group's goals than they could receive through more conventional activities. Publicity may be hard to translate into political influence, however. In the late 1960s, for example, the well-known demonstrations against U.S. involvement in Vietnam had a reverse effect on public opinion. More people supported U.S. involvement after major demonstrations against the war than before. The demonstrations were successful in gaining media attention and probably influenced political leaders. But they failed to influence the public in the intended direction.[12]

The ordinary person contributes to the political system in a variety of ways both actively and passively (see Table 6–4). Most adults watch the evening television news frequently and read about politics in a newspaper at least occasionally. Between a quarter and a third of the people pay close attention to politics. They follow campaigns in the newspapers and watch various television programs on the campaign, such as debates between the presidential candidates.

Attention naturally focuses on activity. Voting, rallies, and demonstrations tell us about the demands made within society. Activity shows that some people want their taxes reduced, others want expanded welfare benefits, and still others want more money for pollution control—the list is endless. Activity also reflects the range of political conflicts. People make demands that conflict with demands made by others. Many people make demands that conflict with some of their other demands. Our attention focuses on political conflict as a special form of activity. Studying political conflict gives important clues to the forces operating in society. The citizens in a democracy reflect the widespread attitudes of support for the political system, as well as the diverse claims that are expressed in political conflict.

TABLE 6–4

How Much Attention Do Americans Pay to Politics?

	Attention to Presidential Campaign
Paid a lot of attention to 1988 campaign	46%
Found the 1984 presidential campaign interesting	56
Watched a good many TV programs about campaign	23
Read a good many newspaper articles about campaign	25
TV commercial for a presidential candidate helped decide how to vote in 1984	12
Talked about presidential election at home a lot	37

Source: 1980 National Election Study, Center for Political Studies; CBS News/*New York Times* Poll, November 18, 1984; recalculated from CBS News/*New York Times* poll data, *New York Times,* November 21, 1988, p. 10.

Passive Participation

Not all forms of citizen involvement are active. Citizens may participate in politics in quiet ways. Passive participation may be just as important as more visible political activities. A crucial form of participation is citizen support of the political system. Public attitudes and feelings may enhance or undermine the government's claim to *legitimacy* or, in other words, its right to govern. The citizens' knowledge of the political system as well as the whole range of approval and disapproval of public affairs constitute the nation's political culture.

American Political Culture

Americans share many beliefs about how the political system should operate, which is to say that Americans share a political culture. There is no agreement on precisely what Americans are most committed to in politics and government, but here are some of the prominent elements:

- *Freedom.* Americans take great pride in and strongly support individual liberty. Americans believe not only in freedom from governmental controls but also that people should not interfere with one another's daily lives.
- *Equality.* Americans believe in political equality, including such fundamental principles as one vote per person. More generally, Americans believe in equal opportunities to participate in political, social, and economic activities while recognizing that the results may be far from equal.
- *Fair play.* Americans believe that everyone is entitled to fair treatment, especially in settling disputes. In our political culture fair play involves the application of known rules in the open, public handling of controversies.
- *Citizenship.* Americans believe they have an obligation to inform themselves, to participate in civic affairs, and to support our political system.

Citizens hold the government and political leaders to standards of performance that implement these broad goals. The public believes in the fundamental values of American democracy, but many other values are widely held. Some are so specific that we might forget them. For example, we take it for granted that the winner of an election will be permitted to take office or that a corrupt public official will be punished. We expect votes to be counted accurately. The elements of political culture are a complex mix of ideas and values about government and politics. Another aspect of political culture is the public's attitudes of support for and opposition to the institutions of democracy.

Popular Support for Democracy

Do people feel satisfied with the government? Is there a sense of loyalty and pride? Are people law-abiding even when they disagree with the law? Do people trust their political leaders? Do they have confidence in political institutions?

Citizenship in a democracy involves both opportunities to express political demands and obligations to support the political system. A democracy always tries to win the support of its citizens by serving, to some degree, their political interests. American citizens seem to support the political system even when they are disenchanted with current leaders. Americans have strong, positive feelings about their country and its democratic institutions. When they are asked about their feelings toward democracy, they give strong, favorable answers.

Almost all Americans believe that democracy is the best form of government. More than half would not change a thing in our system of government, and 80 percent say they would not amend the Constitution. On more specific questions, however, the results differ. A recent poll, for example, found that a majority would amend the Constitution to (1) abolish the electoral college, (2) establish a nationwide primary election to select presidential candidates, (3) provide national referenda on issues, (4) add the Equal Rights Amendment, and (5) require the federal government to balance its budget." [13]

When people are asked about pride in the United States, they turn to political factors. In other countries, people are much more likely to give nonpolitical reasons for their pride. They are likely to say they are proud of their country's economy, culture, or physical beauty, and not nearly so likely to say they are proud of their political system. Americans not only give political reasons for their pride in the United States, but also cite "freedom" or "liberty" as the aspect of the political system that makes them proud.[14]

The political culture in the United States is blended with attitudes toward the performance of the economy and the role of government. A major study of attitudes toward capitalism and democracy found the people most supportive of democratic values are least sure of the fairness of the economic system.[15] But generally Americans strongly support both democracy and free private enterprise. Most believe that a free enterprise economy is fair and efficient and that political freedom and democratic government depend on private enterprise.[16]

At the same time, Americans believe by comparable margins that government regulation of business is essential.[17] In 1988 three-fourths of the public held the view that the "rich just get richer and the poor get poorer." [18]

In the pursuit of particular economic policies, political leaders try to draw on underlying values that support their position. For example, in opposing governmental regulation of business activity, a leader might appeal to the public's support of free enterprise; another leader in supporting the same policy might appeal to the public's belief that sometimes the government should correct the operation of the economy.

There is some tension, if not contradiction, in the public's views of the common ground between the government and the economic system. Americans would like to see improvements in the performance of the capitalist economy and the democratic political system, but they have not considered abandoning either.

Widespread agreement on many basic values does not mean that there is complete uniformity on all political beliefs. Americans are products of such diverse social backgrounds that it is no wonder that they differ on many political values. For example, we often think of variations in political culture in association with geographic areas. Historically, the

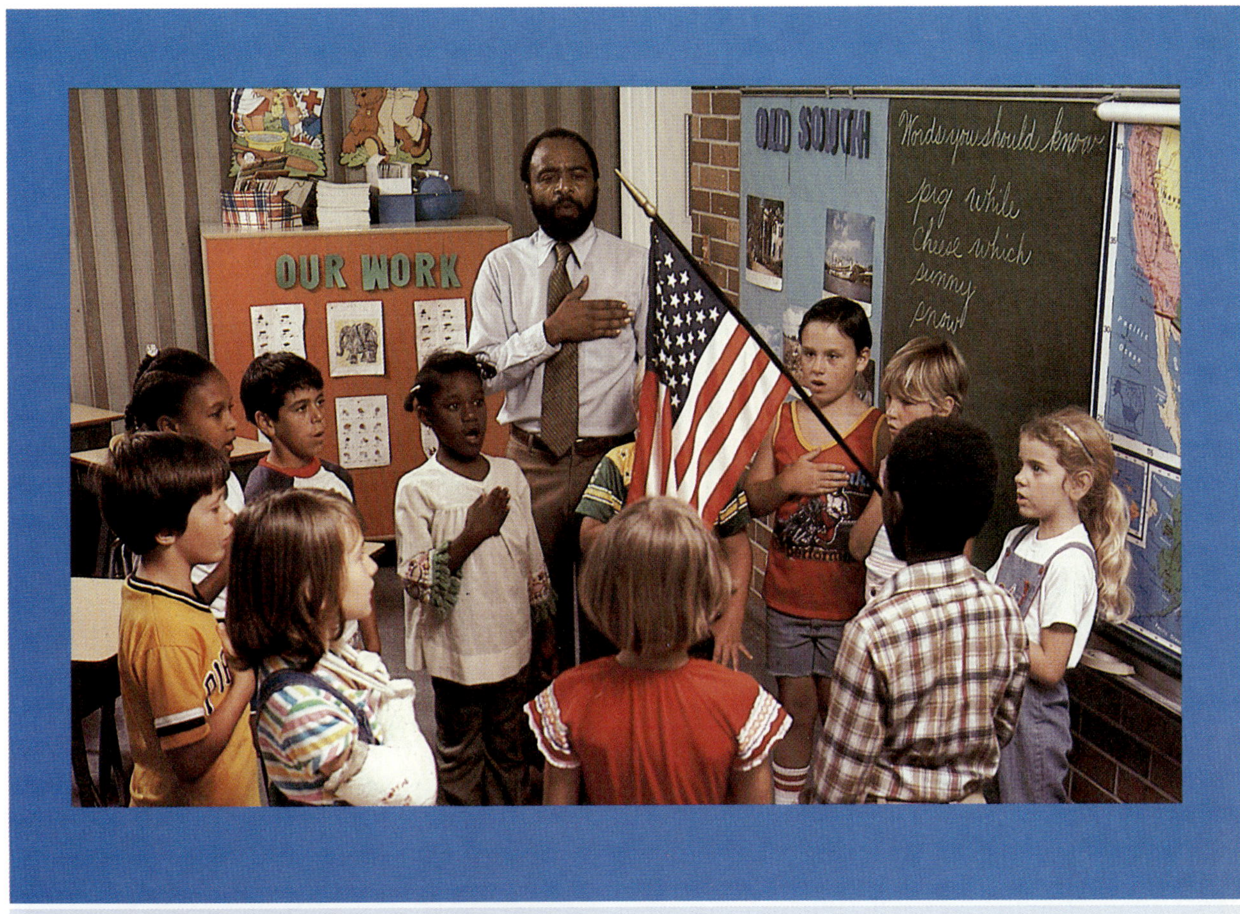

Citizenship training in school teaches political values and ideas from an early age. The Pledge of Allegiance represents a simple message of loyalty in our political culture. Over the years much more complicated, even contradictory, symbols and ideas about politics develop through socialization in school, family, and other social institutions.

South has been viewed as a distinctly different political culture, especially with respect to the role of blacks in the society. Throughout the nation cities contrast with small towns in elements of political culture, but the steady movement of people to and from these areas blurs many of the differences.

Certainly not all views held by Americans completely support their government. By a large margin, Americans believe that the courts are not sufficiently harsh in dealing with criminals. (The public is also opposed overwhelmingly to the use of wiretapping—a fact that may represent conflicting views of justice and freedom.) But overall, the American public takes pride in the nation's political system. In part this reflects basic patriotism, in part attachment to democracy—especially to the value of freedom. The precise meaning of any democratic value to citizens may change as specific issues come to the fore.

Americans learn the values and ideals that constitute political culture during their childhood and for the most part hold to these beliefs throughout their lives. This learning process, called *political socialization,* takes place in families, schools, churches, and other social settings. Indeed, the basic elements of the political culture are so widely shared that it would be difficult to determine when or how they are first acquired. It is more important, perhaps, that Americans are unlikely to hear their basic political values challenged. During their formative years, few are exposed to conflicting views on freedom, equality, or democratic elections.

From the outset, the public schools have been charged with teaching the ideals of citizenship. Almost all studies of public opinion testify to the success of the educational system, which surely explains why those better educated are more committed to democratic values and processes than persons with limited education.

Political Tolerance

Basic democratic values such as freedom, equality, and justice are widely endorsed. But in truth, such values are accepted more in the *abstract* than in their concrete applications.[19] Almost everyone, for example, agrees in freedom of speech, but many would not allow a Communist or a Nazi to speak in their community. Or they may believe in equality generally and yet discriminate against certain people.

Political conflicts are a source of stress in the political system. The more important the clash, the less willing people are to accept defeat and the more hostile they feel toward their political enemies. The norm of political tolerance, an important value in American democracy, runs counter to these feelings of hostility. Political analysts view the public's tolerance of extremists as dependent on how much of a threat they are thought to pose. John Sullivan and others have shown that when people are asked to name a group they particularly dislike and are *then* questioned on their tolerance for that group, levels of intolerance increase. Some people would grant rights to an atheist, but not to a racist. Others would allow a Nazi to speak, but not a Communist. The public has little tolerance for someone who advocates "doing away with elections and letting

Some groups and some points of view strain the public's support of freedom of speech and freedom of assembly. Some views are particularly obnoxious to most Americans. Defending the First Amendment, the Supreme Court has gone to considerable lengths to protect the right of extremists to say what they want to say.

the military run the country." A few years ago Americans were divided 50:50 on letting such a person give a speech. Citizens are considerably more willing to grant extremists the right to free speech than the opportunity to teach in schools.[20]

During the last several decades, public tolerance of unpopular views has increased. Today, for example, a clear majority of Americans believe that an atheist or a Communist should be allowed to speak. Two decades ago, only about one-third held that position. A similar increase in tolerance is found in the public's willingness to see atheists and Communists as college teachers. It may well be, however, that these particular groups are viewed as much less threatening in the 1990s than they were in the early 1950s.

Two well-established patterns describe popular opinion on basic democratic values and processes. First, a number of studies have found that leaders in society express somewhat greater support for values such as freedom and equality than the general public, and also much greater support for their specific applications in the real political world.[21] Second, support for democratic values and procedures among citizens increases sharply with level of education. College-educated Americans profess strong agreement with democratic principles and practices. An equally strong relationship exists between age and commitment to democratic values. On the whole, young people are more tolerant than older people. Furthermore, the young, college-educated population is more supportive of democratic practices than other young people. And they express democratic attitudes more frequently than older, college-educated citizens.

Neither ordinary citizens nor leaders in a political system are likely to be tolerant of extremely threatening groups or ideas. Tolerance should perhaps be seen as a reflection of confidence in the strength and durability of the American democracy.

Trust and Cynicism ■

Americans combine strong support for democratic institutions with strong criticism of the leaders and members of these institutions. People may thus respect the presidency and still believe the president is a fool. People may view political parties as valuable instruments of a democracy and still believe that Democratic and Republican politicians cannot be trusted.

Some alarm has been expressed in recent years over the public's loss of trust and confidence in political leaders.[22] This decline in trust is shown in Figure 6–4. It is not clear how much we should worry about this. Perhaps we should prefer a public that is skeptical of its political leaders but supports the basic institutions of government. Interestingly, it does not appear that a lack of trust leads to apathy and withdrawal from politics. Active, informed participants who are unsure of the wisdom and virtue of their leaders may be exactly what a healthy democracy needs.

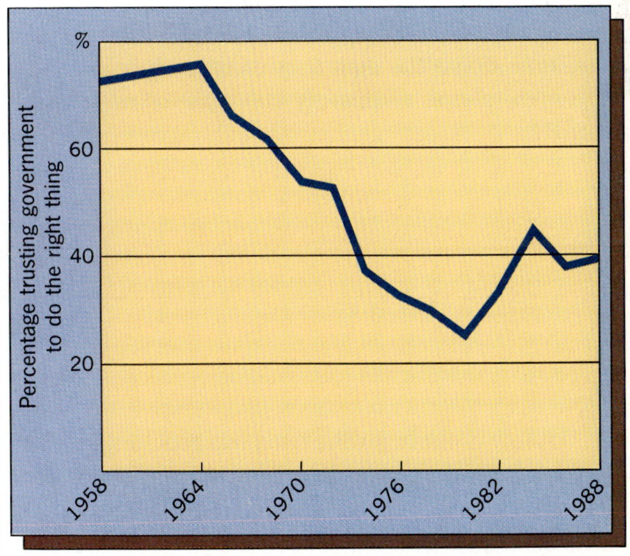

■ **Figure 6–4** Trust in government, 1958–1987: percentage of the public agreeing that the government in Washington can be trusted to do the right thing most of the time or always. Source: National Election Studies, Center for Political Studies; CBS/*New York Times* Poll, October 18–22, 1987.

"Perspectives"

On Citizenship, Voting, and Democracy

"The passive citizen, the nonvoter, the poorly informed or apathetic citizen—all indicate a weak democracy."

—Gabriel Almond and Sidney Verba

"If the survival of the American system depended upon an active, informed, and enlightened citizenry, then democracy in America would have disappeared long ago. . . ."

—Thomas Dye and L. Harmon Ziegler

". . . despite what one may read about backroom political machinations, it is the voters who in large measure shape the men they elect and, in shaping the men, shape ultimately the politics of the nation."

—Richard Scammon and Ben Wattenberg

". . . the masses do not corrupt themselves. If they are corrupt, they have been corrupted."

—V. O. Key, Jr.

"The press . . . may not be successful much of the time in telling people what to think, but it is stunningly successful in telling its readers what to think about."

—Bernard C. Cohen

Sources: Gabriel Almond and Sidney Verba, *The Civic Culture* (Princeton, N.J., Princeton University Press, 1963), p. 474; Thomas Dye and L. Harmon Ziegler, *The Irony of Democracy* (Belmont, Calif.: Duxbury Press, 1981), p. 4; Richard Scammon and Ben Wattenberg, *The Real Majority* (New York: Coward McCann, 1970), pp. 15–16; V. O. Key, Jr., *Public Opinion and American Democracy* (New York: Alfred A. Knopf, 1961), p. 558; Bernard C. Cohen, *The Press and Foreign Policy* (Princeton, N.J.: Princeton University Press, 1963), p. 13.

A low point in public trust was reached in 1980 at the end of the Carter administration. The Reagan years saw some restoration of trust. By 1987 trust was at 40 percent—an increase of 15 percent since the beginning of the Reagan administration. On the other hand, it was far less than the trust shown before the 1970s. These patterns are similar to those connected with the belief that the government is run for the benefit of a few big interests.

Political leaders would prefer a public that is more enthusiastic about them. They work hard to be respected, admired, appreciated, trusted, and reelected. Currently, Americans appear willing to vote for leaders without giving them the full respect and trust they seek. The important point is that public cynicism toward political leaders has not led to a cynical view of the political system.

The loss of confidence in political leaders should be put in perspective. As opposed to "statesmen," politicians have never been held in high regard by the public. Declining trust also shows up in other ways. Numerous surveys, in other countries as well as the United States, have shown a loss of confidence in doctors, lawyers, journalists, teachers, business executives, and other social leaders.[23]

One reason for public discontent appears to be the increased civil violence in society. Riots, demonstrations, and assassinations have taken a toll on the public's sense of well-being. There has been growing doubt that the government can maintain order and domestic peace. New politicians emerge and administrations change, but disorder remains.

Violations of the public trust by political leaders have contributed to the current state of affairs. The decline of over 15 percent in trust between 1972 and 1974, shown in Figure 6–4, is surely due in part to the involvement of the Nixon White House in the Watergate break-in, the subsequent coverup, and the president's resignation. Policy ventures and failures may also appear to violate the public trust. The level of public trust declined by 15 per-

President Nixon prepares to leave for California after resigning office. Events like his resignation, or the coverup of the Watergate break-in that led to it, undermine the public's confidence in political leaders and the institutions of government. Gerald Ford, who became the next president, subsequently pardoned Nixon for any crimes committed in connection with Watergate.

Responding to charges of ethical improprieties, Speaker Jim Wright (D-Tex.) in 1989 became the first Speaker in the history of Congress to resign under pressure; shortly thereafter, he gave up his seat in the House. His successor as Speaker was Thomas S. Foley (D-Wash.), who had served as Majority Leader. Wright's resignation was one phase in a series of political battles over ethical questions raised about both Democratic and Republican leaders. Ethical controversies of this type invariably lead to a decline in popular trust and confidence

cent between 1964 and 1968, a period marked by urban riots and an escalation of American military action in Vietnam—each a major dilemma of the Johnson administration.

The basic explanation for the decline of public trust in officials may be the apparent inability of government to solve public problems. Every administration confronts nagging issues of great variety, involving, for example, unemployment, inflation, race relations, environmental quality, urban decay, foreign policy, and social welfare. When solutions are not forthcoming, public discontent grows. The gap between public expectations and government performance leads inevitably, many observers believe, to declining public trust. Ironically, by their campaign promises, politicians contribute to this result. Nevertheless, President Reagan was almost certainly responsible for raising public confidence in government during his years in office.

Pervasive cynicism, it should be emphasized, has thus far had little effect on citizen political participation.[24] Alienated voters have not withdrawn from politics. They listen to campaign speeches and debates, form opinions, write public officials, discuss politics with friends and neighbors, and go to the polls. All in all, few differences in political behavior appear between citizens who are cynical and those who are not. If this is an anomaly, it is by no means the only one in American politics.

Most Americans feel that they can be effective politically if they make an effort. This "sense of political efficacy," which has been measured for 30 years, is about as high today as in the past.[25] Americans' trust in government has declined, but they continue to believe their political activity counts—that they can influence public decisions. Such a belief is essential to the maintenance of a viable democracy.

Summary

- Political demands from the people move the political system much as popular support keeps it going. The balance between demands and support determines how stable the government will be.
- The eligible electorate has expanded steadily over the past two centuries. The major changes in suffrage since the elimination of property

requirements for white males were extension of voting rights to blacks after the Civil War, women's suffrage in 1920, and the lowering of the voting age to 18 in 1971.

- Turnout in elections in this century has not been high. Recently, only a little over half the eligible electorate has voted in presidential elections; even fewer voters turn out in primaries and local elections. A large proportion of nonvoters are not registered to vote, making registration as well as apathy a barrier to voting.
- A small minority of Americans are highly active in election campaigns. In addition to being more partisan than other people, the actives are older and somewhat better educated.
- Direct attempts to influence particular government policies are as important as electoral activities. Most Americans make some kind of contact with a government official or politician concerning a matter of political interest. Even more people work indirectly through groups that have political goals.
- The institutions and values of democracy enjoy widespread public support. Americans are proud of their political system, especially the freedom enjoyed by the citizenry.
- Intolerance is most likely to be expressed against political enemies who are viewed by the individual as threatening.
- Political leaders and better-educated citizens are more likely to support democratic values and procedures than the rest of the public.
- Although the public supports the institutions of government, it expresses a low level of trust in political leaders. Confidence in leaders has declined during the past two decades, but with no serious effects on the system.

Readings on Citizens, Participation, and Democracy

Almond, Gabriel, and Sidney Verba. 1963. *The Civic Culture.* Princeton, N.J.: Princeton University Press. A classic study of political culture in five nations, including the United States.

Lipset, Seymour Martin, and Martin Schneider. 1983. *The Confidence Gap.* New York: Free Press. A study of the public's views of major social and political institutions and leadership.

McClosky, Herbert, and Alida Brill. 1983. *Dimensions of Tolerance: What Americans Believe About Civil Liberties.* New York: Russell Sage Foundation. An analysis of Americans' attitudes on political tolerance.

McClosky, Herbert, and John Zaller. 1984. *The American Ethos.* A Twentieth Century Fund Report. Cambridge, Mass.: Harvard University Press. Describes the public's attitudes toward capitalism and democracy.

Sullivan, John L., James Piereson, and George E. Marcus. 1982. *Political Tolerance and American Democracy.* Chicago: University of Chicago Press. Surveys tolerance of all unpopular groups and argues that tolerance in the United States is not particularly high.

Tocqueville, Alexis de. 1951. *Democracy in America,* ed. Phillips Bradley, 2 vols. New York: Alfred A. Knopf. The classic study of American political culture.

Verba, Sidney, and Norman Nie. 1972. *Participation in America: Political Democracy and Social Equality.* New York: Harper & Row. Examines forms of participation and their causes.

Wolfinger, Raymond E., and Steven J. Rosenstone. 1980. *Who Votes?* New Haven, Conn.: Yale University Press. A major study of the barriers to turnout and registration.

Chapter 7

Public Opinion and Ideology

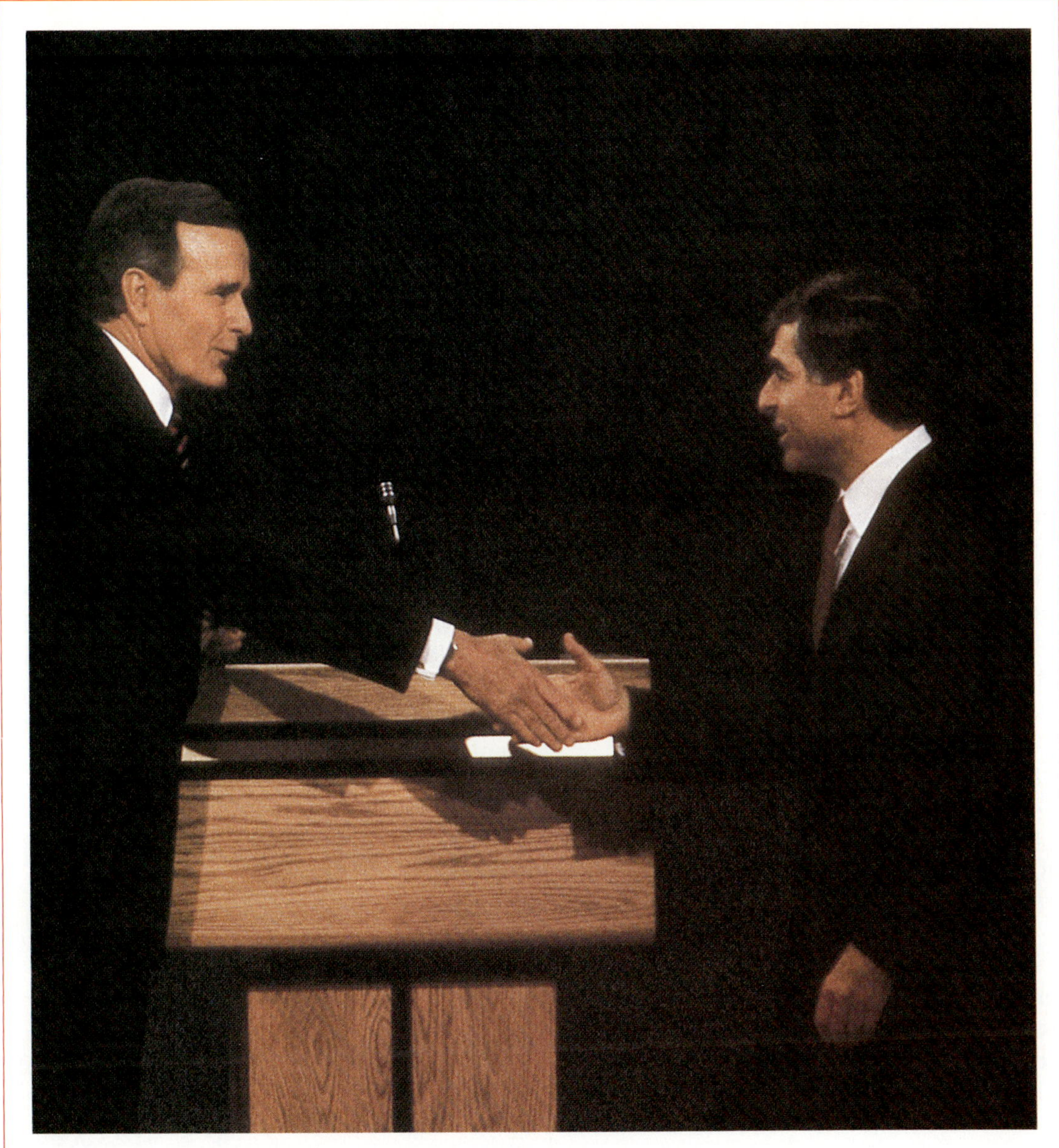

Political organizations are based on people. Their principles, objectives, proposals, and behavior depend on the nature of their followings. Political activity on a large scale requires the support of many people. In American society, one soon learns that people are not an altogether reliable base for political organizations.

Although millions of Americans consider themselves Democrats or Republicans, neither party can count on their supporters to turn out in any particular election. Nor can the parties be confident how their supporters will vote when they do turn out. Few can be relied on to campaign, attend rallies, give money, or do any of the tasks that strengthen political parties as organizations. American voters view the political parties casually; most voters can "take them or leave them."

Interest groups have a similar problem. The leaders constantly appeal to the public to become involved in politics and concerned with issues. More often than not, these appeals are unsuccessful. Citizens go about their own business, often unmindful of the issues that swirl about them. Political leaders face a public that does not know much about current matters, does not listen attentively, and does not seem to care.

These observations should not be misunderstood. Almost all adults are capable of taking an interest in political issues and becoming familiar with them. They simply choose not to do so. People find other things to do, other things to think about. Politics holds no special fascination for most Americans. They are pragmatists; they do not get involved unless they think they can have an impact. People turn their attention to policies reluctantly, only when they believe it is important and bears on their lives.

Most public opinion can be described as *permissive.*[1] This means that a wide range of politics will satisfy the public in solving a problem. On some topics, though, the public has *directive opinions* that express clear demands. There may be a directive opinion that something must be done, but a permissive view on what specifically to do. When people have directive opinions, it is difficult for political leaders not to abide by them. Permissive opinions are less threatening. Of course, leaders would like to inspire the public to demand what the leaders want in the first place.

Political leaders may despair of arousing the public to their causes. For the political system, this has the advantage of making conflicts neither too intense nor too volatile. Ideally, citizens in a democracy respond wisely when necessary and remain calm the rest of the time.

Awareness of Political Issues

In a democracy, citizens are expected to keep informed about government and politics. There is an obligation to know what is going on—perhaps especially what is going wrong. At least citizens should know whether their interests are served by their representatives. One form of citizen participation is simply paying attention to political events.

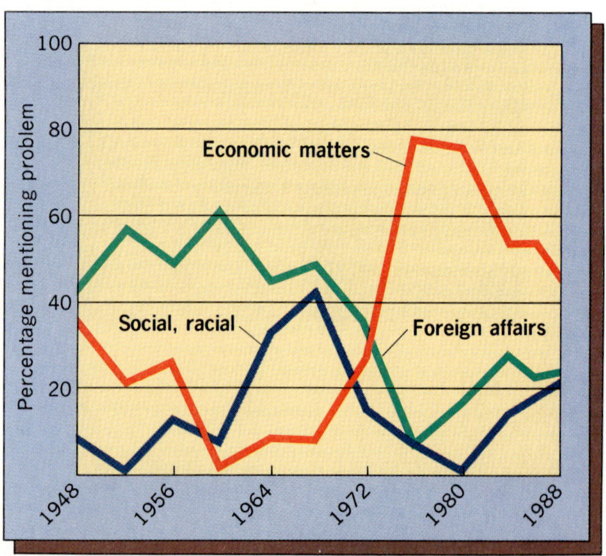

Figure 7–1 Public views of the most important problems facing the nation, 1948–1988. Source: *Gallup Opinion Index* (September 1980), no. 181, p. 11; *Gallup Report* (July 1984, April 1988), no. 226, p. 17; no. 271, p. 7.

In fact, many Americans are poorly informed about issues and uninterested in politics. Americans are ignorant of the details of most issues and unfamiliar with most political leaders.[2] They can, however, make general assessments of the performance of the president, Congress, and the political parties. They can usually judge the overall health of the economy and the general state of foreign affairs; even the most poorly informed know when the country is in a depression or at war.

Most people can become informed on matters they care about intensely. They will understand their own financial status; they will know if they, or people around them, are losing their jobs. They can make connections from one political idea to another on crucial matters. Yet this says nothing about the general ability of the public to analyze political problems. The overall level of information about politics is not high, and political thinking about most matters is far from sophisticated.

Almost every American knows simple facts such as the name of the president or the governor. Only about half know the name of their representative in Congress.

Americans are keenly aware, however, of the major problems in the society. We can capture the mood of Americans in part by examining what they see as the most important problem facing the country. Figure 7–1 shows that concern with the economy has dominated public opinion since the mid-1970s. During the Vietnam War, foreign affairs was the greatest concern. By the late 1980s, more people were beginning to worry about war, international tensions, and social problems than in the early Reagan years. During the Bush administration, drugs and drug abuse came to be seen as the major social problem facing the country.

Figure 7–1 does not indicate what individuals care about personally, only what they believe to be the major problems for the whole society. Also, the data do not reveal the intensity of feelings. Americans have come to view economic problems much more seriously than they did a few years ago. But the personal, intense political concerns of individuals are not so well known.[3] These concerns may be expressed through interest groups.

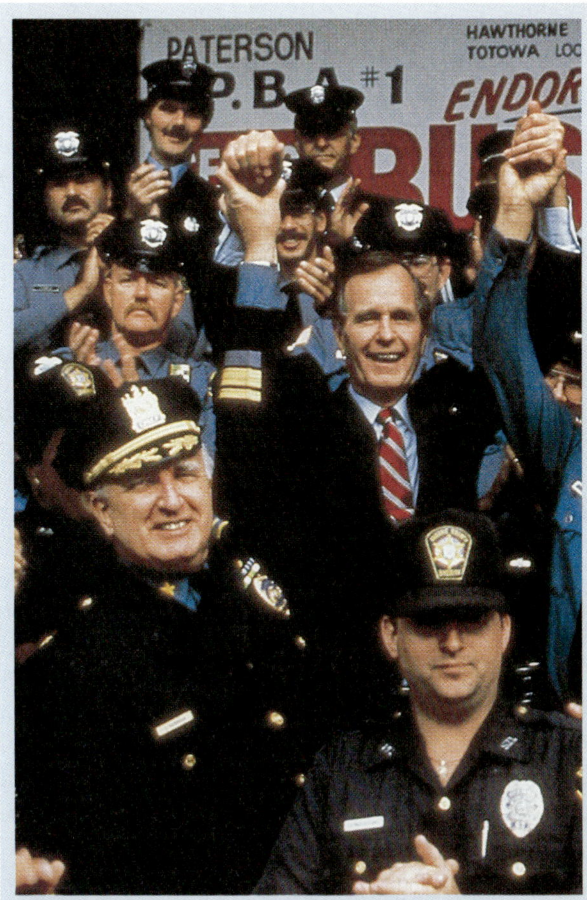

George Bush appearing with New Jersey policemen. Bush campaigned for the presidency on the basis of issue positions such as getting tough on crime. Campaign organizations carefully arrange meetings of this type in order to give the public a visual impression of the candidate's stands through mass media coverage.

Although the average person may not be well informed, some issues are so well understood and important that almost everyone has an opinion. On emotional issues where many people have strong feelings, almost everyone has a position. On the question of abortion, for example, only 2 percent have no opinion. Only 2 percent have no opinion on prayer in public schools.

TABLE 7–1

Issue Awareness

Issues	Percentage of Adults Who Have No Opinion
Government abortion policy	2
Prayer in schools	2
Government aid to blacks	9
Government services and spending	10
Dealing with Russia	10
Defense spending	11
U.S. involvement in Central America	14
Changes in tax laws	57

Source: 1986 National Election Study, Center for Political Studies.

Not all issues generate high public interest.[4] As Table 7–1 shows, many citizens have no views on a major economic issue like the new tax law. One-tenth of the public has no opinion on defense spending or reducing spending on domestic programs.

For most Americans, opinions on political issues are casually held and easily changed. People often hold inconsistent views. It is a rare issue on which people hold strong, hard-to-change views. This means that public opinion ordinarily is permissive or "soft." Political leaders cannot use it to guide them in making decisions. They know that opinions will change with the flow of events and the emergence of new conditions. The weak commitment people feel on most issues is a chance for leaders to shape views and alter public opinion.

Politicians and political commentators often talk as if one type of issue is more important to people than another. This is not true. Sometimes economic issues are dominant, other times foreign policy, and other times race relations

Some issues last longer than others. The boycott of the 1980 Olympics was a short-term issue. The prison furlough program in Massachusetts, which played a prominent role in the presidential campaign of 1988, was of no consequence once the election was over. But issues on relations between blacks and whites have endured. The role of government in the economy has been an issue for over a century. For an issue to provide a basis for political divisions, it must last for quite a while.

Popular Attitudes

Economic Issues

Economic issues are often involved in political clashes. There is almost always some concern with the condition of the economy. In recent decades, economic issues have focused on the role of government in controlling economic activity. Increasingly, political leaders have argued over the role of government in stimulating economic growth. More and more, the president is blamed for unemployment and inflation. A wide range of welfare programs has also led to increased government involvement in the economy.[5]

To a large extent, domestic economic issues have been questions of how much the government should spend on education, medical services, social security, and other programs. During the Reagan administration, expenditures on many social programs were cut back. A public that had supported these programs for years now seemed ready to support their reduction. But the people most affected by spending cuts feel quite differently. The elderly may feel seriously threatened by proposed reductions in social security. Mothers on welfare may be deeply concerned with a different set of programs. Yet there are limits to the self-interest of people as expressed in political attitudes. Only one-third of the unemployed, for example, believe government should try to reduce unemployment if it means increasing inflation. This compares with 20 percent for the public as a whole. Many of the unemployed, in fact, have no opinions on this issue.[6]

Most social programs have broad public support—of the permissive variety. Hence, program reductions or even eliminations may not produce much public reaction. In 1980, 38 percent of the public said they were opposed to reducing services to reduce spending, but this was not an intense view. Twenty-seven percent were willing to reduce services to reduce spending. Most citizens did not demand that programs be cut back to reduce spending. Furthermore, late in 1984 twice as many people believed that government programs have made things better for the poor as rejected the idea. People who voted for Reagan in 1984 were more positive about the success of government programs for the poor than were Mondale supporters.

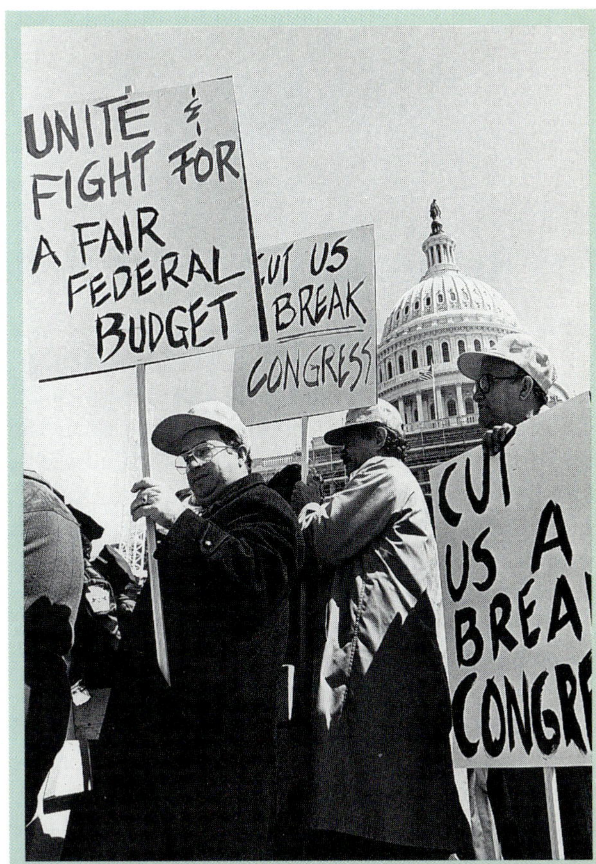

Thousands of people trek to Washington each year to demonstrate for one cause or another. The principal short-run objective of the organizers of these events is to secure media coverage as a way of expanding the conflict and gaining new supporters. Their long-run objective is, of course, to secure favorable public policy. That often means a change in policy.

The Reagan administration made tax reduction a major policy change in 1981. While Democratic and Republican leaders have clashed over tax policy, most have supported tax cuts. In the presidential campaign of 1984, Walter Mondale said he would raise taxes. This was extremely unwelcome to the public, even though many people believed that a tax increase might be necessary. The tax issue was raised in the context of the enormous budget deficits that began to appear in the 1980s. Although most Americans believe the federal government deficit is a serious problem, it has not become the basis for a deep political division. Several reasons account for this. One is that Republicans and Democrats share the view that budget deficits are bad; another is that ordinary citizens have found it difficult to link the deficit with other more familiar economic and social problems.

By 1988 there was widespread public recognition that the budget deficit posed a problem that would have to be dealt with sooner or later. Both George Bush and Michael Dukakis avoided discussions of the deficit and how they would reduce it during the campaign. Most people believed that

The Responsible Uses of Polls

Public opinion polling can be an invaluable tool for assessing the beliefs of the electorate and, more important, for conveying public opinion to political elites. It is a tool, in other words, with the potential for increasing the public's influence in the political system. Through a technique known as *random* or *probability* sampling, survey research firms interview between 1000 and 2000 respondents, who are carefully chosen to be representative of the rest of the country. If the respondents are selected randomly, their answers should reflect the opinions of the broader population. George Gallup, the founder of the famous Gallup Poll, likened the process to stirring a giant kettle of vegetable soup and, before the contents settle to the bottom, dipping a ladle into the kettle and pouring the ladle contents into a bowl. The contents of the bowl should be very similar to the contents of the rest of the kettle.

Poll results nevertheless must be interpreted carefully, with the reader evaluating the poll in light of several considerations:

Question Wording: Responses to questions may vary dramatically depending on how the questions are asked. Adam Clymer found approval of legalized abortions to be much more common when respondents were asked to agree or disagree with the statement: "Abortion sometimes is the best course in a bad situation" (66 percent agreed) than when they were asked whether "abortion is the same thing as murdering a child" (55 percent agreed).

Sampling Error and Confidence Level: There are limitations to the precision of even the most carefully selected sample. A typical poll of 1500 respondents might find that 52 percent of those interviewed approve of the president's performance, with a sampling error of 4 percent and a confidence level of 95 percent. This would mean that if 100 probability samples were selected, the percentage approving of the president would vary between 48 and 56 percent in 95 of the 100 samples. Other things equal, the sampling error decreases and the confidence level increases as the sample size increases.

Date of Interviewing: Responses may be quite different depending on when the respondents are contacted. Preelection polls, for instance, are much more meaningful when taken immediately prior to an election.

Nonattitudes: Respondents are often tempted to pretend that they have a legitimate opinion about an issue when, in fact, they do not. According to Asher (1988), "these nonattitude responses are treated by the analyst as if they represented actual public opinions." For example, one study found that one-third of their sample offered an opinion on the "1975 Public Affairs Act" even though this "act" did not even exist.

To permit the consumer of polls to evaluate them more effectively, many have encouraged the media to disclose just how the poll was taken, including dates and methods of interviewing, the size and nature of the sample, and how the questions were worded and interpreted. But the issue of responsibility will not easily disappear.

Consider, for example, the "trial heat" surveys that provide much of the information on the "horserace" aspects of a political campaign. Hundreds of surveys were conducted during 1988 to assess the relative strength of Bush and Dukakis. The results in the table below show considerable variation from March to November.

Results like these help candidates raise money—if the news is good—and guide their strategy. While most people say that they are not influenced by public opinion polls, the suspicion remains that, at least among indifferent voters, a bandwagon effect exists. Even the most careful and responsible polls—perhaps especially these polls—will be studied for their political impact.

	March	April	May	June	July	Aug.	Sept.	Oct.
Bush	52	45	38	38	41	48	47	50
Dukakis	40	43	54	52	47	44	42	40
Other, undecided	8	12	8	10	12	8	11	10

Sources: Adam Clymer, "One Issue That Seems to Defy a Yes or No," *New York Times,* February 23, 1986, p. 22–E; Herbert Asher, *Polling and the Public* (Washington, D.C.: CQ Press, 1988), p. 21; George F. Bishop, Robert W. Oldendick, and Alfred J. Tuchfarber, "Pseudo-Opinions on Public Affairs," *Public Opinion Quarterly,* 44 (1980), pp. 198–209; Gallup Poll, cited in *Public Opinion* (September/October 1988), pp. 36–37, and in *Minneapolis Star Tribune,* October 26, 1988, p. 15A.

taxes would be increased during the next administration.

Not all opinions on economic matters are as stable as opposition to taxes or enthusiasm for prosperity. An example of shifting opinion is the public's views on government guarantees of a job. Twenty years ago, most Americans supported the idea, but support has declined. Today, there is increased uncertainty about government job guarantees and, in fact, more opposition than support. The political parties have disagreed on this issue, and that division is strongly reflected in public opinion.[7] Perhaps as much as any contemporary issue, the guarantee of a job by the government reflects the Democratic and Republican alignment of the 1930s.

There is some evidence that *both* conservative and liberal leaders have shifted away from using government to solve problems. No similar shift has taken place in the general public. Most people do not believe past government programs have failed; the public is not demanding less government. At the same time, many people are willing to see government programs reduced.

Foreign Policy

Traditionally, when foreign policy issues have become important to Americans, the focus of attention has been war. Despite the public's concern with peace and the threat of war, it often finds other problems more pressing. On occasion, foreign policy matters have dominated public opinion, although these times have been rare in American history.

Recently, economic issues like taxes and the budget deficit have been closely linked to foreign policy. Spending for the military has been a major contributor to federal deficits. And military spending is tied to most aspects of foreign policy. The public's attitudes toward defense spending have varied noticeably in recent years. As Figure 7–2 shows, 1980 was an unusual and brief era of widespread support for increasing military spending. Before and after 1980, Americans have been much less disposed to support defense spending. In the 1988 campaign both Bush and Dukakis talked more about limiting military spending than about increasing it, but on the whole military budgets have not been important concerns for the public.

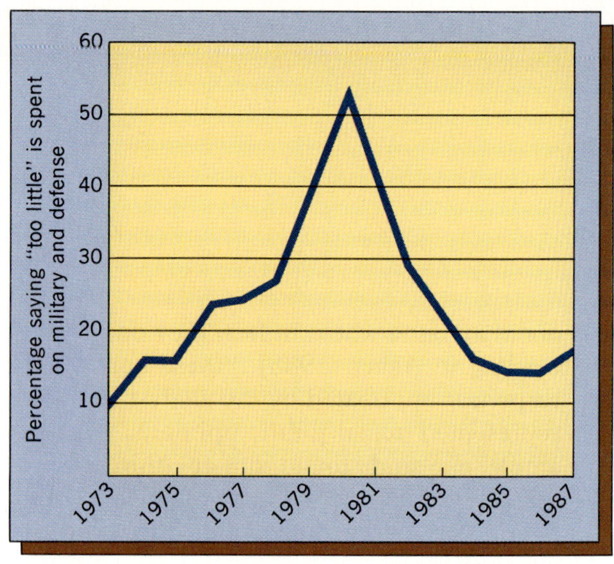

Figure 7–2 Percentage of the public saying that too little is spent on the military and defense. Source: General Social Surveys codebooks, p. 78.

Several episodes a few days apart during the Reagan presidency highlighted foreign relations issues for Americans. One was a success, the other a disaster from the point of view of the public. In October 1983, Americans were stunned by the deaths of over 200 Marines at the Beirut airport. There was confusion in the minds of most people over the role of the United States in the Middle East. Americans generally did not have much information about the conflicts in that region, making it all the more difficult to form opinions about foreign policy.

The invasion of the small Caribbean island of Grenada was a simple episode in military and foreign affairs. Few Americans had heard of Grenada before the invasion; there was no public demand for intervention. For a brief time the public generally approved of the invasion, and a majority took pride in a military triumph that asserted national power. On the other hand, the invasion appeared to make no deep impression on most people.

In the minds of many Americans the most significant development in foreign policy in recent years has been the changing relations between the Soviet Union and the United States. Reagan and Gorbachev were widely credited with reducing tensions between the two countries and improving opportunities for substantial arms reduction. During Reagan's last year in office, the public welcomed the possibility that the Soviet Union might become more of a competitor and less of an enemy.

Attitudes toward foreign countries have been described as *internationalist* or *isolationist.* The internationalist perspective is that the United States needs to be actively involved with other countries. Isolationists prefer policies that disengage the United States from foreign countries. This difference in views has gradually lost its usefulness in explaining public opinion on foreign policy. Another distinction—between an *aggressive* and a *passive* orientation toward foreign affairs—better matches public opinion on current problems.

Aggressive internationalists want to see the United States dominate other countries militarily and economically. This attitude calls for "getting tough"; it views various countries as hostile to the United States. Usually the United States and the USSR are seen as similarly aggressive and on a collision course. Passive internationalists promote

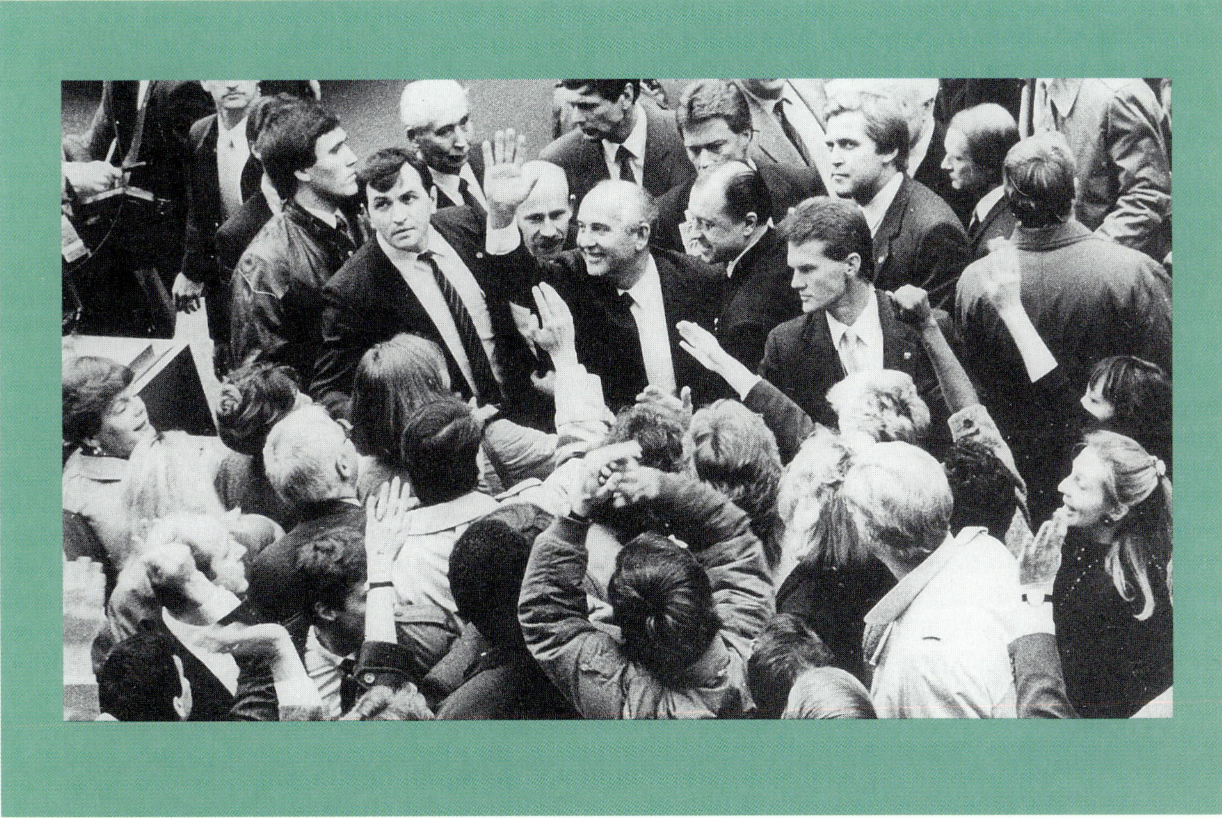

The key to politics is the relationship between leaders and the public. While visiting the United States, Mikhail Gorbachev got out of his car and worked the crowd in the fashion of an American politician. He unquestionably succeeded in making a favorable impression on the American public.

peace and support economic aid to less developed countries. They believe that active, peaceful relations among nations will prevent war and benefit all. Even warlike nations, they believe, will be less menacing if they are not threatened.

Aggressive isolationists are anxious about the military security of the United States. This leads them to support an arms buildup to protect the country from all possible threats. Passive isolationists are a different breed. They call for a withdrawal of American activities from other countries. The United States, in their view, has no business meddling in the affairs of other countries.

For all the commentary on Vietnam and the role of public opinion in the American withdrawal, there is still no clear understanding of popular attitudes toward the war. First, the public followed political leaders in supporting U.S. involvement, and it remained supportive after many leaders began to oppose the war. Second, throughout the 1960s, young people were more "hawkish" on the war than older people. (Some young people did indeed demonstrate against the war, but they were a small percentage of all young people.) Third, although the demonstrations against the war may have impressed political leaders, they appear to have made the general public more—not less—supportive of the war. Fourth, the overall ups and downs in support of the war were directly related to battle reports and casualties. Reports of victories increased support; reported defeats led to declining support.[8]

It has been argued that the "lesson of Vietnam" has influenced public opinion on United States military involvement in Central America. A majority of Americans, for example, were opposed to the Reagan administration's policies in Nicaragua and particularly to sending troops to Central America. However, these feelings were not so important to voters in 1988 that George Bush's support of the Reagan policies was a political liability.

Currently, between one-fifth and one-third of the public appear to be opposed to an aggressive military policy.[9] This segment of the public is particularly concerned to reduce nuclear weapons and to avoid sending U.S. troops overseas. On some military policy issues, public opinion is one-sided. Over two-thirds of the public support the idea of a nuclear freeze, a simple idea that has had widespread support but that has been difficult to translate into actual policies.

Another "new" aspect of foreign affairs is economic policy. In recent years, oil has been an obvious factor in economic relations. The success of foreign products in the United States and the failure to sell American products abroad have been mentioned by people as important aspects of foreign relations. The public has become increasingly concerned over the vulnerability of the American economy in the world. Topics like the trade deficit and foreign capital investment in the United States are now mentioned by Americans as major problems facing the country. Economic protection from foreign imports has won support among only a minority of Americans. Even union members in threatened industries do not strongly support such a policy. Trade deficits, like budget deficits, have proved difficult for most people to understand. In all likelihood, economic crises associated with foreign countries will continue to intrude on American life and public opinion. To a considerable extent, Americans have come to view foreign relations in economic rather than in military or political terms.

Race

Beginning with the issue of slavery, Americans have been torn by seemingly unresolvable racial problems. Although feelings are usually strong on these issues, a gradual shift of opinion has taken place over the past several decades.[10] By the late 1970s, as few as one American in 20 advocated strict segregation of races. Fifteen years earlier, more than one in five supported strict segregation. The data of Figure 7–3 show the gradual acceptance of school integration since World War II. As would be expected, support for school integration was slower to develop in the South than elsewhere. Today the idea of integration of the public schools is widely accepted throughout the nation.

At the same time, the public has not always supported government programs to *promote* in-

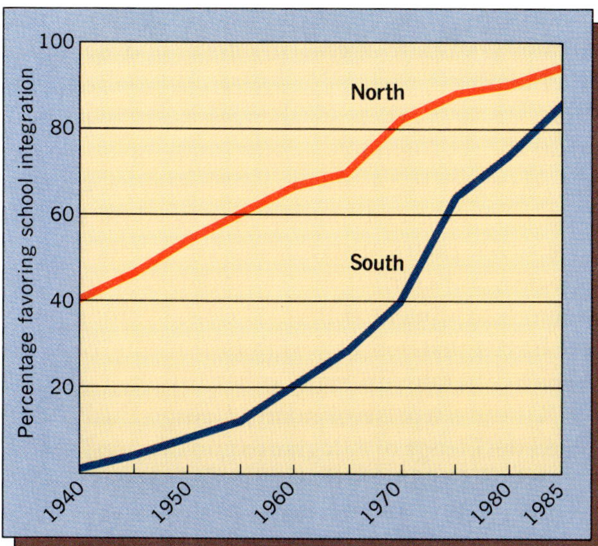

Figure 7–3 Attitudes toward racial integration of public schools, 1942–1985. Source: Tom W. Smith and Paul B. Sheatsley, "American Attitudes Toward Race Relations," *Public Opinion* (October–November 1984), pp. 15, 50; "Opinion Roundup," *Public Opinion* (January–February 1988), p. 28.

tegration. Public support for government efforts to achieve school integration has declined sharply in the last 20 years.[11] Whites are overwhelmingly opposed to busing for school integration. Blacks are not particularly in favor of it either. It is instructive to find that the better-educated and young whites are more supportive of integration than older whites. On balance, most Americans believe blacks and other minorities should be treated equally, but not given special treatment.

The trend toward support for racial equality should not be overemphasized. There are probably two trends: First, younger people are more in favor of racial equality than older people, so there is a steady replacement of people opposed to equality by those who favor it. Second, as a countertrend, some individuals have become opposed to racial equality as they have grown older.

There is only a little evidence on this second pattern. Jennings and Niemi interviewed high school seniors in 1965 and then questioned the same people again in 1973. They found a shift away from support for school integration.[12] Table 7–2 shows that 29 percent of the national sample of young white people switched from favoring school integration to opposing it. All this switching occurred among young white people raised in the North; young white southerners became slightly more accepting of school integration. The parents of these young people were also interviewed in both 1965 and 1973. The parents changed their views little over the eight years, suggesting that younger people are more susceptible to change and more easily influenced by circumstances.

In recent years the race issue has been raised by the political success of Jesse Jackson. Both symbolically and in fact, his campaigns for the presidency have challenged American leadership at the highest levels; in 1988 he attained national political support never enjoyed before by a black leader. Many potential voters, whites as well as blacks, found Jackson a more inspiring, impressive leader than the nominees of the two parties. And although many others were opposed to Jackson, the public increasingly accepted the *idea* of a black as president. By 1987, 79 percent of the public indicated

TABLE 7–2

Attitude Change Toward School Integration Among Young People Between 1965 and 1973

Favor school integration in 1965:	
Still favor integration in 1973	48%
Oppose integration in 1973	29
Oppose school integration in 1965:	
Favor integration in 1973	10
Still oppose integration in 1973	13
Total	100%

Source: 1965 and 1973 Socialization Study, Center for Political Studies.

A former Ku Klux Klan leader, David Duke, won a special election in 1989 for a seat in the Louisiana House of Representatives. Duke ran as a Republican but with the opposition of national leaders like President Bush.

they would vote for a qualified black presidential nominee in their party.[13]

Social and Cultural Values

Issues of individual life-styles, moral values, and religious practices have captured the attention of political leaders and the public alike. Political groups have developed in recent years around goals of family values, sexual freedom, and scores of other matters previously absent from political debates. At times, these clashes have dominated political discussion and election campaigns.

Abortion is an obvious example, as are conflicts over economic and social freedom for homosexuals. Issues surrounding the role of women in society were not settled by the defeat of the Equal Rights Amendment (ERA). The same strong political forces that led to a standoff on the ERA are prepared to take up many other causes.[14]

To the surprise of many, George Bush introduced the Pledge of Allegiance into the presidential campaign of 1988. No major policy controversy had existed on this issue, but once the topic was raised, a clear preference emerged for requiring schoolchildren to start the day with the pledge. Although some social and cultural issues become extremely emotional, there was no real intensity surrounding the pledge issue.

Religious groups have brought many issues to the political system. An old controversy over teaching evolution in the schools has returned to the political agenda. Another issue concerns prayer in public classrooms. About half of the American public supports the idea of beginning the school day with a prayer, but intense support for school prayer is confined to a relatively small group.[15]

As late as 1960, millions of Americans were upset by the thought of a Catholic in the White House. It was as threatening to some Protestants as it was pleasing to most Catholics. For some Protestants, the prospect of a Catholic president signaled that Catholics were becoming more important in society. Others believed the extremist allegation that the Pope would run the government. Whatever the source of apprehension, the issue was real for many voters in the 1960 election, in which Kennedy narrowly defeated Nixon.[16]

There are strong relationships between issues and social characteristics. We can use abortion as an example. Both age and religion are related to positions on abortion. These two patterns are seen in Figure 7–4. Catholics of all ages have about the same views on abortion. Protestants' views, on the

Continuity & CHANGE

America's Growing Acceptance of Women and Minorities

The election of President John F. Kennedy, the nation's first Catholic president, in 1960 dramatized a change in American attitudes toward religious discrimination. But what of the effects of the civil rights and gender equality movements of the 1960s? Are Americans really becoming fairer in their views of women and minorities?

Compared to 50 years ago, we are clearly more likely to extend equal treatment to *both* these groups, at least in the arena of presidential politics. In past decades, a majority would not have voted for women, blacks, or Jews for president, and one-third would not have supported a Catholic like President Kennedy. The likelihood of electing a black president during the 1930s was so minimal that polling organizations did not even ask respondents about it!

Sources: Michael Corbett, *Political Tolerance in America* (New York: Longman, 1982), p. 50; Gallup Report (July 1987), pp. 16–19.

Representative Pat Schroeder (D-Colo.) was one of a large number of candidates for the Democratic presidential nomination in 1988. Like most of the other candidates, she dropped out early because she could not garner adequate support.

Percentages Willing to Vote for a Woman or Minority Candidate for President

Year	Woman	Black	Jew	Catholic
1936–1937	31	—	46	64
1958	55	47	62	68
1969	55	67	86	88
1978	76	77	82	91
1987	82	79	86	—

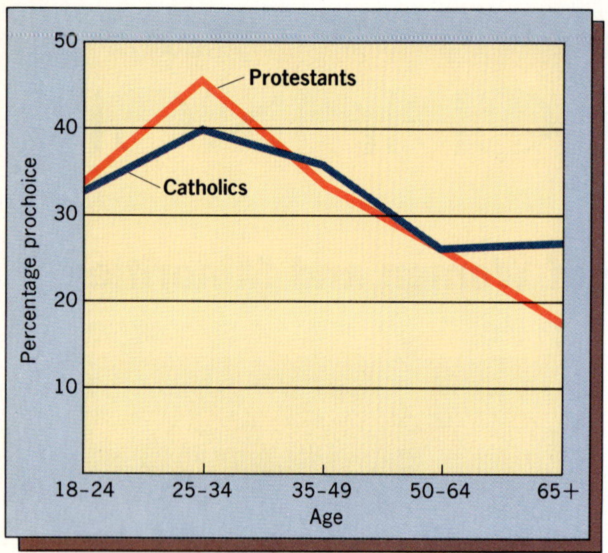

Figure 7–4 Attitudes toward abortion, according to age and religion, 1984. Source: 1984 National Election Study, Center for Political Studies.

other hand, differ with age. Generally younger people have more permissive views than older people.

A major social issue in the past involved the prohibition of the manufacture, sale, and transportation of alcohol. A moral crusade, Prohibition overrode other issues and dominated political campaigns. No compromises between "wets" and "drys" could be reached. In 1919 the Prohibition amendment was adopted. Never observed very fully, it was repealed in 1933.

The political power behind a social issue is frequently an "intense minority"—a small group of people who care intensely about the issue. Gun control is a good example of a current issue with an intense minority on one side and a large, indifferent majority on the other. Nine out of ten Americans favor a seven-day waiting period before purchasing a handgun, and two out of three favor the registration of all guns.[17] Even gun owners share these views with the rest of the public. A small minority holding the opposite views, however, is far more active on the issue, and its visibility creates the impression that public opinion is more evenly divided. (See Chapter 10 for an analysis of the National Rifle Association.)

Determinants of Issue Positions

Many factors contribute to shaping one's political views. The issue of reducing government services to reduce spending has been addressed by both parties for many years; it can serve as an example here. In general, Republican candidates

TABLE 7–3

Attitudes Toward Reduced Government Services and Reduced Spending According to Party Identification

	Democrats	Independents	Republicans
Reduce services to reduce spending	17%	35%	51%
Neither alternative	32	29	27
Increase services	52	36	22
Total	101%	100%	100%
n	345	341	267

Source: 1984 National Election Study, Center for Political Studies.

Flagging hopes for the presidency. Michael Dukakis had great difficulty in dealing with issues such as the Pledge of Allegiance and the pollution of Boston Harbor in his 1988 campaign for the presidency. Republicans used these issues to question his record as governor of Massachusetts.

favor reducing taxes by reducing services, and Democratic candidates favor maintaining (or increasing) services even if increased government spending is required. People would be attracted to a political party because they agree with the positions taken by party leaders. And people who identify with a party would follow the leaders by taking the same issue positions. Table 7–3 shows the expected pattern between party identification and the issue of reduced services. Democrats favor the maintenance of services, while Republicans favor reduced services. Quite strong, the relationship has existed for many years.

On foreign policy and other issues, the differences between Democratic and Republican voters are not so sharp. On some issues, there are really no differences. Democrats and Republicans do not have distinctly different views on overall defense policy or on how to deal with the Soviet Union, but Republicans are more likely to favor higher levels of spending for the military. There are no great differences in the views on abortion or racial equality. Since almost all blacks are Democrats, there is a tendency for Democrats overall to be more in favor of the civil rights movement and policies to help minorities.

"Perspectives"

On Public Opinion and Ideology

"*Our conclusion . . . must be a middle-of-the-road one: voters both here and abroad are neither super-sophisticated nor abysmally ignorant. Individuals form a continuum, with a small group at the very top in knowledge and sophistication, but only a small group as well who are totally uninformed. The only surprise is that it has taken us so long to realize that this truism applies to ideological thinking and all aspects of political knowledge just as it applies to most other subjects.*"

—Richard G. Niemi and Herbert F. Weisberg

"*Americans are not creatures of coherent, wide-ranging ideologies. But their ideas do seem to reflect, in complex ways, preferences of modest scope. They are for some groups, and against others. They desire some values, and oppose others. In this sense, Americans' political beliefs* are *ideological. More generally, American public opinion is of many and diverse pieces, a mosaic of partisan attachments, social relations, values, and personality.*"

—Donald R. Kinder

"*The bulk of the population, perhaps 75 percent, share a homogeneous pattern of opinion and behavior. They are marginally attentive to politics and mildly cynical about the behavior of politicians, but they accept the duty to vote, and they do so with fair regularity. This is the great middle stratum.*"

—W. Russell Neuman

"*Citizens are not as uninvolved, uninformed, and undemocratic as their critics would have us believe, and the nature of citizen politics is changing in ways that should strengthen the democratic process—if political systems respond to these trends.*"

—Russell J. Dalton

Sources: Richard G. Niemi and Herbert F. Weisberg, eds., *Controversies in Voting Behavior,* 2d ed. (Washington, D.C.: CQ Press, 1984), p. 326; Donald R. Kinder, "Diversity and Complexity in American Public Opinion," in *Political Science: The State of the Discipline,* ed. Ada W. Finifter (Washington, D.C.: American Political Science Association, 1983), p. 413; W. Russell Neuman, *The Paradox of Mass Politics* (Cambridge, Mass.: Harvard University Press, 1986), p. 170; Russell J. Dalton, *Citizen Politics in Western Democracies* (Chatham, N.J.: Chatham House, 1988), p. xiv.

The positions people take on issues do not reflect an orderly view of politics. There is little overall consistency—even on issues that appear to be closely related. The general public does not view issues in the same way as do politically active persons. Among the latter, for example, there is likely to be a combination of prolife views on abortion and opposition to the ERA, or prochoice views and support for the ERA. Among ordinary citizens, the relationship between these two issues is weak.

This is not unusual. People take positions on most issues without regard to any broad organizing principles. As a social scientist might say, there is not much *ideological constraint* between issues in

American public opinion.[18] Although liberals tend to take different positions from conservatives, Americans approach issues in a practical rather than an ideological way.

It is appropriate to describe public opinion with respect to specific issues. After all, the connection between popular attitudes and government policies is of great interest to the public, political leaders, and analysts. To some degree, we assess the performance of a democracy by how closely policies coincide with the preferences of the people. On the other hand, we should not be surprised that public opinion is not always translated directly into policy; elected leaders may not agree with public opinion on every matter. Political leaders must decide how closely to follow the demands of the public and when to use their own judgment. Few leaders have any foolproof method of assessing public opinion; it is too difficult and costly to use polls constantly.

Ideology in America

Some people view politics with a broad perspective. A framework of ideas and information about politics that organizes beliefs and values is an *ideology.* In the American political system, an ideology usually focuses on the role of government in regulating the economy and financing social programs. A *liberal* ideology favors more government policies to promote welfare and regulate business. A *conservative* ideology opposes such government involvement and proposes freedom of business from government regulation.

Many issues that divide Americans can be placed on a liberal-to-conservative continuum. For example, a liberal position favors government medical insurance, job guarantees, and school integration; the conservative position opposes these issues. Actually, a number of moral and cultural issues also divide liberals from conservatives in

"Glad you brought that up, Jim. The latest research on polls has turned up some interesting variables. It turns out, for example, that people will tell you any old thing that pops into their heads."

American society today. There are fairly substantial differences on the death penalty, pornography, premarital sex, homosexuality, and legalizing marijuana. On the other hand, there are almost no differences on gun control, busing for integration, and abortion. Not everyone who assumes a liberal or conservative position, though, thinks in ideological terms or is even aware that an ideological position exists.

Ideological Identification

Figure 7–5 shows the ideological composition of the American public. Several major conclusions can be drawn from these periodic readings of the public mind. First, about one-third of the citizenry has no ideological orientation whatsoever. If anything, the public is less ideological today than in the past. Second, conservatives clearly outnumber liberals, typically by a sizable margin. The evidence is plain that liberals have lost ground in American politics. The proportion of conservatives, nevertheless, has fluctuated relatively little during the past decade. And third, the largest gain since the early 1970s has been registered among those citizens for whom ideology carries no meaning. It is interesting to find that the increase in voting for conservative candidates in recent elections, reflected in the composition of Congress and in the presidential victories of Ronald Reagan and George Bush, has not been accompanied by a shift in the ideological coloration of the electorate. The truth is that a surprising number of people appear to be wholly unaffected by the ideological clashes in Congress over public policy issues or by the ideological appeals of presidential contenders.

Ideology and Issues

Americans often describe themselves as liberal on some issues and conservative on others. In other words, individuals are rarely consistent in their ideological preferences. As Table 7–4 shows, however, in the average behavior of the general public there is a clear relationship between ideological identification and attitudes on a wide range of issues. It is important to keep in mind, however, that many people are excluded from Table 7–4 because they do not have an opinion on an issue or lack an ideological orientation.

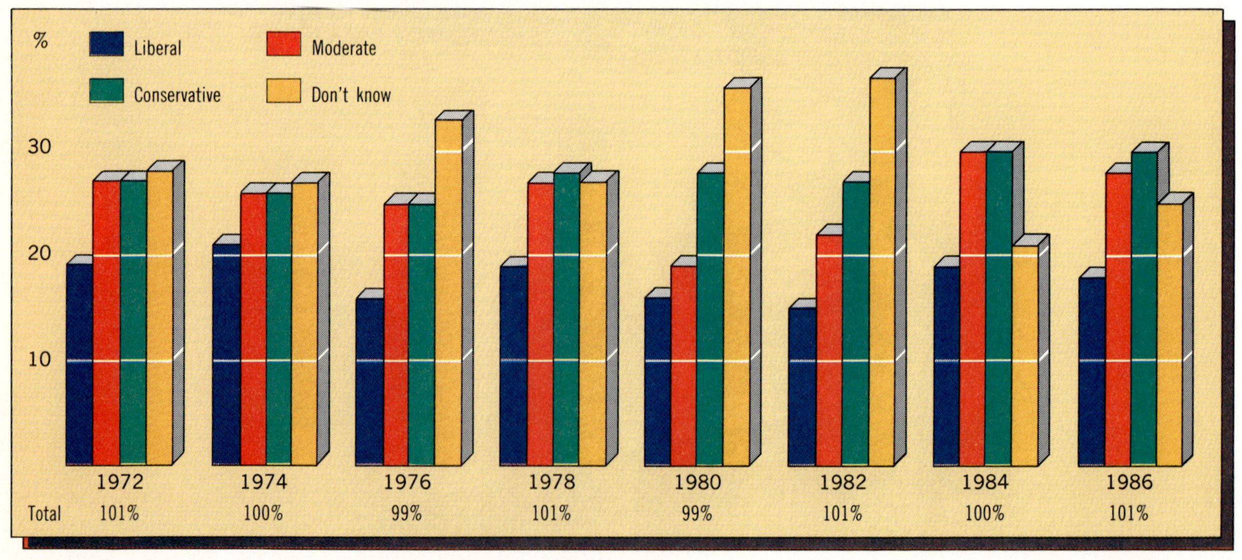

Figure 7–5 Ideological identification, 1972–1986. Source: National Election Studies, Center for Political Studies. (Totals do not add to 100 percent because of rounding.)

TABLE 7–4

Percentage Holding Liberal Positions on Issues According to Ideology, 1972–1984

	Liberal	Middle of the Road			Conservative
Defense spending (1984)	62	43	32	24	19
Maintaining services (1984)	71	68	53	44	35
Abortion (1984)	60	50	39	35	28
Government guarantee of jobs (1984)	52	36	28	20	19
Getting along with Russia (1984)	65	52	34	33	20
Equal Rights Amendment (1980)	91	78	64	48	38
Prayer in schools (1980)	57	41	24	30	14
Protect rights of accused (1976)	59	41	29	22	20
Government medical insurance (1976)	66	45	33	27	16
Legalize marijuana (1976)	60	49	24	24	10
Tax rates (1972)	52	41	36	30	29
Vietnam (1972)	75	61	39	33	27

Source: National Election Studies, Center for Political Studies.

Social Origins of Ideology

Chapter 6 introduced the concept of socialization to describe how people learn the basic elements of political culture. Learning what ideology means and how one feels about liberal and conservative ideas is one aspect of socialization. Ideology, like other political orientations, is often acquired through the family. Liberal families tend to turn out liberal children, while conservative families tend to produce conservative offspring.

As Table 7–5 shows, most social characteristics are unrelated to liberalism *or* conservatism, however. There are no ideological differences between men and women, and practically none between Protestants and Catholics, or between union and nonunion families. Nor is there much ideological variation by region. By contrast, these social characteristics are more highly related to partisanship, as will be seen in Chapter 8.

Young people are more liberal than older people; in fact, the young and blacks are the only categories more liberal than conservative. People over 50 years of age are distinctly more conservative than liberal. This may mean that people become more conservative as they get older—but it is just as possible that the older persons in the population today were always more conservative.

Although it is accepted wisdom that social status is related to liberalism and conservatism, no distinctive relationship appears in our data. Among several indicators of social status in Table 7–5, education, occupation, and income are the most obvious. For none of these is there a simple, consistent relationship to ideology. For education and occupation, both the high- and low-status groups are more conservative than the middle groups. High-income groups are the most conservative, and the lowest-income group is least conservative, but the categories in between are not arranged in an orderly

“ Perspectives ”

On Liberalism

Many different viewpoints claim the label liberal and, indeed, the term has changed meaning over the years. These remarks are taken from a speech by Mario Cuomo, governor of New York, who gave the keynote address to the Democratic National Convention in 1984.

> *Ten days ago, President Reagan admitted that although some people in this country seemed to be doing well nowadays, others were unhappy, and even worried, about themselves, their families and their futures.*
>
> *The President said he didn't understand that fear. He said, "Why, this country is a shining city on the hill."*
>
> *A shining city is perhaps all the President sees from the portico of the White House and the veranda of his ranch, where everyone seems to be doing well.*
>
> *But there's another part of the city, the part where some people can't pay their mortgages and most young people can't afford one, where students can't afford the education they need and middle-class parents watch the dreams they hold for their children evaporate.*
>
> *Maybe if you visited more places, Mr. President, you'd understand. . . .*
>
> *Maybe if you went to Appalachia where some people still live in sheds and to Lackawanna where thousands of unemployed steel workers wonder why we subsidized foreign steel while we surrender their dignity to unemployment and to welfare checks; maybe if you stepped into a shelter in Chicago and talked with some of the homeless there; maybe, Mr. President, if you asked a woman who'd been denied the help she needs to feed her children because you say we need the money to give a tax break to a millionaire or to build a missile we can't even afford to use—maybe then you'd understand. . . .*
>
> *We believe in only the government we need, but we insist on all the government we need. . . .*
>
> *We believe that a society as blessed as ours . . . ought to be able to help the middle class in its struggle, ought to be able to find work for all who can do it, room at the table, shelter for the homeless, care for the elderly and infirm, hope for the destitute.*
>
> *We believe in firm but fair law and order, in the union movement, in privacy for people, openness by government, civil rights, and human rights.*
>
> *We can have a future that provides for all the young of the present by marrying common sense and compassion.*
>
> *. . . for the good of all of us, for the love of this great nation . . .*

Mario Cuomo, Governor of New York.

“ Perspectives ”

On Conservatism

There are many conservative views and interpretations of politics and certainly no authoritative statement of an agreement on principles. These comments were taken from a speech made by William Simon, a former secretary of the treasury, before the Heritage Foundation.

Think back two hundred years or so. How did the world look? The English philosopher Hobbes put it briskly and sharply: human beings could look forward to a life that was "solitary, poor, nasty, brutish and short."

Then something extraordinary happened—something called America. . . . The revolutionary idea was that governments exist to protect liberty. Governments do not bestow rights on their citizens. . . .

Adam Smith challenged the old idea that the wealth of nations is destined to decline or, at best, remain fixed forever. Wealth could be created, the standard of living could be raised—raised beyond even our wildest dreams—but this would require two fundamental changes in the way that we lived.

First, it would require unleashing human creativity; and second, it would require getting the state out of the way of the marketplace. . . .

"Without the Constitution and the Union," Abraham Lincoln said, "we could not have attained the result; but even these are not the primary cause of our great prosperity. There is something back of these, entwining itself more closely about the human heart. That something is the principle of 'Liberty to All'—the principle that clears the path for all—and by consequence, enterprise and industry to all."

William E. Simon, former Secretary of the Treasury.

The formula for success has not changed nor will it: it is freedom and incentives for people to work hard, save and create.

True freedom is not mere absence of restraint; true freedom is not a license to do all we please. The success of the Constitution, the success of America and the American dream, hinge directly on our willingness to couple freedom with a sense of moral responsibility—responsibility to our family; responsibility to our community; responsibility to our country; and ultimately and inescapably, responsibility to our God who rules us all.

TABLE 7–5

Social Characteristics of Liberals, Moderates, and Conservatives, 1986

	Liberals	Moderates	Conservatives
National region	20	46	28
East	19	49	23
Midwest	20	45	31
South	17	48	26
West	26	39	31
Sex			
Male	19	46	29
Female	21	45	27
Age			
18–24	24	47	20
25–29	27	41	26
30–49	20	47	27
50–64	12	47	34
65 and over	17	43	33
Race			
White	19	65	30
Black	26	50	14
Hispanic	23	37	32
Education			
College graduate	23	43	33
Some college	19	51	24
High school	20	47	27
Less than high school	17	39	30
Occupation			
Professional and business	21	47	30
Clerical and sales	21	56	19
Manual workers	22	41	27
Income			
$50,000 and over	23	41	33
$35,000 and 49,999	20	45	33
$25,000 and 34,999	23	50	25
$15,000 and 24,999	18	46	28
$10,000 and 14,999	17	45	29
Under $10,000	21	45	19
Religion			
Protestant	18	46	30
Catholic	21	47	26
Labor union			
Union family	22	46	27
Nonunion family	19	45	29

Source: *Gallup Report,* no. 249 (June 1986), pp. 20–21.

pattern. Race provides another example of mixed ideological patterns: Whites are distributed about as the national average, blacks are quite a bit more liberal, and Hispanics, a relatively low-income group, are more conservative.

The important point is that these social characteristics do not significantly determine ideology. In American society all kinds of people become liberals and conservatives. Ideology is a political, not a social or economic, orientation.

Although there is considerable variation in the relationship between issues and the political parties, Democrats and Republicans differ in their ideologies.[19] Republicans are similar in their ideology; for the most part, they are conservatives. Few are liberals, and not many more are moderates. Democrats are only slightly more liberal than conservative. Both Democrats and independents are about evenly divided into liberals, conservatives, and middle-of-the-roaders. Table 7–6 shows the distribution of party and ideology in 1984. These patterns have not changed much in 20 years. This suggests that there is a fairly strong link between party and ideology. While the parties provide an ideological base of support for the leaders if they choose to seek it, independents are neither strongly liberal nor conservative.

When people are asked where their party stands on ideology, they give conflicting views. Both Democrats and Republicans tend to see their own party as moderate and the other party as rather extreme. Independents believe both parties are extreme. So the overall perception is that Democrat's are strongly liberal and Republican's are strongly conservative. In fact, this corresponds fairly closely to the current party leadership. But it is not an accurate perception of the parties' followers.

Levels of Political Thinking

Most Americans do not think about politics in ideological terms; they do not analyze leaders or political parties with abstract ideas. Their analysis is concrete and down to earth. Politics is understood by most people in terms of who is helped and who is hurt.

Beginning in 1956 with *The American Voter,* a classic study of political behavior, analysts have assessed the public's political thinking.[20] In many national surveys, people have been asked what they think of the political parties and the presidential candidates. Their answers have been classified according to how sophisticated their reasons are for liking or not liking the parties or candidates (see Table 7–7). The most sophisticated individuals gave their answers in ideological terms, describing politics with words like *liberal* and *conservative.*

Somewhat less complicated responses described candidates and parties as helping or hurting groups in society by their policy stands. These "group benefits" reasons are not as sophisticated as ideological answers, yet they are thoroughly political in content. Viewing politics in terms of who gains and who loses makes good sense and should not be thought of as uninformed.

TABLE 7–6

Distribution of Ideology by Party Identification, 1984

	Democrats	Independents	Republicans
Liberal	39%	25%	13%
Middle of the road	36	39	23
Conservative	25	37	64
Total	100%	101%	100%
n	274	276	238

Source: 1984 National Election Study, Center for Political Studies.

TABLE 7–7

Levels of Political Thinking

Levels of Political Thinking	1956	1960	1964	1968	1972	1976	1980
Ideologues	12%	19%	27%	26%	22%	21%	21%
Group benefits	42	31	27	24	27	26	31
Nature of times	24	26	20	29	34	30	31
No issue content	22	23	26	21	17	24	17
Total	100%	99%	100%	100%	100%	101%	100%
n	(1740)	(1741)	(1431)	(1319)	(1372)	(2879)	(1535)

Source: Paul R. Hagner and John C. Pierce, "Conceptualization and Consistency in Political Beliefs: 1956–1976," paper presented at the annual meeting of the Midwest Political Science Association, April 1981, p. 29, table 1; personal communication from John Pierce for 1980.

The last two categories suggest that many people do not have a meaningful basis for evaluating politics. Regardless of the election year and the candidates, about half the public gave basically nonpolitical, uninformed answers.

Table 7–7 presents the levels of political thinking by Americans from 1956 to 1980.[21] The most interesting change is the increase in ideological evaluations by 1964. The first year (1956) was perhaps unusually low in the use of ideological language by the public. It is likely that the public reflects the language used in a campaign.

Many Americans do not have a clear idea of the meaning of "liberal" and "conservative" labels. Thus, there are limits to the influence of ideology on opinions and voting. People who hear that President George Bush is a conservative may decide that they, too, are conservative. But if they have no idea what that means, they are not likely to change their position on issues.

Attitude Change

The stability of public opinion should not be exaggerated. Party loyalties are stable for most people, but political opinions are more changeable. Some change in opinion occurs because circumstances change. But much of the change is made easier because people do not feel too strongly about their views.

An example of a relatively volatile political opinion is the evaluation of the job the president is doing. For all recent presidents, evaluations have varied from strongly positive—usually early in their terms—to at least moderately negative—usually late in their terms. Most people are not intensely committed to their evaluation of the president, so these attitudes are not hard to change. Also, there are huge amounts of information available on which to base an evaluation.

The evaluations of presidents follow the election cycle. Immediately after being inaugurated, a new president enjoys a highly favorable evaluation. This high level of approval gradually declines over the term. Sometimes there are sharp changes. The public's evaluation of President Ford, for example, dropped immediately after his pardon of Richard Nixon. In spring 1981, President Reagan's job rating sharply improved after he was shot. Overall, the trend has been gradual disapproval of presidents the longer they are in office (see Chapter 13).

By the end of his second term in office President Reagan had regained most of the popularity he had lost since early in his administration, and

Youth, Ideology, and Political Volatility

In the United States young people reach voting age with a set of political values that may be changeable. American children learn about politics from their families and perhaps other people in the neighborhood, from television (but generally not newspapers or magazines), and from school and other social institutions. Many will go the rest of their lives without altering the political views they learned in childhood, but others will change.

In the late 1960s and early 1970s, college freshmen were twice as likely to think of themselves as liberal than as conservative. Since then, there has been little change in the number of conservatives, but a significant drop in liberalism. However, the views of today's freshmen can alter, and in recent years the young have changed politically in a way quite unlike the general population.

The table below shows the attitudes of an "age cohort" in 1980, when the individuals were 18 to 29 years old (the youngest members of the electorate), in 1984, and again in 1988, when they were 26 to 37. This group became increasingly Republican and conservative during the eight years of the Reagan administration. In fact, it became more and more like the rest of the general electorate.

Young people are more volatile because they are less set in their ways. They are also less interested in politics and less well informed than older members of the electorate. And this characteristic may be growing. Compared to the 1960s and 1970s, college freshmen today express less interest in political affairs and community action. They are more inclined to think that there is little they can do to change society. (While these attitudes may explain an increasing orientation toward careers in business, an increased interest in financial success is largely found in women, reflecting other changes in society.)

Young people are simply more susceptible to political forces. At various times during the campaign of 1988, the young were viewed as the core of Dukakis's support and the hope of the Republicans for the future. In July the youngest voters favored Dukakis by 53 percent to 34 percent. By October they had switched to Bush, 64 percent to 28 percent. Ultimately, they disappointed both hopes. In November they voted in favor of Bush—by just about the national average.

	18- to 29-Year-Olds in 1980	22- to 33-Year-Olds in 1984	26- to 37-Year-Olds in 1988
Republican	20%	28%	33%
Independent	38	37	32
Democratic	42	35	35
	100	100	100
Liberal	28	24	18
Conservative	25	27	32

Sources: *New York Times,* October 31, 1988, pp. 1, 8; American Council on Education, *National Norms for Entering College Freshmen* (Washington, D.C.: ACE Office of Research, 1967–1972); American Council on Education, *The American Freshman: National Norms* (Los Angeles: UCLA Graduate School of Education, 1974–1987).

he became more popular than other recent presidents. Immediately after the Iran-contra affair made headlines, President Reagan's approval rating dropped 20 percentage points; during his last six months in office he recovered from that loss.[22]

President Reagan often scored lower in specific areas than in his overall job rating. Yet at the end of his term in office, after securing the INF missile treaty, he received high approval (over 70 percent) for his dealings with the Russians. In the public's view, it was a major accomplishment of his presidency.

Although many political opinions are quite stable, evaluations of president's performance serve to illustrate the volatility of political opinion. Shifts in the economy, scandals, or international crises bring on sudden changes. One lesson might be that it is easier to lose popularity than to increase it.

The direct impact of public opinion on political leaders and governmental decisions is hard to judge. But it is clear that the views of large numbers of people can rarely be traced through the policymaking process. The reason is that most opinions are too general and held too casually to compel leaders to take a specific course of action. Policymakers, moreover, are not always sure that what they hear, advanced by the most attentive sector of the public, is in fact what *most* people prefer. Yet in a broad sense, public opinion does set the boundaries within which public decisions are made. It also sets the boundaries within which competing political leaders and organizations contest for power. Those leaders who are clearly out of step with the broad thrust of majority opinion risk re-

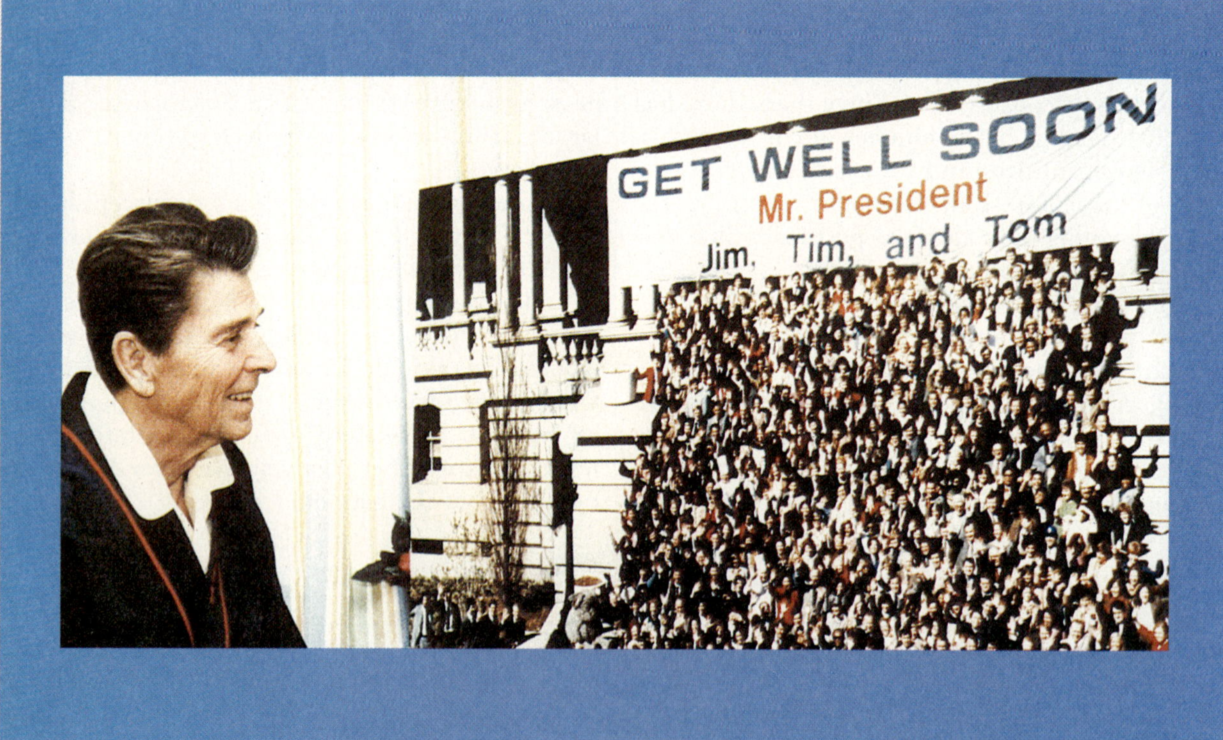

Throughout his eight years in office, President Ronald Reagan enjoyed a great measure of personal popularity. When he suffered personal calamities, such as an assassination attempt or an illness, his popularity increased further. He invariably managed to appear good-natured and humorous in difficult circumstances, and the American public responded positively to his style.

jection and defeat. Their waywardness is an invitation for challengers to instruct the public and to focus a campaign against them. So elections matter: They do more than simply determine winners; they tap certain widely held attitudes and help to reflect, in a generalized way, the dominant values of the public.

Summary

- The public is not grealy interested in or extremely well informed about most political issues. Most people pay very little attention to government affairs.
- A small number of citizens—the attentive public—are aware of most issues and fairly well informed about politics generally. However, most people pay attention to the few issues they care about; they are usually aware of how leaders stand on such issues.
- Different types of issues and problems dominate American politics from time to time. Usually economic issues are important, although foreign affairs, social issues, and racial matters have been the center of attention briefly in recent years.
- Even though economic issues dealing with welfare, government services, and the regulation of business are interrelated, the American public is not particularly ideological. About one-third have never thought of themselves as ideological. There are now more conservatives than liberals, but almost no signs of further shifting in a conservative direction.
- In the absence of a strong ideology, most people rely on party identification to orient their political views and behavior. Most Americans learn to be Democrats or Republicans early in life and maintain those loyalties through their adult years. In the past decade or so, increasingly large numbers of young people have entered the electorate as independents.
- Most attitudes on subjects that people care about remain stable over time. When public opinion changes sharply, it is usually an indication that people are indifferent and poorly informed about that particular issue, or that it is not important to them.

Readings on Public Opinion and Ideology

Abramson, Paul R. 1983. *Political Attitudes in America: Formation and Change.* San Francisco: W. H. Freeman. A broad analysis of public opinion in the United States.

Asher, Herbert. 1988. *Polling and the Public.* Washington, D.C.: CQ Press. An introduction to the methods and analysis of public opinion surveys.

Converse, Philip. 1964. "The Nature of Belief Systems in Mass Publics," in *Ideology and Discontent,* ed. David Apter. New York: Free Press of Glencoe. The major study of political sophistication among leaders and the public.

Delli Carpini, Michael. 1986. *Stability and Change in American Politics.* New York: New York University Press. A study of the attitudes of the 1960s generation.

Erikson, Robert, Norman Luttbeg, and Kent Tedin. 1987. *American Public Opinion.* New York: John Wiley & Sons. A comprehensive survey of work on public opinion.

Hochschild, Jennifer. 1981. *What's Fair?* Cambridge: Harvard University Press. An in-depth study of a small group of people to explore their political and economic values.

Jennings, M. Kent, and Richard G. Niemi. 1974. *The Political Character of Adolescence.* Princeton: Princeton University Press. One of several socialization studies based on interviews with high school seniors and their parents.

Lane, Robert. 1962. *Political Ideology.* New York: Free Press. An in-depth study of 15 men and their orientation to politics.

Pierce, John C., Kathleen M. Beatty, and Paul R. Hagner. 1982. *The Dyamics of American Public Opinion.* Glenview, Ill.: Scott, Foresman. An analysis of popular attitudes toward issues, ideology, and the political system.

Public Opinion, published by the American Enterprise Institute. An interesting journal of analysis, interpretative essays, and public opinion data from many sources.

Chapter 8

Voters and Elections

Elections and the Political System
- Types of Elections
- Election Outcomes
- Electoral College

Characteristics of Elections

Electoral Behavior
- Analysis of Vote Choice
- Partisanship
- Social Characteristics of Partisans and Independents
- Short-Term Forces and Vote Choice

Political Campaigns
- Vote Choice in Primary Elections
- Electoral Competition
- Party Alignments

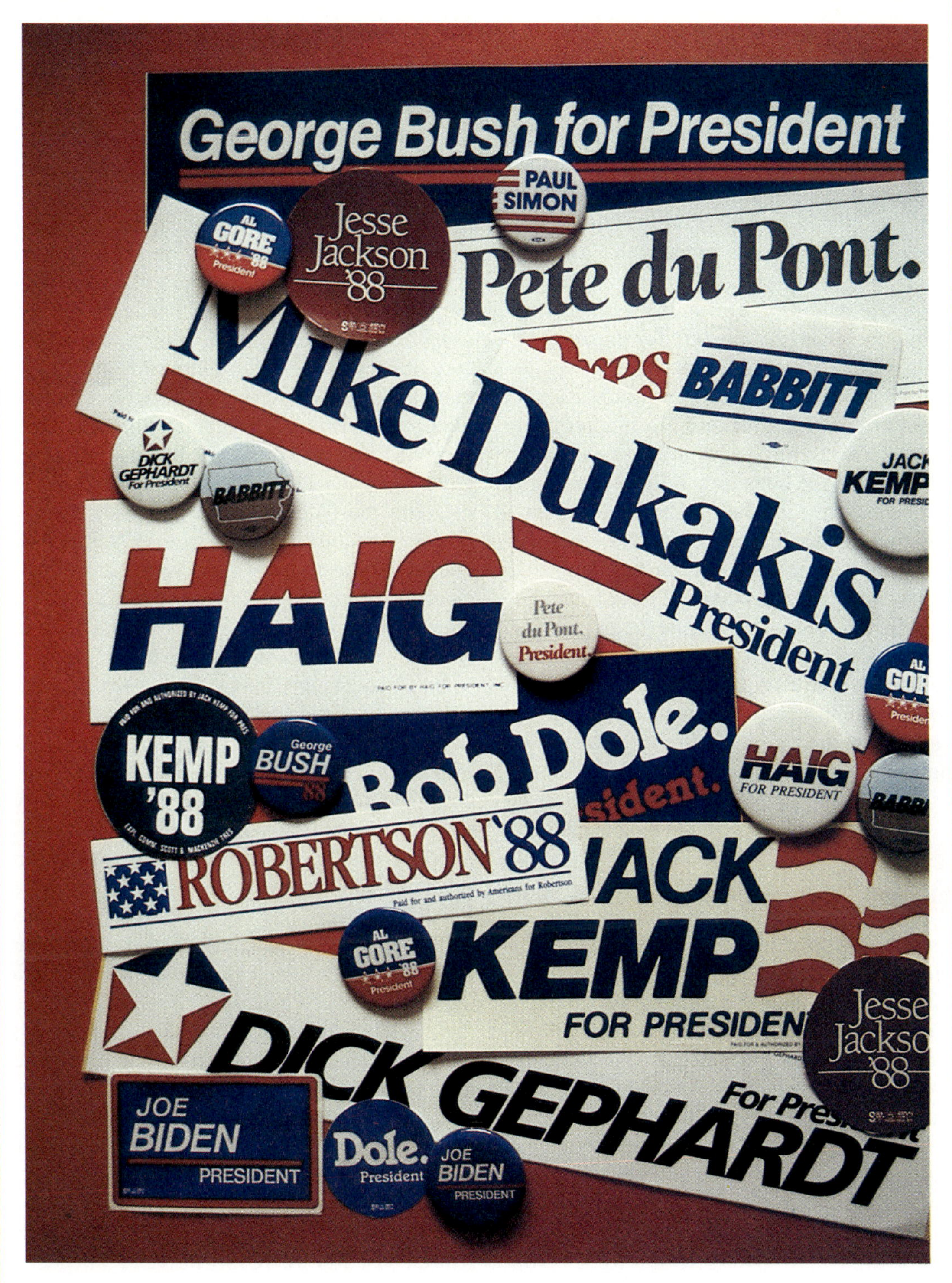

George Bush for President
PAUL SIMON
AL GORE '88 President
Jesse Jackson '88
Pete du Pont.
Mike Dukakis President
BABBITT
DICK GEPHARDT For President
BABBITT
JACK KEMP FOR PRESIDENT
HAIG
PAID FOR BY HAIG FOR PRESIDENT INC
Pete du Pont. President.
AL GORE President
KEMP '88
George BUSH '88
Bob Dole. President.
HAIG FOR PRESIDENT
ROBERTSON '88
Paid for and authorized by Americans for Robertson
JACK KEMP FOR PRESIDENT
AL GORE '88 President
DICK GEPHARDT For President
Jesse Jackson '88
JOE BIDEN PRESIDENT
Dole. President
JOE BIDEN PRESIDENT

Elections are the centerpiece of democratic political systems. They represent the principal means by which the people can hold public officials accountable for their actions. Those in power can be removed from office or entrusted with another term. At the same time, elections give the winners *legitimacy*—the belief that their authority is grounded in popular consent and that the laws they pass must be obeyed. Because democracy rests ultimately on the voluntary consent of citizens, understanding the voter is important for understanding a democratic political system.

This chapter begins with an examination of elections and their characteristics. It then moves to a consideration of the forces that influence electoral behavior—that is, the behavior of individuals and groups in selecting public officials. It closes with an analysis of political campaigns, the competitiveness of the system, and the basic changes in voting behavior that have occurred over time. The popular political forces that support the political system are a combination of long-standing beliefs and loyalities in addition to issues and personalities of the moment. Elections capture these forces as voters express their support for and opposition to the political leaders.

Elections and the Political System

The founders clearly intended to make it difficult for temporary majorities to govern. They provided for the election of officials through several different ways. The president is formally chosen for a four-year term by the electoral college. Senators are elected to six-year terms by statewide constituencies, although originally they were selected by state legislatures. Members of the House of Representatives are elected from districts in the states for two-year terms. State and local officials are elected in still other ways.

These complicated arrangements for electing officeholders mean that many different combinations of voters form majorities. The emergence of these majorities—the base of support for political leaders—may have awkward results. In an election like 1988, the Republicans may win the presidency comfortably but fail to gain a majority in the House. Or a city may elect an independent mayor and a Republican-dominated city council, and send a Democrat to Congress.

Mixed election outcomes cause problems in policy making. The coordination of policy and government activity is made more difficult by divided party control. Majorities are harder to put together; deadlocks occur. Overall, the system of elections contributes to the complexity of American government processes. And this is precisely what the founders intended (see Chapter 2). For better or worse, they did not make it easy for elected officials to govern.

The many different elections in the United States have another consequence. Citizens are expected to vote often. Most citizens have two or three chances a year to vote; in some communities, there may be seven or eight elections in a single year. Also, at each election there are usually many offices to be filled. An ordinary citizen—even a near perfect one—finds it difficult to be well informed about so many contests. Most people do not become well informed about most contests. They need to be encouraged to vote. And if they do vote, they need simple, convenient ways to make choices.

Because they have limited information and face so many choices, voters use guides like party endorsements in deciding how to vote. Of course, many voters are attached to the Republican or Democratic party. Most general elections include candidates endorsed by the parties, so voters can link their party preference to a candidate. This contributes to stable voting patterns. Without the guidance provided by political parties, voting would be much more unpredictable and erratic.

American voting behavior is not especially stable. About one-third of the electorate are political independents who identify with neither party. Some voters switch from party to party or vote irregularly. Party switching serves a purpose. Some voters need to be flexible enough to abandon the party they voted for last time; otherwise, officeholders could stop worrying about the people who

"Try to get in a personal word to the schizophrenics, urging them not to vote a split ticket."

supported them. So elections can change the political system. Voters who are willing to switch sides are the key to that change.[1]

Types of Elections

Citizens do not respond to all elections in the same way. And the results of different types of elections cause variable outcomes for the system.

Of the thousands of elections held in the United States each year, the most important are *general elections,* since they decide who will take office. General elections are usually preceded by *primary elections* to choose each party's nominees for offices. In a one-party area, the primary is the crucial stage in the electoral process. The candidate who wins the primary of the dominant party is almost certain to win the general election.

Primaries are used throughout the political system. Except in rare cases, they do not attract large numbers of voters. A turnout of less than one-third of the electorate is the norm. In most states, voters can vote only in the primary of the party to which they belong (see Chapter 9).

There are also referenda in state and local elections.[2] There is a provision for referenda in some 20 states. In a referendum, there are no candidates; voters indicate that they are for or against a statement or proposition. A *referendum* is like an official polling of public opinion. If a referendum is approved by the voters, it ordinarily becomes law.

The election of the president receives the most

In 1988 eleven candidates sought the Democratic presidential nomination, while six candidates competed for the Republican nomination. Shown here are the leading Democratic candidates: (l to r) Gary Hart, Michael S. Dukakis, Bruce Babbitt, Jesse Jackson, Richard A. Gephardt, Paul Simon, and Albert Gore, Jr. Dukakis won primaries in 22 states and first-round caucuses in 12. Jackson placed second, Gore third.

attention in our political system. We usually describe the political course of the nation in terms of the results of presidential elections. And, of course, the president is the single most important leader in American politics.

Election Outcomes

In a common form of election in the United States, the candidate who receives the *most* votes wins. There is only one winner and it is not necessary to have a majority to win—just one more vote than any other candidate. This is called a *plurality* election. Senators, members of the House of Representatives, governors, and many other officials are elected in this way. The importance of this feature for the party system is discussed in Chapter 9.

Competitiveness is the key in plurality, winner-take-all elections. If elections are close, a small number of voters can change the outcome. Candidates "run scared"; they know that every vote counts and they make an effort to win most voters. Close elections make candidates sensitive to popular impulses. When elections are safe, the leading candidate does not need to worry so much about every voter. And the likely loser has no reason to make a strong effort to win.

The Electoral College: "I Should Have Voted for Kitty"

The electoral college vote in 1988 was 426 for George Bush, 111 for Michael Dukakis, and 1 for Lloyd Bentsen. Lloyd Bentsen? How did it happen that the Democratic party's vice presidential candidate received an electoral vote for president? The answer is that Margarette Leach, a Democratic elector from West Virginia, decided to cast her vote for him instead of Dukakis. She was able to do this because, under the Constitution, electors are free to vote for whomever they wish.

Ms. Leach explained her vote for Bentsen:

> "*I wanted to make a statement about the electoral college. We've outgrown it. And I wanted to point up what I perceive as a weakness in the system—that 270 people can get together in this country and elect a president, whether he's on the ballot or not. . . . When I got home I said to myself, I should have voted for Kitty [Dukakis]. If 270 women got together on the electoral college we could have had a woman president.*"

Of incidental interest, about half of the states have laws that require electors to vote for the presidential and vice presidential candidates who receive a plurality of their state's popular vote. Many constitutional scholars believe, however, that these laws are unenforceable.

Source: *New York Times,* January 4, 1989.

In the United States, many areas are generally safe for Republicans and other areas are generally safe for Democrats. These safe areas protect a party from losing everything in bad years. Even when disaster strikes a party, it manages to win enough elections to keep going. In 1974, the Republican party had a bad year with the Watergate scandal and Nixon's resignation, but the party was not destroyed. By 1980, the Republicans had recovered.

Elections in competitive areas have the opposite effect. Because these areas switch from party to party, they make it possible to remove one party from power and give the other party a chance to govern.

These two types of electoral constituencies—safe and competitive—make the political parties stable and the government changeable. The balance of these two conditions changes through the years. Recently, more and more elections have been close for governors and senators. Elections for U.S. representatives, by contrast, have become safer[3] (see Chapter 12). The House of Representatives has been controlled by Democrats almost continuously since the New Deal.

Electoral College ■

The election of a president is particularly complex.[4] Each state is a unit in the electoral college, and in voting for president it selects a slate of electors pledged to a candidate. The number of electors in a state reflects its size, since there is one elector for each senator and one for each representative. Thus, each state has at least three electoral college

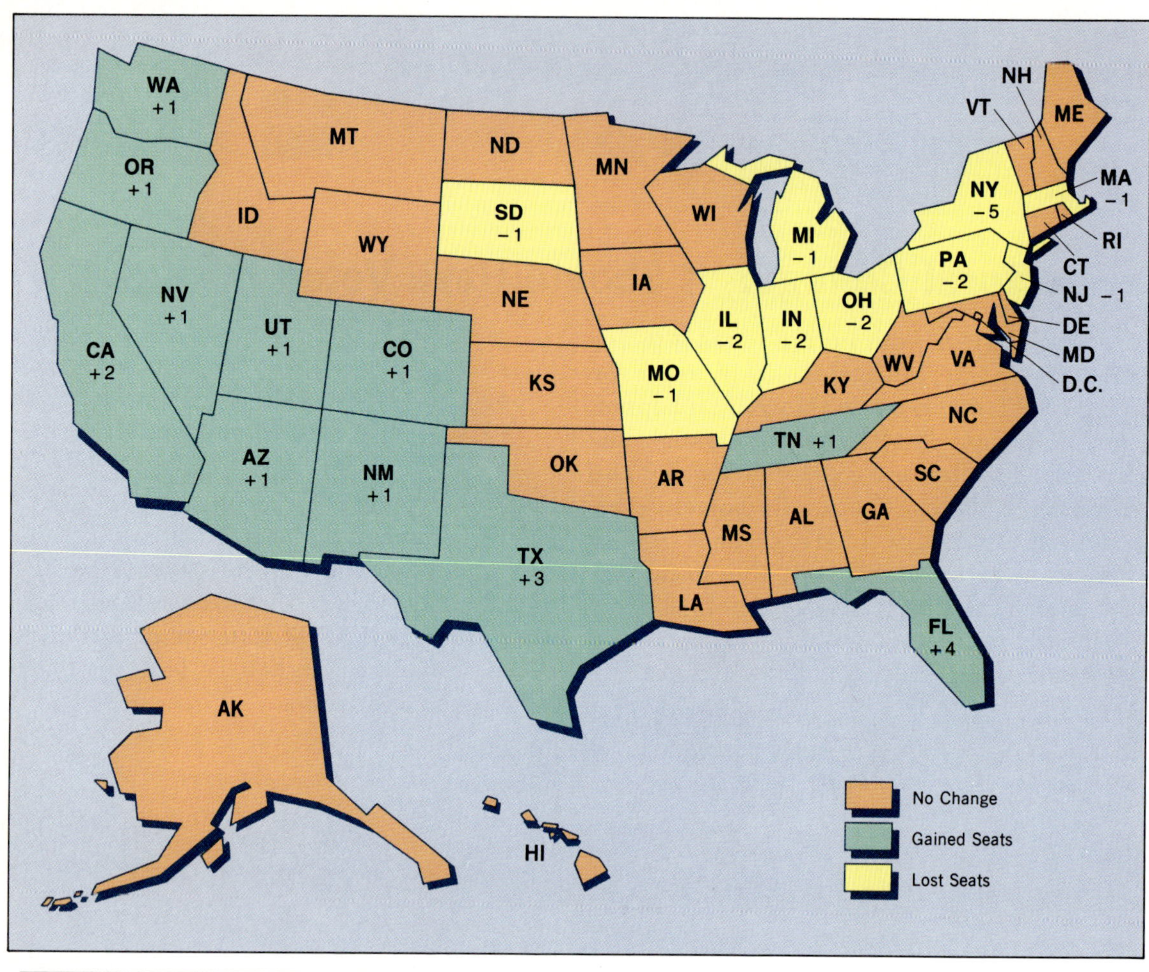

Figure 8–1 Political power shifts South and West.

votes and the District of Columbia is entitled to three electors under the Twenty-third Amendment. States with many congressional districts have many votes in the electoral college. California leads all states with 47 electoral votes, followed by New York with 36.

Every 10 years, the results of a new census cause some states to lose representation in the House of Representatives while other states gain. Following the 1980 census, large states in the Midwest and Northeast lost seats to states in the West and South, reflecting the shifts in population (see Figure 8–1). Population migration toward the South and West continued during the 1980s and will be reflected in the reapportionment of House seats in the early 1990s. These trends represent increasing political power for the "Sunbelt."

All states except Maine award their electoral votes in a block to the presidential candidate who wins a plurality of the popular vote in the state. A presidential candidate can thus have a one-sided victory in the electoral college, with a very close election in popular votes. Indeed, it is possible for a candidate to win in the electoral college and lose in the popular vote. This happened twice in the nineteenth century. Both Rutherford B. Hayes

(1876) and Benjamin Harrison (1888) became president after being outpolled by their opponents. If there is no candidate with a majority in the electoral college, the election shifts to the House of Representatives, where each state delegation casts a single vote. A presidential election has not been decided in the House since 1825.

The unusual method of rewarding state winners in the electoral college leads candidates to try to win votes in large, competitive states. The switching of a few votes can lead to big gains in the electoral college. In 1960, for example, John Kennedy won Illinois by about 9000 votes and Texas by about 56,000, giving him 51 electoral votes. Had some 4500 Illinois voters and 28,000 Texas voters voted Republican rather than Democratic, Richard Nixon would have been elected by a margin of two electoral votes. A switch of less than 8000 votes in Hawaii and Ohio in 1976 would have elected Gerald Ford instead of Jimmy Carter, and nearly 80 million votes were cast in that election.

Of course, in a landslide like 1984, millions of votes would have to change to alter the outcome. Ronald Reagan won 525 electoral votes, carrying every state but Minnesota (10 electoral votes) and the District of Columbia (3 electoral votes). His electoral vote margin was the second largest in history. (Franklin D. Roosevelt defeated Alf Landon in 1936 by a margin of 523 to 8.)

George Bush won a comfortable victory in

Guarded by security personnel, George Bush mixes with a friendly crowd during the 1988 presidential campaign. Bush received 48,886,097 popular votes, or 53.37 percent of the total votes cast. It is safe to say that he did not shake hands with all 48 million supporters, though media coverage sometimes creates such an impression.

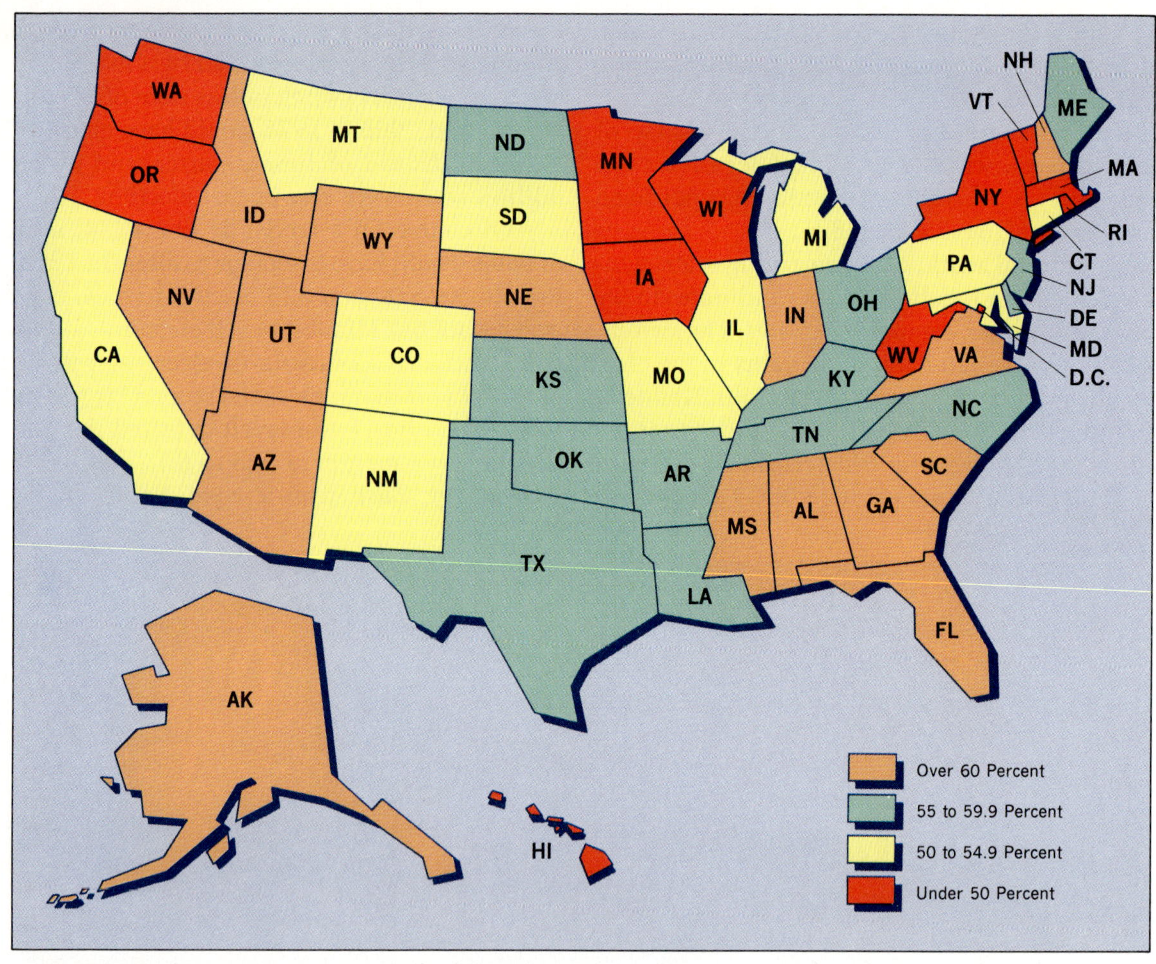

Figure 8–2 The map shows the distribution by state of the popular vote in the 1988 presidential election, showing the percentage for Bush. Source: *New York Times*, November 10, 1988.

1988, with 426 electoral votes against 111 for Michael Dukakis, who won only ten states and the District of Columbia. Nevertheless, the ticket of Dukakis and Bentsen made a strong showing in a number of large states carried by Bush, and they ran significantly better than had Mondale and Ferraro in 1984 (Figure 8–2). Republican presidential candidates have appeared overwhelmingly dominant in southern and Rocky Mountain states for some years. Those states may not provide a majority in electoral votes, but they represent a key advantage for the Republican candidate in a presidential election.

A dozen or so big states are crucial to presidential candidates because of the electoral college. It is much more important to win California with its 47 electoral votes than to win Alaska with 3. Alaska, in fact, may not even be worth a campaign visit. The electoral college invariably skews campaigns and the issues given attention, since the big states differ in many ways from their smaller neighbors. Toward the end of the 1988 campaign both

Bush and Dukakis focused their attention exclusively on large states like California and Illinois.

Characteristics of Elections

American elections have two main characteristics: First, there is sharp variation in turnout; second, there is substantial volatility in party voting. Turnout in off-year elections (those with no presidential contest) is particularly poor. As shown in Chapter 6, nearly two out of three eligible voters stay home during these elections.

Turnout in presidential elections is usually over 50 percent and brings large numbers of independents and weak partisans to the polls. In low-turnout elections, less interested voters are less likely to turn out. Low-turnout elections are more likely to be dominated by strong partisans. In general, voters who turn out in presidential elections are more volatile and more easily influenced than those who vote in low-turnout elections. This is a particular form of the coattail effect—the tendency of voters to continue to vote for one party as they move down the ticket.

To some extent, the attention on turnout is misplaced. Elections are a crucial competitive mechanism for selecting and rejecting leaders, regardless of who votes. Candidates are made more aware of their constituents and more responsive to constituent interests when they must campaign for support. The need to seek the support of the people thus has benefits for the political system that do not depend on turnout. Candidates are reminded of the ultimate power of the people to decide through elections who will rule.

But several factors can limit elections as a means of controlling public officials. One is the absence of competition. If elected representatives are so safe that they need not fear defeat, they may pay less attention to their obligations as an officeholder. Elections can also be undermined by corruption. Corruption usually implies fraudulent handling of the election, but corrupt campaign tactics can have the same effect. The quality of competition is damaged when candidates engage in campaigns of distortion and innuendo. While smear campaigns are probably less common today than in the past, the campaign of 1988 was marred by "negative campaigning."

Virtually all elections give rise to a common problem: interpreting their meaning. Did the voters want to send someone a message? Was a candidate punished or rewarded for a stand? Did most voters merely support their traditional party? Did the winner receive a *mandate* (an "order" from constituents) to pursue a particular course of action? The election of 1988 again raised the question of a mandate. By de-emphasizing issues and attacking Dukakis, it was argued, President Bush forfeited the possibility of a mandate to implement his policy goals. Following the campaign of 1988, a vote for Bush—or a vote for Dukakis, for that matter—seemed to many not to have any relation to issues or policy.

As shown in Figure 8–3, the popular vote for president has varied greatly. In the last 20 years, there have been three very close presidential election: in 1960 between Kennedy and Nixon, in 1968 between Humphrey and Nixon, and in 1976 between Ford and Carter. Those elections could have gone either way. In intervening elections, there have been landslides for the Democrats with Johnson in 1964 and for the Republicans with Nixon in 1972. Reagan scored a substantial victory over Carter in 1980 and an even larger victory over Mondale in 1984.

The presidential election of 1980 was typical of many recent elections. Divided party control of the presidency and Congress resulted; the Republicans won the presidency and the Senate, while the Democrats retained the House. Many voters abandoned their party to vote for a presidential candidate, senator, or respresentative of the other party. And many people—nearly half the eligible voters—did not vote at all. The 1984 election was typical in one respect: An incumbent president was elected to a second term. This has happened consistently for 50 years; the elections of 1980 and 1976 were unusual in that a president was defeated in his bid for a second term.[5]

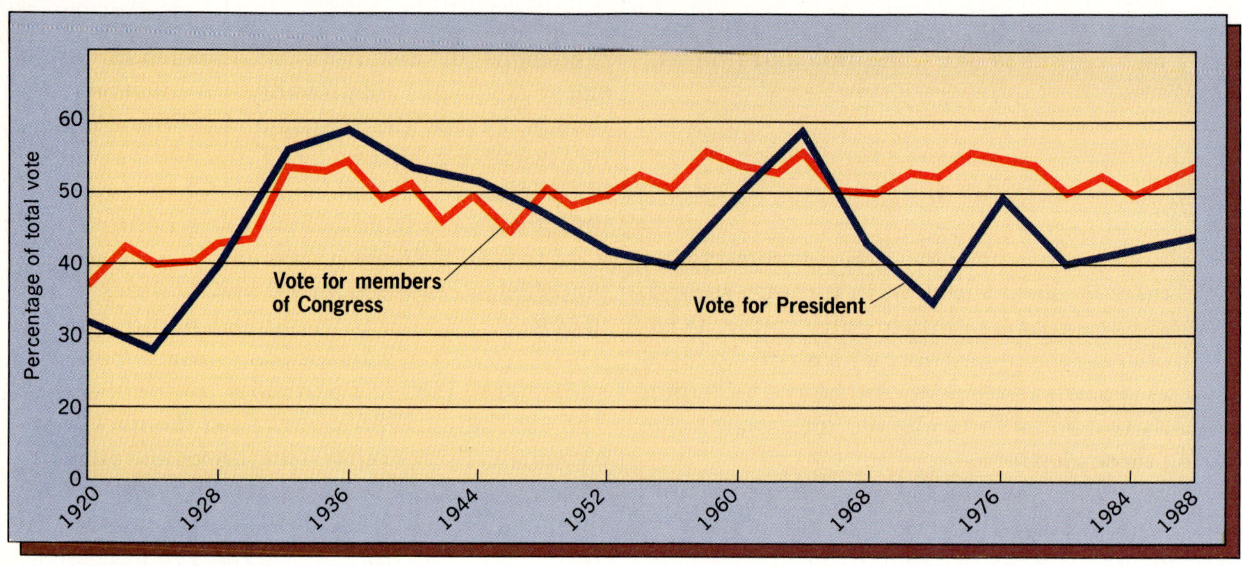

Figure 8–3 Democratic percentage of the total vote for president and for members of the House of Representatives, 1920–1988. Source: Historical Archive of the Inter-University Consortium for Political and Social Research.

In 1988 George Bush won the presidency in the first election without an incumbent since 1968. His near landslide did not carry either the Senate or the House of Representatives, both of which remained safely Democratic. Divided control of the nation's government was once again continued.

Electoral Behavior

People make two decisions in an election. One is whether to vote; the other is for whom to vote. Some people decide they like a candidate and *then* decide to vote. In this section, we will discuss vote choice and the factors that influence it.[6]

Because voting is so crucial in determining who will govern, many studies of voters have been conducted. Of course, not everyone studies voters for the same reasons. Candidates and their advisers want to know how to influence voters. They want to know what they have to do to win the election. Reporters, pundits, and campaign management firms study voters to find out how the campaign is going. Political scientists study voters, usually long after the elections, to learn what influenced them to prefer one candidate over another. These analysts try to figure out what voters are doing and why.

To assess how faithfully elected representatives carry out their mandates, we need to know more about what elections mean. Were voters influenced by the issue appeals of a challenger? Did they simply support the candidate of their party? Did they just pick a name they recognized?

Analysis of Vote Choice

There are two types of influences on voters as they make up their minds. They are affected by *long-term forces,* which are present over the years, and *short-term forces,* which are peculiar to one election. A major long-term force such as party identification accounts for much of the stability in American elections. Short-term forces, such as the issues and personalities of the candidates, provide variability in election outcomes.

Partisanship

Since many people have no ideological orientation to organize their ideas, what other guides to political thinking do they use? By far the most important is identification with a political party. Most Americans think of themselves as either Democrats or Republicans. A substantial minority—about one-third of all adults—does not identify with a party. But party identification does not necessarily determine voting behavior. Even loyal partisans sometimes vote for the other party. Most people are able to switch their votes from time to time without giving up their party identification.

For many decades there have been more Democrats than Republicans and no great change in the strength of either party. In 1988 over 40 percent were Democrats, as can be seen from Figure 8–4. These overall percentages conceal the decline in the number of strong partisans among both Democrats and Republicans. Americans have become less loyal in their support of political parties in the last 20 years.[7]

The overall strength of the parties does not reveal local and regional variations in party strength. Some areas are overwhelmingly Republican; others are strongly Democratic. Most areas are not highly competitive. Many constituencies are fairly safe for one party or the other. And even in a Democratic area, Democrats do not necessarily dominate all elections. The minority party may win elections with the help of independents and dissidents from the other party. In recent decades, there have been landslide victories for both Republican and Democratic presidential candidates. Voting has fluctuated greatly, but party loyalty has changed much less. It is not uncommon to find a Republican landslide in one race and a Democratic landslide in another race—both in the same election in the same state.

Being a Democrat or a Republican is important; people get ideas about what they should believe by knowing what other Democrats or Republicans think.[8] Seeing President Reagan on television urging support for a policy is instructive

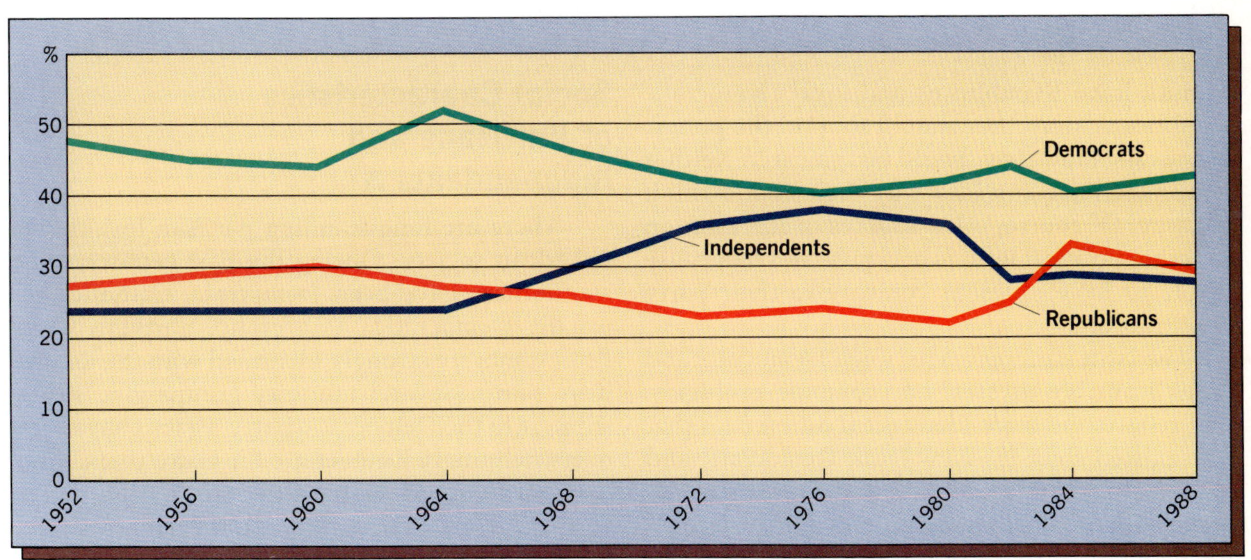

Figure 8–4 Distribution of party identification, 1952–1988. The percentages shown may not add to 100 percent in all years because some people are unwilling or unable to answer the question. Source: Warren E. Miller, Arthur H. Miller, and Edward J. Schneider, *American National Elections Studies Data Sourcebook, 1952–1978* (Cambridge, Mass.: Harvard University Press, 1980), p. 81; Gallup poll release, January 18, 1985, and August 7, 1988.

"We weren't watching—Actually, we're all primaried, caucused, polled, predicted, discussed and analyzed out"

for both loyal Republicans and loyal Democrats. Republicans know they should support the policy; Democrats know they should be against it. Neither group may have any idea why they should think that way. Of course, other sources of information and other political leaders may give cues that cause people to have opinions contrary to their party identification.

The issue differences between Democrats and Republicans are greatest on economic problems. This reflects the basic ideological differences that have existed since the New Deal. Democratic and Republican voters have different views on economic policies; they also see the two parties as having distinctly different positions. The parties have distinct positions on economic issues like health insurance, welfare programs, and job guarantees by government. The parties provide their followers more clear-cut guidance on economic issues than in other policy areas.

Social Characteristics of Partisans and Independents ■

There are long-standing partisan loyalties in American society. During the past century, most southerners have been Democrats. Catholics are usually Democratic. As a group, northern white Protestants are strongly identified with the Republican party. Several minority groups give strong support to the Democratic party. Blacks have been overwhelmingly Democratic for many years. Jews have been almost as one-sided in their affiliation with the Democratic party. And Hispanics have become a more important element in the Democratic coalition.

Since the shifting of party loyalities during the 1930s, most groups have been relatively stable in their support for a party (see Table 8–1). The Democratic party is composed of many separate groups,

TABLE 8–1

Characteristics of Democrats, Republicans, and Independents

	Democrats	Independents	Republicans
Men	40	30	30
Women	45	26	29
Whites	38	30	32
Blacks	75	17	8
Hispanics	51	26	23
18 to 29 years old	38	30	32
30 to 49 years old	43	31	26
50 and over	45	24	31
Less than high school graduate	54	25	21
High school graduate	44	28	28
Some college	39	28	33
College graduate	34	30	36
Under $15,000	51	27	22
$15,000 to $24,999	43	29	28
$25,000 to $39,999	41	29	30
$40,000 and over	34	29	37
Professional or managerial	37	28	35
Other white collar	42	31	27
Blue collar	46	29	25
Protestant	41	27	32
Catholic	46	28	26
East	45	25	30
Midwest	35	34	31
South	46	27	27
West	44	26	30

Source: Gallup Poll, *Minneapolis Star and Tribune*, August 7, 1988, p. 22A. The table is based on 7795 interviews conducted between April 8 and June 27, 1988.

while the Republican party is less varied in composition.[9] The majority party must put together a more diverse collection of people because it is larger. Also, the dominant party appeals to more people in forming its coalition. If the Republican party becomes much larger, it is certain to get a more mixed social composition. For example, in recent years many white southerners have shifted toward the Republicans, broadening the party's base of support in that region. Indeed, among southern whites, there are almost twice as many Republican identifiers today as there were in the 1950s.

Republican strength is greatest among white, middle-class Protestants and Catholics. The wealthy and well educated are also more likely to be Republican. No social groups in America are strongholds of political independence. Although

Candidates like George Bush direct attention to young audiences during their campaigns because so many young people are uncommitted and because political parties are anxious to win or retain the loyalty of young persons.

independents are found throughout society, they are especially numerous among the young and the college educated.

Most Americans grow up in a home where everyone shares the same party identification. A family is likely to be Democratic or Republican, and children learn to emulate their parents.[10] In most families, children usually know at an early age whether they are Democrats or Republicans. Childhood learning about politics is most successful when the parents are highly interested in politics. During the 1930s, when President Roosevelt and the New Deal were extremely popular, party loyalties were acquired with great emotional intensity. In recent years, when enthusiasm for political parties has not been high, more young people have failed to adopt the party of their parents. It is common for young people to enter the electorate as political independents—that is, without party identification.

Since partisan loyalties are the most important long-term force in the American electorate, it is essential to understand the patterns of partisanship and the role of party identification in voting. Ideology is also a long-term force related to vote choice, but it influences fewer voters than partisanship.

Individual party loyalties link ordinary citizens with political leaders. By thinking of themselves as Democrats or Republicans, Americans can recognize leaders who are like them politically. Party identification gives people a basis for evaluating issues, programs, and candidates. It may be the only important information a citizen has when facing a political choice.

The longer voters think of themselves as Democrats or Republicans, the stronger their identification becomes. Persons who identify with a party and usually vote for its candidates develop an emotional attachment to it. They may even get some satisfaction from their opposition to the other party. Politics is often confusing, and party loyalty helps citizens make judgments without too much difficulty. In some states, the use of voting machines strengthens the impact of party, because voters can pull a party lever.

Strong partisans show a high degree of loyalty in most elections. Even an unpopular candidate will receive most of the votes of the party faithful. In the 1988 election, strong Democrats voted for Dukakis. Loyalty to Bush was high among strong Republicans. The real difference in behavior appears among less partisan voters: Weak Democrats abandoned Dukakis to some degree; weak Republicans remained more loyal to Bush. These less partisan voters provide flexibility for the political system. They switch from party to party, thereby permitting one party to replace the other. The strong partisans on each side, by contrast, are a more stable base of support.

Overall, the pattern of defections among Democrats and Republicans in 1988 was similar to that in 1980 and 1984. Almost one-fifth of the Democrats voted for George Bush. Republicans, by contrast, were quite loyal; fewer than one in ten Republicans abandoned Bush to vote for Dukakis.[11] The vote for the House of Representatives was more balanced among partisans. Among both Democrats and Republicans, about one-sixth of the voters defected from their party to vote for a representative from the other party.[12]

Switching is most common among independents. In 1988, they supported George Bush 55 percent to 43 percent. In the same election, independents divided their votes for Congress about evenly. Figure 8–5 shows how independents have voted for president since 1948. With the exception of 1948 and 1964, independents have voted for Republicans. Their vote has fluctuated from 70 percent for Eisenhower in 1956 to 44 percent for Goldwater and Nixon in the 1960s. Most national elections are sufficiently close that the independents hold the balance of power. This was certainly true in 1988.

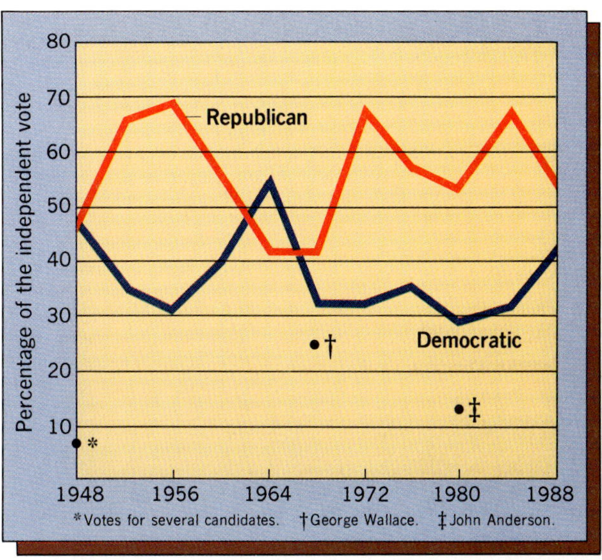

Figure 8–5 Independent voting for president, 1948–1988. Source: "Opinion Roundup," *Public Opinion* (April–May 1984), p. 21; *New York Times,* November 8, 1984, and November 10, 1988.

The social and economic differences in party loyalty are expressed in voting for president as well as in other elections. Table 8–2 shows the 1988 patterns of support for Bush and Dukakis. Some differences are dramatic—for example, blacks, Hispanics, and Jewish voters heavily supported Dukakis. There was a fairly strong relationship between income and voting; high-income voters supported Bush by a margin of two to one. Viewed broadly, however, the voting behavior of groups in 1988 was not marked by major differences. Young voters supported the Republican ticket almost as much as older ones. High-status and low-status white-collar workers both voted for Bush. Blue-

TABLE 8–2

Characteristics of Bush and Dukakis Voters

	Bush	Dukakis
Men	57	41
Women	50	49
Whites	59	40
Blacks	12	86
Hispanics	30	69
18 to 29 years old	52	47
30 to 44 years old	54	45
45 to 59 years old	57	42
60 and over	50	49
Less than high school graduate	43	56
High school graduate	50	49
Some college	57	42
College graduate	62	37
Postgraduate education	50	48
White Protestant	66	33
Catholic	52	47
Jewish	35	64
Family income under $12,500	37	62
$12,500 to $24,999	49	50
$25,000 to $34,999	56	44
$35,000 to $49,999	56	42
$50,000 to $100,000	61	38
Over $100,000	65	32
East	50	49
Midwest	52	47
South	58	41
West	52	46
Professional or managerial	59	40
White-collar worker	57	42
Blue-collar worker	49	50
Homemaker	58	41
Retired	50	49
Unemployed	37	62

Source: *New York Times*/CBS News exit poll, *New York Times,* November 10, 1988.

collar workers were divided evenly, as were high school graduates. In general, Bush's support was greatest among traditional Republican strongholds—the better educated, higher income groups in the electorate.

Throughout the 1980s, there was a noticeable difference in the voting behavior of men and women. In 1988, 57 percent of men and 50 percent of women voted for Bush. The gender gap has received more attention than other aspects of group behavior in elections, but it is not a simple issue. Men and women are indistinguishable in ideology, and within partisan ranks the gender gap disappears. The gap is greatest among independents and among the least *and* best educated, and these relationships have changed from year to year; these results suggest a complex set of causes. Nor is the gender gap large in comparison with the difference in voting behavior found between some other social groups. For example, blacks in recent years have voted overwhelmingly Democratic, whites consistently Republican.

Do Republicans have a gender gap problem with women, or do the Democrats have one with men? Nothing in the data answers that question. In the end, men and women in American society overall have somewhat different values, concerns, and expectations—and that sometimes translates into differences in voting behavior.

Short-Term Forces and Vote Choice

It is important to be aware of voter partisanship when analyzing elections, but outcomes are likely to be determined by short-term forces that reinforce partisan loyalties or cause defections. All candidates look for issues and appeals that will help them or hurt their opponents. So attention naturally focuses on short-term forces even if they eventually cancel out and most voters support their usual party. Campaigns are fought with issues, candidate characteristics, and party images.

Congress and the Incumbency Advantage

Voters who participate in presidential elections often have little information about the candidates and the issues. Their involvement in congressional elections, however, is based on even less information. A majority of voters do not even know the names of both congressional candidates, let alone their positions on issues.

The congressional candidates most likely to be known by the electorate are the incumbents, which helps to explain why they are so difficult to defeat. The scope of their "informational" advantage can be seen in the evidence below.

These advantages are fully reflected in their reelection rates. In every election between 1968 and 1988 except 1974 (the "Watergate" election), more than 90 percent of all House incumbents were reelected. In eight of these eleven elections, more than 94 percent of House incumbents were reelected. An extraordinary 98 percent were returned to Washington by the voters in the elections of 1986 and 1988. These incumbents are now so secure that competition for seats in the House of Representatives is at its lowest level in history.

Comparing House incumbents with their challengers:

Three times	as many voters	recall the incumbent's name.
Twice	as many voters	recognize the incumbent's name.
Twice	as many voters	have had some contact with the incumbent.
Five times	as many voters	have met the incumbent personally.
Six times	as many voters	have attended a meeting where the incumbent spoke.
Four times	as many voters	have received mail from the incumbent.
Twice	as many voters	have read about the incumbent.
Twice	as many voters	have heard the incumbent on the radio or seen him or her on television.
Five times	as many voters	report liking something about the incumbent.

Source: Based on data in Gary C. Jacobson, "Incumbents' Advantages in the 1978 Congressional Elections," *Legislative Studies Quarterly,* 6 (May 1981), p. 186; see also Thomas E. Mann and Raymond E. Wolfinger, "Candidates and Parties in Congressional Elections," *American Political Science Review,* 74 (September 1980), pp. 617–32.

Candidate Appeal. The most important of these three influences is the candidates' personal characteristics. Voters respond to their experience and apparent *competence.* Some of the advantage enjoyed by incumbents is associated with the public's perception that they know what is going on. Most voters have a generous view of elected representatives unless they have specific, unfavorable information. It is disastrous for a candidate to be seen as incompetent and ineffective. In 1980, President Carter lost millions of votes because people viewed him as unable to do anything about the economy and inept in handling foreign affairs. President Carter had an extremely unfavorable image by the end of his four years in office (see also Chapter 13).

A second important element of a candidate's image is his perceived *honesty.* The public's general skepticism about the honesty of political leaders does not apply to each candidate for office. It is, however, not too difficult to raise doubts about the integrity of a candidate. Political leaders are especially sensitive to charges of corruption.

Several times we have mentioned the advantage enjoyed by incumbents—those who already hold office. The advantage of *incumbency* is greatest when the voters do not know much about the candidates. Officeholders have many chances to "make news" and to gain name recognition before a campaign even starts. But unknown opponents must struggle to gain the attention of media and voters.

In 1988 both George Bush and Michael Dukakis acquired unfavorable images by the end of the campaign.[13] Both campaigns attacked the character and competence of the opposing candidate, and while the public professed disapproval of the tactics, it appeared to absorb much of the negative imagery.

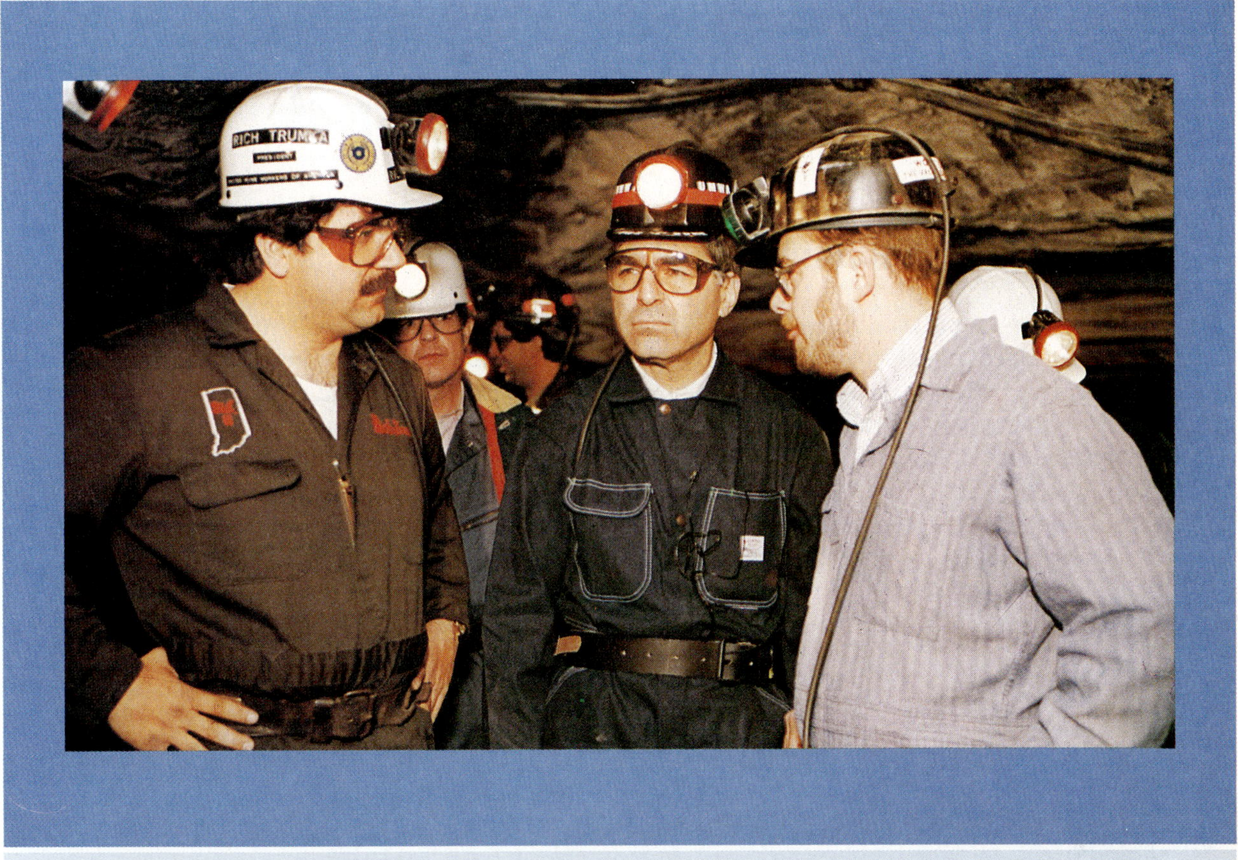

In campaign politics any angle will play. Candidates and their advisers search for "photo opportunities" in the hope that the media will provide news coverage. This photo shows Michael Dukakis, in hard hat, with real hard hats.

Issues and Vote Choice. This was not the first time that candidates were criticized for not facing the issues or not raising the "right" issues. For the most part, candidates face a public that is bored and has little interest in most issues. Even in presidential campaigns, where the issues are peace and prosperity, voters often express slight concern for the topics discussed by the candidates.

The lack of information about or interest in issues has been misunderstood by some campaigners. Voters do care about some issues, and they expect candidates to address them. Voters do not necessarily care about the issues the candidates want to discuss. Also, on some big issues all candidates take about the same stand.

When voters care intensely about an issue, they are capable of selecting the candidate who represents their view. When voters are not concerned about an issue, it is hard for a candidate to use that issue to win votes. It is easy enough for candidates to raise issues, but it is difficult to uncover those that will attract large numbers of voters.

Campaign positions are sometimes misunderstood. In 1968, for example, at the height of the controversy over Vietnam, President Johnson was nearly defeated in the New Hampshire presidential primary by Senator Eugene McCarthy. His poor showing helped force him out of the race. The only significant issue raised by McCarthy was opposition to U.S. involvement in the war. Incredibly,

Continuity & CHANGE

Voting Behavior over Four Decades

What explains how people vote in presidential elections? One approach to an answer is to look for constants in voting behavior throughout the current era. Here are some results over four decades.

Social class does not explain much these days about voting behavior in presidential elections. Voters from the ranks of the professions and business increasingly do not vote much more Republican than the national average. At the other end of the class structure, manual workers are less firmly committed to the Democratic party than before. Nor does Catholic or Protestant religious affiliation matter as much as in the past. The following graph shows that the voting behavior of Catholics and Protestants is becoming increasingly similar—Catholics much less Democratic in their preference, Protestants somewhat less Republican. But a distinct preference for Democratic candidates continues to characterize the voting behavior of blacks and Jews.

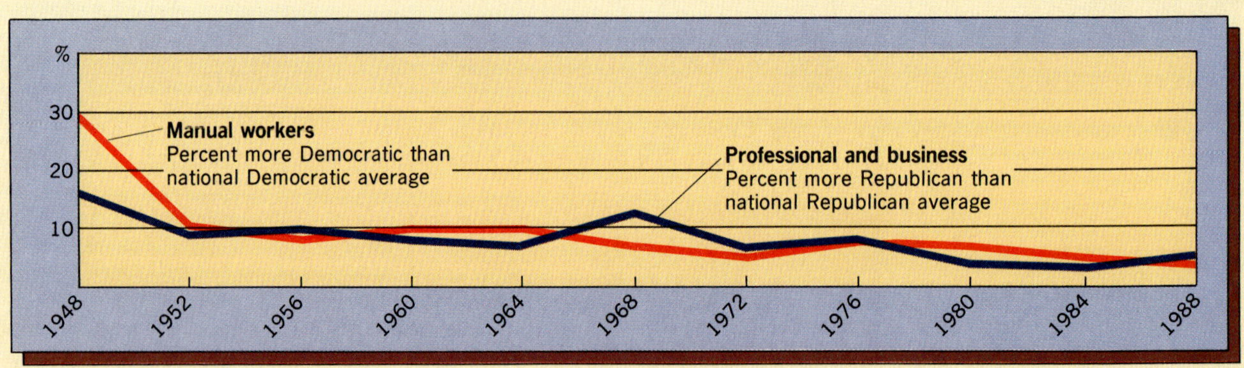

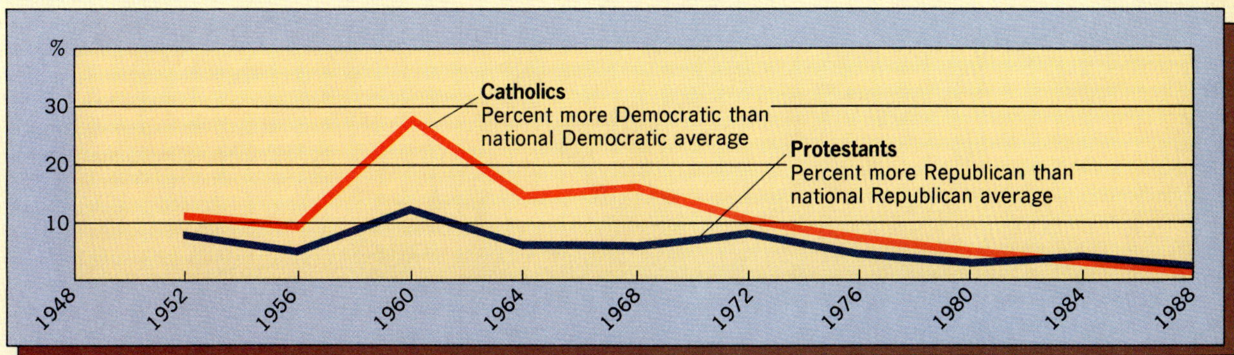

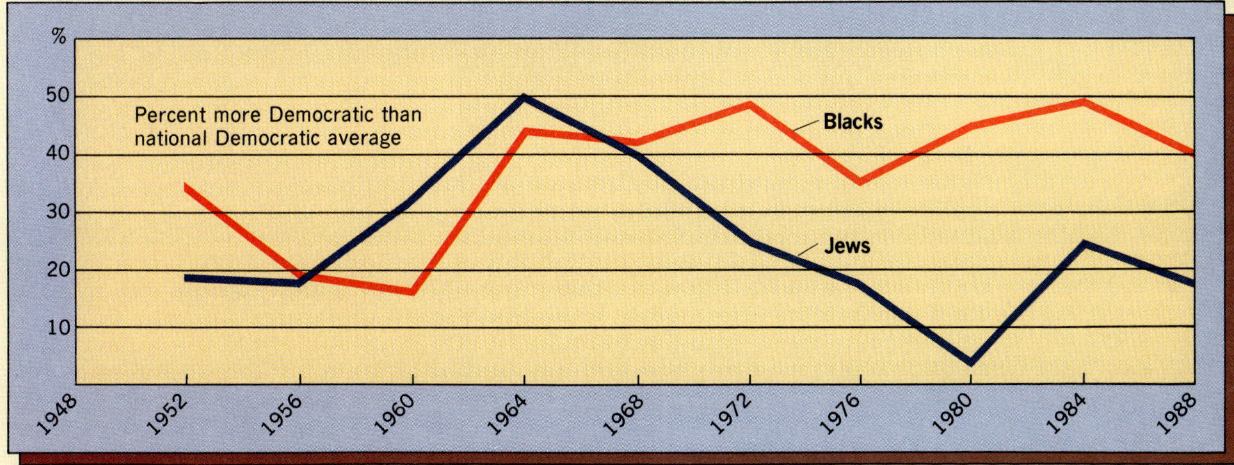

Source: Calculated from data in *Gallup Opinion Index,* December 1980, p. 6; *New York Times*/CBS News Poll, as reported in *New York Times,* November 8, 1984; November 10, 1988. For social class vote in 1948, see Robert R. Alford, *Party and Society* (Chicago: Rand McNally, 1963), p. 352. Data on Jewish vote 1952–1968 drawn from Mark R. Levy and Michael S. Kramer, *The Ethnic Factor* (New York: Simon and Schuster, 1972), p. 103, and for 1972–1980, Robert J. Huckshorn, *Political Parties in America* (Monterey, Calif.: Brooks/Cole, 1984), p. 214; and for 1984, *New York Times*/CBS News Poll. (Note: In 1980, 14 percent of the Jewish vote was cast for John Anderson.)

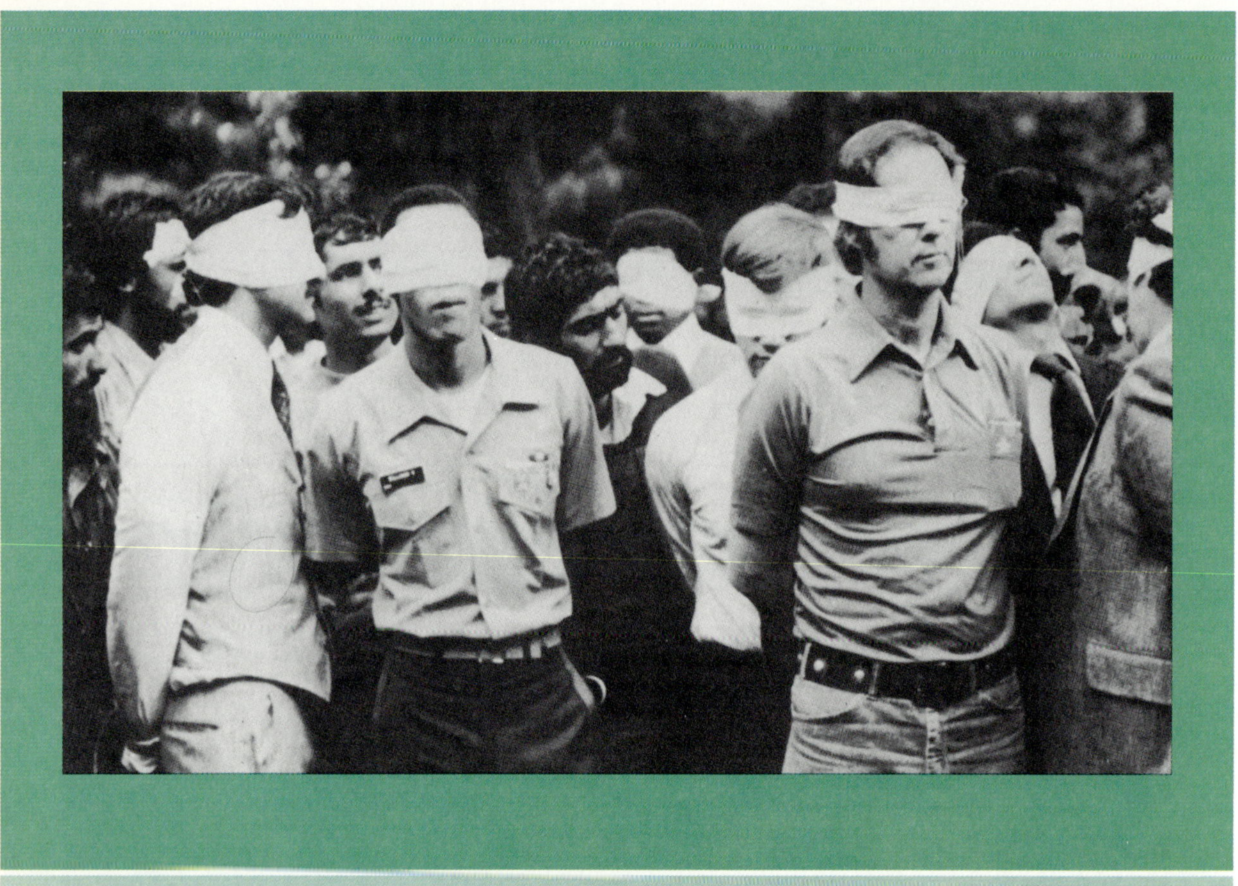

In November, 1979, Americans in the U.S. Embassy in Tehran were taken hostage by Iranian militants. The inability of President Jimmy Carter to free the hostages was a major factor in his defeat by Ronald Reagan in 1980.

more people who voted for McCarthy were for escalating the war than for withdrawal from Vietnam! These voters understood that McCarthy was critical of the president and therefore assumed that he was in favor of more aggressive military action—a position they supported.

Candidates are tempted to make vague statements about issues so they can benefit from the confusion. Candidates who believe they are ahead in a race may be reluctant to take a clear stand that could cost support. Candidates who trail, on the other hand, have every reason to raise many issues, take stands, and force their opponents to do the same.

Sometimes voters correctly perceive the issue positions of candidates and still vote for a candidate with whom they disagree. In 1980 and 1984, many voters disagreed with Reagan on issues but voted for him anyway. In 1972, even more voters supported Nixon while agreeing with McGovern on issues. McGovern, like Carter, suffered from an unfavorable image, and that proved more important than the issues. In 1984, on the other hand, many voters correctly perceived Mondale as proposing a tax increase and did not like the prospect.

More than in most presidential election campaigns, voters in 1988 expressed dissatisfaction with the candidates' handling of issues. Learning from Walter Mondale's experience in 1984, both candidates avoided discussing the possibility that taxes would have to be raised to reduce the federal budget deficit. Consequently, neither discussed the deficit fully, even though the voters considered the issue important for the nation's future. Neither Bush nor Dukakis raised major foreign policy issues either.

In summary, three key conditions must be met if issues are to have an impact on voting behavior. In the first place, voters must be both informed and concerned about an issue. Second, the candidates must take distinguishable stands on this issue. And third, the voters must correctly perceive the candidates' positions in relation to their own.

Party Image and Vote Choice. Candidates may be helped or hurt by their party's reputation; it is a factor over which they have little control. In 1974, after President Nixon's resignation and President Ford's prompt pardon of him, Republican candidates were at a serious disadvantage. The party lost 43 seats in the House of Representatives and 4 in the Senate. Scandals are particularly damaging to a party's image because voters are likely to be aware of them. In 1974, the Republican party's image was badly tarnished by the Watergate break-in and other illegal activities. From time to time a party's reputation suffers from corruption in its midst and its mishandling of the government.

Party loyalty, it has been shown, is generally stable. The way that voters assess the parties, however, tends to change with events and presidential administrations. Figure 8–6 shows some aspects of the public's evaluations of the parties over several decades. During the 1950s, the Republican party was seen as the more likely to keep the United States out of war. President Dwight D. Eisenhower undoubtedly contributed to this view—and benefited from it. From the mid-1970s to the mid-1980s, the Democrats became the party more likely to keep America out of war, but Ronald Reagan dramatically changed that perception once again by 1988.

On the question of which party will do a better job of keeping the country prosperous, the Democratic party typically has enjoyed an advantage. The success of the Reagan administration, however, altered the public view. Currently, the Republicans

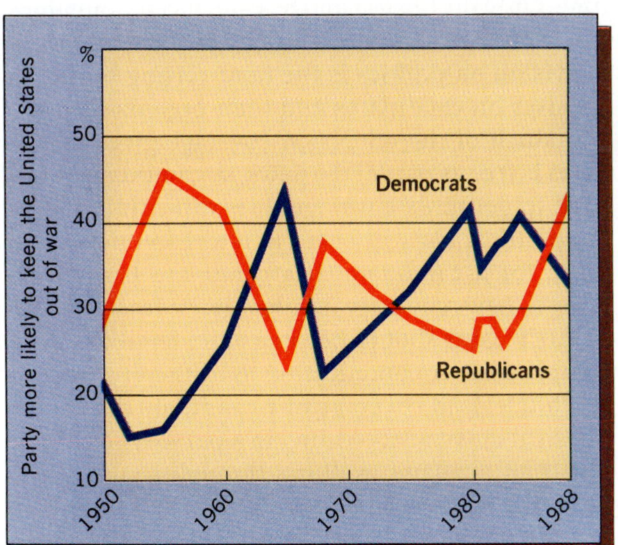

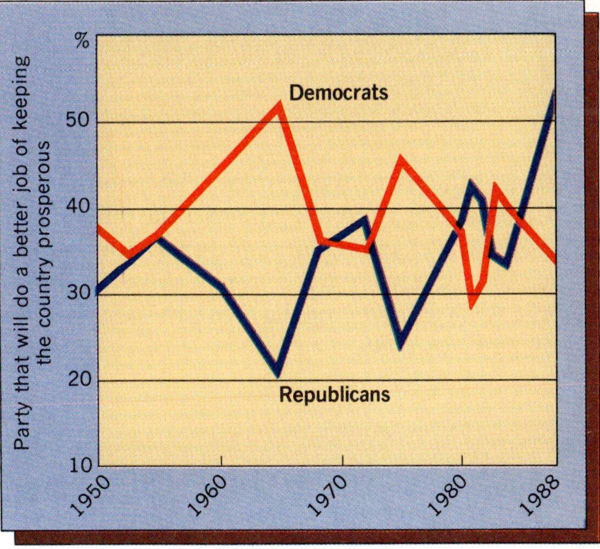

Figure 8–6 The public's view of the political parties, 1950–1988. Source: *Gallup Report* (April 1984), no. 223, pp. 18–19; Gallup poll cited in *Minneapolis Star Tribune,* September 28, 1988.

To attract the media, the conditions have to be right. What better backdrop for a campaign speech, and for the media, than people and flags!

are seen as the party of prosperity. These and other readings cannot, of course, forecast the outcome of a presidential election, but they do provide a rough indication of each party's competitive position. George Bush gained from the favorable perceptions of his party in 1988.

Political Campaigns

Very few voters change their minds during the last months of a campaign. What does happen during a campaign? Does all the time, money, and energy invested have any impact? Very close elections are in doubt to the end; the campaign is critical in determining the outcome. And even though most elections are not very close ultimately, candidates cannot be sure how they will turn out. Thus, intense campaigns are waged in all but the most one-sided races.

Even if very few voters are influenced to switch parties during a campaign, a larger number say they considered voting for more than one candidate. Turnout also may be influenced by the campaign. By encouraging some people to vote and discouraging others, a presidential campaign can affect other races as well. But, although campaign organizations work hard to get out the vote, their biggest impact may be to educate the electorate. Campaign advertising informs people on the stands of candidates and on the issues.

Much has been made of the impact of television on political campaigning.[14] It is true that television has changed campaigns for the presidency; this is one reason campaigns have become so expensive. Some candidates for the U.S. Senate or for governor make considerable use of television, but most candidates for lesser offices do not use it. It is expensive to produce a television commercial and to buy air time. Only the biggest and best-financed campaigns can even consider television. One major impact of television on politics is the fund-raising burden it imposes on candidates and their organizations.

Much of the television coverage given candidates is free as part of the news, so candidates work hard to get news coverage. It is difficult to assess the political consequences of television news coverage for a candidate. If a candidate is not well known, news coverage is valuable. At least the candidate's name should become more familiar. More complicated communication is difficult since so much televised coverage of a candidate deals with physical movement—riding in a parade, getting on or off an airplane, walking through a plant. The brief film footage from part of a speech is not likely to convey much about a candidate's positions on issues.

Naturally, the campaign organizations try hard to control how journalists will cover their candi-

IMPACT

Direct Democracy at Work

In states that permit public referenda, citizens can have a more direct impact on public policy. In such elections, voters decide for or against a particular policy, state constitutional amendment, proposed law, or advisory opinion. These elections can be viewed as pure issue voting.

In 1988, a number of issues were the subject of referenda in various states:

Abortion funding: Voters in Arkansas, Colorado, and Michigan banned state funding of abortions.

AIDS: California voters rejected a proposition requiring doctors to report to the state anyone testing positive for AIDS.

English language: In Arizona, Colorado, and Florida, voters made English the official state language.

Farming: North Dakota voters banned corporate hog farming.

Gun control: Maryland voters supported a law banning cheap handguns. (The National Rifle Association was reported to have spent $4 million to defeat this measure.)

Insurance: Voters in California mandated a 20 percent reduction in insurance rates for automobiles, homes, and businesses.

Nuclear power plants: Massachusetts voters defeated a proposal to close two nuclear power plants.

Seat belts: Voters in Oregon defeated a law requiring motorists to use seat belts.

Smoking ban: Voters in California approved an increase in cigarette taxes from 10 to 35 cents.

date. Their success varies, but if they cannot fully manipulate the news, they have complete control over their huge advertising budgets, and increasingly they depend on television ads to present their candidate's case.

The role of newspapers in political campaigns has not received much recent attention because television seems so important. Nevertheless, research has shown that voters learn more about candidates and issues from newspapers than from television.[15] Readers can find news in a paper or read an article a second time. Television is much less useful because information flashes by and is gone.

During political campaigns, voters learn a lot about the candidates—especially the candidate they prefer. From both news reports and advertising, voters get information about issues and candidates' traits. This information does not usually affect their preferences, but it does lead to a more informed electorate. The campaign strengthens the choices of most voters by giving them more reasons to support their candidates. And television offers some unusual opportunities for making judgments about the candidates. Television debates are the most dramatic campaign events. Millions of people can get an impression of the personalities and issue positions of the candidates. No such opportunity existed prior to television.

Over half the electorate is reported to have paid attention to each television debate in 1988, and a majority of voters said that these debates were helpful in evaluating the candidates. But their major impact was to strengthen voter support for whichever candidate the voter already preferred; few voters switched from one candidate to the other as a result of them.

Campaigning for most elections is done in more traditional ways. Candidates try to meet voters at factory gates and shopping centers. Campaign workers hand out leaflets and brochures; the organization sends out mailings. Billboards, signs, and bumper stickers advertise the candidate's name. A high proportion of the voters in local campaigns are reached in these ways.

The overall impact of campaigns is that: (1) almost everyone is aware that there is an election; (2) people who care about a candidate, party, or issue become aware of the choice they are to make; and (3) even people who do not care about the election learn a great deal about the candidates and their positions.

Modern campaigning has provided new sources of information for voters, so they are no longer dependent on the political parties to tell them how to vote. But the easing of direct party influence should be put in perspective. Most voters still see their choices in terms of party labels. They are also sufficiently informed to use ideas about issue positions and personalities in deciding how to vote. The result is a combination of stability and change.

Political stability emerges from party loyalty, and electoral change stems from the uneven impact of issues and personalities. Voters are less excited about elections than candidates and political actives. Most voters, however, take enough interest in elections to cast a vote that makes sense to them. Voting is not an empty, ignorant act. Voters are well enough informed that candidates must take them seriously. And most voters are not so devoted to political causes that candidates can take them for granted.

Vote Choice in Primary Elections ■

Since more and more states have introduced presidential primaries as a means of selecting delegates to the national conventions, it has become increasingly important to analyze differences between presidential vote choices in general elections and party primaries. One difference, of course, is that partisanship cannot serve as a guide in primaries; ordinarily, all the candidates are either Republicans or Democrats. Competition among candidates of the same party changes the form of vote choice in other ways. Typically the candidates differ less on most issues than in a general election. The result is that their personalities loom important.

Presidential primary elections extend over many months, from February to June, and in the early ones many candidates are not well known. Sometimes a candidate with little national name recognition gets the chance to emerge quickly from obscurity. In 1976 Jimmy Carter came "out of nowhere" to win the Democratic nomination; Gary Hart nearly did the same in 1984. Very few people outside Massachusetts knew Michael Dukakis at the outset of the 1988 nominating season. This lack of knowledge of candidates makes voter opinions during the primaries unusually fluid.[16] (Also see Chapter 9.)

One element unique to a party primary is that voters must decide which candidate will run best against the likely nominee of the opposing party. Partisans may try to select the strongest candidate, as long as that candidate is acceptable in other ways. Public opinion polls may therefore significantly influence what primary voters think by reporting "trial heats" between leading prospects.

Electoral Competition ■

The shifting of support from one political party to another is important in the political system. Whether the shifting alters the outcome of elections, though, depends on the competitiveness of the constituencies. If there are roughly equal num-

TABLE 8–3

Party Systems in the United States

Party System	Critical Realignment	Realigning Issues	Stable Phase	Unstable Years
I	1790s	Federal system	1800–1820	1822–1826
II	1828	Sectional development	1828–1836	1838–1858
III	1860	Slavery and national unity	1860–1872	1874–1894
IV	1896	Industrialization	1896–1910	1912–1930
V	1932	Economy and welfare	1932–1944	1946–1988

bers of Democrats and Republicans in a constituency, a slight shift of voters will change the outcome. When districts are safe for one party, even large shifts will have no effect.

In the last several decades, more and more congressional districts have become safe for one party (but at times safe only for the incumbent). Possibly this is because voters are increasingly aligned with the majority party in the districts. Or perhaps it is a result of incumbents having an advantage through name recognition and superior resources. It may be that both parties in state legislatures have cooperated in drawing district boundaries to create safe districts. Whatever the explanation, voters have shifted considerably in congressional elections without much impact on the party composition of Congress.

Since 1960, the Democrats have done very well in congressional elections, enjoying victories with as much as 57 percent of the nationwide popular vote. During these same years, the Republicans have had several one-sided victories in presidential elections. Voting for other offices such as governor and senator has fluctuated widely. When the 101st Congress convened in January 1989, 21 states were represented by a divided Senate delegation of one Republican and one Democrat.

Almost every large state has had governors and senators from both parties during recent years.

American voters have shown they are willing to turn out and vote in elections on occasion. They have also shown a willingness to split their votes between the parties and to switch from one party to another. The stability in party loyalty provides a base of support for Democrats and Republicans, but the volatility in the electorate creates many opportunities for political change.

Party Alignments

A crucial consideration for a voter is the political party of a candidate. While the party of a candidate is just one factor in a voter's decision, the party of elected officials may have great impact on the government.[17] A basic element of the political system is the dominant party. Because a voter's party loyalty is so important, we want to know which party has the larger following. Since most people remain loyal to one party for a long time, when a party becomes dominant it remains dominant for a long time.

These periods of dominance are called *party eras* or *party systems.*[18] There have been five party systems in American history. Table 8–3 shows the five eras of party dominance, including the most

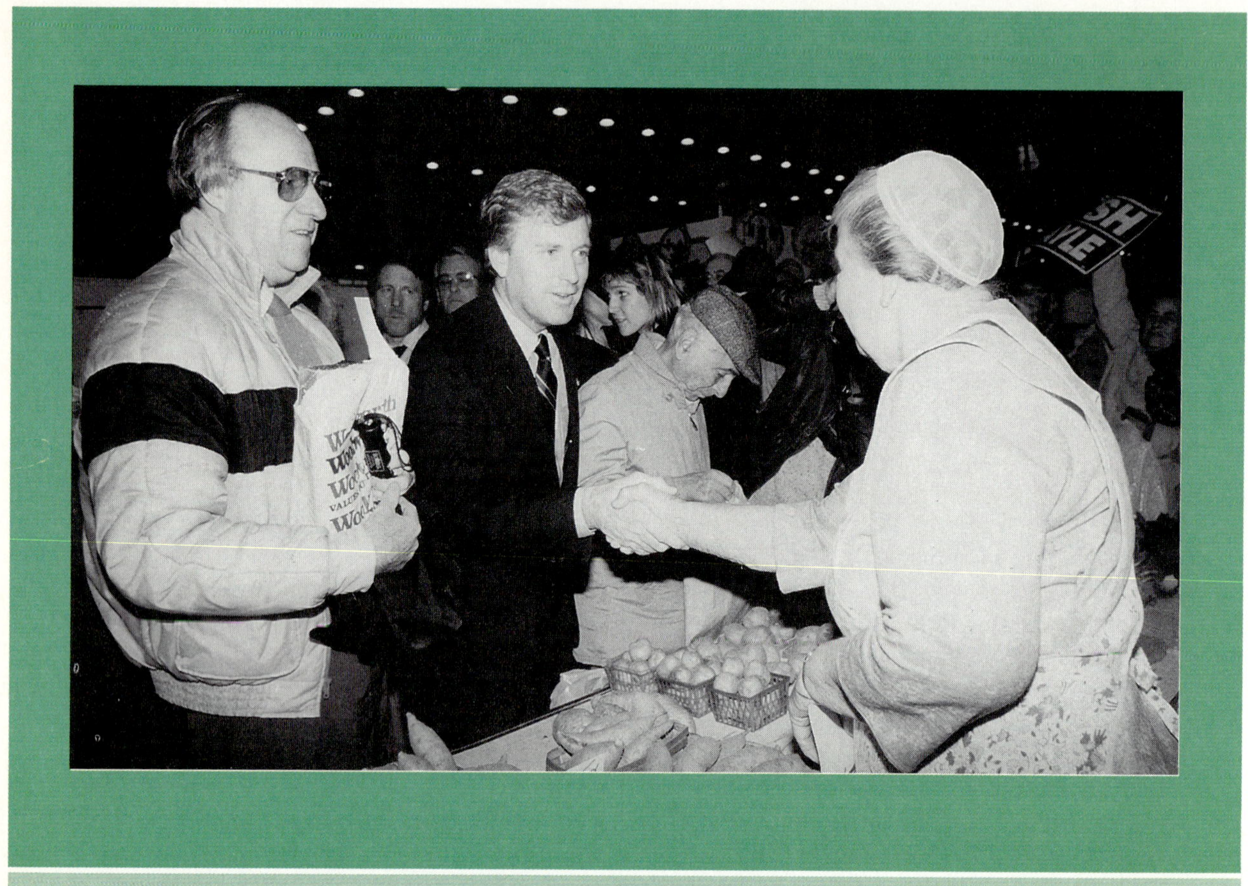

Dan Quayle campaigning in an Amish farmers' market in Pennsylvania. Unless they make a big mistake, candidates for the vice presidency do not make a great "splash" in national news. But they can and do attract regional attention in areas that are not prime targets of the presidential campaign. Vice presidential candidate Quayle focused on rural and small-town America in his 1988 campaign.

recent one beginning in the 1930s. Not all elections are won by the dominant party during these eras, but that party has a clear advantage.

Since the presidential election of 1932, the Democratic party has dominated the political system with a coalition of voters from all parts of society. This New Deal alignment was formed by Franklin Roosevelt to support the Democratic party. The alignment included: (1) southerners who had supported the Democratic party since the Civil War, (2) Catholics who had traditionally voted Democratic, (3) the working class, especially union members in northern cities, and (4) two smaller groups concentrated in northern cities: blacks and Jews.[19] Of course, not everyone in these groups voted Democratic, and in some elections certain groups largely abandoned the coalition. Still, for five decades these groups have been fairly loyal to the Democratic party.

Shifts in party strength that lead from one party system to another are called *partisan realignments.*[20] During partisan realignments, the coalition behind the dominant party changes and the newly dominant party controls the government.

" Perspectives "

On Voting and Voters

"Orthodox democratic theory assumes that every citizen has, or ought to have, thought out for himself certain opinions, i.e., ought to have a definite view, defensible by argument, of what the country needs, of what principles ought to be applied in governing it, of the man in whose hands the government ought to be entrusted. There are persons who talk, though certainly very few who act, as if they believed this theory. . . ."

—Lord Bryce

"Voters are basically lazy, basically uninterested in making an effort to understand."

—Political adviser, the 1968 Nixon campaign

"I do not know how it is with you, but for myself I generally give up at the outset. The simplest problems which come up from day to day seem to me quite unanswerable as soon as I try to get below the surface. . . . My vote is one of the most unimportant acts of my life; if I were to acquaint myself with the matters on which it ought really to depend, if I were to try to get a judgment on which I was willing to risk affairs of even the smallest moment, I should be doing nothing else, and that seems a fatuous conclusion to a fatuous undertaking."

—Judge Learned Hand

"Soft vote is the voters who don't care enough to come vote for you in the rain."

—Jody Powell

"The political behavior of the electorate is not determined solely by psychological and sociological forces, but also by the issues of the day and by the way in which candidates present those issues. If candidates offer clear issue alternatives, voters are more likely to make political issues a criterion for electoral choice."

—Norman H. Nie, Sidney Verba, and John R. Petrocik

"Voters are not fools. To be sure, many individual voters act in odd ways indeed; yet in the large the electorate behaves about as rationally and responsibly as we should expect, given the clarity of the alternatives presented to it and the character of the information available to it. In American presidential campaigns of recent decades the portrait of the American electorate that develops from the data is not one of an electorate straitjacketed by social determinants or moved by subconscious urges triggered by devilishly skilled propagandists. It is rather one of an electorate moved by concern about central and relevant questions of public policy, of governmental performance, and of executive personality."

—V. O. Key, Jr.

Sources: Lord Bryce cited in Bernard Berelson, Paul F. Lazarsfeld, and William N. McPhee, *Voting* (Chicago: University of Chicago Press, 1954), p. 320; from a memorandum prepared for the Nixon campaign in 1968 quoted by Joe McGinniss, *The Selling of the President 1968* (New York: Trident Press, 1969), p. 30; Learned Hand cited in Berelson, Lazarsfeld, and McPhee, *Voting*, p. 312; remark attributed to Jody Powell in Martin Schram, *Running for the President* (New York: Pocket Books, 1976), p. 38; Norman H. Nie, Sidney Verba, and John R. Petrocik, *The Changing American Voter* (Cambridge, Mass.: Harvard University Press, 1976), p. 319; V. O. Key, Jr., *The Responsible Electorate* (New York: Vintage Books, 1966), pp. 7–8.

In 1984 Gary Hart almost won the Democratic presidential nomination, losing narrowly to Walter Mondale. In February of that year, Hart was virtually unknown to the American public. A month later, following the Iowa caucuses and New Hampshire primary, he was running neck-and-neck with Mondale in national opinion polls. Intense coverage by the mass media can catapult candidates into prominence. It can return them to private life just about as rapidly.

When the Democratic party replaced the Republicans as the dominant party in 1932, it controlled the national government until 1946. Although the Republicans have frequently won presidential elections since 1932—seven times since 1952—they have controlled the Senate for only ten years between 1932 and 1990. During the same years, the Republicans have had a majority in the House of Representatives for only four years. Of course, in many years, including the 1980s, Republicans have joined with conservative Democrats (mainly southern) to win votes in Congress (see Chapter 12).

There is a pattern that leads to a partisan realignment. At the beginning of an era, the dominant party controls the government and has widespread support. Over the years, this support declines as electoral switching occurs. No party dominates the government, and often one party wins the presidency and another controls the Congress. The proportion of independents increases and electoral support continues to shift. Sooner or later a crisis—usually economic—leads one party to be thrown out of office and the other party to control the government. If the newly dominant party seems successful in dealing with the crisis, a significant shift in support takes place. A partisan realignment has occurred, and another party system begins.

The conditions necessary for a partisan realignment are present in the American electorate of the 1990s. Many voters have become disengaged from their traditional party attachments. Independents are a major political force—nearly one-third of the electorate. Party switching by voters is common. Ticket splitting often appears to be the norm. Both strong Democrats and strong Republicans have declined in number. Southern Republicans are no longer an oddity—at least one-fourth of all southern whites now regard themselves as Republicans. Voter defections from parties have increased in congressional elections, rivaling those in presidential elections. The American electorate, in a word, has become more volatile as group ties to the parties have weakened, particularly on the Democratic side.

The election of 1980 reflected the sharp disillusion of voters with the Carter administration and the Democratic party. The result was a comfortable victory for Ronald Reagan in 1980 and a

Former President Ronald Reagan kicks off his 1984 bid for reelection at the El Toro Marine Corps Air Station in Irvine, California. An unusually popular president, a skillful communicator, Reagan was not particularly successful in boosting the political fortunes of other Republican candidates or in converting the public to conservatism.

massive victory in 1984. In 1988 George Bush extended the Republican hold on the presidency, while the Democrats continued to control the House and Senate. Still, the loosening of the Democratic party's hold on the electorate does not necessarily mean a partisan realignment.

Despite President Reagan's substantial popularity, there has been no major shift toward conservatism among the voters. The Republican party has more party identifiers than in recent decades, but the Democratic party continues to be the leading party in the electorate. The most that can be said is that a *potential* for realignment exists.

Divided control of government continues to dominate Washington politics. Can the Republican party convert the popularity of presidential candidates into broader bases of support, or will the Democratic party translate its strength in party loyalty and state elections into a presidential victory? Any major and durable shift in the parties' electoral strength is likely to depend on a crisis great enough to disrupt the present stalemate.

Summary

- The many elections in the United States contribute to the diffusion of power and responsibility in the federal structure.
- Most elections for major offices require a plurality, thus discouraging third-party candidates from competing.
- The balance of party loyalties has remained relatively stable since World War II with the Democrats slowly losing their advantage over the Republicans. Through the end of 1989, there were no signs of large shifts. The social groups that distinguish the parties have also remained fairly constant.
- Party loyalty helps to guide voters faced with many choices and to maintain some stability in election outcomes. Party identification is the most important long-term influence on vote choice in American politics.
- The personal characteristics of candidates are usually more important to voters than issues. However, most voters can use issue information in making decisions, and in close elections issues may be decisive.
- Television has increased the cost of campaigning and changed the form of appeals. There is no evidence that television has a great impact on vote choices.
- When underlying party loyalty changes, a partisan realignment occurs that alters the course of government rule and introduces a party system with a new majority coalition.

Readings on Voters and Elections

Abramson, Paul R., John H. Aldrich, and David W. Rohde. 1986. *Change and Continuity in the 1984 Elections.* Washington, D.C.: CQ Press. A solid analysis of recent voting in presidential and congressional elections.

Asher, Herbert B. 1988. *Presidential Elections and American Politics.* Chicago: Dorsey Press. An authoritative survey of many studies in voting behavior.

Bartels, Larry M. 1988. *Presidential Primaries and the Dynamics of Public Choice.* Princeton, N.J.: Princeton University Press. The best work on presidential primaries in recent years.

Burnham, Walter Dean. 1970. *Critical Elections and the Mainsprings of American Politics.* New York: W. W. Norton. A major study of electoral realignment.

Campbell, Angus, Philip E. Converse, Warren E. Miller, and Donald E. Stokes. 1960. *The American Voter.* New York: John Wiley & Sons. The classic study of American voting and still valuable reading.

Clubb, Jerome M., William H. Flanigan, and Nancy H. Zingale. 1980. *Partisan Realignment.* Beverly Hills, Calif.: Sage Publications. A survey of American political history that combines electoral analysis with patterns of governance.

Fiorina, Morris P. 1981. *Retrospective Voting in American National Elections.* New Haven, Conn.: Yale University Press. An important reinterpretation of voting and partisanship.

Nie, Norman H., Sidney Verba, and John R. Petrocik. 1966. *The Changing American Voter.* Cambridge, Mass.: Belknap Press of Harvard University Press. A major study focusing on electoral changes in the early 1960s.

Niemi, Richard G., and Herbert F. Weisberg, eds. 1984. *Controversies in Voting Behavior.* Washington, D.C.: CQ Press. A collection of sophisticated studies of American and European voting behavior.

Silbey, Joel, Allan Bogue, and William Flanigan. 1978. *A History of American Electoral Behavior.* Princeton, N.J.: Princeton University Press. A collection of essays on electoral analysis prior to public opinion polls.

Chapter 9

Political Parties

BUSH
QUAYLE
NEW HAMPSHIRE
GREGG
GOVERNOR
JUDD
CNN

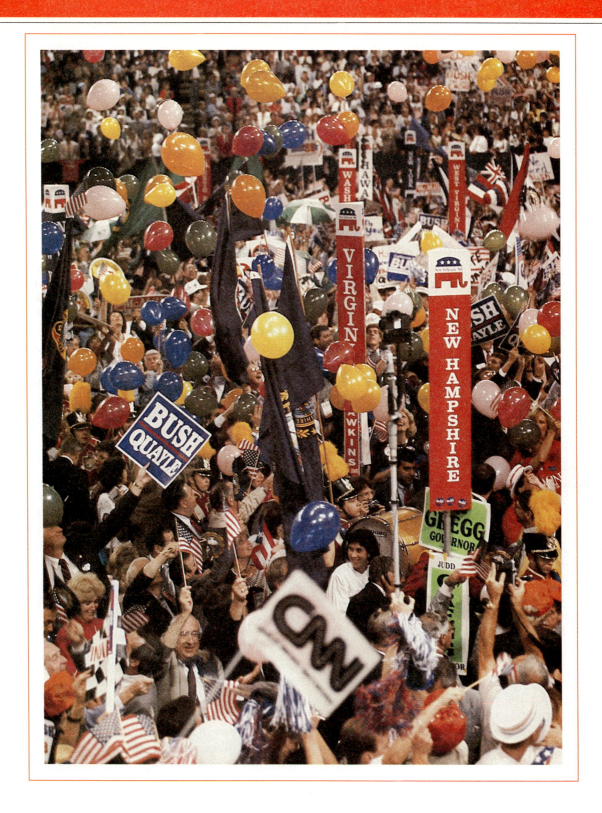

American political parties are not in the best of health. New voters, especially young voters, now often register as independents rather than as partisans. It is common for a majority of voters to split their tickets in presidential elections; even those who consider themselves strong partisans increasingly vote for candidates of the other party. And if typically about 50 percent of the voting-age population now takes the trouble to vote in presidential elections, the most noteworthy fact about party primaries is that most citizens ignore them. Even in Congress party loyalty cannot be taken for granted. Members move in and out of party ranks in committee and floor voting, and biparty coalitions are always poised to upset majority party control. Now and then a member will switch to the other side, seeking reelection under new party colors. From almost any perspective, the parties' loss of vitality is evident.

Not all political actors, though, have suffered from the decline of political parties. Individual candidates have gained increased independence. They compete for the party label and, having won it, are largely free from party control. Political consultants and campaign management firms, paid by individual candidates, provide counsel on issues, strategy, and techniques that party organizations cannot match.

Above all hover the media, especially television, making and unmaking candidates for voters accustomed to obtaining political cues and information by sitting in front of the tube. So important have technology and the mass media become that the parties are often on the sidelines. "Their" candidates, bolstered by personal organizations, struggle for public favor, using all the techniques of mass merchandising.

But party decline must be kept in perspective. American political parties have never been exceptionally powerful, and despite their present difficulties, they are not withering away. At least two out of three voters continue to regard themselves as partisans, and all but a few officeholders are Democrats or Republicans. Nor does the decline of the parties among voters necessarily affect party performance in the government. Congressional Republicans were unusually cohesive during the early years of the Reagan administration, while congressional Democrats drew together during its latter years.

Both parties have gone through bad times and survived. The Democratic party is almost as old as the nation itself, and the Republican party is older than a century. As this chapter will show, tradition is not the only force that maintains them.

The Functions of Parties

Parties are a means of organizing both the electorate and the government. First of all, they are groups, unified in varying degrees. In the electorate, a party is a loose association of voters—individuals who see themselves as party members. Party also refers to the formal organizations of officials who campaign and tend to party business at precinct, city, county, state, and national levels. A third level of party is found in government. It is reflected, for example, in the Republican members of the U.S. House of Representatives, the Democratic members of the Texas state senate, and the Republican governor of Missouri.

Political parties have a simple, practical objective: to win control of government. Nothing else is quite so important; nothing else so thoroughly colors their activities. To gain control of government, parties engage in functions that contribute to the democratization, unity, and rationality of the American political system.

Parties Provide for Popular Control of Government ■

Most students of government find it hard to imagine popular government without political parties. In earlier times, claims to power were based on birth, family, religion, or class. Today, prior claims on power are much less common. To gain control of government, politicians must compete for the votes of the people. Some unpredictability is usually present. Those who win know full well that the next election may bring defeat. And those who lose can usually bank on another chance down the road.

A democratic party system, linked to free elections, permits the people to choose their leaders, to influence government decisions, and in at least some measure, to hold officeholders accountable for their performance. Party is thus an indirect means by which people govern themselves. The broad role of parties in democracies is to provide for the rule of popular majorities.

Parties Foster Consensus ■

The United States is an unusually complex and diverse nation. These attributes have helped to form numerous voting blocs and organized groups representing social, economic, regional, class, religious, and ethnic interests (see Chapter 10).

Conflict among interests is common. Sooner or later, government is called on to take sides in the struggles among groups. Governing consists of making choices. The government may confer advantages on business or labor, on environmentalists or industry, on producers or consumers. Policies can be designed to promote or impede the development of nuclear energy plants or improve the lot of the poor or the wealthy. Virtually all interests look to government for relief or assistance.

A single interest sometimes wins an overwhelming victory in the policy-making process. But it is far more common for policies to be a blend of gains and losses for each of the contending groups. Most public policies reflect major compromises among competing blocs and interests.

Bargaining and compromise are natural to parties and party politicians. Parties stay in business by winning elections. To win, they must develop programs and policies that appeal to all groups and voting blocs. There is nothing exclusionary in the process. Both Democratic and Republican politicians search for support from farmers, city dwellers, business executives, professionals, union workers, white-collar workers, environmentalists, southerners, northerners, women, men, Catholics, Jews, Protestants, blacks, the young, the old, the wealthy, and the poor. No groups are completely ignored.

Within government, the parties act as "brokers." They seek to shape solutions to public problems that will satisfy, at least in some degree, all those interests with claims on them and whose support is important in elections. The advancement of group interests in policy-making bodies (notably legislatures) is not only a key feature of the representative system but also a key function of the major parties.

Parties Recruit and Develop Political Talent ■

Historically, no functions of political parties have been more important than the recruitment of candidates for public office and the organization of campaigns to elect them. During the late nineteenth and early twentieth centuries, party organizations flourished in many areas, especially in the states and major cities of the Northeast and Midwest. Persons ambitious for a career in politics had to work within the party structure, moving up a notch at a time, waiting to get the "nod" from party leaders before seeking office. Nominations were made by caucus-convention systems that, as a rule, were under the tight control of the leaders.

But this has changed. As an agency for recruiting and screening candidates, the party is much less important today. With the development of the direct primary, control over nominations passed from the leaders to the voters. Any candidate who wins a primary is the party's nominee. The primary encourages candidates to make their own strategies and to develop their own followings and sources of campaign funds. At no time in American history have campaigns been more candidate-centered than now.

Although the parties no longer play a dominant role in screening candidates, they make other contributions to the electoral process. Democratic and Republican politicians, as we shall see, differ in their positions on major policy questions; and many voters cast their votes according to party labels. The presence of two major parties both narrows and simplifies the election of public officials. Without parties, many candidates of unknown quality might clog the ballots, making intelligent choice by the voters impossible. Political parties help keep elections from becoming a free-for-all.

"Perspectives"

On Political Parties

"*Political parties constitute a basic element of democratic institutional apparatus. They perform an essential function in the management of succession to power, as well as in the process of obtaining popular consent to the course of public policy. They amass sufficient support to buttress the authority of governments; or, on the contrary, they attract or organize discontent and dissatisfaction sufficient to oust the government.*"

—V. O. Key, Jr.

"*A political party is first of all an organized attempt to get power. . . .*"

—E. E. Schattschneider

"*We Democrats are all under one tent. In any other country we'd be five splinter parties.*"

—Thomas P. ("Tip") O'Neill

"*A party is not . . . a group of men who intend to promote public welfare "upon some principle in which they are all agreed. . . ." A party is a group whose members propose to act in concert in the competitive struggle for political power.*"

—Joseph A. Schumpeter

"*A party isn't a fraternity. It isn't something that you join because you like the old school tie they wear. It is a gathering together of people who basically share the same political philosophy.*"

—Ronald Reagan

"*[A party is] any group, however loosely organized, seeking to elect governmental office-holders under a given label.*"

—Leon Epstein

"*Party is a body of men united, for promulgating by their joint endeavors the national interest, upon some particular principle in which they are all agreed.*"

—Edmund Burke

Sources: V. O. Key, Jr., *Politics, Parties & Pressure Groups* (New York: Thomas Y. Crowell, 1964), p. 9; E. E. Schattschneider, *Party Government* (New York: Holt, Rinehart & Winston, 1942), p. 37; *Washington Post,* June 17, 1975, p. 12; Joseph A. Schumpeter, *Capitalism, Socialism and Democracy* (New York: Harper & Row, 1942), p. 283; *Pittsburgh Post Gazette,* March 20, 1980, p. 9; Leon Epstein, *Political Parties in Western Democracies* (New York: Praeger Publishers, 1967), p. 9; Edmund Burke, *Works* (London: G. Bell and Sons, Ltd., 1897), vol. I, p. 375.

In many states, political parties have played a major role in assimilating and advancing ethnic groups. Successful politicians depend on popular followings; thus, very early they recruited supporters and subleaders from ethnic groups. When opportunities for careers in business and the professions were closed to immigrants and other minorities, the political order was almost wide open. Movement up the political ladder—to a seat on the city council, to the mayor's or governor's office, or to Congress—advanced members of minority groups in society at large. Ambition, political skills, and voting power have been powerful means to overcome discrimination.

Parties Develop Issues and Educate the Public ■

The American public is scarcely ever as attentive, resourceful, or politically involved as classical democratic theory prescribes. Large segments of the public are often indifferent to politics; and public opinion is often inert (see Chapter 7). Political parties, particularly at election time, help to breathe new life into sluggish electorates. The author of a distinguished book on democracy, Robert MacIver, described the educative function of political parties:

> Public opinion is too variant and dispersive to be effective unless it is organized. It must be canalized on the broad lines of some major division of opinion. Party focuses the issues, sharpens the differences between the contending sides, eliminates confusing cross-currents of opinion. . . . The party educates the public while seeking merely to influence it, for it must appeal on grounds of policy. For the same reason it helps to remove the inertia of the public and thus to broaden the range of public opinion. In short the party, in its endeavors to win the public to its side, however unscrupulous it may be in its modes of appeal, is making the democratic system workable. It is the agency by which public opinion is translated into public policy.[1]

Parties Help Manage the Election System ■

The traditional role of the parties in recruiting candidates and mobilizing support in campaigns is well understood. In addition, they provide information to voters concerning where, when, and how to register; they stimulate voting by publicizing candidates; and they participate in the administration of elections by providing members for election boards and watchers to observe the counting of ballots. In a two-party system, the parties check each other on election day, thus lessening the chances for fraud.

Parties Shape the Direction of Government ■

Parties do more than conduct elections. Their major aim is to win control of government—to win its offices. With control of government comes the opportunity to make policies that serve the interests of supporters and reflect the party's idea of the general interest. Using the policy process for these purposes is not easy, though. For one thing, party control of government is often incomplete. From 1952 to 1990, only one-third of all elections produced governments in which both houses of Congress and the presidency were controlled by the same party. When the branches are controlled by different parties, conflict ordinarily is heightened. Deadlocks are common. The success of the president's program will depend on the president's ability to forge bipartisan coalitions in the legislature. As for the public, it finds it difficult and sometimes impossible to hold either party fully accountable for the performance of government.

Even when one party holds both branches, its majority in Congress may be too thin to give it firm control. And conflict among various elements within the majority party may be so intense on some issues that the party is immobilized, unable to find areas of agreement that permit it to act. In recent decades, for example, the influence of congressional Democrats frequently has been reduced by the defections of conservatives in its southern wing.[2]

Whatever the state of party unity, the majority party has a major impact on the course of government. It organizes the chambers of Congress, elects the leaders, controls parliamentary procedures, manages the committee system, and establishes the agenda. And when it can agree on what it wants, it gets its way, at least up to the point of a presidential veto.

Another perspective on the role of party is provided by the platform. One study has shown that

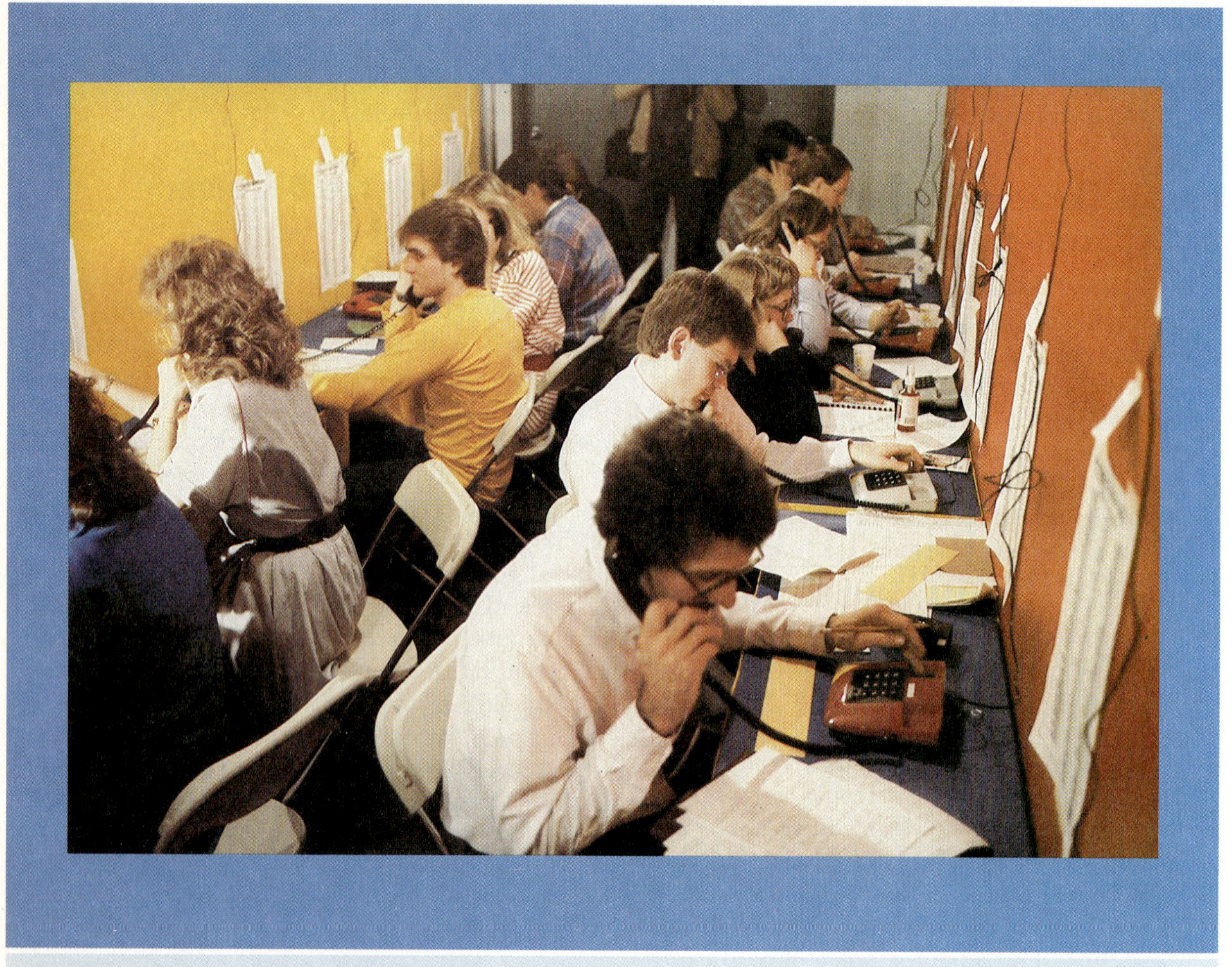

Getting out the vote: A presidential candidate's organization works a bank of telephones, urging voters to turn out for their candidate in the Iowa caucuses, the first opportunity for voters anywhere to express a preference in the nominating process.

platform planks provide a clear indication of the plans of the party. The party that wins the presidency eventually enacts about three-fourths of the programs promised in its platform.[3]

In controlling government, the parties perform another important function. They help to bridge the gap created by the separation of powers—at least when the president and Congress are controlled by the same party. The main reason that deadlock between the branches has not occurred more often is that party platforms and programs, enhanced by party loyalty, have linked executive and legislative leaders to common purposes.

The minority party also helps to shape the direction of government by criticizing the record of the party in power and offering alternatives. The role of the opposition party is vital to a democratic political system. Its leaders can expose abuses of office by majority party politicians and the mismanagement and failures of programs. The opposition party can also serve as a rallying point for citizens unhappy with the performance of the party in power. Eventually, the "outs" replace the "ins," and the process begins anew.

Party Organization

Party organization is not often visible to the average voter—and for a good reason. American parties are not characterized by an imposing and elaborate apparatus. The formal party structure is quite simple. It consists of layers of committees, each largely independent of the others. They stretch from the smallest unit of government, the precinct, to the national agencies, the national convention and the national committee.

Analysts often depict party organization as a pyramid. Thousands of precincts (small voting districts) form the base, while the national committee rests at the pinnacle. Midway up are the state central committees.

The pyramid model, though, is not very useful in explaining real American parties. Its flaw is the suggestion that the national party agencies, perched at the top, run things. In fact, in most respects, state and local party committees are on their own, preoccupied with local matters and capturing local offices. Indeed, one truth about American parties is that they are loose, highly decentralized coalitions. Often they are simply the instruments of local candidates. Only in the presidential nominating process are there major national party controls over state and local organizations—and then only in the Democratic party.

Organizational Levels ■

Precinct, Ward, City, and County Committees. Party organization at the precinct level ordinarily consists of a *precinct committeeman* and *committeewoman.* They are chosen through election by the voters or by a precinct committee of the party. Their principal task is to "deliver" the precinct for the party's candidates on election day. Precinct leaders assist citizens in registration and voting, distribute campaign literature, arrange for meetings with candidates, and help turn out the vote on election day. In some large cities, precinct leaders mediate between citizens and the government—perhaps getting traffic lights, street repairs, better police protection, or jobs in city government. Precincts vary in size from 1000 or 2000 voters in a metropolitan area to less than 50 in a rural area. Taken together, precinct officials in an area make up the *ward organization.*

The next major level of party organization is the *county committee* (or in some communities, the city committee). County committees, made up of all the precinct officials of the county, are usually quite large. The major local party official is the county chairperson, who is ordinarily elected by the county committee. The chairperson may play a major role in recruiting and slating candidates for local and state offices (and occasionally for the U.S. House of Representatives). In jurisdictions where patronage is still important, the chairperson is apt to be deeply involved in its distribution.

State Committees. Lodged above the county committees are the state committees—usually known as *state central committees.* In some states, this committee consists of all the county leaders. This arrangement, at least on paper, links these separate strata. More commonly, state committee members are chosen by party primaries or local conventions. Operating under state law and party rules, state committees may be charged with raising and disbursing campaign money, coordinating statewide campaigns, drafting the party platform, slating candidates for office, arranging for state conventions, and drafting rules for the selection of delegates to the national convention. The state chairperson is commonly selected by the party's gubernatorial candidate. Apart from a major officeholder or two, such as the governor or a U.S. senator, the chairperson is usually the most visible party politician in the state. A few state party leaders, because of their skills or the prominence of their states, also become well known in national politics.

National Party Organization. The highest authority of the party is the *national convention,* yet it governs party affairs only in a very general way. In the first place, it meets for only a few days every four years. And even then, the delegates are preoccupied with selecting the presidential and vice presidential nominees and with shaping the platform. Party governance is not ordinarily a matter of great concern for the convention's prominent politicians. They use their time to gain media attention, to meet with other leaders, and to promote their own careers. Party management by the convention comes down to the passage of a few resolutions to reshape party rules (on delegate selection, for example) and to create commissions to prepare studies and recommendations on structure and procedures.

To the extent that any agency manages the party, it is the *national committee,* which derives its authority from the national convention.[4] Each party's national committee consists of a committeeman and committeewoman from each state, territory, and the District of Columbia, plus other state and local party leaders, such as governors and mayors. Members are chosen in a variety of ways—by primaries, conventions, state committees, or the state's national convention delegates themselves.

One main duty of the national committee is to arrange for the national convention. A convention site must be selected, a temporary roll of delegates compiled, and temporary officers chosen. During presidential election years, the committee coordinates the party's national campaign, raises and allocates campaign funds (of somewhat less importance since the introduction of public financing of presidential elections in the 1970s), and prepares and distributes campaign materials. The Democratic National Committee, working from the blueprints of various study commissions, has been especially active in setting guidelines state parties must follow in selecting national convention delegates.

The one national committee official who matters is the *national chairperson.* Party practices provide for the choice of this official by members of the national committee; usually, however, the chairperson is the personal choice of the party's nominee for the presidency. Seeking to make the office more independent of the presidential nominee, the Democratic National Committee in 1989 changed the chairperson's term to run from election to election rather than from convention to convention.

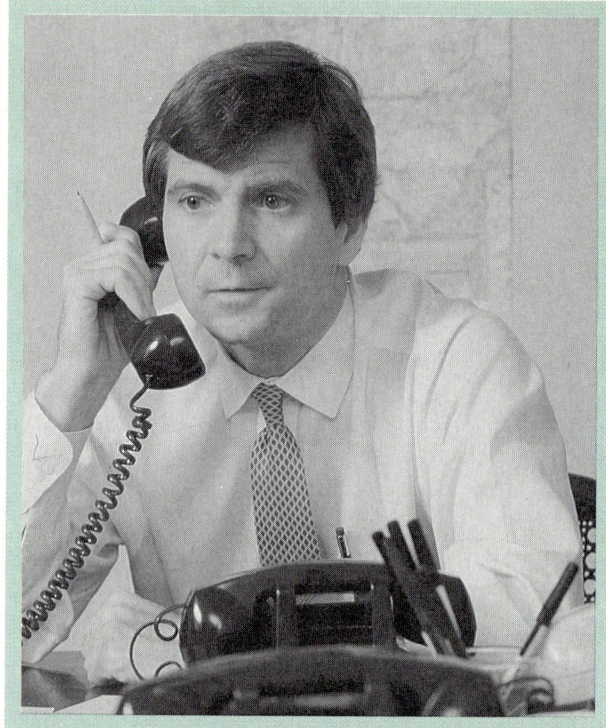

Lee Atwater, selected by George Bush in 1988 to be the Republican National Chairperson.

Men and women chosen for this position often become well-known party figures. They are seen regularly on television during presidential campaigns. Despite their visibility, only a few national chairpersons have had the necessary resources (personality, skills, followings) to become a power in their own right.

The tasks of the national chairperson begin and end with advancing the party's electoral fortunes—especially in the race for the presidency. Supported by a large staff, the chairperson helps to raise funds (sometimes to retire the debts of the previous campaign) and coordinate the activities of regular and volunteer party organizations. All chairpersons face the problem of unifying the party. They seek to create the illusion of a unified movement; and that, in a disjointed party system, is hard to do.

Ron Brown, chosen in 1989 to be the Democratic National Chairperson, is presented the gavel by the outgoing chairperson, Paul Kirk, Jr.

Unlike problems, headaches, and disappointments, satisfactions for the national chairperson are few, which is one reason turnover is high. As a Democratic national chairperson said not long ago, "It's not the sort of job that you lay down in the street and bleed to keep. . . ."[5] Election results also contribute to turnover. The chairperson of the winning party often takes a position in the new administration, while the chairperson of the losing party "takes the rap" and resigns.

There are also party committees in Congress called the *congressional* and *senatorial campaign committees,* one for each party in each house. Independent of the national committees, they assist member campaigns by raising and distributing campaign funds, conducting research, preparing literature, developing and financing television commercials, and advising on campaign strategies. The committees also provide aid to party nominees in states or districts held by the opposition party. The most active and influential of these committees is the National Republican Congressional Campaign Committee. Well organized and well financed, it now has field organizers who travel around the country to advise Republican House candidates on fund-raising, issues, and strategy.

In sum, national party agencies are planning, public relations, research, and fund-raising organizations designed to help elect candidates for national office. They may illuminate party positions and programs, but they do not generate them. Party policy, or what passes as that, is made in Congress.

Characteristics of American Parties

Institutions do not survive simply on the enthusiasm and good intentions of their members or on the skills of their leaders. More is required, including a "good fit" with their environment. An examination of the characteristics of the parties shows the many ways they are in harmony with the political system and society.

Decentralization of Power

There is wide agreement that decentralization of power is the principal characteristic of the American party. This means there is power at all points of the system, leaving national agencies with only limited control over subnational units. The independence and variability of state and local party organizations can be seen in several ways. They differ sharply, for example, in the kinds of candidates they recruit and support, in their relationships with organized interests, and in their ideologies. The Democratic parties of South Carolina and Michigan do not share many traditions; at times they share nothing more than a common name. The Republican parties in the Rocky Mountain states are quite unlike many state Republican parties in the East, particularly in their ideological orientations. The former are conservative; the latter are more liberal. The looseness of this system has led some observers to describe the parties as *confederations* of state and local organizations, joined simply to elect candidates who run under their label.

The voting behavior of members of Congress reflects the decentralized nature of the parties. On certain kinds of policy questions, the majority party finds it difficult to hold its members together. Party lines break as members vote in terms of personal aims or respond to constituency, interest group, or executive agency claims. At times, control of policy formation passes from the majority party to a biparty coalition, such as the well-known "conservative coalition" of southern Democrats and Republicans (see Figure 9–1). The influence of this coalition has waned somewhat in recent years.[6]

The congressional parties, of course, are not always in disrepair. On certain issues, not only do party members vote together, but the parties also present real differences for the voters. On social welfare and labor legislation, for example, most Democrats unite to oppose most Republicans, with Democrats on the liberal side and Republicans on the conservative side. The main point is that party lines collapse often enough to make party control over decision making less than reliable.

Decentralization is also shown in the position of the national party agencies. For the party in control of the administration, the national committee and the national chairperson are mainly the "president's people," concerned with the president's election. National committee leaders have no claim to instruct party colleagues in Congress on policy matters.

Finally, congressional nominations are treated as local matters, to be decided by local standards. (This is especially true on the Democratic side; the National Republican Congressional Committee recently has become more active in recruiting House candidates and in backing nominees in the primaries.) Localism in the nominating process means that the party label is up for grabs: Anyone who wins a Democratic nomination is a Democrat; and anyone who wins a Republican nomination is a Republican. Not surprisingly, some candidates who make their way to national office have little sympathy for national party programs. Recruitment, nomination, and election practices have a profound impact on American parties; in the main, they weaken their unity and enhance their local bias.

Parties as Coalitions

Another major feature of American parties is that they are *coalitions*—that is, associations of various social interests and groups. The outlines of the party coalitions in the electorate are familiar to most observers. In recent decades the Democratic party has attracted a disproportionate number of blacks, Jews, Catholics, southerners, manual (blue-collar) workers, union members, intellectuals, young people, ethnic minorities, persons with lim-

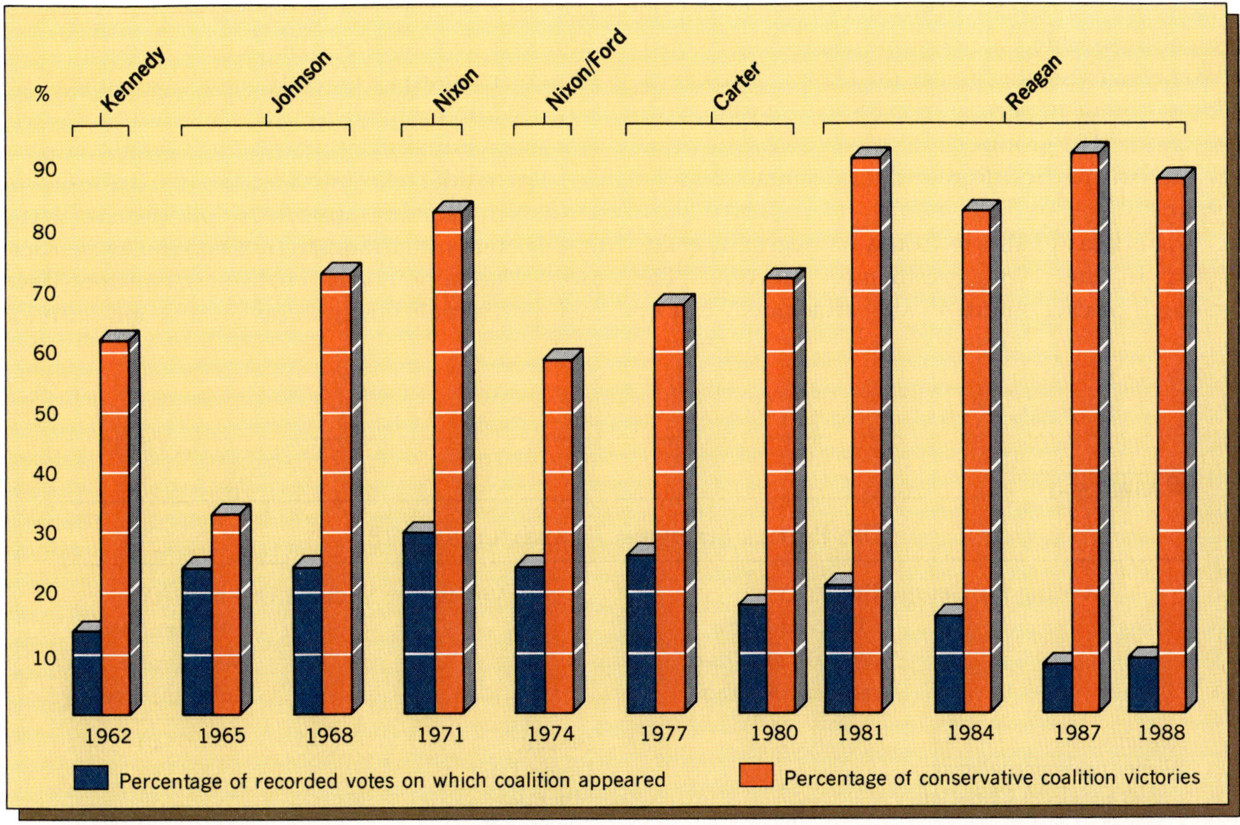

Figure 9–1 Party breakdown in Congress: conservative coalition victories in both houses, 1962–1988. A conservative coalition vote is one in which a majority of voting southern Democrats and a majority of voting Republicans voted opposite a majority of voting northern Democrats. Source: *Congressional Weekly Report,* January 9, 1982, p. 51; October 27, 1984, p. 2821; January 16, 1988, p. 113; November 19, 1988, p. 3349.

ited education, and the poor. In contrast, the Republican party has usually carried special appeal for business executives, industrialists, professionals, farmers, suburbanites, Protestants, college graduates, "old stock" Americans, and the wealthy. In recent years, the split between the races has been dramatic. In the 1988 presidential election, nearly nine out of ten blacks voted Democratic, while six out of ten whites voted Republican. And in southern states, once the center of Democratic strength, white voters overwhelmingly (67 percent) supported the Republican nominee. (Southerners of both races continue to vote heavily Democratic in state and local elections.) Taking the country as a whole, white voters' support for George Bush was only slightly less than their support for Ronald Reagan in the one-sided election of 1984.

Categorizing the groups and social interests that make up the party coalitions can be misleading. First, no group is completely united behind a single party. And second, the coalitions are often in flux. The Democratic coalition has become especially fragile in presidential elections. By no means do all union members vote for Democratic candidates; it is an unusual election, in fact, when less than one-third cast ballots for the Republican nominee. In 1988 union households cast 43 percent of their votes for George Bush. Among the elements in the traditional Democratic coalition, the strongest supporters of Michael Dukakis were blacks, Jews,

Hispanics, the unemployed, and the poor. On the Republican side, many professionals and businesspersons regularly vote for Democratic candidates—about 40 percent in 1988. The most that can be said is that groups tilt toward one or the other of the two parties. Rarely does a party "own" a group.

The data of Table 9–1 show how certain groups voted in the 1988 presidential election. The strength of each group's party attachment can be judged by the extent to which its vote diverged from the overall national vote. Blacks, for example, voted 40 percent more Democratic than the national average, while evangelical Christians voted 27 percent more Republican than the national average.

The moderation of the major parties—shown in their continuing appeal to "middle" or "centrist" voters rather than to those on the extremes—owes something to their coalition character. Since each party coalition contains groups and individ-

TABLE 9–1

The Parties Strongest Supporters in 1988

Voting for George Bush (R)	Percent More Republican Than National Average	Voting for Michael Dukakis (D)	Percent More Democratic Than National Average
Republicans	37	Blacks	40
White fundamentalist or evangelical Christian	27	Democrats	36
Conservatives	26	Liberals	35
White southerners	13	Hispanics	23
White Protestants	12	Jews	18
Income over $100,000	11	Unemployed	16
White men	9	Women with less than high school education	16
Male college graduates	9	Income under $12,500	16
College graduates	8	Union household	11
Income over $50,000	8	Not a high school graduate	10
Whites	5	Full-time student	8
Professional or manager	5	Teacher	5
Southerners	4	Moderates	4
Homemakers	4	Blue-collar workers	4
Independents (men)	4	Men with less than high school education	4
White westerners	4	Women	3
Men	3	Age 60 and over	3
White-collar workers	3	High school graduates	3
White midwesterners	3	Easterners	3
Age 45–59 years	3	Retired	3
Some college education	3	Postgraduate education	2
Bush National vote: 54		Dukakis National vote: 46	

Source: Adapted from exit interview data by *New York Times*/CBS News poll, as reported in the *New York Times*, November 10, 1988.

uals with widely different views, party leaders and candidates must reach compromises that keep the party from flying apart. The Democratic party has not only many liberals, both black and white, but also many conservatives, mainly southern whites. The Republican party has been the home of both conservative midwesterners and liberal easterners. Each party also has "in-between" members, or "moderates." Ideological diversity helps explain why intraparty conflict is sometimes as intense as interparty conflict and why party leaders must be skillful in bargaining.

Party coalitions are always vulnerable to division and exploitation. Each party pursues strategies to crack the opponent's coalition. When Dwight D. Eisenhower ran especially strong in southern states in 1952, for example, he brought a basic change to Republican strategy. Every Republican nominee since then has tried to win the South, to appeal to conservative elements, seeking to break away this large bloc from the Democrats. And the Republicans have had substantial success, as in 1972 (with Richard M. Nixon), in 1980 and 1984 (with Ronald Reagan), and in 1988 (with George Bush). In 1964, a lean year for Republicans, Barry Goldwater nevertheless carried five southern states.

Similarly, Democrats covet Republican followers. The 1976 nomination of Jimmy Carter, a born-again Christian, made the Democratic party more attractive than usual to Protestant voters. Since 1952, among Democratic candidates only Lyndon Johnson received greater support from Protestants than Carter (and Johnson had the good fortune to be matched against Goldwater, a candidate whose support was weak among all groups and all regions except the South). Eschewing the word "liberal" until the closing days of the 1988 campaign, when he switched to a populist message, Michael Dukakis made a strong pitch to win back 1984 Democratic Reagan voters. His strategy was only moderately successful: About half of this large group (one-fifth of all Democratic identifiers) voted for the Republican candidate, George Bush.[7]

Coalition building is never much below the surface in the calculations of party leaders. Group interests, claims, and aspirations are often signaled in the composition of party tickets. The choice of Geraldine Ferraro as the Democratic vice presidential nominee in 1984, for example, reflected an attempt to attract not only the women's vote but also that of Italian Americans and other urban ethnic voters. Other purposes—political, social, even historic—were of course also served.

Expediency and prudence prompt the parties to cast their nets widely, to appeal to as many groups as possible and offend as few as possible. What is sometimes overlooked is the mutuality of this relationship: Groups need the parties as much as the parties need them. Their capacity to shape public policy to their advantage depends on the receptivity of officeholders to their claims.

Votes are exchanged for benefits. Organized labor can expect an attentive hearing from most Democratic officeholders; organized business can expect much the same from most Republican officeholders. At the same time, government becomes more predictable. Groups in the winning coalition have reason to expect better treatment than those in the losing one. If they fail to receive it, they may "think twice" the next time around.

The Concept of Party Membership

The attachment most Americans have for inherited institutions is well known, but in the case of political parties, it leaves something to be desired. About two out of three persons do identify themselves as either Democrats or Republicans, and not many voters ever support a minor party. There are still psychological ties between most voters and the major parties—ties that help preserve the two-party system (see Chapter 8). Self-identification as a partisan, however, falls short of constituting membership in a political party.

The only formal test of party membership is the act of registering to vote. Since registration is governed by state law, membership is an expression of each state's registration provisions. In states with a closed primary, voters ordinarily must indicate their party affiliation, thus entering the public records as a member of a specific party (unless they

Continuity & CHANGE

Race and Voting over Four Decades

Race has not always been a central factor in American voting behavior. The great divide appeared in the 1960s, beginning with the massive shift by blacks toward the Democratic party in 1964 and continuing in 1968 with a significant shift of white voters toward the Republicans.

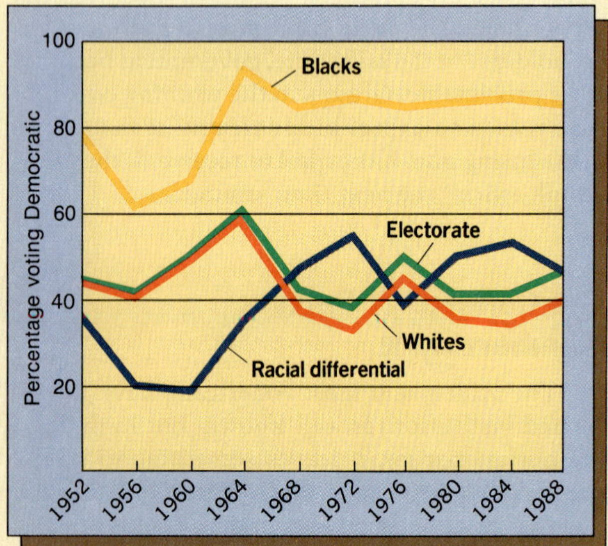

The extraordinary support blacks gave Lyndon Johnson was linked to his commitment to civil rights legislation and to the Republican nomination of Barry Goldwater, a militant conservative and opponent of the 1964 public accommodations law. The Voting Rights Act of 1965, a key part of President Johnson's Great Society program, cemented the relationship between black voters and the Democratic party.

Moving in the opposite direction, the white vote for the Republican candidate exceeded 60 percent in five of the last six presidential elections. Blacks are now the most prominent element in the Democratic coalition—and whites are a large and distinctive part of the Republican coalition. Grounded in socioeconomic policies and civil rights, racial polarization in national politics is unmistakable.

Source: *Gallup Report* (November 1984), pp. 8–9; *New York Times*/CBS poll, as reported in the *New York Times*, November 10, 1988.

What a difference a day makes: Completing the last leg of their 20th anniversary Selma-to-Montgomery voter rights march, civil rights leaders (l to r, Rev. Joseph Lowery, SCLC leader; Rev. John Nettles of Alabama; governor's aide Hezekiah Wagstaff; Atlanta councilman John Lewis; Jesse Jackson) meet with Alabama Governor George C. Wallace in his capitol office. Twenty years earlier he had been their staunchest opponent.

register as an independent). In some states with closed primaries, voters enroll as party members simply by declaring their affiliation at the time of voting in the primary. In states with open primaries, there are no membership requirements. Voters can vote in the primary that interests them, and no one knows their affiliation.

The concept of party membership in the United States is muddled. Parties have no control over who belongs to them and no way of enforcing adherence to their programs. Any person is a Democrat, or a Republican, who professes to be one. Obligations to the party are nonexistent.

> [One] can be a member without applying for admission, a beneficiary without paying dues or contributing to campaigns, a critic without attending meetings, an interpreter without knowing party vocabulary, an apostate without fearing discipline. To the citizen who takes politics casually, it may be the best of all worlds. The typical American is insensitive to the claims, problems, and doctrine of his party. His principal participation in party life is through the act of voting—sometimes for his party and sometimes not.[8]

The Domination of Candidate Organizations ■

American parties suffer from more than a touch of malaise. One sign of this is the emergence of candidate organizations as the dominant force in campaigns. Devising campaign strategies, recruiting campaign workers, raising funds, publicizing issues, mobilizing voters—these activities are now more the responsibilities of officeholders (and candidates for public office) than of party organizations. In many jurisdictions, the party organization is more observer than participant; the real work of campaigning is done by candidates, their families and supporters, and the persons and organizations they hire to assist them.

The decline of party organization does not mean that less attention is paid to winning elections. Rather, "outsiders" have taken over campaign activities that were poorly performed, or not performed at all, by the party apparatus. Campaign management firms, public relations specialists, and political consultants are available for a fee to candidates who need help in organizing their campaigns. Experts are available to conduct public opinion surveys, make films, write speeches, prepare advertising, buy television time, raise money, and offer counsel on issues, image, and strategy. Candidates can be "packaged" and "sold" to voters through public relations campaigns much like products are sold to consumers.

The candidate-centeredness of American politics is especially apparent in matters of money. The parties provide some funds to candidates; using direct-mail fund-raising techniques, national Republican committees have in fact been very successful in raising money for their congressional candidates. But much more is raised by individual candidates, who find the political action committees of interest groups generous contributors. For example, in 1988, 37 percent of the campaign money raised by all House candidates, and 47 percent by House incumbents, came from political action committees (PACs). (See Chapters 10 and 12 for an analysis of PACs.)

At the presidential level, campaigns are financed mainly by public funds—on a matching basis at the nominating stage and fully (but see below) at the election stage. These funds are given to the candidates, not to the parties, except for grants made to each party to meet national convention expenses. The law that introduced public funding to presidential campaigns, the Federal Election Campaign Act of 1974, was designed to favor candidates.

In 1988 each major party presidential candidate organization received $46.1 million from the Treasury to finance its general election campaign. Theoretically, that was the maximum amount that each candidate could spend on his campaign. But the law also permits the parties to raise huge sums of so-called soft money for loosely defined "party building" and "get-out-the-vote" activities at the state level. In practice, much of this private money, which the presidential candidates even help to raise, is used to pay the costs of campaign field operations closely linked to the presidential cam-

"They say to get elected to public office in America one must be rich. Well, my friends, I'm rich. I'm very rich."

paigns—thus circumventing the law's spending limits. With soft money available to meet certain campaign expenses, both Bush and Dukakis used most of their public funds for television advertising. Until the rules are tightened by the Federal Election Commission, national campaigns will continue to be financed in part by private money—a practice clearly in conflict with the public financing provisions of the Federal Election Campaign Act.[9]

Party Characteristics and the Political System

The American party system is much criticized. The major parties are portrayed as too similar, too splintered, and too undisciplined. It is said that their similarities deprive voters of a real choice in elections, that their fragmentation increases the influence of special interests, and that their lack of cohesion prevents voters from holding them accountable.

These complaints are more than a little true. American parties tend to be moderate, party discipline is erratic, and neither party is sufficiently united to always fulfill its campaign promises.

But there is more to the story. In large part, the parties are products of their environment; they are shaped by forces beyond their control. Chief among these is the Constitution, in particular its provisions for federalism and the separation of powers. E. E. Schattschneider described its aims this way:

> The Convention at Philadelphia produced a constitution with a dual attitude: it was proparty in one sense and antiparty in another. The authors of the Constitution refused to suppress the parties by destroying the fundamental liberties in which parties originate. They or

The Public and the Parties

Thinking of the Democratic and Republican parties, would you say there is a great deal of difference in what they stand for, a fair amount of difference, or hardly any difference at all?

A great deal	25%
A fair amount	45
Hardly at all	25
No opinion/don't know	5

What does it mean to you when someone says he or she is a Republican? (leading answers)

Conservative	21%
Money/power	18
Business oriented	13
Agrees with GOP platform	8
Unconcerned with needs of the people	5

What does it mean to you when someone says he or she is a Democrat? (leading answers)

For working people/people oriented	21%
Liberal	18
Person who votes Democratic	9
Spends too much money	7
Cares for poor/disadvantaged	7

The American two-party system has been around for well over a century. Neglected and demeaned, it is nevertheless a survivor. What do the above data tell us about the public and the parties today? First, a significant majority of the public believes that the two parties are not as alike as "two peas in a pod"—one out of four voters, in fact, perceives a "great deal" of difference between the parties. Second, much of the public correctly perceives the parties' ideological thrusts: a conservative, business-oriented Republican party versus a liberal, working-class, labor-oriented Democratic party. Third, even though their ideological development is not particularly acute, the voters are not fools.

Source of data: *The People, Press, and Politics* (Los Angeles: *Times-Mirror,* 1987), pp. 117, 125, as adapted. Note concerning questions two and three in this survey: Some respondents offered more than one answer. About half of the sample consists of "other" (40 percent) and "don't know" (13 percent) responses. For instructive analyses of the position of political parties today, see Leon D. Epstein, *Political Parties in the American Mold* (Madison: University of Wisconsin Press, 1986); David R. Mayhew, *Placing Parties in American Politics* (Princeton, N.J.: Princeton University Press, 1986); and Martin P. Wattenberg, *The Decline of American Political Parties 1952–1984* (Cambridge, Mass.: Harvard University Press, 1986). For a discussion of changes designed to strengthen the parties, see David E. Price, *Bringing Back the Parties* (Washington, D.C.: CQ Press, 1984).

their immediate successors accepted amendments that guaranteed civil rights and thus established a system of party tolerance, i.e., the right to agitate and to organize. This is the proparty aspect of the system. On the other hand, the authors of the Constitution set up an elaborate division and balance of powers within an intricate governmental structure designed to make parties ineffective. It was hoped that the parties would lose and exhaust themselves in futile attempts to fight their way through the labyrinthine framework of the government, much as an attacking army is expected to spend itself against the defensive works of a fortress. This is the antiparty part of the constitutional scheme. To quote Madison, the "great object" of the Constitution was "to preserve the public good and private rights against the danger of such a faction [party] and at the same time to preserve the spirit and form of popular government."

The framers were intent on designing a government system in which no single faction or interest (a party, in the modern sense) could become dominant (see Chapter 2). A partial solution was federalism, with its division of powers between the states and the federal government. The rest of the answer was the separation of powers—an arrangement for the division of power among the legislative, executive, and judicial branches. Under these ingenious arrangements, power checks power; no single faction, whatever its appeal, is likely to win everywhere.

Each arrangement has had a major impact on the party system. Federalism made it inevitable that the party system (as well as the government) would be decentralized, that parties would form around the elective offices of each state. The national Democratic party is basically a coalition of state and local Democratic parties brought together for limited objectives (notably to win the presidency). The Republican party is much the same. Local and state party leaders typically go about their business without paying much attention to national party problems or to the rise and fall of national party fortunes. For them, more important local matters touch directly on their careers and those of other politicians.

The separation of powers has also shaped the parties. Its thrust, like that of federalism, is to disperse power. One of its by-products is "truncated" government: the capture of the presidency by one party and the capture of Congress (perhaps one house) by the other. This has become increasingly common and has afflicted the Republican party in particular. President Eisenhower had to deal with a Democratic-controlled Congress during six of the eight years he was in office (1952—1960), and Presidents Nixon and Ford faced Democratic majorities throughout their terms (1968–1976). President Reagan had to contend with a Democratic majority in the House during both of his terms; he faced a Senate Democratic majority during his last two years in office. George Bush was confronted by even heavier Democratic majorities in both houses of the 101st Congress (1989–1990). When partisan division is added to the normal tensions that exist between president and Congress, cooperation may become impossible. Opportunities for government by party obviously are sharply reduced.

What accounts for the enduring nature of divided party control of government? At least four hypotheses have been suggested:

1. The public prefers divided party control; some national surveys have shown that nearly one out of two voters prefers that the presidency be held by one party while the other party controls Congress.
2. Democratic state legislators, typically in control of a majority of the state legislatures, shape congressional districts to favor the candidacies of their national party colleagues.
3. Fewer voters defect in congressional elections than in presidential elections, and the Democratic party is the majority party in the electorate. Ergo, most Democratic voters vote for Democratic congressional candidates.
4. Voters of both parties prefer incumbents, thus perpetuating Democratic control of Congress.

Perhaps a fifth should be added to explain this governing dilemma: James Madison lives!

Other major elements in the environment of the parties should also be noted. Now used in all states, the direct primary has shifted power over nominations from the party organizations to the voters. Nonpartisan elections, widely used in local elections, weaken the parties by removing party labels from the ballot. Even the diversity of the nation—reflected in social, economic, religious, ethnic, and cultural groups of great variety—poses problems for the party system. Any party that wants to be taken seriously must represent a mixture of interests; hence there is a tendency for each party to become "all things to all people." Accordingly, party doctrine and policies may become indistinct or mushy and party officials adept at straddling tough issues. "Waffling" becomes a form of political survival.

In summary, the fragmentation of American parties owes much to environmental constraints. Whether the parties could have developed much differently (for example, along the centralized lines of European parties) is doubtful given the limits imposed by the system at large.

Dominance of the Two-Party System in America

A leading characteristic of the American system is that it has only two main political parties. By contrast, many European democracies have multiple-party systems, and in still other countries, such as the Soviet Union, the citizens have known only one-party regimes.

The American party system is not strictly two-party, though. There are regions and states, congressional and state legislative districts, and cities and counties so thoroughly dominated by one party that the second party has virtually no chance for victory. Many members of Congress, for example, come from safe (or relatively safe) districts. One-partyism is especially common in local jurisdictions. In many major cities and industrial towns, Republicans occupy a hopeless minority position; and in many small-town, suburban, and open country areas, Democratic officeholders could pass as endangered species. Where one-partyism is entrenched, it is a triumph when the second party even finds a candidate willing to run under its banner.

Despite the presence of many one-party jurisdictions, most citizens are accustomed to election campaigns that are contested by the two major parties. For over a century, they have been the only parties able to generate sustained support among voters.

Why a Two-Party System?

Accounting for the durability of the two-party system is not easy, but reasonable hypotheses can be offered. A major explanation is that the two-party system is supported by one feature of American elections: Members of legislative bodies, notably Congress, are elected from single-member districts (one member to a district). To be elected, a candidate need only secure a *plurality* of votes—that is, simply one more vote than any other candidate for that office. No majority is required, and only one party can win. The combination of single-member district and plurality election weighs heavily on any minor party, since its only chance to win is for its candidate to outpoll both major party candidates. That rarely happens. In practice, votes cast for candidates of lesser parties are usually wasted.

Minor parties are also thwarted by the electoral college system. Each state's electoral votes are cast as a unit for the presidential nominee who obtains a plurality of the popular vote in the state. Thus, the Democratic presidential candidate who gains a plurality of the popular vote in Illinois wins all 24 of that state's electoral votes; the Republican candidate who wins a plurality of the vote in California wins all 47 electoral votes. When George C. Wallace (a powerful Alabama governor) ran as the candidate of the American Independent party in 1968, he received an impressive 5 million popular votes in northern states, but he did not capture a single electoral vote outside the South. Running as an independent in 1980, John Anderson received nearly 6 million popular votes but no electoral

Key Provisions of Federal Election Campaign Act of 1974

Contribution limits
Campaign contributions by individuals to any candidate or candidate committee are limited to $1000 per election. Total contributions by an individual to all federal candidates in one year cannot exceed $25,000.

Political action committees formed by businesses, trade associations, or unions are limited to contributions of no more than $5000 to any candidate in any election. There are no limits on their aggregate contributions.

Expenditure limits
Expenditures in presidential primaries and general elections are limited. In 1988, each candidate could spend up to $23 million in all presidential primaries. The amount that can be spent within each state is also limited. Expenditures in general elections are governed by public financing provisions (see below).

Each national party may make certain expenditures on behalf of its presidential and congressional candidates (for example, 2 cents per voter on behalf of its presidential candidate).

There are no limits on how much House and Senate candidates may collect and spend in their campaigns or on the amount that individuals and groups may spend on behalf of any presidential or congressional candidate, so long as these expenditures are *independent.*

Public financing
Major party candidates for the presidency qualify for full funding prior to the campaign. In 1988, the Democratic and Republican nominees each received $46.1 million in campaign funds. These funds are derived from the federal income tax dollar checkoff.

Minor party and independent candidates qualify for public funds (after the election) if they receive 5 percent of the vote.

Matching federal funds are available for presidential primary candidates after they have first raised $100,000 in private funds ($5000 in contributions of no more than $250 in each of 20 states). Once the $100,000 threshold is reached, the candidate receives matching funds up to $250 per contribution. The maximum amount of matching funds available to any candidate in 1988 was $11.5 million.

votes. To candidates of lesser parties, the American election system must surely appear designed to protect Democrats and Republicans.

Many political scientists believe that if the electoral college were changed to award electoral votes in each state in proportion to the popular votes received by the candidates, minor parties would be encouraged to challenge the major parties. Similarly, in their view, replacement of the electoral college by a direct popular election of the president would weaken the two-party system. Clearly, the two major parties benefit from the "winner-take-all" feature of the electoral college.

A tradition of dualism in political conflict may also help explain the presence of the two-party system. The signs of dualism appeared in the opening struggles between those who favored and those who opposed the Constitution, in the contests between Federalists and Antifederalists and between Democrats and Whigs, and since the middle of the nineteenth century, in the party battles between Democrats and Republicans.[10] Politics conducted within a two-party framework is almost as old as the nation itself.

Election law is another factor in the stability of the two-party system. This is no mystery. Election law is written by state legislators who are themselves Democrats and Republicans. Altruism has not dominated their decisions. In state after state, they have written (and protected) laws that make it difficult for the candidates of minor parties to get on the ballot. (In 1988, 17 independent and

John Anderson, a former Republican member of the U.S. House of Representatives from Illinois, conducts his independent campaign for the presidency in Boston in 1980. Tradition, election law, the political culture, and a shortage of campaign funds make it difficult for third-party and independent candidates to compete for public office, particularly at the national level. Even getting on the ballot is a trial for them!

third-party presidential candidates were on the ballot in at least one state. Only the New Alliance party was on the ballot in all 50 states and the District of Columbia. The typical third party was on the ballot in four or fewer states.[11]) Requirements for early filing and a large number of signatures on petitions, collected in a brief time, have a chilling effect on lesser parties.

Federal law similarly inhibits minor parties. The Federal Election Campaign Act of 1974 provides that minor party candidates for the presidency can qualify for public funding only if they received at least 5 percent of the vote in the previous election. What is more, new parties or parties that received less than 5 percent of the vote four years earlier cannot qualify for public financing until *after* the election (provided they draw 5 percent of the vote).

Minor parties are victims of major party strategy. Although the major parties do not respond to every vagrant spark of popular opinion, they are responsive to the opinions and claims of any important group or voting bloc. The better organized any group is, the greater are the chances that one or both of the parties will consider its case. Parties and officeholders prosper by being flexible—the first principle of politics—and they borrow ideas with little concern for their source. Their capacity to adjust programs to appeal to emerging interests plainly undercuts opportunities for minor parties.

The major parties also attract the best political talent. Not many people who think seriously about a career in politics are willing to tie their fortunes to a party that appears to be lodged on the outskirts of the political system.

Strange as it seems, the nation's two-party system is in certain respects protected by conditions of one-partyism. The existence of one-party states and districts means that the losing party is never wiped out, no matter how poorly it fares in statewide or national elections. Although the country may vote heavily for the Republican presidential candidate, numerous states and districts fall in line for Democratic congressional candidates. Detroit votes heavily Democratic, for example, while much of outstate and upstate Michigan are Republican to the core. Pittsburgh and Philadelphia are dominated by the Democratic party, but Republicans thrive in Pennsylvania's interior counties. Kansas, Wyoming, Idaho, and the Dakotas are as likely to vote Republican as Massachusetts, Missouri, and Maryland are to vote Democratic. One-partyism rarely balances out, but it does immunize the minority party, guarding it from extinction when things are going badly.

Minor or Third Parties

Minor or third parties in the United States tend to have small beginnings and inconspicuous endings. Not many people are even aware of them. Among the minor parties running candidates for president in 1988 were the New Alliance, Libertarian, Populist, Socialist, Socialist Workers, Workers League, Workers World, Prohibition, Consumer, American Independent, Right to Life, and Peace and Freedom.[12] Although many minor parties survive no more than an election or two, a few, such as the Prohibition and Socialist Workers parties, have been around a long time.

It is not often that the total third-party vote for president surpasses 5 percent (see Table 9–2). In 1968, George C. Wallace, candidate of the American Independent party, received 13.5 percent of the national vote (and 46 electoral votes). John Anderson, an independent candidate, gained 6.6 percent of the national vote in 1980. Ordinarily, the combined third-party vote is less than 2 percent, as in 1972, 1976, 1984, and 1988. Even though many voters (more than half in numerous surveys) were dissatisfied with the choice between the major party candidates in 1988, they paid no attention whatsoever to the candidates of the minor parties.

Minor parties are agencies of dissent and agitation, but they are not all alike. Three general types have appeared in American history. One is the *splinter* party that arises from a split in the ranks of a major party. Good examples of splinter or "bolter" parties are the Progressive party of 1912, formed by dissident liberal Republicans who favored Theodore Roosevelt over William Howard Taft, and the States' Rights party (or Dixiecrats) of 1948, a faction of southern Democrats who left the Democratic party in opposition to the nomination of Harry S Truman and the civil rights plank of the Democratic party. The American Independent party also fits generally in the splinter category.

A second type of minor party is an outgrowth of *discontent* with economic conditions. The two leading examples are the Populist party of the late nineteenth century and the Progressive party of 1924. Created to advance the interests of farmers and workers, the Populist party demanded free coinage of silver, a graduated income tax, government ownership of railroads, and other reforms designed to serve the interests of debtor and low-income groups. The Populists ran surprisingly well in 1892, suffered a major defeat in 1896, and went out of business in 1912. (Recently revived, the Populist party's presidential candidate appeared on the ballot in 12 states in 1988.)

Something of the same story could be told about the Progressives of 1924—a party formed to challenge the conservative economic philosophy of the major parties. The Progressive platform called for public ownership of railroads and water power, a strengthened position for organized labor through collective bargaining, popular election of judges, and the direct election of the president. The party received 17 percent of the popular

TABLE 9–2

Third-Party and Independent Presidential Candidates Receiving 5 Percent or More of Popular Vote

Candidate (party)	Year	Percent of Popular Vote	Electoral Votes
John B. Anderson (Independent)	1980	6.6	0
George C. Wallace (American Independent)	1968	13.5	46
Robert M. LaFollette (Progressive)	1924	16.6	13
Theodore Roosevelt (Progressive)	1912	27.4	88
Eugene V. Debs (Socialist)	1912	6.0	0
James B. Weaver (Populist)	1892	8.5	22
John C. Breckinridge (Southern Democrat)	1860	18.1	72
John Bell (Constitutional Union)	1860	12.6	39
Millard Fillmore (Whig-American)	1856	21.5	8
Martin Van Buren (Free Soil)	1848	10.1	0
William Wirt (Anti-Masonic)	1832	7.8	7

Source: *Congressional Quarterly Weekly Report,* October 18, 1980, p. 3147 (as adapted).

vote in 1924, but by the next election it had disappeared.

Minor parties of a third type are usually described as *doctrinaire* or *ideological* parties—that is, parties with highly developed, more or less integrated doctrines designed to interpret the social, economic, and political orders and to justify the introduction of new ideas and systems. Included in this group are the various Marxist parties, such as the Communist and Socialist Workers. There are doctrinaire parties on the "right" wing as well, such as the American and American Independent parties. Right-wing parties usually stress individualism, limited government, and a return to the standards of earlier years; they oppose the "welfare state."

Minor parties share few of the traditions of the major parties. They are impatient advocates of change; their platforms are written in a vocabulary of protest and their pronouncements are weighted with dogma and a sense of urgency. To most Americans, their proposals appear extreme. Although they have not been well rewarded, they have had an impact on the political system. They have illuminated critical problems, sponsored new policy ideas, and sometimes forced the major parties to consider issues they would prefer to avoid. On occasion, the vote given third-party candidates appears to have influenced election outcomes by siphoning off votes from one of the major parties. Overall, their presence and vitality provide clues for judging popular satisfaction with the political order and the major parties.

Parties and the Nominating Process

The roots of the party system are not difficult to uncover. They lie in the nominating process. "He who can make the nominations," E. E. Schattschneider observed in his classic *Party Government,* "is the owner of the party." [13] Throughout much of American history, nominations for public office in many states and cities were controlled by party professionals, by the leaders of the party organizations. Prospective candidates for public office understood the system; they waited in line and their opportunity to run for office came when the "leadership" (the "organization," the "boss") decided it was "time." Being "slated" by the organization—picked in advance of the formal nominating process—was the launching pad for many long careers in government.

Today, slating has a strange ring to it in most parts of the nation. Candidates tend to be self-starters; many never even ask for a party endorsement. Not many candidates, furthermore, are likely to withdraw from a race simply because the leadership has slated someone else. For its part, the organization often remains neutral in the nominating process, apparently willing to take any candidate the voters choose. The relationship between candidates and parties that now exists can be better understood after an examination of the historical methods for making nominations.

Methods of Nomination

Caucus. The earliest method of making nominations in the United States was the *caucus*—an informal group of party leaders that met before the election to nominate candidates. Caucuses were used in local communities well before the Revolutionary War. The most important form came to be the legislative caucus, which was used by party members in the state legislature to nominate governors, lieutenant governors, and presidential electors. At the national level, the congressional caucus, composed of party members in Congress, was used in the early nineteenth century to nominate presidential candidates.

Criticized as undemocratic and unrepresentative, the legislative (or congressional) caucus fell into disfavor; during the 1820s, it was generally replaced by party conventions.

Party Conventions. Party *conventions* gave more representation to the mass of party members in the nomination of candidates. All geographic areas of the state, and hence all party constituencies, were awarded delegates to the state convention; similarly, all states were awarded delegates to the national nominating convention. Representative of local party organizations, the delegates met in public to select party nominees.

Although the convention system was more democratic than the system it replaced, since it enlarged the base of representation, it was subject to heavy criticism. Characterized by abuses in voting practices, fraud, factional conflict, "wheeling and dealing," special interest machinations, and boss domination, the convention became a target of reformers during the latter part of the nineteenth century. They searched for ways to turn the nominating process over to the people.

The Direct Primary. The "democratic" solution was the *direct primary*—the nomination of party candidates by rank-and-file voters in an official election, under state law, and supervised by public officials. Simply put, the primary is an intraparty election to select candidates for the general election. The first state to adopt the direct primary was Wisconsin in 1903. Today all 50 states have some form of primary. Some state laws give the parties a choice of the primary or the older convention method. The convention system survives, if precariously, at the national level.

"Primaries are important. It gives you an opportunity to vote against the party's handpicked candidates!"

The variety of primaries testifies to the ingenuity of American politicians. There are four basic forms (closed, open, blanket, and unitary) and three special forms (runoff, nonpartisan, and presidential). Twenty-six states use the *closed* primary, in which the voter can cast a ballot only in the party to which he or she belongs; membership is ordinarily established through formal registration before the primary election. Laws vary in the ease with which voters can switch back and forth between the parties. Voters in the closed-primary states of Iowa, Ohio, and Wyoming, for example, can change their party registration on election day—which makes their "closed" primary "open" in everything but name. Voters who wish to switch their affiliation in New York, by contrast, must do so 11 months before the primary.[14]

Twenty-one states (not counting those using blanket or nonpartisan primaries) have some form of *open* primary. Not required to register as a party member, the voter is permitted to participate in the primary of the party that interests him or her at the time. In 12 of these states, however, the voter must declare a party preference at the polls to obtain a ballot. In the other nine states, there is no test of party whatsoever.

The *blanket* primary, used in Alaska and Washington, is the most "open" of open primaries. It permits the voter to vote for a candidate of one party for one office and for a candidate of the other party for another office; it thus encourages ticket splitting at the nomination stage.

The most novel form of primary is found in Louisiana, which has an "open elections," or *unitary,* primary. Under this system, all candidates for an office are grouped together in a primary election. A candidate who receives a majority of the primary vote is elected, thus eliminating the need for a general election. If no candidate receives a majority of the votes cast, the top two, irrespective of party affiliation, face each other in a runoff election. The broad effect of the Louisiana law is to combine nominations and general elections into a single election for all offices other than the presidency.

Of these forms, the closed primary (restricting participation in the nominating process to party members) is most in line with the belief that parties stand for something and that each party has a legitimate interest in protecting its label and traditions. Probably most party politicians and political scientists prefer the closed form.

In many states, the nomination of judges, school board members, city council members, and other local officials takes place in *nonpartisan* primaries—those in which the ballot carries no party labels. The members of the unicameral legislature of Nebraska are also chosen on this basis. Nominations go to the two candidates who receive the largest number of votes; they then oppose each other in the general election. Nonpartisanship is an attempt to wall off local offices from the divisiveness of national and state party politics.

Runoff, or second, primaries are common throughout the South. They are especially important in a one-party environment, where candidates flock to the primary of the dominant party. The runoff system provides that if no candidate receives a majority of the votes in the first primary, a second is held between the top two candidates. The second primary thus assures a majority nominee, who usually wins easily in the general election. The growing strength of the Republican party in the South, however, now makes any Democratic nominee's chances in November less than a "sure bet."

In the view of many black political leaders, the runoff system stacks the cards against black candidates in the South. When the choice in a runoff primary is between a white and a black candidate, the argument runs, white voters often cast their ballots along racial lines, usually assuring the nomination of the white candidate. The most prominent opponent of the runoff system is Jesse Jackson. He argues that the candidate who finishes first should be given the nomination, whether or not chosen by a majority. The controversy over runoffs is likely to persist but unlikely to be easily resolved. At the national level, the issue is largely symbolic, since control over election law rests basically with state governments.[15]

Presidential primaries, now used in about two-thirds of the states for testing presidential candidates and for selecting national convention delegates, are discussed later in this chapter.

Primaries, Parties, and Voters. The direct primary was not introduced because reformers had a restless impulse for change. They knew quite clearly what they wanted to do—eliminate the power of political "bosses" by democratizing the nominating process. And they succeeded, probably beyond their expectations.

Politicians and political scientists agree that a main consequence of the primary has been to weaken political parties, reducing or eliminating organization controls over the crucial phase of party activity—candidate selection. Protected by personal followings, courted or pressured by interest groups, and cushioned with personal or outside campaign money, the typical candidate has little reason to pay attention to party leaders or doctrine. Candidates are on their own, free to say (or promise) anything that seems likely to win votes.

Primary elections and candidate-centered politics go hand in hand. The loss of party control over nominations shows in the weakening of party unity in government, especially in legislatures.

There are also other problems with the primary. It is debatable how much the public wants to take part in the nominating process. Voter participation in primaries is low, often embarrassingly low; a 20 to 25 percent turnout is not unusual. Added to this is the high cost of campaigning, for candidates must finance two campaigns. Finally, one wonders about the representativeness of voters who do make it to the polls on primary day. Do they share the same policy views as the general run of party members? Do the candidates they select represent the mass of party members? There are grounds for doubt on both counts.

For citizens who consider the political parties important, the primary is a mixed blessing. Yet a case can be made for primaries. They expand the pool from which candidates are drawn, widen the opportunities for popular elements to press their case by sponsoring candidates, upset cliques, and invite citizens to take part at an early stage in choosing their representatives.

Nominating the President

Continuity and Change

In outward appearance, the process by which presidential (and vice presidential) candidates are nominated is about the same today as in earlier years. Nominations are made by the national convention—a party institution that dates back to the Jacksonian era. Composed of party delegates from the 50 states and the territories, the national convention is the culmination of the nominating phase of the presidential year and the opening of the election campaign.

From its earliest days, the national convention has been a spectacle: large and unwieldy, often boisterous, caught up in oratory and demonstrations, and sometimes torn by factional squabbling and maneuvering. Beneath the surface, however, the convention has changed in two important respects. First, it has declined in importance as a party conclave, one in which leading officials from all over the country meet to take stock of party affairs and work out compromises on leadership and policies necessary to keep the party from breaking apart. Second, the convention has lost much of its independence, becoming less a candidate-*making* institution than a candidate-*ratifying* one.[16]

The composition of state delegations in the convention is much different today. In earlier years, uncommitted delegates were numerous. State leaders served as brokers, bargaining with prominent candidates, exchanging delegation support for some form of advantage, perhaps a promise of appointments in the new administration or the vice presidential nomination for a major state figure. Today, by contrast, the great majority of delegates arrive at the convention pledged to a candidate, which leaves less room for bargaining among leaders. Commonly, in fact, the preconvention struggle determines the nomination, leaving to the convention simply the formality of ratifying the voters' choice. Important votes in the typical convention are few and far between. Speeches, symbol rattling, and committee reports dominate. Through it all, party leaders and well-known public officials sit and watch; their boredom is broken only by observing the antics of delegates or by the interviews they give to the television celebrities and journalists who are looking for an angle that will play.

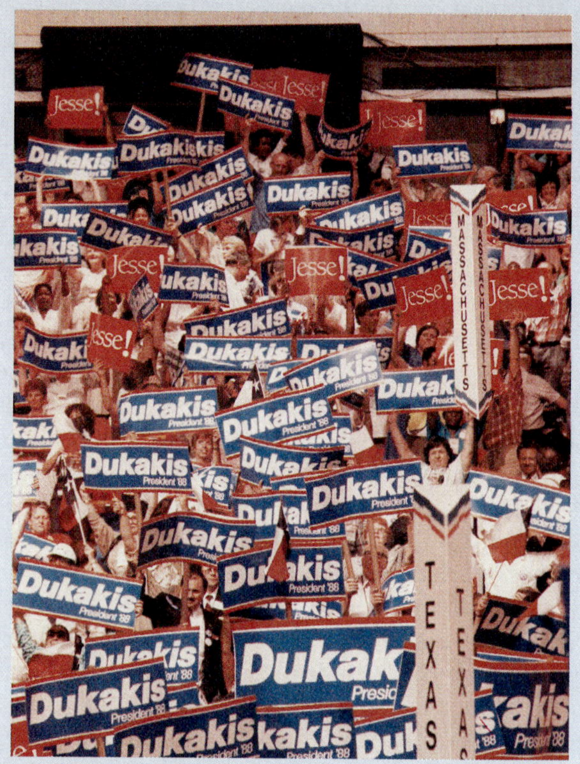

Michael Dukakis and Jesse Jackson signs are thrust up by the convention delegates from Massachusetts and Texas, the states that produced the Dukakis–Bentsen ticket in 1988. Placards, demonstrations, and hoopla are well-known features of the parties' national conventions, but of course no delegate votes are influenced by them. No one knows how voters are affected by convention spectacles.

Other changes flow from the growing democratization of the parties, which is especially pronounced on the Democratic side. The adoption of various rules proposed by reform panels in the 1970s opened up the party to rank-and-file members while cutting the control of party professionals over the presidential nomination.[17] Under these rules, for example, state Democratic parties must have affirmative-action delegate selection programs to encourage "full participation of all Democrats, with particular concern for minority groups, native Americans, women, and youth." To reflect grass roots party interests, 75 percent of all delegates in each state primary must be chosen at the congressional district level or lower. The freedom of individual delegates is protected by a provision that outlaws the *unit rule,* a long-standing Democratic practice under which a majority of a state delegation could bind the minority to vote for the majority's candidate.

National Democratic rules for delegate selection tend to change sharply from one convention to the next. In choosing delegates to the 1980 convention, for example, state parties were required to use a system of proportional representation; a candidate who won 35 percent of the vote in a state caucus or primary was awarded 35 percent of the delegates. For the 1984 and 1988 conventions, state parties could use nonproportional schemes for allocating delegates under which the winning candidate in the state could capture a large share of the delegates. Shortly after the primary season concluded in 1988, however, the Democratic National Committee again changed its rules to require all states to use proportional representation for the 1992 election. This provision was adopted to address charges by Jesse Jackson that nonproportional allocations in major states (Pennsylvania, New Jersey, New York, Ohio, and Florida, for example) had shortchanged him of delegates warranted by his popular support. But how long the party would retain this controversial rule was problematic.

Defining the role of party and public officials in the national convention has also been troublesome for the Democratic party. Its rules during the 1970s clearly favored rank-and-file members and amateur activists over party and public officials. Relatively few members of Congress, for example, were chosen as delegates at that time. To increase the influence of professional politicians, the Democratic National Committee added nearly 600 "superdelegates" (individuals chosen by virtue of their party or public position) to the 1984 convention. For the 1988 convention, the number of reserved seats for these officials was increased to 644. Representing almost 16 percent of all delegates and technically uncommitted, this large bloc was made up of some 250 House and Senate Democrats, all 363 members of the Democratic National Committee, and various governors and senior party figures. Governor Michael Dukakis received particularly strong support from this elite group. In response to initiatives by the forces of Jesse Jackson, who had few superdelegates in his corner, the party cut back their number for the 1992 convention. Automatic seats for the members of the Democratic National Committee, except for certain officers, were eliminated. But this Dukakis–Jackson compromise, which had been worked out at the 1988 convention, did not last long. Asserting its authority in late 1989, the Democratic National Committee voted to make its members automatic delegates once again, thus restoring the importance of uncommitted superdelegates for the 1992 convention.

Selecting the Delegates ■

Two methods are used to choose national convention delegates: presidential primaries and caucus-conventions. Each state chooses its own system.

Managed by the parties, the caucus-convention system provides for the election of delegates by rank-and-file members from one level of the party to the next—ordinarily from precinct caucuses to county conventions to the state convention and from there to the national convention. The first-round caucuses (mass meetings at the precinct level) are crucial, since they establish the delegate strength of each candidate in the conventions to be held later.

In 1988 about one-third of the states, mainly small and medium-sized ones, used the caucus-convention system for the selection of their delegates. The chief criticism of the system centers on low turnouts. Only some 800,000 voters took part in the states' first-round Democratic caucuses in 1988; on the Republican side, caucus participation was even spottier. (For the Republicans, about 200,000 first-round caucus votes were tabulated in ten states; in the remaining states, no votes were even recorded.[18])

The Caucus System: Is It Defensible?

In the 1988 presidential nominating process, participation in first-round caucuses was in sharp contrast with that in the general election. Their widely publicized outcomes also seemed to have little to do with the parties' final preferences. In the table below are some data for selected states.

Is the system defensible? The answer is probably no for those who believe that (1) the parties' caucuses may be captured by intense, segmental, sternly ideological groups; (2) candidates who cannot win in November may be nominated; and (3) a state's national convention delegates should be elected by a relatively large group of voters who are broadly representative of the party.

The answer is probably yes for those who believe that (1) caucuses are a prime test of candidates' organizational capacities; (2) citizens should be willing to spend one evening every four years debating the merits of party candidates for the presidency; (3) voters who fail to attend have no one to blame but themselves if the caucus results disappoint them; and (4) face-to-face, intraparty debate contributes to informed decision making and to overall party vitality.

Source of data: *Congressional Quarterly Weekly Report,* June 4, 1988, pp. 1523–1527.

	Caucus Participants[a]	Caucus Winner	Vote for Party's Candidate in November
Iowa Dem.	126,000 (19%)	Gephardt (31.3%)	667,085
Iowa Rep.	108,838 (20%)	Dole (37.3%)	541,540
Minnesota Rep.	56,563 (6%)	Dole (42.3%)	958,199
Hawaii Rep.	5,000 (3%)	Robertson (81.3%)	158,625
Texas Dem.	100,000 (4%)	Jackson (40.0%)	2,331,286
Washington Rep.	15,210 (2%)	Robertson (39.0%)	800,182
Michigan Dem.	212,668 (13%)	Jackson (53.5%)	1,673,496
Delaware Dem.	4,660 (5%)	Jackson (45.8%)	99,479
Vermont Dem.	6,000 (5%)	Jackson (45.7%)	116,419

[a] In parentheses, as a proportion of the party's vote in the November general election.

Enthusiasm for the caucus-convention system among party regulars appears to be dwindling. This method poses serious problems for them. In some caucus states party regulars have been reduced to bystanders as candidate organizations (and their amateur enthusiasts) vie with one another. Intraparty conflict has also erupted more often in caucus than in primary states. Finally, party leaders are sensitive to the charge that caucus results are not representative of voter sentiment generally. For these reasons, particularly the last one, it would not be surprising to see more states switch to presidential primaries in the 1990s.

Adopted by almost all of the populous states, presidential primaries are easier for the public to understand. A large majority of each state's delegates is chosen on primary day by the direct vote of the people; the remaining delegates are chosen through party processes following the primary. The objective is to shift control over presidential nominations from the party organizations to the public or, to be more precise, to the voters who turn out for the primary election.

More than 65 percent of the delegates to the 1988 party conventions were elected in primaries, with George Bush winning 37 of 38 Republican primaries and Michael Dukakis winning 22 of 37 Democratic primaries.[19] About 35 million people voted in both parties' primaries, a much higher level of participation than in the caucus-convention states. But even 35 million people is not a large number in a nation whose *voting-age* population numbers about 183 million.

The presidential nominating process is dominated by the media. National television crews and the press corps follow the candidates from state to state and from town to town. They interview candidates and average citizens, record debates, speculate on strategy, gauge crowds, forecast victories, and interpret election outcomes. They "zero in" on candidates' mistakes; an ill-chosen remark can become a national issue in a matter of hours. And nothing counts more than the media's interpretation of primary "victories" and "losses." A little-known candidate who receives 25 percent of the vote may be described as the "real" winner; other candidates who receive more votes may be pictured as "in trouble" because they "failed to do as well as expected." (See the discussion of media impact on the parties in Chapter 11.)

Campaigning in the New Hampshire Democratic primary in 1972, Senator Edmund Muskie of Maine loses his composure as he seeks to answer smears made against him and his wife by the state's largest newspaper, the *Manchester Union Leader.* His emotions cost him votes. Although Muskie won this primary, receiving 46 percent of the vote, the press judged his victory unimpressive. George McGovern ultimately won the Democratic nomination. The New Hampshire primary is undeniably important: Every president elected since 1952 has won it!

"Winning" or "placing well" in the first caucus-convention (Iowa), or better yet in the first primary (New Hampshire), can bring a candidate an uncommon amount of national attention and, with it, endorsements, campaign workers, and funds. One good showing sets the stage for the next contest. By contrast, candidates who fare poorly in the early races, and particularly in New Hampshire, are likely to bow out of the race before spring. Less commonly, late primaries are crucial. Nothing is more predictable about the presidential primary system than its unpredictability!

In the choice of national convention delegates, the parties differ in three major respects. First, on the Democratic side, national party rules prescribe in detail the manner in which states are to choose their delegates. To an extent, they even specify who is to be chosen: State delegations are required to reflect accurately the state's population, particularly in terms of representing women, youth, blacks, Hispanics, and Native Americans. Consistent with its federal character, the Republican party is content to let state parties develop their own arrangements, although they are encouraged to find ways to increase the participation of women, young people, minorities, and other groups in the presidential nominating process. (See Table 9–3 for data on the characteristics of the delegates in 1988.) Second, many state Republican parties allocate delegates on a winner-take-all basis, permitting the leading candidate to capture most of the delegates. State Democratic parties, beginning in 1992, are again required to divide delegates in proportion to the presidential candidates' popular vote. And third, the Republican party has no provision for automatic selection of party and public officials—"superdelegates" in Democratic nomenclature.

For both parties, the spread of presidential primaries and the opening up of caucuses have curtailed the influence of party leaders. Voters, not party leaders, control the selection of presidential nominees. In primaries, caucuses, and the convention itself, attention focuses on the candidates and their personal organizations. Prominent party leaders and public officials draw power from their links to candidates. Even the largest state delegations are not of much significance except as they reflect blocs of candidate votes.

In sum, the traditional role of party leaders as power brokers in the convention has been lost; it is rediscovered only when the primaries and caucuses fail to produce a clear-cut front-runner. If the new presidential nominating process fails to produce great presidents, the fault lies mainly with the public (and to some extent, for reasons noted, with the print and broadcast media).

The Work of the Convention

The national convention has three formal responsibilities: select the presidential and vice presidential candidates, adopt the platform, and establish party rules and procedures. To some extent, the convention serves the latent function of uniting

TABLE 9–3

How Democratic and Republican National Convention Delegates Differed in 1988

	Democrats	Republicans
Sex		
Male	50%	65%
Female	50	35
Race/ethnicity		
White	69	91
Black	22	4
Hispanic	6	2
Asian	2	1
Native American	1	1
Education		
Some high school	1	1
High school graduate	8	7
Some college	18	22
College graduate	28	34
Law degree	16	18
Medical degree	0	1
Other advanced degree	27	15
Religion		
Protestant	51	70
White Protestant	31	67
Catholic	30	24
Jewish	6	2
Household income		
\$0–\$9,999	1	0
\$10,000–\$19,999	4	2
\$20,000–\$34,999	16	8
\$35,000–\$49,999	22	16
\$50,000–\$99,999	35	35
\$100,000–\$999,999	14	24
\$1 million and more	0	1

Source: Adapted from survey data in *USA Today,* August 15, 1988, and *New York Times,* August 14, 1988. Percentages may not total to 100 because of rounding and because a few delegates failed to respond to certain questions.

diverse party elements by bringing together representatives of the 50 state parties.

The large size of the conventions (4162 Democratic and 2277 Republican delegates in 1988, plus alternates) requires careful attention to organization. The work of organizing the convention is carried out by four committees. The *committee on credentials* prepares the official membership list of the convention. Most of its work is routine, but occasionally it must decide between the claims of rival slates of delegates bidding to be seated. These decisions can have a crucial impact on the fortunes of certain candidates; they can remove or add blocs of votes pledged to them.

The *committee on permanent organization* chooses the permanent officers of the convention, including the chairperson, the clerks, and the sergeant at arms. The *committee on resolutions,* which begins its work well in advance of the convention, drafts the party platform. Major party leaders, public officials, and representatives of interest groups testify at its hearings, hoping to win acceptance of their views on certain platform planks. When a president is seeking reelection, the platform ordinarily is tailored to his specifications (though it may include a few concessions to his rivals). The *committee on rules* fashions the rules under which convention activities will be conducted (for example, setting the length of nominating and seconding speeches or the procedures for polling state delegations).

The old-fashioned convention under the control of a few party leaders has gone the way of the dodo bird; it is extinct. The "new" convention is noteworthy for the large number of amateur activists and candidate-enthusiasts it attracts. The leaders of candidate blocs (delegates pledged to individual candidates) are the key figures in convention politics and decisions. The most important caucuses are those of the candidates, not those of state delegations as a whole.

In a formal sense, the convention continues to select the presidential ticket. In fact, though, most nominations are settled well before the opening of the convention. First-ballot nominations have become the norm. Neither George Bush's nomination nor Michael Dukakis's was in doubt in 1988. What has happened is that losses in key primary and caucus-convention states take their toll, eliminating one candidate after another until only one is left in each party. The survivor is the nominee.

Of the 16 party conventions since 1960, only the Democratic in 1960 and the Republican in 1976 opened with noticeable uncertainty over the choice of the nominee. In the former, John F. Kennedy emerged as the nominee, having run well in the primary states. In 1976, Gerald R. Ford narrowly won the Republican nomination over Ronald Reagan, who had won 10 primaries to Ford's 17. The intensity of preconvention struggles, marked by the capacity of certain primaries to scuttle candidates, has dimmed the prospects that conventions will reassume their traditional function of choosing the nominee.

The choice of the vice presidential nominee is suspenseful and unpredictable. Although the convention makes the formal nomination, the party's presidential nominee makes the selection. Sometimes disgruntled over this choice, the delegates nevertheless ratify it. The presidential nominee usually selects a person who "balances" the ticket, taking into account factors such as ideology, state, region, ethnicity, religion, age, and (recently) gender and generation.

A well-chosen running mate sometimes can enhance a nominee's strength and offset his weaknesses. In selecting George Bush in 1980, Ronald Reagan chose his main challenger for the presidential nomination. Walter Mondale's choice of Geraldine Ferraro in 1984 broke with major party tradition in more ways than one: Ferraro was the first woman to be nominated for the vice presidency, the first Italian American to be nominated for national office, and the first nominee to be "anointed" prior to the opening of the convention. But she did not help the ticket.

The choice of Senator Lloyd Bentsen, a conservative Texan, by Michael Dukakis in 1988 was designed to bring ideological balance to the ticket and to attract voters in the South (and particularly in Texas with its large cache of 29 electoral votes). Dukakis's "mini" southern strategy, centered around Bentsen, plainly failed, as he lost every southern state. George Bush's surprising selection

Which Presidential Primaries Were Most Important in 1988?

On the Democratic side, consider these states:

New Hampshire (February 16): Critical win for a neighboring state candidate, Massachusetts Governor Michael Dukakis, who had finished third in the Iowa caucuses, behind Congressman Richard Gephardt and Senator Paul Simon. Dukakis received 35.8 percent of the vote, Gephardt 19.8 percent, Simon 17.1 percent, Jesse Jackson 7.8 percent, Albert Gore 6.8 percent, Bruce Babbitt 4.6 percent, and Gary Hart 4.0 percent. Hart's and Babbitt's days were numbered. Once more, this tiny state (whose turnout, for example, was about 10 percent of Pennsylvania's), in which independents are permitted to vote, provided its primary winner with the "big mo" that wins nominations.

"Super Tuesday" (March 8): Fourteen southern primaries (many of them "open"), two New England primaries, and four western caucuses. Predictably, the results narrowed the field. Big losers: Gephardt (12.8 percent of primary vote) and Simon (2.0 percent). Major winners in a still-muddled race: Dukakis (26.3 percent of the primary vote), Jackson (26.6 percent), and Gore (25.7 percent).

Michigan (March 26): Largest state using a pure caucus-convention system in 1988. Three percent of the voting-age population (212,000 out of 6.8 million) took part. Key victory for Jackson—53.4 percent of preference votes to Dukakis's 29.1 percent, Gephardt's 12.8 percent, Gore's 2.1 percent, and Simon's 2.1 percent. Gephardt's campaign ended. Relying on the "lightning may strike" theory—and with nothing better to do—Gore and Simon decided to stay in the race.

Connecticut (March 29): Dukakis defeated Jackson by a 2:1 margin in a diminished field of viable candidates.

Wisconsin (April 5): Crossover primary. Pivotal win for Dukakis (47.5 percent) over Jackson (28.2 percent). Gore (17.4 percent) left twisting in the wind.

New York (April 19): For Jackson the last-chance, must-win state, but Dukakis won with 50.6 percent to Jackson's 37.0 percent. Receiving only 10.1 percent, Gore suspended his campaign. It was all over but the shouting, even though more than one-third of the states had not yet held their primaries or caucuses.

On the Republican side, consider these states:

New Hampshire (February 16): Major win for Vice President George Bush (37.6 percent) over Senator Robert Dole (28.4 percent). Dole had won the Iowa caucuses handily a week earlier. Congressman Jack Kemp and former religious broadcaster Pat Robertson received limited support. Alexander Haig and Pierre du Pont abandoned their campaigns.

"Super Tuesday" (March 8): George Bush swept 16 (mainly southern) primaries, gaining 577 delegates to Dole's 99. Bush received 56.5 percent of the primary vote, Dole 23.7 percent. Kemp fared poorly and soon withdrew. Modest success for southerner Robertson (13.1 percent of the primary vote). Mop-up time: for all intents and purposes, the Republican race was over, even though about two-thirds of the states had not yet taken part in the process.

The most important primaries? For Dukakis: tiny, bucolic New Hampshire and the one-on-one contest in progressive Wisconsin. For Bush: tiny, bucolic New Hampshire and the conservative "Super Tuesday" South.

And what about the impact of Iowa, the first caucus-convention state? Illusory importance in each party.

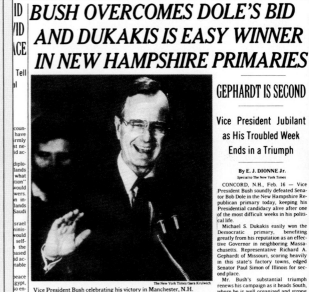

BUSH OVERCOMES DOLE'S BID AND DUKAKIS IS EASY WINNER IN NEW HAMPSHIRE PRIMARIES

GEPHARDT IS SECOND

Vice President Jubilant as His Troubled Week Ends in a Triumph

By E. J. DIONNE Jr.
Special to The New York Times

CONCORD, N.H., Feb. 16 — Vice President Bush soundly defeated Senator Bob Dole in the New Hampshire Republican primary today, keeping his Presidential candidacy alive after one of the most difficult weeks in his political life.

Michael S. Dukakis easily won the Democratic primary, benefiting greatly from his reputation as an effective Governor in neighboring Massachusetts. Representative Richard A. Gephardt of Missouri, scoring heavily in this state's factory towns, edged Senator Paul Simon of Illinois for second place.

Mr. Bush's substantial triumph renews his campaign as it heads South, where he is well organized and strong

The New York Times/Sara Krulwich

Vice President Bush celebrating his victory in Manchester, N.H.

Source of election data: various issues of the *Congressional Quarterly Weekly Report.*

Democratic Vice Presidential candidate Lloyd Bentsen of Texas addresses a group of senior citizens in San Francisco in 1988.

of a younger, telegenic U.S. senator, Dan Quayle of Indiana, reflected his desire to merge conservative and generational appeals. He hoped to satisfy the party's powerful conservative wing, win the attention of the postwar "baby boomers," improve the party's lagging position with women voters, and strengthen its prospects in the Middle West. Many conservatives were pleased with Quayle's selection, to be sure, but undoubtedly he hurt the ticket as a result of prolonged controversies involving his qualifications and National Guard service during the Vietnam War.

Once the vice president is nominated, the convention celebrates the "ticket," listens to the final speeches filled with promises and partisan claims, and adjourns. The delegates head for home; and the campaign begins.

The power of the national convention is largely an illusion. Its role in the nominating process has been eroded by primaries and caucuses, on the one hand, and by the media, on the other. Neither the Democratic nor the Republican convention made an independent decision of importance in 1988. Delegates listened, waved, cheered, grumbled, cried, laughed, roared, sang, affirmed, gave interviews, and posed for television cameras. Not a few of them retreated to their hotel rooms to watch television to find out what was going on. Their authentic decision making consisted of choosing among restaurants and among goodwill hospitality receptions hosted by businesses and other organizations. Their contributions to "coalition formation" were state delegation reciprocal sign-waving agreements.

The work of the delegates consisted of ratifying the voters' preferences for Michael Dukakis and George Bush, ratifying Dukakis's and Bush's selections of Lloyd Bentsen and Dan Quayle as their vice presidential candidates, and ratifying platforms spliced together in advance of the conventions.

The modern convention is cut-and-dried, orchestrated, scripted—a four-night campaign commercial ending with a family sitcom starring the candidates. The convention's loss of power and suspense, coupled with declining voter interest in viewing the proceedings, has prompted the television networks to consider significant reductions in live, prime-time coverage. (Less than one-fourth of the nation's television households, on average, watched the 1988 conventions.) Today, the main function of the convention is simply to provide a setting for political leaders' initiatives to unify the party.

Another Method for Choosing? Presidential Nominees? ■

Is there a better way to select presidential and vice presidential nominees? Some observers believe so. The proposal that has drawn the most attention over the years calls for a *single, one-day national primary.* Each party would hold its own primary. To gain the party's nomination, a candidate would be required to obtain a certain proportion of the popular vote (40 percent in some proposals, a majority in others). A runoff election would follow if no candidate attained the specified level. The names of vice presidential candidates would also appear on the ballot. This leaves to the convention the reduced role of writing the platform.

Other variations represent less extreme departures. One calls for a series of *regional primaries.* All states in a region would hold their primaries on the same day (as southern states did in 1988). The order of the regional primaries, perhaps five altogether, would be determined by lot. The national convention would continue as the formal authority for selecting the presidential ticket; in practical terms, though, this role would be limited to those years in which the primaries are inconclusive.

A modest proposal, designed to lessen the importance of early state victories (or losses), would require any state having a primary to pick one of four dates, ranging from March to June, on which to hold it. No longer would New Hampshire launch the primary season by itself; its results would command the media attention that a state with a handful of delegates and a population of less than a million (about 280,000 primary voters in both parties in 1988) properly deserves.

Advocates of a national primary set great store in the notion of bringing the presidential nominating process under the control of the voters. There is also something to be said for their view that a national primary would simplify and bring order to a "system" that neither candidates nor voters are confident they understand, so confusing is the mix of state law and national and state party rules.

The drawbacks of a national primary, however, are large indeed. First, it would remove the parties from the presidential nominating process, weakening an institution already in trouble. Second, it would add another national election, and possibly a third (runoff), to the burden of the voters. Third, it would lead to greater emphasis on television campaigning because of the need to reach large numbers of voters. With the increased use of television would come heightened campaign costs and, perhaps, the selection of nominees whose main talent is simply a flair for television campaigning. Fourth, a national primary would be an invitation to numerous candidates. One could damage another in unexpected ways, probably increasing the chances that a candidate out of the "mainstream" of the party would win the nomination. Fifth, the prospect would be slim that the voters would select a "balanced" ticket that appeals to divergent people and interests. Finally, a national primary would increase the impact of the media on the outcome itself. Austin Ranney argues:

> In a national primary . . . the only preelection facts relevant to who was winning would be public opinion polls and estimates of the sizes of crowds at candidate meetings. The former are scientifically more respectable than the latter, but neither constitutes hard data in the sense that election returns do. And hard data of that sort would be available only after national primary day. Thus, a one-day national direct primary would give the news media even more power than they now have to influence the outcomes of contests for nominations by shaping most people's perceptions of how these contests were proceeding.[20]

Democratization is a beguiling idea. Proposals of such promise are hard to resist, especially when "reform" is in the air. Even so, the adoption of a national primary is a long way from happening. Many politicians and analysts believe that the current method, for all its awkwardness and flaws, is preferable to one whose adoption might usher in harmful and unforeseen consequences.

The Differences Between the Parties

The hospitality of the major parties to all groups and ideas, except the most extreme, separates them from all other forms of political organization, including minor parties. The parties are *inclusive* rather than exclusive in their appeals for electoral support. For them, the test is not how well any political claim (principle, group) meshes with traditional party programs and values, but whether its acceptance will strengthen the party's position, or at least cut its losses, among the voters. The need to appeal to a wide range of interests leads the parties and their candidates to tone down their doctrine.

The moderation of parties and candidates makes it tempting to argue that there are few differences between Democrats and Republicans. But this temptation should be resisted. There are important differences between the parties in the attitudes of both their members and their officeholders toward major policy questions.

Consider first the electoral parties. The survey data of Table 9–4 show the internal divisions within the parties as well as the broad differences between them. Clearly, neither party is monolithic, in the sense of its members sharing a common set of political beliefs. On certain social issues, such as prayer in the public schools and abortions, certain Democratic and Republican subgroups share the same political space—one broadly defined in this *Times-Mirror* study as intolerance for particular personal freedoms. Differences between party voters, however, loom more important. In their attitudes toward social justice, most Democratic partisans are easily distinguished from most Republican partisans. Democrats are aligned on the side of egalitarianism, social spending, the disadvantaged, and racial equality. The activist side of these social justice questions attracts many fewer Republicans. Rather, Republican voters tend to be dubious of big government, fiscally conservative, probusiness, anticommunist, and pro-defense spending.[21] Significantly, divisions within Republican clusters are less serious than those found on the Democratic side. The most interesting point is of course that the policy views of the parties' "affiliants" differ from one another in important respects. Put another way, the parties clearly do stand for something in the minds of many voters.

Additional evidence on party differences appears in the ideology of Democratic and Republican national convention delegates, as shown in Figure 9–2. To those who see the parties as Tweedledee and Tweedledum, the differences must appear surprising. Thirty-nine percent of the Democratic delegates in 1988 described themselves as liberals, as contrasted with a mere 1 percent of the Republican delegates. At the other ideological pole, the differences are also striking: Conservatives

TABLE 9–4

Differences and Similarities: How Democratic and Republican Voters View Key Social and Economic Issues

	Democratic Groups*				Republican Groups*	
	60s Democrats	New Dealers	Passive Poor	Partisan Poor	Enter- prisers	Moral- ists
Favor constitutional amendment to permit prayers in public schools	52%	83%	83%	81%	69%	88%
Favor mandatory drug test for government employees	39	78	77	69	58	80
Favor changing laws to make it more difficult for a woman to get an abortion	26	54	47	38	40	60
Favor increased spending on programs that assist minorities	50	39	57	60	12	21
Favor death penalty	53	79	78	66	78	85
Favor cutbacks in defense and military spending	69	49	58	57	31	31
Favor increased spending on						
Programs for the homeless	77	73	82	83	38	62
Programs for the unemployed	40	49	62	68	11	30
Improving the nation's health care	76	80	85	84	42	68
Improving the nation's public schools	80	70	77	77	56	65
Aid to farmers	62	69	72	70	29	60
Social Security	62	76	81	85	29	57
Programs for the elderly	79	84	84	87	44	71

* "60s Democrats": well educated, upper middle class, tolerant on personal freedom issues, mainstream Democrats, committed to social justice.

"New Dealers": aging, traditional Democrats, blue collar, union members, less tolerant on personal freedom issues, moderate income.

"Passive Poor": aging, poor, less well educated, uncritical, disproportionately southern, committed to social justice.

"Partisan Poor": firmly Democratic, very low income, poorly educated, urban, disproportionately black, concerned with social justice issues.

"Enterprisers": affluent, well educated, white, suburban, probusiness, antigovernment, tolerant on personal freedom issues.

"Moralists": middle-aged, middle income, white, disproportionately southern, suburban, small cities and rural areas, regular churchgoers, anticommunist, prodefense.

Source: Developed from data in *The People, Press and Politics* (Los Angeles: *Times-Mirror,* 1987), passim.

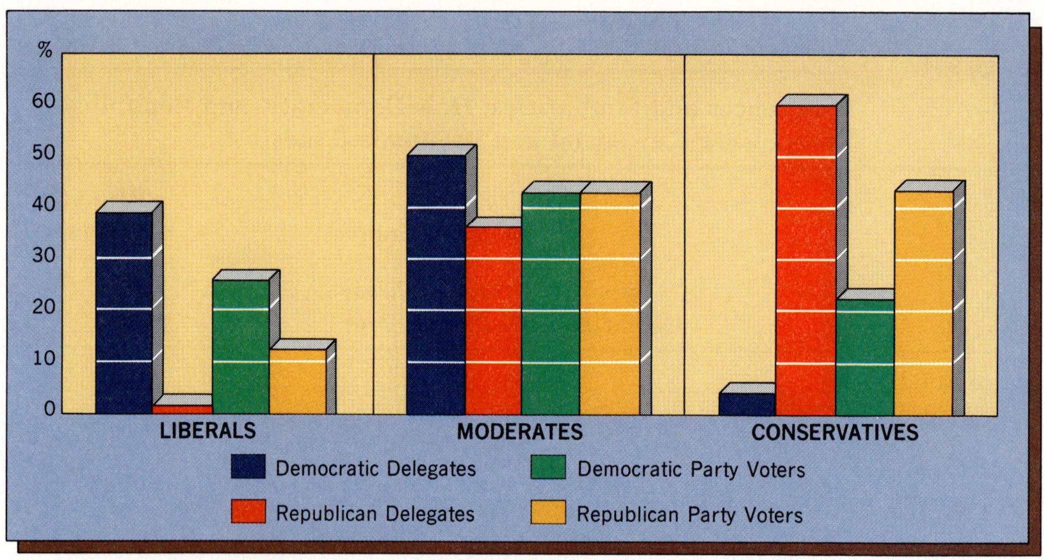

Figure 9–2 Ideology of convention delegates. Contrasted are the ideology of delegates to both parties' conventions in 1988 and the ideology of rank-and-file Democrats and Republicans. Source: Adapted from survey data published by *New York Times*/CBS News; see *New York Times,* July 17, 1988, and August 14, 1988. Ideological positions are based on self-classification. Party voters are self-identified Democrats and Republicans who reported that they were registered to vote. Percentages do not add to 100 because some respondents were unclassified.

made up 4 percent of the Democratic delegates and 60 percent of the Republican delegates. Neither party elite, it should be emphasized, accurately reflected the ideological leanings of average party members: Democratic delegates were more liberal than the average registered Democrat, while Republican delegates were more conservative than the average registered Republican.

Differences in political philosophy translate into differences in public policy views and differences on the role of government. Fifty-eight percent of the Democratic delegates, for example, were in favor of government providing more services; only 3 percent of the Republican delegates favored bigger government. Ninety percent of the Democratic delegates were in favor of increased federal spending on education, as contrasted with 41 percent of the Republican delegates. In terms of the federal role in day care and after-school care for children, 87 percent of the Democratic delegates but only 36 percent of the Republican delegates favored increased program funding. Additionally, Democratic delegates were much more likely to be "prochoice" than Republican delegates, while Republican delegates were much more likely to be "prodefense" than Democratic delegates.[22] The differences between the activists of the two parties are important and unmistakable: One set is clearly liberal, the other is clearly conservative.

Voting in Congress shows the same tilt. Most Democrats vote for social welfare programs (for instance, medical care for the elderly), bills to advance minority rights, proposals supported by organized labor, and measures that provide for government regulation of business. Most Republicans line up on the other side, at times simply because they favor a more gradual approach to the problem or a program of lesser scope. Divison along liberal-conservative lines, reflecting party membership for the most part, is thus fairly common on socioeconomic legislation.

Examination of voting on legislation of concern to major interest groups shows important differences between the parties. Consider the position

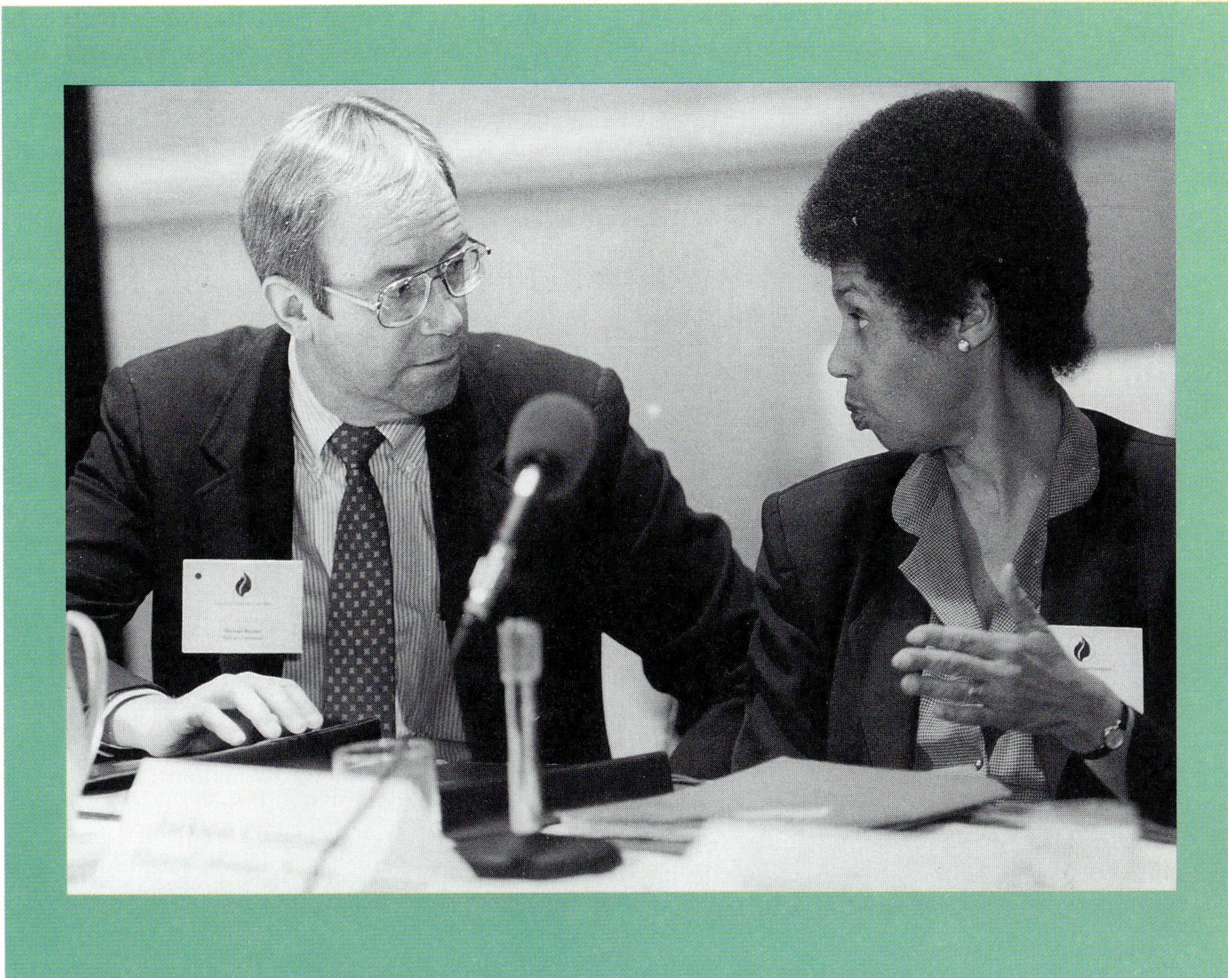

Congressman Michael Barnes, representing the Michael Dukakis organization, confers with Dr. Eleanor Holmes Norton, representing the Jesse Jackson organization, at a meeting of the Democratic Platform Drafting Committee prior to the party's national convention. Typically, platform planks are hammered out in advance of the convention. The losers in these policy struggles, à la Schattschneider, may seek to expand the conflict by carrying the fight to the convention floor—and they sometimes win.

of senators in the 100th Congress on "key votes" selected by organized labor, in this case the Committee on Political Education (COPE) of the AFL-CIO. It is a study in contrasts. More than 90 percent of the Democratic senators voted on the side of labor more than three-fourths of the time. By contrast, 41 percent of the Republican senators were lodged at the lowest level (0 to 25 percent) of support for labor. A small band of Republican moderates and liberals—Weicker (Conn.), Durenberger (Minn.), Danforth (Mo.), Packwood (Ore.), Heinz (Pa.), Specter (Pa.), and Stafford (Vt.)—voted with the AFL-CIO more than three-fourths of the time. What emerges from this analysis is that on various employment and economic issues (and on certain other issues as well), the parties are clearly on opposite sides of the fence. Some "slack" is present in each party's ranks, but not to an extent that obscures the broad contours of Democratic and Republican positions.

Voters who pay attention to politics probably are sensitive to these differences in party philosophies and use their knowledge to make political evaluations. Among ordinary voters, where levels of conceptualization are lower, that is less the case.[23] Yet whether voters realize it or not, the parties do stand for something—almost surely for more than they are given credit.

Summary

- American parties are in a period of decline. The growth in the number of self-professed independents and the increase in ticket splitting are manifestations of party weakness. Public skepticism toward political institutions is high, which not only makes governing more difficult, but also may diminish the legitimacy of government itself.
- Especially pronounced is the loss of party control over nominations. Public choice has largely replaced leadership direction in all areas of the country and from the lowest offices to the nomination of the president. Symbols and trappings aside, the party "presence" in national conventions is less evident now than at any time in the last century.
- The ebbing vitality of party organizations is apparent to the untrained eye. Candidate organizations, geared to political consultants and campaign management firms, are now the key force in campaigns. At the highest level, campaigns have become media events. In selecting the president, especially at the nominating stage, the media have become the new parties.
- Of all party characteristics, decentralization is the most important.
- The American party system is of the two-party variety. It is kept that way by certain institutional supports, including single-member districts, plurality elections, the electoral college, and election laws. Minor parties cluster on the fringe of the political system; they are ordinarily too impotent to play a role in shaping events and all but invisible to most voters.
- The thrust of the major parties is moderate or middle-of-the-road. The parties make appeals to all groups. Nevertheless, there are genuine policy differences between the parties. The policy alternatives presented by the parties—their candidates and officeholders—are greater than most people realize.
- Political parties are the principal means by which the people can control their government. Many students of government believe that parties are indispensable to the preservation of democratic government. By providing a basis for politicians to both cooperate and compete, they lessen the mystery and uncertainty in voting and in government decisions. At the same time, they enhance the public's capacity to hold its representatives accountable.

Readings on Political Parties

American Political Science Association: Committee on Political Parties. 1950. *Toward a More Responsible Two-Party System.* New York: Holt, Rinehart & Winston. A comprehensive series of proposals for revitalizing American parties in keeping with the "party government" model.

Bibby, John F. 1987. *Politics, Parties, and Elections in America.* Chicago: Nelson-Hall. A comprehensive examination of the role and functions of political parties in American politics.

Crotty, William J., and Gary C. Jacobson. 1980. *American Parties in Decline.* Boston: Little, Brown. Describes the diminishing relevance of American parties in government, campaigns, and elections.

Epstein, Leon D. 1986. *Political Parties in the American Mold.* Madison: University of Wisconsin Press. A thoughtful essay on the strengths and limitations of U.S. political parties.

Herrnson, Paul S. 1988. *Party Campaigning in the 1980s.* Cambridge, Mass.: Harvard University Press. An empirical study of the role of political parties in Congressional election campaigns.

Huckshorn, Robert J. 1984. *Political Parties in America.* Monterey, Calif.: Brooks/Cole. A wide-ranging analysis of American parties in transition.

Jones, Charles O. 1970. *The Minority Party in Congress.* Boston: Little, Brown. A suggestive study of the conditions under which minority party influence in congressional decision making is greatest.

Keefe, William J. 1988. *Parties, Politics, and Public Policy in America.* Washington, D.C.: CQ Press. An analysis of parties in the electorate and in the government.

Mayhew, David R. 1986. *Placing Parties in American Politics.* Princeton, N.J.: Princeton University Press. A diagnosis of the health of traditional party organizations in the 50 states.

Polsby, Nelson W. 1983. *Consequences of Party Reform.* New York: Oxford University Press. A criticism of recent electoral reforms and an argument for the strengthening of American parties.

Schattschneider, Elmer E. 1942. *Party Government.* New York: Holt, Rinehart & Winston. A classic work that argues for a responsible party system.

Shafer, Byron E. 1983. *Quiet Revolution: The Struggle for the Democratic Party and the Shaping of Post-Reform Politics.* New York: Russell Sage Foundation. A study of the impact of "democratizing" reforms on the Democratic party.

Sundquist, James L. 1973. *Dynamics of the Party System: Alignment and Realignment of Political Parties.* Washington, D.C.: Brookings Institution. A history of American parties, with special attention to eras of party realignment.

Truman, David B. 1959. *The Congressional Party: A Case Study.* New York: John Wiley & Sons. An imaginative study of the significance of party in roll-call voting in Congress.

Wattenberg, Martin P. 1986. *The Decline of American Political Parties, 1952–1984.* Cambridge, Mass.: Harvard University Press. An analysis of diminishing popular loyalty to American parties.

Chapter 10

Interest Groups

SAVE
THE
FAMILY
FARM

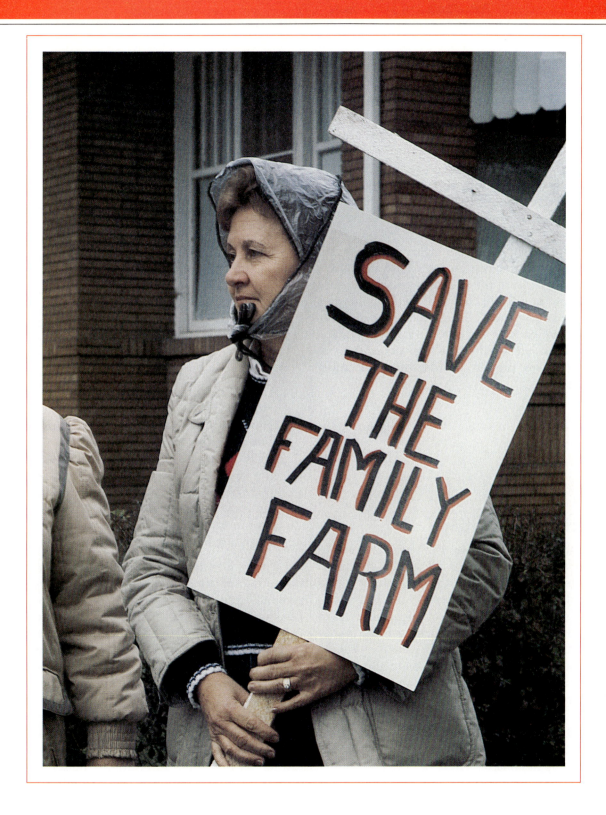

The politics and policies of democracies may be influenced as much by interest groups as by political parties. Interest groups are the product of a free society, where individuals can hold loyalties to groups other than the state. They are key agencies for representing citizen opinions and values. At the same time, interest groups are a valuable source of information for public officials who must weigh alternative policies and estimate how they will affect both the public at large and specific constituencies.

Interest groups are also highly controversial. The influence of interest groups on government is a matter of concern for many Americans because they know intuitively that politics is "who gets what, when, and how." They wonder whether organized groups have too much influence on decision makers and whether the interests of the majority are given proper consideration in shaping public policy.

The Nature of Interest Group Politics

Participation in Groups

Americans are joiners. They are attracted to groups and associations of all kinds. Joining a group is usually a simple matter; forming a new one is almost as easy. Whether a group is likely to leave its mark on history is of slight concern to those who join. The justification for a group is simply its relevance to the lives of its members. People join groups to advance their economic interests; to promote the well-being of their nationality, race, sex, or religion; to serve their social interests; and to achieve community, state, national, and international objectives. Many groups have little or no interest in political activities or public policy. But a surprising number do. Americans engage in politics not just as individuals, but also as members of groups.

The penchant of Americans for joining groups is not new. Analyzing American society in the first half of the 19th century, Alexis de Tocqueville said this about the importance of groups:

> As soon as several of the inhabitants of the United States have taken up an opinion or a feeling which they wish to promote in the world, they look for mutual assistance; and as soon as they have found each other out, they combine. From that moment they are no longer isolated men, but a power seen from afar, whose actions serve for an example, and whose language is listened to. The first time I heard in the United States that a hundred thousand men had bound themselves publicly to abstain from spirituous liquors, it appeared to me more like a joke than a serious engagement; and I did not at once perceive why these temperate citizens could not content themselves with drinking water by their own firesides. I at last understood that these hundred thousand Americans, alarmed by the progress of drunkenness around them, had made up their minds to patronize temperance. They acted just in the same way as a man of high rank who should dress very plainly, in order to inspire the humbler orders with a contempt of luxury. It is probable that, if these hundred thousand men had lived in France, each of them would singly have memorialized the government to watch the public houses all over the kingdom.[1]

For social scientists, group membership offers three kinds of benefits: material, solidary, and purposive. *Material* benefits are tangible. Workers join labor unions because they think wages and working conditions will improve through union negotiations with management. People may join groups for their *solidary* benefits, such as a chance to socialize and gain prestige. These benefits are intangible. Fraternal organizations and religious groups offer solidary benefits. *Purposive* incentives are also intangible. They give members a sense of well-being from joining in a worthwhile cause, such as protecting the environment, reforming political institutions, or improving health care facilities. Many groups provide all three incentives.[2]

The great number of groups in America present rich opportunities to participate. One national sur-

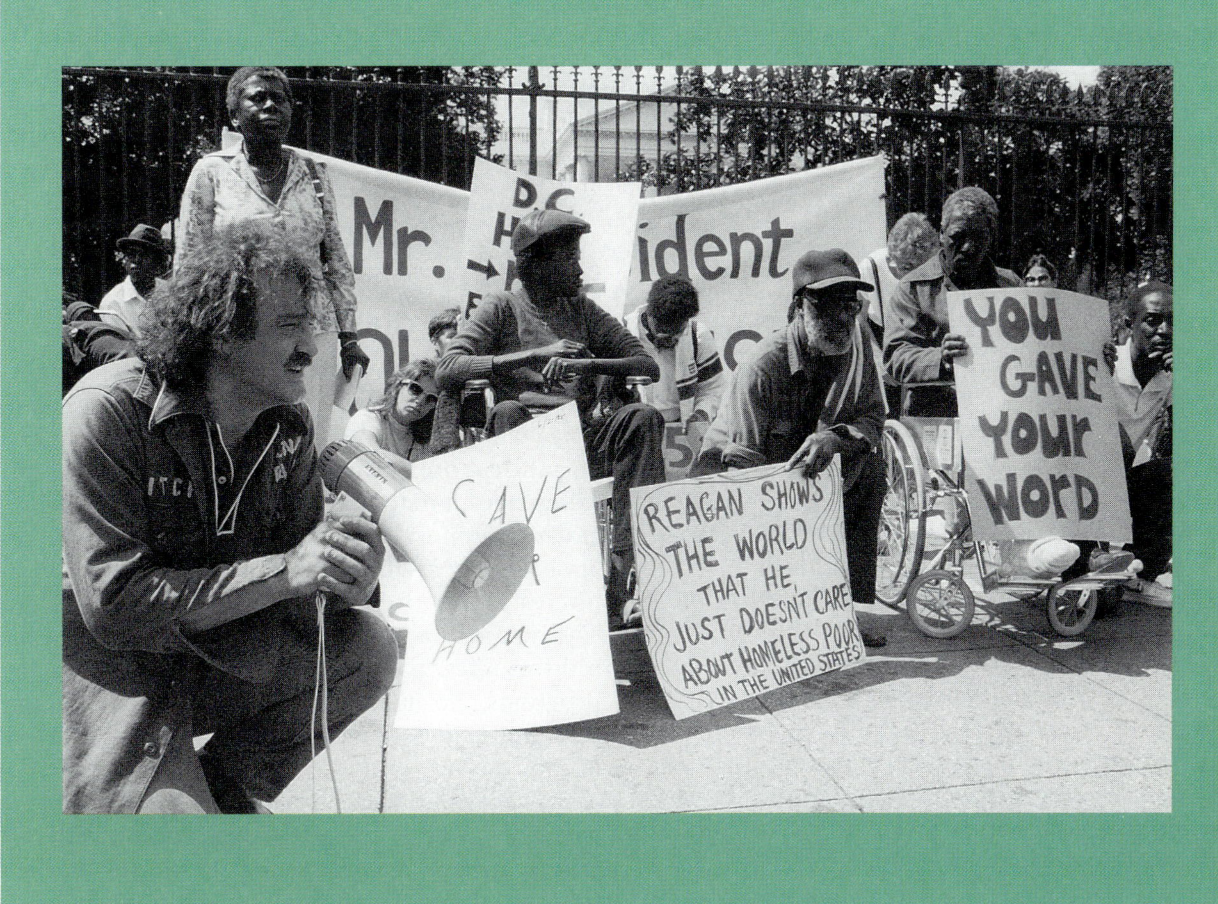

Demonstrations make political statements. Here homeless demonstrators assemble near the White House to protest the Reagan administration's policies concerning the poor. Demonstrations are less important than the media attention they attract.

vey showed that more than 60 percent of all adults belong to at least one group. (Eight percent belong to groups organized for political purposes, such as Democratic or Republican clubs or the League of Women Voters.)[3] Membership is not spread equally across the population, though. Citizens from upper socioeconomic levels are much more apt to join groups than those at lower levels. Physicians, lawyers, and airline pilots routinely join associations. By contrast, most farm workers, migrant workers, domestic aides, and welfare recipients are not active in groups (though there are groups that lobby for the poor, such as the National Anti-Hunger Coalition and the Low-Income Housing Coalition). There is a distinctly upper-class bias in the interest group system.[4]

Organization is a major political resource. By forming groups, individuals are more able to shape decisions that affect their lives. Thirteen million workers in the AFL-CIO have much more power than 13 million workers acting alone to pursue their interests. And so it is with business executives, veterans, ministers, doctors, blacks, teachers, farmers, and others. Because they depend on public support, government officials cannot ignore group claims. Elected officials are notably sensitive to the demands of organized interests.

A Definition ■

Most people have a rough idea of what the term *interest group* means. But it will help our analysis to use a precise definition. An interest group, according to David Truman, is "a shared-attitude group that makes certain claims upon other groups in society. If and when it makes its claims through or upon any of the institutions of government, it becomes a *political interest group.*"[5] These same aggregations are often called pressure groups or lobbies, terms more narrow and value-laden. In the words of Clinton Rossiter, "We call them 'interest groups' when we are feeling clinical, 'pressure groups' when we are feeling critical, and 'lobbies' when we are watching them at work in our fifty-one capitals."[6]

Of the thousands of groups in America, only a small portion function steadily as political interest groups, but many have political potential. A sportsmen's organization, for example, is easily drawn into politics; its members have a stake in state fish and game laws and in the outcomes of statewide referenda to ban trapping or certain forms of hunting. Churches and other religious organizations act as political interest groups when they lobby on legislation involving schools, abortion, foreign policy, or pornography. Operating through such organizations as the National Education Association or the American Federation of Teachers, schoolteachers pressure legislators when public education legislation (especially appropriations) is considered. When highway or water conservation programs are developed, organizations from industry and labor come to the fore, eager to support projects that produce business and jobs.

When Congress sets out to write new legislation on pollution control (involving, say, acid rain, urban smog, or auto tail pipe standards), business interests, such as the auto and coal industries, turn out in force, insisting that more stringent standards will impose an intolerable burden on producers. Environmental groups, of course, are there to support such clean-air legislation. The truth is that scarcely any legislation, rule, or regulation can be proposed that does not activate some groups—those that defend existing conditions as well as those that seek change. Many proposals for change, in fact, are generated by the leadership of organized groups.

Interest Groups and Political Parties ■

Governmental power is sought by both political parties and interest groups—a fact that sometimes clouds the differences between these forms of political organization. But there are important differences. First, interest groups cannot win generalized support from the electorate. Interest group appeal is essentially narrow; it is aimed at a special interest, or set of interests, within the population. The distinction is one of scope. To make a serious bid for office, a party must develop wide-ranging programs. No major party could survive without directing claims, appeals, and promises to a variety of interests.

The second difference is that parties are organized around the election process; interest groups are not. Parties are in business to win elections, to place nominees in public office—in short, to capture government. As a rule, therefore, they field a complete slate of candidates. Interest groups, even the most powerful, are more narrowly ambitious. They too work in elections. They back some candidates and oppose others; but their efforts fall well short of an attempt to take direct control of the government.

The Group Struggle ■

American politics is sometimes seen as a group struggle; that is, groups compete for the advantages government can confer. Policies that benefit one group often (though not always) disadvantage another. A bill to remove all acreage limitations in the production of rice (and thus to increase yields) may benefit consumers and large industrial users of rice, such as brewers and food processors. But it threatens producer lobbies devoted to limited production and high commodity prices. Legislation that increases funds for unemployed workers, veterans, or higher education seems just and desirable to their lobbies; but it causes concern in groups that press for reduced government spending and balanced budgets. Laws that increase employer liability for industrial accidents please labor interests. Business sees them as operating costs. Conflict between groups is common in a democratic system.

Close Ties. At times, groups press their claims with little opposition. Some agricultural policies are shaped in Congress with close cooperation among farm lobbies, key members of agriculture committees, and Department of Agriculture bureaucrats. When these "cozy triangles" or "subgovernments" (see Chapter 17) work out compromises, there is an excellent chance they will be accepted without change by Congress. Thus, in some cases, interest groups, in league with public officials, actually design the public policies from which they benefit. If these policies also reflect broader public interests, that is just coincidence.[7]

Like other crises, unemployment is a stimulus to political organization and political action. This photo depicts a plant closing in Youngstown, Ohio. When plants close, political leaders are stimulated to find solutions, such as tax breaks, protection from imports, and an easing of environmental rules. Because conflicts expand, a Youngstown dilemma can become a national problem almost overnight. (Chapter 1 explains how.)

Formation of Groups. The struggles among groups and between groups and government touch all aspects of American life. What prompts the development of new groups or the activation of dormant ones? We know that specialization and division of labor underlie group formation.[8] Groups develop around a clientele linked to special operations, missions, or fields of competence—the defense industry, the members of the medical or legal professions, the cable news network, the soft drink industry, the ministers of evangelical churches, the opponents of nuclear power, the oil industry, the banking industry, and so forth. As societies become more complex and specialized, groups multiply. And when one side of a controversy organizes, opponents follow suit. In the group struggle, the elementary rule is this: Organization begets organization.

The trigger to group development or activity may be a crisis that affects individuals associated in some way. Unemployment, dropping farm prices, technological innovation, changing status, erosion of traditional values, threat of competition, growing hostility—any disturbance that affects the equilibrium of interacting individuals may be a catalyst to the formation of a group. People affected by the disturbance look for others similarly positioned and seek to restore equilibrium. Discontent, apprehension, change, and maladjustment are the main forces in the creation or activation of interest groups.

Discontent and maladjustment are especially useful in explaining the rise of political interest groups among farmers.

> A factor of great significance in the setting off of political movements is an abrupt change for the worse in the status of one group relative to that of other groups in society. The economics of politics is by no means solely a matter of the poor against the rich; the rich and the poor may live together peaceably for decades, each accepting its status quietly. A rapid change for the worse, however, in the relative status of

> any group, rich or poor, is likely to precipitate political action. Depressions have been closely associated with intensification of farmers' political activity. Agrarian agitation, at times a bit boisterous and disturbing to the conservative elements of society, has not occurred at a uniform pitch but has had its dull periods and its shrill points correlated somewhat with variations in the fortunes of farmers.[9]

An impulse to improve or protect economic position accounts for the formation of many groups. The importance of this was stressed in James Madison's *The Federalist,* no. 10:

> [The] most common and durable source of factions has been the various and unequal distribution of property. Those who hold and those who are without property have ever formed distinct interests in society. Those who are creditors, and those who are debtors, fall under a like discrimination. A landed interest, a manufacturing interest, a mercantile interest, a moneyed interest, with many lesser interests, grow up of necessity in civilized nations, and divide them into different classes, actuated by different sentiments and views. The regulation of these various and interfering interests forms the principal task of modern legislation, and involves the spirit of party and faction in the necessary and ordinary operations of the government.[10]

Not all groups, though, are concerned with economic objectives or measure their success solely by economic advantage. Diverse social and political factors play a role in the formation of interest groups. There are ethnic, racial, cultural, religious, environmental, ethical, patriotic, and reform organizations active in nation and state. Pacifist, interventionist, and isolationist groups vie to shape foreign policies and government attitudes. Their economic basis, if there at all, is normally barely distinguishable.

Finally, interest groups are both created and sustained by government policies. Labor unions grew in number and influence after Congress passed legislation in the 1930s to guarantee the right of employees to organize and bargain collectively. Welfare programs gave rise to organizations of welfare recipients. One result of the Vietnam War was the formation of groups dedicated to peace. And, most recently, international tensions have led to the creation of many new groups (for example, Physicians for Social Responsibility and Lawyers Alliance for Nuclear Arms Control) in support of nuclear disarmament.

Groups proliferate, Hugh Heclo writes, because of the "tendency of successfully enacted policies unwittingly to propagate hybrid interests." Thus, in health care policy, federal funding and regulation

> have not only uncovered but also helped to create diverging interests among hospital associations, insurance companies, medical schools, hospital equipment manufacturers, local health planning groups, preventive medicine advocates, nonteaching research centers, and many others. This does not necessarily mean that every group is in conflict with all of the others all of the time. The point is that [government's activist policies] greatly increase the incentives for groups to form around the differential effects of these policies, each refusing to allow any other group to speak in its name.[11]

Groups and the Political System. Certain aspects of the American political system encourage the participation of groups in politics. First is the structure of government itself. By dividing power between the nation and the states, federalism gives interest groups several points of access and leverage. Some groups focus on state and local levels; others lobby intensively at the national level. A defeat at the national level may be offset by victories in the states. The interest group ignored in Tallahassee or Springfield may get a friendly reception in Washington. Organized labor, for example, has found Congress and the president more responsive to its claims than most governors and state legislatures. And a system of separated powers disperses authority. A decentralized government and vigorous interest group activity go hand in hand.

The political party system also affects the vitality of interest groups. Like the government, the parties are decentralized; power is dispersed throughout the organization. Party discipline is often nonexistent. In no important sense, in fact, do the parties control or defend their candidates. Their fate is their own responsibility. "In the struggle for survival in a highly chaotic political situation," E. E. Schattschneider observed, "the Congressman is thrown very much on his own resources, seeking support wherever he can find it and tending strongly to yield to *all* demands made on him. Any reasonably convincing demonstration of an organized demand for anything is likely to impress him out of all proportion to the real weight or influence of the pressure group." [12]

The influence of interest groups on policy making also is due to the fact that American politics is not characterized by sharp, continuing ideological conflict. Liberals and conservatives are found in each major political party (see Chapter 9). Indeed, differences in political views and attitudes are sometimes as great between members of the same party as between members of the two parties. That has long been true, for instance, on questions about the role of government in the economy. The mix of views within the parties invites interest groups to work both sides of the street—to seek support for their positions from both Democrats and Republicans. They can often splice together bipartisan coalitions. Few groups tie their lobbying fortunes just to one party.[13]

Diversity Within Groups. There is more diversity in interest groups than meets the eye. Groups that represent the same sector of society need not share the same objectives. Few policy questions involving agriculture, for instance, are viewed from the same perspective by all farmers or farm organizations; neither all farmers nor all their special interests are alike. Some farmers raise wheat and others raise corn, cotton, soybeans, or hogs; there are corporate farmers (agribusiness) and sharecroppers, large farm operations and small ones. Legislation that serves the welfare of one segment may harm another. The same is true for labor, business, veterans, and other groups. There are highly skilled workers along with the unskilled, major corporations and Mom and Pop stores, veterans' organizations concerned with the quest for government benefits and those that are "citizens first, veterans second." Policy diversity within these categories is much greater than popular language conveys.

Interest Group Resources. Interest groups vary in their capacity to influence government. Among the factors that shape a group's influence are (1) the size, cohesiveness, and geographic distribution of its membership; (2) its financial base; (3) the skills of its leaders; (4) the prestige or status of its members; (5) the intensity of members' convictions; (6) its access to the media; and (7) the appropriateness of its goals in terms of the traditional values of society. There are great differences in the extent to which groups possess these resources.

Group resources are not always what they seem. Large size, for instance, may not be an advantage. Larger groups, on the whole, have greater problems of organization. Although women, youth, retired persons, and consumers number in the tens of millions, only a fraction of them belong to groups organized to make claims on government. Most people are "free riders"; they gain whatever benefits are available without giving dues, attention, or time and money.[14] All elderly persons gain if Congress increases social security benefits or shapes tax laws to enhance retirement savings; all low-paid workers gain from a hike in the minimum wage. They profit from the efforts of groups in the "gray lobby," such as the American Association of Retired Persons, or those of organized labor. (And, of course, sympathetic members of Congress, often working closely with lobbyists, are crucial in gaining support for group objectives.)

The uneven distribution of resources among groups is at the heart of the controversy between *pluralist* and *elitist* interpretations of American democracy. Theorists in the pluralist school stress that society is composed of many groups, representing diverse interests, attentive to the workings of government, and in conflict with one another. Numerous, competing groups contribute to a policy-making process in which interests struggle and bargain. Each relevant interest is likely to gain

"It's awful the way they're trying to influence Congress. Why don't they serve cocktails and make campaign contributions like we do?"

something; but no one interest is powerful enough to dominate.

Elite theorists see another America in which relatively few people, holding commanding positions outside government, have decisive influence on the major questions of government. Government is the servant of the elite. The general public, in this view, is on the outskirts of power; it is unable through its organizations or through elections to have much impact on central national policies.[15]

Closer to reality is a middle position that sees the American system as a mixture of pluralism and elitism. Elites do exist. Resources are not distributed equally. Some elements of society wield much more influence than others. And some groups win steadily because they have almost no opposition.[16] All that is plain enough. But no one can mistake the array of organized groups that compete with one another, vigorously pressing their claims, leading frequently to public policies that represent a balancing of interests. Clear-cut policy victories for any one element are rare.

The pluralist model, nevertheless, has a special problem. Organization is critical to group success; and some groups have been especially hard to organize. What is more, even organization may not do the trick: The groups in the antipoverty network, for example, could not prevent sharp spending cuts for social programs (welfare, food stamps, and public service jobs) under the Reagan administration. Seeking a significant increase in the minimum wage, low-income, labor, and liberal groups met sharp resistance from the Bush administration in the 101st Congress.

On the whole, blacks, Mexican-Americans, women, consumers, the undereducated, and the poor have not been well served by the interest group system. Most analysts believe that presidents and the courts have been more responsive than Congress to the claims of these groups. (For evidence on the responsiveness of the courts to minority interests, see Chapter 5.) But at times, no organ of government seems to hear them. "The flaw in the pluralist heaven," in the wry observation of E. E. Schattschneider, "is that the heavenly chorus sings with a strong upper-class accent." [17]

The organization of certain categorical groups, such as women and consumers, has been especially difficult because the members' interests diverge. Some women supported the Equal Rights Amendment and others worked to defeat it; and some favor abortion on demand while others oppose it. Conflict between groups representing these views has been intense in recent years.

Major Political Interests

Interest groups of great variety interact with officials at the local, state, and national levels. Almost every important political decision—whether made by a legislature, executive, administrative agency, or court—has an impact on a number of groups. The broad contours of group politics can be sketched by examining the major types of groups that participate actively in politics and seek to gain advantages.

Business Groups

Business has been in politics as long as government has been in business. At no time in American history has business confined its attention simply to the marketplace. Quite the contrary, business has long recognized that government decisions present both risks and opportunities. Public policy can make it easier or harder for firms to do business as well as expand or diminish profits.

Organized business is heavily represented in Washington and the state capitals—it is more fully represented, in fact, than any other economic or social interest. Some large corporations have agents who "work" the corridors of government; in certain respects, Ford, Chrysler, General Motors, and other firms are themselves interest groups. More pervasive are the hundreds of *trade associations,* representing particular trades and industries, that interact with legislators and agency officials about legislation, rules, and regulations that affect their clienteles. They bear such names as the Association of American Railroads, Association of Retail Druggists, American Bankers Association, American Tobacco Institute, American Petroleum Institute, National Coal Association, and National Association of Real Estate Brokers. Not much escapes their attention when their welfare is at stake.

The vast majority of trade associations—now nearly 2000—maintain headquarters in Washington, many only a few blocks from the White House. The migration of trade associations to Washington reflects the increased federal regulation of business. The clothing industry is concerned with regulations involving flammable fabrics, bankers with regulations affecting loans, savings and loan associations with rescuing their industry, insurance firms with product liability regulations, railroads with regulations affecting transportation of hazardous wastes, paint manufacturers with regulations limiting lead in their products, soft-drink manufacturers with regulations on sweeteners, grocers with regulations that specify how meat is to be packaged. The list is endless. Much of the lobbying effort of trade associations focuses on the bureaucracy, the departments and agencies that make rules and regulations. "Every time H.U.D. [the Department of Housing and Urban Development] hiccups," notes one observer," 20 construction industry associations hold a meeting." [18]

The best-known business interest groups are the *United States Chamber of Commerce* and the *National Association of Manufacturers* (see Table 10–1). The U.S. Chamber of Commerce is composed of more than 70,000 firms and individuals; several thousand local, state, and regional chambers; and some 1000 trade and professional associations. Its Washington office has a staff of about 400 people. The National Association of Manufacturers (NAM) has about 13,000 member firms, a Washington staff of 100, and more than a dozen full-time lobbyists.[19]

IMPACT

Lobbyists' Row: K Street in Washington, D.C.

Almost 2000 trade associations and countless corporations and labor unions maintain offices in the nation's capital. Many have impressive research staffs and full-time lobbyists to protect their interests in legislation and the administrative rulings of departments and agencies. Lobbying is the principal growth industry in Washington.

1604 K Street N.W.
National Small Business Assoc.

1608 K Street
American Legion

1612 K Street
American Assoc. of Port Authorities
American Electronics Assoc.
American Industrial Health Council
American Maritime Assoc.
City of San Jose
Control Data Corp.
International Trade and Investment
Korean Institute for Democracy and Unification
National Assoc. of State Alcohol and Drug Abuse Directors
National Engineering Service
Rafshoon Communications
Rocky Mountain Energy and Trade Group

1625 K Street
American Institute of Merchant Shipping
American Recreation Coalition
Council of American Flag Ship Operators
Kerr McGee Corporation
National Assoc. for Milk Marketing Reform
National Petroleum Council

1627 K Street
Armour & Co.
Coca-Cola Co.
Greyhound Corp.
Richard Helms
Institute of Scrap Iron and Steel
Wilbur D. Mills
National Newspaper Assoc.
Northern Illinois Gas Co.

1629 K Street
American Society of Home Inspectors
Americans for Energy Independence
Applied Conservation
National Federation of the Blind
U.S. Hide, Skin, and Leather Assoc.
Carnation Co.
E. I. du Pont de Nemours & Co.
Friends of China
General Mills
Hershey Foods Corp.
International Chemical Co.
Minority Resources
Montana Power Co.
Nabisco
National Assoc. of Black Broadcast Owners
National Assoc. of Insured Persons
National Assoc. of School Psychologists
National Independent Retail Jewelers
National Institute of Graduate Studies
National Investor Relations Institute
National Law and Order Committee
National Organization of State Conservative Parties
National Space Club
Pflow Industries
South Dakota Industrial Development and Expansion Agency
Spra Kleen Company
Tiara Oil Company

1666 K Street
Bell Aerospace Co.
Bell Helicopter Co.
Textron
Wilmer, Cutler & Pickering
National Police Conference

TABLE 10–1

How Business Rates the U.S. Senate

Chief Supporters	Percentage of Votes in Favor of U.S. Chamber of Commerce Positions	Chief Opponents	Percentage of Votes in Opposition to U.S. Chamber of Commerce Positions
Hatch (R–Utah)	100	Gore (D–Tenn.)	90
McCain (R–Ariz.)	100	Dodd (D–Conn.)	87
Armstrong (R–Colo.)	94	Simon (D–Ill.)	87
Boschwitz (R–Minn.)	94	Biden (D–Del.)	83
Garn (R–Utah)	94	Hollings (D–S.C.)	83
Humphrey (R–N.H.)	94	Levin (D–Mich.)	83
Karnes (R–Neb.)	94	Riegle (D–Mich.)	83
Nickles (R–Okla.)	94	Glenn (D–Ohio)	82
Roth (R–Del.)	94	Ford (D–Ky.)	78
Symms (R–Ida.)	94	Fowler (D–Ga.)	78
Warner (R–Va.)	94	Metzenbaum (D–Ohio)	78
Gramm (R–Tex.)	89	Reid (D–Nev.)	78
Helms (R–N.C.)	89	Burdick (D–N.D.)	76
McConnell (R–Ky.)	89	Kennedy (D–Mass.)	76
Quayle (R–Ind.)	89	Rockefeller (D–W.Va.)	76
Trible (R–Va.)	89	Kerry (D–Mass.)	75

Source: Data for 100th Congress, 1st Session, in *Congressional Quarterly Weekly Report,* March 5, 1988, p. 602. Failure to vote does not affect score.

Another important, if less well known, organization is the *Business Roundtable,* an association of the chief executive officers of about 200 giant corporations, including General Motors, General Electric, U.S. Steel, IBM, and AT&T. Formed in 1972, the Business Roundtable supports lobbying by corporation presidents and board chairpersons, people who have easy access to public officials.

Business is not monolithic. At certain levels, in fact, it is sharply divided. Small businesses have objectives that differ from those of giant corporations. What is more, conflict within business is common. Legislation that improves the competitive position of the trucking industry, for example, poses problems for a rival carrier, the railroad industry. Independent oil and gas companies often tangle with "big oil" (the major companies). Public policies that help the electric power industry may harm the natural gas industry. Some businesses gain advantages from international free trade (aircraft and computer industries); others are threatened by foreign competition (steel and automobile industries). And when a tax bill is being drafted, business unity all but disappears. As observed by a member of the House Ways and Means Committee, the tax-writing committee: "Business lobbyists no longer are just pure business lobbyists. Instead, they represent specific interests. In order to protect their interests, they go after someone else's." [20]

Nevertheless, American business organizations do share a common philosophy. With few exceptions, business groups support legislation to reduce the bargaining power of organized labor, to ease taxes on business profits, to lessen government

Steelworkers rally in Washington to urge Congress to find ways to shore up the Social Security system. Labor's political agenda is largely concerned with two kinds of public policy: labor–management relations and social welfare.

regulation of industry, and to provide for government aid to business and industry. Typically, business groups advocate states' rights and are critics of federal power. Proposals to expand social welfare programs find scant support among business groups. No refrain is more common among these groups than the need for economy in government.

Labor Groups

Like business, labor has long been in politics. Yet it took a long time for it to make much headway in the political arena. During the nineteenth century, labor lost many more battles with employers than it won. Prior to Franklin D. Roosevelt's New Deal, unions did not participate aggressively in politics; they focused instead on strengthening their organizations and advancing their interests through collective bargaining. Some unions even opposed government measures to regulate wages and hours; they believed these issues should be settled through negotiation. But all that has changed. Labor now appreciates having government on its side, and few interest groups lobby more vigorously.

Labor's influence is partly a function of numbers. About 17 million men and women belong to labor unions. (Even so, only 17 percent of the nation's wage and salary workers belong to unions.) The largest union is the *American Federation of*

Labor-Congress of Industrial Organizations (AFL-CIO), with a membership of slightly more than 13 million. Some 100 autonomous international unions (garment workers, meat cutters, teachers, musicians, carpenters, government employees, and the like) are affiliated with the AFL-CIO. Also to be reckoned with are such independent unions as the *United Mine Workers,* the *railway brotherhoods,* and the *International Brotherhood of Teamsters.* In 1981, the United Auto Workers rejoined the AFL-CIO, healing a split that began in 1968.

Labor's political role involves both lobbying and electoral (or campaign) politics. The legislative department of the Washington headquarters of the AFL-CIO has a staff of eight lobbyists. The Washington office also has a political department, the Committee on Political Education (COPE), which engages in campaign activities; these include voter registration drives, public opinion polling, campaign organization, fund-raising, and research. Other unions have political arms similar to COPE and their own lobbyists. The interests of unions may differ, but there is substantial cooperation among them.

The large-scale involvement of organized labor in politics is no mystery. In the first place, labor believes that its strength in collective bargaining rests in part on demonstrations of its political clout. Second, labor supports certain social and economic programs that fall outside the range of collective bargaining agreements. And third, like other groups, labor engages in political activities in self-defense—because no group is beyond the reach of government policy.

In legislative politics, labor focuses on two types of measures: labor policy and social welfare legislation. In recent years, it has lobbied Congress on such labor-oriented measures as public works jobs, advance notice for workers before plant closings or mass layoffs, compensation for workers hurt by airline mergers, limits on imports of textiles and shoes, prevailing local wage requirements in military construction contracts, collective bargaining protection for certain classes of workers, food stamps for jobless workers, worker pension benefits, the extension of federal unemployment compensation benefits, and bankruptcy legislation as it affects labor contracts. In social welfare policy, labor has lobbied for increased social security benefits, catastrophic health-care benefits, federal aid to college students, federally assisted housing programs, federally funded day care centers, mandatory controls on hospital costs, consumer protection, and federal education grants for disadvantaged children.

Organized labor has been a leading supporter of civil rights legislation. Occasional foreign policy issues and political reforms also appear on its legislative agenda. The AFL-CIO, for example, has been an important advocate of the public financing of federal elections. The broad point is that labor's policy interests extend well beyond work conditions and union organization.

Overall, labor has found Democrats more responsive to its interests than Republicans (see Table 10–2). In "rewarding its friends," labor channels most of its campaign funds to Democratic candidates. Typically, in recent congressional elections, labor PACs (political action committees) have given more than 90 percent of their contributions to Democratic candidates. Not surprisingly, corporate PACs favor the Republican side—but not to such an overwhelming extent.

Farm Groups

The politicizing of the farmer, leading to the formation of farm pressure groups, can be traced to agricultural unrest. Sharp price declines for agricultural commodities, high freight and tax rates, lack of credit, high prices for products farmers buy, and the ravaging forces of nature have been the main catalysts to farm political organization and action. These factors, especially the prices of agricultural products, now sustain the activity of farm groups in the same way that earlier they prompted the organization of farmer third-party movements.

If solutions to agricultural problems have been scarce, groups organized to seek them have been numerous. State, regional, and national farm organizations represent the interests of American

TABLE 10–2

How Labor Rates the U.S. Senate

Chief Supporters	Percentage of Votes in Favor of AFL-CIO Positions	Chief Opponents	Percentage of Votes in Opposition to AFL-CIO Positions
Biden (D–Del.)	100	McClure (R–Ida.)	100
Bradley (D–N.J.)	100	Wallop (R–Wyo.)	100
Burdick (D–N.D.)	100	Garn (R–Utah)	90
Byrd (D–W.Va.)	100	Gramm (R–Tex.)	90
Dodd (D–Conn.)	100	Nickles (R–Okla.)	90
Ford (D–Ky.)	100	Hatch (R–Utah)	89
Fowler (D–Ga.)	100	Humphrey (R–N.H.)	89
Glenn (D–Ohio)	100	Karnes (R–Neb.)	89
Gore (D–Tenn.)	100	Simpson (R–Wyo.)	89
Graham (D–Fla.)	100	Symms (R–Ida.)	89
Kerry (D–Mass.)	100	Dole (R–Kan.)	80
Kennedy (D–Mass.)	100	Hecht (R–Nev.)	80
Metzenbaum (D–Ohio)	100	Helms (R–N.C.)	80
Mikulski (D–Md.)	100	Kassebaum (R–Kan.)	80
Moynihan (D–N.Y.)	100	Lugar (R–Ind.)	80
Nunn (D–Ga.)	100	McCain (R–Ariz.)	80
Riegle (D–Mich.)	100	Quayle (R–Ind.)	80
Rockefeller (D–W.Va.)	100		
Simon (D–Ill.)	100		

Source: Data for 100th Congress, 1st Session, in *Congressional Quarterly Weekly Report,* March 5, 1988, p. 602. Failure to vote does not affect score.

farmers. The most important farm groups are the *American Farm Bureau Federation,* the *National Grange,* the *National Farmers' Union,* and the *National Council of Farmer Cooperatives.* There are also many special *commodity groups,* such as the National Association of Wheat Growers, the National Potato Council, the National Cattlemen's Association, and the National Cotton Council of America.

Like other interests, organized agriculture is not united. Livestock and poultry producers, for example, oppose high price supports for commodities such as wheat and corn, since higher prices increase feed grain costs. Southern farmers are more disposed to favor price support programs (and thus federal controls) than midwestern farmers. Grape growers and wineries, seeking to protect their industry through legislation to curb inexpensive imports, find that their staunchest opponents are other farm interests—in particular soybean and corn growers, who believe that European countries would retaliate against their commodities.[21]

The major groups also struggle with one another. The Farm Bureau and the Grange are much more conservative than the Farmers' Union. Finding allies in the business community, they seek to lessen government regulation of farming operations and the pricing and production of farm commodities. Responsive to lower-income farm families, the Farmers' Union supports government involvement in agriculture and policies to preserve the "family farm." It is often allied with the AFL-CIO. The Farmers' Union and the Democratic party agree at least as often as the Farm Bureau and the Republican party. Officially, of course, both groups are nonpartisan.

Declining farm population, division within agriculture itself, and heightened political activity by countervailing groups (such as businesses that use agricultural products in manufacturing and consumer groups) have weakened the influence of farm pressure groups. Even so, their successes are substantial. Policymakers and citizens alike believe that a healthy agricultural economy is vital to the nation's strength.

Professional Groups

Many professional associations actively lobby. Associations of teachers, physicians, nurses, dentists, lawyers, psychiatrists, engineers, optometrists, actuaries, pharmacists, chiropractors, osteopaths, personnel consultants, anesthetists, and veterinarians, among others, have lobbyists in Washington and the state capitals. Specialists within these groups may have their own lobby organizations, like dermatologists and gastroenterologists among physicians.

As a rule, the influence of these associations is limited to a narrow band of issues within their sphere of competence. Occasionally, though, professional groups have a major impact on broad public policy—such as teachers' associations that lobby for tax and spending legislation to secure higher teachers' salaries, or medical associations that lobby against government health insurance. Professional associations sometimes war with each other, like the more or less continuous battle between doctors and chiropractors in state legislatures and Congress.

One of the most visible national professional associations is the *American Medical Association (AMA)*. From the late 1940s through the early 1960s, the AMA lobbied successfully against national health insurance ("socialized medicine," in its view). It often spent more money on lobbying than any other group. It suffered a major defeat in 1965 when a social security medical care program was adopted by Congress. Among the AMA's current interests (including measures it opposes as well as those it supports) are health insurance, drug laws, hospital cost control, health planning, intern

Organization increases influence. Women airline pilots at an annual meeting of the International Social Affiliation of Women Airline Pilots. Organizations of this type have two primary objectives: to strengthen the bargaining position of members—seeking to improve salaries, benefits, and conditions of work—and, of broader concern, to promote the interests of the industry by lobbying government officials for favorable public policy.

unionization, prepaid medical plans, anticompetitive medical practices, medical records privacy, and Medicaid and Medicare payments for chiropractic services. The AMA resists government involvement in medicine (so-called political medicine) unless the medical profession is likely to be served. In this respect, it resembles other lobby groups.

Public Interest Groups

The groups that ordinarily command the most attention represent economic interests, such as labor, business, and agriculture. But their voices are not the only ones heard. Recently, so-called *public interest* or *citizen lobbies* have come to the fore; they claim to represent general values within society, such as the environment, consumers, peace, conservation, and "good government." A distinguishing characteristic is that neither these groups nor their members gain material benefits from their political activities. Well-educated, middle-class citizens, concerned with moral and quality of life issues, are the chief supporters of public interest lobbies.[22]

Common Cause is the most visible public interest lobby. Organized in 1970, it now has several hundred thousand dues-paying members. Its lobbying focuses on general policy—such as tax legislation and consumer protection—and on institutional reform—such as public financing of political campaigns, open meetings in Congress and federal agencies, merit selection of federal judges and U.S. attorneys, "sunset" legislation (to establish a fixed expiration date for government programs and agencies), and stringent lobbying disclosure laws. Over the years, its agenda has been dominated by proposals to open up or democratize American political institutions.

Along the lines of Common Cause are the lobbies launched by *Ralph Nader,* the well-known consumer advocate. Included in the Nader apparatus are Public Citizen, Center for the Study of Responsive Law, Critical Mass, Tax Reform Research Group, Health Research Group, the Public Interest Research Group (PIRG), and Congress Watch (the lobby arm). Consumer, health, and environmental policies are the main concerns of these organizations.

Other well-known citizen lobbies are the *League of Women Voters,* the *Consumer Federation of America,* the *American Civil Liberties Union,* the *Sierra Club,* and the *Wilderness Society.* Sternly ideological groups such as the *Americans for Democratic Action* (liberal) and *American Conservative Union* (conservative) reflect another dimension of "citizen politics."

Some critics find the label "public interest group" presumptuous. Not everyone, they note, shares a common view of the public interest. Is the financing of federal elections by tax revenues in the public interest? Is opposition to the spread of nuclear energy plants? Is adoption of strict environmental controls on the development of new coal fields? The answers are complicated; there are compelling arguments on each side.

Public interest groups provide purposive benefits, a form of ideological satisfaction. On the whole, they find it harder to attract and retain members than groups that offer material incentives, such as business and labor.[23]

Government Interest Groups

An interesting phenomenon in interest group politics is the *executive lobby.* This lobby consists of the chief executive, major officials of departments and agencies, and their liaison personnel who meet regularly with legislators. Executive lobbying is done with vigor at both state and national levels. It is especially impressive in Washington, where all cabinet-level departments (and many noncabinet agencies and bureaus too) have congressional relations staffs.

What do administrators want from Congress? A great deal is the answer: goodwill, support for the president's programs, approval of new programs, protection of old ones, and, not least, increased funding of their programs and operations. In practical terms, administrators usually want the members' votes.

Some presidents play a very active role in congressional relations. An insider in President Lyndon Johnson's administration recalls:

> [The president] would say to us, "I want you to go up there today and find out what the members need. What do they need in their district? Do they need the little wife invited down to the White House, or can we help with a constituent?" Then we would go up to the Hill and say, "The president asked me to come see you and ask if you need anything." That was impressive. People felt warmly toward LBJ.[24]

Executive-legislative lobbying is a two-way street. Department liaison offices receive thousands of inquiries and requests from members of Congress each year—for information and for help with problems that trouble their constituents (veterans' benefits, social security payments, emergency military leaves, government contracts, and the like). Handling congressional requests promptly and effectively is essential for smooth agency relations with Congress.

Strange as it may seem, governments lobby each other. Many individual states, cities, and counties have full-time lobbyists (and Washington offices). These agents press Congress and executive agencies for favorable policies and, most important, money. Among the well-known state and local umbrella lobbies are the United States Conference of Mayors, the Governors' Conference, the Council of State Governments, and the National Association of Counties. Protecting federal aid programs (see Chapter 3) is a key task of lower governments. The cost of their lobbying efforts, they reason, is money well spent.

Single-Issue and Cause Groups ■

Interest groups organized around narrow issues play an increasingly important role in American politics. No election of any consequence can be held and no legislative session can take place without the intense involvement of a special form of pressure group: the *cause* group. The bane of many legislators, these groups press hard for favorable decisions on such matters as nuclear power, gun control, public morality, abortion, limitations on government spending, equal rights, environmental protection, and prayer in the public schools. Legislators who vote "wrong" may be severely tested when they seek reelection. The prototype for such groups is the *National Rifle Association;* it has had huge success in resisting gun control legislation, even though the vast majority of citizens favors some form of it (as shown by public opinion surveys).

For many politicians, these special controversies are no-win issues; the statement or vote that pleases one group alienates another. As a U.S. senator said not long ago, "The single-interest constituencies have just about destroyed politics as I knew it. They've made it miserable to be in office—or to run for office—and left me feeling it's hardly worth the struggle to survive." [25]

Lobbying Techniques

Decision Settings ■

The unabashed aim of interest groups and their lobbyists is to influence government decisions. No branch of government escapes their attention. They interact directly with administrators and legislators. Indirectly they become involved in the judicial process by seeking to influence the choice of judges or by bringing cases to court. The National Association for the Advancement of Colored People (NAACP), for example, was instrumental in the legal campaign that led to *Brown* v. *Board of Education,* the historic 1954 public school desegregation decision of the Supreme Court (see Chapter 5). Public interest groups have also been active in litigation, suing businesses to protect the environment or consumers. Failing to win support from the executive or the legislature, groups have often turned to the courts for relief.

Officials of the executive branch are also fair game for lobbyists. Interest groups are concerned not only with how administrators interpret and administer laws, but also with getting them to back

Citizens, Participation, and Washington Lobbies: An Odd Mélange

Washington is a mecca for interest groups. They come there by the hundreds, driven by grim self-interest for the most part, prepared to press for changes in public policy or to resist them. Nothing about them stands out more sharply than their diversity, as the sample below suggests. One would expect to find the well-known groups in this list. But what about the others? Who knew they even existed, let alone what they might want from the government?

Organization	Legislative Interests
American Association of Retired Persons (AARP)	Social security, taxation, nursing home standards, consumer protection, employment of older workers, housing
American Dehydrated Onion & Garlic Association	Agriculture and trade
American Newspaper Publishers Association	First Amendment, Freedom of Information Act, postal rates
Association of Independent Organ Procurement Agencies	Organ transplantation and organ procurement issues
Burdette Road Baby's Association (Bethesda, Md.)	Legislation affecting American babies
California State Teachers' Retirement System	Public pension funds
Consortium of Social Science Associations	Funding of social science research by federal agencies
Consumers for Competitive Fuels	Use and production of alcohol fuels in motor fuels
Damon Corporation	Mammogram legislation

Organization	Legislative Interests
Day-Glo Color Corporation	Temporary suspension of the duty on ortho, para-toluenesulfonamide
Fruit Growers League of Jackson County (Medford, Ore.)	Immigration
Galena Resort Company	Wetlands permit for proposed ski resort
Government of Bangladesh	Foreign assistance
Greyhound Corporation	Opposed to retroactive application of proposed amendments to the RICO (Racketeer Influenced and Corrupt Organizations) statute
Ladies Professional Golf Association	Internal Revenue Code (deferred compensation plans)
McDonnell Douglas Corporation	Space program
National Stone Association	Public works, labor, and tax issues affecting crushed stone industry
Physician Insurers Association of America	Medical malpractice tort reform
Quik Wok Inc.	Food service/food industry
San Gabriel Valley Boys Club of America (El Monte, Calif.)	Gang reduction, AIDS, alcoholism, drug abuse, and teen pregnancy
Sprinkler Pipe Producers Group	The Hotel and Motel Fire Safety Act
Texas Sheep and Goat Ranchers Association	Immigration
The Coalition to Stop the Raid on America	Tender offers and other hostile corporate takeovers
Thrifty Rent-a-Car Systems Inc.	Airport user fees
Toshiba	Trade legislation
Turner Broadcasting System Inc.	Cable television industry
United Transportation Union	Railroad labor
Western Forest Industries Association	Log export
Wilderness Society	Arctic National Wildlife Refuge

their legislative goals. Easing the way for future lobbying, interest groups can sometimes influence the selection of department or agency heads.

Close ties between interest groups and administrative agencies are common. The AFL-CIO usually finds support for its policy goals among the top officials of the Department of Labor (especially during Democratic administrations); the American Legion and the Department of Veterans Affairs cooperate in a similar way. Farm lobbies receive a friendly ear from key bureaucrats in the Department of Agriculture. Housing, low-income, and citizen groups find friends in the Department of Housing and Urban Development. Organized business looks to the Commerce Department and the Treasury. Groups with a stake in health policy watch the programs of the Department of Health and Human Services. The highway lobby focuses on the Department of Transportation; so do the mass transit and railroad lobbies. And so it goes. Few groups, at least few sizable ones, are without friends in the offices of executive agencies.

Cooperation between agencies and interest groups is generated by mutual interest. Bureaucrats need programs to administer, funds to run them, and external political support. Alliances are convenient and instrumental. What helps one participant helps the other. These links furnish the dynamics for a wide range of legislative and executive decisions.

Interest group activity is especially pronounced in the legislative process. Openness, decentralization, lack of hierarchy, weak parties, independent committees, and numerous points of access—the characteristics of legislatures—make them receptive to the overtures of outsiders. Interest groups capitalize on the fact that legislatures are bargaining institutions; no one really controls them. Public policies, as a result, are often the product of accommodation among divergent interests. Individual politicians, essentially on their own in both the legislature and back home, have good reason to be sensitive to the claims of groups whose support may be crucial to their reelection. The independence of legislators from institutional controls, such as the legislative parties, increases their vulnerability to the pressures of organized groups.

The close association of members of Congress with their constituencies—local, state, and regional—is commonly advantageous for interest groups. Concern for their electoral security prompts members to seize every opportunity to advance the interests of individuals and groups whose support in primary and general elections is crucial. James L. Sundquist describes member-constituency relations in a particularly instructive way:

> [Whatever] the merits of the local or regional claim, it must be pressed. Representatives of Texas must see the national interest in terms of oil, those of South Dakota in terms of cattle, and those of Detroit in terms of automobiles. Foreign policy seen through the eyes of a constituency may predispose a representative toward the Greek, the Israeli, or the Irish view of particular problems. The budget appears as a "pork barrel" to be distributed among districts as well as a fiscal program for the country. What weapons the military forces should get are liable to be judged by what factories are located in a state or district. And so it goes across the whole range of policy. Political incentives propel the member—especially the House member who represents more specialized constituencies—from the broad to the narrow perspective.[26]

Lobbying may be either *direct* or *indirect.* The latter is often called grass roots lobbying—lobbying to stimulate the public to contact their representatives. Figure 10–1 shows the interactions in direct and indirect lobbying in a legislative setting (including a special form of indirect lobbying, political campaigning).

Direct Lobbying

This form of lobbying consists of all the direct, face-to-face contacts that lobbyists have with government officials—such as testifying in committee hearings on legislation, consulting with committee staff, or meeting with members and their staff aides. The point of these encounters is to communicate the group's position directly to legislators. Group size has a bearing on the techniques used. Small

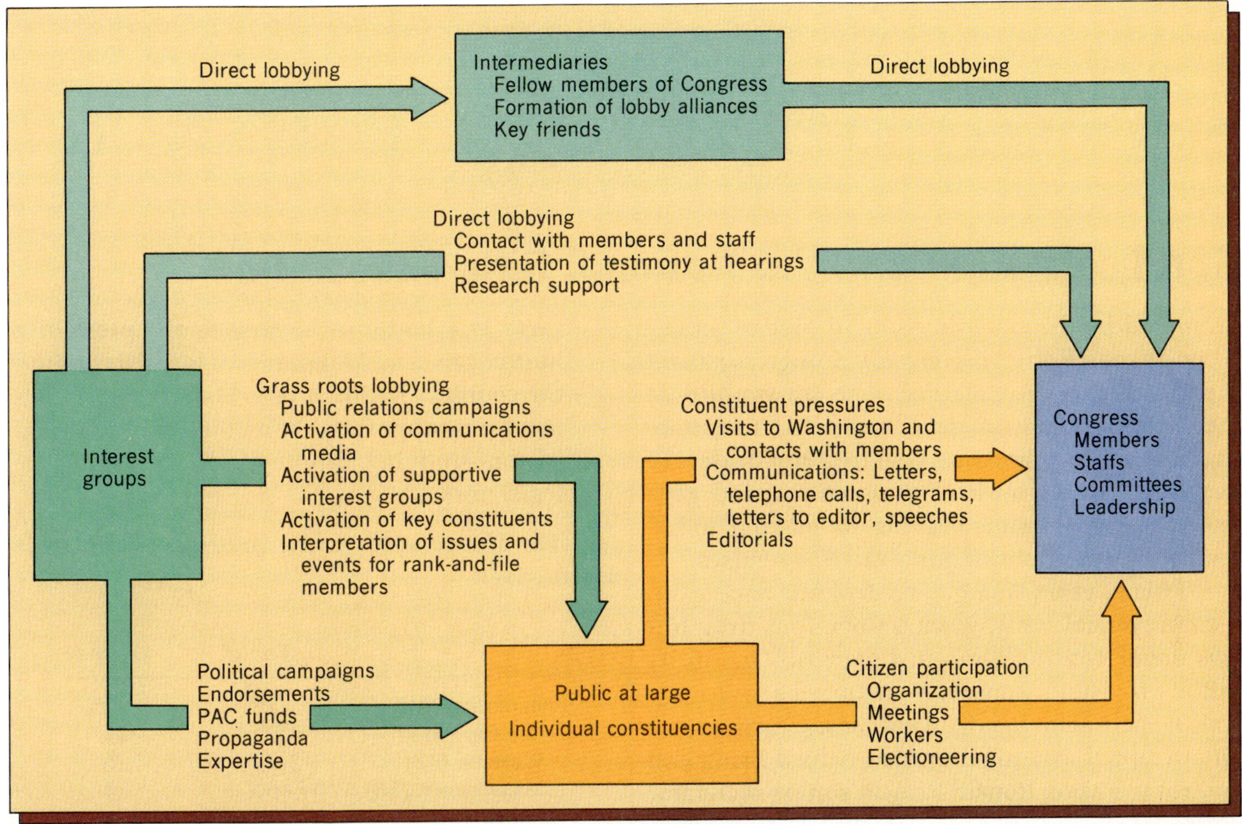

Figure 10–1 Paths of interest group influence.

groups and those with limited budgets concentrate on direct lobbying. Their activity may consist of nothing more than occasionally hiring a lobbyist or law firm to keep track of legislation or to meet with legislators. Large and well-financed groups, such as the Chamber of Commerce and the AFL-CIO, operate from their capital headquarters, well staffed with research, clerical, and lobbying personnel.

Former members of Congress—those who have retired or been defeated—often turn up as lobbyists. In their job of working *on* Congress rather than in it, they have especially good access to members. As one legislator-turned-lobbyist explains:

> When you're talking to somebody you've played paddleball with or played in the Republican-Democratic golf tournament with, or seen regularly in the Capitol Hill Club, there's no question that helps. I think most sitting members go out of their way to be helpful to former members.[27]

Lobbying by celebrities has become common on certain kinds of social issues. Film stars and athletes regularly trek to Capitol Hill, adding glamour to some cause and commanding the attention of the media. When the school prayer amendment was under consideration in the 98th Congress (1983–1984), advocates enlisted Joe Gibbs (Washington Redskins coach), Tom Landry (Dallas Cowboys coach), Roger Staubach (former Cowboys quarterback), Mark Mosely (Redskins placekicker), Rosey Grier (football *and* Hollywood), and others to support the prayer legislation. (It failed, for lack of a few key downfield blocks.) Most lobbying, of course, is done by professional lobbyists.

Continuity & CHANGE

Gun Legislation and the National Rifle Association

Prompted by the assassinations of Martin Luther King, Jr., and Robert F. Kennedy, Congress passed the Gun Control Act of 1968. The law prohibited the interstate sale of guns, restricted interstate transportation of firearms, required gun dealers to keep extensive records of transactions, and gave federal officials wide latitude in making unannounced inspections of gun dealers' premises.

Twenty years later gun control was once again a controversial issue, when an omnibus drug bill was under consideration in Congress. One of its initial provisions would have required a seven-day waiting period for handgun purchases. Again it was an attempted assassination that helped bring gun control to a vote; Ronald Reagan's press secretary, James Brady, was seriously injured in an attempt on the president's life in 1981. But now the Brady amendment *lost,* by a vote of 228–182, despite the support of police groups.

What had changed? Many analysts credited the increased effectiveness of the progun lobby, particularly the National Rifle Association. *Time* described what could be the toughest gun in town:

> Rows of keypunch operators sit in the marble and granite eight-story office of the National Rifle Association in Washington, feeding information into humming computers. Each of the association's 1.8 million members is recorded by zip code, congressional district and past support for the N.R.A. The voting records of Congressmen and Senators, and their answers to an 18-question N.R.A. loyalty test, are also tabulated—and graded from A to F. When there is a battle to be waged, the press of a button can send Mailgrams to loyalists around the country. Within hours, Mailgrams and letters from supporters are on their way to Washington—rallying, cajoling and threatening the legislators.

The House vote on the Brady amendment is instructive:

	Favor	Oppose
Democrats (238)	58%	42%
Eastern (61)	79	21
Western (42)	74	26
Midwestern (58)	66	34
Southern (77)	26	74

	Favor	Oppose
Republicans (172)	26%	74%
Eastern (41)	46	54
Western (38)	18	82
Midwestern (51)	27	73
Southern (42)	12	88

For Republicans generally, the vote on the Brady amendment reflected both party and constituency forces. And for many members, it was a relatively "easy" (nonconflictual) vote, since the party's strength is greatest in nonmetropolitan areas, where the gun culture and the NRA are most likely to thrive.

For the Democrats, the issue was troublesome and divisive. The leadership itself was divided. A

Americans love their guns. But the real reason that it has been so difficult to adopt meaningful gun control legislation is that the National Rifle Association is an exceptionally powerful Washington lobby. Advocates of strict gun controls have had only limited success in organizing popular support for their position—even though most Americans agree with them.

narrow majority of the party (58%) ultimately supported the provision. Southern Democrats were strongly opposed to it, while eastern and western Democrats were most in favor of it. Among northern Democrats, big-city members gave the most support to the waiting-period provision, while members from rural and small-town areas, where sportsmens' groups and the NRA are strongest, were most likely to oppose it. The Brady amendment was defeated by a "conservative coalition" vote—that is, by a majority of voting southern Democrats and a majority of voting Republicans arrayed against a majority of voting northern Democrats.

Source: *Time,* April 20, 1981, p. 22; *Congressional Quarterly Weekly Report,* September 17, 1988, pp. 2620–2621.

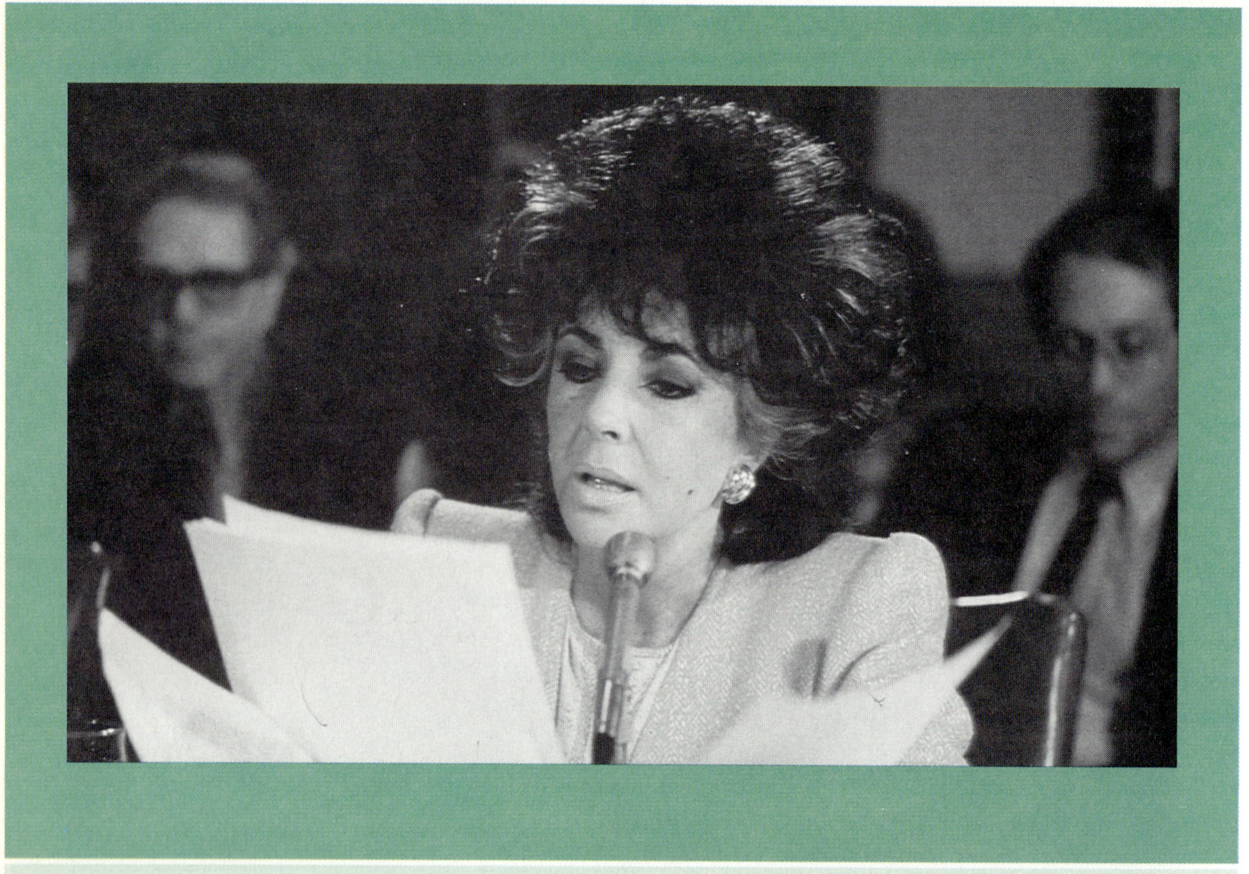

Actress Elizabeth Taylor testifies before a congressional committee on the need for federal programs to combat the AIDS menace. Celebrity witnesses get the attention of members of Congress just as they do the attention of the general public.

Direct lobbying involves services as well as requests. Major lobbies can assist legislators by generating data, developing justifications, producing material for speeches and documents, devising strategies, mediating with other groups, forming coalitions, and drafting legislation. Their services and counsel can help a member "look good" to colleagues and constituents—no small contribution to politicians. The problems interest groups pose for legislators are thus somewhat offset by the resources they make available. *Quid pro quo,* Latin's most useful expression in politics, sums up the relationship.

Groups build support for their positions by forming alliances with other groups. Business organizations such as the Chamber of Commerce often ally with farm organizations such as the American Farm Bureau Federation. Liberal groups join with organized labor to press for social welfare legislation. Conservative groups rally to the side of the American Medical Association to resist federal health care programs. Craft and other unions link up with construction, auto, and trucking trade associations—"strange bedfellows" in other circumstances—to promote federal highway programs.

Alliances are not hard to understand. They are the product of a shared ideology or a willingness to engage in *logrolling*—where one group supports another in return for future support for its own program. Like legislators, groups know that logrolling is often the surest way to splice together a legislative majority.

Logrolling usually ends up in trading votes to advance certain interests. Members expect reciprocity. When threatened by an amendment that would eliminate tobacco sales from the Food for Peace program, a Kentucky House member criticized the amendment's sponsor, a Colorado member representing a district distinguished by its sugar-beet production:

> I recall distinctly that last week, when sugar was in trouble . . . about 20 states which produce tobacco marched right down the road with that gentleman. They do not produce any sugar beets . . . or sugar cane in Kentucky. But when sugar is in trouble, sugar beets and sugar cane, the people in Kentucky are concerned about it.[28]

Interest groups require access to decision makers—the opportunity to present their case. Campaign contributions in the form of funds, workers, and organizational talent open the door for them. Campaign gifts by group political action committees are especially important in financing political campaigns (see Chapter 12). In 1988, nonparty PACs representing corporations, labor, and other organizations contributed $148 million to congressional candidates. Overall, House and Senate incumbents received about eight times as much in PAC funds in 1988 as their challengers.[29] The heightened importance of PACs in financing congressional campaigns is shown by the data of Figure 10–2.

PACs reward their friends and punish their enemies. For many PACs, the principal objective in making contributions is to gain access to officeholders. They care more about officeholders' voting records than about their ideologies. To the dismay of Republicans, many business PACs contribute heavily to Democratic candidates for Congress, because they expect them to win. A key lobbyist for the American Trucking Association makes the point:

> Our local people are businessmen and enamored of the Reagan administration. We'll want to support a guy and they'll say, "Don't do it. He's so left he meets himself coming around." We keep telling them that we can't afford a political philosophy. We'll buy a ticket to anyone's event as long as he didn't vote the wrong way on trucking issues.[30]

The election process, then, is a key point of interaction between interest groups and politicians, particularly legislators. The director of the Washington office of the AMA describes the group's efforts in this way: "We try, and always have tried, to influence the Congress by electing people that we agree with rather than influencing the Congress by buying votes." Thus it is no surprise to find AMPAC, year in and year out, among the leading PAC contributors to congressional candidates. Indeed, a study by Common Cause disclosed that almost 90 percent of the members of a recent Congress had received campaign funds from national and state medical associations. "The major edge that the AMA has as a lobbying group,"

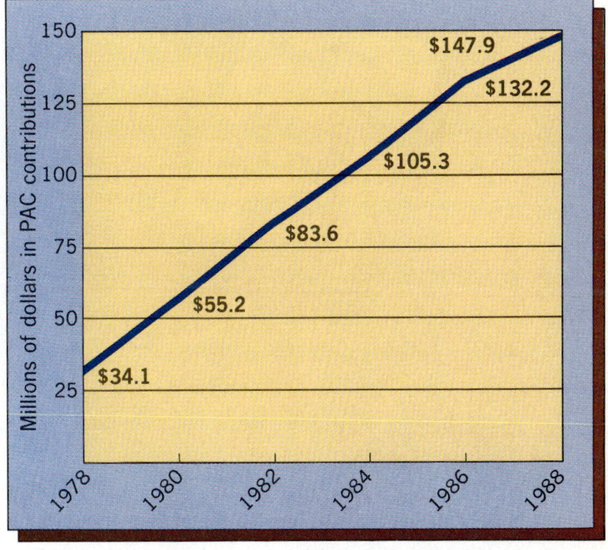

Figure 10–2 PAC contributions to House and Senate candidates, 1978–1988. Source: press releases of the Federal Election Commission, issues of May 10, May 21, 1987, and February 24, 1989. The proportions of congressional candidates' total receipts from PACs were 17 percent in 1978, 22 percent in 1980, 24 percent in 1982, 26 percent in 1984, 28 percent in 1986, and 31 percent in 1988.

observes a member of the House, "is their enormous edge in the amount of contributions they make." [31]

Direct lobbying can include bribes and threats. Both occur, but they are not common. Bribery is risky for all the participants, and not many groups are powerful enough to threaten a legislator with defeat at the polls. Some groups spend money in negative campaigning designed to defeat legislative candidates, but this practice is declining in importance. The vast majority of groups prefers to contribute to candidates who share their values.

Political money has become a major problem in American politics. One veteran Ohio congressman who chose retirement over raising $250,000 for his reelection campaign said: "If you take that dough, you're an ingrate or obligated, and either one is an unsatisfactory position to be in." [32] A recent survey by the Center for Responsive Politics, a Washington research group, reported that about 20 percent of the members of Congress acknowledge that their votes on legislation have been influenced by political contributions.[33]

Finally, groups try to influence government through marches and demonstrations in the capital. Washington has become a "demonstration city" for all kinds of groups—small, large, ragtag, well organized. Who goes there to demonstrate? Almost everyone, it seems: bird watchers (concerned about the preservation of wetlands for nesting), chiropractors (who want their services covered by national health insurance), coal miners, Iranian students, Tibetan-Americans (concerned that their passports list Tibet rather than China as their place

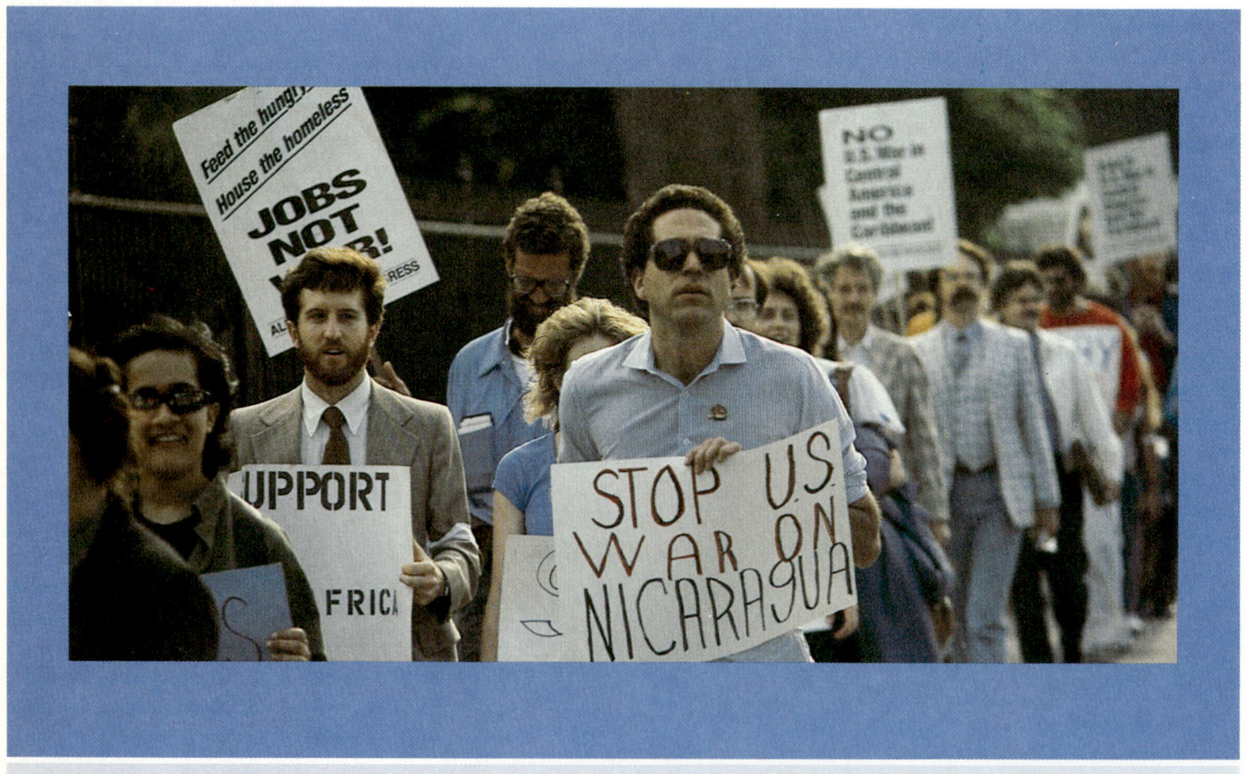

Protests may be organized around a single issue or an assortment of issues. Participants in this march focused on certain foreign policy questions and on the plight of the homeless. Demonstrators hope to convince the broader public to join their "conflict."

“Perspectives”

On Campaign Finance: Is There a PAC Problem?

Political money has long been a troublesome issue in American politics. Currently, the major controversy centers on the heavy flow of PAC money into congressional campaigns. To curb PAC influence, proposals have been introduced to restrict the total amount of such funds that congressional candidates are permitted to accept (perhaps, for example, to $100,000 for House candidates over a two-year election cycle) and to reduce the amount that can be contributed to a candidate per election (now $5000). These proposals thus far have not made much headway. One reason is that congressional Republicans are opposed to these and other limitations, such as spending "caps" or public financing, because they believe that Republican challengers will be unable to defeat Democratic incumbents unless they are able to spend heavily. Another reason, simply, is that members of Congress evaluate PACs in sharply different ways, as these observations show:

“*PACs facilitate the political participation of hundreds of thousands of individuals who might not otherwise become involved in the election of an individual.*”

—Senator John W. Warner (R–Va.)

“*I don't worry about being bought, because I'm not for sale. The truth is I am proud of the PACs and the people who support me.*”

—Senator Phil Gramm (R–Tex.)

“*If you're not able to fund your campaign and keep your responsibility to the people who send you here, you don't belong in office.*”

—Congressman John D. Dingell (D–Mich.)

“*It is fundamentally corrupting. At best, people say they are sympathetic to the people they are getting money from before they get it; at worst, they are selling votes. But you cannot prove cause and effect. I take the money from labor, and I have to think twice in voting against their interests. I shouldn't have to do that.*”

—Congressman Richard L. Ottinger (D–N.Y.)

“*There's a danger that we're putting ourselves on the auction block every election. It's now tough to hear the voices of the citizens in your district. Sometimes the only things you hear are the loud voices in the three-piece suits carrying a PAC check.*”

—Congressman Leon E. Panetta (D–Calif.)

“*I fear we could become a coin-operated Congress. Instead of two bits, you put in $2,500 and pull out a vote.*”

—Senator Barbara Mikulski (D–Md.)

Sources: *Washington Post*, December 5, 1985; *Congressional Quarterly Weekly Report*, December 7, 1985, p. 2568; *Congressional Quarterly Weekly Report*, March 12, 1983, p. 504; *Congressional Quarterly Weekly Report*, March 12, 1983, p. 504; *Time*, March 3, 1986, p. 35; quoted by Larry J. Sabato, *PAC Power: Inside the World of Political Action Committees* (New York: W. W. Norton & Company, 1985), p. 126.

of birth), gays, pacifists, Nazis, bicyclists (who want to bring their bikes into government buildings), farmers (aboard their tractors no less), anarchists, senior citizens, marijuana advocates, equal rights supporters, American Indians, proabortionists, antiabortionists, Marxists, Maoists, religious fundamentalists, Strippers for Christ, and the blind (who want to carry their canes onto airplanes). And that is but a short list. In one recent year, 677 demonstrations took place on the White House sidewalk alone—a symbolic piece of real estate that measures 34 feet by 746 feet. For most groups, demonstrations probably do little to help their cause. Their behavior, in fact, may irritate officials. An antiabortion or equal rights rally that draws 70,000 to 100,000 participants, though, is not so easily dismissed. Politicians can count.[34]

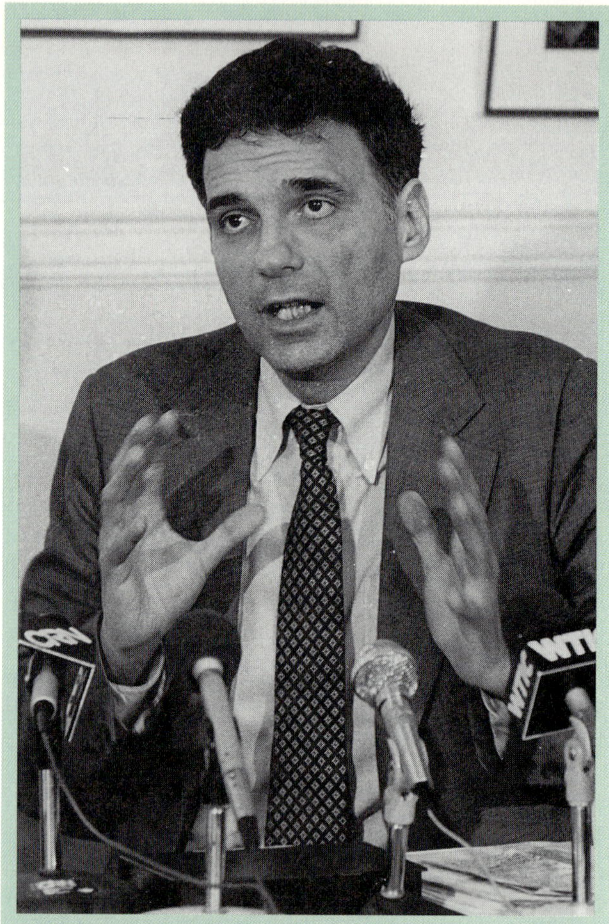

Best known among the lobbyists of the "public interest" genre is Ralph Nader, the consumer advocate. Nader gained prominence in the 1960s by writing a book highly critical of automobile safety standards. Since then he has created a number of organizations, composed mainly of idealistic young professionals and students ("Nader's Raiders"), to do research on public policy questions and to lobby for legislation to protect consumers and the environment.

Indirect Lobbying

Indirect or grass roots lobbying is the other major technique. It seeks to influence government decisions by working through the public—a roundabout but effective approach. The aim is to educate the public or instruct a special clientele through ads in the media, targeted communications, literature mailings, speeches, press releases, editorials, news accounts, and films. Public relations firms often play a large part in orchestrating grass roots campaigns. In recent years, broad-scale campaigns have been waged to convince the public that the energy crisis can be eased if the oil industry is encouraged in its explorations and if government regulation is relaxed, that coal gasification legislation can help solve America's energy problems, and that a trigger-price mechanism (to raise the minimum price at which steel can be imported) can revive the domestic steel industry.

The grass roots efforts of the United States Chamber of Commerce, probably the most respected business lobby, reveal how local pressure is typically organized:

> Four of its lobbyists in Congress watch the progress of each bill that is worrying businessmen, then send an alert when a key legislative action is approaching. The word goes quickly to 1,200 local Congressional Action Committees with some 100,000 members. Through the Chamber's various publications, the alert soon reaches 7 million people. Thus when Washington headquarters signals an "action call"—the time for besieging members of Congress with letters, telegrams, and phone calls—the membership is ready to move. . . .

The Chamber also mans six regional offices in which some 50 operatives study the quirks and pressure points of Senators and Congressmen from their area. They pinpoint what the Chamber calls "Key Resource People," who have special local influence with a legislator. It might be a big campaign contributor, college classmate, or law partner. At a critical moment, these regional staffs are told: "Get the K.R.P.s into the act." The regional offices also clip local editorials for pro-Chamber viewpoints and dispatch them to Washington. Two volumes of newspaper clippings were dumped on congressional desks with heavy impact in the Chamber's successful drive to stall passage of the labor reform bill.[35]

Grass roots lobbying is designed to arouse citizens to action ("Write or call your congressperson") or simply to inform and enhance understanding (to gain long-term public support). Legislators generally agree that grass roots lobbying has a major impact on decision making. A member of the House observes:

> I think the thing that perhaps would be different from the [1950s] is that the most effective lobbyists [today] are the ones back home. I think hospital cost containment got beat not by anybody here in Washington lobbying heavily. It got beat by people who were on the boards of directors of various community hospitals back home who personally wrote you a letter or called you on the phone or stopped by to see you. I think this is indicative that on certain issues, the administration, any administration, is going to have a tough time if the local constituency is in any way, shape, or form organized because of the congressmen being more constituent oriented than party oriented.[36]

Used to the intricacies and expense of advertising, major business groups find grass roots lobbying quite effective. They dominate this form of lobbying. In the view of the president of the Chamber of Commerce of the United States, "it is the only lobbying that counts." [37]

Lobby Impact

Simple and easy to apply, devil theories of politics attract many people. The devil theory of interest groups holds that public officials are under the thumb of powerful lobbies. Government, in this view, is a conveyor belt for moving benefits to private groups in quest of some advantage. In truth, the relationship is much more complex.

First, legislators and bureaucrats come to office with well-developed value systems, conceptions of "good" public policy, established followings, partisan orientations, and minds of their own. Their inclination (or freedom) to respond to the claims of organized groups is thus limited in some measure.

Second, groups win, lose, and draw in their attempts to influence government. Few groups enter any struggle over policy or its implementation thinking they will get exactly (or even most of) what they want. One truth about American government is that public policies usually reflect compromises and trade-offs; most relevant interests gain something and few are completely shut out. Sometimes, of course, the collisions result in a standoff in which there are no policy changes.

Third, public policies are subject to change. A lobby (or lobby alliance) that wins one year may lose the next time around. Losers in the struggle have every reason to look for reinforcements and to intensify their efforts to reverse the settlement.

Fourth, legislators and lobbyists often work together to gain policy objectives. Legislators call on lobbyists for research assistance, advice, and aid in mobilizing support on legislation. What is more, they are not reluctant to ask for campaign contributions. "The amount given," observes a spokesman for the AFL-CIO's Committee on Political Education, "is directly proportional to the amount of pressure he puts on you. You know, they always say they're in trouble." [38]

Fifth, the impact of lobbies is often subtle; it is not easily detected by either insiders or outsiders. Studies of Congress have shown that lobbies are not often successful in *converting* members from one position to another. Trying to change the mind of a staunch opponent is usually a waste of time

"Senator, according to this report, you've been marked for defeat by the A.D.A., the National Rifle Association, the A.F.L.-C.I.O., the N.A.M., the Sierra Club, Planned Parenthood, the World Student Christian Federation, the Clamshell Alliance . . ."

and resources. Hence, lobbies concentrate on *activating* and *reinforcing* members already sympathetic or leaning in their direction. And they take pains to present their case to members who are undecided.[39] All in all, most public officials are probably less vulnerable to interest group pressures than is generally thought. As Congressman Morris K. Udall (D–Ariz.) observed: "A lobbyist can get a bad name around here if he tries to mislead you." [40]

Still, there are many illustrations of interest group victories. By any standards, groups have been successful in protecting (and enlarging) government programs that benefit their clienteles. *Entitlement* programs—under which recipients are legally entitled to benefits from earlier acts of Congress—now represent (by one estimate) nearly 75 percent of the total federal budget. This "uncontrollable" spending (outside the immediate control of Congress) appears in numerous policy areas: defense (retired military personnel pay), agriculture (farm price supports), health (Medicare, Medicaid), income security (old-age and survivors' insurance, disability insurance, civil service retirement, food stamps, unemployment insurance, child nutrition), and veterans (compensation and benefits, readjustment benefits). A major result of entitlements has been the formation and promotion of groups to protect them. Government policies spawn as well as nourish interest groups.

The impact of entitlement programs on federal spending is enormous. In 1967 entitlement spending totaled less than $100 billion; in 1988, spurred in part by inflation, it had grown to more than $500 billion. In medical care, entitlement spending grew from $1 billion in 1965, the year Medicare was enacted, to more than $80 billion in 1988. Any attempt by Congress to reduce entitlements meets fierce opposition by recipient groups. "You've got constituencies that are built into these programs," observes a member of the House Budget Committee. "The reality of it is that you aren't going to cut them off."[41] Nevertheless, entitlement spending stabilized during the Reagan administration.

The effect of lobbying on congressional voting behavior is not easy to measure. Voting decisions on major issues are highly complex. If Congress decides to change the way it does business—establishing ethical codes and financial disclosure requirements for members, open committee meetings, and caucus election of committee chairs—is it simply responding to the demands of reformers, in particular Common Cause? For some members, perhaps. If Congress increases price supports for

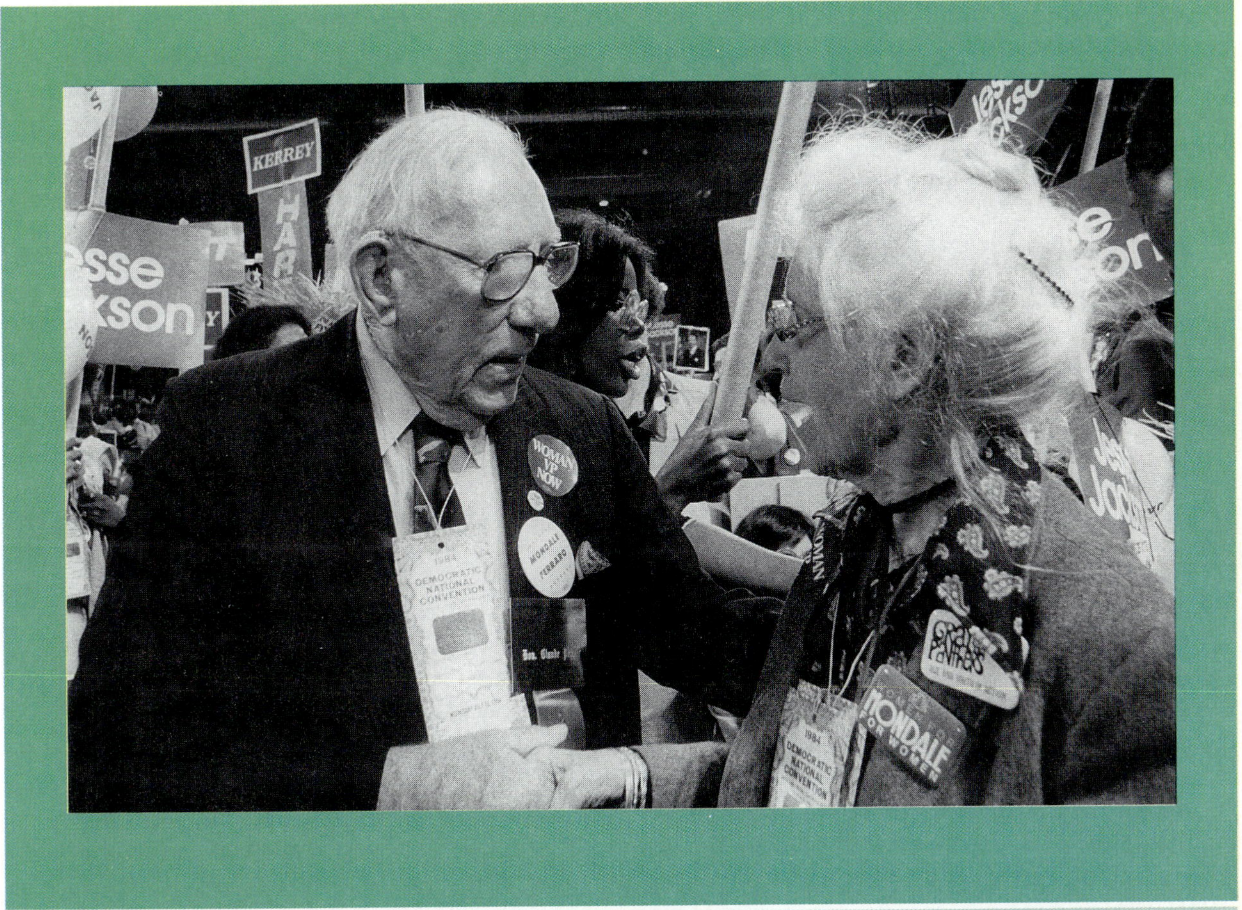

As their numbers have increased, elderly people have become a major political force in American politics. Their leading spokesperson for years was Representative Claude Pepper of Florida, shown in this photo with Maggie Kuhn of the Gray Panthers, an advocacy group for the elderly. When Representative Pepper died in 1989, Congress adopted a resolution providing that the body of this champion of the poor and the elderly would lie in state in the Capitol Rotunda—the highest final honor an American can receive.

sugar and allows direct cash subsidies for sugar farmers, are members merely doing the bidding of the well-organized sugar lobby? For some members, perhaps. If Congress adopts legislation to expand Medicare to provide insurance against catastrophic medical expenses, is it simply currying favor with senior citizen, welfare, labor, and social service organizations? For some members, perhaps. If Congress approves the production of MX missiles, is it simply yielding to heavy pressure from the White House, major MX contractors such as Northrup Corporation and Rockwell International, and aerospace workers? For some members, perhaps. If Congress passes a bill to raise the minimum wage, is it simply capitulating to the demands of the AFL-CIO, other unions, and various church, women's, and civil rights groups? For some members, perhaps. Usually, however, the explanations for votes are considerably more complicated—for reasons noted above and elsewhere (see Chapter 12).

The Regulation of Interest Groups

The First Amendment to the Constitution establishes a firm basis for the activities of political interest groups. "Congress shall make no law," it reads, "abridging the . . . right of the people . . . to petition the Government for a redress of grivances." Petitioning is a basic right of citizens. It is also a key feature of free societies. Hence, not many individuals want to tamper with it—not even those who believe that groups have too much influence in American politics.

How to regulate interest groups without violating the First Amendment has been a persistent public policy problem. One solution is the Federal Regulation of Lobbying Act passed by Congress in 1946. Under its terms, any person or group that solicits, collects, or receives money for the *principal* purpose of influencing congressional decisions on legislation must register with the clerk of the House of Representatives or the secretary of the Senate. In addition, a group must account for its receipts and expenditures. It must file quarterly reports on its lobbying activities, showing, among other things, salaries, expenses, and the proposed legislation it supports or opposes. Many states have adopted similar laws.

The thrust of the 1946 law is clear: to provide control through *public disclosure.* Intrusions on group life are minimal. In upholding the law's constitutionality, the Supreme Court observed that Congress "wants only to know who is being hired, who is putting up the money, and how much."[42]

Few laws have been criticized more than the 1946 disclosure act. For one thing, no agency is charged with its enforcement; thus, there are few prosecutions. Some groups have simply ignored it. Second, the law is vague about the kinds of lobby-legislator interactions that represent lobbying. Third, the act is limited to Congress; it exempts lobby efforts to influence the executive branch. And, most important, the law applies only to individuals and groups whose *principal* purpose is to influence legislative decisions through *direct contacts* with Congress. Groups that concentrate on *grass roots* lobbying are exempt from the registration and reporting requirements.

The 1946 act, as the saying goes, is "more loophole than law." For example, American Telephone & Telegraph, the nation's largest corporation, does not have a single *registered* lobbyist under the law. AT&T contends that its governmental affairs employees in Washington lobby only as a "supplementary activity" and thus are excluded by the "principal purpose" definition.[43]

The lobby law reform issue will neither go away nor be easily settled. At times in the last decade, each house of Congress passed a new lobby law only to see it lost in the other chamber. Who should be required to register? Congress is unsure; it cannot agree on what kinds of lobbying or levels of lobbying activity to illuminate. Should organizations that interact with government but have no paid lobbyist be required to register? Should those that engage in grass roots lobbying be subject to the act? Should groups that lobby the executive branch be covered? Would it be good policy to require groups to disclose their internal operations (including identification of their contributors)?

“ Perspectives ”

On Lobbying

“*Everybody in America has a lobby.*”

—Thomas P. (“Tip”) O'Neill, former Speaker of the U.S. House of Representatives

“*Without lobbying government could not function. The flow of information to Congress and to every federal agency is a vital part of our democratic system. But there is a darker side to lobbying. It derives from the secrecy of lobbying and the widespread suspicion, even when totally unjustified, that secrecy breeds undue influence and corruption.*”

—Joint statement on a lobby disclosure bill by Senators Edward M. Kennedy, Dick Clark, and Robert Stafford

“*I probably spend at least 25 percent of my time listening to lobbyists. A good lobbyist will never try to mislead you on the impact of a proposal, or he immediately loses his credibility.*”

—Former Congressman James C. Corman

“*. . . made me look smart in front of my colleagues. He kept feeding me information on the performance and cost advantages of the F-18—sometimes practically on the House floor—so I could sound off during the debate.*”

—Former Congressman Jim Lloyd

“*It's tough to finance a race without accepting PAC money. If you go out and run for office, it's terribly expensive. . . . One of my objections to PACs is that a candidate inevitably has to turn to them.*”

—Senator Larry Pressler

“*Representative government on Capitol Hill is in the worst shape I have seen in my sixteen years in the Senate. The heart of the problem is that the Senate and the House are awash in a sea of special-interest lobbying and special-interest campaign contributions.*”

—Senator Edward M. Kennedy

“*We've moved a long way since the days when it was all long green. By and large, lobbyists are more ethical and more sophisticated than ever before.*”

—Former Congressman Richard Bolling

Sources: *Time,* August 7, 1978, p. 15; *U.S. News & World Report,* July 25, 1977, p. 30, Copyright 1977, U.S. News & World Report, Inc.; *Business Week,* February 12, 1979, p. 130; *Nation,* November 18, 1978, pp. 537, 538; *U.S. News & World Report,* July 25, 1977, p. 32, Copyright 1977, U.S. News & World Report, Inc.

Will strict reporting requirements be too burdensome, especially for small organizations? And troubling all discussion is this issue: How much regulation is compatible with the free speech and petition guarantees of the First Amendment?

Interest groups are not outlaws in the political system. It is important to recognize not only the problems they create, but also their contributions. First, they represent the views of citizens. Second, they serve an educational function; they inform the public about government and the government about group and constituent preferences. Third, they help to set the government's agenda by illuminating new or persistent problems. Fourth, they offer expertise in public policy analysis. Fifth, they contribute imagination and energy to the political process. Sixth, by entering the policy-making process, they help put together the majorities needed to make decisions. Seventh, their attention to government activities improves the prospect that officials will give careful thought to their decisions.

The main problem of interest groups is thus not their existence, but their excesses. Probably the only satisfactory way to diminish unwholesome pressure politics is to choose officials who will observe customary standards of rectitude and to give them information to evaluate groups and their claims. Solutions to the problems of a democracy, of course, are never complete, neat, or orderly.

Summary

- Groups are a natural outgrowth of a free society; they are an important instrument for the representation of citizen opinions and values. Most Americans belong to at least one group, and many belong to several. The right of groups to participate in politics is assured by the First Amendment.
- American government invites the vigorous participation of groups. Many points of access are available to them, which is the result of federalism, the separation of powers, weak political parties, and decentralized legislatures. The dispersal of power in legislatures is particularly advantageous to groups concerned with defense of the status quo, since a bill can be sidetracked or defeated at any stage in the legislative process.
- The influence of groups extends to all branches of government. Groups that are unable to get favorable outcomes from the legislature or the executive may get relief from the courts.
- The most powerful groups are organized around broad economic interests, particularly business, labor, and agriculture. Certain single-issue groups, however, such as the National Rifle Association, are highly successful in influencing government.
- Groups engage in both direct and indirect (grass roots) lobbying. Only the direct lobbying of Congress is covered by the Federal Regulation of Lobbying Act. Although lobbies and lobbyists are satisfied with the limited scope of this act—and they lobby to protect it—most outside critics and many members of Congress regard it as inadequate. Efforts to write a new lobby law are sure to continue, and to be met with opposition.
- Lobbying is a reciprocal relationship. Interest groups seek favorable decisions from government officials, who in turn use groups to advance their own objectives. Legislator-lobbyist relations are particularly complex: Who is leading and who is being led are not always clear, perhaps not even to the participants.
- Organization is power. Large, well-financed organizations have a great advantage in the struggle over government policy and its implementation.

Readings on Interest Groups

Bauer, Raymond A., Ithiel de Sola Pool, and Lewis A. Dexter. 1963. *American Business and Public Policy: The Politics of Foreign Trade.* New York: Atherton Press. An imaginative study of the role and influence of business organizations on foreign trade policy.

Berry, Jeffrey M. 1977. *Lobbying for the People: The Political Behavior of Public Interest Groups.* Princeton, N.J.: Princeton University Press. A study of the organization and activities of public interest groups.

Milbrath, Lester W. 1963. *The Washington Lobbyists.* Chicago: Rand McNally. A detailed study of the various types of Washington lobbyists and the bases of their influence.

Olson, Mancur. 1971. *The Logic of Collective Action: Public Goods and the Theory of Groups.* Cambridge, Mass.: Harvard University Press. Considers the irrationality of joining groups and the resulting "free rider" problem.

Ornstein, Norman J., and Shirley Elder. 1978. *Interest Groups, Lobbying, and Policymaking.* Washington, D.C.: CQ Press. A description of Washington lobbying practices based on several case studies, concluding with an evaluation of suggested reforms.

Sabato, Larry J. 1985. *PAC Power: Inside the World of Political Action Committees.* New York: Norton. A treatment of the nature and impact of political action committees.

Schattschneider, Elmer E. 1960. *The Semi-Sovereign People: A Realist's View of Democracy in America.* Hinsdale, Ill.: Dryden Press. A classic interpretation of the strategies used by "losers" in political conflicts.

Schlozman, Kay Lehman, and John T. Tierney. 1985. *Organized Interests and American Democracy.* New York: Harper & Row. Interviews with Washington lobbyists.

Stern, Philip M. 1988. *The Best Congress Money Can Buy.* New York: Pantheon Books. A popular account of interactions between political action committees (PACs) and members of Congress.

Truman, David B. 1951. *The Governmental Process: Political Interests and Public Opinion.* New York: Alfred A. Knopf. A classic study of the influence of interest groups.

Chapter 11

Mass Media Politics

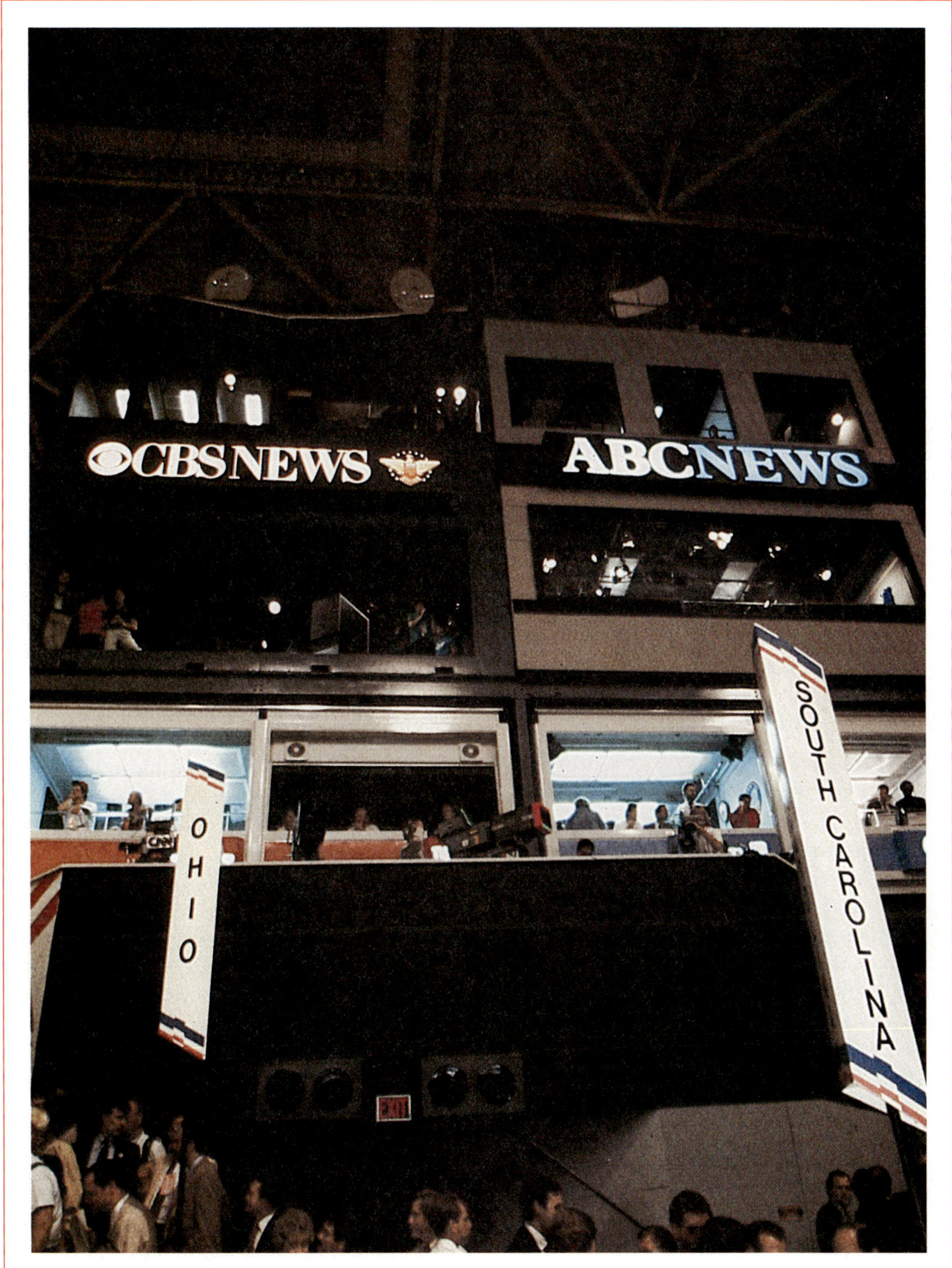
CBS NEWS
ABC NEWS
OHIO
SOUTH CAROLINA

Democracy is a political system rooted in consent: The authority and legitimacy of popularly elected governments are derived from expressions of consent by the governed. No political system places a greater burden on its people. Democratic citizens are expected to judge whether candidates share their outlooks and values on public questions, to evaluate public events they have seen and experienced, to take account of the performance of their leaders, and, through elections, to enforce accountability by empowering or removing public officials.

In a democratic system, the public shapes, in broad contour, what politicians profess and what governments do. Politicians and voters share a complex relationship, as V. O. Key, Jr., observed:

> If politicians perceive the electorate as responsive to father images, they will give it father images. If they see voters as most certainly responsive to nonsense, they will give them nonsense. If they see voters as susceptible to delusion, they will delude them. If they see an electorate receptive to the cold, hard realities, they will give it the cold, hard realities.[1]

The mass media are central to the study of democratic politics because citizens require information to make political judgments. The mass media—newspapers, magazines, television, and radio—provide it. At the same time, they provide a means by which political leaders can communicate with their respective publics. To a significant extent, the media decide which issues will be given major attention and the terms under which they will be considered.

Commentators sometimes describe the print and broadcast media as the "fourth branch of government," suggesting that they rival the legislative, executive, and judicial branches in importance.[2] This chapter will show that there is much to be said for this view.

The influence of the mass media in American politics is assured by the broad declaration of the First Amendment: "Congress shall make no law . . . abridging the freedom of speech, or of the press. . . ." State and local governments are similarly restrained as a result of the Supreme Court's "incorporation" of First Amendment guarantees into the Fourteenth Amendment. (See Chapter 4.)

The right of freedom of speech and press is not absolute. News organizations can be sued by individuals for libel and slander or prosecuted by the government for the publication of material judged libelous, obscene, or seditious or of material ("fighting words") that incites persons to acts of violence. For its part, the Supreme Court steadily has sought to protect the maximum freedom of the press by construing these terms narrowly. Libel suits against a newspaper or magazine, for example, are rarely successful. Press criticism of the government and of public officials (or of public figures generally) is entitled to constitutional protection unless convincing evidence is available that the comment was false, made "with knowledge that it was false or with reckless disregard of whether it was false or not."[3]

This broad protection of the right to criticize public figures—the Sullivan rule—was reaffirmed and extended in 1988. A mock advertisement in *Hustler* magazine had portrayed the Reverend Jerry Falwell, a Baptist television preacher, as an incestuous drunk dallying with his mother in an outhouse. Despite the gross and repugnant cast to this parody, the Supreme Court overturned a decision to award damages to Mr. Falwell for reasons of "emotional distress."[4] Concretely, this ruling means that even wildly outrageous and degrading statements are protected by the free speech–free press guarantees of the First Amendment. The Court's opinion clearly offers substantial protection for editorial writers, cartoonists, and political commentators.

Constitutional protection for the media is also afforded by the Supreme Court's unwillingness to tolerate censorship—any attempt by government to exercise a *prior restraint* on expression. Plainly, American democracy owes much to the judiciary's history of zealous protection of the right of individuals and of the press (both print and broadcast media) to the open expression of opinion. At the same time, the public has known, intuitively as well as empirically, that a free press is indispensable for enforcing responsibility on government officials.

Ownership and Regulation of the Media

Private Ownership

The mass media in the United States are, in the main, privately owned enterprises. Apart from the restrictions imposed on them by libel and antitrust laws, newspapers and magazines enjoy virtually complete freedom from government regulation. Indeed, government subsidizes these businesses to an extent through favorable postal rates. Anyone who can afford to do so is free to launch a newspaper or magazine. By contrast, radio and television operate within a framework of public regulation. The airwaves are a public resource, and broadcasters must obtain a license—in effect, an exclusive privilege—to operate on a specific frequency. Unlike the print media, radio and television cannot function simply as profit-making enterprises; they must also meet certain public interest standards.

The telecommunications industry is not completely private. Under the Public Broadcasting Act of 1967 and subsequent legislation, federal, state, and local funds are made available to support public, noncommercial radio and television stations, particularly to promote innovative, cultural, and public affairs programs.

Concentration of Ownership

One way to describe the American political system is to say that it is *pluralistic.* Political resources, such as money, supporters, and access to the media, are distributed among competing interests. In a pluralistic system, public policy is shaped through bargaining and compromise among competing and shifting interests.

No one claims that a pristine form of pluralism characterizes American democracy. Political power is not distributed equally, and large concentrations of economic resources are present in society. The media are a particularly good example of the concentration of ownership among a limited number of individuals and corporations.

The decline of diversity in media ownership is a paramount fact today. The single publisher who owns a newspaper or the individual broadcaster who owns a radio or television station can still be found, mainly in small-town America, but their numbers have been reduced. Other forms of media ownership are more important. It is common to find single owners of a chain of 20 or 30 newspapers. Cross-media ownership—for example, the ownership of newspapers and television stations—is even more common. The well-known *Chicago Tribune* is only one of 61 media outlets owned by the Tribune Company. The New York Times Company owns 30 newspapers and an assortment of radio stations, television stations, and cable outlets. The nation's principal radio stations are owned by ABC, CBS, NBC, and other conglomerates such as Westinghouse.

Ownership concentration is even more pronounced in the television industry. ABC, CBS, and NBC each owns five television stations serving an audience of some 47 million households in the largest media markets. In addition, the three networks supply about 65 percent of the programming of their local affiliates. Most televised information seen by viewers everywhere is thus based on the choices of network personnel. The networks' parent companies also own a wide range of other media enterprises, including publishing houses, recording companies, movie theaters, and the like.[5]

The great majority of newspapers depend heavily on news stories supplied by the reporters of the Associated Press (AP) or United Press International (UPI). Wire service stories dominate national front page news in virtually all papers; in some papers wire accounts make up three-fourths of all stories. The wires also originate much of the day-to-day domestic news for national television news programs. Wire dependency is a major feature of contemporary journalism.[6] It contributes to the homogeneity of the news, regardless of the newspaper or the section of the country, and limits independent reporting. Only the largest and best-known news organizations, such as the *New York Times* or the *Wall Street Journal,* can afford to assign reporters to "beats" in Washington, other centers of government, or abroad.

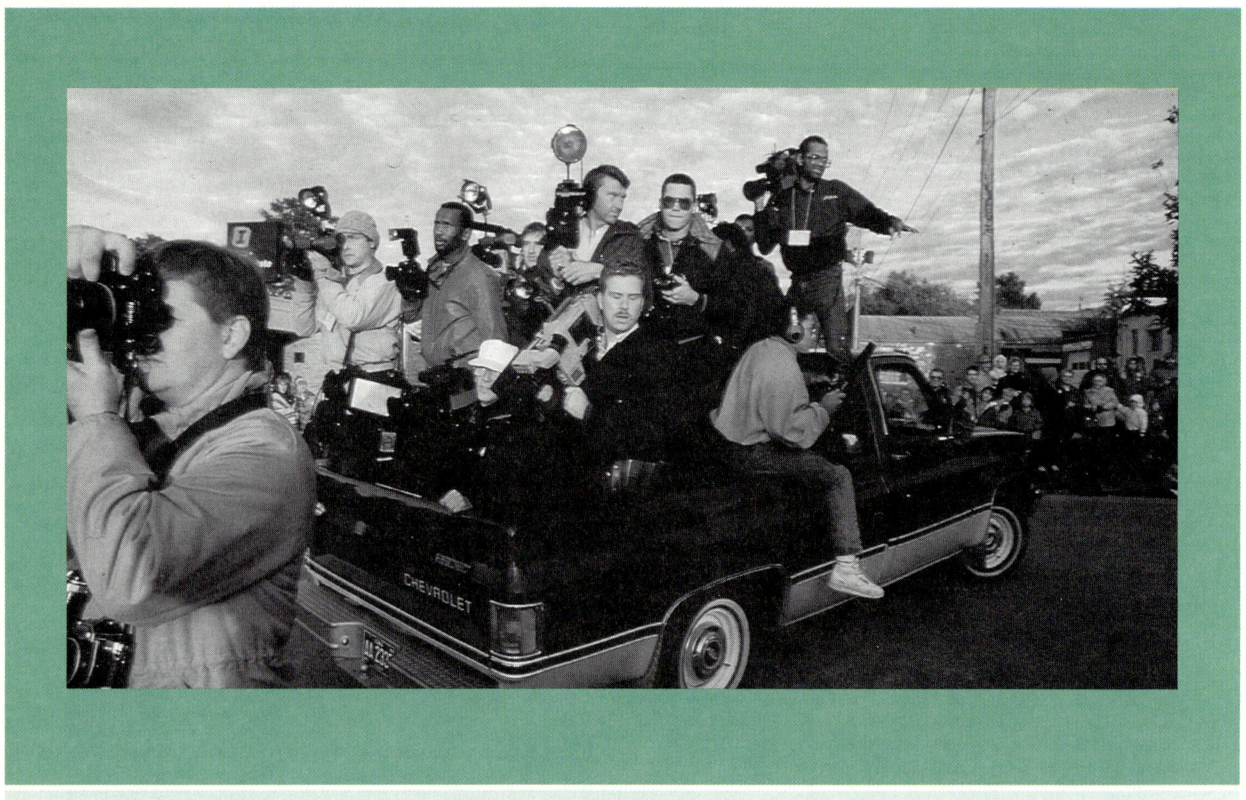

A familiar sight in presidential campaigns: a pack of reporters in search of an interesting photograph of the candidate. After so much time in each other's company, they end up with just about the same photos—and the same views of the campaign. Pack journalism is today a key feature of political reporting.

The media business is big business. The broad consequences of concentrated ownership, linked to minimal regulation, are difficult to establish, but the pattern raises important questions. Staunch conservatives tend to worry about "monopoly power" in the media, while liberals typically are concerned about the public's access to diverse viewpoints.[7] Close observers wonder whether the lack of competitiveness leads to distortions in information and to the manipulation of the public. They also view skeptically the marked uniformity in programming as well as its imbalance stemming from a preoccupation with commercially attractive programs at the expense of public affairs. The media's political power, real and imagined, is an issue that will not go away.

Government Regulation of the Electronic Media

Control over the electronic media rests with the Federal Communications Commission (FCC), created by Congress in 1934 to "serve the public interest, convenience, and necessity." To promote diversity in broadcasting, and thus diversity in the public's information sources, the FCC is empowered to limit the number of stations controlled or owned by a single organization. No corporation, for example, can own more than one radio station or one television station in a single media market; and under FCC rules on cross-media ownership, no person or company can own both a television station and a daily newspaper in the same market.

The FCC occasionally provides exemptions to these rules. In addition, a single person or single company can own a maximum of 12 AM radio stations, 12 FM radio stations, and 12 television stations—an impressive total, nonetheless.

Licenses must be renewed by the FCC every five years for television stations and every seven years for radio stations. In examining renewal applications, the FCC is expected to evaluate whether a station has used the public's property, the airwaves, in a satisfactory manner. Has the station's programming, for example, reflected the needs and interests of the community at large and also those of selected local groups? Has the station allocated sufficient time to public affairs? In point of fact, these and other public interest guidelines are loosely defined, and the performance of stations is not rigorously examined. Hence, it is not surprising that only a few stations ever have had their licenses withdrawn. Typically, license renewal comes easily and automatically.[8]

Numerous court decisions make it clear that newspapers and magazines enjoy virtually complete control over what they will print (or will not print). On the other hand, because they are semi-monopolies, the electronic media operate under different and more generous rules of public access. The two most important access rules have been the equal-time provision and the fairness doctrine.[9]

Equal Time. No station is obligated to make broadcasting time available to political candidates. Section 315 of the Communications Act of 1934 specifies, however, that once a station gives or sells time for campaigning to one candidate for office it must provide the same opportunities to all other candidates seeking that office. To escape the equal-time rule, and thus to maintain internal control over programming, some stations elect not to accept any campaign broadcasts. Currently, the FCC permits the arrangement of television debates among candidates without regard to the equal-time provision; stations can thus exclude minor or fringe candidates from participation.

Fairness Doctrine. From 1949 to 1987 the FCC enforced a regulation requiring broadcasters to observe standards of fairness in return for the privilege of using the nation's airwaves. The doctrine stipulated that broadcasters had to devote a reasonable share of their programming to issues of public importance and, second, to ensure fair coverage of them by including contrasting viewpoints. Fairness, of course, was often difficult to define in specific cases, and many broadcasters believed that the doctrine interfered with their freedom. One unintended result of the rule was that broadcasters tended to shun the discussion of controversial issues because they knew they would face pressure for air time from groups with opposing views. Compliance with the fairness rule would thus affect the station's "bottom line," since the time for regular income-producing programs would be diminished. To some extent the fairness doctrine was softened by FCC regulations (and court rulings) that a station's obligations could be met by airing opposing views in regular news programs.

The fairness doctrine nevertheless has been anathema to the media. The broadcasting industry's long campaign of opposition was vindicated by a federal appeals court ruling in 1986 that the FCC could repeal the fairness doctrine without congressional approval. Seeking to prevent the FCC from abandoning the doctrine, Congress approved legislation in 1987 to put it into law. Democrats in both houses voted overwhelmingly for the law. It was promptly vetoed by President Reagan on the grounds that it was "antagonistic to the freedom of expression guaranteed by the First Amendment." He held that the regulation was unnecessary because of the recent "explosion" in the number of media outlets, which increased opportunities for the expression of diverse and contrasting views on controversial issues.

In late 1987, and in tune with the president, the FCC abolished the fairness doctrine, stating that it was no longer necessary for the protection of free-speech rights. But the issue is not dead. Supporters of the policy continue efforts to reinstitute it through a court challenge to the FCC decision and through legislation. There are both liberal and conservative groups unhappy with deregulation. Broadcasters contend that the new era of deregulation will lead to greater diversity in programming and to enhanced protection of freedom of the press. They assert that a fairness law is unnecessary because broadcasters have "operated at the same high level [as] print journalists."[10] Fairness advocates believe deregulation will lead commercial broadcasters to favor revenue-producing "soaps" and "sitcoms" over public affairs programming, to the exploitation of the public's airways for private profit, and to a constriction of opportunities for public discourse and the expression of contrasting viewpoints.[11] (Repeal of the fairness rule does not affect the FCC's equal-time rule, which governs the allocation of airtime to political candidates.)

The Media and the Public

Mass Appeal

The media are a dominant force in American life. More than 80 percent of all households watch television during the prime-time hours. The average person watches television more than 30 hours a week; households average more than 7 hours a day. About 50 percent of the public regularly watches the news on television. About 80 percent of the people listen to the radio on weekdays. Daily newspaper readers are found in more than 60 percent of all households.[12] America's 1700 daily newspapers have a circulation of over 60 million.

The data confirm what one would suspect. The media appeal to virtually everyone, regardless of age, gender, or status. But certain distinctions can be drawn. Older persons are much more likely than younger ones to view television news and to read newspapers. And social class makes a difference. Better educated and wealthier individuals are much more likely to be newspaper readers than persons with limited education and low-paying jobs. Persons of lower SES (socioeconomic status) watch television news programs in larger numbers than persons of higher SES.

Skepticism and Ambivalence

Television created and depends on "couch potatoes." But the medium does not rank particularly high in public esteem (see Table 11–1). People who have little or no confidence in television are about as numerous as those who have high confidence in it; each group makes up about one-fourth of the public. About half of the public reports only "some" confidence in the "tube." Newspapers fare only slightly better in the public's appraisal. Younger persons, the less well educated, and low-income persons have more confidence in television than their counterparts at the upper end of the scale. And college graduates, professionals, businesspersons, and those with higher incomes trust newspapers more than television.

The public's skepticism toward the media contrasts sharply with its assessment of other institutions. Currently, nearly two out of three Americans express a high level of confidence in the church and the military. About one-half of the public sees the Supreme Court, the banking system, and the public school system in a favorable light. Newspapers, television, and organized labor bring up the rear—less than one-third of the public ex-

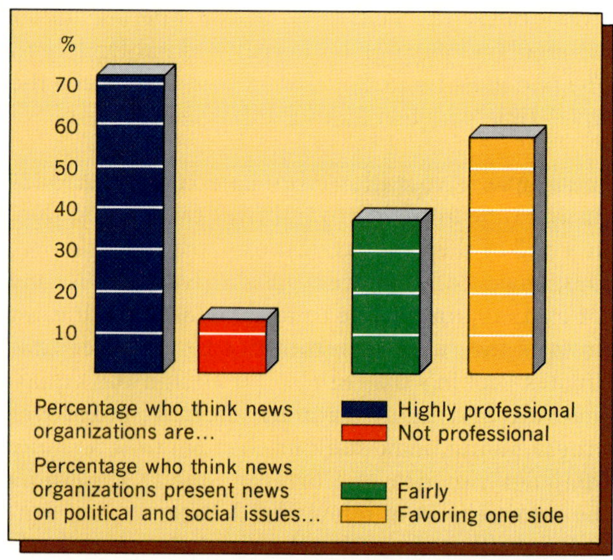

Figure 11–1 The public's perception of the professionalism and fairness of news organizations. Source: adapted from *The People and the Press* (Los Angeles: Times-Mirror, 1986), pp. 6–7. The survey was taken in 1986.

TABLE 11–1

The American Public's Confidence in Television and the Press

	Great Deal or Quite a Lot		Very Little or None	
	Television	**Newspapers**	**Television**	**Newspapers**
National	28%	31%	27%	22%
Age				
18–29 years	33	38	24	19
65 and older	28	32	28	18
Education				
College graduates	19	33	33	20
Not high school graduates	36	28	22	22
Occupation				
Professional and business	24	32	34	23
Blue collar	29	31	25	22
Income				
$40,000 and over	20	29	33	22
Under $15,000	35	31	22	22

Source: *Gallup Report,* August 1987, pp. 8–9 (as adapted). The remainder in each category consists of those people who expressed "some" confidence in television and the newspapers.

presses substantial confidence in these institutions. These patterns are long-standing.[13]

About three-quarters of the public believe that news organizations are "highly professional" (see Figure 11–1). They are seen as organizations that care about the quality of their work. Perceptions of their performance, however, are quite different. Nearly three out of five people believe that reporting is politically biased, thus contributing to a credibility gap. The broad conclusion to be drawn is that the public has a generally favorable attitude toward the news media (print and broadcast) but dislikes their practices.[14] The thrust of the "news" is thus worth exploring.

Characteristics of the News

American news covers a bewildering variety of subjects. Under the right circumstances, virtually any happening can qualify as news and virtually any person can make the news. But there are nevertheless standard patterns of newsworthiness. Doris Graber contends that American news tends to focus on events that are novel and entertaining, that highlight familiar people and situations, and that emphasize conflict and violence.

Partiality: Novel and Entertaining

News personnel instinctively favor stories that are novel and entertaining. Stories in endless procession feature political and personal misadventures, natural and human-made disasters, personal tragedies and triumphs, bizarre and unexpected events, celebrity activities, and ostensibly high-drama occurrences. Preoccupation with novelty and entertainment leads to news stories that stress the trivial aspects of serious developments and the present rather than the past. Complex issues—inflation, unemployment, poverty, disease—are often treated in terms of personal stakes and misfortunes.[15]

As themes in the presentation of American news, novelty and entertainment have never been checked by a condition of popular satiety. This standard cast to news troubles critics. Consider these views from an article published in the *Saturday Evening Post* more than half a century ago (1927):

> And as affairs get harder to understand, the newspapers print relatively less about them, rather than more, because they are harder reading and their subscribers mostly want easy reading. Whatever other objects the newspaper editor may have in mind, attracting readers is his first object. If he gives them, the year through, ten columns of sports and five columns of comic strip to every quarter column of local political affairs—which is probably a very liberal estimate—it is because he has found out that their day-by-day interests run in about that proportion. There is no point in blaming the newspapers.[16]

Partiality: Familiar People and Situations

Those who organize the news also prefer stories that involve familiar people and situations. One result is that coverage is circular. News about familiar people makes them even better known and thus even more newsworthy: news stories beget news stories. Well-known politicians (and "their" agendas) thrive in this information environment, unless scandal is involved, while lesser-known ones struggle for public attention. And second, the news is more parochial than it would be otherwise. A public preoccupied with daily living does not have to work as hard to understand familiar and similar events within its own borders as it does to understand distant and foreign news.

Partiality: Conflict and Violence

Finally, attentiveness to certain kinds of stories is reflected in a heavy emphasis on conflict and violence. Stories of crime, bombings and rioting, assaults, assassinations and murders, investigations, indictments and convictions, and a miscellany of personal calamities crowd the pages of the typical newspaper and the format of television and radio news. Particularly in the big city media and network broadcasting, news is bad news, news is high drama. Coverage of foreign news commonly focuses on violent events. The consequences of the media's hyperattentiveness to conflict and violence are hard to gauge. Doris Graber argues that it leads to a damaging distortion of reality, to the perception that violence is an appropriate way to settle disputes. Political groups may behave violently to obtain news coverage and publicize their cause.

Neglect of Persistent Problems

Media leaders have never believed that public tastes are the only valid criteria for the selection of news. But it sometimes appears this way, and there is no mistaking the fact that the media place heavy emphasis on stories that entertain. Many feel that news organizations neglect the analysis of complex and persistent social, economic, and political problems. Clean water, the argument runs, becomes a news item only when there is a major oil spill, the status of prison conditions only when there is a violent riot, foreign policy only during failures such as the arms-for-hostages Iran-contra scandal. "Stories emphasize the surface appearances, the furious sounds and fiery sights of battle, the well-known or colorful personalities involved—whatever is dramatic," write David L. Paletz and Robert M. Entman. "Underlying causes and actual impacts are little known or long remembered."[17]

Coverage of Political News by Newspapers and Network Television: Similarities and Differences

Both the print and broadcast media have an unabashedly practical aim: to gain and hold an audience (and thus attract advertisers). And, of course, they share other characteristics. A study of news media coverage of presidential campaigns by Michael J. Robinson and Margaret A. Sheehan found that print (represented by the UPI wire service) and network television (represented by CBS) are quite similar in three major respects. First, both are generally committed to "objective reporting" (focusing on observable facts and events, while declining to take explicit positions on candidate qualifications or to draw conclusions or inferences about the events being covered). Second, both tend to emphasize the "horse race" (or competitiveness) aspect of campaigns; "who's winning" evaluations account for almost all of the explicit conclusions drawn by the media. And third, both the wires and networks are generally balanced and generally fair in their treatment of candidates and parties in terms of providing shares of news space and steering clear of partisanship in accounts (though "losers" and minor parties fare poorly in both print and television news).

Differences between the two in campaign reporting nevertheless are substantial. As contrasted with the print media, network television news is:

> *more personal* (more inclined to focus on candidate behavior—especially blunders, gaffes, and scandals);
> *more mediating* (more inclined to tell the audience what the candidates are "up to," not simply what they are doing—in other words, translating rather than transcribing);
> *more analytical* (more inclined to explain and interpret events and behavior);
> *more political* (more inclined to politicize news by portraying leaders as "politicians");
> *more critical* (more inclined to be critical and negative in the treatment of candidates); and
> *more thematic* (more inclined to focus on storytelling, combining various news items into overarching, and perhaps melodramatic, themes).[18]

In political campaigns, particularly in the opening phase, the press sets the media agenda of campaign coverage. As columnist Albert R. Hunt of the *Wall Street Journal* has observed, "Television producers and correspondents scour the newspapers for political insights; the reverse rarely occurs." Once the stories appear in the press, television latches on and dominates the dialogue. Its ascendancy is unmistakable when campaigns are well under way.[19]

Calamities and media coverage go hand in hand. In 1989 the tanker *Exxon Valdez* struck a reef in Alaska's Prince William Sound, releasing 11 million gallons of oil into the water and creating incomparable problems for the environment. While the media are able to show, as here, a cleanup crew at work following the worst oil disaster in U.S. history, the illumination of persistent problems is much more difficult. News commonly needs a "handle."

In the view of Robinson and Sheehan, the networks have developed a new form of campaign reporting:

> While the wires still provide information (who, what, where, when), the networks increasingly offer instruction (why and how). And above all, the networks treat all aspects of politics

> more negatively and critically. . . . In traditional journalism, the news is evidential, detailed and generally respectful. But in network journalism, the news about politics and politicians is more inferential and hostile. Traditional print continually spits out fact-laden news. Much more often network journalism presents a short story, complete with moral.[20]

Journalists themselves see major problems in newsgathering. A study of Washington reporters by Stephen Hess found that reporters believe that too much time is spent on breaking news, that too little time is spent in researching stories, and that news accounts too often focus on personalities. But clearly the most serious problem in newsgathering, as they see it, is the phenomenon of *pack journalism.* As members of the pack, reporters cover the same events, interview the same people or read the same handouts, pool their information, try out interpretations, and write similar stories. Pack journalism imparts a national character to news and, to an extent, shapes the national agenda. It also gives a homogeneous cast to the news while dimming the independent judgment of reporters. No one, including editors, wants to be out of step. The most troublesome aspect of pack journalism is that majority perceptions and interpretations may turn out to be wrong.[21]

Journalists and Their Work

Backgrounds

American journalists are not any closer to representing a cross section of the public than any other national elite. In the main, journalists representing the most prominent national media outlets—such as the *New York Times, Washington Post,* and the television networks—are highly educated white males raised in upper middle-class homes. They are the sons of professionals and businesspeople. Many come from the metropolitan areas of the Northeast, few from small-town middle America. Reporters in this rarefied group commonly make six-figure salaries, while top television anchors make over $1 million annually. The *Washington Post* now requires its reporters and editors to file financial disclosure statements, a sure sign of their "arrival." [22]

At the top of the media heap are the profession's celebrities—reporters who are newsmakers themselves. Recognized wherever they go, they are front-page news when they renew their contracts, switch to another outlet, retire, or encounter some personal problem. A 10-minute "shouting match" (as described by the *New York Times*) between Vice President George Bush and Dan Rather, the CBS news anchor, on live national television was a highlight of the 1988 presidential campaign. People who missed this bristling encounter involving the vice president's role in the Iran-contra affair and his allegations of unfair treatment by CBS could read about it in virtually every newspaper throughout the country the next day. It was front-page news because prominent newscasters are as important as the politicians they cover. The incident also helped to teach the public this key truth: Television news is show business as well as journalism.

Survey data on the ideology and policy views of a sample of journalists, other professionals, and the general public are shown in Table 11–2. This study by the *Los Angeles Times* reveals that journalists are more than twice as likely as the typical voter to see themselves as liberals; in the journalistic fraternity itself, liberals outnumber conservatives by a margin of over three to one. The liberalism of newspeople is pronounced in the case of social issues, such as abortion and school prayer.[23]

The Charge of Political Bias

Does the liberalism of newspeople matter? Does it lead to biased news accounts? A recent national survey finds that about 80 percent of the public perceive an ideological cast to the press. And more important, almost half of the public now perceive the press's political stance to be in conflict with their own. This perception is twice as likely to be held by conservatives as by liberals. The dominant popular view thus holds that the press sides with liberal causes. Among conservatives, there is

TABLE 11–2

The Ideology and Policy Views of Journalists and the General Public

	Public	Journalists	College-Educated Professionals
Ideology			
Consider self			
Liberal	23%	55%	38%
Conservative	29	17	30
Social issues			
Allowing women to have abortions			
Favor	49	82	68
Oppose	44	14	28
Prayer in public schools			
Favor	74	25	58
Oppose	19	67	36
Hiring homosexuals			
Favor	55	89	68
Oppose	31	7	24
Stricter handgun controls			
Favor	50	78	63
Oppose	41	19	34
Economic issues			
Government regulation of business			
Favor	22	49	26
Oppose	50	41	57
Government aid to those unable to support themselves			
Favor	83	95	81
Oppose	11	3	12
Government should reduce income inequality			
Favor	55	50	56
Oppose	23	39	24
Foreign affairs			
Verifiable nuclear freeze			
Favor	66	84	79
Oppose	22	13	17
Increase defense budget			
Favor	38	15	32
Oppose	51	80	63

Source: *Public Opinion* (August/September 1985), p. 7 (as adapted).

a widespread belief that press criticism keeps political leaders from doing their jobs. Strong conservatives appear to be particularly suspicious of television network news departments.[24]

In elections, the liberalism of the media elite translates into support for the Democratic party's candidates. At least 80 percent of the leading journalists typically support Democratic presidential candidates.[25] Among journalists representing the nonprominent media, support for Republican candidates is somewhat higher.[26]

The data on this liberal connection do not necessarily speak for themselves. Evidence that reporters slant the news to conform to their political views is elusive. There are several reasons for believing that systematic political bias is not a problem. First, the liberalism of reporters may be counterbalanced by the conservatism of editors. Editorial endorsements are much more likely to go to Republicans than to Democrats—in about the same proportion in every presidential election. In the four presidential elections between 1972 and 1984 (winners Nixon, Carter, Reagan, Reagan), according to surveys by *Editor and Publisher,* 86 percent of all daily newspapers making candidate endorsements supported the Republican nominee.[27] Second, media leaders are sensitive to their reading (or viewing) audiences and to advertisers, political leaders, and stockholders. Their clientele expect impartiality and evenhanded treatment. Third, tight deadlines and space limitations militate against the introduction of ideological bias in news accounts. And fourth, the professional standards of journalism prescribe that news events be treated

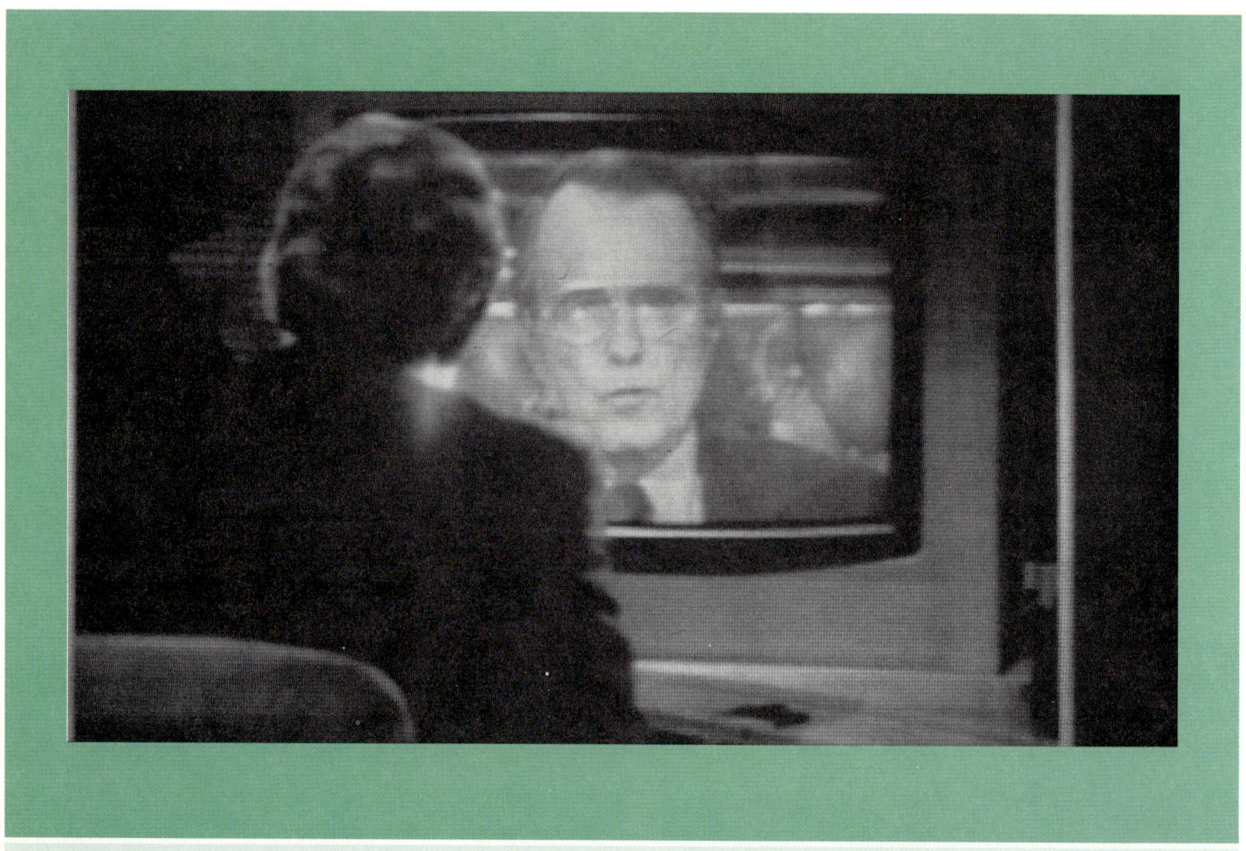

The most spectacular confrontation of the 1988 campaign: the Dan Rather–George Bush "interview."

" Perspectives "

On the Media

"*Instead of promising All the New's That's Fit to Print, I would like to see us say . . . that the newspaper that drops on your doorstep is a partial, hasty, incomplete, inevitably somewhat flawed and inaccurate rendering of some of the things we have heard about in the past 24 hours—distorted, despite our best efforts to eliminate gross bias, by the very process of compression that makes it possible for you to lift it from the doorstep and read it in about an hour.*"

—David S. Broder

"*The problem of journalism in America proceeds from a simple but inescapable bind: journalists are rarely, if ever, in a position to establish the truth about an issue for themselves, and they are therefore almost entirely dependent on self-interested "sources" for the version of reality that they report.*"

—Edward J. Epstein

"*In the past two decades, those of us in the press and television have undergone a startling transformation. . . . We have moved from the sidelines to a place at the center of the action. Inevitably we have become subjects of hot controversy among ordinary people, political leaders, and even in the courts. Inevitably also we have experienced a tension between what we are supposed to do and what we actually do—between myth and reality. This inner tension finds relief in a self-serving creed or ideology—the ideology of the First Amendment. And that ideology implicitly stakes the imperial claim—the claim that what is good for the media is good for America.*"

—Joseph Kraft

"*Television has the large vice of its own great virtue, which is that it is a visual medium and poorly suited to the transmission of ideas.*"

—Lou Cannon

"*A serious discussion of an important issue rarely will get much air time. Network television producers' eyes glaze over at the mere mention of a proposal to address the international debt situation or a welfare program or military reform.*"

—Albert R. Hunt

"*I think television is afraid of being dull.*"

—Peter Jennings

"*[The] modern campaign is mass marketing at its most superficial. It puts a premium on the suggestive slogan, the glib answer, the symbolic backdrop. Television is its medium. Candidates must have razzle-dazzle. Boring is the fatal label. Programs and concepts that cannot be collapsed into a slogan or a thirty-second sound bite go largely unheard and unremembered, for what the modern campaign offers in length, it lacks in depth, like an endless weekend with no Monday morning.*"

—Hedrick Smith

Sources: David S. Broder, *Behind the Front Page* (New York: Simon & Schuster, 1987), p. 14; Edward J. Epstein, *Between Fact and Fiction: The Problem of Journalism* (New York: Vintage Books, 1975), p. 3; Joseph Kraft, "The Imperial Media," *Commentary* (May 1981), p. 36; Lou Cannon, *Reporting: An Inside View* (Sacramento: California Journal Press, 1977), p. 64; Albert R. Hunt, "The Media and Presidential Campaigns," in *Elections American Style,* ed. A. James Reichley (Washington, D.C.: The Brookings Institution, 1987), pp. 57–58; Martin Schram, *The Great American Video Game: Presidential Politics in the Television Age* (New York: William Morrow, 1987), p. 58; Hedrick Smith, *The Power Game: How Washington Works* (New York: Random House, 1988), p. 693.

fairly and objectively. The importance of objectivity is ingrained in the journalism student and the cub reporter. What is more, they learn as journalists that they have fewer problems if they "play it straight." They know their reputations are on the line, and none wants to be simply dismissed as a partisan.

Some critics believe that the news is too objective. Preoccupation with this standard inhibits journalists, it is argued, keeping them from moving beyond direct observation and from drawing logical inferences from the events witnessed. Political campaign reporting in particular is inhibited by the norm of objectivity.[28]

Structural Bias ■

The belief that political bias pervades the news has lived long and dies hard. It is perhaps the major complaint lodged against the media. Academic analysts believe that political bias in the media, whether liberal or conservative, is not really the problem, or surely not the main problem.

Bias exists in television news, Austin Ranney argues, but it is less political than structural bias. As portrayed on television, politics is a game in which individual politicians struggle for advantage and power. Conflict and argument dominate political activity. The focus of reports, moreover, centers on individuals, usually in competition with one another. When the news must deal with organizations, convenience and the medium's pictorial requirements (as well as the economic imperative to hold an audience in an industry of intense competition) lead inexorably to concentration on individuals. Organizations must be personified in newscasts. "Thus, television presents a political party's national nominating convention not as another of a long series of occasions in which the party has met and chosen its standard bearers," says Ranney, "but as this year's contest among candidates, faction leaders, and special interest leaders, with little reference to the past or future."[29]

A study of the Washington press corps by Stephen Hess offers additional support for the thesis of structural bias. Washington reporters appear more as apoliticals than as partisans. "The slant of Washington news," he writes, "is more a product of the angle from which it is observed than from ideology."[30]

In their study of the presidential election campaign of 1980, Robinson and Sheehan found that the evening television news, as contrasted with newspapers, was "less objective, less descriptive, and less respectful of the people and events they covered." But they also concluded that the majority of television news stories were balanced, based closely on sources, and fair. They found no evidence of partisan bias, issue bias, or normative statements.[31] Consistent with the structural bias interpretation, both broadcast and print media "were often superficial, were sometimes petty, and were generally geared to covering events and people instead of institutions, formal process, or public policy."[32]

Consider the presidential campaigns. To begin, the media focus on mainstream candidates and give scant attention to those on the extreme right or extreme left. At most these candidates are "curiosity" figures.[33] Subjective choices enter in other ways. Attuned to the standard of newsworthiness, editors decide which (mainstream) candidates' campaigns warrant full or limited coverage as well as which campaign events should be reported or ignored. And they make decisions to treat some state primaries or caucuses as more important than others. The news *agenda,* in other words, may very well reflect bias.

Structural bias is pronounced in television's decisions on political coverage. For example, of about 100 debates between candidates for the presidency in the 1988 nominating season, only one was televised by a commercial network (NBC). Interestingly, even though this debate received a relatively low viewer rating, its audience was ten times larger than audiences for any of the other debates shown only on public or cable television.[34]

Bias also emerges in the media's preoccupation with negative news, especially in broadcast journalism. In reporting on candidates and campaigns, there is no contest: bad news crowds out good news, regardless of the candidate's party or ideology. A "bad press" simply goes with the territory—"over the long haul the national press is biased against everybody, but in near equal proportions."[35]

"When you quote a Presidential candidate, Gorman, you do not—I repeat—do not roll your eyes."

Reporters do more than transmit news. As Sam Donaldson, ABC's White House correspondent for many years, observed: "So when I ask a question, I think it's important to challenge the president, challenge him to explain policy, justify decisions, defend mistakes, reveal intentions for the future, and comment on a host of matters about which his views are of general concern." [36] Journalists see themselves as "the public's watchdog over government." [37] Or as the late syndicated columnist Joseph Kraft wrote:

> The more august the person the hotter the chase. The more secret the agency the more undiscriminating the attack. The general assumption of most of my colleagues, and I do not suppose I am much of an exception, is that behind every story there is a secret, and that every secret is a dirty secret.. . . Not only have we traded objectivity for bias, but we have also abandoned a place on the sidelines for a piece of the action. We have ceased to be referees and drama critics and become players in the game and actors on the stage.[38]

Although any politician is fair game for skewering, one type attracts unusually heavy criticism: the incumbent, especially the incumbent president. The president has both responsibilities and a record—each an invitation to media scrutiny. The press comes "closest to raw political power," Robinson and Sheehan observe, "when it criticizes to an ever increasing degree the incumbent president. But seemingly, it does that with little regard for the philosophy or politics of the incumbent." The added reality is that this thrust is also negative: "the press tends to unmake incumbents, not make successful candidacies." [39]

A similar account can be sketched in the domain of public policy. In the role of watchdog, the media have a persistent bias in illuminating policy failures rather than policy successes.[40] Failures

Geraldine Ferraro, Democratic vice presidential candidate in 1984, found that troubling problems for her husband and her son preoccupied the media, at times making it impossible for voters to focus on the public policy issues raised in her campaign. Voters also lost sight of her historic role as the first woman major-party candidate for national office. Twenty-first century voters are certain to see women as major party candidates for the presidency and vice presidency.

make more interesting stories. Successes tend to be quiet, more difficult to measure, and at the same time less likely to qualify as "hard news." The job of the journalist is "not to make it easier for government to make and carry out its policies, but to probe deeply and tirelessly into what government is really doing so that the people will know." [41] The media's antiestablishment bias, reflected in pervasive suspicion of individual and organizational power, leads them to focus on decisions and policies that go awry.

Structural bias is a major feature of the media's coverage of the news, and its repercussions are substantial. Evidence suggests that the major news sources, especially the networks, have played a crucial, if unintended, role in the public's growing disenchantment with American politics. As Robinson and Sheehan see it, "Network reporters do seem to want to make the public more aware of the frailties and inadequacies of their elected leadership. . . . If there is one clear-cut example of media power in the age of television news it must be the networks' contribution to our increasing political malaise." [42]

Media bias is a popular issue. But there are other more important aspects of media influence. The interests of political scientists center on two key questions: What is the impact of the media on the political process, especially in terms of political parties, campaigns, elections, and careers? What is the impact of the media on government and public policy? These are difficult questions to answer. Any analysis must lean on scattered evidence, well-reported events, reasonable surmise, and the assessments of close students of the media. Even though the evidence is thin, there is more to these arguments than just imaginings.

Media Impact on the Political Process

Agents of Conflict Expansion

In weighing the political role of the media, it is important not to overlook the obvious: The print and broadcast media have become the principal agents for the expansion (acceleration or enlargement) of political struggles and conflict. "The central political fact in a free society," E. E. Schattschneider wrote, "is the tremendous contagiousness of conflict."[43] Everyone looks for help. Expanding the scope of conflict requires visibility and publicity—the domain of the media.

The media search for news wherever it can be found, and not because they have an axe to grind or a conflict they wish to exploit. Once the media focus on an issue, a candidate, or an officeholder, conflict expansion is inevitable. News spreads, the audience gets involved, people take sides, alliances form, and decisions are made. Nothing looks quite the same in the new media light. Local controversies and new information are transformed into major issues of national concern—sometimes in a matter of hours. And they play out only when the media say they are played out.

The contagiousness of conflict is dramatic. Consider the impact of the media on careers. A presidential candidate wins an unexpected victory (or makes a surprise showing) in an early caucus or primary state; the candidate immediately becomes the center of media attention as well as its grateful beneficiary: free press, free TV, free hype. Momentum takes over. Another presidential candidate engages in an extramarital fling, disclosed as a result of a newspaper stakeout in Washington, and is quickly forced out of the race. Still another candidate bows out following media disclosure (leaked to the press by a rival's campaign manager) of plagiarism in his campaign speeches and, earlier, in law school papers. Upon questioning, a nominee for a Supreme Court seat admits to earlier use of marijuana and withdraws in a rush. An on-air confrontation between a network anchorman and the vice president of the United States leads to an explosion of antimedia resentment ("media bashing") and turns out to be a boon to the vice president's campaign for the Republican nomination. Inquiries into a vice presidential candidate's background disclose that he joined the National Guard during the Vietnam War, thereby avoiding the draft, and that issue drowns out all others, dogging his campaign week after week. The power of the media to make or break careers is matchless.

Conflicts spread because the media pick them up and pick them apart. In pursuit of news and without intention, the media both build an audience for conflict and dramatically assist in its expansion. In a word, the media are active participants in the political process.

Types of Candidates Chosen

Every institution accumulates a distinctive lore. In the cache of media lore is the belief that television has a major impact on the types of candidates who are successful.[44] Candidates for major offices, observers say, have to "come across"—to be able to talk effectively (naturally, informally, conversationally) to their audience. To instill confidence, ideally, they need to look impressive, be telegenic, reflect warmth, appear to be in command, and appear to be sincere. Television deals in appearances, and appearances count.

The media are crucial because campaign coverage turns on "personalization." Candidate style, candidate behavior, and candidate issues are key elements in influencing voters. Image dominates popular perceptions. A nationwide survey by the Hearst Corporation in 1988 found that the single most important standard for judging presidential candidates, chosen by 41 percent of the voters, was honesty.[45] Because voters set great store by this quality, or in reality the appearance of it, the candidate's personality and style must somehow exude it. Some candidates reflect desirable personality qualities, such as honesty and sincerity, better than others. One of the chief reasons for Michael Dukakis's loss to George Bush in 1988, countless political writers opined, was his image impression among voters—his "coldness" and lack of "likability." All this is consistent with the wry observation of columnist Marquis Childs that presidential candidates do not so much "run" for office as "pose" for it.[46]

Media influence also is reflected in the choice of congressional candidates. According to Michael Robinson, there is "a new kind of candidate, a new kind of nominee, and a new kind of incumbent," leading to "a new congressional character—one more dynamic, egocentric, immoderate, and perhaps, intemperate." A new congressional style has emerged, as these harsh observations by a media consultant suggest:

> You look through . . . and you get the guys with the blow-dried hair who read the script well. That's not the kind of guy who'd been elected to [Congress] ten years ago. You've got a guy who is not concerned about issues; who isn't concerned about the mechanics of government; who doesn't attend committee meetings; who avoids taking positions at any opportunity and who yet is a master at getting his face in the newspapers and on television and all that. You get the modern media candidate . . . typical young congressman. . . . He gets elected, he hires a bunch of pros to run his office, sets up a sophisticated constituent contact operation through the mails and through other things. . . . Then he goes out and showboats to get more press so that he gets reelected and is considered for higher office. Those become of much more importance to him than the functioning as a national legislator or part of a branch of government.[47]

Finally, television is firmly linked to the rise of the celebrity candidate. As observed by columnist Hedrick Smith:

> Quite clearly, television has offered a fast track to those with political sex appeal and a knack for personality politics. It has opened the door to celebrities from other walks of life: Jack Kemp, the former Super Bowl quarterback for the Buffalo Bills football team; Bill Bradley, the New York Knicks basketball Hall of Famer; astronaut John Glenn; and regional media personalities such as Jesse Helms, not to mention a Hollywood actor such as Ronald Reagan.[48]

Conduct of Campaigns

"A campaign is not played out anymore so much for people or voters," Peter Hart, a prominent poll taker, recently observed; "it's played out for the media." [49] Candidates and their advisers spend countless hours in shaping plans to gain media attention, establish solid relationships with print and broadcast journalists, and generate favorable stories.

In campaign politics, attracting publicity is one thing, attracting favorable publicity is another. Candidates know that the media's interpretation of events is crucial to their success. In presidential nominating politics, a win is a win is a win—but only if, and to the extent that, the press says it is. Hence, each candidate organization has one or more "spin doctors" on call—aides who offer instant analysis of a campaign event in an effort to shape the interpretation, or "spin," that journalists use in their stories. After the usual presidential debate, for example, spin doctors assemble in the press room to interpret what the reporters have just seen and to explain why and how their candidates "won" the encounter and to amplify or justify their candidates' statements. To some extent they compete with "free spinners"—seasoned political professionals unaffiliated with candidate organizations and sometimes under contract to a television network—who are also on tap to offer their opinions of the debate. Illusion mixes freely with fact and perspective as reporters decide whose spin to buy. Their accounts will in turn deal with who won and why.

Campaign schedules, speeches, and statements all revolve around the media. Candidates fly from one airport tarmac to the next, from one television market to the next, in their quest for press attention and free media time on local television stations. Brief stops are common. During the 1988 nominating campaign preceding "Super Tuesday"—

"Perspectives"

On Reporters and Politicians

"*Reporters are frustrated reformers as television people are frustrated actors. They look upon themselves almost with reverence, like they are protecting the world against the forces of evil.*"

—Julius Duscha

"*Disdain for politicians as unprincipled power-seekers permeates the national media.*"

—S. Robert Lichter, Stanley Rothman, and Linda S. Lichter

"*The candidates this year [1988] proved that, to win throughout the country, they need only treat the media like people with typhoid. Journalists were kept in pens and corralled so far away from the candidate that Bush's press entourage started wearing binoculars. . . . Thus, Bush, and even to some extent Dukakis, succeeded in turning the press corps into an army of stenographers. It would be less expensive if, next time, they could leave the reporters at home and just send their equipment.*"

—Eleanor Randolph

"*The working hypothesis almost universally shared among [television] correspondents is that politicians are suspect; their public images probably false, their public statements disingenuous, their moral pronouncements hypocritical, their motives self-serving, and their promises ephemeral. Correspondents thus see their jobs to be to expose politicians by unmasking their disguises, debunking their claims and piercing their rhetoric. In short, until proven otherwise, political figures of any party or persuasion are presumed to be deceptive opponents. This generalized cynicism toward politicians—who are often called 'frauds,' 'phonies,' and 'liars' in the newsroom—may account for a substantial share of the on-the-air derogation, rather than any partisan politics of the correspondents.*"

—Edward J. Epstein

Sources: Julius Duscha as quoted by Lou Cannon, *Reporting: An Inside View* (Sacramento: California Journal Press, 1977), p. 5; S. Robert Lichter, Stanley Rothman, and Linda S. Lichter, *The Media Elite* (Bethesda, Md.: Adler and Adler Publishers, 1986), p. 115; Eleanor Randolph, "Journalists in Despair over Being Corralled on Campaign Trail," *Washington Post,* November 9, 1988; Edward J. Epstein, *News from Nowhere* (New York: Random House/Vintage Books, 1974), p. 215.

when most of the action was concentrated in the South—some candidates visited five or six states (or more accurately, assorted airports in these states) in a single day, not to see crowds of voters but to secure 20 or 30 seconds of exposure on the local evening news (and, with luck, a snippet on the network news). Candidates who visit a city itself are whisked in and out, there ordinarily only long enough to deliver a speech and, with a television crew present, to shake a few hands at a factory gate or mall. "Photo opportunities" dominate all planning. Whenever possible, major events are scheduled for prime-time television coverage.

The ambiance of presidential campaigns has changed sharply in the new world of videopolitics. Because candidates know that it is difficult to condense their speeches for the evening news programs, they have learned to fashion succinct statements that are virtually certain to catch the attention of producers. Pithiness replaces analysis, in a strategy that focuses on "sound bites," as candidates try to control the content of television reporting. Timing is central. Major policy statements are issued early in the day to improve the chances that network television will pick them up. But that may not do the trick. If they present interesting visuals, minor incidents and disputes still may dominate that day's news.[50] Trivialization of the news apparently is not a problem for most viewers.

The demand of television for news about major campaigns is insatiable. Sometimes no real news is available and sometimes stories are largely contrived. In campaign news, the truth is, significance may not be of significance: if an event produces a good visual, "television is incapable of saying no." Moreover, both candidates and television producers typically skirt the analysis of complicated issues that do not "play well" on the tube. When millions of viewers are watching the networks' evening news programs, Albert Hunt of the *Wall Street Journal* contends, "the medium is at its most superficial." [51]

Television Advertising

Typically, today, the costliest item in major campaigns is television advertising. In an important state primary or caucus, for example, a major candidate is likely to spend between a quarter and a third of a million dollars on television commercials alone. According to New York politicians, it is not unusual for candidate organizations to spend more than $500,000 a week on television commercials in the campaign's closing weeks. Each of the Democratic candidates still in the nominating race at the time of the 1988 New York primary—Michael Dukakis, Jesse Jackson, and Albert Gore—spent between $500,000 and $1 million on television advertising for that crucial primary.[52]

Campaign managers everywhere are accustomed to spending at least half of all receipts for television, and some spend a much higher proportion. U.S. Senate candidates, David Broder estimates, allocate 70 to 80 percent of their funds to paid television, turning them, as one senator put it, into "bag men for the TV operators." [53] One minute of prime-time network advertising now costs almost $250,000.[54] The observations of a prominent New York officeholder, the state comptroller, put the subject in sharp focus: "Television eats money. And the commercials have to be sophisticated, because you're competing with soap and beer commercials. No more candidates with an American flag in the background; the voters go 'click' when they see that." [55]

Television is central to major campaigns because "retail" politics has given way to "wholesale" politics.[56] Candidates do not rely as much on precinct organization as in the past and they have much less time to stand at mill gates, march in parades, or visit an array of plants, businesses, farms, or halls. Another city or state (or airport) is always on that day's agenda. As opportunities for personal visits with voters (including party, civic, labor, and business leaders) have diminished, emphasis has shifted to the wholesale politics of the television commercial, the 15- or 30-second political spot. The mediating function of local leaders, reflected in their assessments of candidates and their interpretations of issues for rank-and-file voters, has atrophied in the face of television dominance.

Television is the new teacher. The fact of the matter is that statewide contests today are nothing quite so much as battles of the airwaves, commercial arrayed against commercial. And negative spots ("comparative advertising," say their users) have become more common. Television ads can be produced overnight to combat the latest one run by the opposition. "The last six weeks is, they throw a grenade, we catch it, throw one back, they catch it," observes a prominent media consultant. "It's a war." [57] The relentless emphasis on negative advertisements in the 1988 campaign undoubtedly was a major explanation for the finding of several polls, shortly before the election, that between half and two-thirds of all voters would have preferred a different set of choices for the presidency.

In the assessment of pollster Lou Harris, Republican spot ads "had an enormous impact" on the outcome of the 1988 presidential election, ranking as more important than any other factor, including the debates, in George Bush's success. The most effective ads portrayed Michael Dukakis as weak on defense, soft on crime, and ineffective in protecting the environment (pollution in Boston Harbor). One Harris survey shortly before the election found that 60 percent of the voters remembered an ad run by the Bush campaign condemning the Massachusetts prison furlough program and featuring a first-degree murderer (Willie Horton, Jr.) who had attacked a couple while on a weekend furlough.[58]

Almost any angle can be exploited in campaign ads. While Speaker of the House, Jim Wright (D–Tex.) once advised his Democratic colleagues to record "testimonials" from constituents who had received assistance from their offices. "The cases," he counseled, "should involve at least some element of drama or human interest. Get about twenty of these little testimonials, schedule them for saturation broadcast in the days immediately prior to the election . . . it will sound as if the congressman has personally helped virtually everyone in town." [59]

Even though many campaign ads contain only vague references to the candidate's position on issues, studies have shown that voters learn more about a candidate's stands from television ads than from television news coverage.[60] That is a striking conclusion. Candidates are familiar with it. What is more, television ads eliminate the risk of gaffes that can occur in live, give-and-take encounters.

Dan Quayle, Republican vice presidential nominee in 1988, speaking at a National Guard convention in St. Louis. The focus of the media on Quayle's service in the Guard during the Vietnam War made that the number one issue of his campaign, often obscuring his positions on public policy.

No participants in contemporary campaigns are more familiar to political insiders than media consultants. And no candidates for major offices feel comfortable without these "hired guns" and assorted "handlers" on their staffs—specialists who know how to win, know the media industry, know the journalists, know the ins and outs of producing television advertisements, know how to gain free media exposure, and know how to present political clients in an attractive light. At times, "managing" the media calls for a strategy of isolating candidates from print and broadcast reporters—as in the case of the hermetically sealed vice presidential campaign of Dan Quayle in 1988. What media specialists practice may be closer to an occult art than to a science, but their work is thought to be indispensable, which places their talents in great demand.

Television gets much of the credit for creating this new and lucrative profession. Media consult-

■ "Meet Willie Horton": the Republican TV commercial that damaged the Dukakis presidential bid. Never could Horton have imagined that his name would become a symbol that the Democratic presidential candidate, who was governor of Massachusetts at the time Horton was furloughed, was "soft" on crime. And were there racist implications in the ad as well, as many charged?

ants now manage most campaigns from top to bottom. They may earn several hundred thousand dollars in a large state campaign since, in addition to their fee of $25,000 to $75,000, they usually receive 15 percent of all money spent to purchase media advertising time. Most consultants work for candidates of only one party.

Linking candidates and consultants resembles a mating dance. Candidates shop for prestigious, high-profile consultants to give luster and credibility to their campaigns, and consultants eye the field of candidates in hopes of signing on with one who can win. The competition among candidates for particular consultants is intense. Candidates want winners. From the perspective of consultants, there is reason to think twice about taking on a long-shot client, but some do. Incumbents pose less risk to the overall winning percentages of consultants. "Incumbents tend to meet the business qualifications more," observes a Republican media consultant, since they offer "a better chance of winning, more certainty of funding, and potential repeat business." A prominent Democratic media consultant offers another view: "The way people establish credibility in this business is very simple. You take on races that are considered to be impossible or very, very difficult, and you win them. Usually you take on the outsiders and you beat the insiders, and then the insiders want you to work for them." Once this dance of calculation and negotiation has ended, the business of selling the candidate begins. Consultants, like candidates, "die" on election night—the swing of a relatively few votes can make or dash a consultant's reputation, just as it can the career of the candidate.[61]

Campaign Dynamics: Horse Races, Front Runners, and Factional Strategies ■

The impact of the print and broadcast media on political campaigns, though inadvertent, is clearly of extraordinary significance. And media involvement is also controversial.

A key charge by critics is that the press and television focus excessively on the competitiveness, or "horse race," aspects of campaigns at the expense of substantive matters, such as the candidates' records and their issue positions. For journalists, horse race stories are easy to generate and easy to report. The public finds them easy to understand. Stories in this mode tell where the candidates have been and where they are going, how crowds and organized groups are responding to them, how politicians size them up, how their strategies have developed, how much money they have raised, how they have dealt with mistakes, who has endorsed them, and, most important, how their campaigns are progressing—that is, who is winning and who is losing.

Drama furnishes the tone for campaign accounts: it is present at the quarter pole, heightened down the back stretch, and dominant in the home stretch; all that is missing for the spectator is a tout sheet and a $2 window. Hyperbole aside, the "race" controls campaign reporting while systematic coverage of issues is downplayed. Complex policy questions are all but ignored by television and by much of the press. The evidence of a variety of studies shows that more than half of all stories on presidential campaigns revolve around hoopla and horse race.[62]

On network news during the crucial first half of the 1988 presidential nominating season—when, for all intents and purposes, all the candidates but George Bush and Michael Dukakis were eliminated—an extraordinary 80 percent of airtime was devoted to horse race stories and only 20 percent to issues. Senator Robert Dole (R–Kans.), one of the campaign's casualties, made these observations on the Senate floor:

> What I witnessed generally on my own campaign plane was an aircraft filled with reporters who became each other's best audience. It was an ultra-insider's game of gossip and nit-picking that turned presidential campaign coverage into trivial pursuits. It was a daily spin from the experts on the state of the campaign, whether it came from a reporter who had been on board for one month, or one stop. . . . Preconceived notions, prewritten stories and premeditated cliches were all confirmed regardless of the facts. And if there was a nice soap opera campaign story out there, it would be kept on the spin cycle for a good week or so. All the while, reporters' necks were craned in the rear of the plane scanning the campaign staff up front for smiles or frowns, or seating arrangements that would somehow reveal the inside story. Meanwhile, the issues disappeared somewhere over Iowa airspace. . . . I just wish I was hounded on the federal deficit as I was on my staff. I just wish I was interrogated about American agriculture as I was about fund-raising. I just wish my voting record was as thoroughly scrutinized as were my wife's personal finances.[63]

The media are also criticized for their preoccupation with the front-runners and their indifference to the other candidates. Horse races and front-runners, of course, go together. The early public opinion polls provide the initial evidence for press and television stories on the front-runners in the presidential nominating race. These early and speculative stories lead to additional coverage of the leaders, even before the first caucus or primary is held. And, of course, the candidates who win or place well in the Iowa precinct caucuses and (or) the New Hampshire primary receive heavy news coverage. A narrow win translates into lopsided victory in terms of coverage in both newspapers and evening news programs. An unexpectedly strong showing by a little-known candidate may catapult him into national prominence—that is the essence of "surprise journalism." [64] Even 15 percent of the vote in a crowded field can sometimes be parlayed into a substantial publicity advantage in the next contest. The candidates who stumble badly in Iowa will receive scant attention from the media and are not likely to be around for long. Their best hope is to surprise the media in New Hampshire by doing better than expected; poor showings there are likely to end their campaigns.

The media's role in the presidential nominating process is decisive, particularly in the early phase. Television and press journalists sort out the candidates, establish performance expectations, boost some campaigns while writing off others, and launch the bandwagons. Quite simply, they create winners and losers. The rewards for capturing the media's attention are all out of proportion to the significance of the contests and, often, to the leading candidates' vote shares as well. Perceptions nevertheless are more important than reality. Winners gain increased visibility, a larger and more attentive following of journalists, front-page stories everywhere, front covers on national newsmagazines and feature stories inside, substantial television news time, endorsements, campaign workers, and a rush of campaign contributions. In a word, early winners and surprise candidates gain momentum in this system of "lotteries driven by media expectations and candidate name recognition." [65] It is not extravagant to argue that in the presidential nominating process the media have largely supplanted the political parties.

Media coverage in the early phase of the pres-

Democratic presidential candidate Michael Dukakis jokes with campaign aides and members of the press on the tarmac of the Green Bay Airport, just prior to a convincing victory in the Wisconsin primary. Every campaign day is a campaign for media attention, including photo opportunities like these. As it turned out, Wisconsin was one of only ten states (along with the District of Columbia) carried by Dukakis in the November election.

idential nominating process sharply affects the strategic decisions of candidates. Basic questions of campaign timing and thrust are involved. Since in large part the media decide who the serious candidates are, candidates feel pressure to enter the opening primaries and caucuses. An early announcement of candidacy, in addition, will generate news coverage that is essential to attract the campaign funds necessary to qualify for matching federal money. The rule is simple: Candidates who are not out of the starting blocks quickly are unlikely to do well. They are second-guessed by the media and perhaps dismissed as serious candidates.

The press and television also play a key role in illuminating the factional appeals of candidates in primaries and caucuses. Increasingly, in the new participatory system, presidential candidates have eschewed coalition building while seeking to mobilize relatively narrow ideological, religious, ethnic, or sectional followings. The more crowded the field, the greater the probability that an active, passionate, well-organized faction can keep the candidate in contention from one Tuesday to the next in the crucial early weeks of the season. Through extensive coverage of the campaign, the media help the candidates to attract, instruct, and mobilize their "natural" factional followings. In a word, they differentiate candidacies. Nelson W. Polsby's analysis is instructive:

> Why must a presidential candidate in the new circumstances created by the proliferation of primaries mobilize his faction rather than

build coalitions? The task of a presidential hopeful, threading a path through the minefield of successive primary elections, is not to win a majority but rather to survive. Survival means gaining as high as possible a rank among the candidates running for election. Coming in first in early primaries means achieving the visibility that ensures that a candidate will be taken seriously by the news media.[66]

Party Vitality

American political parties in the late twentieth century are in trouble. At virtually every stage in the recruitment and election of public officials, the parties have lost power. Campaigns are increasingly candidate centered—candidates, in other words, make the decisions that count. And for many voters, party is no longer of much importance either. Every election attests to the "departisanization" of the electorate as voters evaluate candidates in terms of character and experience while largely ignoring their parties.

Many factors have contributed to the declining significance of political parties (see Chapter 9). But the influence of the media, and particularly television, may be the most important of all. As journalist David Broder contended: "Television has established itself as the prime medium of political communications. The most significant point to be made about television, as compared to printed media, is that it is personality dominated. It deals with political figures, not political institutions. . . . Political parties as such have almost no role in television's portrayal of the political drama." [67]

The media have left their imprint on the parties in several respects. Two deserve special mention. First, the media have played a key role in the weakening of party elites. A candidate's free media time and paid advertising are a much more effective means for influencing mass electorates than working through party leaders and party organizations. The media also provide the best opportunity for candidates, tutored by media consultants, to raise campaign money by capturing public attention. Impressive televised speeches sometimes produce a flood of campaign contributions. It is not stretching the facts to argue that the media are now used to "deliver" votes and money in a way that state and local politicians did a generation ago. As John Sears, a Republican political strategist, put it, "The media stand in a position today, especially in the nomination phase, where the old party bosses used to stand." [68] Virtually everywhere, political consultants and "handlers" have replaced party professionals in running major political campaigns. The hard truth is that party leaders cannot do much either to help or to hurt a candidate's chances for a major statewide or national office. Put another way, media elites are more important than party elites, media politics more important than party politics.

Second, the media have played a major role in the transformation of the national party convention. Today's conventions are dominanted by candidates and their organizations; the influence that party and elected officials wield is a function of their affiliation with one of the candidate organizations. The vast majority of delegates arrive at the convention committed to a candidate, and the convention meets to ratify the voters' choice, expressed in primaries and caucuses, as the presidential nominee. Typically, everyone knows who will win the nomination long in advance of the quadrennial summer conventions. The old "deliberative" convention, marked by high-stakes bargaining among party leaders, with the nomination in suspense, is all but extinct. "In effect," writes Hedrick Smith, "Boss Tube has succeeded Boss Tweed of Tammany Hall, Boss Crump of Memphis, and the Daley machine in Chicago. Television brings politicians right into the living room and lets voters form their own impressions, rather than voters having to depend on what local party bosses, union leaders, church spokesmen, or business chiefs say." [69]

The new party convention is largely a media event. Activities are scheduled at times that will produce maximum television audiences. Controversy is downplayed. Politics is sanitized. Speeches are kept brief. Orchestration and entertainment pervade the convention agenda as leaders strive to showcase their candidates, enhance the party's image, and hold an audience notorious for its short attention span. Elaborate efforts are made to avoid

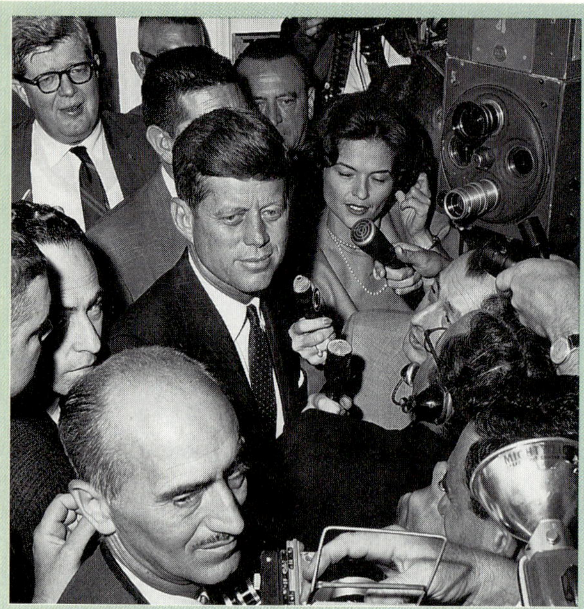

The medium is the message: Swamped by supporters and reporters, Senator John F. Kennedy arrives at the Biltmore Hotel in New York City, site of the Democratic National Convention, in July 1960. He won the nomination on the first ballot. Few candidates, past or present, have used the media more adeptly than Kennedy.

the occasion of cardinal sin, boring the viewers. Convention planners fully appreciate that (in the words of an ABC News vice president) "TV has converted Americans into people who have 12-minute attention spans. Long-form programming has to adjust to the reality that viewers expect a payoff every 12 minutes."[70]

National party conventions have turned into spectacles because they no longer actually choose the candidates, because they are trying to stay in business in a mass-oriented political system, and because the media control the interpretation (and thus the politics) of the preconvention period. Not a great deal is left for the convention to decide.

Marjorie Hershey develops an interesting what-might-have-been argument concerning the parties' loss of influence to the mass media:

> The tremendous expansion of the mass media and other campaign technologies need not have weakened party organizations; if the parties had been firmly rooted in public opinion when these technologies emerged, party organizations might have captured those tools and used them to cement party influence on candidates' campaigns. If the national party organizations had been powerful when television was in its infancy, then they might have been able to claim time for political broadcasts as part of their rightful turf, and been able to distribute that time to loyal candidates.[71]

But this did not happen; it is hard to exaggerate the media's role as kingmaker in presidential nominating politics.

Voter Turnout

Numerous scholars and journalists believe along with Ellen Goodman that the media's election coverage is a major explanation for the decline in turnout of American voters:

> Television has produced a couch-potato constituency. Sitting in front of the set, we expect to be amused, entertained, informed, inactive. Everything comes to us in the same one-way human channel: news and entertainment, political debates and sitcoms. . . . We are comfortable watching, comfortable criticizing. We sink into our role as easily as we sink into the couch. It's hard to get up again. . . . I cannot prove that the rise of politics-as-television is responsible for the decrease of actual real, live voters. But how many viewer-voters have learned from television that they can reject politics because the program is boring? How many think they've done enough when they voted with their fingers?[72]

In all likelihood, television is more responsible for declining voter turnout than newspapers. One study finds, for example, that voters who rely mainly on newspapers for political information are much more likely to see issue differences between presidential candidates than voters who rely

Partisanship and Reliance on the Media

Democratic and Republican voters do not see the world in the same light. Nor do they obtain information on public affairs in exactly the same way. Partisans have distinct preferences: Republicans rely more on newspapers for information, while Democrats rely more on television. This finding is consistent with evidence showing that people who rely more on newspapers than on television are better educated, express more interest in politics, and are more likely to vote. It thus reflects, in part, the social class makeup of the two parties.

Source: Developed from data in *The People, Press, and Politics* (Los Angeles: Times-Mirror, 1987), p. 63.

	Percent of Total Population	Rely Most on . . .	
		Newspapers	Television
Solid Republicans	21%	25%	18%
Independents leaning Republican	18	19	17
Independents leaning Democratic	15	20	12
Solid Democrats	35	30	41
Bystanders (noninvolved)	11	6	12

mainly on television for political news. Consistent with this finding, turnout is much higher among newspaper readers than among the regular viewers of nightly news. By muting the differences between candidates, the argument runs, television has made elections less meaningful. For some, politics is simply one more spectator sport. One effect has been to diminish popular interest and involvement in politics.[73]

By accentuating negative news, the television networks also have contributed to a sharp drop in public affection for the parties' presidential nominees—which would seem to discourage voting. In 1980, for the first time ever, both presidential candidates—Jimmy Carter and Ronald Reagan—received more unfavorable comments than favorable ones. At one time or another in the 1988 campaign, both George Bush and Michael Dukakis were seen about as negatively as positively by the voters.

Turnout also appears to be adversely affected by the television networks' practices in election night reporting. In order to predict election outcomes, each network conducts "exit polls" of a cross section of voters in key precincts around the nation (or state) to learn how they have just voted. The data are then fed into computers and the results analyzed by experts. By late afternoon on election day, long before the polls are closed, the networks usually have an accurate forecast of the outcome.

First used extensively in the presidential election of 1972, exit polls have become both reliable and controversial. The main problem in presidential general elections is that early projections of the results appear to discourage voters from voting in the western states where the polls (on Pacific time) are still open. Awkward developments may occur. Based on network predictions, Jimmy Carter conceded the election to Ronald Reagan in 1980 while the polls were still open in the West; his concession not only led to a falloff in late voting but apparently contributed to narrow losses by several Democratic congresspeople. The networks jumped the gun again in 1984 and 1988.

A partial solution to this problem would be for Congress to adopt a uniform poll closing time for national elections; the polls in the West would thus close at the same time as those in the East. Even "same-time" voting, however, would not prevent the networks from projecting the winner before the polls were closed. Legislation to ban election outcome projections prior to the closing of the polls is another alternative, but it would undoubtedly be challenged as an intrusion on First Amendment freedoms. The best way to solve this problem of vote devaluation would seem to be, quite simply, network restraint in reporting their projections.

Election Outcomes ■

For several reasons, evaluating the impact of media coverage on voter intentions poses difficult problems of analysis. To begin, voting is a complex act. Voters' decisions are affected by such group-based factors as party affiliation, organizational membership, family, and friends; even in today's individualistic political culture many voters find it hard to cut loose from these conventional moorings in casting ballots. Voting behavior is also influenced by ideology, issue preferences, perceptions of candidate qualities, and perceptions of candidate performance in office. The factor of incumbency may also enter the voting calculus. And finally, many voters decide how they will vote before the campaign has even begun (and thus before media information on the campaign is introduced). The net result of this mingling of factors is that media influence on voter preferences is both hard to sort out and, apparently, more limited than might appear at first glance. The American voter is not a blank sheet on which anything can be written.

Nonetheless, the influence of media messages on voter intentions may be reflected in subtle but important ways. Consider these possibilities. First, through sustained reporting on certain issues or problems (for example, crime, corruption in government, drugs, patriotism, domestic or foreign policy failures), the media may create a climate of opinion that molds voter attitudes toward government and politics, which in turn shape their perceptions of candidates and parties. Second, the media help to frame the campaign agenda by directing the voters' attention to certain issues and by ignoring others. Simply put, the media tell the voters what issues are important, thus influencing political debate and analysis in ways that may promote some candidacies and hamper others. And third, by their selective attention to candidates and events the media help to formulate the criteria used by voters in deciding how to vote—perhaps prompting them, for example, to focus on certain qualities such as experience or leadership ability in evaluating candidates.[74] In sum, to borrow from Doris Graber, the media "shape the perceptual environment in which the election takes place." [75]

The media play a major, if unintentional, role in the political process. They are participants. Their impact can be seen in the spread of political conflict, in the types of candidates chosen, in the increasing personalization of campaigns, in the thrust of campaign strategy and decision making, in the huge sums spent on political advertising, in the trivialization of campaign reporting, in the development of issues and candidate images, in the weakening of the party role (but especially in the presidential nominating process), in the treatment of politics as drama and controversy, and in the emergence and consolidation of politics as a spectator sport. Television's impact on these developments has been particularly sizable.

Accompanied by his wife, Senator Joseph Biden (D-Del.) announces his withdrawal from the race for the 1988 Democratic presidential nomination. Biden was plagued by reports of plagiarism, in both his speeches and law school papers, and of having exaggerated his academic accomplishments. Political fatalities are about as numerous as political success stories and, for the media, a vastly more interesting subject for coverage.

Media Impact on Government and Public Policy

The impact on government of the media extends well beyond elections. Of the numerous themes that might be explored, we examine three of special importance: the media's impact on popular trust in government, governmental agenda setting and public policy, and the functioning of the branches of government.

Popular Trust in Government

The American public's confidence in government is much lower today than it was in the 1950s. Opinion surveys in recent years have shown that only one-fourth to one-half of the public believe that the federal government can be trusted to do what is right. Many factors have contributed to the public's disillusionment: assassinations, urban unrest and riots, the Vietnam War, Watergate, the resignation of a vice president and a president, congressional scandals, and a variety of domestic and foreign policy failures, including the wrenching Iranian hostage crisis and the Iran-contra scandal. Obviously, there has been no shortage of discouraging news to frustrate the public.

Television and the print media have also contributed to the erosion of public trust in government by the way they portray politics and politicians "as being motivated mainly or solely by their eagerness to win votes, and seldom or never by any desire to promote the public interest." [76] The result, Michael J. Robinson argues, is "an image of society that tends to be both melodramatic and probably inordinately negative." [77] It is hardly surprising that, in the words of David L. Paletz and Robert N. Entman: "The media's coverage of governmental debate and delay, irresolution and confusion, the implicit and invidious comparison of politics and entertainment on television, do eventuate in public distemper, dismay, dissatisfaction, and discontent." [78]

The Formation of Public Policy

As major agents for the socialization of conflict, the media help illuminate problems for which individuals and groups seek government redress and public policy solutions. Television and the national press played a crucial role in fostering national debate on racial injustice and promoting the civil rights movement in the 1950s and 1960s. Sustained attention by the media made it inevitable that issues like the Vietnam War in the 1960s and 1970s, Watergate in the 1970s, and the arms-for-hostages Iran-contra scandal in the 1980s would be picked up by political elites and gain a prominent place on the federal government's agenda. Television in particular is a major resource available to groups that know how to manipulate it. It is unlikely that the four major civil rights acts passed by Congress between 1957 and 1965, for example, would have been adopted without television's intense and unprecedented attention to the civil rights movement and to the problems of race relations.

Legislation represents a policy response to some kind of problem. That problem must be acute enough to intrude on the well-being of a significant number of people and their organizations or on the well-being of the government itself, conspicuous enough to draw the attention of at least some legislators. In broad terms, legislation is generated by need, apprehension, unrest, conflict, innovation, and events. No institution can or will focus on these conditions more than television. The very conditions that generate legislation lend themselves to television's penchant for news as minidrama and politics as struggle and controversy. Every private-world problem that makes it to the nightly news is a candidate for a solution in public law because 60 million people are going to know about it, and some will try to do something about it.

The national press also plays an important role in analyzing problems and converting them into agenda items. Political elites pay close attention to major stories in prominent papers and to the views of their columnists. Their accounts and reflections are grist for the policy mill. The national audience for any single paper, of course, is quite limited in comparison with the networks' regular viewers.

There is scant mystery concerning the media's role in helping to shape the work of government and public policy itself. Politicians and the media thrive in a symbiotic relationship. The electoral connection requires legislators and executives to develop issues and programs.[79] In search of news, the media can often provide them. The media help to discover issues, give them public saliency, help policy entrepreneurs to communicate with each other, describe policy options, and build support for remedial legislation. Politicians win credit and electoral advantage and the media gain recognition. Journalists are tapped for awards for exposing problems and sometimes achieve celebrity status. Almost everyone profits in a politics in which issues are more important than policy. The policy process need not even be successful. David R. Mayhew has shown that "position taking" (simply making pleasing judgmental statements) by legislators, when linked to popular issues and ample media coverage, can play an important role in ensuring their reelection.[80] The news moves on.

Much like interest groups and parties, the media both promote and impede policy making in America. The "down" side of media involvement appears in an analysis by Austin Ranney. First, by focusing so heavily on the short-term, interesting events and "immediate" results, television has *compressed the time* available for administrations to institute programs and solve problems. Television is "here and now," concerned with dramatic happenings—and so is its audience. It has more difficulty interpreting long-term programs and planning, as well as finding appropriate visuals to use. In public policy terms, administrations must

Mass Media Influence: A Five-Nation Survey

How significant is the media's role in political systems? The broad answer is that there is no broad answer. Concrete evidence is scanty. Media influence, moreover, is inextricably scrambled in all mixtures of institutional decision making.

Perceptions of influence, however, can be gauged. The tble below shows how the public in five countries sees the influence of the media on governmental institutions and the appropriateness of media power.

This survey, by the Louis Harris organization, shows that the American public believes that the media exert a strong influence, particularly on the executive branch of government. Indeed, Americans are much more likely than Western Europeans to see the media as influential in institutional decision making, although citizens in all five countries find a significant influence on public opinion. And Americans are more likely to contend that the media have too much power. Is it surprising that Americans also have much *more* confidence in their institutions, including the media, than the Europeans have in theirs? Other data in the study, not shown, reveal this to be true.

Source: Adapted from tables in an article by Laurence Parisot, "Attitudes about the Media: A Five Country Comparison," *Public Opinion,* January/February 1988, p. 60.

	France	Germany	Britain	Spain	United States
The influence exerted by the media on . . . is large					
Judiciary	46%	29%	40%	32%	69%
Legislature	37	44	48	38	78
Executive branch/ government	48	46	44	41	81
Public opinion	77	71	80	70	88
The media have					
Too much power	29	32	43	46	49
Not enough power	14	6	10	22	10
Just the right amount of power	45	48	41	26	39

get as much as they can as fast as they can. The key is instant success for maximum television impact and for the medium's impatient viewers.

Second, Ranney continues, television coverage tends to *reduce policy options.* Its journalists pry for government's inside information, because there are good stories to be told, and obtain it through leaks from officials with axes to grind. Typically, premature exposure of a policy option dooms it.

Ranney's final point is television's need for a stream of stories from politicians in the executive and legislative branches. Linked to its preoccupation with confrontational politics and the new openness of the institutions, this serves to accentuate the problems of the Madisonian system of fragmented power and to weaken the coalition builders.[81] In Congress, for example, there are more than 200 committees and subcommittees, each with a chairperson seeking TV attention. Political aspirations flourish in this free-for-all political world, and collisions and conflicts are inevitable. Politicians use television to serve their own particularistic purposes rather than to contribute to durable coalitions concerned with comprehensive national programs. The reality is that television is at times nothing quite so much as a vehicle for advancing the parochial interests of imaginative, self-assured politicians. But that, of course, is not all that it is.

The media's capacity to draw the attention of both political elites and the wider public to an issue is extraordinary. Coverage can make political decision making easier or more difficult. Representative Leon E. Panetta (D–Calif.) describes how Congress responded to the drug issue in the 99th Congress (1985–1986):

> While this bill deserves our approval, it disturbs me that we are treating the drug issue as we do so many issues: An event triggers nationwide concern about a problem, three weeks of media coverage and magazine covers follow, quick drafting of legislation occurs followed by passage by the Congress and signature by the president—and then we forget the issue as we move on to another crisis. . . . The attention span of the American people and Congress for national problems is growing shorter and shorter.[82]

Of course, not many issues are dealt with in such a burst of activity. Typically, the key contribution of the media is to help keep an issue alive while politicians try to piece together a policy-making coalition.

President, Congress, and Courts

The politician-media relationship is a two-way street. The media have an extraordinary impact on the institutions of government, especially the executive and legislative branches. By their relentless pursuit of news, the press and television affect not only what government does but also the careers of public officials. They make life easier for them or tougher or, more likely, easier at one time and tougher at another. They simplify or complicate the search for policy solutions to public problems. The media are not simply recorders of public events and conduits for information about them.

By the same token, persons in public life treat the media seriously because of their need to cultivate public opinion. They organize their offices and appoint press aides with the media in mind and devise elaborate plans to draw the media's attention to their achievements. Their objective, of course, is to enhance and prolong their careers through favorable publicity and to advance policies and programs consistent with their goals and philosophies. Politicians and journalists understand each other because each has what the other wants: publicity and visibility on the one hand, access and information on the other.

The most important office in the United States is the presidency. That office is also the focus of political coverage by the print and broadcast media, especially the latter. Proportionately, for example, the television evening news gives about twice as much news space to the White House as do the wire services. "Television news loves the presidency," Michael Robinson writes: "It may not like the incumbent; it may not like any incumbent, but the office of the president has become the *sine qua non* of network journalism." [83] Whatever else it does, television highlights the shortcomings of the president. "The result may be a new sort of equilibrium in which television helps move power toward the office but detracts from the legitimacy of the officeholder." [84]

For several reasons, a study by Fred Smoller shows, portrayal of the president on the evening news programs is frequently negative or unbalanced. One key reason is that news reports must be short and uncomplicated—only 22 minutes altogether are available for news in a 30-minute program. Second, the need for pictures steadily affects what is covered. Complicated stories and complex issues are avoided, while novel and unusual stories (with "interesting" film) are highlighted. Minor happenings get disproportionate attention if they mesh comfortably with ongoing and familiar stories. Third, actions (signing a bill, delivering a speech) are easier to convey in a picture than processes (negotiations, development of policy options) and thus dominate accounts. Compelling visuals of superficial events are common. Fourth, the need for pictures also impels the networks to cover conflict, controversy, and presidential misadventures rather than the routine work of government. "Boring" news must be avoided at all costs, the networks reason, because the audience has a limited attention span. And fifth, analysis and criticism loom much more important than description.

The truncated portrayal of the president is only part of the story. Smoller's examination of newscasts also finds that negative coverage of the president increases as his term ages, that each of the four presidents studied (Nixon, Ford, Carter, and Reagan) received more negative coverage than his predecessor, that presidential "honeymoons" are ending more abruptly and decisively, and that negative television coverage has undermined public support for the president. Overall, coverage of modern presidents is much more likely to be negative than positive. It is important to emphasize again that television's impact on the presidency results from inadvertence and the nature of television news, not from design, partisanship, or malevolence.[85]

Every administration attempts to "manage" the news in ways that will present the president and his programs in the most favorable light. Some control can be effected through press conferences (if the president is skillful), briefings, press releases, scheduling (and contriving) events, radio broadcasts, providing information (and leaking) to selected journalists in the White House press corps and elsewhere, staging ceremonies, arranging for photo opportunities, and delivering presidential addresses and other speeches. The president, after all, can make news—and reporters will always be there to report it. Indeed, they have the president under constant surveillance. Some presidents, such as John Kennedy and Ronald Reagan, have been unusually effective in public relations and in influencing coverage of their administrations. But on the evening news—the principal outlet for information about the president—no president fares very well for very long. On the whole, the televised presidency has done more to erode the authority of the constitutional presidency than to strengthen it.

In the Constitution, Congress is the first branch of government. From the media's perspective, however, it is the second branch—less pivotal, less newsworthy, and less susceptible to analysis than the presidency. Congress is a good place for newsgathering even about the executive branch, because it provides so many sources of information: 535 members and some 15,000 personal and committee staff aides. But it is also a difficult institution to bring into focus, since power is nowhere concentrated. Each member, in a sense, is an entrepreneur running his or her own business, more responsible to a constituency than to Congress as a whole or to any of its subunits. The institution itself is heavily decentralized, with power distributed between two houses and among several hundred committees and subcommittees, committee and subcommittee chairpersons, party leaders and party agencies (such as caucuses and steering committees), and a great variety of informal specialized caucuses.

In a fragmented institution such as Congress, everyone gets a piece of the action. The net result is that Congress cannot speak with a single voice. It has no way to make it clear where the action is or what it means. No one, including reporters, can take Congress for granted because in the last analysis no one knows what Congress will do. Congress

The "Great Communicator" at work: former President Ronald Reagan points to reporters' raised hands during a nationally televised press conference in the East Room of the White House.

itself must wait to know what it will do, if anything, until it has done it—in both houses. Its size, redundancy, unpredictability, and fragmentation make the legislative branch a descriptive and analytic "problem," even for seasoned reporters. But not many of them would want to trade their Capitol Hill "beat" for another assignment.

The truth is that the media generally do not do well in examining Congress as an institution. "Most of us," writes David Broder, "are more comfortable thinking about and writing about individuals than about institutions."[86] Television's treatment of Congress stresses conflict and confrontation—member against member, party against party, legislature against executive. Congressional scandals, of course, get a strong play on television and in both the national and local press. Congressional pay raises drive some newspapers into a frenzy of stories and editorials on "pay grabs." Similar stories erupt over member travel ("junkets" using taxpayer dollars) and the honorarium payments members receive for speeches and articles. And Congress receives more than a little criticism from the media for being too slow, too partisan, too parochial, too preoccupied with pork barrel politics, and too responsive to the initiatives of special interests. Congress in focus, frequently, is Congress out of kilter. For some reporters and some sectors of the media, in fact, Congress-bashing is a major activity.

Instructive treatments of Congress as an institution can often be found in the nation's leading newspapers, such as the *Washington Post,* the *New York Times,* the *Wall Street Journal,* the *Christian Science Monitor,* and the *Los Angeles Times,* and in such weekly journals as the *Congressional Quarterly Weekly Report* and the *National Journal.* Televised public instruction on Congress is also available for those who watch C-SPAN coverage of Congress at work. C-SPAN gives members an opportunity to advertise their wares and viewers an opportunity to learn more about members and public policy questions. Yet the local press, which blankets the nation, has scarcely anything to say about the institutional life of Congress.

Congress fares best in both press and television when it is doing out-of-the-ordinary business—when, for example, its committees appear on television to consider charges in the impeachment trial of President Nixon, or to consider the nomination of Robert Bork to the Supreme Court, or to examine the evidence of a cabal's disdain for the rule of law in the Iran-contra hearings.

The media may treat Congress poorly, but not individual members. Incumbents prosper in the media spotlight, and they are reelected in record numbers, especially in the House. Members are wary of the aggressive, investigative thrust of the national media, but they know that local press and television coverage—the "hometown" coverage that really counts—will be not only extensive but largely sympathetic. Additionally, "in-house" media (including WATS lines, office news prepared by press secretaries and fed to local media, computerized mailings, and multiple radio and television studios for taping programs to be sent to local broadcasters) provide exceptional opportunities for members to communicate with their constituencies. These controlled outlets, bolstered by the "soft" local media, are usually more than enough to offset whatever electoral strains negative reporting by the national press may create.[87]

The media clearly affect congressional careers and the congressional power structure. They contribute to congressional stability through coverage that makes incumbents, especially House members, more secure (notwithstanding the adversarial thrust of the national media). They foster the independence of members and, on the whole, do more to weaken the party leadership than to strengthen it. They preempt the time of legislators (thus augmenting the influence of staffs on policy). And they inflate the significance of interesting mavericks and telegenic younger members. Overall, they contribute in important ways to the deconcentration of power in Congress.

Finally, the media influence congressional strategy and issues. Congressional staffs are knowledgeable about the media, plugged into numerous communications networks, and adept at attracting journalists' attention to member activities and achievements. What is more, Michael Malbin observes, among members and staff there "is a bias in favor of issues that look good in the press"—issues that "sing." "[The] staff looks not only for issues the press will like, but a good entrepreneurial staffer is expected to know how to 'package' what he has in a way the press will find interesting." [88] The next reelection campaign is just around the corner. For many members, in fact, no lull appears between one campaign and the next—serving in Congress is one long campaign for media attention that strengthens the electoral connection.

Least influenced by the media are the courts. Much of their work is done behind closed doors, and judges are not often available for reporters' interviews. The Supreme Court is a special case. It attracts major media coverage at three junctures: when major decisions are announced, when vacancies in its membership occur, and when presidential nominees to fill them are considered by the Senate. For the general run of people, the federal courts are all but invisible, judges little known, the Supreme Court a mystery.

Candidates, officeholders, and politicians in general are sensitive to the media. Yet at the same time, they influence what the media have to say. Few, if any, candidates or officeholders are simply under the thumb of the media—they have power in their own right. And they have become increasingly adept at avoiding "unmanaged" encounters with the media, such as press conferences, where they might make an impromptu response damaging to their campaign. Doubtlessly public officials behave more responsibly because of the fear of exposure by the media; they take greater pains to explain what they are doing or have done. Protected by the First Amendment, the media leave their imprint on politics and government. Their profound contribution to our political system is to provide information so that the public can evaluate issues, policies, candidates, and the performance of officeholders and governments. Almost everyone agrees, however, that the media's performance—in reporting on public affairs and in teaching the public things it needs to know—leaves something to be desired.

Summary

- The mass media perform an indispensable role in democratic political systems. They monitor the affairs of government and educate the public. They are habitually alert to wrongdoing by public officials. In their role of informing the public, they help to convert individuals into citizens. In social science terms, television and newspapers are mediating institutions between citizens and their governments.

- American news has a distinctive tone, mood, and cast. The media favor stories that are novel and entertaining, that highlight familiar people and situations, and that stress conflict and violence. One result of the singular focus of the news is that complicated social, economic, and political problems receive much less attention than their importance warrants.
- In the coverage of political campaigns, television differs from the print media in major ways. It is more personal, more mediating, more analytical, more political, more critical, and more thematic. When campaigns are under way, television thoroughly dominates coverage and popular perceptions of candidates and events. Presidential campaigns are organized around television.
- The media are frequently charged with political bias, but the real problem is structural bias, particularly in the case of television.
- The media play a major, if inadvertent, role in the political process. In search of news, they contribute to the socialization of conflict. They affect the types of candidates chosen, the conduct of campaigns, campaign agendas, and popular perceptions of candidates, issues, and the race itself. Coverage of political campaigns frequently revolves around minidramas featuring entertainment and controversy, miscalculation, and misadventure. Scholars who study the media find that political reporting is laced with negative interpretations, particularly in the case of television. In presidential nominating politics, the media have largely supplanted the political parties. They affect voter intentions and elections in numerous ways. The media's inadvertent importance in politics, whatever else may be said about it, is massively important.
- Finally, the media have a significant impact on public trust in government, the policy-making process, and the careers of politicians and the vitality and stability of government. All of these things result from a basic, if little appreciated, fact: The media are participants in the political process.

Readings on Mass Media Politics

Broder, David S. 1987. *Behind the Front Page: A Candid Look at How the News Is Made.* New York: Simon & Schuster. A critical look at the world of newspapers by one of the nation's eminent journalists.

Cannon, Lou. 1977. *Reporting: An Inside View.* Sacramento: California Journal Press. A noted journalist's insights into how reporters do their jobs—what are their biases, limitations, and decision-making criteria?

Crouse, Timothy. 1973. *The Boys on the Bus.* New York: Ballantine Books. An insightful account of press coverage of the 1972 election, with special emphasis on factors which influenced the coverage.

Epstein, Edward J. 1974. *News from Nowhere.* New York: Random House/Vintage Books. How economic and political considerations (including corporate policy and budgetary restrictions) affect television network news coverage.

Epstein, Edward J. 1975. *Between Fact and Fiction: The Problem of Journalism.* New York: Vintage Books. Problems with which journalists must deal on a daily basis, and some resolutions to the problems.

Graber, Doris A. 1989. *Mass Media and American Politics,* 3d ed. Washington, D.C.: CQ Press. An examination of the media coverage of politics.

Hess, Stephen. 1981. *The Washington Reporters.* Washington, D.C.: Brookings Institution. A study of the characteristics and views of the Washington press corps.

Lichter, Robert S., Stanley Rothman, and Linda S. Lichter. 1986. *The Media Elite: America's New Powerbrokers.* An innovative study of the media environment and how this environment affects news coverage of controversial social issues.

Paletz, David L., and Robert M. Entman. 1981. *Media, Power, Politics.* New York: Free Press. An argument that mass media both manipulate and are manipulated by government officials and politicians.

Patterson, Thomas E., and Robert D. McClure. 1976. *The Unseeing Eye: The Myth of Television Power in National Elections.* A startling analysis of the weaknesses of television coverage of national elections.

Press, Charles, and Kenneth Verburg. 1988. *American Politicians and Journalists.* Glenview: Scott, Foresman. A wide-ranging analysis of the star-crossed romance of politicians and reporters, with each seeking to advance their own careers.

Ranney, Austin. 1983. *Channels of Power: The Impact of Television on American Politics.* New York: Basic Books. An insightful study of the role of television in contemporary politics.

Robinson, Michael J., and Margaret A. Sheehan. 1983. *Over the Wire and on TV: CBS and UPI in Campaign '80.* New York: Russell Sage Foundation. An evaluation of media performance during the 1980 campaign, focusing on differences between electronic and print media.

Part Three

The Structure of Government

"The accumulation of all powers, legislative, executive, and judiciary, in the same hands, whether of one, a few, or many, and whether hereditary, self-appointed, or elective, may justly be pronounced the very definition of tyranny."

— The Federalist

Chapter 12

Congress

Getting Elected to Congress
- The Representative System
- Nominations
- Elections
- Financing Congressional Campaigns

Characteristics of Members

The Organization of Congress
- The Congressional Parties
- The Committee System
- The Staffs and Support Agencies

A Bill Becomes a Law
- The Stages of Lawmaking
- An Overview of Lawmaking

The Voting Behavior of Members of Congress
- Role Orientations and Voting
- Influences on Voting Behavior

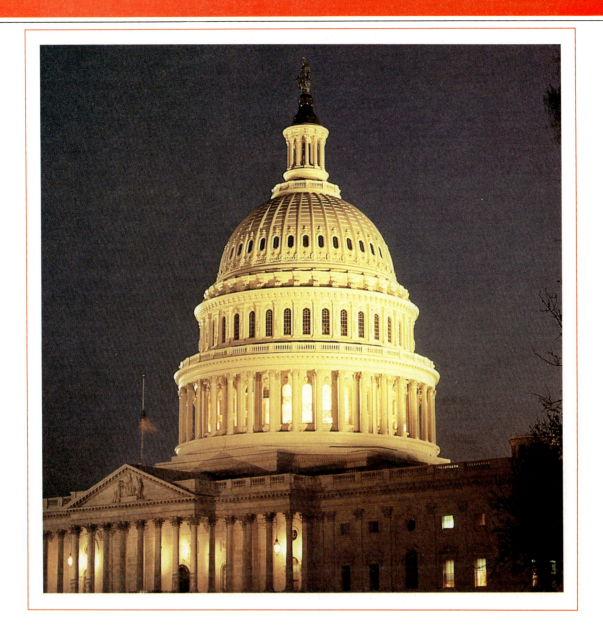

Congress is different things to different people. For citizens in general, it is the nation's chief lawmaking assembly. For blasé Washingtonians, it is a cultural monument that goes unvisited. For the president, it is a dependable partner or a powerful antagonist. For political interest groups, it is a vehicle for protecting the status quo or launching new ventures. For bureaucrats who are worried about their appropriations and programs, it is an incubus or an ally, or something in between. For the courts, it is a source of new business, its legislation grist for the judicial mill. For the political leaders of other nations, it is often an enigma and always a force with which to reckon. For most of the media, most of the time, it appears as an institution less newsworthy than the presidency, as well as one more difficult to bring into focus. For its own members, it is an outlet for political ambition, an opportunity for an important career, and a means of gaining public policy objectives and serving public needs. For democrats of all kinds, it is a genuinely independent and powerful representative institution.

For all these groups, Congress is the center of the American policy-making process. Article I, Section 1 of the Constitution is clear: "All legislative powers herein granted shall be vested in a Congress of the United States, which shall consist of a Senate and House of Representatives." To this broad grant, Article I, Section 8 adds specific powers, such as the authority to declare war, levy taxes, borrow and coin money, regulate commerce, create courts, and create an army and a navy. Article VI, Section 2 declares that the laws of Congress "shall be the supreme law of the land." Congress, in short, enjoys an enviable constitutional position.

This chapter examines how Congress is organized, how it goes about its business, and how it makes decisions. A key feature of Congress will become readily apparent: Like other democratic legislatures, Congress is not a particularly efficient institution, geared to making quick decisions. Rather, it is primarily a *deliberative assembly,* shaped by organizational preferences, procedures, and customs that assure both members and outsiders of abundant opportunities to register their claims and defend their positions. Before examining this and other central elements of Congress, it is necessary to consider how its members are elected. Elections shape Congress in fundamental ways.

Getting Elected to Congress

Our national legislature does not offer many opportunities for persons who aspire to become legislators. Only 535 men and women are elected to it, 435 in the House and 100 in the Senate. Those who manage to join this national elite have one thing in common: They are exceptional politicians. What makes them exceptional is their first nomination and election victories. Numbers tell the story. The 28 million people of California, for example, are represented by only 45 House members and 2 senators, the 12 million people of Florida by only 19 House members and 2 senators. (Each of these rapidly growing states will gain several House seats following reapportionment in 1991.) Aspiring politicians are screened out all along the line—discouraged from challenging the incumbent, ignored by the elements (including party) that recruit and finance candidates, passed over by the voters in the primary, or defeated in the election itself. Often members of Congress are elected only after earlier unsuccessful attempts.

The first election, however, changes matters. The winners gain office and advantages. National party leaders (including the president) get to know them. Lobbyists line up to meet them. Journalists and the media sometimes pay attention to them. Celebrities and the Washington social elite become interested in them. The voters come to recognize their names. Whatever members may contend, staying in Congress is much easier than getting there in the first place.

The Representative System ■

Congress is a *bicameral* legislature; that is, it is composed of two houses. Members of the lower chamber, the House of Representatives, are elected for a two-year term (the length of a Congress). The number of representatives apportioned to each state is determined by its population. As it turns out, more than half the seats in the 435-member House are allocated to the nine largest states. The six least populous states—Alaska, Delaware, North Dakota, South Dakota, Vermont, and Wyoming—have one member each in the House. Each state, irrespective of its population, is awarded two seats in the upper chamber, the Senate. Thus, the residents of sparsely settled Alaska have the same representation in the Senate as the residents of California, even though California has more than 50 times as many people. Senators are elected for a six-year term, with one-third of the membership chosen every two years.

The Constitution provided for senators to be chosen by the legislatures of their states. The Senate, reasoned the founders, would serve as a check on the impulsiveness of the popularly elected lower house. This form of "indirect election," keeping the people at arm's length, lasted for more than a century. Adoption of the Seventeenth Amendment in 1913, however, brought it to an end. Since then, senators have been chosen in the same way as members of the House—by the direct vote of the people.

The boundary lines of congressional districts are drawn by state legislatures. Today all House districts contain about the same number of people (roughly half a million). Prior to the 1960s, however, it was common to find states in which the most populous congressional districts held two, three, or even four times as many people as the smallest districts. This served to underrepresent the interests of the former and to overrepresent the interests of the latter. In general, citizens in rural areas benefited from *malapportionment,* while citizens in urban areas were disadvantaged.

A string of court decisions in the 1960s brought about the fair apportionment of legislative districts. In a major case decided in 1964, *Wesberry* v. *Sanders,* the Supreme Court ruled that the Constitution requires that the vote of one person be worth as much as that of any other person and thus that all congressional districts should contain about the same number of people. The Court's equal-population doctrine—"one man, one vote"—was soon put into effect by all the states, bringing to an end decades of underrepresentation of populous areas. Today, many court decisions later, all legislative districting, state house and senate as well as congressional, is based on the standard of population equality.

The drawing of district lines to reflect population has not eliminated politics from apportionment plans. Districts can still be *gerrymandered* (made to favor a certain party or incumbent) with no violation of the equal-population rule. Two gerrymandering techniques are used. Under one form, the minority party's voting strength is *concentrated* in as few districts as possible, enabling it to win these districts easily but making it hard to win elsewhere. By conceding one or two districts, the majority party may thus win three or four in adjacent areas. Under the other form, the minority party's voting strength is *dispersed* among many districts, thus reducing its overall chances for winning seats. Majority parties everywhere are tempted to gerrymander to improve their electoral position and to protect their incumbents. Extreme partisan gerrymandering, however, appears to be on the way out. In 1986 the Supreme Court refused to invalidate an Indiana reapportionment act that favored the Republican party, observing that this particular gerrymander was not sufficiently offensive to warrant judicial intervention. But the Court warned that gerrymanders will be held unconstitutional "when the electoral system is arranged in a manner that will consistently degrade a voter's or a group of voters' influence on the political process as a whole." [1] State legislatures have thus been given notice that egregious gerrymandering that entrenches the dominant party will not pass constitutional muster.

Nominations

To win a seat in the House of Representatives or the Senate, one must first be nominated, which means winning a district or statewide (Senate) primary election. In areas dominated by one party, there is often more competition in the primary of the dominant party than in the general election. Throughout much of the South and in certain inner-city districts of northern cities, for example, the "real" election occurs in the Democratic primary.

Similarly, in many small-town and agricultural areas of the Midwest and West, the candidates who win the Republican primaries are strong favorites to win in November.

The extent to which congressional primaries are contested (i.e., have two or more candidates) depends in part on the degree of two-party competition in an area. Another factor is *incumbency.* When an incumbent is running for renomination, he or she is often so firmly entrenched that potential challengers are scared off, believing that their chances of winning are too slim to warrant entering the race. They thus concede renomination to the incumbent.

In sum, although the primaries invite competition among candidates, they do not ensure it—and for good reason. Politicians are realists: Why seek a nomination if it is unlikely to lead anywhere?

The capacity of congressional incumbents to withstand primary challengers is striking. In the five elections of the 1970s, only 1.8 percent of all House members and 5.9 percent of all Senate members were defeated at the primary stage. Currently, the defeat of an incumbent in a primary is even less likely. In 1988 only one of 409 House members seeking renomination was defeated, while all Senate incumbents won their primaries. Incumbents cannot, of course, take renomination for granted, unless they have no opposition. Nevertheless, primaries hold few surprises. If incumbents are challenged, the odds are overwhelmingly in their favor.

Other features of the congressional nominating process are also worth noting. Voter turnout in primaries is especially poor. It is common for only 25 percent of the eligible voters to show up at the polls on primary day. A turnout of 40 percent is exceptional, apt to occur only when there are two (or more) well-known, well-financed candidates. Low turnouts probably favor the incumbents, since their personal followings are more likely than other general voters to take their "civic duty" seriously.

It is important to recognize that even though a member of Congress holds a national office, the nomination is largely a matter of state and local politics. Occasionally, national party leaders become involved in the selection process, helping to recruit candidates and even endorsing one candidate over another. This occurs most often in the Republican party. Ordinarily, state and local leaders regard national involvement as an intrusion on their turf.

The inability of the national party to play a major role in congressional nominations, many political scientists contend, is at the root of party disunity in Congress. Democrats and Republicans are chosen according to the standards and vagaries of local constituencies. Inevitably, this leads to some strange ideological mixes: the nomination of conservative Democrats and liberal Republicans, each out of step with most party colleagues.

The localism that surrounds congressional nominations, moreover, contributes to certain national issues being placed on the back burner while members tend carefully to the problems of their constituencies. Pleasing "the folks back home" is what really counts in a decentralized political system. In the grim words of a member of the House, "I'm from an agriculture-producing area, and I'm concerned for farmers' welfare and will look out for them. If New England consumers are suffering, why the hell should I care?" [2]

Elections

Although Congress rests safely this side of Utopia, it is not an institution many members voluntarily leave. Quite the contrary! Once elected to it, the vast majority of members want to stay, and they devote intense effort to this goal. What is more, their work pays off. They win—again and again. Figure 12–1 tells the story of *incumbent* success in recent general elections.

The reelection rate of House members is remarkable. Even in a "bad" year, 90 percent of the incumbents on the general election ballot win. Usually, 95 to 98 percent win. Senators ordinarily do not do as well. Yet more than 90 percent were reelected in 1982 and 1984. In 1988, 85 percent of the Senate incumbents running in the general election were reelected.

Close calls in congressional elections are not the rule. Only about 10 to 15 percent of all House seats are in *marginal* districts—those won by less than 55 percent of the vote. Perhaps one-third of the Senate seats in the usual election meet the test of marginality. Safe seats, by contrast, are numerous. Commonly, a majority of House candidates win with more than 65 percent of the vote. In fact, many House seats are uncontested. In 1988, for example, about 100 of the 435 House members had no opposition in the fall general election.

How is declining competition to be explained? A major factor is incumbency. Studies have shown, for example, that incumbency is more important than party affiliation in shaping voters' decisions in congressional elections. Among voters who cross party lines in congressional elections (defecting from their own party), many more support incumbents than challengers.[3]

David R. Mayhew contends that members of Congress engage in three activities that strengthen their position with voters. First, they are steadily involved in *advertising* their names—through visits back home, newspaper articles, and radio and television appearances. Name recognition undoubtedly helps them in the polling place. Second, they have become adept at *credit claiming.* They can take credit for helping citizens and groups to solve their problems with government and for the public goods, such as new post offices or highway projects, they have helped to secure for the district. Credit, they reason, translates into votes. A third activity is *position taking.* Public office affords members many opportunities to make judgmental statements that please voters. Whether anything happens as a result of taking a position seems not to matter; what *is* important is that the voters like what they hear.[4]

Congressional incumbents have big advantages over their challengers. Countless opportunities are available for them to be in the news. The local media treat them sympathetically (see Chapter 11). They can take many free trips home for speaking engagements, tours around the district, and informal meetings with voters. The franking privilege permits them to send mail to constituents free of charge. (The annual cost of the frank exceeds $200,000 per member—an enormous advantage in advertising.[5]) The members' Washington and district staffs not only provide research assistance and policy guidance but also, and at least as important,

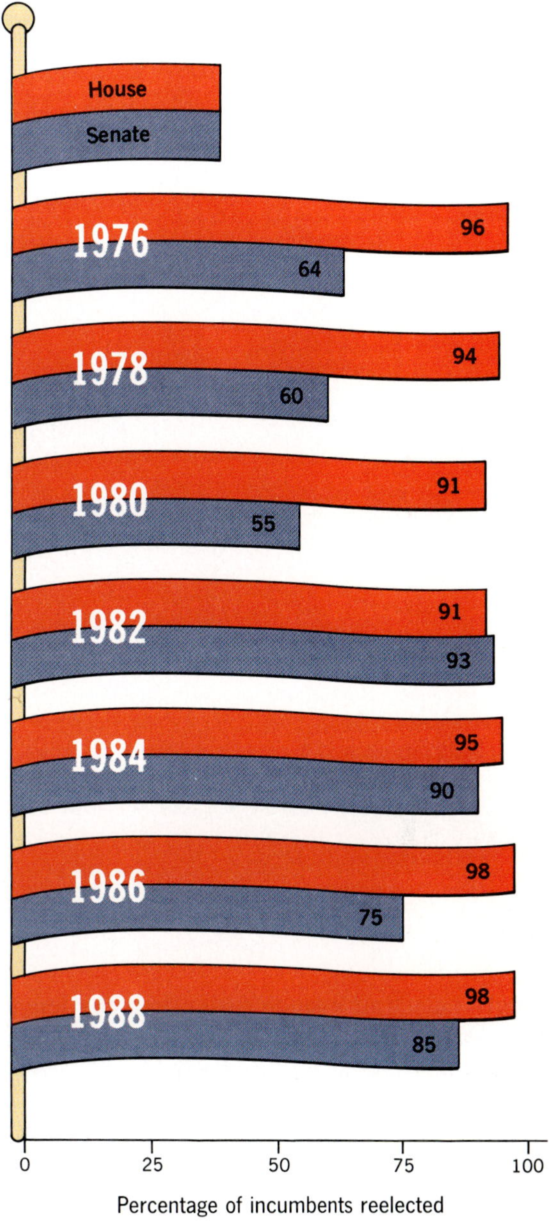

Figure 12–1 Success of congressional incumbents in general elections. Source: various issues of the *Congressional Quarterly Weekly Report.*

handle the requests of constituents. Congressional staffs are key elements in the campaign organizations of members.

Incumbents also have a campaign apparatus in place and a network of supporters and, not sur-

President-elect George Bush talks with Senator Charles S. Robb (D–Va.) shortly after Robb was sworn into office. Robb, who won with more than 70 percent of the vote in 1988, served as governor of Virginia from 1982 to 1986. The governor's office is a good launching pad for a career in the Senate.

prisingly, they find it much easier than challengers to raise campaign funds. The reality today is that a House challenger who cannot raise a half-million-dollar "war chest" has virtually no chance to unseat an incumbent; and even with that sum, the challenger's chances range between slim and none.

The stronger the incumbent, studies have shown, the harder it is to recruit credible challengers.[6] Even the districts in which they run may have been gerrymandered to suit the incumbents. Everything about the situation, including the results of past elections, suggests that incumbents are winners—and there is a winning psychology in elections. Who wants to back a loser? (Surely not most interest groups!)

Incumbents also profit from an anomaly. In the words of Richard F. Fenno, Jr., we "love our congressman . . . [but] not . . . our Congress."[7] An important reason for this is that the public uses different standards for evaluating the institution and the member. Many voters assess the institution in terms of its overall policy accomplishments; when they are disappointed with the results, Congress's public standing suffers. By contrast, few voters evaluate their legislators in a policy context, and they largely ignore the legislators' voting records. Voters judge members in terms of their records of constituency service and their personal attributes.[8] And they obviously like what they see. For incumbents, of course, this is the best of all worlds.

Incumbents fully appreciate the advantages of officeholding. Constituents are always within their reach. In the words of a House member: "It's dramatically easier to run as an incumbent. My opponent made a vicious attack on me in his announcement statement, and I answered it the following day by mailing 220,000 newsletters. . . ."[9] And another member comments:

> The most important part of a campaign is getting out and doing constituent services, and I think that's where you have to look at incumbency. I think in my district, if I go back to the 600 people whom I've helped and they tell their kids and relatives who all live in the same district—you know, she's helped us—I'm better off. They're not going to look at my votes. I am really convinced of that.[10]

Congressional elections are not isolated events. Their outcomes may be influenced by forces beyond the control of the candidates. The popularity of the party's candidate for the presidency, for example, may affect the fortunes of congressional candidates. Straight-ticket voting may secure them votes that ordinarily they would not receive. Likewise, unpopular presidential candidates may hurt their party's chances in certain elections. Not surprisingly, the candidates who are most concerned about how voters view the head of the ticket are those who represent competitive constituencies. President Jimmy Carter's clear-cut defeat by Ronald Reagan in 1980 undoubtedly cost some party members their seats in Congress; 28 of the

“ Perspectives ”

On Incumbents: A Permanent Ruling Class?

“*This institution is not guilty of the charge that it's an ossifying, unchanging place. . . . [Much more turnover] would weaken the institution and would increase the power of the executive and the congressional bureaucracy. . . . The reality is it would decrease the effectiveness of Congress.*”

—Thomas S. Foley, Speaker, U.S. House of Representatives

“*The problem is that the campaign-finance system is so tilted toward incumbents it's hard for a newcomer to crack it. Able men and women who could bring creative new solutions, even if they step forward, have little chance of winning.*”

—Herb Schultz, campaign finance director, Center for Responsive Politics

“*Can you think of a single issue that would be more effectively addressed by having 200 marginal districts?*”

—Alan Ehrenhalt, political editor of *Governing* magazine

“*The combination of a lack of incumbents losing and the fact that most seats aren't contestable sends a warning that something's out of whack here. . . . Everyone understands that the present system for financing and running for office is unfair to challengers. It's gotten to the point where it's a fundamentally corrupt system.*”

—Fred Wertheimer, president, Common Cause

“*Longevity promotes competence. . . . Everything in the government is being professionalized, and if there were enforced or high turnover, members wouldn't have much influence vis-à-vis the executive branch or the institutional congressional bureaucracy. Now members stay around long enough to be able to legislate.*”

—Nelson W. Polsby, political scientist

Source: *Congressional Quarterly Weekly Report,* November 19, 1988, pp. 3362–3365.

31 House incumbents who were defeated were Democrats, as were all 9 incumbent senators who lost. On the other hand, President Reagan's landslide victory over Walter Mondale in 1984 was accompanied by a Republican loss of 2 seats in the Senate and a gain of only 14 in the House. And George Bush's comfortable victory over Michael Dukakis in 1988 carried no payoff in congressional contests: the Republicans lost 1 seat in the Senate and 2 in the House. Most members of Congress, it should be emphasized, represent constituencies that are sufficiently safe (for them if not for their party) that even an unpopular presidential candidate will not threaten their return to Washington.

Midterm elections can prove troublesome for some members of Congress. Those who are most vulnerable are those from marginal districts who belong to the party in control of the administration. It is an unusual midterm election when the administration party increases the number of its seats in Congress. This has occurred only once in this century—in 1934, during the first term of Franklin D. Roosevelt. Administration party losses often are severe. In 8 of the 17 off-year elections between 1922 and 1986, for example, the administration party suffered a net loss of more than 40 House seats. Presidents thus have good reason to approach midterm elections with as much apprehension as do their party colleagues from marginal districts. For the president, the odds are that the new Congress will be less friendly than the previous one.

Although the administration party's midterm sag is expected, the losses are much greater in some years than in others. Research has shown that midterm voters are not evaluating Congress so much as the president. How they evaluate the president determines in large part how they evaluate Congress! The key variables are the president's popularity and the state of the economy. If the public is disenchanted with the president or judges the economy as poor, or both, the midterm losses of the president's party are likely to be severe. With these conditions reversed, losses are likely to be limited.[11] The most vulnerable members of Congress obviously have a special stake in the president's popularity and success in managing the economy. The *president's* problems, it turns out, are *their* problems.

To conclude this analysis of congressional elections, it is important to note that turnout for them is poor, particularly in nonpresidential (off-year, midterm) years. During the 1960s, turnout in midterm House elections reached 45 percent of the nation's voting age population. Since then, it has declined steadily. In 1982 the turnout rate was 37.7 percent, and in 1986 only 33.4 percent. With only one out of three eligible voters casting ballots in 1986, turnout was the lowest of any national election since the mid-1940s.[12] Popular indifference to Congress and its members is a national embarrassment, if not a scandal.

Financing Congressional Campaigns ■

Money is a major element and a major worry in the campaigns of American politicians. Campaigns are expensive and growing ever more so. They cannot be run effectively without substantial funding, at least when major offices are involved; and candidates for Congress know this better than anyone.

In the minds of some citizens, campaign money has some pathology about it. It is tempting to believe that candidates are easily corrupted by money and that contributions buy unusual influence for the donor. Occasional cases of bribery and illegal uses of campaign money reinforce the popular belief that political money is tainted. A little evidence, it seems, goes a long way in shaping people's attitudes about campaign finance.

For most candidates, campaign money is also a problem—more accurately, a series of them. Candidates rarely feel that their campaign treasury is large enough; they spend considerable time and energy trying to add to it; they know that the volume or sources of their funds can become a campaign issue; they wonder what large donors ("fat cats") may expect of them; and they grow uneasy that certain of their funding practices may not comply with campaign finance laws. Whatever else may be said about it, money is trouble in the world of politics. In the words of a veteran Ohio congressman who recently chose to retire rather than wage another campaign: "There isn't a single campaign contribution that isn't a mortgage on the person who receives it. I didn't want to have to incur the high cost of such political mortgages."[13]

Campaign costs have risen rapidly. The data of Figure 12–2 show the total expenditures by *winning* House and Senate candidates in seven congressional elections between 1976 and 1988. Over this period, expenditures by successful House candidates increased by nearly 500 percent and those by successful Senate candidates increased by a whopping 600 percent.[14]

The cost of getting elected to Congress is placed in sharper focus by the data of Table 12–1, showing

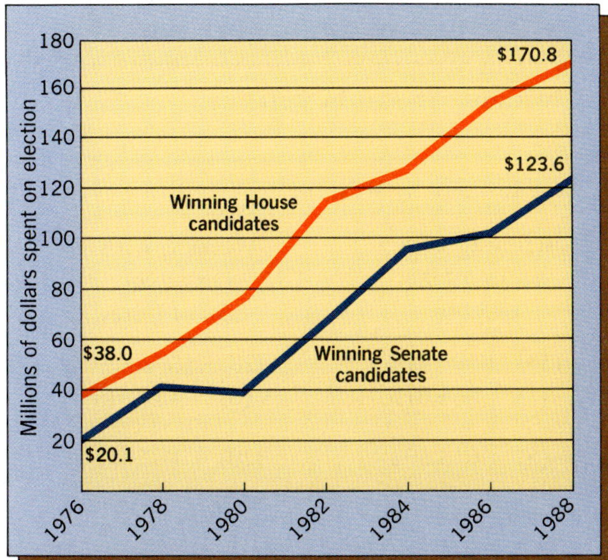

Figure 12–2 Total spending by winning House and Senate candidates. Spending is for all campaigns, including campaigns for the primary, runoff, and general elections—a two-year election cycle for each election from 1976 to 1988. For example, the data for the 1988 election cover the years 1987 and 1988. Source: press release, Federal Election Commission, February 24, 1989.

the 1986 expenditures by winning House candidates in relation to their electoral margins. Several conclusions stand out. First, the biggest spenders are incumbents in relatively competitive races—in 1986 they spent an average of almost $600,000 to win reelection. Second, even incumbents who win easily (by 60 percent or more and perhaps without opposition) spend several hundred thousand dollars on their campaigns; in 1986 their costs averaged $275,000. Third, although few challengers win, those who do spend heavily—on the order of half a million dollars for their campaigns. Necessarily, winners are not pikers!

Some House races are scandalously expensive. Representative Jack Kemp (R–N.Y.) spent $2.6 million in winning reelection in 1986 (and in advertising his presidential wares for 1988). Running for an open seat, Joseph Kennedy (D–Mass.) spent $1.8 million in 1986; he won reelection in 1988 while spending $1.1 million.

Campaign spending in Senate races (not shown in Table 12–1) reflects similar growth. It is now a rare Senate campaign in which a candidate spends less than $1 million, and multimillion-dollar campaigns are commonplace. In 1988, 22 Senate candidates spent more than $3 million each on their campaigns. Pete Wilson (R–Calif.) spent $13 million to win reelection; his Democratic opponent, Leo McCarthy, spent $7 million. Altogether, Democratic incumbents spent an average of $3.4 million in their campaigns, Republican incumbents an average of $4.1 million. The record for Senate campaign spending continues to be held by Jesse Helms (R–N.C.), who spent about $16 million to win reelection in 1984. Money may not buy happiness, but it does help win Senate seats.

Campaign costs have accelerated for three key reasons. First, and most important, candidates are investing more and more heavily in television advertising—and television rates continue to rise. Some U.S. Senate candidates spend three-fourths of their campaign funds on television commercials (see Chapter 11). In winning reelection in 1986, Senator Alan Cranston of California spent more than $7 million simply on television advertising.[15] Second, candidates are now making greater use of expensive, high-technology campaign tools, such as selective direct mail, opinion surveys, and computer analyses of voting behavior. And third, the availability of PAC money prompts candidates to spend freely: "easy come, easy go." Candidates know that every dollar counts, now or later: A large campaign kitty set aside in advance of the election season, for example, helps to scare off potential challengers.

Several sources of campaign funds are available to candidates. Private individuals are the mainstays. About half of the funds raised by House candidates and two-thirds of the funds raised by Senate candidates are given by individuals. Next are the political action committees of interest groups. In recent elections, about one-third of the money received by House candidates and about one-fourth of that received by Senate candidates has come from PACs. And their contributions have been increasing at a steady rate. In 1986 PAC contributions to House and Senate candidates totaled about $148 million, more than four times as much

TABLE 12–1

Costs of Winning U.S. House Elections, Shown in Relation to Electoral Margins, 1986

	Average Expenditures by Winning*					
	Winning with 60% or More of Vote		Winning with 55 to 59.9% of Vote		Winning with Less than 55% of Vote	
Incumbents	(333)	$274,766	(33)	$599,474	(23)	$592,649
Challengers	(1)	382,663	(1)	854,616	(5)	457,046
Candidates for open seats	(15)	586,276	(8)	613,592	(20)	467,371

* The number of House candidates in each category is shown in parentheses. By comparison, the 205 challengers who received less than 40% of the vote had average expenditures of only $92,000. The only way for candidates to get to Washington in any capacity other than visitor is to raise several hundred thousand dollars of campaign funds, and even that amount will probably not do the trick against the usual incumbent.
Source: Data from press release, Federal Election Commission, May 10, 1987.

as in 1978. *Incumbents,* as usual, were the main beneficiaries: for House members, 47 percent of their total receipts came from PACs, and for Senate members, 29 percent. PACs contributed eight times as much money to House incumbents as to their challengers. Congressmen Robert H. Michel (R–Ill.) and Thomas S. Foley (D–Wash.) each accepted $555,000 from assorted PACs.

Political party contributions to congressional candidates rank a distant third, measured in terms of *direct* gifts. Recently, House and Senate candidates have received between 1 and 2 percent of their funds from party committees. This low level of support stems in part from the Federal Election Campaign Act, which limits party gifts to congressional candidates. The law nevertheless does permit the parties to spend relatively large sums on *behalf* of their nominees. Republican party committees are especially active in this regard; they often conduct polls and produce campaign ads to aid their congressional candidates.

An analysis of congressional campaign financing supports several generalizations: (1) Incumbents are much more successful than their challengers in securing campaign funds. Typically, they collect and spend three or four times as much as their challengers. Ample funding helps to account for their success. (2) Spending is usually very heavy when there is an open seat (no incumbent). (3) Winning a seat for the first time, especially in the House, usually involves greater expenditures than winning reelection. (4) Of no surprise, spending is highest in the most competitive districts and states and lowest in those long held by a particular incumbent or party. Politicians and their supporters are realists. (5) Although the vast majority of incumbents are reelected, many of them by lopsided margins, heavy spending by challengers improves their chances for an upset. Challengers who are outspent by incumbents—the usual case—do not often win.[16]

The most troublesome aspect of campaign finance concerns the role of interest groups. Clearly, candidates for Congress have become more reliant on them for campaign money. The worry is simply that this linkage undermines the representative system, giving groups undue influence over public policy. Whether, in fact, some legislators become beholden to the groups that contribute to their campaigns is impossible to say.[17] One member of the House (Jim Leach, R–Iowa) sees the problem

Senator Edward Kennedy (D–Mass.) campaigns on behalf of Senator Alan Cranston (D–Calif.) in the 1986 election. Cranston has held the Senate's second-highest party leadership position—Democratic whip—longer than any predecessor in history. He has been elected to that office seven times, beginning in 1977.

in these terms: "There is an implicit contract between the giver and the recipient of PAC money. It would be going too far to call it bribery, but certainly there is an element of influence peddling that is not trivial." [18] At a minimum, this much is clear: PAC contributions help groups to gain *access*—that is, opportunities to present their views to members who have taken their funds.

Congressional candidates accept (and solicit) PAC money because their campaigns, unlike those of presidential candidates, are privately financed.[19] In fact, one reason for the heavy involvement of interest groups in campaigns for Congress is that presidential candidates who accept public campaign financing cannot accept private contributions. (Groups can, however, spend unlimited amounts on *behalf* of presidential candidates.) In addition, there are no limits on the amount congressional candidates can spend in elections—an inducement for them to collect and spend large sums. Interest groups stand ready to help them amass it.

Characteristics of Members

Congress is made up of successful politicians—men and women who have survived a variety of recruitment, nomination, and election winnowing-out processes. Political ambition, skills, party affiliation, and financial resources, mixed with the personal characteristics of candidates and measures of good fortune, determine who is elected to our national legislature. Those who are chosen, as we shall

see, are in many important respects unlike the voters who choose them. Viewed simply in terms of the backgrounds of its members, Congress is a most unrepresentative body.

The differences between the backgrounds of members of Congress and those they represent are perhaps expected. Consider education. Whereas only about one-fourth of the nation's adult population has attended college, the overwhelming majority of legislators are college graduates. Law and other advanced degrees are common. By any standard, the members of Congress are well educated, much better educated than their constituents.

Consider the occupations of members. In a sense, Congress has been captured by lawyers. In recent Congresses, about half the members have had law backgrounds; the proportion sometimes exceeds two-thirds in the Senate. Members with occupations in business and banking are also numerous; nearly one-third of the members of the 101st Congress (1989–1990), for example, were drawn from those two fields. And many come to Congress from careers in education—recently about 10 percent of the total membership. By contrast, only a few emerge from working-class environments. The prelegislative careers of members of Congress, it is apparent, have little in common with the working lives of most voters.

In terms of sex and race, the membership of Congress also presents a sharp contrast with the population. Both women and blacks are underrepresented—conspicuously in the House, severely in the Senate. In the 101st Congress (1989–1990), for example, there were only 25 women and 24 blacks—all members of the House save two (Senators Nancy Kassebaum, R–Kans., and Barbara Mikulski, D–Md.). Each group has made gains since the 1960s, but neither comes close to winning seats in proportion to its share of the population. Hispanics are also underrepresented in Congress, but not as acutely as women and blacks. In the 101st Congress, there were 12 Hispanic members.

More closely resembling a cross section of the population are the religious affiliations of members. Although much underrepresented in earlier years, Catholics and Jews are now elected in numbers that generally reflect their shares of the population. In recent Congresses, about two-thirds of the members have been Protestants. In terms of their proportions of the population, though, certain high-status Protestant denominations, such as Episcopalian and Presbyterian, are greatly overrepresented in the chambers.

The makeup of Congress can also be examined in terms of party affiliation. Democrats have typically outnumbered Republicans. Until 1980, when they captured the Senate, the Republicans had not won a majority of seats in either chamber since the mid-1950s. Two factors have favored Democratic control of Congress: the party's strength in the electorate and the tendency of voters to reelect incumbents (thus perpetuating Democratic majorities).

In summary, representatives and senators do not closely resemble their constituents. Drawn from the middle and upper classes of society, they are not "average" people. They are overwhelmingly white and overwhelmingly male. They are unusually well educated. Their occupations and incomes testify to their elite status. Nevertheless, data on social background tell only so much. Lawyers, for example, do not vote as a bloc; nor do Episcopalians. Most important, social class characteristics offer no evidence that in forming public policy, members of Congress are preoccupied with passing on benefits to middle- and upper-class interests at the expense of poorer classes. Quite the contrary, how members vote on "class" legislation (for instance, labor-management or social welfare proposals) is influenced much more by their party affiliation than by anything else, including their social status (see Chapter 9).

Barbara A. Mikulski (D–Md.), shown here, and Nancy Landon Kassebaum (R–Kans.) are the only women currently serving in the U.S. Senate. Twenty-five women were elected to the House of Representatives for the 101st Congress (1989–1990). Limited by the seniority rule, no woman chairs a committee in either chamber.

The Organization of Congress

Congress is a complex institution. This is evident in its array of party offices and agencies, in the variety of its informal groups, in its range of committees and subcommittees, and in its infrastructure of staff and other supporting units (Figure 12–3). The complexity of congressional organization, however, has not led to a concentration of power in any one place. Congress, in fact, is characterized

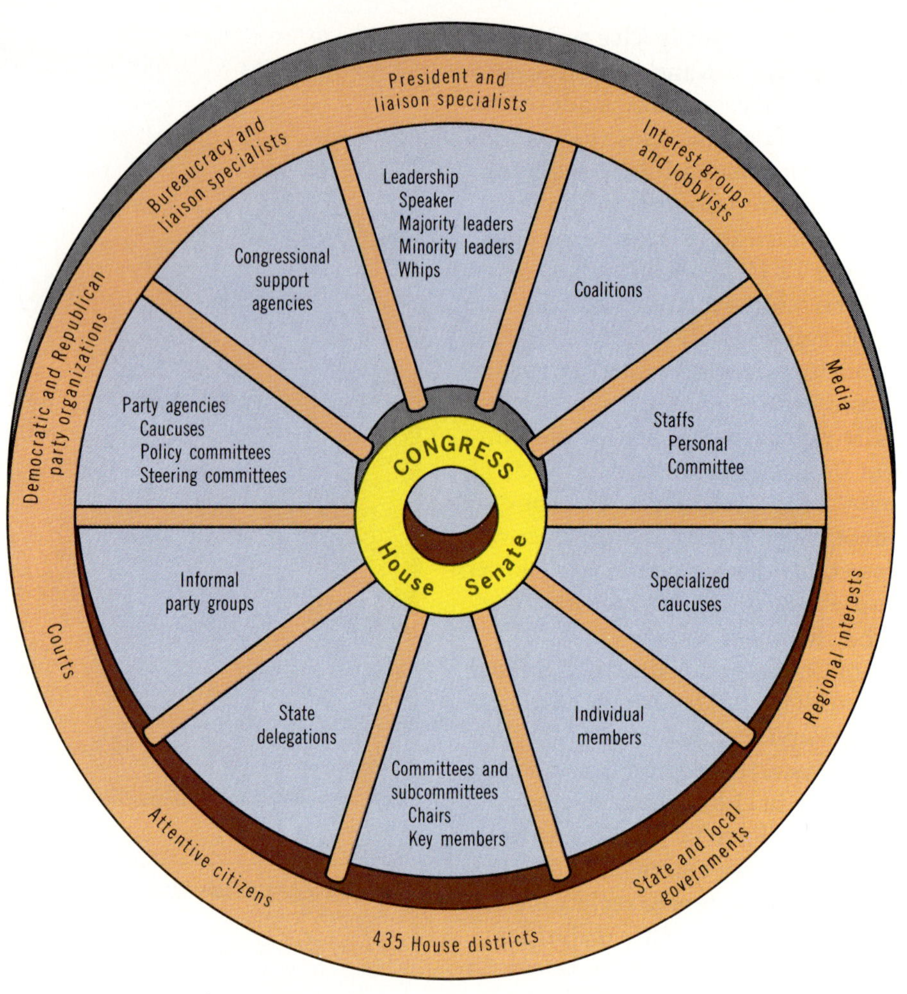

Figure 12–3 Congress: a decentralized institution in a decentralized political system.

by *limited hierarchy.* Party leaders, committee and subcommittee chairs, regional and ideological spokespersons, policy experts, and an assortment of narrow-gauge caucuses (Black Caucus, Congresswomen's Caucus, Steel Caucus, among others), along with individual members, vie to shape new policies and defend old ones. Any member, group, or coalition can usually get a "piece of the action." The most important thing to know about power in Congress is that ordinarily it is *decentralized*—spread among a range of officials and units.

The Congressional Parties

Political party organization is a major element in the structure of Congress. Except for the rare member elected as an independent (running without a party label), all representatives and senators belong to either the Democratic or the Republican party.

The majority party in each chamber is the chief agency for the *centralization* of power. That is not to say that the party, acting through its leadership, is usually successful in convincing its members to vote in common. Often, in fact, party lines collapse despite the efforts of the leaders. The inability of the parties to function as a team is due to many reasons, chief among them the relatively independent position of members and of committees and subcommittees.

Party Leadership. No one really controls Congress, but (majority) party leaders try. They have more at stake than other members in the legislature's record. They are, after all, elected to lead, even if the system makes it hard for them to do so. And it is certain that outside observers, particularly the press, will judge their performance. What is more, the president watches their work closely, since the administration's legislative program is in their hands.

The principal party leaders are the Speaker of the House, the House majority floor leader, and the Senate majority floor leader. The minority party in each chamber also elects a floor leader. Each party elects a whip, a caucus chair, and a policy committee chair. The Republicans in each house also elect the chair of the committee on committees, the panel that makes their party's committee assignments. In addition, the senior member of the majority party in the Senate is elected to the position of president pro tempore—the presiding officer.

Chosen by the majority party caucus, the *Speaker* is the leader of the House and, except for a few members who win recognition as candidates for presidential nomination, the most visible member of Congress. Speakers have an array of informal and formal powers. First of all, the Speaker is the leader of his party in the House. A Speaker whose party controls the administration is likely to be in close touch with the president, to be "in the know" concerning executive plans. No legislator can match the Speaker's access to information—and information is an element of power. The Speaker also gains influence by promoting the interests of individual members. They want good committee assignments, support for their bills, federal projects in their districts, campaign help, information, opportunities to gain publicity, and a string of other favors. In assisting them, the Speaker builds up "credit"—future support when he needs it. These exchanges are as important to the careers of members as they are to the success of the Speaker.

The formal powers of Speakers help them to control the legislative process. These include the power to recognize (or ignore) members who desire to speak on the floor; to appoint members to select, conference, and special committees; to refer bills to committee; to rule on points of order and the germaneness of motions; and to vote to break ties. The Speaker has substantial influence over the scheduling of legislation for consideration on the floor. A party rule adopted in 1975 permits Democratic Speakers to select their party's members of the Rules Committee (subject to caucus approval).

Singly or in combination, however, the Speaker's formal powers are not especially impressive. They do not permit him to command. They offer no assurance that others will follow his lead, setting aside their parochial goals in favor of national purposes. Leadership is more than formal authority. What contributes the most to it, it seems, are various intangible qualities, such as personality and political skill. A close student of congressional leadership, Robert L. Peabody, observes:

> That Speakers like Nicholas Longworth (R–Ohio) and Sam Rayburn (D–Tex.) from time to time have operated effectively has been attributed more to their strong personal characters and persuasive abilities rather than to the limited formal powers available to them. What seems to distinguish strong Speakers from the more mediocre ones has been a willingness to use their limited legislative powers to the hilt, at the same time exploiting other more personal forms of influence with skill and subtlety. They must initiate actions without getting too far out in front of a majority of their followers. They must operate with "controlled partisanship." A Speaker must function in two roles almost simultaneously—first, as the neutral presiding officer to protect the rights of *all* members, majority and minority alike, and second, as partisan leader of the majority party to seek ways to advance the party's policy objectives and continued control of the Congress.[20]

Continuity & CHANGE

How Much Money Do House Incumbents Spend to Be Reelected?

The answer to that question is "plenty." Money is "the mother's milk of politics." Candidates and their staffs spend enormous amounts of time raising it. The following data show the rapid growth of campaign expenditures by House incumbents in the 1980s.

	Average Expenditures		
	1976	1986	1988
Winning Democratic incumbents	$73,000	$312,000	$358,000
Winning Republican incumbents	$86,000	$367,000	$410,000

Source: The 1976 expenditures were calculated from data compiled by Michael J. Malbin and Thomas W. Skladony, as reported in *Money and Politics in the United States: Financing Elections in the 1980s,* ed. Michael J. Malbin (Washington, D.C.: American Enterprise Institute for Public Policy Research, 1984), p. 284; the 1986 and 1988 expenditures were calculated from data appearing in press releases, Federal Election Commission, May 10, 1987, and February 24, 1989.

Party disunity is a nagging problem for legislative leaders, especially in the case of congressional Democrats. The frustrations it creates are reflected in these comments by former Speaker Thomas P. ("Tip") O'Neill:

> You talk about *discipline!* Where discipline should be is in the Democratic caucus! The very fellas who criticize the fact that we don't have discipline, when they have the opportunity to display discipline in the caucus, they don't display it. All the years I've been here, there's only been three chairmen who've ever been ousted. Listen, when I was Speaker of the Massachusetts legislature, I removed a fella from a committee. I had that power. Here, I don't have that power. Here, he's elected by the caucus, and then he's elected by the House. Here, you got conservatives and moderates and liberals! You can't discipline that! I heard [a congressman] on the radio saying we ought to discipline. There'd be *five* parties here if we tried to do that.[21]

The main spokespersons for the legislative parties are the *majority* and *minority leaders,* who are chosen by their respective party caucuses. When the Speakership becomes vacant, the House majority leader ordinarily is elected to the position. When party control shifts—a rare event in recent decades—the minority leader is likely to become Speaker. On the Senate side, the majority floor leader is, in a rough sense, the counterpart of the Speaker, although his formal authority is not so great (see Table 12–2).

The chief duties of the floor leader are to develop his party's legislative program and to build support for his party's position on key proposals. He also plays a major role in scheduling bills for floor consideration. The job is not easy. Working out compromises that will pull the party together requires unusual skill, diplomacy, and imagination. Congressional leaders have an advantage when their party controls the administration, since the president's influence can sometimes be put to use. At times, of course, nothing works.

Like the Speaker, floor leaders are successful when they are effective in persuading members to go along with them; the power of persuasion, in the last analysis, is their principal power. A description of the office by former Speaker Jim Wright (D–Tex.) is instructive: "The majority leader is a conciliator, a mediator, a peacemaker. Even when patching together a tenuous majority he must respect the right of honest dissent, conscious of the limits of his claims upon others." [22]

Assisting the floor leader in party management are the *whips.* Each party in each chamber chooses a whip and a number of deputy (or assistant) whips drawn from various sections of the country. The whip system is basically a communications network for passing information on legislation between

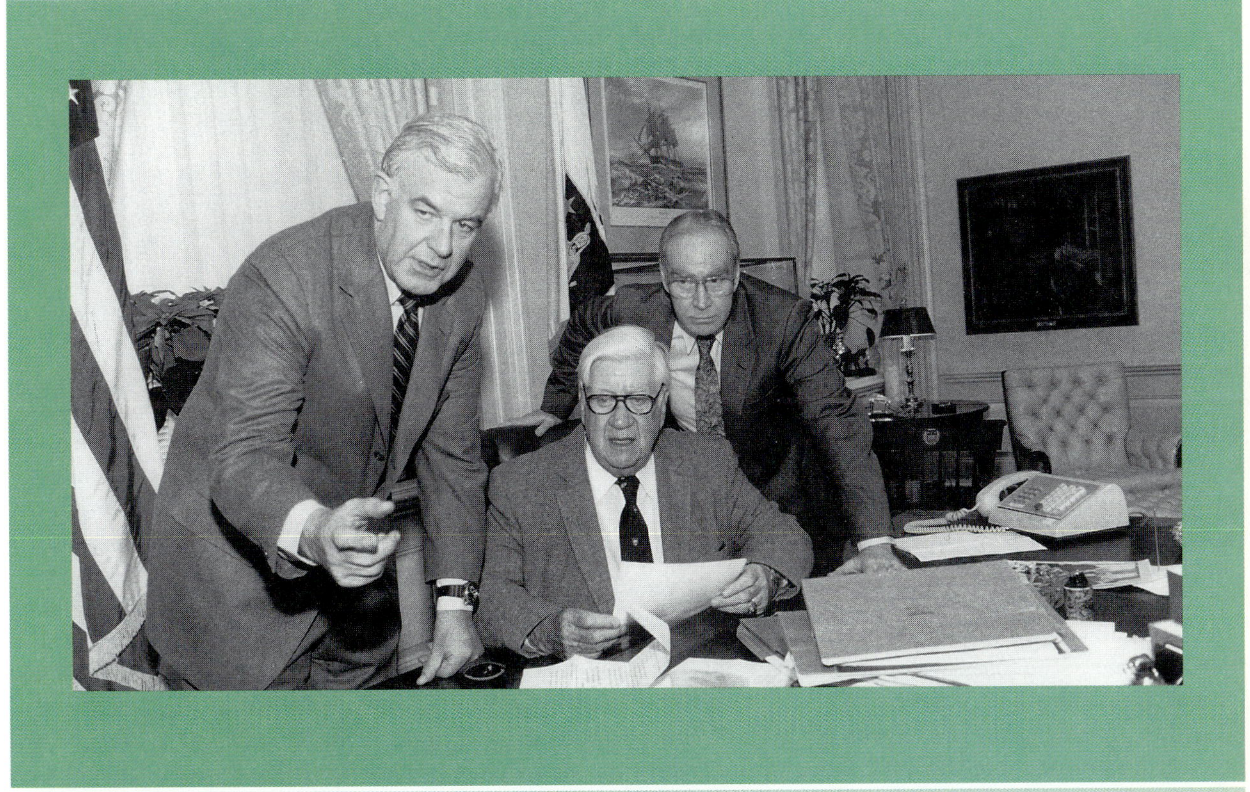

Speakers galore: Thomas P. ("Tip") O'Neill of Massachusetts (center), Speaker for a decade, beginning in 1977. He was succeeded by Jim Wright of Texas (right), who was succeeded by Thomas S. Foley of Washington (left). Foley's election as Speaker in 1989 followed Wright's resignation in the midst of an ethics committee investigation of charges that he had violated House gift and income rules.

TABLE 12–2

Major Differences Between House and Senate

House	Senate
Larger (435 members)	Smaller (100 members)
More formal	Less formal
More hierarchically organized	Less hierarchically organized
Acts more quickly	Acts more slowly
Rules more rigid	Rules more flexible
Debate limited	Debate unlimited
Power less evenly distributed	Power more evenly distributed
More policy specialization	Less policy specialization
More impersonal	More personal
Less "important" constituencies	More "important" constituencies
Less prestige	More prestige

Source: Lewis A. Froman, Jr., *The Congressional Process: Strategies, Rules, and Procedures* (Boston: Little, Brown, 1967), p. 7 (as modified). Copyright © 1967 by Little, Brown and Company (Inc.). But also see an argument by Norman J. Ornstein that these differences are not as large as in the past—in other words, that the House is becoming more like the Senate and the Senate is becoming more like the House: "The House and the Senate in a New Congress," in *The New Congress,* eds. Thomas E. Mann and Norman J. Ornstein (Washington, D.C.: American Enterprise Institute, 1981), pp. 364–371.

leaders and rank-and-file members. On controversial issues, the whip's ability to round up votes can be crucial to the outcome.

Party Agencies. The basis of party organization in each chamber is the *caucus* (or *conference*). Each member automatically becomes a member of his or her party's caucus. Common to legislative organization, caucuses perform three functions: They select party leaders, adopt party rules, and consider and formulate party positions on legislation. In practice, party caucuses are largely concerned with choosing leaders and shaping rules of procedure (such as providing for the caucus election of committee chairs by secret ballot). Developing party positions on legislation is difficult, since members worry less about their party's welfare than about their own. Not many members are willing to go along with colleagues if in doing so they may damage, or seem to damage, the interests of their constituents. At one time (early in this century) King Caucus reigned in the House. Today's independent members, however, would not accept caucus instructions on how to vote.

The other major element in the congressional party apparatus is the *policy committee.* Each party uses its policy committee—an executive committee of the caucus—to discuss party positions on bills and to find ways to gain party unity. Meeting regularly, these committees alert members to the party's side of policy questions—and thus are especially useful for the leadership—but they have never originated party programs. Elected without much help from their party, most members do not have a strong sense of party responsibility. As one member of Congress explained:

> [House members of this generation] have no institutional memory which would give some understanding of what their party, the House

> and the leadership stood for in the past and why some unity and discipline are necessary. As a result, there is little loyalty to the institutions, but only to themselves and their political survival.[23]

Informal Party Groups, State Party Delegations, Caucuses, and Coalitions. Within the array of congressional associations are a number of informal party groups and narrow-gauge caucuses and coalitions. The best-known party group is the House *Democratic Study Group (DSG)*. With about 250 members of liberal to moderate persuasion, the DSG has been in the forefront of efforts to "reform" the House. During the 1970s, the DSG worked successfully to modify the seniority system and to bring about open committee meetings. High on its current list of reforms is legislation to provide for the public financing of House elections. A much smaller Democratic group, the *Conservative Democratic Forum* (Boll Weevils), often joins House Republicans on certain economic issues; mainly southerners, the Boll Weevils supplied key votes in support of President Reagan's economic program. Among the intraparty groups on the Republican side, varying in their goals and ideologies, are the *Republican Study Committee*, the *Wednesday Group*, the *Acorns*, and the *Chowder and Marching Society*. In addition, state party delegations at times have considerable influence on House decisions.

Specialized caucuses and coalitions are also numerous in the House. In recent years, members have formed caucuses and coalitions to promote the policy goals of blacks, women, Spanish-speaking people, steel, coal, ports, shipyards, suburbs, regions, and the environment, among others. The presence of these groups, along with those spawned in the parties, testifies to the parochialism of Congress, to the significance of constituencies, and to the fragmentation of the formal parties. The loyalties of members, it is plain, run in many directions.

No one knows better than party leaders the tenuousness of their hold over today's independent members. The flavor of the leader-follower relationship is suggested in former Speaker Tip O'Neill's advice to President Carter on how to improve his support among Democratic congressmen: "I guess he'll have to go the route I go—come in on bended knee to them." [24]

The Committee System

Congress sets great store by its committee system. Its committees are at the core of the policymaking process. Legislation fashioned by the committees (and their subcommittees) is usually accepted on the floor, although it may be amended there. Legislative proposals that are defeated or ignored in committee are rarely revived by the chamber as a whole. Woodrow Wilson's observations on committee power, made in the late nineteenth century, are still largely accurate:

> The House sits, not for serious discussion, but to sanction the conclusions of its committees as rapidly as possible. It legislates in its committee-rooms; not by the deliberations of majorities, but by the resolutions of specially-commissioned minorities; so that it is not far from the truth to say that *Congress in session is Congress on public exhibition, whilst Congress in its committee-rooms is Congress at work.*[25]

A well-known congressman, writing not too many years ago, gave a graphic description of committee power: "Congress is a collection of committees that come together in a chamber periodically to approve one another's actions." [26]

There are good reasons for the prominence of committees in congressional decision making. First, the volume of bills introduced in Congress is so large (perhaps 10,000 in both sessions) that it would be impossible for the chambers as a whole to sort through them carefully. Committees do the screening, permitting only about 10 to 12 percent of all bills introduced to be reported out for floor action. The chambers can thus concentrate on major legislation and on matters of interest to them. Committees also permit specialization, which not only makes Congress a more self-reliant institution, better able to resist outside pressures, but also enhances the individual member's opportunities for gaining expertise in certain policy fields. For the member, expertise and influence go hand in hand.

Finally, committees play an important role because they are useful political arenas: trade-offs and compromises among competing interests can be hammered out in committees (even more so in subcommittees) that almost certainly would elude the membership as a whole.

Types of Committees. There are three major types of committees in Congress: standing, select, and joint.

The most important committees, the workhorses of Congress, are the *standing* committees. Established in the rules of each chamber and continuing from one Congress to the next, standing committees are organized along functional lines, such as agriculture, appropriations, armed services, judiciary, foreign relations, public works, and veterans' affairs. With rare exception, all measures are referred to a standing committee for consideration. Currently there are 22 standing committees in the House and 16 in the Senate. These 38 committees have about 250 subcommittees. The House Committee on Agriculture, for example, has subcommittees on cotton, dairy and poultry, forests, livestock and grains, and tobacco, among others. The Senate Committee on Finance (revenue legislation) has five subcommittees dealing with energy and agricultural taxation, health, international debt, international trade, and private retirement plans and oversight of the Internal Revenue Service. Most of the detailed work on legislation is done by subcommittees. It is here in particular that members win recognition for their skills in negotiation and reputations as policy experts.

Select committees are temporary panels created to perform a particular task, such as a study or investigation. In recent years, for example, Congress has employed select committees to study problems of the aging, youth and families, hunger, covert arms transactions with Iran, narcotics abuse and control, and the functioning of intelligence agencies.

Designed to promote coordination in a bicameral system, *joint* committees are made up of members from both houses. Congress makes limited use of these committees, except for one—the *conference* committee. Conference committees are formed to iron out differences when the House and Senate have adopted different versions of the same bill. Their decisions are important, since most major bills are routed through a conference committee. No bill can be sent to the president unless it has passed both houses in identical form.

A major development in the committee system since the early 1970s has been the emergence of subcommittees as powers in their own right, especially in the House. Under rules adopted by the majority caucus, subcommittee chairs are now elected by the Democratic members of the full committee (rather than appointed by the committee chair) and are given the authority to hire their own staff. Bills referred to the full committee must be sent promptly to subcommittees. Moreover, no member can serve as chair of more than one subcommittee. The effect of these changes—the Subcommittee Bill of Rights—has been to reduce the control of committee chairs over their committees while dispersing power more widely among members. One result is that the job of party leaders in managing this far-flung system has grown in difficulty.

Committee Assignments. Getting elected is the first order of business for congressional candidates. Once elected, their main objective is to land good committee assignments. For some members who have been reelected, the main aim is to secure a transfer to a more appropriate committee (in terms of the interests of their constituencies) or one that is more prestigious.

Party committees are used to make committee assignments. House Democrats give this job to their *steering and policy committee* (headed by the Speaker when the Democrats are the majority), whereas Senate Democrats use their *steering committee* for this purpose. Republicans employ a *committee on committees* in each house.

Among the factors taken into account in allotting committee seats are the member's preferences, qualifications, region, state, seniority, constituency, and reputation as a legislator. The member's ideological orientation (liberal, moder-

The interior of the Senate Select Committee on Intelligence. This hearing room, located in the Hart Senate Office building, was the site of the hearings on the Iran–contra connection and is normally off limits to the media.

ate, conservative) may also be considered when assignments are made to certain committees. For example, in choosing new members for the House Ways and Means Committee, whose main task is to write tax legislation, Democrats tend to select liberals while Republicans usually select conservatives.[27]

Committee Prestige. Committees differ in their attractiveness and prestige. In general, committees with the greatest appeal have broad, national jurisdictions. At the top of the list for senators are Foreign Relations, Finance, Appropriations, Budget, and Armed Services. In the House, the leading committees are Appropriations, Rules, Ways and Means, Budget, Armed Services, and Foreign Affairs. By contrast, not many members want to serve on Rules and Administration in the Senate or the District of Columbia Committee in the House. Service on these committees is more duty than opportunity. On the whole, members go to "where the action is"—to committees with jurisdictions that may help them win recognition and to those with policy domains important either to them personally or to their districts or states. In addition, speculation runs that, for some members, the attractiveness of a committee may be related to the heavy PAC contributions that flow to its members. The House Committee on Energy and Commerce, whose jurisdiction ranges over major sectors

"Perspectives"

On Congress

"*I have seen in the Halls of Congress more idealism, more humaneness, more compassion, more profiles of courage than in any other institution that I have ever known.*"

—Hubert H. Humphrey, former U.S. senator and former vice president

"*In the district, Congress is held in low esteem, like a used car salesman. As an institution, Congress has never been very popular. Yet people have a high respect for their individual congressman. I didn't fully appreciate that dichotomy till I got here.*"

—Congressman Les AuCoin (D–Oreg.)

"*I see the Senate, where I've served for 12 years, becoming more like the House every day. House members run for reelection every two years and always have to be concerned about the changing public mood. Senators serve six-year terms and should be able to take a longer look at issues. But what's happened is that the Senate has become too short-sighted. We are as influenced by the latest public opinion poll as the House is.*"

—Former Senator Henry L. Bellmon (R–Okla.)

"*It's every man for himself. Every senator is a baron. He has his own principality. Once you adopt that as a means of doing business, it's hard to establish any cohesion.*"

—Former Senator James B. Pearson (R–Kans.)

"*The greatest problem in Congress today is the tremendous pressure of parochial, narrowly defined interests. We seem unable to control the budget. Any group that can organize itself, articulate a problem and propose a solution automatically has a claim on the treasury.*"

—Former Congressman David A. Stockman (R–Mich.; former director, Office of Management and Budget in the Reagan administration)

"*I happen to think that the House is messy, the House will continue to be messy. It was messy under Cannon, under Clay, under Rayburn, under Albert [all former Speakers], and it will be messy under whomever comes along. I think there is a very good reason. It is that the democratic process is messy. . . .*"

—Former Congressman Richard Bolling (D–Mo.)

"*[The] willingness of House members to stand and defend their own votes or voting record contrasts sharply with their disposition to run and hide when a defense of Congress might be called for. Members of Congress run for Congress by running against Congress. The strategy is ubiquitous, addictive, cost-free and foolproof. . . . In the short run, everybody plays and nearly everybody wins. Yet the institution bleeds from 435 separate cuts. In the long run, therefore, somebody may lose.*"

—Richard F. Fenno, Jr., political scientist

"*Some days I had somebody from the state in my office every 15 minutes. Seventy-five percent of my time, or maybe 80 percent, was spent on non-legislative matters. . . . The floor is being used as an instrument of political campaigning far more than it ever has before. People seem to expect that. Constituents judge their senators on how much crap the senator is sending them. The less legislating you do the better legislator you are perceived to be. There isn't much thinking in the Senate any more.*"

—Former Senator Gaylord Nelson (D–Wis.)

"*At one time you'd blow a whistle and say this is what the party wants and the members would line up and say, "Yes sir, yes sir, yes sir." Today they get elected on Monday and they are giving a [floor] speech on Tuesday.*"

—Congressman Joe Moakley (D–Mass.)

"*[People] who want Congress to move quickly and easily don't really want representative government at all. Congress does what's necessary—frequently at the last possible moment after a crisis has already developed. But representative government is always going to be behind the curve. If you understand that, you won't be disappointed in your expectations of our government.*"

—Former Congressman Barber B. Conable, Jr. (R–N.Y.)

"*A congressman's primary job is to legislate. Yet our society and government are so complex that we spend less than a third of our time on legislative matters. A congressman is not only a legislator: he is also an employment agent, passport finder, constituent greeter, tourist agent, getter-outer of the armed services, veterans' affairs adjuster, public buildings dedicator, industrial development specialist, party leader, bill finder, newsletter writer, etc. His typical day will be far more concerned with these problems than with national defense, foreign aid, or appropriations for public works.*"

—Congressman Morris K. Udall (D–Ariz.)

"*There is an absence of a long view. People are running for reelection the day they arrive. It's unbelievable.*"

—Senator John C. Danforth (R–Mo.)

Sources: Stephen K. Bailey, *Congress in the Seventies* (New York: St. Martin's Press, 1970), p. 95; *Congressional Quarterly Weekly Report,* August 2, 1975, p. 1677; *U.S. News & World Report* (November 10, 1980), p. 55, Copyright 1980, U.S. News & World Report, Inc.; *Congressional Quarterly Weekly Report,* September 4, 1982, p. 2181; *U.S. News & World Report* (February 21, 1977), p. 21, Copyright 1977, U.S. News & World Report, Inc.; *Hearings on Committee Organization* in the House before the Select Committee on Committees, U.S. House of Representatives, 93rd Cong., 1st Sess., 1973, II, p. 58; Richard F. Fenno, Jr., *Home Style: House Members in Their Districts* (Boston: Little, Brown, 1978), p. 168; *Congressional Quarterly Weekly Report,* September 4, 1982, pp. 2176–2177; *Congressional Quarterly Weekly Report,* May 27, 1978, pp. 1301–1302; *U.S. News & World Report* (August 20, 1984), p. 30, Copyright 1984, U.S. News & World Report, Inc.; Robert L. Peabody, ed., *Education of a Congressman: The Newsletters of Morris K. Udall* (Indianapolis: Bobbs-Merrill, 1972), p. 248; *Congressional Quarterly Weekly Report,* September 4, 1982, p. 2177.

of the economy, is often cited as an example of a committee "it pays to be on." [28]

Member Goals and the Committee System. The value of a committee assignment varies according to the goals of the individual member. What is an undesirable post for one member may be highly prized by another. A study by Richard F. Fenno, Jr., finds that members have three basic goals: *reelection, influence within the House or Senate,* and *good public policy.* They evaluate committees in terms of the opportunities they present for achieving one of these goals. A member mainly concerned about reelection is apt to seek a seat on a committee whose decisions can have a direct impact on his or her constituency, such as the House committees of Public Works and Transportation, Interior and Insular Affairs, Merchant Marine and Fisheries, and Post Office and Civil Service. For members whose chief goal is influence in Congress, the appropriations and revenue committees in each house are desirable assignments; few decisions are more important than those involving spending and taxing. Finally, such committees as Education and Labor and Foreign Affairs in the House and Foreign Relations in the Senate are attractive to members with policy-oriented goals.[29]

Committee Representativeness. The committees of Congress are sometimes criticized for their unrepresentativeness. Some committees, in other words, are "stacked." This occurs because party leaders pay close attention to the preferences of individual members in making committee assignments. Legislators from farming areas apply for seats on agriculture committees, while those from heavily unionized constituencies request seats on labor committees (House Education and Labor, Senate Labor and Human Resources). Members from western states are concerned with public lands and natural resources, and they flock to the Senate Energy and Natural Resources Committee and to the House Committee on Interior and Insular Affairs. The House Committee on Merchant Marine and Fisheries contains a large number of members from the coastal states. And so it goes. Some committees become "partisans," or special pleaders, for legislation that will distribute benefits to special groups or clienteles. In advancing local interests, committee members may ignore obvious national ones.[30]

To ease the problem of unrepresentative, or "captive," committees, some critics have recommended that committee assignments be rotated every so often, perhaps every four years. Congress, however, has shown little enthusiasm for this proposal, since it would clash with one of its hoary traditions—the seniority system.

The Seniority System. Few traditions are more deeply rooted in the congressional culture than the seniority system. It affects many aspects of congressional life (even the assignment of office space), but its chief importance is that it governs *advancement on committees.* The rule is simple: A member advances in seniority on a committee through continuous service on it. The member who continues to be reelected (perhaps a dozen times in the House) will ordinarily become a committee chair, provided that his or her party holds a majority. When party control shifts, the ranking minority party member on each committee lays claim to the chair. A member who switches from one committee to another must start at the bottom of the party's seniority list on the new committee—a provision that discourages "committee hopping."

Until recently, dissatisfaction with the seniority rule was intense, especially when the Democrats were in power. Beginning with the presidency of Franklin D. Roosevelt in 1932 and continuing through that of Lyndon B. Johnson, which ended in 1968, the seniority rule conferred great advantages on the conservative southern wing of the Democratic party. This occurred because most "safe" Democratic seats were in southern states; voters in these states returned the incumbents to office election after election, adding to their seniority and in effect moving them into the position of chair. When John F. Kennedy became president in 1961, for example, more than 60 percent of the committee chairs were southerners. Few among them supported his New Frontier proposals. Northern party liberals had much less influence on decisions than their numbers warranted.

Today the seniority rule is not a major issue. Typically, southern members chair no more than their fair share of committees (about one-third) when the Democrats are in a majority. Several changes account for the decline in southern power. To begin, Republicans are now winning seats in almost all southern states, which reduces the number of southern Democrats. At the same time, the Democratic party has grown in strength in the North, winning seats that in earlier decades were safely Republican; the Democratic party has become a predominantly northern party. There are now almost twice as many Democratic safe seats in the North as in the South, thus resulting in many more northern chairs. The decline of southern power has taken much of the "heat" out of the seniority issue.

But that is only part of the explanation. The seniority system itself is different. Party rules on seniority adopted in the early 1970s provide for caucus members to cast secret ballots on committee chairs (and ranking minority members) at the opening of each new Congress. Seniority thus no longer automatically governs the allocation of chairs. Committee chairs, moreover, can be removed from office. In 1975, the House Democratic caucus voted to remove three committee chairs who had lost the support of their party colleagues. And in 1985, over the opposition of the Speaker, the House Democratic caucus removed the aging and frail chairman of the Armed Services Committee and picked as his successor the *seventh*-ranking Democrat on the committee. The seniority custom is clearly less powerful today than in the past, but it is in no danger of being discarded.

Finally, the seniority rule is less controversial because the powers of committee leaders have been clipped. No longer can chairs run their committees with an iron hand, personally controlling subcommittees, staff, and decisions. Powers once held by committee chairs are now dispersed. The big gainers in this reshuffling of power, particularly in the House, have been the subcommittees and their chairs.

For some, this new structure of power is attractive because it is more "democratic." Younger members obviously like it, since it increases their influence; it does not take them long to become a subcommittee chair. And autocratic committee chairs have passed from the scene. But there is another side. The dispersal of power has made the institution less cohesive, less manageable, and, as a result, more unpredictable. On the Democratic side, where internal divisions run deep, the management problems of party leaders are sometimes acute.

The Staffs and Support Agencies ■

A major development within Congress over the past two decades has been the growth of a legislative bureaucracy—an array of staff and supporting elements to assist members in doing their jobs. In 1960, appropriations for the legislative branch totaled about $128 million; by 1989, the budget for Congress had grown to about $1.7 billion—a 13-fold increase. In the argot of the press, the country now enjoys a "billion dollar Congress." In all, there are 38,000 congressional employees, including printers, barbers, beauticians, photographers, laborers, television technicians, computer specialists, parking attendants, and professional staff.[31] The most important employees are the *personal* and *committee* staff members of each house.

The congressional bureaucracy is no match for that of the executive branch (with more than 2 million employees), but its growth has been phenomenal. There are about three times as many staff today as in 1960. Currently there are about 11,700 personal staff working in the offices of representatives and senators and about 3000 staff assigned to committees. With an allowance of more than $400,000 a year, each member of the House may hire up to 22 personal aides. Staff allowances for senators are determined by state population, ranging from about $1 million for a senator from a small state to $1.9 million for a member from the largest state—California. There is no limit on the number of employees a senator may hire.

The expansion of congressional staff is, in part, an effort to come to terms with a problem that is central to legislatures: the need for information and expert policy analysis.[32] Committee staffs are organized to gather and analyze information needed

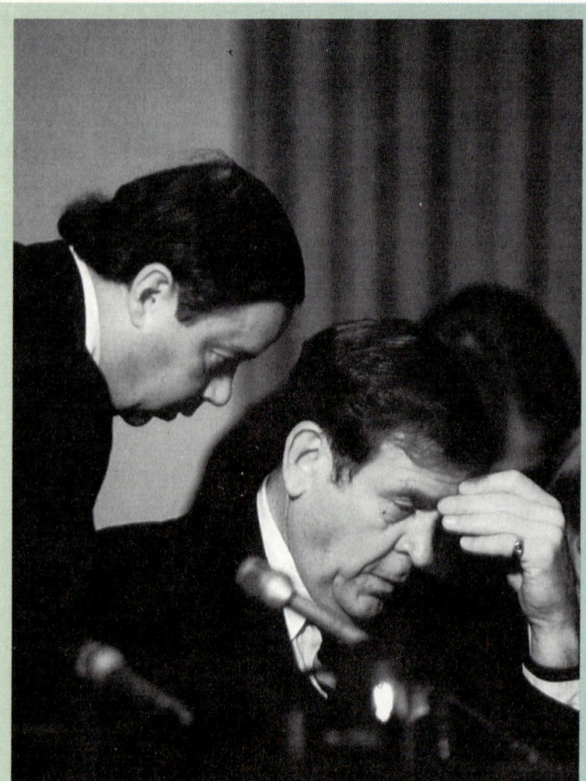

Dan Rostenkowski (D–Ill.), chairman of the powerful House Ways and Means Committee, confers with a staff aide over tax legislation under consideration by the committee.

to shape policy. But more than that, they arrange hearings, structure investigations, frame alternatives, draft legislation, write reports, and interact with lobbyists, legislators, and executive branch personnel. They are often involved in forming a coalition to support a bill. And they are sometimes criticized for taking over the power of members—for writing their own preferences into legislation and otherwise playing too large a role in shaping public policy. As observed by a member of the Senate:

> Members are so burdened with other duties that an increasing amount of committee work is being delegated to staff personnel. As a result, professional staffers are assuming too much power, and in some cases, are making policy rather than merely helping with the technical problems as was intended.[33]

There is no end to the kinds of aid needed by members of Congress. Some personal staff spend considerable time working on legislative matters, such as developing and examining policy options (from the perspective of the member and his or her constituency's interests) and researching and drafting bills. But they spend much more time dealing with constituent requests and activities that promote the member's reelection. Nothing, it seems, is more important than handling constituents' problems with government—matters involving veterans' benefits, social security payments, jobs, program funding, emergency military leaves, immigration, government contracts, and the like. Average persons, community leaders, and organizations of all kinds press hard on legislators for assistance. The office of a senator from a large state, such as California or New York, handles tens of thousands of "cases" each year. *Casework* presents an opportunity for the member to earn credit with the voters and thus to build support for the next election. No member or staff takes it lightly. The fact of the matter is that members *invite* constituents to bring their problems to them, as this newsletter statement by Senator H. John Heinz (R–Pa.) shows clearly:

> Casework is part of my responsibility to ensure that Pennsylvania gets timely and responsive service from the federal government. We are fortunate to have many dedicated people who work in the Senate office full-time on solving your problems. Lost Social Security checks, foul-ups in Black Lung benefits, and problems with military enlistments are just a few of the many problems our 5 in-state Senate offices handle every day. Some problems can be handled quickly, while others take a little more time and persistence. For example, during the Egyptian exhibit at the National Gallery of Art in Washington, we were contacted by the D. T. Watson Home for Crippled Children in Pittsburgh. They wanted to take the children

> to Washington to see the exhibit but the Gallery had refused their request for a special tour because of the huge crowds. A personal call to the Gallery's Director convinced him of the children's special need and the tour was quickly arranged. It has been a pleasure to represent you in the U.S. Senate during the past year. If you ever need help, please do not hesitate to write or call.[34]

Other major duties of the personal staff include answering mail from constituents, meeting with constituents and lobbyists, drafting speeches, writing newsletters and press releases, keeping tabs on political happenings at home, and devising means for gaining media attention. A creative staff that is careful about political detail and opportunity can do much to keep the member in the public eye, enhancing his or her chances for reelection. At the same time, staff support contributes to the member's independence within Congress.

Congressional offices, as much as anything, are campaign offices, working year-round on reelection. And they are effective, which helps explain why so few incumbents are defeated.

The congressional bureaucracy also includes four main research arms: the Congressional Research Service (CRS) of the Library of Congress, the General Accounting Office (GAO), the Congressional Budget Office (CBO), and the Office of Technology Assessment (OTA). These agencies represent the collective staff of Congress, set up to provide basic reference and research services. The GAO, the largest of these agencies with over 5000 employees, is often described as a "watchdog," charged with overseeing the expenditures of executive agencies and evaluating their programs. (See an analysis of the congressional budget process in Chapter 17.)

In matters of organization and structure, Congress knows what it wants. By creating its staff and research infrastructure, its main objective was to develop sources of information and policy analysis, making the institution more self-sufficient and increasing its independence from the executive branch. At the same time, Congress made it easier for its members to cope with the complexities of lawmaking and strengthened their capacity to manage their job, handle constituent requests, and defend constituency interests. An elaborate congressional bureaucracy, it should be clear, serves electoral as well as legislative purposes.

A Bill Becomes a Law

At one time or another, most citizens have come up with an idea they think Congress should turn into law. In the real world of politics, however, individual constituents inspire few laws: Rather, laws are the products of *organized* elements in government and the private sector. They stem in particular from four sources: the executive branch, political interest groups, party programs, and legislators themselves (including their staffs).

The major proposals on the congressional agenda are usually advanced by the president and the agencies of the executive branch (see Chapter 13). But the authorship of many bills is hard to establish. Certain proposals that are regarded as key items in the president's program, for example, may have been discussed in Congress for years. Viewed as the nation's "chief legislator" (as well as chief executive), the president often gets credit for legislation that properly belongs to Congress.

Occasionally, Congress winds up in the driver's seat. Congressional ascendancy in policy making is most likely to develop when the president has been damaged politically (as in the Iran-contra arms scandal), when the president's term in office is nearly over, and when the opposition party holds a commanding majority in each house.

The Stages of Lawmaking ■

Lawmaking involves several stages (Figure 12–4). First, each bill must be introduced by a member of the House or Senate. It is then referred by the presiding officer (in consultation with the parliamentarian) to a standing committee; ordinarily it is then referred to a subcommittee. If the bill is important, hearings will be scheduled (perhaps held on a number of days over several months) at which agents of various interest groups, government officials (including other members of Congress), and interested citizens can offer their views.

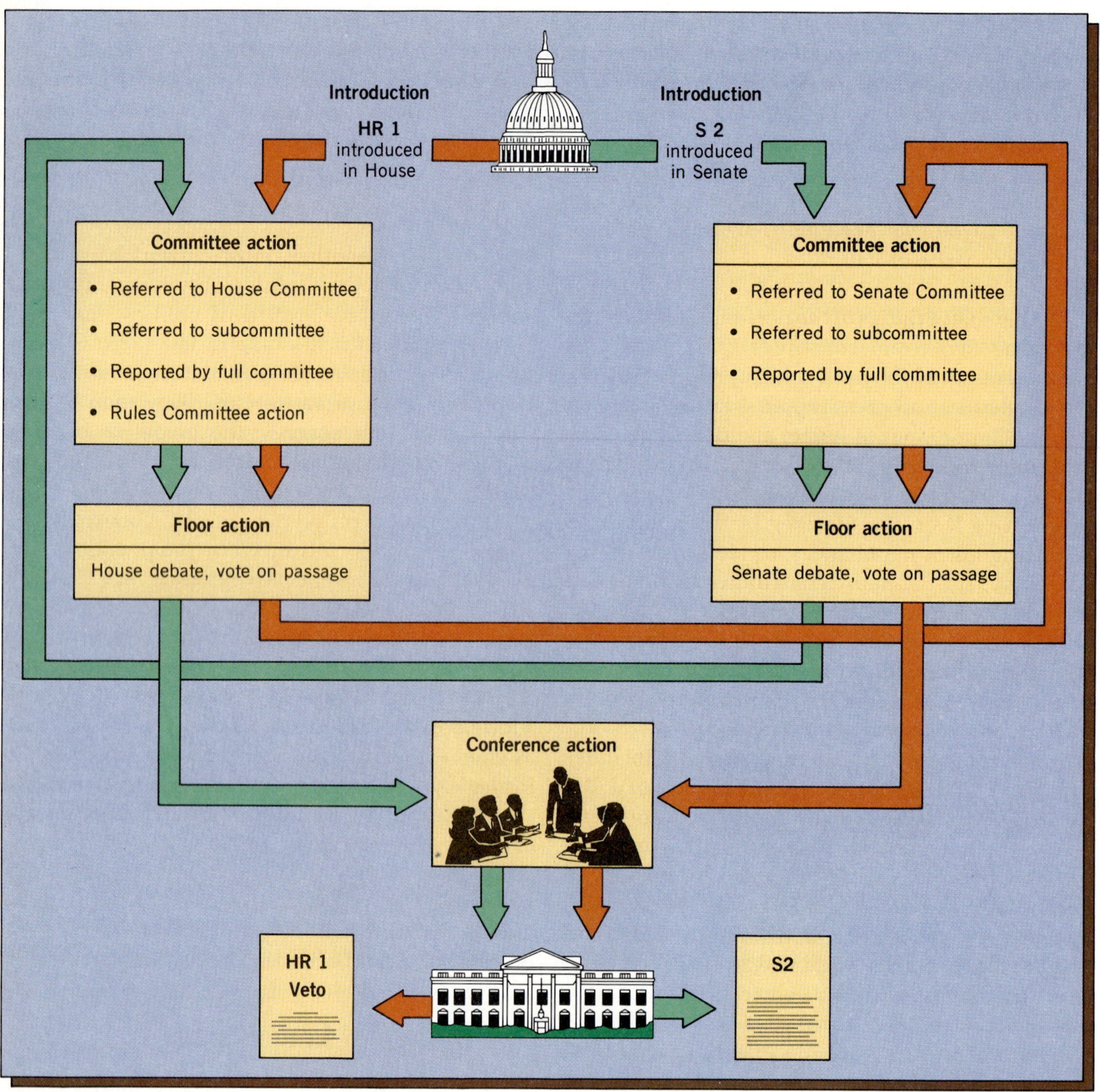

Figure 12–4 How a bill becomes law—the most typical way in which proposed legislation is enacted. There are more complicated, as well as simpler, routes, and most bills fall by the wayside and never become law. The process is illustrated with two hypothetical bills, House bill No. 1 (HR 1) and Senate bill No. 2 (S 2). Each bill must be passed by both houses of Congress in identical form before it can become law. The paths of HR 1 and S 2 are traced separately in the figure. However, in practice most legislation begins as similar proposals in both houses. Source: *Congressional Quarterly.*

Following the hearings, the subcommittee "marks up" the bill, considering it line by line, adding and deleting provisions. Staff research is often critical to the decisions made at this point. Next the bill is considered by the full committee—the last step before it is reported to the chamber as a whole.

Once passed by a committee, a bill is ready for floor consideration. But the process is not automatic. In the House, important bills must first secure a *rule* from the Rules Committee, specifying a time for debate, the division of debate time for proponents and opponents, and whether amendments will be permitted. Occasionally the Rules Committee will refuse to grant a rule, in effect vetoing the bill (unless a House majority votes to take control of the measure—an unlikely action). Scheduling measures in the Senate is a more informal process, done by the majority leader in consultation with the minority leader.

Action on the floor consists of debate, consideration of amendments, and the vote. A major difference between the House and the Senate is that debate is tightly controlled in the House, whereas it is unlimited in the Senate. The Senate's tradition of free debate leads now and then to a *filibuster,* in which a group of senators seeks to defeat a bill by "talking it to death." If the filibusterers can hold the floor long enough, the bill's supporters may decide to throw in the towel, abandoning their bill and freeing the Senate to move on to other business. A filibuster can be halted, however, by the adoption of a *cloture* motion. Under its present cloture rule, in effect since 1975, the Senate requires a three-fifths majority of the membership, or 60 votes (if there are no vacancies), to end debate. Upon the adoption of this motion, the final vote on a bill must be taken within 100 hours, including time spent on debate, quorum calls, and other parliamentary procedures. More cloture votes are successful today than in the past, when a two-thirds vote was required, and filibustering is therefore less of a threat to majority rule in the Senate.

A bill that has passed one house has survived a number of tests, but it must still be passed by the other chamber. The process begins anew: introduction, referral to committee, consideration in subcommittee and committee (including hearings), floor action, and vote on passage. Some bills that command a majority in one house have no chance in the other. In the case of major bills, it is a virtual certainty that the two houses will adopt different versions, thus requiring a conference committee to resolve the differences. For a bill to be sent to the president, a majority of each house must accept the conference report.

The president has several options: sign the bill, permit it to become law without signing it (which happens if the president fails to sign it within ten days while Congress is in session), or veto it. A two-thirds majority of those present and voting in each house may override a presidential veto, thus

Senator Strom Thurmond (R–S.C.) preparing to take the Senate floor in the 1960s to launch a filibuster against a civil rights bill. In 1957 Thurmond set the record for filibustering with a marathon speech of 24 hours, 18 minutes. A one-time Democratic governor, Thurmond was in 1948 the presidential nominee of the States' Rights party (or "Dixiecrats"), which strongly opposed civil rights legislation.

turning the bill into law without his approval (see Chapter 13). Finally, if the president fails to sign a bill passed less than ten days before Congress adjourns, the bill falls victim to a pocket veto.

An Overview of Lawmaking ■

No neat or simple formula exists for passing legislation. In the typical Congress, in fact, only about 5 or 6 percent of the bills introduced are enacted into law.

Committee decisions are critical. A bill that is reported out of committee has an excellent chance of passage, although its provisions may be changed by floor amendments. A bill that is "bottled up" in committee is almost certain to be lost. Although both houses have *discharge* rules—designed to pry a bill out of committee and bring it to the floor—it is rare for them to be used (and even rarer for them to be adopted). Congress may not revere its committees, but it steadily protects them. And, in truth, committees are less arbitrary than they seem: In pigeonholing certain bills, they make life easier for other members who prefer to avoid controversial votes.

Lawmaking in Congress has three main features. First, it is a drawn-out process. It is an unusual bill that moves quickly through both houses to be signed by the president. Under ordinary circumstances, the process of converting a bill into law takes many months, perhaps stretching over both sessions. As Richard F. Fenno, Jr., has pointed out, Congress is "our slow institution." Its slowness is a function of its preference for a consensual mode of decision making. And gaining consensus takes time; there are interests to be accommodated, bargains to be struck, and majorities to be put together. Nothing in this process of adjusting opposing interests is easy, at least when major issues are at hand. Although outside observers often grow impatient with the pace of Congress, slowness has its virtues; an institution that takes such pains to reach agreement is a good candidate, Fenno suggests, to be seen as "the fair institution." [35]

Second, the lawmaking process reflects the basic decentralization of Congress. Power is dispersed. At times it rests with party leaders and agencies, at times with committees and subcommittees (or with their chairs), and at times with members at large. Barber Conable (R–N.Y.), who recently retired from the House after two decades of service, comments on the "power problem" in the institution: "[Throughout] Congress, everybody feels that he has to be a part of every decision that's made. We have a tendency to transfer a lot of the decision making to the floor of the House now. . . . And that means we are deciding things less efficiently and probably with lesser expertise, because everybody wants to be a part of every issue." [36] Viewed in another way, there is a basic tension between the *centripetal* force of the party system and the *centrifugal* force of the committee system, with the former more likely to be linked to national purposes and the latter to local interests. On the whole, the reforms made in Congress in recent years have made the institution more decentralized (see Figure 12–5).

Third, the legislative process has numerous points of access. Members can be influenced by outsiders (chief executive, bureaucracy, interest groups, the media) all along the line—from the drafting of a bill, through its consideration in committee and on the floor, to the vote on its passage. By and large, the openness of Congress increases its vulnerability to outside forces. What is more, because congressional power is diffused, it is easier to defeat legislation than to pass it. A bill can be lost at any stage of the process (even at the outset if referred to a hostile committee).

Passing a bill requires the creation of *successive majorities*—a majority at each stage—in both houses. And even that may not do the job if the president is opposed to it. One of the most important things to know about the legislative struggle is this: The greatest advantages rest with those interests (in and out of the institution) that prefer the status quo.

The Voting Behavior of Members of Congress

Voting is a major activity of Congress. The need to make decisions furnishes the dynamics for com-

Toward decentralization of power	TO IMPROVE CONGRESS IN TERMS OF: Image	Democratization	Lawmaking capabilities	Position vis-á-vis the president	Toward centralization of power
Reduction of powers of committee chairs Changes in seniority system New authority and independence for subcommittees Wider distribution of committee and subcommittee chairs Diminished secrecy: Committee meetings and caucuses open to the public (a "sunshine" reform) Increase in personal and committee staffs	Codes of ethics for members (financial disclosure, limits on outside earned income, limits on franking privilege) Openness of proceedings (open meetings, television coverage of proceedings)	Reduction of powers of committee chairs Subcommittee Bill of Rights Increased visibility for actions: More recorded votes Changes in seniority system Change in cloture rule to make it easier to end debate New authority for minority members of committees	Increase in personal and committee staffs and creation of new research arms (Congressional Budget Office and Office of Technology Assessment) Various procedural reforms Committee consolidation and revamping of jurisdictions	War Powers Act of 1973 (to limit the president's power to send troops abroad without congressional approval) Budget and Impoundment Control Act of 1974 (to strengthen Congress's control over the budget and to limit the president's authority to impound—refuse to spend—funds appropriated by Congress)	Secret caucus votes on committee chairs Creation of Democratic Steering and Policy Committee, headed by Speaker Speaker given authority to nominate members of Rules Committee, subject to caucus approval, and to assign bills to more than one committee Development of new budget procedures

Figure 12–5 The multiple thrusts of modern congressional reform.

mittee, subcommittee, and floor deliberations. Voting reflects earlier bargains, concessions, and compromises. It shapes strategies and reveals the distribution of power. It protects existing law or introduces new policies. It fosters more soul-searching and uneasiness among members than anything else in their jobs. It furnishes editorial writers with "grist for the mill." It provides evidence with which constituents can evaluate their representatives and arms challengers with ammunition to oppose incumbents. Nothing that Congress does is more distinctly legislative than voting.

During a session, each member's vote is recorded on several hundred floor measures. The issues are both simple and complex. Always complex, however, is the attempt to explain *why* members vote as they do. They themselves are not always sure.

This analysis begins by looking at legislative role orientations for clues on voting; it then turns to the consideration of certain factors that influence voting behavior.

Role Orientations and Voting

It should be no surprise that all legislators do not see their responsibilities in the same light. They have, after all, different backgrounds and values and they represent different states and districts. Differences show up in the way they view representation and relate to their jobs. To begin, some legislators believe that their primary role should be that of a *delegate,* one whose obligation is to follow the wishes of his or her constituents. A member thoroughly imbued with the delegate role may

IMPACT

Who Is to Blame for Congressional Policy Failures?

"The last decade of congressional history has written a record of disturbing policy failures. . . . [It] seems fair to ask what role political action committees have played in creating our recurrent legislative paralysis. A moment's reflection supplies the answer: hardly any role at all. . . . Congress fails to solve problems because members routinely sell out to a set of interests more respectable and yet more dangerous than the PACs. They sell out to the pressures of public opinion in the places they represent. . . .

Members of Congress win election through the ceaseless monitoring and cultivation of voter desire. They keep that process up once they are sworn in. It is no accident that the overwhelming majority of staff people in any congressional office work on constituent service, not legislative research. . . . Congress fails for an excess of responsiveness. At no point in recent times has there been so wide a gap between what members are willing to propose in private . . . and what they are willing to endorse in public. . . [They are] desperate to stay in office, and timid about saying or doing anything that might turn a fickle electorate against them. This—not the prevalence of PAC money—is what has rendered Congress so weak in dealing with hard national problems."

Source: Alan Ehrenhalt, "PAC Money: Source of Evil or Scapegoat?" *Congressional Quarterly Weekly Report,* January 11, 1986, p. 99.

at times vote against personal judgment to follow constituency "instructions." Other members see their role as that of a *trustee,* free to follow their own conscience and use their own best judgment in matters that come before them. Still others fit the role of *politico,* the legislator who holds both orientations, alternating between them.

Finding that legislators *perceive* their roles differently, of course, does not establish that they *behave* differently. But it is reasonable to believe that perceptions are linked in a general way to behavior. If so, one would expect members with delegate orientations to be especially responsive to constituency pressures (including interest groups powerful in their home districts). By contrast, members who consider themselves trustees might be expected to take a national view of policy problems and to be more sensitive to stimuli generated outside their constituencies.

Common sense suggests that voting patterns are not static, that they vary from one policy domain to another. In this connection, a study of representative-constituency relationships by Warren Miller and Donald Stokes found evidence for three basic models of representation: the *delegate model* (in which members vote according to their perception of constituency preferences), the *party responsibility model* (in which members vote in line with traditional party positions), and the *trusteeship model* (in which members vote according to their own judgment).

Comparing the policy preferences of constituents (as determined by district opinion surveys) with the attitudes and voting behavior of House members, Miller and Stokes uncovered distinctive links in representation. On social welfare legislation (public housing, aid to education, full employment), the behavior of representatives conformed to the party responsibility model, marked by conflict between liberal Democrats and conservative Republicans. On civil rights legislation (school desegregation, voting rights), they voted as delegates, in keeping with the views of their constituents. In the foreign policy domain (economic and military aid, sending troops abroad), the members' behavior approximated the trusteeship model, with members making up their own minds or else following the lead of the president.[37]

Congressional voting is thus contextual; how members vote, in other words, depends on the situation. As the issue or context changes, so does the behavior of members. On some policy questions, popular control over members' decisions appears to be substantial, as members vote in agreement with constituency preferences or party positions. On other questions, popular control appears to be slight, perhaps even nonexistent. (For evidence on how the public and members of Congress see the role of the legislator, see Table 12–3.)

Influences on Voting Behavior

Weighing the factors that influence a legislator's vote is sometimes as futile as trying to unscramble eggs. Factors blend together, hide behind one another, or reinforce each other. Some are so subtle as to go undetected. Consider this problem: If members vote with their party, is this because *party leaders* exerted pressure on them, because they received counsel from *fellow party members,*

TABLE 12–3

Attitudes of the Public and of Members of Congress Toward the Role of the Representative: A Matter of Some Disagreement

Should a congressman be primarily concerned with looking after the needs and interests of his own district or should he be primarily concerned with looking after the needs and interests of the nation as a whole?

	Public	Members
Own district	56%	24%
Whole nation	34	45
Both equal	—	28
Not sure	9	3

When there is a conflict between what a congressman feels is best and what the people in his district want, should he follow his own conscience or follow what the people in his district want?

	Public	Members
Follow his own conscience	22%	65%
Follow his district	46	5
Depends on the issue	27	25
Not sure	5	4

Source: These surveys were conducted by Louis Harris and Associates. *Final Report of the Commission on Administrative Review,* U.S. House of Representatives, 95th Cong., 1st Sess., 1977, pp. 836, 838, 887, 890. (The totals are not 100 percent due to rounding.)

Four senators who joined in the bipartisan vote to override President Reagan's veto of the $20 billion clean water bill in 1987. From left to right: John Chaffee (R–R.I.), George Mitchell (D–Me.), Quentin Burdick (D–N.D.), and Robert Stafford (R–Vt.). Mitchell was elected Senate Majority Leader prior to the opening of the 101st Congress (1989–1991). He succeeded Robert C. Byrd (D–W.Va.) in this top leadership position.

TABLE 12–4

Importance of Various Actors in Influencing Voting Decisions of Members of Congress

Importance	Constituency	Other Legislators	Party Leadership	Interest Groups	Adminis-tration	Staff	Reading
Determinative	7%	5%	0%	1%	4%	1%	0%
Major importance	31	42	5	25	14	8	17
Minor importance	51	28	32	40	21	26	32
Not important	12	25	63	35	61	66	52
Total percent	101%	100%	100%	101%	100%	101%	101%
Total *N*	222	221	222	222	222	221	221

Source: John W. Kingdon, *Congressmen's Voting Decisions* (New York: Harper & Row, 1981), p. 19.

because the *president* nudged them, because they represent *constituencies* that are typical of those won by their party (thus in voting to advance constituency interests they also vote with their party), or because they hold *psychological attachments* to party programs and positions? Obviously, it is often hard to say.

An interview study of members of the House of Representatives by John Kingdon helps to put voting decisions in perspective. He asked a sample of members to identify the political "actors" who influenced their votes on a series of specific issues. The results appear in Table 12–4.

The leading influences on a member's vote are *other members* and *constituency.* The importance of colleagues is understandable. Members need advice and cues because time is limited, issues are numerous and complex, and political risks are present. They turn to colleagues whom they trust—men and women who have views similar to their own and who can provide not only policy evaluations but also political counsel. "For advice on how to vote," a member is likely to say, "I go to someone whose voting record is like mine." "On something like banking and currency, I don't pretend to be acquainted with it. I just ask ———— or ————. These are people who think exactly like I do, and I don't need to be an expert."[38] "When I come into [the House chamber], particularly on an amendment, when you have been at a committee meeting or whatever, and you don't have any idea what it is, you tend to look around the floor for somebody you know, who is on the committee, whose judgment you respect, and you go to him, somebody who you expect is going to vote pretty much the way you normally would."[39]

The importance of colleagues in influencing voting also shows up in bargaining exchanges. Commenting on his vote to prohibit regulatory agencies from banning cigarette advertising, a member remarked: "This will be sort of a buddy vote. I know cigarettes are harmful and I wouldn't touch them myself. But a lot of my friends are concerned about this, because tobacco means a lot to the economy of their areas. They do things for me when I need it, and I'll do this for them. Frankly, it's just a matter of helping out your friends."[40]

Constituency is a close second to other members in influencing voting. Indeed, *if* a member can identify a constituency preference on an issue, Kingdon's study shows, he or she will vote in line with it about three out of four times. The more intense the constituency interest is perceived to be, the greater the likelihood that members will "vote their district." Members naturally vote to protect a major industry at home:

> I've got many, many families in my district who make a living on tobacco. Now, I never argued that cigarettes are good for your health. . . . If you could show me some way my people are going to eat if I vote against cigarettes, I'll do it. (Interviewer: So you start with the constit-

Senator Bill Bradley (D–N.J.) speaks at the 1988 Democratic National Convention in the Omni Coliseum in Atlanta. Bradley's expertise on tax reform (as well as his ability to move without the ball better than anyone on the Knicks during his NBA years) has broadened his popularity beyond his liberal ideological base. He is now often mentioned as a future nominee for the presidency.

POLITICAL LINKAGE

Ideology and Voting Behavior

What do the members of each of the groups of U.S. senators shown below have in common? The broad answer is ideology, conservative for the first set, liberal for the second set. Section of the country contributes to the explanation, particularly in the case of the South (conservative) and the East (liberal).

Linked to ideology, party membership also plays a significant role in congressional voting. The mean support level of conservative positions for all Democratic senators is 8 percent, and for all Republican senators, 80 percent. On the whole, the Democratic party in Congress represents a liberal ideology, the Republican party a conservative one. But note the ideological cleavages within each party.

These scores show the percentage of votes cast in agreement with positions held by a strongly conservative group, the American Conservative Union (ACU). A senator voting in agreement with the ACU, for example, would have supported measures to require homeless persons receiving medical care under the homeless relief bill to be tested for the AIDS virus, institute mandatory drug testing of federal employees, increase funding for SDI research, and prevent the use of federal funds to pay for abortions in the District of Columbia, while opposing measures to reauthorize the Clean Water Act, impose a moratorium on aid to the Nicaraguan contras, limit development and testing of missile defense systems, limit testing of nuclear warheads, expand Medicare, and authorize additional federal housing programs.

Source: The data for this illustration come from the 100th Congress (1987–1988), 1st Session, as reported in the *Congressional Quarterly Weekly Report,* March 5, 1988, p. 602. Other Senate Democrats with 0% support scores for ACU positions were Cranston (Calif.), Wirth (Colo.), Dodd (Conn.), Inouye (Haw.), Matasunga (Haw.), Sarbanes (Del.), Moynihan (N.Y.), and Pell (R.I.).

> uency factor.) It starts there and it ends there. That's all there is to it. If you don't, you aren't going to be around here very long. Not on something like this, where their livelihood is involved.[41]

The defense of local interests is crucial at the stage of voting. Members build support for their legislation through logrolling—"backscratching," helping each other out, trading votes. These observations by members of the House illustrate how the process of logrolling shapes behavior on legislation with a distinctively local cast:

> It depends on the importance of the bill. On local bills, I think I would [be willing to trade votes]. For example, I am interested in a potato referendum bill . . . and I'm sure that my good friend ———— of New York couldn't care at all about the bill, but he'll probably support it because we're friends. And I'd do the same for him.

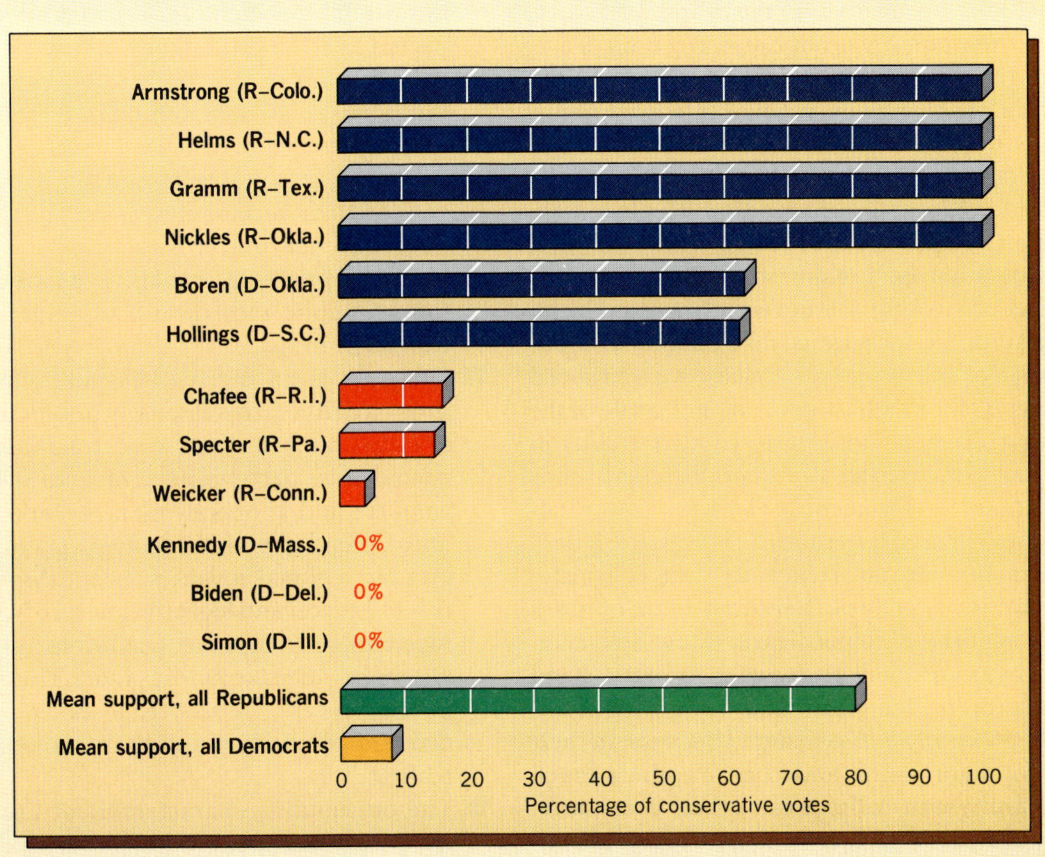

We all support anything that's for Pennsylvania no matter where it goes. You have to in this place with its logrolling.

————'s reclamation project carried by just a few votes. One thing that broke the liberal and big city line against it was the fact that all the boys who played poker and gin rummy with him voted for it. And they took some of the rest of us with them. They said he wasn't going to be so difficult in the future.[42]

Next in importance are *interest groups* and the *administration.* The position of an interest group is most apt to be taken seriously when two conditions are met: the group has a connection with the member's constituency and the issue is highly salient—a "big" issue, in other words. One can conclude from this that a group's influence depends in part on the geographic dispersion of its membership; a group that is strong in many congressional districts (such as the education or veterans' lobbies) has an advantage over one with members concentrated in only a few districts.

As an influence on members' voting decisions, the administration is of moderate importance (see Table 12–4). Among those who heed administration positions are members of the president's party, but even their number is not especially impressive. Overall, the direct influence of the administration and executive branch on voting ranks well below that of other members or constituency.

The other influences on member decisions are party leadership, staff, and reading. The low ranking of party requires clarification. Although party leaders may not be a major source of cues, *party differences* in voting are nevertheless significant. Democrats and Republicans, for example, disagree on a range of socioeconomic issues, such as social welfare and labor legislation, and on the role of the federal government. Interparty conflict results in part because the parties represent different kinds of constituencies (Democratic districts, "lower" socioeconomic levels; Republican districts, "higher" socioeconomic levels). Hence, in "class" legislation, a strong majority of Democrats often opposes a strong majority of Republicans. (Maverick members—those most likely to desert their party—tend to be southern Democrats and eastern Republicans.) Party voting is also fostered because, in their search for information and cues, members touch bases mainly with colleagues of their own party. Party is the silent partner in these transactions.

Thus, party has an impact on congressional decison making even though members may not be especially attentive to the positions of their leaders. What is more, in casting partisan votes, members of the party in control of the presidency often reflect administration positions. Even in the most stringent probing of legislative voting, there is normally more than meets the eye. For complex issues, each vote is more like a bundle of votes, reflecting compromises made along the way and presenting members with varied reasons for voting on one side or the other.

Summary

- Congressional elections are not mysterious. On the whole, Democrats win where they are expected to win and Republicans win where they are expected to win. Safe seats, especially in the House, greatly outnumber competitive seats. Incumbents of both parties are steadily successful in winning reelection. A major reason for their success lies in the advantages of congressional office: staff, travel expenses, franking privilege, visibility, name recognition, a public record, and superior access to campaign funds.
- Congress is an unusually complex organization—a deliberative assembly in which an array of individuals, leaders, staff, committees, subcommittees, party units, and informal groups compete and cooperate to make new policies or to defend old ones. Ideology, party, interest groups, regional loyalties, friendships, executive influence, and logrolling help to bring them together—in temporary coalitions or durable alliances—to make public policy. The openness of the process, moreover, is an invitation to external forces to press their claims on lawmakers.
- The outstanding characteristic of Congress is its decentralization. With power widely dispersed, party leaders have a limited capacity to control House and Senate decisions. Sometimes on their own, sometimes bolstered by the president, they nevertheless win some victories; a popular president, eager to see a program adopted, can be of immense help in fostering party loyalty (particularly during the "honeymoon" period). More commonly, however, the chief architects of public policy are the committees and subcommittees (and the external elements to which they respond). In a real sense, no one really controls Congress.

- The legislative process is a labyrinth. No bill moves easily through its narrow passageways. The vast majority of bills (perhaps nine out of ten) die in committee. Rarely is any bill of consequence signed into law in its original form. Conference committees play a key role in shaping major bills.
- The voting behavior of members of Congress is influenced by a variety of factors—chief among them their colleagues and constituencies. Party affiliation is most likely to affect their decisions on certain kinds of "class" legislation, such as social welfare proposals or labor-management questions.
- Congress in the 1990s is in some ways a new body. It has become more open and democratic. Most committee meetings are now open; many more votes are recorded. More members than ever can lay claim to "a piece of the action." The ultimate control over committee chairs (or ranking members) now rests with the party caucus, thus reducing the impact of seniority. The power of committee chairs has declined, while that of subcommittees has grown. Staff support has been increased to the benefit of both the institution and rank-and-file members. The Senate's cloture rule has been changed to make it easier to end debate. The general impact of the recent reforms has been to make Congress a somewhat more decentralized institution. At the same time, it has become more difficult for party leaders to manage Congress in the interest of developing coherent policies and programs.

Readings on Congress

Dodd, Lawrence C., and Bruce I. Oppenheimer. 1985. *Congress Reconsidered,* 3d ed. Washington, D.C.: CQ Press. An instructive collection of essays on the U.S. Congress.

Fenno, Richard F., Jr. 1978. *Homestyle: House Members in Their Districts.* Boston: Little, Brown. A study of how legislators court their constituents and how their "homestyle" affects Congress as an institution.

Fox, Harrison W., Jr., and Susan Webb Hammond. 1977. *Congressional Staffs: The Invisible Force in American Lawmaking.* New York: Free Press. An examination of the role of legislative professional staff.

Keefe, William J. 1988. *Congress and the American People,* 3d ed. Englewood Cliffs, N.J.: Prentice-Hall. An argument that the more Congress changes, the more it remains the same.

Kingdon, John W. 1981. *Congressmen's Voting Decisions,* 2d ed. New York: Harper & Row. Examines the factors that influence legislators when they cast roll-call votes.

Kozak, David C., and John D. Macartney, eds. 1982. *Congress and Public Policy: A Source Book of Documents and Readings.* Homewood, Ill.: Dorsey Press. A valuable collection of articles, documents, and data pertaining to the U.S. Congress.

Malbin, Michael J. 1980. *Unelected Representatives: Congressional Staff and the Future of Representative Government.* New York: Basic Books. Argues that the expanded role of staff has led to some unforeseen, and undesirable, consequences.

Mayhew, David R. 1974. *Congress: The Electoral Connection.* New Haven, Conn.: Yale University Press. Views legislators as motivated by electoral goals and examines the impact of their behavior on congressional policy making.

Parker, Glenn R., ed. 1985. *Studies of Congress.* Washington, D.C.: CQ Press. A diverse collection of scholarly articles pertaining to Congress.

Peabody, Robert L. 1976. *Leadership in Congress.* Boston: Little, Brown. A study that focuses on congressional leaders and the ways in which they are selected.

West, Darrel M. 1987. *Congress and Economic Policymaking.* Pittsburgh: University of Pittsburgh Press. A study of how Congress modified and legislated President Reagan's policy initiatives.

Wilson, Woodrow. 1956 (originally 1885). *Congressional Government: A Study in American Politics.* New York: Meridian Books. An enduring analysis of the legislative branch.

Chapter 13

The Presidency

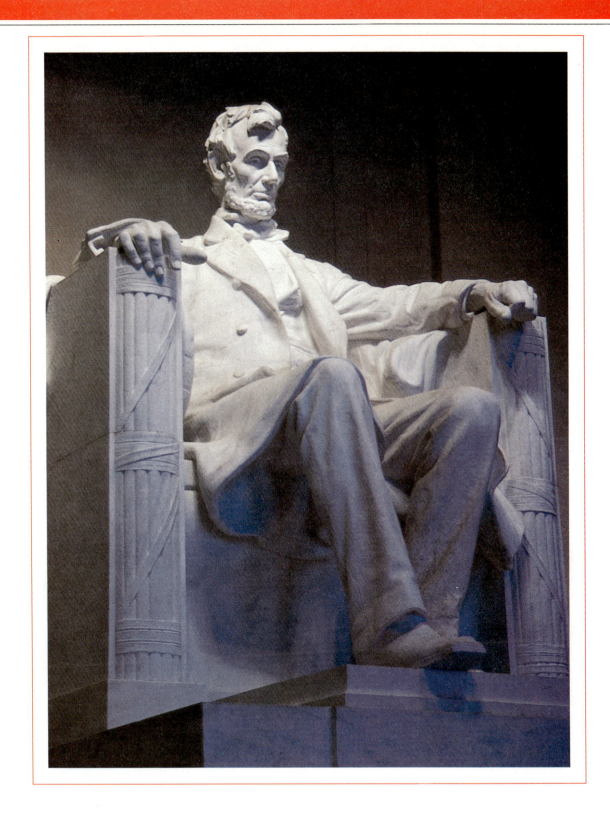

The American president is usually the most visible and powerful political leader in the United States. The president's substantial constitutional authority contributes to his power and status; so does his role as the leader of his political party. But the president has a special status in American society, because the presidency combines instrumental and symbolic leadership; these functions are often separated in other societies. In Great Britain, for example, the king or queen is the symbolic head of the nation; the prime minister runs the government. The vice president too is a nationally elected official, but it is the president alone who serves as both a national symbol and a political leader. This is the basis of his strength—and the source of his difficulties.

The distinctive position of the president is widely recognized. Evidence that the president is someone special comes from many sources. One is the results of public opinion polls. For over 40 years the Gallup Poll has asked Americans to identify the living persons residing anywhere in the world whom they admire most. Presidents or former presidents have won the title in almost every case. The data are shown in Table 13–1.

Americans are also asked regularly whether or not they approve of the way the president is running his office. Presidential popularity is normally high as an administration begins (see Table 13–2). Since the term is just beginning, presidents have not done much on which to be evaluated. It seems likely that high approval flows more from an emotional attachment to this important office and from the candidate's recent electoral victory than from an specific awareness of what the president has done in office. As the president acts in concrete situations, his popularity tends to decrease. Two of the last four presidents have left office with approval ratings of less than 40 percent. President Carter's rating of 21 percent at one stage in his administration seems to be the modern low. The people may love the presidency, but many come to dislike particular presidents whose actions run counter to their own policy preferences and interests. However, most people most of the time think the president is doing a good job, even if they are not exactly sure what presidents do.

The special status of the presidency is illustrated also by the passion with which the media report the most minor details of presidential life: who cuts his hair, what he eats for breakfast, whether he toasts his own muffins, what his golf score was, how long he chopped wood on his ranch. Moreover, presidential statements on football and on the weather are reported, along with pronouncements on arms control and the national debt. No presidential act is too trivial to escape notice.

The broadcast media recognize the special status of the president in other ways. When a president requests television time to address the nation, that time is usually made available. On rare occasions when one television network balks at a request for time, a second request from the White House is usually sufficient stimulus for a change of mind.

The special status of presidents creates problems as well as advantages. Presidents are not dictators. They are able to do much less than they are expected to do. Every president must confront this gap between expectation and reality. President Reagan found it impossible in his first term to cut taxes, balance the federal budget, and reduce government spending all at the same time. He had

TABLE 13–1

Most Admired Man in the World as Perceived by the American Public, 1948–1988

	Number of Years	Percent of Total
U.S. president or former president	33	85
Others	6	15

Note: This question was not asked by the Gallup Organization in 1975 and 1976.
Source: Data from various issues of the *Gallup Report*.

TABLE 13–2

Popular Approval of Presidential Performance in Office, 1961–1988

President	First Poll*	Last Poll*	High Score*	Low Score*	Average Score*
Kennedy	72	58	83	57	70
Johnson	78	49	80	35	54
Nixon	59	24	68	24	48
Ford	71	53	71	37	46
Carter	66	34	75	21	47
Reagan	51	63	68	23	52

* Figures are percentages.
Source: Data from *Gallup Opinion Index.* October–November 1980, supplemented by issues of the *Gallup Report.*

clearly created the impression among some that he could indeed accomplish all this, but many presidents promise too much to get elected. The presidency is an institution destined to create disillusion. When measured by public expectations, presidents are bound to fail. As political scientist Theodore J. Lowi suggests:

> Presidents try to deliver more than they realistically can. Even when they do a fairly good job—which most do by normal standards—they fall so far short of what they themselves expect and what is expected of them that they always will fail. Even if re-elected, they end up in disgrace. And they're less and less likely to get re-elected these days.[1]

The high visibility of presidents and their ability to shape events should not blind us to the crucial limits that context imposes on presidents. Presidents operate under severe constraints. The best way to understand the presidency is to see the president in a context that both enhances and limits his ability to function. (1) Presidential behavior is influenced by social and economic conditions; (2) presidents work in a context of legally specified powers and limits; and (3) presidents operate in a partisan context that may shape their ability. The ability of presidents to act may be sharply bounded by contextual elements, but presidents can and do have an impact on events. What needs to be studied is how large that impact is and under what conditions presidents seem to have a larger or a smaller impact. Because the president can be important in the making and implementing of public policy, the individual's personality, political skill, values, and philosophy of the presidency must be considered.

All presidents must take account of the nation's history and of the presidential institution itself. But the first question in explaining presidential behavior is the narrower one of how they attain office. How candidates are nominated and elected affects what they do after becoming president.

The Presidential Selection Process

Nominations

Presidential candidates are nominated through local caucuses, state party conventions, presidential preference primaries, and finally at the national nominating conventions. This is a massive winnowing-out process. Millions of persons are constitutionally eligible for the presidency; the requirements in Article II, Section 1, are few:

> No Person except a natural born Citizen . . . shall be eligible to the Office of President; neither shall any Person be eligible to that Office who shall not have attained to the Age of thirty five Years, and been Fourteen Years a Resident within the United States.

Yet few citizen get serious consideration; and only one is nominated by each major political party. What does all this achieve? Actually, quite a bit.

Who wins the presidential nomination tells us a great deal about presidents. After the nominations, we know that whoever is elected will accept the values widely held in American society. The nominee will believe in democracy, majority rule, minority rights, political freedom, and a strong measure of political equality. Communists and fascists do not survive the Democratic and Republican nominating processes. In addition, all nominees profess to believe in our constitutional and legal system. Candidates may want to change specific constitutional provisions (for example, a single six-year term for the president), but none will urge a drastic overhaul. The words of two political scientists, Kenneth Prewitt and Alan Stone, describing elite recruitment are applicable here. "The recruitment process filters out only those whose views are 'bizarre': the rabid racist, the 19th-century laissez-faire capitalist, the serious socialist, etc. But having filtered out these odd viewpoints, the recruitment process allows many different viewpoints to find their way into the ruling circles. . . ."[2]

Even on questions of public policy, the similarities in the positions of candidates often outweigh their differences. In 1988 candidates agreed, for example, to keep social security, provide government support for farmers, aid the underprivileged, protect the environment, fight drug abuse, reduce the deficit, and safeguard individual liberties. The normal differences are over how much will be spent, for whose particular benefit, and under what conditions. Preserving minimum wages will seldom be in dispute; the exact level may be the object of controversy, as might be questions of whether minimum wage laws should apply to teenage employees or whether employees in a particular industry should be covered.

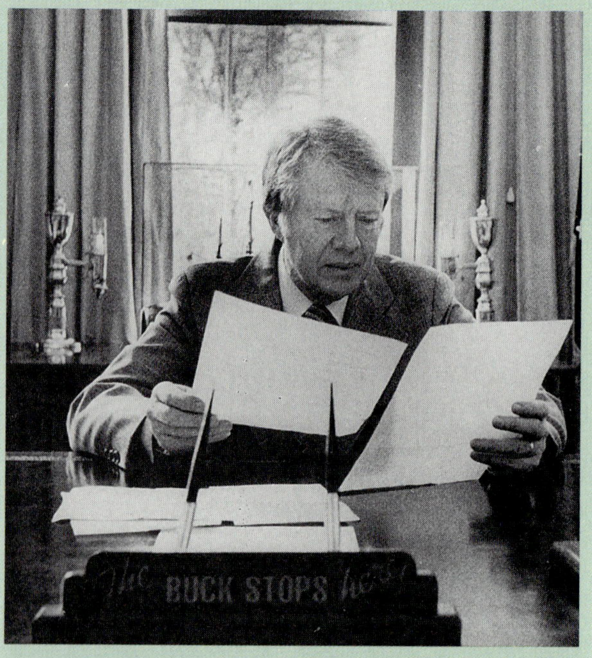

Reflecting his desire to be a strong leader, Jimmy Carter placed a sign previously used by President Harry Truman on his desk. President Carter worked as a "micromanager," involving himself in the details of legislation. Symbols like these are important in establishing the president's style, effectiveness—and power as the incumbent.

The nominating process, then, produces candidates who believe in democracy, candidates who accept the American constitutional system, and candidates who will stand for any policy for which there is a popular consensus. The importance of this outcome cannot be overemphasized. The nominating process helps to promote and maintain the beliefs and values dominant in American society as well as its basic institutions. It exaggerates only a little to say that elections merely fill in the details. If beliefs are relevant to behavior, and most analysts would agree that they are, then understanding how candidates are nominated and which ones are nominated helps explain why presidents act as they do.

An incumbent president seeking renomination has some major advantages. Challenged by Senator Edward Kennedy for the Democratic nomination in 1980, President Jimmy Carter took advantage of his incumbency. In the words of a Democratic leader, "the strongest fact for Carter is that he's President—and that provides powerful insignia and prestige. Patronage helps you with a few individuals and their friends, but not with most voters. The voters are impressed with Air Force One. They're impressed with the office. That's still a lot to go against." [3]

The nominating process helps to produce candidates who will not drastically alter the status quo. Mainly in times of severe domestic crisis do candidates who promise more than that receive the nomination of their party. The candidates who generally emerge will produce what amounts to marginal change. In this way, continuity is enhanced. Presidential elections decide which personality and which political party will occupy the White House. These may be matters of some importance in explaining what presidents do; but much had already been decided before the election result.

Elections

According to the Constitution, presidents are elected by an archaic, quaint device called the *electoral college.* In reality, almost all the time, the action of the electors simply reflects the popular vote.

The framers of the Constitution intended the president to be selected by a group of wise, informed men (the electors) in each state. The electors were to exercise their own best judgment. As the framers saw it, the average voter would not play a direct central role. The electors would meet every four years in their state capitol and vote. Each state would have a number of electoral votes equal to the total number of members from that state in the U.S. House of Representatives and the U.S. Senate. (See Chapter 8 for a more detailed discussion of electoral college procedures.)

Today, no law prevents the system from working as it was originally designed. The electors, in principle, can vote for the person they think is the best choice. Political reality is entirely different. The popular vote in a state normally determines how the electoral vote will be cast. In the more than 20 presidential elections since 1900, the electors have cast over 10,000 electoral votes. Less than 1 percent went to candidates who failed to receive a popular plurality in that state. No presidential election has been decided by "faithless electors" (those who ignore the popular vote in the state and vote their personal preference). The electors abandon their constitutional freedom to decide; they respond to the popular will. Even in the nineteenth century, when the practice was somewhat different, only three elected presidents received fewer popular votes than their defeated opponents.

More democracy in the electoral college has meant a significant change in its workings. In addition, the distribution of electors among the states has continued to change after each census. The thrust of these changes has been to move electoral votes, and hence, potential power, from the Northeast to the South and Southwest. Table 13–3 illustrates a few of these changes.

TABLE 13–3

Changes in the Allocation of Electoral Votes: Some Illustrations, 1960 and 1988

	1960	1988	Gain/Loss
Massachusetts	16	13	
New York	45	36	−20%
Pennsylvania	32	25	
California	32	47	
Florida	10	21	+47%
Texas	24	29	
Illinois	27	24	
Michigan	20	20	−7%
Ohio	25	23	

The electoral college may be a political anachronism, but it remains alive in law. Why? The answers tell us something about the realities of American politics. Gallup poll evidence continues to show that over 70 percent of American voters favor replacing the electoral college with direct popular election of the president.[4] This feeling, however, lacks intensity and depth. Citizens who do not feel strongly frequently fail to act on their beliefs. And in this case, those political leaders who fear the impact of change on their state or political party usually feel more strongly about their views. In American politics, passive majorities often lose to more intense minorities. Where a constitutional amendment is needed (requiring a two-thirds vote in the Congress and ratification by three-fourths of the states), this tendency is even more likely to prevail.

Failure to reform the electoral college also highlights the pragmatic nature of American politics. The potential perils of the electoral college are massive; the actual impact has been slight. So, while reformers argue about what *might* happen, voters tend to focus on what *does* happen. Since 1888, all presidents have been elected with more votes than any opponent. What instructions do the people give to their new leader? Elections seldom provide specific instructions for the winner. First, many potential voters do not actually vote. From 1960 to 1988, voting turnout in presidential elections varied from about 50 percent to slightly over 60 percent. Moreover, as Figure 13–1 shows, in the 14 elections between 1936 and 1988, the winner gained 60 percent or more of the vote in only three. So, in fact, only about 30 percent of those of voting age have actually voted for the new president.

Why did those who did vote select a particular candidate? Seldom because they knew of and approved the specific policies of their favorite candidate. More commonly, voters are expressing satisfaction or dissatisfaction with the results achieved by a previous administration, indicating a general sense that change is needed, or reacting to an attractive candidate such as Franklin Roosevelt or John Kennedy who seems to promise much in vague, general terms. The 1980 presidential election data show no sharp shift in voter issue orientation from 1976; in 1980 more voters labeled the Republicans the best party for prosperity, but more called the Democrats the party best for peace, and the electorate's party affiliation and political philosophy changed little if at all. Yet the voters rejected Jimmy Carter (D) for Ronald Reagan (R). The vote for president in 1980, as usual, reflected a judgment on the past more than an endorsement of specific future policies. The 1984 and 1988 elections were no different. George Bush won comfortably in 1988 even though there were many more voters identified with the Democratic party than the Republican.

The policy significance of the election is obscured because of the reasons that people vote for

Edwin Meese, a long-time associate of Ronald Reagan, wielded influence first within the White House and later as attorney general. He became an example of President Reagan's management by delegation—and its problems, such as presidential isolation and the potential for misuse of power. Meese remains under scrutiny for alleged violation of ethical standards during the Reagan administration.

a particular candidate. One public opinion poll published in 1988 showed that honesty was the single most important criterion for judging presidential candidates.[5] If this report is correct, it confirms previous conclusions that elections rarely resolve specific issue conflicts.

The number of voters, voter motivation, and the nature of campaigns explain the absence of issue mandates for a new president. But all presidents try to act as if their victory did signify voter demand for specific programs they advanced.

In brief, the way presidents gain office affects their ability to govern. Newly elected presidents share the norms of society. They are Democrats or Republicans. They possess political skills and experience; they carry into office the credits and debits acquired during the campaign. Policy positions seldom stray from those widely advocated or accepted in our society. So nominations and elections help the president gain general support from the public. Winning candidates are seldom likely to lead in directions that depart sharply from the status quo. Perhaps the major exceptions in the last 60 years were Presidents Roosevelt in 1933 and Reagan in 1981.

If the largest electoral vote states have common interests, then electoral college arithmetic suggests that presidential candidates be highly attentive to them. After all, the seven largest electoral vote states can supply about 75 percent of the 270 electoral votes needed for victory. The realities of representation are more complex. In landslide victories, the large states tend to vote with everyone else. Thus their distinctive contribution is difficult to discern. In closer presidential races, the large states are typically on the side of the winner but are divided. After all, the president is not accountable to large state interests alone.

Just as the smallest states seldom vote as a distinctive bloc in the Senate, the largest states as a group do not differentiate themselves from the rest of the nation in presidential elections. Just exactly whom the newly elected president represents is seldom clear.

The election results also tell which political party will control the presidency and which will control each house of Congress. The increasing weakness of the national political parties decreases the value of the party factor. A president whose party has a majority in control of each house of Congress gains an edge, but only that. Any predisposition to support the president of one's own party ordinarily pales in the face of sharp policy differences or the pull of constituency interests. Normally a major party affiliation pulls the president toward *centrism.*

Since the office requires a large measure of political skill, presidents have a head start. What may vary tremendously among presidents is how much political skill they have and how they use it. A candidate who can garner a coalition of support strong enough to be elected may not be able to transfer these talents to building coalitions in Congress. The political operatives who thrust their candidate forward successfully may be ill suited to running the White House staff. The obvious advantages of established political skill may fade with the recognition that political skill has many facets; it may not transfer readily across political environments.

The campaign for the nomination and election affects presidential behavior in other ways as well. Jobs have been promised, politically powerful people alienated, policy bargains worked out, and methods of personal interaction established. Campaigns for the presidency also matter because the promises that the candidates make during them are mainly kept. Contrary to popular opinion, the evidence shows that presidents keep their campaign promises well over half the time. Presidents come into office shaped by who they are and how they got there. Few escape the boundaries thus established.

Individuals sometimes come to the presidency without having been elected to the office. When presidents die, resign, or are impeached and convicted, the Constitution provides that the vice president shall succeed to the presidency. If the president is unable, temporarily, to perform the duties of office, the vice president is supposed to act in that role.

These legal provisions do not merely set forth some abstract possibilities. In the last 50 years, three vice presidents have succeeded to the presidency—Truman, Johnson, and Ford. The most important task of the vice president is waiting to act as president should that become necessary. Vice presidents are not trained very well for this possibility. Most presidents do not consistently bring the vice president into the center of the policy-making process. This is partly because vice presidential candidates are normally put on the ticket for political balance. In 1988, Republican vice presidential candidate Dan Quayle provided age and geographic balance. The Democratic vice presidential nominee, Lloyd Bentsen, provided geographic and ideological balance. Vice presidents are not necessarily intimates of the presidential candidate. Presidents more often assign tasks to vice presidents to keep them out of the way than to prepare them for the presidency. Vice presidents are sometimes frustrated by their slight involvement in presidential decision making. Nothing in law or custom forces the president to provide a meaningful apprenticeship for the vice president.

Thus, the nomination and election process for the vice president normally has few policy consequences once the election is over. Vice presidential candidates may on a few occasions make some slight difference in winning or losing an election. Once elected, the vice president fades to whatever obscurity or rises to whatever visibility the president desires. It is not usually harmful to the president to balance the ticket ideologically because the president is free to dispatch the vice president to obscurity once the election is over. Most presidents have done exactly that.

Bases and Limits of Presidential Power: The Societal Context

A president who comes into office determined to achieve substantial change finds massive constraints. The majority that elected the president may not support specific programs. A majority too impressed by campaign rhetoric and filled with political naiveté may expect miracles, a scarce commodity. Public moods are volatile. As Lewis Lapham put it: "The American electorate apparently seeks to elect constitutional deities on whom it confirms absolute power for a brief period of time and then, discovering itself betrayed, it tears the god to pieces." [6]

The size of a president's electoral margin may boost his status with Congress. Figure 13–1 reveals

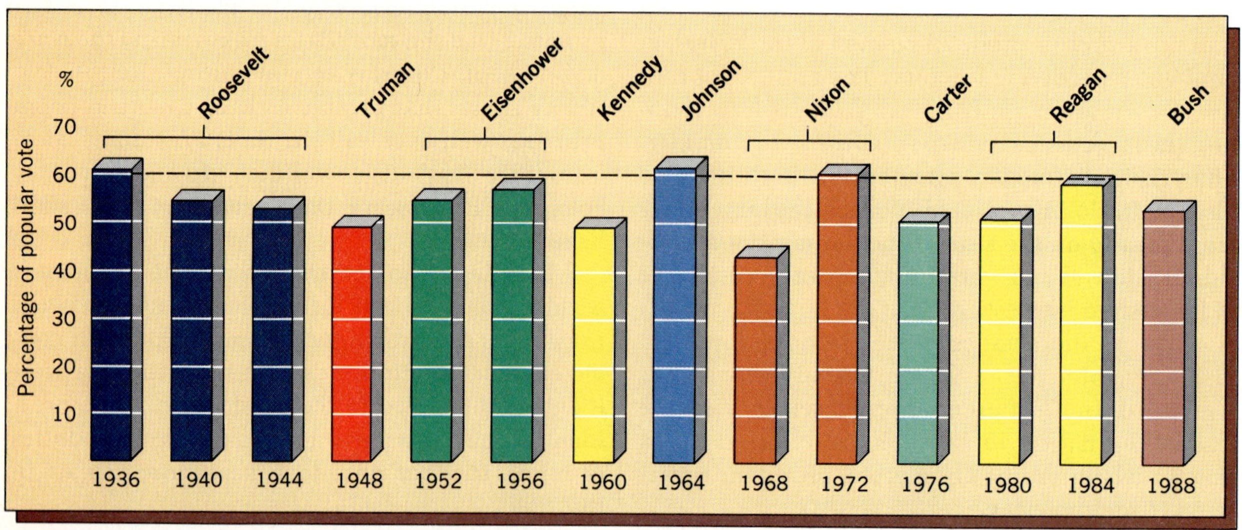

Figure 13–1 Presidential elections, 1936–1988: percentage of popular vote for the winner. A winning margin of 60 percent is often called a landslide victory.

that in the last 50 years fewer than half of the presidents have won their election by a margin large enough to be called a landslide. At the other extreme, a small margin of victory may be inhibiting. President Kennedy's narrow victory reportedly haunted him when he was pressed to put forth and fight for bold new programs, while President Johnson's landslide victory in 1964 encouraged him to press new initiatives. George Bush gained neither solace nor support from the congressional returns that cost Republicans seats in both houses in 1988.

Few presidents can rely on a firm, enduring base of public support. Presidents also find that as they progress from campaign rhetoric to concrete actions, each move angers some people. Thus, a normal aspect of presidential life is an almost inevitable decline in popularity. Although popularity does not necessarily translate into specific policy support, a president who ranks high with the public is less vulnerable to political attack and resistance from other decision makers. Dwight Eisenhower (R), one of the most enduringly popular modern presidents, found the onslaught of Democratic majorities in Congress tempered because his popularity created a fear of public backlash. President Ronald Reagan, in 1981, capitalized on his popularity in pressuring Congress to enact his economic program even though the House was controlled by the Democrats.

In turn, low popularity can erode presidential support. President Nixon and his staff found that invitations were withdrawn, telephone calls were not answered immediately, and support was given less often as his public standing plummeted in the months before his resignation. (See the data on the approval of presidential performance in Table 13–2.) But presidents do have some advantages in building public support. The president has won the nation's only national election. From this he can at least claim generalized mass support.

The general support that presidents gather does not translate automatically into firm political support. The president's chances to build concrete support are greatest when large segments of the public are already predisposed in the direction the president has taken, when the need for support is widely recognized (during a severe international crisis), or when large segments of the public see no immediate impact (especially a negative one) on their own lives.

When President Carter in the late 1970s called the energy crisis the "moral equivalent of war" and repeatedly urged the public to pressure Congress to accept his program, little support was forthcoming. Only a minority of the public saw the energy problem as a genuine crisis. Many saw a direct and negative impact on their life-style if the Carter proposals were passed. Public apathy was the net result. By contrast, when President Reagan in a television address urged voters to pressure members of Congress to "slash federal spending and taxes," "Capitol Hill was promptly inundated with letters and cards." [7]

A second element of the societal context that confronts the president is the intractability of some problems. Most people favor controlling inflation; candidates may get elected partially because they promise to do so. The reality of inflation, though, may be that no experts have effective solutions to offer the president. The easy campaign promise may melt in the face of complex problems. Where are the clear, simple solutions to inflation, unemployment, welfare reform, the Middle East, adequate housing, energy shortages, and crime? The president's abilities to provide solutions may be hampered by the absence of workable and acceptable answers among experts.

An excellent illustration is the problem of drug abuse. Government policy wavers between punishing pushers, punishing users, rehabilitating addicts, keeping drugs off the market, and educational campaigns picturing the horrible consequences of drug use and abuse. Election years especially stimulate a flurry of governmental activity, but these actions and words seldom convey any coherent plan of how to deal with the problem. In the late 1960s and early 1970s, for example, political pressure to control air pollution stimulated governmental action before enough fully reliable knowledge was available as to what to do.

When the experts do offer seemingly reasonable answers, presidents must still go out and gather political support from a diverse public and from a Congress that fully represents this diversity.

Public Opinion and the Presidency: Some High Points and Some Low Points of President Reagan's Popularity

Presidential popularity helps define the context in which the president acts, but it is not the sole basis of presidential power. Even as popular a president as Ronald Reagan had sharp highs and lows in public support. Here are a few.

Popularity high		Popularity low	
May 1981	Honeymoon period	January 1983	Recession deepens
	After assassination attempt	January 1987	Iran-contra episode is publicized
November 1984	Reelection		
August 1985	After surgery for cancerous tumor		
May 1986	Geneva summit with Russians, economy stronger		
	United States bombs Libya		
April 1988	U.S.–USSR tensions eased		

Americans generally agree on basic values; but they may differ sharply on how best to translate this consensus into specific public policy. Successful candidates are often those who can blur issue differences. Specific presidential policy proposals must overcome this diversity of views.

Another quality of American society that affects presidential behavior is public indifference to political issues and actions. This may be either an asset or a liability. Indifference may hinder presidential efforts at mobilization; it may also give leeway that a more active, involved public might not permit. Public apathy or attention may be related to the impact of the media in shaping public perceptions, but in any case, there are severe limits to public awareness. In 1987 five Central American

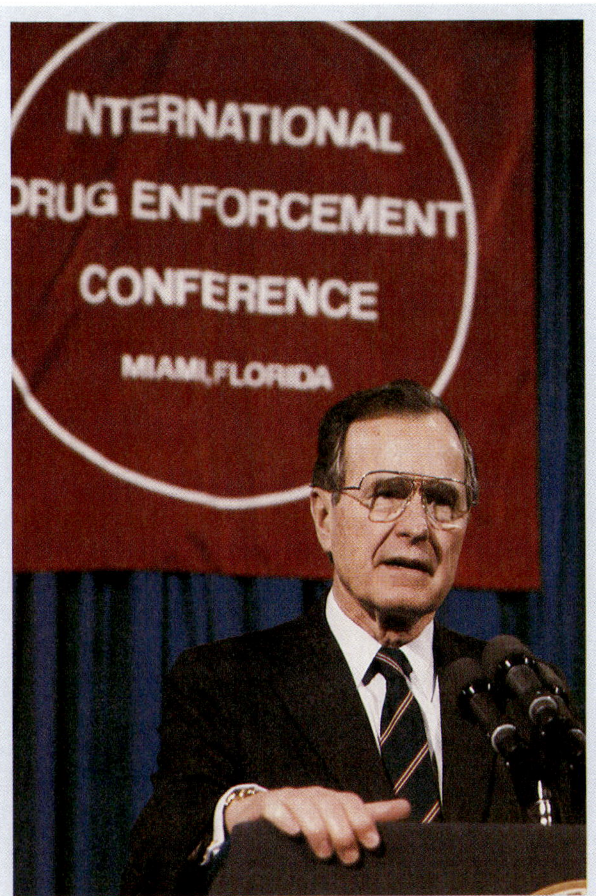

Calling for a war on illegal drug use, George Bush appointed a drug "czar" to coordinate government action. He also relied on the president's public role to promote his aims, as in this nationally televised address on combatting "crack" use. But some charged that he was unwilling to commit enough resources to the fight on drugs. Programs are only as good as the resources allocated to their implementation.

presidents offered a peace plan for Nicaragua, a country much in the headlines in the United States. Several months later a poll showed barely half of the people in the United States had even heard of the plan.

Contextual factors help to place boundaries on what presidents can do and what they think they can do. But sometimes environmental factors enhance presidential discretion and power. The most obvious situation is the nation's involvement in international conflicts such as war. Here previous boundaries broaden as the nation mobilizes its efforts behind the president. Whether war creates new presidential power can be debated. At a minimum, war creates an atmosphere where the boundaries of presidential power can be interpreted more broadly.

A severe economic crisis may yield similar results. When Franklin D. Roosevelt assumed the presidency in 1933, he found economic disaster gripping the nation. Within a few years Congress, under presidential prodding, passed a series of bills that moved America in new directions. The willingness of a majority of people and of Congress to follow the administration's lead grew out of the perceived severity of the economic crisis. The president, they hoped, had discovered some acceptable answers. The previous administration, they thought, had not met this crisis adequately. Similarly, when Ronald Reagan became president in 1981, rates of inflation and unemployment were high. The public seemed to accept his innovative economic doctrines at first partly because of a widespread perception that something new had to be tried.

War and domestic economic disaster are the most obvious examples of social conditions that enhance presidential power. What these events have in common is a general perception of deep *crisis.* Any such situation broadens the president's ability to act. During the Civil War, President Lincoln took unprecedented steps, some of which were legally questionable. In World Wars I and II, Presidents Wilson and Roosevelt, acting as commander in chief, exercised wide-ranging leadership that seemed to expand the scope of presidental power. In negotiating with Iran to free American hostages in 1980–1981, President Jimmy Carter agreed to unfreeze Iranian assets, to cancel lawsuits in U.S. courts by private parties against the Iranian government, and to forbid claims against Iran by the hostages after they were freed. This exercise of power, even though challenged, was upheld by the courts. The crux of the matter was that President Carter had succeeded in obtaining the release of the hostages. Severe crises seem to generate their own interpretations of law.[8]

Bases and Limits of Presidential Power: Legal Powers and Limits

In a democracy, government action must be based or at the very least seem to be based on legal authority. For the president, there are four sources of legal authority: (1) the Constitution itself, (2) acts of Congress, (3) precedents, and (4) court decisions.

Legal Powers and Limits: Authority from the Constitution ■

The Constitution deals with the presidency in some 30 instances. The mentions may be brief and routine, such as requiring the president-elect to take an oath of office, or they may be complex in their implication ("he shall take Care that the Laws be faithfully executed . . ."). The direct constitutional authorizations of power listed in the accompanying box are relatively few. In essence, the president can veto bills passed by Congress, exercise the "executive power," act as commander in chief of the armed forces, grant pardons, sign treaties, make specified nominations and appointments, send messages and recommendations to Congress, and take care that the laws are faithfully executed. Some of this authority is, of course, shared with Congress. Several of these key grants of authority are discussed below.

Veto. One of the president's most important legal powers is the *veto,* defined as a president's refusal to sign a bill passed by Congress within ten days after submission to him. He must return it with reasons for his objections. The president uses the *pocket veto* when he fails to sign a bill that has been submitted to him within ten days of the end of a session of Congress. The bill then cannot be returned to the Congress and so it dies. Unlike the governors in many states, the president cannot use an *item veto*—that is, veto a single section of a bill. The importance of the veto does not derive from its frequent use. From 1961 to 1988, only about 2 percent of the public bills presented to the president were vetoed. Of the vetoes during these years, only 12 percent were overridden. So the president has a potent weapon. Table 13–4 provides data on recent presidential vetoes. The veto is only a tool; it is not the essence of presidential power. President Reagan was spectacularly successful in 1981 in persuading Congress to accept his economic proposals. The veto contributed only marginally to his

TABLE 13–4

Presidential Vetoes and Overrides of Vetoes, 1961–1988

President	Vetoes	Overrides	Percent Overridden
Kennedy (1961–1963)	21	0	0
Johnson (1963–1969)	30	0	0
Nixon (1969–1974)	43	7	16.0
Ford (1974–1977)	66	12	18.0
Carter (1977–1981)	31	2	6.5
Reagan (1981–1988)	78	9	12

Source; *Presidential Vetoes 1789–1976,* compiled by the Senate Library (Washington, D.C.: U.S. Government Printing Office, 1978), p. ix; supplemented by data in *Congressional Quarterly Weekly Report.*

Continuity & CHANGE

The U.S. Constitution and the Presidency

Article	Section	Topic(s)
I	3	Vice presidency, impeachment
I	7	Veto
II	1	Executive power clause; term of office; electoral college; vice presidency; qualifications, removal, death, resignation, inability; compensation; oath of office
II	2	Commander in chief, written opinions from executive department heads, reprieves and pardons, treaties, nominations and appointments: ambassadors/consuls, judges of Supreme Court, officers of the United States
II	3	State of the Union information, recommend measures to the Congress, call special sessions of the Congress, adjourn Congress if the two houses cannot agree on time of, receive ambassadors and ministers, take care that laws be faithfully executed, commission officers of the United States
II	4	Impeachment
VI	3	Oath to support Constitution, no religious test
Amendments		
XII		Modifies election process
XX	1	Date for end of term
XX	3,4	Death, disability, succession
XXII	1	Length of time in office
XXIII		District of Columbia and electoral vote
XXV		Presidential succession

achievement; he used it only twice. Because the veto is so seldom overridden, the threat to use it can be intimidating. There is no way to measure the impact of such a threat; but members of Congress worry about it and seem to be influenced by it. That in itself makes the threat real.

A few overrides of presidential vetoes in recent years have come on very controversial issues, such as a civil rights bill in 1988. Most came on less visible disputes. Occasionally an override comes on an issue that does not threaten to shake the foundations of the republic but seems to many in the Congress to involve a very small-scale but clear wrong. In 1983, the Congress overrode President Reagan's veto of an Oregon land bill involving only about 3 acres of government-owned land and a tiny number of people. Representative Morris Udall (D–Ariz.) articulated a strong sentiment in Congress: "This bill represents such a small act of generosity and such a large dose of simple justice that it is beyond me what the administration thinks it is gaining by vetoing it."[9]

Take Care Clause. No one can state with precision what the constitutional phrase, "he shall take care that the laws be faithfully executed" means. A vigorous, assertive president tries to etch his own definition on history. In practice, each administration views the authority differently. Thus, the Eisenhower administration moved slowly and carefully to implement the civil rights acts of 1957 and 1960. When John Kennedy became president, he urged his advisors to move more swiftly and vigorously to meet the goals of the same legislation. In the 1980s, environmentalists expressed concern over the vigor with which environmental protection laws were being enforced. They argued that the Reagan administration, compared with some of its pred-

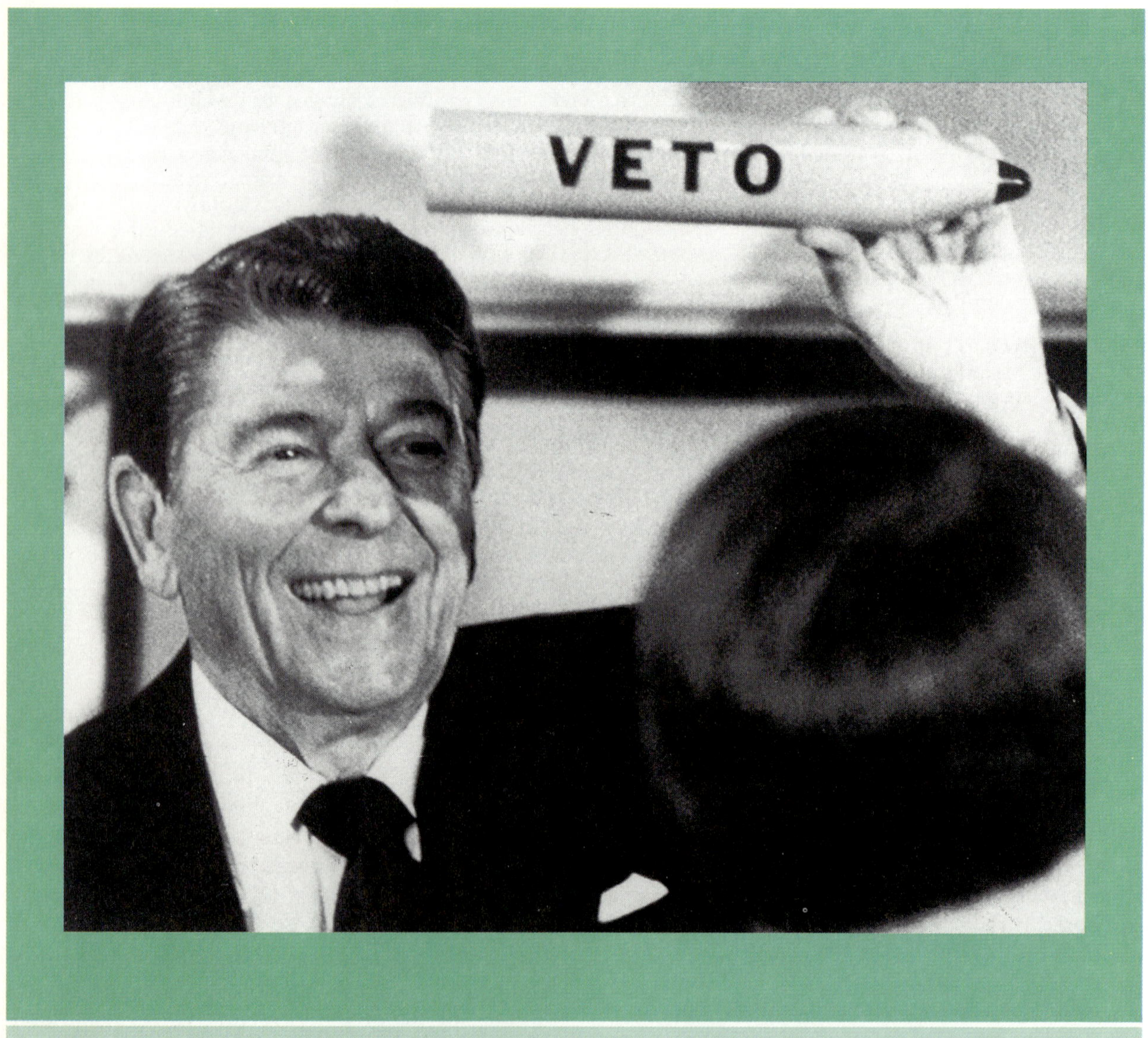

Ronald Reagan vows to defeat Democratic proposals with a veto. President Reagan's mastery of symbol manipulation and the media here depended on educating the public about the inherent powers of his office.

ecessors, was dragging its feet. (By contrast, George Bush, seeking to become "the environmentalist president," proposed major amendments to the Clean Air Act of 1970 that would diminish acid rain, smog created by auto exhausts, and the release of toxic chemicals into the air. Environmentalists were greatly encouraged by his initiative; industries complained about the plan's potential costs.) Vaguely worded grants of authority place great importance on the people in the administration—on their priorities, skills, and energy.

Commander in Chief. The constitutional authority to be commander in chief of the army and navy of the United States also can be interpreted in many ways. Originally, since Congress was given the constitutional authority to declare war, the commander in chief clause was associated with notions of civilian control of the armed forces, military tactics, and conceivably military command. In the hands of vigorous, activist presidents, this clause has become the basis for a widespread assertion of presidential power in foreign affairs. U.S. involvement in Korea during the 1950s was partially based on the commander in chief clause, as was the nation's participation in Vietnam. Presidents now use the commander in chief clause as a basis for asserting initiative in foreign policy matters of such importance that the very survival of the nation may be at stake. This evolution has such extraordinary consequences that it deserves closer inspection.

The original conception of the commander in chief clause was modified substantially during the Civil War when President Lincoln advanced a presidential claim to the *war powers*: the power to defend the United States and its interests as defined by the president whether or not the Congress had declared war. By World War II in the 1940s, President Franklin D. Roosevelt was defining this power as "to take measures necessary to avert a disaster which would interfere with the winning of the war." For example, in February 1942, after the Japanese attack on Pearl Harbor, President Roosevelt ordered the removal of over 100,000 persons of Japanese ancestry from their homes and businesses on the West Coast to inland relocation centers. Two-thirds of them were natural born U.S. citizens. No charges were filed against individuals, nor were they tried in the courts. Several sections of the Bill of Rights were violated, yet Congress and the courts later approved of or acquiesced to the president's action.

If the Civil War and World Wars I and II brought the elaboration and expansion of the commander in chief clause, the cold war era following World War II provided a hospitable environment for even broader claims to presidential power. Presidents sent U.S. armed forces abroad to Korea, Lebanon, the Dominican Republic, and Vietnam with no congressional declaration of war. The commander in chief clause no longer meant simply direction in a declared conflict. It now seemed to provide authority for presidents, acting with no declaration of war, to involve the United States in international conflict. Specific questions abound concerning the president's ability to act unilaterally in sending U.S. troops overseas.

In over 200 instances, presidents have by themselves committed U.S. troops abroad. Most of these incidents involved a few troops, were small in scale, and were limited in time. A qualitative change became apparent after World War II when the United States joined mutual defense organizations such as the North Atlantic Treaty Organization. In these agreements, an attack on one party was to be considered an attack on all. The question for the United States was: Who would decide whether U.S. armed forces would be sent? Although there were extensive debates about this, the reality seemed clear: The president and his advisors would decide. These problems are discussed in more depth in Chapters 14 and 20.

Power to Pardon. The Constitution grants the president the authority to issue pardons for all offenses against the United States except impeachment. A pardon exempts the grantee from the punishment of the laws for an offense he or she has committed or may have committed. Normally this authority is exercised sparingly. The most conspicuous recent example was in 1974 when President Ford pardoned former President Richard Nixon prior to any indictments being issued. Few doubted that President Ford had the legal authority

President Gerald Ford takes the oath of office. He replaced Richard Nixon, who had resigned to avoid impeachment. President Ford added to his difficulties as a president who was not directly elected by pardoning the former president before Nixon was convicted of any crime.

to take this action; many questioned its propriety and political wisdom. That President Ford suffered politically from this decision points up the broad consequences of the exercise of a president's legal authority. His public approval rating plunged from 66 percent before the pardon to about 50 percent just afterward.

Treaty-Making Authority. The president is constitutionally authorized to negotiate treaties with other nations, but they do not become law unless two-thirds of the senators present concur. The many applications of the treaty-making authority include treaties with American Indians, extradition agreements for fugitives, mutual defense agreements, and agreements for arms limitations. Additional discussion of this authority is found in Chapter 20.

Nominations and Appointments. The president nominates Supreme Court judges, ambassadors and ministers, and other public officials whose appointment is not provided for in the Constitution. Congress has augmented this role by authorizing the president to appoint federal judges and heads of executive departments. The advice and consent of the Senate is required. The authority to appoint creates a basis for a cohesive administration and for political patronage. Presidential relations with the federal bureaucracy are discussed at length in Chapter 15.

The president's power to appoint may have an impact on public policy far beyond his term of office. The president appoints judges to the federal courts. These judges' terms are for good behavior; they hold office until they retire or are impeached. Almost every president who serves a full term in office has appointed at least one justice of the Supreme Court (see Table 13–5). President Jimmy Carter (1977–1981) was the exception—but he did appoint 56 judges to appeals courts and 206 to U.S. district courts. Because these are lifetime appointments, the president's impact outlasts his time in office.

President Reagan appointed three justices to the Supreme Court and one chief justice. Overall, President Reagan appointed more than 350 federal judges. This total is the highest for any recent president and is 35 percent higher than that of President Carter. The sharp impact of the Reagan judicial appointees was felt early during the Bush administration in a series of conservative-oriented Supreme Court decisions on abortion, civil rights, capital punishment, and affirmative action (see Chapter 5). Presumably the conservative thrust of this Republican-shaped Court will be felt for many years.

Over 90 percent of federal judges appointed over the last 50 years were of the same political party as the president who selected them. In the Reagan administration, the figure was 97 percent.

Messages and Recommendations to Congress. Presidents are required to inform Congress of the state of the union and to recommend measures to the legislative body. The key here is how presidents exercise this authority. Presidential messages have emerged as part of the presidential leadership effort. They are steps in a bargaining and support-building process rather than instruments for dispensing information. The one who defines the agenda gains a substantial advantage.

Removing the President from Office. The Constitution also specifies the methods for removing a president from office. The most available is the election specified for every four years. Of the nine presidents from Roosevelt to Reagan, only four were elected to a second term. Table 13–6 provides specific information. The voters can turn out a pres-

TABLE 13–5

Partisanship and Presidential Appointments to the Supreme Court, 1930–1988

Dates	Number of Appointments, Including Chief Justices	Number of Appointees of the Same Political Party as the President
1930–1939	7	6
1940–1949	9	7
1950–1959	5	4
1960–1969	5	5
1970–1979	4	3
1980–1988	4	4

Source: Data from Henry J. Abraham, *Freedom and the Court* (New York: Oxford University Press, 1982), pp. 415–416; as supplemented by various issues of the *Congressional Quarterly Weekly Report.*

ident for any reason they choose. The Twenty-second Amendment stipulates in essence that a president can hold office for only two terms. This is true no matter how distinguished his performance in office. The third method of removal—*impeachment*—has been used against presidents only twice in American history. Andrew Johnson (1865–1869) was acquitted of the charges brought; Richard M. Nixon (1969–1974) resigned before the House of Representatives could bring formal charges against him. A president can be impeached by a majority of the House of Representatives. If a president is charged by the House, the U.S. Senate acts as a court to weigh the merits of the impeachment resolution. A two-thirds vote in the Senate is required to convict. If convicted, a president is removed from office.

Presidential Disability. The Constitution provides for succession to the presidency in cases of disability. These provisions are important because there have been assassination attempts against five of the last nine presidents, two have died in office, and others have had major surgery while in office.

Legal Powers and Limits: Legal Authority Through Statutes

Much presidential legal authority derives from acts of Congress. It might be argued, indeed, that most of the specific legal authority of the president derives from *statutes.* Congress has empowered the president to negotiate executive agreements with other countries on such topics as reciprocal trade and supplies for defense. He is authorized to make certain agreements with the United Nations Security Council. In domestic policy, the Congress has at times authorized the president to make appointments in the executive branch, to appoint specified federal judges, to seize railroads during crisis, to impose wage and price controls, to set levels of farm price supports, to apply antitrust laws, to implement labor-management relations acts, to enforce civil rights acts, and to exercise many additional responsibilities.

The statute is the accepted way for Congress to grant authority to the president and to limit its exercise. Much more controversial is the device popularly called the *legislative veto.* The legislative veto is used extensively in overseeing administrative rules and regulations and other actions. Congress sees it as a means to gain some control over the implementation of broad policy initiatives. The legislative veto takes many forms, but in essence, an act of an executive department is deferred or delayed until Congress or some of its committees can block or modify actions with which they disagree. For example, in the War Powers Resolution, if Congress does not support the president's com-

TABLE 13–6

Presidents Elected for One Term or Two Terms, 1932–1988

Presidents Elected for One Term		
Served One Term	**Elected After Succeeding from the Vice Presidency**	**Presidents Elected for Two or More Terms**
Kennedy	Truman	Roosevelt (4 terms)
Carter	Johnson	Eisenhower (2 terms)
Bush		Nixon (2 terms)
		Reagan (2 terms)

Note: President Ford came to the presidency in 1974 after the resignation of Richard Nixon. He ran for election in 1976 but was defeated by Jimmy Carter.

What the Presidency Costs

Congress by statute not only grants powers and sets limits for presidents in office but also sets their salaries. Yet a look at what the presidency actually costs shows the broad power and wide discretion we accord the office. The president's salary and expenses are only a part of the story.

After presidents leave office, Congress can also provide for presidential libraries, office allowances, and Secret Service protection. The expenses for supporting former presidents vary annually, but in recent years the range has been from $25 to $28 million per year.

Salary	$ 200,000
Expenses	50,000
Travel	40,000
Discretionary funds	1,000,000

mitment of troops to an international conflict within 60 days, the troops must be withdrawn. In executive reorganization acts, presidents were authorized to suggest structural changes in the executive branch. If after a fixed number of days Congress had not rejected them, the proposals took effect. Chapter 14 contains a more complete discussion of the implications of the legislative veto.

For executive orders the legal basis is both constitutional and statutory. Early presidents issued executive orders essentially for routine administrative purposes. Beginning with the administration of Franklin D. Roosevelt, these orders have been used for policy purposes in such areas as foreign trade and civil rights. In the nineteenth century, presidents issued an average of less than 20 executive orders each year. Over the last 50 years, the yearly average has been about 120.

While the broad, general grants of presidential legal authority come from the Constitution, much of the president's total legal authority is derived from legislative acts.

Legal Powers and Limits: Authority from Precedent ■

Precedent looms large in determining presidential legal authority. The president's cabinet derives from precedent. So does the use of executive privilege, impoundment, and some executive agreements. Precedent is perhaps even more important in the presidential interpretation of constitutional phrases. The scope of the executive power clause, the commander in chief clause, and the take care clause has been set by the actions of presidents over time.

Using precedent, presidents issue *executive orders* that can have far-reaching consequences. Presidents have by executive order prescribed loyalty-security programs for federal employees. Executive orders have been used frequently in civil rights. President Kennedy in 1962 issued an executive order designed to prevent discrimination in housing when federal funds were involved. During the Korean War, President Truman, by executive order 10340, directed the secretary of commerce to seize steel mills to prevent a strike by steel workers. The Supreme Court declared this action unconstitutional.

What earlier presidents have done affects a president's ability to act. Presidents are not bound by what has been done before, but precedents can help in seeking support. When President Eisenhower sent troops to Little Rock, Arkansas, in 1957 to maintain peace during a conflict over racial integration of the public schools, he supported his action by citing similar behavior by earlier presidents. The legal basis for a similar action by President John Kennedy in Oxford, Mississippi, in 1962 was clearer because of Eisenhower's earlier commitment of troops. To ignore or violate a precedent may place extra burdens on the president. Actions are more easily defended if the president is following familiar paths.

A president who wants to break new ground in the absence of a generally perceived crisis faces obstacles. When President Nixon decided to *impound* money authorized and appropriated by Congress, he created great animosity. Many members of Congress were furious that the president would try to block so many programs he disapproved of by refusing to spend money legally authorized and appropriated by Congress. Subsequently, legislation was passed to limit the president's power to impound. Chapter 14 provides additional discussion of presidential impoundments and congressional responses.

Legal Powers and Limits: Authority from Court Decisions ■

The courts have not consistently played a decisive role in shaping the president's legal authority; but court decisions have helped in the task of definition. There is no single ultimate interpreter of the meaning of the Constitution; but when the courts have ruled and their decisions have been accepted, they become useful agents of interpretation. Thus, the broad legal powers of the president in foreign policy are frequently justified by reference to *U.S.* v. *Curtiss-Wright Corporation* (1936); presidential war powers are reinforced by reference to the Prize cases (1863); and some limits on presidential authority can be derived from *Youngstown Sheet and Tube Company* v. *Sawyer* (1952), decided during the Korean police action. Fearing an interruption of steel production from a prolonged strike, President Truman ordered the seizure of steel mills by the government. The Supreme Court ultimately ruled that the president did *not* have the legal authority to take this action.

Over the years, court decisions have contributed to the definition of presidential legal authority. Despite the importance of this authority, the usual caution must be added: Authority and power are not the same thing. Authority may provide potential power, but the translation from one to the other is not automatic.

Bases and Limits of Presidential Power: The Partisan Context

The president is elected as a partisan and yet is expected to represent the entire nation. That dilemma is eased in two major ways: (1) Both major political parties share the fundamental values of society; (2) neither major party is a cohesive force in opposing the other party. Each party is a coalition of interests. The president finds friends and foes in both parties.

Partisans in Congress may be of some help to the president, but their assistance is neither overwhelming nor certain. Elected mainly on the basis of local issues or personality, members of Congress are more concerned with their constituencies than with the view of any president, even when of their own political party. Moreover, since party leaders may disagree with one another, representatives of the president's own party may dislike both his ideological predispositions and the bargains he strikes

Presidential Leadership and Ethics in Government

Is the American political system in need of reform? Some people think so, including President George Bush. Here is his package of reforms, proposed during the 101st Congress:

- Elimination of political action committees sponsored by corporations, trade associations, or labor unions—which together account for about 90 percent of all PAC campaign contributions.
- Reduction in the amount that ideological and single-issue PACs can contribute to congressional candidates from $5000 to $2500.
- Restrictions on the franking (or free mailing) privilege, which the president described as "mass mailings that amount to political advertising."
- A prohibition on carrying over campaign funds from election to election. Full disclosure of money spent for get-out-the-vote drives and voter registration—so-called "soft" money.
- Legislation to eliminate the gerrymandering of congressional districts.
- An increase in salaries for members of Congress, linked to a ban on honoraria for speeches.
- An increase in the amount that political parties can spend on behalf of congressional candidates.

To no one's surprise, reactions to the Bush package varied. Republicans were enthusiastic; newspapers generally endorsed it; public interest groups, such as Common Cause, found it a step in the right direction. But for Democrats, it was an entirely different matter. Speaker Thomas S. Foley (D-Wash.) contended that the proposals "blatantly favored the Republican party." Democratic National Chairman Ron Brown called the Bush plan "nothing more than a Fat Cat Protection Act."

Designed, said President Bush, to reduce incumbent advantages over challengers and to curb the influence of special interests, the reform package was clearly disadvantageous for the Democratic party—and especially for congressional Democrats. In the first place, Democrats hold a big advantage in number of incumbents. Even most state legislatures, which draw the lines of congressional districts, are controlled by Democrats. And Democratic candidates rely more on PAC contributions than Republicans, who receive more money from large individual contributions. Finally, ideological PACs and single-issue groups—which often favor Republican causes—could continue to make campaign contributions under the Bush plan.

Although long-run prospects for campaign reform appear promising, the eventual settlements in all likelihood will reflect more fully the interests of both parties. Among Democrats there is considerable support for two major proposals not included in the Bush package: public financing of congressional campaigns and spendng caps on House and Senate races.

Sources: *Congressional Quarterly Weekly Report,* July 1, 1989; *New York Times,* June 30, 1989; *Pittsburgh Post-Gazette,* June 30, 1989.

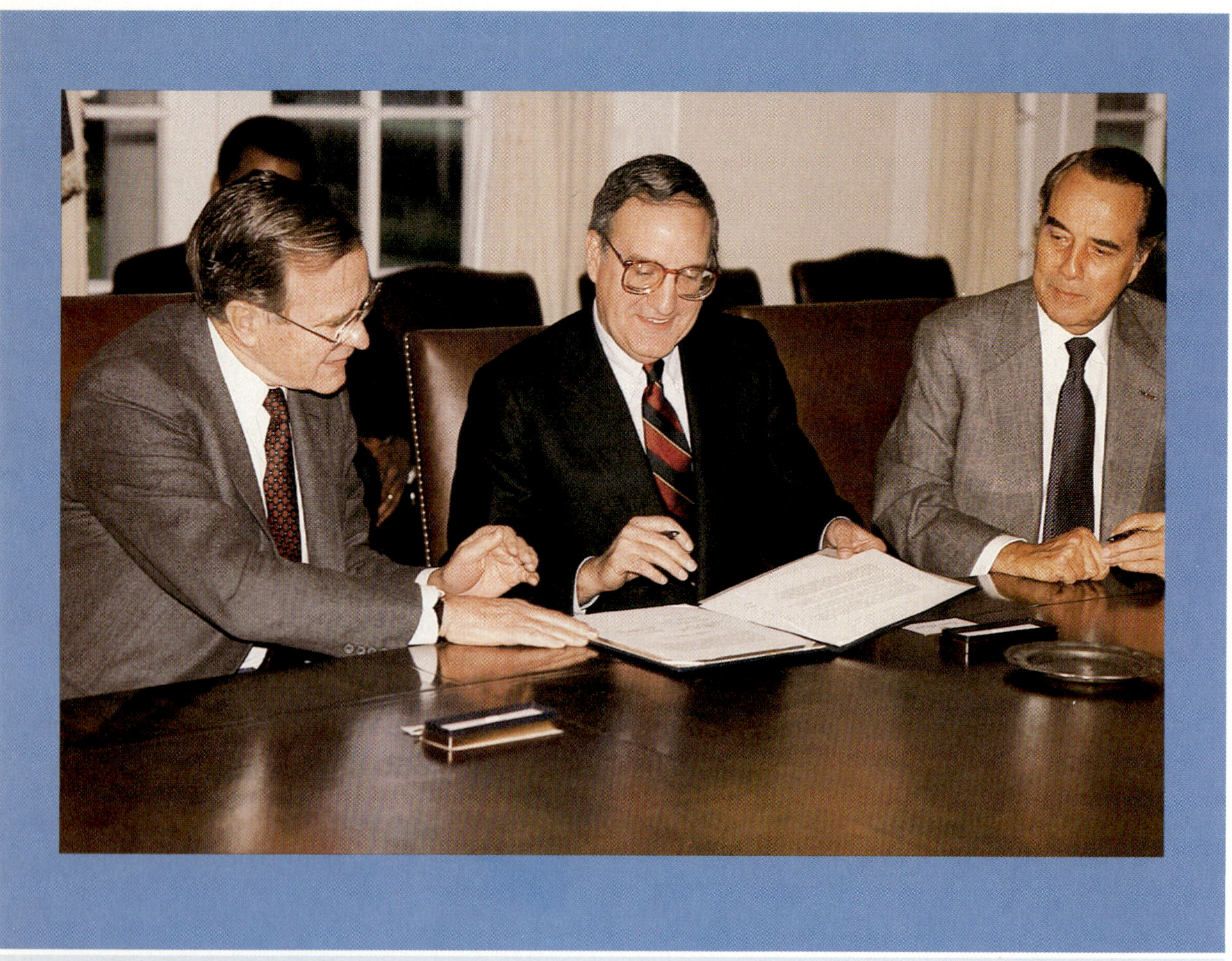

The Reagan administration's policy in Nicaragua consistently faced strong opposition in Congress. President Bush successfully worked toward a compromise with Senate party leaders George Mitchell (D–Me.) and Robert Dole (R.–Kans.). Republican presidents typically face Democratic majorities in both Houses, forcing them to work both sides of the aisle in Congress.

to promote his ends. Normally a president can expect more support in Congress from members of his own party than from the oppositon; but the support is usually a matter of degree. Unanimity and support cannot be predicted; coalitions must be built, not assumed. Sometimes a president needs only a few votes. Then, the party can help.

For the individual member of Congress, the president's standing in his or her own constituency may be important. Presidents who run well ahead of members of the House and Senate in their own districts and states have a better chance of gaining later support from these members of Congress. For most presidents, the coattails are very short. Most members of Congress do not owe their political fate to the president. Recent research suggests a strong connection between a representative's support of president-sponsored legislation and the size of the president's vote in that member's constituency. The popularity of the president in the member's own district may be as central as his standing in national politics.[10]

If the president's party controls Congress, the party leadership may be useful in constructing the coalition the president needs, but even that is a function of the talent of congressional leaders, their own views, and the cohesiveness of their party. During the Carter presidency, the Democratic party had substantial majorities in both House and Senate, yet the party was so fragmented that even Tip O'Neill, a skillful Democratic Speaker of the House, could not deliver majorities consistently for the president's program. As Richard E. Neustadt puts it, "What the Constitution separates, our political parties do not combine." [11]

Conversely, a president facing a Congress controlled in either one or both houses by the opposition party is not doomed in his legislative efforts. From 1968 to 1988, presidents faced an opposition party majority in at least one house of Congress for 16 to 20 years, or 80 percent of the time. Yet on the whole their legislative efforts, as shown in Figure 13–2, yielded results not too dissimilar from those of President Carter, whose political party controlled both houses while he was president.

Bases and Limits of Presidential Power: The Individual President

Perhaps the most elusive element in explaining presidential behavior and its boundaries is the *personal* dimension. As we have seen, presidents are not free agents. The contexts in which they work make a major difference in what they can do. Still, presidential behavior is not completely determined by external forces. Who is president can make a difference. Relevant here are the president's ideology, philosophy of the presidency, and political skills in dealing with both the public and other decision makers.

Presidents are hardly average citizens. All or almost all are male, Caucasian, Anglo-Saxon, Protestant, and college educated. Most had their origins in middle- or upper-class families. A typical career includes service in Congress, and nearly half were state governors. Since 1900, hardly any have served in a president's cabinet. This personal profile provides some insight into how leaders are recruited in the United States. Yet, it reveals little about a president's policies or style of leadership. Other factors must provide more useful keys.

If there are no major social crises and if the president is inclined to maintain the status quo, the course is clear. A president whose ideology points toward change and reform will have a more difficult task unless the nation confronts an imminent, dramatic crisis. American values, societal heterogeneity, and institutional structures promote inaction, so that a president who attempts substantial policy changes has obstacles to overcome. In the long run, of course, both the president and the country may be in worse trouble if change is avoided for reasons of short-run expediency. Balancing long- and short-term considerations is a necessary and vital presidential art.

A president's thinking about his office may shape his behavior. A philosophy supporting vigorous leadership means that the president will be active but not necessarily successful. A president who assumes that his job is largely to execute congressional orders efficiently is likely to experience fewer problems.

A president's political skill is difficult to measure. No one without substantial skill is elected president. Yet, presidents, whatever their skills, are hemmed in by external forces. President Carter was criticized strongly for flooding the congressional agenda with several hundred proposals labeled "top priority" instead of concentrating on a few. Implicit in this criticism was the assumption that a more skillful president would have been more successful in enacting his program. More accurate, perhaps, is that more skills might have ensured passage of more of the president's program.

In examining a president's influence with Congress, George C. Edwards III concluded:

> While we have found that support by Congress for presidents does not necessarily vary with the degree of presidential legislative skills, we are not suggesting that presidents should ignore these skills or that these skills never matter. Certainly, presidents have successfully intervened with a phone call, bargain, threat, or amenity, occasionally winning a crucial vote

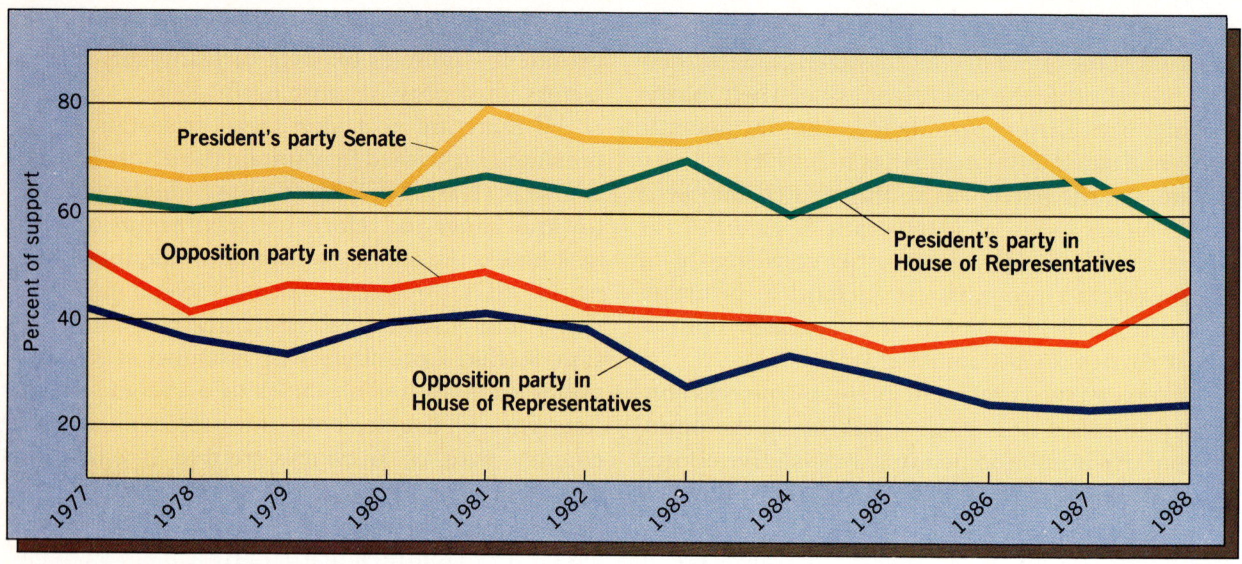

Figure 13–2 Support of the president's program in Congress: the partisan factor, 1977–1988. Source: *Congressional Quarterly Almanac* for each year.

because of such an effort. The important point is that these skills should be placed in their proper perspective. They do not appear to be a predominant factor in determining presidential support in Congress on most roll call votes and therefore, despite commonly held assumptions, they are not a prominent source of influence. Thus, what seems to be the most manipulatable source of presidential influence is probably the least effective.[12]

Despite all the handicaps to success they face, presidents who take a position on an issue frequently get their way in the Congress. Evidence for this proposition is found in Figure 13–3.

Valerie Bunce argues that a political leader such as the president can be most effective as a policy innovator early in a new administration, during the so-called honeymoon period. After that, a smaller impact is often the rule.[13] Evidence from the administrations of Franklin Roosevelt, Lyndon Johnson, and the first term of Ronald Reagan surely points in this direction. Hedrick Smith, then a writer for the *New York Times,* cites the following factors as vital to President Reagan's success in 1981: a national consensus on cutting back on government programs and curbing inflation, clarity of presidential purpose and priorities, a rapid start, skillful and dedicated courting of Congress, clever use of legislative procedures to promote budget cutting, effective appeals to the public, astute political advisers, and building a strong base in his own political party.[14]

Presidents can sometimes receive great attention for lesser accomplishments than the adoption of a legislative program. In 1984, when President Reagan telephoned to congratulate the recipient of an artificial heart, William Schroeder, Mr. Schroeder complained to the president that no action was forthcoming on his efforts to get government disability payments from the Social Security Administration. Schroeder's check was hand-delivered shortly thereafter to his hospital bed. A president can make a difference.

In 1989, immediately following the Supreme Court's decision upholding the constitutionality of flag burning as a form of political protest, President Bush took center stage to propose a constitutional amendment making it a crime to desecrate the American flag. Like the prolonged squabble over the Pledge of Allegiance in the 1988 presidential campaign, this issue was made to order for low-

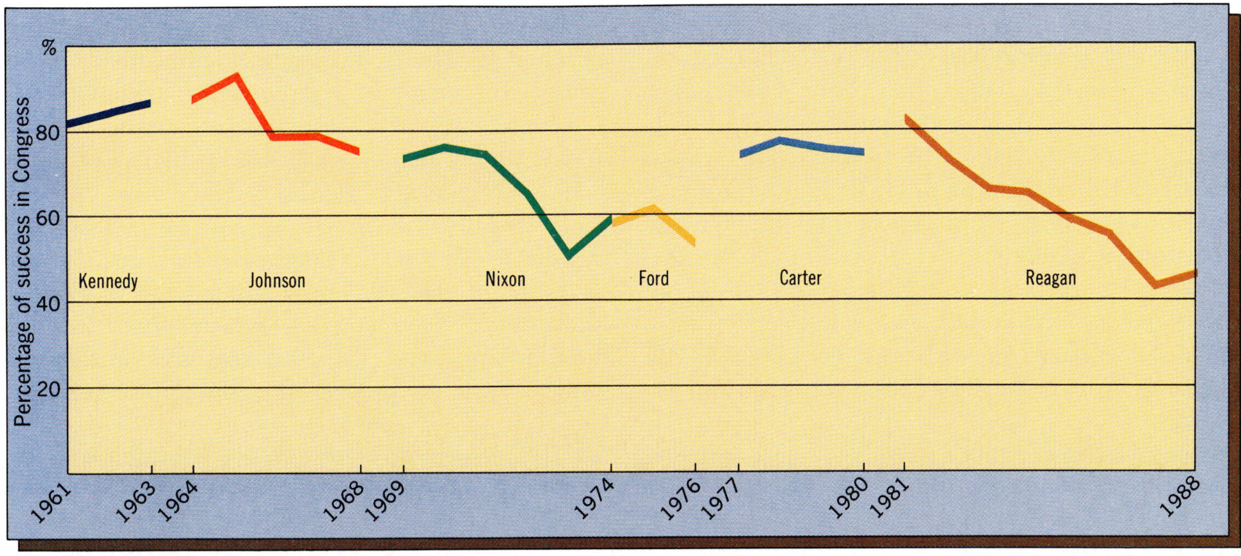

Figure 13–3 Presidential success on votes in Congress, 1961–1988. The percentages shown are based on votes on which the president took a clear position. Source: *Congressional Quarterly Almanac,* 1987; *Congressional Quarterly Weekly Report,* November 19, 1988.

cost, high-return "position taking" and "politicking." The Court's decision also produced a storm of protest and a flood of activity in Congress. And in late 1989 Congress passed a bill to ban flag-burning; preferring a constitutional amendment the president allowed the bill to become law without his signature.

Problems and Dilemmas

The president is expected to speak for all of us—but collectively we do not agree. The president is supposed to represent the majority that elected him—but that is different from representing all of us. The president is supposed to be efficient and yet accountable, a difficult combination. Our system is geared for continuous availability of presidential leadership, but that does not always happen.

Representative of the Whole and Representative of the Majority

The heterogeneity of the nation poses substantial problems for a president who seeks to articulate and promote what the people want. If he cannot speak for all of us, for whom should he speak? One answer is that he should speak for his political party—yet his party, like the public, lacks unified views. A second answer is that he should speak for the majority—but who are they? Those who elected him do not necessarily share his policy views. Polls reported that many voters in 1984 agreed more with Democratic candidate Walter Mondale on specific policy issues, yet voted for the Republican candidate, Ronald Reagan. In addition, the president is expected to be both national leader and party leader, a leader of majorities and protector of minorities. How can he do all this?

On rare occasions, the task is easy. When Japanese planes bombed Pearl Harbor in 1941, the president could defend our national interests with little opposition. The public interest merged with private interests. The president could be both symbolic leader and instrumental leader, both national leader and party leader, both leader of majorities and leader of all. More often, presidents face problems in simultaneously meeting these various obligations.

President Jimmy Carter, for example, headed

a government pledged to expose the hazards to health of smoking tobacco. Yet voters in tobacco-growing states were important to his political fortunes. Moreover, in several states, tobacco growing is important to economic well-being. The resolution of this dilemma provides insight into the workings of the presidency and American politics. While government regulations limit tobacco advertising and require warnings on cigarette packages about the dangers of smoking, government continues to subsidize tobacco growers and President Carter spoke in North Carolina about the beauty of tobacco. Everyone gets something, either symbolic or tangible. There are few neat solutions to basic policy problems in a heterogeneous society.[15]

Presidents can rarely please everyone. In domestic policy matters where the number of competing interests is large, this problem is at its most acute. What is beneficial to some is seen as outrageous to others. The massive indifference of much of the public most of the time may add to a president's burdens in building consensus and seeking popular approval. The idea that the president's greatest asset is the support of the public needs to

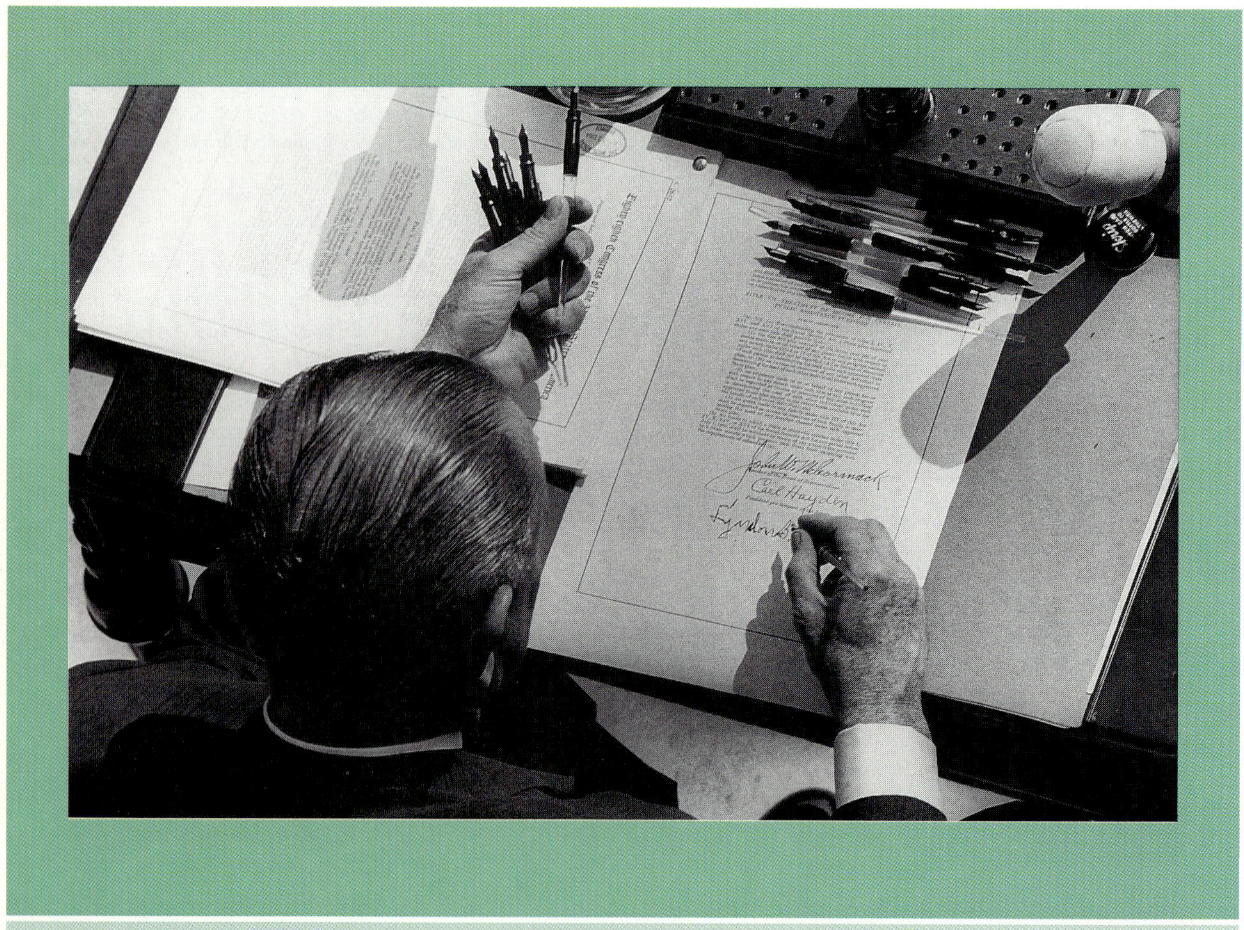

Lyndon B. Johnson's legendary powers of persuasion were never as active as in the early days of his administration, when a president must set new priorities. Here he uses several pens to sign into law his "War on Poverty." He then distributed the pens to members of Congress who played key roles in passing the bill. In the last analysis, the president's chief power is simply the power to persuade.

be considered alongside these grim facts.

The president rarely hears from everyone. Rather, he is regularly told by a variety of interested parties holding contradictory views that they indeed represent the public interest. The major ostensible spokespersons for the public interest are organized private interests.

Efficiency and Accountability

Having won election to the highest political office in the land, the president finds it hard to get many important things done. If effectiveness is difficult to achieve, effectiveness combined with accountability is even harder. Politically unacceptable solutions, no matter how personally attractive to the president, are frequently discarded. The magic lies in coming up with answers that will solve problems (or seem to) and also selling these answers to the Congress and the public. That is no simple task.

Among the barriers presidents encounter are some that they in part create for themselves and some that are seemingly pushed on them by events. One of these is insulation from others and the isolation that results. Presidents are pushed toward isolation from public moods, problems, and official criticism. Isolation begins in their personal life. George Reedy, in his book *The Twilight of the Presidency,*[16] argues that presidents are isolated people in their daily personal lives and in whom they get to talk with. All of the daily burdens that keep the rest of us in touch with reality—traffic jams, waiting in line, the laundry wrecking our shirts—are never encountered by presidents. Food and clothing are brought to them. They are driven or flown everywhere. No crowds bother them as they watch movies in the White House. They need not rush to keep an appointment with a barber; the barber comes to them. Reedy argues that isolation from the daily cares of life makes a president less sensitive to the problems of people in society.

Moreover, Reedy argues, the need to filter letters, telephone calls, and visitors so that the president's time can be conserved gives those who guard that time special advantages. Presidents may hear mainly what those around them want them to hear. Again, the possibility of isolation is raised. Ultimately, Reedy argues, the many-faceted isolation so characteristic of the modern presidency has consequences for the president's ability to be fully accountable. In the Reagan administration, the Iran-contra controversy provided an apt illustration.

The job of the adviser may be to make presidents aware of a wide range of alternative positions and arguments, but the "courtier" role—serving the president by agreeing with him—may be more common. Chester Cooper describes his experience in meetings of the National Security Council during the Johnson administration:

> The President, in due course, would announce his decision and then poll everyone in the room—Council members, their assistants, and members of the White House and NSC Staffs. "Mr. Secretary, do you agree with the decision?" "Yes, Mr. President." "Mr. X, do you agree?" "I agree, Mr. President." During the process I would frequently fall into a Walter Mitty-like fantasy: when my turn came, I would rise to my feet slowly, look around the room, and then directly at the President, and say very quietly and emphatically, "Mr. President, gentlemen, I most definitely do *not* agree." But I was removed from my trance when I heard the President's voice saying, "Mr. Cooper, do you agree?" and out would come, "Yes, Mr. President, I agree." [17]

Presidents are supposed to have unusually good access to sources of information and analysis both in and out of government. Bureaucrats as well as experts outside government are frequently flattered to be sought out by someone in the White House. In practice, these sources are limited by the interest and energy of the president and those around him. Protecting the president's time and energy is important, and yet to expose him to a diversity of opinion and analyses may be equally important. How to accomplish both is a perplexing problem. Presidents, if they are sufficiently alert to the barriers around them, can help themselves at times. Presidents Franklin D. Roosevelt and John F. Kennedy were noted for making such efforts. President Carter attempted to "micro-manage" his

“ Perspectives ”

On the Presidency

“*No one else represents the people as a whole. . . . His is the only national voice. . . .*”

—W. Woodrow Wilson

“*The Presidency is not merely an administrative office. . . . It is preeminently a place of moral leadership.*”

—Franklin D. Roosevelt

“*The Office of President is such a bastardized thing, half royalty and half democracy, that nobody knows whether to genuflect or spit.*”

—Jimmy Breslin

“*The President can't win. If he moves too slow, nothing will pass. If he waits for the second term, it will be too short. If he goes too fast in the first term, the mistakes will cost him reelection. Damn if I know why anyone would want the job.*”

—A Kennedy aide

“*I sit here all day trying to persuade people to do things they ought to have sense enough to do without my persuading them. . . . That's all the powers of the President amount to.*”

—Harry S Truman

“*The worst thing a president can do is to be so paralyzed by propriety that he shrinks from bending the rules when the nation's security requires it.*”

—Raymond J. Price, Jr.

“*It [the presidency] has become 'the fire hydrant of the nation.'*”

—Walter Mondale

“*Even more than the checks of the Constitution, the constraints of the clock are the ultimate limit upon the personal power of a President. The finiteness of time limits what any President can do in the course of a day, a week, or a year.*”

—Richard Rose

“*The essence of the presidency is the responsibility for making decisions and the necessity for making them without peers—with advice and counsel, yes; but also in the sure knowledge that the president alone bears the full and complete burden.*”

—George E. Reedy

"Everybody believes in democracy until he gets to the White House and then you begin to believe in dictatorship, because it's so hard to get things done. Everytime you turn around, people resist you and even resist their own job."

—A Kennedy aide, 1970

"For there is at least one test of the system that is, I think, decisive. There have been five considerable crises in American history. There was the need to start the new republic adequately in 1789; it gave the American people its natural leader in George Washington. The crises of 1800 brought Jefferson to the presidency; that of 1861 brought Abraham Lincoln. The War of 1914 found Woodrow Wilson in office; the great depression resulted in the election of Franklin Roosevelt. So far, it is clear, the hour has brought forth the man. It is of course true, as Bagehot said, that 'success in a lottery is no argument for lotteries.'"

—Harold J. Laski

"Taken by and large, the history of the presidency is a history of aggrandizement."

—Edward S. Corwin

Source: W. Woodrow Wilson, *Constitutional Government in the United States* (New York: Columbia University Press. 1908), p. 68; Franklin D. Roosevelt quoted in Joseph E. Kallenbach, *The American Chief Executive* (New York: Harper & Row, 1966), p. 253; Jimmy Breslin, *How the Good Guys Finally Won* (New York: Ballantine Books, 1975), p. 29; A Kennedy aide quoted in Paul C. Light, "The President's Agenda: Notes on the Timing of Domestic Choice," *Presidential Studies Quarterly,* XI, 1 (Winter 1981), p. 81; Quoted in Robert E. DiClerico, *The American President* (Englewood Cliffs, N.J.: Prentice-Hall, 1979), p. 360; Quoted in Thomas E. Cronin, *The State of the Presidency,* 2d ed. (Boston: Little, Brown, 1980), p. 223; Walter Mondale quoted in Joseph Kraft, "The Post Imperial Presidency," *New York Times Magazine,* November 2, 1980, p. 31; "Government Against Sub-Governments: A European Perspective on Washington," in Richard Rose and Ezra Suleiman, eds., *Presidents and Prime Ministers* (Washington, D.C.: American Enterprise Institute for Public Policy Research, 1980), p. 328; George E. Reedy, *The Twilight of the Presidency,* rev. ed. (New York: New American Library, 1987), p. 52; Harold J. Laski, *The American Presidency, an Interpretation* (New York: Harper & Brothers, 1940); Quoted in the *New York Times,* August 9, 1984, p. 23; Edwin S. Corwin, *The President: Office and Powers* (New York: New York University Press, 1957), pp. 30–31.

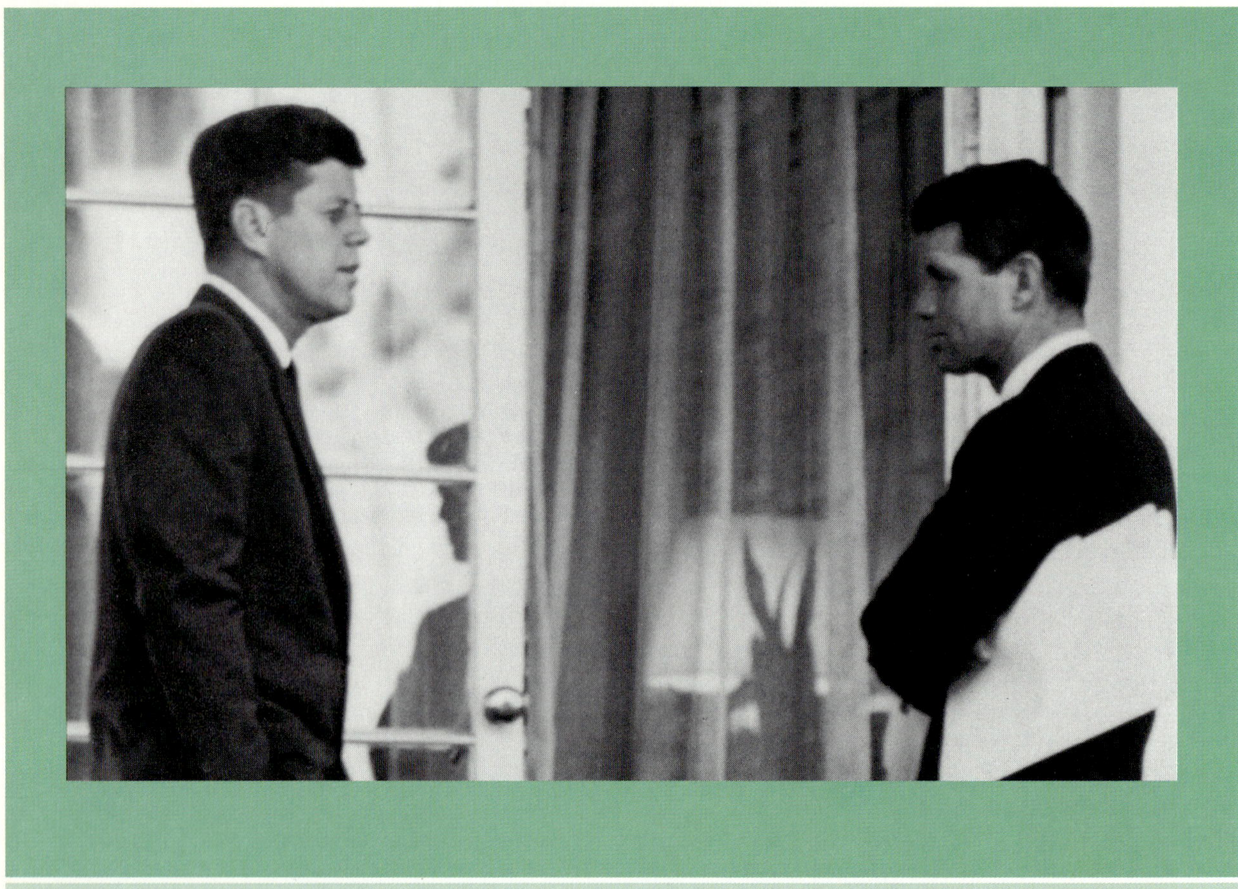

John F. Kennedy meeting with his brother Robert, the attorney general in his administration. Anxious to overcome the presidency's isolation from events and differing opinions, President Kennedy used his brother as one of several channels for maintaining closer contact with the bureaucracy and interest groups.

administration. The problems overwhelmed him. In some ways, President Reagan's inclination to delegate extensively added to the problem. Presidents try to cope in different ways but partial success is their best result. No wonder, then, that Reedy could pose the dilemma but could find few effective solutions.[18]

Accountability is even harder to achieve when the public holds contradictory goals and views: opposition to new taxes, opposition to cuts in programs, but support for a reduction in the budget deficit.

Even virtues can cause problems. Every student of democracy knows the importance of elections. Yet the presidential election cycle means that presidents must spend a significant portion of their time and energy running for their own reelection or supporting members of Congress seeking to return to office. Elections can indeed promote accountability. Yet the time and effort devoted to them must come at the expense of other work. A president running for office or helping others do so is a president distracted from other tasks, and one whose policy decisions may be made with a firm eye toward those whose election support is needed. Serious questions can be raised about whether this behavior always promotes the public interest. A responsive president may not always be an effective one from the perspective of solving problems.

Continuity and Disability

The demands on modern presidents are great. We assume that their services will be continuously available. The age at which presidents enter office, frequently the late fifties, combined with the tensions of the office and the hazards of contemporary public life (the threat of assassination, for one), create the distinct possibility of gaps in continuity. President Reagan's recovery period after he was shot, President Nixon's stress immediately preceding his resignation, President Kennedy's assassination, and President Eisenhower's three serious illnesses are examples.

There are constitutional and statutory solutions to the problem of presidential *disability,* but none is politically effective. If a president dies, the vice president assumes the presidency. The questions here are not about what happens, but about the talents and experience of vice presidents. Vice presidents are seldom nominated because in their party's view they are the second-best person available. The vice president is usually picked to balance the ticket regionally or ideologically. Once in office, most presidents do not anticipate their own death and carefully train their vice presidents for succession. The vice president who is forced to assume the presidency is probably not well prepared to do so. As Eleanor Roosevelt said to Vice President Harry Truman just after President Roosevelt died, ". . . for you are the one in trouble now." [19]

Disability, compared with death or resignation, creates different problems. The mechanism for dealing with disability is specified in the

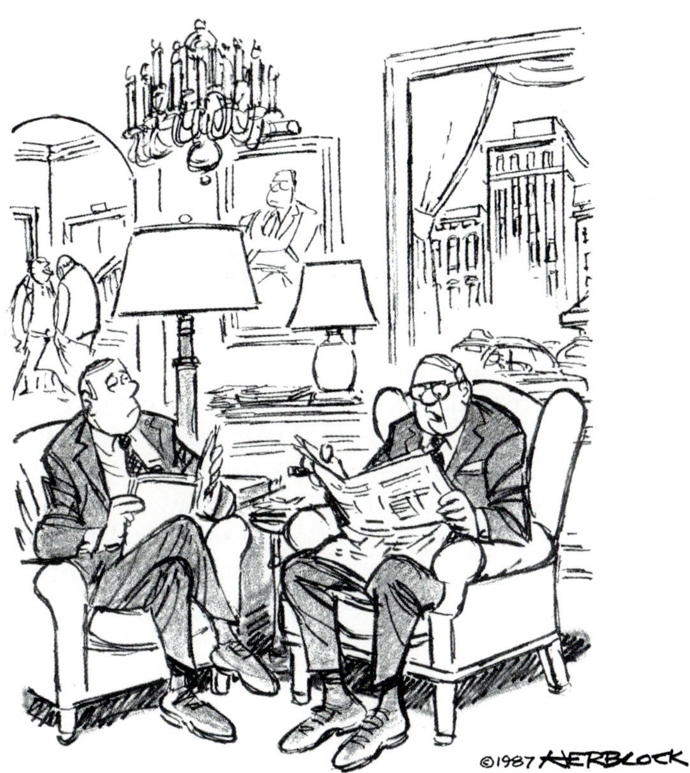

"It's awful that so many people around the president did these things—who in the world hired these people?"

Twenty-fifth Amendment. Good structural solutions are not necessarily good political ones, however. No vice president has ever assumed the presidency during apparent instances of presidential disability; and that is no accident. Vice presidents hesitate to defy precedent, gain the enmity of presidential advisers, and create the appearance of a blatant grab for power. When President Reagan was scheduled for surgery, in July 1985, to remove a malignant growth, he argued that the Twenty-fifth Amendment did not apply to very brief periods of disability. However, he did essentially follow the procedures therein when he authorized Vice President George Bush to serve as acting president during the period of the surgery. President Reagan withdrew this authority about eight hours later after the surgery was completed and the effects of the anesthetic had worn off.

Elections are properly heralded as central to democracy. They can, however, interfere with continuity of leadership. Newly elected presidents and those around them must learn about their new offices and responsibilities. Since the presidency is a unique institution, no amount of experience elsewhere offers fully satisfactory preparation. New presidents need time to adjust and learn. Political and economic realities, both foreign and domestic, may get in the way.

Presidents also need to campaign for reelection. They also find it politically useful to make campaign efforts for their fellow partisans in Congress. More time and energy is thus diverted from other tasks. The virtues of elections for democracies are partially offset by the gaps in continuity of leadership and the warping of priorities that elections inevitably create.

Constitutional limits on presidential service may also hinder continuity of leadership. Under the Twenty-second Amendment to the Constitution, no president may be elected more than twice or serve for longer than ten years. This amendment, heralded by its sponsors as a bulwark against executive tyranny, can have the effect of limiting effective leadership, especially during crises. Apparently, each virtue exacts a price.

Given the problems and limits cited in this analysis how well have presidents performed in office? Popular opinions differ but at least some "experts," historians, have reached a consensus. Historians seems to agree that only a few presidents have been great, and they agree as to who these few are (Table 13–7). Lincoln, Franklin Roosevelt, and Washington are at the top of nearly all the lists. An overwhelming number of presidents have been evaluated by historians as average or above. Hardly any presidents are regarded as failures. Grant and Harding are usually on such lists. For a few presidents, reputations change over time. Only about 30 percent of the people thought that President Truman was doing a good job in office when his term ended in 1952. By the end of the 1980s his stature had risen considerably. The general contours of presidential success and failure are relatively easy to sketch. More precise measures become more complicated. How, for example, should we assess the Reagan presidency? The answer varies with the issue under discussion and the judgment of the assessor.

How all these factors come together can be seen in an analysis of presidential-congressional interaction. Both president and Congress ostensibly speak for the public interest. In this, they have a common objective. Both also attempt to promote their reelection through trying to build majority support. Both, in the main, wish to uphold democratic values and the rule of law. But the bonding agents that tie them together also contain elements for conflict.

The precise meaning of the public interest may be unclear; the president and majorities in Congress may define the term differently. Their common interest in reelection may actually pull them apart, because at least in some cases those who elect the president differ from those who elect the individual member of Congress. Responsiveness to constituency desires is an important idea in a democracy, but what if constituencies differ in what they want? A common desire for reelection enhances cooperation only insofar as constituents want similar things. Sometimes they do not.

The desire to promote common values may provide a common umbrella for president and Congress, but when discussion and the need for action move from the realm of abstract values to that of

TABLE 13–7

Best and Worst Presidents—What the Experts Say

Best	Number of Polls	Number of Mentions in Polls
Jackson	4	3
Jefferson	4	4
Lincoln	4	4
F. D. Roosevelt	4	4
T. Roosevelt	4	4
Truman	4	1
Washington	4	4
Wilson	4	4
Worst	**Number of Polls**	**Number of Polls in Which Rated Low**
Buchanan	3	3
Grant	3	3
Harding	3	3
Pierce	3	3

Source: Data from Robert E. DiClerico, *The American President* (Englewood Cliffs, N.J.: Prentice-Hall, 1979), table 9–1.

concrete policy, consensus may well turn into conflict. Agreement that a good education for our children is desirable does not guarantee that all will want school busing to be used to achieve racial integration in the public schools. If we agree that the rights of citizens should be defended, we will not necessarily concur that illegally obtained evidence should not be admissible in a court of law. If we share a belief in the importance of protecting individual privacy against government intrusion into our lives, we will not necessarily agree that government should have no policy concerning abortion.

So the bonds of unity tend to dissolve in some specific policy contexts. What unites the president and the Congress may also pull them apart.

Further complicating the problem of executive-legislative conflict and cooperation is the fact that neither branch always speaks with one voice. Much executive-legislative interaction occurs when departments and bureaus work with just a few members of Congress and their staffs in committees and subcommittees. (Chapters 15 and 17 provide additional discussion of this point.) Time, energy, concern, and priorities limit the number of issues that rise to the attention of each branch. And although each branch may have been designed to speak for the whole, it frequently ends up speaking for itself and for the interests it represents.

Executive-legislative cooperation and conflict are genuinely multidimensional. On the very few issues where a general public consensus translates into agreement on the details of public policy, both the executive and the legislative branches will reflect this agreement. When a president seems to have captured mass support, such as Roosevelt in 1933, Johnson in 1964, and Reagan in 1981, Congress may go along. But these are exceptional situations. In most cases, the normal disagreements in society will be reflected in how the executive and

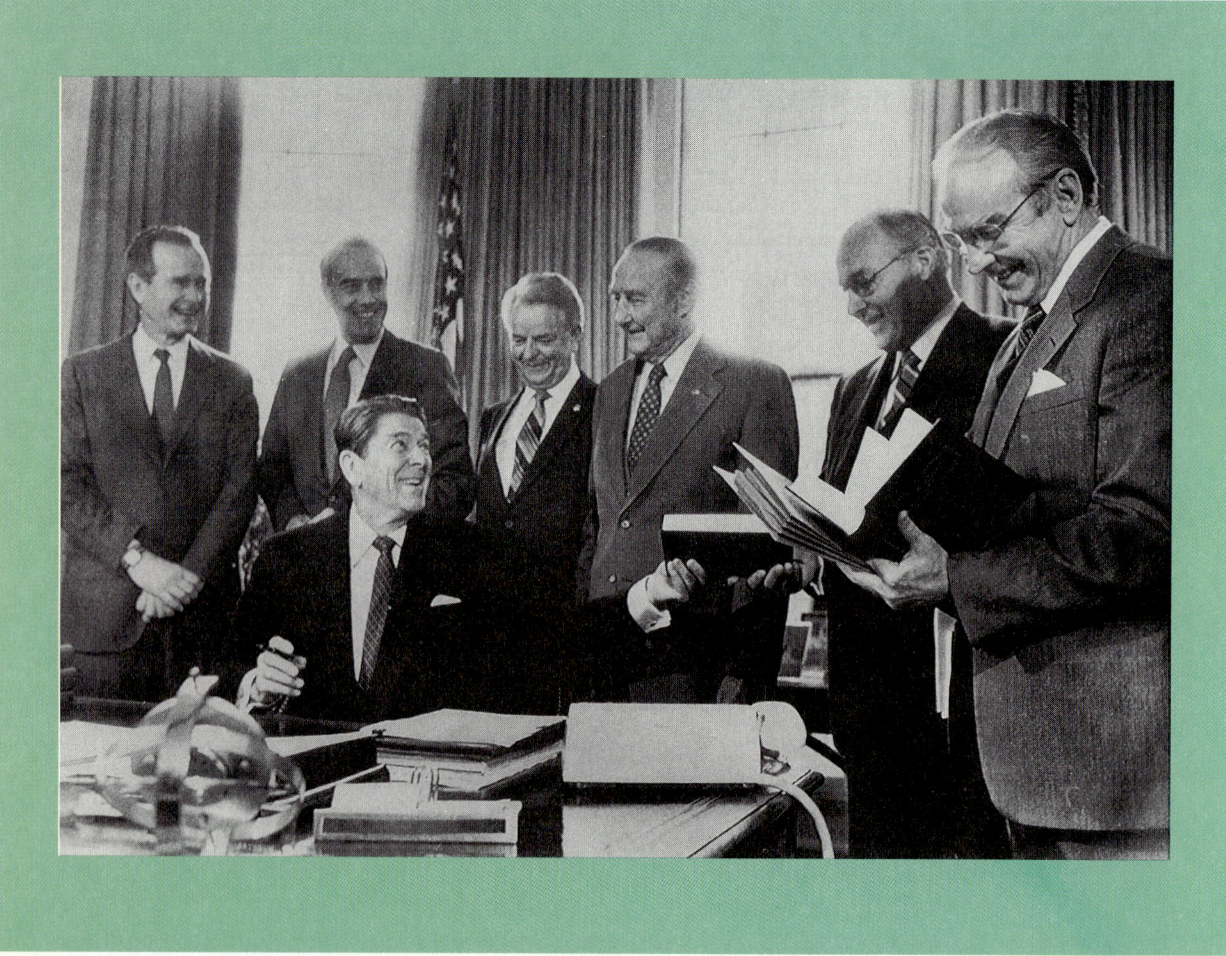

President Ronald Reagan often used his genial personality to build support for his programs. "Schmoozing" may not be enough by itself to guarantee success. But this kind of friendly exchange with leaders of both parties in Congress is crucial to the equation of presidential power.

legislative branches interact. Conflict as well as cooperation is normal in American government and politics.

Summary

- The presidency holds a unique status in American government and politics. Presidents are both national symbols and political leaders. Presidents are thus potentially powerful.
- One negative consequence of this dual status is that most people expect presidents to do more than is humanly possible. If a problem such as unemployment or inflation arises, the president is expected to solve it, or at least to provide solutions for others such as Congress to adopt. Even if the difficulties are beyond the president's ability to control, an absence of solutions will mean public disfavor.
- How presidents are nominated and elected affects what they do in office. Informal qualifi-

cations are more important than those set by the Constitution in determining who is nominated and elected. Candidates are screened carefully in some ways—especially for ideology and political party—but the screening process is imperfect.

- The bases and limits of presidential power are established as societal, legal, and partisan factors interact with the individual who is president. Much of what presidents can do is determined by the conditions in which they work. Who is president is always relevant, but seldom decisive.
- The vagueness of key constitutional provisions leaves room for individual presidents and circumstances to shape presidential powers and limits. Constitutional terms such as "executive power" and "commander in chief" are defined mainly by experience. There is no single meaning for these phrases; they gain meaning as political solutions are worked out.
- All presidents face basic problems such as how to represent the majority that elected them and yet speak for all the people, and how to be both effective and responsible. No president has solved these puzzles. But then no president can fully do so, for they are inherent in leadership in a democratic society.

Readings on The Presidency

Edwards, George C. 1983. *The Public Presidency: The Pursuit of Popular Control.* New York: St. Martin's Press. The presidents' pursuit of popular support.

Jones, Charles O., ed. 1988. *The Reagan Legacy: Promise and Performance.* Chatham, N.J.: Chatham House Publishers. Differing perspectives on the long-term impact of the Reagan administration.

Kernell, Samuel. 1986. *Going Public: New Strategies of Presidential Leadership.* Washington, D.C.: CQ Press. How presidents increasingly "go public" in appealing for policy support.

Neustadt, Richard E. 1980. *Presidential Power: The Politics of Leadership from FDR to Carter.* New York: John Wiley & Sons. A classic treatment of how presidents can, and do, seek influence once in the White House.

Pfiffner, James P. 1988. *The Strategic Presidency: Hitting the Ground Running.* Chicago: Dorsey Press. How governmental power is transferred from one administration to the next.

Reedy, George E. 1987. *The Twilight of the Presidency,* rev. ed. New York: New American Library. An argument that modern presidents are far too insulated if they are to be effective *and* accountable.

Rockman, Bert A. 1984. *The Leadership Question: The Presidency and the American System.* New York: Praeger Publishers. The relationship between presidents and the constraints of the political system.

Schlesinger, Arthur M., Jr. 1973. *The Imperial Presidency.* Boston: Houghton Mifflin. The view that modern presidents have become aloof, arrogant, and out of touch with the American electorate.

Watson, Richard A., and Norman C. Thomas. 1988. *The Politics of the Presidency,* 2d ed. Washington, D.C.: CQ Press. An up-to-date survey text on the American presidency.

Wayne, Stephen J. 1988. *The Road to the White House: The Politics of Presidential Elections,* 3d ed. New York: St. Martin's Press. A guide to the system to presidential selection.

Chapter 14

Executive-Legislative Relations

Governments can be democratic or dictatorial. They can also be categorized as presidential or parliamentary. Underlying such efforts is the assumption that how the executive and legislative branches interact tells us a great deal about the politics of the country. That conclusion is certainly warranted for the United States, where the president and Congress sometimes cooperate, sometimes fight, and usually do some of each.

The central fact about the presidency and Congress is that they are separate institutions required by law and prodded by necessity to work together. For that reason, the unifying theme of this chapter is executive-legislative cooperation and conflict.

The Presidency and Congress: Separate Institutions

In many democratic countries, the president or prime minister is selected by the legislature. The chief executive is closely tied to the legislative branch. He or she can be removed or strongly challenged through legislative votes of no confidence. In the United States, the president and Congress are independently created and selected. They also have independent powers. Taken together, these facts tell us much about what happens in the national government and why.

The framers of the Constitution believed that separating executive and legislative powers provided a good defense against tyranny. So they designed the governmental system that way. Article I of the Constitution deals with the legislative branch: Article II is concerned with the presidency. Thus each is created legally independent of each other. Both stem directly from the Constitution.

Independence begins in the Constitution and is physically and psychologically reinforced by where the branches are housed in Washington, D.C. The distance from Capitol Hill, the home of Congress, and the White House, the home of presidents, is a short drive or a long haul, depending on circumstances. Architecture reflects legal autonomy. The building are apart; the physical distance sometimes mirrors political and policy distance. The president is not a creature of Congress, just as Congress does not only serve at the president's pleasure. Each must live with the other. The way in which each is selected affects their relationship.

Selecting the President and Congress

The president is nominated and elected on a national basis. Congress, with one minor exception, plays no role in the process. Primary elections and caucuses in the states are the usual means for selecting delegates to the national nominating conventions, where the presidential nominees of the two major parties are legally selected. In recent years the decision has been made, however, before the conventions actually begin. Presidents are then elected through the constitutionally prescribed electoral college. Only if no candidate wins a majority of the electoral vote is presidential selection given over to the House of Representatives. Congress has been involved in deciding such inconclusive elections only three times in American history and never in the twentieth century. In other words, Congress plays no formal role in the nomination and election of presidents over 90 percent of the time.

Similarly, presidents have nothing to do legally with the selection of members of Congress. Members of the Senate are selected from their states. Members of the House of Representatives are selected from districts within their states. The procedure is constitutionally prescribed. In law, the president has nothing to say about this process. Even politically, the president's influence is usually very small. Individual members of Congress may be helped if a president campaigns for them, but the president is rarely a decisive figure. Congressional candidates are elected mainly for state and local reasons.

The few presidential attempts to purge the Congress for not supporting the administration have been notoriously unsuccessful. Even as popular a president as Franklin Roosevelt or Ronald Reagan could not win this battle. In recent elections almost all members of the House of Representatives

TABLE 14–1

President and Congress, Party Control, 1900–1988

	Number of Elections	Percent of Total
Same party controls the presidency and Congress	29	64.4
Same party controls the presidency and one house of Congress	5	11.1
Different parties control the presidency and Congress (both houses)	11	24.4

who have sought reelection have won. Most senators who seek to retain their office do so but the figures are not as great as they are for the House. Only in marginal districts, often less than 10 percent of the total, may the president's impact be more than peripheral.

Not only the constituencies but also the terms of office of the president and members of Congress differ. Presidents serve for four years and may run for reelection once. Members of the House have two-year terms and senators have six-year terms. Electorates may have different attitudes and preferences at each of these times. Both the type of constituency and the length of term may add to the possibility of executive-legislative differences.

The net effect of separate elections for the president and members of Congress is that members feel little obligation to the president for their electoral success. The impact of this feeling on subsequent behavior is clear. State or district interests determine how members of Congress behave far more than a president's preferences, even if the president is a member of the same political party.

Separate selection also raises the possibility of different political parties controlling the presidency and the Congress (see Table 14–1). In recent years, divided government has been the rule. Congress has normally been controlled by Democrats, the presidency by Republicans. This situation provides an additional invitation to struggle. Legal differences can be reinforced by political ones. Table 14–2 shows that in some recent elections senators of a president's party may indeed get more votes in their state than does the president. Legislative autonomy is enhanced by such results.

Constitutionally prescribed separate elections also mean that presidents cannot turn what they

TABLE 14–2

Presidents and Senators of the Same Political Party: Comparative Electoral Margins

	1976	1980	1984	1988
Number of states in which senators of the same political party as the president ran ahead of the president	18	7	10	10
Number of states in which the president ran ahead of a senator of the same political party	3	14	7	4

Andrew Johnson was the first president to face a serious attempt at impeachment. The Senate failed to convict him by only one vote. The difficulties of checking a president through impeachment are immense. Since President Johnson (1865–1869), only Richard Nixon has come close to being impeached.

consider a fractious Congress out of office. Congress, in turn, can remove a president only through the impeachment process. This requires the House of Representatives to vote articles of impeachment and the Senate by a two-thirds vote to convict. No president has ever been removed from office through impeachment. In only two cases has the effort come close. President Andrew Johnson narrowly escaped conviction following the Civil War. In the twentieth century, President Nixon resigned the presidency in the face of near certainty of impeachment and conviction.

Under the Twenty-fifth Amendment to the Constitution, Congress does have a role to play in filling a vacancy in the vice presidency. If that office becomes vacant, the president appoints a replacement subject to congressional confirmation. This provision has been used twice. After Vice President Spiro Agnew resigned in the Nixon adminstration, the president appointed Gerald Ford to replace him. When Ford became president after Nixon's resignation, he appointed Nelson Rockefeller to assume the position of vice president. Both were confirmed with no great difficulty by the Congress.

Separation of Powers

The Constitution not only prescribes separate selection processes for the presidency and the Congress, it also grants each institution independent powers. For example, Congress is authorized to lay and collect taxes, to borrow money, to regulate commerce, to provide for a monetary system, to establish lower federal courts, to declare war, and to maintain the armed forces. The president is given the authority to exercise the executive power, to be commander in chief of the armed forces, to issue pardons, to take care that the laws are faithfully executed, and to commission officers of the United States. The key problem here is that many of these grants of authority are ambiguous both in their core meaning and in their scope. Ambiguity invites interpretation and interpretation invites conflict. Such conflicts have been a part of our entire historical experience and in many instances remain unresolved today.

Constitutional ambiguity is a virtue in that it facilitates adapting to new circumstances and accommodating to changes in societal values and preferences; its liability is that conflict is regularly generated. In the absence of clarity and certainty of meaning, individuals, interests, and institutional representatives can each assert their own version of truth. Conflicting views create a need for methods of reconciliation. What these are will be addressed shortly.

The difficulties arising from independent powers and ambiguity in meaning are compounded by shared powers. For example, creating budgets involves both the executive and legislative branches; laws are passed mainly through cooperative efforts between the executive and legislative branches; key appointments such as federal judges and members of the president's cabinet require executive and legislative cooperation. Shared powers invite conflict; they create the necessity for cooperation. Both branches need to act together, yet legal and political pressures can pull them apart. Let us first look at some areas where cooperation is required by law or by the force of events. We shall then discuss when, how, and why some measure of cooperation is achieved.

The Necessity for Cooperation

Lawmaking

With rare exceptions the president and Congress work together to pass laws. Presidents can, of course, veto bills passed by Congress and Congress in turn can override these vetoes. Statistically, such incidents are rare. The normal pattern is for the president to sign the bills that Congress passes. Only a small percentage of bills are vetoed. Table 13–4 shows that the number of vetoes for the last six presidents has been between 21 and 66, a tiny fraction of the total number of bills passed. But when a president does veto a bill, the veto usually stands. Generally less than one of five vetoes is overridden.

Because the two branches need to, and usually do, cooperate to pass laws, each is subject to the influence of the other. An environment for bargaining is created. Presidential influence is seen in agenda setting and in attempts to shape votes.

Congress is free to set its own agenda and sometimes actually does so. Yet the usual situation is for Congress to consider most of the items that the president thinks are the most important. The representative status of the president, perhaps the size of his election victory, his ability to command public attention through the media, and his party leadership combine to make him potentially a major force in the legislative process. As discussed in Chapter 13, how successful he is in these efforts can be observed by seeing whether Congress talks about what he asks it to. The answer is often yes. If the question is whether Congress actually enacts what the president wants it to, the answer is only sometimes. Figure 13–3 suggests that the presidents often see Congress pass much of what they request but that the results are uneven. As shown in this figure for the last six presidents, presidential success ranges from 43 to 93 percent.

If the president's requests are not enacted or if Congress passes a bill that the president does not approve of and if he cares enough about the issue, then he can exercise the constitutionally given power of veto. As the data in Chapter 13 show, the veto is highly effective since so few are overridden. At the end of the session of Congress the pocket veto is even more effective, since Congress, having adjourned, gets no chance to override. Recall that the veto is hardly ever used by presidents. It is used as a last resort.

Presidential influence over legislative outcomes is limited by his short political coattails, his limited patronage, the lack of unity in his own political party, his own abilities to persuade, and broader contextual factors. Sometimes these can work to the advantage of the president. As former Democratic Speaker of the House Tip O'Neill once stated:

> . . . Despite my strong opposition to the President's program, I decided to give it a chance to be voted on by the nation's elected representatives.
>
> For one thing, that's how our democracy is supposed to work. For another, I was afraid that the voters would repudiate the Democrats if we didn't give the President a chance to pass his program. After all, the nation was still in an economic crisis and people wanted immediate action. . . .
>
> I was less concerned about losing the legislative battle in the spring and summer of 1981 than I was with losing at the polls in the fall of 1982. I was convinced that if the Democrats were perceived as stalling in the midst of a national economic crisis, there would be hell to pay in the midterm elections.[1]

Presidents win some and lose some, but dramatic, innovative, far-reaching collections of programs enacted into law are rare in the American experience. In the last 60 years, only the first few years of the Roosevelt administration, the first several years of the administration of President Lyndon Johnson, and 1981 for President Reagan were exceptions to the norm. Government and policy as the president wants it is a rarity in U.S. politics.

Implementation of the Law: Congress Oversees The Bureaucracy

Once laws are passed, policies must be implemented. Primarily an executive branch function, implementation can be of interest to Congress. The reasons are legal, political, electoral, ideological, and sometimes personal. What tools does Congress have to control the bureaucracy, how are they used, and with what results?

The tools available to Congress are many, since the authority to oversee bureaucratic activity is as broad as such activity itself. If the bureaucracy does it, Congress can check up on it. The Legislative Reorganization Act of 1946, for example, gives committees of the Congress instructions to:

> . . . exercise continuous watchfulness of the execution by the administrative agencies concerned of any laws, the subject matter of which is within the jurisdiction of such committee.

What Congress or, more accurately, parts of it can do ranges from informal contacts to gain information about certain actions—probably hundreds of telephone calls are made every day to the executive branch departments asking questions about particular programs and policies—to more formal letters and memos that go forth daily seeking written replies from the executive branch.

The main work of legislative oversight of the bureaucracy occurs in congressional committees. Each committee is charged by law to monitor the activities of the departments and agencies that come under its jurisdiction. Committee staffs, like individual members and their staffs, place telephone calls and write letters and memos. In addition, they can mount formal investigations into the conduct of bureaucrats. Witnesses can be called to testify. Committees can require that departments and agencies report regularly to them in writing. Always lurking in the background is the possibility of changes in legislation affecting the bureaucratic unit and changes in the amount of money that will be made available for executive branch programs.

There are many techniques for legislative control of the bureaucracy and many actors in the Congress to use these techniques. Several committees may be concerned with one issue—for example, how the administrative departments and agencies are dealing with the problem of shortages of oil—because many committees may be involved in providing the program authority and funds that departments and agencies require. Program authority may come from the authorizing committees, such as Agriculture; administrative budgets are affected by the appropriations committees and the budget committees. Many committees may find legitimate reasons for overseeing the same executive program.

Even if the legislative authority for oversight of the bureaucracy is broad and the techniques for doing so are many, the inevitable result is not that Congress oversees in a comprehensive way. Only a small fraction of bureaucratic activity receives close congressional attention on a systematic basis. The results of oversight efforts are generally uneven. A few administrative activities receive close attention; some receive notice but not much attention; and most are not subject to extensive congressional review. Members of Congress and their staffs are simply burdened with too many responsibilities to carry out each of them with complete effectiveness. Shortages of time and energy mean that choices will have to be made. Someone has to decide which issues will be pressed and which will be given little attention or ignored. In making these decisions, the priorities of the members will be vital. What they think is most important to them is what they will attend to. How do they decide? Many would argue that they do so with an eye firmly fixed on what will help them get reelected. One useful rule is this: What benefits their careers moves quickly to the top of the priority list.

To wrestle with ethics in government, Congress regularly sets up committees, sponsors special studies, and, from time to time, tries to write new rules. But even when such a committee works hard, as this House Committee led by Julian C. Dixon (D.-Calif.) did in 1989, its results can fail to satisfy fully its members and the public.

The results of all these efforts to oversee the bureaucracy range from remarkably effective to inconsequential. A few investigations may lead to significant changes in administrative behavior; others may lead to executive evasions and delay in the hope that congressional attention may soon wander off to other issues. In brief, the results are mixed. Very hard to document but probably of great importance to control of the bureaucracy is the working of "the law of anticipated reactions." That is, bureaucrats, knowing that Congress *might* monitor any of their activities, will be sensitive to congressional concerns even if those concerns do not always manifest themselves in action. The fear or anticipation of oversight may be as central to control of the bureaucracy as actual congressional efforts to do so.

Congress, or units of it, may promote or impede coordination in the executive branch. Congressional resistance to administrative efforts at coordination may impose formidable roadblocks. The President's Private Sector Survey on Cost Control (the Grace Commission) reported in 1984 that congressional involvement in the administration of programs can prevent or delay steps needed to achieve maximum efficiency in the executive branch. This group estimated, for example, that congressional interference in the routines of administration might carry a dollar cost over three years of some $7.8 billion.[2] Some areas identified

“ Perspectives ”

On Executive-Legislative Relations

“*No political truth is certainly of greater intrinsic value, or is stamped with the authority of more enlightened patrons of liberty, than that on which the objection is founded. The accumulation of all powers, legislative, executive, and judiciary, in the same hands, whether of one, a few, or many, and whether hereditary, self-appointed, or elective, may justly be pronounced the very definition of tyranny.*”

—James Madison, *The Federalist*, no. 47

“*The doctrine of the separation of powers was adopted by the Convention of 1787, not to promote efficiency, but to preclude the exercise of arbitrary power.*”

—Justice Louis Brandeis

“*While the Constitution diffuses power the better to secure liberty, it also contemplates that practice will integrate the dispersed powers into workable government.*”

—Justice Robert Jackson

“*The federal judiciary should not decide constitutional questions concerning the respective powers of Congress and the President* vis-à-vis *one another; . . . their final resolution should be remitted to the interplay of the national political process.*”

—Jesse H. Choper

“*The executive seeks broad discretion; Congress seeks to control the particulars.*”

—Allen Schick

“*Needless to say, there are no automatic formulas that can be invoked to preserve congressional power in all contingencies.*”

—Randall B. Ripley

“*The men and women in Congress love nothing better than to hear from the head guy, so they can go back to their districts and say, "I was talking to the President the other day. . . ."*”

—Thomas P. O'Neill, Speaker of the House

“*You've got to give it all you can, that first year. Doesn't matter what kind of majority you come in with. You've got just one year when they treat you right, and before they start worrying about themselves. The third year, you lose votes; if this war goes on, I'll lose a lot of 'em. A lot of our people don't belong here, they're in Republican seats, and the Republicans will get them back. The fourth year's all politics. You can't put anything through when half the Congress is thinking how to beat you. . . .*”

—President Lyndon B. Johnson

Sources: Louis Brandeis in *Myers* v. *United States* (1927); Robert Jackson in *Youngstown Sheet and Tube* v. *Sawyer* (1952); Jesse H. Choper in *Judicial Review and the National Political Process* (Chicago: University of Chicago Press, 1980), p. 263; Allen Schick in "Politics Through Law," in *Both Ends of the Avenue*, ed. Anthony King (Washington, D.C.: American Enterprise Institute for Public Policy Research, 1983), p. 157; Randall B. Ripley in "Congress and Foreign and Defense Policy," *Mershon Center Quarterly Report* (Summer 1988), pp. 6–7; Thomas P. O'Neill in *Man of the House* (New York: Random House, 1987), pp. 341–342; Lyndon B. Johnson, quoted in Harry McPherson, *A Political Education* (Boston: Little, Brown, 1972), p. 268.

as prime candidates for cost reduction except for the meddling of the Congress were the number of Defense Department installations (over 5000), military commissaries in the United States (over 200), special wage scales in the Government Printing Office, and low-priority weather stations. Whether the Grace Commission was correct in its assessment is not the issue here. What is central is the vast and substantial congressional involvement, for good or ill, in executive branch decision making.

In conducting oversight, congressional limits are partly self-imposed. During the Iran-contra controversy in the second term of the Reagan administration some observers wondered why Congress had not been more diligent in supervising the ban that they had imposed on sending military aid to the dissidents called the contras in Nicaragua. Some of the congressional difficulties stemmed from lying and deception practiced by some members of the executive branch. Neglect also flowed from congressional attention to many other duties. Some senators saw the key in deliberate attempts by the executive branch to mislead. Congress cannot cope effectively with this in the short run. Congress can only hope that executive branch officials will not regularly practice deception partly because they fear that they will be found out in the long run.

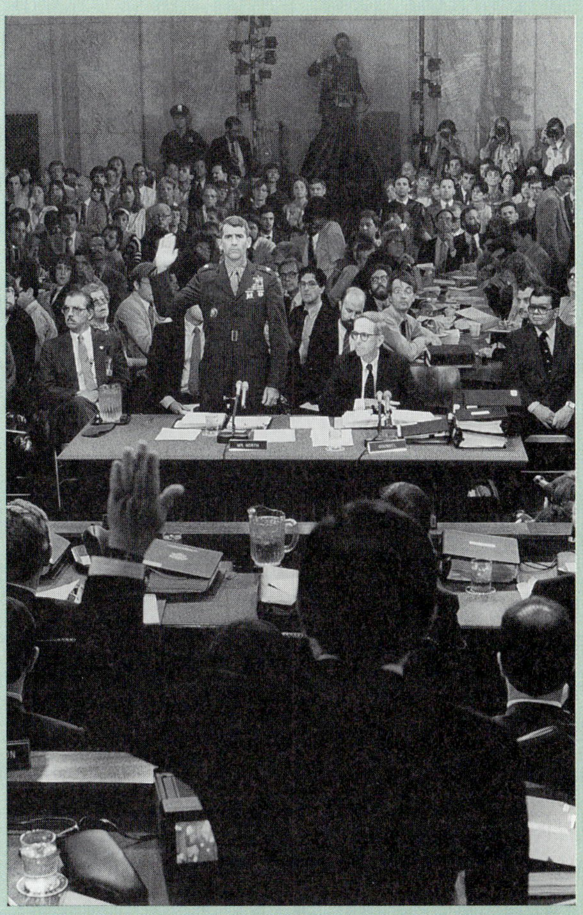

Lt. Col. Oliver L. North, the central figure in the Iran–contra affair (secret arms sales to Iran in 1985 with diversion of the profits to the Nicaraguan Contra guerrillas), is sworn in before the Senate Iran–Contra Committee. The Committee concluded that White House behavior was marked by "secrecy, deception and disdain for the rule of law" and that President Reagan was responsible for the North-led "cabal of zealots."

The Budget

Creating a budget is a third area where the law requires executive-legislative cooperation. Presidents submit budget proposals to Congress. Congress considers, amends, accepts, or rejects these proposals and then submits a budget for the president's signature or veto. Normally then the law requires cooperation between the branches of government in budget making.

Making a budget is, at its core, a political act. Budgets make policy. This fact is fully realized by all of the participants in the process. Procedures are adapted as political necessity requires. Political leaders in both branches are caught between cross-pressures for additional benefits from government and an unwillingness to pay for these through new taxes. In such a highly charged political atmosphere, Allen Schick suggests that "the script is written as the relationship progresses."[3]

In his first year as president, Ronald Reagan was extremely successful in manipulating the budget process for his own ends. Later, President Reagan complained, "It's called the President's budget, and yet there is nothing binding in it. It is submitted to the Congress and they don't even have to consider it."[4]

Congress and the President's Cabinet

In March 1989, the U.S. Senate rejected John Tower, President George Bush's nominee to become the Secretary of Defense. By a party-line vote of 53–47 (only three Democrats voted for Tower, and only one Republican voted against him), the Senate refused to confirm the appointment. Republicans charged that the rejection was entirely "political." Democrats and other critics contended that Tower, a former Republican senator from Texas, was unfit for the position because of his history of drinking and amorous pursuits and his close ties to defense contractors.

Even though the U.S. Constitution (Article II, Section 2) permits the president to appoint the Cabinet with the "Advice and Consent of the Senate," only eight nominations before Tower had ever been rejected by the chamber. According to Joseph P. Harris, author of a definitive study on the subject, the president is generally given little trouble with his Cabinet nominations because "it is recognized that unless he is given a free hand in the choice of his Cabinet he cannot be held responsible for the administration of the executive branch." The details (below) of the nine departures from this norm provide an interesting lesson in the art of politics.

The *majority* of these rejections had little to do with the qualifications of the nominee. Rather, they stemmed from attempts to embarrass the president. The most blatant examples occurred during the last two years of the John Tyler administration. Tyler, who had deserted the Democratic party to accept the Whig nomination for the vice presidency in 1840, became the president upon the death of President Harrison in 1841. But when Tyler broke ranks with the Whig leaders in Congress, he was not accepted back in the Democratic party and, consequently, found himself to be a man without a party. Because of the animosity between Tyler and both major parties, the Senate not only rejected four cabinet appointments, but also denied the

Nomination	Year	President	Position
Roger B. Taney	1834	Jackson	Secretary of the Treasury
Caleb Cushing	1843	Tyler	Secretary of the Treasury
David Henshaw	1844	Tyler	Secretary of the Navy
James M. Porter	1844	Tyler	Secretary of War
James S. Green	1844	Tyler	Secretary of the Treasury
Henry Stanberry	1868	A. Johnson	Attorney General
Charles B. Warren	1925	Coolidge	Attorney General
Lewis L. Strauss	1959	Eisenhower	Secretary of Commerce
John Tower	1989	Bush	Secretary of Defense

president four Supreme Court nominations, the ambassadorships of France and Brazil, and dozens of other lower-level appointments.

Similar motives led to the defeat of Andrew Johnson's Attorney General nomination two decades later. Henry Stanberry served as Attorney General until 1868, when he resigned in order to serve as Johnson's private counsel during the impeachment proceedings of that year. When the Senate failed to convict Johnson after the House had impeached him, the president renominated Stanberry for his old position. But the Senate, still angered by Johnson's acquittal, rejected him.

The other rejections occurred for a variety of reasons. The Senate rejected Roger Taney because he had agreed to President Andrew Jackson's plans to withdraw federal funds from the Bank of the United States after Jackson had given Taney an interim appointment as the Treasury Secretary. Charles Warren was denied the leadership of the Justice Department because, as counsel for sugar producers from 1902 to 1906, he was believed to have violated provisions of the Sherman Antitrust Act. (This defeat could have been prevented if Vice President John Dawes had broken the first vote, a 40:40 tie, instead of taking a nap in his hotel room.) And President Dwight D. Eisenhower's choice of Lewis Strauss as the Secretary of Commerce was rejected because, as the chair of the Atomic Energy Commission, Strauss was seen as both too conservative and as uncooperative and deceptive in his dealings with the Joint Atomic Energy Committee in Congress.

John Tower defends his appointment by President Bush to the position of Secretary of Defense.

Sources: Joseph P. Harris, *The Advice and Consent of the Senate: A Study of the Confirmation of Appointments by the United States Senate* (Berkeley, Calif.: University of California Press, 1953), p. 259; *Congressional Quarterly Almanac* (Washington, D.C.: Congressional Quarterly 1959), Vol. XV.

Ultimately, the overall figures in the budget passed by Congress do not often look very different from those in the president's initial submission. The figures in some of the parts may be altered dramatically, however.

Presidential Appointments

Many of the principal officials in the executive branch as well as federal judges are appointed by the president and must be confirmed by the Senate. Most presidential appointees are confirmed without great controversy. Political conflict varies with the office and the situation. For example, the last presidential nominee to a cabinet position that was not confirmed was John Tower, nominated by President Bush to be Secretary of Defense in 1989. Almost all nominees to the Supreme Court are also confirmed.

For federal judges in the lower courts, most nominees are confirmed, but this is because of an extensive system of prior clearance with the relevant senators before the nomination is made. Even in administrations where many such appointments are made, the rule still holds. In the Reagan administrations, for example, the president appointed nearly half of the judges on the district and appeals courts, yet his confirmation figure remained high.

The occasional dramatic executive-legislative confrontation such as that over the nomination of Robert Bork for the Supreme Court in 1987 does not alter the rule. Such incidents merely attest to the potential power, infrequently exercised, that Congress possesses.

Near the end of a president's time in office, Congress, especially if controlled by a political party different from the president's, may delay consideration of appointees in the hope that the next election will yield a presidential victory for their own party and hence different appointees when the new president takes over. Such was the fate of President Lyndon Johnson's appointee, Abraham Fortas, to be chief justice of the Supreme Court. Similarly, in the last few months of the Reagan administration, the confirmation of a series of ambassadorial appointees was slowed apparently for this reason. The election to the presidency of George Bush, Reagan's vice president, made the Democratic strategy less effective. President Reagan's staff was reportedly not surprised at the stalling tactic. They seemed to regard this as a normal part of politics.

Treaties

Under the Constitution, treaties signed by the president must receive a vote of approval from two-thirds of the Senate. Few treaties are formally defeated in the Senate—only some 20 in all U.S. history—but others were blocked in committee or withdrawn without a vote.

As U.S. involvement in foreign policy increased in the twentieth century, presidents began to rely more on executive agreements which do not necessarily require Senate approval. The changing usage of treaties and executive agreements is shown in Table 14–3.

Events and Crisis

Executive-legislative cooperation is sometimes driven by the force of events. Especially in time of war, Congress tends to acquiesce in executive in-

TABLE 14–3

Treaties and Executive Agreements: Uses of

	Executive Agreements	Treaties*
Through 1800	0	9
1801–1850	15	88
1851–1900	107	231
1901–1950	1875	610
1951–1980	6781	866

* Includes protocols and conventions.

Sources: Data obtained from Gary King and Lyn Ragsdale, *The Elusive Executive: Discovering Statistical Patterns in the Presidency* (Washington, D.C.: Congressional Quarterly, 1988), pp. 131–140.

itiatives more than is usually the case. During the Civil War, World War I, and World War II, executive-legislative animosities rooted in policy, party, and personal differences receded in the face of crisis. Similarly, in the 1930s, as the Roosevelt administration tried to cope with the Great Depression, Congress served as a vehicle for presidential success rather than as an obstacle to change. Such a congressional response is more likely if a vigorous, popular president is in office. The experience of the Reagan administration in 1981 in dealing with substantial inflation and unemployment also illustrates unusual congressional compliance. A severe economic crisis set the tone. President Reagan's perceived popular mandate, effective legislative liaison by the administration, and a sure sense of strategy built on the perceived crisis to foster legislative success.

Bases for Cooperation

Common Values ■

Law and crisis push the executive and legislative branches toward cooperation. What factors enhance this possibility? First, value agreement is important. Presidents and members of Congress agree on the basic values and legal foundations of our society and politics. They may disagree on appropriate means to achieve these goals but an underlying consensus helps form a common ground.

The Merits and Nature of the Issue ■

Agreement on the merits of an issue may also contribute to cooperation. People in both branches may come to agree on the best way to deal with a problem. Also, some types of issues promote cooperation more than others. For example, some argue that cooperation is easier to achieve on foreign policy questions than on domestic issues. Aaron Wildavsky's two-presidencies thesis rests on this distinction.[5] What is argued is that the president has basic advantages in getting agreement from Congress on foreign policy issues. The necessity for speed and secrecy in decision making, information superiority, and national interests at stake are all alleged to contribute.

Whether Wildavsky's distinction is valid has been debated by scholars for some 25 years. Some see no major foreign-domestic policy differences relevant to executive-legislative relations. Others find more cooperation on foreign policy issues but only under selected conditions. The most convincing finding is that foreign/domestic differences in cooperation are closely related to the political party affiliation of the president. Over the last 30 years, when a Democrat has held the White House, differences in cooperation on foreign and domestic issues were minimal. Only for Republican presidents does cooperation vary depending on whether the issue is one of foreign or domestic policy. An explanation for this is not hard to find. Democratic majorities in Congress, the normal condition for over 50 years, can come to agree with Republican presidents on foreign policy issues yet have more difficulty in doing so on domestic issues, where the pull of party and constituency is stronger. For Democratic presidents, Democratic majorities in Congress are supportive across both dimensions of public policy.[6]

Political Parties ■

The nature of the major political parties can also help in achieving executive-legislative cooperation. Political parties are usually discussed in terms of conflict. But neither party is monolithic. Each contains liberals, moderates, and conservatives. So when a president seeks support in Congress, some members of each political party will usually provide it. Chapter 13 discussed the evidence concerning party differences in supporting the president.

The experience during the 100th Congress, 1987–1988 shows that divided government does not necessarily mean inactive government. President Reagan was a Republican, and both houses of Congress were controlled by the Democrats. An inventory of accomplishments at the end of the 100th Congress showed major legislation passed dealing with international trade, welfare reform,

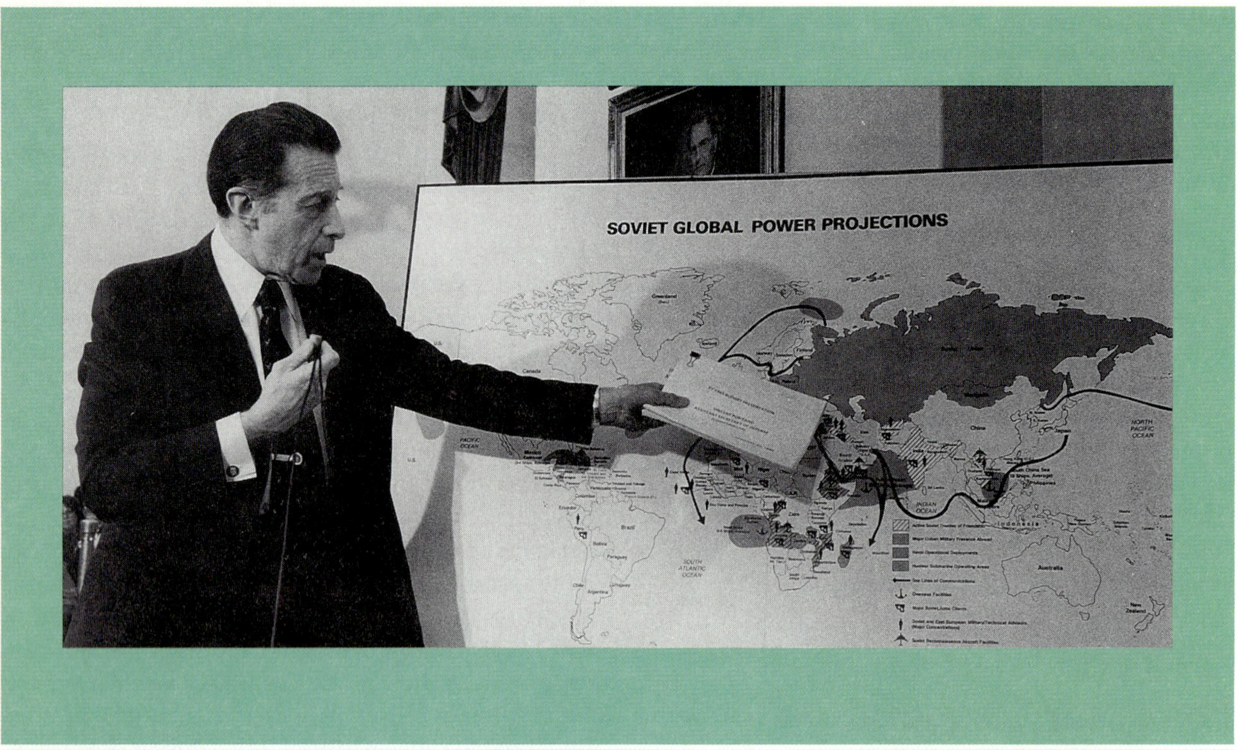

When it comes to foreign policy, any administration tends to have superior information to that of Congress. And with that information comes added powers of persuasion. Here Casper Weinberger, Secretary of Defense in the Reagan cabinet, gives his view of Soviet global power projections. He hoped to use this to pry more money for defense out of Congress.

catastrophic health insurance, sewage treatment, and veterans' affairs.

How is this atypical phenomenon to be explained? The answers are found in unusually vigorous leadership in the House, a presidency somewhat stained by the Iran-contra scandal, a crisis atmosphere created by the stock market crash of October 1987, and major improvements in U.S.-Soviet relations. In other words, contextual, institutional, and personal factors combined in distinctive ways to form an explanation.

Public Support

Public support can push the president and Congress to cooperate. When the United States invaded Grenada in 1983 quite a few members of Congress initially expressed shock and hostility to administration policy. As it became clear quickly that the public overwhelmingly supported the Reagan initiative, congressional hostility rapidly disappeared.

Similarly, presidential election victories do not guarantee that the president will be able to deal successfully with Congress, though a perceived landslide can bolster the chief executive's efforts. If the public seems strongly united behind a president, congressional cooperation is more likely to be forthcoming.

Prestige may serve similar ends, but its importance is not entirely clear. Scholars generally perceive the relevance of public support but assign it different weights. For some, it is another item; for others, it is a central element.

Presidential Skills

Finally, presidential skills at politics may help smooth over policy differences with Congress. After the bitter campaign for the presidency in 1980, President Reagan rapidly moved to smooth over differences with the Democratic majority in the House of Representatives. President George Bush, elected in 1988, faced the same problem and moved in the same direction. Political skills may indeed help a president take advantage of contextual elements but usually cannot alter societal and institutional forces very much. When issues are close, a skillful president can make a difference.[7]

Conversely, a president who asks the Congress to do too many things at once and does not set clear priorities, and who neglects to build an effective lobbying presence in Congress, diminishes the possibility of congressional cooperation. The case of President Jimmy Carter is instructive. Elected as an outsider to politics, Carter, a serious, intelligent, and hardworking person, expected Congress to react positively to his proposals because they were right. Feeling that he represented the people and that Congress was populated by parochials, Carter neglected the normal presidential tactics of persuasion through political bargaining. His programs suffered in Congress accordingly.[8]

When presidents come close to settling differences with Congress, personal involvement may make a difference. With the budget dominating the policy agenda, that skill becomes more important than ever. Members of Congress expect to hear the views of the president and his advisors.

How Are Executive-Legislative Disputes Resolved?

Bargaining and Compromise

If cooperation is possible and conflict is inevitable, how are executive-legislative disputes actually resolved? One answer is through direct bargaining and compromise. Deals are struck mainly outside the glare of public inspection. As one writer puts it, "Private understandings, privately concluded, are the essence of political exchange for presidents in need of legislators' assistance."[9]

The tools of bargaining are varied. Jobs offered, publicity, promises of future assistance on legislation are regularly involved. Rarely are exchanges so blunt as one reported in the 1960s:

> Senator Russell B. Long . . . summoned me to his office and demanded that I accommodate a request of one of his constituents. "You'd better take care of him," Long said, "or I won't let the President's tax bill get through my committee."[10]

Some of the forms of executive-legislative bargaining and compromise can be seen in three brief case studies: the controversy over the closing of military bases in the United States, disputes over executive privilege, and efforts to reorganize the executive branch.

Closing Military Bases. The Vietnam War brought a major military buildup in the United States. Following that conflict, several hundred military bases in the United States were closed. The congressional outcry over these closings, which caused jobs and revenue to be lost in congressional districts, led to legislation that made it more difficult to close additional bases. These laws were so effective that no major military bases were closed for over a decade.

In the 1980s, however, increased pressures to cut government spending revived pressure to save money by closing bases. One estimate was that more than $2 billion would be saved if bases not needed for our defense effort were closed. At issue was a conflict between saving money, which members of Congress favored, and keeping money flowing into their districts, which members also favored. As one senator put it:

> There is something in the heart of every politician that loves a dam, or a harbor, or a bridge or a military installation. They want the money coming into the area and they defend to the death the continuation of a base.[11]

To resolve this dilemma, Congress and the Reagan administration agreed in 1988 to authorize an independent commission to study the problem and to recommend which bases should be closed. Congress would have to vote on the whole list at once, thus relieving political pressures on the affected members. Also, no base would be closed for over a year.

The net result was a policy representing a generally acceptable compromise. The administration could close some bases and save money. Yet the political heat from the closing of any one base was relieved. Congressional desires to have a form of veto over base closings were met, but not for individual bases. Only the whole list could be voted up or down. If everyone was not deliriously happy, most on balance were at least satisfied. Politics is mostly "satisficing" (finding answers good enough for people to accept), and less often optimizing.

Executive Privilege. One of the longest-running disputes in executive-legislative relations centers around the question of executive privilege. Presidents and their top advisers have always claimed that they could legitimately withhold certain kinds of information from the Congress. One example was the record of advice given by the president's advisers. Over half of the presidents have asserted such claims and have refused to turn over materials requested by Congress. In turn, members of Congress have frequently objected to the practice of executive privilege. Congress argued that it had a legitimate right to see the documents that its members asked for.

Since the Constitution is not explicit about executive privilege, and since the courts through most of our history have avoided addressing the problem, the president and Congress have continued to press their own interpretations of what is permissible. The normal method for settling these differences has been negotiation. Congress would often get to see some documents but not all that it asked for. Sometimes only selected members of Congress would get to see sensitive materials.

Two dramatic episodes in recent history illustrate exceptions to standard practice. During the Watergate controversies in the Nixon administration, the Supreme Court ordered President Nixon to supply materials needed in the criminal prosecution of some of the Watergate figures, and he complied. More characteristically, the Court refused to order the president to turn over materials to a Senate committee.

More recently, during the Iran-contra controversy in 1987, President Reagan refused to invoke executive privilege and urged full cooperation with the congressional investigations.

These two episodes stand in sharp contrast to the normal situation where deals are struck, no one completely wins, and no principles are resolved but an accommodation is reached.

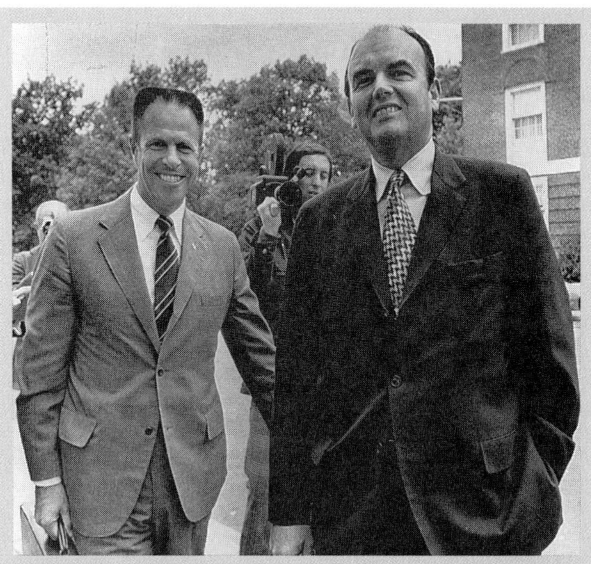

Two of President Nixon's top advisers, H. R. Haldeman and John Erlichman, arrive to discuss the Watergate scandal with attorneys for a Senate committee. It was widely assumed that neither told all they knew. Both faced possible criminal indictments, and both were trying to protect an administration that claimed "executive privilege."

Executive Branch Reorganization. Creating a new department in the executive branch normally involves bargaining over many years. An apt illustration is the creation of a new Department of Veterans Affairs in 1988. This unit became the fourteenth cabinet-level department. (See Chapter 15 for additional discussion of the president's cabinet.)

The idea of a Department of Veterans Affairs was an old one in Washington. It goes back over 50 years to pre-New Deal days. But all of this discussion was not translated into action until President Reagan in 1987 embraced the idea. Previous pressure on Congress from veterans' groups was not a sufficient stimulus. Faced with an endorsement from a popular president, a forthcoming election, *and* substantial lobbying from veterans' groups, Congress now found it relatively easy to act. Ignored were assessments suggesting that there was no strong administrative reason for creating the department.

The political pressure brought to bear on Congress was based on the assumption that a cabinet-level department would mean better access and more influence on legislation and policy affecting veterans. Yet congressional support for veterans' causes had traditionally been strong. Perhaps creating a symbol was a central element.

At a less visible level, executive reorganization is an ongoing process. Congress, through law, sets the basic structure of the executive branch. But changes within departments and transfers of functions among departments sometimes can take place under executive branch stimulus. Once established, departments can be reorganized. For over 40 years (but not from 1973 until 1977), Congress authorized the president to propose reorganization plans subject to its veto. From 1949 to 1981, presidents submitted 103 reorganization plans to Congress; 83 have been implemented. This authority lapsed in 1981.

The decision of the Supreme Court in *Immigration and Naturalization Service* v. *Chadha*

President Bush names Louis W. Sullivan to lead the Department of Health and Human Services, a position that has evolved over several cabinet-level reorganizations. Sullivan's appointment turned controversial when it became clear that his views, especially on abortion, did not always agree with those of some of the president's key conservative supporters.

(1983), apparently banning the legislative veto, a device commonly used in reorganization statutes for many years, forced a new examination of the entire issue. Congress resolved this dilemma temporarily in 1984, when it renewed the reorganization authority of the president until the end of the year and provided that both houses of Congress must approve any presidential proposal for reorganization.

Conflict Resolution and International Crises

The norm for resolving executive-legislative conflict is through bargaining and negotiation. In foreign policy crises, the events themselves push toward unity in government. In these situations, the president assumes a dominant role. Congress recognizes that rapid and decisive action means presidential action. One example illustrates how events inspire cooperation.

In May 1975, the U.S.-owned merchant ship SS *Mayaguez* was seized by Cambodian armed forces near their coast. President Ford responded quickly and decisively. He ordered the ship and its crew to be rescued. Legislation passed in the wake of the Vietnam War prohibited the United States from spending money for military purposes in that area. The War Powers Resolution of 1973 suggested that presidents consult with Congress before sending U.S. military forces into combat situations. Such consultation did not occur. Yet majorities in Congress vocally supported this questionable presidential action. Only months later did this comity unravel when congressional investigators discovered that more lives were lost in the rescue effort than were saved.

Not all foreign policy issues are matters of crisis. In more routine situations such as foreign trade and foreign aid, Congress is assuredly of more importance, and conflict between the two branches of government becomes more visible and protracted just as it does on some domestic policy issues.

Conflict Resolution Through Outsiders

The Courts. The courts only rarely play a decisive role in resolving executive-legislative conflict. Legal scholar Jesse Choper argues that it ought to be that way.[12] When the courts do get involved as they decide cases before them, their decisions can be noteworthy. The discussion below of several of these cases provides additional insight.

In 1952, during the Korean War, the threat of a strike in the steel industry pushed President Truman to seize and operate the steel mills. He feared that a strike would harm our military efforts in the Korean conflict. The administration defended this unusual action by claiming an inherent presidential power to act. Some owners of steel mills, angry at the seizure, sought help in the courts. The case came to the Supreme Court on appeal. The Court, in *Youngstown Sheet and Tube* v. *Sawyer,* refused to accept the inherent powers argument. The Court pointed out that Congress had indicated no desire to incorporate the seizure power into legislation. The Court also found no clear, direct constitutional basis for this presidential action. The president, the Court argued, had available clearly legal alternative courses of action.

On its face, the Court decision seemingly rebuked President Truman partly because the administration had ignored alternatives provided by Congress. A dissenting judge, however, posed a crucial question. Was the decision really based on the administration's failure to prove that the crisis was severe enough to justify an extraordinary action such as seizing steel mills? The implication was that if the crisis at hand was severe enough, perhaps the judicial decision might be different.

Did the Court decide that the president needed specific constitutional or legislative authorization to act even in a severe crisis? Or did the Court hint that the type and degree of executive discretion vary with the severity of the crisis and that presidents can take unusual actions as long as they can show that such action is necessary in a particular situation?

In *Immigration and Naturalization Service* v. *Chadha,* 1983, the Supreme Court addressed the constitutionality of the legislative veto. Increases in the scope and amount of governmental activity had stimulated Congress to search for new ways to cope. One such device was the legislative veto. Congress would write legislation in general terms. The bureaucracy, it was assumed, would spell out details as it dealt with specific situations. How then could Congress maintain some control? One answer was the legislative veto, which allowed Congress or its committees to prevent a particular exercise of executive discretion. For over 40 years, Congress increasingly used this device. From 1955 to 1960, 24 legislative acts stipulated it. In the 1970s the figure was 248.[13] Presidents object to the legislative veto on policy grounds and as an attack on what they see to be executive prerogatives. They argue that Congress can act with no opportunity for the president to challenge their decision. To majorities in Congress, the legislative veto seemed to provide a useful tool for dealing with practical problems.

In 1983 the Supreme Court ruled that such legislative vetoes were unconstitutional. They argued that Congress could not constitutionally engage in policy implementation, an executive function. The view of the majority was that there is a clear-cut separation of powers between the executive and legislative branches. In Chief Justice Warren Burger's words;

> Explicit and unambiguous provisions of the Constitution prescribe and define the respec-

Continuity & CHANGE

Conflict over Foreign Policy in Different Administrations

From time to time, Congress attempts to reassert its authority in the foreign policy arena. The most recent wave of reassertion took place during the early and middle 1970s. Vietnam and Watergate were the most visible catalysts. A sampling of legislative initiatives (some still operative, and others now inoperative) includes:

1973: Case Act on Executive Agreements: requires the secretary of state to submit to the Senate any international agreements made by executive agreement.

War Powers Resolution: urges that presidents consult with Congress and notify Congress regarding commitment of U.S. forces abroad into areas where hostilities are present or imminent; also gives the legislature authority to terminate the use of troops.

1974: Congressional Budget and Impoundment Control Act: augments the legislature's participation in budget preparation and permits Congress to block presidential attempts to impound funds.

1975: Foreign Assistance Act: attempts to restrict military and economic assistance to foreign nations.

1976: Arms Export Control Act: places restrictions on armaments sent abroad.

International Security Assistance Act: restricts military operations in, and assistance to, Angola and Chile.

National Emergencies Act: terminates numerous presidential powers that resulted from previous national emergencies since the 1930s.

1977: International Development Act: prohibits assistance to Vietnam, Cambodia, Laos, and Cuba.

International Security Assistance Act: prohibits aid or military operations in Zaire unless the President certifies that such aid is in the U.S. national security interest.

1978: Foreign Aid Appropriations Act: places numerous restrictions on the use of U.S. foreign aid.

Source: Thomas E. Cronin, *The State of the Presidency* (Boston: Little, Brown, 1980), chap. 6.

tive functions of the Congress and of the Executive in the legislative process.

Executive functions, the Court stated, could not be performed by Congress and thus the legislative veto, whereby Congress reserved for itself some role in the process of executing the law, was unconstitutional.

The Court's definition of the separation of powers seemed in error to a dissenting judge. Justice Byron White argued, "The Constitution does not directly authorize or prohibit the legislative veto." Generations of experience were to be sacrificed to doctrinal purity. Congress had always been involved in some executive functions; the president had played a substantial role in the legislative process.

The Supreme Court confronted the meaning of the separation of powers doctrine again in 1988 in *Morrison* v. *Olson.* A majority of the judges saw no violation of the separation of powers doctrine in legislation creating independent prosecutors to investigate charges of misconduct by high officials in the executive branch. This time, a minority opinion argued for the clear separation that the majority had seen in the 1983 Chadha case.

These cases suggest that the lines of authority between the president and Congress are seldom precisely clear. Courts sometimes seem to clarify an issue for the moment but they provide few permanent solutions. Executive-legislative boundaries remain a problem requiring repeated and continuing attention by all parties concerned.

Elections and Public Opinion. In the short run, elections and public opinion rarely resolve executive-legislative conflict. Most elections yield no specific policy directions that the president and Congress think they must follow. Most incumbents in Congress are reelected whether or not Congress is fighting with the president. On most issues, public opinion is neither firm nor united. Various groups express firmly held views. These are relevant to particular members of Congress but not to Congress as a whole. If there is a clear, firm, and enduring opinion across the nation on a particular topic, that view will be reflected throughout the government. Such circumstances are rare. An apathetic public and divided interest groups hardly provide a solid base for executive-legislative cooperation.

In 1948 President Truman campaigned against the Republican-dominated 80th Congress. The election of Truman with Democratic majorities in both houses of Congress still did not give precise guidance on how executive-legislative disputes were to be settled.

In 1988 the Republican candidate for the presidency, George Bush, was elected, but the same public increased Democratic majorities in both houses of Congress. What this result did to solve problems of the homeless, the budget deficit, problems of health care, international trade imbalances, and the weakness of the dollar was far from obvious. The public voted for whom it wanted both at the presidential and the congressional level, but the candidates were not given specific orders as to what to do. Thus the message for both the president and Congress was murky.

On rare occasions, public opinion does produce executive-legislative harmony. When the United States invaded Grenada in 1983, some members of Congress harshly criticized President Reagan's action. These reservations disappeared in the wake of a torrent of positive public opinion.

If elections and public opinion seldom resolve executive-legislative conflict in the short run, the long-range relationships may be even more subtle and complex. In the 1964 presidential election, President Johnson campaigned on a program of essentially preserving the status quo on the U.S. role in Vietnam. Most of Congress and the public seemingly agreed. By 1968, strong congressional and public challenges to administration policy were mounted. In the election of 1972, presidential candidates Nixon and McGovern, majorities in Congress, and a majority of the public seemed to want the United States to get out of Vietnam. In a complex series of steps both branches of government and public opinion had shifted from their 1964 positions. Historians continue to debate over who or what caused these views to shift and in what order. What is clear is that all parties did shift and that their changes in view were in the same direction.

Conflict Resolution Through Law

Disputes not resolved informally through bargaining, crisis, or court intervention or by outbursts of public opinion or election mandates are sometimes mitigated through formal action to change the law. In extreme cases, Congress simply ignores presidential suggestions and passes their own version of legislation. Bills passed that are vetoed can be made into law through an override. Not all parties to a legislative-executive dispute need agree on

Acting as commander-in-chief of the armed forces, President Reagan ordered U.S. forces to invade Grenada. He said that he was concerned for the safety of American citizens there, and he raised the question of Soviet influence in the western hemisphere. Congress may have the power to declare war, but it followed public opinion in applauding the president's action.

the particular legal solution for that solution to become law. Attempts at conflict resolution through law can be assessed by studying two examples: impoundment and the war powers.

Impoundment. Many presidents have decided not to spend all of the money appropriated by Congress. Perhaps the task had already been accomplished with other funds. Or perhaps new conditions would dictate the wisdom of waiting to spend the money. Money not spent at the end of the fiscal year was returned to the U.S. treasury (impounded). The practice of impoundment has been widely used for certain administrative purposes and not because of sharp policy conflicts. Especially in the Nixon administration, the motive for using impoundments switched from administration to policy. Impoundment was used largely because the president simply did not like some programs. President Nixon's extensive use of impoundment for policy purposes stimulated Congress to respond by passing the Congressional Budget and Impoundment Control Act of 1974. This law set up formal rules to determine the conditions under which a presidential impoundment could stand. Under its provisions, a president who wanted to delay spending appropriated money (deferral) could do so unless Congress formally disapproved. A 1977 statute tightened this restriction. Presidents can now defer expenditures in essence

Separation of Powers and the Judiciary

Executive-legislative relations take place against a background of judicial review and the constitutional framework. The Supreme Court has wrestled with the meaning of separation of powers at several points in recent history. Key decisions over the last 40 years have altered the balance of power between the executive and legislative branches, and the role of the courts in the conflict has increased since the Nixon administration.

Youngstown Sheet and Tube v. *Sawyer,* 1952	President Truman attempts to seize and operate steel mills during the Korean War. The Court rules that the president lacks that authority.
Buckley v. *Valeo,* 1976	The Federal Election Commission, as created by law, is held unconstitutional. The Court rules that congressional appointees cannot serve on a body performing executive functions.
Nixon v. *Administrator of General Services,* 1977	Congress directs the administrator of general services to hold and screen presidential papers, and the Court upholds congressional action.
Immigration and Naturalization Service v. *Chadha,* 1983	The Court rules that the legislative veto violates the doctrine of separation of powers.
Bowsher v. *Syner,* 1986	Congress invokes mandatory cuts in the federal budget to handle a rapidly growing deficit; the law makes the comptroller general responsible for calculating the cuts. The Court rules the act unconstitutional, because an official removable by Congress cannot perform such executive functions.
Morrison v. *Olson,* 1988	The president fails in a challenge to Congress's power, as the Court upholds the authority to appoint a special prosecutor to investigate charges of misconduct in the executive branch.

only if the program's objectives have been met elsewhere.

If a president wants to cancel rather than delay spending appropriated money, the action is called a rescission. If Congress does not formally act to accept the rescission, the president must spend the money. The shape of executive-legislative relations on budget and spending matters was altered through law.

Changing the law did not necessarily solve the

problem. Routine deferrals made for administrative purposes have been accepted by Congress almost all the time. In contrast, deferrals made on policy grounds have been allowed to stand about half the time. Congress has approved rescissions only about one-third of the time.[14] Table 14–4 shows exactly what happened from 1975 to 1988.

Presidential success in achieving policy goals through impoundment has been uneven. President Carter was more successful than President Ford. President Reagan's early record of success in impounding funds did not persist through the last six years of his administrations. A central variable is presidential standing. Popular presidents with strong political support in and out of Congress reach their objectives through impoundment more than do presidents with less standing and support. Although law may alter executive-legislative balance, politics governs outcomes. Law distributes advantages; politics resolves contentious issues or precludes their settlement.

The War Powers Resolution of 1973. The constitutional uncertainty about the extent of the president's ability unilaterally to commit troops abroad historically has resulted in executive-legislative skirmishes rather than bitter divisions. As late as the decade between 1955 and 1965, Congress raised no major objections to presidential commitments of troops abroad. It was the experience with the Vietnam War and administration justifications for U.S. involvement that raised the level of tension between the president and majorities in Congress. It seemed to many that legal justification was simply rationalizing what had been done. The legal advisor to the Department of State in the administration of Lyndon Johnson could argue:

> Under the Constitution the President, in addition to being Chief Executive, is Commander in Chief of the Army and Navy. He holds the prime responsibility for the conduct of United States foreign relations. These duties carry very broad powers, including the power to deploy American forces abroad and commit them to military operations when the President deems such action necessary to maintain the security and defense of the United States.
>
> . . . Under our Constitution it is the President who must decide when an armed attack has occurred. He has also the constitutional responsibility for determining what measures of defense are required when the peace and safety of the United States are endangered. If he considers that deployment of the United States forces to South Vietnam is required, and that military measures against the source of Communist aggression in North Vietnam are necessary, he is constitutionally empowered to take these measures.[15]

TABLE 14–4

Presidents and Impoundments, 1975–1988

President	Percent of Rescissions Accepted by Congress	Percent of Deferrals Accepted by Congress: Routine	Percent of Deferrals Accepted by Congress: Policy
Ford	7.2	99.9	59.2
Carter	37.1	99.9	56.7
Reagan	38.1	99.2	47.8

Source: Data from Allen Schick, "The Disappearing Impoundment Power," *Tax Foundation, Tax Features* (October 1988), p. 4.

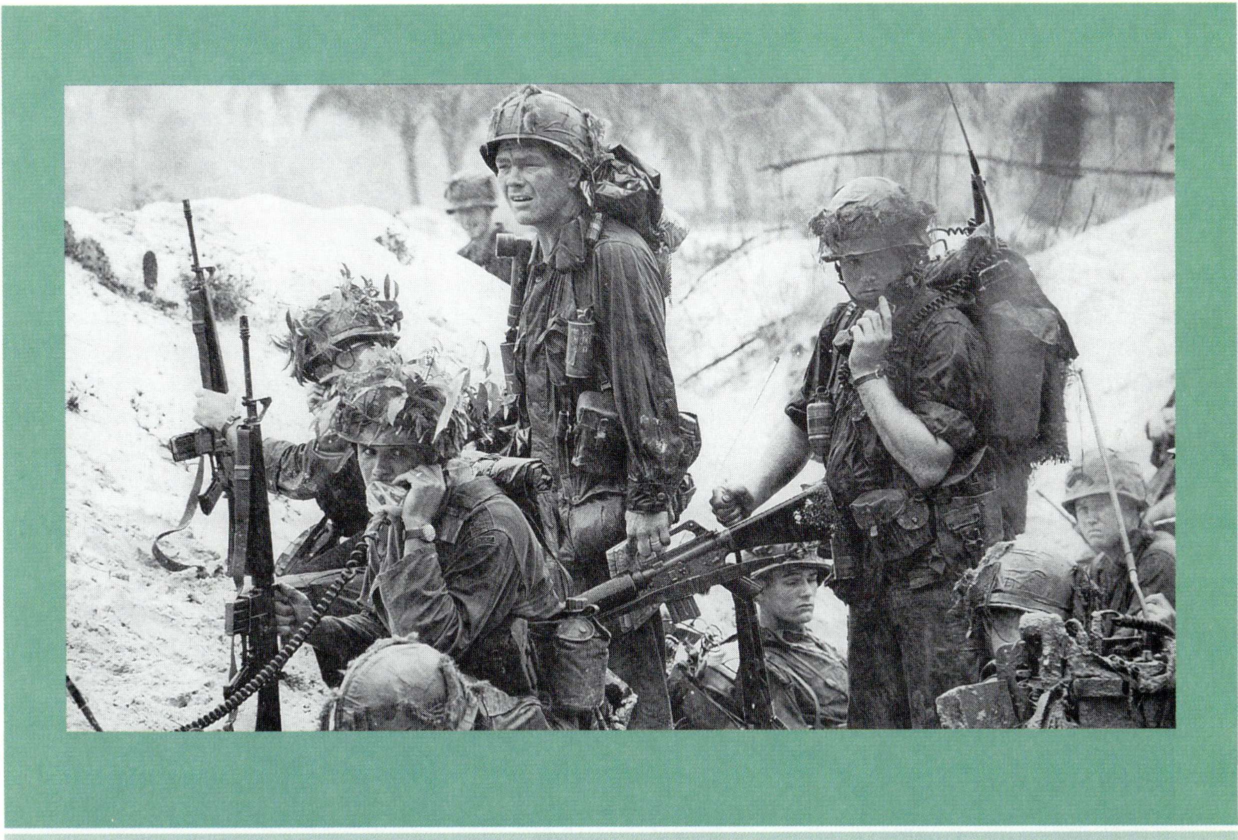

The U.S. involvement in Vietnam triggered a long, bitter controversy over the president's right to commit troops without consulting Congress. The war's severe consequences—for both foreign policy and domestic politics—led many in Congress to demand more power to consent to future global commitments.

The consequences of the Vietnam involvement, both domestic and international, were such that many came to view our participation as tragic. How could such disasters be prevented in the future? How could presidents have the discretion they need to be effective in protecting U.S. interests and yet be limited to minimize the possibility of irresponsible presidential action? Congress confronted this dilemma in the extensive debates culminating in the *War Powers Resolution* of 1973. This resolution was vetoed by President Nixon and then passed over his veto. There are as yet no conclusive answers about the effectiveness of the War Powers Resolution, but there is growing evidence which suggests that its impact may be rather slight. Even in its own formal application, the case of the United States marines in Lebanon in 1983, the Congress seemed to think that the resolution was operative, while President Reagan denied its applicability.

What was originally intended in the resolution was a judicious marriage between effectiveness, efficiency, and responsibility. The substantial opportunities for presidents to exercise discretion would enable them to defend the interests of the United States as necessity seemed to demand. Few wanted to erase presidential flexibility. The crux of the matter was to allow presidents to do what needed to be done, but yet to place bounds on presidential behavior that would create substantial limits. If events have suggested that that goal will not

The War Powers Resolution of 1973

Congress, in passing the War Powers Act over a presidential veto, intended to do three things: (1) to involve Congress in foreign policy decision making by urging prior consultation between the president and key legislators; (2) to keep Congress abreast of foreign policy initiatives by requiring presidents to report to Congress within 48 hours whenever U.S. troops are sent to hostile or potentially hostile environments; and (3) to permit Congress to force the withdrawal of troops after a 60-day period. In reality, although the second provision has generally been successful, the War Powers Act has not given Congress the opportunity to influence foreign policy initiatives prior to execution. Neither has it forced the withdrawal of troops.

Events	Prior Consultation?	Report?	Withdrawal of Troops?
Nixon administration			
Evacuation of U.S. citizens from Cyprus (1974)	No	No	No
Aerial resupply of Cambodia (1974)	No	No	No
Reconnaissance missions over Cambodia (1974)	No	No	No
Ford administration			
Sealift of refugees from Danang to safer areas of Vietnam (1975)	No	Yes	No
Evacuation of Cambodia (1975)	No	Yes	No
Evacuation of Vietnam (1975)	No	Yes	No
Recapture of SS *Mayaquez* (1975)	No	Yes*	No
Evacuation of Americans from Lebanon (1976)	No	No	No
U.S. forces to Korea (1976)	No	No	No
Carter administration			
Support for French/Belgian rescue operations in Zaire (1978)	No	No	No

Events	Prior Consultation?	Report?	Withdrawal of Troops?
Mission to rescue American hostages held by Iran (1980)	No	Yes	No
Reagan administration			
Sending of U.S. advisors to El Salvador (1981)	No	No	No
U.S. enforcement of peace treaty between Egypt and Israel (1982)	No	Yes	No
U.S. Marines to assist PLO withdrawal from Lebanon (1982)	No	Yes	No
U.S. Marines to restore Lebanese government (1982)	No	Yes	No
Reconnaissance in Chad (1983)	No	Yes	No
Lebanon peacekeeping mission (1983)	No	Yes	No
U.S. aircraft to Chad (1983)	No	Yes	No
Training exercises in Central America and Caribbean (1983)	No	No	No
U.S. invasion in Grenada (1983)	No	Yes	No
Presence in Gulf of Sidra (1986)	No	Yes	No
Retaliation against Libya (1986)	No	Yes	No
U.S. ships to Persian Gulf (1987–)	No	Yes	No

* This is the only instance where a president has reported to Congress in a manner which starts the 60-day time clock.

Sources: Robert D. Clark, Andrew M. Egeland, Jr., and David B. Sanford, *The War Powers Resolution: Balance of War Powers in the Eighties* (Washington, D.C.: National Defense University Press, 1985); Daniel P. Franklin, "War Powers in the Modern Context," *Congress and the Presidency* (Spring 1987), pp. 77–92.

War Powers Resolution of 1973 (Public Law 93-148)

It is the purpose of this joint resolution [to] insure that . . . the constitutional powers of the President as Commander in Chief to introduce United States armed forces into hostilities, or into situations where imminent involvement in hostilities is clearly indicated by the circumstances, are exercised only pursuant to (1) a declaration of war, (2) specific statutory authorization, or (3) a national emergency created by attack upon the United States, its territories or possessions, or its armed forces. . . .

The President in every possible instance shall consult with Congress before introducing United States armed forces into hostilities or into situations where imminent involvement in hostilities is clearly indicated by the circumstances, and after every such introduction shall consult regularly with the Congress until United States Armed Forces are no longer engaged in hostilities or have been removed from such situations. . . .

In the absence of a declaration of war, in any case in which United States armed forces are introduced (1) into hostilities or into situations where imminent involvement in hostilities is clearly indicated by the circumstances; (2) into the territory, airspace or waters of a foreign nation, while equipped for combat, except for deployments which relate solely to supply, replacement, repair, or training of such forces; or (3) in numbers which substantially enlarge United States armed forces equipped for combat already located in a foreign nation; the President shall submit within 48 hours to the Speaker of the House of Representatives and to the President pro Tempore of the Senate a report, in writing, setting forth (a) the circumstances necessitating the introduction of United States armed forces; (b) the Constitutional and legislative authority under which such introduction took place, and (3) to the estimated scope and duration of the hostilities to involement. . . .

Within 60 calendar days after a report is submitted or is required to be submitted pursuant to Section 4 (A) (1), whichever is earlier, the President shall terminate any use of United States armed forces with respect to which such report was submitted (or required to be submitted), unless the Congress (1) has declared war or has enacted a specific authorization for such use of United States armed forces, (2) has extended by law such 60-day period, or (3) is physically unable to meet as a result of an armed attack upon the United States. Such 60-day period shall be extended for not more than an additional 30 days if the President determines and certifies to the Congress in writing that unavoidable military necessity respecting the safety of United States armed forces requires the continued use of such armed forces in the course of bringing about a prompt removal of such forces. . . .

For purposes of this joint resolution, the term "Introduction of United States armed forces" includes the assignment of members of such armed forces to command, coordinate, participate in the movement or accompany the regular or irregular military forces of any foreign country or government when such military forces are engaged, or there exists an imminent threat that such forces will become engaged in hostilities. . . .

Nothing in this joint resolution (1) is intended to alter the Constitutional authority of the Congress or of the President, or the provisions of existing treaties; or (2) shall be construed as granting any authority to the President with respect to the introduction of United States armed forces into hostilities or into situations wherein involvement in hostilities is clearly indicated by the circumstances which authority he would not have had in the absence of this joint resolution.

be reached, the resolution remains as a reasonable *legal* answer to an enduring dilemma. Perhaps what the experience with the resolution tells us most clearly is that problems of war and military commitments abroad in times of crisis will not be dealt with primarily as legal problems. The appearance of legality must be maintained in a constitutional democracy, but the necessity of survival sometimes makes that task quite difficult.

Presidents in crisis situations seem to do what they feel is necessary and appropriate and then search for plausible legal defenses. Given the special status of the presidency and the tendency to rally behind presidential decisions in crisis situations, presidents have a great advantage in confronting international crises. The net impact of the War Powers Resolution may be more psychological than legal: Presidents may worry a bit more about possible reactions to what they do and may work harder to articulate a defense of their actions. Perhaps that is the most that can be expected in a democracy. The provisions of the War Powers Resolution excerpted in the accompanying box provide a basis for further discussion of this vexing and vital problem.

Cooperation and Conflict

Both cooperation and conflict are characteristic of executive-legislative relations. The mix is what changes with different issues, personalities, and contexts. Routine issues are discussed and resolved on a daily basis with neither publicity nor political bloodletting. On more controversial issues, experience varies. The president and Congress, at times, work together with speed and efficiency. Admittedly, these periods are rare. The first 100 days of the Roosevelt administration in 1933, the Johnson administration on domestic issues in 1964 and 1965, and the Reagan administration in 1981 are the only three modern examples. What that means is that most of the time executive-legislative relations are a mixed bag of cooperation and conflict. Even within the same administration, the pattern varies. Contrast the early Roosevelt success with the struggles later; contrast the Reagan victories in 1981 with problems later in the Reagan administration.

Few modern presidents fail to achieve some rapport with Congress. Few Congresses totally dominate their presidents. Mixed patterns of influence are the rule. This is not an accident of particular periods in history; it is an intended result. Those who framed the Constitution knew what they wanted, and for over 200 years they have achieved their goal. Power and ambition are matched against power and ambition. Charles O. Jones estimates that in the twentieth century one institution, either the presidency or the Congress, dominated the relationship less than one-third of the time. Mixed patterns predominate.

The system was designed to achieve controlled tension. The design has worked. What are the implications of this for American government and politics?

1. Policy will seldom change rapidly.
2. When changes are made, they will often be incremental in nature.
3. Periods of passion will be scarce. Periods of calm and passion will alternate but this will not occur in fixed cycles.
4. Policy will generally be moderate ideologically.
5. Most policy results will be achieved through bargaining and compromise.
6. It is not clear that either the president or Congress is the normal depository of wisdom. In the words of Willmoore Kendall: ". . . we have two *conceptions* of higher principle about which reasonable men may legitimately differ." [6]

Some see this as an undesirable situation. The passion for change always burns deeply for a few. But the desire for change neither guarantees that it will occur or, if it does, that it will be successful. There are many proposed changes and reforms. Few such proposals are seriously considered and even fewer are adopted. Those that are adopted almost never seriously alter the contours of executive-legislative relations. Those who would augment cooperation by instituting a parliamentary system presume that new institutional patterns can be imposed on the same society. This is surely a dubious proposition. Little but wish supports that hope. On a smaller scale, proposals for an item veto for the president or a guaranteed balanced budget may surely alter the shape of executive-legislative relations but, again, not their basic patterns. When the Supreme Court in 1983 declared the legislative veto to be unconstitutional, a rash of devices appeared to achieve similar ends. The power of adaptation in American politics is large. Practice rises above and beyond particular forms.

Summary

- An intergrated, smooth executive-legislative relationship is unlikely for more than a very short period. Conflict *and* cooperation are built into the relationship.
- Cooperation is promoted by the pressure of problems in foreign policy, the constitutionally imposed necessity for cooperation, shared values, and a pragmatic political culture.
- The external environment strongly shapes the nature of executive-legislative relations. The greatest periods of executive-legislative cooperation come in times of deep crisis, either domestic or international. Conflict is more common at other times.
- Periods of strong one-party dominance increase the odds for executive-legislative cooperation. The last several decades have not looked like that. In our present era, no single political party dominates national politics. Republicans have won the presidency in five of the last six elections. In that same quarter-century, the Democrats have controlled at least one house of the Congress almost all of the time. The potential for executive-legislative conflict grows under such circumstances.
- The heterogeneity of American society, the constitutional system of separation of powers and checks and balances, and the nature of the party system make executive-legislative conflict inevitable. The system was designed that way and it works.
- Cooperation and conflict in executive-legislative relations maintain an uneasy coexistence. The relationship is regularly altered in its details but cannot be readily changed in its basics.
- Patterns of executive-legislative interaction reflect the characteristics of the entire political system. They are best studied from the perspective of this context.

Readings on Executive-Legislative Relations

Aberbach, Joel D., Robert D. Putnam, and Bert A. Rockman. 1981. *Bureaucrats and Politicians in Western Democracies.* Cambridge, Mass.: Harvard University Press. A comparative study of the characteristics and attitudes of bureaucrats and political leaders in Western democracies.

Binkley, Wilfred E. 1962. *President and Congress,* 3d rev. ed. New York: Vintage Books. Classic treatment of the constitutional powers of the president *vis-à-vis* Congress.

Crabb, Cecil V., and Pat M. Holt. 1984. *Invitation to Struggle: Congress, the President, and Foreign Policy,* 2d ed. Washington, D.C.: CQ Press. An explanation and five case studies of the legislative-executive "struggle" to make foreign policy.

Craig, Barbara H. 1988. *Chadha: The Story of an Epic Constitutional Struggle.* New York: Oxford University Press. An account of the Supreme Court's decision to overturn the legislative veto.

Edwards, George C. 1980. *Presidential Influence in Congress.* San Francisco: W. H. Freeman. An empirical study of the president's impact on the legislative branch.

Fisher, Louis. 1987. *The Politics of Shared Power: Congress and the Executive,* 2d ed. Washington, D.C.: CQ Press. Argues that, despite the system of checks and balances, authority in government is not so much checked as shared.

Holtzman, Abraham. 1970. *Legislative Liaison: Executive Leadership in Congress.* Chicago: Rand McNally. A study of executive branch personnel who link the White House with Congress.

Ripley, Randall B., and Grace A. Franklin. 1987. *Congress, the Bureaucracy, and Public Policy,* 4th ed. Chicago: Dorsey Press. Examines how Congress and the federal bureaucracy interact in different policy areas.

Schick, Allen. 1980. *Congress and Money: Budgeting, Spending, and Taxing.* Washington, D.C.: Urban Institute. How Congress makes money decisions.

Wayne, Stephen J. 1978. *The Legislative Presidency.* New York: Harper & Row. Presidential involvement in the formulation, coordination, and implementation of legislative policy.

Chapter 15

The Bureaucracy

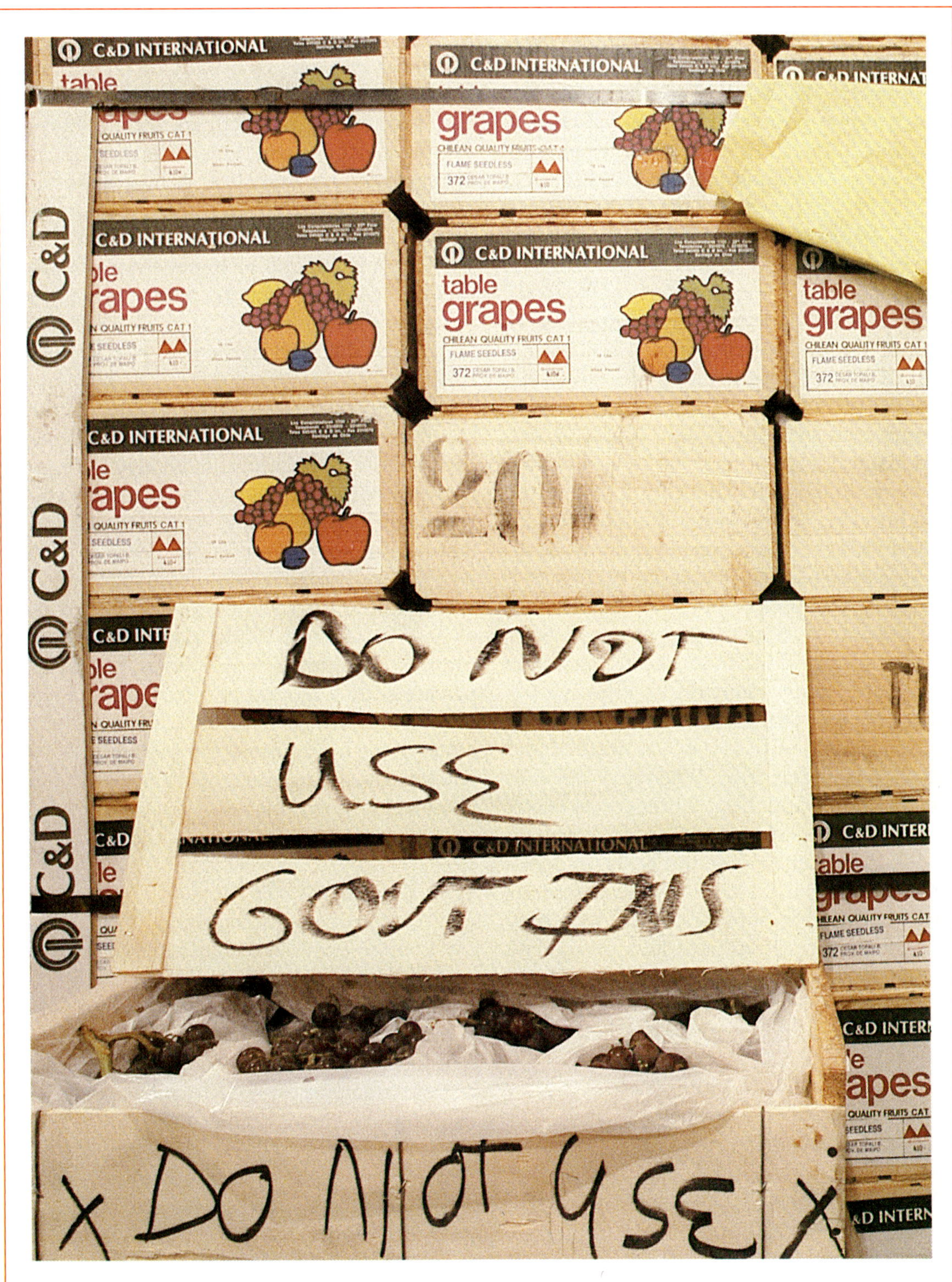
C&D INTERNATIONAL
table grapes
CHILEAN QUALITY FRUITS CAT 1
FLAME SEEDLESS
372
C&D
20
DO NOT
USE
GOVT INS
x DO NOT USE x

The president, Congress, and the courts make the dramatic decisions of government. The media watch as they pass tax increases, send troops abroad to protect American interests, and make and implement laws concerning racial segregation and integration. Most of the actual work of the national government, however, is done by the federal bureaucracy in the executive branch of government. Processing social security applications and checks, monitoring loans for college students, attending to the claims of veterans, testing pesticides, issuing passports, regulating atomic energy installations, administering price supports for farmers, urging foreign tourists to visit the United States, developing and maintaining national parks, and buying supplies for military bases are only a few of the duties the bureaucracy performs. Bureaucrats are vital to the routines of government and are significant in the policy-making process.

In carrying out policy, bureaucrats can contribute to shaping it. Sometimes policy, politics, and administration are hard to separate. Those who implement policy must interpret its meaning because policy is often written in general terms that gain precise meaning only as they are applied and interpreted in particular cases. When they discover problems in implementation, bureaucrats make suggestions to alter and perhaps improve policy. These suggestions can become the basis for legislation and administrative action. For these reasons we need to know what bureaucrats do, who they are, how they are organized, and how they relate to the president and Congress.

Bureaucracy: Characteristics and Growth

The executive branch extends beyond the president and his immediate advisers. The federal bureaucracy consists of about 3 million civilian employees in some 75 departments and agencies. Only a small number, about 11 percent, work in or near Washington, D.C. The services they perform range from influencing policy to working as clerks, typists, and messengers.

What bureaucrats usually do is similar to work in the private sector. They type and send letters and memorandums, process forms, answer telephones, and go to meetings. In terms of professions, bureaucrats are chemists, demographers, intelligence analysts, civil engineers, economists, and agronomists. Almost all of them keep their jobs whether a Democrat or Republican wins the presidential election and no matter which political party has the majority in Congress. The bureaucrats are indeed the most permanent part of the government.

Bureaucrats, like their private counterparts, have varied training, experience, and capabilities. Perhaps the most important change in recent times is the growing number of bureaucrats who are in technical or professional occupations. Some estimate the number to be one-third of the bureaucracy, a significantly higher proportion than in the private sector. Table 15–1 shows some of these differences as of 1981, along with the pay of white-collar employees. Compared with similar positions in the private sector, federal government compensation, salary, and fringe benefits tend to be somewhat better at the lower levels, but private sector salaries outstrip those in government for the higher, more responsible positions.

The Bureaucrats

What are the characteristics of the typical federal civilian employee? One report puts it this way for full-time nonpostal employees in 1987: the average age is about 42; the average length of service in the government is about 13 years; about 33 percent have attained a B.A. or B.S. degree; about 58 percent are male; about 73 percent are Caucasian.

The executive branch is organized into departments, agencies, government corporations, and commissions. The basic organization is set by Congress, and what Congress creates, usually only Congress can eliminate. Early in his administration, President Reagan wanted to abolish two executive departments, Energy and Education. When Congress refused to accept his recommendation, the president abandoned the effort. Congress establishes the basic structure of the executive branch;

TABLE 15–1

Federal Employees: Occupations and Salaries

Occupation Group	Number of Employees (Rounded)	Pay Grades for White-Collar Employees*	1985 Salaries	Number of Employees (Rounded)
Professional	330,400	GS 16–18	$61,296–$84,157	1,000
Administrative	400,600	GS 13–15	37,599–67,940	231,100
Technical	346,600	GS 11–12	26,381–41,105	388,000
Clerical	392,500	GS 7–10	17,824–31,211	377,000
Blue collar	452,070	GS 1–6	9,339–20,855	563,000
Other	42,700			

* General schedule (GS) pay classification grades.
Sources: *Statistical Abstract of the United States,* 1984, p. 337; 1988, p. 309.

the administration can fill in any blanks by specifying rules and details. Proposals for new departments and agencies, of course, may be suggested to Congress by the administration.

Changing values and new technologies may lead to more government. If there is pressure for more regulation, the size of government may increase. In recent decades demands for a cleaner environment, more safety on the job, consumer product safety, and more equal opportunities in employment have had this effect.

Congress provides the bureaucracy with policy as well as structure. The Fulbright exchange of scholars program, food stamps, farm subsidy programs, federal mortgage guarantees, the interstate highway program, foreign aid, quotas on imports, research on water resources, training programs for youth, protection against unsafe foods, and promoting environmental quality—all have roots in legislation.

Basic personnel policies are also derived from legislation. Congress may set pay classification systems, salary ceilings, hiring and firing policies, and policies for promotion. The Civil Service Reform Act of 1978 created a new senior executive service of top-level bureaucrats who can move among units and be given bonuses for superior work. The implementation of personnel policies is largely a task of the executive branch.

Bureaucratic Growth

Government has grown immensely in scope and expenditures in the twentieth century. Changes in the size and duties of government are mirrored in the federal bureaucracy. In 1900, only 5 of the cabinet departments existed. The total outlay of funds by the federal government rose from about $520 million to over $1 trillion in 1988. This figure is expected to persist in the early 1990s. The number of paid civilian employees has also increased sharply since 1900. Figure 15–1 shows a rise from about 240,000 employees in 1900 to about 3 million throughout the 1980s. Over the last 50 years, public employment at the state and local levels has quadrupled from about 3 million to over 13 million. But if we compare these figures with those for the entire U.S. population, the perspective changes. Federal government employees made up less than 1 percent of the population in 1901. The figure in 1990 is still about 1 percent.

Another way to measure the growth of government is to compare federal government expenditures with the size of the gross national product.

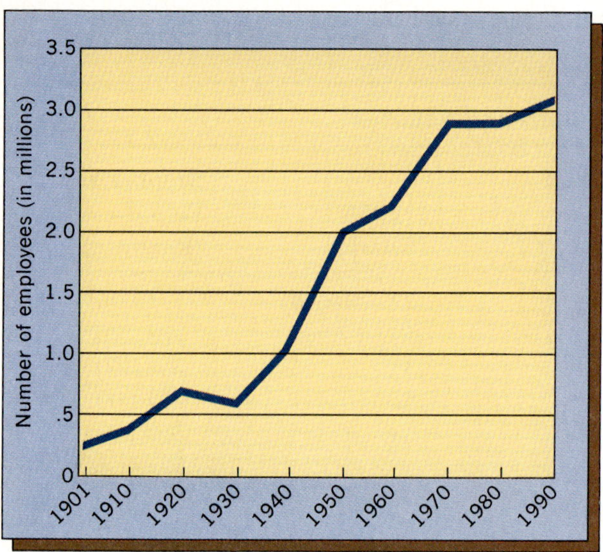

Figure 15–1 Increase in federal government employees, 1901–1990. Source: U.S. Bureau of the Census, *Historical Statistics of the United States, Colonial Times to 1957* (Washington, D.C.: U.S. Government Printing Office, 1960), p. 710; *Statistical Abstract of the United States,* 1988, p. 307.

Figure 15–2 reveals the relationship from 1970 to 1987. By this measure, the effort of the Reagan administration to reduce the "size" of the federal government in the economy has been less than fully successful.

By contrast, federal regulatory efforts in the 1980s seem to have decreased. The *Federal Register,* a compilation of regulations and legal notices issued or proposed by federal agencies, grew dramatically in the 1970s from about 20,000 pages to over 70,000 pages. The efforts of the Reagan administration to reduce federal regulation are reflected in the figures: under 58,000 pages for 1983, less than 50,000 in 1986. During the eight years of the Reagan administration, the reductions amounted to about 45 percent.

Public Images of Bureaucrats

In the midst of these changes in size, scope, activity, and expenditures, one constant remains. The public image of the federal bureaucracy is not a very good one. A national poll in 1981 showed that citizens thought about 42 cents of every dollar collected by the national government was wasted. About 67 percent thought federal workers were better paid and had more benefits than their counterparts in the private sector. But they thought government employees didn't work as hard.[1] Whether confidence, trust, or efficiency is measured, the typical reaction is to rank federal bureaucrats low. One obvious paradox in American politics is that a group of people performing such vital tasks is viewed this way by the public. And strangely enough, Daniel Katz and associates reported in 1975 that public evaluations of direct, specific experiences with government agencies were higher than were evaluations of government agencies and bureaucrats in general.[2]

Bureaucrats could find some slight solace in a poll reported in 1986. More people reportedly had confidence in them than in the leaders of organized labor.[3]

The public image of bureaucrats is reinforced by politicians who find it easy to use the bureaucracy as a target in their campaigns for reelection. In the presidential campaigns in 1976 and 1980 the winning candidates for the presidency, Democrat Jimmy Carter and Republican Ronald Reagan, successfully used negative criticism of the bureaucracy to gain electoral support. Members of Congress find the same technique useful in their campaigns and exploit it endlessly.

Public attitudes toward the bureaucracy were reinforced by conclusions reached in the report issued by the President's Private Sector Survey on Cost Control, popularly called the Grace Commission after its chairman, J. Peter Grace. The commission, established by President Reagan in 1982, made some 2500 recommendations on nearly 800 issues. Its two-volume summary report ran to over 600 pages and concluded that savings and revenue enhancements of some $424 billion in the federal budget would be possible if waste was reduced, if system failures were corrected, if personnel management was improved, and if structural deficiencies were attacked. The commission did emphasize that about 73 percent of these changes would require the approval of Congress. Clearly, controlling

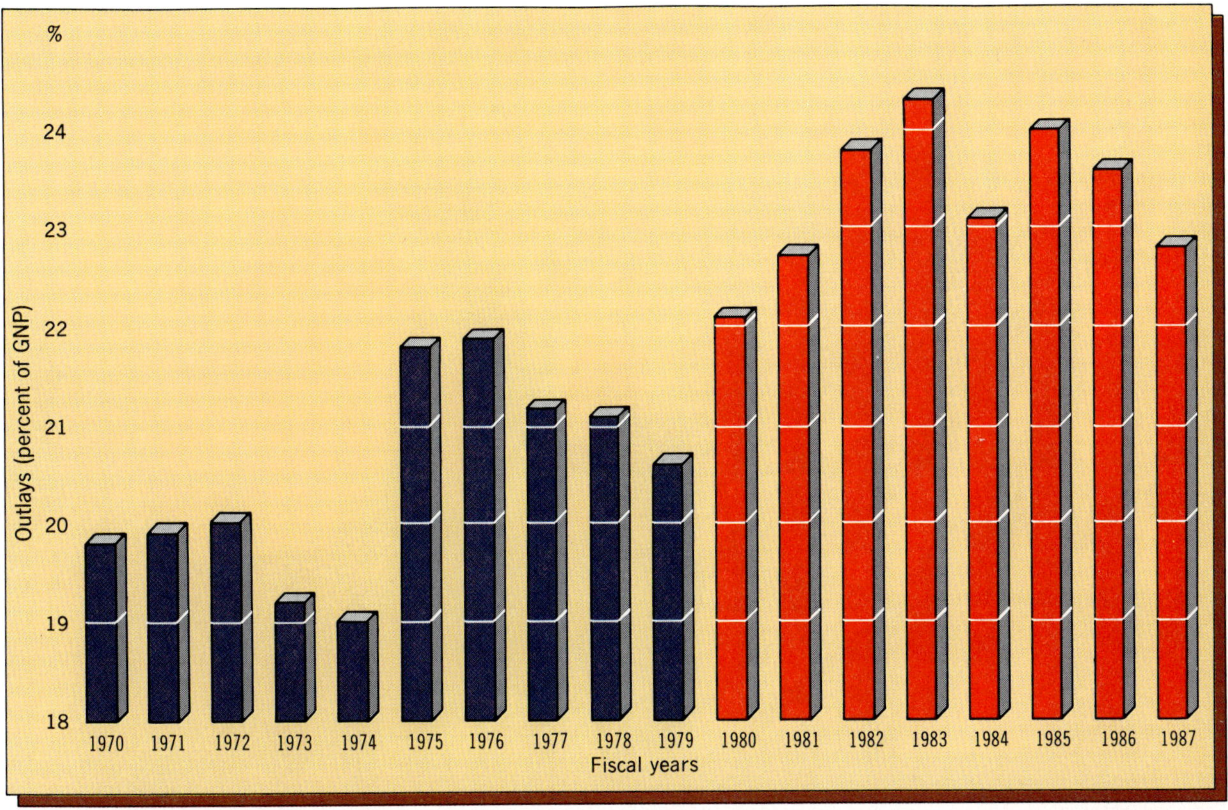

Figure 15–2 Federal outlays as a percentage of GNP, 1970–1987. Source: *Budget of the United States Government, Fiscal 1989,* p. 6g–39.

the bureaucracy is not just the job of the president and his advisers. The Congress is intimately involved.

The accuracy of the Grace Commission's estimates were questioned in a joint report issued by the Congressional Budget Office and the General Accounting Office, which found these estimates to be excessively high. Other critics charged that the commission was really recommending basic policy changes under the heading of better management. The correct amount of possible savings cannot be readily established. The commission's reports were given wide publicity. They provided additional fuel for those with negative images of government.

But even compared with state and local governments, another survey reported, the federal government is not well regarded. When asked from which level of government they got the most for their money, 35 percent cited local government, 27 percent state government, and only 24 percent cited the national government.[4]

Selection of Bureaucrats

This large bureaucracy is supposed to be accountable to the president and Congress. The way in which most bureaucrats are selected may complicate that task. Most bureaucrats are selected by a merit system. New administrations replace only a tiny portion of executive branch employees. Merit systems dating from the Pendleton Act of 1883 are designed to select employees based on competence only. Initially, merit systems covered only a small part of the federal work force. But the system has expanded in this century. By 1930 about 77 percent of federal employees were covered. In the 1980s,

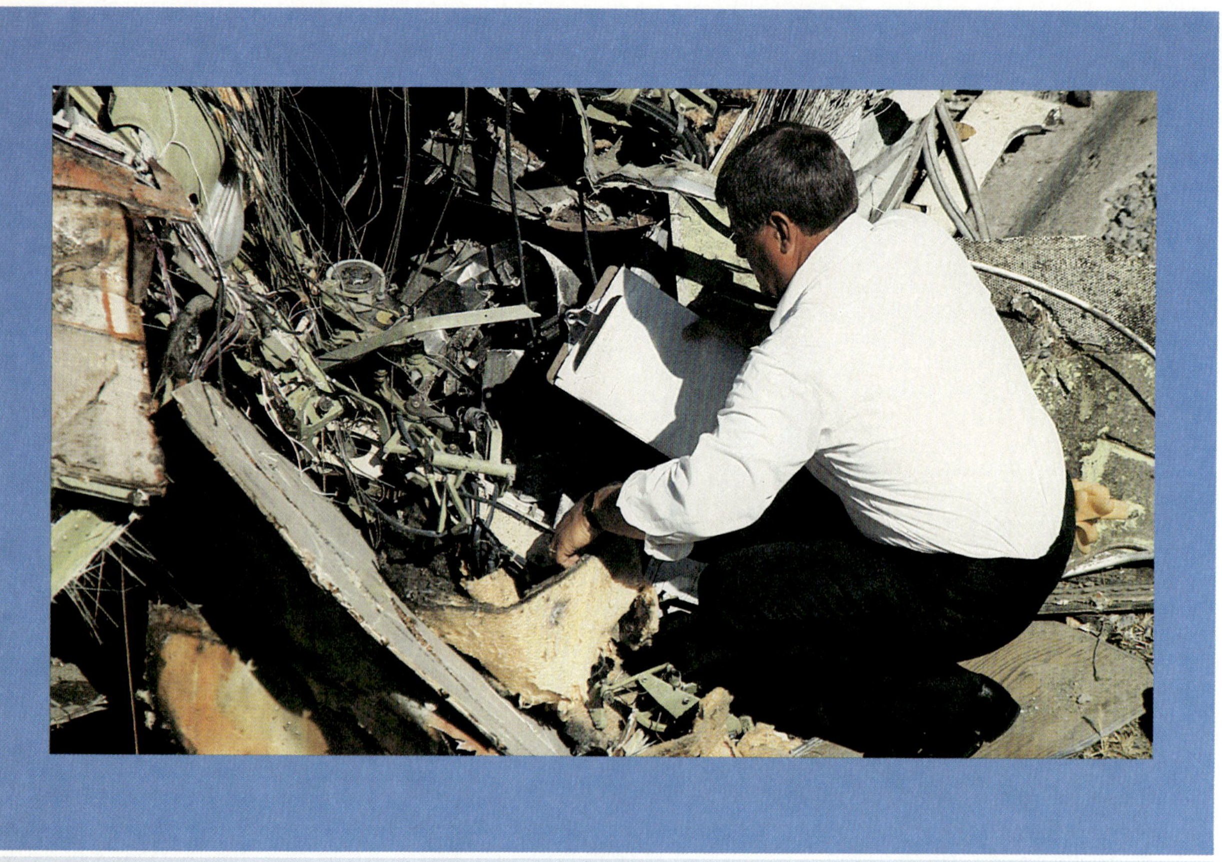

A government inspector examines wreckage from a commercial airliner at an airport outside Detroit, Michigan. He is searching for clues to the causes of the crash. Many in government are highly skilled specialists, in a remarkable variety of professions.

the figure exceeded 90 percent. The goal of the merit systems in the national government is to depoliticize the bureaucracy. Once hired, bureaucrats cannot be replaced at the whim of a new administration. Technical competence and employee continuity are promoted, but the cost may be responsiveness to the programs of a new administration.

To enhance their job protection, bureaucrats are barred from many forms of political activity. The theory is that they cannot then be coerced by their superiors into providing political support. By the end of the 1980s the pendulum was swinging toward allowing bureaucrats to participate outside of working hours in a wider range of political activity. How to balance the rights of bureaucrats as citizens, their on-the-job protection, and the desire for a politically neutral professional civil service remains perplexing.

The merit system for employee selection is now so well established that any sharp change in personnel policy stimulates a strong reaction. In 1985 the Reagan administration decided to abandon a long-standing preference for hiring full-time employees and urged departments and agencies to fill positions with temporary employees. The stated purposes of this move were to save the government some fringe benefit costs and to ease the difficulties in firing unneeded employees. Critics immediately proclaimed this a blow at the merit system.

A new administration focuses on only the relatively few positions it can fill. In Hugh Heclo's words,

> Presidents and department heads make few choices that are more important than those concerning the type of people who will serve with them in the administration. In affecting the everyday work of government, these hundreds of personnel selections add up to a cumulative act of choice that may be at least as important as the electorate's single act of choice for president every four years.[5]

Presidents often pick their closest advisers from persons familiar to them or highly recommended by those who are. Positions less close to the president, such as cabinet members, are mainly held by strangers. President Reagan articulated some guidelines he used to select top government personnel.

> My basic rule is that I want people who don't want a job in government. I want people who are already so successful that they would regard a government job as a step down, not a step up.
>
> I don't want empire builders, I want people who will be the first to tell me if their jobs are unnecessary.
>
> Out there in the private sector there is an awful lot of brains and talent in people who haven't learned all the things you can't do.
>
> [We will have] a new restructuring of the Presidential Cabinet that will make Cabinet Officers the managers of the national administration—not captives of the bureaucracy or special interests in the departments that they are supposed to direct.[6]

In selecting cabinet members, the Carter, Reagan, and Bush administrations wrote job descriptions and made lists of "qualified" candidates. The selection process was well under way before inauguration day. American political parties have no set of leaders ready to step into cabinet positions; cabinet personnel may be personal friends, such as James A. Baker III and John Sununu in the Bush administration, whose advice and experience the president values. They may be appointed as a political payoff, perhaps for support given during the nomination or election process. They may be known for their expertise in a particular field.

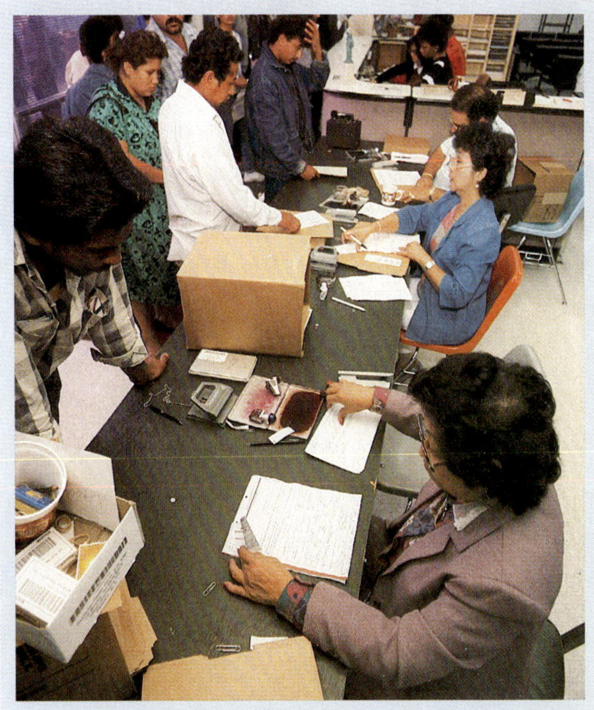

Policy changes often mean government taking on new tasks—and new employees. For example, laws allowing more aliens to receive legal status has added to the demands on officials at this alien amnesty office. Changes in response to important policy problems help fuel the growth of government.

Cabinet selection is seldom a tidy process. Richard F. Fenno captures its essence:

> The process of Cabinet selection is a subprocess, related to every point to the American political system as a whole, and revealing something of the reactive nature of the Cabinet as an institution. The process finds its underlying consistency in the fundamental pluralism of American politics. Until such time as the basic contours of the system change, Cabinet appointment will continue to frustrate those who seek a neatly rational scheme of selection to which they can apply equally well-structured systems of prediction and judgment.[7]

The way cabinet members are picked tells much about how they will work with the president. These department heads—often picked for reasons other than personal closeness and loyalty—are expected by presidents and their advisers to serve the administration with loyalty. That wish is destined to remain at least partially unfulfilled.

Appointments to the position of department head must be confirmed by the Senate, and that requirement has seldom posed a major hurdle. The Senate rarely rejects nominees to such policy-making positions. Over the course of American history, only about 2 percent have been turned down. Only three such appointments since 1900 have not won confirmation in the Senate; the last one was John Tower, nominated by President Bush to be Secretary of Defense; the second last was Lewis L. Strauss, nominated by President Eisenhower to be Secretary of Commerce in 1959.[8] The overall Senate record in confirming presidential appointees at all levels of the bureaucracy is similar. Table 15–2 provides data from 1975 to 1987. During this period, an average of about 98 percent of the nominations submitted were confirmed.

Presidents have trouble controlling the appointment process. There are three reasons for this: (1) The president's political party has no coherent leadership that can move into governing positions.

TABLE 15–2

Senate Confirmation of Presidential Nominations, 1975–1988

Years	Nominations Proposed	Nominations Confirmed	Percent Confirmed
1975–1976	132,151	131,378	99
1977–1978	137,504	124,730	91
1979–1980	154,797	154,665	99
1981–1982	186,264	184,844	99
1983–1984	97,893	97,262	99
1985–1986	99,614	95,811	96
1987–1988	89,193	88,721	99

Source: Data from the *Congressional Record* for the relevant years.

(2) Some appointees come from lucrative, prestigious jobs outside of government. Some of them may see government service as only a temporary interlude before returning to private life. Their careers are not tied to the success of the president or the political party. (3) Some appointees are picked to pay off political obligations. Loyalty to the president is not their first priority.[9]

Organization charts tell us that department heads are subordinate to the president. The selection process tells us that the relationship is much more complicated. Department heads may be selected because of their ties to other factions of the president's party. They may be chosen because of their links to interest groups that do not share all the president's goals. They may be picked because of their intimacy with key members of Congress. Moreover, close congressional relations may oil their path to success. All these relationships may create cross-pressures. Yet the effective functioning of the administration is related to how these problems are worked out.

> The success of your presidency depends on the views of those who hold the top jobs in your administration. People make policy. And if the key individuals in your government are not dedicated, demonstrated, energetic advocates of your positions on the issues, your views will not prevail.[10]

Conduct of Bureaucrats

The conduct of bureaucrats is influenced by their organizational status, their professional training, their own views and personalities, their relationships with politically selected leaders in the executive branch, and their interactions with members of Congress and interest groups. Yet despite this diversity of influences, several common problems emerge for those in middle and high positions. One is conflict of interest.

Many bureaucrats do rise through the ranks, but the amount of lateral movement between the private sector and the high levels of the executive branch is unusual for Western democracies. Willful corruption may be a statistical rarity, but the loyalties and standards of behavior established in the business community are hard to forget during a brief period of government service. Moreover, if one's career is pointed toward returning to the private sector, it is difficult while in the government to avoid thinking of one's future advantage. In either case, bureaucrats run up against the problem of how to separate their private gain from what is

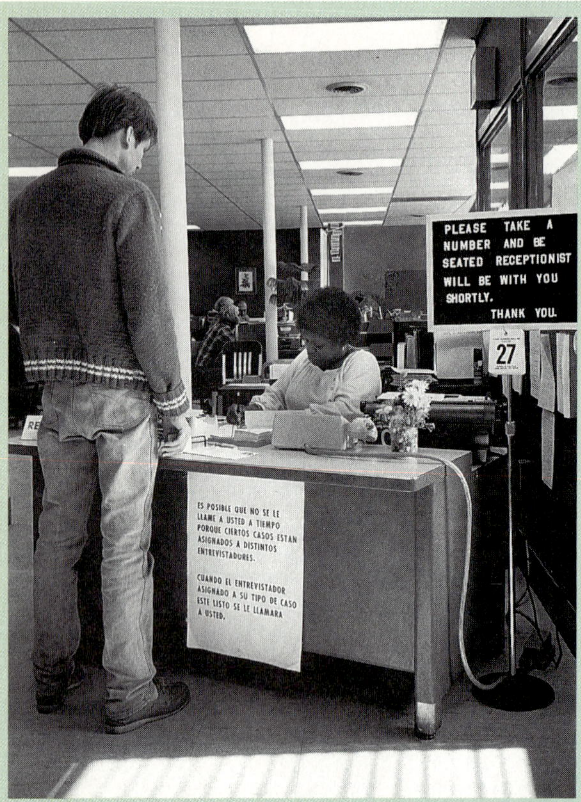

The many demands on government mean a bureaucracy with almost endless formal procedures, like those facing this applicant at a social security office. Programs such as old-age assistance, old-age survivors' disability insurance, unemployment compensations, and aid to families with dependent children make up the largest single item in the federal budget.

TABLE 15–3

Laws to Promote Ethics in Government

- Financial disclosure rules for top-level officials in the executive branch, federal judges, members of Congress, and nominees to top-level positions in the executive branch.
- Establishment of an Office of Government Ethics to set rules and regulations concerning conflict-of-interest and other ethical problems and to monitor compliance with federal ethics laws.
- Restrictions on federal officials who leave government service—including their lobbying efforts on matters in which they had a substantial interest while on the government payroll.
- Mechanisms for the appointment of special prosecutors to investigate allegations of corruption against high-level government officials.
- Rules requiring the reporting of any gifts valued above a specified amount of money.

presumed to be the public interest. The Reagan administration was hounded by this problem. More than 100 high-level officials, including some very prominent in the administration, faced probes questioning whether their actions had violated standards of ethical conduct prescribed in law. Table 15–3 lists some current laws regulating ethics in government.

Government service as an interlude in a private career has come under special scrutiny as it affects relations within the bureaucracy. Leadership often requires knowledge and expertise. These are hard to come by for political appointees who at the subcabinet level stay in government for only about 18 months on the average.

Structure of the Bureaucracy

The executive branch is a complex structure; it has been called a monster. Some 75 units are arranged with clarity only on paper (see Figure 15–3).

There are 14 departments headed by officials who form the president's cabinet. These departments, created by acts of Congress, are headed by a single person appointed by the president and confirmed by the Senate. Each department deals with a wide range of government activity.

The independent regulatory commissions are outside the regular executive departments. The president selects the members (usually between 5 and 11), who must be confirmed by the Senate. Unlike department heads, commissioners serve for

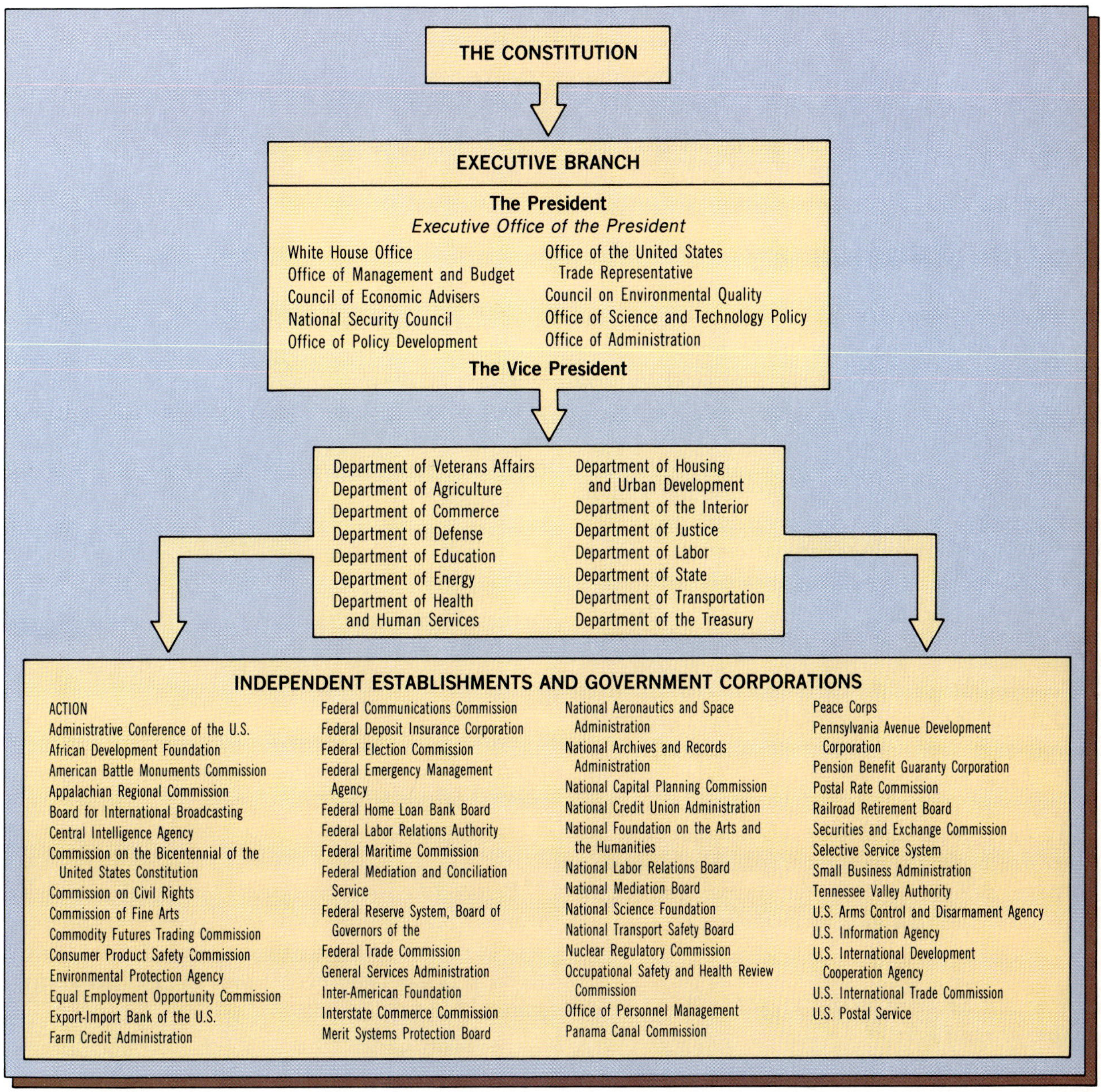

Figure 15–3 Executive branch. This chart tries to show only the more important agencies of government in 1988.

a fixed term and cannot be fired at the pleasure of the president. Some of the major commissions are the Interstate Commerce Commission, the Federal Trade Commission, the Securities and Exchange Commission, and the Federal Communications Commission.

These agencies set rules for the sectors of the economy they regulate. They also bring charges against violators. The agencies exist because the economy is so large and complex that Congress and regular executive agencies cannot keep up with daily problems and needs; also, they cannot rule

"Perspectives"

On the Bureaucracy

"*Bureaucrats favor cutting red tape lengthwise. . . . [I'm for] busing some of the bureaucrats in Washington out into the country to meet the real people.*"

—Ronald Reagan

"*The President does not strictly speaking 'run the government.' He makes the key decisions, but the Government is 'run' in the departments and agencies.*"

—Aide to Edwin Meese, III, former White House counselor

"*Reorganization of the Government is like cutting the Federal Budget. Everybody is for it in general as long as it doesn't affect them specifically.*"

—Walter Mondale

"*We have no discipline in this bureaucracy. We never fire anybody. We never reprimand anybody. We never demote anybody. We always promote the sons-of-bitches that kick us in the ass.*"

—Richard Nixon

"*It would be good if the President fired a few people around here.*"

—A senior Carter White House aide

"*The Treasury is so large and far-flung and ingrained in its practices that I find it almost impossible to get the action and results I want. But the Treasury is not to be compared with the State Department. You should go through the experience of trying to get any changes in the thinking, policy, and action of the career diplomats and then you'd know what a real problem was. But the Treasury and State Departments put together are nothing compared with the Navy. To change anything in the Navy is like punching a feather bed. You punch it with your right and you punch it with your left until you are finally exhausted, and then you find the damn bed just as you left it before you started punching.*"

—Franklin D. Roosevelt

"*I thought I was the President, but when it comes to these bureaucracies, I can't make them do a damn thing.*"

—Harry S Truman

"*Bundy and I get more done in one day than they do in six months at State. The State Department is a bowl full of jelly.*"

—John F. Kennedy

"*Before I became president, I realized and I was warned that dealing with the federal bureaucracy would be one of the worst problems I would have to face. It has been even worse than I had anticipated.*"

—Jimmy Carter

Sources: Quoted in Theo Lippman, Jr., "Reagan Wit Ranked High," *Pittsburgh Press,* March 27, 1982, p. B3; Steven R. Weisman, "The President as Chairman of the Board," *New York Times National Economic Survey,* January 10, 1982, p. 24; *New York Times,* March 2, 1979, p. A11; Nixon and a Carter aide quoted in Thomas E. Cronin, *The State of the Presidency,* 2d ed. (Boston: Little, Brown, 1980), p. 223; Roosevelt, Truman, Kennedy, and Carter quoted in G. Calvin MacKenzie, "Personnel Appointment Strategies in Post-War Presidential Administrations," paper delivered at the annual meeting of the Midwest Political Science Association, Chicago, April 24, 1980.

free from partisan and electoral considerations. Independent regulatory agencies were designed to remove important areas of policy making and adjudication from the direct control of the president and the Congress, the most obviously political branches of the government. The desire to insulate commission activities from the political process is reflected in the structure and procedures of the commissions. Whether that can be achieved is less certain. Experience with the actual operation of the commissions gives mixed evidence.

Government corporations are agencies that administer business enterprises and generate revenue. They are formed to handle such activities as insuring bank deposits (Federal Deposit Insurance Corporation, FDIC) and delivering mail (U.S. Postal Service).

About 50 other agencies complete the picture. These include units such as the Board for International Broadcasting, Selective Service System, Office of Personnel Management, and the Railroad Retirement Board.

Departments and agencies vary greatly in size. Table 15–4 shows the largest departments. In contrast, the Arms Control and Disarmament Agency has about 200 employees, the American Battle Monuments Commission has about 400, the Railroad Retirement Board has about 1600, and the Selective Service System has about 300.

George Bush introduces his new chief of staff. John Sununu, former New Hampshire governor, was a close friend and political associate. Although Sununu lacked Washington experience, his appointment pleased conservative Republicans. They wanted assurance that their interests would be defended in President Bush's inner circle.

TABLE 15–4

Civilian Employees in the National Government: The Five Largest Departments in the Executive Branch, 1986

Department	Number of Employees
Defense	1,067,974
Treasury	135,628
Health and Human Services	133,842
Agriculture	113,147
Interior	73,980

Source: Data from the *Statistical Abstract of the United States 1988*, p. 310.

Matters of structure are frequently matters of politics. Proposals to create a new cabinet-level department such as Veterans Affairs or to abolish a department such as Education seldom stem from abstract theories of administration. Departments and agencies are created, transferred, combined, or dissolved mainly for political, policy, or ideological reasons.

Coordination of the Executive Branch

In the last 50 years, two developments have been paramount: the greater scope and complexity of modern government and the increasing importance of foreign policy. Presidents have responded by creating full-time coordinating staffs to work directly for them. In 1939 a labyrinth of offices called the Executive Office of the President (EOP) came into being. Figure 15–4 shows the structure of the EOP in 1988. The White House Office contains some of the president's closest advisers. Its structure is shown in Figure 15–5.

The EOP now has some 1500 employees, the White House Office some 400. Assisting the president and coordinating the activities of the executive branch requires a lot of people, time, and effort. Why is this the case?

Difficulties in Coordination—Why?

The president needs the executive office for help that does not come readily from the regular bureaucracy. Why that is the case requires careful analysis of the complex and ambivalent relations between the chief executive and the federal bureaucracy. The consequences that flow from these relationships also require attention.

How bureaucrats are selected and the structure in which they work give some hints of the need for coordination. Presidents think their popular election means their programs should be accepted and implemented. Some bureaucrats, along with Congress and interest groups, do not agree. The president's desire for loyalty was expressed by John Ehrlichman, a top aide to President Nixon. In describing Nixon's new appointees for his second term, he was reported to have said: "When we say jump, they will only ask, how high?" [11]

Size of the Bureaucracy. The obstacles to an executive branch marching in unison behind the president are many. Sheer size is one. Some 3 million persons of diverse backgrounds and experience are hard to bring together. The size of the bureaucracy frequently leads to slowness and difficulty in coordination; on occasion, it results in total confusion. Thus, in the Reagan administration, Secretary Samuel R. Pierce, Jr., of the Department of Housing and Urban Development met with assembled members of his department to answer their questions.

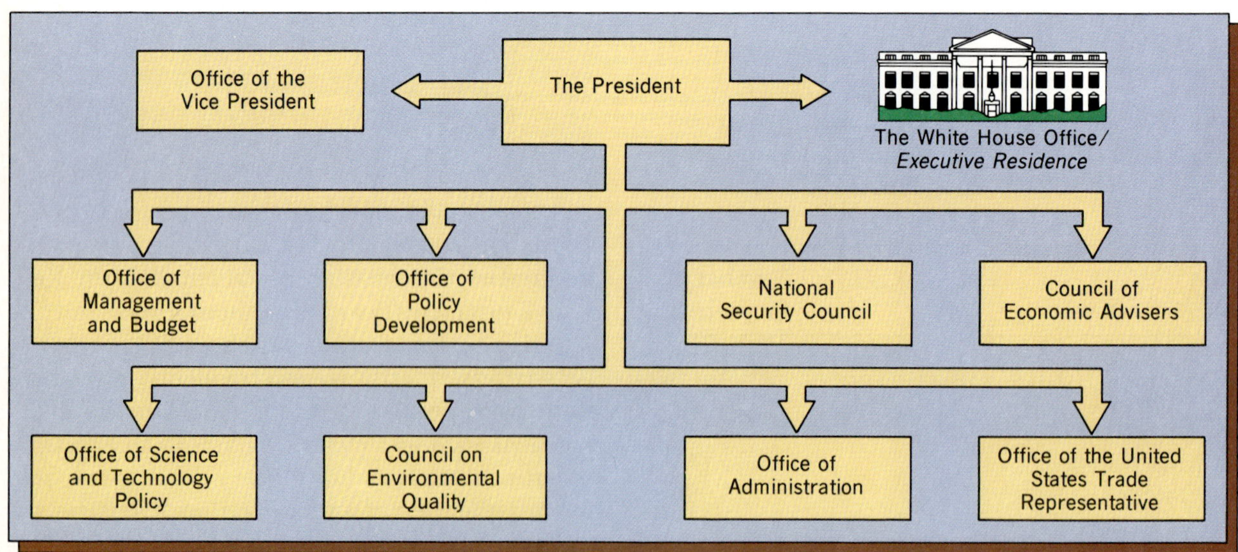

Figure 15–4 Executive office of the president.

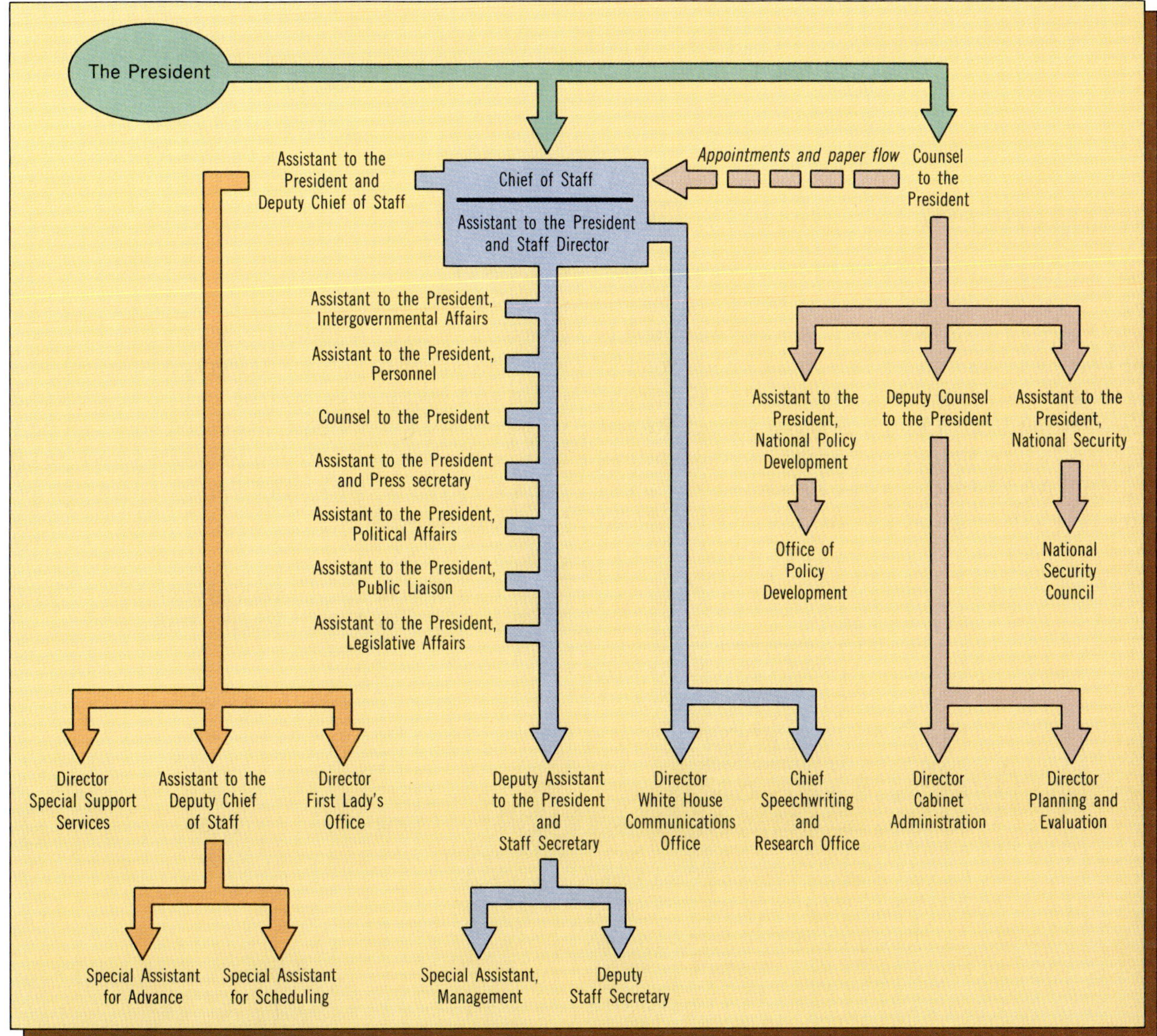

Figure 15–5 White House office.

When time ran out, he promised to answer in writing any remaining questions submitted. Shortly thereafter, an employee received a memo directing him to prepare answers for the secretary. The employee in sorting through the questions found that he himself had submitted two of them.[12]

Bureaucratic Diversity. Diversity is a second factor. Differing units in the bureaucracy have their own interests and agendas. Each thinks its work is vital. Each seek to maintain the status quo or to push its priorities higher on the executive agenda. R. Douglas Arnold argues that for some agencies the main goal is to preserve the budgets; serving the public interest is a lesser goal.[13] This possibility is promoted because it is often difficult to know what the public interest actually is. Reasonable persons can disagree on what that crucial but elusive concept means. In conflicts between concrete, more

Independent Regulatory Commissions

The independent regulatory agencies in the executive branch have the power to set the rules for broad sectors of the economy. Among the oldest is the Federal Communications Commission. Created in 1934, well before the media became a dominant force in political life, it was assigned additional regulatory jurisdiction under the Communications Satellite Act of 1962. As just a sample of its activities, the FCC regulates both AM and FM radio stations and television stations, and it issues construction permits, operating licenses, renewals, and transfers. It also regulates common carrier communications by telephone, telegraph, satellite, and radio and oversees compliance with the laws and with commission policies. Its seven commissioners now oversee some 2000 employees in six regional offices. Here are some other independent regulatory commissions.

Commission	Year Created	Employees—March 1988
Consumer Product Safety Commission	1972	522
Environmental Protection Agency	1970	13,367
Equal Employment Opportunity Commission	1965	3,253
Federal Trade Commission	1914	1,036
Interstate Commerce Commission	1887	719
Securities and Exchange Commission	1934	2,050

Source: U.S. Office of Personnel Management, *Federal Civilian Workforce Statistics, Employment and Trends,* March 1988, pp. 27–29.

precise interests and vaguely defined, more general goals, bureaucrats often tilt toward the specific. The rule is simple: Not everything can be a top priority. The result is conflict over attention and resources. Survival means jobs, income, status, and program promotion.

Complex Issues. The effects of diversity are reinforced by the complexity of issues and their administration. Questions of barriers to foreign trade may involve the Defense, State, Commerce, and Treasury Departments as well as other agencies. In his message to Congress of March 25, 1971, President Nixon pointed out that 29 departments and agencies of the federal government were involved in educational matters, 15 departments and agencies dealt with health, 3 departments handled water resources, and federal recreation areas were administered by 6 agencies in 3 departments. Inertia, protecting one's turf, and conflict are the almost inevitable results. One report noted that in 1982 federal rules governing the ingredients in pizza filled about 40 pages of government documents with some 310 regulations.

Cross Pressures. How bureaucrats are selected may push them away from exclusive concern with presidential priorities. Bureaucrats may want to help and cooperate with the president, but that is not likely to be their first priority. Protection of their jobs, programs, and agencies may supersede loyalty to the president.

Even the president's appointees are subject to these considerations. Heads of departments need cooperation from their subordinates to be effective. If presidential priorities do not match department ambitions, problems arise. As Shirley Hufstedler, secretary of education in the Carter administration, put it:

> Enormous problems of budget, organization, legislation, and regulation will confront you constantly. Each problem will be worthy of your undivided attention, but none will ever get it. You must keep all of these balls in the air at the same time, or one of them is sure to hit you on the head. While you juggle, you must contend with hundreds of interest groups, ranging from advocates for more sex education to those who are horrified at what children are already being taught.
>
> All the while, you must obey, simultaneously, the President, the Congress and the courts—even when they are moving in different directions. And you must explain to the nation, through the media, what it is that you are doing and why on earth it is necessary.[14]

James Watt, Secretary of the Interior under Ronald Reagan, quickly came under fire for his extreme conservative views on the environment (and other issues). Later, critics alleged his involvement in influence peddling for federal housing programs. Ethical concerns about the Department of Housing and Urban Development continued during the Bush administration.

President Nixon appointed Robert Finch to be secretary of health, education, and welfare because he expected Finch, a close personal and political associate, to place strict controls on spending. Finch, in turn, was caught in a cross-fire between his desire to serve the president and his interest in promoting sound programs. The pressure became so intense that he resigned after 18 months.

Cabinet members may disagree not only with the president or their own subordinates but also with their peers. Each department head has an interest in protecting his or her department. Thus, the perspectives of the secretary of defense and the secretary of state may differ on issues such as nuclear disarmament, military and economic aid to other nations, and policy toward Israel. These differences are to be fully expected. How and from where one approaches a problem affect one's analysis and conclusions.

Mismatched Incentives. The president, his immediate advisers, the heads of the executive departments, and the bureaucrats seek to serve the public interest, administration interests, department or agency interests, ideological interests, and individual interests. General incentives will be similar for all of these groups; specific incentives are not. In fact, there may be many sharp differences be-

tween presidents and civil servants. For the president and those around him, the short run is vital. Creating symbolic satisfaction may be as important as solving problems. The appearance of problem solving may indeed replace actually addressing a problem.

Bureaucrats have a variety of incentives, but only a few of them can lead to support for the president's priorities. The time frame for many bureaucrats is the long run. Their primary concern may be problem solving rather than the outcome of the next election. Programs in most departments and agencies have been developed over a long period of time. Most bureaucrats will still be at their jobs whatever the result of the next election. And their programs will still be operating. These differences in perspective can be vital. Presidents and top officials in the executive branch want quick, visible results—for which they can take credit. Bureaucrats may not be concerned primarily with either aim. The answers that *they* seek may sometimes be for altogether different problems.

Thus, serious, hardworking people trying to do their best may generate conflict because their visions of what is appropriate, necessary, and timely may not match.

Cross-pressures and inefficiencies of size, complexity, and diversity are not isolated problems; they may be the norm on a wide range of issues. To these problems must be added an open political culture, one which assumes that having many individuals and groups with access to most elements in the political process is a desirable situation. This can lead to many different organizations trying to influence different parts of the government, to a system of weak political parties, and to institutional fragmentation. The president and the Congress do not always speak with one voice because they may represent differing elements in the society. The framers of the Constitution intended to build executive-legislative conflict into the political process. In this respect, they succeeded brilliantly.

How Presidents Try to Coordinate: The Executive Office of the President

If the president cannot count on support and coordination, where can he get help to correlate advice and information from diverse sources and where can he get objective advice? The answer of every president in the last 50 years has been the Executive office of the President and his own advisers in the White House Office. The growth of these units mirrors the need of presidents for help in achieving their goals.

The EOP consists of units such as the White House Office, the Office of Management and Budget, the Council of Economic Advisers, the National Security Council, and the Office of Policy Development. In 1988 the executive office had about 1600 employees.

The White House Office serves the president directly. The staff helps the president communicate with congressional leaders and individual members, heads of executive programs and agencies, the media, and the public. A president's most visible

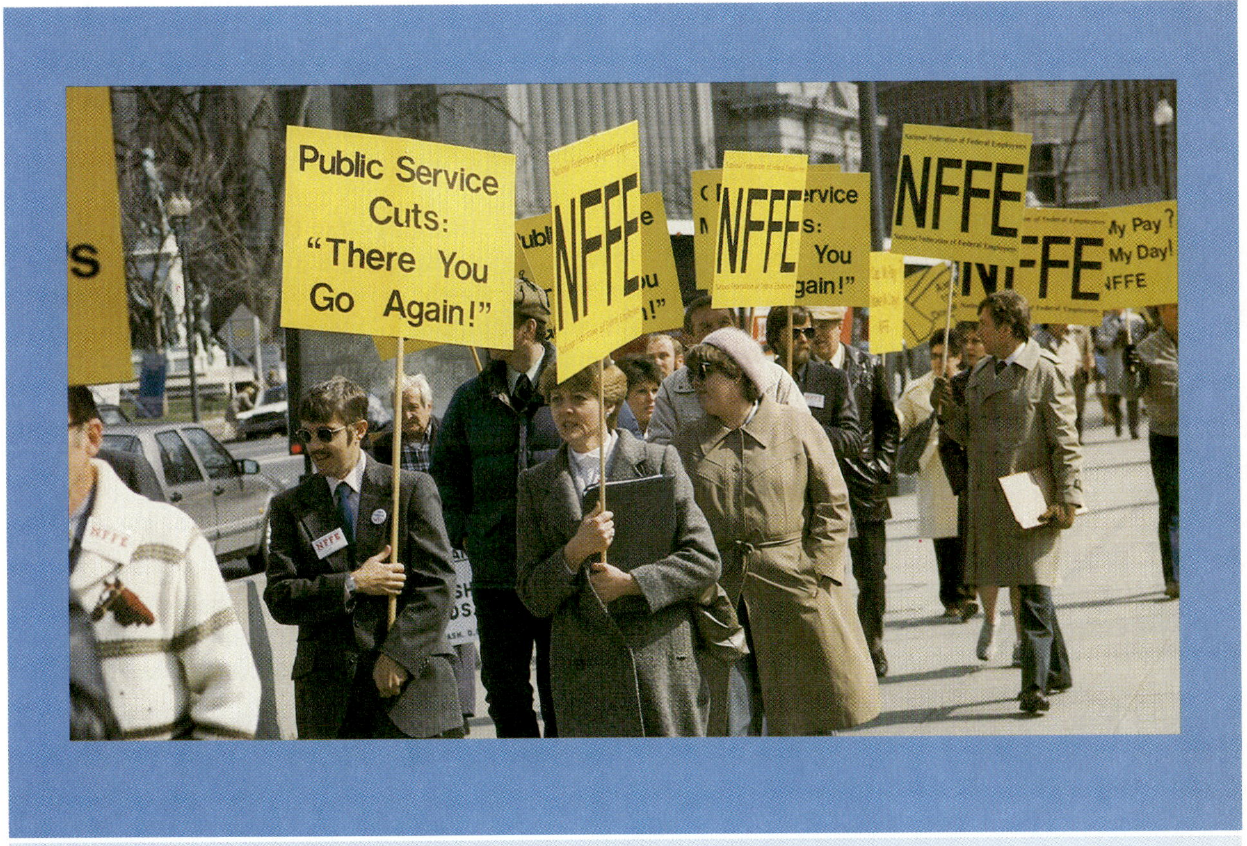

Whenever government tries to spend less, programs are hurt—and so are individuals. Here government workers march to protest the Reagan budget cuts. Programs create their own support. Some become so entrenched that it is all but impossible to reduce spending on them.

David Stockman, Ronald Reagan's energetic Director of the Budget. Stockman provided ideas and energy that helped drive a new economic agenda through Congress. Later Stockman, who had returned to Wall Street, wrote a book revealing that the programs were based on questionable assumptions, but to many he still stood for the struggle to control the growth of government.

advisers are likely to be here. In the first Reagan administration, top advisers such as Edwin Meese III, Michaeal Deaver, and James A. Baker III worked in the White House Office. In the second Reagan administration, the White House Office was the official home of Donald Regan and Howard Baker. Following the 1988 presidential election, President Bush moved to select his top assistants. Included were Richard G. Darman, Brent Scowcroft, and John H. Sununu.

As James Pfiffner puts it, "No one questions that the modern presidency needs an active White House staff.. . . the president cannot operate without a staff to protect his political interests and keep the administration focused on the central agenda." [15]

The Office of Management and Budget reviews government structures and procedures with an eye toward improving them. It promotes cooperation and coordination among executive departments and agencies. It supervises budget preparation and implementation. It compiles and assesses department advice on proposed legislation. It seeks to help the president determine whether program objectives have been met. Overall, it promotes the president's priorities in policy development and implementation.

The Council of Economic Advisers has three members. It analyzes the national economy and advises the president on how changes relate to his programs. The council recommends policies to promote both a stable economy and economic growth.

The National Security Council helps the president integrate foreign policy with defense and domestic policy. Its membership, established by law, includes the vice president, the secretary of state, and the secretary of defense. The chairman of the Joint Chiefs of Staff and the director of the Central Intelligence Agency advise the council in their areas.

The Office of Policy Development was a new name in the Reagan administration for the president's domestic policy staff. Among its functions are coordination of domestic policy options and review of major domestic policies.

Presidents have used the Executive Office of the President to achieve coordination and control through at least four means:

1. Formulating and presenting a coordinated budget to Congress.
2. Presenting a legislative program to Congress that represents the administration's efforts, rather than those of individual departments.
3. Monitoring the implementation of legislation from a presidential perspective.
4. Centralizing regulatory activity.

Coordination Through the Budget. A complex process of coordinating executive budget proposals takes place each year. In 1921, Congress passed the Budget and Accounting Act. The president is

Continuity & CHANGE

The Cabinet

The expansion of federal governmental activities over two centuries is clearly reflected in the growth in size of the president's cabinet. Here is how the cabinet stood in three administrations, with the year of establishment of each cabinet-level department.

The Commerce and Labor Departments, established in 1913, were originally created as a single Department of Commerce and Labor in 1903. The Defense Department was consolidated in 1949 from separate Departments of War and the Navy. And the Departments of Education and of Health and Human Services were created from the single department of Health, Education and Welfare established in 1953. Promoting an agency to cabinet-level status, as with the Veterans Affairs Department in 1989, can gain political support for a president, his political party, or for a set of issues. Attempting to abolish a department can yield the same result or, at times, backfire on a president. The departments of education and energy still exist despite President Reagan's stated desire to abolish them. The political reality of Washington is that a president cannot always get what he wants—either in terms of public policy or in the organization of the executive branch.

President Abraham Lincoln	President Woodrow Wilson	President George Bush
State (1789)	State	State
Treasury (1789)	Treasury	Treasury
Attorney General (1789)	Justice (renamed, 1870)	Justice
War (1789)	War	} Defense (1949)
Navy (1798)	Navy	
Interior (1849)	Interior	Interior
	Agriculture (1889)	Agriculture
	Commerce (1913)	Commerce
	Labor (1913)	Labor
		Housing and Urban Development (1965)
		Transportation (1966)
		Energy (1977)
		Education (1979)
		Health and Human Services (1979)
		Veterans Affairs (1989)

required to submit an "executive budget" to Congress. The Bureau of the Budget, the predecessor of the Office of Management and Budget, originally coordinated the requests from executive departments and agencies. Since money is frequently the key to policy, the authority to coordinate budget requests is no trivial grant.

Each department and agency proposes a budget to achieve its goals. But when these requests are added up, the total is always too high. Decisions must be made about which proposals to support. That difficult task falls initially to the Office of Management and Budget (OMB). Only a few of the most critical decisions reach the president's desk. The OMB, sometimes with the president's advisers, does the rest.

In the Reagan administration, OMB was used perhaps to an unprecedented degree to coordinate efforts to impose budget cuts on the executive departments. The administration succeeded at first, but its widely publicized manipulation of the budgetary process contributed to later congressional resistance. Several administration budgets presented to Congress after 1981 were pronounced "dead on arrival." The price of more administration budgetary coordination and control may have been less credibility afterward.

Further frustrating administration attempts to use coordination to achieve policy objectives is that so much of the budget, about 75 percent, is relatively uncontrollable in any one year. That is because much of the money had previously been committed. Benefits have been authorized, contracts have been made, and interest on the national debt must be paid.

Coordination Through Program Clearance. Coordinating executive department and agency proposals for policy is no simple task. The OMB helps in several ways. It reviews department reports to Congress on proposed or pending legislation. It reviews agency proposals to see if they are "in accord with the program of the president." It advises the president on whether to sign or veto a certain bill sent by Congress. Until the 1960s, central clearance was done largely within the Bureau of the Budget (now OMB). Beginning with the Kennedy administration (1961–1963), the White House staff began to play a more central role in the clearance of major items. Clearing more routine items remains in the Office of Management and Budget.

Centralizing Regulatory Activity. Presidents since the administration of Richard Nixon have attempted to bring some measure of coordination into the regulatory activities of the executive departments and agencies. Presidents Nixon and Carter contributed especially to this trend. However, it was the Reagan administration that made such attempts a central tool in reducing the scope and number of federal regulations. Coordination became a rather obvious means for promoting policy preferences.

Coordination Through Program Implementation. If presidential programs are to be effective, they need to be coordinated in implementation as well as formulation. But this is difficult. A shortage of White House time and energy, political constraints, and low political payoffs force more attention on creating programs. Thus, there are incentives for presidents and their top advisers to do something else. Stephen Wayne describes this problem:

> The president has a management dilemma. The government is simply too large and too complex for the chief executive and a few personal aides to run it alone. That is why there are departments and agencies. But how can these departments and agencies be kept responsive to the president's interests and needs? In the policy-making sphere, the answer seems to lie in the influence of sizable presidential staffs and agencies and centralized coordinating and clearing processes. In the policy implementation sphere, the staffs are not nearly as involved or as influential and the processes not nearly as centralized nor controlling. How to oversee the executive branch without overinvolving the White House and OMB and without overwhelming the departments and agencies is a critical problem that every contemporary president has and will continue to face.[16]

Coordination Through Structural Change. Some students of government policy in the area of science have long despaired over the confusion and disarray displayed by the government. Problems relating to science and technology arise in almost every department, but they are perhaps most prominent in seven major units: the Department of Commerce, the Department of Health and Human Services, the Department of Energy, the National Science Foundation, the National Oceanic and Atmospheric Administration, the Bureau of Standards, and the National Aeronautics and Space Administration.

Proposals to improve coordination surface intermittently. In the mid-1980s the argument was over whether to create a cabinet-level department of science and technology. Discussion of this proposal uncovered serious disputes over coordination and control and exposed the intimate relationships among structure, interests, and public policy. What some see as a useful reform, others see as a power grab or a distortion of priorities. The links between structure and policy tend to remain obscure until major proposals for structural change begin to gain attention. Then, the truth emerges. Structural change, insiders come to realize, really involve arguments about public policy and political power.

Coordination and Control

Problems of coordination are closely related to problems of control. The ability of an administration to control the bureaucracy is limited. White House aide Michael Balzano offered in 1972 an extreme but partially correct assessment:

> President Nixon doesn't run the bureaucracy; the civil service and the unions do. It took him three years to find out what was going on in the bureaucracy. And God forbid if any President is defeated after the first term, because then the bureaucracy has another three years to play games with the next President.[17]

In the few matters to which the president and his advisers give top priority, they are more likely to get their way. Such items, though, cover only a tiny part of total bureaucratic activity.

Efforts at control are also inhibited because each cabinet member faces limits in dealing with his or her own unit. (1) Most members of the cabinet do not control the jurisdiction of their agency, its structure, the appropriations they receive, or the selection of personnel within their agency. (2) Subordinates have networks of political supporters. They are tied to congressional committees and subcommittees, individual members of Congress, and interest groups. On matters of importance to them, they are not easily moved. (3) New appointees and even those with some experience have limited knowledge of how a department operates. The tenure of top executive branch officials averages less than two years. This always means relative inexperience at the top. (4) Department heads have dual obligations. They must support the president *and* promote the programs of their departments. If a president advocates programs that a department judges to be undesirable, the secretary's life becomes complicated. (5) Department heads are regularly undercut by the Executive Office of the President. Its sole concern is working for the president; it does not have to deal daily with the problems of individual departments.

Every president faces the same problems. But some encounter more difficulty than others. Richard Nixon, in nearly two terms, tried to assert more control over the executive branch. He abandoned the idea of a cabinet with balanced political interests for one populated by loyalists. He paid more attention than most presidents to getting "his people" appointed to subcabinet positions. He reorganized the Executive Office of the President. He tried to cope with diversity by appointing supersecretaries for domestic affairs. He withheld funds for entire programs of which he disapproved. In brief, he wanted more control over not only large policy matters but also daily government operations. The events connected with Watergate reduced his ability. But well before that, President Nixon had expressed his frustration with the bureaucracy.[18]

President Reagan made an even stronger effort through sharp funding cuts, personnel reductions,

Federal Spending and the Bureaucracy

It is commonly assumed that the president and Congress make a great deal of difference in establishing budgetary priorities and in shifting governmental spending patterns. But an examination of three typical departments reveals far more stability than change in spending. Budgets for three important departments—Defense, Agriculture, and Housing and Urban Development—are listed below over three decades. The dollar amounts spent by each department, of course, have increased dramatically. Yet the proportion of total federal outlays spent by each department (in parentheses) has remained remarkably consistent over a 30-year period. Does that mean that the bureaucracy is out of control? One exception is the reduction in the proportion of the budget devoted to the Pentagon after 1970; throughout the 1960s, the defense budget was abnormally high due to the Vietnam War involvement.

	Defense	Agriculture	Housing and Urban Development
1965	$ 51,371 (43.5%)	$ 6,940 (5.9%)	$ 492 (0.4%)
1970	$ 84,187 (43.1%)	$ 8,412 (4.3%)	$ 2,432 (1.2%)
1975	$ 93,148 (28.0%)	$15,556 (4.7%)	$ 7,512 (2.3%)
1980	$146,073 (24.8%)	$34,785 (5.9%)	$12,735 (2.2%)
1985	$263,924 (27.9%)	$55,523 (5.9%)	$28,720 (3.0%)
1990 (estimate)	$322,295 (28.1%)	$48,199 (4.2%)	$22,555 (2.0%)

Figures in millions of dollars.

Source: Executive Office of the President: Office of Management and Budget. *Historical Tables, Budget of the United States Government, Fiscal Year 1989* (Washington, D.C.: U.S. Government Printing Office, 1988).

close monitoring of the process for making political appointments, increased use of OMB, more stress on coordinating mechanisms, and, overall, an emphasis on "control from the top." Edwin Meese, then counselor to President Reagan, assessed the administration's situation as follows: (1) 10 to 20 percent of bureaucrats will oppose the administration generally and have to be politically isolated; (2) 10 to 20 percent will be eager to serve a president with Reagan's ideas; and (3) the rest will do what they are told.

A Reagan appointee to the Labor Department

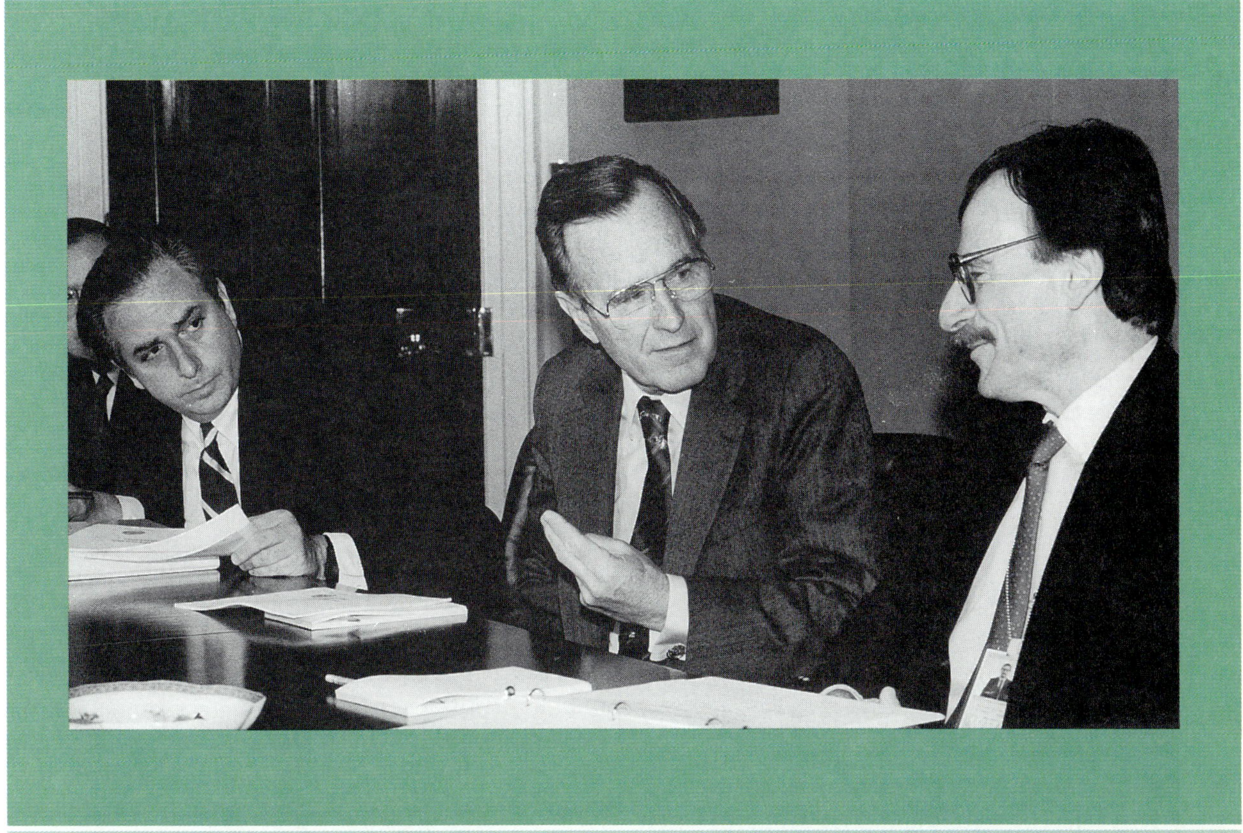

Like his predecessors, President Bush was faced with the task of promoting his program not just in Congress, but in the executive as well. On the budget, he relied on a working group that included Budget Director Richard Darman, at left, and Michael Boskin, chairman of the Council of Economic Advisors. Budget problems now dominate presidential agendas.

saw his problem this way: "I can't trust advice from a dedicated government activist when we're trying to curb programs." [19]

Any president, and especially one who seeks major changes, finds some foot-dragging and hostility in the bureaucracy. In the Reagan administration, lawyers in the Civil Rights Division of the Department of Justice protested against attempts to gain tax exemptions for segregated schools. The administration, in effect, told them to support the president or quit. Most of them were protected from being fired by civil service regulations; they chose to continue in their positions and still protest.

Newly elected President George Bush indicated even before he assumed the presidency that he would be more of a "hands-on" president than was Ronald Reagan. Each president faces similar problems; each reacts in his own way.

One example of the problem in coordinating the executive branch is helpful. Historically, the Department of State has played a central role in advising the president on foreign policy. President Woodrow Wilson had Colonel House as a personal adviser, and President Franklin Roosevelt used Harry Hopkins. The growth of substantial White House concern with coordination dates from after World War II and especially from the Kennedy administration. Then presidential advisers began to play a central role in formulating foreign policy. The inevitable result is controversy between the

State Department and White House foreign policy advisers over creating and implementing foreign policy.

Some of these conflicts arise from differences over policy; some come from battles over status and access to the president; and some result from clashes of perspective: For national security advisers in the White House, the job is seen as promoting the president's foreign policy program as part of his overall objectives, both foreign and domestic. For the State Department, the main concern is understanding and improving our relations with other countries. Most recent administrations have begun with the desire to minimize this conflict. Most end by trying to live with what is called "this inherent conflict." [20]

Leslie Gelb, who served in the Department of State, assesses the problems of coordination in foreign policy:

> There are two iron laws that govern relations between the White House, on the one hand, and the State Department and the Defense Department on the other. The first is that things won't work well with a strong national security advisor to the President. The second is that without a strong advisor, things won't work at all.[21]

Every president must find ways to coordinate and at times control the bureaucracy. Yet, experts on bureaucracy remind us:

> One of the major functions, in short, of the permanent apparatus is to serve presidents by helping them avoid stupid mistakes that threaten their political viability. The urge to command and to centralize often fails to recognize that political impulses should be subjected to tests of sobriety.[22]

Congress further complicates the picture. Like the executive branch leadership, Congress possesses potential weapons to influence bureaucrats. Congress provides the basic structure, funds, and program authority for the executive branch. This massive legal authority over the bureaucracy and the bureaucrats encourages members of Congress to see that the structure works and to check whether policy is implemented faithfully and money is spent efficiently and wisely. Partisan motives may push members of Congress to act when the president is of the opposite political party. Hostility to particular administration policies may stimulate congressional interest in particular examples of implementation. Constituent pressures may push in the same direction. A member of Congress whose district or politically significant parts of it are affected by bureaucratic activity finds strong reasons to develop an interest. What matters then is where the member of Congress is situated. Committee and subcommittee assignments shape the member's behavior.

The conflicts that develop are not always between the president and Congress as a whole; Congress is specialized, as is the executive branch. No member of Congress can perform all his or her tasks, for the job is just too big. So specialization and division of labor are guaranteed. From these, a measure of reciprocity follows. In all but the most unusual cases, members of Congress will look for cues about what to do from those of their colleagues who know more about what is going on in a particular situation. Key committees and subcommittees often play a decisive role in dealing with policy implementation in a department or agency. Day-to-day contacts and discussions are usually between the relevant committees and subcommittees of the Congress, their staffs, and the relevant departments, bureaus, or agencies in the executive branch. On most issues, most of the time, most members of Congress and top-level administrators in the executive branch are not involved. So interest groups concentrate their attention on persons and units in both branches who they think will make a difference in achieving their purposes.

"Cozy triangles," "iron triangles," or "whirlpools of power" are formed among those in Congress, the executive branch, and interest groups who maintain continuing concern and activity on a particular subject. These alliances or networks are extraordinarily important in public policy making and implementation. Only on the most controversial issues or those that capture general attention—a small number—do the whirlpools recede in importance (see Chapter 18). And legislative concern with what the bureaucracy does almost inevitably follows. The reasons are legal, political, electoral, ideological, and sometimes personal. What tools does Congress have to control the bureaucracy, how are they used, and with what results?

The ability of any administration to promote efficient and responsible behavior in the bureaucracy may be limited, but there are other forces that work in the same direction. The media can monitor and expose errant behavior in the bureaucracy. Congressional investigations may serve similar ends. The professional standards and ethics of the bureaucrats themselves may contribute, as may the efforts of "whistle-blowers"—bureaucrats who go to Congress, the media, the public, or their own superiors to expose alleged wrongdoing by other bureaucrats.

General societal values, the belief that those who abuse the powers of their office should be exposed, laws providing protections for whistle-blowers, and the political interests of some members of the Congress all seem to encourage the practice. The reality is something different. The protections for whistle-blowers may seem substantial, but their fate has not been a kind one. Because whistle-blowers violate an important bureaucratic norm—do not make the organization look bad—they assume substantial risks.

Moreover, whistle-blowing has its negative side. Peter Drucker states this view clearly and sharply:

> "Whistle-blowing," after all, is simply another word for "informing." And perhaps it is not quite irrelevant that the only societies in Western history that encouraged informers were bloody and infamous tyrannies—Tiberius and Nero in Rome, the Inquisition in the Spain of Philip II, the French Terror, and Stalin.[23]

The government official who by law is required to defend those who blow the whistle advised bureaucrats to work quietly within their organizations and not to publicize their charges. "Unless you're in a position to retire or are independently wealthy, don't do it. Don't put your head up because it will get blown off."[24] The recent experience of even the most visible whistle-blowers seems to confirm the accuracy of this warning.

Elizabeth Dole, Secretary of Labor in the Bush cabinet, greets labor leader Lane Kirkland. Cabinet members end up spending much of their time with groups affected by their departments. Of course, Dole also keeps up with Congress. Her husband, Robert Dole, is Senate Republican leader and was an opponent of George Bush for the presidential nomination in 1988.

The record of governmental abuses, scandals, and poor management revealed by whistle-blowers has been sufficiently impressive to stimulate reactions to attempts at punishing them for going public. Private organizations have sprung up to help guard whistle-blowers against reprisals. Congress is moving in similar directions. Still, the fate of the whistle-blower remains rather precarious. Dissent in and out of government has its price to be paid.

Consequences

What are the consequences of how bureaucrats are selected and the way the bureaucracy is structured? There are sharp limits on the ability of presidents and their advisers to coordinate and control the bureaucracy. Also, bureaucratic inertia is common. During the Cuban missile crisis in 1962, President Kennedy discovered that his previous desires to remove U.S. missile bases from Turkey had not been carried out.

Political responsibility is difficult to pin down if the president does not have full control. Policy and its administration tend to get mixed. Administration in the executive branch is a political art as well as a science. Presidents and those close to them have trouble getting a full and objective picture of events and alternatives.

What is to be done about this? For that matter, can anything be done about it? Should it?

Presidents, students of public administration, pundits, editorial writers, and others tend to think progress is always probable. Attempts to purge personnel, select political appointees more carefully, and get stronger cabinet appointees continue. At times these have some impact, but it is seldom decisive.

Organizational changes such as revitalizing the cabinet, restructuring the Executive Office of the President, and augmenting or reducing the autonomy of the independent regulatory agencies continue to be proposed. Most such ideas have insufficient support and much opposition. The status quo favors certain individuals, groups, and organizations. Those who benefit from this see no point in altering the status quo. Occasional reorganizations such as creating a separate Department of Health, Education, and Welfare in 1953 can make some difference, but the basic reality remains.

Another suggestion is to alter bureaucratic attitudes by broadening concern with the president's program and minimizing parochialism.[25] This is noble, but bureaucratic attitudes do not arise in a vacuum. The pluralism of American society, its fragmented political institutions, and weak political parties push the federal bureaucracy toward its present status. These powerful forces can be channeled somewhat, but they are unlikely to be overcome.

Summary

- Most routine work of government and much of its policy-making activity involve the bureaucracy. Bureaucrats therefore are important cogs in governing. Who they are, how they are organized, and what they do make a great difference.
- The increase in government functions in the last 60 years has been accompanied by growth in the number of executive branch units, the number of government employees, and government expenditures. The increase in size of the bureaucracy, however, is small when compared with the growth of the budget and the U.S. population.
- Despite the organization charts, the president does not have total control of the executive branch. Executive branch size, structure, authority, and financial resources depend on Congress. Both the president and Congress can be deeply involved in bureaucratic activity. Administration thus becomes politicized, not merely a technical activity.
- A new administration can fill very few positions in the executive branch with its own choices. About 90 percent of the personnel are selected by merit systems; therefore, they are not subject to political appointment and removal. This frustrates presidents who wish to institute new policies and programs.
- Even the president's appointees for department heads develop department and agency loyalties. If the president's desires differ from agency or department desires, he cannot count on full support from his own appointees.
- The size, complexity, and diversity of the executive branch create a need for centralized coordination and control. Presidents in the last 50 years have developed coordinating mechanisms in the Executive Office of the President and personal advisers. But no president has

built a completely centralized executive branch.

- Presidents and their advisers gain some control through coordinating the budget sent to Congress, instituting central clearance for department legislative proposals, and monitoring how legislation is implemented in departments and agencies. Still the time and energy of presidents and their advisers are limited. The payoffs in the political arena from these efforts are low. In this context more coordination and control are always possible, but a unified executive branch is not.

Readings on The Bureaucracy

Berman, Larry. 1979. *The Office of Management and Budget and the Presidency, 1921–1979.* Princeton, N.J.: Princeton University Press. Describes the evolution and politicization of the OMB.

Campbell, Colin. 1986. *Managing the Presidency: Carter, Reagan, and the Search for Executive Harmony.* Pittsburgh: University of Pittsburgh Press. A study of the interaction between the president and the federal bureaucracy.

Destler, I. M. 1972. *Presidents, Bureaucrats, and Foreign Policy: The Politics of Organizational Reform.* Princeton, N.J.: Princeton University Press. A study of the federal bureaucracy in foreign policy making.

Fisher, Louis. 1976. *Presidential Spending Power.* Princeton, N.J.: Princeton University Press. Argues that crucial spending decisions are often made by administrative officials rather than by Congress.

Hart, John. 1987. *The Presidential Branch.* New York: Pergamon Press. Considers the complicated problems of presidential staffing.

Heclo, Hugh. 1977. *A Government of Strangers: Executive Politics in Washington.* Washington, D.C.: Brookings Institution. An analysis of relations between bureaucrats and political appointees.

Nathan, Richard P. 1983. *The Administrative Presidency.* New York: John Wiley & Sons. Argues that presidents should play a large role in managing the bureaucracy in order to realize their policy objectives.

Porter, Roger B. 1980. *Presidential Decision Making: The Economic Policy Board.* New York: Cambridge University Press. Describes the structure and operation of an important advisory body during the Ford administration.

Rourke, Francis E., ed. 1985. *Bureaucratic Power in National Policy Making,* 4th ed. Boston: Little, Brown. Readings on the federal bureaucracy.

Seidman, Harold, and Robert Gilmour. 1986. *Politics, Position, and Power: From the Positive to the Regulatory State,* 4th ed. New York: Oxford University Press. Examines the implications for the administration as the government becomes increasingly regulatory.

Chapter 16

The Judiciary

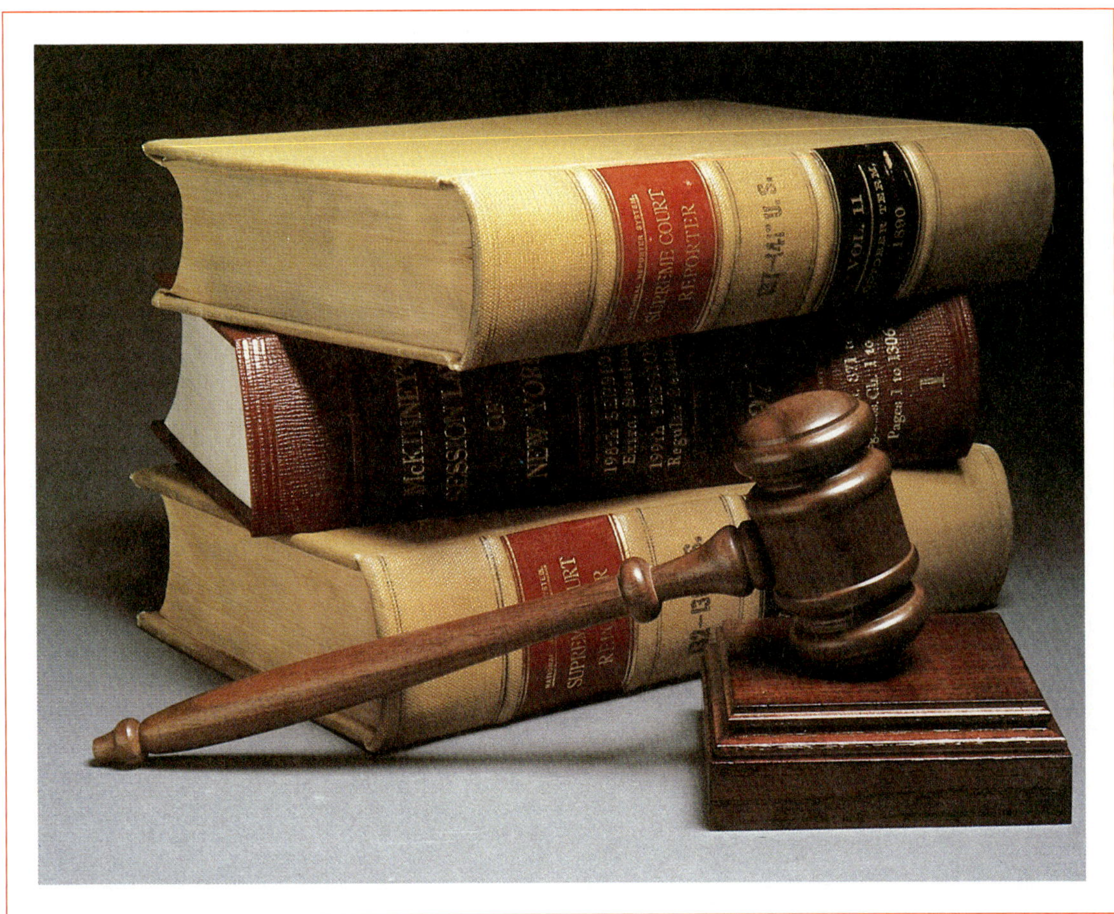
SUPREME COURT
REPORTER
VOL. 11
1890
NEW YORK
Pages 1 to 1306

Sooner or later, Alexis de Tocqueville observed over 150 years ago, in American democracy every issue is taken to court. Propelled by three-quarters of a million lawyers, we are still doing precisely that.[1] Whatever its merits, our reliance on the courts to settle political disputes is a central part of our governmental process.

To understand the political struggle in the United States, we must remember that our system is based on the concept of the separation of powers, modified by checks and balances. At times, these safeguards may seem to exist more in theory than in practice, especially the first. But the separation of powers is an essential and often powerful aspect of our government process. Separation of powers is one of the cardinal characteristics of what many observers have seen as the mysteries of American politics. Arthur Guiterman explains them in these words:

> Providence that watches over children, drunks, and fools,
> With silent miracles and other esoterica,
> Continue to suspend the ordinary rules,
> And take care of the United States of America.[2]

The chief weapon of the government's judicial branch against other branches—to whom the poem may well apply more accurately—at either the national or state level is the power of *judicial review.* The court systems of more than 60 other countries—usually those with a federal government structure—are also supposed to possess this power. Only a few, however, such as in Australia, Canada, and India, actually have it. It does not exist in unitary democratic states such as Britain. Even though their courts can interpret laws and pass judgment, they cannot veto legislative or executive action.

In a court system that possesses the power of judicial review, any court of record, high or low, can decide that any law, or any official action based on it, is unconstitutional and hence unenforceable. It can also decide that a public official's action is illegal, if after careful consideration of past legal decisions the judges decide it goes against the basic law. In our land, this is the *written* Constitution. Of course, judicial review also denotes the *positive* judicial power to uphold government actions, but the power of veto is the more drastic application. By using its power of judicial review, a court applies the superior of two laws. In the American democracy, this means that the written Constitution takes precedence over a law or a decision made by an executive or administrative official. Remembering that fact, we shall look at how the judicial branch of the government is set up, how it works, and who its judges are.

Courts: The Institutional Framework

Most Americans know less about their government's judicial branch than about the other two branches. This is unfortunate, because Americans are turning more and more to the courts to solve problems and settle disputes the legislative and executive branches are unable or unwilling to handle. The legislature has been especially guilty of avoiding public problems (although, of course, to do nothing is also a decision). It has publicly denounced the courts for making the laws instead of passing judgment on them. But the legislature has clearly been eager to "pass the buck." Racial segregation is an obvious example. The American tendency, encouraged by lawyers, to rely on the courts for important decisions has resulted in a glut of court cases. It is a fact of governmental life that will surely continue.

Since our government is a federal one, the 50 states must cooperate with the national government to make, enforce, and interpret the law. Thus, one may explain the American court system as either 2 or 51 separate systems. It is appropriate to think of the federal judiciary as a two-part system; one part is created by the federal Constitution and the other by state constitutions. Each system acts according to its own interpretation of the law.

The Supreme Court exercises its authority over the state courts only when a case in the state court raises a substantial federal question. The Supreme Court itself decides whether the question is indeed important to the nation and whether its "federal" nature is "substantial." Those who bring a case to federal court must first have tried every possible

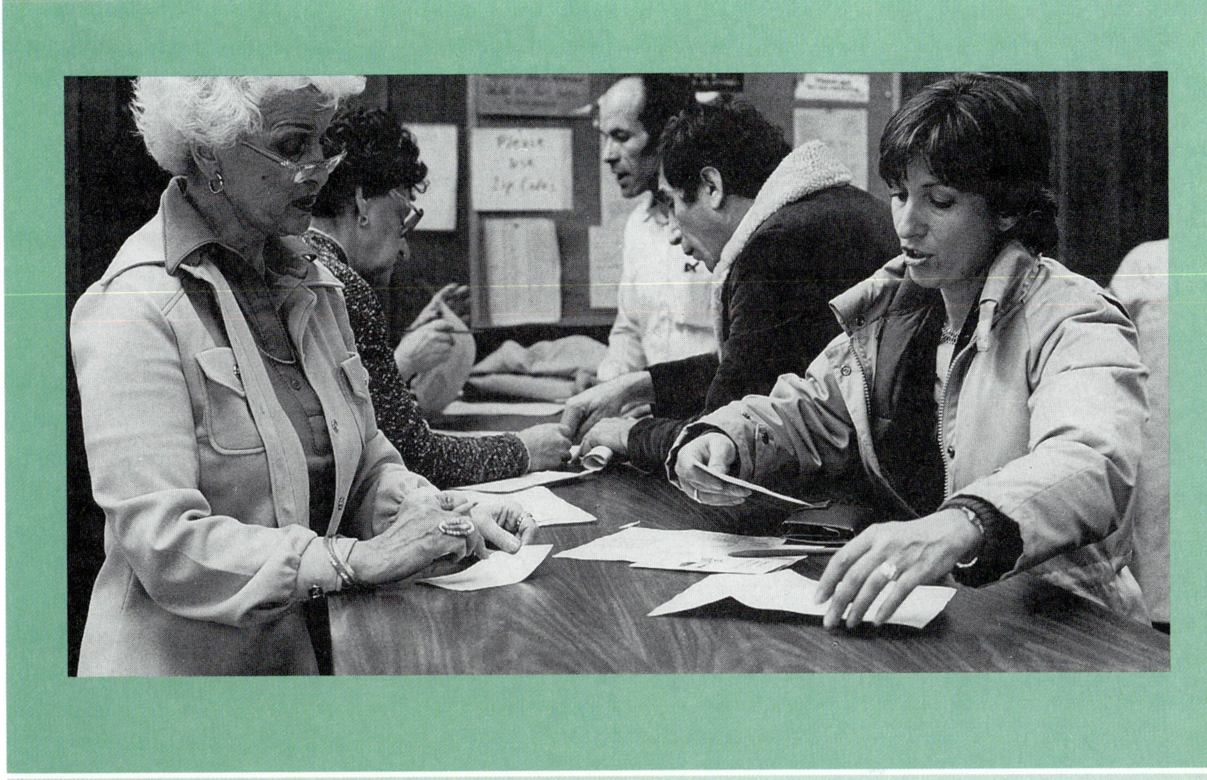

Americans today are increasingly demanding their day in court, all but overwhelming the judiciary. Here citizens file applications to small claims court. This and other kinds of courts, some quite specialized, help keep up with the stream of litigation. They have the obligation to handle the ever-growing load of cases swiftly and efficiently.

way of settling it at the state court level. Of course, if the issue was a national one, it would have begun in a federal court. In all but a few cases, the highest court of the land has complete discretion to accept or reject a case for review.

Thus, except for appeals to the Supreme Court and other special cases, the state and federal systems are separate and are expected to respect each other's authority. However, Congress does have the power to alter the limits of that authority either by legislation or by way of a constitutional amendment.

State Courts

Each state establishes its court system by constitutional or legislative command. Courts are organized in various ways, but no matter how many different courts a state has, and whatever they are called, they usually have three levels. The first is a trial court, then an intermediate appellate court, and at the top a supreme court.

Most states use the justice of the peace for the bulk of basic legal matters. This title dates back to the fourteenth century, although sometimes a justice of the peace was called squire or magistrate. The justice of the peace is either appointed or elected and is not always a lawyer. He or she is a jack-of-all-trades in minor civil matters and certain criminal offenses. Between the justice of the peace and the basic trial court level, or next to it, there are special courts such as the police court, small claims court, night court, traffic court, or simply municipal court. Designed to provide rapid and

Continuity & CHANGE

The Litigiousness of the American Culture

"*There is hardly a political question in the United States which sooner or later does not turn into a judicial one.*"

—Alexis de Tocqueville, 1835

"*Hand an American a problem and he immediately takes it to court. Half the population over the age of 30 is at law because it lacks the ingenuity to solve such humdrum problems as how to live with somebody who snores or dislikes your taste in television, and how to divide up the dishes, the children, the house and the jewelry before plodding on into middle age.*"

—Russell Baker, 1977

Almost a century and a half before columnist Russell Baker commented on the tendency of Americans to turn to the courts to solve their problems, the extraordinarily perceptive Alexis de Toqueville made the same observation. In part, this litigious spirit is fueled by a large number of attorneys, of which the United States has far more per capita than any other nation in the world. And, as shown below, the growth of this profession has, if anything, accelerated over the past few decades.

	U.S. Population	Number of Lawyers	Lawyers per Person
1951	154,000,000	221,605	1:695
1960	179,323,000	285,933	1:627
1970	203,302,000	355,242	1:572
1980	226,546,000	542,205	1:418
1990	249,731,000	805,000	1:310

Source: Barbara A. Curran, *The Lawyer Statistical Report: A Statistical Profile of the U.S. Legal Profession in the 1980s* (Chicago: American Bar Foundation, 1985). The 1990 figure is an estimate. Quotations are from Richard D. Heffner, ed., *Democracy in America* by Alexis de Tocqueville (New York: Mentor, 1956) and "The Courts of First Resort," *New York Times,* July 26, 1977, p. 30.

relatively inexpensive proceedings, these courts perform a significant service in solving problems.

Trial Courts and Juries. Most cases become visible at the trial court level. This court not only has the most cases but also uses the *trial jury,* also known as *petit jury.* This brings citizens into the judicial process. *State juries* may be used in both civil and criminal cases. *Civil* cases do not have to involve a state jury, if the parties to the suit and the presiding judge decide a jury is not needed. Juries in *criminal* cases at the state level are made up of 6 to 12 persons. Juries are now generally chosen at random from lists of voters and are selected in

The trial court, the workhorse of our system of justice. Here a jury—that intriguing, often maddening democratic institution—is called on to render a judgment. The composition and size of juries varies from state to state. In criminal cases at the federal level, their twelve members—a jury of one's peers—must reach a unanimous verdict.

court. Opposing attorneys are allowed total freedom to challenge potential jurors for *cause* and to make limited *peremptory* challenges. The defense usually gets more peremptory challenges than the prosecution. A peremptory challenge can get rid of a prospective juror because he or she is considered undesirable to pass judgment; this accusation does not have to give any valid basis, although in a 7:2 decision the Supreme Court held in 1986 that the equal protection of the laws clause of the Fourteenth Amendment "forbids the *prosecutor* (though apparently not the *defense*) to challenge potential jurors solely on account of their race."[3]

Most trial courts are at the county level. With broad civil and criminal authority, the county court is the workhorse of the state court system. On the same level, often working with the county court, are courts with old Anglo-Saxon or French names such as quarter sessions, common pleas, oyer and terminer, orphans, probate, juvenile, equity, domestic relations, surrogate, chancery, district, and circuit courts.

Intermediate Appellate Courts. Most states provide an intermediate court for appeals from trial or lower-level courts. Yet it is sometimes possible to go directly to the highest state court. Again, the names of intermediate courts vary, with the following being most common: appellate division, superior court, state appellate court, and intermediate court of appeals.

Final Courts of Appeals. Each state has a supreme court at the top of the judicial structure. Sometimes cases can begin there (original jurisdiction), but the vast majority of its cases are appeals from lower state courts. Like courts at other levels, the highest state courts have various names, although supreme court is the most common. Other names are court of appeals (New York), supreme judicial court (Maine), and supreme court of appeals (West Virginia). The state's highest court declares state law; its decisions bind all lower courts. Only if all state remedies have been tried, and if it can be argued that the issue involved is a federal question of substance, can state litigants ask to have their case heard again by the U.S. Supreme Court. State appeals cases involving federal issues can go directly to the U.S. Supreme Court, unless federal law directs a case to a lower federal court, and if the U.S. Supreme Court will agree to accept the case. To all intents and purposes, it enjoys all but total discretion to accept or reject a case on appeal.

Federal Courts: Two Types

The federal judicial structure is relatively simple. There are two types of federal courts: the *constitutional* courts, created under Article III of the Constitution (the judicial article), and the *legislative* courts, created under Article I (the legislative article). They differ in the following ways:

1. Legislative courts have judicial tasks and also certain nonjudicial or quasi-judicial functions, such as administration, and other jobs that are only partly legislative. Constitutional courts carry out strictly judicial functions.
2. Although the legislative courts are part of the appeals system established by the Constitution, their function is to ensure that specific congressional laws are enforced. Examples are laws covering taxation and aspects of military justice. This does not mean that cases cannot be appealed to constitutional courts.

"It's nothing personal, Prescott. It's just that a higher court gets a kick out of overruling a lower court."

3. Constitutional courts cannot render advisory opinions unless there is a "case or controversy" according to Article III. But legislative courts have this power. They may decide whether government action is right or called for by the Constitution, even if there is no bona fide case or controversy. Both types of courts are allowed by law to make so-called *declaratory judgments.* These differ from advisory opinions because they apply to an actual controversy, whereas an advisory opinion deals with an abstract or hypothetical question. In other words, a declaratory judgment enables either type of court to enter a final judgment between litigants in an *actual controversy;* it defines their respective rights under a law, contract, will, or other official document. However, it cannot add any consequential or coercive relief to that otherwise binding judgment. An example was the Alabama Power Co.'s contracts with the Tennessee Valley Authority; in *Ashwander* v. *T.V.A.,* 297 U.S. 288 (1936), the Court answered in the affirmative the question whether the Congress-created Tennessee Valley Authority could constitutionally create and sell electric power it generated in competition with, and at lower rates than, private industry.

4. Probably the most important difference between the two types of courts stems from the Article III safeguards on tenure and salary for constitutional judges. Constitutional court judges may keep their jobs and may not have their salaries reduced while in office if they maintain "good behavior." Legislative judges serve under terms set by Congress—usually for 15 years—and their salaries could, in theory, be "diminished" during their service.

Federal Legislative Courts. Article I, Section 8, Clause 9 of the Constitution gives Congress authority "to constitute tribunals inferior to the Supreme Court." A number of such courts have come into being throughout our history.

This clause was used to establish the U.S. Customs Court (now also known as the Court of International Trade). This was the first legislative court to be changed by Congress into a constitutional one. The old U.S. Court of Claims was similarly changed, but it was reconstituted into a legislative court in 1982 and is now called the U.S. Claims Court. Courts that the U.S. Supreme Court sees as having "mixed" functions are the federal courts in the District of Columbia and the territorial courts in Guam, Puerto Rico, the Virgin Islands, and the Northern Mariana Islands.

The three most visible legislative courts are the U.S. Court of Military Appeals, the U.S. Tax Court, and the recently established U.S. Court of Veterans' Appeals. The first was created by Congress in 1950 to "make rules for the government and regulation of land and naval forces" (Article I, Section 8, Clause 14). It is an appeals court for military personnel convicted of certain offenses and sometimes convicted by court martial. The tax court, once without much power, was made into a legislative court in 1969 through Congress's power of taxation. It holds trials throughout the United States when taxpayers challenge the decisions of the Internal Revenue Service. The new (1988) Veterans' tribunal has exclusive jurisdiction to review decisions of the Board of Veterans' Appeals. It promises to be a busy court.

Federal Constitutional Courts. From time to time, courts created by Article III of the Constitution have included certain specialized tribunals, such as the U.S. Court of Customs and Patent Appeals. But the most important federal constitutional courts are the *U.S. district courts,* the *U.S. courts of appeals,* and the *U.S. Supreme Court.* Since the U.S. Supreme Court is the only one expressly mentioned in the Constitution, Congress had to establish the rest of the federal court system. Thus, one of its first pieces of legislation was the Judiciary Act of 1789.

Jurisdiction. As Table 16–1 shows, Article III, strengthened by congressional legislation, spells out in precise detail the jurisdiction of the federal courts. Section 2 makes clear that the federal judicial power extends "to *all Cases* in law and equity,[4] arising under the Constitution, the Laws of the United States, and Treaties made or which shall be made under their Authority. . . ." *All cases*

TABLE 16–1

The Jurisdiction of the Federal Constitutional Courts

1 *Supreme Court of the United States,* nine judges, has:
Original jurisdiction in actions or controversies:
- *1. Between the United States and a state.
- 2. Between two or more states.
- *3. Involving *foreign* ambassadors, other *foreign* public ministers, and *foreign* consuls or their "domestics or domestic servants, not inconsistent with the law of nations."
- *4. *Commenced by a state against* citizens of another state or aliens, or *against* a foreign country. (If these actions are *commenced by the citizen or alien against a state,* or by a foreign country *against* a state, the suit must *begin in state court,* according to the provisions of Amendment 11.)

Appellate jurisdiction from:
1. All lower federal *constitutional* courts; most, but not all, federal *legislative* courts; and the *territorial* courts.
2. The highest state courts having jurisdiction, when a "substantial federal question" is involved.

13 *U.S. (circuit) courts of appeals,* 168 (not counting "senior," i.e., retired) judges, have
Appellate jurisdiction *only* from:
1. U.S. district courts.
2. U.S. territorial courts, the U.S. Tax Court, and some District of Columbia courts.
3. The U.S. Court of Appeals for the Federal Circuit.
4. The U.S. independent regulatory commissions.
5. Certain federal administrative agencies and departments (for review, but also for *enforcement* of certain of their actions and orders).

94 *U.S. district courts,* approximately 576 (not counting "senior," i.e., retired) judges, have
original jurisdiction *only*† over:
- 1. All crimes against the United States.
- 2. All civil actions arising under the Constitution, laws, or treaties of the United States, wherein the matter in controversy exceeds $50,000 (unless the U.S. Supreme Court has jurisdiction as outlined above).
- *3. Cases involving citizens of different states or citizens and aliens, provided the value of the controversy is in excess of $50,000.
- 4. Admiralty, maritime, and prize cases.
- *5. Review and *enforcement* of orders and actions of certain federal administrative agencies and departments.
- 6. All such other cases as Congress may validly prescribe by law.

Note: These are the three major constitutional courts created under Article III of the Constitution. Two special constitutional courts are omitted—the old U.S. Customs Court, now the U.S. Court of International Trade, and the Foreign Intelligence Surveillance Court.

* *Jurisdiction not exclusive*—while cases, according to Article III of the Constitution, are to originate here, legal arrangements may be made to have them handled by a different level court. For example, Congress has the power to give the federal district courts *concurrent original jurisdiction* over cases affecting foreign ambassadors.

† A case can be made for the contention that it also has a measure of *appellate* jurisdiction, involving certain actions tried before U.S. commissioners (one of whom is authorized for each federal district).

Source: Adapted from Henry J. Abraham, *The Judiciary: The Supreme Court of the United States in the Governmental Process* (Boston: Allyn & Bacon, 1987), pp. 16–17.

While a judge presides over a trial, it is up to the jury to come to a verdict. In other countries, judges and other professionals often conduct a trial without a jury, as in this Australian court. Of course, our system also includes what are known as *collegial bodies*—higher courts in which judges sit together. The best known is the nine-member U.S. Supreme Court.

points to the central requirement that the jurisdiction of federal constitutional courts is limited to bona fide "cases" (and "controversies," spelled out in a later segment of Section 2). In effect, it means that there must be a genuine case or controversy with two or more litigants on opposite sides of an issue clearly clashing. Unlike the other two branches, the judiciary is not "self-starting." Cases come to it; it neither "shops" for them, nor does it—except on very rare occasions—invite or encourage potential litigants.

Beyond that first requirement of a case or controversy, the judiciary article carefully identifies the kinds of authority given to the courts. These differ according to the nature or character of (1) the *subject matter* involved and (2) the *parties* to the suit. Jurisdiction determined by subject matter applies to cases and controversies arising (1) under the Constitution, a federal law, or a treaty; or (2) under maritime or admiralty laws. Jurisdiction determined by the parties involved applies to five types of cases and controversies: *if* (1) the United States is a party to the suit; (2) one of the 50 states is a party to the suit—*unless,* under the Eleventh Amendment, the suit was first brought or prosecuted *against* the state *by* any individual or a foreign country, who must sue in *state* court; (3) the suit is between citizens of *different* states (known as "diversity of citizenship" cases); (4) the suit affects *foreign* ambassadors and other officially recognized foreign diplomats; and (5) the suit arises between citizens of the *same* state because of a dispute involving land claimed by two or more states.

Federal constitutional courts are not the only courts that can try cases that fall into these several categories. Congress may give some such cases to the state courts, either as supplements to the work of the federal courts or in place of them. Diversity of citizenship suits are an example. Congress has decided that before a case can begin in a federal court, the value of the property involved must be at least $50,000; otherwise, the suit must be filed in the state courts. Even when $50,000 or more is at stake, Congress permits either federal or state courts to hear such cases, depending on the wishes of the parties. Indeed, Congress has given state and federal courts the same authority in several kinds of cases. If a case is appealed, though, the federal courts have final authority under Article VI, the "supremacy clause" of the federal Constitution.

The Two Lower Federal Constitutional Courts ■

Because of the glamor and visibility of the Supreme Court, it has overshadowed the lower-level federal courts. But to ignore these other courts is unwise and denies the nature of the judicial process. We need to know something about what these lower courts were set up to do.

U.S. District Courts. The busiest of the three types of courts are the 94 U.S. district courts. These are the workhorses of the federal judiciary, staffed by 1 to 27 judges per district (totaling 576 in 1989). They handle some 600,000 civil, criminal, and bankruptcy cases each year. They are the action, the trial courts; here the typical federal suits begin, from mail fraud to contempt to civil rights to kidnapping cases. These courts can call a federal trial jury, because anyone accused in a criminal case that could bring a jail or prison term (even for misdemeanors or petty crimes) is entitled to a jury by the Constitution. However, a jury can be omitted if the parties to the suit and the judge agree. Unlike trial juries in *state* criminal cases, a *federal* trial jury must have 12 members and they must agree unanimously to find the defendant either guilty or not guilty. Failing to agree on either, the jury will be "hung," and the case can either be dropped or retried. Federal *civil* cases do not have to involve a jury if the value of the controversy is less than $20, or by common agreement. A jury in a civil case may have as few as six members, and its decision apparently need not be unanimous if at least six agree on a verdict.[5] Although many cases are appealed to the next higher court, most federal cases begin and end in one of the U.S. district courts.

U.S. Courts of Appeals. The 13 U.S. courts of appeals are often still called circuit courts of appeals because they cover large geographic areas. They constitute the intermediate appeals level of the federal court system. With certain exceptions,[6] appeals from the U.S. district courts, most federal legislative courts, independent regulatory commissions, and certain other federal administrative agencies and departments come for a final decision to the courts of appeals.

Increased to 132 active members during the Carter administration and to 168 during Reagan's first term—not counting "senior," that is, retired judges, who may still be serving on a part- or even full-time basis—judges sit in panels ranging from 3 to 15 in 11 geographically divided circuits plus one for the District of Columbia (see Figure 16–1). A greatly increasing number of appeals—close to 30,000—reach these courts each year. Each court has a chief judge, who must step down as chief at the age of 70 but need not retire. As in the old days of "circuit riding," which lasted until roughly the end of the Civil War, each of the 12 circuits is theoretically headed by one of the nine justices of the U.S. Supreme Court. Each justice has authority to act on certain pleas that arise from court actions in his or her circuit. A thirteenth, nongeographic, court of appeals (with 12 additional judges) was established in 1982.

Proceedings in the courts of appeals are conducted on the basis of evidence submitted to the lower courts, such as one of the U.S. district courts or an administrative agency. Except for the Second Circuit Court of Appeals (covering New York, Connecticut, and Vermont), which has always heard

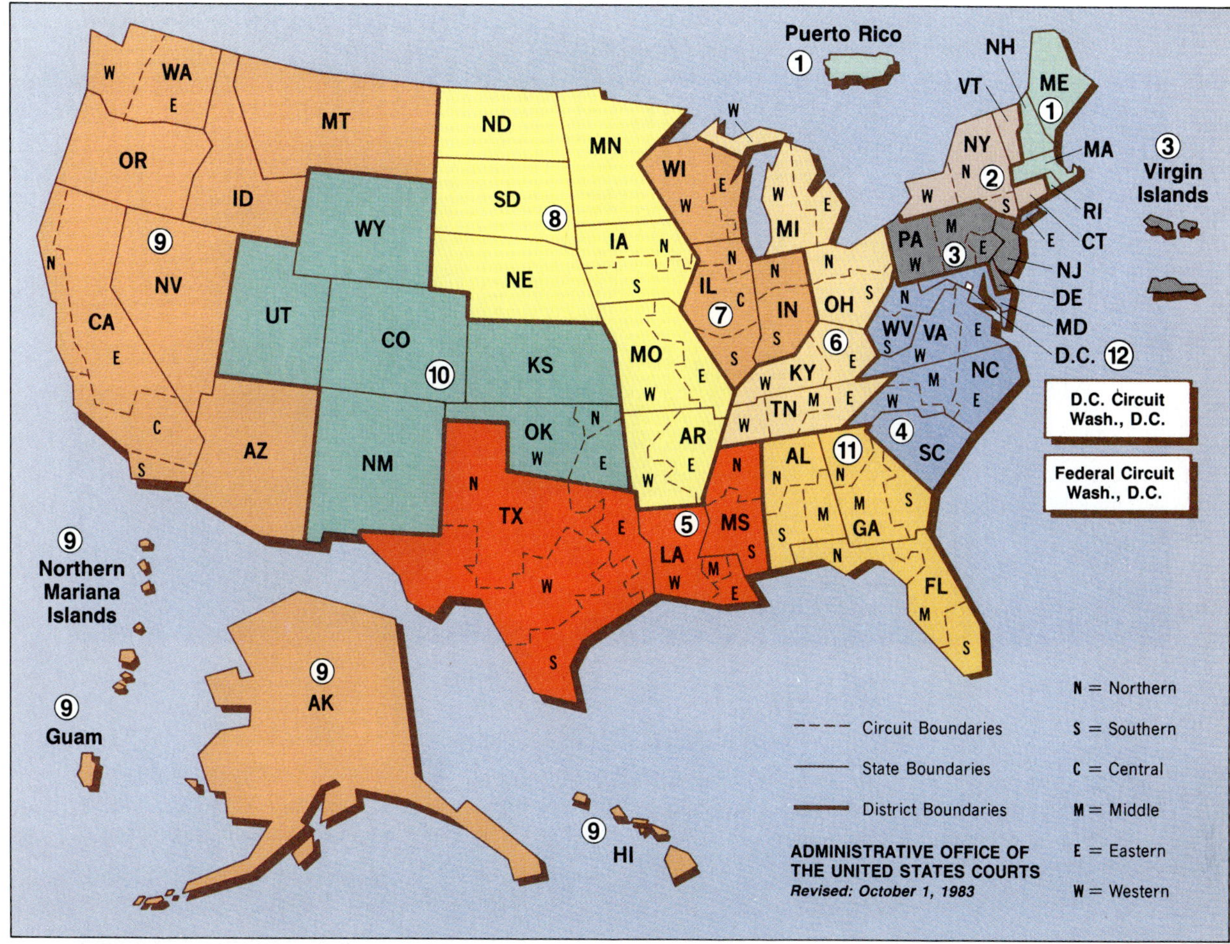

Figure 16–1 U.S. circuit courts of appeals and district courts. Districts for the courts of appeals are numbered, and their boundaries are shown by the heavy black lines. Thinner black lines indicate state borders, while broken lines show jurisdictional boundaries of district courts in states having more than one district. The 12th Circuit Court, not numbered on the figure, is confined to the nation's capital and is known as the U.S. Circuit Court for the District of Columbia. The 13th, created in 1982, is the U.S. Court of Appeals for the Federal Circuit; it combines all the functions of the old U.S. Court of Customs and Patent Appeals and the appellate functions of the old U.S. Court of Claims. (Most of the latter's other functions are retained in a new U.S. Court of Claims.) Source: Administrative Office of the U.S. Courts, 1983.

oral argument in appeals cases, oral argument is heard only in cases regarded as most important. All other cases are decided on the basis of submitted documents. Theoretically, *new* evidence may not be presented at the appeals level, because all evidence should have been submitted at the trial stage, but trial lawyers are masters of ingenuity.

The U.S. Supreme Court

The Supreme Court, often simply called the Court, is the only court mentioned in the Constitution; it stands at the apex of the judicial structure. Its chief justice's title is not Chief Justice of the Supreme Court but Chief Justice of the United

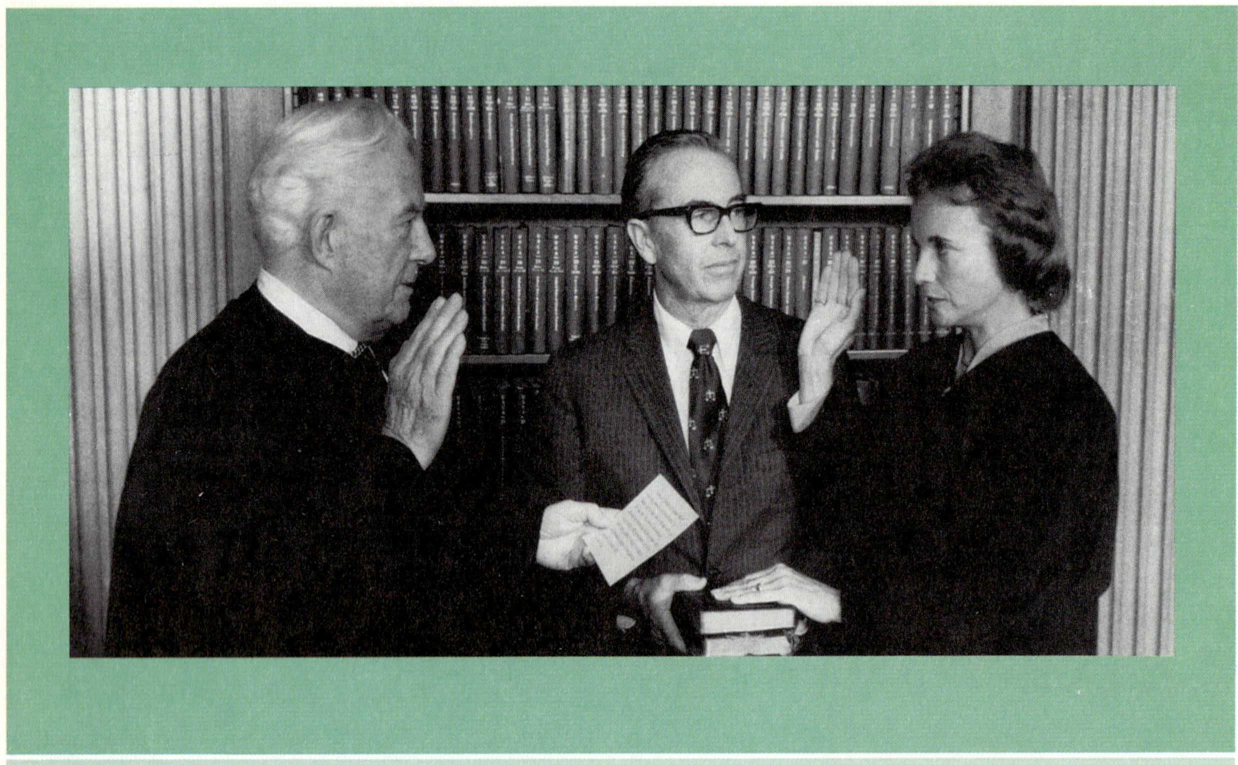

Sandra Day O'Connor, the first woman on the U.S. Supreme Court. She was confirmed 99:0 by the Senate in President Reagan's first year in office. Here O'Connor, then an Arizona state judge, is sworn in by Chief Justice Warren Burger as her husband watches. Many believe that there is no more powerful position in government than justice of the Supreme Court.

States. Since 1869, the Court has had nine members—the chief justice and eight associate justices—but it has had as few as five (1789) and as many as ten (1863). Its size is subject to appropriate legislation under Article III of the Constitution. So is its jurisdiction.

Jurisdiction. The Court has both original and appellate jurisdiction. The rules that govern what cases *begin* in the Supreme Court can be changed only by constitutional amendment; those regulating appeals cases can be changed by law. Original jurisdiction, as outlined in Article III, is rarely used—averaging once or twice per term. One reason cases seldom begin in the Supreme Court is the Eleventh Amendment, which prohibits suits against a state "by citizens of another state, or by citizens or subjects of any foreign state." [7] Another is the Court's practice of extending some responsibilities to the federal trial courts. Today the Court exercises original jurisdiction *exclusively* only in cases involving two or more states; examples are boundary squabbles between Texas and Louisiana in 1973 and between Ohio and Kentucky in 1980.

The Supreme Court, then, is basically an appeals court. Congress has the power to change the Court's power in appeals cases, but it has done so rarely. Only once did it use this power vindictively—in a famous post-Civil War case, the *McCardle* case of 1869.[8] It deprived the Court of jurisdiction to hear the kind of habeas corpus appeals involved there. However, this potential weapon is recognized by the Court in its general tendency to defer to Congress's power and lawmaking authority.

As Table 16–1 outlines, appeals cases reach the Court from state courts as well as lower federal courts. There are three ways of appealing a case to the Supreme Court:

1. Most often, on a *writ of certiorari;*
2. Rarely, on a direct *writ of appeal;*
3. Seldom, by certification—in essence, a lower court's "inquiry" of, or request to, the high court, usually asking for technical instructions.

The writ of appeal represents the theoretical right of bringing a case to the Supreme Court. This right is granted by law (and, of course, is removable by law) to those who want the Court to review a case. However, since the Court determines the "substantiality" of the question presented by the appellant, it does not have to accept the case. In 1988 Congress yielded to the Court's repeated requests that, with only a handful of exceptions from three-judge district courts, the writ of appeal be abolished in favor of the most frequently granted writ, *certiorari*—or *cert.,* as it is simply called by the profession. This writ has been totally at the discretion of the Court since the Judges Bill of 1925. Writs of *certiorari* (translated as "made more certain") are governed by the rule of four: Unless four justices vote to review a case, it will not be heard and will simply appear among the "*certiorari* denied" petitions, the largest component of the Court's dispositions. Some insist that a denial of *cert.* means that the Supreme Court agrees with the results; others insist that the denial means only that the Court, for whatever reason, simply did not wish to accept the case. One thing is clear: A denial of *cert.* means that the petitioner has failed and must be content with becoming a listing in the Court's annals.

Today the Supreme Court handles more than 5000 cases a year. However, most of them are denied review, or a lower court's decision is simply affirmed or reversed. Attention focuses on about 150 cases a year. Those are the ones Justice Oliver Wendell Holmes called "the trouble cases." In them, the justices hear oral argument in the Court's magnificent chambers. The remainder merely find a place in the *United States Reports*—the Court's official record.

The Supreme Court at Work: In Front of the Purple Curtain. Unless it is called into special session (as, for example, in *Cooper* v. *Aaron,* the 1958 case involving the Little Rock, Arkansas, school desegregation crisis), the Court sits formally from early October through June, three days a week (usually two weeks of each month), from 10:00 to 12:00 noon and 1:00 to 3:00 P.M. However, if the Court thinks it necessary, as it did in the 1971 *Pentagon Papers* case and the 1974 *Nixon Tapes* case, it may extend its session.

The lovely white-marbled Court building at 1 First Street, S.E., contains a splendid, high-ceilinged court chamber seating 300 (188 seats for the public and 112 for the case participants and their supporters). Attending a Supreme Court session is awe-inspiring. The justices are seated "on high," with the chief justice in the center and the associate justices flanking the chief justice in descending order of seniority (see Figure 16–2). They listen to the counsel, often interrupting and peppering them with questions during the 30 minutes each side is usually allotted. The cases being heard have been briefed by all sides and submitted to the Court well in advance, according to specific rules and regulations. Oral argument is still far more than window dressing; although the justices are presumably already familiar with the case, oral argument may well influence their ultimate decision. A Supreme Court case is a fascinating example of the living judicial process.

The Supreme Court at Work: Behind the Purple Curtain. In addition to disposing of the petitions for review that were denied oral argument, the Court's most crucial business is to decide on the roughly 150 cases it chooses to review each year. The first step, after a case is heard, is the plenary Wednesday afternoon or Friday conference, when the cases that have just been heard are discussed. The justices meet alone in a securely locked, stately room in which no one but the nine justices is permitted. After shaking hands with one another and taking their seats around the large mahogany table, the

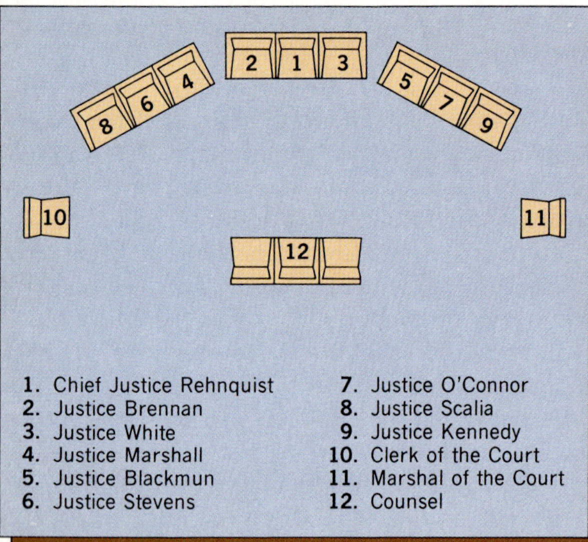

Figure 16–2 How justices are seated on the Supreme Court, 1988–1989. Source: Office of the Marshal, Supreme Court building, 1 First Street, S.E., Washington, D.C.

nine argue and discuss the issues. Usually the chief justice's view is stated first, followed by the others in descending order of seniority. The same order is used for the subsequent *tentative* vote. Each justice records all votes in a hinged, lockable red leather docket book. Then the Court proceeds to the next stage—writing opinions.

When the justices agree unanimously, or when the chief justice is on the majority side of a case, the chief justice writes the opinion or assigns it to one of the justices on the majority side. But if the chief justice is in the minority, the *majority opinion* is assigned by the senior associate justice on that side. In only about a fourth of the cases is the Court's vote unanimous; most cases produce concurring and dissenting opinions. A *concurring opinion* agrees with the result reached by the majority but does not agree with the reasoning of the opinion. A *dissenting opinion* disagrees with the view of the majority. Many a memorable dissenting opinon has ultimately become the voice of the Court's majority; an example is Justice John Marshall Harlan's lonely dissent in the 1896 *Plessy* v. *Ferguson case* (see Chapter 5). His rejection of the "separate but equal" decision became the law of the land some six decades later in the 1954–1955 *Brown* v. *Board of Education* desegregation cases. Many of Justice Oliver Wendell Holmes's dissents were later vindicated also. (The champion dissenter to date is Justice William O. Douglas, who wrote 586 dissenting opinions during his record $36\frac{1}{2}$ years on the Court.)

However the justices vote, the final opinion is carefully prepared behind the scenes. Each justice participates in at least some phase of the process. Drafts are exchanged, and persuasion is applied. Bright young law school graduates—law clerks (each justice usually selects four, the chief justice five)—do research and other legwork for "their" justice. Reaching an opinion may involve much bargaining and give-and-take. This may even result in a justice changing sides and the opinion being written by a different author. The "chief's" leadership abilities are very important here. John Marshall, Roger Taney, William Howard Taft, Charles Evans Hughes, and Earl Warren have been the most successful in persuading others to follow them.

When the Court's decision is ready, the opinion or opinions are printed by its own print shop. An announcement is then made publicly from the bench. Once confined to what was known as "opinion Monday," opinions may now be handed down on any of the Court's oral argument days—Monday, Tuesday, or Wednesday. The justices may read them in full (a practice the chief justice usually frowns on), summarize them, read excerpts from them, or simply declaim them.

Because the decision is now the law of the land, it is vital to distinguish between the controlling opinion's *ratio decidenci* and its *obiter dictum,* if any. The *ratio decidendi* means the point of law settled by the decision, the legal rule henceforth to be obeyed, the *res judicata* (e.g., that indigent defendants in criminal cases are entitled to a court-appointed attorney). An *obiter dictum* is a nonessential, extra comment expressing a viewpoint, observation, warning, or exhortation that its author believed to be important. John Marshall was famous for his *dicta,* as in *Marbury* v. *Madison,* where they took up 20 of the 27 pages of his opinion. Earl Warren was another devotee of *dicta.*

"The vote is 16 to 4. One of you has voted twelve times."

Although enforcement of the Court's decisions does not always follow automatically, the rule of law means compliance with Supreme Court decisions. Most decisions are promptly and properly complied with, even when they are unpopular and have aroused contention. But our history has also witnessed both delays and defiance of the Court's rulings—especially on such emotion-charged issues as desegregation, criminal justice, and public school prayer—often accompanied by harsh criticism of judges.

Judges and Justices: How and Why They Reach the Bench

Although much folklore surrounds the selection of judges, there is nothing sinister or mysterious about how those who sit on state and federal benches are nominated and confirmed. Our system is perhaps less rational or professional than those of England, Germany, and France, however.

In England, judges are appointed by the Crown from a small (about 5000) distinguished group of elite lawyers, called barristers. In France, the president selects judges from graduates of a professional school—the Ecole Nationale de la Magistrature, which students must attend for 28 months. In West Germany, judges are elected by Parliament.

In the United States, the nearly 30,000 state and 1500 plus federal judges (except bankruptcy judges) are elected or appointed by the political branches, or both. All *federal* judges are selected and nominated by the president and confirmed by a simple majority vote of the Senate. There are *neither* constitutional *nor* statutory requirements for membership on the federal bench, although no one not admitted to the bar has ever been a federal judge. State judges are elected by the voters or legislators or appointed by the governor with or with-

The Chief Justice: Earl Warren and a History-Making Decision

Brown v. *Board of Education,* the case that outlawed segregated public schools, was to shake the nation—and Chief Justice Earl Warren knew it. His work to achieve unanimity inside the Court illustrates the qualities that made him, in the mind of many, an outstanding chief justice. Later he described just what happened:*

> Ordinarily, the Justices, at our Friday conferences stated their positions, offered debate and then voted. But in *Brown* we were all conscious of the case, so I held off a vote from conference to conference, while we discussed it. If you'll remember, *Brown* was argued in the fall of 1953, and I did not call for a vote until the middle of the following February, when I was certain we would be unanimous. We took one vote and that was it.
>
> I assigned myself to write the decision, for it seemed to me that something so important ought to issue over the name of the Chief Justice of the United States. In drafting it, I sought to use low-key, unemotional language and to keep it short enough so that it could be published in full in every newspaper in the country. I kept the text secret (it was locked in my safe) until I read from the bench.

Here are the others whose leadership has helped shape the high court.

Chief Justice	Appointed by President	Judicial Oath Taken	How Term Ended	Years of Service
John Jay	Washington	1789	Resigned	5
John Rutledge	Washington	1795	Not confirmed by Senate	½
Oliver Ellsworth	Washington	1796	Resigned	4
John Marshall	Adams, J.	1801	Death	34
Roger Brooke Taney	Jackson	1836	Death	28
Salmon Portland Chase	Lincoln	1864	Death	8½
Morrison Remick Waite	Grant	1874	Death	14
Melville Weston Fuller	Cleveland	1888	Death	21
Edward Douglass White	Taft	1910	Death	10
William Howard Taft	Harding	1921	Retired	8
Charles Evans Hughes	Hoover	1930	Retired	11
Harlan Fiske Stone	Roosevelt, F.	1941	Death	5
Frederick Moore Vinson	Truman	1946	Death	7
Earl Warren	Eisenhower	1953	Retired	15
Warren Earl Burger	Nixon	1969	Retired	17
William H. Rehnquist	Reagan	1986	—	—

*Source: *New York Times,* July 11, 1974, p. A35.

out legislative consent, by commissioners, or, in a few cases, even by courts alone. Increasingly, various combinations of the appointive and elective processes are used. In most states, but not at the federal level, judges are required to be lawyers.

State Judges

Today almost all states appoint judges to at least some of their courts, most states elect judges to certain courts, and about half of the states use a combination of appointments and elections (see Figure 16–3). Elections vary from state to state. In 1988 they ranged from direct popular election (as in Arkansas and Alabama) to election by the legislature (South Carolina and Virginia).

Candidates may run on partisan tickets (West Virginia and New Mexico) or nonpartisan ones (Michigan and Washington), but judges usually must run as a member of one party or the other. The term of office for most elected judges averages 6 to 10 years; but for some it is 15 (Maryland) and for others it is life (Rhode Island). In a few states, it is the practice to support the sitting judge when he or she is up for reelection. Massachusetts's judges, except for justices of the peace, are selected by a commission and serve for life, "conditioned upon good behavior." In New Jersey, judges are

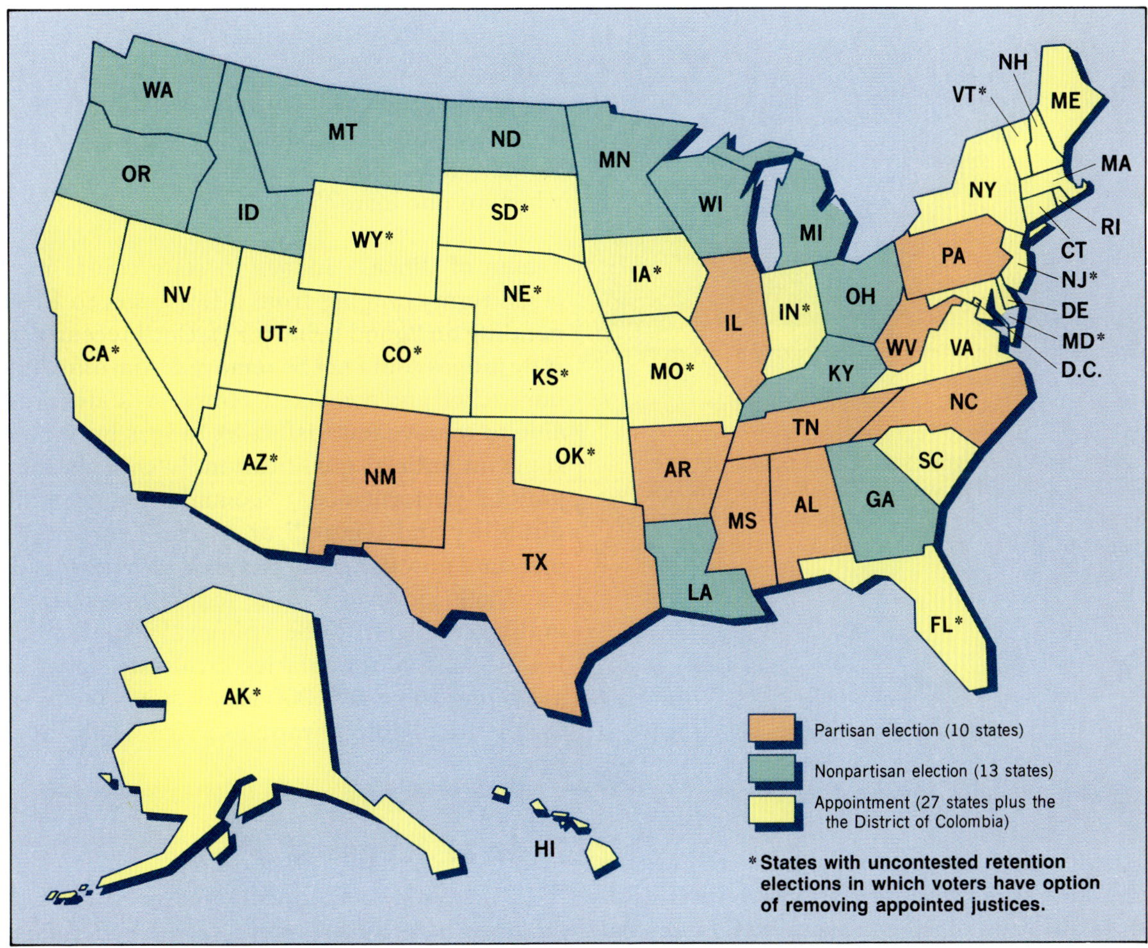

Figure 16–3 How states pick supreme court justices. Source: *New York Times,* January 22, 1988.

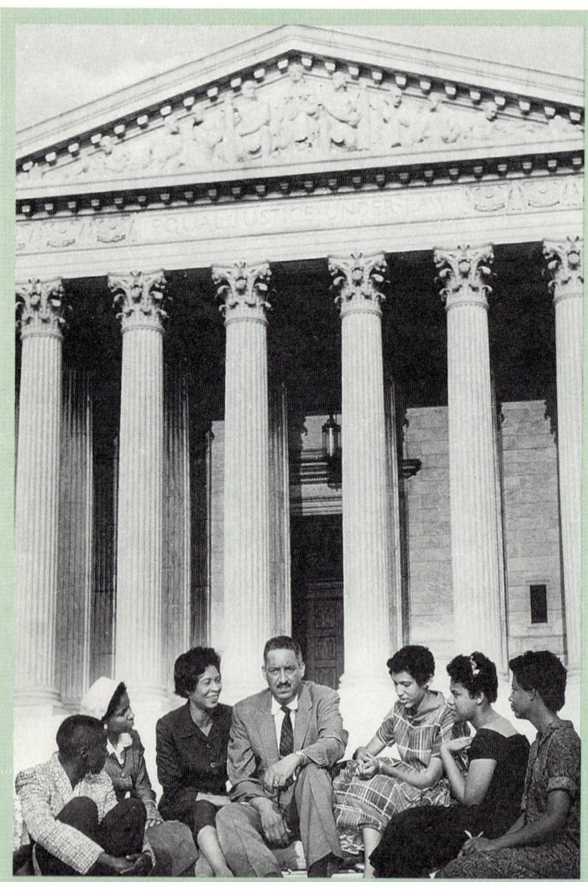

Thurgood Marshall as a young attorney on the steps of the Supreme Court, where he was the winning counsel in *Brown* v. *Board of Education,* the landmark desegregation case. Great-grandson of a slave, and son of a steward at an exclusively white country club, he rose to become in 1967 the first nonwhite ever to serve on this nation's highest court.

selected by the governor for seven-year terms; if they are reappointed, they receive life terms if they demonstrate "good behavior."

The Combination Compromise. Because both the elective and appointive methods have been criticized, California and Missouri designed and adopted compromise arrangements in 1934 and 1940, respectively. Half of the states have since adopted versions of those two plans for at least some of their courts. In California, the governor nominates one prospective judge to a Commission on Judicial Appointments. If approved, the successful nominee serves until the next general election. At that time, running unopposed and on a nonpartisan ballot, the incumbent may be elected for a 12-year term. In Missouri, a nonpartisan nominating board, known as the Appellate Commission, selects three candidates for each vacant judgeship. The governor appoints one of these for a probationary term, not less than one year, until the next general election is held. As in California, the candidate then runs unopposed on a nonpartisan ballot for a 12-year term. Missouri voters are asked, simply: "Shall judge——of the——Court be retained in office?"

Voters have been pleased with these mixed plans. Indeed, in the roughly 55 years of retention elections of the California and Missouri type, only 36 judges of some 16,000 running have been defeated. No wonder some have asked: Who wins when no one loses?[9]

Tenure of Office. Judges in state courts may be given terms ranging from a few years to life (depending on "good behavior"). Until recently, most state judges could not be removed from office unless impeached and convicted. However, states are now able to remove unsatisfactory judges by "commissions on judicial qualification," "commissions on judicial performance," "commissions on judicial disability and tenure," or special courts. All but one state now use these methods to remove judges.

State judgeships, like federal ones, are generally considered to be "plums." This is perhaps less because of the salaries involved—now (1989) averaging about $55,000 for all state courts—than for the intangible rewards: service, visibility, and power.

Federal Judges

The power and prestige enjoyed by federal judges surpass those of state judges. Federal judges may seem to have only the power to persuade, in Alexander Hamilton's words, since financial and military power are in other hands; but their prestige, authority, and political power extend their role far beyond mere persuasion. By 1989, their once-modest salaries had risen to $89,500 for a U.S. district court judge and $115,000 for the Chief Justice of the United States, with future increases almost certain. A federal judgeship is not very likely to be shunned when opportunity beckons!

Tenure of Office. Federal judges, with the exception of some legislative court judges, are appointed for good behavior, which generally means for life (or until voluntary resignation or retirement). Except for those whose terms are limited by Congress, as set up by Article I (legislative court judges), no federal judge can be compelled to retire, although retirement laws encourage some to do so. The sole method of removal is impeachment and conviction. As spelled out in Article II, Section 4, charges are limited to "Treason, Bribery, or other high crimes and misdemeanors." [10] To date (mid-1989) thirteen federal judges have been impeached, of whom seven have been convicted and removed.

Although impeachment and conviction remains the sole method of removal of federal judges, in 1980 Congress passed a law designed to discipline, but not remove, all Article III judges formally accused of misconduct except for Supreme Court judges. It gives the judicial councils of the 13 judicial circuits the power to discipline their judges in specific ways. This law strikes a compromise between giving Congress power to create a special court to try misconduct and disability cases and granting that power to each judicial circuit.

Selection Procedures and Politics. In theory, the president has *carte blanche* to appoint judges to the federal bench, subject only to Senate "advice and consent." In practice, though, the president's power is limited for at least three reasons. First, it is virtually impossible for the president to appoint a judge to a federal court and get confirmation without approval from the senators of the state concerned, especially if they are members of the president's party. "Senatorial courtesy" is the practice of not selecting individuals politically objectionable to home-state senators. It must always be observed to maintain goodwill both with the Senate and in one's own party. Although the practice applies there, too, the staffing of the Supreme Court has always been considered the president's particular province. However, the rejection of Nixon nominees Clement F. Haynsworth, Jr., in 1969 and G. Harrold Carswell in 1970, and of President Reagan's choice of Robert H. Bork in 1987, showed that the Senate does take seriously its obligation of "advice and consent." By 1988, the Senate had rejected 28 Supreme Court nominees out of a total of 142, although all but 5 were rejected in the last century.[11]

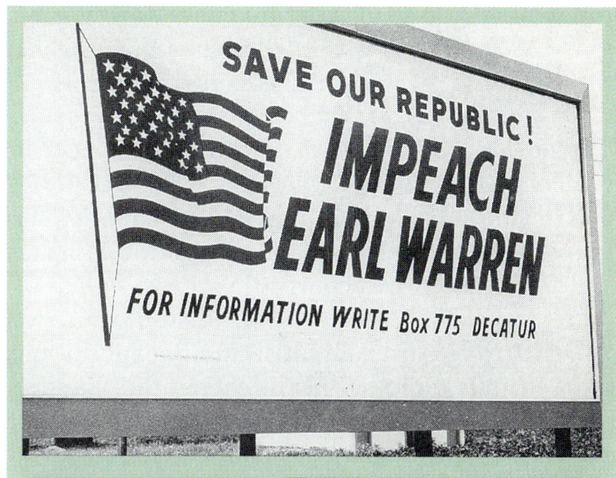

In Earl Warren's 16-year term as Chief Justice, the Supreme Court expanded civil rights and civil liberties for all Americans. A former governor of California and unsuccessful nominee for vice president before his appointment by President Eisenhower in 1953, he was a constant subject of praise and attack for the historic changes under "the Warren court."

As a potentially revolutionary change in the politics of appointing federal judges, the Federal Omnibus Judgeship Act of 1978 gave President Carter the opportunity to appoint 152 new judges, in addition to about the same number of appointments made necessary by normal attrition. Carter nominated almost 300 judges, more than any other president in our history. It had a momentous impact on the judiciary. Because of a Carter campaign promise, some 100 of these nominees were women, blacks, and Hispanics, of whom there had been a total of only 29 when Carter assumed office in 1977 (see Table 16–2).

To carry out his resolve to "depoliticize" the judiciary, Carter took two steps: One was to establish the U.S. Circuit Judge Nomination Commission to help him fill vacant judgeships. For each vacancy in the circuit courts, this commission submitted five names to the president. The commission lived up to the Carter administration's expectations by identifying and suggesting heretofore "underrepresented" elements in the population. At the same time, the nominees' political identity, including those picked for the district courts, was close to 98 percent Democratic. (This was higher than any other president's record except Woodrow Wilson's.) The commission arrangement was terminated by President Reagan in 1981. Carter's second major change in the appointment process was to ask senators to establish merit advisory groups in their home states that would select nominees to the federal district courts to be sent to the president. By 1981, 40 senators in 30 states had moved to adopt the plan (although there had been some support for it before the Carter administration's drive). It was a "new ballgame" but it did not detract from the ultimate power of the Senate.

The second influence limiting the president's power to appoint federal judges is the 15-member American Bar Association (ABA) Committee on Federal Judiciary. This committee has played an unofficial role in the appointment process since 1946. It scrutinizes and rates nominees to the bench and assigns each to one of four categories: "exceptionally well qualified," "well qualified," "qualified," and "not qualified." The bar's disapproval is not a veto, though; both the president and the Senate have ignored some of its recommendations: President Carter nominated six individuals rated "not qualified" by the bar committee, and three were approved by the Senate. But the committee is a major force to be reckoned with, notwithstanding Carter's reforms, which reduced its impact temporarily. Table 16–3 shows the ABA ratings of the judicial nominees of recent presidents—from Eisenhower to Reagan.

A third limitation on the president is becoming

TABLE 16–2

Judicial Nominees and Group Representation

	Women	Blacks	Hispanics
U.S. Court of Appeals			
Johnson	2.5%	5.0%	n.a.
Nixon	0	0	n.a.
Ford	0	0	n.a.
Carter	19.6	16.1	3.6%
Reagan	5.1	1.3	1.3
U.S. District Court			
Johnson	1.6%	4.1%	2.5%
Nixon	0.6	3.4	1.1
Ford	1.9	5.8	1.9
Carter	14.4	13.9	6.9
Reagan	8.3	2.1	4.8

Sources: The Johnson, Nixon, and Ford statistics are from studies by Sheldon Goldman, *Judicature* (April–May 1985 and 1989). The Carter and Reagan percentages were compiled by the *Congressional Quarterly* based on figures from the Justice Department and the Senate Judiciary Committee; see also Goldman, *Judicature* (April–May 1987); and *Congressional Quarterly* (November 26, 1988).

TABLE 16–3

How Qualified Are Federal Judges? The ABA Ratings

	Exceptionally Well Qualified	Well Qualified	Qualified	Unqualified
Eisenhower	17.1%	44.6%	32.6%	5.7%
Kennedy	16.6	45.6	31.5	6.3
Johnson	12.2	43.3	41.7	2.8
Nixon	6.3	42.8	50.9	0
Ford	3.0	47.0	48.5	1.5
Carter	6.1	49.6	43.1	1.2
Reagan	7.1	48.1	44.8	0

Sources: The Eisenhower, Kennedy, and Johnson statistics are adapted from Harold W. Chase, *Federal Judges: The Appointing Process* (Minneapolis: University of Minnesota, 1972), pp. 178–180. The later statistics were compiled by the *Congressional Quarterly* based on data from the American Bar Association. See also Sheldon Goldman's studies in *Judicature* (April–May 1985, April–May 1987, and April–May 1989).

increasingly evident: It is the influence, however subtle, of sitting judges. This is shown at the appeals court level and is especially strong in appointments to the Supreme Court. There was much behind-the-scenes politics by Chief Justices Taft (the most aggressively active), Hughes, Stone, Vinson, Warren, and Burger and Associate Justices Harlan I, Miller, Van Devanter, Brandeis, and Frankfurter.[12]

Qualifications and Characteristics. Although it is difficult to account for the selection of federal court judges, certain characteristics have emerged as essential.[13] No requirements are set up either by the Constitution or by law; according to custom and politics, though, a federal judge must have a law degree. This may be the only prerequisite that all agree on. Judicial experience is also important, but not inevitably so; had it been a requirement, such Supreme Court giants as Chief Justices Taney, Fuller, and Warren and Associate Justices Story, Brandeis, Sutherland, Frankfurter, Robert Jackson, and Powell could not have been appointed. Of course, experience as a judge is significant proof of objective professional merit. Other considerations are political "availability," (i.e., is the selectee politically "reliable?") ideological "appropriateness," personal attractiveness, plus friendship with the president. Recently, "equitable" or "representative" factors have been increasingly emphasized: geographic origin, religion, and most important, ethnic background, race, and sex.

In theory, the only consideration should be demonstrable professional merit, but in the political world other characteristics must be weighed. Since nonwhites and women rarely served as judges on courts of any level until quite recently, it is not surprising that these and other groups have insistently demanded judicial positions. This raises the intriguing question of whether the judiciary was intended by the founders to be "representative." The most that can be said is that the idea never entered their debates.

Judicial Power and Responsibility

Like the pope, judges have no army to enforce their decisions, yet they possess the power of moral au-

Congress Checks the Judiciary: Judicial Impeachment and Conviction

Like Congress and the president, the federal judiciary is subject to the checks and balances of the other two branches. Judicial appointments are made by the president (with the advice and consent of the Senate), and Congress has the ultimate power of impeachment and conviction of members of the federal bench—the only method by which such judges can be removed against their will. Specifically, a vote by the House will *impeach* a judge, while a vote of two-thirds of the senators will result in the judge's *conviction.* To date, thirteen federal judges have been impeached, but only seven of these individuals have been removed from office through conviction:

1. 1803: U.S. District Court Judge John Pickering: Impeached for drunkenness and profanity on the bench and for unlawful decisions. Convicted by Senate.
2. 1804: Supreme Court Justice Samuel Chase: Impeached for malfeasance, but acquitted in the Senate.
3. 1830: U.S. District Court Judge James Peck: Impeached for abusing contempt-of-court powers, but acquitted in the Senate.
4. 1862: U.S. District Court Judge West Humphreys: Impeached for supporting secession and for acting as a judge of the Confederate District Court. Convicted by Senate.
5. 1873: U.S. District Court Judge Mark Delahay: Impeached for misconduct in office and unsuitable personal habits (e.g., intoxication). Resigned before Senate trial.
6. 1904: U.S. District Court Judge Charles Swayne: Impeached for padding expense accounts and using property in receivership for personal gain, but acquitted in the Senate.
7. 1912: U.S. Commerce Court Judge Robert Archbald: Impeached for corrupt alliance with coal mine owners and railroad officials. Convicted by Senate.
8. 1926: U.S. District Court Judge George English: Impeached for taking an interest-free loan from a bank of which he was director. Resigned before Senate trial.
9. 1933: U.S. District Court Judge Harold Louderback: Impeached for favoritism in naming receivers, but acquitted in the Senate.
10. 1936: U.S. District Court Judge Halsted Ritter: Impeached for secretly taking a fee from a former law partner. Convicted by Senate.
11. 1986: U.S. District Court Judge Harry Claiborn: Impeached 406:0 for income tax evasion. Convicted by Senate.
12. 1988: U.S. District Court Judge Alcee L. Hastings: Impeached 413:3 for high crimes and misdemeanors (most notably, bribery). Convicted by Senate.
13. 1989: U.S. District Court Judge Walter L. Nixon: Impeached 417:0 for lying to federal investigators and a federal grand jury. Convicted by Senate.

Source: *Washington Post,* August 9, 1988, p. A9 and *New York times,* May 11, 1989, p. A8.

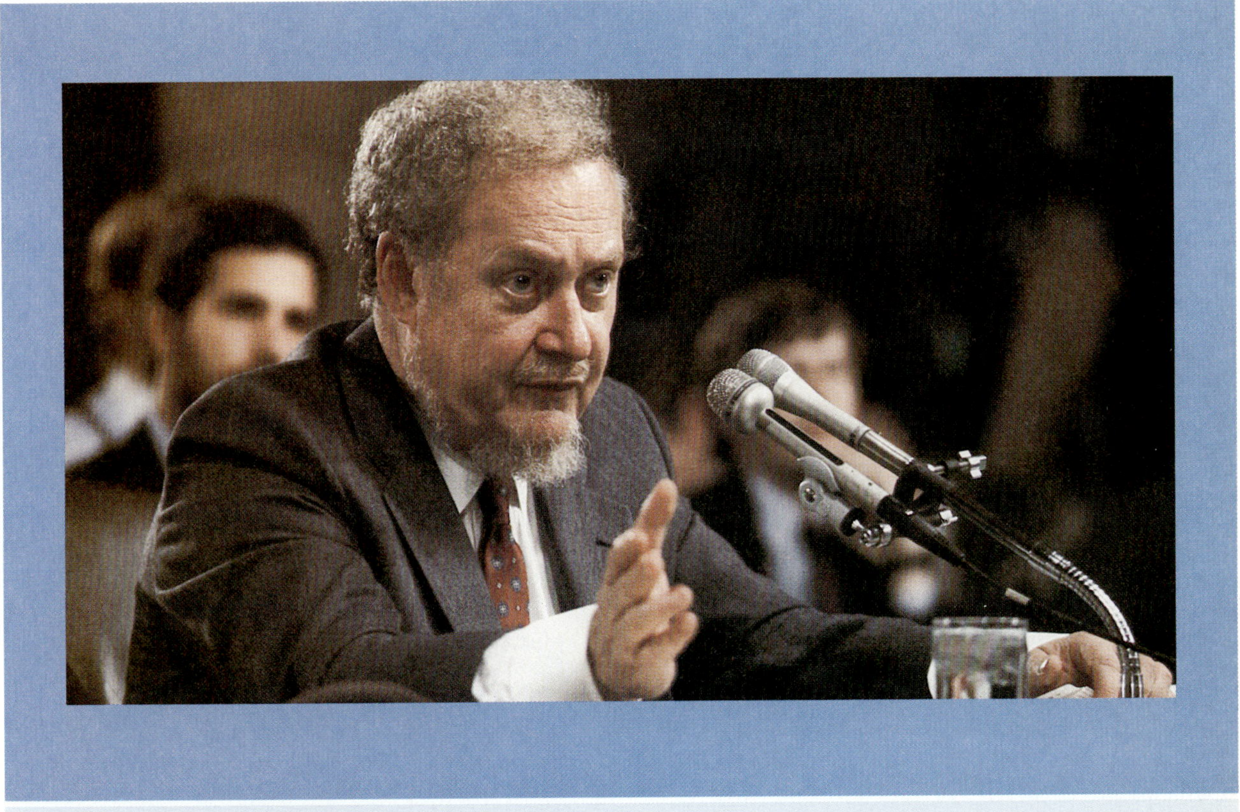

In 1987, U.S. Court of Appeals Judge Robert Bork became the fifth nominee to the Supreme Court in this century to be rejected by the Senate. Just two Democrats voted for him, only six Republicans against him. Lobbying played a role in his defeat, and so did his outspoken Senate testimony. Many—on both sides—felt that Bork would be decisive in moving the Court away from support for civil rights and liberties.

thority, which far surpasses the force of arms. This is essentially persuasive power, but it represents the law of the land, is delineated in the Constitution, and is overwhelmingly supported by the American public. Because the courts clarify and explain the law, the public naturally turns to the judicial branch to solve problems. A prime example is the Watergate tapes case, *United States* v. *Nixon,* which compelled the president to turn over his recordings to the courts (and ultimately resulted in his resignation).

While the U.S. district courts are very important, they are the courts of first instance. Thus, they are less involved in interpreting the Constitution and the law conclusively than are the appeals courts—the U.S. courts of appeals and the U.S. Supreme Court. But all federal courts, primarily the three levels of constitutional courts, exercise judicial authority. This inevitably raises profound questions about the role of the courts. The power of judicial review is the judiciary's most controversial weapon. As we have seen, it gives the courts the power to say no as well as yes to the other branches of government. And no is more of a problem than yes.

Judicial Review

Although the power of judicial review is not mentioned specifically in the Constitution, the

After Robert Bork's rejection, President Reagan chose Douglas Ginsburg for the Supreme Court. His nomination never reached the Senate. The administration's background check had missed some skeletons in Ginsburg's closet, including "pot" use as a law professor. Reagan's third choice, Judge Anthony M. Kennedy of the U.S. 9th Circuit Court of Appeals, easily won Senate approval.

founders discussed at length the need for a final arbiter in the political system. Judicial review is implied by various sections of the Constitution, such as Article VI (the supremacy clause) and Article III, which describes court power in detail. The founders realized the need for judicial review because of their experience as colonists at the mercy of the Privy Council. Hamilton's contributions to the *Federalist* and Section 25 of the Judiciary Act of 1789 both pointed to the need for judicial review. John Marshall, fourth chief justice of the United States, finally gave it constitutional validity in *Marbury* v. *Madison* (1803).

***Marbury* v. *Madison*.** The case of *Marbury* v. *Madison* has a curious history: Justice Marshall had direct personal involvement in the case; he should have disqualified himself from participating in it; and he certainly should not have written the opinion. The case could readily have been disposed of without meeting the constitutional issue and it might have been dismissed on jurisdictional grounds. Finally, Marshall's construction of the issues was unnecessarily complex. Nevertheless, the case comes down to us because Marshall ruled that "an act repugnant to the Constitution is void" and that "it is emphatically the province and the duty of the judicial department to say what the law is."

“ Perspectives ”

On the Judges' Role: Finding or Making Law

“*We are not final because we are infallible, but we are infallible only because we are final.*”

—Justice Robert H. Jackson

“*We have a legislative body, called the House of Representatives, of over 400 men. We have another legislative body, called the Senate, of less than 100 men. We have, in reality, another legislative body, called the Supreme Court, of nine men; and they are more powerful than all the others put together.*”

—Senator George W. Norris (R–Neb.)

“*They [courts and judges] make no law, they establish no policy, they never enter the domain of popular action. They do not govern. Their function in relation to the state is limited to seeing that popular action does not trespass upon right and justice as it exists in written constitutions and natural law.*”

—Justice David J. Brewer

“*While unconstitutional exercise by the executive and legislative branches is subject to judicial restraint, the only check on our own exercise of power is our own sense of self-restraint.*”

—Justice Harlan Fiske Stone

“*We are under the Constitution, but the Constitution is what the judges say it is.*”

—Governor Charles Evans Hughes of New York

“*Like other mortals, judges, though unaware, may be in the grip of prepossessions. The only way to relax such a grip, the only way to avoid finding in the Constitution the personal bias one has placed in it, is to explore the influences that have shaped one's unanalyzed views . . .*”

—Justice Felix Frankfurter

“*Judicial power, as contradistinguished from the power of the law, has no existence. Courts are the mere instruments of the law and can will nothing.*”

—Chief Justice John Marshall

“*I saw where justice lay, and the moral issue decided the court half the time; and I then sat down to search the authorities. . . . I might once in a while be embarrassed by a technical rule, but I almost always found principles suited to my views of the case . . .*”

—Chancellor James Kent of New York

Sources: Justice Jackson in *Brown* v. *Allen,* 334 U.S. 443 (1953), at 540, concurring opinion; George Norris, *Congressional Record* (February 13, 1930), p. 35666; Justice Brewer, address to the New York State Bar Association (1893); Justice Stone, in *United States* v. *Butler,* 297 U.S. 1 (1936), at 62, dissenting opinion; Charles Evans Hughes (1908), *Addresses* (New York: Harper's, 1916), p. 185; Justice Frankfurter, in *Haley* v. *Ohio,* 332 U.S. 596 (1948), concurring opinion; Chief Justice Marshall, in *Osborn* v. *United States Bank,* 9 Wheaton 739 (1824), majority opinion; James Kent (1810), in Willian Kent, ed., *The Memoirs and Letters of James Kent* (Boston: Little Brown, 1898), pp. 158–159.

POLITICAL LINKAGE

The Courts and Separation of Powers: Maxims of Judicial Restraint

Judicial activism has become a controversial issue, yet the Supreme Court has generally followed consistent principles that serve as a check on its powers. While these rules are not necessarily always followed, here are some "maxims" of judicial restraint:

1. Before the Court will glance at a particular issue or dispute, a definite "case" or "controversy" at law or in equity between bona fide adversaries under the Constitution must exist, involving the protection or enforcement of valuable legal rights, or the punishment, prevention, or redress of wrongs directly concerning the party or parties bringing the justiciable suit.
2. The party or parties bringing suit must have "standing."
3. The Court does not render advisory opinions, i.e., judicial rulings upon the constitutionality of governmental action in the absence of a case or controversy requiring such a ruling for its disposition.
4. Not only must the complainant in federal court expressly declare that he is invoking the Constitution of the United States, but a specific live rather than dead constitutional issue citing the particular provision on which he relies in that document must be raised by him; the Court will not entertain generalities.
5. The Court will not pass upon the constitutionality of a statute at the instance of one who has availed himself of its benefits but then decides to challenge its legality anyway.
6. All remedies in the pertinent lower federal and state courts must have been exhausted, and prescribed lower court procedure duly followed, before making application to the U.S. Supreme Court for review.
7. The federal question at issue must be substantial rather than trivial; it must be the piv-

By his apparent cautiousness, this brilliant Machiavellian seized the ultimate judicial power. In what is generally viewed as the most important decision in the Court's history, Marshall ruled that since Section 13 of the Judiciary Act had given the Supreme Court the power to issue a writ of *mandamus* by mere legislation, thus altering the constitutionally limited *original jurisdiction* of the Supreme Court, that segment of the law was necessarily null and void. Changes in the Constitution's wording may be brought about only by constitutional amendment. As one observer commented: "John Marshall snatched from the majority and offered to our courts, the function of rendering our political decencies and aspirations into immanent law. What we owe to Marshall is the otal point of the case; and it must be part of the plaintiff's case rather than part of his adversary's defense.

8. Questions of fact—as distinct from questions of law—are not normally accepted as proper bases for review.

9. The Court has never held itself absolutely bound by its precedents.

10. The Court has been inclined to defer to certain legislative or executive actions by classifying an issue otherwise quite properly before it as a political question—hence refusing to come to grips with it.

11. In the event of a validly challenged statute, the presumption of its constitutionality is always in its favor.

12. If a case or controversy can be decided upon any other than constitutional grounds—such as by statutory construction, which constitutes the greatest single area of the Court's work, or if it can rest on an independent state ground—the Court will be eager to do so.

13. The Court will not ordinarily impute illegal motives to the lawmakers.

14. If the Court does find that it must hold a law unconstitutional, it will usually try hard to confine the holding to that particular section of the statute which was successfully challenged on constitutional grounds.

15. A legislative enactment—or an executive action—may be unwise, unjust, unfair, undemocratic, injudicious, ". . . if you like . . . tyrannical," or simply stupid, but still be constitutional in the eyes of the Court.

16. The Court is not designed to serve as a check against inept, unwise, emotional, unrepresentative legislators; its responsibility is constitutional authority.

Source: Summarized from Henry J. Abraham: *The Judicial Process* (Copyright © 5th ed., 1986, by Oxford University Press, Inc., New York), pp. 369–392. Used by permission.

opportunity he gave us of combining a reign of conscience with a republic." [14]

After *Marbury* v. *Madison*. Although the Supreme Court is the final institutional judicial authority, it has rarely invoked its power of judicial review. Like lower courts, it prefers statutory construction. As of late 1988, of some 95,000 public and private laws passed by Congress, the Supreme Court had struck down as unconstitutional some or all of only 137 or 138 provisions of federal laws.[15] However, since 1789 it has thrown out some or all of more than 1000 state and local laws and provisions of state constitutions. After John Marshall's coup in *Marbury* v. *Madison,* no other federal legislation was declared unconstitutional by his Court (and only 36 state laws fell) during the rest of his 34 years on the high bench.

Just a year after *Marbury,* in the *Flying Fish* case (1804), Marshall made certain that the Court had judicial authority over the executive branch as well as the legislative branch. He ruled that President Adams had exceeded his powers in ordering the navy to seize vessels bound *to* or *from* a French port; Congress had authorized seizure of ships only going *to* French ports. Even without judicial review, though, the Marshall Court wielded awesome power. Three passive or uninspiring chief justices (John Jay, John Rutledge, and Oliver Ellsworth) had done little to bring respect to the judicial branch. But under the assertive Marshall, it did more than either of the other two branches to make the young United States strong, vigorous, and powerful and to render its Constitution a living, effective, elastic basic law.

It was not until 1857 that another federal law was struck down by the Supreme Court, in its disastrous decision in *Dred Scott* v. *Sandford.* Chief Justice Taney's historic ruling was intended to stem the tide of the oncoming war, but it had precisely the opposite effect.

The greatest crisis caused by the Court's use of judicial review occurred under the so-called nine old men of the Hughes Court (dominated by the doctrinaires Sutherland, Van Devanter, Butler, and McReynolds). This Court declared unconstitutional no fewer than 13 crucial New Deal laws, sponsored by the Franklin Roosevelt administration, between 1934 and 1936, many by 5:4 votes; yet these laws had been overwhelmingly endorsed by the government's legislative and executive branches as well as the public. Since then, only 65 provisions of congressional statutes have fallen (as of mid-1988). All were nullified since 1943, and all except eight because the Court said they infringed on civil rights or liberties granted by the Constitution.

Are Jurists "Judges" or "Legislators"?

The power of the courts does not depend merely on the power of judicial review. The courts' more frequent function is to interpret the law and state and federal executive actions. Do judges, in making decisions, "judge" each case on its own merits or do they "legislate"? Do they "find" or "make" the law? Theoretically, a court only judges a case or controversy and reaches a decision according to the law. Yet judges, especially those of the Supreme Court, are frequently accused of "legislating" rather than "judging," of "playing God," of being "social engineers," "power usurpers," and "busybodies." Critics agree that judges must have power to interpret legislation and executive action, and, if "absolutely justified," even strike down what is beyond "rational question" unconstitutional or illegal. However, many insist on drawing a line between judicial *judgment* and the exercise of judicial *will,* or "legislating." But can we draw such a line?

The debate between judicial activism and judicial restraint grows more heated each year as cases on race and such issues as abortion bring the Court to settle controversial political matters. Sometimes these opinions depend on "whose ox is being gored." However, it is not quite that simple. Reactions to judicial decisions are often subjective and judges themselves differ about their roles; "activists" like Justices Douglas and Brennan, for example, are much different from "conservatives" like Justices Frankfurter and Harlan II.

Obviously, judges do make law. Even Justice Holmes, an advocate of judicial restraint, recognized that judges do and must "legislate." (More than once he joked, "Why, I made some [laws] myself, just last Monday!") But he insisted that judges "can do so only interstitially; they are confined from molar to molecular motions." [16] By this he meant that while judges had ample decision room, they must not go beyond authorized limits. "Judges are men, not disembodied spirits; as men they respond to human situations," said Justice Frankfurter. Justice McReynolds insisted that a judge should not be "an amorphous dummy unspotted by human emotions"—and he assuredly was "spotted." And as Justice Cardozo wrote so eloquently, "The great tides and currents which engulf the rest of men do not turn aside in their course and pass the judges by." [17]

Yet human or not, a qualified and conscientious judge is not a free agent. Judges are "rigidly bound within walls that are unseen" by outsiders. They are governed by a long heritage: the spirit of the Anglo-Saxon law, the impact of past cases, and the regard for *stare decisis* (Latin, meaning "to stand by an earlier decision"). The sense of continuity with the past, as Holmes said, "is not a duty, it is only a necessity." [18] To Holmes, "A page of history was worth more than a volume of logic." Finally, the tradition of the Anglo-Saxon law, which includes a mass of unwritten laws, practices, rules, and customs, also dictates judicial self-restraint.

Judges know two other cardinal facts: First, only the president has the power to enforce their decisions—as, for example, when Presidents Eisenhower and Kennedy sent troops to Little Rock, Arkansas, Tuscaloosa, Alabama, and Oxford, Mississippi to support court orders to desegregate public schools and universities. Second, judicial decisions may be reversed, more or less effectively,

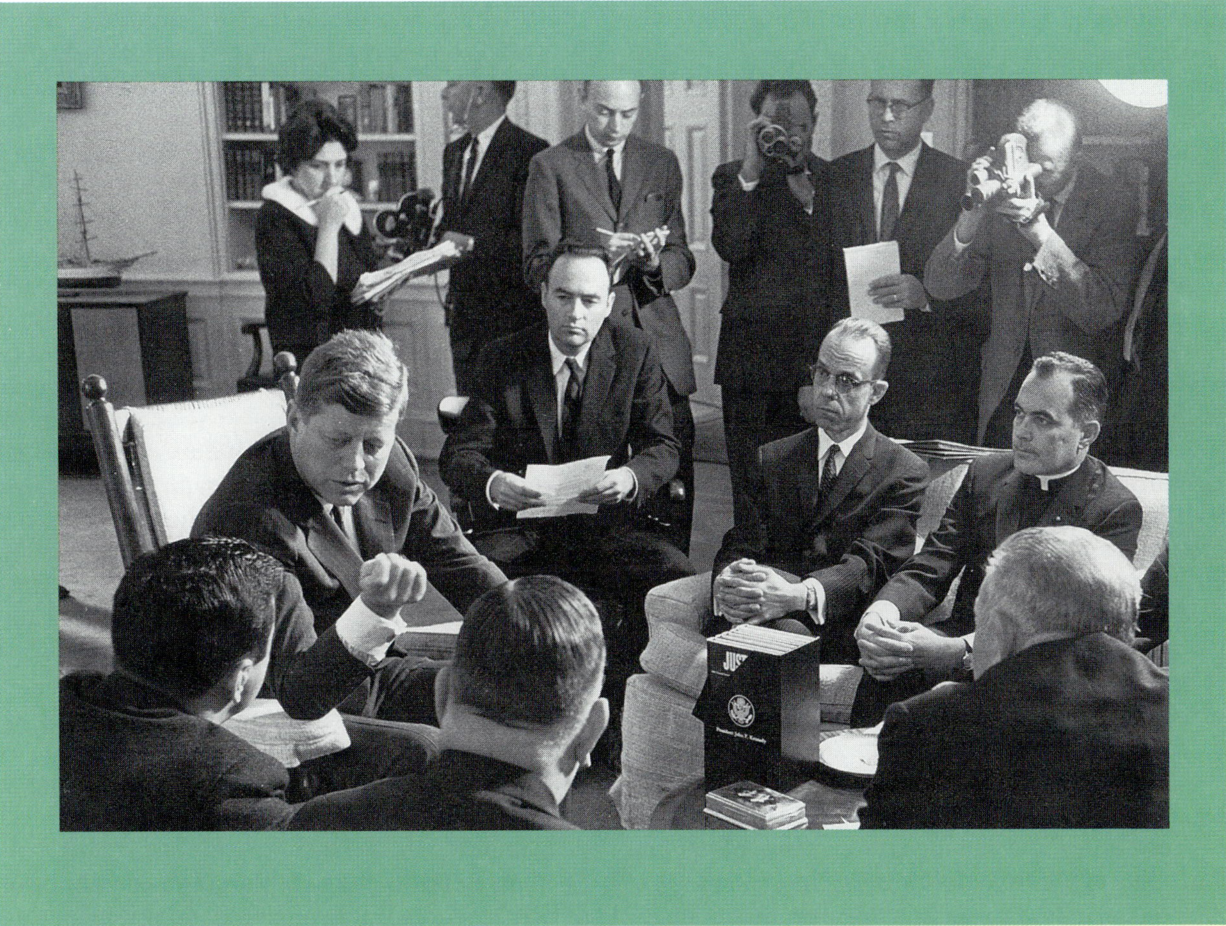

The judiciary's only power is moral suasion. The power of the purse and the sword are in other hands—Congress and the president. Here John F. Kennedy confers with aides and civil rights leaders before using force to support court desegregation orders in Oxford, Mississippi, and Tuscaloosa, Alabama, starting in 1961. Three years earlier, President Eisenhower sent troops to Little Rock to back the Court's ruling.

by legislation or by constitutional amendment. As Alexander Hamilton observed, the judiciary's only power is its power to persuade; purse and sword are in other hands.

But perhaps we expect the judicial branch to settle policy issues that the other branches ought to handle, such as desegregation, reapportionment, criminal justice, protection of privacy, and separation of church and state. Commented veteran court watcher Anthony Lewis: "Judicial interventions on fundamental issues are most clearly justified when there is no other remedy for a situation that threatens the nation fabric—when the path of political change is blocked." [19] This view assumes constitutional authority, however. Thus, while the Constitution gives clear authority to outlaw racial segregation and legislative malapportionment, it may well be fair to ask whether the courts have gone too far, especially in forced school busing, racial pairing, "reverse discrimination," and crabbed mathematical preciseness in legislative districting and apportionment. It is tempting to pass the buck. Yet the Constitution did not make the courts the nation's primary lawmakers.

Of course, the judicial branch, led by the Supreme Court, is engaged in politics. In Justice Frankfurter's words, though, the Court is "the Nation's ultimate judicial tribunal, not a super-legal-aid bureau." [20] Neither is it "a panacea for every blot upon the public welfare, nor should this Court, ordained as a judicial body, be thought of as a general haven for reform movements," to quote Justice John Marshall Harlan II.[21] Of course, the justices, who are "inevitably teachers in a vital national constitutional seminar," [22] consult their own policy preferences. But a "constitutional *seminar*" is not a "constitutional *convention.*"

Judges must maintain high standards of integrity, intelligence, logic, reflectiveness, and consistency. They must demonstrate a sense of history and a knowledge of public affairs; they must follow "the hunch of intuition about the inner life of American democracy." [23] They must heed the "felt necessities of the time," [24] although this is basically the legislature's job, while holding to constitutional fundamentals. They should resolutely shun *prescriptive* policy making.

Summary

- The federal court system is well designed and functions adequately. State court systems are perhaps less adequate. But our court system is burdened by a growing number of cases. Lawyers appear to be taking advantage of our liberal adversary system; they encourage clients to go to court when disputes could be settled otherwise.
- The tendency to turn questions of public policy into judicial ones weakens the role of the legislature. It gives more importance to the courts at the expense of the republican ideal.
- The power of judicial review makes the courts essential arbiters in resolving disputes among the three branches of government. It also arbitrates between the federal government and the states and establishes the difference between social and individual rights.
- Theoretically, courts—especially appeals courts—merely decide the constitutionality of a challenged law or executive action. Yet judges are also humans, subject to the same forces as other persons. They are not free from value commitments.
- Judges disagree about the nature of the judicial role. Some may be charged with "legislating" rather than "judging." But the line between those two concepts is difficult to draw. Certain maxims of judicial self-restraint—such as classifying an issue as "political" and thus refusing to tackle it—have evolved to define the judicial role.
- Judges are well paid, prestigious, powerful, and politically influential. States choose judges in three ways: election, appointment, and a combination of the two, as in California and Missouri, which use the appointment plus popular retention election plan. The constitutionally mandated plan of presidential nomination and senatorial confirmation for federal judges is broadly regarded as preferable.
- Presidents may well value professional merit over political affiliation in choosing judges. But presidents have always appointed a very large

majority of judges from their own party. Ford chose the fewest from his own party, yet 81.2 percent of his appointments were Republicans. Democrat Wilson's appointees were 98.6 percent from his own party, a record that still stands.

- President Carter changed the way lower federal court judges were selected and nominated to open up the federal bench. He appointed almost 300 judges—a record—including many women, blacks, and Hispanics. Carter's changes reflected a "representative" concept, which, while not new, had never been followed before. Carter did not have any opportunity to appoint Supreme Court justices, however. When the initial vacancy during the Reagan administration occurred, the president appointed the first woman to sit on the Supreme Court—Sandra Day O'Connor of Arizona. The next two Reagan appointees, Antonin Scalia and Anthony Kennedy, as well as his promotion of Justice Rehnquist to chief justice, opted for "conservative" jurisprudence. President Bush was expected to follow a similar course, if vacancies arose.

Readings on The Judiciary

Abraham, Henry J. 1985. *Justices and Presidents: A Political History of Appointments to the Supreme Court,* 2nd ed. New York: Oxford University Press. Examines presidential motivations in the selection of all justices from Jay through O'Connor, how they fulfilled their nominator's expectations, and how they performed on the high bench.

Abraham, Henry J. 1986. *The Judicial Process: An Introductory Analysis of the Courts of the United States, England, and France,* 5th ed. New York: Oxford University Press. Examines and evaluates the nature of the judicial process comparatively, with particular emphasis on its modus operandi in the United States.

Bickel, Alexander M. 1978. *The Supreme Court and the Idea of Progress,* rev. ed. New Haven, Conn.: Yale University Press. A sophisticated analysis and critique of the role of the U.S. Supreme Court in the governmental process.

Cardozo, Benjamin N. 1921. *The Nature of the Judicial Process.* New Haven, Conn.: Yale University Press. Still the leading interpretation of the appropriate role of judges and justices, written with elegance and stylistic brilliance.

Choper, Jesse. 1980. *Judicial Review and the National Political Process.* Chicago: University of Chicago Press. Grapples with the elusive line between judicial "judging" and "legislating" and suggests a controversial solution.

Ely, John Hart. 1979. *Democracy and Distrust: A Theory of Judicial Review.* Cambridge, Mass.: Harvard University Press. An interesting but contentious attempt to draw the line between judicial activism and restraint by focusing on "process" as the solution.

Holmes, Oliver Wendell, Jr. 1881. *The Common Law.* Boston: Little, Brown. The classic treatment of the Anglo-Saxon common law, its meaning, and its application, by the famed justice.

Lusky, Louis. 1975. *By What Right? A Commentary on the Supreme Court's Right to Revise the Constitution.* Charlottesville, Va.: Michie Co. A learned, if controversial, endeavor to present a solution for the elusiveness of the appropriate "line" in judicial review.

McDowell, Gary L. 1988. *Curbing the Courts: The Constitution and the Limits of Judicial Power.* Baton Rouge: Louisiana State University Press. An engaging effort to harness judicial power by perceived constitutional authority to curb the courts through various procedural arrangements.

Rehnquist, William H. 1987. *The Supreme Court: How It Was, How It Is.* New York: William Morrow. A comprehensive, expert account of the operation of the U.S. Supreme Court, written in readable style by the sixteenth chief justice of the United States.

Part Four

Public Policy

"The citizen of the United States does not acquire his practical science and his positive notions from books. . . . The American learns to know the laws by participating in the act of legislation; and he takes a lesson in the forms of governing from governing."

— Alexis de Tocqueville

Chapter 17

Domestic Policy Processes

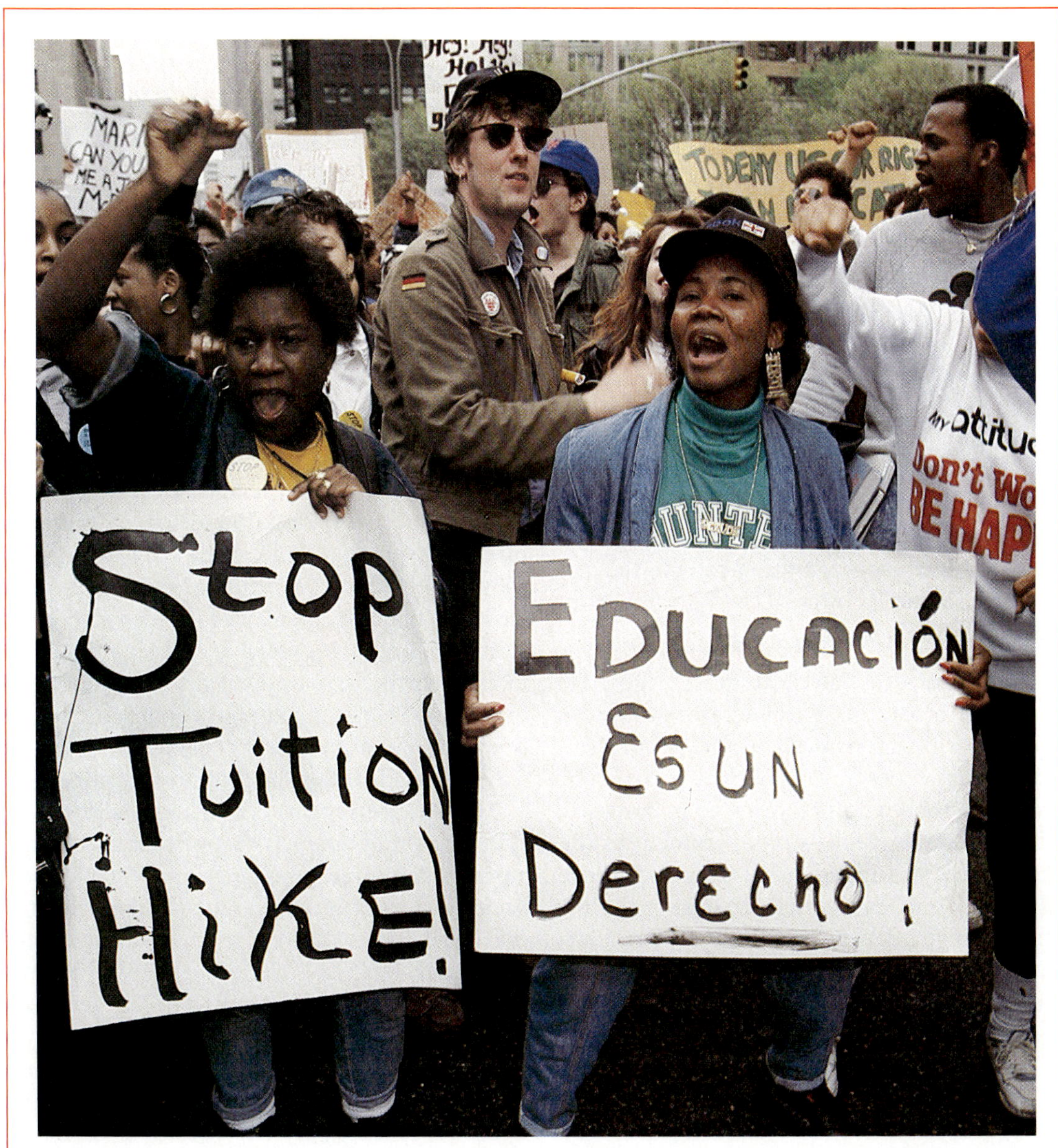
Stop Tuition Hike!
Educación Es un Derecho!
my attitude
Don't Wo
BE HAP

In one of his final addresses as president, Ronald Reagan discussed a concept familiar to students of public policy—the "iron triangle."

> It sometimes seems to many Americans that what might be called a triangle of institutions—parts of Congress, the media, and special-interest groups—is transforming and placing out of focus our constitutional balance. . . . Some have used the term "iron triangle" to describe something like what I am talking about. . . .
>
> When I came to office, I found the presidency a weakened institution. I found a Congress that was trying to transform our government into a quasi-parliamentary system. And I found a Washington colony that—through the iron triangle—was attempting to rule the nation according to its interests and desires more than the nation's.[1]

The president did not quite get it right. He substituted the media for bureaucratic groups as the third corner of the triangle. But he expressed the concerns that many have about the policy connections among those vitally interested in domestic issues. The iron triangle, or subgovernment as the phenomenon will be labeled here, is one response to the complications caused by separating the institutions. What gets divided by the president, Congress, and the courts is joined through communication within subgovernments. Before discussing this phenomenon in more detail, however, it is important to review the nature of the policy process in more general terms.

Making public policy is a frustrating and very human process. Its complexities are rooted in the Constitution and the vast institutional structure of government; its effects are felt in every aspect of our lives. Yet whatever the impediments to smooth-running decision making, and they are many, the fact is that we still pass laws and implement them. This chapter discusses how that happens, with special attention to the budget-making process that has grown so intricate in recent times.

At one time, the word *policy* was used to mean government. It has also been used to mean management, or prudence in management. Today the common meaning is a settled program adopted and followed by a government, institution, body, or individual. How does a program get adopted and followed by a government? That is the central question for this chapter. We will focus on the *policy process*—that is, the means by which programs are developed, put into effect, and then evaluated for their merit.

Networks of Policymakers

It is important to stress the democratic quality of our policy process. Settling on a plan to be followed by government is complicated by a devotion to public participation in decision making. Americans are often willing to sacrifice efficiency in order that those affected by government can have their say. To be sure, no one knows exactly how much public participation is required to achieve democracy—but we are likely to know it if some group feels left out. And Americans appear to support having an *opportunity* to participate, even if they do not always take advantage of that opportunity.

There are several consequences of the American version of democratic policy making. First, as a practical matter, participation often will be quite limited—typically confined to those with the expertise or direct interest in the issue at hand. Second, there is always the possibility of greatly expanded participation should a policy gain national attention. Third, policy designs prepared by a few normally have to be approved by those representing the many. And fourth, a whole government (typically represented by the president or his party) may be evaluated in an election for how well it manages participatory values.

Studying the policy process is different from studying specific government institutions like the presidency, Congress, or the courts. Here the focus is on public problems and how government deals with them. For example, the spread of AIDS during the late 1980s is clearly a major public problem. Who did what in government to act on that problem? What conflicts among participants can be identified? In proposing policy action some propose treatment and research for cures; others favor widespread testing of individuals. This type of controversy distinguishes a problem from an *issue*—a controversial public problem.

Focusing on issues leads to studying action in the political institutions that exist to resolve them. Only rarely can one explain all of what happens on a major issue by observing just one institution. Bureaucrats, legislators, presidents and their appointees, and even judges may be involved along the way. Frequently different branches of government interact to form *a network of decision makers*—a minigovernment for a particular issue. These policy networks of contact and communication underlie the policy process. They existed long before President Reagan acknowledged them in 1988.

When government expands, the number and complexity of policy networks become greater. Picture the national government as a huge mosaic of networks, with thousands of communications lines crisscrossing the major political institution. Viewing government in this way reveals roadblocks to policy change, especially to reducing government programs. Policy networks tend to become permanent features of government. Douglass Cater refers to these networks as *subgovernments:*

> In one important area of policy after another, substantial efforts to exercise power are waged by alliances cutting across the two branches of government and including key operatives from outside. In effect, they constitute subgovernments of Washington comprising the expert, the interested, and the engaged. . . . The subgovernment's tendency is to strive to become self-sustaining in control of power necessary to its purposes. Each resists being overridden.[2]

Various names are used to refer to these interactions among government officials and private interests. They are called "subsystems," "whirlpools," "cozy little triangles," or President Reagan's "iron triangles." To simplify matters, we will use Cater's term "subgovernment."

Figure 17–1 shows some of the subgovernment for policy issues associated with elementary and secondary education. When a specific problem arises within this broad set of issues, participants from the executive, Congress, and the affected groups will react and interact. Executive participants will probably be drawn from the Department of Education's unit on elementary and secondary education or possibly its unit on aid for federally impacted areas (an example would be those areas of the country where military bases are located—one impact of which is to reduce the local tax base for school support). The Office of Management and Budget (OMB), located in the Executive Office of the President, will also be involved when the issue is budgetary. Congressional participants are drawn from the House and Senate subcommittees that have been created to deal with federal aid to schools. Subcommittee members and staff will be involved in the issues for which they have expertise or special interest. Finally, the interest groups will be represented by professional lobbyists and others from national, state, and local groups who come to Capitol Hill to testify and otherwise seek to convince legislators to support their views. The source for the information in Figure 17–1 is a document called the *Washington Information Directory.* It could easily be labeled a "Handbook of Subgovernments" since it lists over 500 major issues and identifies the executive, legislative, and interest group units that are associated with these issues. Such a *Directory* is a proper supplement to the Constitution for understanding how democracy works in this nation.

If a group has gained a government subsidy, tax break, competitive advantage, or other favorable policy, it will naturally resist change that threatens its present status. Often the group can expect support from the legislators and bureaucrats who were instrumental in the original decision. The reason is simple. Members of Congress and administrators tend to identify with a program they supported originally. Presumably it was designed initially to solve a problem judged to be serious enough to require federal action. Thus, they perceive benefits for their constituents or clienteles from its continuation. Furthermore, rewards are involved. Legislators may be reelected when they are viewed as delivering benefits to their constituents; government agencies may receive support from appreciative interest groups when they administer these benefits. This is not to say that all in gov-

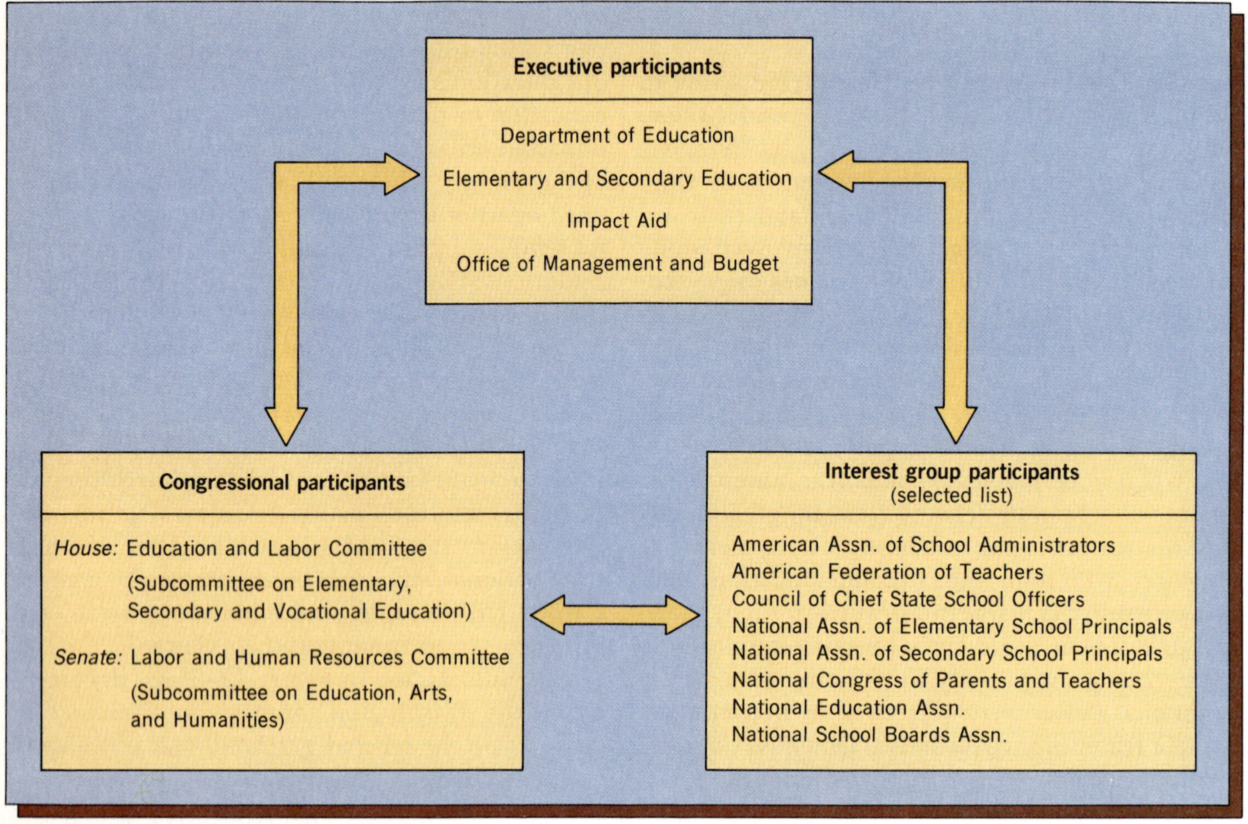

Figure 17–1 An elementary and secondary subgovernment. Source: Congressional Quarterly, *Washington Information Directory, 1984–1985* (Washington, D.C.: Congressional Quarterly, Inc., 1984) pp. 101–103.

ernment are cynical and self-interested. It simply recognizes the realities of how programs begin and are sustained over time, as well as the understandable reluctance of people to give up benefits.

The integrity of subgovernments was severely challenged in the 1970s. Active citizens' groups like Common Cause and the Ralph Nader organization were joined by numerous organizations concerned with the rights of women and minorities, environmental issues, nuclear power and its effects, and the Vietnam War. These groups often demand increased participation in government decision making. They express dissatisfaction with the "cozy little triangle" concept of governing as basically undemocratic. Further, the environmental, energy, and economic issues of the 1970s and 1980s were simply too large in scope to be dealt with effectively by subgovernments. The result was the emergence of what one scholar has called *issue networks.* Issue networks are less tightly drawn than subgovernments for they "comprise a large number of participants with quite variable degrees of mutual commitment or of dependence on others in their environment; in fact it is almost impossible to say where a network leaves off and the environment begins." [3] Compared to the cozy little triangles, networks seem like "sloppy large hexagons." [4]

Subgovernments can be directly threatened by legislative proposals. There are literally thousands of examples of this happening. Sometimes legislation is so broad in scope that it cuts across the interests represented within subgovernments. On these rare occasions subgovernment participants

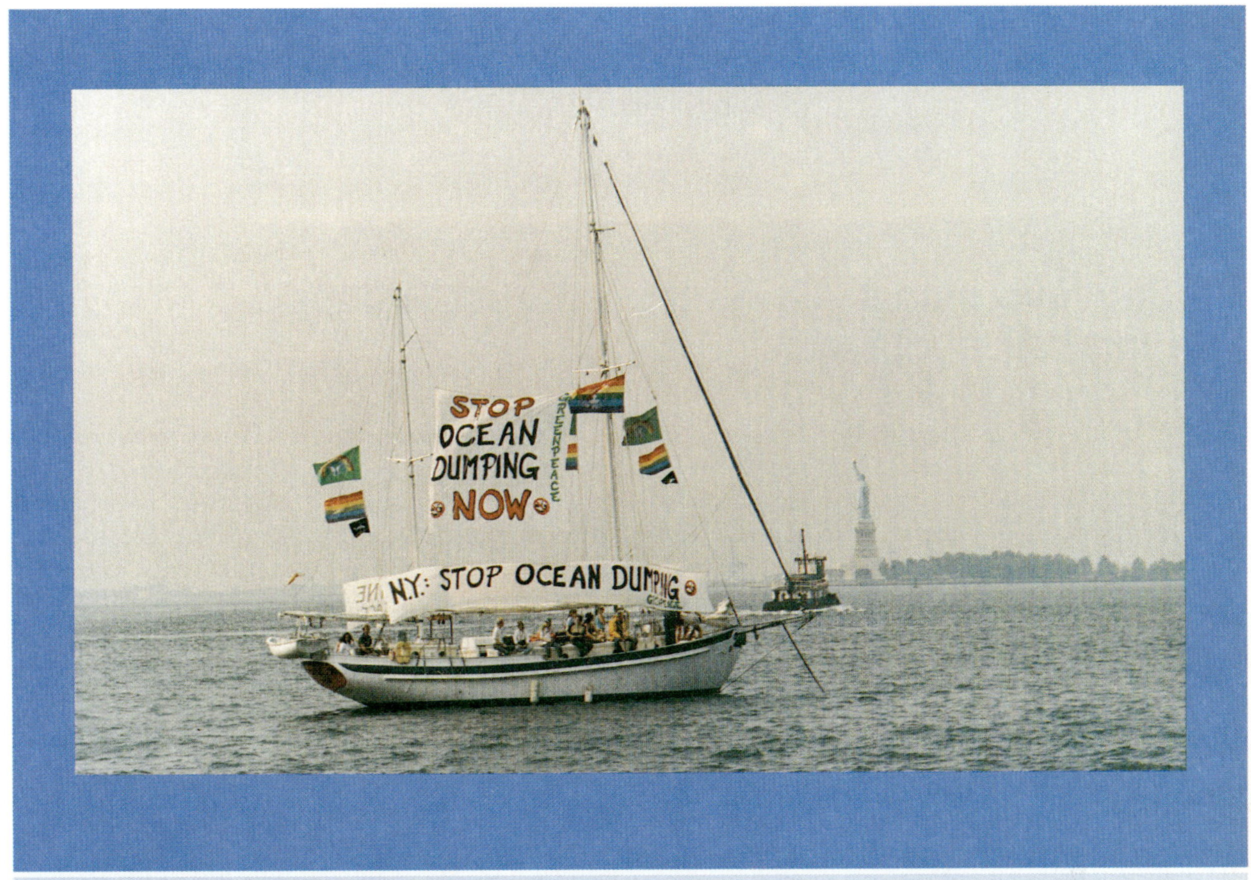

The recent rise of citizen groups has challenged subgovernment politics. This group has taken to sailboats—to show concern for the environment—in their protest against the dumping of wastes in ocean waters. Citizen actions like this one near New York City have become common, often attracting media attention and leading to policy change.

may all be drawn to Capitol Hill at the same time—if not always united in their response to the legislative threat. Jeffrey H. Birnbaum and Alan S. Murray describe such a case in their book *Showdown at Gucci Gulch: Lawmakers, Lobbyists, and the Unlikely Triumph of Tax Reform.* The federal taxing system had been the object of full-scale reform for decades. But with so many powerful interests involved, only cosmetic changes were possible, many of which only made the tax code worse. Former Treasury Secretary Donald T. Regan, a principal proponent of reform during the Reagan administration, described the situation this way:

The tax system was complicated, inequitable, expensive to administrate, and so filled with loopholes that it was entirely unnecessary to cheat on taxes in order to avoid them. Some individuals earned millions of dollars in a given year, reported every penny of this income and, by taking advantage of tax shelters and other provisions provided by law, paid no federal income tax at all. The inequity was even more glaring in the case of corporations. The underground economy alone, conducted in cash and unrecorded transactions, probably cost the Treasury at least $90 billion a year in

"Perspectives"

On Subgovernment: Congress, Interest Groups, and Executive Agencies

"*Nothing is more natural than for interested individuals or groups to cluster about those government agencies whose decisions affect them directly. With the rise of the welfare state and its attendant philosophy of positive government, these relationships were formalized and invested with theoretical underpinnings of 'interest group liberalism.'*"

—Roger H. Davidson

"*The resolution of policy issues tends often to be relegated to secondary levels of the political setting. Policy-making is often left essentially to subordinate units of the Administration and of Congress. The parties often similarly tend to leave issue politics to interest groups. Thus the relative autonomy of bureaus, committees, and interest groups in special areas of policy is encouraged by being 'farmed out' to the organizations most immediately concerned.*"

—J. Leiper Freeman

"*First, subsystems provide stability for existing equilibriums among interests. . . . Second, subsystems provide continuous access and superior opportunities for influence to high-quantity, aggregated interests. . . . Third, subsystems provide some access and representation to interests that are not dominant. . . . Fourth, substantial changes in the balances among interests served by subsystems can be expected to occur only through macropolitical intervention that modifies the rules and roles operating in the systems.*"

—Emmette S. Redford

"*I don't believe too much in the momentum theory any more. I believe in institutional inertia. Two months of response can't beat fifteen years of political infrastructure. I'm talking about K Street and all of the interest groups in this town, the community of interest groups.*"

—David Stockman

"*There are three types of policy networks. . . . The cozy little connection is restricted to contacts between those who want a favor and those with authority to grant it. . . . The cozy little triangle also is characterized by limited participation and access. . . . The principal function of the triangle is to stabilize policy. . . . Finally, the sloppy large hexagon describes those interactions on highly visible, public issues for which there is considerable demand that large numbers of public figures be involved. Access is virtually unlimited.*"

—Charles O. Jones

Sources: Roger H. Davidson, "Breaking Up Those 'Cozy Triangles': An Impossible Dream?" in *Legislative Reform and Public Policy* eds. Susan Welch and John Peters (New York: Praeger, 1977), p. 30; J. Leiper Freeman. *The Political Process* (Garden City, N.Y.: Doubleday, 1955), p. 10; Emmette S. Redford, *Democracy in the Administrative State* (New York: Oxford University Press, 1969), pp. 102–105; William Greider, "The Education of David Stockman," *Atlantic Monthly* (December 1981), p. 51; Charles O. Jones, *The United States Congress: People, Place, and Policy* (Homewood, Ill.: Dorsey Press, 1982), p. 361.

> unpaid taxes on an estimated $500 billion in unreported earnings.[5]

According to Regan, he got President Reagan's attention on this matter by asking him: "What does General Electric have in common with Boeing, General Dynamics, and fifty-seven other big corporations?" The president said he did not know.

> "What these outfits have in common is that no one of them pays a penny in taxes to the United States government."
>
> *What?* the President said.
>
> His shock was genuine. A dumbfounded silence settled over his economic advisers. What unconventional idea was I trying to plant in the President's mind now?
>
> "Believe it or not, Mr. President," I continued, "your secretary paid more federal taxes last year than all of those giant companies put together." [6]

As the idea of tax reform gained momentum on Capitol Hill, even the chairman of the Committee on Ways and Means, Dan Rostenkowski (D–Ill.), may have failed to appreciate the enormity of undertaking tax reform. Ways and Means top tax lawyer Robert Leonard tried to give a hint. He approached his chairman several times in early 1985 bearing a copy of the Internal Revenue Code of 1954, the standard text at the time. It was hundreds of pages in small print. "Boss," Leonard told him, "that's what we're going to change." After he had done that a couple of times, Rostenkowski said, "It began to penetrate this thick skull. I said, 'Holy Jesus, this is a monstrous task.' But by then we were already in it; you get to the point of no return." [7]

Both President Reagan and Rostenkowski—later to be joined by the chairman of the Senate Finance Committee, Robert Packwood (R–Ore.)—decided that the time had come to make major changes. It was a remarkable demonstration of bipartisan leadership that sent lobbyists scurrying to Capitol Hill.

> With billions of dollars of tax breaks on the line, major corporations, trade associations, and pressure groups hired the biggest names in Washington to protect themselves. . . . Many of the lobbyists were former members of Congress and former aides, whose stock-in-trade was their expertise in the system and their access to old colleagues and bosses.[8]

These were the highly paid, well-tailored, and Gucci-shoed representatives of those in danger of losing their tax breaks. They lined up every morning outside the Committee on Ways and Means—in the halls of the Longworth House Office Building, which came to be known as Gucci Gulch. "The line sometimes stretched the entire length of the hallway, a city block long, and then wrapped around the corner. There were so many people that it looked like the committee was giving something away—which, at times, it was." [9] Eventually the most comprehensive tax reform bill in history passed both houses and was signed by the president.

National political institutions interact to make policy decisions—occasionally as comprehensive in scope as the 1986 tax reform. Those who make up subgovernments may prefer to make decisions informally—perhaps even out of public view. But they are subject to the actions of the institutions of government. Approval may be merely formal in many cases, but it is almost always required.

Stages of the Policy Process

What happens when government acts on a public problem? First, the problem is identified, defined, and judged to be significant enough for government action. Second, options for solving the problem are reviewed, followed by the selection of the best choice. Third, this option must gain the approval of those elected to their positions of authority. Fourth, policy solutions are applied to the problem. Fifth, the results are measured to determine whether it was all worthwhile, whether the policy actually solved the problem. Sixth, adjustments are made after evaluating impacts. No wonder that, most often, the end result is a relatively small change in an existing policy!

These six stages are common to most deci-

IMPACT

Organized Interests and the Gasoline Tax

What issue pits General Motors against Chrysler? Southern and western states against northeastern and midwestern states? The answer: an increase in the gasoline tax for the purpose of reducing the federal budget deficit. One proposal facing Congress would provide for an increase of 10 cents per gallon in the next five years. Immediately, interest groups began taking sides.

The current tax, about 25 percent of the price of fuel, is far below the average of 68 percent in Europe and Japan. The bill's supporters note that every penny of increase would reduce the deficit by about a billion dollars. By encouraging Americans to drive less, a tax could also help the environment and reduce dependence on foreign oil. But a diverse coalition of interest groups ranged against it gives the bill only an outside chance:

- Representatives of southern and western states, where citizens drive more to cover the greater distances between towns, claim that the tax would unfairly hurt their drivers. Governors and state departments of transportation also oppose an increase in the federal fuel tax because it would become harder to increase *state* fuel taxes (currently between 7.5 and 20.9 cents per gallon).
- The Road Information Program—which includes asphalt makers, road builders, and the Automobile Association of America—opposes diverting money from the construction and repair of highways and bridges. Right now most gasoline tax revenues are earmarked for the federal Highway Trust Fund. Using this money for nonhighway purposes, such as deficit reduction, might establish a precedent, leading to other raids on the HTF and, ultimately, to a deterioration of the nation's roads.
- The Coalition Against Regressive Taxation rejects any sales tax. Such a tax is regressive, since if two drivers use the same amount of gasoline, the one with lower income pays a greater *portion* of income in tax.
- The Fuel Users for Equitable Levies (FUEL)—including everything from California grape growers to rural Vermont letter carriers—argues that the deficit should not be balanced at the expense of those whose work requires them to use more gas.
- Tourist-related industries worry that fewer families would travel if fuel prices increase.

The proposal has one perhaps surprising ally. Chrysler is the only American auto manufacturer heavily invested in smaller and more efficient cars; an increase in the gasoline tax would encourage motorists to buy Chrysler cars. Yet clearly advocates of an increase in the fuel tax face a real challenge in their efforts to reduce the federal budget deficit.

Source: *Congressional Quarterly Weekly Report,* January 7, 1989, pp. 24–27.

sionmaking processes in or out of government. We will look at each stage in detail.

Identifying the Problem

Why do some problems get to government and others not? Some people believe that government responds to pressure from interest groups. According to one scholar:

> The range of organized, identifiable, known groups is amazingly narrow; there is nothing remotely universal about it. . . . *Pressure politics is essentially the politics of small groups.* . . . The system is skewed, loaded and unbalanced in favor of a fraction of a minority.[10]

By this view, the problems that get to government are those defined by a relatively few groups, those with the financial and other resources to engage in pressure politics. As a result the agenda tends to be biased to favor certain groups or classes in society.

Others propose that those in authority may try to prevent certain problems from getting to government. Problem identification and definition are controlled by those groups with special access to public officials. Reference is made to "nondecisionmaking"—that is, efforts to prevent government acknowledgement of certain problems.

> A nondecision . . . is a decision that results in suppression or thwarting of a . . . challenge to the values or interests of the decision-maker. To be more nearly explicit, nondecision-making is a means by which demands for change in the existing allocation of benefits and privileges in the community can be suffocated before they are even voiced; or kept covert; or killed before they gain access to the relevant decision-making arena.[11]

These interpretations ring true to some, especially to those who cannot get their problem before government. In fact, public opinion can play an important role in determining the priorities among problems or in building support for major changes in government programs. It is generally acknowledged that the lack of public support for the Vietnam War was important in our eventual withdrawal; domestic priorities were more important. In a more recent example, the Reagan administration had a difficult time selling aid to the contras as a national policy toward Nicaragua. Public opinion tended to be very skeptical even though aid was supported by a popular president.

Yet there is little question of the importance—and political nature—of the first stage of the policy process. Getting a problem on the agenda is a crucial first step in seeking government relief. If politics is about power, then control of the agenda is a critical element in the political process.

It is not in the least surprising that major economic interests in society will act to protect their advantage. A good example is car safety for automobile manufacturers. Once safety is identified as an important problem requiring government action, there is little the manufacturers can do to fight new regulations. How can anyone oppose improving the safety of motor vehicles? The nondecisionmaking approach is to prevent the issue of safety from getting to the government in the first place.

Major changes in the agenda of government tend to come during periods of government expansion, like Roosevelt's New Deal during the 1930s or Johnson's Great Society during the 1960s. More often, however, new problems grow out of those already treated by government, leaving little room for problems to come from outside. Or programs may grow so fast that they command most of the available resources; this too precludes new initiatives. Therefore a mature government may generate its own agenda.

The huge deficits piled up during the Reagan administration illustrate the difficulty in getting public support for action on a major domestic problem. Since the economy was doing well, neither the president nor Congress was willing to take dramatic actions to forestall future effects of the deficit. Lacking public interest or support, public officials were reluctant to act, though all acknowledged the significant problems that resulted. The growth of debt during the Reagan period was not even a major issue in the 1988 presidential election despite agreement among experts as to its importance for the new administration and the 101st Congress.

POLITICAL LINKAGE

Public Opinion and Public Policy

Does public opinion really matter? Consider popular opposition to the war in Vietnam. In each year from the mid-1960s until American troops withdrew in 1974, a sample of public opinion was asked this question:

> In view of the developments since we entered the fighting in Vietnam, do you think the United States made a mistake sending troops to fight in Vietnam?

Here are the results.

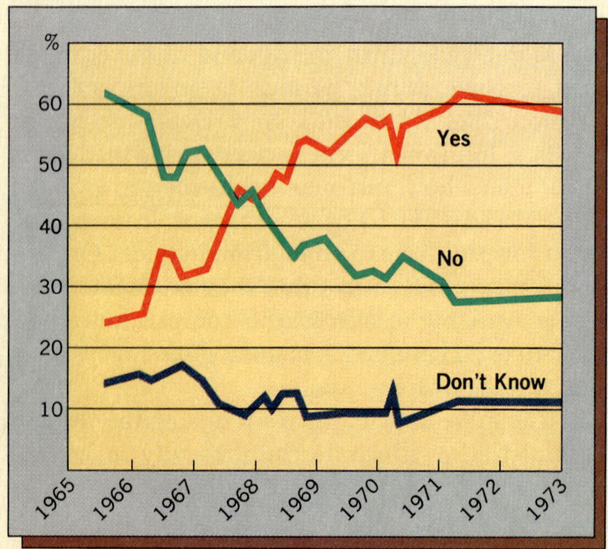

While the public began to disapprove of U.S. involvement at least as early as 1965, its changing attitude in the following years was much more important to the policy-making process. It became increasingly difficult for the government to explain and justify its foreign policy. Public opinion does not always influence policy decisions—but when citizen attitudes become crystallized and emotional, government leaders are hesitant to ignore them.

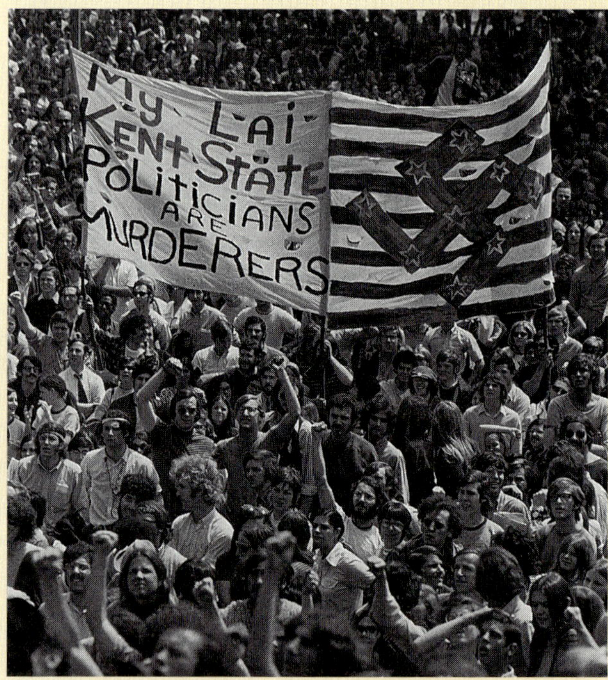

As the Vietnam War grew more controversial, government faced frequent protests—and new constraints on policy making. A touchstone was Kent State University, where National Guard soldiers fired on students, killing four. The students had gathered in protest after American soldiers massacred civilians at My Lai, a village in Vietnam.

Source: Harold W. Stanley and Richard G. Niemi, *Vital Statistics on American Politics* (Washington, D.C.: Congressional Quarterly Press, 1988), p. 299.

Choosing an Option

Once a problem that merits government action is identified, proposals must be designed to cope with it. Developing these options is not a politically neutral process. One person's good alternative may be another's worst choice. People differ dramatically in how they view policy issues and their solutions.

Consider the financial problems of colleges and universities. Solutions may include direct subsidies from government to the institutions, tax credits to parents for tuition payments, increased tuition, loans to needy students, and loans to all students. Which solution is "good" depends on how one sees the effects of aiding institutions, either directly or through the consumers (parents or students). Those effected are also likely to have opinions about whether such support is best administered at the federal or state level. Criteria for making these judgments are typically based on each person's experience and personal situation. Conflict among these judgments makes the ultimate selection political.

The development of options, even the final choice among them, is often left to a subgovernment. But even experts in a bureaucracy, an interest group, or a legislative committee have definite preferences of their own. Sometimes they favor what has been done in the past; sometimes they search for analogies to determine what was done in similar cases. Often they choose the option on which they have the most complete information or for which there is strong pressure.

The process of choosing the best option may be simple or incredibly complex. It may depend on

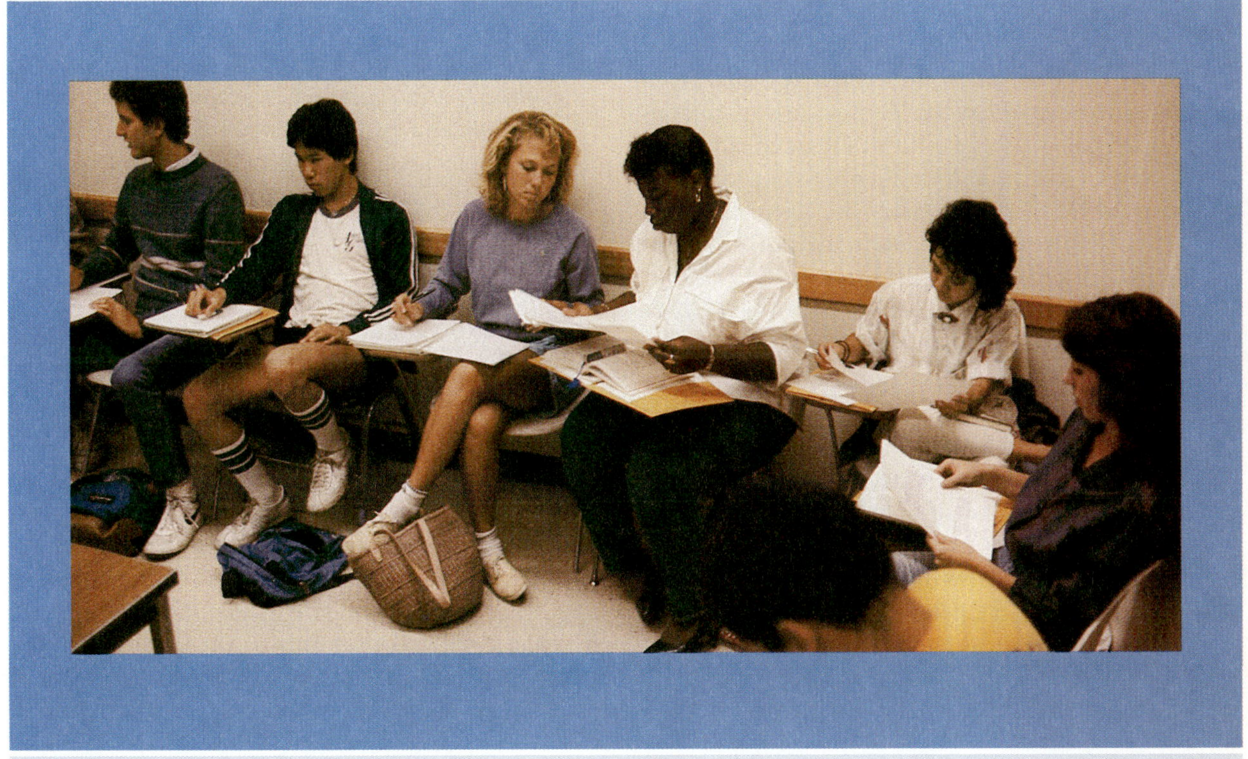

Methods for financing higher education in the United States are as diverse as students themselves. Federal, state, and local governments may be involved. So may private sources, including foundations, business, labor—and, of course, above all, the family. No other nation has such a varied system of support.

the nature of the issue, the number of interests affected, whether or not a government program is already on the books, and the levels of government involved. Selecting the best site for the local library is normally simple; it involves relatively few people and limited choices. Determining how to reduce trade imbalances is an enormously complex undertaking. Thus, for example, in 1988 President Reagan resisted various congressional initiatives in regard to foreign trade, fearing retaliation by other nations. He vetoed one bill only to have the Congress pass a second with the support of many of his own party.

One advantage of democracy is presumed to be this competition between proposed solutions. In theory, a large number of participants searching for the best choice should produce the best possible policy. It does not always work out, but few advocate reducing participation.

Getting Approval ■

Once the best possible option for solving a problem has been selected, the next task is to convince others to go along with it. Democratic political systems—unlike autocratic ones—require that plans be public and invite criticism. The finest plan cannot be implemented without legislative, organizational, or professional support.

The most familiar approval process is *lawmaking in legislatures.* It is fundamental to a democratic system—the process by which all other approval procedures are authorized. In legislatures a proposal must receive majority support, normally a simple majority of 50 percent plus one, but sometimes more. In a bicameral legislature like Congress, majorities must be built in both houses. Getting this support begins in subcommittees. Each stage of the legislative process may require different tactics to build and maintain agreements. Few proposals become law without changes along the way. And opponents to legislative action can take advantage of the many stages to force compromise or prevent approval altogether.

Government bureaucracies and private organizations share a different approval process. In a hierarchical or pyramidlike structure, typically only a few people get the right to say yes or no. Reaching and persuading the right official isn't always easy, especially when several organizations are involved. In very complex issues, a proposal may take years just to get before a legislature.

Frequently government agencies have authority to make important choices with the force of law. The agency must then develop means for making these choices, including ways to get approval. The National Historic Preservation Act provides a good example. It authorized the secretary of the interior "to establish a program of matching grants-in-aid to states for projects having as their purpose the preservation for public benefit of properties that are significant in American history, architecture, archeology, and culture." But how were these grants to be made? Congress provided few details. Rather, the act gave the secretary of the interior wide discretion:

> SEC. 102 (a) No grant may be made under this Act—
>
> (1) unless application therefore is submitted to the Secretary in accordance with regulations and procedures prescribed by him;
>
> (2) unless the application is in accordance with the comprehensive statewide historical preservation plan which has been approved by the Secretary . . .
>
> (3) for more than 50 per centum of the total cost involved, as determined by the Secretary and his determination shall be final.[12]

Note that the secretary was directed to develop regulations and procedures—to establish a small policy process that would identify options and select those that would gain approval. Majority approval of all those involved may not be needed; on a highly technical issue of this type, a secretary may want the concurrence of experts. Thus, *expertise or professionalism* may also be the basis of getting approval. Later, members of Congress may evaluate the judgment of the experts, determining whether it suits their original intent.

Applying the Solution ■

Passing laws may be only the start of problem solving. With program implementation, govern-

"Now, if you're the adventurous type, here's a little beauty that was turned out before there were any government safety standards."

ment returns to where it started—the problem. The policy has to prove itself effective.[13] One scholar explained it this way:

> Public policies are rarely self-executing. . . . If a policy is inappropriate, if it cannot alleviate the problem for which it was designed, it will probably be a failure no matter how well it is implemented. But even a brilliant policy poorly implemented may fail to achieve the goals of its designers.[14]

To be implemented policies require organization and resources. While often the agency that originated the proposal is given the responsibility for administering it, many programs create new government units, like the National Aeronautics and Space Administration, created along with the space program in 1958, or the Consumer Product Safety Commission, created in 1972. Other units may be reorganized into a new agency, like the Departments of Education and Energy, both created by the Carter administration, or the Department of Veterans Affairs, created in the Reagan administration.

Once an organization is in place with enough authority, personnel, and money, it must determine what to do. Often the law is simple to apply. For example, the Highway Act of 1956—the largest public works project in history—left few doubts about what was supposed to happen next. The result was the interstate highway system. But the purposes of many social, environmental, and economic programs are not so straightforward. For example, the stringent drug bill passed in the heat of an election campaign in 1988 required careful implementation, since fervor for tough measures often subsides after an election.

Sometimes a program has multiple, mixed, conflicting, or unstated goals. Tax law may seek to change behavior as well as raise revenue. For example, a tax on gasoline may be to conserve fuel; a tax on cigarettes may be a health measure to reduce smoking. Some may hope that economic development programs will reduce racial unrest by creating jobs. Leaders in Congress sold the Gramm-Rudman-Hollings deficit reduction proposal in 1986 as a "gun to the head" of Congress—to force legislators to act responsibly on the budget or suffer

New government functions result in new government agencies. The venture into space could be sponsored only through the National Aeronautics and Space Administration (NASA). Future exploration will have implications for commerce and defense, and that is likely to require further reorganization in government.

severe cuts in programs favored by their constituents.

The point is that those involved in implementing the law must first interpret it. They must judge the intentions of the lawmakers. They must also be sensitive to changes in public and political support. Legislators meanwhile must oversee the decisions made by bureaucrats and other policy implementors. These judgments may be as important as the law itself.

Measuring the Results

It is logical that those who press for the passage of a program should want to know whether it is successful. Did it, in fact, solve the problem? Astonishingly, however, "it is a very recent development in the practice of governments to seriously ask questions about the impact of policy, and to expect or even hope to get a scientific answer." [15]

More often, one federal program is piled on another, with little feedback on the effectiveness of what went before. Alice M. Rivlin, the economist who served as the first director of the Congressional Budget Office, drew the startling conclusion in 1970 that *"little is known about how to produce more effective health, education, and other social services."* Worse yet, "neither social service systems nor federal programs are organized to find out." [16] In her view, government does not know how to find out how to be more effective.

In recent years, Congress, the bureaucracy, and the public have put much more effort into measuring the effectiveness of the government programs. The result has been a growing expertise in policy measurement. The explosion of federal programs and large budget deficits also have fed the demand for oversight—and made it far more complex.

Note that demands for evaluation decreased when budget deficits forced cutbacks in the 1980s. Policymakers may try to be more efficient, but competition naturally increases when resources are limited. Those who want more, or seek to keep what they have, may insist that other programs be tested. And if one program is evaluated for its effectiveness, then those who support that program will want others to be analyzed as well.

As with implementation, where the goals are clear, it is easy to measure success. In the decades after the Highway Act, for example, it was simple to determine how many miles of asphalt and concrete had been laid. (Quality is another matter, of course.) If the goal is 50,000 miles and 30,000 miles are in place, 60 percent of the job is done. But where the goals are improved housing, better educational opportunities, or healthier citizens, measuring the results is difficult. Even the social and economic effects of highways are hard to predict and understand. Highway construction can create barriers between neighborhoods if not destroy them altogether, encourage suburban growth, or bypass cities and towns.

Often the rhetoric behind a social program

raises expectations. These high expectations then serve as an unrealistic basis for evaluating progress. For example, federal transportation policy for the disabled did give hope, and certain goals were realized. But there was also disappointment. According to Robert A. Katzmann:

> Given its complexity, devising transportation policy for disabled people requires considerable time before it can be fully implemented; during this period, there must be a sense of consistency. At minimum, if objectives are to be achieved, there must be guidance from federal policymakers. . . . What emerged were mostly confused signals from a fragmented Congress and inconsistent direction from the Department of Transportation, sharing responsibility with the Department of Health, Education, and Welfare. . . . The effect on state and local bodies was perhaps predictable: if the federal thrust kept changing, then those governments had little incentive to devote their energies to devising programs to satisfy soon-to-be outdated requirements.[17]

Part of the problem may stem from how much government personnel know—or can know—about what works. Rivlin gives an example:

> That educated people are less likely to be poor and that children from poor families tend to perform badly in school were known facts. That extra resources spent to "compensate" for lack of intellectual stimulation at home would improve the performance of poor children in school and break the cycle of poverty was a tenet of faith. No one really knew *how* to run a successful compensatory education program. There were hunches and theories, but few facts.[18]

Measuring the impact of policy can be a highly political process, as one group seeks to win out over

"The Food and Drug Administration is really cracking down. Now we have to list all the ingredients in our potions."

"Perspectives"

On the Policy Process

"*Policy analysis is an art. Its subjects are public problems that must be solved at least tentatively to be understood. Piet Hein put this thought-twister, 'Art is the solving of problems that cannot be expressed until they are solved.' Policy analysis must create problems that decision makers are able to handle with the variables under their control and in the time available.*"

—Aaron Wildavsky

"*Large-scale policy objectives . . . are not easily reconciled to the dominant political environment of pluralist bargaining and scarce resources. The danger looms that many important policy objectives will fail to be realized because they will prove to be large-scale objectives for which commitment and resources could not be obtained at requisite levels. Large-scale policies are extremely vulnerable to the compromise and reduction processes of distributive politics.*"

—Paul R. Schulman

"*The decline of Congress, the decline of independence among regulatory agencies, the general decline of law as an instrument of control are all due far more than anything else to changes in the philosophy of law and the prevailing attitude toward laws. Admittedly the complexity of modern life forces Congress into vagueness and generality in drafting its statutes. Admittedly the political pressure of social unrest forces Congress and the president into premature formulations that make delegation of power inevitable. But to take these causes and effects as natural and good, and then to build the system around them, is to doom the system to its present slide toward its lowest common accomplishment.*"

—Theodore J. Lowi

"*Who makes income maintenance policy, or crime control policy, or mental health policy? The answer, of course, is that in our system of government there is no single, authoritative policy maker. In the case of most social issues, the power to influence or shape policies and programs is fragmented among the executive branch, the legislature, the judiciary, and organized private interest groups—at all levels of government. . . . Policy making that takes place within the framework of an adversary process can hardly be scientific or rational. Policy decisions are made through bargaining and compromise by participants with widely dissimilar perspectives.*"

—Laurence E. Lynn, Jr.

"*Each type of policy generates and is therefore surrounded by its own distinctive set of political relationships. These relationships in turn help to determine substantive, concrete outcomes when policy decisions emerge.*"

—Randall B. Ripley and
Grace A. Franklin

"*The politicians who make economic policy operate under conditions of political competition. The simple fact of competition, especially when that competition is informed by political ideology, explains a great deal of what goes on in the political world and, I would argue, in important parts of the economic world also.*"

—Edward R. Tufte

Sources: Aaron Wildavsky, *Speaking Truth to Power* (Boston: Little, Brown, 1979), pp. 15–16; Paul R. Schulman, *Large-Scale Policy Making* (New York: Elsevier, 1980), p. 20; Theodore J. Lowi, *The End of Liberalism,* 2d ed. (New York: W. W. Norton, 1979), p. 125; Laurence E. Lynn, Jr., ed., *Knowledge and Policy* (Washington, D.C.: National Academy of Sciences, 1978), pp. 15–16; Randall B. Ripley and Grace A. Franklin, *Congress, the Bureaucracy, and Public Policy,* rev. ed. (Homewood, Ill.: Dorsey Press, 1984), p. 20; Edward R. Tufte, *Political Control of the Economy* (Princeton, N.J.: Princeton University Press, 1978), p. x.

another. "Policy evaluation is . . . frequently the arm of politics, not just the judge or spectator." [19]

Making Adjustments ■

Systematic measurement of impacts can lead to adjustments in policy. Ideally, a continual process of testing and tinkering would take place until a program was on course and had sufficient support to sustain it. Under such ideal circumstances, the program would end when it met its goals, when the problem it was designed to treat was solved.

We do not live in such a perfect world. The problems of measuring impacts make it unlikely that changes will be so predictable. Even when the evidence is clear—and often it is fragmentary or contradictory—it may be ignored. Some failed programs come to serve purposes not originally foreseen, perhaps purposes as political as a senator's reelection. Thus, even failing programs may, in a sense, succeed.

The simplest adjustment is just to do a little more of what has been done in the past. Referred to as *incrementalism,* the gradual expansion of existing programs characterizes much of American policy making. If we knew what was truly effective in solving domestic problems, government could act swiftly, even comprehensively. But such knowledge is not available. So our efforts tend to be piecemeal—a little more here, a little more there. Lack of planning capability may also encourage those in government "to identify situations or ills from

■ Building roads has long been one of the federal government's most important jobs. The Highway Act of 1956 authorized an especially monumental task—building an interstate highway system. That system is now virtually completed. Goals like these are clearly measurable, and today we probably take our superhighways for granted.

which to move *away* rather than goals *toward* which to move."[20]

Figure 17–2 summarizes the policy process. It is a logical progression from problem to program, back to problem for administering the program, and finally to results or impacts. In practice, however, one activity does not have to be completed for another to begin. Government often tries to solve problems that are not well defined. Why? Sometimes the pressure to act overwhelms the need for adequate information. For example, the fear of drug use in the late 1980s led to dramatic proposals based on dubious conclusions about cause and effect. And President Bush's anticrime package, offered early in his administration, was criticized for its emphasis on the punishment of criminals over the prevention of crime.

Second, while certain activities are associated with institutions (e.g., approval with a legislature, application with the bureaucracy), participants from different institutions may be involved at every stage. Both the courts and legislatures often play a role in policy administration. And, as illustrated earlier, a bureaucratic agency often enters the approval stage. This constant interaction between officials in government and interest groups is the basis for subgovernments.

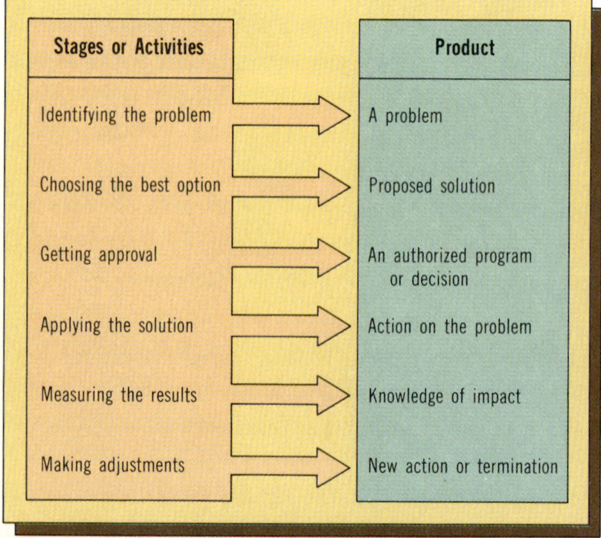

Stages or Activities
Product
Identifying the problem
A problem
Choosing the best option
Proposed solution
Getting approval
An authorized program or decision
Applying the solution
Action on the problem
Measuring the results
Knowledge of impact
Making adjustments
New action or termination

Figure 17–2 The policy process.

The Constitution and the Policy Process

Constitutional Arrangements

The founders hoped to divide responsibility among the major institutions of government. Citing the French philosopher Montesquieu, they saw a separation of powers into three major branches: executive, legislative, and judicial. They could *not* foresee an enormous and powerful bureaucracy. For the framers, however, the legislature was to do more than simply make the laws, the executive to administer them, and the courts to interpret them. The framers designed a more complex system. With Montesquieu they were anxious to prevent tyranny, but they doubted that mere separation of powers was enough. They gave each branch some control over the others. As James Madison described it in the *Federalist:*

> The magistrate in whom the whole executive power resides cannot of himself make a law; though he can put a negative on every law [the veto power]; nor administer justice in person, though he has the appointment of those who do administer it. The judges can exercise no executive prerogative, though they are shoots from the executive stock; nor any legislative function, though they may be advised with by the legislative councils. The entire legislature can perform no judiciary act, though by the joint act of two of its branches the judges may be removed from their offices [impeachment], and though one of its branches is possessed of the judicial power in the last resort. The entire legislature, again, can exercise no executive prerogative, though one of its branches constitutes the supreme executive magistracy, and another, on the impeachment of a third, can try and condemn all the subordinate officers in the executive department.[21]

Besides separating, checking, and balancing national government power, the framers sought to preserve an active role for state governments. Federalism was a practical necessity for getting the new

Constitution approved (see Chapter 3). But the idea of state and local rights was also strongly embedded in the American Revolution and the antipathy for a distant monarch.

These doctrines of separated powers, checks and balances, and federalism have shaped the American policy process, making it unique in the world. The ideas have considerable force in political rhetoric and policy action. No day passes in the nation's capital without a practical expression of these fundamental principles. All three branches seek to protect their prerogatives and monitor the exercise of power by the others. Policy proposals emanating from the executive are normally sensitive to the role of the states; if not, then members of Congress, themselves representatives of the states, will react critically.

Separating the elections for the executive and legislature permits split-party control, an important factor in policy making. Since World War II, the president's party has been a majority in both houses of Congress less than half the time. Presidents Truman, Eisenhower, Nixon, Ford, Reagan, and Bush all worked with Congresses controlled by the other party. Between 1981 and 1987, even the Congress had divided party control, with the Democrats a majority in the House of Representatives, the Republicans in the Senate. The American voter has gone Madison one better—adding partisan division to the separation of institutions. As constitutional doctrines have become incorporated into political institutions, they have also had an everyday impact on the policy process:

1. *Difficulty in making sweeping changes in existing policy*—follows from the lack of concentrated authority.

2. *Encouragement of strong lobbies*—follows from the need to pursue goals among several institutions (legislative, executive, judicial) and possibly at different levels (national, state, local).

3. *Weak policy role for political parties*—follows from independent means of selecting legislators and presidents.

4. *Encouragement of compromise and bargaining*—follows from all the above.

5. *Refusal of groups to take no for an answer*—follows from the many appeal possibilities in a divided system.

These add up to a formal system that shapes the context for making policy decisions. Americans continue to be suspicious of too much power concentrated in one branch of government. But the associated costs include fragmented, incremental policy results. The American political system is often criticized for its failure to produce comprehensive and integrated policy programs. But it is hard to see how we can have it both ways. As long as we favor dividing responsibility, we have to live with the fragmentation that follows.

So the Constitution is the natural starting point for understanding how policy activities are done. It sets the stage on which policy players will act. It also creates the structure within which the script is written. We next consider that structure and its impact on the policy process.

Institutions and the Policy Process

The separation of powers and federalism are more than theories. Several chapters in this book describe how the executive (including the bureaucracy), Congress, and the courts are organized and do their work. When these institutions act on domestic issues, they are normally sensitive to their counterparts at the state and local levels. Often national actions address issues that have been treated at these other levels. Thus, there must be institutional awareness in Washington of what has been done in the states. Further, national decision makers often intend programs to be administered by state and local officials.

Thus, our institutions and levels of government are both independent and dependent—just as the framers intended. For example, Congress has authority to pass laws, but is dependent on the executive to put them into effect. The national government has full authority to act in many domestic spheres, but frequently must rely on the states to help administer its programs. Institutions at all levels create formal processes that accommodate what is done elsewhere. Whereas much work may be done informally by networks of decision makers (or subgovernments), formal approval is necessary within the institutions.

Consider this example at a national level. Tobacco producers may work out a subsidy program with Department of Agriculture bureaucrats and crucial members of House and Senate committees on agriculture. But that agreement must then go through a formal process of approval within Congress, the executive, or both. Formal approval may be automatic; perhaps there are permanent tradeoffs between supporters of tobacco subsidies and other programs. Or new bargains may have to be struck to get approval. The point is that formal, institutional processes do affect policy making.

Figure 17–3 is a simplified view of the connections between the early stages of the policy process and formal institutions. As shown, those most directly involved in the issue (the subgovernment) may have reached agreement. But if they want the presidential stamp of approval, they have to feed their proposal into a legislative clearance process managed by the Office of Management and Budget. The purpose of this is straightforward. A president does not want proposals to be transmitted to Congress from the executive branch without his approval. Therefore a clearance process is required:

> Beginning in the 1930s this centralized clearance process was extended to include all ex-

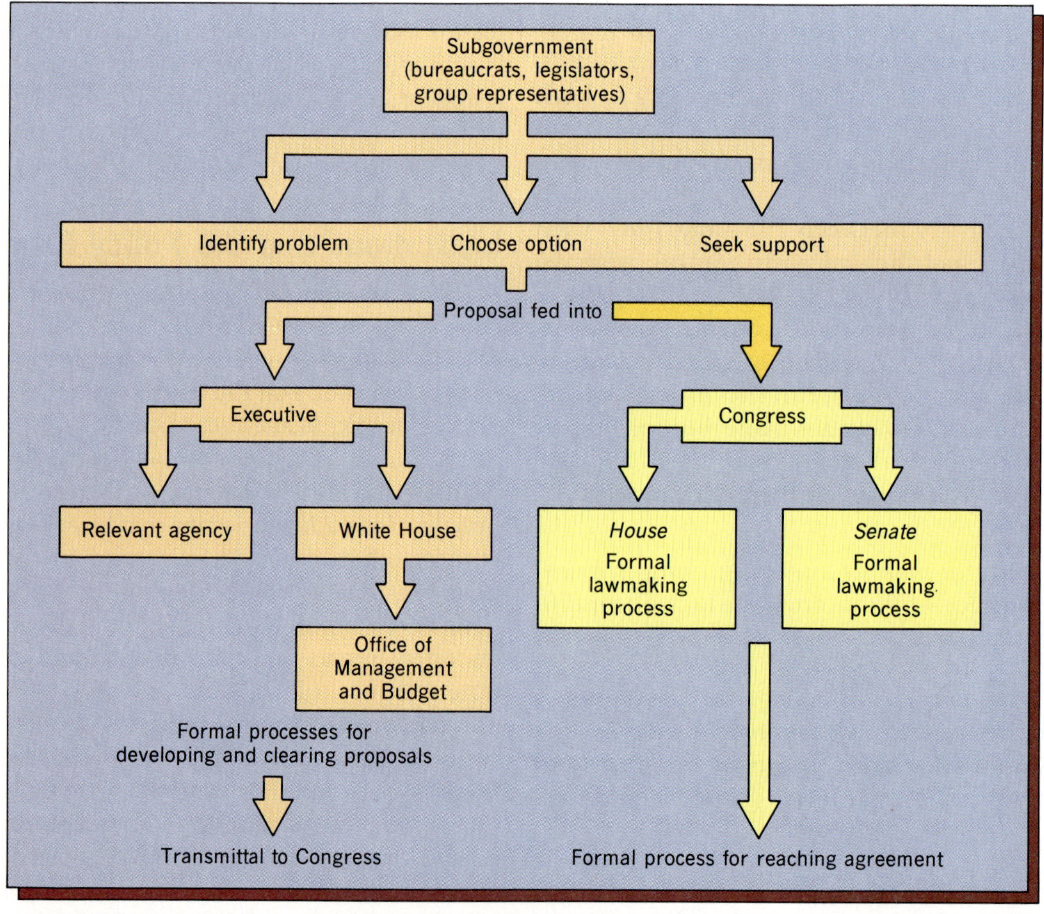

Figure 17–3 Feeding the work of subgovernments into formal institutions.

ecutive branch requests for legislation, regardless of whether or not money would be expended. In each case, the budget officials had to decide whether the proposal was in accord with the president's legislative program. If it was not, then it could not be submitted to Congress by executive departments and agencies.[22]

The demand that a proposal from an agency clear OMB influences its development. Those who help develop a proposal will be more sensitive to the president's priorities if they know his support is needed.

All is not lost if OMB will not clear a proposal. With sufficient congressional support, the proposal may still become law. Even a presidential veto can be overridden in Congress. But Figure 17–3 shows that one does not avoid institutional processes by turning to Congress. Far from it. The formal lawmaking processes in the House and the Senate are elaborate. Those who wish to have a policy agreement translated into law must be prepared to sustain their arguments through many stages of the legislative process.

It is because of their constitutional power of approval that legislators are drawn into early stages of the policy process. In other political systems, legislatures have restricted authority—often limited to rubber-stamping executive proposals. Such legislators play a much smaller role in the policy process than do members of Congress.

Changing Issues and the Domestic Policy Process

The domestic policy agenda has changed dramatically in the past few decades. The flood of new government programs in the 1960s was followed by consolidation and even contraction during the 1980s. These shifts have affected every stage of the policy process:

1. *Identifying the problem*—tends to be limited to problems with existing programs; new problems not invited.
2. *Choosing the best option*—typically restricted to the option likely to reduce costs or ensure better management.
3. *Getting approval*—support limited to proposals that are justified as reducing costs and improving effectiveness.
4. *Applying the solution*—strong emphasis on efficiency and effectiveness, doing more with less.
5. *Measuring the results*—large increase in program evaluation, with emphasis on negative rather than positive results.
6. *Making adjustments*—more than the usual number of terminations.

In the politics of consolidating or reducing federal responsibilities new social programs take a back seat to procedural maneuvers. Except to react to severe crisis, most subgovernments are preoccupied with maintaining their programs at current levels.

Other trends are at odds with a reduced federal government. The public has come to expect the federal government to act on issues like welfare, education, farm production and prices, and labor-management relations. Other issues that were national in scope are now international, including energy, the environment, economic problems, and human rights. The 1973 Arab oil embargo and the long Iran–Iraq War in the Middle East showed that small nations can cause severe domestic problems in this country. Americans learned that they are no longer self-sufficient in energy resources. The trade imbalances of the 1980s revealed weaknesses in the nation's industrial might.

Budget Making and the Policy Process ■

Government programs cannot be put into effect without money. Getting money and determining how it will be spent are important aspects of the policy process. "If money is the lifeblood of government, the national budget is its circulatory system," as one scholar put it.[23] Budgets are an annual stocktaking of national commitments; they reveal

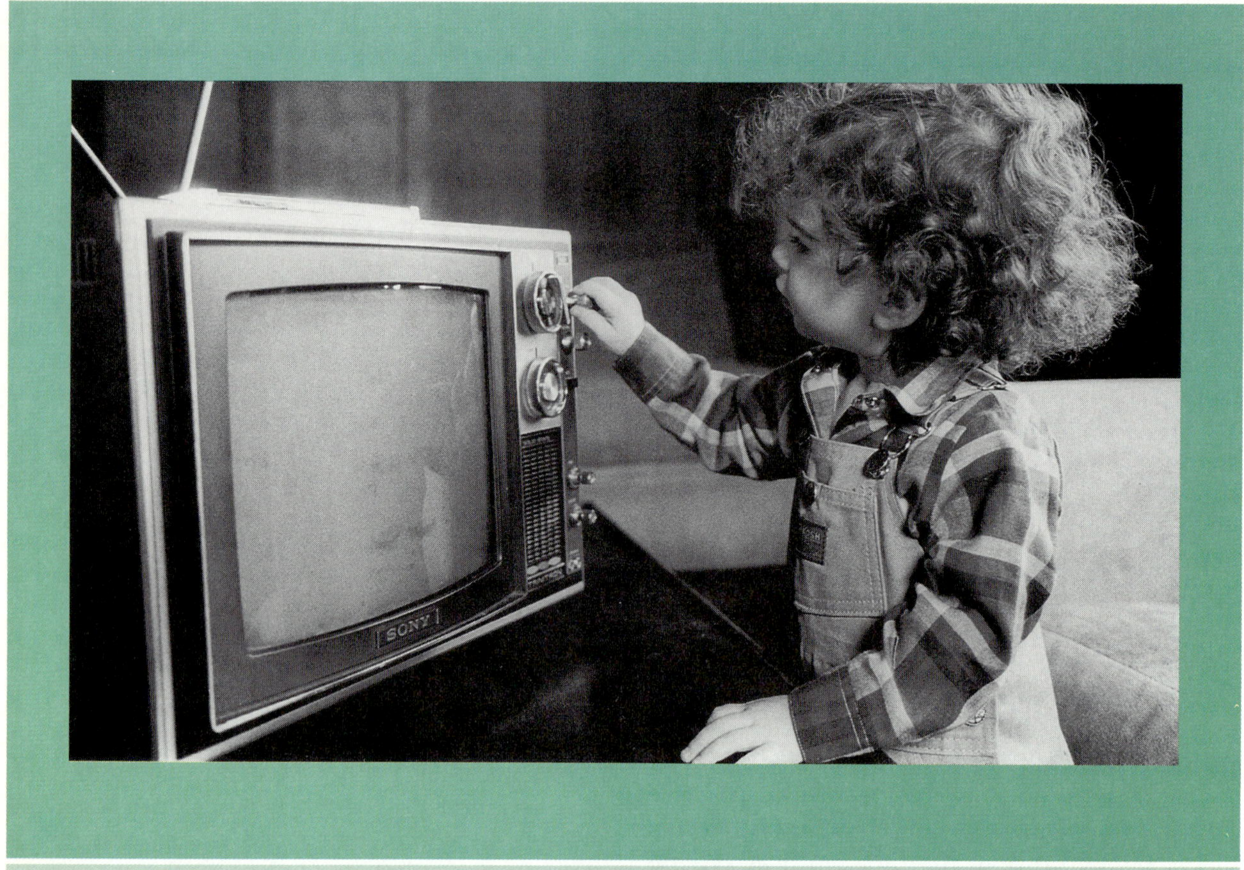

Look at the name on the electronic gadgets in your own home, and you will know why there is a trade imbalance. Much of the equipment will have come from Japan, Korea, or Taiwan. Even workers who suffer directly from foreign competition tend to buy imported goods. When they do, they help profoundly alter the American economy.

which public problems will receive major attention. Aaron Wildavsky, a leading scholar of the budget process, explains it this way:

> At one level a budget is a prediction. A budget contains words and figures that propose expenditures for certain objects and purposes. The words describe types of expenditures (salaries, equipment, travel) or purposes (preventing war, improving mental health, providing low-income housing), and the figures are attached to each item. Presumably, those who make a budget intend there to be a direct connection between what is written in it and future events. If requests for funds are granted, if they are spent in accordance with instructions, and if the actions involved lead to the desired consequences, then the purposes stated in the document will be achieved. *Budgets thus become links between financial resources and human resources and human behavior in order to accomplish policy objectives.*[24]

Budgets are political documents. They reflect judgments about what government should do. Budget politics become particularly intense in a period of huge deficits. When revenue is scarce, conflict dominates.

Despite its importance, the budget-making process is not directly addressed in the Constitution. Revenue—that is, money—is mentioned several times, but not a procedure for executive-con-

“ Perspectives ”

On the Budget Process

“Anyone who wants to understand American politics must first understand social security. Those who care about budget deficits must know something about the single largest program on the domestic ledger; those who care about electoral politics must know something about the central concern of older voters; those who care about trust in government must know something about the lack of confidence in social security among young and old Americans alike; those who care about poverty must know something about the most important program for helping elderly women and minorities.”

—Paul Light

“Somehow we have got to force our colleagues to stop talking thrift one day and complaining about the excessive expenditures and deficit, but then spending the remainder of the year voting for every program that comes down the pike—adding expenditures to the government's budget because of good ideas or humane ideas, or ideas that are thought worthwhile and which they cannot oppose.”

—Robert N. Giaimo, former chairman,
House Committee on the Budget

“Between the lofty rhetoric of statesmen and the daily tasks of bureaucrats lie money and its politics: how it is raised and how it is spent. As Alexander Hamilton noted two centuries ago, money sustains the essential functions of government. The Constitution of the United States conferred upon Congress the power of the purse, but a glance at history reveals that the executive branch gradually became dominant in the fiscal affairs of the nation.”

—Lance T. LeLoup

“Can government continue on a business-as-usual basis if the economy no longer produces the goods as in the past? The answer . . . is no. The reason is simple: past commitments to future spending threaten to overload government, requiring it to spend more money than can be provided by the fruits of economic growth. . . . Governments must then put the brakes on public spending or else cut the take-home pay of its citizens. If it decides to cut rather than protect take-home pay, it faces the prospect of political bankruptcy.”

—Richard Rose and Guy Peters

“People who sought stern budgetary discipline and spending cutbacks have been discouraged by continuing deficits and spiraling expenditures; they have disregarded the fact that the Budget Act permits Congress to adopt any budget policy it deems appropriate. People who sought to extensively revamp national priorities to match their own preferences have been disappointed by the slow pace of change, as if a budget process alone could uproot interest group politics in the United States or change the basic political function of Congress in resolving conflicts among claimants on the public purse.”

—Allen Schick

Sources: Paul Light, *Artful Work: The Politics of Social Security Reform* (New York: Random House, 1985), p. ix; Kenneth A. Shepsle, ed., *The Congressional Budget Process* (St. Louis: Center for the Study of American Business, Washington University, 1980), p. 57; Lance LeLoup, *The Fiscal Congress* (Westport, Conn.: Greenwood Press, 1980), p. 3; Richard Rose and Guy Peters, *Can Government Go Bankrupt?* (New York: Basic Books, 1978), p. 9; Allen Schick, *Congress and Money* (Washington, D.C.: Urban Institute, 1980), p. 566.

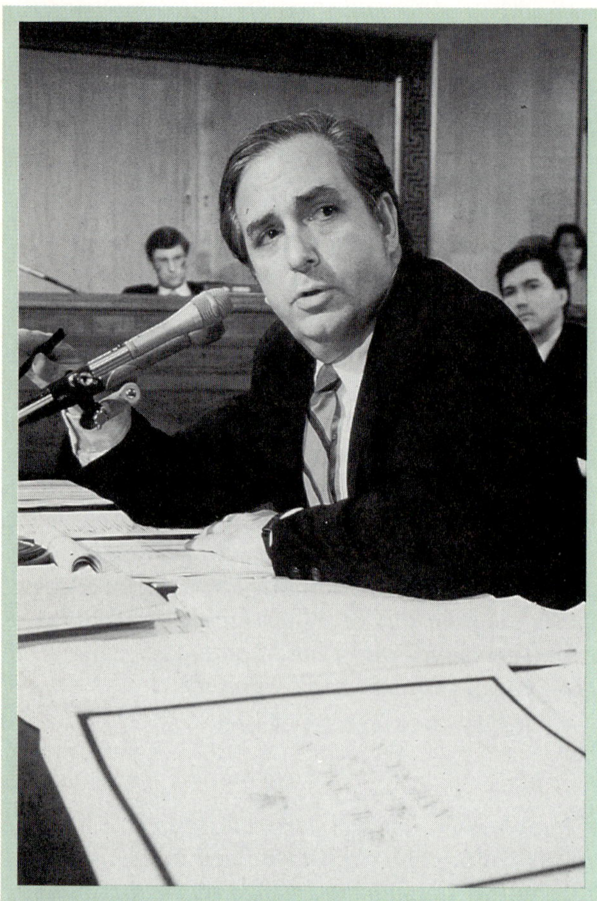

Richard Darman, director of the Office of Management and Budget (OMB) in the Bush administration, as he testifies before Congress. Darman holds one of the hottest seats in national government. He has responsibility for preparing a budget that reflects the president's priorities and will not contribute to the deficit.

gressional budget development. For over a century there was no single national budget. Individual departments and agencies submitted their requests for appropriations directly to Congress. In 1921 Congress passed a Budget and Accounting Act that concentrated budget making in the presidency. A new Bureau of the Budget was to help the president coordinate the budget requests. At first this office was in the Department of the Treasury, but in 1939 President Roosevelt placed it within the executive office of the president. In 1970 a reorganization initiated by President Nixon changed the name from the Bureau of the Budget to the Office of Management and Budget.

As government grew, the budget became central to the domestic policy process. Throughout the Reagan administration, budget making was the focus of domestic policy debate. Why was this so? First, budgeting becomes more important when an administration seeks to cut back on government. All eyes focus on eliminating programs and managing them more efficiently. Second, subgovernments came into conflict. Survival often means attack as, for example, when farm policy advocates react to cuts in their programs by criticizing budget increases for new weapons systems. Subgovernments may expand in mutual support but cut back in mutual animosity. Finally, the sheer magnitude of the deficits compelled policymakers to concentrate on the budget.

The Bush years, like the Reagan era before them, will probably be known as the era of budget making. Like it or not, and most did not, official Washington in the 1980s began and ended each day with budget talk. The status of the federal balance sheet permeated the 1988 policy agenda even while the presidential candidates avoided confronting it directly in the campaign. Budget issues continued to dominate policy politics from the start of the Bush administration, and they should do the same into the 1990s (see Chapter 19).

An Overview of Budget Making

Budget making in democracies typically requires participation by executive policymakers and elected representatives. First, analysts propose a taxing and spending plan in accordance with the policy goals of the chief executive. Congress then reviews and approves the plan, though seldom in the form submitted. Congress will change a budget even when a majority of its members are of the same party as the president. Since World War II, however, when presidents and Congresses have more often than not been of different parties, budget conflict has often been intense and protracted.

During one of these periods of split party control, Congress dramatically changed its budget-

the small society **by Brickman**

making procedures. In 1972 President Nixon, a Republican, won reelection by one of the greatest landslides in history. Meanwhile, Democrats retained their majorities in both the House and Senate. Nixon challenged Congress by recommending programmatic cuts in his budget and refusing to spend appropriated money if the cuts were restored (thus impounding the funds). These confrontations encouraged Congress to reform its budgeting procedures and limit the president's impoundment authority. The Budget and Impoundment Control Act of 1974 was the most dramatic reform in congressional budgeting in history:

1. New deadlines for congressional action encouraged prompt review of budgets.
2. Both the House and Senate created standing committees on the budget.
3. A new Congressional Budget Office (CBO) of professional analysts would serve the budget committees and House and Senate leaders.
4. A congressional budget resolution was to be passed in both houses. It would serve as a guideline for the standing committees—in essence, as a congressional budget.

With these changes Congress could produce an alternative to the president's budget. However, this greater independence also carried with it certain disadvantages. Though now less dependent on the executive, the legislature created expectations that were not easy to meet. It helped President Reagan and others criticize Congress for not meeting its own deadlines—or producing a budget.

Figure 17–4 provides an eagle's eye view of the budget cycle. Note that the various steps are keyed to the *fiscal year*—a term used by accountants to refer to the dates in which accounts are opened and closed. The 1974 act changed the fiscal year from July 1–June 30 to October 1–September 30. Of course, both branches must start early in preparing for the beginning of the fiscal year. As shown in the figure, executive formulation begins a full 19 months in advance; congressional work begins at least 9 months in advance. In fact, today's budget process is continuous, with both branches engaged in planning a future budget, approving that for the upcoming year, implementing the one currently in effect, and auditing the previous fiscal year. One of the essential oddities of our system is that an outgoing president prepares the budget for a new president. If they are not of the same party, a first order of business for the new president is to prepare a budget virtually on a crash basis. What normally takes many months must be accomplished in a matter of weeks.

A new budget was expected of George Bush in 1989 even though he was a Republican like his predecessor, Ronald Reagan. The Democratic Congress demanded that he identify his priorities as distinct from those of Reagan. In fact, President

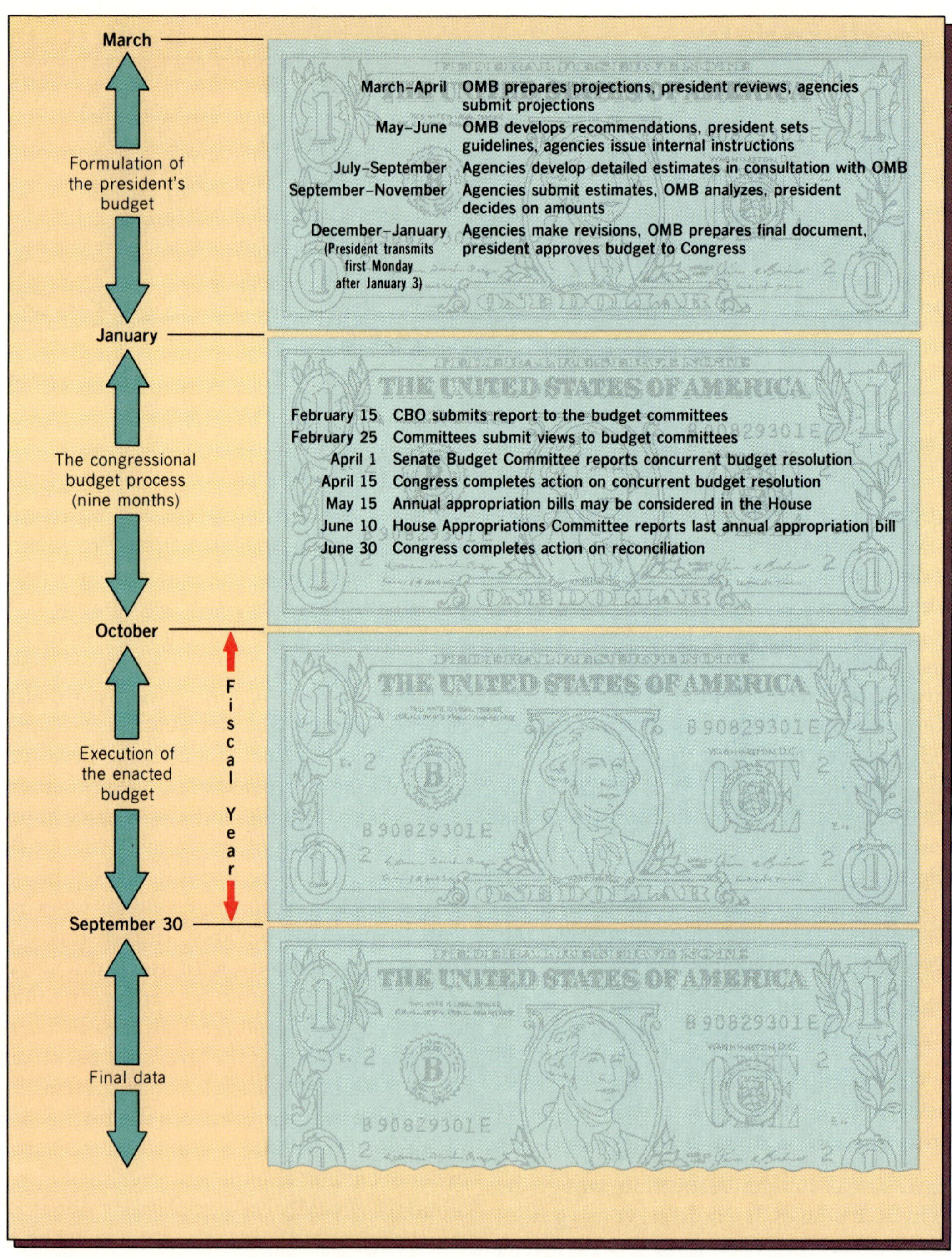

March
Formulation of the president's budget
March–April OMB prepares projections, president reviews, agencies submit projections
May–June OMB develops recommendations, president sets guidelines, agencies issue internal instructions
July–September Agencies develop detailed estimates in consultation with OMB
September–November Agencies submit estimates, OMB analyzes, president decides on amounts
December–January (President transmits first Monday after January 3) Agencies make revisions, OMB prepares final document, president approves budget to Congress
January
The congressional budget process (nine months)
February 15 CBO submits report to the budget committees
February 25 Committees submit views to budget committees
April 1 Senate Budget Committee reports concurrent budget resolution
April 15 Congress completes action on concurrent budget resolution
May 15 Annual appropriation bills may be considered in the House
June 10 House Appropriations Committee reports last annual appropriation bill
June 30 Congress completes action on reconciliation
October
Execution of the enacted budget
Fiscal Year
September 30
Final data

Figure 17–4 The federal budget-making process. Source: Office of Management and Budget, *The United States Budget in Brief* (Washington, D.C.: U.S. Government Printing Office, 1988), p. 90; *A Glossary of Terms Used in the Federal Budget Process* (Washington, D.C.: U.S. General Accounting Office, 1981), pp. 10–11; U.S. House of Representatives, Committee on Ways and Means, *Background Material and Data on Programs within the Jurisdiction of the Committee on Ways and Means, 100th Congress,* 2nd session, 1988, pp. 1013–1014.

Bush and congressional Democratic leaders worked out a bipartisan agreement on the budget that passed Congress.

Executive Preparation and Submission

Executive budget making involves continual interaction among the president, his domestic policy aides, the Office of Management and Budget, and the departments and agencies. Figure 17–4 shows the timetable. The president sets policy priorities. The OMB then translates presidential policy goals and determines whether the requests from the agencies of government are consistent with these goals. The departments and agencies seek support for what they have done in the past and what they would like to do in the future. They try to show that their requests are consistent with presidential priorities.

The early months of budget preparation (March–June) include a review of the current status of spending. The process begins with the general outlook of the economy, including the effects of government spending. This stage culminates in the budgetary targets that are conveyed to the departments and agencies.

The next months (July–September) are devoted to preparing detailed estimates within the departments and agencies. These estimates become the basis for extended analysis by OMB during the period between September and November. The OMB holds hearings with agency representatives to help reassess the economic impacts. In the remaining months, the president makes the decisions, and a final document is prepared. The president transmits the budget to Congress on the first Monday after January 3, along with a message justifying it.

The executive budget now projects spending and revenues for four fiscal years beyond the budget year. These projections serve as guidelines for agencies in future planning as well as for Congress in estimating what's ahead. They also provide information about the long-term effects of current spending. Like all economic projections, however, such estimates are not accurate predictions of the future. For example, in 1982 it was estimated that the deficit in 1986 would be $159 billion. In fact it was $221 billion. That $62 billion difference was nearly equal to the whole budget in 1952.

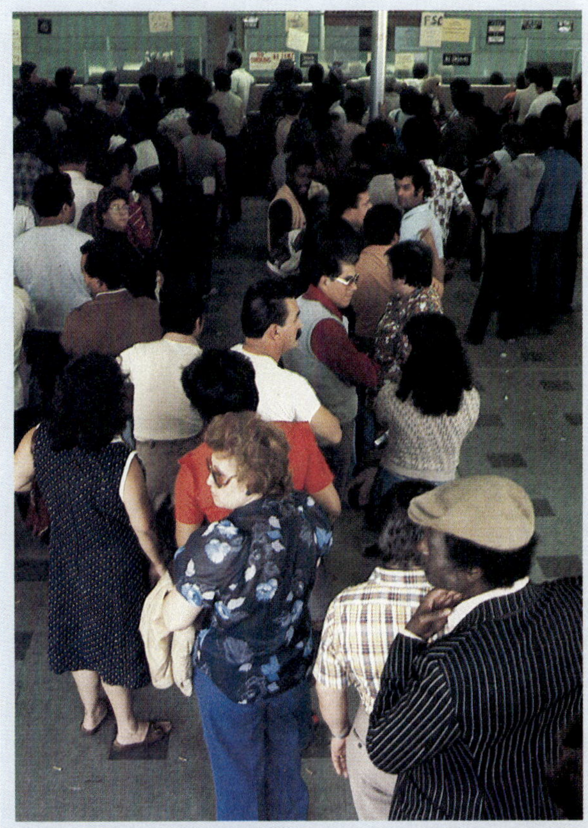

Curbing inflation often puts more people out of work. Unemployment, in turn, increases government spending while reducing federal revenues. After all, those without jobs pay less in taxes. The result—a bigger deficit and a tougher job of budget making. Early in the Reagan administration, unemployment rose as the country experienced a recession.

Projections can never be accurate predictions because so many factors can upset budget calculations. An unexpected increase in unemployment can increase government spending by billions of dollars as unemployment compensation is paid out. Those out of work do not pay taxes, so revenue estimates are also affected. Inflation can have a serious impact on budget estimates as government pays more for goods and services; welfare checks also are indexed to the inflation rate. Defense costs can soar during international crises or because of cost overruns in weapons development. Mistakes in accounting alone may amount to billions of dollars. The public finds it hard to believe such errors are possible. Yet a $1 billion error—a huge amount to the ordinary citizen—is *one-tenth of 1 percent in a trillion-dollar budget.*

The Congressional Budget Process

Before the Budget and Impoundment Control Act of 1974 was passed, it was difficult to identify a congressional budget process. Although the fiscal year (then July 1 to June 30) provided a timetable of sorts, it was seldom met. The reason was simple. Congress had no way to integrate its budget decisions. Once the president transmitted a budget to Capitol Hill, its various parts went to committees and subcommittees. It was never reassembled as a whole document. It simply disappeared, though its many parts worked their way through the House of Representatives and the Senate.

The 1974 act set in place a more orderly process. With the help of the Congressional Budget Office, the House and Senate committees on the budget begin work on the new budget even before they receive it from the president. The basis of this work is the greatly increased flow of economic and budgetary information and analysis from the CBO and the budget committee staffs. Periodic economic forecasts and spending projections issued by the CBO are of major importance for congressional budget building. Like OMB on the executive side, the CBO provides five-year projections. The existence of the CBO makes Congress much less dependent on the executive, in terms of both data and analysis.

Figure 17–4 includes the deadlines for congressional action on the budget. After receiving the president's budget in January, the House and Senate budget committees hold public hearings to collect the information they will need later to prepare a budget resolution. This resolution will serve as Congress's response to the president's budget. The Congressional Budget Office prepares its report of the president's budget, as well as an independent analysis of spending and revenues, by February 15. Standing committees report budget estimates for programs within their jurisdiction to the budget committees by February 25 (much the same way that departments and agencies report on the executive side). Meanwhile, the two appropriations committees and the two taxing committees (Ways and Means in the House, Finance in the Senate) begin work on spending and revenue bills, respectively. Since 1987 the timetable requires that Congress pass the first budget resolution by April 15.

The budget resolution sets targets for spending and revenue. These targets are guidelines for the standing committees in their work. Presidential approval is not required, though, as in 1989, the president may reach agreement with congressional leaders in advance. The budget committees also monitor and coordinate the work of the other committees. Congress then completes action on all spending bills and prepares a second budget resolution.

The new process greatly improved the information and advice available to Congress for budget making. Even more important was the creation of the CBO and the budget committees to monitor developments in the other committees. A problem soon developed, however, in realizing the benefits of the new system. A reconciliation process was to follow passage of the second budget resolution, formerly set for September 15. By this process, adjustments were to be made in individual programs so that total spending did not exceed the limits set in the budget resolution. Coming so late, however, the reconciliation process was not effective. As budget scholar Allen Schick pointed out:

> By the time reconciliation was supposed to be completed [late September], the new fiscal year was about to start. It was unreasonable to expect the House and Senate to reopen appropriations issues that had been decided only weeks earlier or to take away funds that were

> about to be spent. Moreover, the Budget Act provided only ten days between adoption of the second resolution and final passage of a reconciliation bill. This was not sufficient time.[25]

Such problems convinced the budget committees to have reconciliation follow passage of the first budget resolution. This was done for fiscal year 1981 and subsequently. As Schick says:

> The shift from the second to the first resolution is much more than a matter of timing; it also changes the focus of reconciliation. Rather than targeting reconciliation on actions taken during the current session, Congress now uses it to change legislation enacted in previous years.[26]

Not all problems were solved with this change. It worked to President Reagan's advantage when he first entered office, since it provided him with a mechanism to enforce budget cuts. However, conflicts between Reagan and congressional Democrats soon made it tough for reconciliation to work.

Typically, the House of Representatives acts first on money matters. Disagreements between the

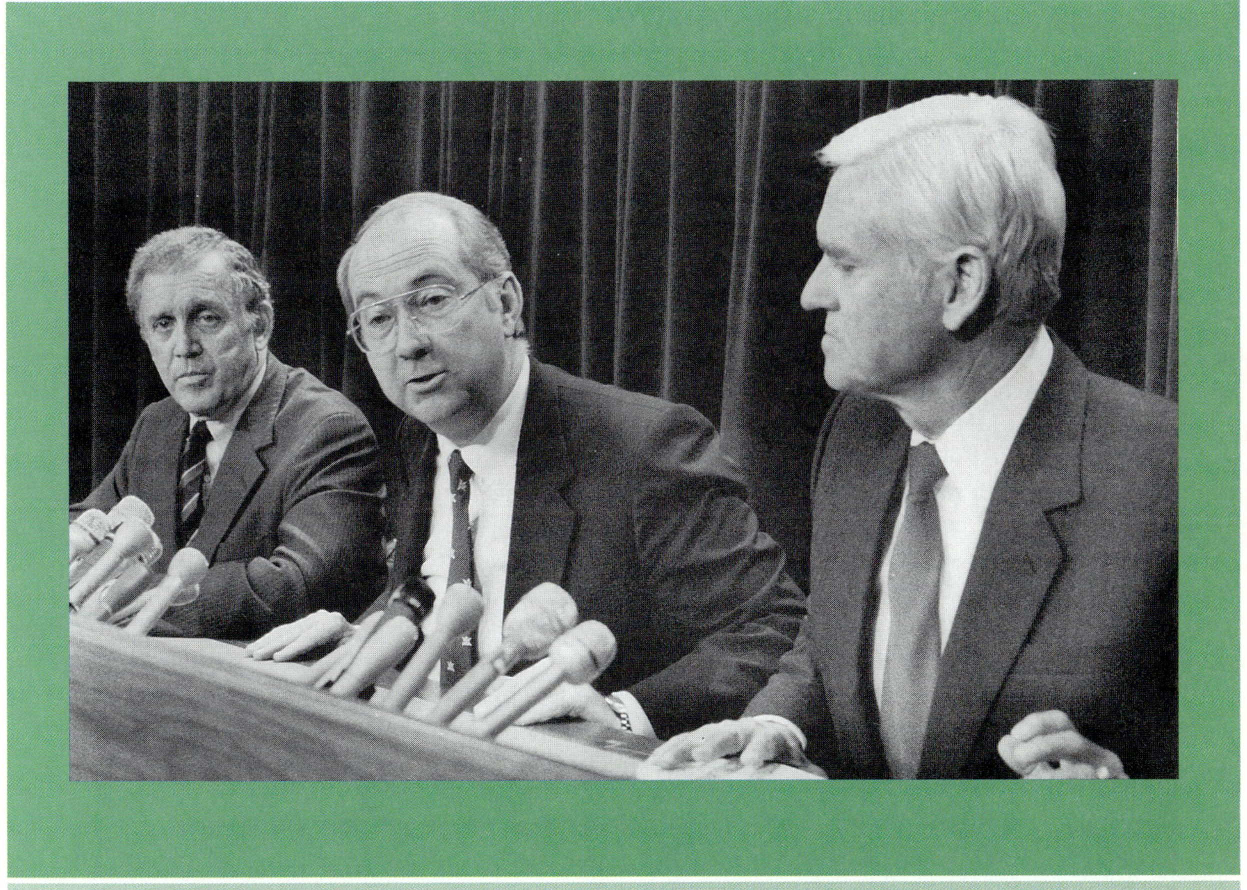

The Gramm-Rudman-Hollings Act sought to reduce the budget deficit in stages. The authors of the bill, from left to right, were Warren Rudman (R.–N.H.), Phil Gramm (R.–Tex.), and Ernest Hollings (D.–S.C.). Their bipartisan effort has at least encouraged budget makers to look for ways to cut expenditures, find new revenue sources, and reduce loopholes in the tax laws.

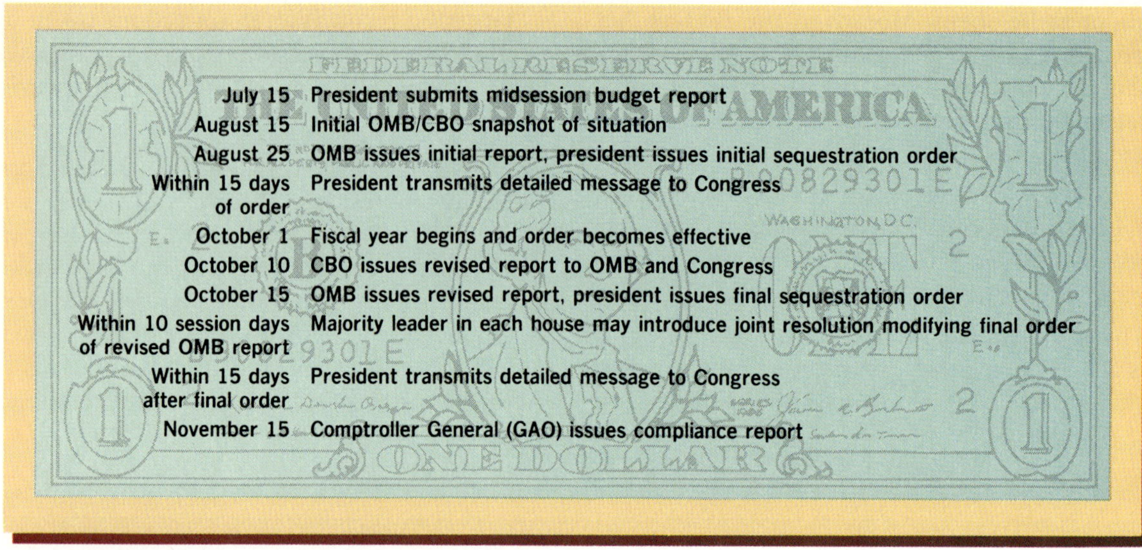

July 15	President submits midsession budget report
August 15	Initial OMB/CBO snapshot of situation
August 25	OMB issues initial report, president issues initial sequestration order
Within 15 days of order	President transmits detailed message to Congress
October 1	Fiscal year begins and order becomes effective
October 10	CBO issues revised report to OMB and Congress
October 15	OMB issues revised report, president issues final sequestration order
Within 10 session days of revised OMB report	Majority leader in each house may introduce joint resolution modifying final order
Within 15 days after final order	President transmits detailed message to Congress
November 15	Comptroller General (GAO) issues compliance report

Figure 17–5 The Gramm-Rudman-Hollings timetable. Source: U.S. House of Representatives, Committee on Ways and Means, *Background Material and Data on Programs within the Jurisdiction of the Committee on Ways and Means,* 100th Congress, 2nd session, 1988, pp. 1000–1001.

House and Senate are resolved in conferences, with reports sent back for approval to each chamber. After passage by both houses, appropriations and revenue bills are sent to the president for approval or veto. If Congress fails to complete the process before the start of the new fiscal year, continuing resolutions are passed to provide authority for departments and agencies to spend money in the interim. It has become common practice in recent years for Congress to wait until the last minute, or beyond, and then pass large, omnibus continuing resolutions. In fact, critics charge that the congressional budget process has broken down.

The Budget and Deficits

Growing concern about huge deficits and the failure of the president and Congress to propose and enact balanced budgets led to passage of a Balanced Budget and Emergency Deficit Control Act in 1985. The act was known popularly as Gramm-Rudman-Hollings after its cosponsors, Senators Phil Gramm (R–Tex.), Warren Rudman (R–N.H.), and Ernest Hollings (D–S.C.). It set declining deficit limits over a period of six years, culminating in a balanced budget by 1991 (see Table 17–1). The Office of Management and Budget and the Congressional Budget Office were to analyze spending, revenue, and economic conditions to determine whether the deficit targets for the next fiscal year would be met. On the basis of this analysis, the General Accounting Office (GAO) was directed to specify reductions, if required to meet targets. The president was then required to issue a so-called *sequestration order* to enforce the GAO reductions. By this new process, Congress hopes to force the president and its own members to make budget cuts so as to reduce deficits.

On July 7, 1986, the Supreme Court ruled in *Bowsher* v. *Synar* that the type of authority given to the GAO was executive in nature. Congress has the power to initiate removal of the comptroller general, who heads GAO. Therefore, the Court ruled that "Congress in effect has retained control over the Act's execution and has unconstitutionally intruded into the executive function.[27] Fearing that this section might in fact be judged to be unconstitutional, the sponsors provided for an alternative procedure whereby the cuts required by the sequestration procedure would be approved by Congress and the president—in other words, through a more or less regular legislative process.

The alternative procedure was not automatic. In essence it brought the whole budget-cutting exercise back to the halls of Congress, where the Gramm-Rudman-Hollings supporters did not want it. Thus in September 1987, revised deficit limits were enacted (see Table 17–1), with a balanced budget projected for 1993. And a new automatic process was devised, as shown in Figure 17–5. OMB, in consultation with CBO, was given authority to issue a report on reductions should the budget as passed not meet the target for the fiscal year in question. The new process also provided for congressional action subsequent to sequestration. Congress had time to make the necessary cuts so as to avoid automatic reductions (see Figure 17–6).

TABLE 17–1

Gramm-Rudman-Hollings Deficit Targets

	Target (billion of dollars)	
Fiscal Years	**1985**	**1987**
1986	$172	—
1987	144	—
1988	108	$144 (+36)
1989	72	136 (+64)
1990	36	100 (+64)
1991	0	64 (+64)
1992	0	28 (+28)
1993	0	0

Source: Derived from data in Elizabeth Wehr, "Doubtful Congress Clears Gramm-Rudman Fix," *Congressional Quarterly Weekly Report,* September 26, 1987, p. 2311.

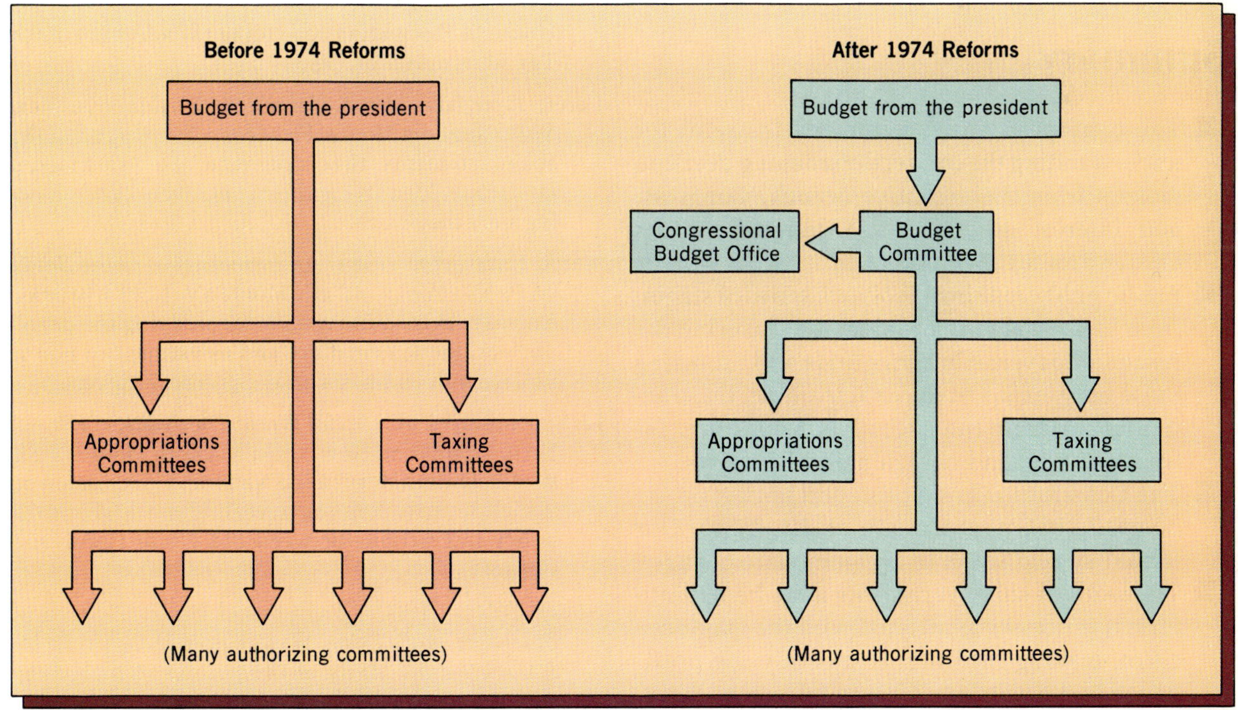

Figure 17–6 Congressional budget process before and after reform.

Major reforms in the budget process have occurred in the last 15 years. Driven by partisanship, huge deficits, and the sheer complexity of budget policy issues, Congress passed the Budget and Impoundment Control Act in 1974 and two Gramm-Rudman-Hollings budget reduction acts in 1985 and 1987. As one student of the process concludes:

> Reforms have increased the number of budgetary participants, made the budget process more open, created a more independent congressional budgeting process, forced the President and the Office of Management and Budget to work more closely with Congress, gave Congress more budget information through the Congressional Budget Office, and established a coherent and constitutional method of congressional review over presidential impoundments. The budget process is more complex, open, and democratic, but more conflictual and difficult for the President.[28]

Summary

- The concept of subgovernments is useful for understanding the connections among decision makers from the executive branch, Congress, and interest groups. These subgovernments cluster around specific issues.
- Public policy making involves a series of stages, from identifying the problem to measuring the results of government programs and adjusting those programs. Often participants in these activities are from the executive, legislature, interest groups, and occasionally the courts.
- The Constitution has a profound impact on the domestic policy process in all its stages. Our formal system seeks to accommodate change.
- The work of subgovernments must be fed into formal processes associated with the major decision-making institutions (notably the presidency and Congress). This requirement determines how subgovernments do their work.
- The shift from an expansive to a contractive domestic agenda has reshaped the domestic policy process. The debate centers on organizational, procedural, and budget matters associated with the effectiveness and cost of existing programs. Therefore, the substantive issues on the agenda are different from those associated with earlier government initiatives.
- The budget process has come to be of primary importance in a time of contractive issues and growing deficits. New congressional procedures permit more informed debate on the budget. Budget reforms have dramatically altered the process of budget making for both Congress and the president.

Readings on Domestic Policy Processes

Birnbaum, Jeffrey H., and Alan S. Murray. 1987. *Showdown at Gucci Gulch.* New York: Random House. A fascinating account of the adoption of the Tax Reform Act of 1986.

Cater, Douglass. 1964. *Power in Washington.* New York: Random House. Provides a description of the subgovernments that dominate the Washington landscape, identifying their components and showing how they work.

Jones, Charles O. 1984. *An Introduction to the Study of Public Policy,* 3d ed. Monterey, Calif.: Brooks/Cole. Provides a framework for studying the development, implementation, and assessment of public policy, with emphasis on the political aspects.

Light, Paul C. 1985. *Artful Work: The Politics of Social Security Reform.* New York: Random House. Tells the fascinating story of the National Commission on Social Security Reform, revealing much about the policy interactions between the White House and Congress.

Schick, Allen. 1980. *Congress and Money: Budgeting, Spending, and Taxing.* Washington, D.C.: Urban Institute. Careful study of the politics of budgeting, with a focus on the Budget and Impoundment Control Act of 1974.

Smith, Hedrick. 1988. *The Power Game: How Washington Works.* New York: Random House. A massive study of how politics and policy making take place in Washington, described as an elaborate set of power games.

Wildavsky, Aaron. 1988. *The New Politics of the Budgetary Process.* Glenview, Ill.: Scott, Foresman. Offers a realistic description of the way budgets are prepared and approved, with an emphasis on the politics involved.

Chapter 18

Domestic Policy Growth

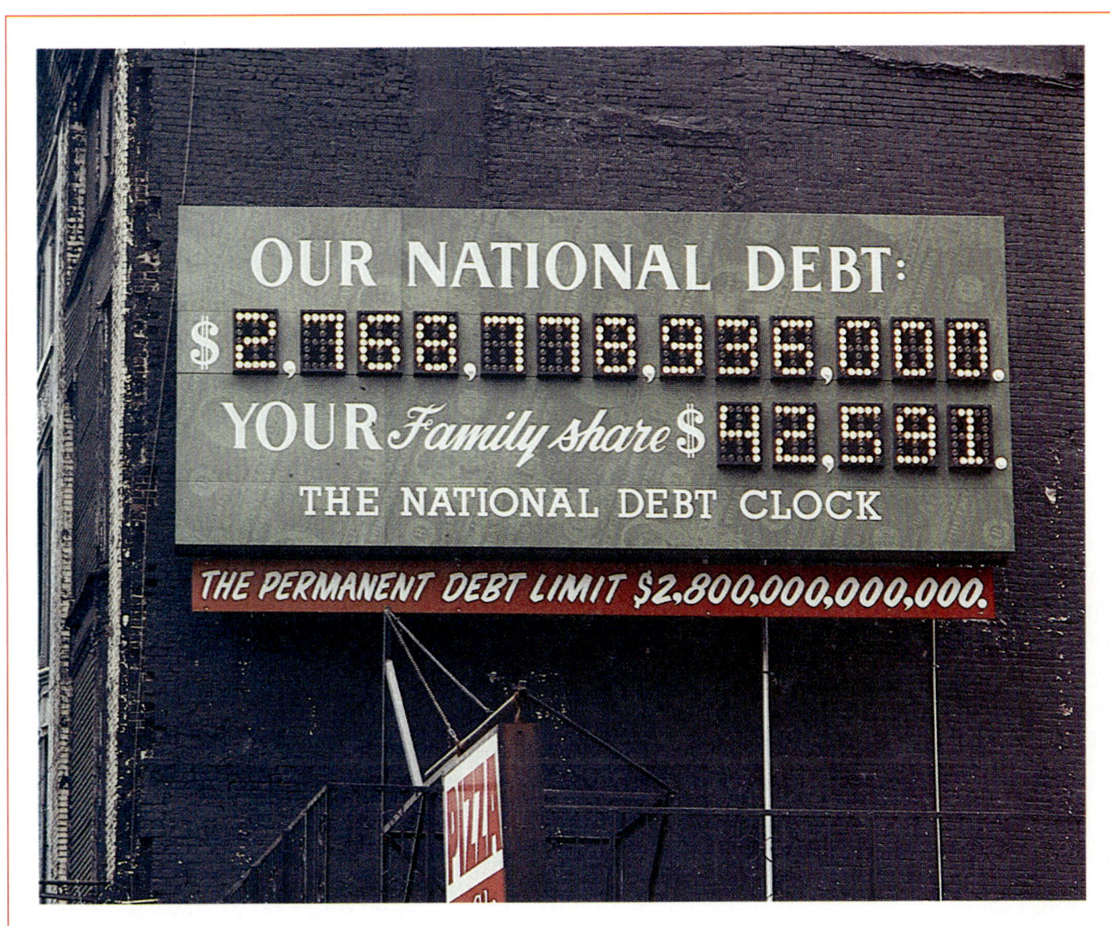
OUR NATIONAL DEBT:
$2,768,778,936,000.
YOUR Family share $42,591.
THE NATIONAL DEBT CLOCK
THE PERMANENT DEBT LIMIT $2,800,000,000,000.
PIZZA

I am certain that my fellow Americans expect that on my induction into the Presidency I will address them with a candor and a decision which the present situation of our Nation impels. This is preeminently the time to speak the truth, the whole truth, frankly and boldly. . . . Values have shrunken to fantastic levels; taxes have risen; our ability to pay has fallen; government of all kinds is faced by serious curtailment of income; the means of exchange are frozen in the currents of trade; the withered leaves of industrial enterprise lie on every side; farmers find no markets for their produce; the savings of many years in thousands of families are gone.

More important, a host of unemployed citizens face the grim problem of existence, and an equally great number toil with little return. Only a foolish optimist can deny the dark realities of the moment.[1]

Franklin D. Roosevelt, speaking at his first inauguration, March 4, 1933, was describing one of the darkest hours in American history. Domestic policy problems overwhelmed government in the early 1930s. The 1932 election marked the end of an era of limited government and the start of a new era of public policy. This chapter identifies the cycles of national policy action since the emergence of modern government in the Roosevelt years.

The 1930s seem very long ago. Yet the time since is just a fourth of the life of our young republic. Over 50 million people in the United States are 55 years or older and thus can make personal comparisons between then and now. For those who are younger, here are illustrative facts and figures about what has happened just in regard to travel and communication.[2]

Travel

1. The Automobile Revolution In 1930 about one of three persons over 20 owned a car; now the ratio is nearly one car for every person over 25. The federal government alone provides over four times as many highway miles as in 1930; people travel by car nearly six times as far (1.5 trillion miles annually). The annual production of cars is well over twice the number of babies born.

2. The Rail Devolution In 1930, 775 operating railroads carried over 700 million passengers; today Amtrak carries about 25 million passengers annually. The number of passenger train cars has decreased 20-fold since 1930.

3. Taking to the Air In 1930 there were about 500 aircraft in commercial service, carrying about 385,000 passengers. Now there are five times that many aircraft carrying 400 million passengers.

Communication

1. Person-to-Person and Place-to-Place Some 41 percent of the 30 million households in 1930 had telephones; now that number has increased to well over 90 percent of nearly 90 million households. The actual number of telephones has increased from 20 million to 200 million, the number of *daily* conversations from 80 million to well over a trillion.

2. Hearing Sounds and Voices About 4 million radios were produced in 1930; 30 percent of the households had at least one. Now a staggering 30 million radios are produced, with most households having several (an average of over five).

3. Watching Pictures No one had a television set in 1930. Now all but a very few households have at least one set; the average is almost two per household. World events, both tragic and joyous, now are instantly viewable in the home.

Other dramatic changes have occurred in industrial production, energy consumption, consumer buying, education, recreation, and personal income. Social and economic life is very different from that in the 1930s, and so have been the demands made on the federal government. The growth in the federal budget illustrates at a glance what has happened. Federal budgets today are beyond what any one dreamed in the 1930s. Then the word "trillion" was used mostly in speaking of distances to the stars. Now we have expenditures over $1 trillion and debt of nearly $3 trillion.

Transportation has changed dramatically in the last 50 years, with profound effects on how we live, work, and do business. It has been personalized with the growth in ownership of automobiles, speeded up with jet travel. Airports today are as crowded as railroad stations were in the past. Changes in how Americans live ultimately change the agenda of government.

Nowhere is that emergence more dramatic than in the escalation of expenditures over the past five decades. As shown in Figure 18–1, it was not until the 1940s that the national government spent over $10 billion, not until the 1960s that it spent over $100 billion (though it came close during World War II), and not until the 1970s that it spent over $200 billion. During the 1970s spending began to increase rapidly in spite of the efforts of a succession of presidents—Nixon, Ford, Carter, Reagan—all dedicated to cutting back. Expenditures nearly tripled in the 1970s, from less than $200 billion to just under $600 billion and nearly doubled in the 1980s to just under $1.2 trillion.

Much of this stunning increase was explained by the high inflation of the 1970s. But even after adjustment for inflation, outlays increased by 67 percent between 1971 and 1990. On the other hand, as a percentage of gross national product (that is, the worth of all goods and services produced in the nation), federal government outlays did not increase greatly—from 19.8 percent in 1970 to an estimated 20.4 percent in 1990, after a significant increase in the mid-1980s. By this measure, big government was matching an upscale economic and industrial system of production.

We turn, then, to an analysis of the several phases of policy making from the 1930s to the pres-

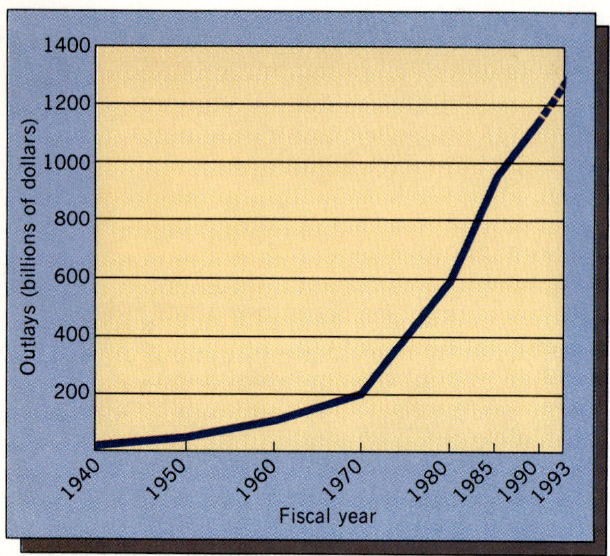

Figure 18–1 Growth in federal outlays, 1940–1993. Source: Office of Management and Budget, *The United States Budget in Brief* (Washington, D.C.: U.S. Government Printing Office, 1988).

ent. We will observe a period of expansion, then consolidation, another expansion, another effort at consolidation, then an effort at contraction. With each period has come a change in the agenda of government.

The Agenda of Government

The word *agenda* means simply "things to be done." But what *are* the things to be done in government? A great deal of effort is typically required to convince the government to do something for you or a group to which you belong. Success can be highly rewarding, defeat very costly. There are winners and losers in any process of choosing among problems to be treated. If your group fails this first test, it is excluded from subsequent policy making.

Listing those things to be done is a crucial first step for government officials. Setting priorities makes their job easier by focusing attention on a few issues. Not surprisingly, "there is a strong status quo bias in any existing system, and the legal machinery of that system is designed and operates to reinforce and defend that bias." [3] This statement means that getting government officials to accept a new issue may be difficult. It suggests further that once government has become an enterprise in excess of $1 trillion, its agenda will be filled with issues growing out of current programs.

The following historical review of domestic policy issues shows a steady expansion of the national government agenda until it becomes so crowded that little room is left for additional demands. In a sense, the agenda becomes self-perpetuating, with most issues being associated with extending, reforming, or reducing programs already on the books. How this occurred is basic to understanding current policy issues. The review starts in the 1930s—the period of dramatic federal government expansion; a period that laid the basis for modern government.

The Growth of Government

Dominant Domestic Issues Before 1945

This chapter began by comparing life in the 1930s with life today. The starting point has to be 1930 because of its importance in the history of national domestic policy. It was the first full year of the Great Depression—an event that led to a dramatic increase in the very role of the national government. The depression produced a huge agenda of social and economic problems. No one doubted what problems had to be acted on, and Washington was never the same again.

It is interesting to return to the period just before the depression to see what the president judged to be the important issues. In his memoirs, President Herbert Hoover said:

> I came to the White House with a program of vigorous policies in three directions.
>
> I was determined to carry forward the reconstruction and development measures in which I had participated as Secretary of Commerce.
>
> There was urgent need for reforms in our social and business life. . . . Little had been

> done by the Federal government in the fields of reform or progress during the fourteen years before my time.
>
> The third field was to reorient our foreign relations. . . .[4]

President Hoover listed issues of interest to him when he served as secretary of commerce (1921–1928). Development of water resources, conservation, improvement of highways, better housing, and child welfare are a few of these. He also wrote of "my ideas on reform," citing law enforcement, executive branch organization, veterans affairs, tariffs, regulation of business, and social programs as deserving attention. Throughout his discussion, one is impressed with the extent to which the president's own experience determined the priorities. The chapter in his memoirs on child welfare begins as follows: "While in the White House, I carried on the work of the American Child Health Association, which I had founded ten years before." [5] Events had not yet taken over the agenda of government. The president was able to fashion a program from his own experiences. But then came the depression. As President Hoover observed: "Instead of being able to devote my four years wholly to my purposes I was to be overtaken by the economic hurricane which sprang from the delayed consequences of the World War I." [6]

President Hoover was overwhelmingly defeated by Franklin D. Roosevelt in 1932. This event itself was destined to ensure a new domestic agenda in the 1930s. At the time, however, newly elected presidents had to wait four months before taking office (from November until March). The pressures on Roosevelt during this period were considerable. Historian Frank Freidel explains:

> All the divergent pressures, from those wishing to preserve the old order and those eager for a "new deal," converged upon Roosevelt: liberals and conservatives in the Democratic party and the Republican, the unemployed and the rich, the farmers, laborers, and white-collar workers, members of the Brain Trust who had advised him during the campaign, and members of Congress determined to protect their own power, even the outgoing President. All of them wanted to commit the President-elect in advance to one or another course of action.[7]

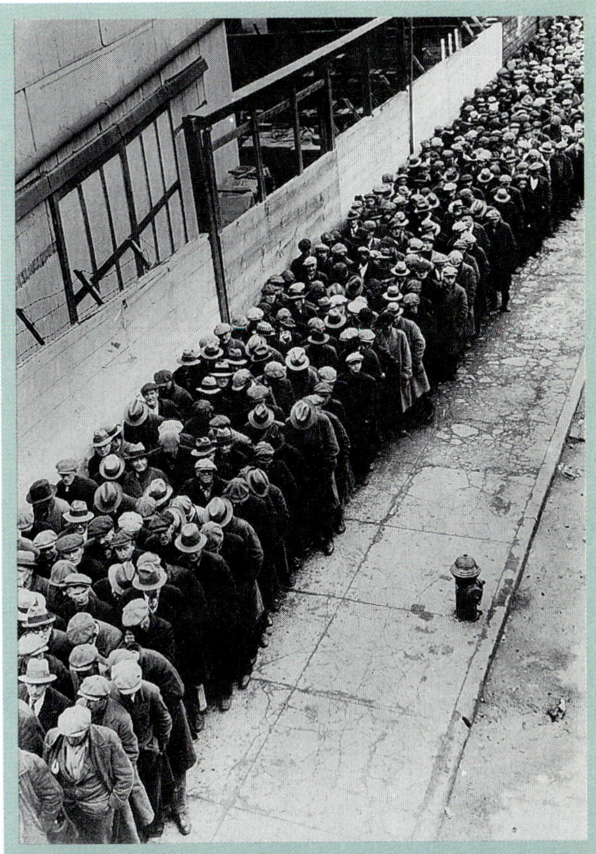

The Great Depression, which left millions unemployed, led to growth in government. In its first 100 days, the Roosevelt administration enacted programs to save failing banks, stabilize the economy, and create new jobs. As a result, the federal government continues to play a greater role in the economy and the lives of Americans.

The leisurely personal pace described by Hoover in 1929 was not possible in 1932–1933. The economic problems were massive and government had to respond. Thus, a new and active national government was created in the brief time of 100 days.

What was accomplished? And what followed these early days of the Roosevelt administration? Table 18–1 lists an impressive outpouring of legislation. Note the variety of topics and targets that

“ Perspectives ”

On Presidential Views of Domestic Policy

“In 1953 we had seen the end of the Korean War. In 1954 we had won out over the economic hazard of a recession. With these problems behind us, we in the United States entered a new era of unprecedented peace and unprecedented prosperity. The slogan ‘Peace, Progress, and Prosperity,’ which was applied to the first-term years and was used in the campaign of 1956, perhaps seems platitudinous. But compared with any years of the two preceding decades, these surely must have seemed miraculous to most Americans. Not in the lifetime of millions of our citizens—children, adolescents, and men and women entering adult life—had we previously had peace, progress, and prosperity all at one time.”

—President Dwight D. Eisenhower, in Mandate for Change, 1963

“First, justice was the promise that all who made the journey would share in the fruits of the land. In a land of great wealth, families must not live in hopeless poverty. In a land rich in harvest, children just must not go hungry. In a land of healing miracles, neighbors must not suffer and die unattended. In a great land of learning and scholars, young people must be taught to read and write. For the more than 30 years that I have served this nation, I have believed that this injustice to our people, this waste of our resources, was our real enemy. . . . But change has given us new weapons. Before this generation of Americans is finished, this enemy will not only retreat—it will be conquered.”

—President Lyndon B. Johnson, inaugural address, 1965

“We have learned that ‘more’ is not necessarily ‘better,’ that even our great nation has its recognized limits, and that we can neither answer all questions nor solve all problems. We cannot afford to do everything, nor can we afford to lack boldness as we meet the future. So together, in a spirit of

were affected—the economy, banking, transportation, farms and farmers, housing, public works, securities, communication, currency, taxes, employment, and social security. Additional legislation was enacted in the second Roosevelt administration (1937–1941), but the main thrust of the new agenda was set in the first. The Supreme Court found much of Roosevelt's domestic program too creative to suit its reading of the Constitution (see Chapter 16). Many programs were declared unconstitutional, and the president found it necessary to enact them in different form. The president even tried to increase the number of Supreme Court justices. Since he had not been able to appoint any justices in his first term, Roosevelt was concerned that a Court from another era was interfering with his efforts to shape a new agenda. Roosevelt lost his bid to “pack” the Court, but retirements in the *individual sacrifice for the common good, we must simply do our best."*

—President Jimmy Carter, inaugural address, 1977

"If I am elected, I shall regard my election as proof that the people of the United States have decided to set a new agenda. No problem that we face today can compare with the need to restore the health of the American economy. . . . The people have not created this disaster in our economy: the federal government has. It has overspent, overestimated, and overregulated. It has failed to deliver services within the revenues it should be allowed to raise from taxes. . . . The key to restoring the health of the economy lies in cutting taxes. At the same time, we need to get the waste out of federal spending."

—President Ronald W. Reagan, official announcement to seek Republican nomination, 1979

"My friends, we have work to do. There are the homeless, lost and roaming—there are the children who have nothing, no love, no normalcy—there are those who cannot free themselves of enslavement to whatever addiction—drugs, welfare, the demoralization that rules the slums. There is crime to be conquered, the rough crime of the streets. There are young women to be helped who are about to become mothers of children they can't care for and might not love. They need our care, our guidance, and our education; though we bless them for choosing life. The old solution, the old way, was to think that public money alone could end these problems. But we have learned that that is not so. And in any case, our funds are low. We have a deficit to bring down. We have more will than wallet; but will is what we need."

—President George Bush, inaugural address, 1989

next two and a half years gave him a chance to appoint several new judges.[8] His agenda—a new agenda for the federal government—was then firmly in place.

World War II interrupted any further plans Roosevelt had to expand national domestic activities. The change in domestic policy he had achieved during the 1930s did carry over to the postwar period, though. Driven by the economic collapse of 1929, social and economic programs were created as a new base for the expansion of the national government. Breakthroughs occurred in many issue areas. The question was no longer *whether* the national government should be involved but *how* it should be involved. From the public's perspective, new expectations regarding the role of government were created. Laissez-faire, the doctrine that government should not interfere

TABLE 18–1

An Outpouring of Legislation: Building a New Domestic Agenda in the First Roosevelt Administration

I. The First 100 Days	
March 9	Emergency Banking Relief Act (introduced, passed, signed in less than eight hours).
March 20	Economy Act (cut pensions and salaries; reorganized agencies).
March 22	Beer and Wine Revenue Act (legalized the sale of wine and beer).
March 31	Civilian Conservation Corps Reconstruction Relief Act (jobs for young men).
April 19	Abandonment of the gold standard.
May 12	Federal Emergency Relief Act (FERA) (half allocated to the states).
May 13	Agricultural Adjustment Act (AAA) (designed to raise farm prices).
May 18	Tennessee Valley Authority Act (authorized construction of dams and power plants on Tennessee River).
May 27	Federal Securities Act (registration of new securities with the Federal Trade Commission).
June 13	Home Owners Refinancing Act (authorized refinancing of nonfarm mortgage debts).
June 16	National Industrial Recovery Act (established regulatory codes for industries; established Public Works Administration to reduce unemployment).
June 16	Banking Act of 1933 (created the Federal Bank Deposit Insurance Corporation to guarantee bank deposits).
June 16	Emergency Railroad Transportation Act (established greater coordination of railroads).
June 16	Farm Credit Act (reorganized agricultural credit programs).
II. Subsequent First-Term Actions	
1933	Issued a number of executive orders associated with putting legislation into effect.
	Approved codes for specific industries.
1934	
January 31	Farm Mortgage Refinancing Act (authorized refinancing of farm debts).
February 15	Civil Works Emergency Relief Act (authorized a civil works and direct relief program under FERA).

with economic and social life, was no longer the dominant public philosophy.

Post-World War II Domestic Issues and Programs

Domestic programs were put on hold during World War II. The war required a total national commitment. The end of the war brought domestic issues to the forefront once more. Problems of employment, labor-management relations, housing, inflation, industrial conversion, farm surpluses, transportation, veterans' benefits, and social welfare dominated the government's agenda in the immediate postwar period. Some of these problems were carried over from the 1930s; others were a

February 23	Crop Loan Act (loans to agricultural producers).
April 21	Cotton Control Act (state and county quotas on cotton).
April 28	Home Owner's Loan Act (guarantees for refinancing of home mortgages).
May 18	Crime Control Acts.
June 6	Federal Securities Exchange Act [established Securities and Exchange Commission (SEC)].
June 19	Communications Act of 1934 [established Federal Communications Commission (FCC)].
June 19	Silver Purchase Act (authorized purchase of silver equal to one-third the Treasury's gold holdings).
June 27	Railway Labor Act (upheld rights of workers to organize and bargain).
June 28	National Housing Act [established Federal Housing Administration (FHA) to insure loans].
1935	
April 8	Emergency Relief Appropriation Act [established Works Progress Administration (WPA)].
April 27	Soil Conservation Act (established soil conservation service).
July 5	Wagner-Connally Act [established National Labor Relations Board (NLRB)].
August 9	Motor Carrier Act [placed interstate buses and trucks under authority of Interstate Commerce Commission (ICC)].
August 14	Social Security Act (first major national social security law).
August 30	Revenue Act of 1935 (more stringent taxes on the wealthy).
1936	
February 29	Soil Conservation and Domestic Allotment Act (replaced the AAA, which had been declared unconstitutional).
June 20	Federal Anti-Price Discrimination Act (prohibited low prices by chain stores engaged in interstate commerce).
June 26	Merchant Marine Act (established Maritime Commission).

Source: Compiled from chronological listing in Tim Taylor, *The Book of Presidents* (New York: Arno Press, 1972), pp. 393–406.

result of the war itself. Unquestionably, the war had a positive effect on the national economy. Unemployment all but disappeared and consumer demand increased. Americans were ready to work and play—to build houses, produce food, buy cars, travel, spend money. The problem was how to shift the work force to a peacetime basis while absorbing thousands of returning veterans.

Despite the apparent good economic times ahead, no one proposed rescinding the New Deal programs. These programs were the basis for the national government's domestic policies. Most of the domestic legislation enacted during the Truman and Eisenhower administrations was an extension or amendment to laws passed during the Roosevelt administrations of the 1930s. Thus, Roosevelt's agenda continued to influence national decision making.

At the same time, President Eisenhower showed little disposition to propose new federal programs. As James L. Sundquist, who worked on Capitol Hill in the late 1950s, points out "His career had at no time immersed him in domestic matters."[9] While he did not intend to repeal the New Deal, neither was he moved to expand it. Meanwhile, according to Sundquist, the Democrats were preparing a large number of proposals to be introduced and passed if they regained control of the White House. The Democrats were in a majority in Congress during six of the eight years of the Eisenhower administrations (1955–1961), and they sought to enact "the activist program on domestic issues inherited from twenty years of the Franklin Roosevelt and Truman administrations."[10] When John F. Kennedy was elected in 1960, he could rely on an elaborate program of new policy initiatives prepared by fellow Democrats.

> The Democratic tradition the voters endorsed [in 1960] was, in a word, one of activism. It was the activism approach to public problems—open-minded, innovative, willing to employ the powers of government . . . —that characterized the Democratic program developed in the 1950s and both the attitude and the substance of the Kennedy campaign. The election cannot be interpreted as a clear endorsement of all of the specific policy proposals in the Democratic program. But it was a clear endorsement of an approach to domestic problems, of a governing temper—and tempo. That was the mandate Kennedy asked for. That was the mandate he was given.[11]

As it happened, however, President Kennedy won by the narrowest of margins, less than 120,000 votes in a total vote of over 68 million. And though the Democrats retained substantial margins in both the House and Senate, the Republicans gained seats in both chambers in the 1960 election. Therefore, congressional Democrats were not beholden to the president and he had difficulties in enacting his programs. Still, the Kennedy administration prepared policy proposals in a number of domestic

Government action usually means a great deal of paperwork. Aid to education was one of President Kennedy's major successes. But tuition support is not for everyone, and these forms are needed to help determine who is eligible and deserving.

areas and began to build support on Capitol Hill. For example, the president was determined to tackle the thorny issue of federal aid to education. Previous efforts to pass a comprehensive bill had failed, in part due to the stranglehold of the southern Democrats on the House Committee of Rules. Kennedy supported a move to expand the membership of the committee—adding two liberal Democrats so as to get a majority for his program.

When Lyndon B. Johnson assumed the presidency on the death of Kennedy, he was successful in getting the bills passed. A second wave of social legislation reset the agenda—perhaps to a degree equal to that of the New Deal during the Roosevelt administrations.

Clearing the Agenda in the 1960s

President John F. Kennedy's inaugural address on January 20, 1961, was among the most positive ever delivered. He implored Americans to get involved in the business of governing. "Ask not what your country can do for you; ask what you can do for your country." But the series of legislative recommendations was not immediately endorsed by Congress. In his last news conference in

1963, he observed that "I am looking forward to the record of this Congress [the 88th], but . . . this is going to be an 18-month delivery." [12] The pace of action in Congress was slow before his assassination, and the president was criticized for his inability to get Congress moving.

But Congress also was judged at fault by many. Cumbersome procedures and lack of strong party leadership on Capitol Hill were cited as problems. Lyndon B. Johnson later reflected:

> Congress is jealous of its prerogatives. All too often that jealousy turns into a stubborn refusal to cooperate in any way with the Chief Executive.
>
> The Congress had been in such a mood from the first day that John Kennedy took office in 1961, and the situation had been getting worse instead of better. . . . An entire program of social legislation proposed by President Kennedy—from aid to education to food stamps to civil rights—remained bottled up in committee, while the Congress defiantly refused to budge or act in any way.
>
> This situation had grown so intolerable that when I assumed office, a month before the end of the year, more than half of the appropriations bills remained unpassed. . . . We had not faced a similar situation in thirty-two years. I remember telling Senator Dirksen [R–Ill.] that "we're going to be in a hell of a shape if the Congress won't even pay its own bills." [13]

Following the assassination, the new president decided to move the legislative program despite the problems with Congress. Here is the way he put it in his memoirs:

> If any sense were to come of the senseless events which had brought me to the Office of the Presidency, it would only come from my using the experience I had gained as a legislator to encourage the legislative process to function as the modern era required. I felt that if we were going to move we would have to move quickly. . . .[14]

Table 18–2 shows some of the more important programs enacted during 1964–1965. To the Kennedy proposals, President Johnson added many of his own and fashioned what he called the Great Society. During 1964, his notable successes were the Civil Rights Act and the Economic Opportunity Act. Enacting the former was more difficult, but the president was determined to see the bill become law as a tribute to President Kennedy. In speaking to Congress a week after the assassination, President Johnson stated: "First, no memorial oration or eulogy could more eloquently honor President Kennedy's memory than the earliest possible passage of the civil rights bill for which he fought so long."[15]

A coalition of Republicans and Democrats passed the bill in the House by a large margin. But there are two houses of Congress, and in the Senate 19 southern Democrats and one Texas Republican tried to talk the bill to death. The filibuster lasted for 57 days! Finally, bipartisan support for a motion to end debate killed the filibuster and the bill was subsequently passed. It was the first time in history that the Senate had stopped a filibuster on a civil rights bill.

If the Civil Rights Act was a tribute to John Kennedy, the Economic Opportunity Act was a mark of what to expect from Lyndon Johnson. It was the first of the Great Society programs. "The poverty program . . . was my kind of undertaking," Johnson said.[16] In his State of the Union address on January 8, 1964, the president announced: "This administration today, here and now, declares unconditional war on poverty in America." This program was the first broad-scale attack on the roots of poverty and was therefore highly innovative.

The pace of legislation proposed by President Johnson and enacted by Congress quickened considerably in 1965, after Johnson was elected by one of the largest landslides in history. In Congress, Democrats now had better than two-to-one majorities in both houses. And whereas Democrats had a net loss of seats in the House and Senate with Kennedy's narrow win in 1960, they had a net gain of 38 House and 2 Senate seats in 1964. Here was a Congress prepared to do the president's bidding.

In his first State of the Union message as an elected president, Johnson stated that "we are only

TABLE 18–2

The Johnson Record, 1964–1965: Clearing the Agenda of the 1960s

1964
- Civil Rights Act (the most comprehensive legislation since Reconstruction)
- Revenue Act (major reduction in taxes)
- Food Stamp Act (begun as an agricultural surplus disposal program)
- Economic Opportunity Act (the "war on poverty"—a major Johnson initiative)
- Extension of Hill-Burton Act (grants for hospital construction and modernization)
- Nurse Training Act (grants for training and construction of nursing schools)
- Omnibus Housing Act (extension of current programs plus four new initiatives)
- National Wilderness Preservation System (designated land for the system and established regulations)

1965
- Medicare (provided health benefits for the aged)
- Elementary and Secondary Education Act (most sweeping federal education act in history)
- Higher Education Act (aid for students and colleges)
- Creation of a Department of Housing and Urban Development (HUD)
- Older Americans Act (created an Administration on Aging and authorized grants to states)
- Voting Rights Act (federally enforced registration of voters in areas of discrimination)
- Housing and Urban Development Act (most far-reaching since the 1949 act)
- Community Mental Health Centers Act Amendments (grants for staffing)
- Law Enforcement Assistance Act (aid for local law enforcement officials)

Source: Compiled from descriptions in Congressional Quarterly, *Congress and the Nation:* vols. I and II (Washington, D.C.: Congressional Quarterly, Inc., 1965, 1969).

at the beginning of the road to the Great Society." He then listed goals to be achieved. These goals were followed by a record number of legislative proposals—469 in all. Table 18–2 lists the most significant bills that were enacted. Medicare and the Elementary and Secondary Education Act were particularly notable since both had been on the agenda for a long time. But the volume of legislation passed was as impressive as any one accomplishment. Of the 469 proposals submitted, 323 were passed in some form by Congress!

By the end of Johnson's term, the federal government was deeply involved in many aspects of social life. What had been started during the depression was essentially completed during the 1960s. Education, civil rights, a direct attack on the causes of poverty, and a large-scale program of health benefits were carryovers from the pre-World War II agenda. All were treated during the 1960s. The country entered the 1970s with a varied catalog of government programs. The goals included a new range of government action:

Research: Identify problems and possible solutions through government-sponsored research and development.

Stimulate nongovernment solutions: Provide grants, loans, subsidies, or tax incentives to the private sphere.

Stimulate state and local government solu-

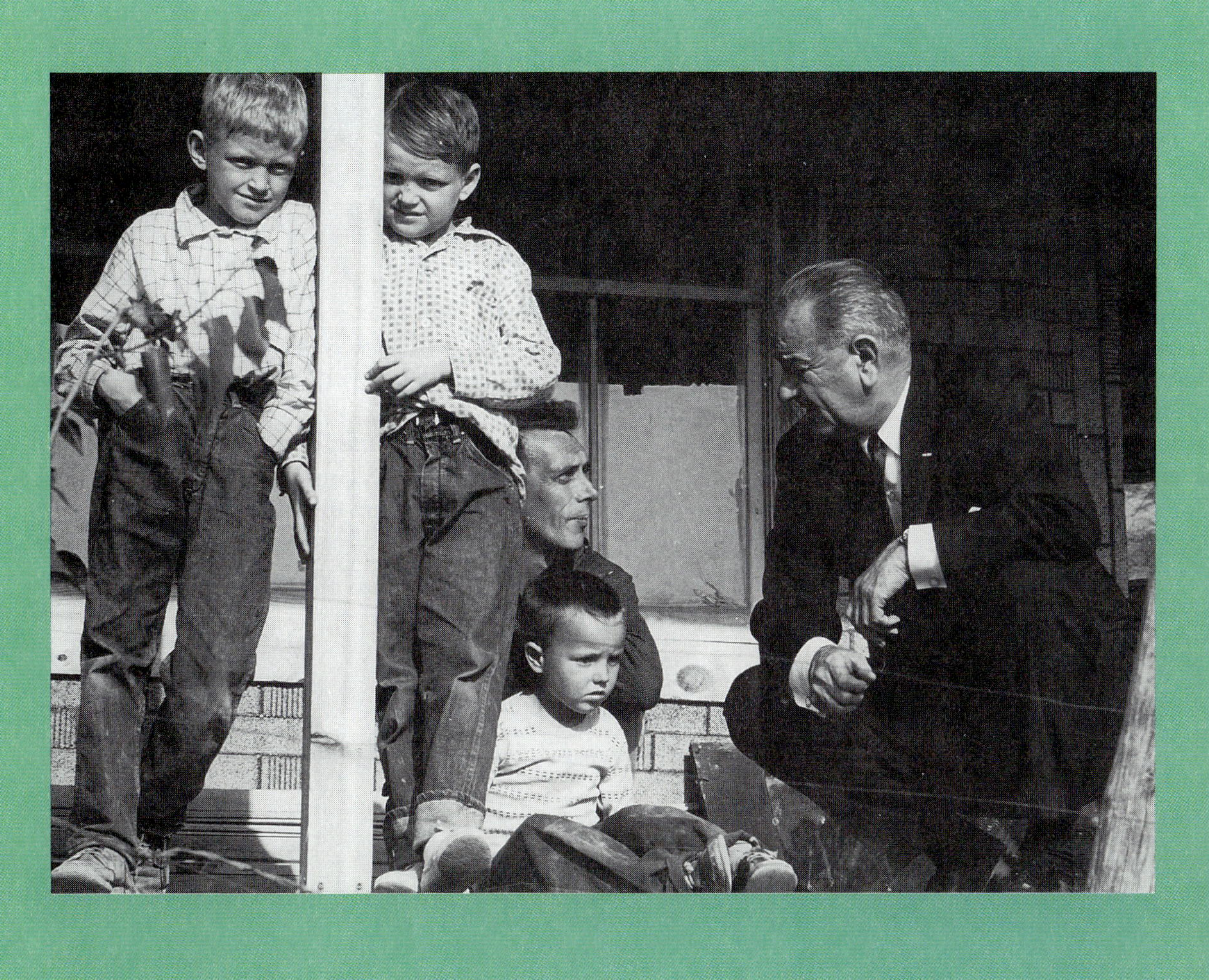

President Lyndon B. Johnson visiting a family in eastern Kentucky, one of the "poverty pockets" to which his Economic Opportunity Act of 1964 was directed. This father of eight explained to the president that he had been out of work for two years, earning just $400 in 1963.

tions: Provide grants or loans to state and local governments to encourage them to act on a problem (see Chapter 3).

Regulate: Seek to control the bad effects of existing social, political, and economic practices.

Prevent: Seek to prevent a bad effect from occurring.

Provide a service: Offer education, training, health care for those unlikely to get it otherwise.

Provide physical improvement: Build highways, bridges, dams, where the private sphere is unlikely to act.

Preserve land: Provide parks, control use of public land.

Provide income: Offer payments to those meeting certain criteria of need (to include pensions).

Provide technology: Actually develop technologies where the private sphere is unlikely to act (as with space exploration).

Tax Burdens in Western Democracies

Americans, like citizens everywhere, complain endlessly about taxes. And the tax burden in the United States—$4740 per person—is greater than in most Western democracies. A closer look, however, may put that tax burden in perspective. The second column shows taxes as a percentage of gross domestic product (GDP) for 20 nations. The GDP, or gross national product minus the value of goods produced outside the country, is a measure of the total worth of all the goods and services the country produces. When taxes are examined as a percentage of GDP, it becomes clear that citizens in the United States actually pay very little by international standards.

So which column best measures the American tax burden? Answering that question is part of setting the domestic policy agenda.

Source: *Statistical Abstract of the United States, 1988* (Washington, D.C.: U.S. Government Printing Office, 1988), p. 810.

	Per Capita Taxes (U.S. dollars)	Tax Revenues (percent of GDP)
Sweden	$6064	50.5%
Denmark	5573	49.2
Norway	6668	47.8
Belgium	3854	46.9
France	4216	45.6
Netherlands	3879	45.0
Austria	3714	42.5
United Kingdom	3025	38.1
West Germany	3869	37.8
Finland	4116	37.3
Greece	1178	35.1
Italy	2565	34.7
New Zealand	2304	34.3
Canada	4621	33.1
Switzerland	4554	32.1
Portugal	676	31.1
Australia	3213	30.3
UNITED STATES	4740	29.2
Spain	1226	28.8
Japan	3107	28.0

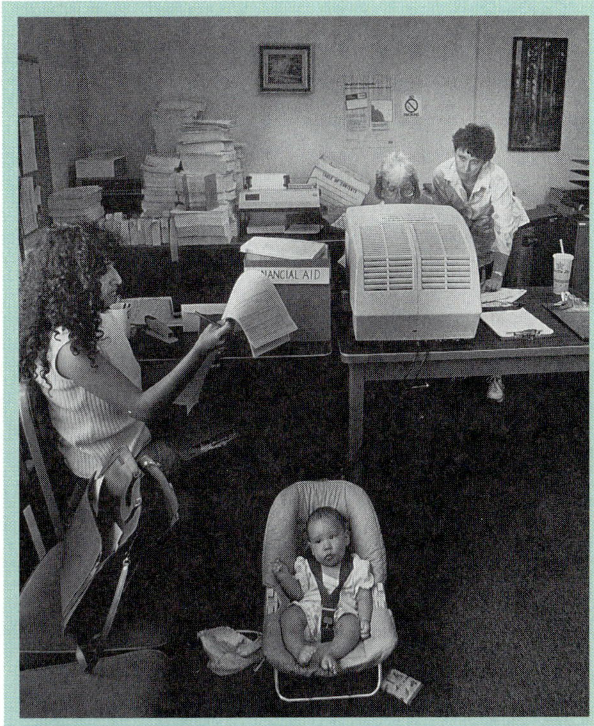

Administering welfare has become an important function of government at all levels. This applicant is finishing off the paperwork while a check is made of computerized data. Although payments to individuals constitute a large portion of the federal budget, most go *not* to young mothers like this, but to older Americans.

This list is remarkable for more than its length. For many of these activities the federal government provides the money—either directly with grants and payments or indirectly with tax credits and other tax relief measures. According to Frederick C. Mosher, "considerably less than one tenth of the federal budget is allotted to domestic activities *that the federal government performs itself.*" [17] In other words, many federal programs set conditions under which the federal government gives money to others to spend. If the conditions apply, the money is either paid out or not taken in.

For example, if you as an individual qualify for unemployment benefits, food stamps, Medicare, or retirement income, you are entitled to receive support from the government. These provisions are properly referred to as *entitlement* programs, and they now constitute a large portion of the federal budget. They are also labeled "uncontrollable" because they tend to be open-ended. Often no limit is put on the amount to be allocated by these programs. With unemployment benefits, for example, if the number of jobless doubles due to an economic downturn, then all those eligible receive checks based on the current formula. Therefore, in a recession, government expenditures increase and revenues decrease, thus contributing to large deficits. "These open-end programs have grown from about 27 percent of the budget in fiscal 1967 to an estimated 48 percent in fiscal 1982. . . ." [18]

Another type of benefit that is uncontrollable shows up on the revenue side of the ledger. Tax credits, that is, credits against your tax bill for engaging in certain types of activity, and deductions on taxable income have an impact on balancing a budget. For example, in being able to deduct interest payments or depreciation on property or equipment, individuals and business firms receive an enviable benefit—money they don't have to send to the government at all. As with entitlement programs, if you qualify, you get the benefit. If anything, these so-called tax expenditures are more uncontrollable than the entitlement programs and probably involve as much or more fraud.

Clearing the agenda in the 1960s has turned out to be expensive. The actual cost of the programs is less worrisome to many people than the fact that the costs escalate on their own. Reductions cannot be made without changing the laws—that is, changing the eligibility for receiving benefits. Table 18–3 shows the increases in budget outlays for the past two decades. The figures are adjusted for inflation, which gives a more accurate picture of government costs. Thus, as estimated for 1990, instead of the actual current-dollar spending of over $1 trillion, the total in constant dollars (using 1982 as a base) was $848.6 billion. Even adjusting for inflation, the increases are impressive—particularly so given that all four presidents during the period were self-proclaimed budget cutters.

One can observe several impacts of the Great Society programs in Table 18–3, as well as the effects of President Reagan's efforts to cut back. First,

TABLE 18–3

The Growth in Government: Federal Outlays Since 1981

	Federal Government Outlays (billions of 1982 dollars)					Percent Change	
	1971	1976	1981	1986	1991 (est.)	1971–1986	1971–1991
National defense	$202.7	$153.6	$171.4	$228.7	$245.6	+12.8%	+21.2%
Nondefense spending							
Payments to individuals	181.0	291.7	344.3	389.4	439.9	+115.1%	+143.0%
Other grants	43.3	64.3	61.3	50.7	38.3	+17.1%	−11.5%
Interest	34.0	43.0	73.7	117.9	117.4	+246.7%	+245.3%
Other	75.8	80.1	106.0	94.6	82.2	+24.8%	+8.4%
Total nondefense spending *	$306.7	$456.2	$555.2	$619.3	$646.1	+101.9%	+110.7%
Total outlays *	$509.4	$609.8	$726.5	$848.0	$891.6	+66.5%	+75.0%

* Columns do not total exactly due to undistributed offsetting receipts.
Source: Compiled from data in *The United States Budget in Brief* (Washington, D.C.: U.S. Government Printing Office, 1988), p. 103.

the growth of nondefense programs from 1971 to 1990 is dramatic—nearly doubling. By contrast, defense programs have increased by just over one-fourth, and they actually declined in constant dollars during the mid-1970s. Second, the two areas of greatest growth were in "payments to individuals" and "net interest" on the debt. The first represents the many retirement programs, unemployment compensation, and other direct welfare payments. The estimated increase for these programs by 1990 is over 125 percent. The second reflects the huge deficits that developed in the Reagan administration. Note that these interest payments on the debt have increased by well over 200 percent.

Third, the proportions of defense and nondefense programs have changed. In 1971, the split was defense 40 percent, nondefense 60 percent. In 1990 it is estimated that defense will constitute 30 percent, nondefense 70 percent. And actually that represents an increase for defense, which had slipped to just 24 percent of the total budget outlays in 1981.

Finally, Table 18–3 identifies the principal area of cutting back during the Reagan administration. Whereas there was a decrease in the *rate* of increase in payments to individuals, there was significant decline in all other grants—nearly 12 percent in constant dollars between 1971 and as estimated for 1990. Unfortunately for the goal of a balanced budget, the other grants were too small a proportion of total spending (less than 5 percent in 1990) to make much difference. Thus Table 18–3 provides a nice summary of the growing debt problem—significant increases in defense and payments to individuals without compensatory cuts in other programs.

By the end of the 1960s, no one questioned whether the national government had a full agenda of domestic issues. Self-expanding programs were in place. Budgets grew on their own. Presidents and Congresses were left with only marginal choices for starting new programs. Further, new issues developed out of a growing public concern for the environment and our dependence on foreign oil. The consequence of these developments was a reshaping of the national domestic agenda in the 1970s.

New Issues and Politics

The Rise of a New Agenda

The decade of the 1960s was one of the most turbulent in American history. Blacks demanded a share of the economic prosperity, young people demanded an end to American involvement in the Vietnam War, and by the end of the decade, middle-class Americans were insisting on a clean environment. Demonstrations, some of them quite violent, almost became a way of life. By the end of the decade, sociologist Amitai Etzioni concluded:

> The rise in the number, frequency, scope, and "respectability" of demonstrations and their close link with television all suggest that demonstrations, as a major means through which protest can be expressed, are now and will remain part and parcel of the country's political processes and will not disappear when the war in Vietnam is over or the needs of the poor are met. For good or bad, they are now part of our system.[19]

Molly Yard, president of the National Organization for Women (NOW). The women's movement has grown rapidly in recent years. Today NOW lobbies for women's issues at all levels of government. It places special emphasis on equal pay, employment opportunities, and the pro-choice position in regard to abortion. It even explored forming a third party in 1989.

In his State of the Union address in 1970, President Nixon acknowledged that "the decade of the sixties was . . . a period of . . . the greatest social unrest in America in 100 years. Never has a nation seemed to have had more and enjoyed it less." The president declared that the government itself was at fault.

> At heart, the issue is the effectiveness of government.
>
> Ours has become as it continues to be—and should remain—a society of large expectations. Government helped to generate these expectations and undertook to meet them. Yet, increasingly, it proved unable to do so.
>
> As a people, we had too many visions—and too little vision.
>
> Now, as we enter the seventies, we should enter also a great age of reform of the institutions of American government.[20]

In essence, President Nixon announced the end of government expansion and the beginning of a period of reorganization and consolidation. His program was made more explicit in his 1971 State of the Union address. He announced a six-part package. Three of the six goals were consolidative—welfare reform, revenue sharing with state and local governments, and federal government reorganization. One proposal—improved health care—appeared to be an effort to upstage Senator Edward Kennedy's (D–Mass.) national health care plan. The environmental programs were offered to ride the crest of what had become a very popular issue. And the sixth goal—new job opportunities—was a hardy perennial.

Following the enactment of the Great Society programs, policy attention in Washington was directed to curbing further growth in government. At the same time, major environmental programs enacted during the early 1970s expanded the reach of government in another way. Major regulatory programs were developed and new agencies were created. Table 18–4 shows the outpouring of legislation during a relatively short time—all enacted just before the Arab oil embargo that catapulted another major issue onto the agenda of the national government.

The effect of many environmental regulations was to increase energy consumption. Therefore, a clash between environmental and energy goals was inevitable.

> In 1973 America awoke to an energy crisis. After years of seemingly unlimited supplies of energy products at low prices, it suddenly appeared that the oil wells had run dry. Gas stations were closed on Sundays and often early on other days, absurdly long lines formed at their pumps, heating oil was rationed, plane flights were canceled for lack of fuel, farmers had no fuel to plow their fields or to dry their crops, and truckers, angry at high fuel prices and delays, went out on strike.[21]

The event that triggered the crisis was an embargo on oil shipments by the Organization of Petroleum Exporting Countries (OPEC). The decision was made on October 17, 1973, at a meeting in Kuwait and was imposed the next day. The OPEC action was a response in part to the pro-Israeli posture of the United States and certain European nations during the Arab-Israeli war.

The embargo continued until March 18, 1974. Several developments converged to produce the crisis. First was our growing dependence on foreign oil. Oil imports rose steeply just before the embargo and continued to increase afterward, finally peaking in 1977. A second development was a significant increase in the price of imported oil. The average price per barrel before the embargo was just over $3. That price nearly quadrupled in one year and continued to increase until it reached nearly $22 in 1979.[22] Figure 18–2 shows that these price increases had a dramatic effect on the cost of crude oil in this country. Note that there were *two* steep increases. The first one hit immediately after the

TABLE 18–4

The Federal Government and the Environment: National Legislation Enacted 1969–1972

Year	Legislation	Comment
1969	National Environmental Policy Act	Established Council on Environmental Quality
1970	Environmental Quality Improvement Act	Established Office of Environmental Quality
1970	Reorganization Plans Nos. 3 and 4	Established Environmental Protection Agency and National Oceanic and Atmospheric Administration
1970	Clean Air Amendments	Most comprehensive regulation ever enacted
1970	Water Quality Improvement Act	Reauthorization of earlier program
1970	Resource Recovery Act	Grants for solid waste disposal
1972	Federal Water Pollution Control Act	Major expansion of existing program
1972	Noise Control Act	New federal regulations
1972	Federal Environmental Pesticide Control Act	New federal regulations

The oil embargo imposed by the Organization of Petroleum Exporting Countries (OPEC) resulted in long lines of frustrated drivers. Many gasoline stations were open for just a few hours a day. Some pumped gas until it ran out. This energy crisis changed the domestic policy agenda, as Americans learned that they were no longer self-sufficient in energy.

embargo; then a leveling off occurred (1975–1977) and an even more dramatic rise followed (1979–1980), coinciding with the fall of the Shah of Iran and the crisis that ensued. These trends were important in and of themselves, but were not critical if Americans could have shifted easily to other fuel sources. Unfortunately, no such shift was possible in the short run. In fact, just the opposite was happening. In 1920 petroleum constituted 14 percent and in 1973 nearly half (47 percent) of all fuel use.[23] Well over half of the petroleum used in the 1970s was for the fuel tanks of the more than 150 million cars, trucks, and buses in the United States. Motor vehicles cannot easily use other fuels, which brings us to the long gas lines that made this crisis very personal to millions of Americans.

These developments dramatically challenged the American political and economic systems. The United States is the world's greatest consumer of energy—using nearly 30 percent of all fuel consumed in the world. The economy naturally was affected in many ways by oil shortages and price increases, but so were politics and social life. Even more important, however, may have been the realization that America was no longer independent. The oil embargo merely drew attention to changes that were occurring. Public perception began to catch up with reality in the mid-1970s. And the reality was that small nations, far from our shores, could have a significant impact on our domestic agenda.

The profound change from energy independence to dependence was acknowledged by Presidents Nixon, Ford, and Carter. Each struggled to develop plans that would reestablish energy self-sufficiency. They offered proposals that touched

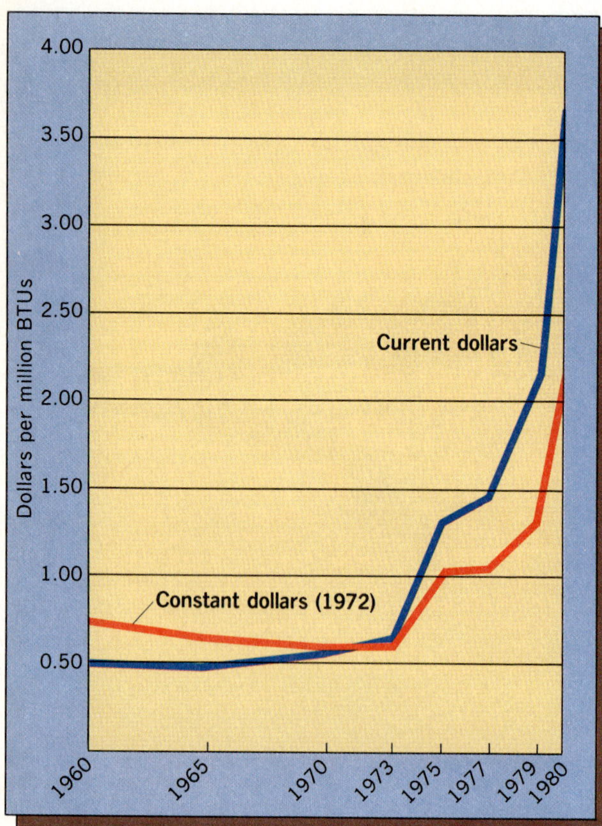

Figure 18–2 Crude oil prices in selected years from 1960 to 1980. Source: *Statistical Abstract of the United States, 1982–1983* (Washington, D.C.: U.S. Government Printing Office, 1982), p. 573.

almost every aspect of energy supply, distribution, and consumption. Presidents Nixon and Ford stressed increasing supply; President Carter stressed conservation. Energy issues had such massive impact on the American political and economic system that they came to dominate the government's agenda. According to Walter A. Rosenbaum, "governmental authority over the energy sector expanded so greatly during the 1970s that practically no domain of energy management remained unaffected by 1980." He also observed: "the nation's energy future is becoming increasingly the creation of public *management*." [24]

The agenda in the 1970s was characterized by problems of government management. Efforts were made to consolidate the social programs of the Johnson administration and to bring more order to a whole set of complex energy, environmental, and economic issues. Obviously, programs designed to provide better control, more coordination, and the like are much less glamorous than those offering new initiatives. And even the new emphasis on controls, regulation, and management was not successful in curbing government expenditures. Thus, still another agenda was forming during the 1970s—one with roots in the early Nixon administration, one that was etched more clearly in the Carter administration, one that dominated the 1980 election campaign between Carter and Reagan, and one that is with us still in the Bush administration.

Government as the Problem

In his inaugural address, President Ronald Reagan repeated a statement he had made often in his several campaigns for the presidency: "Government is not the solution to our problem. Government is the problem." Presidential rhetoric aside, it did seem that another significant shift had occurred in the agenda of the national government. Ronald Reagan was elected in an electoral college landslide (his popular vote total was much less impressive), the Republicans won a majority in the Senate for the first time in 28 years, and House Republicans increased their numbers by 33 seats. In the 1980 campaign, Reagan emphasized cutting government expenditures, reducing the size of the national government, shifting responsibilities to state and local governments, and stimulating the economy by cutting taxes and eliminating regulations. His was a contractive agenda in regard to domestic policy, and the election results appeared to give him an overwhelming mandate.

In its way, President Reagan's first year in office, 1981, was as important to domestic policy as President Roosevelt's was in 1933.[25] The two leaders sought to move government in different directions, however. Roosevelt, in the New Deal, expanded the role of the national government in the domestic sphere. Reagan, on the other hand, was determined to reduce, and possibly reverse, the rate of government growth. He had remarkable success

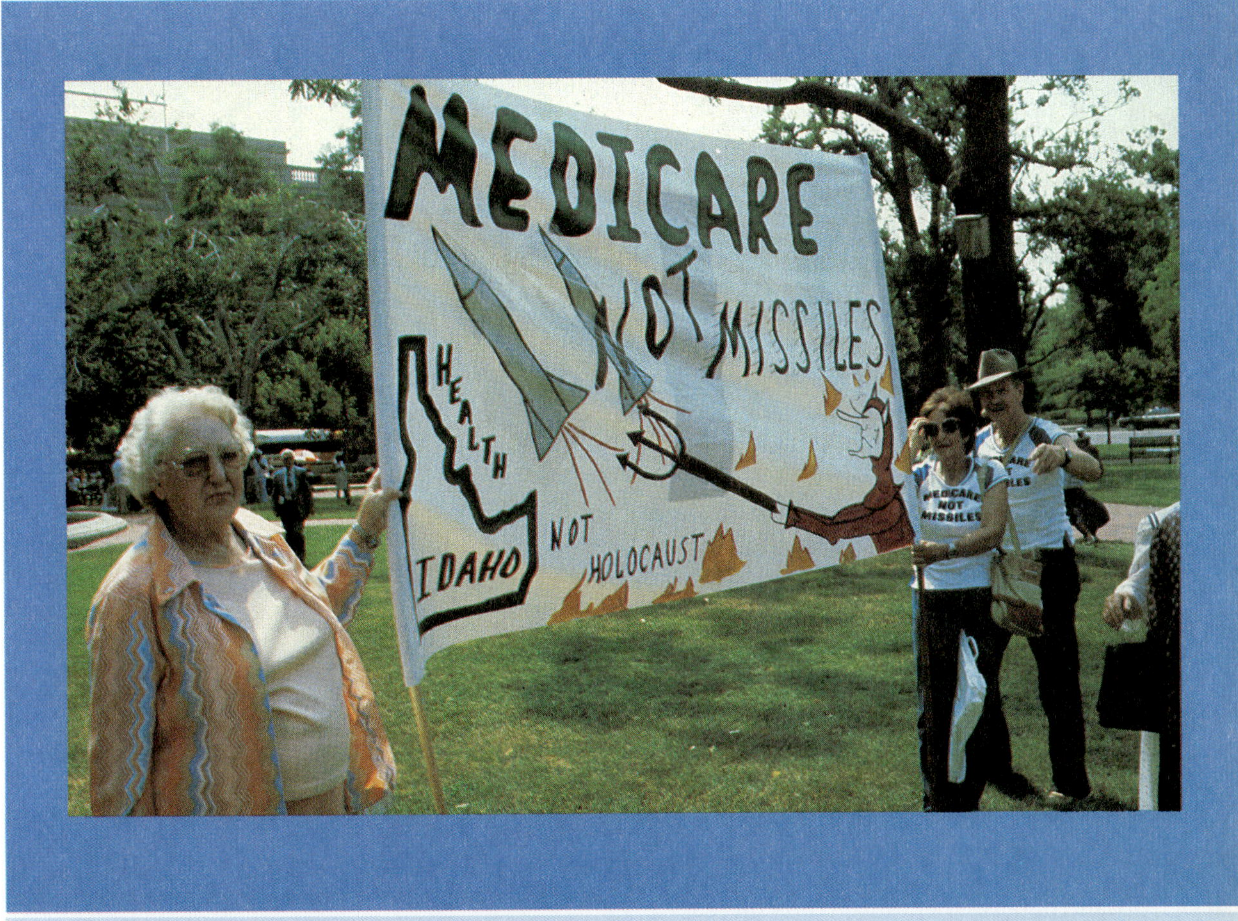

The elderly have become one of the most powerful groups in America. Since they have the time and resources to lobby, members of Congress listen. The most powerful interest group representing senior citizens is the American Association of Retired Persons (AARP). Groups like this have succeeded in gaining important retirement benefits and resisting cuts.

in getting congressional support for his program in 1981. Here is what happened:

1. A three-year tax cut was proposed by President Reagan to stimulate the economy—so-called supply-side economics. Congress approved much of what the president asked for.
2. Severe cuts in some domestic programs were requested, and many were approved by Congress.
3. An overhaul of the social security system was proposed but rejected by Congress. Later, in 1983, reforms were enacted following a study by an independent commission.
4. Significant increases in defense spending were requested, and most were approved by Congress.

Note that the president identified very large issues—the economy, budget growth, social security, and defense. A major consequence of his successes, when combined with his failure in 1981 to reform social security, was to produce unprecedented deficits. The tax cuts reduced revenue, the

Continuity & CHANGE

Past Spending and the Headache of the Federal Debt

One of President Bush's major challenges is the federal deficit. Yet, contrary to common belief, growth in the deficit need not be a consequence of the government spending more on federal programs today than it collects in taxes. In 1988 the federal treasury took in only $5 billion less than was spent on tangible programs and services—and estimates for 1989 projected a surplus of tax revenues over spending for those programs.

The explanation? We have to look at *past* as well as present spending. In order to pay the interest on past years' deficits, the government must continue to borrow even more heavily, resulting in further increases in the debt. Here is how continued interest payments on past debt enter the picture, as shown by the deficit and net interest (both as a percent of GNP):

When Bush served as vice president, taxes were cut sharply and defense spending greatly increased. As a result, in 1983, for example, government programs exceeded income by $118 billion. Because Congress and the Reagan administration then refused to increase taxes to pay for the massive Pentagon buildup, the debt tripled between 1980 and 1989.

The result is that the federal government spent more than $160 billion in 1989 simply for interest payments on the debt. Borrowing charges seem likely to grow in the 1990s. While economists, political leaders, and other Americans differ on the danger of the spiral of borrowing, to break out of it, Congress and the White House would have to make draconian cuts in domestic or military spending programs—or else increase taxes.

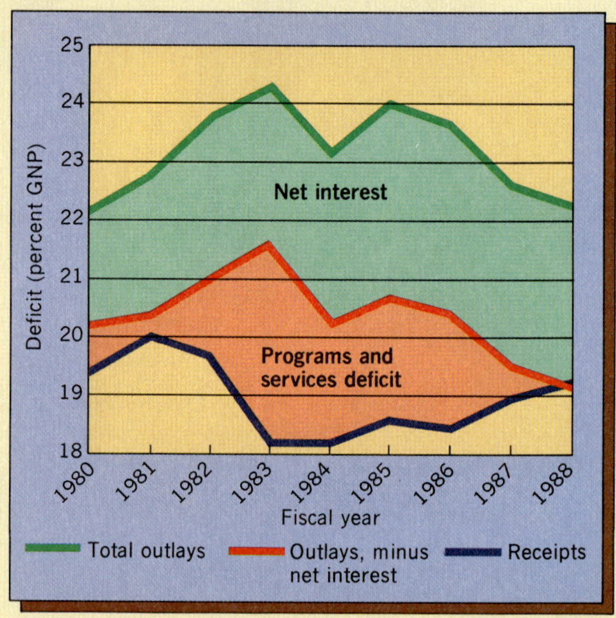

Source: Data from *Congressional Quarterly Weekly Report,* September 10, 1988, pp. 2491–2494.

defense buildup increased expenditures, and the budget cuts for domestic programs were not sufficient to make up the difference. As budget analyst Allen Schick put it: "Ronald Reagan won the battles but lost the budget." [26] It was hoped that tax cuts would correct the nation's economic ills and thus produce more revenue by increasing profits and putting the unemployed back to work. That hope was not realized in the short run, however, and by January 1983, serious questions were raised about President Reagan's political future. Unemployment and interest rates remained high, thus stifling economic growth. The president's program was in jeopardy.

Yet ironically it was the record deficits of this conservative president that secured his new agenda. Policy conversation in Washington changed dramatically after 1981. Few public officials proposed new domestic programs; policymakers focused on the budget. Policy analyst Richard P. Nathan explains:

> The Reagan administration seized the moment in 1981. Under the impetus of budget revisions, the administration achieved a major change of direction in national policy for domestic, and particularly social, programs. The decay rate of the administration's legislative success in this area has been commented upon. . . . However, in my view, these setbacks do not have as much importance as do the fundamentally changed tone and approach to domestic policy-making and its execution that were brought about under Reagan. Reagan's conservative movement, I would argue, has had its greatest success in the field of domestic policy.[27]

How large were the deficits? They exceeded anything ever experienced: 1981—$79 billion; 1982—$128 billion; 1983—$208 billion; 1984—$185 billion. The total for these 4 years equaled that for the previous 38 years! The situation did not improve during the second term. Deficits exceeded $200 billion in 1985 and 1986 and were then estimated to decline with the implementation of the Gramm-Rudman-Hollings deficit limitation procedures (see Chapter 17). Even with the reductions, however, the deficit exceeded the whole federal government budget of a typical year in the 1960s.

Naturally, these record-setting deficits sent the total federal debt skyrocketing. Figure 18–3 tells the story. The total debt exceeded $1 trillion for the first time in 1981, exceeded $2 trillion just five years later, and will reach $3 trillion early in the 1990s. Small wonder that the budget came to take center stage in domestic policy making during the 1980s.

Reducing government is a difficult and highly conflictual process (see Chapter 17). Groups that benefit from existing programs naturally resist cuts. Whereas group A may support group B as govern-

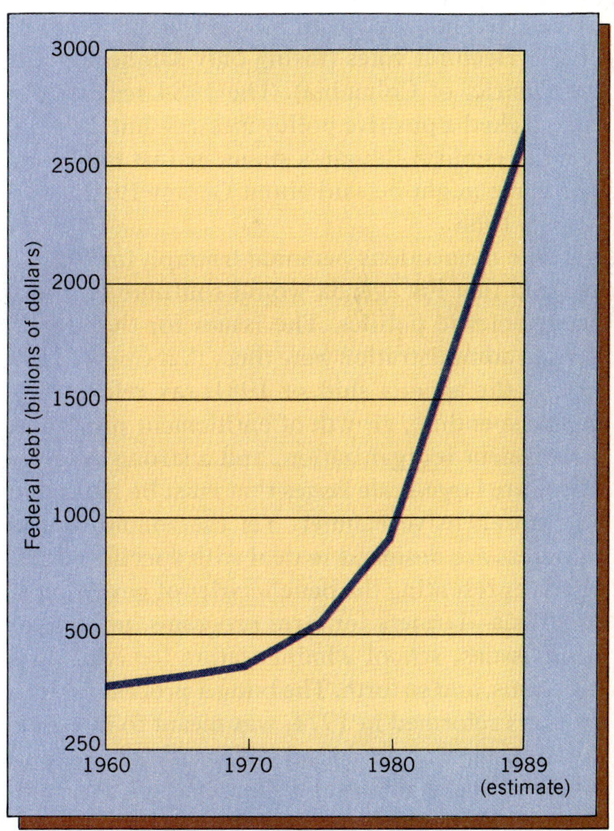

Figure 18–3 Growth in the federal debt, showing selected years from 1960 to 1985. Source: *The United States Budget in Brief, Fiscal Year 1987* (Washington, D.C.: U.S. Government Printing Office, 1988), p. 97.

ment expands ("You scratch my back and I'll scratch yours"), each group tends to be competitive when cuts are necessary. That is, A will agree to cuts for B if A can be spared and vice versa. But no one wants to go it alone with cuts. Therefore groups are likely to pay more attention to what is happening to others during periods of budget cuts. The Reagan agenda introduced this combative politics into domestic policy making.

As it happened, economic conditions improved steadily from the low point in January 1983, and the deficit did not really become a negative issue for President Reagan in 1984. Interest rates declined, the employment situation improved, and the inflation rate remained low. Democratic presidential candidate Walter F. Mondale stressed the deficit issue during the 1984 campaign—even promising a tax increase. But the voters rejected his appeal, and the president won 525 of 538 electoral votes (losing only Minnesota and the District of Columbia). The 1984 results may have lacked a positive policy message but they did seem to confirm Reagan's stand against tax hikes. The same might be said about George Bush's victory in 1988.

The tremendous personal triumph for Reagan ensured that his agenda would continue to dominate domestic politics. The issues for the second Reagan administration were those that emerged following the agenda shift of 1981: tax reform, domestic spending, growth of entitlement programs, government reorganization, and a strong defense. These are large-scale issues that must be treated in a comprehensive manner. Yet the committees in Congress are designed to deal with specific issues, often representing the beneficiaries of government programs—farmers for farm programs, unions for labor issues, school administrators for education programs, and so forth. The budget process in Congress, as reformed in 1974, was meant to integrate decision making on broad policy issues—to pull together that which gets pulled apart in the committees. It therefore became an increasingly important, if severely tested, process during the Reagan era (see Chapter 17).

President Reagan was not entirely successful in getting his program enacted. The Democrats retained their majority in the House of Representatives during the first term and acted as a counterforce to the president and the Senate Republican majority. In the Reagan landslide of 1984, the Senate Republicans had a net loss of two seats and the House Republicans did not gain enough seats to threaten Democratic control of that chamber. Then in 1986 Democrats recaptured control of the Senate by a 55 to 45 margin. Prospects were not encouraging for cooperative presidential-congressional relations during the last years of the Reagan administration.

Transition to a New Agenda ■

Expectations of stalemate between the president and Congress were not fully realized during the 100th Congress. First, a sobering event occurred on October 19, 1987. The Dow-Jones industrial average, a major indicator of stock market performance, plunged a record 508 points. It was estimated that $500 billion in paper value was lost in this one day. People worried about a repeat of the 1929 stock market crash that precipitated the Great Depression.

As a result of this stunning event and its reverberations in the world's economy, there were demands that the Republican president and the Democratic Congress set aside their partisan differences and reach an agreement on the budget. It took nearly two months of sometimes bitter wrangling between the White House and Capitol Hill, but in the end an agreement was forged. Congress passed the package just before Christmas. It included spending cuts and tax increases, the latter inaugurating a new era—a fiscal agenda in which policymakers turned to the revenue side of the ledger.

The 1987 agreement established the budget limitations for 1988, thus essentially removing the normally contentious budget politics from election year campaigning. The White House and Congress agreed to follow the guidelines set down by the 1987 plan. This then permitted policymakers to turn to other issues. The result was that the 100th Congress was considerably more productive than expected. For the first time in many years, major

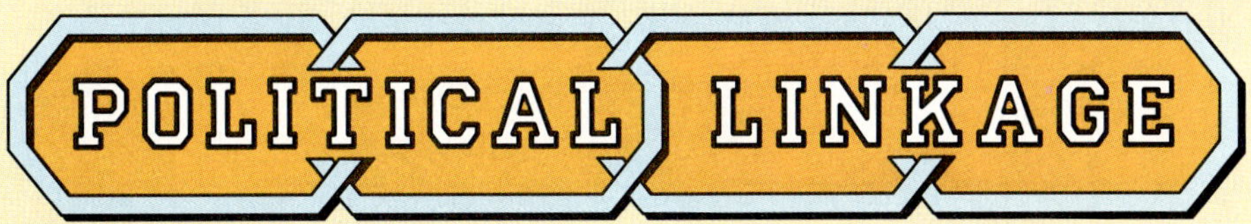

Domestic Policy and the Inconsistencies of Public Opinion

How do elected officials act on public preferences? Opinion polls may be of some help, yet often they are more confusing than enlightening. During the 1988 presidential campaign, for instance, George Bush frequently cited polls to back his claim that liberal views have gone out of style in the American polity. But was the Republican candidate correct that the American public was demanding a conservative approach to government?

One poll did, in fact, find that only 18 percent of respondents described themselves as liberal, with 44 percent and 32 percent labeling themselves moderate and conservative, respectively. These figures seem to lend credence to Bush's argument.

On the other hand, Americans' views on specific issues may suggest a different consensus. The table below shows the views—from the same poll—on perhaps the biggest issue in the campaign, federal spending.

The conservative agenda generally calls for high levels of spending for national defense, low levels of spending for most domestic programs. The data here suggest that a majority of Americans actually favor *increased* domestic spending, and a plurality supports holding Pentagon spending at its present level.

In the end, it may be easier to campaign on public opinion than to assess firmly public preferences and use them as a basis for policy.

Source: CBS News/*New York Times* press release, July 11, 1988.

Federal Spending Should Be . . .

	Increased	Decreased	Kept the Same
Military and defense	17%	28%	49%
Education programs	71	3	21
Day care and after-school care	52	10	30
Combating illegal drugs	75	6	14
Helping the homeless	68	4	23

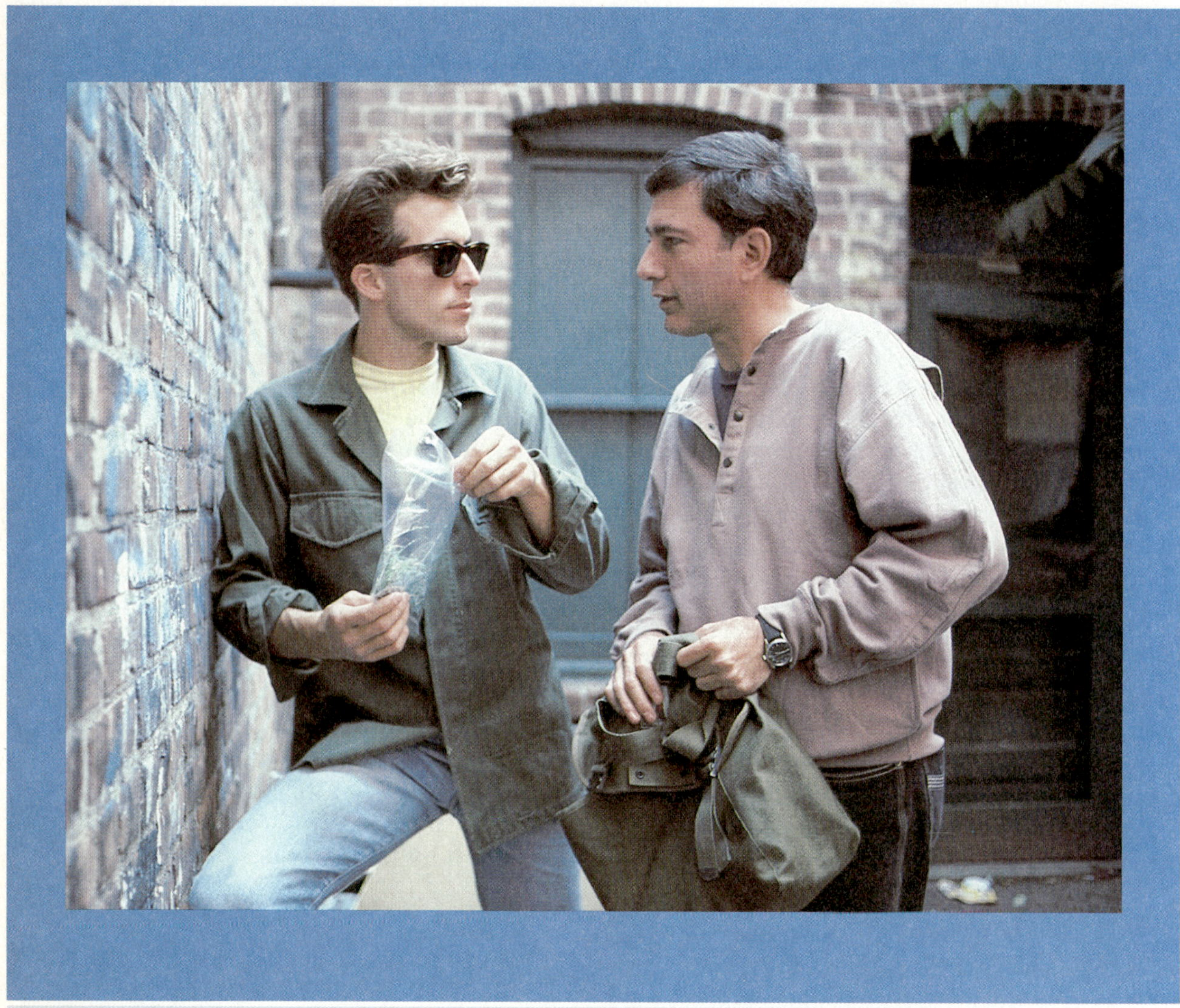

Drug use attracts public attention like no other item on the domestic policy agenda. President Bush and members of Congress are equally alarmed by its effects on health, crime, families, and education. Congress enacted an antidrug act in 1988, and the president appointed a drug czar in 1989. All agree that the problem will test policy makers for some time to come.

attention was directed to problems other than the budget—like the serious drug problem, trade imbalances, catastrophic health insurance, and welfare reform. Thus the Reagan administration ended with the prospect of inaugurating a post-contractive policy agenda. What form it would take was not altogether clear, but revenue, trade, energy, the economy, and still more government reorganization appeared to be among the priorities as George Bush entered the White House.

The 100-day evaluations of the Bush administration criticized the president's failure to be more forceful in agenda setting. Though elected in an impressive 40-state victory, Bush was said to lack a mandate. Under these circumstances, the president favored a bipartisan approach. He met

"It's been like this ever since that report on pesticides in apples . . ."

frequently with congressional Democratic leaders to formulate policy proposals for dealing with major issues like the budget. Proposing a new agenda proved difficult to Bush in the face of mounting deficits.

Domestic Issues: An Overview

A great deal of history has been incorporated into this brief treatment of domestic policy issues. Several patterns emerge. First, as is shown in Figure 18–4, it is possible to identify broad trends in government actions on domestic policy issues. The Roosevelt administration witnessed a major breakthrough in domestic programs; it provided a full social agenda at the national level for the first time. The Truman and Eisenhower administrations were much less active, concentrating more on consolidating the initiatives of the earlier period. The Kennedy-Johnson years provided another quantum increase in government programs, particularly in social welfare. These programs were possibly greater in their impact than those of the 1930s. Again we witnessed a period of consolidation during the Nixon, Ford, and Carter administrations, a period in which government effectiveness and management were emphasized. In addition, an array of economic, energy, and environmental issues developed which spawned new government regulations. This second period of consolidation differed from that under Truman and Eisenhower for two reasons: (1) Expenditures continued to grow at seemingly uncontrollable rates, and (2) government regulations increased to the point that both public and private officials expressed concern. These developments explain why this period is labeled "consolidation with government growth" in Figure 18–4.

The sizable growth in government expenditures and regulation despite presidents determined

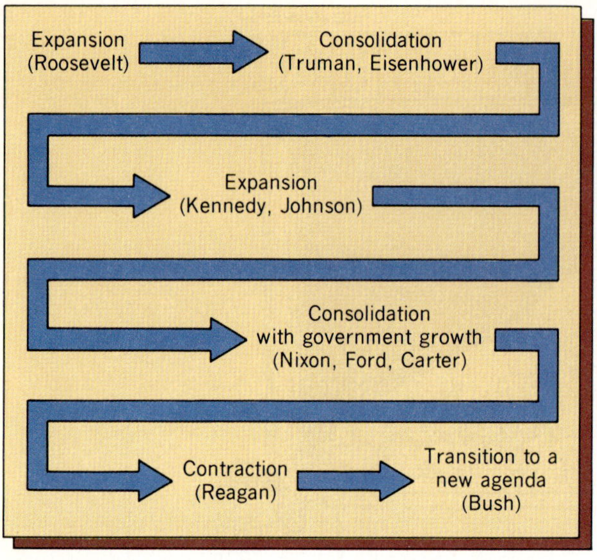

Figure 18–4 Trends in the domestic policy agenda.

to manage this growth may have contributed to the Reagan presidency. All three presidents during the 1970s stressed balancing the budget. If anything, the Democrat, Jimmy Carter, was the most emphatic. Yet the deficits mounted. Perhaps more than anything else, this apparent uncontrollability led to support for the contraction of government.

A second observation growing out of the material in this chapter is that different politics are associated with the various phases of domestic policy. There are shifts between the political parties in the White House, varying presidential-congressional relationships, and changes in public mood. At the very least, these changes warn us that comparing one presidential administration with another is tricky unless we account for domestic policy demands.

Before the Reagan administration, it appeared that the domestic policy agenda in Washington had cycles of expansion and consolidation. One might even go back to the presidency of Woodrow Wilson as an example of expansion, followed by the consolidative administrations of Presidents Harding, Coolidge, and Hoover. What the Reagan administration proposed to do, however, was to reverse gears: provide less revenue (at least in the short run), cut back on the growth of expenditures, and give the state and local governments more authority. The president's bold plan was successful enough to force official Washington to adopt a new agenda. His reelection guaranteed continuity of the Reagan domestic issues of taxation, size and effectiveness of government, and budgetary control. As we look ahead, it is apparent that a new agenda is now emerging. What form it will take is not now apparent—though attention to the fiscal matters growing out of historic deficits is surely demanded. President George Bush is the manager of the new agenda. As in the last two years of the Reagan administration, he faces Democratic majorities in both houses of Congress. Bush promised not to raise taxes—"read my lips, no new taxes"—but the prospect of economic instability pressured him to act on the fiscal issues dominating the agenda.

We can be certain of one thing. In 1930 the national government in Washington was a relatively small and placid enterprise. Fewer than 75,000 federal employees worked in Washington, D.C. Though the demands on government were building, they were still relatively few. Today the scene is quite different. More than 335,000 federal employees work in Washington, and complex worlds of domestic policy have grown up within the capital. In the relatively brief period of 60 years, a huge government apparatus has emerged to cope with the problems of the most advanced and complex society in the history of the world.

Summary

- The past 60 years have witnessed staggering changes in the number and scope of domestic issues. Government expanded to meet the challenges of these changes.
- The 1930s and 1960s, in particular, produced the greatest number of domestic programs. Social, economic, and political conditions in each era supported major expansions of the domestic policy agenda.
- Each period of expansion was followed by a

period of consolidation in which attention was on improving the effectiveness of government programs. The politics of consolidation vary considerably from the politics of expansion. The second consolidative phase (under Presidents Nixon, Ford, and Carter) was characterized by continued government growth (particularly in economic regulatory programs and welfare expenditures).

- For the first time, the nation appears to be entering a period during which there is support for contraction of government programs. Driven by huge deficits and a $2 trillion national debt, policymakers' attention is directed to reduced spending and/or increased revenue.
- The Reagan era produced a legacy of debt that constrains future agendas. It will likely result in attention to fiscal issues in the immediate future, forcing the Bush administration to consider raising more revenue.

Readings on Domestic Policy Growth

Cobb, Roger, and Charles, Elder. 1972. *Participation in American Politics: The Dynamics of Agenda Building.* Boston: Allyn & Bacon. An analysis of the politics of getting problems to government, with many practical illustrations.

Congressional Quarterly. 1965, 1969, 1973, 1977, 1981, 1985. *Congress and the Nation,* vols. I–VI. Washington, D.C.: Congressional Quarterly, Inc. Provides details of the domestic problems and policies of each of the post-World War II administrations—Truman through Reagan. A basic reference.

Jones, Charles O., ed. 1988. *The Reagan Legacy: Promise and Performance.* Chatham, N.J.: Chatham House Publishers. A recounting of politics and policy issues of the Reagan years, with discussions of the impact of that era.

Kingdon, John W. 1984. *Agendas, Alternatives, and Public Policies.* Boston: Little, Brown. An analysis of the ways in which issues win a place on the agenda of government.

Leuchtenburg, William. 1963. *Franklin D. Roosevelt and the New Deal, 1932–1940.* New York: Harper & Row. A full account of the growth of government during the Roosevelt period, a time in which much of the present domestic agenda was set in place.

Polsby, Nelson W. 1984. *Political Innovation in America.* New Haven, Conn: Yale University Press. An insightful analysis of how public policy innovations come to be adopted.

Sundquist, James L. 1968. *Politics and Policy: The Eisenhower, Kennedy, and Johnson Years.* Washington, D.C.: The Brookings Institution. A detailed review of the emergence of issues during the 1950s and 1960s and how each administration tried to manage its agenda.

Chapter 19

Domestic Policy Issues: The 1990s

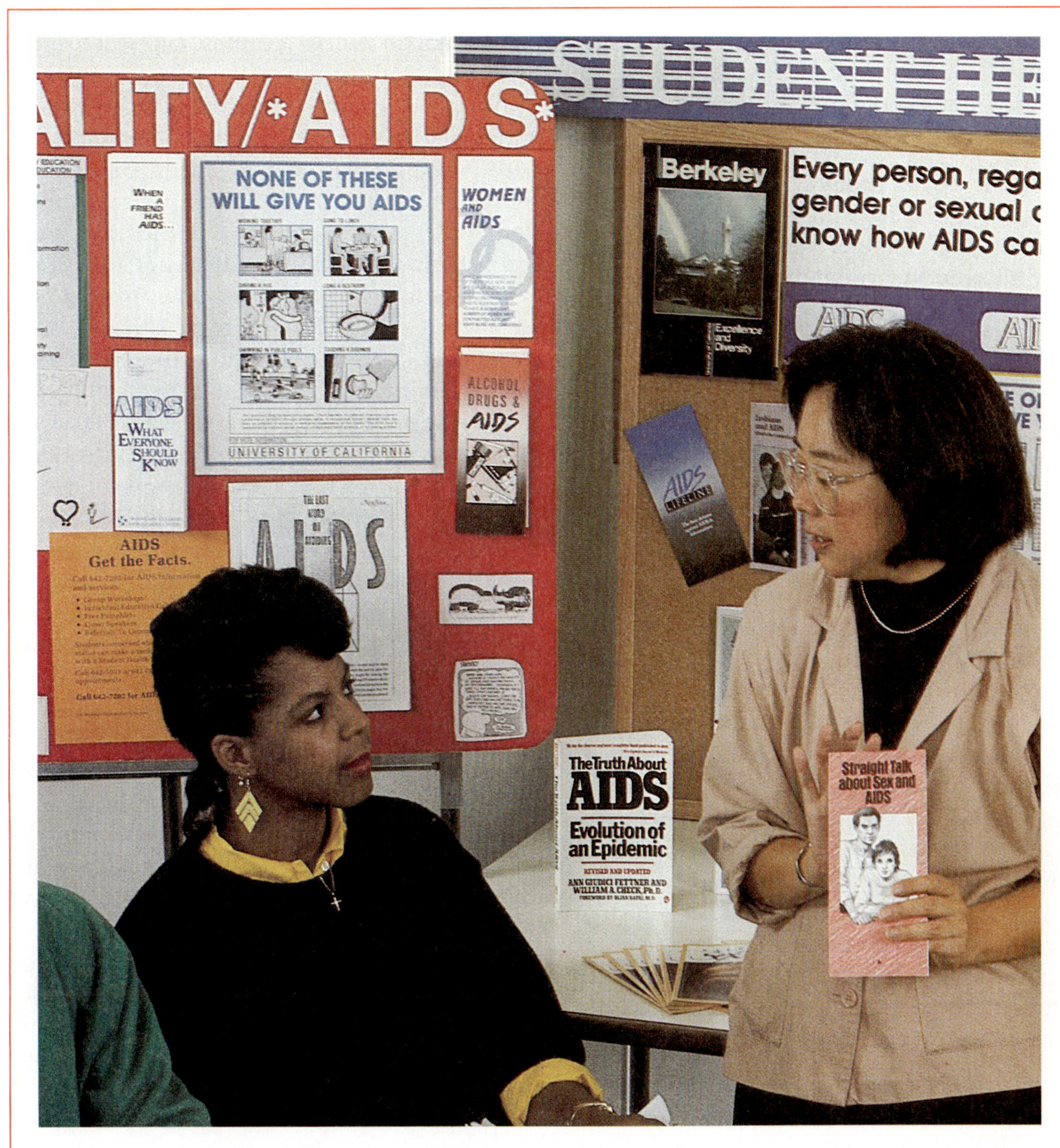

ALITY/*AIDS*
STUDENT HE
WHEN A FRIEND HAS AIDS...
NONE OF THESE WILL GIVE YOU AIDS
UNIVERSITY OF CALIFORNIA
WOMEN AND AIDS
ALCOHOL DRUGS & AIDS
AIDS WHAT EVERYONE SHOULD KNOW
AIDS Get the Facts.
Berkeley
Excellence and Diversity
Every person, rega
gender or sexual
know how AIDS ca
AIDS LIFELINE
The Truth About AIDS
Evolution of an Epidemic
REVISED AND UPDATED
ANN GIUDICI FETTNER AND WILLIAM A. CHECK, Ph.D.
Straight Talk about Sex and AIDS

In their acceptance speeches, the 1988 presidential candidates touched on many of the basic domestic issues facing the United States in the 1990s. George Bush reached out to many Americans when he said:

> America is not in decline. America is a rising nation. . . . But let's be frank. Things aren't perfect in this country. There are people who haven't tasted the fruits of the expansion. I've talked to farmers about the bills they can't pay and I've been to the factories that feel the strain of change. And I've seen the urban children who play amidst the shattered glass and the shattered lives. And, you know, there are the homeless. . . . They're there, and we have to help them.

Michael Dukakis also looked to America's future:

> It's time to meet the challenge of the next American frontier—the challenge of building an economic future for our country that will create good jobs at good wages for every citizen in this land. . . . It's time to rekindle the American spirit of invention and of daring: to exchange voodoo economics for can-do economics.. . . It's time . . . to see that young families in this country are never again forced to choose between the jobs they need and the children they love: time to be sure that parents are never again told that no matter how long they work or how hard their child tries, a college education is a right they can't afford.

Even these brief excerpts mention income inequalities, the homeless, structural unemployment, child care, and education. The campaign itself was an inventory of issues—health care, the deficit, crime, drugs, the environment, and housing, to name but a few.

This chapter reviews the current domestic policy agenda—the principal federal government programs and the issues they generate. It will illustrate a point made in Chapter 18: the agenda arises from programs already on the books, with little space left for new problems or experimentation with new ideas. This is not to say that the government can never act on AIDS or the epidemic of drug use. But given budget deficits, it may take such crises to justify new programs.

Federal programs address three broad categories of issues. First, *resource* issues include the wide range associated with managing natural resources, food production, energy use, transportation, and research. These activities contribute to our personal and industrial strength.

Second, *welfare* issues refer to the government's role in providing income security and such social services as health, education, housing, and safety. These include programs for the *many* as well as those for the *needy*. For example, the Medicaid program is targeted to low-income Americans who do not qualify for social security and cannot afford to be in a private health care program. Medicare, on the other hand, is available to *all* the aged who have contributed to the social security system for the requisite number of quarters. The income of the patient is not a criterion for participation.

The third category includes *economic* issues. Programs in all categories have economic implications, to be sure. But this group of issues concerns direct decisions by the government regarding the economy. Increasingly, government is expected to play a large role in stabilizing the economy. While economic policy does not itself count for much of the budget, it is a result of the large role that the budget plays in the economy.

Government actions on these issues vary in significant ways. *Distributive* programs are those that benefit a large segment of the public. A public highway is a classic example of a distributive program. *Redistributive* programs, in contrast, benefit those with limited income. Other government programs are *regulatory*—seeking to control social and economic behavior in some way. Some regulations are designed to increase or manage business or industrial competition; others are aimed at protecting the public (e.g., from false advertising).[1]

Resources

For most of our history, public policy has been to encourage the use, even the exploitation, of our natural resources. America seemed a nation with boundless resources—land, game, forests, and minerals in abundance, even oil and natural gas. Perhaps the greatest achievement of the government under the Articles of Confederation was passage of the Northwest Ordinance in 1787. This act provided for the settlement and, eventually, statehood of western lands north of the Ohio River. Laws passed during the next century enticed Americans to move west. One historian, Frederick Jackson Turner, even found that this vast land frontier contributed to the nation's political development:

> American democracy . . . came out of the American forest, and it gained new strength each time it touched a new frontier. Not the constitution, but free land and an abundance of natural resources open to a fit people, made the democratic type of society in America for three centuries while it occupied its empire.[2]

As Turner wrote these words in the early part of this century, he acknowledged the need for a change in national policy.

> The national problem is no longer how to cut and burn away the vast screen of the dense and daunting forest; it is how to save and wisely use the remaining timbers. . . . The cry of scientific farming and the conservation of natural resources replaces the cry of rapid conquest of the wilderness.[3]

With the closing of the frontier, national resource policy, in a sense, doubled back on itself. Still, despite efforts to conserve land and to produce more from that land, as new resources were discovered, federal policy either did not interfere with exploitation or actively encouraged it. Examples are the tax breaks to the oil industry and the creation of a private nuclear power industry.

The resource agenda today shows that important changes have occurred. No longer confident in the abundance of the land, we face the problems of maintaining our high standard of living without permanently endangering future generations. Managing those conflicting goals is no simple task.

Total expenditures for the resources identified here do not come close to matching welfare or defense spending. Policy is not well integrated across these many issues. Nor is much attention paid to the effects on our resources of defense, urban development, or other policies. Unquestionably, however, resource policy is growing. We may expect future environmental, energy, and technological crises to result in even greater federal responsibilities in this domain.

Energy Resources ■

National energy policy changed substantially during the Reagan years. During the crisis caused by the embargo on oil shipments by the Organization of Petroleum Exporting Countries (OPEC), government enacted a substantial energy program. Federal policy of the 1970s encouraged the development of new sources of energy—solar, synthetic, geothermal, and advanced nuclear sources. Conservation was also stressed, through pricing, education, and tax incentives. Because oil shortages posed threats to national defense, petroleum reserves were enlarged. In the 1980s, however, no longer threatened by shortages from the Middle East, the new administration quickly acted on pressure to allow market forces to work once again.

In 1981 the budget for energy programs was over $15 billion. By the end of the decade the budget was approximately one-fifth that amount. Most money in current budgets goes for research and development, primarily for nuclear power; very little is allocated for conservation.

The problems of the future are not too different from those of the recent past—continued dependence on foreign oil, the safety of nuclear power plants and the disposal of nuclear waste, the environmental effects of energy use, and the rising cost of energy. Many specialists believe that we have not fully prepared for a repeat of the energy crises of the 1970s, that we have slipped back into old practices of ignoring the inevitable shortages to come. Others contend that we are in a better position to manage a future crisis. We now have a Department of Energy and committees in both houses of Congress to act quickly should serious problems develop. An OPEC agreement in 1988 to reduce the oil supply will test how well prepared we are.

Environmental Protection

The last two decades witnessed a vast increase in federal programs to protect the environment. During the late 1960s, public pressure helped create an outpouring of legislation, regulating how we use air, water, and land (see Table 18–2). An affluent, technological society now paid attention as never before to the waste it produced. Many judged that industrial progress itself was poisoning the land. Even efforts to protect ourselves—for example, by conditioning the air inside buildings or by moving farther away from polluted cities—have contributed to the deterioration of the environment.

Future environmental problems will not be as easy to finesse as energy issues. Not even the Reagan administration could ignore them, though it sought to reduce the federal government's role. Research has revealed the serious hazards of chemical dumping, pesticide use, solid waste in landfills, radioactive waste disposal, raw sewage discharged into natural waters, and burning coal and oil. The process of cleaning up hazardous waste sites (Figure 19–1) has scarcely begun. Acid rain now falls on areas that do not themselves contribute the pollutants that soil the clouds. And some scientists warn of a "greenhouse effect" by which significant increases of carbon dioxide may result in a warming trend that could melt the polar ice cap and result in severe flooding.

We may expect more federal government involvement in environmental protection in the future. Though the Environmental Protection Agency (EPA) is criticized for its interference in industrial management, few now believe that the state and local governments can manage these issues. In fact, international cooperation is required in areas from ocean pollution to nuclear power disasters (as in Chernobyl in the Soviet Union). Acid rain is a subject of continuous negotiation between the United States and Canada, and was one target of an extensive clean air plan offered by the Bush administration in 1989.

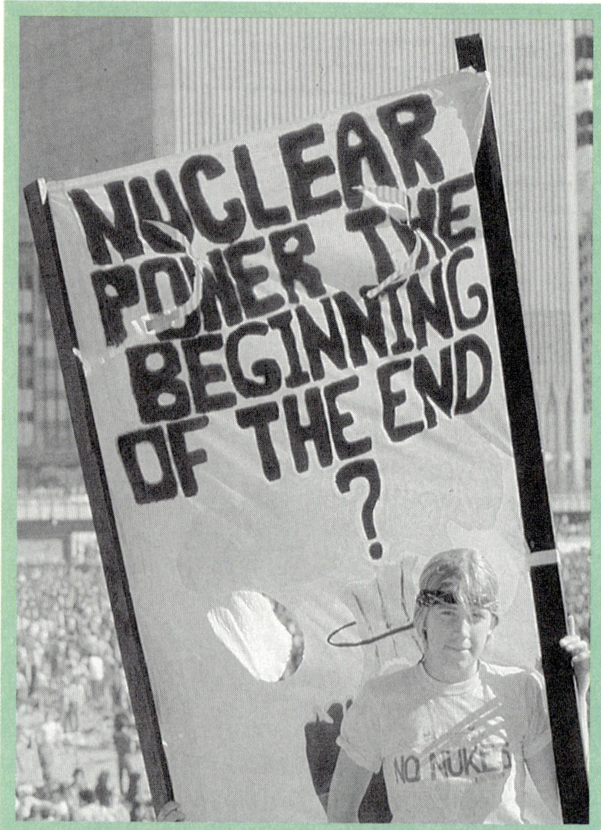

Americans are great consumers of energy. At one time, nuclear power promised an inexhaustible supply to meet the nation's private, industrial, and defense needs. We now know more about the costs of nuclear power stations—to consumers and the environment. Accidents at Three Mile Island in Pennsylvania and Chernobyl in the Soviet Union demonstrated the potential dangers.

Agriculture

Farming has always been a risky venture. Too much rain, too little rain, pest infestation, the market, foreign competition—so many variables are beyond the control of any farmer. Small wonder that the farm population has decreased. In 1920 nearly 32 million people lived on farms—about 30 percent of the population. Now just about 2 percent remain—a little over 5 million. Yet farm output has increased during the same period.

Though few in numbers, farmers have been well represented in Washington. Presidents and Congresses consistently support programs to ease risks for farmers. Techniques have included price supports for commodities (usually the difference

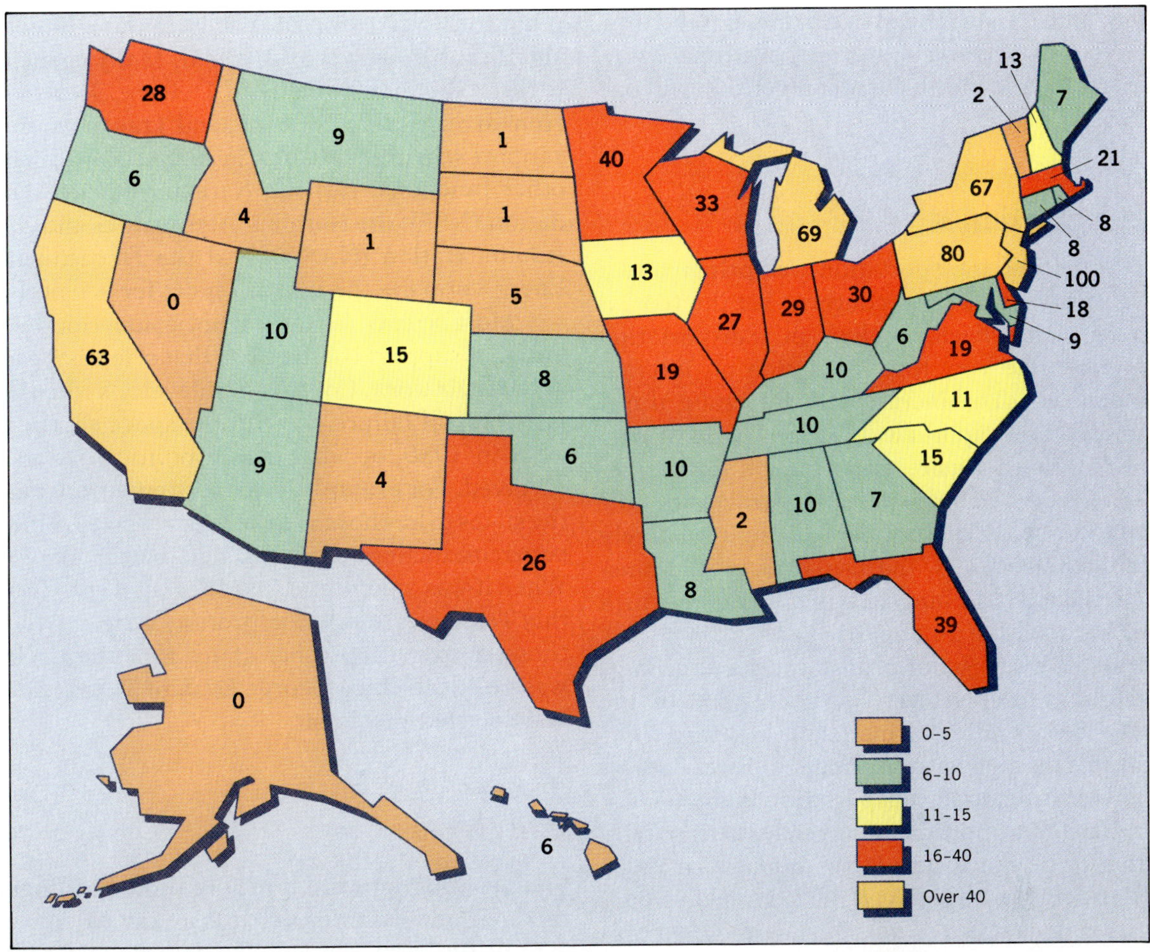

Figure 19–1 Hazardous waste sites in the United States. In June 1987 the federal government designated 942 hazardous waste locations (including eight in Puerto Rico and one in Guam). Source: *Statistical Abstract of the United States, 1988* (Washington, D.C.: U.S. Government Printing Office, 1988), p. 193.

between the market price and a target price), production controls to maintain or increase the market price, loans, research, soil conservation, economic analysis, and rural development, including electrification programs.

The Reagan administration espoused a free-market approach to farm problems. Presumably farmers would be able to compete in world markets if government everywhere reduced its role—that was the dream. Reagan's director of the Office of Management and Budget, David A. Stockman, expressed this view: "The worst nonsense of all in the budget . . . was farm subsidies. The nation's agriculturalists had never been the same after the New Deal turned the wheat, corn, cotton, and dairy business into a way of life based on organized larceny." [4] Were they successful in freeing the farm market? According to Stockman: "We ended up spending $60 billion over five years rather than $10 billion. It was another case of missing the revolution by a country mile." [5]

The future problems in agriculture are not significantly different from those of the recent past. Reducing the government's role is difficult indeed to achieve. In theory, agricultural production in the United States should contribute to solving another major problem—the trade deficit. But that cannot happen if the market price is too high. Meanwhile, farmers must plan ahead and, understandably, worry about whether a shift from government support to free worldwide market competition will pay their bills.

Transportation

At one time transportation was principally a subject of state and local concern. Yet the federal government has been involved in transportation policy from the very first legislation on internal improvements. The increases in interstate travel and in defense requirements since World War II have encouraged a more active federal role. Highways, railroads, waterways, and air travel are now all subjects of national policy. Though relatively new to cabinet status, the Department of Transportation has a large budget, typically ranking fifth or sixth among the 14 departments.

The Highway Act of 1956 authorized the largest public works project in the history of the world—41,000 miles of interstate highways. Expenditures on highways continue to be the largest portion of the federal transportation budget. Only a very small proportion of the interstate system remains to be constructed, but highway maintenance and repair are costly. Railroad use, on which the nation once relied so heavily, has declined dramatically with the increase in automotive and air travel; the principal federal role is now related to safety.

Other issues are related to the development of mass transit systems in large cities and the improvement of airports and the air traffic control system. Controversies involve safety, such as the use of air bags in automobiles; the use of the highway trust fund, originally intended for highways only; and the relative contributions of the federal government and the states. But transportation issues are not presently as contentious as those in other policy areas.

Science

Science policy issues include support for research, development of technology, and space exploration. Allocations for science have increased significantly since World War II. Many agencies—such as the Departments of Defense, Health and Human Services, Education, and Transportation—support scientific research in connection with their other functions. But the National Science Foundation (NSF), the National Aeronautics and Space Administration (NASA), and the Department of Energy provide the most support for science.

Most science issues are not contentious. Government support is offered so that scientists can go about their work. Controversy develops when there is a colossal failure, as with the space shuttle disaster in 1986, or when major political stakes are involved. For example, intense competition among the states to be chosen as the site for the $4.4 billion superconducting supercollider began in 1987. When it was announced just after the 1988 election that Texas was the choice, protests were heard from those representing other states that the decision was political, since George Bush of Texas had just been elected president.

Welfare

Welfare programs are typically thought to benefit the poor and disabled. That is a very narrow concept of the term *welfare.* The federal government has scores of programs aimed toward improving the health, happiness, or general well-being of all its citizens, not just the unfortunate. In fact, programs for the many constitute the larger share of welfare costs. The old-age, survivors, and disability insurance (OASDI) programs alone constitute about one-fifth of the total federal outlays—approaching $250 billion.

Welfare programs vary greatly in the public support they receive. Those designed to assist the middle class, such as the Social Security system, are popular; those aimed specifically at the needy are typically under fire and often the object of reform. Welfare reform is a hardy staple of the policy agenda. As Martin Anderson, an adviser to President Nixon, put it: "If you were going to run for President of the United States, you had to have a welfare reform program." [6]

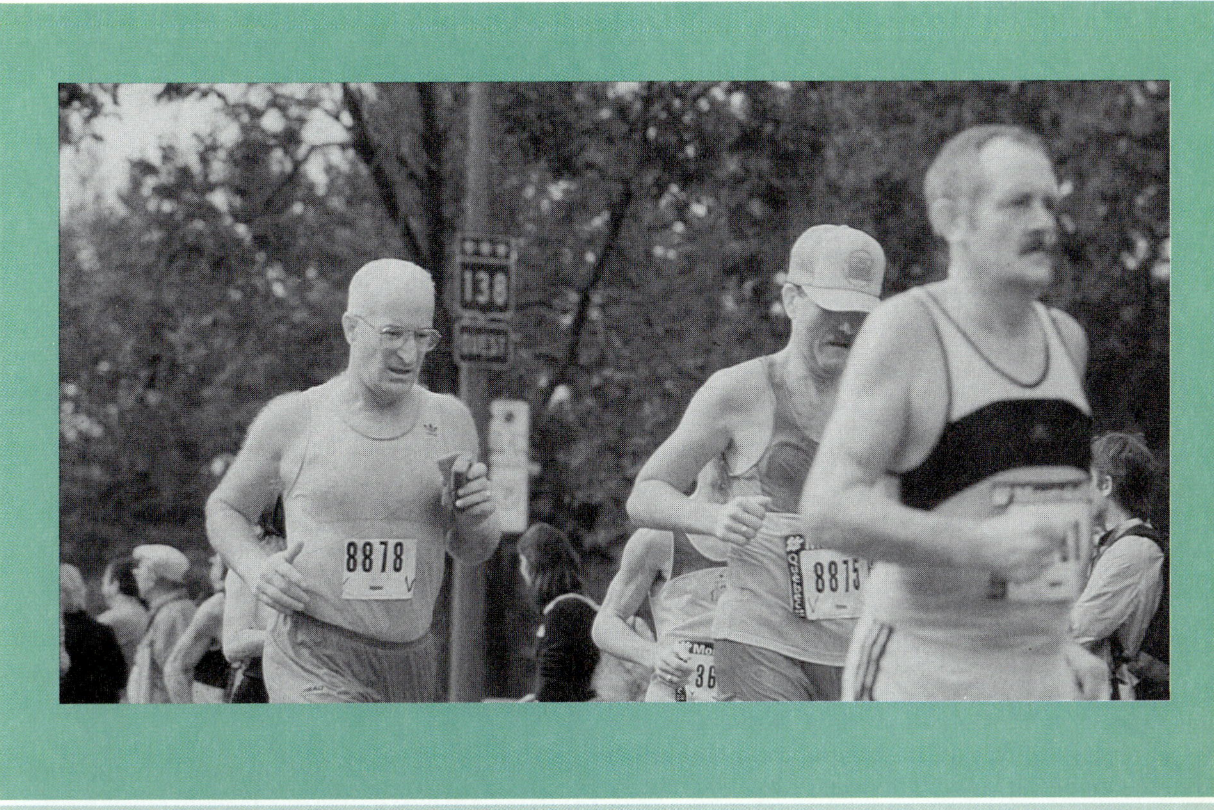

Americans are living longer. Already by far the largest welfare expenditure is in the form of pensions and health care costs for those in retirement. Given current trends, these costs will continue to rise, making it hard to enact new programs for other groups in need of public support.

Unquestionably the greatest social welfare program enacted in American history was the Social Security Act of 1935. Remarkably, "the United States was . . . the last major industrial nation to adopt a general social security system covering most of the population." [7] The stimulus was "the eruption of the most serious national economic crisis the United States had ever experienced." [8] This sweeping legislation included old-age insurance, assistance to the aged poor (who did not qualify for insurance), aid to the blind, aid to dependent children, and unemployment insurance. Its purpose was to identify those needing help and either establish a contributory system to provide assistance when needed (as with the aged or unemployed) or offer direct benefits to those who are in no position to contribute to their own welfare.

Welfare Programs for the Many

Welfare for the many continues to be a substantial part of the annual federal budget. Most of the programs are not threatened by controversy. Such benefits as retirement income, Medicare, housing support, and college loans have widespread public support. The Bush administration may attempt to make reductions as part of a deficit reduction package. But most Americans would rather pay more in taxes than lose such standard benefits.

Retirement

For most Americans the term "social security" means retirement income. As indicated above, the

the small society
by Brickman
THE GOVERNMENT ASSUMES RESPONSIBILITY FOR THE HEALTH, WELFARE AND HAPPINESS OF ALL ITS CITIZENS—
EXCEPT THE TAXPAYERS—
10-16
BRICKMAN
© 1980 King Features Syndicate, Inc. World rights reserved.

OASDI programs account for the largest share of all welfare expenditures, nearly $100 billion more than all other income security programs. OASDI is funded by payroll taxes on earnings (up to a maximum), with the employer and the employee each contributing. The tax rate has increased sharply in recent years to meet funding crises (to 12.4 percent in 1990—half paid by workers, half by employers). So has the maximum amount of salary to be taxed (up to $50,000 in 1990).

Though the system is referred to as "insurance," it is not, in fact, actuarially sound. Instead, the president and Congress respond to warnings of future crises by enacting changes from time to time—most recently in 1983, overcoming a political stalemate between the Republican president, Ronald Reagan, and the Democratic House of Representatives. A special bipartisan commission, formed in 1982, was charged with responsibility for defining the problem and developing ideas for change. After tough political and policy conflict, the commission's recommendations won the support of President Reagan and the Speaker of the House, Thomas P. O'Neill (D–Mass.). Paul C. Light studied how the two sides reached an agreement:

> The system had remained in limbo on social security for three years, unable to move forward in the congressional subcommittees or in the budget process. The system could not work without a consensus, and none existed. There was no agreement on either the size of the coming crisis or the appropriate solutions. Congress and the President could reach a compromise only by leaving the normal process for a secret negotiating gang.[9]

For the time being, the social security retirement system is sound. Large *surpluses* are projected—well into the next century. The next crisis may occur when the baby boom generation reaches retirement age, roughly in the years 2015 and 2020. A large number of retirees and fewer people in the work force due to the lower birth rate in the 1960s, 1970s, and 1980s will mean sharply fewer workers per beneficiary. In 1960 the ratio was 5.1 to 1, in 1990 3.3 to 1; in 2020 the number of workers per beneficiary will be 2.1 to 1, and in 2035 just 1.9 to 1.[10] "Obviously today's workers pay for yesterday's workers' retirement, while looking to the contributions of the next generation to secure their own retirement." [11] There are many political ramifications of these changes. Those in the work force may begin to question whether they should pay high retirement benefits. They may also worry whether the program will survive until their retirement.

Certain of the changes made in 1983 adjust for an aging and more affluent population. For example, the age for receiving full benefits will be raised from 65 to 66 in 2009 and to 67 in 2027. Beneficiaries with high incomes in retirement, either those still at work or those with other retirement income, will have to pay taxes on part of what they receive from social security. Unquestionably, other adjustments will be needed to react to demographic and economic changes. And because of partisan and generational differences, each change can be expected to result in intense conflict.

Health Care

If the issue of retirement through social security has moderated, that of national health care is as intense as ever. Perhaps no set of problems evokes more conflict in domestic politics. Rapidly rising costs, projected to increase further by as much as three or four times between 1980 and 1990, have taxed the capacity of individuals and their health insurance programs to pay. Recent increases have been more than double the inflation rate—a 9.8 percent increase in 1987 and 8.2 percent and 9.1 percent in 1988 and 1989, respectively. The total bill these days is about $600 billion. Figure 19–2 shows the steep rise between 1970 and 1988. About 60 percent of these costs are paid for by the private sphere (individuals or insurance programs), the rest by government programs.

The major federally supported health care program is *Medicare.* Paid for out of social security taxes, Medicare is available to an estimated 32 million aged (those over 65 who have paid the requisite amount of social security taxes) and disabled persons. Supplementary insurance is available at extra cost to pay a large portion of doctors' fees.

Medicare was enacted in 1965 as a part of President Johnson's Great Society. Originally, the system worked through cost reimbursement. Hospitals and physicians submitted bills directly to the government. In 1984 this was replaced by a prospective payment system. To help control the skyrocketing costs, the reasonable payment for treatment of an illness or injury is now calculated in advance.

While these and other changes have helped to curb the costs of health care, with increasing longevity and diagnostic improvements the problem is still acute. The Reagan administration proposed several changes. These include a voucher system, by which beneficiaries could choose other health plans in the private sphere; increased contributions to be paid by future recipients of supplementary medical insurance; and measures to encourage more cost-effective pricing policies by hospitals and physicians.

Dealing with the health care dilemma has not been easy. In 1988 Congress enacted legislation significantly expanding Medicare. Called the Medicare Catastrophic Coverage Act, this law provided that *all* hospitalization costs would be covered after the patient had paid an annual deductible fee. It also placed ceilings on personal expenses for physicians, with the government paying the rest. Even a portion of outpatient prescription drugs would be paid for by Medicare.

Fee increases would be required to pay for these benefits. In addition, a new supplemental premium, or surtax, would be levied on eligible individuals who pay federal income tax of $150 or more. Initially, the annual supplemental premium was to be capped at $800 per person.

The surtax provoked a storm of controversy among the elderly. Many seniors believed, mistakenly, that all beneficiaries would be required to pay the $800 maximum premium. Others contended that the benefits duplicated those already provided by their private Medigap policies. Seniors were also incensed that the beneficiaries alone were required to pay for these new benefits. By late 1989, opposition to the "seniors-only surtax" had become so intense that it was inevitable that Congress would either repeal the act entirely or substantially pare its most costly benefits, including doctor bills and prescription-

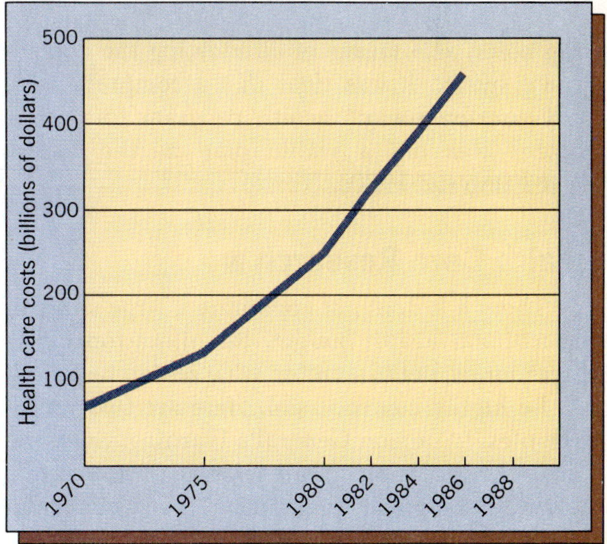

Figure 19–2 Costs of public and private health care in the United States for selected years from 1970 to 1987. Source: *Statistical Abstract of the United States, 1988* (Washington, D.C.: U.S. Government Printing Office, 1988).

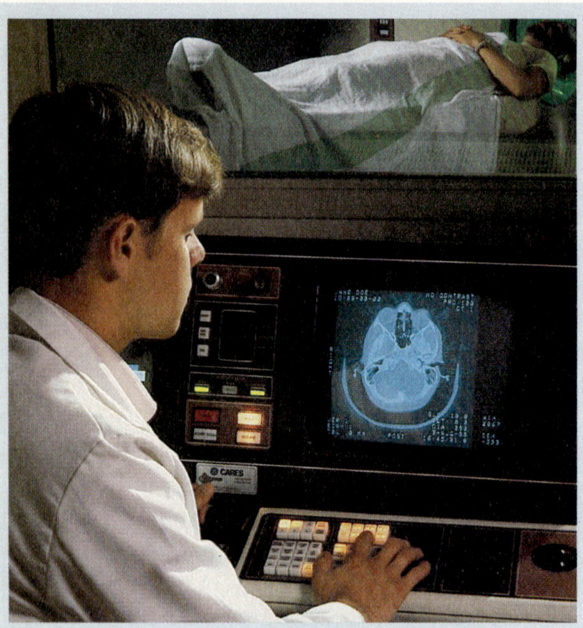

Health care costs are rising significantly faster than the rate of inflation. Technology is one reason behind the trend. Doctors use—and patients demand—the most advanced diagnostic equipment. It will be difficult to control these spiraling costs without interfering with the relationship between patient and physician.

drug costs, as a means of eliminating the controversial surtax. It was clear that a comprehensive "pay-your-own-way" health program for senior citizens was not a viable plan as the nation moved into the 1990s.

Health Care Research

Though it does not constitute a large share of the national health budget, the allocation of research funds, not to mention what researchers find, can be highly controversial. Here are two recent examples. "Surgeon General's Warning: Smoking Causes Lung Cancer, Heart Disease, Emphysema, And May Complicate Pregnancy." The warning label on a pack of cigarettes or in a tobacco advertisement is a direct consequence of federally sponsored research. The tobacco industry may still dispute that research, but the consequences of policy actions are very real. Fewer people smoke, and those who do cannot always do it where they wish.

A second example is research into AIDS—acquired immune deficiency syndrome. This disease, still so fatal and so poorly understood, threatens to infect as many as 5 million people by 1991. AIDS is transmitted through intimate sexual contact, blood transfusions, and the sharing of hypodermic needles. It is therefore closely linked to patterns of drug use in America's inner cities. Originally thought by many to affect only gay men and drug users, AIDS has spread, current evidence shows, among other heterosexuals as well. Not surprisingly, fears of an epidemic, combined with the absence of medical solutions, have led to strong public reactions. There has even been talk of a quarantine for high-risk groups. And as those most at risk come under greater public scrutiny, they too react strongly, with concern for both their safety and their privacy.

In the late 1980s the federal government acted to define the scope of the AIDS problem. At the same time, it sharply increased research funds and began to educate the public about the real, as opposed to imagined, dangers of the disease. A national commission appointed by President Reagan issued a strong call for action. And in 1988 Congress passed a comprehensive bill that further expedited AIDS research and provided funds for public education, anonymous blood testing, and some health services for patients. The bill also authorized a new national commission to monitor the AIDS problem.

Coming at the end of the session, the AIDS bill was packaged along with several other health measures. President Reagan did not favor other sections of the bill, and he had objections to the AIDS provisions as well. Although ultimately he did not veto the measure, the controversy surrounding AIDS legislation is likely to persist. No doubt support for research will continue. But unless public fears are allayed, we can expect demands for extreme measures—ones that may discriminate against those with a high risk of carrying the disease-causing virus.

Housing

Congress takes up housing policy in its banking committees. Not surprisingly, then, the major programs guarantee loans for prospective homeowners with a steady income but without the funds to make large down payments. Beginning in 1934, the newly created Federal Housing Administration (FHA) convinced banks to reduce down payments and provide long-term loans. If the homeowner defaulted, the FHA paid the loan and took title to the house. A similar program was available to veterans after World War II, with even more generous terms.

Homeowners can deduct the interest payments and property taxes from their gross income, reducing their taxes substantially. This deduction amounts to a subsidy of many billions of dollars. Many Americans have taken advantage of it—some to own second or third homes, becoming landlords in the process. Even those purchasing vacation homes had this tax break. The Tax Reform Act of 1986 limited deductions to interest on two homes, curbing some of the abuse.

Today most people get conventional home loans. Yet many homeowners still depend on a government-guaranteed loan, and future housing policy is unlikely to make substantial changes in loan guarantees. Owner-occupied housing units now constitute 65 percent of all housing. They have increased by nearly 25 million units just in the last 25 years.[12]

Other government policies seriously affect home buying as well. For example, when interest rates rise, fewer Americans can afford to build or purchase homes, with predictable negative effects on the entire economy. This is an excellent example of the ripple effects of government policy in a market economy. It suggests that monetary policy, as set by the Federal Reserve Board, can have a large impact on how we live and whether we work.

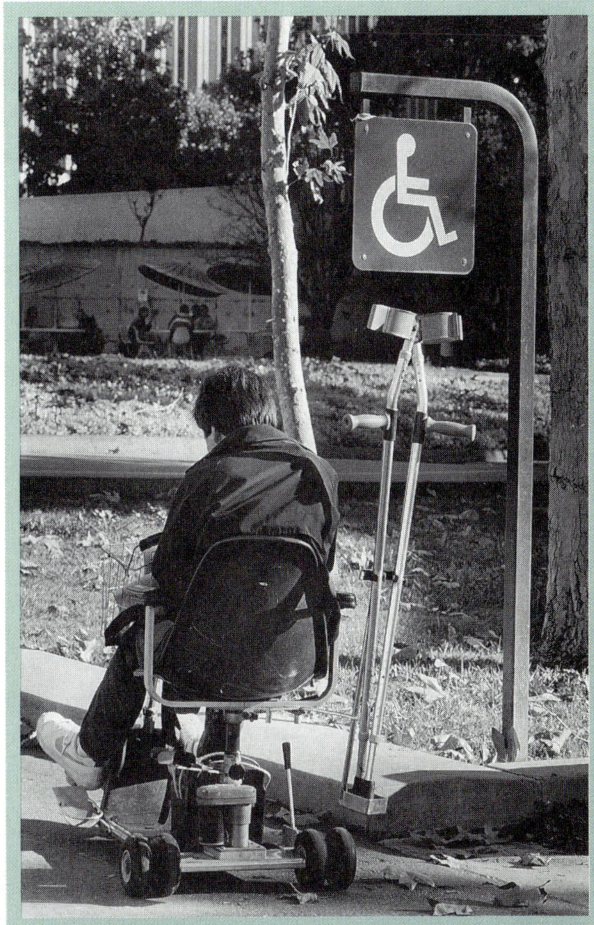

Governments at all levels have acted to improve the quality of life for the handicapped. The now-familiar wheelchair symbol shows that special provisions have been made, including ramps and special elevators. Public buildings, like here at the University of California, Irvine, have had to meet new standards to facilitate access for the disabled.

Education

The federal government's role in education still pales when compared with that of state and local governments. A Department of Education was created in 1867 but was not of cabinet-level status; in fact, it was little more than a record-keeping bureau in the Department of the Interior.[13] It was not until 1978 that a full-fledged Department of Education was authorized, a response to the significant growth in education programs following the passage of the Elementary and Secondary Education Act of 1965. Even with this increase in federal activity and in status, the Department of Education's budget is less than 15 percent of the amount spent on education by state governments.

Most of the federal government's education programs are designed to assist the needy and will be discussed in the next section. Historically, however, there has been federal support of various

Continuity & CHANGE

Welfare for the Needy, Welfare for the Many

As we saw in the previous chapter, nowhere is the growth in the agenda of government clearer than in federal payments directly to individuals. In the postwar years these outlays have skyrocketed—from $1.6 million in 1940, when the New Deal expansion was already in place, to over half a trillion dollars in 1990. In fact, their growth has been so rapid that it is far from easy to represent it in a single picture, although the figure below comes close.

Depicted here are the four key components of federal outlays to the individual: *retirement* programs, such as social security; *medical care;* programs for housing, food, and other forms of *public assistance;* and such *other* programs as unemployment insurance and student loans. Be careful to note that the scale is chosen differently on the right side of the figure, where spending is much, much greater.

The graph shows the change in the federal agenda in the postwar years. For example, the unusual prominence given to unemployment insurance and student aid in 1950 reflects conditions right after World War II; at that time many returning veterans were continuing their education, and the nation still experienced a postwar economic downturn. Since then, however, the growth of programs has clearly been driven by something other than external conditions—the agenda itself.

But the figure also makes clear that what many people think of as "welfare" is only one component—and hardly the largest or the fastest growing component—of federal welfare programs. Today, more and more Americans benefit from welfare for the many.

Source: *Historical Tables: Budget of the United States Government, Fiscal Year 1990* (Washington, D.C.: U.S. Government Printing Office, 1989), pp. 197–233.

kinds for all schools. The Land Ordinance of 1785 provided that in disposing of the lands in the western territory, "surveyors . . . shall proceed to divide the . . . territory into townships of six miles square. . . . There shall be reserved the lot No. 16, of every township, for the maintenance of public schools within the said township." And in the Northwest Ordinance of 1787, Article 3 of the articles of compact for admission of new states declared that "religion, morality, and knowledge, being necessary to good government and the happiness of mankind, schools and the means of education shall forever be encouraged." [14]

These basic laws for settling and governing the new territories assume state and local management of education. The federal government's role has traditionally been merely to supplement that effort. Examples are support for colleges of agriculture, vocational education, and schools in areas with sizable federal land or many government employees.

In 1958 the largest program of direct federal aid to the schools was passed. The National Defense Education Act was designed to improve the teaching of science, mathematics, and foreign languages. This aid was stimulated by the success of the Soviet space program, specifically the orbiting of the Sputnik satellite, and the failure of American satellite launchings.

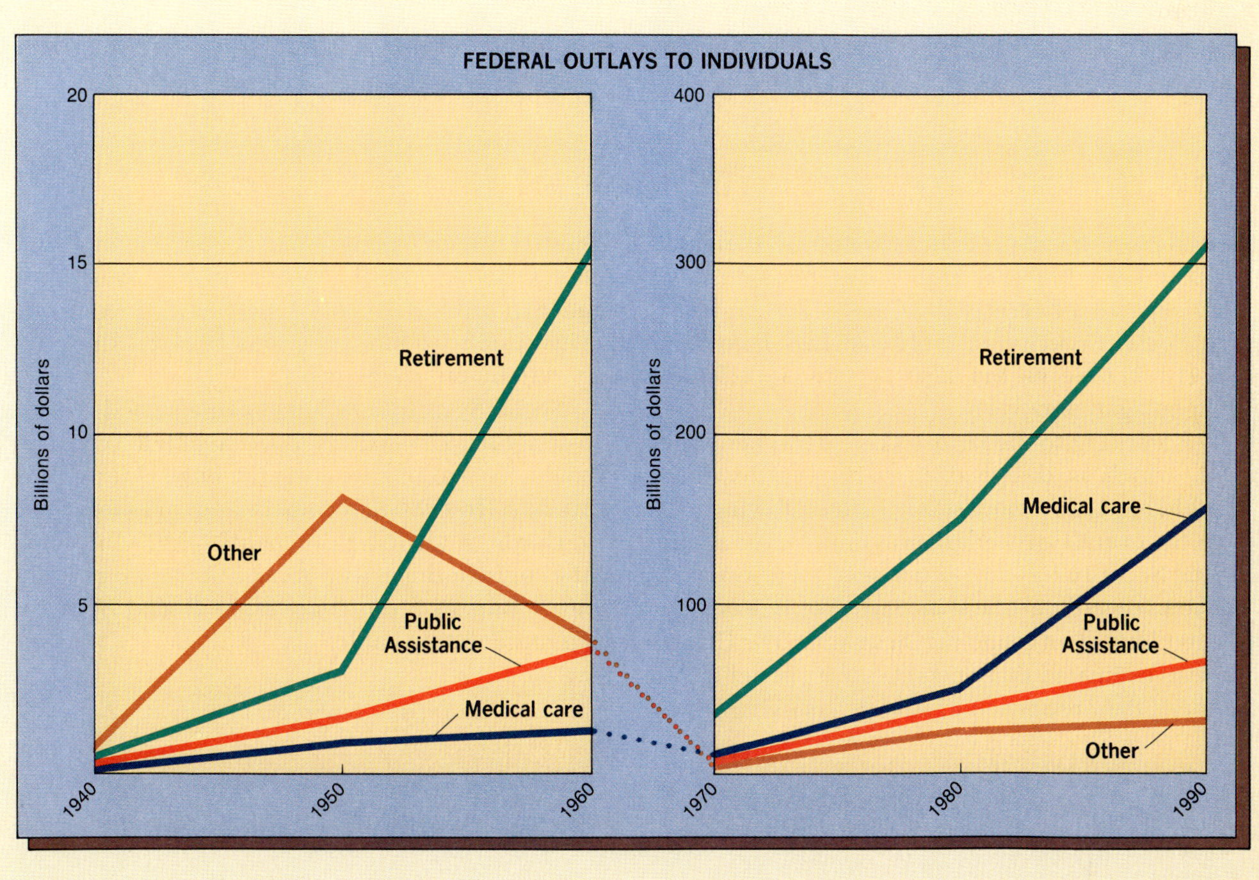

Accompanying the school aid provisions of the 1958 act was a graduate fellowship program. Aid to college students has since become an important part of federal education policy. Benefits for World War II veterans included financial aid for attending college—the GI Bill of Rights. Similar benefits were provided to Korean War veterans. During the 1970s low-interest loans were offered to students from middle-income families. Millions of students took advantage of the program before it was restricted by the Reagan administration.

The role of the federal government in education will continue to be controversial. A reduction in federal spending to educate the general population seems likely in the Bush years, despite the new president's public commitment to education. Today's deficits force those with new programs to produce strong and persuasive reasons for their adoption.

Veterans' Benefits

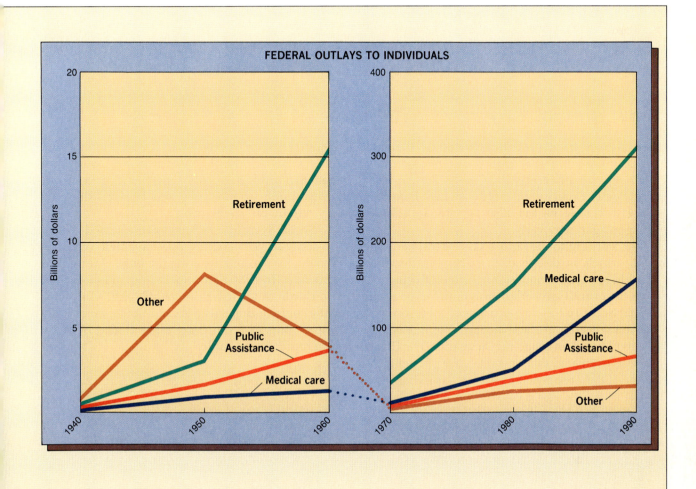

The United States has been generous in providing benefits for those who serve in the armed forces, particularly following World War II. The Veterans Administration, finally given departmental status in 1988, has typically been responsible for more spending than most of the cabinet de-

Government Programs: The Case of Social Security

Not all government programs accomplish their aim. Occasionally, however, policies accomplish *more* than expected. Recently the Census Bureau found that Social Security not only provides income to elderly Americans but also acts as an effective weapon against poverty.

According to the report, the federal tax structure, which is designed in part to redistribute wealth, has only a modest impact on relieving poverty. So, overall, do welfare programs for the needy. Social Security has no "means test"; it is available without regard to one's income. Yet it has a far greater impact on economic inequality. The Census Bureau estimated that Social Security benefits had reduced the proportion of Americans living below the poverty level from 21.2 to 14.9 percent by 1986. Among the elderly, the reduction was even more dramatic, from 47.5 to 14 percent. By contrast, means-tested welfare programs reduced the poverty rate by only 1 percent.

Social Security has long been a sacred cow in Washington. Lawmakers have avoided reducing benefits for fear of alienating the huge elderly constituency. (In 1986 that constituency got more than two-thirds of all federal benefits—$200 billion—while contributing only $60.7 billion in taxes.) The Census Bureau report may make Social Security even more untouchable.

Source: *New York Times,* December 28, 1988, pp. 1, 12.

partments. The Servicemen's Readjustment Act, popularly called the "GI Bill of Rights," was passed in 1944 to assist the millions of veterans to return to civilian life. Payment was to compensate for losses in employment, education, job advancement, and housing, along with security for those injured during the war. Many benefits were then extended to Korean War and Vietnam War veterans, and even to those serving in peacetime.

Total veterans' benefits cost nearly $30 billion annually. The two largest expenditures are for medical care and compensation. Many categories of veterans are eligible for care in the nation's largest medical care system. VA hospitals are a familiar sight in our largest cities. Veterans with service-connected disabilities and their survivors receive compensation. Expenditures have leveled off with the passage of time. For example, some 400,000 fewer World War II veterans and survivors are eligible for benefits than in 1970.[15]

The other major veterans' benefits are pensions and support for education. Pensions have been controversial because veterans may also receive retirement benefits from social security and private pension plans—sometimes called double or triple dipping. Expenditures for veterans' education meanwhile continue to decrease as those eligible exhaust their benefits.

Welfare Programs for the Needy

Most people think of welfare as the response of a well-meaning governing body to the needs of the poor and disabled. Programs for the needy include direct money payments to assist those without jobs or prospects of employment, services of various kinds, commodities like food and housing, and education.

In striking contrast to programs for the many, the beneficiaries of these programs have relatively little influence on their design or administration. The Economic Opportunity Act of 1964, commonly referred to as the War on Poverty, was, therefore, very special: It authorized Community Action Agencies to formulate programs at the grass roots level—where the poor experience poverty. Unfortunately, the programs and the structure failed to win widespread support. By the 1980s only a few of these initiatives survived.

Income Security

The original Social Security Act provided assistance for several categories of needy Americans: the aged who did not qualify for retirement benefits, women with dependent children and no husband, the blind, and the seriously disabled. The states administered these programs with matching contributions from the state and federal governments. Benefits varied, primarily owing to differences in state subsidies. In 1974 the programs for the aged, blind, and disabled were reorganized as Supplemental Security Income (SSI), which set uniform minimum benefits. Initially, managing SSI was a monumental challenge to the Social Security Administration. "Errors in determination of eligibility or in payments occurred in about a fourth of the cases; overpayments approached a billion dollars a year; applicants waited hours for service at area offices."[16] This is not too surprising, given the tasks that had to be performed, but it did fuel criticism of welfare programs.

Aid to Families with Dependent Children (AFDC) continues to be administered by the states, supported by federal matching grants. AFDC has been one of the most heavily criticized welfare programs. Great disparities exist among the states in the payments made to the recipients. Critics argue that the program tends to contribute to the conditions that lead to poverty—illegitimacy, one-parent families, and limited incentives to seek employment. Their evidence includes the increasing numbers of participants and escalating costs. Yet as indicated in Figure 19–3, monthly payments under either SSI or AFDC are modest.

Attempts to encourage AFDC mothers to get jobs began in 1971, when they were required to sign up for work training programs. Unfortunately, however, the programs were often inadequate and there were too few day-care centers. In a major overhaul of the program passed in 1988, Congress required the states to establish programs to train recipients for permanent jobs. The state programs have to guarantee child care, transportation, and other services so that recipients can participate. Money for child support is withheld from the absent parent's paycheck. It remains to be seen whether this latest change will be effective in re-

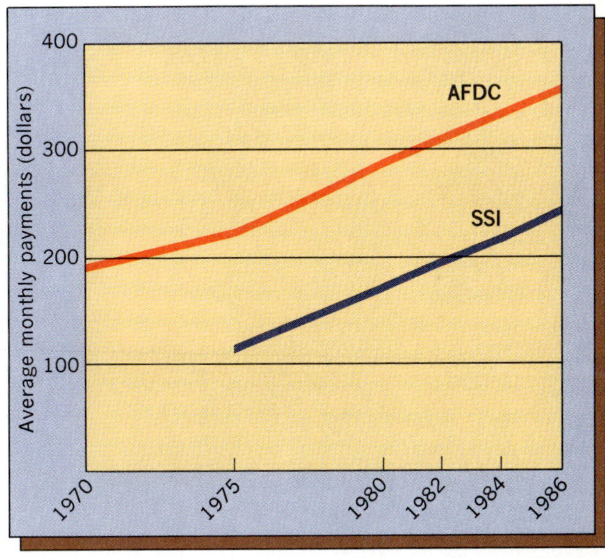

Figure 19–3 Public aid to the needy. Shown here are federal outlays under the two most important programs of welfare for the needy, for selected years from 1970 to 1986. The graph indicates the payment per family under AFDC, or Aid to Families with Dependent Children, and the payment per recipient under SSI, or Supplemental Security Income (which was not yet in existence in 1970). Source: *Statistical Abstract of the United States, 1988* (Washington, D.C.: U.S. Government Printing Office, 1988).

ducing the number of people who receive government assistance—and in silencing critics.

Another income security program is unemployment compensation. Also a part of the original Social Security Act, this program virtually required states to participate. No one questions the need for some system of unemployment insurance. Rather, the debate typically centers on who is eligible and how much they benefit. In periods of high unemployment, as in 1982, the period of coverage may be extended. In 1988 an estimated 2.2 million workers received benefits each week, down from nearly 4 million in 1982.

Health Care

Medicare, discussed in the last section, provides health care for the elderly under the Social Security Act. But not only the elderly face medical problems and limited resources. Congress therefore authorized *Medicaid,* a medical assistance program for the needy of all ages. Medicaid was to be administered by the states with contributions from the federal government.

Not unexpectedly, Medicaid costs have soared along with the increasing costs of health care—up in 1990 to more than two-thirds of direct outlays

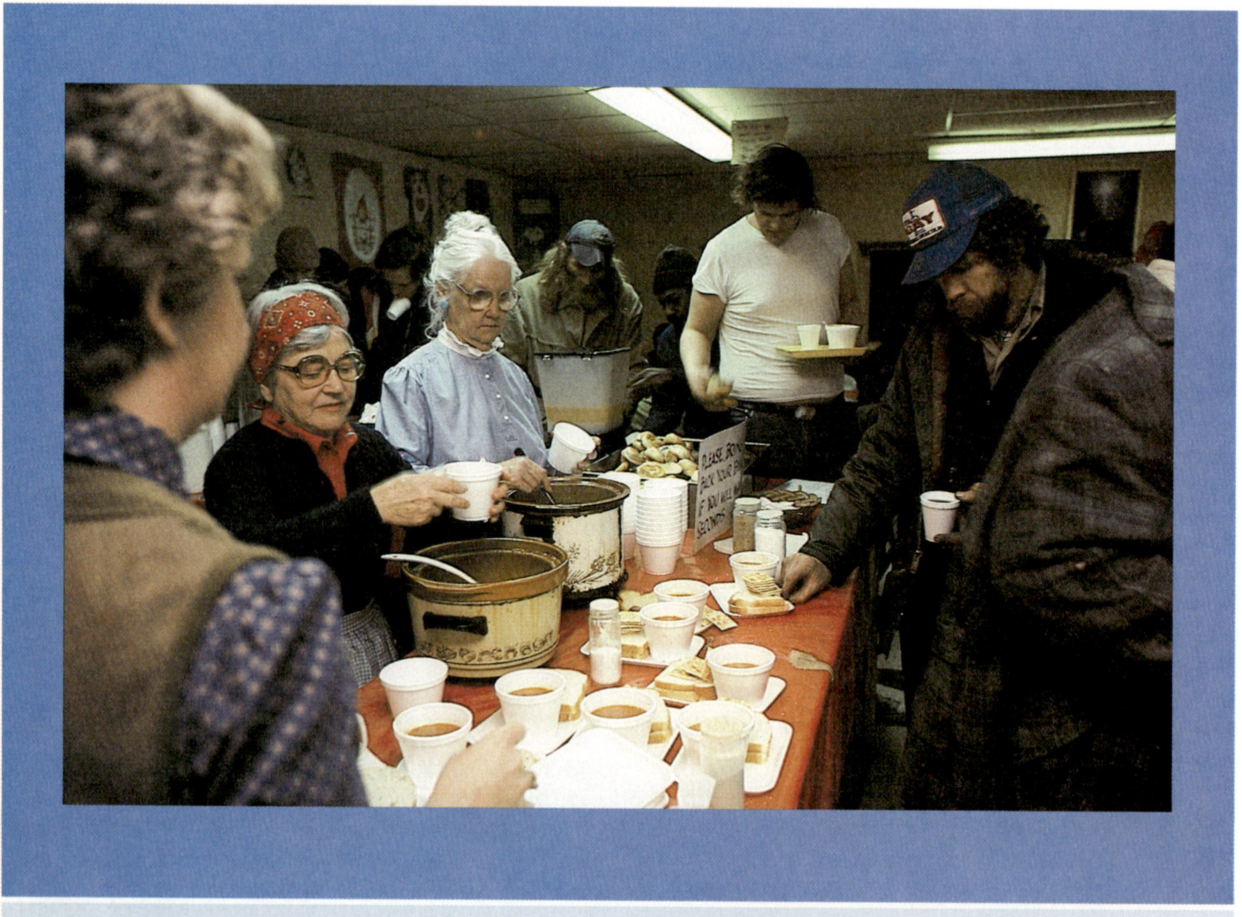

America is a wealthy nation, yet there remain many inequities that government seeks to redress. Numerous agencies, both public and private, provide food to the needy. The food stamp program, for example, allows recipients to purchase food in markets. Other programs, like this one, offer meals directly to those in need.

Public Policy, Public Opinion, and Civil Liberties: The Case of AIDS

Often what seems like good public policy to some threatens the civil liberties of others. One major problem associated with the treatment and prevention of acquired immune deficiency syndrome (AIDS), for example, is that many of the policy options interfere with the rights of those afflicted. And the conflict between policy and liberty leads to a great deal of ambivalence on the part of the American public.

The Gallup Poll has found that a vast majority of Americans believe that "AIDS sufferers should be treated with compassion." But because of the perceived severity of the problem, 90 percent also feel that immigrants should be tested for the AIDS virus, and nearly as large majorities support testing for prison inmates, members of the armed forces, applicants for a marriage license—even visitors from foreign countries. In fact, a narrow majority of the people polled favor testing *all* American citizens.

As the policies become more invasive of privacy, however, majorities oppose them. Should employers have the right to dismiss an employee with AIDS? By 64 to 25 percent, Americans don't think so, and fewer still favor isolating AIDS victims or allowing landlords to evict them. Yet more than half believe that AIDS victims should be forced to carry an identification card indicating the nature of their illness.

We can expect controversies like these to reach the public policy agenda in the 1990s. And on the right of privacy, it may be that in the end the courts must decide.

Source: *Gallup Report,* no. 261 (June 1987), pp. 2–13; nos. 268–269 (January–February 1988), pp. 30–41.

for health by the federal government. And that excludes Medicare, which, again, is part of social security. Some 24 million people receive Medicaid benefits.

The reforms in Medicare, principally the prospective reimbursement system, have also changed Medicaid. The problem is that states administer the program, and not all have acted to make changes. President Reagan proposed that the federal government take over the administration of Medicaid, in exchange for other programs going to the states. His proposal met with skepticism on Capitol Hill (see Chapter 3). Reductions in federal funding, resulting in changes within state programs, have made a complicated health care system even more complicated. Government administrators, health care professionals, and the poor interact in such different ways among the 50 states that it is hard to describe exactly what Medicaid means as a national program.

Housing and Food Assistance ■

Housing is important to Americans. A large

majority want to own their own home; the poor cannot. Because housing is so personal, associated with how we live, work, and socialize, government policy is bound to be controversial. State and local efforts have been limited. And, of course, judgments are most likely to be made for those least well represented in decision making—those with the greatest housing needs.

In 1937 Congress passed the first long-range public housing program. It provided financial encouragement for local housing authorities to construct and operate low-income rental housing units. However, reduced housing construction during World War II and the return of millions of veterans after the war soon created an acute shortage of housing.

The Housing Act of 1949 declared as a goal "a decent home and suitable living environment for every American family." It included an urban renewal program and support for 810,000 units of low-rent housing for low-income families. Unfortunately, in the eyes of most observers, the program failed. The slums were not cleared, nor were the 810,000 units built. Here is one assessment: "If public agencies are judged by the policies they generate and the policies in turn are evaluated by reference to their human consequences, then the people of the United States have a monstrosity on their hands—blundering, incompetent, insensitive, expensive, and unable or unwilling to learn and improve."[17] Many public housing projects became simply high-rise slums, and some were destroyed. Yet others successfully housed low-income families, and a few projects are still being built.

Subsequent programs have sought to keep government from deciding how and where low-income people should live. In the late 1960s the federal government supplemented rental payments for approved housing rather than building the units; at the same time, mortgage subsidy programs reduced interest payments for the poor. (Later, aid was extended to those with higher incomes.) Scandals hit both programs as unscrupulous developers took advantage of the poor and the government.

To correct these problems, the Reagan administration sought to reduce further the role of the federal government. A pilot program now offers vouchers that low-income families can use for rent. Reagan also reduced housing subsidies, forcing low-income families to pay a larger percentage of their income for housing. Funding for the construction of low-income housing units was also reduced drastically.

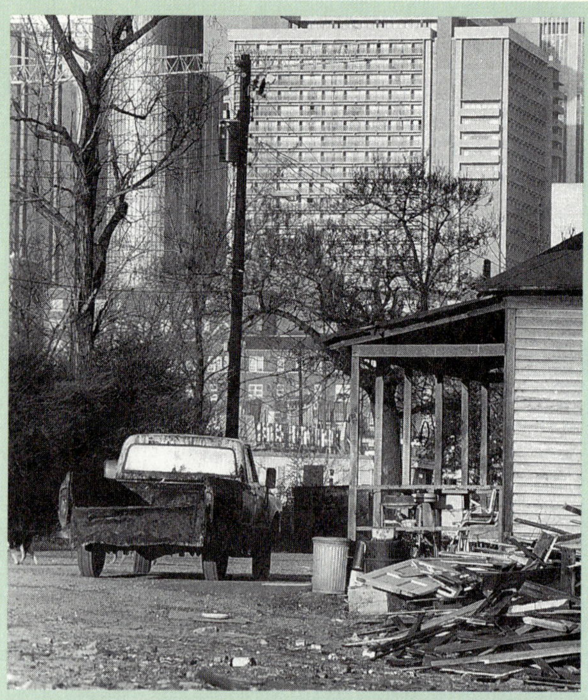

Most American cities can match Atlanta in this striking contrast of slums and sleek new buildings. Housing continues to be among the most difficult public policy issues. Urban renewal may have broad support, but private development often occupies sites where the poor once lived. The loss of housing has unfortunately not been matched by new construction.

Housing policy became so controversial in the Reagan years that no extensive bill passed until 1987—and even then only at the very last minute. The latest legislation includes such experiments as interest-free loans for those displaced by federally aided community development projects. Another initiative was aid to the homeless. The 100th Congress authorized money for emergency shelters and food assistance. Not all of the money was actually appropriated, however, because of budget constraints. Federal housing policy for the needy is a

“ Perspectives ”

On Health Care: The Cost of National Well-Being

“At this time, some 30 to 40 million Americans are without protection against the financial ravages attending serious illness. Close to half of these are full-time workers. Close to one third are children under the age of 18. . . . Some of the uninsured could undoubtedly afford to purchase health insurance out of their own resources, if affordable individual policies were actually available.”

—Uwe E. Reinhardt, Princeton University

“Health care costs will rise probably even more rapidly in 1989 than in 1988. The average jump in premiums could hit 30 percent in 1989. But at the same time, we are getting less for it.”

—Joseph Califano, former secretary of health, education, and welfare

“With technology even when something is cheaper we will be using it more. Wages are also interesting. This problem is dramatically illustrated by the shortage of nurses and lab technicians. Wages are going up, and we will have to pay people more to maintain the current levels of quality. I am skeptical about anyone bringing down costs.”

—William B. Schwartz, Tufts University

“There are no easy answers to cutting health care costs. . . . One quarter of them stem from technology, one quarter from the aging of the population, and one half from the basic mismanagement of the health care system. . . . It is that last half of the increase that you can target. . . . We have to begin influencing physicians' practice patterns. And we have to start challenging hospitals about how they deliver care.”

—Charles O. Schetter, director, health care practice, McKinsey & Company

Sources: Uwe E. Reinhardt, testimony before the Committee on Ways and Means, U.S. House of Representatives, September 22, 1988; others quoted in the *New York Times*, November 27, 1988.

sort of time capsule, containing remnants of past policies and current experiments. Severe housing problems remain, but the budget deficit and past experience make future large-scale projects unlikely. Further scandals were revealed in 1989—resulting in the suspension of several housing programs by HUD secretary Jack Kemp.

Food is as important as shelter, and the federal government has provided aid since the 1930s. The first school lunch and food stamp programs were designed to distribute agricultural surpluses. So was a 1954 school milk program. Under the Johnson administration, however, in 1964, food stamps became one of the most popular programs in Washington. Farmers, food producers, and suppliers join in its support, and some 20 million poor persons now regularly participate, at an annual cost of approximately $11 billion.

In striking contrast to housing programs, the problems with food stamps are few—mostly matters of administrative fine-tuning. If conservatives worry about possible fraud and have succeeded in tightening eligibility requirements, few would go so far as to advocate dropping the program. Among other contributions, it has helped the unemployed during periods of economic recession, such as in 1982.

Education

For decades racial, religious, and ideological issues made a broad program of federal aid to education impossible. The 1965 antipoverty program achieved a breakthrough agreement, including support to schools with a substantial number of students from low-income families. The formula provided aid to most schools "to meet the special educational needs of educationally deprived children." [18] How this was to be done was left to local school districts.

At first, local school districts often spent money to meet their own needs rather than those of the "educationally deprived." It was not until 1976 that the Office of Education, the precursor to the Department of Education, tightened the guidelines and closely monitored their application. As a result, schools had more success in meeting the original intent of the legislation, as measured by various achievement tests.

President Reagan sought to reduce the federal role in education by combining various programs into block grants to the states, which would then have more flexibility in spending the funds. He was unsuccessful in eliminating the 1965 program and a special program for handicapped children. In the 1988 election both George Bush and Michael Dukakis emphasized education, and that same year Congress authorized more expenditures than the president had requested. It was apparent that there will be no retreat in the federal government's role in elementary and secondary education support for low-income and handicapped students. It is also clear that no sizable expansion can be expected in the near future.

Education programs of a different order are those "designed to improve individuals' abilities to obtain and retain jobs by developing job skills and to support services that match individuals with jobs." [19] These include programs for the unemployed, for those displaced by changes in the economy, for disadvantaged youth, and for mothers receiving AFDC payments.

Job training programs have come and gone in the last 20 years. A series of changing names tells the story: Manpower Development and Training, Neighborhood Youth Corps, Operation Mainstream, Job Opportunities in the Business Sector (JOBS), Youth Conservation Corps, and public employment programs. The Comprehensive Employment and Training Act of 1973, known as CETA, consolidated many of these. Substantially reduced by President Reagan, CETA was itself superseded by the Job Training Partnership Act of 1982 (JTPA). Its principal sponsor was Senator Dan Quayle of Indiana, now vice president.[20] Where earlier programs were administered almost entirely through state and local governments, JTPA sought to involve the private sphere much more in job creation.

It may well be that the federal government has finally hit on a successful formula for job training. Still, as with housing, health, and other education programs, the personal, and therefore highly variable, nature of the problem makes it a sensitive policy issue. As with so many domestic issues, the variation is best managed through a federal system, with state and local governments accommodating the differences in cooperation with the private sphere, where most of the jobs are found. This tension between local variation and the federal bureaucracy's concern for standardization remains a dilemma.

Helping students from low-income families to higher education has broad political support. The Economic Opportunity Act of 1964 established a work-study program, while the Higher Education Act of 1965 provided "educational opportunity grants" for needy college students. The Reagan administration created a needs test for these grants—known as Pell grants, after the principal sponsor, Senator Claiborne Pell (D–R.I.)—and cut them substantially. Such programs will continue to absorb budget cuts in periods of high deficits—perhaps even more than their proportionate share—but they will survive. A persuasive case can be made that one route out of poverty is through education.

Welfare programs directed to problems of the poor have never had the same sound political footing as those for the many. Since others—mostly middle- and upper-class white men—define social and economic problems for the poor, program experimentation and reform are inevitable. The diagnosis of what the problems are may change, too. That is not to say these programs are in danger of being dropped. Rather it is to emphasize that they are always subject to reform.

The Economy

On each of these issues, we have seen the federal government try to devise solutions and authorize, then appropriate, money to pay for them. Government decisions on the economy may have greater long-run effects. Actions such as changes in interest rates by the Federal Reserve Board typically do not cost many federal dollars, but they profoundly affect employment, resources, the cost of goods and services, and the general welfare.

Despite the importance of the government's role, there is no Department of the Economy. Rather, several agencies directly set or significantly influence economic policy:

The *Department of the Treasury* recommends tax policy, advises the president on fiscal and economic policy, and manages the debt.

The *Department of Commerce* advises the president on international trade and domestic economic development and provides data on private sector productivity and other economic indicators.

The *Department of Labor* advises the president on policies related to wages and employment opportunities and conditions and also provides data on labor economics (including the unemployment rate).

The *Council of Economic Advisers* analyzes the economy on a continuing basis, advises the president on economic policy and the economic implications of other policies, and prepares the annual economic report for Congress.

The *Federal Reserve Board* establishes monetary policy by setting the reserves for banks, determining discount rates, regulating credit, and purchasing and selling securities.

The *Office of Management and Budget* prepares the annual budget, in consultation with the departments and agencies, and advises the president on budgetary and other economic matters.

The *Economic Policy Advisory Board* advises the president on domestic and international economic issues and oversees general economic policy.

All of these, save the Federal Reserve Board, serve the president. Their top executives are appointed by and advise the president, and they implement the president's decisions. The Federal Reserve Board, or Fed, as it is popularly called, is an independent regulatory commission. Although the president names its seven-person board of governors, including its powerful chairman, with the consent of the Senate, the governors' 14-year terms overlap so that no one president can appoint the whole board. The Fed is unusually influenced by its chairman (as compared with other regulatory commissions or even other government agencies).[21]

Most of these executive agencies have legislative counterparts in Congress's taxing, appropriations, banking, and labor committees. The Joint Economic Committee receives the annual economic report of the Council of Economic Advisers and makes recommendations to Congress. Since 1974 Congress also has had its own budget office, which provides independent analysis of the economic effects of budget revenues and expenditures (see Chapter 17).

Fiscal Policy ■

Fiscal policy includes the use of taxing and spending to stimulate or stabilize economic growth. Chapter 17 looked in detail at the budget—now a trillion dollar enterprise that is consistently out of balance. Economists warn that the deficit threatens the status of the dollar in competition with other currencies, increases our indebtedness to foreign

The Federal Deposit Insurance Corporation (FDIC) protects bank deposits. But it may also close banks that can no longer meet their obligations. A crisis in the savings and loan industry in 1988–1989 led to further controls, linked to a massive bailout of failing "thrifts," or savings banks, by the federal government.

nations, and contributes to serious trade imbalances. The Bush administration started work immediately on these issues, constrained by the president's campaign promise of no new taxes. The president's economists were also reluctant to make substantial changes as long as such economic indicators as unemployment, interest rates, and inflation remained favorable.

Today's budget deficit is extraordinary. In times past, White House economic planners had more flexibility in determining how to intercede. During a recession, or when a recession was threatened, taxes might be cut to stimulate private spending, or government spending might be increased to inject more money into the economy. Conservatives tend to favor the former approach, liberals the latter. "Supply-side" economists believe that because tax cuts stimulate the economy and put more people to work, they actually produce more revenue. In practice, the supply-side experiment of 1981 did not produce enough additional revenue to balance the budget.

If the economy is overstimulated, persistent inflation may result. To reduce inflation, presidents have tried wage and price controls, with variable success. In some cases, voluntary cooperation was sought from business and labor. President Nixon imposed wage and price controls. His direct government intervention into the marketplace was unpopular. In addition, problems developed when controls were removed and pent-up demand was released.

Monetary Policy

Monetary policy is very much what one would imagine from the term itself—policy governing the supply and flow of money in the economy. The Fed is the principal governmental agency for setting monetary policy. Donald F. Kettl describes its role this way:

> Unquestionably the Fed has enormous power over the American economy. Like other central banks, it has the job of keeping the currency stable by managing the nation's supply of money and credit. To nearly everyone, that means controlling interest rates, and the Fed has used that function to gain great influence over the nation's—and increasingly the world's—economy.[22]

When President Reagan entered the White House in 1981, inflation exceeded 13 percent, the prime interest rate (the rate that is charged to banks) was nearly 19 percent (with consumer rates exceeding 20 percent), and unemployment stood at over $7\frac{1}{2}$ percent (see Figure 19–4). Reagan's fiscal policy was to cut taxes and reduce domestic expenditures. The Fed imposed tight money policies to reduce inflation. Kettl describes what happened:

> Fed policy stayed extremely tight throughout 1981 and into 1982, and interest rates remained at more than 20 percent through most of 1981. Inflation proved stubborn; it slowed only slightly from 13.5 to 10.4 percent, while unemployment grew to near 10 percent in the worst recession since the Depression. Not until 1982 did the inflation rate convincingly head downward, to 6.1 percent for the year. Interest rates for 1982 retreated to about 11.5 percent by the end of the year, but unemployment hovered near 10 percent for the year.[23]

It is a good example of fiscal and monetary policies working in opposite directions. The mounting deficits contributed to inflation; tight controls on money kept interest rates high, preventing economic growth. Both the president and members of Congress criticized Fed Chairman Paul Volcker, but eventually inflation did decline, and confidence in business was restored. Volcker, who was reappointed when his term came to an end in 1983, was actually credited with much of the success of Reagan's economic policy in the first term.

Volcker's replacement in 1987, Alan Greenspan, issued what were already familiar warnings about the deficit and its effects following the 1988 election. It was a challenge to the new president, George Bush, to deal forcefully with the deficit. Initially Bush proposed a "flexible freeze" by which spending would be held at the inflation rate except for "true national priorities."

As is evident from this review, setting monetary policy outside the normal political process has certain advantages. The Fed is protected by its independent status and long terms of office. Thus it presumably can withstand the short-run political pressures and concentrate on what is best for the economy. Nevertheless, the Fed can withstand criticism only up to a point. Its decisions so directly affect the market—business, labor, and consumers—that elected public officials are bound to

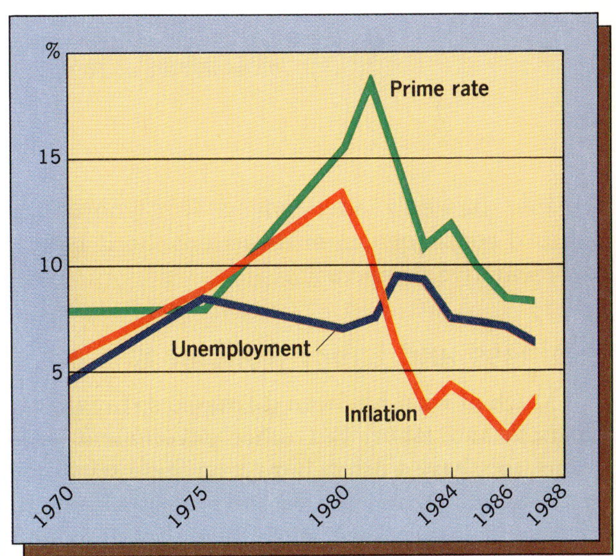

Figure 19–4 Monetary policy and the state of the economy. Shown are three important economic indicators—unemployment, inflation, and the prime interest rate—in selected years from 1970 to 1988. (The prime rate is the rate of interest charged to banks.) Source: *Statistical Abstract of the United States, 1988* (Washington, D.C.: U.S. Government Printing Office, 1988).

"You'll notice that when some things are up, others are down, and when the things that are up go down, the things that are down go up."

threaten the Fed's independence if it ignores the political consequences of its actions. So it is in a representative democracy.

Business and Labor Policies ■

Much of what has been discussed so far affects business and labor. But other government programs, too, have a direct impact on these segments of the economy. Direct subsidies to business go back to the last century, when the railroads gained millions of acres of land. Other aids to business include tax breaks, such as the depletion allowance for the oil industry, and government loans or loan guarantees, like the $1.5 billion in loan guarantees to bail out the Chrysler Corporation in 1979.

Government regulation of business and industry ranges from antitrust and trade rules to matters of safety and health, environmental practices, and energy use. Many of these laws are administered and enforced by the independent regulatory commissions. Politics help to shape each of these sets of regulations, with interaction among industries, their lobbyists, members of Congress, and the regulatory bodies. In recent years the politics of regulation has been overshadowed by the politics of deregulation. Martha Derthick and Paul Quirk have described this change as "procompetitive reform." The process, most notably in both the airline and trucking industries, was a type of policy escalation:

> When change is in the air, no one knows with any precision what will constrain which actors or how far change will go. Under such circumstances, office holders play a kind of leapfrog,

IMPACT

The American Policy Agenda

"**The Budget Deficit** *The federal debt, now $2.8 trillion and mounting at the rate of about $12 billion every month, is not an abstraction; in real dollars it works out to a debt of about $37,000 for every family in America. . . .*"

"**The Savings and Loan Crisis** *An estimated 500 individual savings and loan associations are . . . insolvent by generally accepted accounting principles, and another 400 are in such difficulty that they are likely to fail. . . . The insurance division of the Federal Home Loan Bank Board that regulates the thrift industry is short by an estimated $50 to $100 billion of the amount it needs to pay off depositors. . . .*"

"**Children at Risk** *In the United States today, one child in five is poor. . . . Children make up the biggest single segment of the 32 million Americans who live below the official poverty line. . . .*"

""**The Greenhouse Effect** *The ozone and global warning problems are real. Scientific evidence is now irrefutable that there is a depletion of the ozone layer which shields us from the ultraviolet rays of the sun. Without an adequate ozone layer, rates of cancer will accelerate and some plants and animals would be threatened. . . .*"

"**Drugs** *Drugs are spreading fear in American life—fear that a child will be hooked at school or on the playground, fear that a drug gang could move into the neighborhood, fear that a drug addict will commit violence to someone in your family. . . . The country spends $140 billion a year for drugs, and consumes 60 percent of the world's drug supply.*"

Source: *American Agenda: Report to the Forty-First President of the United States of America* (Los Angeles: Times Mirror Company, 1989).

each one outdoing the other in a series of small jumps, until a limit is reached. The game of leapfrog may be driven by collective excitement and enthusiasm, with the players competing to see who will be first to attain some preconceived line of finish.[24]

Regulation continues to be an important method for government control of business. Corporate takeovers, insider trading, and stock market practices are all subjects of congressional concern and likely further regulation. A crisis in the savings and loan industry in 1988 encouraged greater government control to prevent future insolvency of the thrift institutions. President Bush proposed a plan early in his administration to restore confidence in the savings and loan system. The 101st Congress, too, acted quickly on this issue.

Federal labor legislation has sought to protect workers against exploitation by business and industry, to promote equality of opportunity and civil rights, to assure the rights of workers to organize and bargain collectively, to prohibit unfair labor union practices, and to promote harmonious labor-management relations. Early struggles to unionize in the first decades of this century were bitter and violent. Gradually, unions developed impressive political power, which aided them in increasing wages and improving working conditions.

Today labor issues are very different. A smaller proportion of the work force now belongs to unions. Threatened by foreign trade and faced with a changing work force, labor unions often face a disadvantage in their lobbying efforts. Foreign competition has rendered strikes less effective, transforming the union's negotiating position. Plant closings have led to high unemployment in certain regions. A 1988 law requires 60 days notice

Federal regulations are designed to protect the health and safety of Americans. Here workers in New Jersey remove radioactive soil from homes built on a former industrial site. Federally sponsored research reveals new hazards all the time, and the likely outcome is further regulations.

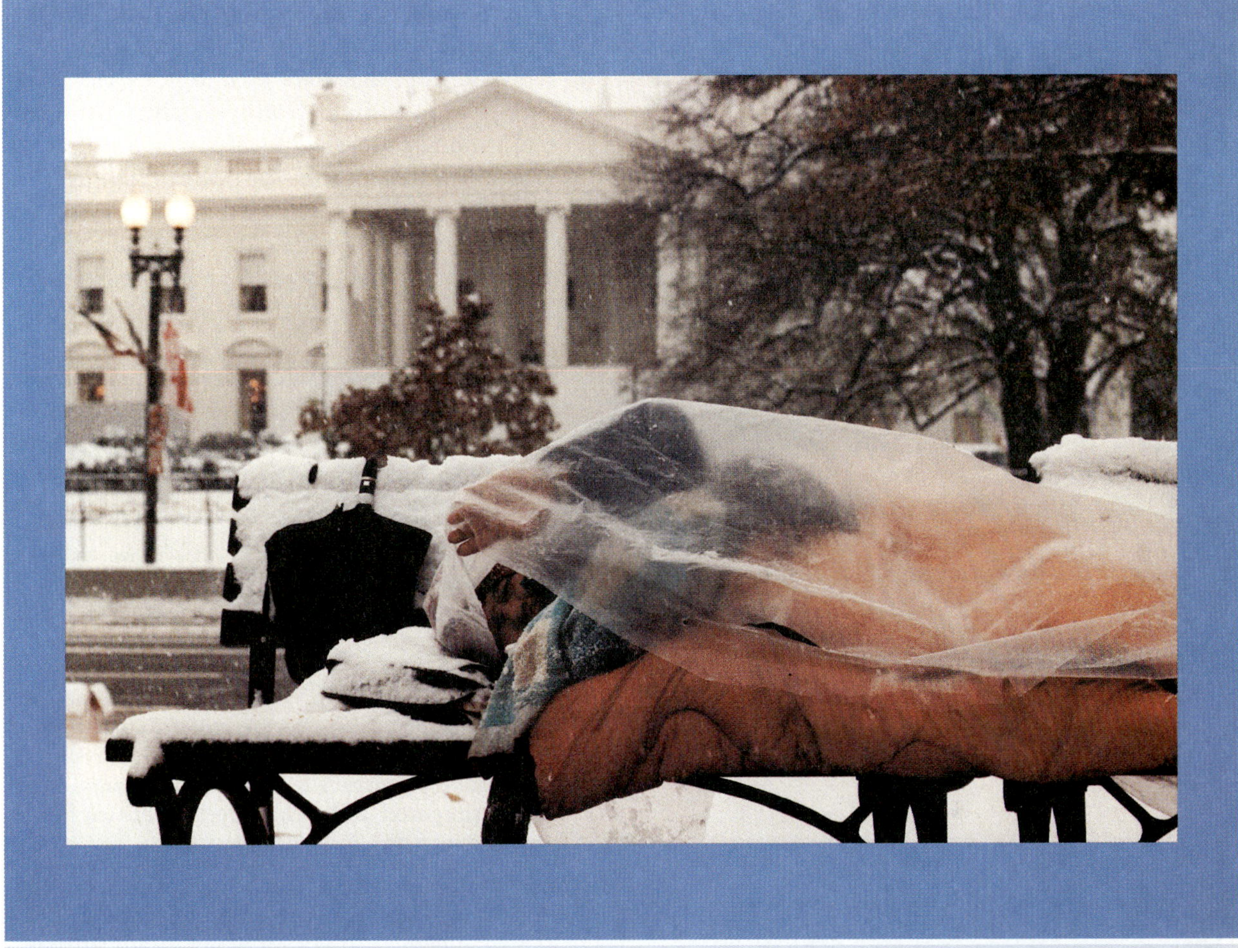

An individual sleeping near—but not in—a famous house. The plight of the homeless has forced itself on national attention, but the problem remains acute. The 100th Congress enacted legislation to aid the homeless, and elected officials agree that more must be done. Finding solutions to persistent problems is part of the agenda of government for the 1990s.

before closing a plant (for any business with 100 or more employees). Other issues resulting from the trade imbalance are bound to be on future labor agendas.

The characteristics of those doing the work of business and industry have changed, and so has the work itself. Consider the role of women. In 1970 approximately 30 million women were employed, representing 38 percent of the total work force. In 1985 over 47 million women were employed—44 percent of the work force. Different workers in different jobs result in different issues. Today, child care is a labor issue, for example, as is parental leave.

The Domestic Policy Agenda

It was said that the 1988 election was issueless. While it is true that the aura of peace and prosperity led to few policy confrontations between the candidates, still an agenda of issues awaits any president. Those domestic issues constitute the continuing commitments of the federal government.

Current federal programs concerning resources, welfare, and the economy will generate much of the agenda of the 1990s. The huge deficit creates an enormous issue in and of itself, one that challenged the Bush administration even before the inauguration. Bush limited his options during the campaign by advising Congress to "read my lips: no new taxes." But he met with congressional leaders before taking office and worked out a budget agreement in cooperation with the Democratic Budget Committee Chairmen early in 1989.

A large deficit means a very special agenda:

1. Policy initiatives can succeed only if they are financially self-supporting.
2. Significant program expansion or new programs require a crisis.
3. Government must evaluate existing programs carefully to make them more efficient and effective.

The best place to look for issues in the 1990s is within the federal government itself. Major resource issues center on energy supply, environmental repair, and farm production and pricing more accommodated to the world market. Welfare issues derive directly from budget problems. Programs for the many have broad public support and will be cautiously revised. Health care costs continue to escalate. The AIDS crisis is just beginning to unfold and continues to occupy policymakers. Welfare programs for the needy continue to be the subject of reform. Finally, fiscal and monetary issues emanate from budget and trade imbalances as America attempts to stabilize its position in the world economy.

Summary

- The growing recognition of limited resources has led to an increase in government regulation. Determining the effects of one resource policy on another continues to be important.
- Welfare programs start with high expectations and great promise. They overestimate the federal capacity to solve problems, leading to an ever-unfolding process of policy change.
- Welfare programs generate dependency for those receiving the benefits. Programs for the many become too entrenched to change easily, while those for the needy are regularily subject to reform.
- Economic issues now dominate the domestic policy agenda, limiting government's capacity to act on other programs. Increasingly, international events affect the domestic economy.

Readings on Domestic Policy Issues: The 1990s

American Agenda, Inc. 1989. *American Agenda: A Report to the Forty-First President of the United States of America.* Los Angeles: Times Mirror. A review of the most critical issues facing the government in the 1990s, prepared under the direction of two former presidents—Ford and Carter.

Anderson, James E., David W. Brady, Charles S. Bullock, and Joseph Stewart. 1984. *Public Policy and Politics in America,* 2d ed. Monterey, Calif.: Brooks/Cole. An issue-by-issue treatment of the major domestic problems and policies of the last half century.

Anton, Thomas J. 1989. *American Federalism and Public Policy.* New York: Random House. A conceptual treatment of the relationship between federalism and public policy in the United States. Examines modern federal politics in terms of the interactions among national, state, and local governments.

Brewster, Lawrence G. 1987. *The Public Agenda: Issues in American Politics.* New York: St. Martin's Press. An analysis of the major policy problems facing the nation in the last decade of the twentieth century. Included are the political economy, energy, health, toxic wastes, crime, immigration, and the arms race.

Chubb, John E., and Paul E. Peterson, eds. 1989. *Can the Government Govern?* Washington: Brookings Institution. An analysis of the capacity of present political institutions to manage the policy issues of the time, with recommendations for change.

Congressional Quarterly Weekly Report and the *National Journal* are two weekly publications that provide a review and analysis of the policy agenda as it is acted on by the White House, Congress, the agencies, and the courts.

Derthick, Martha. 1979. *Policymaking for Social Security.* Washington, D.C.: Brookings Institution. A masterful review of the complex world of social security issues and programs.

Shuman, Howard E. 1988. *Politics and the Budget.* Englewood Cliffs, N.J.: Prentice Hall. A focus on the nation's number-one policy problem: the budget.

Tufte, Edward R. 1978. *Political Control of the Economy.* Princeton, N.J.: Princeton University Press. A study that examines how "political" considerations affect governmental decisions concerning the economy.

Wilson, James Q., ed. 1980. *The Politics of Regulation.* New York: Basic Books. An interesting series of case studies on the politics of the regulatory process.

Chapter 20

Foreign Policy

A foreign policy that protects the nation is a prerequisite for peace. But do American political institutions enable our leaders to conduct an effective foreign policy? Writing in the 1830s, after his visit to the United States, the astute French aristocrat Alexis de Toqueville captured the problem:

> Foreign politics demand scarcely any of the qualities which are peculiar to a democracy; they require, on the contrary, the perfect use of all those in which it is deficient. . . . [A] democracy can only with great difficulty regulate the details of an important undertaking, persevere in a fixed design, and work out its execution in spite of serious obstacles. It cannot combine its measure with secrecy or await their consequences with patience.[1]

Yet the United States today has commitments around the world. Its foreign policy during the last four decades has focused on its principal competitor, the Soviet Union. Soviet-American problems, however, are by no means the only ones it faces. Increasingly, the world is beset by regional rivalries—Arab-Israeli conflicts, the Iran-Iraq war, instability in such close neighbors as Nicaragua, and racial conflict in South Africa, to name just a few. In addition, more and more of the problems facing the United States are economic ones that deeply affect its ability to play a global role. This chapter looks at U.S. foreign policy as it enters the 1990s after a decade in which American commitments have grown, while our ability to support those commitments has drastically shrunk.

The Goals of Foreign Policy

The Search for Security

All nations need a foreign policy. Unlike individuals in an organized society, nations fear for their security, if not their survival. A government in a country usually provides at least some degree of law and order so that most persons do not continuously worry about threats to their lives. However, there is no world government with an authority superior to that of the individual national governments. The result is frequently called anarchy. This does not mean chaos, but rather the absence of government institutions to make and enforce order and allow for peaceful change.

So nations in the international system feel insecure; with no higher authority that can protect all of them, each regards other nations as potential adversaries rather than as friends. The fundamental rule of states—each independent and yet interdependent with one another—is to protect themselves.[2] To forget this task is to risk endangering the state. If a nation wishes to enjoy its way of life in peace, it must at all times be on guard. The reason for maintaining military strength follows logically. Power will restrain power if a balance is preserved.

If danger comes, a nation cannot call the international equivalent of the local police; there is no such thing. Distrust is widespread in an anarchical international system. When one state extends the hand of friendship, the other wonders why. Where their security and possibly their survival are at stake, states are cautious and careful. All nations proclaim they are peace-loving but suspect that other states are not.

Since American foreign policy is primarily concerned with ensuring the nation's securty, we will refer to the specific policies that seek to achieve this as *security* policies. These include (but are not limited to) such areas as the defense budget, arms control, limited war, alliances, arms transfers to allies and other countries, economic and technical aid, and intelligence operations against other states. Most of these policies are continuing because they involve long-term interests. The United States, as one of the world's two nuclear superpowers, has a continuing interest in balancing Soviet military strength; but it also has an interest in arms control—reducing the intensity of the arms competition and stabilizing the balance in an environment of rapid innovation and change in weapons. Foreign aid programs and arms transfers go on from year to year, although the recipients and the amounts they receive may change. When wars have occurred, as in Vietnam, they have lasted for years and required major commitments of people, arms, and money.

In contrast to security policies, there are also *crisis* policies. Crises are distinguished by their relative infrequency and short duration. But they make up for their lack of numbers by the great danger they present. Frequently a surprise, a crisis is characterized by a high perception of threat to the nation's vital interests and a lack of time the policymakers have to deal with it. If they do not act quickly, the situation will go against them. The most critical element of a crisis is the possibility of the use of force or actual violence, which underlies much of traditional international politics. In short, the likelihood of war erupting suddenly becomes a real danger. In the case of a Soviet-American crisis, even if the initial clash involves only threats or low levels of force, the possibility of escalation to a nuclear confrontation is always present. The art of crisis management is therefore defending the interests threatened (usually by invoking the threat of force) while simultaneously avoiding nuclear war—a most difficult and demanding task.

The Goal of Prosperity

Security, while fundamental, is not a nation's only goal. Prosperity is another. The major *domestic* reason for growth in government, and especially growth in executive power, has been the increasing demand for jobs, prosperity, and social services. Governments all over the world, but especially in democratically elected countries, are held responsible for the welfare of their people. Security issues, except in crises or wars, rarely touch the mass of the electorate personally; many voters are not even aware of important events in foreign policy. But unemployment, salaries, and prices affect their pocketbooks. These bread-and-butter issues, normally considered domestic issues, arouse them quickly, or at least in time for the next election.

The problem is that most nations do not have the natural resources or the industrial and agricultural capacity to ensure their own prosperity. They must import raw materials, manufactured goods, and food. The result is that nations trade with one another. In the West, trade has been carried on largely by private enterprise and has not generally been seen as a foreign policy matter. But as nations and economies have become more interdependent, even a government like that of the United States no longer controls its economic destiny. The nation has many of the resources it needs, an enormous industry, and productive agriculture, but its standard of living and style of life are profoundly affected by events overseas.

Since 1973, when the Organization of Petroleum Exporting Countries (OPEC) quadrupled oil prices, it has been clear that our prosperity can depend on decisions made abroad. The collapse in 1979 of Iran's pro-Western shah—one man in a country most Americans could probably not find on a map—resulted in a further sharp rise in oil prices. The subsequent recession was convincing evidence of how much overseas events can dislocate an entire economy. Issues once seen as foreign policy have become domestic concerns, as well as the other way around.

The 1980s reinforced that lesson. President Reagan's tax cuts created a huge budget deficit and drove up the value of the dollar. The result: U.S. goods were priced out of world markets; foreign goods, from Japanese VCRs to German-made machine tools, flooded the American market. The United States suffered bankruptcies and unemployment in farming and industry and a growing trade deficit, and it became the largest debtor nation in history.

In the 1990s the United States continues to face a shrinking and increasingly uncompetitive economy, making its global commitment harder to support, because Japan and Third World countries have added American mass-production techniques to their lower labor costs. Because the distinction between international and domestic policies and politics has been disappearing, and most economic issues now involve elements of both, we call them *intermestic* issues.[3] Table 20–1 lists some examples of intermestic concerns across the president's entire cabinet.

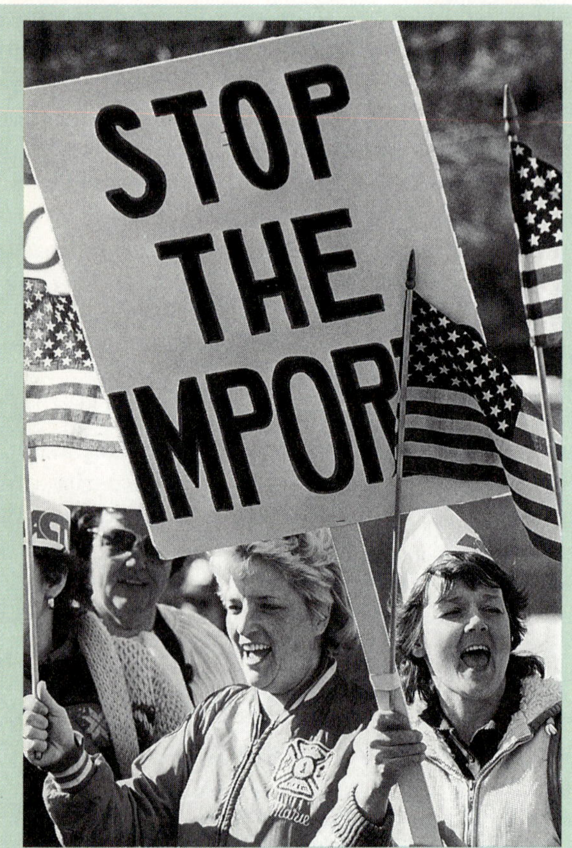

American industry now often finds itself unable to compete not only for foreign markets, but even at home. Faced with low-priced (and often more innovative) imports, companies are shifting production overseas, to benefit from cheaper labor. Americans concerned about the loss of their jobs, like these garment workers, form part of a growing protectionist movement.

America as a Global Power

Ironically, it was only after the war in Vietnam that America emerged as a global power with extensive international involvement. For decades its foreign policy had been characterized by the word *containment*—a reaction to the growing power of the Soviet Union after World War II. Allied by necessity against Nazi Germany, the United States and the Soviet Union found themselves the only two great powers after Germany's defeat, France's failure to recover from its own defeat in 1940, and great Britain's exhaustion after the allied victory. The resulting conflict, known as the Cold War, has become one of the longest in history. Already is it longer than the 31 years from the start of World War I in 1914 to the end of World War II in 1945.

The Cold War began as the Soviet Union sought to expand its influence. Already it had established its shadow over all of Eastern Europe, as the Red Army advanced toward Berlin, Germany's former capital, in 1945. Now it turned first south—to Iran, Turkey, and Greece—and then to a weak and fearful postwar Western Europe. In 1950 it permitted its satellite North Korea to invade South Korea. Meanwhile, America began to make commitments of its own. The Truman Doctrine asserted American support for Turkey and Greece; the Marshall Plan and the North Atlantic Treaty Organization (NATO) extended American aid for the economic recovery and military protection of Western Europe. In the Korean War, America committed troops to stop the Communist invasion. After the coming to power of the Chinese Communists in 1949, the United States sought to contain the apparently united Sino-Soviet, or Chinese and Soviet, bloc, which seemed to extend from Central Europe to the Pacific Ocean. But American alliances in the Middle East and Southeast Asia proved to be weak instruments of containment, and the latter resulted in our tragic intervention in the Vietnam War, beginning in the 1960s.

Since that long conflict, the United States has met with leaders of Communist China to exploit its schism with the Soviet Union. And despite a growing disillusionment after Vietnam with America's role in the world, that role has continued to grow. In the wake of the Soviet invasion of Afghanistan in December 1979, President Carter extended U.S. protection to the oil sheikdoms in the Persian Gulf. In addition, after the Sandinistas came into power in Nicaragua that same year, the United States became increasingly involved in Central American affairs. During the Vietnam War, the United States was often criticized for trying to play "the world's policeman" in far-away countries. Yet today, issues in every area of the world affect American security and economic interests.

TABLE 20–1

The Increasing Prominence of Intermestic Issues: Some Issues with Both Foreign and Domestic Impact Facing the Executive

Department of Agriculture	Commodity trading; crop import and export quotas
Department of Commerce	International trade
Department of Drug Enforcement	Drug trade
Department of Education	Bilingual education
Department of Energy	Petroleum imports; OPEC nations; energy independence
Department of Health and Human Services	World health concerns; income maintenance for new immigrants
Department of Housing and Urban Development	Housing concerns of immigrants
Department of the Interior	Acid rain; protection of endangered marine wildlife
Department of Justice	Immigration; civil and criminal treatment of immigrants
Department of Labor	Product (e.g., automobile) imports
Department of Transportation	International air traffic
Department of the Treasury	Value of the dollar in relation to foreign currencies; U.S. trade deficits with foreign nations

The Constitution and the Conduct of Foreign Policy

The Separation of Powers Problem

During the cold war with the Soviet Union after World War II, there was considerable worry about how well the United States could perform in foreign policy. At the heart of this concern was the separation of powers.[4] The Constitution gave the federal government sole responsibility for the conduct of foreign policy, but it divided authority in this area, as in the domestic one, between the president and Congress. The president could receive and send ambassadors, but the Senate had to give its advice and consent to treaties by a two-thirds majority and confirm all major political, diplomatic, and military appointments. The president was commander in chief of the nation's armed forces, but only Congress could declare war, appropriate funds for the military, and regulate commerce with other countries. Congress could also investigate the executive department's conduct of foreign policy.

The Constitution was founded on the belief that the concentration and exercise of power could lead to an abuse of power and that only a system of checks and balances would prevent such abuses and preserve the liberties of the people from a tyrannical government (see Chapter 2). Thus, executive-legislative conflict was built into the system; Congress's task was to restrain the presidency. But the conduct of foreign policy required a centralization of power in the executive.[5] In an anarchical international system, a nation often has to act with speed, secrecy, continuity of purpose, and flexibility. This means that the president, as the nation's chief diplomat and commander in chief, must have the necessary authority to conduct an effective foreign policy. In fact, from 1941 to 1945, the balance between the president and Congress was virtually

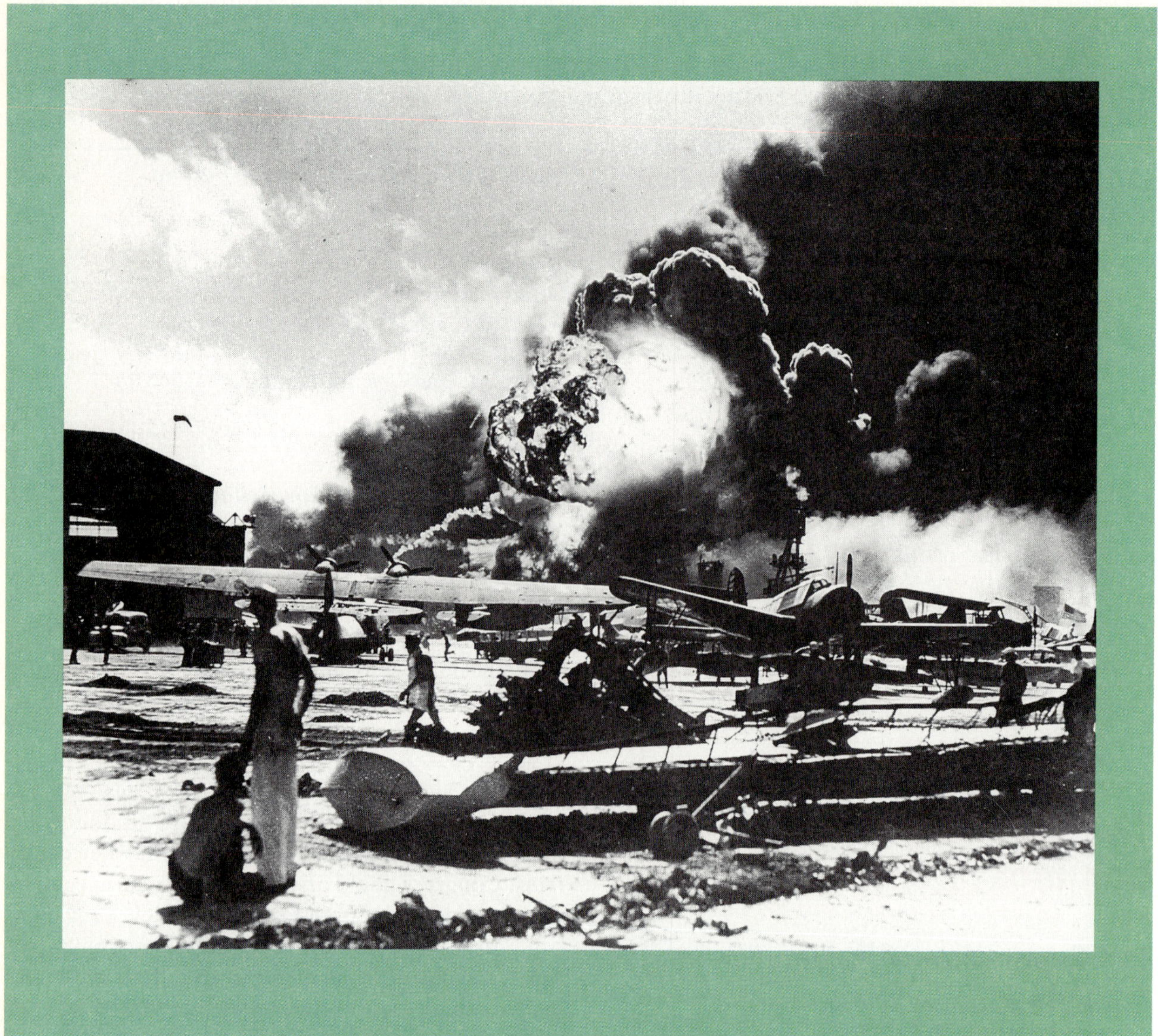

Pearl Harbor: December 7, 1941. The attack by Japan on the American fleet ended two years of bickering between Congress and President Roosevelt over increasing U.S. involvement in World War II. The country rallied behind the president in defeating first Germany, then Japan. After the war, the new perception of a Soviet threat prolonged bipartisan cooperation.

suspended, and the president was given emergency powers until the end of World War II. After the hostilities had ended, this grant of virtually authoritarian power (sometimes referred to as "democratic Caesarism") ended. Now executive-legislative relations returned to a more nearly normal form of institutional and partisan conflict.

However, the postwar Soviet-American conflict was neither war nor peace, as these words are normally understood; nor was this conflict, called the Cold War, either hot or cold, but a bit of both. It was not a conflict lasting just a few years, but rather a long-term conflict with no end in sight. Thus, the president needed to exercise emergency powers on a more permanent basis. This required congressional support and executive-legislative coordination.

The concern after World War II was that the president and Congress would be unable to work together. History reinforced this concern because, symbolically, the first foreign policy involvement in this century—foreshadowing the more intense and continuous involvement in international politics just over two decades later—ended in a disaster.[6] The Versailles peace treaty after World War I ended the war with Germany and established the League of Nations (the predecessor of the United Nations) as a peacekeeping organization. It was defeated in the Senate, even though a majority of Americans favored the treaty right after the war. This rejection of President Wilson and the League was later thought to be a major reason why the peace did not last and World War II broke out. It had taken American participation on the side of England and France to defeat Germany; without American power, the two European states were too weak to deter further German aggression.

Thus, the fear was that presidents would often find their foreign policies destroyed, blocked, or weakened for several reasons:

1. Congress, with its frequent elections—one-third of the Senate and all of the House every two years—reflects the frequently irrational changes of public mood from a too passionate involvement to no involvement at all. The resulting swings of policy would undermine any possible continuity and steady policy.

2. Members of Congress represent their constituencies and thus the short-run interests of the voters (if they wish to be reelected) of their districts or states. The president, nationally elected, can speak for broader and longer-run national interests (see Chapter 13).

3. The opposition party may control one or both houses of Congress.

4. Even if the president's party controls the Senate or the House, lack of party discipline and loyalty means that the president cannot be sure of getting policies through Congress. This was especially true of treaties, with their extraordinary requirement of a two-thirds majority.

5. Presidents have to appeal to the opposition party for support; they may not get it, but if they do, they have to pay the price by adopting some of its policy positions despite any reservations they might have.

6. Congress, being so highly decentralized, and parties being weak, is unduly influenced by interest groups concerned only with advancing their own narrow interests.

7. The president (like Wilson) may not be very good at establishing and maintaining good relations with Congress, a body sensitive to institutional slights and quick to arouse to anger. Perhaps in domestic policy we could still afford "politics as usual." But in foreign policy, where in the nuclear age one major mistake might be one too many, we could not.

The Bipartisan Solution

A widespread recommendation to overcome this executive-legislative barrier was *bipartisan* (or nonpartisan) support for the president in foreign policy.[7] This emphasis on support from *both* parties was a recognition of the obstacles the American political system poses for a rational, coherent, and consistent policy toward the rest of the world: namely, the institutional barrier between the executive and legislative branches of government and the failure of the party system to overcome this barrier by tying them together.

Thus, in foreign policy, the "national interest" was to be placed above party interests. "Politics should stop at the water's edge." America should face the world united. Partisanship should have no place in foreign policy decisions. Abandoning the political considerations usual in domestic politics was the patriotic thing to do. Executive-legislative conflict and party controversy over foreign affairs would weaken the stability and continuity of American policy, make it impossible to speak to other countries with one voice, and erode the nation's

Foreign Policy Leadership

Political leaders in the United States often feel obliged to take positions on issues that differ from the views of the public. Especially on foreign policy, they may suspect that the public does not pay enough attention to the issues to have an informed opinion, or that the public does not really care. In what issues does this kind of leadership matter? The table here shows that while many citizens are reluctant to become involved in international affairs, leaders generally recognize the importance of a more active American role. That difference is especially clear when military involvement is at issue.

	Public	Leaders	Difference
1. Best to take an active role in world affairs	71%	99%	28%
2. Vietnam War was not wrong or immoral	29	57	28
3. Favor foreign military aid	36	78	42
4. Favor aid for foreign economic development and technical assistance	60	93	33
5. Favor exchanging scientists with USSR	59	86	27
Favor sending U.S. troops if:			
6. Soviets invade Western Europe	68	93	25
7. Soviets invade Japan	53	82	29
8. Arabs invade Israel	32	57	25
9. North Korea invades South Korea	24	64	40

Source: Chicago Council on Foreign Affairs, 1986.

credibility in its relationships with allies and enemies.

Note the distinction made between domestic and foreign policy. The rationale for the American party system is that the "outs" must hold the "ins" responsible and that to do so they must scrutinize administration policy and be free to criticize it and advance alternatives. Yet in the conduct of foreign policy, this role of the opposition was to be abandoned; in the name of patriotism, the "outs" were to support the "ins." Yet, wasn't foreign policy more important than domestic policy—if only because in the nuclear era America's survival was certainly at stake? Doesn't this require the opposite of blind support for policies that the "in" party claimed were in the "national interest"?

In foreign policy, then, the political system was to operate differently than in the domestic area. Congress was to rally behind the president and, in turn, it was to help rally the country behind the president, as in World War II. Indeed, the more normal peacetime pattern of executive-legislative conflict was avoided because the peace after 1945 was abnormal. The American-Soviet rivalry was not named the Cold War for nothing. It may not have been a hot war, but it was war in the sense that Russia, as the other superpower, was perceived as a great threat to American security. This threat existed not only because of Russia's great military power, but also because its Communist values and beliefs were hostile to American democracy. The Russian challenge was therefore seen as fundamental in terms of physical and political survival. It was at least as dangerous as Nazi Germany's threat in World War II.

More basic were the widespread beliefs about America's role and aims in the world: that the central conflict in the world was between the Communist bloc led by Russia and the "free world" led by the United States; that any Communist expansion of influence was a loss of influence for the United States; that the basic American purpose was to oppose this expansion; and that force, as well as diplomatic and economic means, was legitimate for achieving this goal. The president, the bureaucracy, and Congress agreed on fundamental objectives. Disagreements were largely confined to how to achieve these objectives (with the major exception of American policy in Asia). While this perception of high threat and consensus on foreign policy lasted, the president was the clear leader in foreign policy, and Congress played a largely secondary and supportive role.

The Cold War and Presidential Power

Presidents have been prominently associated with American foreign policy: Washington's farewell address, the Monroe Doctrine, Theodore Roosevelt's "Big Stick," Wilson's Fourteen Points, Franklin Roosevelt's Good Neighbor policy, and the "doctrines" almost all postwar presidents have promoted—from the Truman Doctrine (committing the United States to the defense of Greece and Turkey at the beginning of the Cold War) to the Reagan Doctrine (promising support for anti-Marxist government guerillas in Afghanistan and other countries).

Presidential Leadership in Foreign Policy

One reason for this presidential prominence is that the Constitution granted the president specific authority with a great potential for expansion. These grants, such as that of making the president commander in chief, were written so that they were open to interpretation as circumstances changed. In a real sense, what was *not* in the Constitution "proved ultimately more important than what was." [8] Often called the Constitution's "great silences," they gave strong presidents freedom to do what they thought they needed to do in unprecedented circumstances on behalf of the nation's interests, as they defined them, and to test the powers and limits of the office.

There were also "missing powers" in the Constitution. For example, the Constitution did not say who had the power to recognize other states or to proclaim neutrality. If the president and Senate must cooperate in the negotiation and ratification of a treaty, did they both have to agree when terminating a treaty? If Congress must declare war, does it also make peace? Who proclaims neutrality—the president, as commander in chief, or Congress because of its authority to declare war and regulate commerce? One way of determining who exercises these powers has been to assume that the foreign affairs powers explicitly granted imply other powers. Washington interpreted the president's power to appoint and receive ambassadors, for example, as implying that he also had the power to recognize or withhold recognition from other states.

The implied powers doctrine, however, leaves considerable room for struggles between the executive and legislative branches for control of the conduct of foreign affairs, especially as presidents enhanced their powers during this century. As Louis Henkin has noted, the powers specifically allocated to the president are so few that "a stranger reading the Constitution would get little inkling of such large presidential authority, for the powers

In the 1970s the United States formed a strategic relationship with China, which increasingly was in conflict with the Soviet Union. President Bush, a former ambassador to China, was eager to maintain that virtual alliance. Here he meets with Chinese party leader Zhao Ziyang soon after taking office. Later in 1989, he was criticized for reacting too leniently when China cruelly crushed a student-led pro-democracy movement.

explicitly vested in him are few and seem modest, far fewer and more modest than those bestowed upon Congress."[9] He continued, "It seems incredible that these few meager grants support the most powerful office in the world and the multivaried, wide-flung web-work of foreign activity of the most powerful nation in the world."[10]

Presidents in this century, especially since Franklin Roosevelt and World War II, have been particularly assertive. Facing external threats far graver than those of their predecessors, they generally did what they felt had to be done unless it was specifically forbidden by the Constitution, the courts, or Congress. (This is opposed to the theory that a president can do only what is specifically permitted.) In short, their constitutionally assigned and implied powers allowed presidents to act.

The second reason for presidential ascendancy is the ability to take the initiative diplomatically and, even more so, militarily. A president can express support for a nation so often that it virtually amounts to a defense treaty (for example, Israel);

can visit a beleaguered city like West Berlin, thus reaffirming America's commitment; can negotiate a treaty with friends or foes and place the Senate in the awkward position of repudiating the president and the nation's honor if it does not give its consent (which it does occasionally); can journey to a former adversary, thereby signaling a shift in relations (for example, Nixon's trip to China and later Russia); and can use the armed forces at will. It was the president who first sent troops into Korea to resist North Korean aggression, who ordered supplies sent in 1948 to a West Berlin blockaded by the Soviet Union, who commanded the blockade of Cuba during the "missile crisis" of 1962 to force the Soviets to withdraw their missiles. It was Presidents Kennedy and Johnson who saw a need to defend South Vietnam against the North in that divided country. Presidents have also sent military advisors into El Salvador and ordered the Central Intelligence Agency to overthrow governments they saw as hostile—including Iran, Guatamala, Chile, Cuba, and Nicaragua.

A third reason for the president's preeminence is access to enormous bureaucratic expertise. Congress has usually relied on executive information and interpretation of events; presidential knowledge equaled presidential leadership. The principal executive agencies outside the White House are the senior foreign policy departments—the State Department (chiefly responsible for conducting the nation's foreign relations), the Department of Defense (mainly responsible for the training, organizing, and use of the armed forces), and the CIA (with the functions of intelligence collection and evaluation and covert operations). The junior departments are the International Communications Agency or ICA (propaganda), the Agency for International Development (its initials, AID, state its purpose), and the Arms Control and Disarmament Agency or ACDA (whose title defines its tasks). In addition, the president can call on agencies whose jurisdictions are primarily domestic but who have an interest in special areas of foreign policy, such as Agriculture (food exports), Commerce (trade), Treasury (the value of the U.S. dollar), and Energy (oil imports and alternative sources of energy).

Foreign Policy and the Selection of Presidents ■

A reflection of the increasing importance of foreign policy and the president's role in it is the presidential candidates selected in both parties. From the Civil War to World War II, many governors became presidents—Hayes, Cleveland, McKinley, Theodore Roosevelt, Wilson, Harding, Coolidge, and Franklin Roosevelt. After World War II and until Vietnam, however, candidates were generally senators. Truman had been picked by Roosevelt as his vice president and succeeded on the president's death. He was elected in his own right over the favored Governor Dewey in 1948. Eisenhower was, of course, the exception. He was the general who had led the allied armies in the invasion of continental Europe and had become the first commander of the North Atlantic Treaty Organization (NATO). He thus had considerable diplomatic and military experience. He twice easily beat the Democratic presidential candidate, Governor Stevenson (1952 and 1956). After Eisenhower, Senators Kennedy, Johnson, and Nixon became presidents.

Why did so many of the postwar presidents and vice presidents (Barkley, Nixon, Johnson, and Humphrey) as well as many of the competing candidates in both parties come from the Senate? The answer appears to be that the Senate, as the upper body, has been most active in foreign policy. The Senate Foreign Relations Committee has long been its most prestigious committee. Senators are exposed to debates on foreign policy issues. Indeed, those who ran successfully for their party's presidential or vice presidential nomination were all members of either the Foreign Relations Committee or the Armed Services Committee. Those who ran unsuccessfully the first time to be their party's top candidates and were successful the second time had all joined one of these committees in the meantime. Senators, in short, had "Washington experience" and some exposure to foreign policy issues.

Governors had only domestic experience, which was enough before the United States became a world power. While a few governors had foreign policy exposure, only two became presidential candidates (as noted, Dewey and Stevenson). One (Agnew) did not run, but was chosen by Nixon in 1968. Others tried but failed to become their party's leaders. Carter in 1976 was the first successful governor since World War II. He became the Democratic standard-bearer after the Vietnam War and the disillusionment with America's global role, the Watergate scandal, and the increased attention to domestic problems (especially civil rights and poverty). Washington experience was the last thing the country wanted, which was ideal for a virtually unknown ex-governor.

Another ex-governor, Ronald Reagan, used the same anti-Washington theme successfully against Carter himself four years later, at a time when high inflation and unemployment made the economy a prime issue. But with Walter Mondale's defeat in 1984 and the end of President Reagan's term in office, most of the candidates in both parties for the presidency have again come from the Washington establishment. The Republican contest for the presidential nomination in 1988 came down to Vice President Bush and Robert Dole, the Senate majority leader.

Still, if foreign policy experience definitely matters, the 1988 election was probably the first since World War II in which the Soviet threat was not a major issue. Michael Dukakis approved of the Reagan administration's moves toward arms control, and he promised continuity in Soviet-American relations. Bush made much of his experience as vice president and tried to portray Dukakis as weak on foreign and defense policy. He cited Dukakis's previous support of a "freeze" in

Politicians often travel abroad to gain media publicity and boost their prestige in the United States. Dan Quayle, shown here in Southeast Asia, has also visited Central America. Foreign travel helps keep vice presidents out of the president's hair. It also provides them with knowledge that may be useful some day should they succeed the president.

the development of nuclear weapons; a freeze, he argued, would have eliminated Soviet incentive to negotiate the elimination of an entire class of arms, intermediate-range nuclear weapons. On the whole, Bush succeeded in conveying an impression that Dukakis was too moralistic on foreign policy to keep and use American military strength, but what was more striking was that American-Soviet relations had been placed on the back burner. A majority of Americans believed that the economic competition with our allies posed a greater threat to national security. President Bush's first appointment was symbolic. By naming James Baker, the former secretary of the treasury, to be his secretary of state, he recognized that economic issues have become a critical ingredient of foreign policy.

Executive Organization for Foreign Policy

Presidents can call on considerable bureaucratic expertise in formulating foreign policy. The problem for presidents is the diversity of viewpoints and policy recommendations they receive. Each department and agency has its own specific perspective on policy; indeed, different groups within each department view the world and what the United States should do from their own vantage point. Thus, State Department and Defense Department views are likely to be different because foreign service officers and military officers are trained differently and see foreign policy issues in different ways. But State is further divided into regional and functional bureaus. Defense, in turn, is divided into Army, Navy, and Air Force; each of these is further subdivided by the branches of each service. Thus, there are many "actors."

There is rarely a correct point of view on any single foreign policy issue; there are only competing versions of the correct policy from each actor. The result is called *bureaucratic politics:* conflict among the actors participating in a specific decision and, on the opposite side, efforts to reconcile these conflicting views by negotiating compromises to arrive at some decision. This may, of course, be impossible. Then a stalemate results, and no decision is made because no single policy attracts a majority of actors. Or the result may be a compromise so vaguely written that each actor continues to act independently. Or an agreement may allow policy to move only one step ahead on the path it has been moving on for months, if not years, already. No fundamental change in policy is likely to occur, even though circumstances may have altered and the old policy may no longer respond adequately to the new conditions.[11] The danger of bureaucratic participation and conflict is that the policy that is produced may not be the best policy for the problem it was intended to deal with. Yet the compromises were probably necessary to reach a decision at all.

How, then, is a stalemate or paralysis to be avoided? How can old policies be changed as circumstances change? How, above all, can presidents impose their priorities and viewpoints on a decentralized bureaucracy? And how, by the time a decision reaches them, can presidents avoid lower-level bureaucratic compromises that may not be the best way of dealing with the issue at hand and may leave them no real policy choices? Every president is likely to have strong feelings about specific policies toward certain countries or problems. And most presidents want to be sure they hear all sides of an issue before deciding which alternative proposal to accept.

Who will take the leadership role in daily policy making? Presidents are busy, often occupied with other political, domestic policy, or ceremonial tasks. The bureaucracy, left to itself, will continue to function, but its policies may lack coherence, avoid some problems, fail to deal adequately with others, and not reflect the president's preferences. Who, on the behalf of the president, will be the prime spokesperson and director of foreign policy making? Presidents have generally adopted one of two strategies: placing the secretary of state in charge, or assigning the role to the president's national security assistant in the White House.[12]

The Secretary of State as Policy Chief ■

The secretary of state is, in a way, the obvious individual to be the administration's top figure on

"Perspectives"

On Foreign Policy

"*I long ago made up my mind that no treaty . . . that gave room for a difference of opinion could ever pass the Senate . . . there will always be 34% of the Senate on the backguard side of every question. . . . A treaty entering the Senate is like a bull going into the arena; no one can say just how or when the blow will fall—but one thing is certain—it will never leave the arena alive.*"

—John Hay, secretary of state under President McKinley

"*I confess to increasingly serious misgivings about the ability of the Congress to play a constructive role in our foreign relations. . . . The trouble with the resurgent legislature of the late 1970s is not so much that it has gone too far, as that it has gone in the wrong direction, carping and meddling in the service of special interests but scarcely asserting itself through reflective deliberation on basic issues of national interest.*"

—Senator J. William Fulbright, former chairman, Senate Foreign Relations Committee

"*. . . Congress has strengths as well as weaknesses in its foreign policy-making role. The activism and assertiveness of Congress in foreign policy can be viewed positively. The representativeness of Congress and its accessibility remain its major sources of strength, and have ensured a healthy input of the people's opinions into foreign policy-making. They often convey directly to the executive the doubts and the confusions about policy as well as approval or disapproval. . . . When issues of peace, aid and recognition are subject to intense debate and discussion in a collegial body, policy is often strengthened.*"

—Lee H. Hamilton (U.S. House of Representatives from Indiana and chairman of the Subcommittee on Europe and the Middle East of the House Foreign Affairs Committee) and Michael H. Van Dusen (staff director of the subcommittee)

foreign policy issues. Foreign policy is, after all, the State Department's business, and the secretary is in charge of the department and the senior cabinet member. If the president makes it clear that the secretary is the prime foreign policy adviser and has the president's confidence—prerequisites for the strategy of placing the secretary in charge—the secretary will take a broad view and coordinate policy among the participating departments. Ideally, the nation's foreign policy should be consistent with its military and economic policies. Three postwar presidents—Truman, Eisenhower, and Ford—relied exclusively on strong secretaries of state—Acheson, Dulles, and Kissinger, respectively.

This strategy has its limits and may not work. The State Department has a reputation of being cautious, frequently timid, unimaginative, and slow to make decisions. One reason for this is its division along regional lines. The Department is

"[The] security of free peoples and the growth of freedom both demand a restoration of bipartisan consensus in American foreign policy. We disagree on some policy choices. But we are convinced that the American national purpose must at some point be fixed. If it is redefined—or even subject to redefinition—with every change of administration in Washington, the United States risks becoming a factor of inconstancy in the world. The national tendency to oscillate between exaggerated belligerence and unrealistic expectation will be magnified. Other nations—friends or adversaries—unable to gear their policies to American steadiness will go their own way, dooming the United States to growing irrelevance."

—Henry Kissinger and Cyrus Vance

". . . It appears that agreement with the administration even having a majority in the Congress often counts for little. It comes out that having reached agreement with the administration, one ought then to enter into separate external relations with the American Congress, and renegotiate . . . the agreement reached.

. . . With whom in America can we have dealings? . . . it is still not clear who exactly in the U.S. can speak in international relations on behalf of the United States."

—Genrikh A. Trofimenko, a Soviet observer (*commenting on the Senate's failure to consent to SALT II*)

Sources: Thomas A. Bailey, *A Diplomatic History of the American People,* 7th ed. (New York: Appleton-Century-Crofts, 1964), pp. 487–488; *New York Times,* April 7, 1984; "Making the Separation of Powers Work," *Foreign Affairs* (Fall 1978), pp. 31, 39; Henry A. Kissinger and Cyrus Vance, "Bipartisan Objectives for American Foreign Policy," *Foreign Affairs* (Summer 1988), p. 899; "Too Many Negotiators," *New York Times,* July 13, 1979.

therefore deeply divided on virtually any policy (e.g., the European desk versus the African desk), which hampers its ability to make clear-cut decisions. Another reason is that the department has no permanent constituency. It may attempt to define the "national interest," but foreign news is too often bad news. The department is often regarded suspiciously as a promoter of *foreign* views. It therefore has little popular support.

The contrast with the Defense Department is striking. While State is generally referred to as Foggy Bottom (a reflection on what many people conclude is its state of thinking), the military has more generally been identified with national pride and partriotism. This public appeal gives Defense an enormous advantage in bureaucratic struggles; and this advantage is reinforced because it has specific, well-organized constituents—veterans' groups, industries (business associations and labor unions) that produce weapons, and senators and representatives from states and districts that hold these industries, as well as military bases. The State Department is generally a "weak" department in terms of influence. Thus, State may not be in a position to provide foreign policy leadership and impose coherence on American policy. Even when presidents initially wanted State to play that role, their irritation with the department has often led them to look to someone else to assume this role. During the Kennedy-Johnson period, the secretary of defense emerged as the principal adviser.

An Alternative: The National Security Assistant

The other principal person in a position to advise the president is the national security assistant (NSA). Shortly after World War II, Congress established the National Security Council (NSC) by statute to ensure that all views on foreign issues would be heard and brought to the president's attention. In addition to the president and vice president, its members are the secretaries of state, defense, and treasury; the chair of the Joint Chiefs of Staff; the directors of the CIA and the Office of Management and Budget; and the chair of the Council of Economic Advisers. The president can also invite others to attend, such as the directors of ACDA and ICA. Presidents have not always paid much attention to the NSC, depending on their decision-making styles.

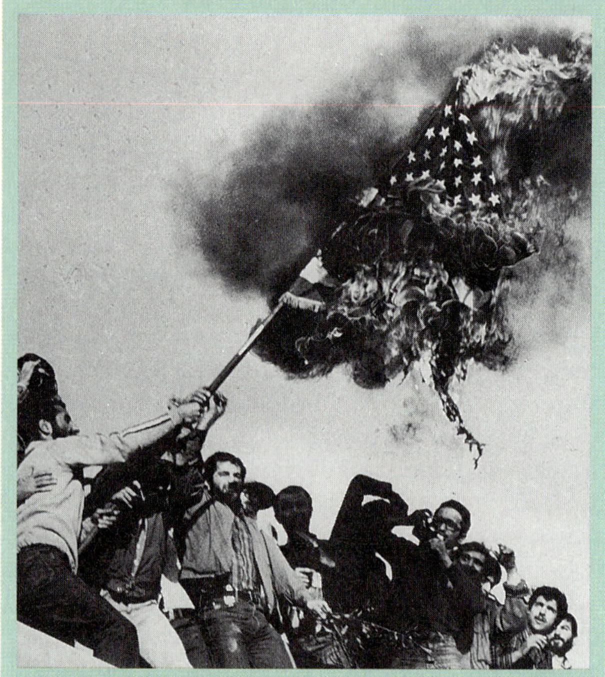

Iranian militants shortly after their takeover of the U.S. embassy in Teheran. The embassy staff was held hostage for 444 days, while the Carter administration appeared helpless to gain their release from the Shiite fundamentalist government of Iran. These events, which followed the 1979 collapse of the Shah, were a searing experience for Americans. One result was President Carter's defeat by Ronald Reagan in 1980.

Nevertheless, the NSA, who is the NSC staff director, has gained great publicity and prominence. As the United States has become more involved in international politics in this century, presidents have found it necessary and useful to have a foreign policy assistant in the White House whom they trust and to whom they feel personally or intellectually close. Long before the NSC was established in 1947, Wilson had Colonel House and Franklin Roosevelt had Harry Hopkins. But it was Kennedy who first appointed a prominent academic, McGeorge Bundy of Harvard, as his NSA. Lyndon Johnson kept Bundy on after Kennedy's assassination and after Bundy's resignation appointed W. W. Rostow of MIT (now at Texas).

But it was Nixon's appointment of Henry Kissinger, also from Harvard, that made the NSA visible and powerful. Kissinger clearly took charge; even before his later appointment as secretary of state, he was secretary in all but name. Who can recall the name of Nixon's first secretary of state? In contrast to the relative anonymity of Bundy and Rostow, Kissinger handled the strategic arms control talks (SALT), the opening to Communist China, and the Vietnam and Middle East peace negotiations—often with humor and style.[13] He became something of a public hero.

In contrast to Truman, Eisenhower, Ford, and Reagan, Kennedy and Nixon wanted to be their own secretaries of state. They therefore appointed weak secretaries. This trend toward presidents being their own secretaries of state reflects the fact that world events have forced presidents to devote more time to foreign affairs, whether they wish to do so or not. As this responsibility has grown and the bureaucracy has been unresponsive or divided on what to do, most presidents have looked for the "brilliant academic" who sat in an office down the hall from the Oval Office. This person was frequently available to discuss external problems, policy alternatives, and their pros and cons, and to anticipate future problems and find the weaknesses in the various bureaucratic positions.

No One in Charge: Disorganization in the Executive ■

When the president is unable to decide on a chief advisor, policy declarations can be confusing and inconsistent. President Carter did not want another Kissinger.[14] In Cyrus Vance, he appointed as secretary of state a respected figure who would be his number one man in foreign policy. But the NSA, Zbigniew Brzezinski, soon began to play a more visible role as his concerns about Soviet military strength in the Third World grew. The Soviet invasion of Afghanistan in December 1979 ended Vance's influence. He resigned shortly thereafter because the president went ahead with a failed attempt to rescue American diplomats held as hostages in the American Embassy in Iran. Carter himself had become a hard-liner.

President Reagan also wished to avoid public quarrels between the NSA and the secretary of state. He appointed a strong secretary of state, Alexander Haig, and a less well-known and assertive figure, Richard Allen, as NSA. Allen, a former business consultant, was supposed to play the role originally designed for his position—a largely neutral manager. He was to ensure that the president received all the necessary information and a full range of options to make decisions, coordinate the work of all the departments involved, and see that Reagan's decisions were carried out. But it was difficult to do this without authority, and Allen's influence in the White House was not great. Previous NSAs had direct access to the president, whom they briefed each morning and consulted with several times in a day. In turn, the bureaucracy knew that the NSA had the confidence of the president. Allen could get to the Oval Office only through Ed Meese. Totally inexperienced in foreign policy, Meese was the president's closest advisor and the real power in the White House. Allen's tasks became difficult to carry out.

His successor, William Clark, a former California judge and a long-time friend of the president, had direct access. The difficulty now was Clark's lack of knowledge, competence, and experience in foreign policy. This should have made him a good manager of conflicting positions among the president's advisors, and it might have strengthened the secretary of state's primacy. Instead, Haig was himself, as he put it, "mortally handicapped" by lack of regular access to a president uncomfortable with foreign policy issues. He too resigned.[15]

The White House staff had suspected Haig of trying to overshadow the president. His successor, George Schultz, an expert in international economics, but not politics, appeared to be more of a "team player." Clark became increasingly assertive on arms control, the Middle East, and Central American issues, and Schultz was saved from being overshadowed only when Clark resigned to become secretary of the interior.

Neither of Clark's successors had political experience or competence in foreign policy. Robert ("Bud") McFarlane, an ex-Marine and competent staff officer, could again reach the president mainly through his chief of staff, Meese's successor, Donald Regan. Frustrated as well by continuous conflict between the secretaries of state and defense, paralysis on key issues, and the president's lack of interest in foreign policy and short attention span, McFarlane quit after two years. He was replaced by acting admiral John Poindexter, who had no foreign policy experience whatsoever.

Like many in the post-Vietnam military, Poindexter distrusted the press and Congress, and he believed strongly in covert action. He conducted two on behalf of President Reagan. The first came when pro-Iranian terrorists seized a half-dozen American hostages in Lebanon.[16] Despite the president's firm public stance that the United States would not deal with terrorists, he decided to try to gain the hostages' release by a trade of arms. The

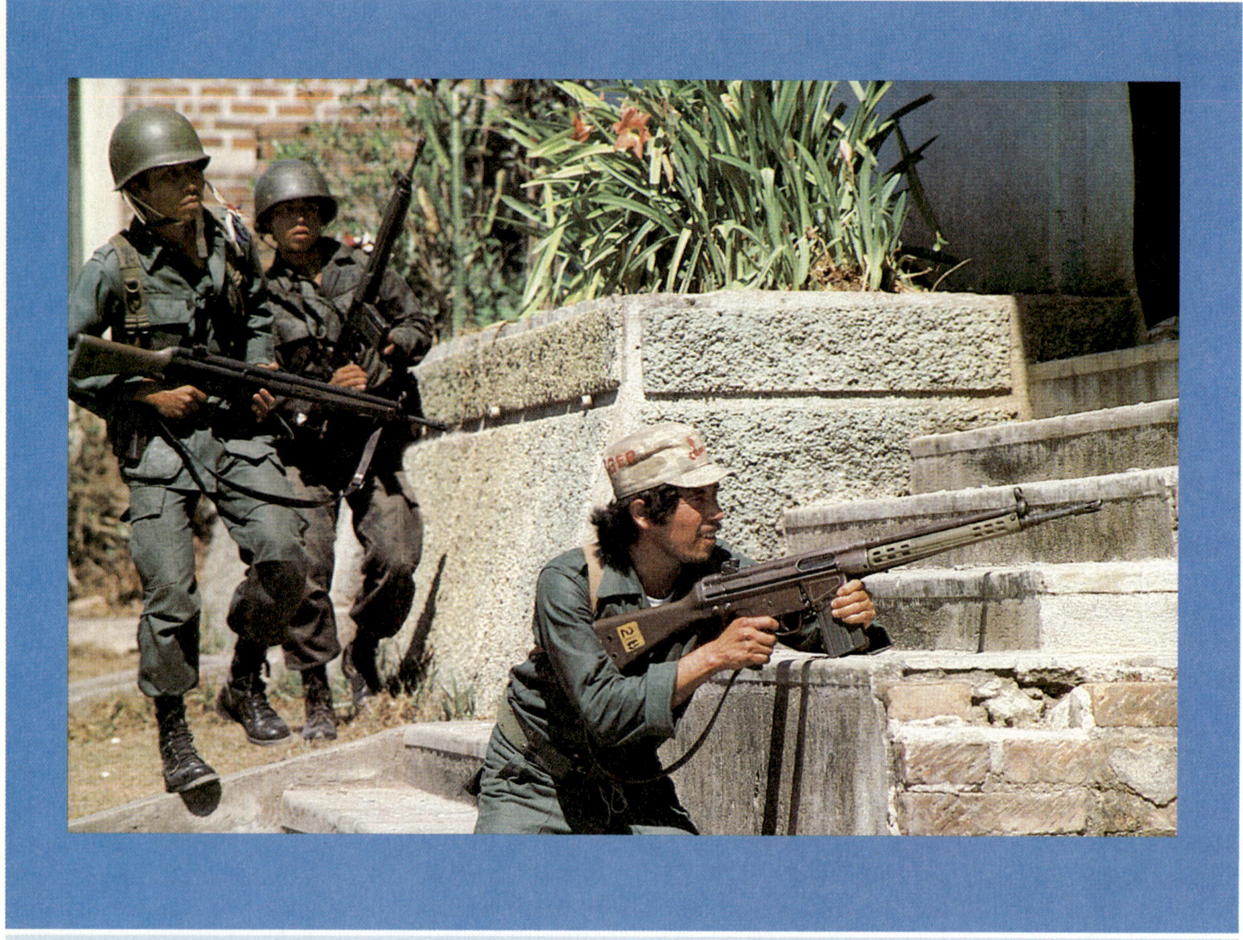

After the Sandanistas came to power in Nicaragua in 1979, they aligned themselves with the Soviet Union. Ronald Reagan, unlike earlier presidents, was constrained by public sentiment after Vietnam. He could neither use U.S. forces nor quietly conduct covert action to overthrow a foreign government. His Contra war led to failure, opposition in Congress, and Irangate.

trade had to be kept utterly secret. If it became known, it could undermine Reagan's credibility and weaken America's leadership; it would send shock waves through America's Arab friends, mainly oil sheiks afraid of an Iranian victory in its war with Iraq.

Poindexter was also in charge of the president's "covert war" against Nicaragua's Sandinista government after Congress opposed that action. The Sandinistas had come to power after a popular revolution overthrew a pro-American dictator. Now, turning on the business community, trade unions, the Catholic church, and other groups who had been their allies, they suppressed other parties, increased ties with Cuba and the Soviet Union, and helped the guerrillas fighting the government of neighboring El Salvador. In the wake of these events, the CIA organized and financed the contras, whom President Reagan called "freedom fighters." The CIA's stated purpose was to pressure the Sandinistas to halt supplies to the Salvadorean guerrillas; the real purpose, as became clear, was to overthrow the Sandinistas.

Opposition in Congress to the covert war grew. Especially in the Democratically controlled House, many feared another Vietnam. Others expressed sympathy, at least initially, for the Sandinista regime's ideological commitment to improving the lives of the mass of Nicaraguans; some leaders of the contras were said to be loyal followers of the former dictator and to disregard human rights. A series of sabatoge attacks by the CIA—without the knowledge and consent of Congress's intelligence committees—now enraged even the Republican Senate. A result was the Boland amendment, in which the House cut off military aid for the contras in 1984. The amendment prohibited the CIA, the Pentagon, or any other intelligence "entity" from militarily aiding the contras "directly or indirectly." Aid was restored only in 1986.

At the time of passage, Congress's intent seemed clear. No one in the administration then claimed that Boland did not apply to the president. The chief executive swears on taking office to execute the laws faithfully, even if Congress does not fund a preferred policy. No one claimed that officials could solicit money from wealthy Americans or foreign governments to finance the contras. But they did just that. The president later argued that he was not responsible—and anyway Boland never explicitly mentioned the NSC. It could not have done so; the NSC had never been an operating agency until the administration "privatized" the conduct of foreign policy!

What earned the affair such names as Irangate, Iranamuck, and Contradeception was that the two covert actions were deeply connected. Funds diverted from the sale of arms to Iran went to support the contras, even after it became clear that the Iranians were discouraging the release of all the hostages. (For every one released, the terrorists in Lebanon seized another.) President Reagan still wanted the hostages freed, and his NSA had a vested interest in continuing the arms sales to earn money for the contras.

The investigation in Congress never made clear whether the CIA chief was behind the scandals, although it seems plausible. What is known is that Poindexter and Lt. Col. Oliver North were deeply involved in both. They lied to Congress and bypassed the secretaries of state and defense (both of whom objected strongly to the arms deal with Iran). North secretly ran the war out of the NSC, which raised funds and recruited former military and CIA employees to take over the "private war." The NSC was never intended to be used for covert activities, which continued without regular review, even by the NSA's own staff. The covert action was very profitable to the arms dealers, but what aroused more concern was a dangerous precedent: A president who could not mobilize support for his policies bypassed Congress.

The discovery seriously weakened an administration already in its closing years, when presidents often become "lame ducks." The nation remembered how Iran had humiliated the United States for 444 days after it seized the U.S. embassy in 1979. Polls showed that a majority of Americans believed that the president knew of the diversion of funds to the contras, but a "smoking gun" was never found. Poindexter admitted that he normally went over his plans with the president before implementing them, but he took responsibility in this instance—and lost his job.

In 1986 Frank Carlucci became the fifth NSA in five years. A man with long experience in intelligence and defense matters, his task was to ensure that the NSC did what it was supposed to do. But the sudden resignation of Secretary of Defense Caspar Weinberger led to Carlucci's departure. General Colin Powell became NSA number six; competent, he lasted until the end of Reagan's term.

But the lesson of how not to run the NSC was secondary to the central problem—a "hands-off" president. President Reagan set broad goals but was unwilling to involve himself in the critical details of policy. Committed to ideological preconceptions, he refused to exercise real leadership on key issues, and until his last two years, he allowed neither the NSA nor the secretary of state to be his foreign policy leader. As in the Kennedy years, the secretary of defense was the primary force behind foreign policy; his focus was the military buildup and opposition to arms control.

Continuing Competition in the Conduct of Foreign Policy

It is understandable why presidents at the outset of their term express preference for either the secretary of state or the NSA—usually the former—to be chief advisor. Conflicting policy statements raise questions among friends and foes alike about what the foreign policy of the United States is and who is in charge. A further result is tension with Congress, which does not confirm the NSA's appointment. As a president's assistant, the NSA, again unlike a cabinet officer, cannot be called on to testify before congressional committees, even though all NSAs give television or newspaper interviews. At best, the assistant meets informally with, say, the Senate Foreign Relations Committee or individual members of Congress. But perhaps the greatest danger is that an NSA with strong policy preferences will not ensure that all points of view reach the president.

Public quarrels about the control of policy between the NSA and the secretary of state may be hard to avoid—and so may the increasing prominence of the assistant, for several reasons.[17] First, like other departments, State views policy from its own perspective. By contrast, the assistant, sitting in the White House at the apex of the government's structure, is in a better position to integrate the many strands of foreign policy.

Second, as we have noted, recent presidents have felt that they could not depend on State for quick, sound advice. They have seen that department as too often timid, unimaginative, unwilling to take risks. Presidents have therefore wanted the judgment of someone besides the secretary of state. The NSA has been that person.

Third, the State Department lacks expertise in areas that ought to be its strengths. Foreign service officers may lack knowledge of a particular region, despite frequent rotation there, or of foreign languages, especially Russian, Chinese, Japanese, and Arabic languages. State also can miss the skills needed to hold its own in areas of increasing specialization, such as science and technology, international economics, or even politics and the military.

Fourth, even if it could be the primary speaker on policy, it might not be the only one, or the most powerful. As economic issues become more prominent, Agriculture, Treasury, and Commerce as well as Defense tend to become powerful voices. Each represents a major sector of society, be it farming, the defense industry, or the banking and business community. All have political influence and can mobilize support for their views in Congress and among the public. State's chances of determining policy through coordinating these varying views are not great.

Fifth, many of its most essential skills may not help in a policy struggle. Diplomacy requires foreign service officers to be sensitive to the concerns of the countries in which they are posted. The State Department, after all, represents the American desire to get along with other nations. Its skills are in compromising differences and accommodating conflicting interests. Influence in Washington, however, requires an aggressive style.

Lastly, the NSA sits with the president at the critical juncture where foreign and domestic policies—and politics—intersect. Only the president can estimate the trade-off, especially the cost in domestic support of a particular foreign policy. The NSC assistant, right down the corridor from the Oval Office, can help the president decide. The NSA and the president can develop a relationship in which they speak frankly about all aspects of policy.

No president, in any event, can now do without the NSA. A strong NSC assistant—which does not necessarily mean one in the public limelight—is critical for effective foreign policy, even if it occasionally means some friction with other key figures. A new president may lack experience in foreign policy or prefer to focus on the domestic arena, but the stakes in foreign policy—the nation's security and prosperity—are too great. Reluctantly or eagerly, the president is forced to make critical decisions on foreign policy issues. It is the president's preeminence in foreign affairs that has elevated the NSA to current prominence. It will be interesting to watch President Bush, who claims foreign policy expertise, deal with his secretary of state, James Baker, and NSA Brent Scowcroft—both strong, knowledgeable, and experienced.

Crisis, Security, and Intermestic Policies[18]

Crises are characterized by surprise, perception of a great threat, a short time in which to act, and, above all, the likelihood of a military confrontation that could escalate to a nuclear clash. These characteristics ensure that crises are not handled either in routine fashion or by the bureaucracy. Rather, because vital interests are involved, the danger of war has risen enormously, and, in all probability if the crisis erupted unexpectedly, it would immediately "rise to the top"—to the president and the president's advisers. In extraordinary circumstances, standard operating procedures are largely bypassed.

The president is the central figure in crisis decision making. Presidents will quickly decide, as Truman did during the Berlin blockade in 1948 or Kennedy when informed of Russian missiles in Cuba in 1962, whether such actions constitute a threat, how grave the threat is, and whether the United States should react and how. Obviously, they consult their advisers. Some, like the secretaries of state and defense and chair of the Joint Chiefs of Staff, are members of the NSC. Others may not be. Presidents do not like to be told whom they must consult, as the congressional statute creating the NSC did in defining NSC membership. Kennedy created an Executive Council, composed of not only the above foreign policy officials but also members of his White House staff, other cabinet members, and ex-government officials whose judgment he trusted. Some presidents have consulted members of Congress they respect. Others, like Nixon in the spring of 1972 when the North Vietnamese launched a large-scale conventional invasion of South Vietnam after U.S. ground forces had been withdrawn from battle, consulted mainly with the national security assistant, the vice president, and the secretary of the treasury.

Given the brevity of crises, Congress and public opinion do not have time to criticize; indeed, criticism at such a time is generally condemned as unpatriotic. Thus, the separation of powers has no impact on crisis decision making. Nor, it must be added, do bureaucratic self-interest and conflicts usually erupt at such time. This is because the decisions are made at the top and the bureaucracy gets busy carrying out the president's decisions to defend American interests and avoid a military confrontation.

Security and intermestic policies are also formulated basically by the executive branch, but the president relies heavily on the various departments involved in a particular issue. In contrast to crises, these types of policies involve Congress and interest groups. They require the Senate's consent (treaties) or congressional approval, frequently because these policies require funding; because the law requires it (the War Powers Resolution requires such support if the president wants to use force); or because the president wants the support of congressional majorities to show the world the nation is united on a specific action, as in congressional resolutions. To avoid trouble later, a president may consult key legislative leaders and committees and seek their input. Sometimes some of these people, especially senators, attend negotiations. The assumption is that if they are in on the takeoff, Congress will have a vested interest in an issue and support that policy.

On intermestic issues, Congress is even more active because these are not only foreign policy issues but also domestic ones. While the foreign policy bureaucracies and congressional committees in both houses participate, so do the more numerous domestic executive agencies and legislative committees. Interest groups are also active. On security issues they are less active than on intermestic ones, but when key issues like the Panama Canal or SALT II become symbolic liberal-conservative issues, single-issue groups become very active, especially those who are opposed to the direction the issue is taking. On policies that affect the economy and society, more interest groups are active.

Thus, on crisis policy, presidents exercise the most leadership and influence. On security policies they still lead, although more bureaucratic politics are involved in the decision making; Congress, interest groups, and segments of public opinion are involved, although the extent of participation varies with the issue. And on intermestic policies, presidential leadership may be restrained even more—and may become nonexistent—because of the extensive roles played by congressional leaders, committees and subcommittees, interest groups, and public opinion.[19] In short, presidential leadership tends to be inversely related to the number of other

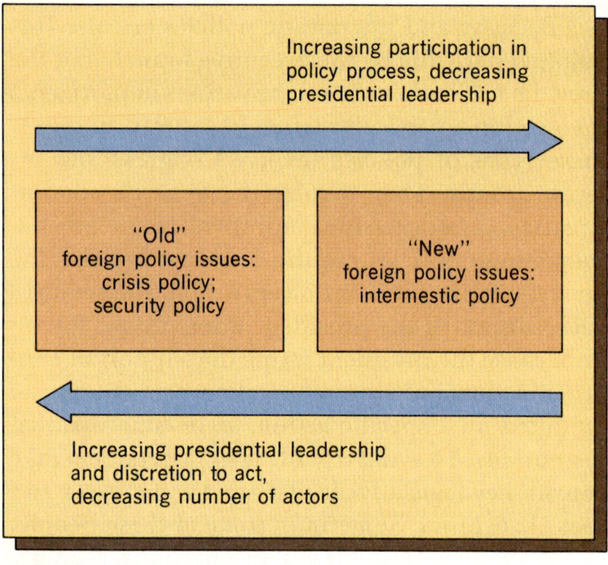

Figure 20–1 Presidential leadership on foreign policy.

executive and legislative actors interested in an issue (see Figure 20–1).

Congress and Foreign Policy After Vietnam

In the post-Vietnam period, a more assertive congressional role was generally welcomed. The war, which had bitterly divided the nation, was blamed on the executive. During the Cold War, when presidents had led the nation, they had accumulated too much power. They made life-and-death decisions virtually by themselves; indeed, the interventions in the Korean and Vietnamese wars had occurred in the absence of congressional declarations of war. The United States, it was often said, had become overcommitted. Congress ought therefore be more energetic in holding presidents accountable for their foreign policies. It should ensure that, instead of being a "global policeman," the United States would play a more responsible and limited role in the world. Restraints were placed on the president's ability to use force (the War Powers Act), on the CIA's covert operations, and on executive agreements as a way of getting around the treaty process.

During the Cold War the executive-legislative consensus on foreign policy had held the two branches of government together and permitted the president to exercise foreign policy leadership. With the major exception of policy toward Communist China and Asia in general, where there were genuine differences over policy, president and Congress tended to agree on policy after they forged their agreement on the containment policy in the late 1940s. Differences were mainly over tactics and the means to achieve specific goals, not over the purposes of the policy itself. Within the context of this shared consensus and congressional willingness to play a subordinate and secondary role, the institutional causes of executive-legislative conflict were overcome by bipartisanship. The Cold War was considered an emergency situation, comparable to a hot war, requiring strong and clear presidential direction and discretion in the conduct of policy. Vietnam, which suggested that for all the foreign policy expertise of the executive branch it had blundered badly, shattered the consensus on foreign policy.

In this new circumstance, the obstacles to executive-legislative cooperation now came to the fore: institutional rivalry, partisanship, the different electoral systems for the president and Congress, lack of party discipline and loyalty, the decentralized organization of Congress, and the resulting potential influence of interest groups. Indeed, the obstacles had become greater. Many of the reasons have been studied earlier in this book. The weakening of party leaders, along with mushrooming congressional subcommittees and their staffs, helped members of Congress gain the expertise to challenge the president. Where the Senate had traditionally overshadowed the House in foreign policy matters, now even House members commented that Congress had become 535 secretaries of state. The splintered subcommittee system also aided the growing power of interest groups, many with ideological agendas. Because bills had to go through several stages, well-financed economic interests, foreign governments, and single-interest lobbyists could bring pressure to bear at more points.

Presidential leadership became increasingly

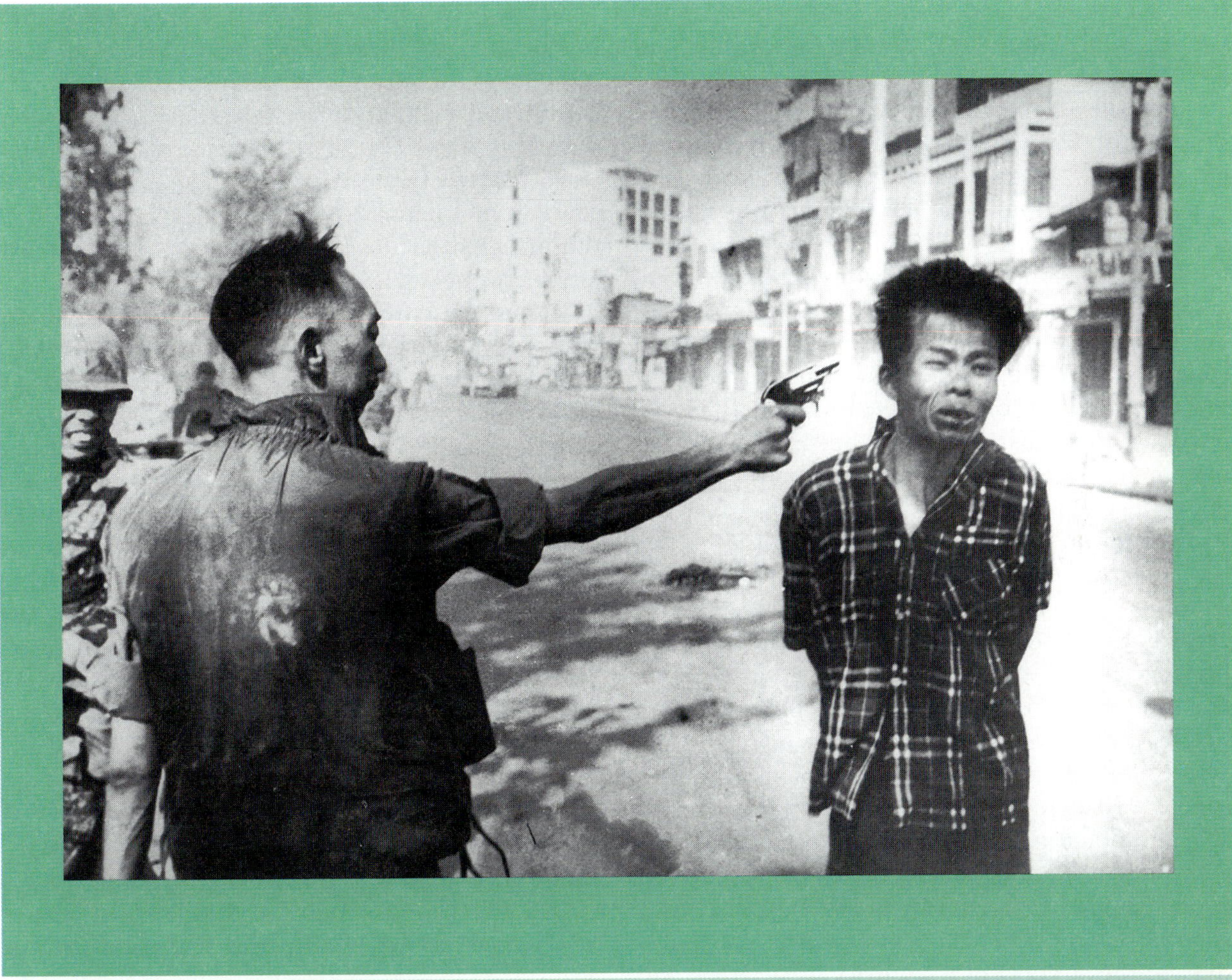

This widely publicized photo of South Vietnam's chief of police killing a Vietcong guerilla symbolized to many a war with no clear victory in sight. Vietnam shattered the Cold War policy consensus between Congress and the president as it bitterly divided America. Will the reemergence of a U.S.–Soviet detente reduce differences over foreign policy in the 1990s?

tested. The more open process meant the president could no longer rely on a few congressional leaders but had to organize broad coalitions on almost every initiative, and it became easier then ever to amend, delay, weaken, or kill policy recommendations in Congress (see Chapter 13).

How did all this translate into policy after Vietnam?[20] For one thing, it allowed Congress to weaken the executive's hand in pursuit of détente with the Soviet Union—a policy that Congress generally favored. Meanwhile, since the United States no longer held clear strategic superiority, the risks and costs of using force had become greater. The approach to containment of the Soviets had to change as well. Both Presidents Nixon and Ford sought to supplement military with economic power and to pursue such tactics as alignment with China, the other large Communist power, against Moscow. Given the Soviet failures in agriculture and industry, the administration wished to use food, technology, and credit—commercial agreements—to give Moscow incentives for détente and self-restraint.

But then Senator Henry Jackson (D–Wash.) proposed to allow trade between the two countries only if more Russian Jews were allowed to emigrate. Jackson, long a friend of Israel, was getting ready to seek the nomination for president, and he hoped to consolidate his support among Jewish voters. The Russians turned the trade agreement down. As a result, many contracts went to European countries, and the United States lost a powerful tool to moderate Soviet policy: If trade had developed, the Russians would have been fearful of losing items on which their economy had become dependent. Russian-Jewish emigration instead actually fell off.

The Senate also undermined arms control. Nixon, Ford, and Carter pursued strategic arms control to stabilize the deterrent balance; they hoped to slow a Soviet arms buildup at a time when the American program was essentially limited to putting more warheads on its missiles. The first Strategic Arms Limitation Talks had produced a set of SALT agreements in 1972 restraining offensive and defensive arms. All three presidents now continued negotiations. In 1979 Carter and Soviet leader Leonid Brezhnev initiated a treaty, but SALT II never received the Senate's two-thirds consent—despite the support of a majority of senators and the public and seven years of negotiations by three presidents, all of whom felt a treaty was in the national interest. It was finally withdrawn by Carter when the Soviets invaded Afghanistan.

President Carter used the Soviet action to save himself from a humiliating defeat, for which his own blunders were only partly responsible. He had closely involved the Senate in the process of negotiations, replaced a liberal head of the Arms Control and Development Agency (ACDA) with a conservative retired general, and placed a close ally of Senator Jackson, a powerful voice on arms control issues, on the negotiating team. Nevertheless, the SALT II treaty went down to defeat. The repudiation by one part of government of a popular commitment signed by the president as chief policymaker can happen only in the American system of separate institutions with shared powers.

Conservative Republicans were particularly hostile to SALT II. Ironically, it was President Reagan who was finally weaned from his dislike of arms control and who in 1987 arrived at an agreement with Moscow to eliminate intermediate-range missiles. The treaty passed by the huge margin of 93 to 4, but not before long Senate hearings at which the principal critics were some of Reagan's most ardent supporters.

Even policies that had little or nothing to do with the Soviet Union fell afoul of the executive-legislative tug of war. The Panama Canal treaty passed by only one vote after lengthy hearings and debates, despite considerable Senate participation in the treaty process. These treaties demonstrate why presidents since 1940 have preferred to avoid the Senate's power of consent and resorted instead to executive agreements.

Negotiations on the Middle East also ran into frequent congressional opposition. The United States, in seeking to mediate an Arab-Israeli peace, repeatedly found itself unable to press Israel to be more conciliatory. Two reasons were a largely uncritical view of Israeli lobby, perhaps the best organized in Washington.

While presidents were also pro-Israel, they realized that making peace in the Middle East required a more evenhanded U.S. role. As a former NSC expert on the Middle East has said:

> On-the-job training is the only way to learn about the problems with dealing with the press, Congress, and the pro-Israeli lobby when U.S. policy is seen as tilting too far toward the Arabs. On the substance of the Arab-Israeli dispute, the result of learning about the Middle East tends to move a president toward what might be called an evenhanded position. . . . By contrast, the result of gaining experience with the realities of domestic politics is to reinforce a president's tendency to emphasize one-sided support for Israel—particularly in election years and in public statements. . . . With a four-year presidential term, the effect of these two learning processes is to make the second and third years the best time for steady policymaking on the Middle East.[21]

The *intifada,* or uprising, which has continued since 1987 in the Israli-occupied West Bank and Gaza Strip. The struggle of Arab Palestinians for statehood led the Palestinian Liberation Organization (PLO) to offer to negotiate with Israel. It also paralyzed the Israli government, unable to decide whether to exchange territory for peace. The United States has tried to promote peace negotiations.

The brief 1967 Arab-Israeli war ended with Israeli occupation of considerable Arab land. An American-sponsored peace treaty returned the Sinai desert to Egypt in 1979, but Israel kept the West Bank and the Gaza strip and annexed other captured territories, including East Jerusalem. It also opposed the creation of a Palestinian state. Most of the Arab states felt that Egypt had "sold out" by making peace with Israel before the territorial and Palestinian issues were resolved. Because of Israel's almost complete dependence on the United States for military, economic, and political support, they held the United States responsible for not pressuring Israel to more compromises so that a comprehensive regional peace could be negotiated.

In 1988, for example, the Senate placed restrictions on arms sales to Kuwait because of con-

Voters, Elections, and Foreign Policy

One reason that Michael Dukakis lost his bid for president in 1988 was George Bush's experience in foreign policy. Even on foreign policy issues where citizens traditionally give Democrats the edge, voters felt that Bush would do a better job than his rival. And on issues where the Republican party is held superior, such as maintaining a strong national defense, Bush held an overwhelming advantage.

	Percent Believing That . . . Would Do a Better Job on the Issue			
	Democrats	**Republicans**	**Dukakis**	**Bush**
Establishing policies toward South Africa	45%	27%	34%	41%
Handling military spending	45	32	39	49
Persuading our allies to pay more of their own defense	40	38	37	45
Dealing with the situation in Central America	39	36	28	57
Keeping us out of war	37	38	36	47
Solving the crisis in the Mideast between Israel and its Arab neighbors	37	39	26	53
Dealing with terrorism	30	41	26	57
Negotiating arms control agreements	31	44	22	64
Handling relations with the Soviet Union	31	44	22	67
Guarding against Soviet aggression	27	48	24	62
Maintaining a strong national defense	26	52	22	66

Source: Americans Talk Security surveys no. 3 (The Daniel Yankelovich Group, February 1988, pp. 61–64); no. 4 (Marttila & Kiley, Inc., March 1988, p. 69); no. 11 (The Daniel Yankelovich Group, November 1988, pp. 190–198).

cerns about Israel's safety. That very day Saudi Arabia contracted with Britain to buy a $25 billion package of arms plus two British-designed air bases. The Saudis claimed that they were tired of being humiliated as Congress denied or restricted their arms requests; London did not exclude specific weapons or arms features. After the loss of Saudi business, the Senate and the executive worked out the arrangement for the Kuwaiti sale. But it was not just $2 billion at stake; it was influence with states which are generally pro-American and moderate, which control much of the world's oil reserves, and which with better weapons could more ably share the burden of regional defense. In the United States, unlike London, Paris, or Beijing, arms and other agreements involve a long, open political process—one that the conservative Arab monarchies find demeaning.

Congress and the Military

By the time the Reagan administration took office, public concern about the growing Soviet military strength had already resulted in a turnabout of the antimilitary mood of the early and middle 1970s. President Carter already had increased the defense budget. But after initial support in Congress for further armaments, executive-legislative conflict again broke out. At issue were Reagan's commitments to an almost $2 trillion military modernization program, a simultaneous tax cut, and his initial opposition to arms control. The battle became especially intense over the president's 1983 Strategic Defense Initiative (SDI) plan.

SDI was conceived to protect the nation's population against Soviet missiles. Once *both* nations had SDI in place—for Reagan offered to share American technology if the Russians could not come up with their own—missiles would become "impotent and obsolete."

Congressional opposition was strong, especially from the Democrats controlling the House. Critics worried that SDI would have to work perfectly—and work under the shock of a sudden attack that could destroy the United States forever. If even 20 percent of Soviet warheads got through, cities would be devastated. And that would amount to a high rate of success for a complex defense shield that could never be tested until the day it was necessary to use it. Worse, even assuming that scientists could invent the exotic laser and particle beams and place them on space stations, it would be only the beginning of a new defensive arms race. The Soviets would not only want their own SDI, they would also expand their offensive weapons to overcome ours. SDI would neither end the arms race nor abolish missiles. Instead it could destabilize the mutual deterrence between the superpowers—and at an enormous expense, during a time of growing budget deficits. Within the executive branch, the Joint Chiefs of Staff remained skeptical. They feared that the enormous budget for SDI could cut into all other military programs.

By 1986 opposition had spread to Republicans in the Senate, and funding for SDI was cut. The confrontation focused on the 1972 Anti-Ballistic Missile (ABM) treaty. More than any other agreement, it had become a symbol of arms control and restraint. Senator Sam Nunn (D–Ga.), who became chair of the Senate Armed Services Committee in 1986, reviewed the record of the ABM treaty negotiations. He concluded that it would prohibit tests of SDI in space; the administration would have to confine research to the laboratory. All but one of the negotiators of the treaty agreed with this interpretation. Since the Senate had consented to the ABM treaty, Nunn informed the White House that a change by the United States alone would lead to a constitutional crisis.[22]

Just to make sure, the Senate Armed Services Committee voted an amendment to the defense appropriations bill. With this, the defense budget itself blocked any testing of SDI before the end of President Reagan's term of office. Republicans argued that the amendment unconstitutionally restricted the president; the Democrats replied that they were protecting the Senate's role in making treaties.

Faced with continued confrontation and reductions in defense funding, President Reagan pushed for early deployment of SDI—to begin before he left office. He feared that if he could not in this way commit his successor and Congress to SDI, it would be downgraded to a bargaining chip in arms talks with the Soviet Union. He may well have been correct. The 1987 budget forced sharp cutbacks in key development projects.

That same year, early deployment was set back even further. A panel of leading physicists declared that it could not even be known if a system were feasible for at least ten years, perhaps not until the next century. The panel included scientists from the government's own laboratories, with access to SDI research. The House followed by rejecting an amendment to begin deployment by 1994; the vote was 302 to 121. When the Air Force general in charge of the program resigned, the Reagan administration announced a radical reduction in plans for deployment.

If there was any consensus by 1988, it was for continued research and development, but no decision to deploy SDI. Many in the Senate and the Defense Department advanced a partial system, to protect America's increasingly vulnerable land-based missiles. Senator Nunn himself, somewhat surprisingly, took that position. But Congress's nonpartisan Office of Technology Assessment lent support to critics. It concluded that a complex missile defense shield would probably suffer a "catastrophic failure" at the very moment it was needed.

From the start, SDI had been the president's "baby." It had no real bureaucratic or congressional lobby inside government, no major think-tank support outside. President Reagan had mobilized some support among military officials in charge of the program, industries involved in development, and loyal Republicans. Yet by the end of his term in office, its fate hinged on the outcome of the 1988 presidential election. Vice President Bush could hardly disavow it, but he talked of a more limited system in the face of growing budget constraints. Michael Dukakis opposed it. The result of their positions was to undermine further SDI's value as a bargaining chip with the Soviets.

Ironically, SDI may have brought the Soviet Union back to the bargaining table after they had walked out of arms control talks with President Reagan. Moscow was well aware of its inferiority in high technology, and it could not afford another expensive arms race. With the Russians eager to reach agreement, Reagan had the opportunity to maximize Soviet concessions in return for promising to restrict SDI research and delay deployment. But he refused to consider that compromise, even after early deployment had become impossible. Every study doubted that scientists would know if such exotic defenses as laser beams could be feasible until well into the next century. The administration that had created a potent bargaining tool had also largely wasted it.

President Bush will have to decide how to use SDI in Strategic Arms Reductions Talks (START). Any START agreement would greatly limit the Soviet missiles that SDI was designed to fight—while relegating SDI to a research program.

The War Powers Resolution

Congress had already asserted a stronger role in the making of foreign policy in 1974, shortly before President Nixon resigned his office, when it enacted the War Powers Resolution. Passed by just four votes over Nixon's veto, the resolution embodied the public's disillusionment with foreign military intervention after Vietnam. It required the president to report to Congress within 48 hours whenever American forces are sent into conflict or "where imminent involvement in hostilities is clearly indicated by the circumstances." If Congress does not approve the action within 60 days—or within 90 if the president cites "unaviodable necessity"—U.S. forces must be withdrawn.

No president has accepted the constitutionality of the War Powers Resolution. They have considered it an infringement of their power as commander in chief. They have informed Congress, as the resolution demands, when they have used force—but only when they have agreed that the situation involves "imminent involvement in hostilities." President Ford, for instance, announced that he had used the military to recover the U.S. merchant ship *Mayaguez,* seized in 1975 by Cambodia on the high seas. But he did not consult with the legislature any more than did his predecessors. President Carter did not notify Congress at all when, in 1980, he attempted the rescue of hostages held in Iran. He believed that a leak would have

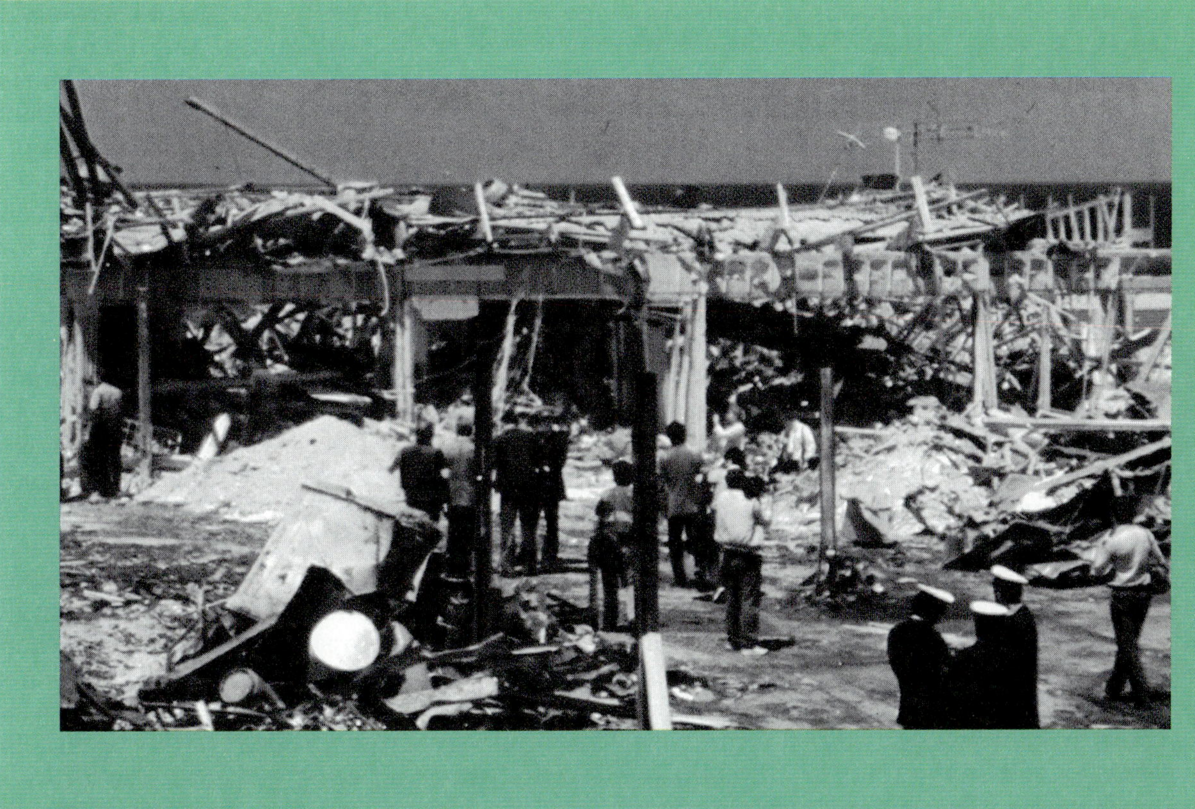

Was Libya's Col. Muammar Qaddafi behind the attack on a West Berlin disco in which American servicemen died? The Reagan administration thought so—and retaliated. Although Libya then restrained its anti-American campaign, two U.S. bombers were lost in the raid. President Reagan refused to invoke the War Powers Act, claiming that he already had the needed authority as commander-in-chief.

endangered the operation, and so he defined the use of American forces as humanitarian, not military. Since the rescue failed, no one in Congress was willing to make an issue over the War Powers Resolution.

President Reagan was even more determined to use force when he judged it necessary. He wanted to send Moscow and others a message that the post-Vietnam days of "isolationism" were over. Humiliations like the Iranian taking of hostages would no longer be tolerated, and further efforts by the Soviet Union to extend its influence in the Third World—as in Angola, Ethiopia, and South Yemen—were unacceptable. In key decisions the president refused to invoke the War Powers Resolution.

Some of Reagan's actions were popular. One was the 1983 invasion of Grenada, where U.S. troops overthrew a pro-Cuban regime. Another was a 1986 air attack, meant to punish Colonel Muhammar Qaddafi of Libya for alleged involvement in terrorist attacks on Americans. Both actions were brief; neither involved heavy casualties. Most important, they were judged successes. (In fact, thousands of troops could hardly have failed in Grenada against a few hundred Cuban construction workers. Nor could U.S. bombers against a small, relatively weak country like Libya, despite its Soviet equipment—although Qaddafi and other Libyan leaders emerged unharmed.) When Democrats in Congress sought to apply the War Powers Resolution to Grenada, they quickly changed their minds in the face of public acclaim for the intervention. The resolution had been passed to prevent another drawn-out conflict like Vietnam. It had no effect on quick strikes in Libya and Grenada, where success created its own support.

Nor has it applied to military assistance or to unofficial, "covert" war. In El Salvador, for example, the administration decided to oppose what it saw as Soviet, Cuban, and Nicaraguan intervention on behalf of Marxist guerrillas. It sent military and economic aid to government forces, along with 50 military advisors. Many in Congress opposed the administration. They felt that the roots of civil war in El Salvador were years of poverty, social injustice, and political oppression, not external assistance. The government's inability to control the "death squads," which eliminated many who hoped for change, became a symbol of what critics called the real problem—right-wing violence. Nevertheless, the administration persisted. Eventually, a more reform-minded government came to power in El Salvador, gained more of the military's support, improved the army's capacity to fight, and began to demonstrate some respect for human rights. While the issues of that civil war remained, early fears that the United States might be drawn into another Vietnam faded.

Similar fears did not go away so easily in Nicaragua. As we have seen, President Reagan believed that Nicaragua had become a "Cuba on the mainland," a center for subverting its Central American neighbors.[23] The administration organized and supported the contras, maneuvered the U.S. fleet off the Nicaraguan coasts, and sent troops on "exercises" in neighboring Honduras. When Congress in 1984 cut off military assistance in Nicaragua, the president instructed his staff to keep the contras together "body and soul." The result was the Iran-contra affair. Determined to overthrow the Sandinista government, the administration ignored Congress and the law by private conduct of foreign policy.

Memories of Vietnam hung heavily over Congress, which called intermittently, both before and after the Iran-contra affair, for invoking the War Powers Resolution. Many feared that U.S. troops would be involved in combat if the contras failed. Yet Congress was understandably reluctant to insist.[24] Directly challenging a president's power might restrain the commander in chief's ability to act in the future. Congress also feared blame for any policy failure if it compelled the withdrawal of U.S. forces.

Yet the resolution has had a double effect. Presidents may be restrained by awareness that Congress can invoke the War Powers Resolution. More important, however, they also know that Congress is watching—and is very sensitive to any acts that may result in hostilities. Consider the president's 1983 commitment of 1200 marines in Beirut, Lebanon, as part of an international peacekeeping force. The action followed an Israeli invasion of that country, its occupation by Israeli and Syrian forces, and fighting among the various factions—mainly Maronite Christian and Muslim. Reagan managed to gain from Congress 18 months to help stabilize the government of Lebanon and to get Syria and Israel to withdraw. In return, Congress required him to sign legislation authorizing the marines to stay; the act included a provision that the War Powers Resolution was in force, since marines had been fired on. Despite his signature, the president disavowed the act, saying that he could not cede authority he possessed as commander in chief. Yet shortly after 241 marines were killed by a single suicidal terrorist, who drove a truck loaded with explosives into a marine barrack, he withdrew U.S. forces.

The nation is simply unready for protracted intervention, with high costs in lives and money and without certain victory. That is why President Reagan, while publicly opposed to the Sandinistas, resorted to covert war. Unable to mobilize support for his policy from a majority of the country, he knew that to send forces into Nicaragua would cause an uproar in the United States. As his pullback of marines from Lebanon also showed, he was acutely aware of popular opposition to any long-term military commitment. He knew too that in 1984 he would again be running for president, and he could not afford a situation where he could no longer withdraw or stop the bleeding sore.

Despite the War Powers Resolution, however, Congress and the president remained in potential conflict. Reagan's leadership and willingness to commit the United States continued, and so did Congress's watchfulness. Both were illustrated in 1987, when the administration decided to reflag 11 Kuwaiti oil tankers and to provide them with a naval escort. Public hearings had given full publicity to the arms trade with Iran. The deal shocked the Arab world, especially oil sheiks living near Iran in the Persian Gulf. If Iran were to win its war with Iraq (then in its seventh year), the generally moderate, pro-Western Arab regimes might be in jeopardy. Kuwait, one of the sheikdoms, and an ally of Iraq in all but name, turned to Moscow to defend its tankers. Iraq, fearing a long war of attrition it would probably lose, had begun to attack oil tankers on the way to or from Iran; it hoped to cut off Iran's principal source of revenue for the war—oil exports. Kuwait asked for protection against Iran's air attacks in return, and Moscow responded positively. Washington now saw a chance to reassure the Arab oil kingdoms and to minimize Soviet influence in an area vital to the Western industrial democracies. It thus agreed to have the United States shield the Kuwaiti tankers.

Congress viewed the reflagging and the naval escort with apprehension. The administration calculated that the three or four warships stationed in the Gulf could safeguard the few tankers, but it ended up with almost 30 warships on the spot by early 1988. It made no plans for landing rights for American fighter planes or for ship repair facilities in the Arab states. Embarrassingly, America's preoccupation with high technology meant that it had no modern minesweepers; our European allies had to send some of theirs when Iran responded by laying mines left over from World War I. But Congress's main concern was American involvement: How long and deep would it become?

Both houses of Congress suggested that the administration postpone reflagging. When that failed, they repeatedly objected to the president's refusal to invoke the War Powers Resolution. It seemed that hostilities were indeed "imminent." The Navy paid sailors extra money for dangerous duty in the Gulf, and several shooting incidents with Iran did occur. However, Reagan feared that, under the resolution, Congress would compel withdrawal in 60 days if Iran attacked an American ship with major loss of life. In fact, if the War Powers Resolution were in place, it might even give Iran incentive to attack in order to force the United States to pull back.

The war ended in 1988, and the navy withdrew some of its ships. Nevertheless, the War Powers Resolution continued to raise concerns among friends and allies who depend on American protection. They questioned the reliability of U.S. commitments and, despite the Persian Gulf involvement, our steadfastness under fire. The resolution also remained a point of contention between the branches of government. On both sides, frustration ran high. The president refused to accept the authority of the War Powers Resolution, while the Senate wanted it rewritten so that Congress could not be shunted aside in the basic decisions of war and peace. It remains on the books in the Bush administration.

Democratic-Republican Differences on Foreign Policy ■

Executive-legislative conflict has been symptomatic of a deeper set of differences between the two parties. Vietnam destroyed the bipartisan consensus of the Cold War period, a consensus in which Democratic administrations had given priority to the East-West struggle and had not hesitated to use force (Korea, Vietnam) or the threat of force (Berlin, Cuba) in pursuit of containing Soviet-led communism.[25] Since Vietnam, it has been Republican administrations that still hold the traditional view of the Soviet Union as an aggressive, expansionist state and propose the need for containment, if necessary with the use or threat of force. Even more important, Soviet and proxy (mainly Cuban) interventions in Angola, Ethiopia, and South Yemen have been viewed as the result of Moscow's reading of a lack of will in Washington. The Democrats, as the Carter administration showed repeatedly in the days before the Soviet invasion of Afghanistan in

1979, no longer shared these perceptions. While Democrats admitted that the Soviet Union could not be wished away, they explained Soviet intentions and the growth of Soviet power more as defensive reactions to U.S. policies than as innate Soviet ambitions. Thus the counsel was for a more restrained U.S. policy. Arms control became the focus of policy toward Moscow.

More broadly and significantly, the Democrats tended to look at the world less in East-West terms than in terms of North and South: the Western industrial world and the Third World. Soviet interventions in the Third World were explained in terms of regional, national, or domestic racial and socio-economic tensions. If these local problems could be resolved, there would be no opportunities for the Soviets to exploit.

This shift from an East-West to a North-South perspective, from security and military to socio-economic issues, especially the gap between the rich and poor nations of the world, from balance of power to "world order" concerns, reflected in part a reaction to Vietnam, which the Democrats had led the country into and which had bitterly divided the party afterward and resulted in the losses of the presidential elections of 1968 and 1972. Another key reason for the shift was the Democrats' base among the poorer elements of society in this country. In a more constrained economy, which could no longer afford simultaneously high wages, large welfare payments, and sizable defense expenditures, Reagan rearmed the nation and cut social services. The Democratic party's emphasis was on providing more butter even if this entailed fewer guns. This anti-interventionist position, plus concern for preserving the social services for their constituents, explains the Democrats' strong position against the MX missile, which the president claimed was necessary to modernize the U.S. deterrent force. (This did not mean that there was no constituency within the Republican party for a slower defense buildup, for the business community was fearful of the Reagan deficits as well as the higher taxes that might be necessary to reduce them.)

Explaining Soviet policy essentially in defensive terms, with the overtone that if the United States acted with greater restraint Moscow would follow suit, and focusing on arms control in order to reduce the possibilities of an arms race and of increased tensions and possibly war became the basis for a concentration on the poor-rich nations gap that fitted the Democratic party well. Long the speaker for the less privileged at home, concerned for their welfare, the party in the 1980s became the home for many non-Cuban Hispanic voters; its older black constituency strengthened this orientation, as aggressive leaders like the Reverend Jesse Jackson in 1984 and even more effectively in 1988 articulated Third World views with their emphasis on the international order's injustice, the West's responsibility for this injustice, and the need to uplift the world's poor. This emphasis on helping the poor was psychologically more congenial to the party than "power politics."

The former foreign policy consensus had ironically been the product of an effort by Cold War liberals within the Democratic party. They had pursued a hard-line policy toward the Soviet Union. Precisely because the party was liberal, concerned with issues of individual freedom and dignity and social justice at home, it was also hawkish vis-á-vis a totalitarian Soviet Union. Freedom and justice were at stake internationally too. But Cold War liberals largely ceased to exist within the party after Vietnam, and the label became a contradiction in terms. To be a liberal in the 1970s and 1980s was to be critical of the hard-line foreign policy stances and large defense budgets so characteristic of the earlier Truman, Kennedy, and Johnson administrations and now the Republican administrations. In the words of the 1984 Democratic platform, the principal threats to the nation which, it admitted, provided opportunities for Soviet intervention, are "poverty, repression and despair. Against adversaries such as these, military force is of limited value." As we have frequently seen, the 1988 presidential campaign suggested that these interparty differences remain largely intact.

Foreign Policy and the Democratic Dilemma ■

The concern at the end of World War II that America's political institutions might not be able to cope effectively with foreign policy does not

Secretary of State James Baker negotiating with Soviet President Mikhail Gorbachev in the Kremlin. Given an economy unable to provide the Soviet people with such basics as soap, butter, and meat, Gorbachev sought to relax the Cold War. Moscow's need to cut heavy military expenditures may promise new arms control agreements—on both nuclear and conventional forces.

seem unwarranted in retrospect. During the Cold War, it was clear who the enemy was; there was broad agreement about what to do. The "clear and present" danger united the nation and led to extensive executive-legislative cooperation. These exceptional conditions no longer exist in a considerably more complex world in which the Soviet Union is only one—though still widely considered the most important—country or issue with which the United States must cope. Today, in the post-Vietnam era, comes the real test of de Tocqueville's prophesy: Will America's political institutions work together responsibly? When the two branches, the executive and the legislative, pull in opposite directions frequently and over a prolonged period of time, American foreign policy is bound to lose coherence, effectiveness, and—in foreign eyes, allied and hostile—credibility. It may well be that, as has been said, the Constitution is an invitation to struggle over foreign policy, but no one can "foresee . . . the consequences of that struggle in the nuclear age." [26] Presidentially appointed bipartisan commissions to bridge executive-legislative differences, as on Social Security, the MX, the Central America during the Reagan administration, are not long-run solutions. And it is clear that the American people like a divided government. In 1988, while electing a Republican president for the fifth time in the last six elections—and the seventh in the last ten—they strengthened the Democratic majority in Congress.

Inherent in this institutional rivalry is the more basic democratic dilemma. For the problem is not only the conduct of an effective foreign policy; more fundamentally, it is the preservation of our democratic values. On the one hand, our democracy is deliberately based on checks and balances, intended to prevent a concentration of power so vast that it would lead to an abuse of power and to domestic tyranny. On the other hand, foreign policy requires a powerful executive to protect American democracy from external threats. The key question is whether America's democratic domestic order is compatible with an executive powerful enough to protect the nation so that it can be secure and continue to enjoy its democratic way of life. Will the nation lose its democratic soul in trying to protect its security, or will its security become endangered as the nation becomes the victim of its democratic organization?

America's governmental institutions were designed to check domestic tyranny and preserve liberty. Are they also capable of making policy to deal with external threats to this nation's security and well-being while simultaneously preserving democracy at home at a time when the two parties disagree fundamentally on foreign policy—when they no longer see the world in the same way? Is it true, as a former Democratic presidential assistant has written:

> A particular shortcoming in need of remedy is the structural inability of our government to propose, legislate and administer a balanced program for governing. In parliamentary terms, one might say that under the U.S. Constitution it is not feasible to "form a government." The separation of powers between the legislative and executive branches, whatever its merits in 1793, has become a structure that almost guarantees stalemate today. As we wonder why we are having such a difficult time making decisions we all know must be made, and projecting our power and leadership, we should reflect on whether this is one big reason.[27]

It has been said that a house divided against itself cannot stand. Can our national government? Will it be able during the 1990s to govern, to make the tough choices it must make? Or will confrontation and stalemate be the basic pattern of the Bush administration? Ironically, it may be the Soviet Union's efforts to solve its domestic problems that may reduce executive–legislative conflicts on the role of the United States in the world.

While the United States, Japan, and Western Europe move into a postindustrial phase, the Soviet Union finds that its economy, able to produce only a plentiful supply of arms, can neither feed its people adequately, provide them with the necessities of life—even such items as soap and razor blades—nor keep up technologically with the West. Faced with the need to restructure (*perestroika*) its economic and political systems, and not lose its superpower rank, Mikhail Gorbachev, the dynamic Soviet leader since 1985, found it necessary to shift gears on Soviet foreign policy. Eliminating the Western perception of the Soviet Union as a threat, and achieving nuclear and conventional arms control agreements to save money that could then be invested in the ailing Soviet economy, he also sought to attract Western credits, technology, and trade to help revitalize his country. In addition, he withdrew Soviet troops from Afghanistan, and pressured Cuba to end its intervention in both Angola and Southern Africa, and Vietnam to withdraw its forces from Cambodia.

But, and perhaps most unexpectedly, Gorbachev fought to unburden Moscow of Eastern Europe. Because preserving Eastern Europe was economically costly and intermittently required military suppression of popular efforts to get rid of the Communist-imposed governments there, Gorbachev chose to tolerate domestic changes within Eastern Europe if the countries there remained members of the Warsaw Treaty Organization, which protected Soviet security. In 1989, Poland became the first eastern European country to install a non-Communist government; Hungary changed its name from People's Republic to simply Republic of Hungary; and the Communist party, in order to compete in free elections scheduled for 1990, changed its name to a democratic socialist one.

Most surprising of all, in response to thousands of East Germans fleeing their country to West Germany, and mass demonstrations in several of its cities, East Germany changed its leader and half its politboro, and, in a most dramatic move, opened up the Berlin Wall. Built in 1961, and ever since a symbol of the Cold War's underlying theme—freedom versus tyranny—its opening represented the current trend in Eastern Europe: "de-communization." The shift of the Eastern European community has been increasingly toward greater political pluralism and the use of market forces to recover economically.

As the old Cold War tensions died and the Soviet Union found itself absorbed domestically, a long remission of the Cold War, if not its end, appeared likely. With it the institutional and political concerns about the conduct of American foreign policy declined as well. The key issue became presidential leadership and the wisdom of American policy in the creation and management of a post-Cold War world.

Summary

- The decision-making processes and the actors involved in foreign policy differ according to whether the policy is a crisis, security, or intermestic issue.
- The "old" foreign policy, revolving around security issues, is still mainly made by a relatively small group of political leaders and professional officers in the major foreign policy bureaucracies. The "new" foreign policy, revolving around economic issues, includes many bureaucracies whose prime jurisdiction is domestic, as well as interest groups and Congress, whose prime interests are domestic.
- The central figure in executive decision making, the president, chooses whether to organize it around the secretary of state or the national security assistant. The degree of presidential leadership possible on a particular issue reflects the kind of policy being pursued; the number of executive, legislative, and interest-group actors involved in the policy process; and the presence or absence of consensus.
- In a period of consensus, Congress and public opinion follow presidential leadership. In a period of disagreement on fundamental policy, including disagreement on key issues between the two parties, the executive-legislative conflict is accentuated. Every major issue becomes a matter of controversy, division, and indecision. Each lead to inaction, to ineffective action, or even to unilateral—and, as in the Iran-contra affair, illegal—executive action.
- Its decentralized structure makes Congress virtually incapable of forming a timely, coherent policy. It makes it easier for Congress to weaken or stop a policy.
- The policy process has become more democratized by including more participants. However, the degree of participation in policy by Congress, interest groups, and public opinion depends on the issue. Intermestic policies mobilize all three to great activity and are therefore the most difficult to resolve. In a crisis, the president dominates policy making. Security policy falls between these two types; the president exercises leadership but no longer has a "free hand."
- The separation of powers is critical to the conduct of U.S. foreign policy. It may well also be the weakest link in the policy process, an obstacle to what de Toqueville called the perseverence of a fixed design in foreign policy.

Readings on Foreign Policy

Cheever, Daniel S., and H. Field Haviland. 1952. *American Foreign Policy and the Separation of Powers.* Cambridge, Mass.: Harvard University Press. An early assessment of the conduct of the early days of the containment policy and the successes and failures of bipartisanship.

Crabb, Cecil V., Jr. 1957. *Bipartisanship Foreign Policy.* New York: Row, Peterson. A review and evaluation of how the separation of powers and bipartisanship affected American foreign policy through the mid-1950s.

Destler I. M. 1974. *Presidents, Bureaucrats, and Foreign Policy.* Princeton, N.J.: Princeton University Press. An analysis of how the "bureaucratic politics" in the executive branch can most effectively be harnessed for the making and carrying out of foreign policy.

Destler, I. M., Leslie H. Gelb, and Anthony Lake. 1984. *The Unmaking of American Foreign Policy.* New York: Simon & Schuster. An easy-to-read account of the post-Vietnam direction of the Cold War consensus and how it has made the conduct of foreign policy much more difficult.

George, Alexander L. 1980. *Presidential Decisionmaking in Foreign Policy.* Boulder, Colo.: Westview Press. An instructive analysis that focuses on the need for presidents to be surrounded by a "multiple advocacy" system and not become the prisoners of one single point of view on policy.

Holsti, Ole R., and James N. Rosenau. 1984. *American Leadership in World Affairs.* Boston: Allen & Unwin. A detailed analysis of three separate schools of thinking about the nature of the post-Vietnam world and the role the United States should play in it.

Inderfurth, Karl F., and Loch K. Johnson, eds. 1988. *Decisions of the Highest Order.* Pacific Grove, Calif.: Brooks/Cole. A collection of readings that provide a superb perspective on the National Security Council, its evolution, its directors, and its performance.

Kissinger, Henry A. 1979. *White House Years.* Boston: Little, Brown. A book unsurpassed for its insights into American and foreign policymakers and the difficulties of conducting U.S. foreign policy.

Quandt, William B. 1986. *Camp David.* Washington, D.C.: Brookings Institution. A detailed case study by a participant in the negotiations leading to the Egyptian-Israeli peace, showing how much domestic politics affects—and hinders—the making and execution of foreign policy.

Spanier, John. 1988. *American Foreign Policy since World War II,* 11th ed. Washington, D.C.: Congressional Quarterly Press. An analysis of U.S. foreign policy through the first two years of the second Reagan administration.

Spanier, John, and Eric Uslaner. 1989. *American Foreign Policy and the Democratic Dilemmas.* Pacific Grove, Calif.: Brooks/Cole. An examination of the principal actors making foreign policy: the White House, the executive bureaucracies, the Congress, interset groups and political action committees, and public opinion.

Appendix

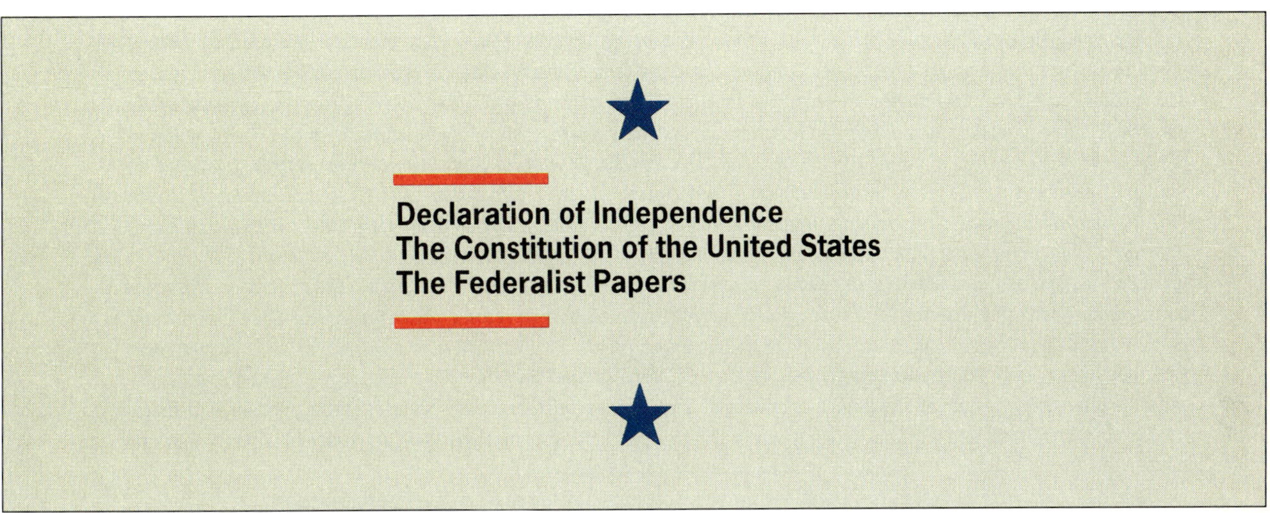
Declaration of Independence
The Constitution of the United States
The Federalist Papers

The Declaration of Independence

in Congress, July 4, 1776

The unanimous Declaration of the thirteen united States of America,

When in the Course of human events, it becomes necessary for one people to dissolve the political bands which have connected them with another, and to assume among the Powers of the earth, the separate and equal station to which the Laws of Nature and of Nature's God entitle them, a decent respect to the opinions of mankind requires that they should declare the causes which impel them to the separation.

We hold these truths to be self-evident, that all men are created equal, that they are endowed by their Creator with certain unalienable Rights, that among these are Life, Liberty and the pursuit of Happiness. That to secure these rights, Governments are instituted among Men, deriving their just powers from the consent of the governed. That whenever any Form of Government becomes destructive of these ends, it is the Right of the People to alter or to abolish it, and to institute new Government, laying its foundation on such principles and organizing its powers in such form, as to them shall seem most likely to effect their Safety and Happiness. Prudence, indeed, will dictate that Governments long established should not be changed for light and transient causes; and accordingly all experience hath shown, that mankind are more disposed to suffer, while evils are sufferable, than to right themselves by abolishing the forms to which they are accustomed. But when a long train of abuses and usurpations, pursuing invariably the same Object evinces a design to reduce them under absolute Despotism, it is their right, it is their duty, to throw off such Government, and to provide new Guards for their future security.—Such has been the patient sufferance of these Colonies; and such is now the necessity which constrains them to alter their former Systems of Government. The history of the present King of Great Britain is a history of repeated injuries and usurpations, all having in direct object the establishment of an absolute Tyranny over these States. To prove this, let Facts be submitted to a candid world.

He has refused his Assent to Laws, the most wholesome and necessary for the public good.

He has forbidden his Governors to pass Laws of immediate and pressing importance, unless suspended in their operation till his Assent should be obtained; and when so suspended, he has utterly neglected to attend to them.

He has refused to pass other Laws for the accommodation of large districts of people, unless those people would relinquish the right of Representation in the Legislature, a right inestimable to them and formidable to tyrants only.

He has called together legislative bodies at places unusual, uncomfortable, and distant from the depository of their Public Records, for the sole purpose of fatiguing them into compliance with his measures.

He has dissolved Representative Houses repeatedly, for opposing with manly firmness his invasions on the rights of the people.

He has refused for a long time, after such dissolutions, to cause others to be elected; whereby the Legislative Powers, incapable of Annihilation, have returned to the People at large for their exercise; the State remaining in the meantime exposed to all the dangers of invasion from without, and convulsions within.

He has endeavoured to prevent the population of these States; for that purpose obstructing the Laws for Naturalization of Foreigners; refusing to pass others to encourage their migrations hither, and raising the conditions of new Appropriations of Lands.

He has obstructed the Administration of Justice, by refusing his Assent to Laws for establishing Judiciary Powers.

He has made Judges dependent on his Will alone, for the tenure of their offices, and the amount and payment of their salaries.

He has erected a multitude of New Offices, and sent hither swarms of Officers to harass our people; and eat out their substance.

He has kept among us, in times of peace, Standing Armies without the Consent of our legislatures.

He has affected to render the Military independent of and superior to the Civil Power.

He has combined with others to subject us to a jurisdiction foreign to our constitution, and unacknowledged by our laws; giving his Assent to their acts of pretended Legislation:

For quartering large bodies of armed troops among us:

For protecting them, by a mock Trial, from Punishment for any Murders which they should commit on the inhabitants of these States:

For cutting off our Trade with all parts of the world:

For imposing taxes on us without our Consent:

For depriving us in many cases, of the benefits of Trial of Jury:

For transporting us beyond Seas to be tried for pretended offences:

For abolishing the free System of English Laws in a neighboring Province, establishing therein an Arbitrary government, and enlarging its Boundaries so as to render it at once an example and fit instrument for introducing the same absolute rule into these Colonies:

For taking away our Charters, abolishing our most valuable Laws, and altering fundamentally the Forms of our Governments:

For suspending our own Legislatures, and declaring themselves invested with Power to legislate for us in all cases whatsoever.

He has abdicated Government here, by declaring us out of his Protection and waging War against us.

He has plundered our seas, ravaged our Coasts, burnt our towns, and destroyed the lives of our people.

He is at this time transporting large armies of foreign mercenaries to compleat the works of death, desolation and tyranny, already begun with circumstances of Cruelty & perfidy scarcely paralleled in the most barbarous ages, and totally unworthy the Head of a civilized nation.

He has constrained our fellow Citizens taken Captive on the high Seas to bear Arms against their Country, to become the executioners of their friends and Brethren, or to fall themselves by their Hands.

He has excited domestic insurrections amongst us, and has endeavoured to bring on the inhabitants of our frontiers, the merciless Indian Savages, whose known rule of warfare, is an undistinguished destruction of all ages, sexes and conditions.

In every stage of these Oppressions We have Petitioned for Redress in the most humble terms: Our repeated Petitions have been answered only by repeated injury. A Prince, whose character is thus marked by every act which may define a Tyrant, is unfit to be the ruler of a free people.

Nor have We been wanting in attentions to our British brethren. We have warned them from time to time of attempts by their legislature to extend an unwarrantable jurisdiction over us. We have reminded them of the circumstances of our emigration and settlement here. We have appealed to their native justice and magnanimity, and we have conjured them by the ties of our common kindred to disavow these usurpations which, would inevitably interrupt our connections and correspondence. They too have been deaf to the voice of justice and of consanguinity. We must, therefore, acquiesce in the necessity, which denounces our Separation, and hold them, as we hold the rest of mankind, Enemies in War, in Peace Friends.

We, therefore, the Representatives of the united States of America, in General Congress, Assembled, appealing to the Supreme Judge of the world for the rectitude of our intentions, do, in the Name, and by authority of the good People of these Colonies, solemnly publish and declare, That these United Colonies are, and of Right ought to be Free and Independent States; that they are Absolved from all Allegiance to the British Crown, and that all political connection between them and the State of Great Britain, is and ought to be totally dissolved; and that as Free and Independent States, they have full power to levy War, conclude Peace, contract Alliances, establish Commerce, and to do all other Acts and Things which Independent States may of right do. And for the support of this Declaration, with a firm reliance on the Protection of Divine Providence, we mutually pledge to each other our Lives, our Fortunes and our sacred Honor.

John Hancock
(Massachusetts)

New Hampshire
Josiah Bartlett
William Whipple
Matthew Thornton

Massachusetts
Samuel Adams
John Adams
Robert Treat Paine
Elbridge Gerry

Delaware
Caesar Rodney
George Read
Thomas McKean

New York
William Floyd
Philip Livingston
Francis Lewis
Lewis Morris

New Jersey
Richard Stockton
John Witherspoon
Francis Hopkinson
John Hart
Abraham Clark

North Carolina
William Hooper
Joseph Hewes
John Penn

Maryland
Samuel Chase
William Paca
Thomas Stone
Charles Carroll of Carrollton

South Carolina
Edward Rutledge
Thomas Heywood, Jr.
Thomas Lynch, Jr.
Arthur Middleton

Rhode Island
Stephen Hopkins
William Ellery

Connecticut
Roger Sherman
Samuel Huntington
William Williams
Oliver Wolcott

Pennsylvania
Robert Morris
Benjamin Rush
Benjamin Franklin
John Morton
George Clymer
James Smith
George Taylor
James Wilson
George Ross

Virginia
George Wythe
Richard Henry Lee
Thomas Jefferson
Benjamin Harrison
Thomas Nelson, Jr.
Francis Lightfoot Lee
Carter Braxton

Georgia
Button Gwinnett
Lyman Hall
George Walton

The Constitution of the United States

We the People of the United States, In Order to form a more perfect Union, establish Justice, insure domestic Tranquility, provide for the common defense, promote the general Welfare, and secure the Blessings of Liberty to ourselves and our Posterity, do ordain and establish this Constitution for the United States of America.

Note: Marginal notes explain certain constitutional passages.

ARTICLE I

Section 1. All legislative Powers herein granted shall be vested in a Congress of the United States, which shall consist of a Senate and House of Representatives.

Congress, a bicameral legislature, the first branch of government.

Section 2. The House of Representatives shall be composed of members chosen every second Year by the People of the several States, and the Electors in each State shall have the Qualifications requisite for Electors of the most numerous Branch of the State Legislature.

A two-year term for members of the House of Representatives.

No person shall be a representative who shall not have attained to the Age of twenty five Years, and been seven Years a Citizen of the United States, and who shall not, when elected, be an Inhabitant of that State in which he shall be chosen.

Qualifications for House members: citizenship, 25 years of age.

Representatives and direct Taxes shall be apportioned among the several States which may be included within this union, according to their respective Numbers, which shall be determined by adding to the whole Number of free Persons, including those bound to Service for a Term of Years, and excluding Indians not taxed, three fifths of all other Persons. The actual Enumeration shall be made within three Years after the first Meeting of the Congress of the United States, and within every subsequent Term of ten Years, in such Manner as they shall by Law direct. The Number of Representatives shall not exceed one for every thirty Thousand, but each State shall have at Least one Representative; and until such enumeration shall be made, the State of New Hampshire shall be entitled to chuse three, Massachusetts eight, Rhode-Island and Providence Plantations one, Connecticut five, New York six, New Jersey four, Pennsylvania eight, Delaware one, Maryland six, Virginia ten, North Carolina five, South Carolina five, and Georgia three.

Apportionment of representatives among states on basis of state population. Except for several small states, each representative today represents more than 500,000 people. A decennial (10-year) census is taken to determine the number of House seats to be awarded each state. States may win or lose seats following the census.

When vacancies happen in the Representation from any State, the Executive Authority thereof shall issue Writs of Election to fill such Vacancies.

Governor given authority to call an election to fill a House vacancy.

The House of Representatives shall chuse their speaker and other Officers; and shall have the sole Power of Impeachment.

The Speaker of the House, chosen by the majority party, presides over the chamber. The impeachment process (to remove federal officials from office) begins in the House of Representatives.

Section 3. The Senate of the United States shall be composed of two Senators from each State, chosen by the Legislature thereof, for six Years; and each Senator shall have one Vote.

Two senators from each state, 6-year term, one-third of the Senate elected every two years. Since the passage of the Seventeenth Amendment, senators have been popularly elected—a democratizing reform.

Immediately after they shall be assembled in Consequence of the first Election, they shall be divided as equally as may be into three Classes. The Seats of the Senators of the first Class shall be vacated at the Expiration of the second Year, of the second Class at the Expiration of the fourth Year, and of the third Class at the Expiration of the sixth Year, so that one third may be chosen every second Year; and if Vacancies happen by Resignation, or otherwise, during the Recess of the Legislature of any State, the Executive thereof may make temporary Appointments until the next Meeting of the Legislature, which shall then fill such Vacancies.

Governor may make a temporary appointment to fill a Senate vacancy.

No Person shall be a Senator who shall not have attained to the Age of thirty Years, and been nine Years a Citizen of the United States, and who shall not, when elected, be an Inhabitant of that State for which he shall be chosen.

Qualifications for Senate members: citizenship, 30 years of age.

The Vice President of the United States shall be President of the Senate, but shall have no Vote, unless they be equally divided.

Vice president may vote to break a tie in Senate.

The Senate shall chuse their other Officers, and also a President pro tempore, in the Absence of the Vice President, or when he shall exercise the Office of the President of the United States.

Presiding officer of the Senate is the president *pro tempore,* traditionally the senior member of the majority party.

The Senate shall have the sole Power to try all Impeachments. When sitting for that Purpose, they shall be on Oath of Affirmation. When the President of the United States is tried, the Chief Justice shall preside: And no Person shall be convicted without the Concurrence of two thirds of the Members present.

Judgment in Cases of Impeachment shall not extend further than to removal from Office, and disqualification to hold and enjoy any Office of honor, Trust or Profit under the United States: but the Party convicted shall nevertheless be liable and subject to Indictment, Trial, Judgment and Punishment, according to law.

Second stage of the impeachment process: Senate acts as a court to try a federal official impeached (accused) by the House. Conviction (and removal from office) requires two-thirds vote of members present. The impeachment process is a "gun behind the door," a deterrent to the waywardness of federal officials.

Section 4. The Times, Places and Manner of holding Elections for Senators and Representatives, shall be prescribed in each State by the Legislature thereof; but the Congress may at any time by Law make or alter such regulations, except as to the Places of chusing Senators.

Congressional elections held on first Tuesday after first Monday in November in even-numbered years.

The Congress shall assemble at least once in every Year, and such Meeting shall be on the first Monday in December, unless they shall by Law appoint a different Day:

Opening of congressional session changed by Twentieth Amendment to January 3.

Section 5. Each House shall be the Judge of the Elections, Returns and Qualifications of its own Members, and a Majority of each shall constitute a Quorum to do Business; but a smaller Number may adjourn from day to day, and may be authorized to compel the Attendance of absent Members, in such Manner, and under such Penalties as each House may provide.

Each House may determine the Rules for its Proceedings, punish its Members for disorderly Behaviour, and, with the Concurrence of two thirds, expel a Member.

Each House shall keep a Journal of its Proceedings, and from time to time publish the same, excepting such Parts as may in their Judgment require Secrecy; and the Yeas and Nays of the Members of either House on any question shall, at the Desire of one fifth of those Present, be entered on the Journal.

Neither House, during the Session of Congress, shall, without the Consent of the other, adjourn for more than three days, nor to any other Place than that in which the two Houses shall be sitting.

House and Senate may refuse to seat a member judged to be improperly elected. Majority of members required to transact business. Each house establishes its own rules of procedure. Two-thirds vote required to expel a member.

Section 6. The Senators and Representatives shall receive a Compensation for their Services, to be ascertained by Law, and paid out of the Treasury of the United States. They shall in all Cases, except Treason, Felony and Breach of the Peace, be privileged from Arrest during their Attendance at the Session of their respective Houses, and in going to and returning from the same; and for any Speech or Debate in either House, they shall not be questioned in any other Place.

Congressional salary established by members. Members enjoy a considerable measure of freedom of speech as well as immunity from arrest. Congressional "immunity" contributes to the independence of the legislative branch and its members.

No Senator or Representative shall, during the Time for which he was elected, be appointed to any civil Office under the Authority of the United States, which shall have been created, or the Emoluments whereof shall have been encreased during such time; and no Person holding any Office under the United States, shall be a Member of either House during his Continuance in Office.

A member of Congress cannot hold a position in another branch of government. Reaffirms principle of separation of powers.

Section 7. All Bills for raising Revenue shall originate in the House of Representatives; but the Senate may propose or concur with Amendments as on other Bills.

Tax legislation originates in the House of Representatives but may be changed in the Senate.

Every Bill which shall have passed the House of Representatives and the Senate, shall, before it become a Law, be presented to the President of the United States; If he approve he shall sign it, but if not he shall return it, with his Objections to that House in which it shall have originated, who shall enter the Objections at large on their Journal, and proceed to reconsider it. If after such Reconsideration two thirds of that House shall agree to pass the Bill, it shall be sent, together with the Objections, to the other House, by which it shall likewise be reconsidered, and if approved by two thirds of that House, it shall become a Law. But in all such Cases the Votes of both Houses shall be determined by Yeas and Nays, and the Names of the Persons voting for and against the Bill shall be entered on the Journal of each House respectively. If any Bill shall not be returned by the president within ten Days (Sundays excepted) after it shall have been presented to him, the Same shall be a Law, in like Manner as if he had signed it, unless the Congress by their Adjournment prevent its Return, in which Case it shall not be a Law.

The presidential veto, a basic element in the doctrine of checks and balances. A bill vetoed by the president may be overridden (and thus become law) by a two-thirds majority in both houses. The president can exercise a "pocket veto" by refusing to sign a bill sent to him within the last 10 days of a session.

Every Order, Resolution, or Vote to which the Concurrence of the Senate and House of Representatives may be necessary (except on a question of Adjournment) shall be presented to the President of the United States; and before the Same shall take Effect, shall be approved by him, or being disapproved by him, shall be repassed by two thirds of the Senate and House of Representatives, according to the Rules and Limitations prescribed in the Case of a Bill.

Constitutional amendments adopted by Congress are not subject to presidential veto. Rather, they are ratified (or rejected) by state legislatures or state conventions.

Section 8. The Congress shall have Power To lay and collect Taxes, Duties, Imposts and Excises, to pay the Debts and provide for the common Defence and general Welfare of the United States; but all Duties, Imposts and Excises shall be uniform throughout the United States;

To borrow Money on the credit of the United States;

To regulate Commerce with foreign Nations, and among the several States, and with the Indian Tribes;

To establish an uniform Rule of Naturalization, and uniform Laws on the subject of Bankruptcies throughout the United States;

To coin Money, regulate the Value thereof, and of foreign Coin, and fix the Standard of Weights and Measures;

To provide for the Punishment of counterfeiting the Securities and current Coin of the United States;

To establish Post Offices and post Roads;

A major section of the Constitution, Article I, Section 8, lists the *express* or *enumerated* powers of Congress. These include, among others, the power to tax, borrow money, regulate commerce, provide for a monetary system, establish provisions for naturalization, establish lower federal courts, declare war, and maintain armed services.

To promote the Progress of Science and useful Arts, by securing for limited Times to Authors and Inventors the exclusive Right to their respective Writings and Discoveries;

To constitute Tribunals inferior to the supreme Court;

To define and punish Piracies and Felonies committed on the high Seas, and Offences against the Law of Nations;

To declare War, grant Letters of Marque and Reprisal, and make Rules concerning Captures on Land and Water;

To raise and support Armies, but no Appropriation of Money to that Use shall be for a longer Term than two Years;

To provide and maintain a Navy;

To make Rules for the Government and Regulation of the land and naval Forces;

To provide for calling forth the Militia to execute the Laws of the Union, suppress Insurrections and repel Invasions;

To provide for organizing, arming, and disciplining, the Militia, and for governing such Part of them as may be employed in the Service of the United States, reserving to the States respectively, the Appointment of the Officers, and the Authority of training the Militia according to the discipline prescribed by Congress;

To exercise exclusive Legislation in all Cases whatsoever, over such District (not exceeding ten Miles square) as may, by Cession of particular States, and the Acceptance of Congress, become the Seat of the Government of the United States, and to exercise like Authority over all Places purchased by the Consent of the Legislature of the State in which the Same shall be for the Erection of Forts, Magazines, Arsenals, dock-Yards, and other needful Buildings;-And

To make all Laws which shall be necessary and proper for carrying into Execution the foregoing Powers, and all other Powers vested by this Constitution in the Government of the United States, or in any Department or Officer thereof.

The famous "necessary and proper" clause, also known as the "elastic" clause. Permits Congress to exercise many powers not expressly granted in Article I, Section 8.

Section 9. The Migration or Importation of such Persons as any of the States now existing shall think proper to admit, shall not be prohibited by the Congress prior to the Year one thousand eight hundred and eight, but a Tax or duty may be imposed on such Importation, not exceeding ten dollars for each Person.

Presages a ban on importation of slaves, which took effect in 1808.

The Privilege of the Writ of Habeas Corpus shall not be suspended, unless when in Cases of Rebellion or Invasion the public Safety may require it.

No Bill of Attainder or ex post facto Law shall be passed.

No Capitation, or other direct, Tax shall be laid, unless in Proportion to the Census or Enumeration herein before directed to be taken.

No Tax or Duty shall be laid on Articles exported from any State.

No Preference shall be given by any Regulation of Commerce or Revenue to the Ports of one State over those of another: nor shall Vessels bound to, or from, one State be obliged to enter, clear, or pay Duties in another.

The writ of *habaeas corpus,* a basic protection of personal liberty, is the right of an imprisoned person to be brought before a judge to decide the legality of his or her detention. A *bill of attainder* is a legislative act declaring a person or persons guilty of a crime and meting out punishment for that crime. An *ex post facto* law is a criminal law that takes effect after the fact—retroactively, in other words.

No Money shall be drawn from the Treasury, but in Consequence of Appropriations made by Law; and a regular Statement and Account of the Receipts and Expenditures of all public Money shall be published from time to time.

No Title of Nobility shall be granted by the United States: And no Person holding any office of Profit or Trust under them, shall, without the Consent of the Congress, accept of any present, Emolument, Office, or Title, of any kind whatever, from any King, Prince, or foreign States.

Congress controls the "purse strings" of the nation—no legislative power is more important.

Section 10. No State shall enter into any Treaty, Alliance, or Confederation; grant Letters of Marque and Treaty; Alliance, or Confederation; grant Letters of Marque and Reprisal; coin Money; emit Bills of Credit; make any Thing but gold and silver Coin a Tender in Payment of Debts; pass any Bill of Attainder, ex post facto Law, or Law impairing the Obligation of Contracts, or grant any Title of Nobility.

Prohibitions on the states: the states, for example, cannot make treaties with foreign nations, coin money, pass bills of attainder, or pass *ex post facto* laws.

No State shall, without the Consent of the Congress, lay any Imposts or Duties on Imports or Exports, except what may be absolutely necessary for executing its inspection Laws: and the net Produce of all Duties and Imposts, laid by any State on Imports and Exports, shall be for the Use of the Treasury of the United States; and all such Laws shall be subject to Revision and Control of the Congress.

No State shall, without the Consent of Congress, lay any Duty of Tonnage, keep Troops, or Ships of War in time of Peace, enter into any Agreement or Compact with another State, or with a foreign Power, or engage in War, unless actually invaded, or in such imminent Danger as will not admit of delay.

ARTICLE II

Section 1. The executive Power shall be vested in a President of the United States of America. He shall hold his Office during the Term of four Years, and, together with the Vice President, chosen for the same term, be elected, as follows

Nowhere defined in the Constitution, the "executive power" is a broad grant of authority to the president. Presidential actions and court decisions have helped to explain the meaning of this vague grant of power.

Each State shall appoint, in such Manner as the Legislature thereof may direct, a Number of Electors, equal to the whole Number of Senators and Representatives to which the State may be entitled in the Congress: but no Senator or Representative, or Person holding an office of Trust or Profit under the United States, shall be appointed an Elector.

Each state receives as many presidential electors as it has representatives and senators. Today, electors are popularly elected; a presidential candidate who wins a *plurality* of popular votes in a state wins *all* of that state's electoral votes.

The Electors shall meet in their respective States, and vote by Ballot for two Persons, of whom one at least shall not be an Inhabitant of the same State with themselves. And they shall make a List of all the Persons voted for, and of the Number of Votes for each; which List they shall sign and certify, and transmit sealed to the Seat of the Government of the United States, directed to the President of the Senate. The President of the Senate shall, in the Presence of the Senate and House of Representatives, open all the Certificates, and the Votes shall then be counted. The Person having the greatest Number of Votes shall be the President, if such Number be a Majority of the whole Number of Electors appointed; and if there be more than one who have such Majority, and have an equal Number of Votes, then the House of Representatives shall immediately chuse by Ballot one of them for President: and if no Person have a Majority, then from the five highest on the List the said House shall in like Manner chuse the President. But in chusing the President, the Votes shall be taken by States, the Representation from each State having one Vote; A quorum for this Purpose shall consist of a Member or Members from two thirds of the States, and a Majority of all the States shall be necessary to a Choice. In every Case, after the Choice of the President, the Person having the greatest Number of Votes of the Electors shall be the Vice President. But if there should remain two or more who have equal Votes, the Senate shall chuse from them by Ballot the Vice President.

The Twelfth Amendment replaces this clause. Under this amendment, separate ballots are cast for president and vice president. No more ties, as in the case of Jefferson and Burr. (Jefferson eventually won.)

The Congress may determine the Time of chusing the Electors and the Day on which they shall give their Votes; which Day shall be the same throughout the United States.

No Person except a natural born Citizen, or a Citizen of the United States, at the time of the Adoption of this Constitution, shall be eligible to the Office of President; neither shall any person be eligible to that Office who shall not have attained to the Age of thirty five Years, and been fourteen Years a Resident within the United States.

Qualifications for the presidency: natural-born citizen, 35 years of age, 14 years a resident within the United States.

In case of the Removal of the President from Office, or of his Death, Resignation, or Inability to discharge the Powers and Duties of the said Office, the Same shall devolve on the Vice President, and the Congress may by Law provide for the Case of Removal, Death, Resignation or Inability, both of the President and Vice President, declaring what Officer shall then act as President, and such Officer shall act accordingly, until the Disability be removed, or a President shall be elected.

Vice president succeeds to the presidency in the event of the president's death (or resignation, as in the case of Richard M. Nixon). The Twenty-fifth Amendment deals with presidential disability.

The President shall, at stated Times, receive for his Services a Compensation, which shall neither be encreased nor diminished during the Period for which he shall have been elected, and he shall not receive within that Period any other Emolument from the United States, or any of them.

Before he enter on the Execution of his Office, he shall take the following Oath or Affirmation:- "I do solemnly swear (or affirm) that I will faithfully execute the Office of President of the United States, and will to the best of my Ability, preserve, protect and defend the Constitution of the United States."

The president's oath of office.

Section 2. The President shall be Commander in Chief of the Army and Navy of the United States, and of the Militia of the several States, when called into the actual Service of the United States; he may require the Opinion, in writing, of the principal Officer in each of the executive Departments, upon any Subject relating to the Duties of their respective Offices, and he shall have power to grant Reprieves and Pardons for Offences against the United States, except in Cases of Impeachment.

Civilian supremacy: the president is commander in chief of the armed forces. Department heads appointed by the president; collectively, they now comprise the *cabinet.* A *pardon* permits the president to forgive persons for all offenses against the United States, except in cases of impeachment. A *reprieve* simply delays punishment.

He shall have Power, by and with the Advice and Consent of the Senate, to make Treaties, provided two thirds of the Senators present concur; and he shall nominate, and by and with the Advice and Consent of the Senate, shall appoint Ambassadors, other public Ministers and Consuls, Judges of the supreme Court, and all other Officers of the United States, whose Appointments are not herein otherwise provided for, and which shall be established by Law; but the Congress may by Law vest the Appointment of such inferior officers, as they think proper, in the President alone, in the Courts of Law, or in the Heads of Departments.

Presidential treaties and appointments require the approval of the Senate—an important "check and balance."

The President shall have Power to fill up all Vacancies that may happen during the Recess of the Senate, by granting Commissions which shall expire at the end of their next Session.

The president may make "recess appointments" while the Senate is not in session.

Section 3. He shall from time to time give to the Congress Information of the State of the Union, and recommend to their Consideration such Measures as he shall judge necessary and expedient; he may, on extraordinary Occasions, convene both Houses, or either of them, and in Case of Disagreement between them, with Respect to the Time

A "legislative" power of the president: messages to Congress describing his program and recommending the passage of legislation.

of Adjournment, he may adjourn them to such Time as he shall think proper; he shall receive Ambassadors and other public Ministers; he shall take Care that the Laws be faithfully executed, and shall Commission all of the officers of the United States.

Section 4. The President, Vice President and all civil Officers of the United States, shall be removed from Office on Impeachment for, and Conviction of, Treason, Bribery, or other High Crimes and Misdemeanors.

Removal of the president from office through impeachment proceedings.

ARTICLE III

Section 1. The judicial Power of the United States, shall be vested in one supreme Court, and in such inferior Courts as the Congress may from time to time ordain and establish. The Judges, both of the supreme and inferior Courts, shall hold their Offices during good Behaviour, and shall, at stated Times, receive for their Services, a Compensation, which shall not be diminished during their Continuance in Office.

The Constitution establishes a Supreme Court, with other federal courts to be created by Congress. Federal judges, whose appointments must be confirmed by the Senate, hold office for life, assuming "good behavior."

Section 2. The judicial Power shall extend to all Cases, in Law and Equity, arising under this Constitution, the Laws of the United States, and Treaties made, or which shall be made, under their Authority;-to all Cases affecting Ambassadors, other public Ministers and Consuls;-to all Cases of admiralty and maritime Jurisdiction;-to Controversies to which the United States shall be a party;-to Controversies between two or more States; between a State and Citizens of another State;-between Citizens of different States;-between Citizens of the same State claiming Lands under Grants of different States, and between a State, or the Citizens thereof, and foreign States, Citizens or Subjects.

The types of cases and controversies that make up the jurisdiction of federal courts. These include, for example, diplomatic cases, admiralty and maritime cases, controversies between two or more states, and cases between citizens of different states.

In all Cases affecting Ambassadors, other public Ministers and Consuls, and those in which a State shall be Party, the supreme Court shall have original Jurisdiction. In all the other Cases before mentioned, the supreme Court shall have appellate Jurisdiction, both as to Law and Fact, with such Exceptions, and under such Regulations as the Congress shall make.

Original jurisdiction: the types of cases that *start* in the Supreme Court. Original jurisdiction cases are rare. The Supreme Court is basically an appeals court, with cases appealed to it from state courts, as well as lower federal courts.

The Trial of all Crimes, except in Cases of Impeachment, shall be by Jury; and such Trial shall be held in the State where the said Crimes shall have been committed; but when not committed within any State, the Trial shall be at such Place or Places as the Congress may by Law have directed.

The right to a trial by jury.

Section 3. Treason against the United States, shall consist only in levying War against them, or in adhering to their Enemies, giving them Aid and Comfort. No Person shall be convicted of Treason unless on the Testimony of two Witnesses to the same overt Act, or on Confession in open Court.

The Congress shall have Power to declare the Punishment of Treason, but no Attainder of Treason shall work Corruption of Blood, or Forfeiture except during the Life of the Person attainted.

The crime of treason.

ARTICLE IV

Section 1. Full Faith and Credit shall be given in each State to the public Acts, Records, and judicial Proceedings of every State. And the Congress may by general Laws prescribe the Manner in which such Acts, Records, and Proceedings shall be proved, and the Effect thereof.

Each state is required to recognize the civil rulings of the other states. For example, private contracts made under the laws of one state must be upheld by other states.

Section 2. The Citizens of each State shall be entitled to all Privileges and Immunities of Citizens in the several States.

States cannot favor their own citizens by discriminating against citizens of other states. The citizens of one state, for example, may acquire property in another state, engage in normal business there, and have access to that state's courts.

A Person charged in any State with Treason, Felony, or other Crime, who shall flee from Justice, and be found in another State, shall on Demand of the executive Authority of the State from which he fled, be delivered up, to be removed to the State having Jurisdiction of the Crime.

This provision deals with the process of *extradition.* A person accused of a crime who flees across a state line (under ordinary circumstances) will, when captured, be surrendered to the state from which he or she fled.

No Person held to Service or Labour in one State, under the Laws thereof, escaping into another, shall, in Consequence of any Law or Regulation therein, be discharged from such Service or Labour, but shall be delivered up on Claim of the Party to whom such Service or Labour may be due.

Obsolete, since the Thirteenth Amendment abolished slavery.

Section 3. New States may be admitted by the Congress into this Union; but no new State shall be formed or erected within the Jurisdiction of any other State; nor any State be formed by the Junction of two or more States, or Parts of States, without the Consent of the Legislatures of the States concerned as well as of the Congress.

The Congress shall have Power to dispose of and make all needful Rules and Regulations respecting the Territory or other Property belonging to the United States; and nothing in this Constitution shall be so construed as to Prejudice any Claims of the United States, or of any particular State.

Procedures for admitting new states. Alaska and Hawaii were the last states to be admitted to the Union.

Section 4. The United States shall guarantee to every State in this Union a Republican Form of Government, and shall protect each of them against Invasion; and on Application of the Legislature, or of the Executive (when the Legislature cannot be convened) against domestic Violence.

A *republican* form of government is one in which the majority rules through the election of representatives.

ARTICLE V

The Congress, whenever two thirds of both Houses shall deem it necessary, shall propose Amendments to this Constitution, or, on the Application of the Legislatures of two thirds of the several States, shall call a Convention for proposing Amendments, which, in either Case, shall be valid to all Intents and Purposes, as Part of this Constitution, when ratified by the Legislatures of three fourths of the several States, or by Conventions in three fourths thereof, as the one or the other Mode of Ratification may be proposed by the Congress; Provided that no Amendment which may be made prior to the Year One thousand eight hundred and eight shall in any Manner affect the first and fourth Clauses in the Ninth Section of the first Article; and that no State, without its Consent, shall be deprived of its equal Suffrage in the Senate.

Amendments to the Constitution are *proposed* by a two-thirds vote of both houses of Congress or by a convention called by Congress in response to the request of two thirds of the states. Amendments are *ratified* by three fourths of the state legislatures or by constitutional conventions in three fourths of the states.

ARTICLE VI

All Debts contracted and Engagements entered into, before the Adoption of this Constitution, shall be as valid against the United States under this Constitution, as under the Confederation.

This Constitution, and the Laws of the United States which shall be made in Pursuance thereof; and all Treaties made, or which shall be made, under the Authority of the United States, shall be the supreme Law of the Land; and the Judges in every State shall be bound thereby, any Thing in the Constitution or Laws of any State to the Contrary notwithstanding.

The *supremacy clause* provides that if a federal and a state law are in conflict, the federal law prevails.

The Senators and Representatives before mentioned, and the Members of the several State Legislatures, and all executive and judicial Officers, both of the United States and of the several States, shall be bound by Oath or Affirmation, to support this Constitution; but no religious Test shall ever be required as a Qualification to any Office or public Trust under the United States.

State and national officials are bound to support the Constitution. Religion may not be a qualification for holding public office.

ARTICLE VII

The Ratification of the Conventions of nine States shall be sufficient for the Establishment of this Constitution between the States so ratifying the Same.

Adoption of the Constitution required the consent of only 9 of the 13 states.

Done in Convention by the Unanimous Consent of the States present the Seventeenth Day of September in the Year of our Lord one thousand seven hundred and Eighty seven and of the Independence of the United States of America the Twelfth. In witness whereof We have hereunto subscribed our Names.

[The first 10 Amendments were ratified December 15, 1791, and form what is known as the Bill of Rights.]

AMENDMENT 1

Congress shall make no law respecting an establishment of religion, or prohibiting the free exercise thereof; or abridging the freedom of speech, or of the press; or the right of the people peaceably to assemble, and to petition the Government for a redress of grievances.

Key constitutional liberties of citizens: freedom of religion, speech, press, association, assembly, and petition. Many of the most important and best-known Supreme Court decisions deal with the protection of these individual liberties.

AMENDMENT 2

A well regulated Militia, being necessary to the security of a free State, the right of the people to keep and bear Arms, shall not be infringed.

States empowered to maintain an armed militia (national guard, in today's terminology).

AMENDMENT 3

No Soldier shall, in time of peace be quartered in any house, without the consent of the Owner, nor in time of war, but in a manner to be prescribed by Law.

The army's right to place soldiers in private homes is limited.

AMENDMENT 4

The right of the people to be secure in their persons, houses, papers, and effects, against unreasonable searches and seizures, shall not be violated, and no Warrants shall issue, but upon probable cause, supported by Oath or affirmation, and particularly describing the place to be searched and the persons or things to be seized.

A warrant (legal order from a judicial officer) is required before a person's house or place of business can be searched.

AMENDMENT 5

No person shall be held to answer for a capital, or otherwise infamous crime, unless on a presentment or indictment of a Grand Jury, except in cases arising in the land or naval forces, or in the Militia, when in actual service in time of War or public danger; nor shall any person be subject for the same offence to be twice put in jeopardy of life or limb; nor shall be compelled in any criminal case to be a witness against himself, nor be deprived of life, liberty, or property, without due process of law; nor shall private property be taken for public use, without just compensation.

A person accused of a serious crime must first be *indicted* (accused) by a *grand jury.* No person can be subjected to *double jeopardy* (tried twice for the same crime). Persons are also protected from *self-incrimination*—that is, from having to answer questions that might subject them to criminal prosecution. The "due process of law" clause protects individuals from arbitrary treatment by government.

AMENDMENT 6

In all criminal prosecutions, the accused shall enjoy the right to a speedy and public trial, by an impartial jury of the State and district wherein the crime shall have been committed, which district shall have been previously ascertained by law, and to be informed of the nature and cause of the accusation; to be confronted with the witnesses against him; to have compulsory process for obtaining witnesses in his favor, and to have the Assistance of Counsel for his defense.

A defendant in a criminal case is guaranteed a trial without undue delay, a reasonable length of time to prepare his or her case, the right to be informed of the charges, and the right to confront hostile witnesses.

AMENDMENT 7

In Suits at common law, where the value in controversy shall exceed twenty dollars, the right of trial by jury shall be preserved, and no fact tried by a jury, shall be otherwise reexamined in any Court of the United States, than according to the rules of the common law.

A jury trial is required in federal courts in cases involving 20 or more dollars. Jury trial can be waived by the parties to the dispute, permitting a judge to settle the case.

AMENDMENT 8

Excessive bail shall not be required, nor excessive fines imposed, nor cruel and unusual punishments inflicted.

General limits on arbitrary government.

AMENDMENT 9

The enumeration in the Constitution, of certain rights, shall not be construed to deny or disparage others retained by the people.

The rights of the people are not limited simply to those specifically enumerated in the Constitution.

AMENDMENT 10

The powers not delegated to the United States by the Constitution, nor prohibited by it to the States, are reserved to the States respectively, or to the people.

An amendment that has sometimes been used to limit the power of the national government. From one perspective, the Tenth Amendment is simply a truism.

AMENDMENT 11
[Ratified February 7, 1795]

The Judicial power of the United States shall not be construed to extend to any suit in law or equity, commenced or prosecuted against one of the United States by Citizens of another State, or by Citizens or Subjects of any Foreign State.

A state cannot be sued in the federal courts by a citizen of another state or by a citizen of a foreign country.

AMENDMENT 12
[Ratified July 27, 1804]

The Electors shall meet in their respective states and vote by ballot for President and Vice-President, one of whom, at least, shall not be an inhabitant of the same state with themselves; they shall name in their ballots the person voted for as President, and in distinct ballots the person voted for as Vice-President, and they shall make distinct lists of all persons voted for as President, and of all persons voted for as Vice-President, and of the number of votes for each, which lists they shall sign and certify, and transmit sealed to the seat of the government of the United States, directed to the President of the Senate;-The President of the Senate shall, in the presence of the Senate and House of Representatives, open all the certificates and the votes shall then be counted;-The person having the greatest number of votes for President, shall be the President, if such number be a majority of the whole number of Electors appointed; and if no person have such majority, then from the persons having the highest numbers not exceeding three on the list of those voted for as President, the House of Representatives shall choose immediately by ballot, the President. But in choosing the President, the votes shall be taken by states, the representation from each state having one vote; a quorum for this purpose shall consist of a member or members from two-thirds of the states, and a majority of all the states shall be necessary to a choice. And if the House of Representatives shall not choose a President whenever the right of choice shall devolve upon them, before the fourth day of March next following, the Vice-President shall act as President, as in the case of the death or other constitutional disability of the President.-The person having the greatest number of votes as Vice-President, shall be the Vice-President, if such number be a majority of the whole number of Electors appointed, and if no person have a majority, then from the two highest numbers on the list, the Senate shall choose the Vice-President; a quorum for the purpose shall consist of two-thirds of the whole number of Senators, and a majority of the whole number shall be necessary to a choice. But no person constitutionally ineligible to the office of President shall be eligible to that of Vice-President of the United States.

Changes the original method by which the president and vice president were selected by requiring presidential electors to cast separate ballots for these offices. If no presidential candidate receives a majority of the electoral votes (270 out of 538), the House of Representatives chooses from among the top three candidates. In this process, each state delegation casts one vote. If no vice presidential candidate receives a majority, the Senate chooses from among the top two candidates.

AMENDMENT 13
[Ratified December 6, 1865]

Section 1. Neither slavery nor involuntary servitude, except as a punishment for crime whereof the party shall have been duly convicted, shall exist within the United States, or any place subject to their jurisdiction.

Slavery abolished.

Section 2. Congress shall have the power to enforce this article by appropriate legislation.

AMENDMENT 14
[Ratified July 9, 1868]

Section 1. All persons born or naturalized in the United States, and subject to the jurisdiction thereof, are citizens of the United States and of the State wherein they reside. No State shall make or enforce any law which shall abridge the privileges or immunities of citizens of the United States; nor shall any State deprive any person of life, liberty, or property, without due process of law; nor deny to any person within its jurisdiction the equal protection of the laws.

Former slaves are accorded full citizenship. As a result of decisions of the Supreme Court, state governments as well as the federal government are limited by the Bill of Rights. State governments must observe the principles of "due process of law" and grant all persons "equal protection of the laws." This latter clause became the basis for the Supreme Court's decision outlawing segregated public schools in 1954 (*Brown* v. *Board of Education of Topeka*).

Section 2. Representatives shall be appointed among the several States according to their respective numbers, counting the whole number of persons in each State, excluding Indians not taxed. But when the right to vote at any election for the choice of electors for President and Vice President of the United States, Representatives in Congress, the Executive and Judicial Officers of a State, or the members of the Legislature thereof, is denied to any of the male inhabitants of such State, being twenty-one years of age, and citizens of the United States, or in any way abridged, except for participation in rebellion, or other crime, the basis of representation therein shall be reduced in the proportion which the number of such male citizens shall bear to the whole number of male citizens twenty-one years of age in such State.

Intended to force southern states to permit blacks to vote by threatening to reduce their representation in the House, this section of the Constitution was never applied.

Section 3. No person shall be a Senator or Representative in Congress, or elector of President and Vice President, or hold any office, civil or military, under the United States, or under any State, who, having previously taken an oath, as a member of Congress, or as an officer of the United States, or as a member of any State legislature, or as an executive or judicial officer of any State, to support the Constitution of the United States, shall have engaged in insurrection or rebellion against the same, or given aid or comfort to the enemies thereof. But Congress may by a vote of two-thirds of each House, remove such disability.

Officials of the Confederacy were disqualified from becoming federal officials, unless exempted by Congress.

Section 4. The validity of the public debt of the United States, authorized by law, including debts incurred for payment of pensions and bounties for services in suppressing insurrection or rebellion, shall not be questioned. But neither the United States nor any State shall assume or pay any debt or obligation incurred in aid of insurrection or rebellion against the United States, or any claim for the loss or emancipation of any slave; but all such debts, obligations and claims shall be held illegal and void.

The federal civil war debt is declared legal.

Section 5. The Congress shall have power to enforce, by appropriate legislation, the provisions of this article.

AMENDMENT 15
[Ratified February 3, 1870]

Section 1. The right of citizens of the United States to vote shall not be denied or abridged by the United States or by any State on account of race, color, or previous condition of servitude.

Section 2. The Congress shall have power to enforce this article by appropriate legislation.

Blacks were given the right to vote by this amendment, but its passage had little effect at the time. The Voting Rights Act of 1965, arguably the most important civil rights legislation in American history, finally brought black citizens into the electorate on a large scale; it delivered what the Fifteenth Amendment promised.

AMENDMENT 16
[Ratified February 3, 1913]

The Congress shall have power to lay and collect taxes on incomes, from whatever source derived, without apportionment among the several States, and without regard to any census or enumeration.

Nullifying a Supreme Court decision, this amendment gave Congress the power to levy an income tax.

AMENDMENT 17
[Ratified April 8, 1913]

The Senate of the United States shall be composed of two Senators from each State, elected by the people thereof for six years; and each Senator shall have one vote. The electors in each state shall have the qualification requisite for electors of the most numerous branch of the State legislatures.

When vacancies happen in the representation of any State in the Senate, the executive authority of such State shall issue writs of election to fill such vacancies; *Provided,* That the legislature of any State may empower the executive thereof to make temporary appointments until the people fill the vacancies by election as the legislature may direct.

This amendment shall not be so construed as to affect the election or term of any Senator chosen before it becomes valid as part of the Constitution.

Henceforth, senators would be popularly elected, like members of the House, rather than chosen by state legislatures—a democratizing reform.

AMENDMENT 18
[Ratified January 16, 1919]

Section 1. After one year from the ratification of this article the manufacture, sale, or transportation of intoxicating liquors within, the importation thereof into, or the exportation thereof from the United States and all territory subject to the jurisdiction thereof for beverage purposes is hereby prohibited.

Prohibition of liquor manufacture, sale, or transportation. The experiment failed; repealed by the Twenty-first Amendment.

Section 2. The Congress and the several States shall have concurrent power to enforce this article by appropriate legislation.

Section 3. This article shall be inoperative unless it shall have been ratified as an amendment to the Constitution by the legislatures of the several States, as provided in the Constitution, within seven years from the date of the submission hereof to the State by the Congress.

AMENDMENT 19
[Ratified August 18, 1920]

The right of citizens of the United States to vote shall not be denied or abridged by the United States or by any State on account of sex. Congress shall have the power to enforce this article by appropriate legislation.

Finally, gender politics: Women are given the right to vote.

AMENDMENT 20
[Ratified January 23, 1933]

Section 1. The terms of the President and Vice President shall end at noon on the 20th day of January, and the terms of Senators and Representatives at noon on the 3d day of January, of the years in which such terms would have ended if this article had not been ratified; and the terms of their successors shall then begin.

Changes the dates for the beginning of presidential and congressional terms from March to January, provides for succession to the presidency, and empowers Congress to extend the line of succession.

Section 2. The Congress shall assemble at least once in every year, and such meeting shall begin at noon on the 3d day of January, unless they shall by law appoint a different day.

Section 3. If, at the time fixed for the beginning of the term of the President, the President elect shall have died, the Vice President elect shall become President. If a President shall not have been chosen before the time fixed for the beginning of his term, or if the President elect shall have failed to qualify, then the Vice President elect shall act as President until a President shall have qualified; and the Congress may by law provide for the case wherein neither a President elect nor a Vice President elect shall have qualified, declaring who shall then act as President, or the manner in which one who is to act shall be selected, and such person shall act accordingly until a President or Vice President shall have qualified.

Section 4. The Congress may by law provide for the case of the death of any of the persons from whom the House of Representatives may choose a President whenever the right of choice shall have devolved upon them, and for the case of the death of any of the persons from whom the Senate may choose a Vice President whenever the right of choice shall have devolved upon them.

Section 5. Sections 1 and 2 shall take effect on the 15th day of October following the ratification of this article.

Section 6. This article shall be inoperative unless it shall have been ratified as an amendment to the Constitution by the legislatures of three-fourths of the several states within seven years from the date of its submission.

AMENDMENT 21
[Ratified December 5, 1933]

Section 1. The eighteenth article of amendment to the Constitution of the United States is hereby repealed.

Repeals the Eighteenth Amendment.

Section 2. The transportation or importation into any State, Territory, or Possession of the United States for delivery or use herein of intoxicating liquors, in violation of the laws thereof, is hereby prohibited.

Section 3. This article shall be inoperative unless it shall have been ratified as an amendment to the Constitution by conventions in several States, as provided in the Constitution, within seven years from the date of the submission hereof to the States by the Congress.

AMENDMENT 22
[Ratified February 27, 1951]

Section 1. No person shall be elected to the office of the President more than twice, and no person who has held the office of President, or acted as President, for more than two years of a term to which some other person was elected President shall be elected to the office of the President more than once. But this Article shall not apply to any person holding the office of President when this Article was proposed by the Congress, and shall not prevent any person who may be holding the office of President, or acting as President, during the term within which this Article becomes operative from holding the office of President or acting as President during the remainder of such term.

Limiting popular choice: A president may serve only two full terms plus two years of the previous president's term—in other words, 10 years maximum.

Section 2. This article shall be inoperative unless it shall have been ratified as an amendment to the Constitution by the legislatures of three-fourths of the several States within seven years from the date of its submission to the States by the Congress.

AMENDMENT 23
[Ratified March 29, 1961]

Section 1. The District constituting the seat of Government of the United States shall appoint in such manner as the Congress may direct:
A number of electors of President and Vice President equal to the whole number of Senators and Representatives in Congress to which the District would be entitled if it were a state, but in no event more than the least populous State; they shall be in addition to those appointed by the States, but they shall be considered, for the purposes of the election of President and Vice President, to be electors appointed by a State; and they shall meet in the District and perform such duties as provided by the twelfth article of amendment.

Awards the District of Columbia three electoral votes.

Section 2. The Congress shall have power to enforce this article by appropriate legislation.

AMENDMENT 24
[Ratified January 23, 1964]

Section 1. The right of citizens of the United States to vote in any primary or other election for President or Vice President, for electors for President or Vice President, or for Senator or Representative in Congress, shall not be denied or abridged by the United States or by any State by reason or failure to pay any poll tax or other tax.

Outlaws the poll tax as a requirement for voting in *federal* elections. The poll tax was a tax on the right to vote. In 1966, the Supreme Court outlawed poll taxes in *all* elections.

Section 2. The Congress shall have power to enforce this article by appropriate legislation.

AMENDMENT 25
[Ratified February 10, 1967]

Section 1. In case of the removal of the President from office or of his death or resignation, the Vice President shall become President.

Prescribes the succession route to the presidency, provides for the selection of the vice president in the case of a vacancy in that office, and develops procedures to be used in the event of the president's inability to discharge the powers and duties of his office.

Section 2. Whenever there is vacancy in the office of the Vice President, the President shall nominate a Vice President who shall take office upon confirmation by a majority vote of both Houses of Congress.

Section 3. Whenever the President transmits to the President pro tempore of the Senate and the speaker of the House of Representatives his written declaration that he is unable to discharge the powers and duties of his office, and until he transmits to them a written declaration to the contrary, such powers and duties shall be discharged by the Vice President as Acting President.

Section 4. Whenever the Vice President and a majority of either the principal officers of the executive department or of such other body as Congress may by law provide, transmit to the President pro tempore of the Senate and the Speaker of the House of Representatives their written declaration that the President is unable to discharge the powers and duties of his office, the Vice President shall immediately assume the powers and duties of the office as Acting President.

Thereafter, when the President transmits to the President pro tempore of the Senate and the Speaker of the House of Representatives his written declaration that no inability exists, he shall resume the powers and duties of his office unless the Vice President and a majority of either the principal officers of the executive department or of such other body as Congress may by law provide, transmit within four days to the President pro tempore of the Senate and the Speaker of the House of Representatives their written declaration that the President is unable to discharge the powers and duties of his office. Thereupon Congress shall decide the issue, assembling within forty-eight hours for that purpose if not in session. If the Congress, within twenty-one days after receipt of the latter written declaration, or, if Congress is not in session, within twenty-one days after Congress is required to assemble, determined by two-thirds vote of both Houses that the President is unable to discharge the powers and duties of his office, the Vice President shall continue to discharge the same as Acting President; otherwise, the President shall resume the powers and duties of his office.

AMENDMENT 26
[Ratified June 30, 1971]

Section 1. The right of citizens of the United States, who are eighteen years of age or older, to vote shall not be denied or abridged by the United States or by any State on account of age.

Eighteen-year-old citizens are given the right to vote in all elections.

Section 2. The Congress shall have the power to enforce this article by appropriate legislation.

The Federalist Papers

The collection known as *The Federalist Papers* consists of 85 essays written by Alexander Hamilton, John Jay, and James Madison under the pen name Publius and published in New York newspapers in 1787 and 1788 to support ratification of the Constitution. Excerpts from *Federalist* Nos. 10, 51, and 78 are reprinted here.

JAMES MADISON: Federalist No. 10

Among the numerous advantages promised by a well constructed Union, none deserves to be more accurately developed than its tendency to break and control the violence of faction. The friend of popular governments never finds himself so much alarmed for their character and fate as when he contemplates their propensity to this dangerous vice. He will not fail, therefore, to set a due value on any plan which, without violating the principles to which he is attached, provides a proper cure for it. The instability, injustice, and confusion, introduced into the public councils, have, in truth been the mortal diseases under which popular governments have everywhere perished; as they continue to be the favorite and fruitful topics from which the adversaries to liberty derive their most specious declamations. The valuable improvements made by the American constitutions on the popular models, both ancient and modern, cannot certainly be too much admired; but it would be an unwarrantable partiality, to contend that they have as effectually obviated the danger on this side, as was wished and expected. Complaints are everywhere heard from our most considerate and virtuous citizens, equally the friends of public and private faith, and of public and personal liberty, that our governments are too unstable; that the public good is disregarded in the conflicts of rival parties; and that measures are too often decided, not according to the rules of justice, and the rights of the minor party, but by the superior force of an interested and overbearing majority. However anxiously we may wish that these complaints had no foundation, the evidence of known facts will not permit us to deny that they are in some degree true. It will be found, indeed, on a candid review of our situation, that some of the distresses under which we labor, have been erroneously charged on the operation of our governments; but it will be found, at the same time, that other causes will not alone account for many of our heaviest misfortunes; and, particularly, for the prevailing and increasing distrust of public engagements, and alarm for private rights, which are echoed from one end of the continent to the other. These must be chiefly, if not wholly, effects of the unsteadiness and injustice, with which a factious spirit has tainted our public administrations.

By a faction, I understand a number of citizens, whether amounting to a majority or minority of the whole, who are united and actuated by some common impulse of passion, or of interest, adverse to the rights of other citizens, or to the permanent and aggregate interests of the community.

There are two methods of curing the mischiefs of faction: The one, by removing its causes; the other, by controlling its effects.

There are again two methods of removing the causes of faction: the one, by destroying the liberty which is essential to its existence; the other, by giving to every citizen the same opinions, the same passions, and the same interests.

It could never be more truly said, than of the first remedy, that it was worse than the disease. Liberty is to faction what air is to fire, an aliment, without which it instantly expires. But it could not be a less folly to abolish liberty, which is essential to political life because it nourishes faction, than it would be to wish the annihilation of air, which is essential to animal life, because it imparts to fire its destructive agency.

The second expedient is as impracticable, as the first would be unwise. As long as the reason of man continues fallible, and he is at liberty to exercise it, different opinions will be formed. As long as the connection subsists between his reason and his self-love, his opinions and his passions will have a reciprocal influence on each other; and the former will be objects to which the latter will attach themselves. The diversity in the faculties of men, from which the rights of property originate, is not less as insuperable obstacle to a uniformity of interests. The protection of those faculties is the first object of government. From the protection of different and unequal faculties of acquiring property, the possession of different degrees and kinds of property immediately results; and from the influence of these on the sentiments and views of the respective proprietors, ensues a division of the society into different interests and parties.

The latent causes of faction are thus sown in the nature of man; and we see them everywhere brought into different degrees of activity, according to the different circumstances of civil society. A zeal for different opinions concerning religion, concerning government, and many other points, as well of speculation as of practice; an attachment to different leaders, ambitiously contending for preeminence and power; or to persons of other descriptions, whose fortunes have been interesting to the human passions, have, in turn, divided mankind into parties, inflamed them with mutual animosity, and rendered them much more disposed to vex and oppress each other, than to cooperate for their common good. So strong is this propensity of mankind, to fall into mutual animosities, that where no substantial occasion presents itself, the most frivolous and fanciful distinctions have been sufficient to kindle their unfriendly passions, and excite their most violent conflicts. But the most common and durable source of factions has been the various and unequal distribution of property. Those who hold, and those who are without property, have ever formed distinct interests in society. Those who are creditors, and those who are debtors, fall under a like discrimination. A landed interest, a manufacturing interest, a mercantile interest, a moneyed interest, with many lesser interests, grow up of necessity in civilized nations, and divide them into different classes, actuated by different sentiments and views. The regulation of these various and interfering interests forms the principal task of modern legislation, and involves the spirit of party and faction in the necessary and ordinary operations of government.

No man is allowed to be a judge in his own cause; because his interest will certainly bias his judgment, and, not improbably, corrupt his integrity. With equal, nay, with greater reason, a body of men are unfit to be both judges and parties at the same time; yet what are many of the most important acts of legislation, but so many judicial determinations, not indeed concerning the rights of single persons, but concerning the rights of large bodies of citizens? And what are the different classes of legislators, but advocates and parties to the cause which they determine? Is a law proposed concerning private debts? It is a question to which the creditors are parties on one side, and the debtors on the other. Justice ought to hold the balance between them. Yet the parties are, and must be, themselves the judges; and the most numerous party, or, in other words, the most powerful faction, must be expected to prevail. Shall domestic manufactures be encouraged, and in what degree, by restrictions on foreign manufactures? are questions which would be differently decided by the landed and the manufacturing classes; and probably by neither with a sole regard to justice and the public good. . . .

It is in vain to say, that enlightened statesmen will be able to adjust these clashing interests, and render them all subservient to the public good. Enlightened statesmen will not always be at the helm; nor, in many cases, can such an adjustment be made at all, without taking into view indirect and remote considerations, which will rarely prevail over the immediate interest which one party may find in disregarding the rights of another, or the good of the whole.

The inference to which we are brought is, that the *causes* of faction cannot be removed; and that relief is only to be sought in the means of controlling its *effects.*

If a faction consists of less than a majority, relief is supplied by the republican principle, which enables the majority to defeat its sinister views, by regular vote. It may clog the administration, it may convulse the society; but it will be unable to execute and mask its violence under the forms of the constitution. When a majority is included in a faction, the form of popular government, on the other hand, enables it to sacrifice to its ruling passion or interest, both the public good and the rights of other citizens. To secure the public good, and private rights, against the danger of such a faction, and at the same time to preserve the spirit and the form of popular government, is then the great object to which our inquiries are directed. Let me add, that it is the great desideratum, by which alone this form of government can be rescued from the opprobrium under which it has so long labored, and be recommended to the esteem and adoption of mankind.

By what means is this object attainable? Evidently by one of two only. Either the existence of the same passion or interest in a majority, at the same time must be prevented; or the majority, having such coexistent passion or interest, must be rendered, by their number and local situation, unable to concert and carry into effect schemes of oppression. If the impulse and the opportunity be suffered to coincide, we well know, that neither moral nor religious motives can be relied on as an adequate control. They are not found to be such on the injustice and violence of individuals, and lose their efficacy in proportion to the number combined together; that is, in proportion as their efficacy becomes needful.

From this view of the subject, it may be concluded, that a pure democracy, by which I mean a society consisting of a small number of citizens, who assemble and administer the government in person, can admit of no cure from the mischiefs of faction. A common passion or interest will, in almost every case, be felt by a majority of the whole; a communication and concert, results from the form of government itself; and there is nothing to check the inducements to sacrifice the weaker party, or an obnoxious individual. Hence it is, that such democracies have ever been spectacles of turbulence and contention; have ever been found incompatible with personal security, or the rights of property; and have, in general been as short in their lives, as they have been violent in their deaths. Theoretic politicians, who have patronized this species of government, have erroneously supposed that by reducing mankind to a perfect equality in their political rights, they would, at the same time, be perfectly equalized and assimilated in their possessions, their opinions, and their passions.

A republic, by which I mean a government in which the scheme of representation takes place, opens a different prospect, and promises the cure for which we are seeking. Let us examine the points in which it varies from pure democracy, and we shall comprehend both the nature of the cure and the efficacy which it must derive from the union.

The two great points of difference, between a democracy and a republic, are, first, the delegation of the government, in the latter, to a small number of citizens elected by the rest; secondly, the greater number of citizens, and greater sphere of country, over which the latter may be extended.

The effect of the first difference is on the one hand, to refine and enlarge the public views, by passing them through the medium of a chosen body of citizens, whose wisdom may best discern the true interest in their country, and whose patriotism and love of justice, will be least likely to sacrifice it to temporary or partial considerations. Under such a regulation, it may well happen, that the public voice, pronounced by the representatives of the people, will be more consonant to the public good, than if pronounced by the people themselves, convened for the purpose. On the other hand, the effect may be inverted. Men of factious tempers, of local prejudices, or of sinister designs, may by intrigue, by corruption, or by other means, first obtain the suffrages, and then betray the interests, of the people. The question resulting is, whether small or extensive republics are most favorable to the election of proper guardians of the public weal; and it is clearly decided in favor of the latter by two obvious considerations.

In the first place, it is to be remarked, that however small the republic may be, the representatives must be raised to a certain number, in order to guard against the cabals of a few; and that however large it may be, they must be limited to a certain number, in order to guard against the confusion of a multitude. Hence, the number of representatives in the two cases not being in proportion to that of the constituents, and being proportionally greatest in the small republic, it follows that if the proportion of fit characters be not less in the large than in the small republic, the former will present a greater option, and consequently a greater probability of a fit choice.

In the next place, as each representative will be chosen by a greater number of citizens in the large than in the small republic, it will be more difficult for unworthy candidates to practice with success the vicious arts, by which elections are too often carried; and the suffrages of the people being more free, will be more likely to center in men who possess the most attractive merit, and the most diffusive and established characters. . . .

The other point of difference is, the greater number of citizens, and extent of territory, which may be brought within the compass of republican, than of democratic government; and it is this circumstance principally which renders factious combinations less to be dreaded in the former, than in the latter. The smaller the society, the fewer probably will be the distinct parties and interests composing it; the fewer the distinct parties and interests, the more frequently will a majority be found of the same party; and the smaller the number of individuals composing a majority, and the smaller the compass within which they are placed, the more easily they will concert and execute their plans of oppression. Extend the sphere, and you take in a greater variety of parties and interests; you make it less probable that a majority of the whole will have a common motive to invade the rights of other citizens; or if such a common motive exists, it will be more difficult for all who feel it to discover their own strength, and to act in unison with each other. . . .

Hence, it clearly appears, that the same advantage, which a republic has over a democracy, in controlling the effects of faction, is enjoyed by a large over a small republic—is enjoyed by the union over the states composing it. Does this advantage consist in the substitution of representatives, whose enlightened views and virtuous sentiments render them superior to local prejudices, and to schemes of injustice? It will not be denied, that the representation of the union will be most likely to possess these requisite endowments. Does it consist in the greater security afforded by a greater variety of parties, against the event of any one party being able to outnumber and oppress the rest? In an equal degree does the increased variety of parties, comprised within the union, increase this security? Does it, in fine, consist in the greater obstacles opposed to the concert and accomplishment of the secret wishes of an unjust and interested majority? Here, again, the extent of the union gives it the most palpable advantage.

The influence of factious leaders may kindle a flame within their particular states, but will be unable to spread a general conflagration through the other states; a religious sect may degenerate into a political faction in a part of the confederacy; but the variety of sects dispersed over the entire face of it, must secure the national councils against any danger from that source; a rage for paper money, for an abolition of debts, for an equal division of property, or for any other improper or wicked project, will be less apt to pervade the whole body of the union, than a particular member of it; in the same proportion as such a malady is more likely to taint a particular country or district, than an entire state.

In the extent and proper structure of the union, therefore, we behold a republican remedy for the diseases most incident to republican government. And according to the degree of pleasure and pride we feel in being republicans, ought to be our zeal in cherishing the spirit, and supporting the character of Federalists.

JAMES MADISON: Federalist No. 51

To what expedient then shall we finally resort, for maintaining in practice the necessary partition of power among the several departments, as laid down in the constitution? The only answer that can be given is, that as all these exterior provisions are found to be inadequate, the defect must be supplied, by so contriving the interior structure of the government, as that its several constituent parts may, by their mutual relations, be the means of keeping each other in their proper places. . . .

In order to lay a due foundation for that separate and distinct exercise of the different powers of government, which, to a certain extent, is admitted on all hands to be essential to the preservation of liberty, it is evident that each department should have a will of its own; and consequently should be so constituted, that the members of each should have as little agency as possible in the appointment of the members of the others. . . .

It is equally evident, that the members of each department should be as little dependent as possible on those of the others, for the emoluments annexed to their offices. Were the executive magistrate, or the judges, not independent of the legislature in this particular, their independence in every other, would be merely nominal.

But the great security against a gradual concentration of the several powers in the same department, consists in giving to those who administer each department, the necessary constitutional means, and personal motives, to resist encroachments of the others. The provision for defense must in this, as in all other cases, be made commensurate to the danger of attack. Ambition must be made to counteract ambition. The interest of the man must be connected with the constitutional rights of the place. It may be a reflection on human nature, that such devices should be necessary to control the abuses of government. But what is government itself, but the greatest of all reflections on human nature? If men were angels, no government would be necessary. If angels were to govern men, neither external nor internal controls on government would be necessary. In framing a government, which is to be administered by men over men, the great difficulty lies in this: You must first enable the government to control the governed; and in the next place, oblige it to control itself. A dependence on the people is, no doubt, the primary control on the government; but experience has taught mankind the necessity of auxiliary precautions.

This policy of supplying by opposite and rival interests, the defect of better motives, might be traced through the whole system of human affairs, private as well as public. We see it particularly displayed in all the subordinate distributions of power; where the constant aim is, to divide and arrange the several offices in such a manner, as that each may be a check on the other; that the private interest of every individual, may be a sentinel over the public rights. These interventions of prudence cannot be less requisite to the distribution of the supreme powers of the state.

But it is not possible to give to each department an equal power of self-defense. In republican government, the legislative authority necessarily predominates. The remedy for this inconvenience is, to divide the legislature into different branches; and to render them by different modes of election, and different principles of action, as little connected with each other, as the nature of their common functions, and their common dependence on the society will admit. It may even be necessary to guard against dangerous encroachments, by still further precautions. As the weight of the legislative authority requires that it should be thus divided, the weakness of the executive may require, on the other hand, that it should be fortified. An absolute negative on the legislature, appears, at first view, to be the natural defense with which the executive magistrate should be armed. But perhaps it would be neither altogether safe, nor alone sufficient. On ordinary occasions, it might not be exerted with the requisite firmness; and on extraordinary occasions, it might be perfidiously abused. May not this defect of an absolute negative be supplied by some qualified connection between this weaker department, and the weaker branch of the stronger department, by which the latter may be led to support the constitutional rights of the former, without being too much detached from the rights of its own department?

ALEXANDER HAMILTON: Federalist No. 78

We proceed now to an examination of the judiciary department of the proposed government.

In unfolding the defects of the existing confederation, the utility and necessity of a federal judicature have been clearly pointed out. It is the less necessary to recapitulate the considerations there urged; as the propriety of the institution in the abstract is not disputed; the only questions which have been raised being relative to the manner of constituting it, and to its extent. To these points, therefore, our observations shall be confined.

The manner of constituting it seems to embrace these several objects: 1st. The mode of appointing the judges; 2nd. The tenure by which they are to hold their places; 3rd. The partition of the judiciary authority between different courts, and their relations to each other.

First. As to the mode of appointing the judges: This is the same with that of appointing the officers of the union in general, and has been so fully discussed . . . that nothing can be said here which would not be useless repetition.

Second. As to the tenure by which the judges are to hold their places: This chiefly concerns their duration in office; the provisions for their support; the precautions for their responsibility.

According to the plan of the convention, all the judges who may be appointed by the United States are to hold their offices *during good behavior;* which is conformable to the most approved of the state constitutions. . . . The standard of good behavior for the continuance in office of the judicial magistracy is certainly one of the most valuable of the modern improvements in the practice of government. In a monarchy, it is an excellent barrier to the despotism of the prince; in a republic, it is a no less excellent barrier to the encroachments and oppressions of the representative body. And it is the best expedient which can be devised in any government, to secure a steady, upright, and impartial administration of the laws.

Whoever attentively considers the different departments

of power must perceive, that, in a government in which they are separated from each other, the judiciary, from the nature of its functions, will always be the least dangerous to the political rights of the constitution; because it will be at least in a capacity to annoy or injure them. The executive not only dispenses the honors, but holds the sword of the community. The legislature not only commands the purse, but prescribes the rules by which the duties and rights of every citizen are to be regulated. The judiciary, on the contrary, has no influence over either the sword or the purse; no direction either of the strength or of the wealth of the society; and can take no active resolution whatever. It may truly be said to have neither FORCE NOR WILL, but merely judgment; and must ultimately depend upon the aid of the executive arm for the efficacious exercise even of this faculty.

This simple view of the matter suggests several important consequences: It proves incontestably, that the judiciary is beyond comparison, the weakest of the three departments of power, that it can never attack with success either of the other two: and that all possible care is requisite to enable it to defend itself against their attacks. It equally proves, that, though individual oppression may now and then proceed from the courts of justice, the general liberty of the people can never be endangered from that quarter; I mean so long as the judiciary remains truly distinct from both the legislature and executive. For I agree, that "there is no liberty, if the power of judging be not separated from the legislative and executive powers." It proves, in the last place, that as liberty can have nothing to fear from the judiciary alone, but would have everything to fear from its union with either of the other departments; that, as all the effects of such a union must ensue from a dependence of the former on the latter, notwithstanding a nominal and apparent separation; that as, from the natural feebleness of the judiciary, it is in continual jeopardy of being overpowered, awed or influenced by its coordinate branches; that, as nothing can contribute so much to its firmness and independence as PERMANENCY IN OFFICE, this quality may therefore be justly regarded as an indispensable ingredient in its constitution; and, in a great measure, as the CITADEL of the public justice and the public security.

The complete independence of the courts of justice is peculiarly essential in a limited constitution. By a limited constitution, I understand one which contains certain specified exceptions to the legislative authority; such, for instance, as that it shall pass no bills of attainder, no *ex post facto* laws, and the like. Limitations of this kind can be preserved in practice no other way than through the medium of the courts of justice, whose duty it must be to declare all acts contrary to the manifest tenor of the constitution void. Without this, all the reservations of particular rights or privileges would amount to nothing.

Some perplexity respecting the right of the courts to pronounce legislative acts void, because contrary to the constitution, has arisen from an imagination that the doctrine would imply a superiority of the judiciary to the legislative power. It is urged that the authority which can declare the acts of another void, must necessarily be superior to the one whose acts may be declared void. As this doctrine is of great importance in all the American constitutions, a brief discussion of the grounds on which it rests cannot be unacceptable.

There is no position which depends on clearer principles than that every act of a delegated authority, contrary to the tenor of the commission under which it is exercised, is void. No legislative act, therefore, contrary to the constitution, can be valid. To deny this would be to affirm, that the deputy is greater than his principal; that the servant is above his master; that the representatives of the people are superior to the people themselves; that men, acting by virtue of powers, may do not only what their powers do not authorize, but what they forbid.

If it be said that the legislative body are themselves the constitutional judges of their own powers, and that the construction they put upon them is conclusive upon the other departments, it may be answered, that this cannot be the natural presumption, where it is not to be collected from any particular provisions in the constitution. It is not otherwise to be supposed that the constitution could intend to enable the representatives of the people to substitute their *will* to that of their constituents. It is far more rational to suppose that the courts were designed to be an intermediate body between the people and the legislature, in order, among other things, to keep the latter within the limits assigned to their authority. The interpretation of the laws is the proper and peculiar province of the courts. A constitution is, in fact, and must be, regarded by the judges as a fundamental law. It must therefore belong to them to ascertain its meaning, as well as the meaning of any particular act proceeding from the legislative body. If there should happen to be an irreconcilable variance between the two, that which has the superior obligation and validity ought, of course, to be preferred; in other words, the constitution ought to be preferred to the statute, the intention of the people to the intention of their agents.

Nor does this conclusion by any means suppose a superiority of the judicial to the legislative power. It only supposes that the power of the people is superior to both; and that where the will of the legislature declared in its statutes, stands in opposition to that of the people declared in constitution, the judges ought to be governed by the latter, rather than the former. They ought to regulate their decisions by the fundamental laws, rather than by those which are not fundamental. . . .

It can be of no weight to say, that the courts, on the pretense of a repugnancy, may substitute their own pleasure to the constitutional intentions of the legislature. This might as well happen in the case of two contradictory statutes; or it might as well happen in every adjudication upon any single statute. The courts must declare the sense of the law; and if they should be disposed to exercise WILL instead of JUDGMENT, the consequence would equally be the substitution of their pleasure to that of the legislative body. The observation, if it proved anything, would prove that there ought to be no judges distinct from the body.

If then the courts of justice are to be considered as the bulwarks of a limited constitution, against legislative encroachments, this consideration will afford a strong argument for the permanent tenure of judicial officers, since nothing will contribute so much as this to that independent spirit in the judges, which must be essential to the faithful performance of so arduous a duty.

This independence of the judges is equally requisite to guard the constitution and the rights of individuals, from the effects of those ill-humors which the arts of designing men, or the influence of particular conjunctures, sometimes disseminate among the people themselves, and which, though they speedily give place to better information, and more deliberate reflection, have a tendency, in the meantime, to occasion dangerous innovations in the government, and serious oppressions of the minor party in the community. . . . Until the people have, by some solemn and authoritative act, annulled or changed the established form, it is binding upon themselves collectively, as well as individually; and no presumption, or even knowledge of their sentiments, can warrant their representatives in a departure from it, prior to such an act. But it is easy to see, that it would require an uncommon portion of fortitude in the judges to do their duty as faithful guardians of the constitution, where legislative invasions of it had been instigated by the major voice of the community.

But it is not with a view to infractions of the constitution only, that the independence of the judges may be an essential safeguard against the effects of occasional ill-humors in the society. These sometimes extend no farther than to the injury of the private rights of particular classes of citizens, by unjust and partial laws. Here also the firmness of the judicial magistracy is of vast importance in mitigating the severity, and confining the operation of such laws. It not only serves to moderate the immediate mischiefs of those which may have been passed, but it operates as a check upon the legislative body in passing them; who, perceiving that obstacles to the success of an iniquitous intention are to be expected from the scruples of the courts, are in a manner compelled by the very motives of the injustice they meditate, to qualify their attempts. . . .

That inflexible and uniform adherence to the rights of the constitution, and of individuals, which we perceive to be indispensable in the courts of justice, can certainly not be expected from judges who hold their offices by a temporary commission. Periodical appointments, however regulated, or by whomsoever made, would, in some way or other, be fatal to their necessary independence. If the power of making them was committed either to the executive or legislature, there would be danger of an improper compliance to the branch which possessed it; if to both, there would be an unwillingness to hazard the displeasure of either; if to the people, or to persons chosen by them for the special purpose, there would be too great a disposition to consult popularity to justify a reliance that nothing would be consulted but the constitution and the laws.

There is yet a further and a weighty reason for the permanency of judicial offices, which is deducible from the nature of the qualifications they require. It has been frequently remarked, with great propriety, that a voluminous code of laws is one of the inconveniences necessarily connected with the advantages of a free government. To avoid an arbitrary discretion in the courts, it is indispensable that they should be bound down by strict rules and precedents, which serve to define and point out their duty in every particular case that comes before them; and it will readily be conceived, from the variety of controversies which grow out of the folly and wickedness of mankind, that the records of those precedents must unavoidably swell to a very considerable bulk, and must demand long and laborious study to acquire a competent knowledge of them. Hence it is, that there can be but few men in the society, who will have sufficient skill in the laws to qualify them for the stations of judges. And making the proper deductions for the ordinary depravity of human nature, the number must be still smaller, of those who unite the requisite integrity with the requisite knowledge. . . .

Glossary

ABA Committee on Federal Judiciary: The American Bar Association's influential 14-member committee that evaluates all federal judicial nominations and renders judgments as to the individual's qualifications on the basis of EWQ (exceptionally well-qualified), WQ (well-qualified), Q (qualified), and NQ (not qualified).

Accountability: The concept underlying representative democratic government that elected officials are responsible to the people for their actions.

Active political participation: Participation in politics that requires the expenditure of time and energy by citizens in pursuit of political goals. Includes voting, campaigning, and direct attempts to influence political decision makers.

Administration party: The party of the current president.

Advisory opinion: A formal opinion by a judge or judges about a question of law submitted by a legislature or by an executive (administrative) officer, but not actually presented to the court in a concrete lawsuit.

Agenda: Literally, "things to be done." The agenda of government is the list of issues to be acted on; what government works on.

Anti-Federalists: Name used by Federalists for opponents of ratification of the new Constitution. The opponents generally feared the powers of the proposed national government, but they lacked a concrete counterproposal, except for retention of the Articles of Confederation. They were also less well organized than the Federalists.

Apathy: Lack of interest in politics and a feeling that neither the individual nor the government makes much difference.

Appellate court: A court that primarily hears appeals from lower courts. The Supreme Court can be considered an appellate court, though we normally reserve the specific term for *intermediate* appellate courts in both the state and federal court systems.

Approval processes: The means by which a proposal is authorized to be put into effect. Such processes include majority-building in a legislature, getting the approval of the relevant person in a hierarchy, or convincing an expert to agree that the proposal is feasible.

Article I, Section 8 of the Constitution: The part of the Constitution that enumerates the powers of the national government. Examples: powers to tax, declare war, and coin money.

Articles of Confederation: First national constitution, drafted in November 1777, but not approved by the last state, Maryland, until March 1781. It provided for a weak central government with no executive or judiciary. The states were supreme, each having one vote in the Congress; Congress had neither the power to levy taxes nor the power to regulate commerce.

Attentive public: The relatively small number of citizens who are aware of most public issues and who are generally well informed about politics.

Bad tendency test: Less strict test for limiting freedom of expression developed in *Gitlow* v. *New York* (1925). Verbal and written expression may be curbed if it has a bad tendency to "corrupt public morals, incite to crime, and disturb the public peace."

Balance of power: A relationship whereby nations strive to maximize their security through the establishment of an approximate power equilibrium in the international system, thus reducing the probability of warfare or domination by another nation. In short, power checks power.

Bargaining: The attempt by two or more parties to come to an agreement, often through compromise or exchange of favors or trade-offs.

Beauty contest primary: A presidential primary in which voters choose among the presidential candidates without electing delegates, who are chosen in party caucuses and conventions.

Bicameral legislature: A legislative body composed of two chambers. In the United States, the House of Representatives is the lower house and the Senate is the upper house.

Bill: The written proposal in either the House or the Senate that constitutes the first step in creating a new law.

Bill of attainder: A legislative act declaring a person or persons guilty of a crime and meting out punishment for that crime.

Bill of Rights: First ten amendments to the Constitution, ratified in 1791. These amendments place limitations on the federal government and affirm the rights of the people and of the states.

Bipartisanship: Sometimes referred to as nonpartisanship, the term refers to the support of both major parties for foreign policy, regardless of which party occupies the White House. The assumption is that foreign policy should not be subject to partisan attack and exploitation.

Biparty coalition: A voting coalition of Democratic and Republican members in Congress. The most durable of these alignments is the "conservative coalition," composed of Republicans and southern Democrats.

Blanket primary: An "open" open primary that allows citizens to split their votes between parties on an office-by-office basis. For example, a citizen may vote in the Democratic primary for senator and in the Republican primary for governor.

Block grants: Grants-in-aid that commit funds to a broad functional area, rather than to a specific category or project. The grants have fewer details, carry fewer requirements, and require less paperwork than categorical grants. Block grants are ordinarily favored by Republican members of Congress.

***Brown* v. *Board of Education of Topeka* (1954):** Historic unanimous Supreme Court decision holding the "separate but equal" concept to be an unconstitutional violation of the equal protection of the laws clause of the Fourteenth Amendment. Overruled the long-standing contrary precedent of *Plessy* v. *Ferguson* (1896). *Brown* wrought a major sociopolitical revolution.

Budget: For the national government, a document setting spending limits for departments, agencies, and programs. In doing so, the budget reflects policy choices. It is also an instrument for promoting accountability.

Budget and Accounting Act of 1921: The law that established a coordinated federal government budget and auditing system and created the Bureau of the Budget (now the Office of Management and Budget) to assist the president in working with the new system.

Budget and Impoundment Control Act of 1974: Act whereby Congress reformed its budgetary process. It established a new fiscal year and budget timetable, created a Congressional Budget Office, and formed a budget committee in each house.

Bureaucracy: Any administrative system that carries out the day-to-day tasks of government using standardized procedures and rules and that is divided according to specialization of duties.

Bureaucratic politics: Term given to a style of policy making characterized by conflict among political actors who occupy positions in bureaucratic organizations or other political institutions. Every actor has political views, which often represent the needs of the organization. Conflict among the many competing views often results in some compromise acceptable to the majority of participants.

Cabinet: The term used to describe the collective heads of the executive branch departments. The cabinet serves largely as an informal advisory group to the president. Its membership is a matter of presidential discretion, but by custom the cabinet includes the heads of major departments, the vice president, and the director of the Central Intelligence Agency. Some presidents, including Ronald Reagan, have also included the U.S. ambassador to the United Nations.

Candidate appeal or candidate image: Personal characteristics of candidates that affect voters' evaluations. Voters respond to candidates' experience and apparent competence as well as to their honesty and integrity.

Candidate-centered campaign: An election campaign run largely by a political organization loyal to a single candidate, primarily for the benefit of that candidate. Little regard is given to the regular party organization or to the party ticket.

Casework: Services that members of Congress provide for their constituents. Casework may involve anything from helping constituents with social security problems to assisting local government officials in obtaining federal funds. Providing constituency assistance is a major activity of congressional offices.

Categorical grants: Grants awarded for specific purposes. Most of these grants require that recipient governments also contribute some matching funds and that state and local governments conform to detailed regulations regarding the use of the funds. These grants account for approximately 85 percent of all funds for grants-in-aid.

Caucus-convention nominating system: A system in which national convention delegates are chosen by the participants at caucus and convention meetings which begin at the precinct level—so-called first round caucuses. Here the basic delegate strength of the candidates is established. The selection process then moves to county conventions, to the state convention, and then to the national convention. The other form for the selection of delegates is the presidential primary.

Central clearance: The process of coordinating all executive branch legislative proposals through the Office of Management and Budget and other units within the Executive Office of the President.

Certiorari: The order by a higher court to a lower court to send up a case for review. Petitions for writ of *certiorari* are the most common means of appeal to the U.S. Supreme Court, whereby the claimant asks the Court to make the case "more certain" in the eyes of the Constitution. Also known simply as *cert.*

Checks and balances: Powers distributed among separate branches of government in a manner designed to protect each branch from interference by the others. In Madison's words: "Ambition must be made to counteract ambition. The interest of the man must be connected with the constitutional rights of the place."

Civil Rights Act of 1964: Landmark civil rights legislation in this century which included provisions to end discrimination in voting, public accommodations, public education, and employment.

Civil rights and civil liberties: Fundamental rights and liberties usually described in a constitution or bill of rights. These secure persons, personal property, and personal opinions from arbitrary interference by government. *Civil rights* concern equal protection and due process of the law for all groups, while *civil liberties* concern exercise of freedoms of speech, assembly, religion, petition, the press, criminal justice, and the like.

Clear and present danger test: Doctrine established in *Schenk* v. *United States* (1919) that freedom of expression can be limited in circumstances where such expression would create a clear and present danger of substantive evil that Congress has a right to prevent.

Closed primary: A form of primary election that requires voters to declare their party affiliation when registering or prior to casting their ballot. Citizens can vote only in the primary election of the party with which they affiliate. (See also Open primary.)

Cloture: A procedure by which debate in the Senate can be terminated. (See also Filibuster.)

Code of Federal Regulations: A U.S. government publication that contains a codified list of all federal rules and regulations first published in the *Federal Register.*

Cold War: A term to describe the tension and hostility between the United States (the West) and the Soviet Union (the Soviet-led Communist bloc) after World War II.

Combination compromise: A procedure whereby state judges are first appointed to the bench by the governor or some state commission until the next general election. In the election, the candidate then runs unopposed on a nonpartisan ballot that asks the voters whether the judge should or should not be retained. This procedure is an attempt to answer the criticisms of both the appointive and elective methods of selecting state judges.

Commander in chief clause: The constitutional provision that grants to the president authority over the nation's armed forces. This clause has been expanded with time to grant the president wide-ranging powers in the area of foreign policy.

Concurrent: "Running together"; having the same authority; at the same time. For example, courts have concurrent jurisdiction when each one has the power to deal with the same subjects and cases, and concurrent sentences are prison terms that run at the same time.

Concurring opinion: When a justice agrees with the majority vote on a case, but not with the reasons behind the majority opinion. These opinions do not have the force of law, but they are important as guides to future decisions.

Confirmation of appointments: Approval by a legislative body of some appointments to executive and judicial positions. This potential check on presidential appointments is performed at the national level by the Senate.

Congressional Budget Office (CBO): Authorized in 1974 to assist Congress in the preparation of budget resolutions and to provide independent analysis of the president's budget.

Connecticut Compromise: Compromise between nationalism and state sovereignty that resolved the differences between Virginia and New Jersey plans at the Constitutional Convention. It proposed a bicameral legislature with the House elected by the people based on population, and equal representation in a Senate elected by the state legislatures, with two senators for each state.

Consensus: Widespread agreement on basic values and procedures that provide the foundation for democratic government.

Conservatism: A philosophy that stresses individual and private initiative and a need for limitations on the powers of government.

Conservative coalition: A voting alliance in Congress of southern Democrats and Republicans in opposition to northern Democrats.

Consolidation: The period following government expansion. Emphasis is on consolidative issues: balancing the budget, reorganization, making government work better.

Constant dollars: A means for correcting inflationary impacts by recalculating current prices into the worth of a dollar in a particular year (such as 1990 prices in terms of the dollar's worth in 1972).

Constituency: The voters, or "people back home," whom the member of Congress represents. For the member of the House of Representatives, the constituency is an electoral district based on population; for the senator, it is the state from which he or she is elected.

Constitutional Convention: Meeting in Philadelphia in the summer of 1787 authorized by Congress to revise the Articles of Confederation. Instead, it produced the Constitution of the United States.

Constitutional court: A federal court created under Article III of the Constitution that carries out strictly judicial functions. Federal constitutional courts include the U.S. District Courts, the U.S. Courts of Appeals, and the U.S. Supreme Court.

Cooperative federalism: Term used to describe the efforts of national, state, and local governments to cooperate in meeting public problems and providing services to the citizens.

Cozy triangle: A grouping or "subgovernment" consisting of interest groups, bureaucrats who deal with the interest groups, and key members of congressional committees that develop legislation of concern to the interest groups and bureaucrats. Public policy for the area of concern is worked out through negotiations among the participants in the cozy triangle, and it usually is accepted by Congress and the president.

Crisis policy: The policy created in an intense, usually relatively brief confrontation that involves vital national interests. From a policy-making perspective, a crisis is characterized by little planning time, elite executive-level deliberations, the central role of the president, lack of reliable information, and the perceived need to react quickly and decisively. Congress plays little role in a crisis, generally supporting the president.

Critical election: An election that brings a new ruling coalition into power; often associated with a social or economic crisis. Sometimes called a "realigning election." A critical election launches a long period of control by one political party.

Declaration of Independence: Document formally severing ties between Great Britain and the American Colonies. Drafted by Thomas Jefferson, it argues that government is designed to secure the rights of its citizens and that proper government rests on the consent of the governed.

Declaratory judgment: A type of advisory opinion that pertains to a specific case. The court passes judgment between claimants in an actual controversy and defines their respective rights, but does not assign payment of damages. These judgments often remove the need for lengthy and expensive legal proceedings.

De facto: In fact; actual; a situation that exists in fact whether or not it is lawful.

Deficit: The extent to which a government's expenditures exceed its revenues.

De jure: Of right; legitimate; lawful, whether or not true in actual fact. For example, a president may be the de jure head of a government even if the army takes actual power by force.

Delegate role: The orientation of legislators who follow closely the wishes of their constituents. Contrast with trustee role.

Delegated powers: The powers awarded the national government by the Constitution, set forth in both specific and general terms. General powers include "all legislative powers" to Congress (Article I), "executive power" in the president (Article II), and "the judicial power" in the Supreme Court and such inferior courts as Congress establishes (Article III).

Democratic party: One of two major political parties in the country and since the 1930s the party having the larger, more diverse following. Today's party is based on the Democratic-Republican party founded by Thomas Jefferson and others almost 200 years ago.

Democratic Study Group: The largest of the many informal party organizations in Congress, the DSG is a group of 150 or so moderate to liberal House Democrats.

Democrats: Followers of or sympathizers with the Democratic party and its candidates. Currently Democrats outnumber Republicans. They are a coalition of minorities, most notably blacks, Jews, and Catholics in addition to union members and lower-income individuals in society.

Demonstration: Violent or peaceful activity by the public that expresses political views.

Diffuse support: Mass support of a generalized variety. (Contrast this with *concrete support* for specific programs.)

Direct lobbying: Face-to-face contacts by lobbyists with public officials, such as testifying in congressional hearings or meeting with members of Congress or their staffs. (See also Grass roots lobbying.)

Direct primary: Election held to nominate the candidates of a party. (Democratic and Republican nominees then oppose each other in the general election held in November.)

Directive opinion: A distribution of public opinion on a given political question or problem that expresses clear demands which leaders' policy choices are expected to satisfy.

Discharge petition: A move on the floor of either house to force a bill out of committee for floor consideration. Rarely successful.

Dissenting opinion: Opinion by a justice who disagrees with the view of the majority. Dissenting opinions have no force of law, but many have become important in themselves as guides to future decisions. Many dissenting opinions later become the Court's majority opinion, as was the case with Justice Harlan's dissent in *Plessy* v. *Ferguson* (1896).

Districting (or redistricting): The process by which state legislatures draw congressional election districts according to population distribution. Usually occurs every 10 years, following the census. (See also Gerrymandering.)

Divided party control: Condition in which one party controls the presidency and the other party controls one or both houses of Congress. A common situation in recent decades, particularly when the presidency is held by the Republican party.

Domestic policy trends: The various phases of government policy activity from expansion to consolidation to contraction, possibly returning once again to expansion.

Double jeopardy: Trying a person a second time for the same criminal offense for which he or she has already been acquitted.

Due process of law: Protection against arbitrary actions of government that violate a person's civil liberties or civil rights. *Procedural due process* concerns the propriety and fairness of the manner in which the legislative or administrative process is carried out. *Substantive due process* concerns the reasonableness and appropriateness of the subject matter or content of a law or executive ordinance.

Electoral college: Constitutional method of indirect election of president and vice president—a compromise. Electors, equal in number to senators and representatives in Congress to which each state is entitled, meet in their respective states on a specific day determined by Congress to cast ballots for president and vice president. The original intention was to have chief executives chosen dispassionately by community leaders; but the party system has made members of the electoral college into party stalwarts pledged to cast votes for their party's nominees. The state legislatures have power to determine how the electors are chosen, but today all are popularly elected in the following manner: The entire slate of electors nominated by the party whose candidate for president wins the most votes (a plurality) in the state become members of the college for that state.

Electoral mandate: An order or command from constituents for winning candidates to pursue a particular course of action. This "order" is normally not given specifically, but is inferred from the issue positions taken by the winning candidates.

Elitist interpretation: An analysis of interest-group politics in the United States which contends that pressures and power are too concentrated among special interests—usually large corporations and key executive departments, such as Defense—so that ordinary citizens and their representatives have little effective say in the development of important policies that affect employment, inflation, the environment, energy, and peace.

Eminent domain: The superior dominion of the government over property within the state. Government may appropriate private property for necessary public use, provided that owners are given reasonable compensation for their loss.

Entitlement program: A program whereby benefits (money payments or provision of services) are automatically distributed to persons who qualify under the conditions set down by law. Government cannot control the expenditures of these programs except by changing the law governing the entitlement; such programs are therefore referred to as "uncontrollable." Examples include Medicare, social security pensions, food stamps, and unemployment compensation. Currently, about 75 percent of the federal budget is relatively uncontrollable.

Equal time: A provision of the Communications Act of 1934 providing that if a station gives or sells time for campaigning to one candidate for office, it must give equal time to other candidates seeking that office. Under rules of the Federal Communications Commission, however, minor party candidates can be excluded from television debates between Democratic and Republican presidential candidates.

Exclusionary rule: (1) A reason why even relevant evidence will be kept out of a trial. (2) "The exclusionary rule" often means the rule that illegally gathered evidence may not be used in a criminal trial.

Executive agreement: An agreement between the president and another nation that has the force of law but, unlike treaties, does not require senatorial approval. Executive agreements are useful in routine foreign policy matters or those that require quick decisions.

Executive lobby: Officials of the executive branch who seek to influence the decisions of members of Congress.

Executive Office of the President: Office established in 1939 to assist presidents in carrying out their duties. It contains such units as the Council of Economic Advisers, the Office of Management and Budget, and the National Security Council. These offices, set up to serve the president directly, normally do not have programs to run. Instead, they coordinate the work of others.

Executive order: A rule or regulation, issued by the president, that has the effect of law without the need for congressional approval. Executive orders are usually used to carry out constitutional provisions or statutes.

Executive privilege: The claim by the president or the executive branch to withhold from other units of government information that would breach confidentiality within the executive branch or endanger national security.

Ex post facto law: A criminal law that takes effect after the fact. That is, actions taken in the past are declared to be criminal, even though they were not crimes at the time they were committed.

Fairness doctrine: A Federal Communications Commission regulation requiring radio and television stations to provide fair coverage of all sides of public issues. Nudged by the Reagan administration, the FCC abolished the doctrine in 1987.

Faithless elector: An elector who does not vote for the presidential candidate of his or her party who has carried the state. Of some 17,000 electors chosen since the first presidential election, only about a dozen, including one in 1988, have been "faithless."

Federal Communications Commission: Created by the Communications Act of 1934, the FCC is an independent agency charged with the regulation of television, radio, wire, and cable communications. It develops regulations for the industry, including the number of stations that can be controlled or owned by a single organization. Stations are required periodically to renew their licenses with the FCC.

Federal Election Campaign Act of 1971 and Amendments of 1974: The federal act providing for public financing of presidential elections and for regulation of campaign contributions and expenditures in federal elections.

Federal Register: A U.S. government publication that contains all presidential proclamations, reorganization plans, and executive orders, as well as all notices of proposed administrative rules and regulations. The *Federal Register* was initiated by an act of Congress in 1935. It is published five times each week.

Federal Regulation of Lobbying Act: Basic law that regulates groups in their activities designed to influence congressional decisions. Adopted in 1946, the law requires groups to register and to identify the legislation they support or oppose.

Federalism: The division of governmental powers between strong and independent state governments and the national government.

Federalist: Name adopted by proponents of the new Constitution; connoted that the proponents favored a constitutional federation of states, later called *federalism,* even though the new Constitution created a stronger central government relative to that of the Articles of Confederation.

Federalist: Also called *The Federalist Papers,* this is the collected essays of James Madison, Alexander Hamilton, and John Jay written in support of ratification of the new Constitution. Originally published in New York newspapers, this collection provides an authoritative interpretation of the intentions of the founders, and it stands as a major statement of American political thought.

Filibuster: "Talking a bill to death" in the Senate; when a senator or group of senators seeks to stop a bill by delaying a vote through open debate. A filibuster, in essence a marathon speech, can succeed unless the Senate passes a motion of *cloture* that will stop debate and force a vote on the bill. Cloture motions require a three-fifths majority of the Senate (or 60 votes).

First Continental Congress: A meeting in Philadelphia with delegates from all colonies except Georgia from September 5 through October 26, 1774. The Congress sought to redress colonists' grievances that acts of the British Parliament and of the militia had violated their rights.

Fiscal year: The period in which accounts are opened and closed for accounting purposes. In 1974, the government's fiscal year was changed from July 1–June 30 to October 1–September 30.

Food stamps: A Great Society program (Lyndon Johnson administration) that issues stamps to persons who qualify; these stamps may then be used for the purchase of food products. (See also Entitlement program.)

Foreign policy: The agenda of issues with which a government must deal, because nations live together with over 150 other nations in an international system in which each must look out for its own security and prosperity.

Franchise: The right to vote.

Franking privilege: Rule that allows members of Congress to send mail to their constituents free of charge. This privilege is particularly helpful in election years.

Free rider: Term used to describe individuals who gain benefits from government programs without belonging to the groups that lobby for them. All low-paid workers, for example, benefit from the efforts of groups that lobby Congress to raise the minimum wage.

Full faith and credit: A provision of the Constitution that requires each state to recognize the civil rulings of the other states.

General elections: Elections that decide who will take office. These elections normally have larger turnouts than do primary elections.

Gerrymandering: Drawing a congressional district to favor one party or the other in upcoming elections. Gerrymandered districts often resemble oddly shaped animals like salamanders (whence a portion of the term derives). (See also Malapportionment.)

***Gitlow* v. *New York* (1925):** Supreme Court case that first applied the freedom of press provisions of the First Amendment of the Bill of Rights to the states by means of the Fourteenth Amendment. This case also established the bad tendency test regarding freedom of expression. (See Bad tendency test.)

GOP Committee on Committees: The Republican party version of the Steering and Policy Committee in both the House and the Senate.

Government corporation: A unit of government that conducts activities like those of a business; for example, the Tennessee Valley Authority creates electric power, and the Federal Deposit Insurance Corporation insures the deposits in member banks.

Grants-in-aid: Grants from the federal government to state and local governments to assist them in providing governmental services.

Grass roots lobbying: An effort by groups to influence and inspire the public to bring pressure on their representatives. Grass roots lobbying is not regulated by the 1946 Federal Regulation of Lobbying Act. This form of lobbying is also known as indirect lobbying.

Great Depression: The period of economic upheaval during the 1930s that drastically altered the agenda of government and led to major social and economic programs.

Great Society: Label given to the social and economic programs initiated during the Johnson administration (1964–1969), such as the Economic Opportunity Act, Medicare, the Elementary and Secondary Education Act, and the Voting Rights Act.

Habeas corpus: The right of an imprisoned person to be brought before a judge to decide the legality of his or her detention.

Hierarchy: The structure of authority within administrative or corporate organizations. According to this principle, each person or organizational unit is under the authority of and responsible to someone at the next highest level. In hierarchical structures, certain persons are granted the power to say yes or no by virtue of their position in the organization.

Ideology: A more or less consistent and interrelated set of views concerning politics and governmental policies. In the American context, the ideology of *liberals* generally includes a belief in the need to use government to solve social and economic problems, a disposition to favor federal governmental action over state and local action, and a belief that government should promote equality among individuals. *Conservatives,* by contrast, generally favor individual and private initiative, limited government, a heavy emphasis on national defense, and states' rights.

Imminence test: Standard designed to maximize freedom of expression, developed in *Whitney* v. *California* (1927). A clear and present danger exists only if "the evil apprehended is so imminent that it may befall before there is opportunity for full discussion."

Impeachment: A constitutional grant of authority to Congress that provides for the removal of the president (or other federal officials) for "high crimes and misdemeanors." The House of Representatives first votes articles of impeachment against the accused by a majority vote. The Senate then acts as a court to decide on the merits of the articles. If the Senate, by a two-thirds majority, agrees with the articles of impeachment, the accused is removed from office.

Implied powers: The doctrine that the congressional power "To make all Laws which shall be necessary and proper for carrying into Execution the foregoing [specific] powers'' (Article I, Section 8) implies that Congress can pass legislation on subjects not specifically listed in the Constitution. Such legislation must, of course, be related to carrying out specific grants of power, and it must not be forbidden otherwise by the Bill of Rights or other constitutional provisions.

Impoundment: The process whereby the president ''refuses'' to spend money authorized and appropriated by Congress for specific programs. President Nixon's attempt to use impoundment to block programs that he disliked led Congress to pass legislation limiting presidential impoundment powers.

Incorporation: The ''nationalization'' of the Bill of Rights by judicial rulings, thus ''absorbing'' it and making it applicable to all 50 states.

Incrementalism: A principle of decision making whereby only small or marginal changes are made in existing policies or programs because decision makers lack sufficient information or other capabilities to make more comprehensive changes.

Incumbent: The current officeholder. Incumbents seek reelection; nonofficeholders seek election.

Independent regulatory commission: A unit of government, not part of a regular executive department such as transportation or energy, whose job is to regulate a specified area of economic activity. These units are designed to be somewhat independent of president and Congress and hence are sometimes called semiautonomous agencies.

Independents: Nonpartisan members of the electorate who may or may not be interested in politics and public affairs but who are not loyal to a political party.

Indictment: A formal accusation of a crime, made against a person by a grand jury on the request of a prosecutor.

Indirect election: The method by which senators originally were selected by state legislatures and not directly by the voters. Senators are now elected by direct or ''popular'' vote, as are members of the House of Representatives.

Inherent powers: Powers in foreign affairs arising from the status of the United States as a sovereign nation, necessarily engaged in external relations with other nations. Such powers are not limited to express powers, such as those of declaring war or making treaties.

Interest group: A group of people who share common goals and who seek to influence the formation and administration of public policy. Interest groups ''lobby'' the various branches of government, but especially the legislature.

Intermestic policy: Issues that embrace both international and domestic politics, such as food production or access to raw materials, especially oil. Similar to domestic policy in that Congress, interest groups, and the various publics play a larger role in its formulation and the executive a lesser one than in other foreign policy decisions.

International or state system: The interactions of the independent national political units within a global context of cultural and institutional anarchy.

Isolationism: A view (especially before World War II) that the United States should withdraw from world affairs and not become involved with other nations.

Issue awareness: Attention to matters of public policy and political debate. Most Americans have some information about major issues.

Issue network: An expanded and less exclusive version of a subgovernment that is associated with larger issues.

Issue voting: Vote choice made on the basis of agreement with one or more of the issue stands of a candidate.

Joint committees: Bodies composed of members of each chamber that serve to promote coordination between the two houses. *Conference committees* are the most common type of joint committee; they are formed to iron out differences between House and Senate versions of the same bill.

Judicial review: The doctrine that permits the federal courts to declare acts of Congress, the president, and the states to be unconstitutional and therefore null and void. This power applies to all courts, although the Supreme Court is regarded as the final judge.

Jurisdiction: Authority granted to the courts to hear and decide a case. This authority is different for different types and levels of courts. The U.S. Supreme Court, for example, has original jurisdiction in cases involving two or more states.

Justiciable: Proper to be decided by a court; for example, a ''justiciable controversy'' is a real dispute that a court may handle.

Law: A statute passed by Congress and signed by the president or passed over the president's veto. Laws set policy, establish structures, protect rights, and set penalties. They limit the discretion of government officials.

Legislative caucus (or conference): The primary party organization in each chamber, to which each party member automatically belongs. Party caucuses select party leaders, adopt party rules, and try to formulate party positions on issues.

Legislative court: Any federal court created by Congress under Article I of the Constitution. Legislative courts are often created for specific functions besides their judicial ones, such as tax administration. Legislative courts include the U.S. Tax Court and the Court of Military Appeals.

Legislative oversight of bureaucracy: Congressional activity to see if the executive branch, or parts of it, is faithfully, efficiently, and effectively implementing law.

Legislative veto: A provision used by Congress whereby the executive branch is given discretion to act subject to various forms of congressional review when that discretion is exercised in particular instances. The legislative veto was declared unconstitutional by the Supreme Court in 1983.

Legitimacy: The ability of governmental officials to have citizens accept their authority as a matter of right.

Liberalism: A view of the role of government that supports efforts to regulate business and to provide programs for education, medical care, welfare, and so on.

Literacy tests: Tests of reading ability that citizens were required to pass prior to registering to vote. In many areas, particularly in the South, these tests were administered in a manner that discriminated against blacks and other minority groups.

Lobbying: The efforts of an individual or a group to influence legislative or executive decisions.

Logrolling: A form of alliance by which one group agrees to support another's program or legislation in return for the second group's support of its program or legislation.

Long-term forces: Influences at work on voters that tend to remain constant over a series of elections. Common long-term forces include the party identification and socioeconomic status of a voter.

Loophole primaries: Presidential primaries in which a candidate who wins a plurality (more votes than any other candidate) can win all (or a disproportionate number) of the delegates, rather than sharing them with the candidates who place second or third.

Madisonian political system: A term often used to describe the main features of the American political system, such as the separation of powers, checks and balances, and federalism. Each is a device for limiting the concentration of power in a single entity. As James Madison argued, "ambition must be made to counteract ambition" in order "to control the abuses of government." Madisonian arrangements may also make it difficult to make decisions and to fix responsibility for actions.

Majority and minority leaders: The party leaders on the floor of each chamber of Congress. The floor leaders are selected by their respective party caucuses, work to develop party strategies, and try to maintain party loyalty in Congress.

Malapportionment: The practice of drawing congressional districts in a way that provides disproportionate numbers of representatives for some segments of the population, notably rural districts prior to the 1960s. (See also Gerrymandering.)

Mandamus: A court order that compels some person or institution to perform an act, particularly one that the person or institution has a clear legal duty to perform.

Mandate: An instruction by voters in elections to the winning candidate to act in particular policy areas in specific ways. Presidents who win by large majorities frequently argue that mandates exist for the programs they present to Congress. Given the differences within electoral majorities, the lack of public attention to the specifics of policy, and the roots of some voting in personality and partisanship, specific mandates rarely exist.

***Marbury* v. *Madison*:** An 1803 Supreme Court decision in which Chief Justice John Marshall established the doctrine of judicial review regarding acts of Congress.

Marginal seats: Congressional districts (or states, for the Senate) where neither party has a clear and dominant majority. Elections in such districts or states are usually very competitive, whereas there is a relative lack of competition in one-party or "safe" seats.

Markup: The decisions of a committee or subcommittee in revising a bill. During the markup stage, a bill is put in final form for floor action.

Mass media: Television, newspapers, and, to a lesser extent, radio and magazines. Sources of political news and advertising for large audiences.

***McCulloch* v. *Maryland*:** Supreme Court decision in 1819 that established the doctrine of implied powers.

Medicare: A program to provide health care benefits for the elderly as an extension of social security benefits. (See also Entitlement program.)

Merit system: A procedure whereby all career civil servants in the U.S. government are hired according to their competence. The merit system was first created in the Pendleton Act of 1883 and was designed to remove federal employees from political pressure.

Midterm elections: Congressional elections held in the second year of a presidential term. Voters often use these elections to express their support or dissatisfaction with the person (and party) in the White House. Typically, the president's party loses seats in Congress in off-year elections.

Miranda warning: The warning that must be given to a person arrested or taken into custody by a police officer or other official. It includes the fact that what you say may be held against you and the right to remain silent and to contact a lawyer.

Montesquieu: Baron Charles de Secondat Montesquieu (1689–1775), a French noble whose principal work, *The Spirit of the Laws,* published in 1748, contained a defense of the separation of powers and of checks and balances that influenced the framers of the Constitution.

Multimember district: A constituency with two or more representatives elected in a single election.

National interest: An ordering of priorities in accordance with national goals.

National Security Assistant: The director of the NSC staff who has increasingly become one of the president's chief foreign policy advisers, often rivaling, and occasionally surpassing, the secretary of state.

National Security Council: Unit established in 1947 to advise the president on the relationships among foreign, military, and domestic policy. Its precise duties have evolved with each new president.

National supremacy clause: Article VI, Clause 2, which declares that the Constitution, the laws of the United States, and all treaties shall be the supreme law of the land. Anything in the constitutions and laws of the states must conform to the national Constitution and the national laws. If there is a conflict between state and national constitutions or laws, the national position prevails.

Necessary and proper clause: That clause in Article I, Section 8 of the Constitution which provides for the implied powers of Congress.

Negative campaigning: Campaign tactics that attack a candidate for office, sometimes unfairly. Some negative campaigns are conducted in the absence of a candidate to support.

New Deal: The public policy program of Franklin D. Roosevelt's administration, beginning in 1933. It featured far-reaching government programs to deal with the crisis of the Great Depression and to provide for the general welfare. Examples of New Deal programs are the Social Security Act, the National Industrial Recovery Act, the Agricultural Adjustment Act, and the National Housing Act.

New Jersey Plan: The basic plan for a new government favored by the small states at the Constitutional Convention. It proposed a unicameral national legislature based on equal representation of all states. This plan also called for a plural national executive to be appointed by Congress. The executive would then appoint the judiciary. (See also Connecticut Compromise.)

Nondecisions: Decisions made by powerful actors to prevent certain issues from getting on the agenda of government. In this view, for example, the automobile industry prevented motor vehicle safety from getting on the agenda, since it would be difficult to control once the problem was acknowledged.

Nonpartisan election: An election in which there are no party labels on the ballot. Many local officials are elected in this manner as are state legislators in Nebraska.

Obiter dictum: Extra comments, viewpoints, or warnings expressed in a judicial opinion. *Dicta* do not have the force of law, but are views their authors believe to be important to add to the opinion.

Office of Management and Budget (OMB) in the Executive Office of the President: Established originally as the Bureau of the Budget, OMB has the responsibility for preparing the president's budget.

Oil embargo: Action taken by the OPEC states in 1973 to stop oil shipments to the United States, thus precipitating a major energy crisis.

One-party state: A state in which one party regularly controls nearly all public offices. Southern states have long been known as one-party Democratic states. Republican strength, however, is growing in the South, and is especially apparent in presidential elections.

OPEC: The Organization of Petroleum Exporting Countries (Saudi Arabia, Algeria, Qatar, Kuwait, Libya, Iraq, Iran, United Arab Emirates, Nigeria, Indonesia, Venezuela, and Ecuador), a cartel whose purpose is collectively to fix levels of production and the price of crude oil on the world market.

Open political culture: A set of widely held ideas about politics that stresses citizen opportunities to have access to and influence on many units of government, such as Congress and the bureaucracy.

Open primary: A form of primary election that allows citizens to vote in the primary election of any party; no declaration of affiliation is required. (See also Closed primary.)

Open seat: A legislative district in which the incumbent is not running for reelection.

Opinion leadership: Function performed by members of the attentive public, who inform friends, relatives, co-workers, and others about political affairs.

***Palko* v. *Connecticut* (1937):** Supreme Court case in which the Court attempted to distinguish fundamental rights that applied to both state and federal governments from less important or "formal" rights that need not apply to the states. This was later amended when nearly all rights, although not all, were made applicable to the states.

Pardon: The constitutional grant of authority that allows the president to forgive persons for all offenses against the United States except impeachment. The pardon exempts the recipient from any punishment for the federal offense that was or may have been committed.

Participatory democracy: A view of politics that places a high value on widespread involvement by all citizens. Town meetings in which all citizens discuss and vote on issues are cited as models of participatory democracy.

Partisan realignments: Shifts in party strength that lead from one party system to the next.

Party caucus: A meeting of party leaders for the purpose of nominating party candidates for office; earliest method of nomination. This term is now often used synonymously with *party convention* at the local level.

Party convention: A public meeting of party members or officials for the purpose of nominating candidates for public office. May also be used to draw up party rules, elect party officers, and adopt party platforms.

Party identification: Self-proclaimed partisan loyalty to a political party. Americans almost always identify as Democrats or Republicans. About one third of the American people claim no party identification, however; they declare themselves "independents."

Party platform: A statement of party principles and proposals drawn up at election time. The national party platforms adopted by the national conventions are predictive of proposals and policies that parties' presidential nominees and members of Congress will support. Only some states bother to adopt state party platforms; in any case, state platforms are usually ignored by the parties' nominees and the mass media.

Party responsibility: A system of "responsible parties" characterized by centralized, unified, and disciplined parties committed to the execution of programs offered at elections and held accountable by the voters for their performance.

Party systems or party eras: Periods of stable party alignment in which one party normally is dominant.

Party voting: Vote choices made on the basis of partisan identification; voting a straight ticket is a form of party voting, ticket-splitting is a form of defection.

Party whips: Assistants to the majority and minority floor leaders who act as links between the party leadership and regular party members. They also work to develop members' support for party positions on major bills. Whip organizations are particularly elaborate in the U.S. House of Representatives.

Passive political participation: Feelings and attitudes held by citizens that express their support or lack thereof for governmental institutions. Widespread popular support for American political institutions enhances the government's claim to legitimacy.

Patronage: The practice of awarding jobs, contracts, or other favors to supporters, friends, and other party members.

Pendleton Act (Civil Service Act of 1883): Law that sets basic principles for appointment to government positions through an open competitive process on the basis of merit. This law was a key step in building a merit system for hiring in the national government.

Peremptory challenge: An objection (by either side in the case) to having a prospective juror sit because that person is considered undesirable. No reason for the challenge need be given by the objecting side, but the *number* of such challenges is limited.

Permissive opinion: A distribution of public opinion on a given political question or problem that permits leaders a number of policy choices that will satisfy the public.

Pluralist interpretation: An analysis of interest group politics in the United States which contends that resources and power are spread sufficiently so that no single group or small number of groups can exercise undemocratic control of public policy.

Plurality election: An election in which the winner is the candidate who polls the most votes, regardless of whether or not these votes amount to a majority of votes cast in the election.

Pocket veto: Failure of the president to sign a bill into law that was passed by Congress with fewer than 10 days left in the congressional session. The bill is thus lost.

Policy: A settled course adopted and followed by a government, institution, body, or individual. In other words, it is the output of government action.

Policy evaluation: The process of measuring results, of determining whether the policy works. Evaluation is crucial during consolidative phases of domestic policy.

Policy implementation: The process of applying a solution to a problem. In this stage or process, a government agency may learn of the feasibility of its programs.

Policy process: The means by which government programs are developed and put into effect. The process typically includes several stages—identifying the problem, choosing an option, getting approval, applying the solution, measuring the results, and making adjustments.

Political action committee (PAC): A committee set up by a union, corporation, trade association, or other interest group to collect funds and disburse them for political purposes. Unions and corporations are forbidden by law from making direct contributions to political candidates. Funds raised by PACs on a voluntary basis from members, employees, officers, and stockholders, however, can be used for any legal political purpose.

Political culture: A widely shared set of ideas, values, and beliefs about government and politics.

Political efficacy: The estimate of one's ability to achieve his or her political goals through active political participation.

Political machine: A state or local party organization tightly controlled by the leadership. Patronage is typically the cement that keeps the organization together.

Poll tax: A tax citizens must pay before being allowed to cast their votes. Banned by the Twenty-fourth Amendment (1964).

Power (among states): The ability to influence other nations in the state system to behave in a certain manner or to prevent them from taking a particular action.

Precedent: An action that affects future decisions in similar situations. Supreme Court decisions and presidential actions over the years have provided precedents that have either expanded or limited presidential power in certain ways, such as foreign policy.

President pro-tempore: A senior member of the majority party in the Senate who acts as the presiding officer of that body in the absence of the vice president. This is a largely honorary position, since most power is in the hands of the Senate majority leader.

Presidential coattails: The effect of a president's presence on the vote received by other, lesser candidates of the same party. Popular presidents strengthen the vote for the entire ticket.

Presidential disability: Incapacity of the president that makes it impossible to carry out the powers and duties of the office. There is little agreement on the criteria to use in making this judgment. The Twenty-fifth Amendment (1967) outlines the procedures to be followed when disability is invoked.

Primary election: An intraparty election in each party for the choice of party nominees for office. Party primaries are regulated by state law and administered by public officials.

Privileges and immunities clause: Found in Article IV of the Constitution, this clause prevents states from favoring their own citizens by discriminating against citizens of other states.

Project grants: Special categorical grants designed to handle specific problems. These grants are made selectively on the basis of written proposals submitted by agencies of state and local governments. The federal government issues guidelines and specifications for submitting the proposals.

Proportional-representation primary: A presidential primary in which all candidates who reach the threshold, usually about 15 percent of the vote, are awarded their proportionate share of the delegates. Candidates who fail to reach the threshold receive no delegates.

Public interest group: A group that claims to represent the interests of the general public. Examples: Common Cause, American Civil Liberties Union, League of Women Voters.

Public opinion polls: Interviews with a sample of people to get their views of issues and to find out how they plan to vote. Candidates may use polls to help plan their campaigns.

Quid pro quo: Literally, "something for something," or reciprocity: the delivery of something in return for considerations given. Lobbyists and legislators often relate to one another on the basis of quid pro quo.

Racism: An attitude of hostility toward a race that leads to discriminatory or intolerant action.

Random sampling: A method of choosing persons or objects from a given population in such a manner that each person or object has an equal chance of being selected.

Ranking member: Term used to describe the member of the minority party with longest uninterrupted service on each committee. When party control of a chamber shifts, the ranking member ordinarily becomes the committee chair.

Ratio decidenti: The point of law settled by a Supreme Court (or other appellate court) decision. This point becomes the rule of law.

Reagan's New Federalism: A proposal to transfer more than 100 categorical grants-in-aid, including Aid to Families with Dependent Children and the food stamp program, back to the states. The federal government would take over Medicaid in exchange, and it would also provide some special funding to help states meet additional costs over a 10-year period. By 1991, the transfer process would be concluded. The federal government would have less overall responsibility and the state governments would have greater responsibilities and greater freedom from federal standards and regulations in meeting those responsibilities. The plan to swap programs was not approved.

Realignment: A major change in the political loyalties of voters, reflected in their shift of allegiance from one party to the other.

Recall: Removal of elected officials from office by a vote of the people.

Reconciliation: The congressional process of ensuring that actual spending levels are in line with the goals set in budget resolutions. The process is complicated by the fact that so many committees and subcommittees are involved in acting on the budget.

Referendum: An election in which voters indicate approval or disapproval of a statement or proposition.

Remand: A judgment or decision of an appellate court that requires a return of the case before it to the lower court from which it came in order to comply with the higher court's ruling. Used predominantly in instances where the appellate tribunal overrules or reverses the lower court.

Representative democracy: Called a "republican" form of government by the founders, this is a system of government in which the majority rules through the election of representatives. The founders contrasted this form of government with "democracy." Democracy was government in which the majority ruled directly through such means as mass meetings. This method of governance was impractical for a large country. Besides that, the founders observed that direct democracy had been associated historically with turbulence, excess, and disorder.

Republican form of government: A government based on the idea that those who hold political power are responsible to the voters who elect them; in other words, the key element in this form of government is representation.

Republican party: One of the two major political parties in the country. It was formed during the Civil War era as the war party of the North. Republican candidates for the presidency have won all but four elections since World War II.

Republicans: Followers of or sympathizers with the Republican party and its candidates. The Republican coalition of voters is overwhelmingly white and disproportionately middle-class Protestants. Republicans are generally better educated and wealthier than Democrats.

Reserved powers: Powers not delegated to the United States, which the Tenth Amendment declares are "reserved to the States or to the people." These powers are not specifically defined; traditionally they have included power over the education, health, safety, and morals of citizens. (The latter three are called "police powers.")

Revenue sharing: Eliminated in 1986, this was a program that returned federal tax dollars to state and local governments based on local population, tax effort, and per capita income. Grants had few strings, and matching funds were not required. Revenue sharing was designed to produce greater independence and decentralization among governmental units in the federal system. At its peak, revenue sharing accounted for about 5 percent of all federal aid.

Rule: A decision from the House Rules Committee that sets the time and length of House floor debate on a bill and the extent to which amendments to the bill will be allowed. Used for major bills.

Rule of four: The rule that the Supreme Court will grant no "certs" unless four or more Justices agree to review the case. This rule ensures that only a small percentage of all appeals are heard each year.

Rules Committee of the House of Representatives: A standing committee of the House that controls the flow of legislation from other standing committees to the floor; this committee plays a key role in establishing the House agenda.

Runoff primary: A second primary held between the top two candidates if no candidate receives a majority of the vote in the first primary. Of central importance in southern states dominated by the Democratic party.

Safe district: Electoral constituency in which candidates from a dominant party normally win with ease. Opposite of competitive (or marginal) district.

Safe seat: A legislative seat held more or less continuously by the same party or incumbent.

SALT II: The second Strategic Arms Limitation Treaty negotiated between the United States and the Soviet Union during the 1970s. Although the chief executives of both nations agreed to SALT II, President Carter was unable to generate Senate approval for the treaty, as required by the Constitution.

Sampling error: The expected variation in estimates about a population. When using a pure random sample, it is possible to calculate sampling error with precision.

Second Continental Congress: Congress that met in Philadelphia on May 5, 1775, after Britain refused to acknowledge the grievances in the petition of the first Congress. Rebellion was already in progress, and the Second Congress voted to raise a Continental Army and to appoint George Washington as commander in chief. On July 4, 1776, the Congress adopted the Declaration of Independence. On November 17, 1777, it approved the Articles of Confederation.

Security policy: Noncrisis foreign policy decisions involving bargaining among the White House staff, foreign policy bureaucracies, Congress, interest groups, and the public, although the executive branch generally possesses the greater influence.

Select committee: Temporary congressional committee created for a special purpose, such as an investigation into some national problem. Examples: Senate Indian Affairs, Senate Intelligence, House Aging, House Hunger, House Narcotics Abuse and Control. Occasionally, a select committee is awarded permanent status, such as Senate Indian Affairs in 1984.

Self-perpetuating agenda: Circumstances in which government programs generate future agenda issues, with little or no room for other issues.

Senatorial courtesy: The tradition that presidents consult with the senator or senators of their party from a state before making an appointment to the federal bench (or other higher office) from that state. Presidents rarely appoint a person opposed by the senators from that state. Should a president do so, a senator may ask the "courtesy" of the Senate to oppose the president's choice publicly.

Seniority system: A tradition, now somewhat less powerful, that awards committee chairs to members with the longest continuous service on each committee.

Separation of powers: The intentional division of the executive, legislative, and judicial powers into separate branches of government, designed to prevent concentration of the powers of government in the hands of any single group or faction.

Seventeenth Amendment: Adopted in 1913, this amendment provides for the direct election of members of the U.S. Senate. Prior to its adoption, senators were chosen by the legislatures of their states.

Short-term forces: Particular influences that affect voters at a single election. Typical short-term forces are candidates' personal characteristics, issue positions, and the current reputations of the party organizations.

Single-member district: A system in which only one legislator is elected in a district. All members of the U.S. House of Representatives are elected from single-member districts.

***Smith* v. *Allwright* (1944):** Supreme Court case that declared white primaries—primary elections conducted by "private" political parties in a manner designed to exclude nonwhites—unconstitutional. A major contribution of the Court to the democratization of elections and political parties.

Socialization: Political beliefs and orientations that are acquired during childhood; these beliefs usually last through the adult years.

Socialization of conflict: A political strategy based on the idea that the outcome of political conflicts is determined by the participation of the audience. The losing side in political struggles seeks to widen the scope of conflict by gaining reinforcements. By getting the audience involved in the fight, the losing side hopes to alter the balance of power. The winning side, by contrast, attempts to limit the expansion of conflict. This theory was developed by E. E. Schattschneider, a former president of the American Political Science Association.

Speaker of the House: The presiding officer of the House of Representatives, who is also head of the majority party in the House. The Speaker is chosen by the majority party caucus and is formally elected by the whole House.

Specific, express, or enumerated powers: Delegated powers specifically enumerated in Article I, Section

8 of the Constitution. These include the power to tax, to borrow and coin money, to declare war, to regulate interstate and foreign commerce, to raise and support an army, to maintain a navy, and to establish post offices and post roads.

Split-ticket voting: A vote cast for candidates of different parties for different offices in the same election. A voter who votes for a Republican candidate for president and a Democratic candidate for senator casts a split ticket.

Standing committees: The permanent and major committees of each chamber, organized according to functional areas (such as agriculture). These committees handle all legislation introduced in each chamber.

Stare decisis: A Latin term for precedent. The judicial reference—some regard it as an obligation—to abide by an earlier decision, unless the passage of time or other seemingly compelling circumstances justify overruling or reversing an established precedent.

State of the Union message: A constitutional provision that requires the president to report to Congress annually on the state of the nation. This message is now used as a major vehicle for suggesting new programs or directions.

States' rights: A political doctrine which holds that the powers of the national government are limited to those expressly listed in Article I, Section 8 of the Constitution. Proponents of states' rights resist the development of new national programs or the expansion of old ones. On the whole, Republicans and southern Democrats are most likely to espouse this doctrine.

Statutes: Acts of Congress that become law after they are signed by the president. Many congressional statutes have expanded the president's legal authority to act in certain circumstances—for example, the power to make executive agreements with other nations.

Steering and Policy Committee: A Democratic party organization in the House of Representatives that assigns Democratic members to various committees. The Senate version of this is called the Steering Committee.

Straight-ticket voting: A vote cast for all the candidates of one party.

Subcommittee Bill of Rights: Title given to a collection of congressional "reforms" that took place during the mid-1970s and reduced the power of standing committee chairs and dispersed power to subcommittees.

Subgovernment: A network of policy actors joined by their common interest in an issue or program. A typical subgovernment includes interest group representatives, bureaucrats, and members (and staff) of Congress, and is sometimes referred to as a "cozy little triangle."

Suffrage: The right to vote in political matters; also called the franchise.

Superdelegates: Delegates to the Democratic National Convention who are selected because they are prominent party or public officials, such as members of Congress. These positions were created to increase the influence of professional politicians in the national convention.

Surge and decline: The pattern of high and low turnout associated with presidential and off-year elections. High-turnout elections attract more voters with little interest in politics, in contrast to low-turnout elections, which are dominated by strong partisans.

Take care clause: A constitutional provision that the president shall "take care that the laws be faithfully executed." This clause is somewhat vague in its meaning, and each administration tends to interpret it in different ways.

Third party: A party that challenges the two major parties. Also called "minor" party. Examples: American Independent, Socialist, Libertarian.

Tolerance: Attitude of acceptance and fairness toward other participants in a political system, especially toward one's opponents.

Treaty: A formal, written agreement between two or more nations normally signed by the president or his subordinates. The signed document must then be approved by the Senate by a two-thirds vote. A treaty once ratified has the status of law both internationally and within the United States.

Trial heat: Public opinion poll that asks people how they would vote "if the election were held today" to estimate the strength of candidates.

Trust: Feelings and attitudes of faith in and approval of leaders and institutions; often discussed as the opposite of cynicism.

Trustee role: The orientation of legislators who believe that their main obligation to constituents is to use their own best judgment in making decisions; contrast with *delegate role.*

Turnout: Proportion of voting-age population that actually casts ballots in an election.

Unicameralism: A legislature with only one house. Of the 50 states, only Nebraska has a unicameral legislature.

United States Reports: The official publication of Supreme Court decisions and opinions, both majority and dissenting. All recorded decisions of the Court can be found in this publication.

Veto: A constitutional power vested in the president to refuse to sign any bill passed by Congress. On receiving a bill, the president may (1) sign it into law; (2) not sign it, whereupon it becomes law after ten congressional working days; (3) veto it and send it back to the house of origin; (4) issue a *pocket veto* by refusing to sign a bill passed within ten days of congressional adjournment (the bill cannot be sent back to Congress and dies for lack of a signature).

Virginia Plan: Major proposal for a new central government, written mainly by James Madison. It proposed a bicameral national legislature, an executive, and a judiciary for the national government. Principles of representation in the plan favored states with greater population and wealth.

Voter registration: The requirement that those with the franchise certify their eligibility to vote on an official list prior to casting their vote in an election. Designed to prevent electors from casting more than one vote in an election.

Voting Rights Act of 1965: An act of Congress that suspended state and county voter qualification devices, such as literacy tests, which were being used to keep blacks from voting. One of the most important civil rights acts in the history of the nation.

Wall of separation: The constitutional doctrine, first enunciated by Thomas Jefferson, designed to ensure a strict separation between Church and state under the "nonestablishment of religion" concept of the First (and Fourteenth) amendments to the Constitution. Discussed at considerable length and depth in the modern era in *Everson* v. *Board of Education of Ewing Township* (1947).

War on Poverty: The popular name given to programs of the Economic Opportunity Act of 1964. President Johnson referred to it as "my kind of undertaking."

War Powers Resolution of 1973: A congressional action requesting presidents to consult with Congress before committing the armed forces abroad into areas where hostilities are present or likely. If such forces are sent, presidents must report to Congress within 48 hours. These forces must be withdrawn within a specified period of time unless Congress has taken action to support presidential commitments.

Ways and Means Committee: A standing committee in the U.S. House of Representatives whose main function is to write tax legislation.

***Wesberry* v. *Sanders* (1964):** Supreme Court decision declaring malapportionment unconstitutional. This "one person, one vote" decision declared that all congressional districts must be approximately equal in population.

White House Office: Unit within the Executive Office of the President that directly assists the president in carrying out the duties of the office. The president's closest advisers are usually located here.

Winner-take-all: As applied in the electoral college, a system that awards all of a state's electoral votes to the candidate who receives the most popular votes.

Winner-take-all primary: Also known as a "loophole" primary, this is a presidential primary in which voters cast ballots directly for convention delegates who may be pledged to candidates or uncommitted. In the usual outcome, the leading candidate in this primary wins all the delegates in a district. Used by populous states to magnify the importance of their primaries. Democrats eliminated this form of primary for 1992.

Writ of habeas corpus: A court order requiring an official holding a prisoner to present that prisoner in court and to show cause for the prisoner's continued detention.

Notes

Chapter 1

1. V. O. Key, Jr., *Politics, Parties, and Pressure Groups* (New York: Thomas Y. Crowell, 1952), pp. 4–5. Key defined politics in this way: "Politics deals with human relationships of superordination and subordination, of dominance and submission, of the governors and the governed. The study of politics is the study of these relationships of power; the concern of the practicing politicians is the acquisition and retention of political power."

2. Harold Lasswell, *Politics: Who Gets What, When, and How* (Cleveland: Meridian Books, 1958). This book was first published by McGraw-Hill Book Co. in 1936.

3. See M. Margaret Conway, *Political Participation in the United States* (Washington, D.C.: CQ Press, 1985), especially chaps. 1 and 2. Also see William H. Flanigan and Nancy H. Zingale, *Political Behavior of the American Electorate* (Boston: Allyn & Bacon, 1983), chap. 1.

4. David B. Truman, *The Governmental Process* (New York: Knopf, 1953), p. 21. (Emphasis added.)

5. Harvey Fergusson, *People and Power* (New York: Morrow, 1947), pp. 101–102.

6. E. E. Schattschneider, *The Semisovereign People: A Realist's View of Democracy in America* (Hinsdale, Ill.: Dryden Press, 1975), pp. 39, 65.

7. Schattschneider, *The Semisovereign People*, pp. 2–3.

8. Schattschneider, *The Semisovereign People*, p. 39.

9. *USA Today*, March 28, 1983.

10. *Washington Post* (National Weekly Edition), December 10, 1984.

11. *Washington Post* (National Weekly Edition), December 10, 1984.

12. See Hedrick Smith, *The Power Game: How Washington Works* (New York: Random House, 1988), especially pp. 36–39.

13. Smith, *The Power Game*, pp. 83–84.

14. For an analysis of the Reagan years, see Charles O. Jones, *The Reagan Legacy: Promise and Performance* (Chatham, N.J.: Chatham House, 1988).

15. James L. Sundquist, "Congress and the President: Enemies or Partners?" in *Congress Reconsidered*, eds. Lawrence C. Dodd and Bruce I. Oppenheimer (New York: Praeger, 1977), p. 240.

16. Robert A. Dahl, *A Preface to Democratic Theory* (Chicago: University of Chicago Press, 1956), pp. 146, 151.

Chapter 2

1. Alfred H. Kelly and Winfred A. Harbison, *The American Constitution: Its Origins and Development* (New York: Norton, 1948), p. 94.

2. John P. Roche, "The Founding Fathers: A Reform Caucus in Action," *American Political Science Review*, 55 (December 1961), pp. 812, 815–816.

3. There is a number of excellent studies of the Constitution and its formation. As a starter, see Max Farrand, *The Framing of the Constitution of the United States* (New Haven, Conn.: Yale University Press, 1913); David G. Smith, *The Convention and the Constitution* (New York: St. Martin's Press, 1965); Clinton Rossiter, *1787: The Grand Convention* (New York: Macmillan, 1966); Seymour Martin Lipset, *The First New Nation* (New York: Basic Books, 1963); Charles S. Hyneman and George W. Carey, *A Second Federalist: Congress Creates a Government* (New York: Appleton-Century-Crofts, 1967); Edward S. Corwin, *The Constitution and What It Means Today* (New York: Atheneum, 1963); and C. Herman Pritchett, *The American Constitution* (New York: McGraw-Hill, 1977). Concerning the thesis that the Constitution was written to protect the delegates' property interests, see two opposing views: Charles A. Beard, *An Economic Interpretation of the Constitution* (New York: Macmillan, 1913), and Robert E. Brown, *Charles A. Beard and the Constitution* (Princeton, N.J.: Princeton University Press, 1956).

4. Joseph M. Bessette, "Deliberative Democracy: The Majority Principle in Republican Government," in *How Democratic Is the Constitution?* eds. Robert A. Goldwin and William A. Schambra (Washington, D.C.: American Enterprise Institute, 1980), p. 107. For an intriguing view of modern democracy, see Michael Margolis, *Viable Democracy* (Middlesex, Eng.: Penguin Books, 1979).

5. Alexander Hamilton, John Jay, and James Madison, *The Federalist* (New York: Modern Library, 1937), p. 59.

6. The Constitution empowered state legislatures to provide for the manner in which presidential electors are chosen. Originally, electors were chosen by the legislatures themselves in certain states. Before long, however, all were elected by popular vote.

7. Hamilton, Jay, and Madison, *The Federalist*, p. 337. (Emphasis added.)

8. Arthur N. Holcombe, *Our More Perfect Union* (Cambridge, Mass.: Harvard University Press, 1950), p. 236.

9. Hamilton, Jay, and Madison, *The Federalist*, p. 339. (Emphasis added.)

10. Holcombe, *Our More Perfect Union*, p. 10.

11. Martin Diamond, "The Revolution of Sober Expectations," in *America's Continuing Revolution*, eds. Irving Kristol et al. (Washington, D.C.: American Enterprise Institute, 1975), p. 38.

12. Alfred F. Young, "Conservatives, the Constitution, and the 'Spirit of Accommodation,' " in *How Democratic Is the Constitution?*, p. 118. For a view that the Constitution is essentially elitist, designed to curb democratic politics, see Michael Parenti, "The Constitution as an Elitist Document," in *How Democratic Is the Constitution?*, pp. 39–58.

13. Herbert Agar, *The Price of Union* (Boston: Houghton Mifflin, 1950), p. xiv.

Chapter 3

1. J. W. Peltason, *Corwin and Peltason's Understanding the Constitution* (New York: Holt, Rinehart & Winston, 1979), p. 123.

2. *Hammer* v. *Dagenhart*, 247 U.S. 251 (1918).

3. *United States* v. *Darby*, 312 U.S. 100, 124 (1941). This case overruled *Hammer* v. *Dagenhart.*

4. *United States* v. *Curtiss-Wright Export Corporation*, 299 U.S. 304 (1936).

5. C. Herman Pritchett, *The American Constitution* (New York: McGraw-Hill, 1977), pp. 70–72.

6. See an account of this dispute in the *New York Times*, March 27, 1984, p. 12.

7. *McCulloch* v. *Maryland*, 4 Wheaton 316 (1819).

8. Advisory Commission on Intergovernmental Relations, *The Federal Role in the Federal System: The Dynamics of Growth, An Agenda for American Federalism—Restoring Confidence and Competence* (Washington, D.C.: U.S. Government Printing Office, 1981), p. 30. (Emphasis added.)

9. Terry Sanford, *Storm Over the States* (New York: McGraw-Hill, 1967), p. 1.

10. Ira Sharkansky, *The Maligned States* (New York: McGraw-Hill, 1978), p. 95.

11. Advisory Commission on Intergovernmental Relations, *The Federal Role in the Federal System: The Dynamics of Growth, A Crisis of Confidence and Competence* (Washington, D.C.: U.S. Government Printing Office, 1980), p. 4.

12. Morris P. Fiorina, *Congress: Keystone of the Washington Establishment* (New Haven, Conn.: Yale University Press, 1977), p. 71.

13. *Garcia* v. *San Antonio Metropolitan Transit Authority*, 469 U.S. 528 (1985).

14. Martin Shapiro, "The Supreme Court: From Warren to Burger," in *The New American Political System*, ed. Anthony King (Washington, D.C.: American Enterprise Institute, 1978), p. 179.

15. The states' reliance on the sales tax, though still heavy, is less today than in the past. Currently, 37 states use *both* the personal income tax and the general sales tax. In 1950, only 17 states used both taxes. Advisory Commission on Intergovernmental Relations, *Significant Features of Fiscal Federalism 1978–79* (Washington, D.C.: U.S. Government Printing Office, 1980), p. 51.

16. Michael D. Reagan, *The New Federalism* (New York: Oxford University Press, 1972), pp. 33–44.

17. See E. E. Schattschneider, *The Semisovereign People: A Realist's View of Democracy in America* (Hinsdale, Ill.: Dryden Press, 1975), especially chap. 1.

18. Reagan, *The New Federalism*, p. 18.

19. Daniel J. Elazar, *American Federalism: A View from the States* (New York: Thomas Y. Crowell, 1966), p. 53. (Emphasis added.)

20. For instructive analyses of the grant-in-aid system, see Reagan, *The New Federalism*, pp. 54–88; and Deil S. Wright, *Understanding Intergovernmental Relations* (North Scituate, Mass.: Duxbury Press, 1978), pp. 128–147.

21. "Special Analysis H," in *Special Analyses, Budget of the United States Government, Fiscal Year 1989* (Washington, D.C.: U.S. Government Printing Office, 1988), pp. H-1–H-20.

22. Reagan, *The New Federalism*, pp. 66–72.

23. *South Dakota* v. *Dole,* 107 S.Ct. 2793 (1987).

24. Edward C. Banfield, "Revenue Sharing in Theory and Practice," in *The Uneasy Partnership,* eds. Richard D. Feld and Carl Grafton (Palo Alto, Calif.: National Press Books, 1973), p. 70.

25. *Congressional Quarterly Weekly Report,* February 7, 1981, pp. 275–278.

26. Roger Friedland and Herbert Wong, "Congressional Politics, Federal Grants, and Local Needs: Who Gets What and Why?" in *The Municipal Money Chase: The Politics of Local Government Finance,* ed. Alberta M. Sbragia (Boulder, Colo.: Westview Press, 1983), pp. 213–244.

27. George E. Peterson, "Federalism and the States: An Experiment in Decentralization," in *The Reagan Record,* eds. John L. Palmer and Isabel V. Sawhill (Cambridge, Mass.: Ballinger, 1984), p. 230.

28. See an interesting essay on the politics of federal aid by Raymond E. Owen, "Managers and Politicians: The Politics of Spending Federal Money," in *The Municipal Money Chase: The Politics of Local Government Finance,* pp. 185–211.

29. "Special Analysis H," in *Special Analyses, Budget of the United States Government, Fiscal Year 1989* (Washington, D.C.: U.S. Government Printing Office, 1988), p. H-22.

30. James Sterling Young, *The Washington Community: 1800–1828* (New York: Harcourt Brace Jovanovich, 1966), pp. 30–31.

31. Advisory Commission on Intergovernmental Relations, *The Federal Role in the Federal System: The Dynamics of Growth, a Crisis of Confidence and Competence,* pp. 82–88.

32. Ibid., p. 88.

33. Reagan, *The New Federalism,* p. 145.

34. Robert Gleason, "Federalism 1986–87: Signals of a New Era," *Intergovernmental Perspective,* (Winter 1988), p. 9.

35. Richard P. Nathan, Fred C. Doolittle, and associates, *Reagan and the States* (Princeton, N.J.: Princeton University Press, 1987), p. 356.

36. David R. Beam, "New Federalism, Old Realities: The Reagan Administration and Intergovernmental Reform," in *The Reagan Presidency and the Governing of America,* eds. Lester M. Salamon and Michael S. Lund (Washington, D.C.: Urban Institute Press, 1984), p. 440.

37. John Shannon, "The Faces of Fiscal Federalism," *Intergovernmental Perspective,* (Winter 1988), p. 17.

38. Nathan, Doolittle, and associates, *Reagan and the States,* p. 362.

Chapter 4

1. *West Virginia Board of Education* v. *Barnette,* 310 U.S. 624 (1943), at 642.

2. Aspects of these two chapters are based on author Henry J. Abraham's *Freedom and the Court: Civil Rights and Liberties in the United States,* 5th ed. (New York: Oxford University Press, 1988), and *The Judiciary: The Supreme Court in the Governmental Process,* 7th ed. (Boston: Allyn & Bacon, 1987). With permission.

3. Howard's monograph was published by the National Governor's Association Center for Public Research, Washington, D.C., 1980.

4. *Chicago, Burlington and Quincy Railroad* v. *Chicago,* 166 U.S. 226 (1897), a unanimous opinion written by Justice John Marshall Harlan I.

5. See Chapter 16. The case was *Gitlow* v. *New York,* 268 U.S. 652 (1925). The decision was 7:2, with Justices Holmes and Harlan dissenting. Gitlow lost and went to jail, but the principle of the "incorporation" of the Bill of Rights had been established.

6. 302 U.S. 319 (1937). (The dissenter was Justice Butler, but he wrote no opinion.)

7. 16 Wallace 36 (1873), at 74.

8. 109 U.S. 3.

9. *Plessy* v. *Ferguson,* 163 U.S. 537 (1896), at 551.

10. Ibid., dissenting opinion, at 559.

11. Professor Alpheus T. Mason's words, quoted in Abraham, *Freedom and the Court,* p. 419.

12. See ibid., chap. 7, "Race: The American Dilemma," especially pp. 413–419.

13. *Fletcher* v. *Peck,* 6 Cranch 87 (1810), and *Dartmouth College* v. *Woodward,* 4 Wheaton 51 (1819).

14. As of Black's ascent, the New Deal could usually count on, in addition to Black's, the votes of Justices

Cardozo, Brandeis, Stone, and—after their 1937 "conversion"—Chief Justice Hughes and/or Justice Owen J. Roberts. President Roosevelt appointed nine justices. Only President Washington appointed more: 10 (actually 14, but 4 did not serve).

15. Loren P. Beth, "The Case for Judicial Protection of Civil Liberties," *Journal of Politics,* 17 (February 1955), p. 112.

16. Hugo L. Black, "The Bill of Rights," *New York University Law Review,* 35 (April 1960), pp. 867, 874. As he put the matter elsewhere: "I think that state regulation [of economic affairs] should be viewed quite differently than where it touches or involves freedom of speech, press, religion, assembly, or other specific safeguards of the Bill of Rights. It is the duty of this Court to be alert to see that these constitutionally preferred rights are not abridged." Dissenting opinion, *Morey* v. *Doud,* 354 U.S. 457 (1957), at 471.

17. 304 U.S. 144 (1938), at 152.

18. *Minersville School District* v. *Gobitis,* 310 U.S. 586 (1940).

19. *West Virginia State Board of Education* v. *Barnette,* 319 U.S. 624 (1943), at 606–607.

20. *Ferguson* v. *Skrupa,* 372 U.S. 726 (1963), at 732.

21. As quoted by Charles P. Curtis in *Lions Under the Throne* (Boston: Houghton Mifflin, 1947), p. 281.

22. As told by Francis Biddle, *Justice Holmes, Natural Law, and the Supreme Court* (New York: Macmillan, 1961), p. 9.

23. See Robert H. Jackson, *The Supreme Court in the American System of Government* (Cambridge, Mass.: Harvard University Press, 1955), p. 82.

24. The exact quote, penned in *United States* v. *Rabinowitz,* 339 U.S. 56 (1950), was: "It is a fair summary of history to say that safeguards of liberty have been forged in controversies involving not very nice people."

25. *Culombe* v. *Connecticut,* 367 U.S. 568 (1961).

26. *Miranda* v. *Arizona,* 384 U.S. 436 (1966). (Miranda was killed in a barroom brawl in 1976; the police subsequently used a "Miranda card" to read the prime suspect his rights prior to arrest.)

27. See the contentious property tax application case of *San Antonio Independent School District* v. *Rodriguez,* 411 U.S. 1 (1973), and the related *Kadremas* v. *Dickinson Public Schools,* 56 LW 4777 (1988).

28. For example, *Harper* v. *Virginia Board of Elections,* 383 U.S. 663 (1966).

29. For example, *Shapiro* v. *Thompson,* 394 U.S. 1 (1967).

30. For example, *Loving* v. *Virginia,* 388 U.S. 1 (1967).

31. For example, *Graham* v. *Richardson,* 403 U.S. 365 (1971), and *Plyler* v. *Doe,* 457 U.S. 202 (1982).

32. See Chapter 5 for details.

33. As it did successfully in the highly controversial *Korematsu* v. *United States,* 323 U.S. 214 (1944), the famed "Japanese exclusion from the West Coast" World War II case. But that decision was overruled 40 years later.

34. *Olmstead* v. *United States,* 277 U.S. 438 (1928), at 478.

35. Justice Black's enumeration in his dissenting opinion in *Harper* v. *Virginia Board of Education,* 383 U.S. 663 (1966), at 677–679.

36. 13 N.Y. 358 (1856), declaring a law banning the sale of liquor unconstitutional.

37. *Papachristou* v. *City of Jacksonville,* 405 U.S. 156 (1972).

38. 342 U.S. 165 (1952), at 173.

39. *Malloy* v. *Hogan,* 378 U.S. 1 (1964).

40. 372 U.S. 355 (1963), 378 U.S. 478 (1964), and 384 U.S. 436 (1966), respectively.

41. Paul A. Freund, *The Supreme Court of the United States: Its Justices, Purposes, and Performance* (Cleveland: World, 1981), p. 87.

42. See E. V. Rostow, *The Sovereign Prerogative: The Supreme Court and the Quest for Law* (New Haven, Conn.: Yale University Press, 1962), chap. 3.

43. See the classification of privacy developed in P. Allan Dionisopoulos and Craig Ducat, *The Right to Privacy: Essays and Cases* (St. Paul, Minn.: West Publishing Co., 1976); the authors are two leading students of the issue.

44. *New Jersey* v. *T.L.O.,* 469 U.S. 325 (1985).

45. *Stanley* v. *Georgia,* 394 U.S. 557 (1969), at 565.

46. *Garger* v. *New Jersey,* 429 U.S. 922 (1976).

47. *Time, Inc.* v. *Hill,* 385 U.S. 374 (1967).

48. See, for example, *Cox Broadcasting Corp.* v. *Cohn,* 420 U.S. 469 (1975).

49. *Griswold* v. *Connecticut,* 381 U.S. 479 (1965), at 485.

50. *Roe* v. *Wade,* 410 U.S. 113 (1973).

51. *Doe* v. *Commonwealth Attorney,* 425 U.S. 901 (1978), and *Enslin* v. *Bean,* 436 U.S. 912 (1978), respectively.

52. *Bowers* v, *Hardwick,* 478 U.S. 186 (1986). The decisive vote was cast by Justice Powell.

Chapter 5

1. *Cantwell* v. *Connecticut,* 310 U.S. 296.

2. *Gillette* v. *United States* and *Negre* v. *Larsen,* 410 U.S. 437, at 469.

3. *Everson* v. *Board of Education of Ewing Township,* 330 U.S. 1, at 15–16.

4. *Engel* v. *Vitale,* 370 U.S. 431 (1962), at 425. Justices Frankfurter and White did not participate.

5. *Abington Township* v. *Schempp* and *Murray* v. *Curlett,* 374 U.S. 203 (1963).

6. *Wallace* v. *Jaffree,* 472 U.S. 38.

7. *Lemon* v. *Kurtzman* and *Earley* v. *Dicenso,* 403 U.S. 602 (1971), at 625.

8. *Lynch* v. *Donnelly,* 465 U.S. 668 (1984).

9. For a detailed analysis and interpretation of the religion clauses, see Henry J. Abraham, *Freedom and the Court: Civil Rights and Liberties in the United States,* 5th ed. (New York: Oxford University Press, 1988), chap. VI, "Religion," pp. 277–392.

10. *Schenck* v. *United States,* 249 U.S. 47, at 52.

11. As quoted by Zechariah Chafee, Jr., in his classic *Freedom of Speech in the United States,* 6th printing (Cambridge: Harvard University Press, 1967), p. 110. Chapter 3 in this epic work on freedom of expression fully describes the circumstances surrounding the *Abrams* case (pp. 108–140). See also Richard Polenberg's *Fighting Faiths: The Abrams Case, the Supreme Court, and Free Speech* (New York: Viking Press, 1988).

12. *Abrams* v. *United States,* 250 U.S. 616 (1919), at 630.

13. *Gitlow* v. *New York,* 268 U.S. 652 (1925).

14. *Whitney* v. *California,* 274 U.S. 356 (1927), at 376–378.

15. *Dennis* v. *United States,* 341 U.S. 494 (1951), at 510–511.

16. Ibid., at 581.

17. 369 U.S. 186 (1962).

18. *Gray* v. *Sanders,* 372 U.S. 368 (1963), at 381. (Italics added.)

19. *Reynolds* v. *Sims,* 377 U.S. 533 (1964), and five companion cases (377 U.S. 633–713). Warren's statement is at 562 and 567.

20. *Karcher* v. *Daggett,* 462 U.S. 725 (1984).

21. There are 11 "southern" states: Virginia, North Carolina, South Carolina, Georgia, Florida, Alabama, Louisiana, Mississippi, Texas, Arkansas, and Tennessee. Six are commonly classified as "border" states: Maryland, Delaware, West Virginia, Kentucky, Oklahoma, and Missouri.

22. 163 U.S. 537, at 544, 551.

23. Ibid., at 559.

24. *Sweatt* v. *Painter,* 339 U.S. 629.

25. *Brown* v. *Board of Education of Topeka,* 347 U.S. 483, and *Bolling* v. *Sharpe,* 347 U.S. 497.

26. 347 U.S. 483, at 495–497.

27. Ibid., 349 U.S. 294 (1955).

28. *Watson* v. *Memphis,* 373 U.S. 526.

29. *Alexander* v. *Holmes County, Mississippi, Board of Education,* 396 U.S. 19, at 20.

30. The Watts riots lasted six days and resulted in 34 deaths, 1032 injuries, the arrest of 3952 persons, and $40 million in property damage (more than 600 buildings were damaged and 200 totally destroyed). The Detroit riots of 1967 were even worse. That bloodiest uprising in the country in half a century lasted five days and resulted in 43 deaths, 1347 injuries, 3800 arrests, 5000 made homeless, 1300 buildings reduced to rubble, and $500 million in damages. See Abraham, *Freedom and the Court,* p. 398.

31. *Swann* v. *Charlotte-Mecklenburg Board of Education,* 402 U.S. 1, at 15, 30. (Italics added.) For some interesting background analysis, heavily critical of the chief justice's role, see Bernard Schwartz, *Swann's Way: The School Busing Case and the Supreme Court* (New York: Oxford University Press, 1986).

32. *Swann* v. *Charlotte-Mecklenburg Board of Education,* at 28.

33. *Bradley* v. *School Board of the City of Richmond,* 338 F. Supp. 67; followed by *School Board of the City of Richmond* v. *Bradley,* 462 F. 2d 1058 and *Bradley* v. *State Board of Education of the Commonwealth of Virginia,* 411 U.S. 913 (1973).

34. Title VII, and Sec. 703 (j).

35. *De Funis* v. *Odegaard,* 416 U.S. 312, at 320 ff.

36. *Washington* v. *Davis,* 426 U.S. 229 (1976).

37. *McDonald* v. *Santa Fe Transportation Co.,* 427 U.S. 273 (1976).

38. *Regents of the University of California* v. *Bakke,* 438 U.S. 265 (1978).

39. June 29, 1978, p. 1.

40. *Steelworkers* v. *Weber,* 442 U.S. 193 (1979).

41. Ibid., at 255.

42. *United Steelworkers of America* v. *Weber,* 443 U.S. 193 (1979), at 473, 476, and 482.

43. Ibid., at 532.

44. Ibid., at 545, 552, fn. 30, and 534.

45. *Firefighters Local Union* v. *Stotts,* 467 U.S. 561.

46. 476 U.S. 267 (1986).

47. *Firefighters* v. *Cleveland,* 478 U.S. 501, and *Sheet Metal Workers* v. *EEOC,* 478 U.S. 421 (1986).

48. 480 U.S. 149 (1987).

49. *Johnson* v. *Transportation Agency, Santa Clara County,* 480 U.S. 616 (1987).

50. *City of Richmond* v. *J. A. Croson Co.,* 57 LW 4132 (1989).

51. *Muller* v. *Oregon,* 208 U.S. 412 (1908).

52. *Rostker* v. *Goldberg,* 453 U.S. 57 (1981), and *Wayte* v. *United States,* 470 U.S. 598 (1985).

53. *County of Washington* v. *Alberta Gunther,* 452 U.S. 161.

54. Comment from the bench, June 22, 1964, as quoted in the *New York Times,* June 23, 1974, p. 16, in connection with the Court's holding in *Bell* v. *Maryland,* 378 U.S. 226, at 328, dissenting opinion.

55. *Reitman* v. *Mulkey,* 387 U.S. 369.

56. Stat. 437.

57. *Daniel* v. *Paul,* 395 U.S. 298 (1969).

58. *Palmer* v. *Thompson,* 403 U.S. 217 (1971).

59. *Moose Lodge #107* v. *Irvis,* 407 U.S. 163. The dissenting justices were Douglas, Brennan, and Marshall. This holding was reconfirmed in 1973 when the Court, 8:1, let stand a decision below that upheld the right of a New Orleans hotel to bar women from its men's grill, under a state ordinance that licenses bars but does not forbid sexual discrimination in places of public accommodation (*Millenson* v. *New Hotel Monteleone, Inc.,* 414 U.S. 1011). But *Golden* v. *Biscayne Bay Yacht Club,* 429 U.S. 872 (1976), *certiorari* denied, went the other way.

60. *Roberts* v. *U.S. Jaycees,* 465 U.S. 555 (1984) and *Board of Directors of Rotary International* v. *Rotary Club of Duarte,* 481 U.S. 537 (1987).

61. *New York State Club Association* v. *New York,* 56 LW 4653.

62. *Runyon* v. *McCrary,* 427 U.S. 160.

63. 427 U.S. 160, at 194, 195, 215.

64. *Bob Jones University* v. *United States* and *Goldsboro Christian Schools* v. *United States,* 461 U.S. 574 (1983).

65. *Patterson* v. *McLean Credit Union,* 56 LW 3735.

Chapter 6

1. Chilton Williamson, *American Suffrage from Property to Democracy, 1760–1860* (Princeton, N.J.: Princeton University Press, 1960).

2. Jerrold D. Rusk and John J. Stucker, "The Effect of the Southern System of Election Laws on Voting Participation," in *The History of American Electoral Behavior,* eds. Joel Silbey, Allan Bogue, and William Flanigan (Princeton, N.J.: Princeton University Press, 1978). See also J. Morgan Kousser, *The Shaping of Southern Politics* (New Haven, Conn.: Yale University Press, 1974).

3. Raymond E. Wolfinger and Steven J. Rosenstone, *Who Votes?* (New Haven, Conn.: Yale University Press, 1980), p. 78.

4. Much of the data on the American public in this and the next two chapters come from the national election studies conducted by the Center for Political Studies at the University of Michigan. These data were made available by the Inter-university Consortium for Political and Social Research.

5. 1980 National Election Study.

6. Paul Abramson and John Aldrich, "The Decline of

Electoral Participation in America," *American Political Science Review,* 76 (September 1982), pp. 502–521.

7. Angus Campbell, "Surge and Decline: A Study of Electoral Change," in *Elections and the Political Order,* eds. Angus Campbell et al. (New York: John Wiley & Sons, 1966), pp. 40–62.

8. Sidney Verba and Norman Nie, *Participation in America: Political Democracy and Social Equality* (New York: Harper & Row, 1972), chap. 4.

9. Ibid.

10. These data are from the 1973 General Social Survey conducted by the National Opinion Research Center at the University of Chicago.

11. Survey by ABC News/*The Washington Post* Poll cited in *Public Opinion* (April/May, 1981), p. 35.

12. Milton J. Rosenberg, Sidney Verba, and Philip Converse, *Vietnam and the Silent Majority* (New York: Harper & Row, 1970).

13. Ibid.

14. "Opinion Roundup," *Public Opinion,* 2 (1979), p. 35, from a poll by the Roper Organization in April–May 1979.

15. Herbert McClosky and John Zaller, *The American Ethos.* A Twentieth Century Fund Report. (Cambridge, Mass.: Harvard University Press, 1984).

16. Ibid., Table 5–1, p. 133.

17. Ibid., Table 5–7, p. 147.

18. Gallup survey, May 13–22, 1988, cited in *Public Opinion* (September/October 1988), p. 30.

19. James W. Prothro and Charles M. Grigg, "Fundamental Principles of Democracy: Bases of Agreement and Disagreement," *Journal of Politics,* 22 (1960), pp. 276–294.

20. James Piereson, John L. Sullivan, and George Marcus, "Political Tolerance: An Overview and Some New Findings," in *The Electorate Reconsidered,* eds. John C. Pierce and John L. Sullivan (Beverly Hills, Calif.: Sage Publications, 1980), pp. 157–178.

21. Herbert McClosky, Paul J. Hoffman, and Rosemary O'Hara, "Issue Conflict and Consensus Among Party Leaders and Followers," *American Political Science Review,* 54 (1960), pp. 406–429; and Samuel A. Stouffer, *Communism, Conformity and Civil Liberties* (Garden City, N.Y.: Doubleday, 1955).

22. Arthur H. Miller, "Political Issues and Trust in Government: 1964–1970," and Jack Citrin, "Comment," *American Political Science Review,* 68 (1974), pp. 951–988.

23. Seymour Martin Lipset and William Schneider, *The Confidence Gap* (New York: Free Press, 1983).

24. Miller, "Political Issues," and Citrin, "Comment."

25. Warren E. Miller, Arthur H. Miller, and Edward J. Schneider, *American National Elections Studies Data Sourcebook 1952–1978* (Cambridge, Mass.: Harvard University Press, 1980), p. 268.

Chapter 7

1. V. O. Key, *Public Opinion and American Democracy* (New York: Alfred A. Knopf, 1961), chaps. 2–5.

2. Contrary to frequent commentary, Americans are better informed and more interested in politics than citizens in other democracies; see Gabriel Almond and Sidney Verba, *The Civic Culture* (Princeton, N.J.: Princeton University Press, 1963).

3. For many years, surveys have revealed that health and medical problems dominate personal concerns. To get people to talk about other problems, it is necessary to focus the question on the neighborhood, community, nation, and so on.

4. Angus Campbell et al., *The American Voter* (New York: John Wiley & Sons, 1960), chap. 8.

5. Everett Ladd with Charles Hadley, *Political Parties and Political Issues* (Beverly Hills, Calif.: Sage Publications, 1973).

6. Based on analysis of the 1984 National Election Study data.

7. The discussion of the realignment of American politics usually focuses on demographic changes (see Chapter 8), but a case could be made that the real change is issue based and ideological.

8. John E. Mueller, *War, Presidents and Public Opinion* (New York: John Wiley & Sons, 1973), chap. 3.

9. "Opinion Roundup," *Public Opinion* (April–May 1984), p. 37, citing a survey by *Time*/Yankelovich, Skelly and White from December 1983.

10. Two elements need to be distinguished. One is the changing attitudes toward issues involving race and the other is the changing impact of race and characteristics associated with race on issue positions.

11. Warren E. Miller, Arthur H. Miller, and Edward J. Schneider, *American National Election Studies Data Sourcebook, 1952–1978* (Cambridge, Mass.: Harvard University Press, 1980), pp. 174–176.

12. Kent Jennings and Richard Niemi, *The Political Character of Adolescence* (Princeton, N.J.: Princeton University Press, 1974), is the major publication from this project. The data are available from the Inter-university Consortium for Political and Social Research.

13. *Gallup Report,* no. 262 (July 1987), p. 19.

14. For an analysis of the defeat of the ERA see Jane J. Mansbridge, *Why We Lost the ERA* (Chicago: University of Chicago Press, 1986).

15. The Gallup Poll found that in mid-1988, 70 percent of the public supported the idea of prayer in the schools [*Gallup Report,* no. 274 (July 1988), p. 15]. When the question becomes a *common* prayer, support drops below 50 percent.

16. Although Kennedy's Catholicism cost him votes in 1960, the heavy losses were mainly in the South, where the normal Democratic advantage helped him to win some states anyway. His Catholicism helped him in the North, where slight gains tipped the balance in some close states. See Angus Campbell et al., *Elections and the Political Order* (New York: John Wiley & Sons, 1966), chaps. 5 and 6.

17. Gallup Poll cited in *Minneapolis Star and Tribune,* October 30, 1988, p. 15A.

18. A controversy over the degree of constraint in the public has developed in recent years. See John Sullivan et al., "Ideological Constraint in the Mass Public," *American Journal of Political Science* (May 1978), pp. 233–249.

19. Gerald Pomper, *Voter's Choice: Varieties of American Electoral Behavior* (New York: Dodd, Mead, 1975), chap. 8.

20. Campbell et al., *The American Voter,* chap. 10.

21. For the published work, see John C. Pierce and Paul R. Hagner, "Changes in the Public's Political Thinking: The Watershed Years, 1956–1968," in *The Electorate Reconsidered,* ed. John C. Pierce and John L. Sullivan (Beverly Hills, Calif.: Sage Publications, 1980).

22. William C. Adams, "Recent Fables About Ronald Reagan," *Public Opinion* (October–November 1984), p. 9.

Chapter 8

1. For an analysis that focuses on switchers, see V. O. Key, Jr., *The Responsible Electorate* (Cambridge, Mass.: Belknap Press of Harvard University Press, 1966).

2. Relatively little study has been made of referenda. A good survey is David Butler and Austin Ranney, eds., *Referendums: A Comparative Study of Practice and Theory* (Washington, D.C.: American Enterprise Institute for Public Policy Research, 1978).

3. David R. Mayhew, "Congressional Elections: The Case of the Vanishing Marginals," *Polity,* 6 (1974).

4. For more commentary on the electoral college and the selection of a president, see *Winner Take All, Report of the Twentieth Century Fund Task Force on Reform of the Presidential Election Process* (New York: Holmes and Meier, 1978).

5. President Ford was defeated in an election bid but he was appointed, not elected, to office.

6. The major studies of vote choice are Angus Campbell et al., *The American Voter* (New York: John Wiley & Sons, 1960); Norman H. Nie, Sidney Verba, and John R. Petrocik, *The Changing American Voter* (Cambridge, Mass.: Harvard University Press, 1976). For a good survey of many studies, see Herbert Asher, *Presidential Elections and American Politics,* rev. ed. (Homewood, Ill.: Dorsey Press, 1980).

7. Jerome M. Clubb, William H. Flanigan, and Nancy H. Zingale, *Partisan Realignment* (Beverly Hills, Calif.: Sage Publications, 1980), chap. 4.

8. Gerald Pomper, *Voter's Choice* (New York: Dodd, Mead, 1975), chap. 8.

9. Nie et al., *The Changing American Voter,* chaps. 13 and 14.

10. Kent Jennings and Richard Niemi, *The Political Character of Adolescence* (Princeton, N.J.: Princeton University Press, 1974).

11. *New York Times,* November 10, 1988, p. 18.

12. *New York Times,* November 10, 1988, pp. 22–24.

13. It is ironic that immediately after the election the public's images of Bush and Dukakis improved so much that they became favorable for the first time in months. *New York Times*/CBS News poll data cited in the *New York Times,* November 21, 1988, p. 17.

14. For example, see Thomas E. Patterson and Robert D. McClure, *The Unseeing Eye* (New York: G. P. Putnam's Sons, 1976).

15. Thomas E. Patterson, *The Mass Media Election* (New York: Praeger Publishers, 1980), pts. III and IV.

16. For an excellent discussion of this topic see Larry M. Bartels, *Presidential Primaries and the Dynamics of Public Choice* (Princeton, N.J.: Princeton University Press, 1988).

17. This point is taken for granted in almost all studies. For historical perspective, see James L. Sundquist, *Dynamics of the Party System* (Washington, D.C.: Brookings Institution, 1973).

18. Walter Dean Burnham, "Party Systems and the Political Process," in *The American Party Systems: Stages of Political Development,* ed. William N. Chambers and Walter Dean Burnham (New York: Oxford University Press, 1975).

19. See Everett C. Ladd, "The Shifting Party Coalitions—1932–1976," in *Emerging Coalitions in American Politics,* ed. Seymour Martin Lipset (San Francisco: Institute for Contemporary Studies, 1978).

20. For a discussion of these patterns, see Clubb et al., *Partisan Realignment.*

Chapter 9

1. Robert MacIver, *The Web of Government* (New York: Macmillan, 1947), p. 213.

2. For a study of conflict within the Democratic party in Congress, see William R. Shaffer, *Party and Ideology in the United States Congress* (Lanham, Md.: University Press of America, 1980).

3. Gerald M. Pomper, *Elections in America: Control and Influence in Democratic Politics* (New York: Dodd, Mead, 1971), p. 186.

4. A particularly useful study of the national committee is by Cornelius P. Cotter and Bernard C. Hennessy, *Politics Without Power: The National Party Committees* (New York: Atherton, 1964).

5. *Congressional Quarterly Weekly Report,* January 14, 1978, p. 58.

6. Recent political and demographic changes in the South have weakened the conservative coalition. See an instructive article by Alan Ehrenhalt, "Changing South Perils Conservative Coalition," *Congressional Quarterly Weekly Report* (August 1, 1987), pp. 1699–1705.

7. See the data of the *New York Times*/CBS News exit poll, *New York Times,* November 10, 1988.

8. William J. Keefe, *Parties, Politics, and Public Policy in America* (Washington, D.C.: CQ Press, 1988), pp. 71–72.

9. In the lexicon of the *New York Times,* "soft" money is described as "sewer" money. Both campaigns hoped to raise at least $50 million in soft money in 1988. See an editorial on this underground financing of presidential campaigns in the *Times* issue of October 21, 1988.

10. V. O. Key, Jr., *Politics, Parties & Pressure Groups* (New York: Thomas Y. Crowell, 1964), pp. 207–208.

11. *Congressional Quarterly Weekly Report,* November 5, 1988, p. 3184.

12. Ibid., p. 3184.

13. E. E. Schattschneider, *Party Government* (New York: Holt, Rinehart & Winston, 1942), p. 64.

14. See an analysis of closed and open primaries by Craig L. Carr and Gary L. Scott, "The Logic of State Primary Classification Schemes," *American Politics Quarterly,* 12 (October 1984), pp. 465–476.

15. A useful summary of the arguments concerning runoff primaries appears in the *Congressional Quarterly Weekly Report,* May 5, 1984, pp. 1033–1035. The effects of abolishing runoff primaries are hard to predict. Would more black candidates win nomination? The answer is yes if white voters split their vote among several candidates. Would more black candidates be elected? The answer is uncertain. Some white Democratic voters might vote for the Republican candidate rather than their party's black nominee.

16. See William R. Keech and Donald R. Matthews, "Patterns in the Presidential Nominating Process, 1936–1976," in *Parties and Elections in an Anti-Party Age,* ed. Jeff Fishel (Bloomington: Indiana University Press, 1978), pp. 203–218.

17. For instructive analyses of party reform, see Austin Ranney, *Curing the Mischiefs of Faction: Party Reform in America* (Berkeley: University of California Press, 1975); William J. Crotty, *Political Reform & the American Experiment* (New York: Thomas Y. Crowell, 1977); and Everett C. Ladd, Jr., *Where Have All the Voters Gone?* (New York: W. W. Norton, 1982).

18. See an excellent analysis of the caucus-convention system by Rhodes Cook and Dave Kaplan in the *Congressional Quarterly Weekly Report,* June 4, 1988, pp. 1523–1527.

19. *Congressional Quarterly Weekly Report,* July 9, 1988, p. 1892. North Dakota is included in the states won by Michael Dukakis because he won the write-in vote; no names were listed on the ballot. New York is included in the string of primary victories of George Bush; although the state held no preference vote on the Republican side, Bush won a large majority of delegates.

20. Austin Ranney, *The Federalization of Presidential Primaries* (Washington, D.C.: American Enterprise Institute for Public Policy Research, 1978), p. 37.

21. *The People, Press and Politics* (Los Angeles: *Times-Mirror,* 1987), especially pp. 35–40, 95–101.

22. See the evidence on these and other policy views held by Democratic and Republican delegates in the *New York Times,* August 14, 1988.

23. At most, about one-quarter of the electorate has sufficient political sophistication to evaluate parties and candidates in terms of ideology and issues. The evaluations of the large majority of citizens carry very little political content. See Norman H. Nie, Sidney Verba, and John R. Petrocik, *The Changing American Voter* (Cambridge, Mass.: Harvard University Press, 1976), p. 118.

Chapter 10

1. Richard D. Heffner, ed., *Democracy in America* (New York: New American Library, 1956), p. 201. The classic work by de Tocqueville was first published in 1835.

2. See an analysis of these forms of benefits by Peter B. Clark and James Q. Wilson, "Incentive Systems: A Theory of Organizations," *Administrative Science Quarterly,* 6 (September 1961), pp. 219–266.

3. Sidney Verba and Norman H. Nie, *Participation in America: Political Democracy and Social Equality* (New York: Harper & Row, 1972), p. 41.

4. See the analysis of E. E. Schattschneider, *The Semisovereign People* (Hinsdale, Ill.: Dryden Press, 1975), especially chap. 2.

5. David B. Truman, *The Governmental Process* (New York: Alfred A. Knopf, 1951), p. 37. (Emphasis added.)

6. Clinton Rossiter, *Parties and Politics in America* (Ithaca, N.Y.: Cornell University Press, 1960), p. 21.

7. See an instructive study by Roger H. Davidson, "Breaking Up Those 'Cozy Triangles': An Impossible Dream?" in *Legislative Reform and Public Policy,* ed. Susan Welch and John G. Peters (New York: Praeger Publishers, 1977), pp. 30–53. The links between interest groups, legislators, and administrative agencies are explored at length in J. Leiper Freeman, *The Political Process: Executive Bureau–Legislative Committee Relations* (New York: Random House, 1965).

8. Truman, *The Governmental Process,* pp. 26–33.

9. V. O. Key, Jr., *Politics, Parties, and Pressure Groups* (New York: Thomas Y. Crowell, 1958), p. 28.

10. *The Federalist,* no. 10 (1787).

11. Hugh Heclo, "Issue Networks and the Executive Establishment," in *The New American Political System,* ed. Anthony King (Washington, D.C.: American Enterprise Institute, 1978), p. 96.

12. E. E. Schattschneider, "Pressure Groups Versus Political Parties," *The Annals,* 259 (September 1948), pp. 18–19.

13. For further development of these themes, see William J. Keefe and Morris S. Ogul, *The American Legislative Process: Congress and the States* (Englewood Cliffs, N.J.: Prentice-Hall, 1989), pp. 276–277.

14. See Mancur Olson, *The Logic of Collective Action: Public Goods and the Theory of Groups* (New York: Schocken Books, 1968), pp. 76–91.

15. The best way to understand the pluralist and elitist doctrines is to consult certain key works. For the pluralist position, see Truman, *The Governmental Process,* and Robert A. Dahl, *Who Governs?* (New Haven, Conn.: Yale University Press, 1961). For the elitist perspective, see C. Wright Mills, *The Power Elite* (New York: Oxford University Press, 1956), and G. William Domhoff, *Who Rules America?* (Englewood Cliffs, N.J.: Prentice-Hall, 1967).

16. Michael T. Hayes, "The Semi-Sovereign Pressure Groups: A Critique of Current Theory and an Alternative Typology," *Journal of Politics,* 40 (February 1978), pp. 134–161.

17. Schattschneider, *The Semisovereign People,* pp. 34–35.

18. *New York Times,* March 4, 1978.

19. The data on interest groups in these paragraphs are from Norman J. Ornstein and Shirley Elder, *Interest Groups, Lobbying and Policymaking* (Washington,

D.C.: Congressional Quarterly Press, 1978), especially chap. 2.

20. *Congressional Quarterly Weekly Report,* June 25, 1983, p. 1279.

21. See an interesting account of this intra-agriculture conflict in *Congressional Quarterly Weekly Report* (March 31, 1984), pp. 507–509.

22. See the studies of Andrew S. McFarland, *Public Interest Lobbies: Decision Making on Energy* (Washington, D.C.: American Enterprise Institute, 1976), and Jeffrey M. Berry, *Lobbying for the People* (Princeton, N.J.: Princeton University Press, 1977).

23. An especially useful analysis of the problems of groups that deal mainly in purposive incentives can be found in Robert H. Salisbury, "An Exchange Theory of Interest Groups," *Midwest Journal of Political Science,* 13 (February 1969), pp. 1–32.

24. *Congressional Quarterly Weekly Report,* March 4, 1978, p. 586.

25. *Washington Post,* September 13, 1978.

26. James L. Sundquist, "Congress and the President: Enemies or Partners?" in *Congress Reconsidered,* eds. Lawrence C. Dodd and Bruce I. Oppenheimer (New York: Praeger Publishers, 1977), p. 230.

27. *Congressional Quarterly Weekly Report,* December 27, 1980, p. 3646.

28. *Congressional Quarterly Weekly Report,* August 6, 1977, p. 1654.

29. For comprehensive data on PAC contributions, see the press releases of the Federal Election Commission, issues of February 24 and April 9, 1989.

30. *Congressional Quarterly Weekly Report,* November 21, 1981, p. 2269.

31. *Congressional Quarterly Weekly Report,* January 7, 1984, p. 19.

32. *New York Times,* March 6, 1978.

33. This evidence appears in Philip M. Stern, *The Best Congress Money Can Buy* (New York: Pantheon Books, 1988), p. x.

34. *Washington Post,* August 21, 1978.

35. *Time,* August 7, 1978, pp. 17–18.

36. John F. Bibby, ed., *Congress Off the Record* (Washington, D.C.: American Enterprise Institute for Public Policy Research, 1983), p. 34.

37. *New York Times,* April 17, 1978.

38. *Congressional Quarterly Weekly Report,* November 21, 1981, p. 2270.

39. See Donald R. Matthews, *U.S. Senators and Their World* (Chapel Hill: University of North Carolina Press, 1960), chap 8; and Raymond A. Bauer, Ithiel de Sola Pool, and Lewis A. Dexter, *American Business and Public Policy* (New York: Atherton Press, 1963), pp. 350–357.

40. *U.S. News & World Report,* September 19, 1983, p. 65. For lobbyists' methods, see also Bauer et al., *American Business and Public Policy.*

41. See the discussion of entitlement programs in *Congressional Quarterly Weekly Report,* January 19, 1980, pp. 117–124. The quotation is from p. 122.

42. *U.S.* v. *Harriss et al.,* 347 U.S. 612 (1954).

43. *Congressional Quarterly Weekly Report,* July 26, 1980, p. 2089.

Chapter 11

1. V. O. Key, Jr., and Milton C. Cummings, *The Responsible Electorate* (New York: Vintage Books, 1966), p. 6.

2. See, for example, Douglass Cater, *The Fourth Branch of Government* (Boston: Houghton Mifflin, 1959).

3. *New York Times Co.* v. *Sullivan,* 376 U.S. 254 (1964).

4. *Hustler Magazine* v. *Falwell,* 108 S.Ct. 876 (1988).

5. This discussion of media ownership is based largely on Doris A. Graber, *Mass Media and American Politics* (Washington, D.C.: CQ Press, 1984), especially pp. 39–44.

6. Michael J. Robinson and Margaret A. Sheehan, *Over the Wire and on TV* (New York: Russell Sage Foundation, 1980), p. 15.

7. *Congressional Quarterly Weekly Report,* April 25, 1987, p. 785.

8. See Graber, *Mass Media and American Politics,* pp. 47–51.

9. Ibid., pp. 106–109.

10. *New York Times,* December 23, 1987.

11. For analysis of the recent struggles over the fairness doctrine, see various issues of the *Congressional Quar-*

terly Weekly Report, including those of April 25, June 27, and August 8, 1987. For a wide-ranging analysis of government regulation of the media, see Steven J. Simmons, *The Fairness Doctrine and the Media* (Berkeley: University of California Press, 1978).

12. Bureau of the Census. *Statistical Abstract of the United States* (Washington, D.C.: U.S. Government Printing Office, 1987), p. 531.

13. *Gallup Report,* August 1987, pp. 8–9.

14. *The People and the Press* (Los Angeles: Times-Mirror, 1986), part 2, pp. 6–9.

15. This discussion of the characteristics of news is based largely on Graber, *Mass Media and American Politics,* pp. 89–93.

16. Will Payne, "Local Politics," *Saturday Evening Post,* April 30, 1927, p. 44.

17. David L. Paletz and Robert M. Entman, *Media Power Politics* (New York: Free Press, 1981), p. 17.

18. Robinson and Sheehan, *Over the Wire and on TV,* pp. 207–215.

19. Albert R. Hunt, "The Media and Presidential Campaigns," in *Elections American Style,* ed. A. James Reichley (Washington, D.C.: The Brookings Institution, 1987), pp. 58–59.

20. Robinson and Sheehan, *Over the Wire and on TV,* p. 216.

21. Stephen Hess, *The Washington Reporters* (Washington, D.C.: The Brookings Institution, 1981), especially pp. 130–137.

22. S. Robert Lichter, Stanley Rothman, and Linda S. Lichter, *The Media Elite* (Bethesda, Md.: Adler and Adler Publishers, 1986), pp. 21–27.

23. See an analysis of this survey by William Schneider and I. A. Lewis, "Views on the News," *Public Opinion,* (August/September 1985), pp. 6–11.

24. *The People and the Press* (Los Angeles: Times-Mirror, 1986), part 3, pp. 9–10.

25. Lichter et al., *The Media Elite,* pp. 28–29.

26. Graber, *Mass Media and American Politics,* p. 60.

27. These surveys of editorial endorsements are made by *Editor and Publisher* immediately prior to the election. The 1984 data appear in the November 3, 1984, issue, pp. 9–12. Typically, about one-fourth of all dailies do not endorse presidential candidates.

28. See the development of these themes in Robinson and Sheehan, *Over the Wire and on TV,* pp. 60–62.

29. Austin Ranney, *Channels of Power: The Impact of Television on American Politics* (New York: Basic Books, 1983), p. 56.

30. Hess, *The Washington Reporters,* p. 115.

31. Robinson and Sheehan, *Over the Wire and on TV,* p. 295.

32. Ibid., p. 303.

33. Ibid., p. 54.

34. Curtis B. Gans, "Is TV Turning off the American Voter?" *New York Times,* July 3, 1988.

35. Michael J. Robinson, "Just How Liberal Is the News?" *Public Opinion* (February/March 1983), p. 59.

36. Sam Donaldson, *Hold On, Mr. President* (New York: Random House, 1987), p. 7.

37. Ranney, *Channels of Power,* p. 61.

38. Joseph Kraft, "The Imperial Media," *Commentary* (May 1981), pp. 41, 43.

39. Robinson and Sheehan, *Over the Wire and on TV,* p. 302.

40. Ibid., p. 294.

41. Ranney, *Channels of Power,* p. 61.

42. Robinson and Sheehan, *Over the Wire and on TV,* p. 302.

43. E. E. Schattschneider, *The Semisovereign People* (New York: Holt, Rinehart & Winston, 1960), p. 2. See an explication of the "socialization of conflict" model in chap. 1.

44. See Ranney, *Channels of Power,* pp. 101–105, and Graber, *Mass Media and American Politics,* pp. 184–186.

45. *The American Public's Experience with Recent Presidential Elections: A National Survey of Public Awareness and Personal Opinion* (New York: Hearst Corporation, 1988), p. 24.

46. Quoted in Graber, *Mass Media and American Politics,* p. 185.

47. Michael J. Robinson, "Three Faces of Congressional Media," in Thomas E. Mann and Norman J. Ornstein, *The New Congress* (Washington, D.C.: American Enterprise Institute for Public Policy Research, 1981), pp. 93–94.

48. Hedrick Smith, *The Power Game: How Washington Works* (New York: Random House, 1988), p. 37.

49. Quoted in Hunt, "The Media and Presidential Campaigns," p. 53.

50. David S. Broder, *Behind the Front Page: A Candid Look at How the News Is Made* (New York: Simon & Schuster, 1987), pp. 240–241.

51. Hunt, "The Media and Presidential Campaigns," p. 58.

52. See the *New York Times,* issues of March 15, 21, and 24, 1988, and *USA Today,* April 14, 1988.

53. *Washington Post,* June 15, 1987.

54. *Chicago Tribune,* January 24, 1988.

55. *New York Times,* March 21, 1988.

56. See a column by R. W. Apple, Jr., in the *New York Times,* February 11, 1988.

57. *Congressional Quarterly Weekly Report,* December 19, 1987, p. 3145.

58. *Pittsburgh Post Gazette,* October 24, 1988.

59. *Congressional Quarterly Weekly Report,* June 10, 1978, p. 1463.

60. See evidence assembled by Charles Press and Kenneth Verburg, *American Politicians and Journalists* (Glenview, Ill.: Scott, Foresman, 1988), p. 233. The importance of television ads in campaigns is not surprising. It may be hard to believe but the average American is exposed to about 3000 ads a day in newspapers, billboards, and the like and spends a whopping year and a half of his or her life viewing television commercials. See an article on advertising clutter by syndicated columnist (and ABC news commentator) George F. Will, appearing, among other places, in the *Pittsburgh Post-Gazette,* December 28, 1987.

61. This analysis is based mainly on an article by Peter Bragdon in the *Congressional Quarterly Weekly Report,* December 19, 1987, pp. 3143–3146, quotations on p. 3143 and p. 3144.

62. See Graber, *Mass Media in American Politics,* pp. 200–208, and Thomas Patterson, *The Mass Media Election: How Americans Choose Their President* (New York: Praeger Publishers, 1980), especially pp. 21–25.

63. *Congressional Record,* 100th Congress, 2d Session, April 26, 1988, pp. S4734–4735 (daily edition). The data on horse race versus issue airtime are derived from a study commissioned by *USA Today,* as reported in the issue of April 22, 1988.

64. See Robinson and Sheehan, *Over the Wire and on TV,* pp. 89–90.

65. Henry E. Brady and Richard Johnston, "What's the Primary Message: Horse Race or Issue Journalism?" in *Media and Momentum,* eds. Gary R. Orren and Nelson W. Polsby (Chatham, N.J.: Chatham House Publishers, 1987), p. 128.

66. Nelson W. Polsby, *Consequences of Party Reform* (New York: Oxford University Press, 1983), p. 67.

67. David S. Broder, "Of Presidents and Parties," *Wilson Quarterly,* 2 (Winter 1978), pp. 109–110.

68. Hunt, "The Media and Presidential Campaigns," p. 54.

69. Smith, *The Power Game,* p. 36.

70. *USA Today,* January 19, 1988.

71. Marjorie Randon Hershey, *Running for Office: The Political Education of Campaigners* (Chatham, N.J.: Chatham House Publishers, 1984), p. 148.

72. Ellen Goodman, "Turning on Television's Viewer/Voter," *Pittsburgh Post-Gazette,* March 10, 1988.

73. Joseph Wagner, "Media Do Make a Difference: The Differential Impact of Mass Media in the 1976 Presidential Race," *American Journal of Political Science,* 27 (August 1983), pp. 407–430.

74. See Paletz and Entman, *Media Power Politics,* p. 241.

75. Graber, *Mass Media and American Politics,* p. 213.

76. Ranney, *Channels of Power,* p. 76.

77. Michael J. Robinson, "Television and American Politics: 1956–1976," *Public Interest,* 48 (Summer 1977), p. 28.

78. Paletz and Entman, *Media Power Politics,* p. 251.

79. Political routines, such as elections, generate the need for policy alternatives. See an interesting framework developed by Nelson W. Polsby to explain the acceptance of policy innovation in *Political Innovation in America* (New Haven, Conn.: Yale University Press, 1984), especially chap. 5.

80. David R. Mayhew, *Congress: The Electoral Connection* (New Haven, Conn.: Yale University Press, 1975), especially pp. 61–77.

81. See Ranney, *Channels of Power,* pp. 124–147.

82. *Congressional Record,* 99th Congress, 2d Session, September 10, 1986, p. H6598 (daily edition).

83. Robinson and Sheehan, *Over the Wire and on TV,* p. 191.

84. Robinson, "Television and American Politics," p. 22.

85. Fred Smoller, "The Six O'Clock Presidency: Patterns of Network News Coverage of the President," *Presidential Studies Quarterly,* 16 (Winter 1986), pp. 31–49.

86. Broder, *Behind the Front Page,* p. 215.

87. See an unusually interesting essay by Michael J. Robinson, "Three Faces of Congressional Media," in *The New Congress,* eds. Thomas E. Mann and Norman J. Ornstein (Washington, D.C.: American Enterprise Institute for Public Policy Research, 1981), pp. 56–96.

88. Michael J. Malbin, *Unelected Representatives: Congressional Staff and the Future of Representative Government* (New York: Basic Books, 1980), p. 44.

Chapter 12

1. *Davis* v. *Bandemer,* 106 S.Ct. 2810 (1986).

2. John W. Kingdon, *Congressmen's Voting Decisions* (New York: Harper & Row, 1981), p. 37.

3. See, for example, Warren Lee Kostroski, "Party and Incumbency in Postwar Senate Elections," *American Political Science Review,* 67 (December 1973), pp. 1213–1234; Candice J. Nelson, "The Effect of Incumbency on Congressional Elections, 1964–1974," *Political Science Quarterly,* 93 (Winter 1978–1979), pp. 665–678; and Albert D. Cover and David R. Mayhew, "Congressional Dynamics and the Decline of Competitive Congressional Elections," in *Congress Reconsidered,* eds. Lawrence C. Dodd and Bruce I. Oppenheimer (New York: Praeger Publishers, 1981), pp. 73–78.

4. David R. Mayhew, *Congress: The Electoral Connection* (New Haven, Conn.: Yale University Press, 1974), pp. 49–77.

5. *Congressional Quarterly Weekly Report,* July 2, 1983, p. 1354.

6. Concerning incumbents and their challengers, see Gary C. Jacobson, "The Marginals Never Vanished: Incumbency and Competition in Elections to the U.S. House of Representatives, 1952–82," *American Journal of Political Science,* 31 (February 1987), pp. 126–141; Jon R. Bond, Gary Covington, and Richard Fleisher, "Explaining Challenger Quality in Congressional Elections," *Journal of Politics,* 47 (May 1985) pp. 510–529; and Lyn Ragsdale, "Incumbent Popularity, Challenger Invisibility, and Congressional Voters," *Legislative Studies Quarterly,* 6 (May 1981), pp. 201–218.

7. Richard F. Fenno, Jr., "If, as Ralph Nader Says, Congress Is 'The Broken Branch,' How Come We Love Our Congressman So Much?" in *Congress in Change: Evolution and Reform,* ed. Norman J. Ornstein (New York: Praeger Publishers, 1975), p. 278.

8. Glenn R. Parker and Roger H. Davidson, "Why Do Americans Love Their Congressmen So Much More Than Their Congress?" *Legislative Studies Quarterly,* 4 (February 1979), pp. 53–61.

9. John F. Bibby, ed., *Congress Off the Record* (Washington, D.C.: American Enterprise Institute for Public Policy Research, 1983), p. 46.

10. Ibid., p. 45.

11. Edward R. Tufte, "Determinants of the Outcomes of Midterm Congressional Elections," *American Political Science Review,* 69 (September 1975), pp. 812–826.

12. *Congressional Quarterly Weekly Report,* March 14, 1987, pp. 484–485.

13. *New Kensington Valley News Dispatch* (Pennsylvania), October 8, 1980, p. 8.

14. The 1988 data on campaign receipts and expenditures in this section are drawn from press releases of the Federal Election Commission, February 24, and April 9, 1989. The 1986 data are taken from the Commission's press releases of May 10, and May 21, 1987.

15. *New York Times,* July 3, 1988.

16. On the critical importance of campaign spending by congressional challengers, see Gary C. Jacobson, "The Effects of Campaign Spending in Congressional Elections," *American Political Science Review,* 72 (June 1978), pp. 469–491.

17. For an argument that PAC contributions (and lobbying activities in general) affect legislative outcomes only at the margins, see Michael J. Malbin, "Looking Back at the Future of Campaign Finance Reform," in *Money and Politics in the United States* (Washington, D.C.: American Enterprise Institute for Public Policy Research, 1984), pp. 265–268.

18. *U.S. News & World Report,* May 28, 1984, p. 47.

19. In addition to providing for public financing of presidential campaigns, the Federal Election Campaign Act

of 1974 placed limitations on the personal and total campaign expenditures of candidates for Congress. But these did not last long. A Supreme Court decision in 1976, *Buckley* v. *Valeo,* ruled that both limitations were unconstitutional, in violation of the free speech and free association guarantees of the First Amendment. With these restrictions lifted, congressional campaign spending has grown at a rapid pace. Now the sky is the limit.

20. Robert L. Peabody, *Leadership in Congress: Stability, Succession, and Change* (Boston: Little, Brown, 1976), pp. 41–42.

21. Dotson Rader, "Tip O'Neill: He Needs a Win," *Parade* (September 27, 1981), p. 7.

22. *Congressional Quarterly Weekly Report,* December 11, 1976, p. 3293.

23. *New Republic,* December 16, 1977, p. 11. The statement was made by Congressman David Obey (D–Wis.).

24. *New York Times,* June 4, 1979, p. D10.

25. Woodrow Wilson, *Congressional Government* (New York: Meridian Books, 1956), p. 69. (Emphasis added.) This classic work was first published in 1885.

26. Clem Miller, *Member of the House* (New York: Charles Scribner's Sons, 1962), p. 110.

27. John Manley, *The Politics of Finance: The House Committee on Ways and Means* (Boston: Little, Brown, 1970), p. 40.

28. See an analysis of the Energy and Commerce Committee (and its PAC connections) in the *Congressional Quarterly Weekly Report,* March 12, 1983, pp. 501–508.

29. Richard F. Fenno, Jr., *Congressmen in Committees* (Boston: Little, Brown, 1973).

30. Roger H. Davidson, "Representation and Congressional Committees," *The Annals,* 411 (January 1974), pp. 48–62.

31. *Congressional Quarterly Weekly Report,* November 24, 1979, p. 2631.

32. For instructive analyses of congressional staffs, see Harrison W. Fox, Jr., and Susan Webb Hammond, *Congressional Staffs: The Invisible Force in American Lawmaking* (New York: Free Press, 1977); Kenneth Kofmehl, *Professional Staffs of Congress* (West Lafayette, Ind.: Purdue University Press, 1977); and Michael J. Malbin, *Unelected Representatives: Congressional Staff and the Future of Representative Government* (New York: Basic Books, 1980).

33. *Hearings before the Temporary Select Committee to Study the Senate Committee System,* 94th Cong., 2d Sess., 1976, p. 117. The statement was made by Senator Robert Dole (R–Kans.).

34. *John Heinz Reports,* April 1978.

35. Richard F. Fenno, Jr., "Strengthening a Congressional Strength," in *Congress Reconsidered,* eds. Lawrence C. Dodd and Bruce I. Oppenheimer, p. 263.

36. *Congressional Quarterly Weekly Report,* November 3, 1984, p. 2870.

37. Warren E. Miller and Donald E. Stokes, "Constituency Influence in Congress," *American Political Science Review,* 57 (March 1963), pp. 45–65.

38. Kingdon, *Congressmen's Voting Decisions,* p. 77.

39. Bibby, *Congress Off the Record,* p. 22.

40. Kingdon, *Congressmen's Voting Decisions,* p. 100.

41. Ibid., p. 37.

42. These quotations are drawn from Herbert B. Asher, "The Learning of Legislative Norms," *American Political Science Review,* 67 (June 1973), p. 503; Barbara Deckard Sinclair, "State Party Delegations in the United States House of Representatives—an Analysis of Group Action," *Polity,* 5 (Spring 1973), p. 330; Charles L. Clapp, *The Congressman: His Work as He Sees It* (Washington, D.C.: Brookings Institution, 1963), p. 15.

Chapter 13

1. "Is the Presidency Too Big for One Person?" interview with Theodore J. Lowi, *U.S. News & World Report,* February 2, 1981, p. 24.

2. Kenneth Prewitt and Alan Stone, *The Ruling Elites* (New York: Harper & Row, 1973), pp. 150–151.

3. Quoted in the *New York Times,* October 12, 1979, p. A20. © 1979 by The New York Times Company. Reprinted by permission.

4. The *Gallup Opinion Index* for April 1977, p. 12, provides data for 1966–1977. The highest support for direct popular election was in 1968, when 81 percent approved.

5. *The American Public's Experience with Recent Presidential Elections: A National Survey of Public Awareness and Personal Opinion* (New York: Hearst Corporation, 1988), p. 25.

6. Lewis H. Lapham, "Edward Kennedy and the Romance of Death," *Harper's* (December 1979), p. 41.

7. Drummond Ayres, Jr., "G.O.P. Keeps Tabs on Nation's Mood," *New York Times.* November 16, 1981, p. A18.

8. A fascinating discussion of this crucial problem is in Clinton Rossiter, with notes and additional text by Richard P. Longaker, *The Supreme Court and the Commander in Chief* (Ithaca, N.Y.: Cornell University Press, 1976), expanded edition.

9. Quoted in *Congressional Quarterly Weekly Report,* October 29, 1983, p. 2240.

10. For some interesting comments on this and related points, see George C. Edwards III, *Presidential Influence in Congress* (San Francisco: W. H. Freeman, 1980), pp. 70–81.

11. Richard E. Neustadt, *Presidential Power* (New York: John Wiley & Sons, 1980), p. 26.

12. Edwards, *Presidential Influence in Congress,* p. 202.

13. *Do New Leaders Make a Difference?* (Princeton, N.J.: Princeton University Press, 1981).

14. "The President as Coalition Builder: Reagan's First Year," in *Rethinking the Presidency,* ed. Thomas E. Cronin (Boston: Little, Brown, 1982), pp. 271–286.

15. See an interesting discussion by Bert A. Rockman, "Carter's Troubles," *Society* (July–August 1980), pp. 34–40.

16. George Reedy, *The Twilight of the Presidency* (New York: New American Library, 1987).

17. Chester L. Cooper, *The Last Crusade; America in Vietnam* (New York: Dodd, Mead, 1970), p. 223.

18. Reedy, pp. 178–180.

19. Quoted in Cabell Phillips, *The Truman Presidency* (Baltimore: Penguin Books, 1969), p. 6.

Chapter 14

1. Charles O. Jones, ed., *The Reagan Legacy* (Chatham, N.J.: Chatham House Publishers, 1988), p. 34.

2. President's Private Sector Survey on Cost Control, *Report on the Cost of Congressional Encroachment,* 1984, provides detailed information on this subject.

3. Allen Schick, *Crisis in the Budget Process* (Washington, D.C.: American Enterprise Institute for Public Policy Research, 1986), p. 16.

4. Quoted in Schick, p. 14.

5. Aaron Wildavsky, "The Two Presidencies," *Trans-Action,* 4 (December 1966).

6. Richard Fleisher and Jon Bond, "Are There Two Presidencies? Yes, but Only for Republicans," *Journal of Politics,* 50 (August 1988), pp. 747–767.

7. Nigel Bowles, *The White House and Capitol Hill* (Oxford: Clarendon Press, 1987), p. 247. For a somewhat different perspective see, George C. Edwards III, *Presidential Influence in Congress* (San Francisco: W. H. Freeman, 1980).

8. Charles O. Jones, *The Trusteeship Presidency* (Baton Rouge, La.: Louisiana State University Press, 1988).

9. Bowles, *The White House and Capitol Hill,* pp. 246–247.

10. Lawrence C. McQuade, "Being There," *New York Times Magazine,* September 22, 1988, p. 82.

11. Quoted in *Congressional Quarterly Weekly Report,* October 15, 1988, p. 2999.

12. Jesse H. Choper, *Judicial Review and the National Policy Process* (Chicago: University of Chicago Press, 1980).

13. Clark F. Norton, *Congressional Review, Deferral, and Disapproval of Executive Actions* (Washington, D.C.: Congressional Research Service, 1976), p. 8. Barbara Hinkson Craig, *The Legislative Veto* (Boulder, Colo.: Westview Press, 1983), p. 27.

14. Allen Schick, "The Disappearing Impoundment Power," *Tax Features, Tax Foundation* (October 1988), p. 4.

15. Leonard C. Meeker, "The Legality of United States Participation in the Defense of Viet-Nam," *Department of State Bulletin* 54, no. 1396 (March 28, 1966), pp. 484–485.

16. Willmoore Kendall, "The Two Majorities," *Midwest Journal of Political Science,* 4 (November 1960), p. 345.

Chapter 15

1. *Gallup Opinion Index,* September 1977, pp. 20–24.

2. Daniel Katz, Barbara A. Gutek, Robert L. Kahn, and Eugenia Barton, *Bureaucratic Encounters* (Ann Arbor: Survey Research Center, Institute for Social Research, University of Michigan, 1975), p. 120.

3. *Public Opinion,* May/June 1987, p. 27.

4. Survey by the Advisory Commission on Intergovernmental Relations in May 1984, as reported in the *National Journal* (July 14, 1984), p. 1374.

5. Hugh Heclo, *A Government of Strangers: Executive Politics in Washington* (Washington, D.C.: Brookings Institution, 1977), p. 88. Copyright © 1977 by the Brookings Institution, Washington, D.C.

6. Quoted in G. Calvin Mackenzie, "Cabinet and Subcabinet Selection in Reagan's First Year: New Variations on Some Not-So-Old Themes," paper presented at the annual meeting of the American Political Science Association, New York, 1981, p. 5.

7. Richard F. Fenno, Jr., *The President's Cabinet* (New York: Vintage Books, 1959), p. 87.

8. Two thorough discussions of presidential appointments are by Joseph P. Harris, *The Advice and Consent of the Senate* (Berkeley: University of California Press, 1953), and G. Calvin Mackenzie, *The Politics of Presidential Appointments* (New York: Free Press, 1981).

9. For a more complete discussion, see Mackenzie, *Politics of Presidential Appointments,* especially pp. 247–254.

10. Dom Bonafede, "New Right Preaches a New Religion and Ronald Reagan Is Its Prophet," *National Journal* (May 2, 1981), p. 779.

11. Quoted in Richard P. Nathan, *The Plot That Failed, Nixon and the Administrative Presidency* (New York: John Wiley & Sons, 1975), p. 81.

12. This incident, presumably genuine, was reported in "Briefing," *New York Times,* February 19, 1982, p. A14.

13. R. Douglas Arnold, *Congress and the Bureaucracy* (New Haven, Conn.: Yale University Press, 1979).

14. "Open Letter to a Cabinet Member," *New York Times Magazine,* January 11, 1981, p. 38. © 1981 by the New York Times Company. Reprinted by permission.

15. James P. Pfiffner, *The Strategic Presidency* (Chicago: Dorsey Press, 1988), p. 37.

16. Stephen J. Wayne, *The Legislative Presidency* (New York: Harper & Row, 1978), p. 196.

17. Quoted from the *Wall Street Journal* in Nathan, *The Plot That Failed,* p. 83.

18. The extreme efforts in the Nixon administration to control the bureaucracy are detailed in Nathan, *The Plot That Failed.*

19. Quoted in "A War Reagan's Winning: Taming the Bureaucracy," *U.S. News & World Report* (April 5, 1982), p. 26.

20. An excellent discussion of the relations between the National Security Council and the Department of State is in Bert A. Rockman, "America's Departments of State: Irregular and Regular Syndromes of Policy Making," *American Political Science Review,* 75 (December 1981), pp. 911–927.

21. The *New York Times,* January 7, 1982, p. A20. © 1982 by the New York Times Company. Reprinted by permission.

22. Joel D. Aberbach and Bert A. Rockman, "Mandates or Mandarins?" *Public Administration Review* (March/April 1988), p. 610.

23. Peter F. Drucker, "What Is 'Business Ethics'?" *The Public Interest* (Spring 1981), p. 33.

24. Quoted in *Congressional Quarterly Weekly Report,* November 3, 1984, p. 2872.

25. See Bradley H. Patterson, Jr., "On Federal Management and the Presidency," *Management* (Fall 1980), pp. 2–5.

Chapter 16

1. "The Courts of First Resort," *New York Times,* July 26, 1977, p. 30c.

2. As quoted in M. Judd Harmon, ed., *Essays on the Constitution of the United States* (Port Washington, N.Y.: Kennikat Press, 1978), p. 61.

3. *Batson* v. *Kentucky,* 476 U.S. 79.

4. *Law,* broadly speaking, represents the rules of conduct that pertain to a given political order of society, rules backed by the organized force of the community. As it has evolved through the centuries, law has been

made either by the political representatives of the people or by jurists. The former type of law is generally known as *statutory law,* the latter as *common law.* The crucial distinction is between codified, written (*statutory*) law and unwritten (*common*) law. *Equity* is a supplement to the common law. It begins where the law ends, taking the form of a judicial decree (rather than a judgment of yes or no).

5. See *Krause and Scheuer, et al.* v. *Rhodes and White, et al.* (one of the "Kent State cases," decided August 27, 1975).

6. See Henry J. Abraham, *The Judicial Process: An Introductory Analysis of the Courts of the United States, England, and France,* 5th ed. (New York: Oxford University Press, 1986), pp. 168–171.

7. Ratified in 1798.

8. Abraham, *The Judicial Process,* pp. 327–329, 362. (*McCardle's* citation is 7 Wallace 506.)

9. See William Jenkins, Jr., "Retention Elections: Who Wins When No One Loses?" *Judicature,* 61 (August 1977), pp. 79–86.

10. See Abraham, *The Judicial Process,* pp. 44–50.

11. See Henry J. Abraham and Edward M. Goldberg, "A Note on the Appointment of Justices of the Supreme Court of the United States," *Journal of the American Bar Association,* 46 (February 1960), pp. 147–150.

12. See Henry J. Abraham and Bruce Allen Murphy, "The Influence of Sitting and Retired Justices on Presidential Supreme Court Nominations," *Hastings Constitutional Law Review,* 3 (Winter 1976), pp. 37–63.

13. See Henry J. Abraham, *Justices and Presidents: A Political History of Appointments to the Supreme Court,* 2d ed. (New York: Oxford University Press, 1985).

14. Charles P. Curtis, "Review and Majority Rule," in *Supreme Court and Supreme Law,* ed. Edmond Cohn (New York: Simon & Schuster, 1971), p. 198.

15. See the tables and accompanying text in Abraham, *The Judicial Process,* pp. 292–308.

16. *Southern Pacific Co.* v. *Jensen,* 224 U.S. 205 (1916), at 22.

17. Benjamin N. Cardozo, *The Nature of the Judicial Process* (New Haven, Conn.: Yale University Press, 1921), p. 169.

18. As quoted by Alpheus T. Mason and William M. Beaney in *American Constitutional Law,* 6th ed. (Englewood Cliffs, N.J.: Prentice-Hall, 1978), p. XXVI.

19. *New York Times,* November 15, 1971, p. 41.

20. *Uveges* v. *Pennsylvania,* 335 U.S. 437 (1948), at 437.

21. *Reynolds* v. *Sims,* 377 U.S. 533 (1964), at 624, dissenting opinion.

22. Eugene V. Rostow, "The Democratic Character of Judicial Review," *Harvard Law Review,* 66 (1952), p. 195.

23. Judge Hutcheson of Texas, as quoted by Eugene V. Rostow in *The Sovereign Prerogative: The Supreme Court and the Quest for Law* (New Haven, Conn.: Yale University Press, 1963), p. 110.

24. Oliver Wendell Holmes, Jr., *The Common Law* (Boston: Little, Brown, 1881), p. 1.

Chapter 17

1. Farewell address to political appointees, December 13, 1988.

2. Douglass Cater, *Power in Washington* (New York: Random House, 1964), p. 17.

3. Hugh Heclo, "Issue Networks and the Executive Establishment," in *The New American Political System,* ed. Anthony King (Washington, D.C.: American Enterprise Institute, 1978), p. 102.

4. Charles O. Jones, *The United States Congress: People, Place, and Policy* (Homewood, Ill.: Dorsey Press, 1982), p. 363.

5. Donald T. Regan, *For the Record: From Wall Street to Washington* (New York: Harcourt Brace Jovanovich, 1988), p. 194.

6. Ibid., p. 193.

7. Jeffrey H. Birnbaum and Alan S. Murray, *Showdown at Gucci Gulch: Lawmakers, Lobbyists, and the Unlikely Triumph of Tax Reform* (New York: Random House, 1987), p. 102.

8. Ibid., p. 177.

9. Ibid., p. 178.

10. E. E. Schattschneider, *The Semisovereign People* (New York: Holt, Rinehart & Winston, 1960), pp. 30, 55.

11. Peter Bachrach and Morton S. Baratz, *Power and*

Poverty: Theory and Practice (New York: Oxford University Press, 1970), p. 44.

12. Oscar Gray, *Cases and Materials on Environmental Law* (Washington, D.C.: Bureau of National Affairs, 1973), p. 733.

13. Jeffrey Pressman and Aaron Wildavsky, *Implementation,* 2d ed. (Berkeley: University of California Press, 1979), pp. xx, xxi.

14. George C. Edwards, III, *Implementing Public Policy* (Washington, D.C.: Congressional Quarterly Press, 1980), p. 1.

15. James S. Coleman, "Problems of Conceptualization and Measurement in Studying Policy Impacts," in *Public Policy Evaluation,* ed. Kenneth M. Dolbeare (Beverly Hills, Calif.: Sage Publications, 1975), p. 19.

16. Alice M. Rivlin, *Systematic Thinking for Social Action* (Washington, D.C.: Brookings Institution, 1971), p. 7.

17. Robert A. Katzmann, *Institutional Disability: The Saga of Transportation Policy for the Disabled* (Washington, D.C.: Brookings Institution, 1986), p. 202.

18. Rivlin, *Systematic Thinking,* p. 80.

19. Fred Frohock, *Public Policy: Scope and Logic* (Englewood Cliffs, N.J.: Prentice-Hall, 1979), p. 184.

20. David Braybrooke and Charles E. Lindblom, *A Strategy of Decision* (New York: Free Press, 1963), p. 102.

21. *Federalist* no. 47 (New York: Modern Library, 1937), p. 315.

22. Stephen J. Wayne, *The Legislative Presidency* (New York: Harper & Row, 1978), pp. 71–72.

23. Lance LeLoup, *Budgetary Politics* (Brunswick, Ohio: King's Court, 1980), p. 3.

24. Aaron Wildavsky, *The New Politics of the Budgetary Process* (Glenview, Ill.: Scott, Foresman, 1988), pp. 1–2.

25. Allan Schick, *Reconciliation and the Congressional Budget Process* (Washington, D.C.: American Enterprise Institute, 1981), p. 5.

26. Ibid., p. 7.

27. *Bowsher* v. *Synar,* 106A S.Ct. 3181 (1986), at 3192–3193.

28. James A. Thurber, "The Politics of Spending: Congressional-Presidential Relations in an Era of Budget Reform," paper prepared for the 14th American Politics Group Annual Conference, Oxford University, Oxford, England, 1988, p. 31.

Chapter 18

1. *Inaugural Addresses of the Presidents of the United States* (Washington, D.C.: U.S. Government Printing Office, 1952), p. 225.

2. Statistics taken from Bureau of the Census. *Historical Statistics of the United States: Colonial Times to 1970,* vols. 1 and 2 (Washington, D.C.: U.S. Government Printing Office, 1975); and Bureau of the Census, *Statistical Abstract of the United States* (Washington, D.C.: U.S. Government Printing Office, 1987).

3. Roger W. Cobb and Charles D. Elder, *Participation in American Politics: The Dynamics of Agenda-Building* (Boston: Allyn & Bacon, 1972), p. 11.

4. Herbert Hoover, *Memoirs: The Cabinet and the Presidency, 1920–1933,* vol. 2 (New York: Macmillan, 1952), p. 223.

5. Ibid., p. 259.

6. Ibid., p. 223.

7. Frank Freidel, *Franklin D. Roosevelt: Launching the New Deal* (Boston: Little, Brown, 1973), p. 15.

8. See William E. Leuchtenburg, *Franklin D. Roosevelt and the New Deal: 1932–1940* (New York: Harper & Row, 1963), pp. 231–239.

9. James L. Sundquist, *Politics and Policy: The Eisenhower, Kennedy, and Johnson Years* (Washington, D.C.: Brookings Institution, 1968), p. 419.

10. Ibid., p. 386.

11. Ibid., p. 470.

12. Quoted in Congressional Quarterly, *Congress and the Nation,* vol. 1 (Washington, D.C.: Congressional Quarterly, Inc., 1965), p. 49.

13. Lyndon B. Johnson, *The Vantage Point: Perspectives on the Presidency, 1963–1969* (New York: Holt, Rinehart & Winston, 1971), p. 34.

14. Ibid., p. 35.

15. Quoted in *Congressional Quarterly Weekly Report,* November 29, 1963, p. 2089.

16. Johnson, *Vantage Point,* p. 71.

17. Frederick C. Mosher, "The Changing Responsibilities and Tactics of the Federal Government," *Public Administration Review,* 40 (November–December 1980), p. 542.

18. Joseph A. Pechman, ed., *Setting National Priorities: The 1982 Budget* (Washington, D.C.: Brookings Institution, 1981), p. 46.

19. Amitai Etzioni, *Demonstration Democracy* (New York: Gordon and Breach, 1970), pp. 14–15.

20. Quoted in *Congressional Quarterly Weekly Report,* January 23, 1970, p. 246.

21. Barry Blechman et al., *Setting National Priorities: The 1975 Budget* (Washington, D.C.: Brookings Institution, 1974), p. 133.

22. Craufurd D. Goodwin, ed., *Energy Policy in Perspective* (Washington, D.C.: Brookings Institution, 1981), p. 696; and Congressional Quarterly, *Congress and the Nation,* vol. IV (Washington, D.C.: Congressional Quarterly, Inc., 1977), p. 202.

23. Energy Policy Project, Ford Foundation, *Exploring Energy Choices: A Preliminary Report* (New York: Ford Foundation, 1974), p. 69.

24. Walter A. Rosenbaum, *Energy, Politics and Public Policy* (Washington, D.C.: Congressional Quarterly, Inc., 1981), p. 4. (Emphasis added.)

25. See Norman J. Ornstein, ed., *President and Congress: Assessing Reagan's First Year* (Washington, D.C.: American Enterprise Institute, 1982).

26. Allen Schick, "How the Budget Was Won and Lost," in Ornstein, *President and Congress,* p. 14.

27. Richard P. Nathan, "The Reagan Presidency in Domestic Affairs," in *The Reagan Presidency: An Early Assessment,* ed. Fred I. Greenstein (Baltimore: Johns Hopkins Press, 1983), p. 78.

Chapter 19

1. See Randall B. Ripley and Grace A. Franklin, *Congress, the Bureaucracy, and Public Policy* (Chicago: Dorsey Press, 1987).

2. Frederick Jackson Turner, *The Frontier in American History* (New York: Henry Holt and Company, 1921), p. 293.

3. Ibid., pp. 293–294.

4. David A. Stockman, *The Triumph of Politics: Why the Reagan Revolution Failed* (New York: Harper & Row, 1986), pp. 152–153.

5. Ibid., p. 154.

6. Martin Anderson, *Welfare: The Political Economy of Welfare Reform in the United States* (Palo Alto, Calif.: Hoover Press, 1978), p. 14.

7. Congressional Quarterly, *Congress and the Nation, 1945–1964,* vol. 1 (Washington, D.C.: Congressional Quarterly, Inc., 1965), p. 1225.

8. Charles McKinley and Robert W. Frase, *Launching Social Security: A Capture-and-Record Account* (Madison: University of Wisconsin Press, 1970), p. 3.

9. Paul C. Light, *Artful Work: The Politics of Social Security Reform* (New York: Random House, 1985), p. 231.

10. Peter T. Kilburn, "The Temptation of the Social Security Surplus," *New York Times,* November 27, 1988, p. e5.

11. James E. Anderson, David W. Brady, Charles S. Bullock III, and Joseph Stewart, Jr., *Public Policy and Politics in America,* 2d ed. (Monterey, Calif.: Brooks/Cole, 1984), p. 194.

12. Bureau of the Census, *Statistical Abstract of the United States, 1987* (Washington, D.C.: U.S. Government Printing Office, 1986), p. 710.

13. Congressional Quarterly, *Congress and the Nation, 1977–1980,* vol. V (Washington, D.C.: Congressional Quarterly, Inc., 1981), p. 664.

14. Both quotations from Henry Steele Commager, ed., *Documents of American History* (New York: Appleton-Century-Crofts, 1949), pp. 124, 131.

15. Bureau of the Census, *Statistical Abstract,* p. 333.

16. Martha Derthick, *Policymaking for Social Security* (Washington, D.C.: Brookings Institution, 1979), p. 32.

17. Eugene J. Meehan, *The Quality of Federal Policymaking: Programmed Failure in Public Housing* (Columbia: University of Missouri Press, 1979), p. 194.

18. Congressional Quarterly, *Congress and the Nation, 1965–1968* (Washington, D.C.: Congressional Quarterly, Inc., 1969), p. 710.

19. Office of Management and Budget, *The United States Budget in Brief: Fiscal Year 1988* (Washington, D.C.: U.S. Government Printing Office, 1987), p. 70.

20. For details see Richard F. Fenno, Jr., *The Making of a Senator: Dan Quayle* (Washington, D.C.: Congressional Quarterly Press, 1989), chaps. 2 and 3.

21. Donald F. Kettl, *Leadership at the Fed* (New Haven, Conn.: Yale University Press, 1986), p. 13.

22. Ibid., p. 1.

23. Ibid., p. 180.

24. Martha Derthick and Paul J. Quirk, *The Politics of Deregulation* (Washington, D.C.: Brookings Institution, 1985), p. 95.

Chapter 20

1. Alexis de Tocqueville, *Democracy in America* (New York: Alfred A. Knopf, 1948), vol. I, pp. 234–235.

2. See John Spanier, *Games Nations Play,* 6th ed. (New York: Holt, Rinehart & Winston, 1987), pp. 110–140, for a more detailed analysis of the international system. For a survey of American foreign policy, see John Spanier, *American Foreign Policy since World War II,* 11th ed. (Washington, D.C.: Congressional Quarterly Press, 1988).

3. Bayless Manning, "The Congress, the Executive and Intermestic Affairs: Three Proposals," *Foreign Affairs* (January 1977), pp. 306–324.

4. James McGregor Burns, *Congress on Trial* (New York: Harper & Row, 1949), and George B. Galloway, *Congress at the Crossroads* (New York: Thomas Y. Crowell, 1946), are good examples of a general concern about Congress. Daniel S. Cheever and H. Field Haviland, *American Foreign Policy and the Separation of Powers* (Cambridge, Mass.: Harvard University Press, 1952), is more specifically directed toward the foreign policy process.

5. Paul Seabury, *Power, Freedom and Diplomacy* (New York: Vintage Books, 1967), pp. 184–196.

6. See Thomas A. Bailey, *Woodrow Wilson and the Lost Peace* and especially *Woodrow Wilson and the Great Betrayal* (New York: Macmillan, 1944 and 1948, respectively).

7. Cecil V. Crabb, Jr., *Bipartisan Foreign Policy* (New York: Row, Peterson, 1957), and H. Bradford Westerfield, *Foreign Policy and Party Politics* (New Haven, Conn.: Yale University Press, 1955).

8. Seabury, *Power, Freedom and Diplomacy,* p. 196.

9. Louis Henkin, *Foreign Affairs and the Constitution* (Mineola, N.Y.: Foundation Press, 1973), p. 37.

10. Ibid., p. 41.

11. I. M. Destler, *Presidents, Bureaucrats, and Foreign Policy* (Princeton, N.J.: Princeton University Press, 1972), pp. 64, 74.

12. Ibid., pp. 83–94, 256–264. Also see Henry Kissinger, in *White House Years* (Boston: Little, Brown, 1979), where he recommends that the secretary of state be the president's principal adviser—after first appointing a national security assistant. See pp. 24–48.

13. Kissinger, *White House Years,* and *Years of Upheaval* (Boston: Little, Brown, 1982).

14. Zbigniew Brzezinski, *Power and Principle* (New York: Farrar, Straus, Giroux, 1983), and Cyrus Vance, *Hard Choices* (New York: Simon & Schuster, 1982).

15. Alexander M. Haig, Jr., *Caveat* (New York: Macmillan, 1984).

16. See the final Senate and House Intelligence Committees report, *The Iran-Contra Affair* (Washington, D.C.: U.S. Government Printing Office, 1987), and excerpts from the presidentially appointed Tower Commission study of the National Security Council in the *New York Times,* February 27, 1987. Also see Jane Mayer and Doyle McManus, *Landslide: The Unmasking of a President* (Boston: Houghton Mifflin, 1987).

17. Duncan L. Clarke, "Why It Can't Lead," *Foreign Policy* (Spring 1987), pp. 108–142. Also see the memoirs by Kissinger and, especially, Brzezinski on the NSA's role, including the latter's article, "The NSC's Midlife Crisis," *Foreign Policy* (Winter 1987–1988), pp. 94–99.

18. For detail, see John Spanier and Eric Uslaner, *Foreign Policies and the Democratic Dilemmas,* 5th ed. (Homewood, Ill.: Dorsey Press, 1989), chaps. 7 and 8.

19. Donald A. Peppers, " 'The Two Presidencies': Eight Years Later," in *Perspectives on the Presidency,* ed. Aaron Wildavsky (Boston: Little, Brown, 1975), pp. 448–461.

20. Some of the examples mentioned are detailed in original case studies in John Spanier and Joseph Nogee, eds., *Congress, the Presidency and American Foreign Policy* (New York: Pergamon Press, 1981); Cecil V. Crabb, Jr., and Pat M. Holt, *Invitation to Struggle,* 2d ed. (Washington, D.C.: Congressional Quarterly Press, 1984); and Thomas M. Franck and Edward Wiesband, *Foreign Policy by Congress* (New York: Oxford University Press, 1979).

21. William B. Quandt, *Camp David* (Washington, D.C.: Brookings Institution, 1986), pp. 12–13.

22. See Nunn's arguments in "The ABM Reinterpretation Issue," *Washington Quarterly* (Autumn 1987), pp. 45–57, and the administration's response by Abraham Sofaer, "The ABM Treaty: Legal Analysis in a Political Cauldron," ibid., pp. 59–75. On the background to SDI see Philip M. Boffey, William J. Broad, et al., *Claiming the Heavens* (New York: Times Books, 1988).

23. Roy Gutman, *The Making of American Policy in Nicaragua 1981–87* (New York: Simon & Schuster, 1988).

24. Tom Wicker, "A Law That Failed," *New York Times,* January 7, 1988.

25. Ole R. Holsti and James N. Rosenau, *American Leadership in World Affairs* (Boston: Allen & Unwin, 1984), examine the breakdown of the consensus in great detail. Also see their update in *International Studies Quarterly,* December 1986.

26. Murray Marder, "Hill Fights Reagan for Soul of Foreign Policy," *Washington Post,* September 2, 1984. For a somewhat different perspective see I. M. Destler, Leslie H. Gelb, and Anthony Lake, *The Unmaking of American Foreign Policy* (New York: Simon & Schuster, 1984).

27. Lloyd N. Cutler, "To Form a Government," *Foreign Affairs* (Fall 1980), pp. 126–127. Also see James McGregor Burns, *The Power to Lead* (New York: Simon & Schuster, 1984).

Picture Credits

CHAPTER 1: (opener) p. 3, Bettmann Newsphotos; p. 4, *The New Yorker Magazine;* p. 6, Charles Kennard/Stock, Boston; p. 7, Historical Pictures Service; p. 11, J. L. Atlan/ Sygma; p. 12, Bernard Schoenbaum/*The New Yorker Magazine*/February 4, 1985; p. 16. Peter Yates/The Picture Group; p. 18, Freda Leinwand/Monkmeyer Press Photo; p. 21, Bettmann Newsphotos; p. 23, Wide World Photos; p. 24, Wide World Photos; p. 27, Gamma Laison.

PART ONE: (opener) p. 31, Four By Five.

CHAPTER 2: (opener) p. 33, Bettmann Newsphotos; p. 35, Weber, *The New Yorker Magazine*/May 15, 1988; p. 36, The Granger Collection; p. 38, P. Steiner/*The New Yorker Magazine;* p. 39, The Bettmann Archive; p. 40, The Bettmann Archive; p. 43, The Bettmann Archive; p. 46, The Bettmann Archive; p. 51, Bettmann Newsphotos; p. 54, Hovovitch/ Gamma Laison; p. 60, Bettmann Newsphotos.

CHAPTER 3: (opener) p. 65, Paul Conklin/Monkmeyer Press Photo; p. 69, Bettmann Newsphotos; p. 71, Bettmann Archive; p. 74, Murray Lemmon/Photo Researchers, Inc.; p. 76, George Goodwin/Monkmeyer Press Photo; p. 78, Bettmann Newsphotos; p. 80, Wide World Photos; p. 82, Ferry/ Gamma Laison; p. 83, *The New Yorker Magazine*/Dana Fradon; p. 86, © Tom McHugh/Photo Researchers, Inc.; p. 92, Paul Conklin/Monkmeyer Press Photo.

CHAPTER 4: (opener) p. 97, Sudhir/The Picture Group; p. 99, © Pamela Price/The Picture Group; p. 103, Bettmann Newsphotos; p. 105, Wide World Photos; p. 111, Tannenbaum/Sygma; p. 112, © Jan Halaska/Photo Researchers, Inc.; p. 115, Wide World Photos; p. 116, William Thompson/The Picture Cube; p. 118, © Yvonne Hemsey/Gamma Laison; p. 119, © The Los Angeles Times Syndicate.

CHAPTER 5: (opener) p. 123, John Marmaras/Woodfin Camp & Associates; p. 125, Wide World Photos; p. 131, Wide World Photos; p. 138, © John Chiasson/Gamma Laison; p. 141, Bettmann Newsphotos; p. 143, Bettmann Newsphotos; p. 144, Carl Iwasaki/*Life Magazine* © 1953/ Time Inc.; p. 151, Bettmann Newsphotos; p. 152, Wide World Photos; p. 164, Bettmann Newsphotos.

PART TWO: (opener) p. 169, © 1989 Michael Geissinger/ Comstock.

CHAPTER 6: (opener) p. 171, © Andrew Popper/The Picture Group; p. 173, Wide World Photos; p. 176, Bettmann Newsphotos; p. 179, Dick Hanley/Photo Researchers, Inc.; p. 182, © Sidney Harris; p. 185, © Alan Carey/The Image Works, Inc.; p. 188, Bettmann Newsphotos; p. 191, Michel Heron/Monkmeyer Press Photo; p. 192, Jim Anderson/ Woodfin Camp & Associates; p. 195, Bettmann Newsphotos; p. 196, Bettmann Newsphotos.

CHAPTER 7: (opener) p. 199, Pamela Price/The Picture Group; p. 201, Cynthia Johnson/Time Pix Syndication; p. 203, Teresa Zabala/Monkmeyer Press Photo; p. 207, Wide World Photos; p. 210, Bettmann Newsphotos; p. 212, Wide World Photos; p. 213, Ron Dirito/Sygma; p. 215, *The New Yorker Magazine*/September 3, 1984; p. 221, Sygma Paris; p. 222, Bettmann Newsphotos; p. 223, Bettmann Newsphotos.

CHAPTER 8: p. 229, © Sidney Harris; p. 230, Wide World Photos; p. 233, © Don Heiny/The Picture Group; p. 238, © 1984 Herblock. From Herblock: *Through the Looking Glass* (W. W. Norton, 1984); p. 240, © Don Heiny/The Picture Group; p. 244, The Star Tribune Syndicate; p. 245, © Steve Liss/Gamma Laison; p. 246, Bettmann Newsphotos; p. 250, Steve Liss/Time Pix Syndication; p. 254, Wide World Photos; p. 256, Bettmann Newsphotos.

CHAPTER 9: (opener) p. 261, Wally McNamee/Woodfin Camp & Associates; p. 266, Weiner/Gamma Laison; p. 268, © Cynthia Johnson/Gamma Laison; p. 269, Wide World Photos; p. 275, Bettmann Newsphotos; p. 277, Dana Fradon/*The New Yorker Magazine;* p. 282, Wide World Photos; p. 286, Courtesy of Cowles Syndicate, Inc.; p. 288, Bettmann Newsphotos; p. 292, NYT Pictures; p. 296, *The New York Times;* p. 297, Wide World Photos; p. 301, Wide World Photos.

CHAPTER 10: (opener) p. 305, © Max Winter/The Picture Group; p. 307, Bettmann Newsphotos; p. 308, Bettmann Newsphotos; p. 313, © 1968, Herblock, from *The Herblock Gallery* (Simon and Shuster, 1968); p. 316, Robert Scurlock/ Superstock; p. 319, Wide World Photos; p. 327, Susan Greewood/Gamma Laison; p. 328, Wide World Photos; p. 330, Wally McNamee/Woodfin Camp & Associates; p. 332, Wide World Photos; p. 334, Dana Fradon/*The New Yorker Magazine,* April 7, 1980; p. 335, Wide World Photos.

CHAPTER 11: (opener) p. 341, Jacques Chenet/Woodfin Camp & Associates; p. 344, © Kenneth Jarecke/Contact Press Images; p. 349, Bettmann Newsphotos; p. 352, Gamma Laison; p. 355, Stevenson/*The New Yorker Magazine;* p. 356, Vyto Starinskas/Sygma; p. 361, Wide World Photos; p. 362, Erich Hartman/Magnum; p. 364, Wide World Photos; p. 366, Bettmann Newsphotos; p. 369, Wide World Photos; p. 374, Bettmann Newsphotos.

PART THREE: (opener) p. 379, Wally McNamee/Woodfin Camp & Associates.

CHAPTER 12: (opener) p. 381, Stuart Cohen/Comstock; p. 386, Bettmann Newsphotos; p. 391, Wide World Photos; p. 393, © Eugene Richards/Magnum; p. 397, Bettmann Newsphotos; p. 401, Bettmann Newsphotos; p. 406, Wally McNamee/Woodfin Camp & Associates; p. 409, Bettmann Newsphotos; p. 414, Bettmann Newsphotos; p. 415, Larry Downing/Woodfin Camp & Associates.

CHAPTER 13: (opener) p. 421, Obrmeski/The Image Bank; p. 424, Wide World Photos; p. 426, B. Markel/Gamma Laison; p. 430, Larry Downing/Woodfin Camp & Associates; p. 434, Wide World Photos; p. 436, Wide World Photos; p. 441, Diana Walker/Gamma Laison; p. 445, Bettmann Newsphotos; p. 447, John F. Kennedy Library; p. 448, from *Herblock at Large* (Pantheon, 1987); p. 453, Paul Hosefros/NYT Pictures.

CHAPTER 14: (opener) p. 457, Wally McNamee/Woodfin Camp & Associates; p. 460, Bettmann Archives; p. 463, © Larry Downing/Woodfin Camp & Associates; p. 465, Bettmann Newsphotos; p. 467, R. Maiman/Sygma; p. 470, Wide World Photos; p. 471, Wide World Photos; p. 473, Bettmann Newsphotos; p. 474, Johnson/Gamma Laison; p. 478, Wide World Photos.

CHAPTER 15: (opener) p. 489, © M. Abramson/Woodfin Camp & Associates; p. 494, A. Tannenbaum/Sygma; p. 495, © Paul Howell/Gamma Laison; p. 496, from *Herblock Through the Looking Glass* (W. W. Norton, 1984); p. 498, Alan Carey/The Image Works, Inc.; p. 501, Wide World Photos; p. 505, Wide World Photos; p. 506, Stayskal/The Chicago Tribune; p. 507, © Al Stephenson/The Picture Group; p. 508, © 1984, Kenneth Garrett/Woodfin Camp & Associates; p. 513, Wide World Photos; p. 515, Wide World Photos.

CHAPTER 16: (opener) p. 519, Four by Five; p. 521, Rhoda Sidney/Monkmeyer Press Photo; p. 523, Billy E. Barnes/Stock Boston; p. 524, Sidney Harris; p. 527, © Rick Smolen/Sygma; p. 530, Bettmann Newsphotos; p. 533, Sidney Harris; p. 536, Bettmann Newsphotos; p. 537, Wide World Photos; p. 541, © Brad Markel/Gamma Laison; p. 542, Larry Downing/Woodfin Camp & Associates; p. 547, Bettman Newsphotos.

PART FOUR: (opener) p. 551, © Adam Woolfit/Woodfin Camp & Associates.

CHAPTER 17: (opener) p. 553, R. Maiman/Sygma; p. 557, Wide World Photos; p. 562, Ellis Herwig/The Picture Cube; p. 563, Ellis Herwig/The Picture Cube; p. 564, Sidney Harris; p. 566, Hank Morgan/Photo Researchers, Inc.; p. 567, Sidney Harris; p. 569, © Tom Myers/Photo Researchers, Inc.; p. 574, Elizabeth Crews/Stock Boston; p. 576, Brad Markel/Gamma Laison; p. 577, © King Feature Syndicates; p. 579, Tannenbaum/Sygma; p. 581, Wide World Photos.

CHAPTER 18: (opener) p. 587, Beryl Goldberg; p. 589, Gabe Palmer/The Stock Market; p. 591, Bettmann Newsphotos; p. 596, © Jerry Gay; p. 599, Wide World Photos; p. 601, Spencer Grant/Monkmeyer Press Photo; p. 603, Wide World Photos; p. 605, Patricia Hollander Gross/Stock Boston; p. 607, © Al Stephenson/The Picture Group; p. 612, Richard Hutchings/Photo Researchers, Inc.; p. 513, K. C. Statz/The Los Angeles Times Syndicate.

CHAPTER 19: (opener) p. 617, © James D. Wilson/Woodfin Camp & Associates; p. 620, Richard Steedman/The Stock Market; p. 623, Monkmeyer Press Photo; p. 626, © Grant LeDuc/Monkmeyer Press Photo; p. 627, Spencer Grant/Monkmeyer Press Photo; p. 632, Mike Maple/Woodfin Camp & Associates; p. 634, Allen Green/Photo Researchers, Inc.; p. 638, © Skip O'Rourke/The Image Works, Inc.; p. 640, Sidney Harris; p. 642, A. Tannenbaum/Sygma; p. 643, Bettmann Newsphotos.

CHAPTER 20: (opener) p. 647, © Doug Menuez/The Picture Group; p. 650, Wide World Photos; p. 652, Bettmann Newsphotos; p. 656, Bettmann Newsphotos; p. 658, © Narunart Prapanya/Gamma Laison; p. 662, Wide World Photos; p. 664, © Oliver Rebbot/Contact Press Images; p. 669, Wide World Photos; p. 671, Bettmann Newsphotos; p. 675, Wide World Photos; p. 679, Wide World Photos.

INDEX

About the Authors

William J. Keefe is professor of political science at the University of Pittsburgh, where he served as department chair from 1968 to 1976. A graduate of Illinois State University, he received his M.A. from Wayne State University and his Ph.D. from Northwestern University. Along with various articles, he has published *The American Legislative Process* (with Morris S. Ogul), *Parties, Politics, and Public Policy in America,* and *Congress and the American People.* Dr. Keefe has served as Chairman of the Advisory Committee of the Congressional Fellowship Program, as Chairman of the Program Committee for the national meeting, and as Treasurer of the American Political Science Association. He is now a member of the Association's Trust and Development Fund Board and a member of the executive board of the section on political parties.

Henry J. Abraham, James Hart professor of government and foreign affairs at the University of Virginia, has been named by the Commonwealth of Virginia as outstanding teacher in the social sciences and won the Thomas Jefferson Award, his school's highest honor. Previously at the University of Pennsylvania (where he earned his Ph.D.), CCNY, the University of Colorado, Columbia University, and Swarthmore College, he has also lectured frequently abroad. Among his 12 books are *The American Judicial Process, Freedom and the Court,* and *The Judiciary,* now entering its eighth edition. He has written chapters in edited volumes and some 85 professional articles. A consultant to the U.S. Senate committee on the judiciary and a member of the Virginia commission on the U.S. bicentennial, he has headed the faculty senates at Virginia and Pennsylvania.

William H. Flanigan is professor of political science at the University of Minnesota and past president of the Social Science History Association. He received his B.A. from Wabash College, his M.A. and Ph.D. from Yale University. Dr. Flanigan is co-author of *Political Behavior of the American Electorate* (with Nancy H. Zingale) and co-editor of *The History of American Electoral Behavior* (with Joel H. Silbey and Allan G. Bogue). With Jerome Clubb and Professor Zingale, he also has written *Partisan Realignment* and edited the volume *Analyzing Electoral History.*

Charles O. Jones is Hawkins Professor of Political Science, University of Wisconsin–Madison, where he also received his Ph.D. He previously taught at the University of Virginia. Formerly chair of the executive committee of the Social Science Research Council and national president of ΠΣΑ, the political science honor society, he has been a consultant for the House ways and means committee and has testified before the House budget and rules committees. Along with his many articles on Congress, the presidency, public policy, political parties, and elections, he has written *An Introduction to* *the Study of Public Policy, United States Congress: People, Place, and Policy,* and, most recently, *The Trusteeship President: Jimmy Carter and the United States Congress.* From 1977 to 1981, he served as managing editor of the *American Political Science Review.*

Morris S. Ogul, professor of political science at the University of Pittsburgh, was its department chair from 1980 to 1984. He received his Ph.D. at the University of Michigan. The author of *Congress Oversees the Bureaucracy* and co-author (with William J. Keefe) of *The American Legislative Process,* he has also contributed to the Congressional Quarterly's *Congress Reconsidered* (edited by Lawrence C. Dodd and others) and to numerous scholarly journals. Dr. Ogul has been a consultant to committees of both the House and U.S. Senate and to the U.S. Office of Personnel Management. He has frequently participated in seminars at the Executive Seminar Centers in Kingspoint, New York, and Oak Ridge, Tennessee.

John W. Spanier, professor of political science at the University of Florida, received his A.B. and M.A. at Harvard and his Ph.D. at Yale University. He has worked as a consultant on arms control and lectured at such institutions as the Air Command Staff College, the Foreign Service Institute, West Point, and the Naval War College. His books include *American Foreign Policy Since World War II* (the first volume on U.S. foreign policy officially published in China), *Games Nations Play: How to Analyze International Politics, How American Foreign Policy Is Made, World Politics in an Age of Revolution,* and *The Truman–MacArthur Controversy and the Korean War* (one of only 2,000 books in the presidential library). He has also contributed chapters to several edited books and written many articles and book reviews.

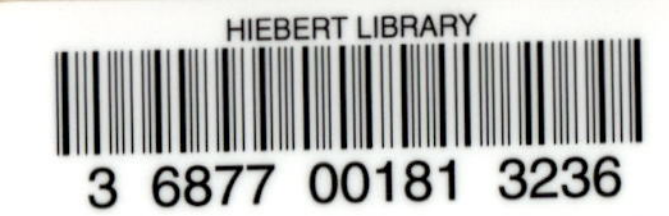

DATE DUE

Participation in Elections: The 1988 Presidential Election

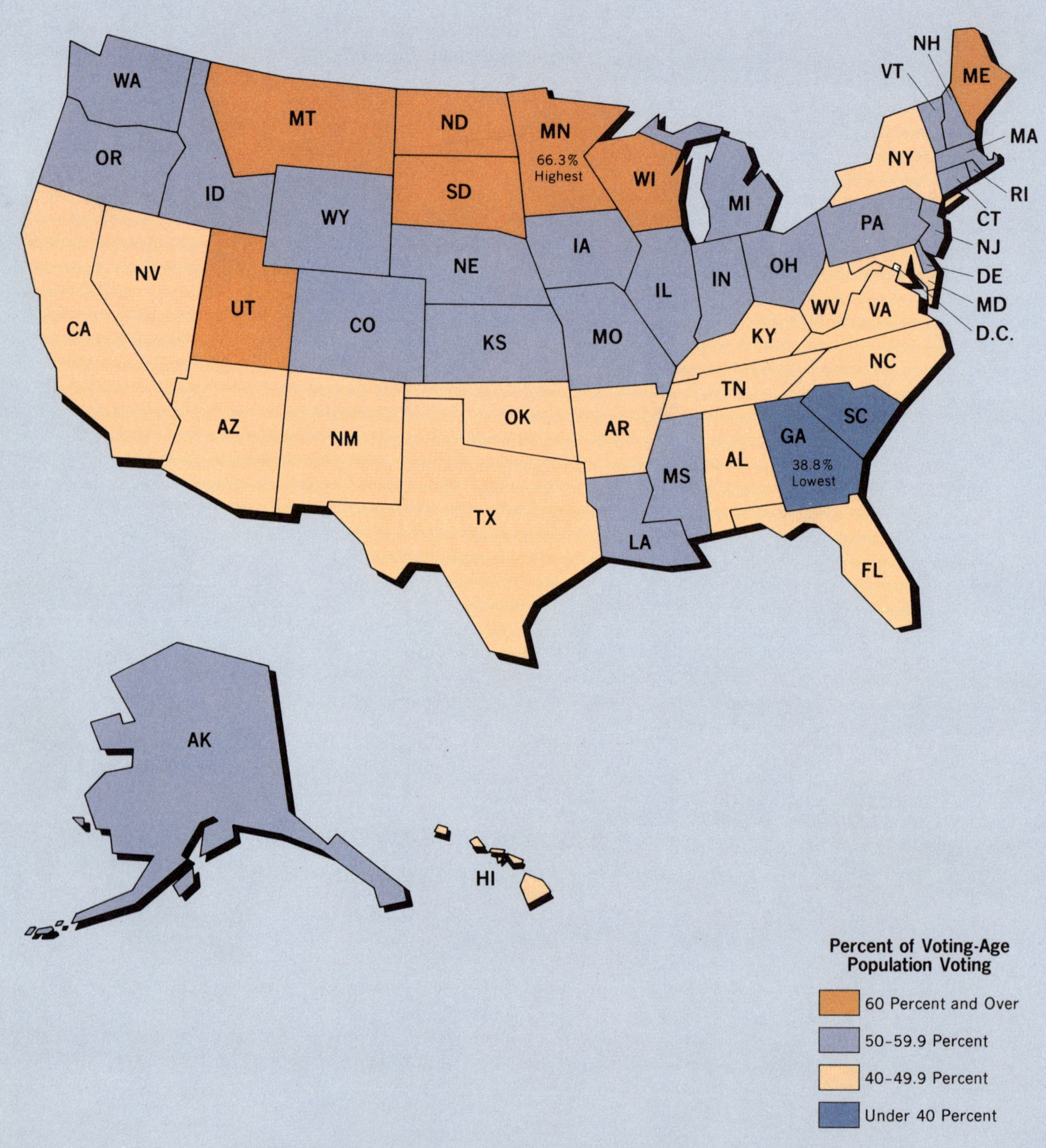

Percent of Voting-Age Population Voting

- 60 Percent and Over
- 50–59.9 Percent
- 40–49.9 Percent
- Under 40 Percent